SCHUBERT'S COMPLETE SONG TEXTS

Volume I

With

International Phonetic Alphabet Transcriptions
Word for Word Translations
and
Commentary

By

BEAUMONT GLASS

LEYERLE PUBLICATIONS

SCHUBERT'S COMPLETE SONG TEXTS

Volume I

By

BEAUMONT GLASS

Copyright © Leyerle Publications 1996
ISBN 1-878617-19-2

LEYERLE PUBLICATIONS
Executive Offices
28 Stanley Street
Mt. Morris, New York 14510

This book may be ordered directly from

**LEYERLE
PUBLICATIONS**

Box 384
Geneseo, New York 14454

DEDICATION

*To the lieder singer I most admire,
my wife, EVANGELINE NOËL*

im Dezember 1965/

LOTTE LEHMANN
4565 VIA HUERTO
HOPE RANCH PARK
SANTA BARBARA, CALIFORNIA

Beaumont Glass hat durch mehrere Saisons meine Liederklassen in der Musik Aka=
demie in Santa Barbara(California)begleitet - und ich habe ihn als einen sehr
sensitiven,serioesen und musikalischen Begleiter schaetzen gelernt.Er ist wirk=
lich viel mehr als das:er durchdringt die Seele der Lieder nachschoepferisch
und ist fuer den Singenden eine wahre Inspiration.
Ich kann ihn nur waermstens und aufrichtigst empfehlen.

[signature: Lotte Lehmann]

English Translation

From Lotte Lehmann, December 1965:

Beaumont Glass has for several seasons accompanied my lieder classes at the Music Academy in
Santa Babara [California] -- and I have learned to esteem him as a very sensitive, serious, and
musical accompanist. He is really much more than that: he penetrates into the soul of the songs
re-creatively and is for the singer a true inspiration. I can only recommend him most warmly and
most sincerely.

Lotte Lehmann

ABOUT THE AUTHOR

Professor Beaumont Glass is at present the Director of Opera Theater at the University of Iowa, Iowa City, where he has coached and staged thirty full-scale productions, including *Boris Godunov*, which was telecast in its entirety by Iowa Public Television, and Handel's *Agrippina*, taken on tour to Europe in 1985. He directed *Lucia di Lammermoor*, with Roberta Peters in the title role, for the Utah Opera Company, and *The Magic Flute, Fidelio, The Marriage of Figaro, The Barber of Seville*, and *The Abduction from the Seraglio* for the Cedar Rapids Symphony. He has translated eighteen complete operas, and his translations have been performed by Boston Lyric Opera, the Opera Theater of Springfield, Illinois, the University of Maryland, the Cedar Rapids Symphony, and Anoka Opera, Minnesota, as well as by the University of Iowa.

Before coming to the University of Iowa in 1980, Glass was "*Studienleiter*" (Director of Musical Studies, head of the coaching staff, in charge of the musical preparation of all the operas) at the Zurich Opera, his home theater for nineteen years. He was coach, harpsichordist, and recital accompanist at the Festival of Aix-en-Provence for four summers. In addition to staging forty-eight different operas in Europe and the United States, he has accompanied lieder recitals in the Salzburg, Aix, and Holland Festivals, as well as on tour with Grace Bumbry, Martina Arroyo, and Simon Estes. Glass speaks German, Italian, and French.

He is the author of a biography of soprano Lotte Lehmann, published by Capra Press, Santa Barbara, in 1988. Glass had been Lehmann's assistant for several years at the Music Academy of the West, Santa Barbara, both in art song and in opera. Earlier, he had assisted Maggie Teyte at her studio in London. Glass has written articles for *The Opera Quarterly* and the San Francisco Opera program book, and he has given lectures on opera and art song in Switzerland and in America, including the "Presidential Lecture" at the University of Iowa for the year 1988. Four times in 1994 he was the guest lecturer on the weekly radio program "*Opera Fanatic*" in New York, station WKCR-FM.

Glass made his professional debut as a stage director for the Northwest Grand Opera in Seattle, where his first production was Verdi's *La traviata*, starring Dorothy Kirsten. He has subsequently worked with many of the best-known singers in the world of opera, either as coach or as stage director, or as both.

He is at present preparing a complete edition of the texts of all of Franz Schubert's songs in two volumes, with word-for-word translations, international phonetic alphabet transcriptions, and notes on interpretation, variants, special words, etc., to be published in 1996 and 1997 by Leyerle Publications. He has also created over 150 singing translations of German, French, Spanish, Russian, Finnish, and Norwegian art songs.

Glass is a graduate of Phillips Exeter Academy and the U.S. Naval Academy, Annapolis.

Franz Schubert

Schubert and his Songs
A Brief View

Franz Schubert was born in the Viennese suburb of Lichtenthal on January 31, 1797, the son of a schoolmaster and a domestic servant. The home of his boyhood was filled with music: He learned how to play the violin from his father, the piano from his brother Ignaz; his choirmaster taught him singing, the organ, and basic principles of harmony. When he was eleven he entered the *Stadtkonvikt*, a sort of conservatory-school where specially selected boys were trained to sing in the choir of the Imperial Chapel. He wrote a Fantasy in G for Piano Duet when he was thirteen, his first string quartet at fifteen, his first symphony at sixteen, and, at seventeen, a miraculous, fully mature masterpiece, "*Gretchen am Spinnrade*" from Goethe's *Faust*. A year later came *Erlkönig*, another of his most famous songs. He had been writing songs, copiously, since the age of fourteen. During his adolescence he studied counterpoint and voice with Antonio Salieri, Mozart's notorious rival. An earlier teacher had said of Schubert: "I have nothing more to teach him; he has been taught by God." Papa Schubert expected his son to keep music as an avocation and to prepare for some more practical profession. There was a serious rift between father and son; then Schubert's mother died. A reconciliation took place, but Schubert left home to take up lodgings with various individual friends. Ever since his time at the "Convict," he had enjoyed the company of a wide circle of devoted and admiring young bohemians, poets, and painters, who were drawn to him through his music, especially through his songs. Several of them provided him with lyrics. He was amazingly prolific: on October 19, 1815, for example, he composed seven songs in one day! He wore glasses even while sleeping, so that he could write down an inspiration the moment he woke up. Music, poetry, nature, and convivial friends were everything to him; he ate too much, smoked too much, drank too much (though no one ever saw him drunk), and cared perhaps too little about personal fastidiousness. He was nicknamed "*Schwammerl*"—"Little Sponge." He had a sweet nature, free of cruelty or cynicism. Schubert lived in the city but sang of the country: he and his friends often arranged excursions to the fields and woods just outside Vienna. And in the evening there would be a "*Schubertiade*" at someone's house and Franz would perform his latest compositions and then play for his friends to dance. A distinguished and famous singer, Michael Vogl, took an interest in Schubert's songs and made it his mission to promote them whenever he could in Viennese musical circles. He recognized Schubert's unique ability to capture the essential mood of a poem in his music and to bring the words to new and vivid life. These songs have a remarkable spontaneity and youthfulness, overflowing with feeling, whether joyful, serene, melancholy, or desperate; no matter how sad the subject, there is pain without bitterness. But such songs were ahead of their time. The Viennese aristocrats liked what they knew; the publishers found Schubert's music too difficult, non-commercial. Out of more than a thousand compositions, only a little over one hundred were published during his lifetime. Schubert lived on the borderline of poverty; fame came only after death, a tragically early death before he had reached the age of thirty-two. Today he is recognized as the most significant creator of an art form we call the German *Lied*. He was not the first; *Das Veilchen* by Mozart, for example, and Beethoven's beautiful song cycle, *An die ferne Geliebte*, are worthy precursors. But *Gretchen am Spinnrade* and *Erlkönig* were truly something new and could not have been written by anyone before him. His response to poetry was enthusiastic and instinctive, and he happened to live in an era of poets whose romantic sensibilities reveled in the celebration of nature and in the unashamed expression of personal feelings. If today some of their poems seem overly sentimental, or perhaps too preoccupied with death, too prone to self-pity, we will nevertheless appreciate their best qualities and enjoy them more sympathetically if we can return in imagination to the time that gave them birth. The "Age of Reason" had ended in the chaos of revolution. Political ideologies were ruthlessly suppressed by the censors. But the individual human heart could be explored in poetry. Schubert's songs— he wrote well over six hundred!— represent the German *Lied* in its purest form. They inspired the other great lieder composers who came after him, Robert Schumann, Johannes Brahms, Hugo Wolf, and Richard Strauss. The greatest of Schubert's songs are immortal treasures.

Thoughts on Interpreting Lieder

The singer is an indispensable partner of the composer and of the poet. The singer gives life and expression to the notes and the words and—above all!—to the feelings behind them, the feelings that *inspired* them. This requires, besides a beautiful voice, a rich imagination and the power to communicate. Every poem was born out of a special experience (the mundane and the ordinary are best left to prose); that *specialness* stirred the composer to set it to music. It is our task to try to find—or to imagine—that original, motivating spark of inspiration, and then to illuminate the song from within.

Study the poem, immerse yourself in it! Be sure that you understand its message exactly (one misunderstood word can sometimes alter everything, can even reverse the meaning). Who is speaking those words? Where should you imagine the speaker to be? To whom is he or she addressing those words, and in what frame of mind? Why *that* word, and not another? Why that phrase? What clue to the poet's meaning, what insight do they give us? Every singer is simultaneously an actor, communicating words with the most effective and appropriate expression, ready to move us, to shatter or to charm. But no matter how expressive, the words must be understood: clarity of diction is essential. Even the most exquisite verbal nuance is wasted if the word is not being received by the listener. But clear diction does not mean "spitting out" the consonants in little explosions that break up the line of the melody. Consonants need to be resonantly projected, but not exaggerated, and those voiced consonants that lend themselves to *legato* (especially l, m, n, ng) should be lovingly cherished, to compensate for the many that do not.

The words came first, of course. But the music lifts the words to another realm of the imagination, adding a new dimension, new colors, an intensified spiritual resonance. the union of words and tones is what makes a song; in a truly great *Lied* the combination of poem and music surpasses what either could accomplish alone. In performance, each element must get its individual due and yet be blended in harmony with its counterpart. The consonants and vowels—their sheer sound, apart from the meaning of the word they form,— become part of the musical fabric, the musical effect. Be sensitive to the musical possibilities of the language itself.

To understand the song the singer must study the accompaniment as well as the vocal line. The piano part is full of clues; look for them! The prelude, the postlude, the interludes—they are your world of the moment, your surrounding atmosphere; often they are *you*, your feelings, the "subtext" behind the words you sing. Your eyes, your bearing, your entire expression must be in harmony with what is coming to you from the piano. Imagine where you are, what you see before you, what you are feeling. And communicate all of that to the audience as eloquently as you can, without overstepping the boundary between stage and concert platform. Be totally expressive—but not "theatrical." A great lieder singer invites the audience into the world of the song, to share in moments of beauty and flights of the spirit that the poet and the composer have created and that the interpreter must always endeavor to re-create anew.

It is not nearly enough simply to sing the indicated pitches and note values and to pronounce the words clearly and correctly, no matter how beautiful the voice. Live with the song. Explore its world. Without a special contribution from the imagination, the personality, and the very *soul* of the singer, the performance would at best offer flowers without any fragrance.

Schubert and his poets were deeply sensitive to nature, in all its moods. The Romantics still had a classical education; living as they did among monuments of history and art, they absorbed a rich cultural awareness, which is reflected in their works. Spend time in nature; visit museums; study paintings and literature of the period; listen to recordings by Dietrich Fischer-Dieskau, Elisabeth Schwarzkopf, Lotte Lehmann, Elly Ameling, and other great interpreters of lieder.

Format and Phonetics
An Explanation and Introduction

Format:

The song texts are in alphabetical order by title.

The German text of each song or aria is printed in **bold type**; *above* each word is a transcription of the pronunciation in the characters of the International Phonetic Alphabet ("IPA"); *beneath* each word of the German text is an English word that is as close as practicable to the literal meaning, chosen from among the possible choices offered in a comprehensive German-English dictionary; beneath *that*, usually, in a *fourth* line, is the meaning of the line as it might be expressed in English, with its very different syntax.

Example (from *Die Forelle*, "The Trout"):

ɪn ˈlaenəm ˈbɛçlaen ˈhɛlə, daː ʃos ɪn ˈfroːɐ(r) laᷝel di ˈlɑonɪʃə foˈrɛlə foˈryːbɐ
In einem Bächlein helle, da schoss in froher Eil die launische Forelle vorüber
In a brooklet clear, there shot in happy haste the capricious trout past
(In a clear little brook, in happy haste, the capricious trout shot past...)

Often different interpretations may be possible; the translator has made a choice according to his own feeling for the language and his own understanding of the poem. A number of definite errors have been discovered in various otherwise excellent books of translations.

After the title, and a translation of the title, the opus number, if any, the year of composition, and the name of the poet are given. Variants in the text are noted beneath or beside the relevant line, with pronunciation (in IPA) and translation of any words different from those in the line. After the end of each song there is a more or less brief commentary, consisting of observations about the nature of the song, with perhaps a hint about the interpretation, some possibly useful background information, an explanation of discrepancies or unusual references, or similar points.

Phonetics:

The pronunciation suggested is based on a combination of two authoritative sources, *Duden—Das Aussprachewörterbuch*, and *Siebs—Deutsche Hochsprache*.

The **diphthongs**, for example, are taken from Siebs, since that version works better for singers, a̯e, ɑo, ɔø (Siebs) instead of ai, au, ɔy (Duden). The treatment of the unaccented ending "**er**" (as in "*Mutter*" or "*aber*") and words or syllables **ending in r** (such as "*der*," "*nur*," "*mehrfach*," "*verlor*") is as recommended in Duden. When the following word or syllable starts with a vowel, it is often advisable *in singing* to pronounce the r, for the sake of clarity and a smoother *legato*. Where that is the case, this collection offers a choice, e.g.: deːɐ/deːr, or ˈoːdɐ(r). The more formal the mood of the song, the more rhetorical or archaic the wording, the heavier the accompaniment, the more likely that the r's will be sounded distinctly. Some familiarity with current practice among the best German singers is a desirable guide in such, as in all cases.

In general, the pronunciation given is that which would be used in *speaking* the words (an exception: when the composer has given a note to a vowel that would ordinarily be non-syllabic in speech, e.g: eˈlyːziʊm—four syllables—instead of eˈlyːzjʊm—three syllables). **Double consonants** within a word are not pronounced in speech, but may be treated differently in singing, depending on the length of the note values and the importance of the word itself. For instance, in singing a word like "*Wonne*" (ecstasy) in a slow tempo, the n will be prolonged, both for expressive purposes and to counteract the abnormal rhythm of the word that is dictated by the music, since in speech it would be pronounced quickly with a very short and open ɔ. This subtle distinction has not been observed in the present compilation, and is left to the singer's discretion. If a short vowel is to be sung on a relatively long note, some compromise must be made between the normal pronunciation in quick speech and the demands of the music: this is usually accomplished by doubling the consonant that follows the vowel, to indicate its shorter value. "*Kann*" (can), for instance, must be distinguished from "*Kahn*" (boat).

To remind singers (and speakers) that **t, k, and p** are more or less strongly **aspirated** in German (indicated by Duden only in the introductory pages, later merely assumed), certain IPA symbols have been added to indicate the degree of aspiration: tʰ, kʰ, pʰ strongly aspirated, t', k', p' lightly aspirated. When a word ends with the t, k, or p sound, and the next begins with the same sound, or its voiced equivalent (d, g, or b) the final t, k, or p is *not* aspirated, unless a pause is made between the words (a musical rest, for example). The directors and coaches of German opera houses are very particular about such matters. German audiences expect to understand the words.

A note on the sources:

The compiler and translator has attempted to include the texts of all the solo vocal pieces found in the leading collections of Schubert's lieder, as well as those more recently discovered. Schubert was astoundingly prolific during his tragically brief life. There are 615 different poems or prose poems in these volumes, and many of them he set to music more than once.

The various currently available editions of Schubert's songs are derived, for the most part, from one or the other of two major publications: (1) the *Gesamtausgabe* ("Complete Edition") as edited by Eusebius Mandyczewski and published in 1894 by Breitkopf & Härtel, Leipzig, under the title *Franz Schubert's Werke*, Series 20, in ten volumes; and (2) the more familiar *Edition Peters*, Frankfurt, New York, London, edited by Max Friedländer, in seven volumes. There are many differences between those two publications, and those differences are dealt with in this collection. In many cases, the *Gesamtausgabe* reflects what Schubert actually wrote in the original manuscripts, whereas the Peters edition is often based on the first *published* version, with variants that may or may not have been authorized by the composer himself. Sometimes, where there are discrepancies between Schubert's wording and that of the original poem, the text has been changed by Friedländer (in the Peters edition) to conform with the latter.

Eighteen of the songs included here do not appear in either of the leading collections mentioned above, either because they were lost, or because they were left incomplete by the composer. Performable versions of those songs were completed by Reinhard van Hoorickx and privately published.

The translations:

The translator has endeavored to make the meaning of the text as clear as possible, without any concern for elegance or poetic beauty in the English wording. Some of the original poems are quite straight-forward; others are subject to various interpretations; still others need to be lived in for a while before they yield up a sense of their message. Some German words are encountered only in poetry today; dictionaries usually label them "poetic." But perfectly ordinary words still in daily use are translated into their English equivalents; "*Mädchen*," for example, is usually going to be "girl" rather than "maiden," unless a medieval atmosphere is an integral factor in the effectiveness of the poem. "*Du*" will be "you" rather than "thou," unless the poem is a prayer.

German diction:

Vowels:

One striking feature of German is the marked **difference in duration** between **long** and **short** vowels. "*Abend*" ('aːbənt' - evening), for example, has a long ah; in "*Nacht*" (naxtʰ - night) the *a* is very short. Yet a singer may find the word *Nacht* on a much longer note than the first syllable of *Abend*. How to be true to the sound of the word? No matter how short the note, the *aː* in *Abend* must give the impression of duration through the quality and intensity of the vowel. The *a* in *Nacht* must be prolonged without weight or stress, and the *ch* should be pronounced slightly earlier than if the word were "*nach*" (naːx - after, toward) for instance, which has a relatively long *a*. Another characteristic of German is the obligatory use of the **glottal stop** [ǀ] to separate the end of one word from a following word that begins with a vowel, or to separate certain word elements within a word. Examples: *sie entehren ihn* (ziː ǀɛntˈǀeːrən ǀiːn - they dishonor him), *du und ich* (duː ǀʊntˈ ǀɪç - you and I), *vereinen* (fɛɐ̯ǀaɛnən/fɛrǀaɛnən - to unite).

—[a] is the IPA symbol for the usual *a* in German. It is basically a brighter, more forward vowel than our American "ah" (except, perhaps, an "ah" in Boston). The *a* in "*Vater*" ('faːtˈɐ - father) or "*haben*" ('haːbən - have) is long; in "*Gevatter*" (gəˈfatˈɐ - godfather) the *a* is short.

—[ɑ] is a darker version of *a*, slightly lower and farther back in the mouth; it occurs in the diphthong represented in normal print as *au* and in the IPA as ɑo. Examples: *Baum* (bɑom - tree), *Haus* (hɑos - house).

Besides the difference in duration between "long" and "short," there is a strong phonetic **difference** between the following "**closed**" and "**open**" vowels:

—[e] is a very **closed** vowel that does not exist in American English, and is usually one of the last to be mastered by singers who are not French or German (it is identical with the French *é*). [e] is closer to the position of [i] in the mouth than its nearest approximation in standard English. Examples: *ewig* ('eːvɪç - eternal), *Seele* ('zeːlə - soul). The difference between "*Leben*" ('leːbən - life, to live) and "*lieben*" ('liːbən - to love) is slight but crucial.

—[ɛ] is similar to the short open *e* in such English words as "let," "egg." It can be long or short; its long version, [ɛː], is identical to the vowel in "air" without the *r*, and is written as *ä* in German. It is the same sound as *è* in French. That sound must be **avoided** when the [ɛ] is short, as in *Herz* (hɛrts - heart), *Herr* (hɛr - Sir, Mr.), in both of which the vowel is as in "head" and **not** as in "hair" (an important distinction); *ä* can also be short, pronounced [ɛ].

—[ə] is a slightly darkened version of [ɛ] and **should not sound like the English [ʌ]**, the vowel in "love," which in German is only found in the ending *er*, as in *Mutter* ('mʊtˈɐ - mother) or *aber* ('aːbɐ - but), and is represented in the IPA as [ɐ].

—[i] is a closed vowel identical to the *ee* in "see."

—[ɪ] is open and short, as in "it" or "if" in English. Some Americans do not distinguish between [ɪ] and [ɛ] in everyday speech, making "bin," "been," and "Ben" sound the same. They must guard against making the same **error** in German. Examples: *ich* (ɪç - I), *bin* (bɪn - am).

—[o] is a **very closed** vowel that, like [e] does not exist in English, but does in French (spelled *ô, au,* or *eau*). It is closer to the mouth position of [u] than its nearest approximation in American English, which is usually a diphthong [ʌo]. Examples: *ohne* ('oːnə - without), *Tod* (tʰoːtˈ - death), *Boot* (boːtʰ - boat).

—[ɔ] is very open, almost as much as in French, and always short (whereas the nearest sound in American speech, the vowel in "awe" is generally long). Examples: *noch* (nɔx - still), *Sonne* ('zɔnə - sun). There is a big difference between the sound of *offen* ('ɔfən - open) and *Ofen* ('oːfən - oven).

—[u] is closed and similar to the vowel in "moon." Examples: *du* (duː - you), *Ruhe* ('ruːə - rest, peace), *tun* (tʰuːn - to do).

—[ʊ] is open and short, similar to the vowel in "foot" or "look" (if pronounced according to standard English; many Americans have a **problem** with this sound in German as in their own regional vernacular). Examples: *Mutter* ('mʊtˈɐ - mother), *und* (ʊntˈ - and), *Kuss* (kʰʊs - kiss).

—[ø] is closed and does not exist in English. It is pronounced by forming the lips to make a very closed [o] and at the same time trying to say a closed German (or French) [e]. Examples: *schön* (ʃøːn - beautiful), *hören* ('høːrən - to hear), *König* ('kʰøːnɪç - king). Most Americans make too open a sound when attempting this vowel. It must be distinguished from its open counterpart:

—[œ], the open version of [ø], made by forming the lips to make an open [ɔ] while trying to say [ɛ]. The sound exists in English in "girl," "world," "bird," etc. (before the *r* is added). Examples: *möchte* ('mœçt'ə - would like), *Götter* ('gœt'ɐ - gods), *Töchter* ('tʰœçt'ɐ - daughters).

—[y] is closed and does not exist in English. It is made by rounding the lips as if to say [u] and trying to pronounce [i]. Examples: *grün* (gryːn - green), *früh* (fryː - early), *süss* (zyːs - sweet). It is easier than [ø] for Americans because [u] and [i] exist in English, whereas pure [o] and [e] do not.

—[ʏ] is the open version of [y], made by rounding the lips as if to say [ʊ] and trying to pronounce [ɪ]. Examples: *jünger* ('jʏŋɐ - younger), *Küsse* ('kʰʏsə - kisses), *Glück* (glʏkʰ - luck).

Diphthongs are always pronounced short in German speech, but may be notated long in music, in which case the first of the two vowel sounds must take up most of the duration of the note (as when singing English diphthongs) Examples: *Wein* (va͜ɛn - wine), *Haut* (ha͜ʊtʰ- skin), *Freude* ('frɔ͜ødə - joy).

Consonants:

When the last letter in a word (or word element) is *b, d, g, v,* or *s* that final consonant is unvoiced in German. That means that [b] becomes [p], [d] becomes [t], [g] becomes [k], [v] becomes [f], [z] becomes [s] (exception: when *ich* follows a verb that has lost its final *e* through contraction, as in "*hab' ich,*" the final consonant of the shortened verb may keep its voiced sound). Americans have a particular problem with a final *s* after a voiced consonant, as in *Herzens* ('hɛrtsəns - heart's), *Lebens* ('leːbəns - life's), *niemals* ('niːmaːls - never), because in English an *s* after a voiced consonant is usually voiced (as in "lens"), unless the sound is spelled with a *c*, as in "fence" or "dance." Watch out for this **common fault**! *P, t,* and *k* are usually aspirated in German (that is, mixed with the sound of *h*); this will be indicated by a following [ʰ] if strongly aspirated, or by ['] if slightly aspirated. When *b, d,* and *g* become *p, t,* and *k* at the end of a phrase, they are not as strongly aspirated as the final consonant would be in words actually spelled with *p, t,* or *k*. Example: the difference between *tot* (tʰoːtʰ - dead) and *Tod* (tʰoːt' - death), if the word happens to end a phrase (otherwise both words sound the same).

—*ch* has two pronunciations: [ç] "front *ch*" follows a "front" vowel (*i, e, ä, ö, ü*) or a consonant. It is a light hissing sound, (the lips are not moved, as they are for *sh*). Examples: *ich* (ɪç - I), *Milch* (mɪlç - milk), *durch* (dʊrç - through), *manch* (manç - many a). "Back *ch*" [x] follows a "back" vowel (*a, o, u*). Examples: *ach* (ax - ah!), *noch* (nɔx - still), *Buch* (buːx - book). There are two **common errors** in pronouncing [x]: either it sounds too much like [ç] or too much like [k]. Example: *Nacht* (naxtʰ - night) must not sound like *nackt* (nak'tʰ - naked).

—*j* [j] is pronounced like *y* in English; sometimes it is aspirated with an *h* for expressive reasons. Examples: *ja* (jaː or hjaː - yes), *jung* (jʊŋ or hjʊŋ - young). The possible aspiration has not been indicated in this collection.

—*l* [l] is articulated with the tongue farther toward the front of the mouth than in American speech (but not past the teeth, as in some Russian words). It is a light, lyrical sound, and one of the **problems** for most American speakers. Examples: *Liebe* ('liːbə - love), *Welt* (vɛltʰ - world).

—*m* [m], *n* [n], and *ng* [ŋ] are hummed very resonantly in German singing. Final *n* in the ending *en*, however, is only lightly touched, since such endings serve a grammatical rather than an expressive function.

—*nk* is pronounced [ŋk], as in *denken* ('dɛŋk'ən - to think), *Dunkel* ('dʊŋk'əl - dark).

—*qu* is pronounced [kʰv]; that is why German singers often have trouble in Italian with "*questo*" or "*qui*". Examples: *Quelle* ('kʰvɛlə - spring, source), *Qual* (kʰvaːl - torment).

—*r* is uvular in speech (as in French) but trilled or "flipped" by the tongue in singing. Final *r* is a special case, as discussed above under the heading "Phonetics." After a long vowel, in the prefixes *er, ver, zer,* and in the endings *er, ern,* etc., it is barely indicated and rarely flipped or rolled in modern German speech. Examples: *nur* (nuːɐ̯ - only), *er* (eːɐ̯ - he), *vergessen* (fɛɐ̯ˈgɛsən - to forget), *Mutter* (ˈmʊtˈɐ - mother). Final double r, as in *starr* (ʃtˈar - rigid) is rolled.

—*st* and *sp* at the beginning of a word element are usually pronounced as if the *s* were *sh* [ʃ]. Examples: *Strasse* (ˈʃtˈraːsə - street), *sprechen* (ˈʃpˈrɛçən - to speak). If *st* or *sp* follow a vowel, or if the *s* and the *t* or *p* belong to different syllables, then the pronunciation is normal. Examples: *erst* (eːɐ̯stˈ - first), *lispeln* (ˈlɪspˈəln - to whisper, to lisp).

—*v* is usually pronounced like *f,* but there are exceptions, especially in names. Venus (ˈveːnʊs) keeps the *v* sound; Eva can be pronounced both ways, with [f] for Eve in paradise or the heroine of Wagner's *Die Meistersinger* (eːfa); with [v] for a modern woman, such as Hitler's mistress (eːva). Note that the final *a* is a pure [a] and never [ə] or [ʌ].

—*w* is pronounced [v]. Examples: *Welle* (ˈvɛlə - wave), *wenn* (vɛn - when, if).

—*z* is pronounced *ts* [ts̠]. Examples: *zu* (ts̠uː - to, too), *zwei* (ts̠vae̯ - two).

Because there are so many consonants in German, and because they often need to be articulated very strongly and sharply, the singer who wants to sing a beautiful *legato* line must be alert to every opportunity to take advantage of those consonants that lend themselves to *legato* singing, especially *l, m, n, ng.* Those consonants, especially when double, offer the possibility of making a *portamento* or **slur on the consonant itself,** which can give a much needed curve to the otherwise overly angular effect of short choppy syllables bristling with consonants. Seize every chance to exploit those curves! Examples: *Wonne* (ˈvɔnnə - rapture), *Kummer* (ˈkʰʊmmɐ - sadness), *Wange* (ˈvaŋə - cheek), *helle* (ˈhɛllə - bright). Note that in these examples the *n, m,* and *l* have been doubled in the suggested pronunciation, to illustrate the point. They are not doubled in speech, and therefore not in the phonetic transcriptions in this collection. Doubling at the discretion of the singer is often done for expressive reasons, to add intensity to key words, such as *Liebe!* (ˈlliːbə - love!), *Mutter!* (ˈmmʊtˈɐ - Mother!), *Süsse!* (ˈzzyːsə - sweet one!), etc. Lotte Lehmann, in her master classes, used to call out to her students: "Ten l's!" when they were to sing the word "*Liebe*" in a particularly rapturous phrase.

Stressed syllables: primary stress is indicated with the IPA symbol ['] in front of the syllable; in cases of possible ambiguity, a secondary stress may be indicated with [ˌ].

Some abbreviations:

Op. ... , No. ... = Opus ... , Number ...
GA = *Gesamtausgabe* (ten volumes of Series XX of Schubert's Collected Works,
         as first published by Breitkopf & Härtel, Leipzig)
P . = Peters Edition (a six-volume collection)
p. = poem (the poet's words, if different from Schubert's text)
subj. = grammatical subject
obj. = grammatical object
obs. = obsolete

Note: *Lieder* means "songs," the plural of the German word for song which is *das Lied.* In English we can say "lieder singer" or "he sang several lieder," but not "a lieder": the term would be "a *Lied.*" The plural form has become a part of our language, but not yet the singular.

'aːbənt'
Abend
Evening

Five-page sketch [composed 1819] (poem by Johann Ludwig Tieck)

viː lɪst' lɛs dɛn, das tʰryːp' lʊnt' ʃveːɐ̯ zoː   'laləs kʰɔmt', foˈryːbɐ tsiːt',
Wie ist es denn, dass trüb und schwer so   alles kommt, vorüber zieht,
How is it then, that dreary and heavy practically all comes, by passes,
(Why is it then that practically everything that comes and goes turns out to be dreary and heavy,)

ʊnt' 'vɛksəlnt', 'kʰvɛːlənt', 'lɪmɐ leːɐ̯, das 'larmə hɛrts lɪn zɪç fɛɐ̯'glyːt'ʰ?
und wechselnd, quälend,   immer leer,   das arme Herz in sich verglüht?
and changing, tormenting, always empty, the poor heart in itself ceases glowing?
(and that the poor heart, changing, tormenting itself, always empty, ceases glowing inside?)

kʰɑɔm gəˈkʰɔmən zɔl lɪç 'ʃaedən, kʰɑɔm lɛnt''glɔmən 'lœʃən   'viːdɐ 'lalə 'frɔ̷ødən,
Kaum gekommen soll ich scheiden, kaum entglommen löschen   wieder alle Freuden,
Barely come, am I to depart, barely kindled are extinguished again all joys,
(Barely come, I have to depart; barely kindled, all joys are extinguished again,)

ʊnt deːɐ̯ 'laedən   'dʊŋk'lə 'vɔlkə zɛŋt' zɪç 'niːdɐ.
und der Leiden   dunkle Wolke senkt sich nieder.
and the sufferings' dark cloud sinks itself down.
(and the dark cloud of suffering descends.)

ɑɔs den 'lɪçt'ɐn lɪn di naxt', lɑɔs den 'lɑɔgən, diː miːɐ̯ 'tʰaːgən,
Aus den Lichtern in die Nacht, aus den Augen, die mir tagen,
From the lights into the night, from the eyes, that for me dawn,
(From light into the darkness of night, from the eyes that are the dawn to me,)

diː maen 'gantsəs hɛrts dʊrç'laxt',   bin lɪç 'viːdɐ(r) 'lalən 'pʰlaːgən,
die mein ganzes Herz durchlacht,   bin ich wieder allen Plagen,
that my whole heart through-laughs, am I again to all miseries,
(that smile through my whole heart, I am once again given back to all the miseries,)

dem 'dyrən 'leːbən tsu'rʏkgəgeːbən. viː 'flʏçt'gə 'lɑɔgənblɪk'ə maen 'glʏk'ə!
dem dürren Leben zurückgegeben. Wie flücht'ge Augenblicke mein Glücke!
to the arid life given back. Like fleeting moments (is) my happiness!
(given back to an arid life, my happiness like fleeting moments!)

viː 'laŋə, 'laŋə 'dɑɔɐ deːɐ̯ 'tʰrɛnʊŋ 'dyːst'rə 'ʃveːrə 'tʰrɑɔɐ! —
Wie lange, lange Dauer der Trennung düstre schwere Trauer!—
What long, long duration the separation's gloomy, heavy grief! —
(How long, how long the gloomy, heavy grief of separation lasts! —)

tsu'rʏk' tsuː 'kʰeːrən lʊnt dɪç lɛnt''beːrən! loː lals lɪç dɪç nɔx nɪçt' gəˈzeːn,
Zurück zu kehren und dich entbehren! O als ich dich noch nicht gesehn,
Back to return and you to be without! Oh, when I you yet not (had) seen,
(To have to go back and be without you! Oh, when I had not yet seen you,)

2

daː 'dʊrftʻə 'zeːnzʊxtʻ ba͜e miːɐ̯ za͜en, ḷa͜en 'hɔfnʊŋsvɪntʻ ḷɪn 'ma͜enən 'vʏnʃən veːn,
da durfte Sehnsucht bei mir sein, ein Hoffnungswind in meinen Wünschen wehn,
then could longing with me be, a hope- wind in my wishes blow,
(then at least I could yearn, a breeze of hope could blow through my wishes,)

di 'tsuːkʰʊnft vaːɐ̯/vaːr ḷa͜en 'hɛlɐ ʃa͜en: jɛtstʻ mʊs ḷɪç fɔm ḷɛɐ̯'ɪnən/lɛrʻɪnən 'kʰa͜ofən,
die Zukunft war ein heller Schein: jetzt muss ich vom Erinnern kaufen,
the future was a bright gleam: now must I from the remembering buy)
(the future was a bright gleam; now I must buy from my memory)

vas ḷɪç kʰa͜om tsɛɐ̯'ʃtʻrɔøtʻ ḷɛm'pfant'; 'viːdɐ dʊrç di 'vyːstʻən 'ha͜ofən,
was ich kaum zerstreut empfand; wieder durch die wüsten Haufen,
what I scarcely dispersed experienced; again through the desolate heaps,
(that which I once experienced undispersed; again through desolate heaps,)

dʊrç ḷa͜en ḷʊnbə'voːntʻəs lantʻ, zɔl ḷɪç 'ḷɪrə, 'kʰlaːgəntʻ, 'ʃva͜efən,
durch ein unbewohntes Land, soll ich irre, klagend, schweifen,
through an uninhabited land, must I lost, lamenting, stray,
(through an uninhabited land, I have to stray, lost and lamenting,)

ʊnt dɛs 'glʏkʻəs 'gɔldnə 'ʃtʻra͜efən ḷa͜ox di 'lɛtstʻən, 'ḷapʻgəvantʰ .
und des Glückes goldne Streifen auch die letzten, abgewandt.
and the happiness's golden streaks even the last, turned away from.
(turned away from the golden rays of happiness, even from the very last of them.)

nɔx fyːl ḷɪç 'da͜enə hantʻ, nɔx viː ḷɪm 'tʰra͜omə 'da͜enə 'kʰʏsə,
Noch fühl' ich deine Hand, noch wie im Traume deine Küsse,
Still feel I your hand, still as in the dream your kisses,
(I still feel your hand, still feel, as if in a dream, your kisses,)

nɔx 'fɔlgən miːɐ̯ di 'hɔldən 'blɪkʻə, ḷʊnt di ḷɛm'pfɪndʊŋ, das ḷɪç 'ḷaləs 'mɪsə,
noch folgen mir die holden Blicke, und die Empfindung, dass ich alles misse,
still follow me the lovely glances; and the feeling that I everything miss
(those lovely glances still follow me; and the feeling that I miss everything)

bla͜epʻtʻ ba͜e miːɐ̯ tsu'rʏkʻə. loː 'hɔfən, 'ʃmaxtʻən, 'liːbəsla͜etʻ ḷʊntʻ 'zeːnən,
bleibt bei mir zurücke. O Hoffen, Schmachten, Liebesleid und Sehnen,
remains with me back. O hope, languishing, love- sorrow and yearning,
(stays behind with me. O hoping, languishing, love's sorrow, and yearning,—)

viː dʏrstʻ ḷɪç naːx den 'zyːsən 'tʰrɛːnən! loː 'tʰrøːstʻə mɪç dɔx, 'ḷa͜etʻləs 'vɛːnən,
wie dürst' ich nach den süssen Tränen! O tröste mich doch, eitles Wähnen,
how thirst I for the sweet tears! O comfort me, do, idle imagining,
(how I thirst for your sweet tears! Oh comfort me, do, idle imagination,)

zoː leːɐ̯ duː bɪstʻ, zoː tʰoːtʻ, zoː 'nɪçtʻɪç! fɛɐ̯'lastʻ liːɐ̯/liːr 'ḷalə mɪç zoː 'flʏçtʻɪç?
so leer du bist, so tot, so nichtig! Verlasst ihr alle mich so flüchtig?
as empty (as) you are, as dead, as futile! Abandon you all me so hastily?
(however empty you are, however dead, however futile! Do you all abandon me so hastily?)

[oː 'geːgənvartʻ, viː bɪst duː ʃnɛl! fɛɐ̯'gaŋənha͜etʻ, viː bɪst duː kʰla͜en!
[O Gegenwart, wie bist du schnell! Vergangenheit, wie bist du klein!
[O present, how are you fast! Past, how are you small!
[(Oh present, how fast you are! Past, how small you are!)

oː ˈtsuːkʰʊnftˈ, viː vɪrst duː ʊnˈlɛntˈlɪç zae̯n?
O Zukunft, wie wirst du unendlich sein?
O future, how will you endless be?
(Oh future, how will you be, endlessly?)

ʊnˈlɛntˈlɪç viː lam ˈhɪməlsboːɡən di ˈʃtˈɛrnə lɪn di ˈleːvɡən ˈrɔ̯ømə ˈʃtˈae̯ɡən,
Unendlich wie am Himmelsbogen die Sterne in die ew'gen Räume steigen,
Endlessly, as on the heavenly arch the stars into the eternal spaces rise,
(Endlessly, as the stars rise up into their eternal places on the arch of heaven,)

zoː fyːl lɪç ˈʃtˈʊndən, ˈtʰaːɡə, ˈmoːndən ˈheːɐ̯ɡətsoːɡən, lʊnt dʊrç mae̯n ˈtʰiːfstˈəs zae̯n
so fühl' ich Stunden, Tage, Monden hergezogen, und durch mein tiefstes Sein
thus feel I hours, days, moons hither drawn, and through my deepest being
(thus I feel the hours, days, months pass by, and through the very depths of my being)

das ˈtʰryːbə ˈʃvae̯ɡən, lʊm mɪç lae̯n lʊnfɛɐ̯ˈɡɛŋlɪç meːɐ̯ fɔn ˈʃvartsən ˈvoːɡən,
das trübe Schweigen, um mich ein unvergänglich Meer von schwarzen Wogen,
the dreary silence, around me an imperishable sea of black waves,
(feel the dreary silence; all around me there is an everlasting sea of black waves,)

lʊntˈ lax! kʰae̯n ˈɡryːnəs ˈluːfɐ vɪl zɪç ˈtsae̯ɡən!]
und ach! kein grünes Ufer will sich zeigen!]
and ah! no green shore wants itself to show!]
(and, ah! no green shore can be seen!)]

[Schubert left a five-page sketch of his proposed setting of this poem, with only the first few words written in, and occasional indications for the accompaniment. A performable version has been made and privately printed by Reinhard van Hoorickx. The poem was published in 1802 in the *Musenalmanach* ("Almanac of the Muses"), lacking the last verse (in brackets, above).]

ˈaːbəntˈbɪldɐ
Abendbilder
Evening Images

Published posthumously [composed in 1819] (poem by Johann Peter Silbert)

ʃtˈɪl bəˈɡɪnts lɪm hae̯n tsuː tʰao̯ən, ˈruːɪç veːpˈt deːɐ̯ ˈdɛmrʊŋ ˈɡrao̯ən
Still beginnt's im Hain zu tauen, ruhig webt der Dämmrung Grauen
Quietly begins it in the grove to dew, peacefully weaves the twilight's greying
(Quietly the dew begins to fall in the grove, peacefully the dimming twilight weaves)

dʊrç di ɡluːtˈ ˈzanftˈɐ fluːtʰ, dʊrç das ɡruːn lʊmˈbʊʃtˈɐ[r] ˈlao̯ən,
durch die Glut sanfter Flut, durch das Grün umbuschter Auen,
through the glow of gentle inundation, through the green of bush-encircled meadows,

zoː di ˈtʰrʊŋkˈnən ˈblɪkˈə ˈʃao̯ən. ziː! deːɐ̯ ˈraːbən ˈnaxtˈɡəfiːdɐ
so die trunknen Blicke schauen. Sieh! der Raben Nachtgefieder
so the intoxicated glances look. See! the ravens' night-plumage
(as the eye looks on, entranced. See! The raven-black plumage of night)

4

rɑ͜ʊʃt‘ lɑ͜ʊf 'fɛrnə 'la͜eçən 'niːdɐ. 'balzaːmdʊft‘ hɑ͜ʊçt di lʊftʰ;
rauscht auf ferne Eichen nieder. Balsamduft haucht die Luft;
rustles onto distant oak-trees down. balm-fragrance exhales the air;
(sifts down onto distant oak-trees. The air exhales a balmy fragrance;)

filo'meːləns ˌtsɑ͜ʊbɐliːdɐ 'halət tsartʰ di 'lɛço 'viːdɐ.
Philomelens Zauberlieder hallet zart die Echo wieder.
Philomela's* magic songs sounds delicately the echo again.
 (the echo delicately repeats the magic songs of the nightingale.)

hɔrç! dɛs 'laːbəntglœk‘la͜ens 'tʰøːnə 'maːnən ɛrnst deːr 'eːɐdə 'zøːnə,
Horch! des Abendglöckleins Töne mahnen ernst der Erde Söhne,
Hark! the evening little bell's tones remind gravely the earth's sons,
(Listen! The tones of the little vesper bell gravely remind the sons of earth,)

das liːɐ hɛrts 'hɪməlvɛrts,
dass ihr Herz, himmelwärts,
that their heart, heavenwards,

'zɪnənt‘ ɔp‘ deːɐ 'ha͜emaːt‘ 'ʃøːnə, zɪç dɛs 'eːɐdəntʰants lɛnt‘'vøːnə.
sinnend ob der Heimat Schöne, sich des Erdentands entwöhne.
reflecting on the homeland's beauty, itself of the earthly bauble wean.
(reflecting on the beauty of their homeland, should wean itself away from worldly trumpery.)

dʊrç deːɐ 'hoːən 'vɔlk‘ən 'riːgəl 'fʊŋk‘əln 'tʰɑ͜ʊzənt‘ 'hɪməlsziːgəl, 'luːnas bɪlt‘
Durch der hohen Wolken Riegel funkeln tausend Himmelssiegel, Lunas Bild
Through the high clouds' bars sparkle [a] thousand heaven- seals, Luna's image
(Through the strata of high clouds a thousand stars, seals of heaven, are sparkling, Luna's image)
                                                              [Luna was the Roman goddess of the moon]

'ʃt‘rɔ͜øət‘ mɪlt‘ ɪn deːɐ 'fluːt‘ən 'kʰlaːrən 'ʃp‘iːgəl 'ʃɪmɐnt‘ gɔlt‘ lɑ͜ʊf fluːr ʊnt‘ 'hyːgəl.
streuet mild in der Fluten klarem Spiegel schimmernd Gold auf Flur und Hügel.
strews gently in the floods' clear mirror shimmering gold upon field and hill.
(in the clear mirror of the waters gently strews shimmering gold onto field and hill.)
          [*Peters & poem:* **klaren** (Schubert's change, in the *GA*, makes better grammatical sense)]

fɔn dɛs 'fɔlmoːnts 'viːdɐʃa͜enə 'blɪtsət das bə'moːst‘ə, kʰla͜enə 'kʰɪrçəndax. aːbɐ lax!
Von des Vollmonds Widerscheine blitzet das bemooste, kleine Kirchendach. Aber ach!
From the full moon's reflection flashes the mossy little church roof. But ah!
(The moss-covered little roof of the church sparkles as it reflects the full moon's light. But ah!)

rɪŋs'ʊm 'dɛk‘ən 'la͜eçənʃt‘a͜enə deːr lɛnt‘'ʃlʊmɐt‘ən gə'ba͜en.
ringsum decken Leichensteine der Entschlummerten Gebein.
all around cover grave-stones the sleepers' bones.
(all around grave-stones are covering the remains of those who have passed away.)
          [*poem:* **ringsum decken kühle** ('kʰyːlə, cool) **Steine... Gebeine**]

ruːt‘, loː 'tʰrɑ͜ʊt‘ə! fɔn den 'veːən, bɪs ba͜em 'groːsən 'ɑ͜ʊfleʃt‘eːən lɑ͜ʊs deːɐ naxt‘
Ruht, o Traute! von den Wehen, bis beim grossen Auferstehen aus der Nacht
Rest, O dear one! from the pains, until at the great resurrection out of the night,
(Rest, O dear one, from the pains of life, until, at the great resurrection, out of the night,)

'gɔt'əs maxt' |aenst' |ʊns ruːft', |ɪn 'zaenɐ 'høːən 'leːvgə 'vɔnən |aentsugeːən.
Gottes Macht einst uns ruft, in seiner Höhen ewge Wonnen einzugehen.
God's might one day us calls, into His heights' eternal blisses in togo.
(God's might calls us one day to enter into the eternal bliss of His empyrean heights.)

[*Philomela, the daughter of a king of Athens in Greek mythology, was transformed into a nightingale by the gods to save her from a violent death. Her name has become a poetic synonym for nightingale.]

'aːbənt'liːt' / deːɐ̯ moːnt' |ɪst' '|ɑofgə'gaŋən
Abendlied / Der Mond ist aufgegangen
Evening Song / The Moon Has Risen

Posthumously published [composed in 1816] (poem by Matthias Claudius)

deːɐ̯ moːnt' |ɪst' 'lɑofgə'gaŋən; di 'gɔldnən 'ʃt'ɛrnlaen 'praŋən
Der Mond ist aufgegangen; die goldnen Sternlein prangen
The moon has risen; the golden little stars glitter

|am 'hɪməl hɛl |ʊnt' kʰlaːɐ̯; deːɐ̯ valt' ʃt'eːt' ʃvarts |ʊnt' 'ʃvaegət',
am Himmel hell und klar; Der Wald steht schwarz und schweiget,
in the sky brightly and clearly; the forest stands black and is silent,

|ʊnt' |ɑos den 'viːzən 'ʃt'aegət deːɐ̯ 'vaesə 'neːbəl 'vʊndɐbaːɐ̯.
und aus den Wiesen steiget der weisse Nebel wunderbar.
and from the meadows rises the white mist wondrously.

viː |ɪst di vɛlt' zoː 'ʃt'ɪlə, |ʊnt' |ɪn deːɐ̯ 'dɛmrʊŋ 'hʏlə zoː 't̯ʰrɑoliç |ʊnt' zoː hɔlt'!
Wie ist die Welt so stille, und in der Dämmrung Hülle so traulich und so hold!
How is the world so quiet, and in the twilight's cover so homelike and so lovely!
(How quiet the world is, and under the mantle of twilight how homelike and how lovely,)

als 'laenə 'ʃt'ɪlə 'kamɐ, voː liːɐ̯ des 't̯ʰaːgəs 'jamɐ fɛɐ̯'ʃlaːfən |ʊnt' fɛɐ̯'gɛsən zɔltʰ.
als eine stille Kammer, wo ihr des Tages Jammer verschlafen und vergessen sollt.
like a quiet chamber, where you the day's distress sleep away and forget shall.
(like a quiet bedroom where you can sleep away and forget the distress of the day.)

zeːt' liːɐ̯ den moːnt' dɔrt' 'ʃt'eːən? |eːr |ɪst' nuːɐ̯ halp' t̯su 'zeːən,
Seht ihr den Mond dort stehen? er ist nur halb zu sehen,
See you the moon there stand? It is only half to be seen,
(Do you see the moon there? It appears as a half-moon,)

|ʊnt' |ɪst' dɔx rʊnt' |ʊnt' ʃøːn! zoː zɪnt' voːl 'mançə 'zaxən,
und ist doch rund und schön! so sind wohl manche Sachen,
and is yet round and beautiful! So are indeed many things
(and yet the moon itself is round, and beautiful! So are indeed many things)

di: viːɐ̯ gə't̯ʰroːst' bə'laxən, vael 'lʊnzrə 'lɑogən ziː nɪçt' zeːn.
die wir getrost belachen, weil unsre Augen sie nicht sehn.
which we confidently laugh at, because our eyes them not see.
(which we confidently laugh at, because our eyes do not see them as they really are.).

viːɐ̯ ˈʃtˈɔltsə ˈmɛnʃənkʰɪndɐ   zɪnt ˈlaɛtˈəl ˈlarmə ˈzʏndɐ, lʊnt ˈvɪsən gaːɐ̯ nɪçt fiːl.
Wir stolze Menschenkinder sind eitel   arme Sünder, und wissen gar   nicht viel.
We proud human beings   are merely poor sinners and know at all not   much.
(We proud human beings are merely poor sinners and do not know very much at all.)

viːɐ̯ ˈʃpˈɪnən ˈlʊftˈgəʃpˈɪnstˈə lʊnt ˈzuːxən ˈfiːlə ˈkʰʏnstˈə, lʊnt ˈkʰɔmən ˈvaɛtˈɐ fɔn dem tsiːl.
Wir spinnen Luftgespinnste und suchen viele Künste, und kommen weiter von dem Ziel.
We spin   air-webs   and seek   many arts,   and come   farther from the goal.
(We spin webs made of air and seek out many arts, and yet we only end up farther than ever from our goal.)

gɔt, las daɛn haɛl   lʊns ˈʃaɒən, lɑɒf nɪçts fɛɐ̯ˈgɛŋlɪçs ˈtʰrɑɒən,
Gott, lass dein Heil   uns schauen, auf nichts vergänglich's trauen,
God, let Thy salvation us behold, in nothing ephemeral   trust,
(God, let us behold Thy salvation, let us put our trust in nothing ephemeral,)

[poem: Gott, lass uns d e i n Heil schauen]

nɪçt ˈlaɛtˈəlkʰaɛtˈ lʊns frɔø̯n! las lʊns ˈlaɛnfɛltˈɪç ˈveːɐ̯dən,
nicht Eitelkeit   uns freun! lass uns einfältig   werden,
not vanity   us gladden! Let us simple   become,
(let us not take pleasure in vanity! Let us become simple,)

lʊntˈ foːɐ̯ diːɐ̯ hiːɐ̯/hiːr lɑɒf ˈleːɐ̯dən viː ˈkʰɪndɐ frɔm lʊntˈ ˈfrøːlɪç zaɛn!
und vor   dir hier   auf Erden wie Kinder fromm und fröhlich sein!
and before Thee here   on earth   like children devout and cheerful be!
(and before Thee here on earth be as innocent and cheerful as children!)

[This song is a gentle meditation on God and man, inspired by the beauty of a quiet evening.]

ˈaːbəntˈliːtˈ / groːs lʊntˈ ˈroːtˈlɛntˈflamətˈ
Abendlied / Gross und rotentflammet
Evening Song / Large and Flaming Red

Posthumously published [composed 1815] (poem by Friedrich Leopold, Graf zu Stolberg)

groːs lʊntˈ ˈroːtˈlɛntˈflamətˈ ˈʃveːbət nɔx di ʒɔn lam ˈhɪməlsrant,
Gross und rotentflammet schwebet noch die Sonn' am   Himmelsrand,
Large and red-inflamed   hovers   still the sun   at the heaven's rim,
(Large and flaming red the sun is still hovering at heaven's rim,)

ʊntˈ lɑɒf ˈblɑɒən ˈvoːgən ˈbeːbət nɔx liːɐ̯/liːr ˈlapˈglants   bɪs tsʊm ʃtˈrant;
und auf blauen Wogen bebet   noch ihr Abglanz   bis zum Strand;
and on blue   waves trembles still its   reflected splendor until to the shore;
(and its reflected splendor still trembles on blue waves as far as the shore;)

ɑɒs dem ˈbuːxənvaldə ˈheːbət zɪç deːɐ̯ moːntˈ, lʊntˈ ˈvɪŋkˈətˈ ruː ˈzaɛnɐ ˈʃvɛstˈɐ/ʃvɛstˈɐr
aus dem Buchenwalde hebet sich der Mond, und winket Ruh seiner Schwester
out of the beech   woods raises itself the moon, and signals rest its   sister
(the moon rises out of the beech woods and signals rest to its sister,)

ˈleːɐ̯də tsuː. ɪn ɡəˈʃvɔlnən ˈvɔlkən ˈbalət ˈdʊŋkˈlɐ zɪç di ˈroːtˈə ɡluːtʰ,
Erde zu. In geschwollnen Wolken ballet dunkler sich die rote Glut,
Earth to. In swollen clouds bunches darker itself the red glow,
(the Earth. In swollen clouds the red glow contracts and grows darker,)

ˈtsartˈɐ ˈfarbənvɛksəl ˈvalət lɑ̯ɔf deːɐ̯ ˈrɔɡənblyːtˈə fluːtʰ;
zarter Farbenwechsel wallet auf der Roggenblüte Flut;
delicate color- changing undulates on the rye- blossom flood;
(a succession of delicate colors undulates upon the flood of blossoming rye;)

ˈtsvɪʃən ˈʃvaŋkˈən ˈhalmən ˈʃalət ˈreːɡɐ ˈvaxtˈəln ˈhɛlɐ ˈʃlaːkˈ, ʊnt deːɐ̯ ˈhɪrtˈə
zwischen schwanken Halmen schallet reger Wachteln heller Schlag, und der Hirte
among supple stalks sounds lively quails' bright song, and the shepherd
(the bright song of lively quails sounds from among supple stalks, and the shepherd)

p̯faɛ̯ftˈ liːm naːx. ˈvoːlɡərʊx ɛntˈʃtˈaɛ̯kˈt den ˈlɑ̯ɔən dɔrtˈ ɪn ˈtsaːɐ̯(r)tˈɡəvʊndnəm
pfeift ihm nach. Wohlgeruch entsteigt den Auen dort in zartgewundnem
pipes it after. Pleasant fragrance rises from the meadows there in delicately spiralling
(imitates it on his pipe. Pleasant fragrance rises from the meadows there in delicately spiralling)

dʊftʰ, lʊnt di ˈjʏŋstˈən ˈʃtˈɑ̯ɔdən ˈtʰɑ̯ɔən ˈkʰyːləs ˈlaːpzaːl dʊrç di lʊftʰ;
Duft und die jüngsten Stauden tauen kühles Labsal durch die Luft;
perfume and the youngest shrubs dew cool refreshment through the air;
(perfume, and dew dropping from the youngest shrubs spreads cool refreshment through the air;)

ˈjeːdəs ˈblyːmçən zɑ̯ɔkˈtˈ mɪtˈ ˈlɑ̯ɔən ˈlɪpˈən, lʊnt das ˈɡrɛːsçən zɪŋkˈtˈ
jedes Blümchen saugt mit lauen Lippen, und das Gräschen sinkt
each little flower sucks with warm lips, and the little grass sinks
(each little flower sucks up that cool refreshment with warm lips, and the grass droops)

ˈʊntˈɐ ˈpʰɛrlən, diː lɛs tʰrɪŋkˈtʰ.
unter Perlen, die es trinkt.
beneath pearls which it drinks.
(beneath the weight of the liquid pearls that it is drinking.)

ˈiːrə ˈrɪŋəltʰɑ̯ɔbən ˈɡɪrən nɔx di ˈtʰɔ̯øbɐ zanftˈ lɪn ruː, ˈdyːstˈrə ˈfleːdɐmɔ̯øzə
Ihre Ringeltauben girren noch die Täuber sanft in Ruh, düstre Fledermäuse
Their ring- doves coo still the cock pigeons gently into rest, dark bats
(The cock pigeons are still cooing their ring-doves gently to sleep, dark bats)

ˈʃvɪrən nuːn dem ˈɡlatˈən ˈtʰaɛ̯çə tsuː, ʊnt deːɐ̯ ˈkʰɛːfɐ ˈʃaːrən ˈlɪrən,
schwirren nun dem glatten Teiche zu, und der Käfer Scharen irren,
whir now the smooth pond toward, and the beetles' troops go astray,
(are now whirring toward the smooth pond, and troops of beetles stray about,)

lʊnt deːɐ̯/deːr ˈluːhu, nuːn lɛɐ̯ˈvaxtʰ, ˈtsiːətˈ ˈhɔ̯øləntˈ lɑ̯ɔf di vaxtʰ.
und der Uhu, nun erwacht, ziehet heulend auf die Wacht.
and the owl, now awakened, goes hooting onto the watch.
(and the owl, now awakened, hooting, goes on guard-duty.)

mɪt dem ˈkʰœpfçən lɪm ɡəˈfiːdɐ, ˈʃlʊmɐn ˈlʊnzrə ˈzɛŋɐ nuːn,
Mit dem Köpfchen im Gefieder, schlummern unsre Sänger nun,
With the little head in the feathers, sleep our singers now,
(With their little heads tucked under their wings, our songbirds are now asleep,)

8

ɛs fɛɐ̯ˈʃtʼʊmən ˈliːrə ˈliːdɐ, zɛlpst di ˈlɑʊtʼən ˈʃtʼaːrə ruːn
es verstummen ihre Lieder, selbst die lauten Stare   ruhn
it   become silent their songs, even the loud   starlings rest
(their songs have become silent, even the loud starlings are resting)

ɑʊf den ˈʃvaŋkʼən ˈbɪnzən ˈviːdɐ, nuːɐ̯ di ˈnaxtʼɪgal laˈlaen froø̯tʼ zɪç nɔx
auf den schwanken Binsen wieder, nur die Nachtigall allein freut   sich noch
on the supple   rushes again, only the nightingale alone delights itself still
(on supple rushes again; only the nightingale still takes delight)

ɪm ˈmoːndənʃaen. viː, lɑʊx ɪn deːɐ̯ ˈʃtʼɪlə ˈreːgə, mɪt dem ˈlanbəgɪn deːɐ̯ naxtʰ,
im   Mondenschein. Wie, auch in der Stille rege, mit dem Anbeginn der Nacht,
in the moonlight.   How, even in the quiet alert, with the beginning of the night,
(in the moonlight. How, alert even in the quiet, at the very beginning of the night,)

naːx deːɐ̯ ˈmanɪçfaltʼgən ˈpfleːgə, nuːn di ˈmʊtʼɐ lɪstʼ bəˈdaxtʰ,
nach der mannigfalt'gen Pflege, nun die Mutter ist bedacht,
after the manifold   care,   now the mother is mindful,
(after the many things she must take care of, —how attentive now the mother is,)

das ziː ˈliːrə ˈkʰɪntʼlaen ˈleːgə;   viː ziː ˈjeːdəs   ˈlɛtstʼən gruːs nɔx bəˈloːntʼ
dass sie ihre Kindlein   lege;   wie sie Jedes   letzten Gruss noch belohnt
that she her little children lay down; how she each one's last greeting still rewards
(as she lays her little children into their beds; how she again rewards each one's last "good night")

mɪtʼ ˈvaeçəm kʰʊs; ˈalzo, naːx dɛs tʰaːks gəˈtʰʏməl ʃɑʊt deːr ˈleːvgən ˈliːbə blɪkʰ
mit weichem Kuss; also, nach des Tags Getümmel schaut der ew'gen Liebe Blick
with soft   kiss; thus, after the day's bustle   looks the eternal love's gaze
(with a soft kiss; thus, after the bustle of the day, the gaze of Eternal Love looks)

dʊrç den ˈʃtʼɛrnənfɔlən ˈhɪməl lɑʊf di ˈleːɐ̯də nɔx tsuˈrʏkʰ; fryː
durch den sternenvollen Himmel auf die Erde noch zurück; früh
through the star- full   heaven onto the earth still back; early
(through the star-filled heavens back to the earth again; in the early morning)

fɛɐ̯ˈnɪmtʼ ziː   das gəˈvɪməl deːɐ̯/deːr lɛɐ̯ˈvaxtʼən ˈleːɐ̯tʼ, lʊntʼ ʃpʼɛːtʼ
vernimmt sie   das Gewimmel der   erwachten Erd', und spät
perceives it (Eternal Love) the swarming of the awakened earth, and late
(Eternal Love perceives the swarming of the awakened earth, and at the end of the day)

høːɐ̯tʼ ziː   deːn, deːɐ̯/deːr ˈlaenzaːm fleːtʰ.   vɛn di ˈnaxtʼɪgalən
hört sie   den, der   einsam fleht.   Wenn die Nachtigallen
hears it (Eternal Love) him, who   in solitude supplicates. When the nightingales
(hears the one who prays in solitude. When the nightingales)

ˈfløːtʼən, ˈheːbə dɪç,   maen gaestʼ, lɛmˈpʰoːɐ̯! bae dɛs ˈjʊŋən tʰaːks lɛɐ̯ˈrøːtʼən
flöten, hebe dich,   mein Geist, empor! Bei des jungen Tags Erröten
warble, lift yourself, my spirit, up!   At the young day's reddening
(are warbling, lift yourself up, my spirit! At the dawning of each new day,)

naekʼ, loː ˈvaːtʼɐ, miːɐ̯ daen loːɐ̯! fɔn deːɐ̯/deːr leːɐ̯tʼ lʊntʼ ˈliːrən ˈnøːtʼən
neig', o Vater, mir dein Ohr! Von der   Erd' und ihren Nöten
bend, O Father, to me your ear! From the   earth and its troubles
(bend your ear to me, O Father! From the earth and its troubles)

ʃt'aek', loː gaest'! viː dʊft   deːɐ̯/deːr lao,   zent'/zɛnd lʊns, 'vaːt'ɐ, 'daenən tʰao!
steig', o Geist! Wie Duft   der   Au,   send'   uns, Vater, deinen Tau!
rise,   O spirit! Like fragrance of the   meadow send   to us, Father, your   dew!
(rise up, O my spirit! Like the fragrance of the meadow, Father, send us Thy dew!))

[This musically simple strophic song is one of the seven poems by Stolberg that Schubert set.]

'aːbənt'liːt' / zanft' glɛntst di 'laːbənt'zɔnə
Abendlied / Sanft glänzt die Abendsonne
Evening Song / Gently Gleams the Evening Sun

Posthumously published [composed 1816] (poet unknown)

zanft' glɛntst di 'laːbənt'zɔnə laof 'diːzə 'ʃt'ɪlə fluːɐ̯
Sanft glänzt die Abendsonne auf diese stille Flur
Gently gleams the evening-sun onto this quiet meadow
(The evening sun sheds its light gently onto this quiet meadow)

ʊnt' 'ʃt'raːlət' ruː   lʊnt' 'vɔnə   laof 'jeːdə kʰrea'tuːɐ̯.
und strahlet Ruh und Wonne auf jede Kreatur.
and beams   peace and   bliss   upon every living creature.

ziː 'tsaeçnət lɪçt' lʊnt' 'ʃat'ən   laof di bə'blyːmt'ə lao,
Sie zeichnet Licht und Schatten auf die beblümte Au,
It delineates light and shadow on the flowered   pasture,

ʊnt' laof den 'gryːnən 'mat'ən   blɪtst   deːɐ̯ k'rɪst'ʰalnə tʰao.
und auf den grünen Matten blitzt   der kristallne Tau.
and on the green   meadows sparkles the crystal   dew.
(and the crystal dew sparkles on the green meadows.)

hiːr lɪn deːɐ̯ 'tseːfyːɐ̯n ['tseːfiːɐ̯n] 'ʃp'iːlə baem 'froːən 'foːgəlkʰoːɐ̯,
Hier in der Zephyrn [Zephirn] Spiele beim frohen Vogelchor,
Here in the zephyrs'   games to the happy chorus of birds,
                    ["*Zephyr*" is an older, more classical form of "*Zephir*"]

hiːɐ̯ 'ʃt'aegən 'hoːxgəfyːlə lɪn 'maenɐ brʊst' lɛm'pʰoːɐ̯.
hier steigen Hochgefühle in meiner Brust empor.
here rise   high feelings in my   breast upwards.
(here sublime feelings rise up in my breast.)

ɪç 'laːt'mə 'zyːsə 'frɔødən laof 'diːzəm 'tʰɛmp'ə laen,
Ich atme   süsse Freuden auf diesem Tempe ein,
I breathe sweet joys   on this   Tempe in,
(I inhale sweet feelings of joy in this Vale of Tempe,)
          [The "Vale of Tempe" is a beautiful valley in Thessaly, Greece, sacred to Apollo]

mɪç 'fliːən   graːm lʊnt' 'laedən lɪm   'mɪldən 'laːbənt'ʃaen.
mich fliehen Gram und Leiden im   milden Abendschein.
me flee   grief and sorrows in the mild   evening-shine.
(grief and sorrow flee from me in the mild sunset glow.)

10

diːɐ̯, deːɐ̯ di ˈlaːbənt'rø:t'ə lam ˈhɪməl ˈl̥aosɡəʃpantʰ
Dir, der die Abendröte am Himmel ausgespannt
To You, who the sunset in the sky spread out
(To You, who have spread out the sunset across the sky)

ʊnt' ˈzyːsəs ˈnaxt'ɡəflø:t'ə l̥aof 'diːzə fluːɐ̯ ɡəˈzantʰ,
und süsses Nachtgeflöte auf diese Flur gesandt,
and sweet night-fluting onto this meadow sent,
(and sent sweet flute-like sounds at night onto this meadow,)

diːɐ̯ zae diːs hɛrts ɡəˈvaeət, das 'raenɐ daŋk' dʊrçˈɡlyːtʰ,
dir sei dies Herz geweihet, das reiner Dank durchglüht,
to You be this heart consecrated, which with pure gratitude through-glows,
(to You may this heart be consecrated, which glows through and through with pure gratitude,)

ɛs ˈʃlaːɡə nɔx lɛɐ̯ˈfrɔøət', vɛn l̥aenst das 'leːbən fliːtʰ.
es schlage noch erfreuet, wenn einst das Leben flieht.
it beat still gladdened, when someday the life flees.
(and may it beat still gladdened, when someday life will flee.)

[This musically unpretentious but pretty strophic song expresses the unacknowledged poet's gratitude to God for the happy feelings inspired by the loveliness of a sunset.]

ˈaːbənt'liːt deːɐ̯ ˈfyrst'ɪn
Abendlied der Fürstin
Evening Song of the Princess

Posthumously published [composed 1816] (poem by Johann Mayrhofer)

deːɐ̯ ˈlaːbənt' ˈrø:t'ət' nuːn das tʰaːl, mɪlt' ˈʃɪmɐt ˈhɛsp'erʊs,
Der Abend rötet nun das Tal, mild schimmert Hesperus,
The evening reddens now the valley, gently shimmers Hesperus,
(The red of sunset is now coloring the valley, Hesperus, the evening star, is gently shimmering,)

di 'buːxən ˈʃt'eːən ʃt'ɪl tsuˈmaːl lʊnt' ˈlaezɐ raoʃt deːɐ̯ flʊs.
die Buchen stehen still zumal und leiser rauscht der Fluss.
the beech trees stand still especially and more softly murmurs the river.
(the beech trees stand especially still and the river murmurs more softly.)

di 'vɔlk'ən 'zeːɡəln 'ɡɔlt'bəzɔømt' lam 'kʰlaːrən fɪrmaˈmɛntʰ;
Die Wolken segeln goldbesäumt am klaren Firmament;
The clouds sail gold-bordered in the clear firmament;

das hɛrts, lɛs ʃvɛlk't, das hɛrts, lɛs tʰrɔømt' fɔn 'eːɐ̯dəŋkʰvaːl ɡəˈtʰrɛntʰ.
das Herz, es schwelgt, das Herz, es träumt von Erdenqual getrennt.
the heart, it revels, the heart, it dreams from earthly pain severed.
(the heart revels; severed from any sense of earthly pain, the heart dreams.)

am 'ɡryːnən 'hyːɡəl 'hɪŋɡəʃt'rɛk't' ʃlɛːft' voːl deːɐ̯ 'jɛːɡɐ(r) laen.
Am grünen Hügel hingestreckt schläft wohl der Jäger ein.
On the green hill stretched out falls asleep perhaps the huntsman -- .
(Stretched out on the green hillside, the huntsman has perhaps fallen asleep.)

["*einschlafen*" = to fall asleep; *original poem:* **Auf grünem... schläft sanft** (gently)]

dɔx ˈpʰlœʦlɪç liːn deːɐ̯ ˈdɔnɐ vɛkˈtʰ, ʊntˈ ˈblɪʦə ˈʦɪʃən drae̯n.
Doch plötzlich ihn der Donner weckt, und Blitze zischen drein.
But suddenly him the thunder wakes, and lightnings hiss inside it.
(But suddenly thunder wakes him, and lightning flashes make a hissing sound.)

voː bɪst duː, ˈhae̯lɪç ˈlaːbəntˈroːtˈ, voː ˈzanftˈɐ ˈhɛspˈerʊs?
Wo bist du, heilig Abendrot, wo sanfter Hesperus?
Where are you, holy sunset? Where, gentle Hesperus?

zoː ˈvandəlt dɛn lɪn ʃmɛrʦ ʊntˈ noːtˈ zɪç ˈjeːkˈlɪçɐ gəˈnʊs.
So wandelt denn in Schmerz und Not sich jeglicher Genuss.
Thus transforms then in pain and distress itself every pleasure.
(Thus every pleasure is transformed into pain and distress.)

[*original poem:* **Es wandelt sich... ein jeglicher Genuss**]

[A rather pessimistic poem! The pastoral 6-8 melody of Schubert's setting is interrupted by a brief musical thunderstorm in the middle section. The text changes are by Schubert himself.]

ˈaːbəntˈliːtˈ fyːɐ̯ di lɛntˈˈfɛrntˈə
Abendlied für die Entfernte
Evening Song for the Distant One

Op. 88 [1825] (August Wilhelm Schlegel)

hɪˈnao̯s, mae̯n blɪkˈ! hɪˈnao̯s lɪns tʰaːl! daː voːntˈ nɔx ˈleːbənsfʏlə;
Hinaus, mein Blick! hinaus ins Tal! da wohnt noch Lebensfülle;
Outward, my gaze! out into the valley! there dwells still life's abundance;

daː ˈlaːbə dɪç lɪm ˈmoːndənʃtˈraːl ʊntˈ lan deːɐ̯ ˈhae̯lgən ˈʃtˈɪlə.
da labe dich im Mondenstrahl und an der heilgen Stille.
there refresh yourself in the moon-ray and at the holy stillness.
(there refresh yourself in a ray of moonlight and with the holy stillness.)

daː hɔrç nuːn ˈlʊngəʃtˈøːɐ̯tˈ, mae̯n hɛrʦ, daː hɔrç den ˈlae̯zən ˈkʰlɛŋən,
Da horch nun ungestört, mein Herz, da horch den leisen Klängen,
There listen now undisturbed, my heart, there listen to the soft sounds,

diː, viː fɔn fɛrn, ʦuː vɔn lʊntˈ ʃmɛrʦ, zɪç diːɐ̯/diːr lɛntˈˈge̯gən ˈdrɛŋən.
die, wie von fern, zu Wonn und Schmerz, sich dir entgegen drängen.
which, as if from afar, to rapture and pain, themselves you toward press.
(which, as if from afar, hurry toward you, inspiring feelings of rapture and pain.)

ziː ˈdrɛŋən zɪç zoː ˈvʊndɐbaːɐ̯, ziː ˈreːgən lal mae̯n ˈzeːnən.
Sie drängen sich so wunderbar, sie regen all mein Sehnen.
They urge themselves so wondrously, they stir all my yearning.

oː zaːkˈ miːɐ̯/miːr ˈlaːnʊn, bɪst du vaːɐ̯? bɪst duː lae̯n ˈlae̯tˈləs ˈveːnən?
O sag mir, Ahnung, bist du wahr? bist du ein eitles Wähnen?
O tell me, presentiment, are you true? are you an idle fancy?

vɪrtˈ lae̯nstˈ mae̯n lao̯kˈ lɪn ˈhɛlɐ lʊstˈ, viː jɛʦtˈ lɪn ˈtʰreːnən, ˈlɛçəln?
Wird einst mein Aug in heller Lust, wie jetzt in Tränen, lächeln?
Will one day my eye in bright pleasure, as now in tears, smile?

vɪrt' ḁenst di lɔft' lɛm'pʰøːɐ̯t'ə brʊstʰ miːɐ̯ 'zeːlgə ruː lʊm'fɛçəln?
Wird einst die oft empörte Brust mir selge Ruh umfächeln?
Will one day the often indignant breast for me blessed peace around fan?
(Will my often indignant breast one day fan around me an air of blessed peace?)

vɛn 'laːnʊŋ lʊnt' lɛr'lɪnɐʊŋ/lɛɐ̯'lɪnɐʊŋ foːɐ̯/foːr 'ʊnzɐm blɪk' zɪç 'gat'ən,
Wenn Ahnung und Erinnerung vor unserm Blick sich gatten,
When presentiment and memory before our gaze themselves unite,
(When presentiment and memory unite themselves before our gaze,)

dan 'mɪldɐt' zɪç ts̻ʊr 'dɛmɐʊŋ deːɐ̯ 'zeːlə 't'iːfst'ɐ 'ʃat'ən.
dann mildert sich zur Dämmerung der Seele tiefster Schatten.
then mitigates itself to the twilight the soul's deepest shadow.
(then the soul's deepest darkness becomes mitigated to twilight.)

ax, 'dʏrft'ən viːɐ̯ mɪt 't'ʰrɔɣ̞mən nɪçt di 'vɪrk'lɪçkʰḁet' fɛɐ̯'veːbən,
Ach, dürften wir mit Träumen nicht die Wirklichkeit verweben,
Ah, were allowed we with dreams not the reality to interweave,
(Ah, if we were not allowed to entwine reality with dreams,)

viː larm lan 'farbə, glants̻ lʊnt' lɪçt' veːɐ̯st duː, o 'mɛnʃənleːbən!
wie arm an Farbe, Glanz und Licht wärst du, o Menschenleben!
how poor in color, radiance, and light would be you, O human life!
(how poor in color, radiance, and light you would be, O human life!)

[*original poem:* **wärst dann** (dan, then) **du Menschenleben**]

zoː 'hɔfət 't'ʰrɔɣ̞lɪç lʊnt' bə'hart das hɛrts̻ bɪs hɪn ts̻ʊm 'graːbə;
So hoffet treulich und beharrt das Herz bis hin zum Grabe;
So hopes faithfully and steadfastly the heart until onward to the grave;
(So the heart hopes faithfully and steadfastly as long as we live;)

mɪt' liːp' lʊm'fasts̻ di 'geːgənvart', lʊnt dʏŋk't' zɪç rḁeç lan 'haːbə.
mit Lieb umfasst's die Gegenwart, und dünkt sich reich an Habe.
with love clasps it the present time, and thinks itself rich in possessions.
(with love it clasps the present time, and thinks itself rich in possessions.)

di 'haːbə, diː lɛs zɛlpst' zɪç ʃaft', maːk' liːm kʰḁen 'ʃɪk'zaːl 'rɑo̯bən;
Die Habe, die es selbst sich schafft, mag ihm kein Schicksal rauben;
The possessions which it itself for itself creates may from it no fate steal;
(May no fate steal from the heart those possessions which it has created for itself by itself;)

lɛs leːp't' lʊnt' veːp't' lɪn verm lʊnt' kʰraftʰ. dʊrç 'ts̻uːfɛɐ̯zɪçt' lʊnt' 'glɑo̯bən.
es lebt und webt in Wärm und Kraft, durch Zuversicht und Glauben.
it lives and weaves in warmth and strength, through trust and faith.
 [*"lebt und webt"* = is full of life, is full of activity]

ʊnt' veːɐ̯/veːr lɪn naxt' lʊnt' 'neːbəldampf lɑo̯x 'laləs rɪŋs lɛɐ̯'ʃt'ɔrbən,
Und wär in Nacht und Nebeldampf auch alles rings erstorben,
And were in night and mist- vapor even everything all around died away,
(And even if everything all around were to die away in a misty night,)

diːs hɛrts hatˈ lɛŋstˈ   fyːɐ̯ ˈjeːdən kʰampf zɪç   ˈlaenən ʃiltˈ lɛɐ̯ˈvɔrbən.
dies Herz hat längst   für jeden Kampf sich   einen Schild erworben.
this heart has long since for any   battle for itself a   shield gained.
(this heart has long since gained for itself a shield that will serve in any battle.)

mɪtˈ ˈhoːəm tʰrɔts   ɪm ˈlʊngəˈmax tʰrɛːkˈtˈ lɛs vas liːm bəˈʃiːdən.
Mit hohem Trotz   im Ungemach trägt   es, was ihm beschieden.
With high defiance in the hardship bears it what to it (was) allotted.
(With high fearlessness in hardship it bears whatever has been allotted to it.)

zoː ˈʃlʊm   rɪç laen, zoː veːɐ̯d lɪç vax, ɪn lʊstˈ nɪçtʰ, dɔx ɪn ˈfriːdən.
So schlummr' ich ein, so werd   ich wach, in Lust   nicht, doch in Frieden.
So fall asleep I ... , so become I awake, in pleasure not, yet in peace.
(In that way I fall asleep, in that way I awake, not in pleasure, perhaps, but still at peace.)

[Again a meditation upon the mysteries of the human soul is inspired by the stillness and beauty of an evening alone out in nature. Schubert omitted one stanza of the poem (the third of six).]

ˈaːbəntˈrøːtˈə
Abendröte
Sunset

Posthumously published [composed in 1823] (poem by Friedrich von Schlegel)

tʰiːfɐ zɪŋkˈətˈ ʃoːn di ˈzɔnə, lʊntˈ lɛs ˈlaːtˈmət ˈlaləs   ˈruːə,
Tiefer sinket schon die Sonne, und es atmet alles Ruhe,
Deeper sinks already the sun, and there breathes everything tranquillity,
(The sun is sinking deeper already, and everything breathes an air of tranquillity,)

tʰaːgəs   ˈlarbaetˈ lɪstˈ fɔlˈlɛndətʰ, lʊnt̩ di ˈkʰɪndɐ ˈʃertsən ˈmʊntˈɐ.
Tages Arbeit ist vollendet, und die Kinder scherzen munter.
(the) day's work is completed, and the children are joking merrily.

gryːnɐ glɛntst di ˈgryːnə ˈleːɐ̯də, leː di ˈzɔnə gants fɛɐ̯ˈzʊŋkˈən;
Grüner glänzt die grüne Erde, eh die Sonne ganz versunken;
Greener glistens the green earth, before the sun (has) entirely sunk;
(The green earth glistens greener before the sun has entirely set;)

ˈmɪldən ˈbalzaːm ˈhɑoxən   ˈlaezə ɪn di ˈlʏftˈə nuːn di ˈbluːmən,
milden Balsam hauchen leise in die Lüfte nun die Blumen,
mild balm breathe out quietly into the breezes now the flowers,
(the flowers are now quietly breathing out a mild balm into the breezes,)

deːɐ̯ di ˈzeːlə tsartˈ   bəˈryːrətˈ, vɛn di ˈzɪnə ˈzeːlɪç tʰrʊŋkˈən.
der die Seele zart   berühret, wenn die Sinne selig trunken.
which the soul delicately touches, when the senses blissfully (are) intoxicated.
(which delicately touches the soul when one's senses are blissfully intoxicated.)

ˈkʰlaenə ˈføːgəl, ˈfɛrnə ˈmɛnʃən, ˈbɛrgə hɪməlˈlan gəˈʃvʊŋən,
Kleine Vögel, ferne Menschen, Berge himmelan geschwungen,
Little birds, distant people, mountains heavenwards whirled,

14

ʊnt deːɐ̯ ˈɡroːsə ˈzɪlbɐʃtˈroːm, deːɐ̯/deːr ɪm ˈtʰaːlə ʃlaŋk ɡəˈvʊndən,
und der grosse Silberstrom, der   im   Tale   schlank gewunden,
and the   great   silver stream, which   in the valley slender wound,
(and the great silver river, which winds about in the valley in a slender line,)

ˈaləs   ʃaɛntʰ dem ˈdɪçtɐ ˈreːdənt, dɛn leːɐ̯ hat den zɪn ɡəˈfʊndən,
alles   scheint dem Dichter redend, denn er hat den Sinn gefunden,
everything seems to the poet   speaking, for he has the sense found,
(everything seems to be speaking to the poet, for he has found the meaning,)

ʊnt das ʔal,   ʔaɛn ˈʔaɛntsɪç kʰoːɐ̯, ˈmançəs liːtʰ ʔaɔs ˈʔaɛnəm ˈmʊndə.
und das All,   ein einzig Chor, manches Lied aus   einem Munde.
and the universe (seems) one single chorus, many a song out of one   mouth.

[When the senses are drunk with the beauty of a sunset, the soul of the poet is gently stirred, and
it seems to him that all of nature is singing together in one sublime harmony. Note that in the
original German each of the above lines ends in a stress on the dark vowel u (u or ʊ). In the
accompaniment Schubert has illustrated the trills of the birds, the murmur of the balmy breeze,
the majesty of the mountains, and the swirling silvery flow of the river.]

ˈaːbəntʃtˈɛmtˈçən: ʔan ˈliːna
Abendständchen: An Lina
Evening Serenade: To Lina

Posthumously published [composed 1815] (poem by Gabriele von Baumberg)

zaɛ zanftˈ viː ˈliːrə ˈzeːlə, ʊntˈ ˈhaɛtˈɐ viː ˈliːɐ̯ blɪkʰ,
Sei sanft wie ihre Seele, und heiter wie ihr Blick,
Be gentle as her soul, and serene as her gaze,

oː ˈaːbəntˈ, ʊntˈ fɛɐ̯ˈmeːlə mɪtˈ ˈzɛltˈnɐ tʰrɔø   das ɡlʏkʰ.
o Abend, und vermähle mit selt'ner Treu   das Glück.
O evening, and marry   with rare   faithfulness the happiness.
(O evening, and unite happiness with rare faithfulness.)

vɛn ˈaləs ʃleːftˈ. ʊntˈ ˈtʰryːbə di ˈʃtˈɪlə ˈlampˈə ʃaɛntʰ,
Wenn alles schläft, und trübe die stille Lampe scheint,
When all   sleeps, and dimly the silent lamp   is shining,
(When everyone is asleep, and the silent lamp is dimly shining,)

ʊntˈ ˈhɔfnʊŋsloːzə ˈliːbə ɔftˈ ˈhɛlə ˈtʰreːnən vaɛntʰ,   [*poem:* **noch** (nɔx, still) **helle Tränen**]
und hoffnungslose Liebe oft   helle Tränen weint,
and hopeless   love often bright tears   weeps,
(and hopeless love is often weeping bright tears,)

vɪl ɪç, las miːɐ̯s ɡəˈlɪŋən, tsuː ˈliːrəm ˈfɛnstˈɐ ɡeːn,
will ich, lass mir's gelingen, zu ihrem Fenster gehn,
want I,   let to me it succeed, to her   window go,
(I want to go to her window--oh, may my plan succeed!--)

ʔaɛn liːtˈ fɔn ˈliːbə ˈzɪŋən ʊntˈ ˈʃmaxtˈəntˈ   naːx liːɐ̯ zeːn.
ein Lied von Liebe singen und schmachtend nach ihr sehn.
a   song of love   sing   and languishingly for her look.
(and sing a love song and languishingly look for her.)

fiˈlae̯çt,   das ˈkʰlaːɡətʰøːnə fɔn ˈmae̯nəm ˈzae̯tʰənʃpʰiːl
Vielleicht, dass Klagetöne von meinem Saitenspiel
Maybe,   that lament-tones from my   stringed instrument
(It may be that tones of lament from my guitar)

meːɐ̯ ˈvɪrkʰən   ɑo̯f di ˈʃøːnə,   meːɐ̯ ˈrae̯tsən liːɐ̯ ɡəˈfyːl;
mehr wirken   auf die Schöne,   mehr reizen ihr Gefühl;
more have effect upon the beautiful one, more stir up   her emotion;
(will have more effect upon that beautiful woman, will stir her emotion more;)

fiˈlae̯çt,   das ˈmae̯nə ˈzae̯tʰən lʊntʰ ˈmae̯nə fantaˈziːən
vielleicht, dass meine Saiten und meine Phantasien
maybe,   that my   strings and my   fantasies
(it may be that my strumming and my fantasies)

ae̯n hɛrts tsuːɐ̯ ˈliːbə ˈlae̯tʰən, das ˈʊnlɛmpfɪntʰlɪç ʃiːn.
ein Herz zur   Liebe leiten, das unempfindlich schien.
a   heart to the love lead,   that unfeeling   seemed.
(can lead toward love a heart that seemed to be unfeeling.)

vɛn ziː, lɪm ˈzanftʰən ˈʃlʊmɐ   dʊrç ˈliːdɐ ɡɛrn   ɡəˈʃtøːɐ̯tʰ,
Wenn sie, im   sanften Schlummer durch Lieder gern   gestört,
If   she, in the gentle   slumber   through songs willingly disturbed,
(If she, willingly disturbed in her gentle slumber by the sound of songs,)

halpʰˈtʰrɔ̯øməntʰ ˈmae̯nən ˈkʰʊmɐ(r) lʊntʰ ˈmae̯nə ˈlae̯dən høːɐ̯tʰ;
halbträumend meinen Kummer und meine Leiden hört;
half-dreaming   my   grief and   my   sorrows hears;
(half dreaming, hears my grief and my sorrow,)

dan baŋ,   lʊntʰ ˈɪmɐ bɛŋɐ,   fɔn ˈliːrəm ˈlaːɡɐ ʃtʰae̯kʰtʰ,
dann bang,   und immer bänger,   von ihrem Lager steigt,
then anxiously, and ever   more anxiously, from her   couch rises,
(then anxiously, and ever more anxiously, rises from her couch)

ʊntʰ vas leːɐ̯ lɪtʰ, liːɐ̯ ˈzɛŋɐ, zɪç   ˈzɛlbɐ(r) lyːbɐ̯ˈtsɔ̯økʰtʰ:
und was er litt,   ihr Sänger, sich   selber überzeugt:
and what he suffered, her singer, for herself herself to convince:
(and goes herself to see for herself what he, her singer, has suffered:)
                              [*"sich selber/selbst überzeugen"* = to go to see for oneself]

dan lɔ̯øçtʰ lɑo̯s ˈdae̯nɐ ˈhøːə hɛˈrapʰ, ɡəˈliːpʰtʰɐ mɔːntʰ!
dann leucht' aus deiner Höhe herab, geliebter Mond!
then shine   from your   height down, beloved   moon!
(then shine down from your heights, beloved moon,)

das lɪç di ˈtʰrɛːnən ˈzeːə, diː ˈmae̯nən ʃmɛrts bəˈloːntʰ.
dass ich die Tränen sehe, die   meinen Schmerz belohnt.
that I the tears see, which my   pain   (have) rewarded.
(so that I may see the tears that will be the reward for my pain.)

[The melody of this strophic song, composed in 1815, seems to belong to the eighteenth century.
There is a misprint in the voice part: the last note of the second phrase should be c, not b flat.]

'aːbənt' ʃt'ɛrn
Abendstern
Evening Star

Posthumously published [1824] (poem by Johann Mayrhofer)

vas vaelst du 'laenzaːm lan dem 'hɪməl, loː 'ʃøːnɐ   ʃt'ɛrn? lʊnt' bɪst' zoː mɪlt';
Was weilst du einsam   an dem Himmel, o schöner Stern? und bist so mild;
Why linger you lonesome in the sky,   O beautiful star? and are   so mild;
(Why do you linger alone in the sky, O beautiful star, you who are so gentle?)

va'rʊm lɛnt''fɛrnt das 'fʊŋk'əlndə gə'vɪməl deːɐ̯ 'bryːdɐ zɪç fɔn 'daenəm bɪlt'?
warum entfernt das funkelnde Gewimmel der   Brüder sich von deinem Bild?
Why   withdraws the sparkling swarm   of the brothers itself from your   image?
(Why does the sparkling swarm of your brother stars stay away from you?)

 ɪç bɪn deːɐ̯ 'liːbə 'tʰrɔø̯ɐ ʃt'ɛrn, ziː 'halt'ən zɪç   fɔn 'liːbə fɛrn.
"Ich bin der Liebe treuer Stern, sie   halten sich   von Liebe fern."
"I am the love's faithful star,   they hold   themselves from love   far off."
(I am love's faithful star; they keep themselves far off from love.")

zoː 'zɔlt'əst du tsuː 'liːnən 'geːn, bɪst duː deːɐ̯ 'liːbə,   'tsao̯drə nɪətʰ!
So   solltest du zu ihnen gehen, bist du der Liebe,   zaudre nicht!
Then should you to them go,   are you the love(-star), hesitate not!
(Then you should go to them; if you are the star of love, do not hesitate!)

veːɐ̯ 'mœçt'ə dɛn diːɐ̯ viːdɐ̯'ʃt'eːən? duː 'zyːsəs, 'laegənzɪnɪç lɪçtʰ!
Wer möchte denn dir widerstehen? du süsses, eigensinnig Licht!
Who might   then you resist?   you sweet, self-willed   light!
(Who then would want to resist you, you sweet, independent-minded light?)

 ɪç 'zeː, 'ʃɑo̯ə 'kʰaenən kʰaem lʊnt' 'blaebə 'tʰrɑo̯ɐnt' ʃt'ɪl da'haem.
"Ich säe, schaue keinen Keim und bleibe trauernd still   daheim."
"I sow, see   no   bud,   and remain grieving quietly at home."

[This song is a dialogue between the poet and the evening star. Why does it shine all alone in the evening sky, avoided by the other stars, if it is the star of love? The love-star answers with sorrow and bitterness that, although it plants the seeds of love, no buds are seen to be sprouting.]

'aːbənts 'lʊnt'ɐ deːɐ̯ 'lɪndə
Abends unter der Linde
In the Evening under the Linden Tree

Posthumously published [two versions, both composed 1815] (poem by Ludwig Kosegarten)

vo'heːɐ̯/vo'heːr, loː 'naːmənloːsəs 'zeːnən, das den bə'kʰlɛmt'ən 'buːzən prɛstʰ?
Woher,   o namenloses Sehnen, das den beklemmten Busen presst?
Whence,   O nameless   longing, that the uneasy   bosom oppresses?
(Where do you come from, O nameless longing that oppresses the uneasy bosom?)

vo'heːɐ̯/vo'heːr, liːɐ̯ 'bɪt'ɐzyːsən 't^hrɛːnən, diː liːɐ̯ das 'l̩ɑ̯ogə 'dɛmɐnt' nɛst^h?
Woher,   ihr bittersüssen Tränen, die   ihr das Auge dämmernd nässt?
Whence,   you bittersweet tears,   who you the eye   dimmingly moisten?
(Where do you come from, you bittersweet tears, you who moisten and dim the eyes?)

oː 'laːbənt'roːt', loː 'moːndənblɪts,   flɪmt' 'blasɐ(r)   lʊm   den 'lɪndənzɪts!
O Abendrot,   o Mondenblitz,   flimmt blasser   um   den Lindensitz!
O sunset,   O moon- lightning, glimmer more palely around the   linden- seat!

ɛs 'zɔ̯øzəlt' lɪn dem lɑ̯op' deːɐ̯ 'lɪndə; lɛs 'flʏst'ɐt' lɪm   la'k^haːt͡sj̩ənʃt'rɑ̯ox.
Es säuselt in dem Laub der Linde; es flüstert im   Akazienstrauch.
It rustles in the foliage of the linden; it whispers in the acacia bush.
(The foliage of the linden tree is rustling; the acacia bush is whispering.)

miːɐ̯ 'ʃmɑ̯eçəlt' zyːs,   miːɐ̯ 'ʃmɑ̯eçəlt' 'lɪndə dɛs 'grɑ̯oən 'laːbənt͡s 'lɑ̯oɐ hɑ̯ox.
Mir schmeichelt süss,   mir schmeichelt linde des grauen Abends   lauer Hauch.
Me flatters   sweetly, me caresses   gently the grey   evening's warm breath.
(The warm breath of twilight flatters me sweetly, caresses me gently.)

ɛs ʃp'rɪçt' lʊm   mɪç, viː 'gɑ̯aest'ɐgruːs; lɛs veːt' mɪç lan, viː 'lɛŋəlk^hʊs.
Es spricht um   mich, wie Geistergruss;   es weht mich an, wie Engelkuss.
It speaks   around me,   like ghost- greeting; it blows me   at,   like angel-kiss.
(I hear voices around me, speaking a ghostly greeting; I feel someone blow me an angel's kiss.)

ɛs glɛnt͡st', lɛs glɛnt͡st' lɪm 'naxt'gəfɪldə. deːɐ̯ 'lɪndə 'grɑ̯oɐ 'ʃɑ̯et'əl beːp't^h --
Es glänzt, es glänzt im   Nachtgefilde. Der Linde   grauer Scheitel bebt --
It gleams, it gleams in the night-fields. The linden's grey   crown   quivers --
(Something is gleaming in the nocturnal fields; the grey crown of the linden tree is quivering...)

fɛɐ̯k^hleːɐ̯t'ə 'hɪmlɪʃə   gə'bɪldə, zɑ̯et' liːr lɛs, diː liːɐ̯ mɪç lʊm'ʃveːp't^h?
verklärte   himmlische Gebilde, seid ihr es, die ihr mich umschwebt?
transfigured heavenly   creatures, are   you it, who you me   hover about?
(transfigured heavenly creatures, is it you who hover about me?)

lç 'fyːlə 'lɔ̯ørəs 'laːt'əms k^hʊs, loː juːljə! loː le'miːljʊs!
Ich fühle eures Atems Kuss, o Julie! o Emilius!
I   feel   your breath's kiss, O Julia! O Emilius!
(I feel the kiss of your breath, O Julia! O Emilius!)

blɑ̯ep't' 'zeːlgə, blɑ̯ep't' lɪn 'lɔ̯ørəm 'leːdən! dɛs 'leːbəns hɑ̯ox bleːst' ʃveːr lʊnt' ʃvyːl
Bleibt Sel'ge, bleibt in eurem Eden! Des Lebens Hauch bläst schwer und schwül
Stay   blest, stay   in your Eden! The life's   breath blows hard   and sultry
(Stay blest, stay in your Eden! Life's breath blows hard and oppressively)

dʊrç 'ʃt'ʊmə 'lɑ̯eçənfɔlə 'øːdən, le'lyːziʊm lɪst' mɪlt' lʊnt' k^hyːl.
durch stumme leichenvolle Öden. Elysium ist mild und kühl.
through mute   corpse- full wastes. Elysium is   mild and cool.
(through wastes strewn with corpses. Elysium is mild and cool.)

e'lyːziʊm lɪst' 'vɔnəfɔl --   faːɐ̯t' voːl, liːɐ̯ 't^hrɑ̯ot'ən! 'faːrət' voːl!
Elysium ist   wonnevoll -- fahrt wohl, ihr Trauten! fahret wohl!
Elysium is   blissful -- farewell,   you dear ones! farewell!

18

[The poet feels the presence of beloved ghosts in the mysterious twilight. Schubert made two melodically and rhythmically different strophic settings of this poem, on two successive days. The last three lines (after "Öden," above) are as follows in the original poem: *Bei euch nur walten dämmernd Kühl / Und tiefe Ruh. Drum fahret wohl! / Für heut und morgen fahret wohl!*"]

Abschied / Ade! du muntre, du fröhliche Stadt see *Schwanengesang*

'apˈʃiːtˈ, naːx 'laenɐ 'valfaːɐ̯tslaːrjə / lʊnts, 'loːdɐ 'lapˈʃiːtˈ
Abschied, nach einer Wallfahrtsarie / Lunz, oder Abschied
Farewell, after a pilgrimage melody / Lunz, or Farewell

Posthumously published [arranged "after a pilgrimage melody" in 1816]
(poem by Johann Mayrhofer)

'yːbɐ di 'bɛrgə   tsiːtˈ liːɐ̯ fɔrtʰ; kʰɔmtˈ   lan 'mançən 'gryːnən lɔrtʰ,
Über die Berge   zieht ihr fort; kommt   an manchen grünen Ort,
Over the mountains go   you forth; (you) come   to   many   a   green   place,
(You are going away over the mountains; you will come to many a green spot,)

mʊs   tsuˈrʏkˈə gants laˈlaen; 'leːbətˈ voːl! lɛs mʊs zoː zaen.
muss   zurücke ganz allein; lebet wohl! es muss so sein.
(I) must back   all   alone; farewell!   it must so be.
(I must remain behind all alone. Farewell! It must be so.)

'ʃaedən,   'maedən, vas man liːpˈtʰ, lax viː vɪrt   das hɛrts bəˈtʰryːpˈtʰ!
Scheiden, meiden, was man liebt, ach wie wird   das Herz betrübt!
To part,   to avoid what one loves, ah   how becomes the heart troubled!
(To part, not to be near what one loves, ah! how the heart becomes troubled!)

oː 'zeːənʃpˈiːɡəl, valtˈ lʊntˈ 'hyːɡəl 'ʃvɪndən   lal;
O Seenspiegel, Wald und Hügel schwinden all;
O Lake-mirror, forest and hill   disappear   all;
(Oh, the reflections in the lake, forest and hill, all disappear;)

hø̆ːɐ̯   fɛɐ̯ˈʃvɪmən   'lɔ̆ø̆ɐ 'ʃtˈɪmən 'viːdɐhal. 'leːpˈtˈ voːl! kʰlɪŋtˈ 'kʰlaːɡəfɔl.
hör   verschwimmen eurer Stimmen Widerhall. Lebt   wohl! klingt klagevoll.
(I) hear become blurred your   voices'   echo.   Farewell! (it) sounds lamentation-full.
(I hear the echo of your voices become blurred. Farewell!--that word sounds full of lamentation.)

[A feature of this song is the echo, an octave lower, of the four opening and closing phrases. The poem was entitled *Lunz*, after the name of a village in the Vienna Woods. Schubert himself added the line "*Lebt wohl! klingt klagevoll*," and rearranged some of the words.]

'apˈʃiːtˈ fɔn deːɐ 'leːɐ̯də
Abschied von der Erde
Farewell to the Earth

Posthumously published "Melodrama" [1826?] (Adolph Pratobevera, Freiherr von Wiesborn)

leːpˈ voːl, duː 'ʃøːnə   'leːɐ̯də! kʰan dɪç leːɐ̯stˈ jɛtstˈ fɛɐ̯ˈʃtˈeːn,
Leb wohl, du schöne Erde!   Kann dich erst   jetzt verstehn,
Farewell,   you beautiful earth! (I) can   you only   now   understand,
(Farewell, you beautiful earth! Only now can I understand you,)

voː 'frɔødə lʊntʼ voː 'kʰʊmɐ lan lʊns foˈryːbɐ veːn.
wo Freude und wo Kummer an uns vorüber wehn.
where joy and where sorrow to us past blow.
(where joy and where sorrow blow past us.)

leːpʼ voːl, duː 'ma_est'ɐ 'kʰʊmɐ! daŋkʼ diːɐ mɪtʼ 'nasəm blɪkʰ,
Leb wohl, du Meister Kummer! Dank dir mit nassem Blick,
Farewell, you, Master Sorrow! (I) thank you with wet gaze,
(Farewell, Schoolmaster Sorrow! I thank you with moist eyes,)

mɪtʼ miːɐ neːm lɪç di 'frɔødə, dɪç las lɪç hiːɐ tsuˈrʏkʰ.
Mit mir nehm ich die Freude, dich lass ich hier zurück.
With me take I the joy, you leave I here behind.
(I take the joy with me; *you* I leave behind.)

zae nuːɐ laen 'mɪldɐ 'leːrɐ, fyːɐ 'lalə hɪn tsu: gɔtʰ.
Sei nur ein milder Lehrer, führ Alle hin zu Gott.
Be only a gentle teacher, lead all from here to God.
(Just be a gentle teacher, lead everyone toward God.)

tsaekʼ lɪn den 'tʰryːpʼstʼən 'nɛçtʼən laen 'ʃtʼraeflaen 'mɔrgənroːtʰ.
Zeig in den trübsten Nächten ein Streiflein Morgenrot.
Show in the most troubled nights a little streak (of) dawn.

'lasə ziː 'liːbə 'laːnən, zoː 'daŋkʼən ziː diːɐ nɔx,
Lasse sie Liebe ahnen, so danken sie dir noch,
Let them love surmise, so thank they you yet,
(Let them feel a sense of the presence of love; they will thank you for that yet,)

deːɐ 'fryːɐ lʊnt deːɐ 'ʃpʼeːtʼɐ, ziː 'daŋkʼən 'vaenənt dɔx.
der früher und der später, sie danken weinend doch.
this one earlier and that one later, they thank weeping nevertheless.
(this one earlier and that one later, they all will thank you, weeping, nevertheless.)

dan glɛntst das 'leːbən 'haetʼɐ, mɪltʼ 'lɛçəltʼ 'jeːdɐ ʃmɛrts,
Dann glänzt das Leben heiter, mild lächelt jeder Schmerz,
Then sparkles the life serenely, gently smiles every pain,
(Then life will sparkle serenely, every pain will smile gently,)

di 'frɔødə hɛltʼ lʊmˈfaŋən das 'ruːgə 'kʰlaːrə hɛrts!
Die Freude hält umfangen das ruh'ge klare Herz!
The joy holds embraced the peaceful clear heart!
(joy will hold the pure and peaceful heart in its embrace!)

[*Abschied von der Erde* is not a song. It is a "melodrama," that is, a composition in which the speaking voice is accompanied by music. It is Schubert's only effort in that form, which was used very effectively in Beethoven's opera *Fidelio*, and was later exploited by Schumann, Liszt, and Richard Strauss, among others. The poem, a fragment from *Der Falke* ("The Falcon"), a one-act verse play, expresses the insight of someone near to death that suffering teaches human beings a spiritual truth that cannot be learned through pleasure alone. The poet asks "Schoolmaster Sorrow" to offer his pupils at least a ray of hope in the dark night of the soul, and a glimpse of love, on their way toward spiritual growth, toward God; then their pain will be benign and kindly, and their grateful hearts will feel a truly enduring joy.]

ˈlapˈʃiːtˈ fɔn deːɐ̯ ˈharfə
Abschied von der Harfe
Farewell to the Harp

Published posthumously [composed 1816] (poem by Johann Gaudenz von Sallis-Seewis)

nɔx ˈaenmaːl tʰøːn, oː ˈharfə, diː nuːɐ̯ ɡəˈfyːlə tʰøːntʰ!
Noch einmal tön, o Harfe, die nur Gefühle tönt!
Yet once sound, O harp, which only feelings sounds!
(Resound one more time, O harp that only sounds feelings,)

fɛɐ̯ˈhalə tsaːɐ̯tˈ ʊntˈ ˈlaezə nɔx ˈjeːnə ˈʃvaːnənvaezə,
verhalle zart und leise noch jene Schwanenweise,
die away delicately and softly still that swan- melody,
(may that swan-melody still die away delicately and softly,)

diː aof deːɐ̯ fluːt dɛs ˈleːbəns ʊns mɪt deːɐ̯ noːtˈ fɛɐ̯ˈzøːntʰ!
die auf der Flut des Lebens uns mit der Not versöhnt!
which on the river of life us with the misery reconciles!
(which reconciles us with misery on the river of life!)

ɪm ˈmɔrɡənʃaen dɛs ˈleːbəns ɛɐ̯ˈkʰlaŋst duː raen ʊntˈ hɛl!
Im Morgenschein des Lebens erklangst du rein und hell!
In the morning-glow of the life sounded you pure and bright!
(In life's morning-glow you sounded pure and bright!)

veːɐ̯ kʰan deːn kʰlaŋ fɛɐ̯ˈvaːrən? dʊrç ˈfɔrʃən ʊntˈ ɛɐ̯ˈfaːrən
Wer kann den Klang verwahren? durch Forschen und Erfahren
Who can the sound preserve? through searching and learning
(Who can hold onto that sound? In our searching and learning)

fɛɐ̯ˈha120 ... fɛɐ̯ˈhalətˈ ʊntˈ fɛɐ̯ˈziːkˈtˈə dɛs ˈliːdəs ˈraenɐ kʰvɛl.
verhallet und versiegte des Liedes reiner Quell.
dies away and dries up the song's pure source.
(the pure source of song dies away and dries up.)

ɪn ˈʃpˈɛːtˈɐn ˈjuːɡəntˈjaːrən haltˈ lɛs ʃoːn tsaːɐ̯tˈ ʊntˈ baŋ,
In spätern Jugendjahren hallt es schon zart und bang,
In later youth- years sounds it already frail and fearful,
(In later years of youth it already sounds frail and fearful)

viː ˈfɪŋkˈənʃlaːkˈ ɪm ˈmɛrtsə; mɪt dɛs ɛntˈkʰnɔspˈəns ˈʃmɛrtsə
wie Finkenschlag im Märze; mit des Entknospens Schmerze
like finches' song in the March; with the de-budding's pain
(like the song of the finch in March; with the pain of emerging from the bud)

ɛɐ̯ˈbeːbən hɛrts ʊntˈ ˈzaetˈən fɔl ˈliːbə ʊntˈ ɡəˈzaŋ!
erbeben Herz und Saiten voll Liebe und Gesang!
tremble heart and harpstrings full of love and song!
(heart and harpstrings tremble full of love and song!)

am ˈzɔmɐtʰaːk' dɛs ˈleːbəns fɛɐ̯ˈʃt'ʊmt das ˈzaet'ənʃp'iːl!
Am Sommertag des Lebens verstummt das Saitenspiel!
In the summer-day of the life becomes silent the string-play!
(In the summertime of life the play of the strings becomes silent!)

ɑos ˈzeːnzʊxt̯sfɔlɐ ˈzeːlə lɔk't̯s nɔx viː filoˈmeːlə,
Aus sehnsuchtsvoller Seele lockt's noch wie Philomele,
Out of yearningful soul draws it still like Philomela (the nightingale),
(Out of the soul full of yearning it still draws, like the nightingale,)

ʃoːn ˈzɛlt'nɐr, ˈlaːbɐ ˈryːrɐnt', nuːɐ̯ ˈʃveːɐ̯muːt' ʊnt' gəˈfyːl.
schon seltner, aber rührend, nur Schwermut und Gefühl.
admittedly more rarely, but movingly, only melancholy and feeling.

oː ʃlaːk' ɪm ˈdʊŋk'lən ˈbuːzən deːɐ̯/deːr ˈɛrnst'ən ˈlaːbənt̯tsaetʰ!
O schlag im dunklen Busen der ernsten Abendzeit!
O blow in the dark bosom of the solemn evening-time!

vɪl ʊm das ˈløːdə ˈleːbən dɛs ˈʃɪk'zaːls naxt' zɪç ˈveːbən,
Will um das öde Leben des Schicksals Nacht sich weben,
Will about the desolate life the destiny's night itself weave,
(If destiny's night will weave itself about desolate life,)

dan ʃlaːk' ʊnt' ˈvɛk'ə ˈzeːnzʊxt' naːx deːɐ̯/deːr ʊnˈʃt'ɛrp'lɪçkʰaetʰ.
dann schlag und wecke Sehnsucht nach der Unsterblichkeit.
then strike and waken longing for the immortality.
(then strike and waken longing for immortality.)

[The song of life becomes fainter as we grow older; may its last dying echo awaken our longing for the life to come.]

ˈap'ʃiːt' fɔn ˈlaenəm ˈfrɔø̯ndə
Abschied von einem Freunde
Farewell to a Friend

Posthumously published [1817] (poem by the composer)

ˈleːbə voːl! ˈleːbə voːl! duː ˈliːbɐ frɔø̯nt'! ˈtsiːə hɪn ɪn ˈfɛrnəs lant',
Lebe wohl! lebe wohl! du lieber Freund! Ziehe hin in fernes Land,
Farewell! Farewell! you dear friend! Go off into distant land,
(Farewell! Farewell, you dear friend! Go off to a distant land,)

nɪm deːɐ̯ ˈfrɔø̯nt'ʃaft tʰrɑot'əs bant', ʊnt' bəˈvaːɐ̯s/bəˈvaːrs ɪn ˈtʰrɔø̯ɐ hant'!
nimm der Freundschaft trautes Band, und bewahr's in treuer Hand!
take the friendship's intimate bond, and preserve it in faithful hand!
(take with you the intimate bond of friendship, and preserve it faithfully!)

høːr ɪn ˈdiːzəm ˈtʰrɑoɐzaŋ ˈmaenəs ˈhertsəns ˈlinɐn draŋ,
Hör in diesem Trauersang meines Herzens innern Drang,
Hear in this song of grieving my heart's inner distress,

tʰøːnt' leːɐ̯ dɔx   zoː dʊmpf ʊnt' baŋ.   'ʃae̯dən hae̯st   das 'bɪt'rə vɔrtʰ,
tönt er doch so dumpf und bang.   Scheiden heisst das bittre Wort,
sounds it   though so dull   and anxious. Parting   is called the bitter word,
(though it sounds so dull and anxious. The bitter word is "parting,")

veː! lɛs ruːft dɪç fɔn lʊns fɔrtʰ, hɪn lan deːn bə'ʃt'ɪmʊŋslɔrtʰ.
Weh! es ruft dich von uns fort, hin an den Bestimmungsort.
Alas! it calls you from us   away, away to the destination.
(Alas! it calls you away from us, away to your destination.)

[vɛn   diːs liːt dae̯n hɛrts lɛɐ̯'grae̯ft', 'frɔøndɛs 'ʃat'ən   'nɛːɐ̯ ʃvae̯ft',
[Wenn dies Lied dein Herz ergreift,   Freundes Schatten näher schweift,
[If   this song your heart stirs,   friend's shadow nearer wanders,
[(If this song touches your heart, your friend's shadow will hover nearer to you,)

'mae̯nɐ 'zeːlə 'zae̯t'ən ʃt'rae̯ftʰ. 'leːbə voːl, duː 'liːbɐ frɔønt'!]
meiner Seele Saiten streift.   Lebe wohl, du lieber Freund!]
my   soul's strings grazes. Fare well, you dear friend!]
(and will lightly brush the harpstrings of my soul. Farewell, dear friend!)]

[This is the only song that Schubert composed to a poem of his own. He wrote it for his friend Franz von Schober, who had to travel to Sweden and would be away from Vienna for a year. The Peters edition gives only three verses; the *Gesamtausgabe* adds the fourth (in brackets, above).]

adela'iːdə
Adelaide
Adelaide

Posthumously published [composed 1814] (Friedrich von Matthisson)

'ae̯nzaːm 'vandəlt dae̯n frɔønt' lɪm 'fryːlɪŋsgartən,
Einsam wandelt dein Freund im   Frühlingsgarten,
Lonely wanders your friend in the spring-   garden,
(Your friend wanders, lonely, in the springtime garden,)

mɪlt' fɔm 'liːp'lɪçən 'tsɑobɐlɪçt' lʊm'flɔsən,
mild vom   lieblichen Zauberlicht umflossen,
gently by the lovely   magic- light encircled,
(gently bathed in lovely, magical light,)   ["*von Licht umflossen*" = bathed in light]

das   dʊrç   'vaŋk'əndə 'blyːt'əntsvae̯gə tsɪt'ɐtʰ, adela'iːdə!
das   durch wankende Blütenzweige   zittert, Adelaide!
which through swaying   blossom-branches trembles, Adelaide!
(which trembles through swaying branches in blossom, Adelaide!)

ɪn deːɐ̯ 'ʃp'iːgəlndən fluːt', ɪm   ʃneː   deːɐ̯/deːr 'alp'ən,
In der spiegelnden Flut, im   Schnee der   Alpen,
In the   reflecting   stream, in the snow   of the   Alps,

ɪn dɛs 'zɪŋk'əndən tʰaːgəs 'gɔlt'gə'vœlk'ən, ɪm   gə'fɪldə deːɐ̯ 'ʃt'ɛrnə   [*GA:* **Goldgewölke**]
in des sinkenden Tages Goldgewölken, im   Gefilde der   Sterne
in the sinking   day's gold-clouds,   in the fields   of the stars
(in the golden clouds of the departing day, in the fields of stars)

ʃtˈraːlt dₐɛn ˈbɪltˈnɪs, adelaˈiːdə! ˈlaːbəntˈlʏftˈçən ɪm ˈʦaːɐ̯tˈən ˈlₐobə ˈflʏstˈɐn;
strahlt dein Bildnis, Adelaide! Abendlüftchen im zarten Laube flüstern;
radiates your image, Adelaide! Evening breezes in the delicate foliage whisper;
(your image is radiating, Adelaide! Evening breezes whisper in the delicate foliage;)

ˈzɪlbɐɡlœkˈçən dɛs mₐɛs ɪm ˈɡraːzə ˈzɔɸzəln;
Silberglöckchen des Mais im Grase säuseln;
silver bells of the May in the grass rustle;
(silver bells of May rustle in the grass;)

ˈvɛlən ˈrₐoʃən ʊntˈ ˈnaxtˈɪɡalən ˈfløːtˈən : adelaˈiːdə! ˈlₐɛnstˈ,
Wellen rauschen und Nachtigallen flöten: Adelaide! Einst,
waves murmur and nightingales warble: "Adelaide!" Some day —

loː ˈvʊndɐ, lɛntˈblyːtˈ lₐof ˈmₐɛnəm ˈɡraːbə ˈlₐɛnə ˈbluːmə deːɐ̯/deːr ˈlaʃə ˈmₐɛnəs ˈhɛrʦəns;
o Wunder, entblüht auf meinem Grabe eine Blume der Asche meines Herzens;
O wonder, blooms on my grave a flower from the ashes of my heart;
(O wonder! — a flower will bloom on my grave from the ashes of my heart;)

ˈdɔɸtˈlɪç ˈʃɪmɐtˈ lₐof ˈjeːdəm ˈpʰʊrpˈʊrˈblɛtˈçən : adelaˈiːdə!
deutlich schimmert auf jedem Purpurblättchen: Adelaide!
clearly shimmers on every purple little petal: Adelaide!
(on every purple petal the name Adelaide will shimmer clearly!)

[This poem had already been set by Beethoven in a much more famous song with the same title.]

ˈaːdəlvɔltˈ ʊntˈ ˈlɛma
Adelwold und Emma
Adelwold and Emma

Posthumously published [composed 1815] (ballad by Friedrich Anton Bertrand)

hoːx, ʊntˈ ˈleːɐn ʃiːɐ̯ fɔn ˈdₐoɐ, raːktˈ lₐɛn ˈrɪtˈɐʃlɔs lɛmˈpʰiːɐ̯.
Hoch, und ehern schier von Dauer, ragt ein Ritterschloss empor.
High, and brazen nearly in durableness, towers a knight-castle upwards.
(High, and nearly as perdurable as brass, a knight's castle is towering toward the sky.)

ˈbeːrən ˈlaːɡən lan dem tʰoːɐ̯, ˈbɔɸtˈə ˈʃnₐobəntˈ lₐof deːɐ̯ ˈlₐoɐ,
Bären lagen an dem Tor, Beute schnaubend auf der Lauer,
Bears lay at the gate, prey snorting on the look-out,
(Bears used to lie at the gate, on the look-out and sniffing for prey,)

ˈtʰʏrmə ˈʦɪŋəltˈən di ˈmₐoɐ, ɡlₐɛç den ˈriːzən—
Türme zingelten die Mauer, gleich den Riesen—
Towers ringed the walls, like the giants—
(Towers ringed the walls, looking like giants—)

ˈbaŋə ˈʃₐoɐ ˈveːtˈən ˈbrₐozəntˈ, viː lₐɛn meːɐ̯, fɔn den ˈtʰanənvɪpfəln heːɐ̯.
bange Schauer wehten brausend, wie ein Meer, von den Tannenwipfeln her.
fearful showers blew, raging like a sea, from the fir-tree-tops hither.
(the wind, roaring like the sea, blew down fearful showers from the fir-tree-tops.)

[*The old knight is introduced:*]

24

'aːbɐ 'fɪnstˈrɐ 'kʰʊmɐ 'naːkˈtˈə, 'muːtˈfɛɐ̯tseːrənˈtˈ ʊm ʊntˈ lan,
Aber finstrer Kummer nagte, mutverzehrend um und an,
But dark grief gnawed, courage-consuming around and at,
(But dark grief was gnawing, consuming his courage from all sides,)

hiːɐ̯/hiːr lam 'vakˈɐn 'dɔɤ̯tʃən man, dem kʰaɛn faɛnt tsuː 'tʰrɔtsən 'vaːkˈtˈə;
hier am wackern deutschen Mann, dem kein Feind zu trotzen wagte;
here at the valiant German man, whom no enemy to defy dared;
(was gnawing here at the valiant German man whom no enemy dared to defy;)

ɔftˈ, nɔx leː deːɐ̯ 'mɔrgən 'tʰaːkˈtˈə, fuːɐ̯/fuːr leːɐ̯/leːr lɑɤ̯f fɔm tʰrɑɤ̯m ʊntˈ 'fraːkˈtˈə,
oft, noch eh' der Morgen tagte, fuhr er auf vom Traum und fragte,
often, still before the morning dawned, jumped he up from the dream and asked,
(often, even before the morning dawned, he would jump up from his dream and ask,)

ɪtstˈ mɪtˈ 'zɔɤ̯ftsɐ, ɪtstˈ mɪtˈ ʃraɛ, voː zaɛn 'tʰɔɤ̯rɐ 'lɛtstˈɐ zaɛ?
itzt mit Seufzer, itzt mit Schrei, wo sein teurer Letzter sei?
now with sigh, now with cry, where his dear last one be?
(now with a sigh, now with a cry, where his dear last son might be?)

[*Emma, his daughter:*]

'faːtɐ, 'ruːfə nɪçt dem 'liːbən; 'flʏstˈɐtˈ 'laɛnstˈəns 'lɛma draɛn,
"Vater, rufe nicht dem Lieben;" flüstert einstens Emma drein,
"Father, call not the dear one"; whispered once Emma thereinto,
("Father, do not call our dear one," Emma whispered, interrupting him,)

ziː, leːɐ̯ ʃleːftˈ lɪm 'kʰɛmɐlaɛn zanftˈ ʊntˈ ʃtˈɔlts, vas kʰan liːn 'tʰryːbən?
"sieh, er schläft im Kämmerlein sanft und stolz, was kann ihn trüben?"
"See, he sleeps in the little chamber gently and proudly; what can him trouble?"
("See, he is sleeping in his tomb, quiet and proud; what can trouble him there?")

ɪç nɪçtˈ 'ruːfən?—zɪntˈ nɪçtˈ 'ziːbən 'maɛnɐ zøːn lɪm kʰampf gə'bliːbən?
"Ich nicht rufen?—sind nicht sieben meiner Söhn' im Kampf geblieben?
"I not call?— are not seven of my sons in the battle left (on the battlefield)?
("I should not call?—have not seven of my sons fallen in battle?)

vaɛntˈ lɪç nɪçtˈ ʃoːn 'fʏnftseːn jaːɐ̯/jaːr lʊm das vaɛpˈ das lɔɤ̯ç gə'baːɐ̯?
Weint' ich nicht schon fünfzehn Jahr um das Weib das euch gebar?"
Wept I not already fifteen years for the woman who you bore?"
(Have I not already spent fifteen years weeping for the woman who gave you birth?)

'ɛma høːɐ̯ts lʊntˈ ʃmiːkˈtˈ mɪtˈ 'beːbən 'vaɛnəntˈ zɪç lan 'zaɛnə brustʰ:
Emma hört's und schmiegt mit Beben weinend sich an seine Brust:
Emma hears it and presses with trembling weeping herself against his breast:
(Emma hears that and, trembling and weeping, presses herself against his breast:)

'faːtˈɐ! ziː daɛn kʰɪntˈ! lax fryː vaːɐ̯ daɛn 'baɛfal maɛn bə'ʃtreːbən!
"Vater! Sieh' dein Kind! ach früh war dein Beifall mein Bestreben!"
"Father! See your child! Ah, early was your approval my aspiration!"
("Father, look at your child! Ah, since childhood I have ever aspired to earn your approval!")

viː vɛn 'tʰroːst'əsvɔrt ʦuː 'geːbən 'boːt'ən 'gɔt'əs 'niːdɐʃveːbən,
Wie wenn Trosteswort zu geben Boten Gottes niederschweben,
As if comfort-word to give messengers of God down-float,
(As if messengers of God were floating down to earth to give words of comfort,)

fyːɐt deːɐ 'hɔldən reːt' ʊnt blɪk' 'nɔøə kʰraft' ɪn liːn ʦu'rʏkʰ.
führt der Holden Red' und Blick neue Kraft in ihn zurück.
leads the lovely one's speech and look new strength into him back.
(the speech and the look of his lovely daughter bring new strength back to him.)

'haet'ɐ pʰrɛst' leːɐ ziː lans 'hɛrʦeː loː fɛɐ'giːp', das lɪç fɛɐ'gaːs,
Heiter presst' er sie ans Herze: "o vergib, dass ich vergass,
Cheerfully pressed he her to the heart: "O forgive, that I forgot,
(Cheered, he pressed her to his heart: "Oh forgive me, that I forgot,)

'vɛlçən ʃaʦ lɪç nɔx bə'zaːs, ly:bɐ'mant' fɔn 'maenəm 'ʃmɛrʦə.
welchen Schatz ich noch besass, übermannt von meinem Schmerze.
what a treasure I still possessed, overcome by my pain.
(overcome by my pain, what a treasure I still possess—in *you*.)

'aːbɐ ʃp'raːxst duː nɪçt' lɪm 'ʃɛrʦə, voːl dan! bae dem ʃaen deːɐ 'kʰɛrʦə
Aber sprachst du nicht im Scherze, wohl dann! bei dem Schein der Kerze
But spoke you not in the jest, well then! by the gleam of the candle
(But if you were not speaking in jest, very well then! By candle-light)

'vandlə mɪt' miːɐ/miːr 'laenən gaŋ ʃt'raks den 'dyːst'ɐn veːk' lɛnt'laŋ!
wandle mit mir einen Gang stracks den düstern Weg entlang!"
walk with me a stretch right now the dark passageway along!"
(walk with me a stretch right now along the dark passageway!")

[*The knight takes his daughter to the family tomb, where her seven brothers are buried:*]

'ʦɪt'ɐnt' 'fɔlk't'ə ziː, balt' gə'laŋən ziː ʦur 'halə, graos ʊnt tʰiːf,
Zitternd folgte sie, bald gelangen sie zur Halle, graus und tief,
Trembling followed she, soon arrived they at the hall, gruesome and deep,
(She followed him, trembling; soon they arrived at the hall, gruesome and deep,)

voː di ʃaːɐ deːɐ 'fɛːt'ɐ ʃliːf; rɪŋs lɪm kʰraes lan 'zɪlbɐʃp'aŋən
wo die Schar der Väter schlief; rings im Kreis an Silberspangen
where the troop of the ancestors slept; all around in the circle on silver clasps
(where the troop of ancestors were sleeping; around in a circle, suspended from silver clasps,)

ʊm laen 'laxt'əs 'heːɐgə'haŋən 'lɔøçt'ət'ən mɪt' 'blaeçəm, 'baŋən 'graːbəsʃɪmɐ
um ein achtes hergehangen leuchteten mit bleichem, bangen Grabesschimmer
around an eighth (lamp) hung lighted with pale, fearful grave- shimmer
(hung about an eighth lamp, with a pale, fearful, funereal shimmer)

fɔrt' lʊnt' fɔrt' 'ziːbən 'lɛmp'laen 'diːzəm lɔrt.
fort und fort sieben Lämplein diesem Ort.
forth and forth (= continually) seven little lamps this place.
(seven little lamps lighted the place, continually.)

26

'ʊnt'ɐn ˈlɛmp'laen vaːɐs fɔn ˈʃt'aenən... tʰrɑon! lɛɐˈtseːlən kʰan lɪçs nɪçtʰ,
Untern Lämplein war's von Steinen... Traun! erzählen kann ich's nicht,
Beneath the little lamps was it of stones... Truly! tell can I it not,
(Beneath the little lamps there were gravestones.... Truly, I can not tell the rest,)

vaːɐs zoː ˈtʰrɑorɪç ˈtsuːgərɪçt', vaːɐs zoː ˈlaːdənt' ax tsʊm ˈvaenən.
war's so traurig zugericht, war's so ladend ach zum Weinen.
was it so mournfully prepared, was it so inviting ah to the weeping.
(it was so mournfully arranged, ah, it invited one to weep.)

bae den ˈhaelɪgən gəˈbaenən, ˈvɛlçən ˈdiːzə ˈlamp'ən ˈʃaenən,
"Bei den heiligen Gebeinen, welchen diese Lampen scheinen,"
"By the sacred bones upon which these lamps are shining,"

ruːft' leːɐ lɑot', bəˈʃvøːɐ/bəˈʃvøːr lɪç dɪç, ˈtʰrɑot'ə ˈtʰɔxt'ɐ, ˈhøːrə mɪç!
ruft er laut, "beschwör' ich dich, traute Tochter, höre mich!
called he loudly, "implore I you, dear daughter, hear me!
(he called loudly, "I implore you, dear daughter, listen to me!)

maen gəˈʃlɛçt' zaet' ˈgrɑoən ˈtsaet'ən, vaːɐ, viː ˈrɪt'ɐsmɛnɐn tsiːmtʰ,
Mein Geschlecht seit grauen Zeiten, war, wie Rittersmännern ziemt,
My kin since grey times, was, as for knightly men is seemly,
(Since olden times my kin, as is seemly for men of the knightly class, has been)

kʰɛk', gəˈʃt'rɛŋ lʊnt' fast' bəˈryːmtʰ. lɪn dɛs ˈgraːbəs ˈdʊŋk'əlhaet'
keck, gestreng und fast berühmt. In des Grabes Dunkelheit
bold, austere, and almost renowned. Into the grave's darkness

zaŋk' di rae fɔn ˈbiːdɐlɔøt'ən, ˈzaŋk'ən diː, zoː mɪç lɛɐˈfrɔøt'ən,
sank die Reih' von Biederleuten, sanken die, so mich erfreuten,
sank the row of honorable people, sank those who so me gladdened,
(sank that row of men of honor, sank those in whom I so rejoiced,)

bɪs laenst deːɐ poˈzɑonə hal ziː vɪrt' ˈvɛk'ən ˈlaltsuˈmaːl.
bis einst der Posaune Hall sie wird wecken allzumal.
until one day the trombone's peal them will awaken all at once.
(until one day the final trumpet's peal will awaken them all at once.)

niː fɛɐˈgaːsən ˈdaenə ˈbryːdɐ ˈdiːzɐ ˈgroːsən ˈlaːnən veːɐtʰ,
Nie vergassen deine Brüder dieser grossen Ahnen Wert,
Never forgot your brothers these great forebears' merit,
(Your brothers never forgot the merit of those great forebears.)

raeç lʊnt' ˈkʰaezɐ ʃɛtst' liːɐ ʃveːɐtʰ viː laen ˈdɛk'əndəs gəˈfiːdɐ.
Reich und Kaiser schätzt* ihr Schwert wie ein deckendes Gefieder. [*Schubert's error?]
Realm and emperor values their sword as a covering plumage.
(The realm and the emperor value their swords as a protective covering of plumage.)

[*poem:*Reich und Kaiser *schützt'* (ʃytst') ihr Schwert wie ein deckendes Gefieder.]
[*better sense:*(Their sword *protected* the realm and the emperor like a sheltering wing.)]

[*The knight beseeches his daughter to marry only a valiant knight of noble stock:*]

giːpʻ ziː, ˈtʰɔxtʻɐ, giːpʻ ziː ˈviːdɐ miːɐ̯ ɪm ˈvakʻɐn ˈbrɔø̯tʻɪgam
Gib sie, Tochter, gib sie wieder mir im wackern Bräutigam
Give them, daughter, give them again to me in the valiant bridegroom

diːɐ̯/diːr lɛɐ̯ˈkʰiːstʻ ḷɑos ˈhɛldənʃtʻam! ˈlaːbɐ fluːx! ḷʊntʻ mɪt dem ˈvɔrtʻə,
dir erkiest aus Heldenstamm! Aber Fluch!" und mit dem Worte,
for you chosen out of hero- stock! But curse!" and with that word,
(chosen for you from heroic stock! But curse...!" And with that word,)

glɑe̯ç lals ʃrɛkʻtʻ liːn naxtʻ ḷʊntʻ grɑos, t͡soːkʻ leːɐ̯ ˈpʰlœt͡slɪç ziː hɪˈnɑos
gleich als schreckt' ihn Nacht und Graus, zog er plötzlich sie hinaus
just as if frightened him night and horror, pulled he suddenly her out
(just as if night and horror had frightened him, he suddenly pulled her)

ḷɑos dem ˈʃɑoɐfɔlən ˈlɔrtʻə. ˈlɛma ˈvaŋkʻtʻə dʊrç di ˈpfɔrtʻə:
aus dem schauervollen Orte. Emma wankte durch die Pforte:
out of the dreadful place. Emma staggered through the entrance:

ˈɛndə nɪçt di ˈʃrɛkʻənsvɔrtʻə! dɛŋkʻ ḷan ˈhɪməl ḷʊntʻ gəˈrɪçtʰ!
"Ende nicht die Schreckensworte! denk' an Himmel und Gericht!
"Finish not the frightening words! Think of heaven and judgment!
("Do not finish that terrible thought! Think of heaven and divine judgment!)

[The knight's page, Adelwold, who secretly loves Emma, is introduced:]

oː fɛɐ̯ˈvɪrf, fɛɐ̯ˈvɪrf mɪç nɪçtʰ! blɑe̯ç, viː ziː, mɪtʻ ˈbaŋən ˈt͡saːgən
O verwirf, verwirf mich nicht!" Bleich, wie sie, mit bangem Zagen
Oh reject, reject me not!" Pale, as she, with anxious trepidation
(Oh do not reject me, do not condemn me!" Pale, like her, with anxious trepidation)

leːnt dɛs ˈrɪtʻɐs ˈkʰnapʻə hiːɐ̯, viː dem ˈzʏndɐ vɪrt͡s liːm ʃiːɐ̯,
lehnt des Ritters Knappe hier, wie dem Sünder wird's ihm schier,
leans the knight's page here, as to the sinner becomes it to him almost,
(the knight's page reels; he feels almost like a sinner)

deːn di ˈʃrɛkʻən ˈgɔtʻəs ˈʃlaːgən, kʰɑom t͡suː ˈlaːtʻmən tʰɛːtʻ leːɐ̯ ˈvaːgən,
den die Schrecken Gottes schlagen, kaum zu atmen tät er wagen,
whom the terrors of God strike, scarcely to breathe does he dare,
(who is struck by the fear of God; he scarcely dares to breathe,)

kʰɑom di ˈkʰɛrt͡sə ˈfoːɐ̯t͡sutʰraːgən ˈhatʻə matʻ ḷʊntʻ ˈfiːbɐhaftʻ ˈzae̯nə ˈrɛçtʻə nɔx di kʰraftʰ.
kaum die Kerze vorzutragen hatte matt und fieberhaft seine Rechte noch die Kraft.
barely the candle before to carry had weak and feverish his right hand still the strength.
(his right hand, weak and feverish, had barely still the strength to carry the candle before them.)

[Flashback: Adelwold was brought to the castle as an orphan child.]

ˈaːdəlvɔldən braxtʻ ḷals ˈvɑe̯zə ˈmɪtʻlae̯t͡sfɔl ḷɑof ˈzae̯nəm rɔs
Adelwolden bracht' als Waise mitleidsvoll auf seinem Ross
Adelwold [object] brought as orphan compassionately on his horse
(On his horse the knight compassionately brought Adelwold, an orphan child,)

ˈaenst deːɐ̯ ˈrɪtˀɐ naːx dem ʃlɔs haem fɔn ˈaenɐ ˈfɛrnən ˈraezə,
einst der Ritter nach dem Schloss heim von einer fernen Reise,
one day the knight [subject] to the castle home from a distant journey,
(home to the castle one day, after a journey to distant lands,)

ˈp͡fleːkˀtˀə zaen mɪt tʰraŋkˀ ʊntˀ ˈʃpˀaezə, tʰɛːtˀ liːn ˈheːɡən ɪn dem ˈkʰraezə ˈzaenɐ ˈkʰɪndɐ;
pflegte sein mit Trank und Speise, tät ihn hegen in dem Kreise seiner Kinder;
tended him with drink and food, did him shelter in the circle of his children;
(nurtured him with food and drink and sheltered him in the circle of his own children;)

ɔftˀ ʊntˀ fiːl vaːɐ̯/vaːr leːɐ̯ ˈtʰʊməlntˀ liːɐ̯ ɡəˈʃpˀiːl. ˈaːbɐ ˈɛma....
oft und viel war er tummelnd ihr Gespiel. Aber Emma....
often and much was he romping their playfellow. But Emma....
(very often he was their playfellow, romping with them. But Emma....)

ˈzaenə ˈɡant͡sə ˈt͡sartˀə ˈzeːlə veːpˀtˀ ʊm ziː... vaːɐ̯/vaːr lɛs ˈfryːə zʏmpˀˈatʰiː?
seine ganze zarte Seele webt um sie.... war es frühe Sympathie?
his entire tender soul weaves about her... was it early fondness?
(his entire tender soul hovers about her... was it the first signs of love?)

[*Now Adelwold is a young man, a knight by training but without aristocratic ancestry.*]

froː lʊmˈvantˀ ziː ˈzaenə ˈlant͡sə lɪm tʰʊrˈniːɐ̯ mɪtˀ ˈlaenəm ˈkʰrant͡sə,
froh umwand sie seine Lanze im Turnier mit einem Kranze,
gladly entwined she his lance in the tourney with a garland,
(Gladly she entwined his lance with a garland at the tourney,)

ˈʃveːpˀtˀə ˈlaeçtˀɐ dan lɪm ˈtʰant͡sə mɪt dem ˈrɪtˀɐ kʰɛkˀ lʊnt tʰrɔø,
schwebte leichter dann im Tanze mit dem Ritter keck und treu,
floated more lightly then in the dance with the knight bold and loyal,
(dancing with the bold, loyal knight she floated more lightly)

lals das ˈlʏftˀçən ˈʃveːpˀtˀ lɪm mae.
als das Lüftchen schwebt im Mai.
than the breeze hovers in the May.
(than a breeze in May.)

ˈroːzɪç laof t͡sʊm ˈjʏŋlɪŋ ˈblyːtˀə balt deːɐ̯ ˈniːdrə fɔn ɡəˈʃlɛçtʰ;
Rosig auf zum Jüngling blühte bald der Niedre von Geschlecht;
Rosy up to the young man blossomed soon the low-born of family;
(The low-born child soon blossomed into a healthy, handsome young man;)

ˈeːdlɐ ˈloːntˀə niː laen kʰnɛçt ˈzaenəs ˈp͡fleːɡɐs ˈvaːtˀɐɡyːtˀə,
edler lohnte nie ein Knecht seines Pflegers Vatergüte,
more nobly rewarded never a vassal his guardian's fatherly kindness,
(no vassal ever rewarded more nobly his guardian's fatherly kindness,)

[*Adelwold tries to suppress his love for Emma, recalling her father's curse:*]

ˈaːbɐ haes lʊntˀ ˈhaesɐ ˈɡlyːtˀə, vas t͡suː ˈdɛmp͡fən leːɐ̯ zɪç ˈmyːtˀə,
aber heiss und heisser glühte, was zu dämpfen er sich mühte,
but hot and hotter burned that which to extinguish he himself troubled,
(but the flame that he struggled to extinguish burned hotter and hotter,)

'fɛst'ɐ   kʰnʏp͡ft' li:n, 'fɛst'ɐ   lax! ɭan das 'frɔ͡ølaen 'je:dɐ tʰa:k';
fester   knüpft' ihn, fester   ach! an das Fräulein   jeder Tag;
more firmly bound   him, more firmly ah! to the young lady every day;
(every day bound him more firmly, ah, still more firmly to the young lady;)

fɛst' ɭʊnt' 'fɛst'ɐ   zi: ɭan 'li:rən 'zy:sən, 'tʰrɑ͡ot'ən 'la:dəlvɔlt'.
fest und fester   sie an ihren süssen, trauten Adelwold.
firmly and more firmly her to her   sweet, dear   Adelwold.
(every day bound her firmly and more firmly to her sweet, dear Adelwold.)

vas zɪnt' 'vap'ən,   lant' ɭʊnt' gɔlt', zɔlt' ɭɪç 'larmə   dɪç fɛɐ̯'li:rən?
"Was sind Wappen,   Land und Gold, sollt' ich Arme   dich verlieren?
"What are   coat of arms, land and gold, should I   poor woman you lose?
("What use are coat of arms, land, and gold, if I, poor woman, should lose you?)

vas di 'flɪt'ɐ,   zo: mɪç 'ʦi:rən? vas baŋ'kʰɛt'ə ba͡e tʰʊr'ni:rən?
Was die Flitter,   so mich zieren? Was Bankette bei Turnieren?
What the tinsels, (that) so me   adorn? What banquets   with jousting?
(What use are the fancy frills that adorn me? What use banquets with jousting?)

'vap'ən,   lant', gə'ʃmʊk'   ɭʊnt' gɔlt' lo:nt'   ɭa͡en tʰrɑ͡om fɔn 'la:dəlvɔlt'!
Wappen,   Land, Geschmuck und Gold lohnt   ein Traum von Adelwold!"
Coat of arms, land, jewelry   and gold is worth a   dream of Adelwold!"
(One dream about Adelwold is worth any coat of arms, any land or jewelry or gold!")

zo: das 'frɔ͡ølaen,   vɛn de:ɐ̯ 'ʃla͡eɐ   'grɑ͡oɐ 'nɛçt'ə zi: ɭʊm'fɪŋ.
So das Fräulein,   wenn der Schleier grauer Nächte sie umfing.
So the young lady, when the veil   of grey nights   her surrounded.
(So thought the young lady, when the dark veil of night surrounded her.)

[Adelwold, certain that his love is hopeless, decides to make a pilgrimage to the Holy Land:]

dɔx mɪt' ɭa͡ens—ɭals 'ɛma 'hɔ͡øt'ə ʃp'ɛ:t' nɔx 'be:t'ət', va͡ent' ɭʊnt' vaxtʰ,
Doch mit eins— als Emma heute spät   noch betet, weint und wacht,
But with one— as Emma today late   still prays, weeps and wakes,
(But all at once—as Emma is still awake, saying her prayers and weeping, late this evening,)

ʃt'e:t' gə'hʏlt' ɭɪn 'pʰɪlgɐtʰraxt' 'la:dəlvɔlt' ɭan 'li:rɐ 'za͡et'ə:
steht gehüllt in Pilgertracht Adelwold an ihrer Seite:
stands wrapped in pilgrim-garb Adelwold at her   side:
(—Adelwold stands at her side, dressed in pilgrim's robes:)

'ʦʏrnə   nɪçt', gəbene'da͡et'ə! dɛn mɪç tʰra͡ep'ʦ, mɪç tʰra͡ep'ʦ ɭɪns   'va͡et'ə;
"Zürne   nicht, Gebenedeite! denn mich treibt's, mich treibt's ins   Weite;
"Be angry not,   blessed one! for   me drives it, me   drives it into the distance;
("Do not be angry, blessed lady! Something within me impels me to go away into distant lands;)

'frɔ͡ølaen, dɪç bə'fe:l   ɭɪç gɔt', da͡en ɭɪm 'le:bən ɭʊnt' ɭɪm tʰo:t'!
Fräulein, dich befehl'   ich Gott, dein im   Leben und im   Tod!
Lady,   you commend I (to) God, yours in the life   and in the death!
(Lady, I leave you in the hands of God; I am yours in life and in death!)

30

'laet'ən zɔl mɪç 'diːzɐ 'ʃt'rɛk'ən hɪn   ɪn 'tsiːɔns 'haelgəs lant',
Leiten soll mich dieser Stecken hin   in Zions heilges Land,
guide shall me this staff   hence into Zion's holy   land,
(This staff shall guide me hence into the holy land of Zion,)

voː fi'laeçt' laen 'hɔøflaen   zant' balt den 'larmən vɪrt' bə'dɛk'ən;
wo   vielleicht ein Häuflein   Sand bald den Armen   wird bedecken;
where perhaps a   little mound (of) sand soon the poor man will cover;
(where perhaps a little mound of sand will soon cover me, poor man;)

'maenə 'zeːlə mʊs lɛɐ̯'ʃrɛk'ən, dʊrç fɛɐ̯'raːt' zɪç tsu: bə'flɛk'ən lan   dem man,
meine Seele muss erschrecken, durch Verrat sich zu beflecken an   dem Mann,
my   soul must be frightened, through betrayal itself to stain   against the man,
(my soul must recoil from staining itself through betrayal of the man)

deːɐ̯ mɪlt' lʊnt' groːs, heːɐ̯ mɪç t^hruːk' lɪn 'zaenən ʃoːs.   ['zaenəm]
der mild und gross, her mich trug   in seinen Schoss. [*poem:* in seinem Schoss]
who, gentle and great, hither me   brought into his   lap.   [in his   lap]
(who, so gentle and so great, brought me here into the bosom of his family.)

'zeːlɪç   t^hrɔømt' lɪç laenst' lals 'k^hnaːbə. 'lɛŋəl! lax, fɛɐ̯'giːp' lɛs miːɐ̯!
Selig   träumt ich einst als Knabe.... Engel! ach, vergib es mir!
Blissfully dreamed I   once as boy.... Angel! ah, forgive it me!
(As a boy I once blissfully dreamed.... Angel! Ah, forgive me for that!)

dɛn laen 'bɛt'lɐ bɪn lɪç ʃiːɐ̯, nuːɐ̯ diːs hɛrts lɪst' 'maenə 'haːbə!
denn ein Bettler bin ich schier, nur dies Herz ist   meine Habe!"
for a   beggar am I   nearly, only this heart is   my   possession!"
(For I am practically a beggar; this heart of mine is my only possession!")

'jʏŋlɪŋ,   lax, lan 'diːzəm 'ʃt'aːbə fyːɐ̯st du: 't^hrɔøloːs mɪç tsʊm 'graːbə,
"Jüngling, ach, an diesem Stabe führst du treulos   mich zum Grabe,
"Young man, ah, with that staff lead you faithlessly me   to the grave,
("Young man, ah, with that staff you faithlessly lead me to the grave,)

du: 'vʏrgəst', gɔt' fɛɐ̯'tsae lɛs diːɐ̯! diː   dɪç 'liːp't'ə, fyːɐ̯/fyːr lʊnt' fyːɐ̯!
du würgest, Gott verzeih' es dir! die   dich liebte, für   und für!"
you strangle, God forgive it you! her who you loved, for   and for (= for ever)!"
(you slay—God forgive you for that!—the one who loved you for ever and ever!")

ʊnt' ʃoːn 'vaŋk't'ə deːɐ̯/deːr lɛnt'tsʏk't'ə, lals dɛs 'frɔølaens 'k^hɔøʃɐ larm,
Und schon wankte der   Entzückte,   als des Fräuleins   keuscher Arm,
and already wavered the   enchanted one, as the young lady's chaste   arm,
(and already the enchanted young man wavered as the young lady's chaste arm,)

ax, zoː vaes, zoː vaeç lʊnt' varm zanft' liːn hɪn   tsʊm 'buːzən 'drʏk't'ə!
ach, so weiss, so weich und warm sanft ihn hin   zum Busen drückte!
ah, so white, so soft   and warm gently him hence to the bosom pressed!
(ah, so white, so soft and warm, gently pressed him to her bosom!)

[Adelwold recalls her father's half-uttered curse at the tomb of his sons:]

ˈlaːbɐ ˈfʏrçtˈɐliçɐ ˈblɪkˈt'ə, vas liːm ʃiːɐ liːɐ kʰʊs lɛntˈˈrʏkˈt'ə,
Aber fürchterlicher blickte, was ihm schier ihr Kuss entrückte,
But more frightful looked that which from him sheerly her kiss took away,
(But that which sheerly took away her kiss from him looked more frightful than ever,)

ʊntˈ fɔm ˈhɛrtsən, das liːm ʃluːkˈ, rɪs liːn ʃnɛl dɛs ˈfaːt'ɐs fluːx.
und vom Herzen, das ihm schlug, riss ihn schnell des Vaters Fluch.
and from the heart that for him beat, tore him quickly the father's curse.
(and her father's curse tore him away from her heart that was beating only for him.)

[Adelwold has left the castle; Emma suffers immeasurably:]

ˈlɪndrə, ˈfaːt'ɐ, ˈmaɛnə ˈvʊndə! ˈkʰaɛnən lɑọtˈ lɑọs ˈdaɛnəm ˈmʊndə!
"Lindre, Vater, meine Wunde! keinen Laut aus deinem Munde!
"Alleviate, Father, my wound! No sound out of your mouth!
("Father, alleviate my wound! I hear not a sound from your mouth!)

ˈkʰaɛnə tsɛːɐ/tsɛːr lɪn ˈdiːzə ˈʃt'ʊndə! ˈkʰaɛnə ˈzɔnə, diː miːɐ blɪkˈtʰ!
Keine Zähr' in dieser Stunde! Keine Sonne, die mir blickt!
No tear in this hour! No sun, which for me shines!
(Not a tear at this hour! No sun to shine for me!)

ˈkʰaɛnə naxt, diː mɪç lɛɐˈkʰvɪkˈtʰ!
keine Nacht, die mich erquickt!"
no night, which me refreshes!"
(No night to refresh me!")

gɔltˈ, gəˈʃt'aɛn lʊntˈ ˈzaɛdə ˈnɪmɐ, ʃvøːɐt' ziː, fɔrt tsuː ˈleːgən an,
Gold, Gestein und Seide nimmer, schwört sie, fort zu legen an,
Gold, precious stones and silk never, swore she, henceforth to put on,
(Gold, precious stones and silk she swore never again to put on,)

ˈkʰaɛnə ˈtsoːfə darf liːɐ naːn, lʊntˈ kʰaɛn ˈkʰnap'ə, jɛtstˈ lʊntˈ ˈnɪmɐ.
keine Zofe darf ihr nahn, und kein Knappe, jetzt und nimmer.
no maid-servant may her approach, and no page, now and never.
(no maid-servant may come near her, nor any page, now or ever.)

ɔftˈ baɛ ˈtʰrɑọt'əm ˈmoːndəsʃɪmɐ valtˈ ziː ˈbaːɐfuːs ˈlyːbɐ ˈtʰrʏmɐ,
Oft bei trautem Mondesschimmer wallt sie barfuss über Trümmer,
often by intimate moon- shimmer walked she barefoot over ruins,
(often in the intimacy of moonlight she walked barefoot over ruins)

vɪltˈ fɛɐ'vaksən, ʃt'aɛl lʊntˈ rɑọ, nɔx tsur ˈhoːxgəloːp't'ən frɑọ.
wild verwachsen, steil und rauh, noch zur hochgelobten Frau.
wildly overgrown, steep and rough, still to the high-praised Lady.
(that were wildly overgrown, steep and rough, to the shrine of our blessed Lady.)

[Emma has lost her will to live:]

ˈrɪt'ɐ! lax, ʃoːn veːtˈ fɔm ˈgraːbə ˈdaɛnɐ ˈɛma ˈtʰoːt'ənlʊftʰ!
Ritter! ach, schon weht vom Grabe deiner Emma Totenluft!
Knight! Ah, already blows from the grave of your Emma death-air!
(Knight! Ah, already the air of death is blowing from the future grave of your Emma!)

32

ʃoːn lʊmˈʃvɛrmt deːɐ̯ ˈfɛːtʰɐ grʊftʰ ˈlaːnəntʰ ˈkʰɔøtslaen, lɔøl lʊntʰ ˈraːbə.
schon umschwärmt der Väter Gruft ahnend Käuzlein, Eul' und Rabe.
already swarm around the ancestors' tomb expectantly little screech-owl, owl, and raven.
(already the owl and the raven are hovering expectantly around the tomb of your forebears.)

veː diːɐ̯! veː! lan ˈzaenəm ˈʃtaːbə fɔlktʰ ziː ˈvɪlɪç liːm tsʊm ˈgraːbə hɪn,
Weh dir! weh! an seinem Stabe folgt sie willig ihm zum Grabe hin,
Woe to you! Woe! beside his staff follows she willingly him to the grave hence,
(Woe to you! Woe! As if beside his staff, she willingly follows him toward the grave,)

voː meːɐ̯ den hɛlm lʊntʰ ʃiltʰ, ˈliːbə, tʰrɔø lʊntʰ ˈtʰuːgəntʰ gɪltʰ!
wo mehr denn Helm und Schild, Liebe, Treu' und Tugend gilt!
where more than helmet and shield, love, loyalty and virtue counts!
(where love, loyalty, and virtue count for more than the helmet and shield of a knight!)

zɛlpʰst dem ˈrɪtʰɐ tʰeːtʰ zɪç ˈzɛŋkʰən tʰiːf lʊntʰ ˈtʰiːfɐ jɛtst das haopʰtʰ,
Selbst dem Ritter tät sich senken tief und tiefer jetzt das Haupt,
Himself to the knight does itself sink deep and deeper now the head,
(The knight himself now bows his head lower and lower;)

kʰaom das leːɐ̯ deːɐ̯ meːɐ̯ nɔx glaopʰtʰ: ˈzɔøftsən tʰeːtʰ leːɐ̯ lɪtstʰ, lɪtst ˈdɛŋkʰən,
kaum dass er der Mär noch glaubt: seufzen tät er itzt, itzt denken,
scarcely that he the tale still believes: sigh does he now, now think,
(he scarcely still believes the tidings [that Adelwold has left them]: one moment he is sighing, the next he is lost in thought,)

vas den ˈjʏŋlɪŋ ˈkʰɔntʰə ˈkʰrɛŋkʰən? lɔpʰ laen ʃpʰiːl fɔn naetʰ lʊntʰ ˈrɛŋkʰən?
was den Jüngling konnte kränken? ob ein Spiel von Neid und Ränken?
what the young man could offend? Whether a game of envy and intrigues?
(wondering what could have offended the young man, whether envy and intrigue were involved.)

ɔpʰʔ?... viː laen gəˈʃpʰɛnst deːɐ̯ naxtʰ, ʃrɛkʰtʰ liːn, vas leːɐ̯/leːr lɪtstʰ gəˈdaxtʰ...
Ob?..... Wie ein Gespenst der Nacht, schreckt ihn, was er itzt gedacht.....
Whether?... Like a phantom of the night frightens him what he now thought of....
(Could it be...? What he now remembered frightens him like a phantom of the night....)

[The castle is suddenly on fire:]

ˈheːɐ̯gəˈfyːɐ̯tʰ laof ˈʃvyːlən ˈvɪndən, mʊs laen ʃtʰraːl di bʊrkʰ lɛntˈtsʏndən:
Hergeführt auf schwülen Winden, muss ein Strahl die Burg entzünden:
Brought hither on sultry winds, must a flash (of lightning) the castle set afire:
(Brought on by sultry winds, a lightning flash must have set the castle on fire:)

ˈtʰoːzəntʰ glaeç den ˈvoːgən ˈvalən rɪŋs di ˈgluːtʰən—ˈkʰraxəntʰ ˈdrɔøən
tosend gleich den Wogen wallen rings die Gluten— krachend dräuen
roaring like the waves seethe all around the fires— cracking threaten
(roaring like mighty waves, the flames are seething all around—cracking,)

zɔøl lʊntʰ ˈvœlbʊŋ, balkʰ lʊntʰ ʃtʰaen, ʃtraks lɪn ˈtʰrʏmɛn tsuː tsɛɐ̯ˈfalən;
Säul' und Wölbung, Balk' und Stein, stracks in Trümmern zu zerfallen;
column and vault, rafter and stone, immediately into fragments to crumble;
(column and vault, rafter and stone threaten to tumble down into fragments at any moment;)

'aŋst'ru:f |ʊnt' fɛɐ̯'tsvaeflʊŋ 'ʃalən 'graozənt dʊrç di 'vaet'ən 'halən,
Angstruf und Verzweiflung schallen grausend durch die weiten Hallen,
fear-cry and despair resound horrifyingly through the broad halls,
(cries of terror and despair resound horrifyingly through the broad halls,)

ʃt'ʏrmənt drɛŋt' |ʊnt' 'la:t'əmlo:s kʰnɛçt' |ʊnt' 'jʊŋk'ɐ |aos dem ʃlɔs.
stürmend drängt und atemlos Knecht und Junker aus dem Schloss.
stormingly rush and breathlessly knave and nobleman out of the castle.
(servants and noblemen rush tumultuously and breathlessly out of the castle.)

'rıçt'ɐ, |ax, fɛɐ̯'ʃo:nə! ru:ft de:ɐ̯ graes mıt' ʃt'arəm blɪkʰ,
"Richter, ach, verschone!" ruft der Greis mit starrem Blick,
"Judge, ah, spare!" calls the old man with staring gaze,
("Heavenly Judge, spare us!" cries out the old man, his gaze fixed and staring,)

gɔt'! maen kʰınt', |ɛs blaep't tsu'rʏkʰ! 'rɛt'ət, das |ɔøç gɔt' |aenst' 'lo:nə!
"Gott! mein Kind, es bleibt zurück! Rettet, dass euch Gott einst lohne!
"God! My child, it remains back! Rescue, that you God someday reward!
("God! My child remains behind in the burning castle! Rescue her, men, may God reward you!)

gɔlt' |ʊnt' 'zɪlbɐ, lant' |ʊnt' 'fro:nə, 'je:də bʊrk', di: |ıç bə'vo:nə,
Gold und Silber, Land und Frone, jede Burg, die ich bewohne,
Gold and silver, land and bondsmen, every castle that I inhabit,

'li:rəm 'rɛt'ɐ tsum gə'vın, zɛlp'st di:s 'le:bən ge:p' |ıç hın fy:ɐ̯ zi:!
ihrem Retter zum Gewinn, selbst dies Leben geb' ich hin für sie!"
to her rescuer as the prize, itself this life give I away for her!"
(my life itself, everything I give away to her rescuer as a prize!")

'glaet'ən |ap' fɔn 't'ʰaobən 'lo:rən t'ʰɛ:t dɛs 'ho:xbədrɛŋt'ən ʃrae.
Gleiten ab von tauben Ohren tät des Hochbedrängten Schrei.
Glide off from deaf ears does the highly-oppressed one's cry.
(The stricken man's cry falls upon deaf ears.)

[Suddenly a rescuer appears—it is Adelwold:]

'a:bɐ 'pʰlœtslıç ʃt'ʏrtst hɛɐ̯'bae,, de:ɐ̯/de:r |i:ɐ̯ 't'ʰrɔøə 'tsu:gəʃvo:rən,
Aber plötzlich stürzt herbei, der ihr Treue zugeschworen,
But suddenly dashes hither, he who to her loyalty (had) sworn,
(But suddenly he who had sworn eternal faithfulness to Emma, Adelwold, dashes hither,)

ʃt'ʏrtst' na:x den |ɛnt'flamt'ən 't'ʰo:rən, gi:p't' mıt' 'frɔødən zıç fɛɐ̯'lo:rən.
stürzt nach den entflammten Toren, gibt mit Freuden sich verloren.
dashes toward the flaming gates, gives with joys himself lost.
(dashes toward the flame-engulfed gates, joyfully gives himself up for lost.)

'je:dɐ 'ʃt'aonənt', fɛrn |ʊnt' na:, vɛ:nt |aen 'blɛnt'vɛrk, vas le:ɐ̯ za:,
Jeder staunend, fern und nah, wähnt ein Blendwerk, was er sah,
Everyone astonished, far and near, imagines a mirage, what he saw,
(Everyone, far or near, is astonished and imagines what he saw to be a mirage,)

glu:t' |an glu:t', |ʊnt' 'je:dəs ʃt're:bən ʃi:n fɛɐ̯'ge:bəns—
Glut an Glut, und jedes Streben schien vergebens—
Fire upon fire, and every effort seemed in vain—

34

'ɛnt'lɪç fast' leːɐ̯ di 't^hɔ̯ørə, 'zyːsə last', k^halt', lʊnt' 'zɔndɐ ʃp'uːɐ̯ fɔn 'leːbən;
Endlich fasst er die teure, süsse Last, kalt, und sonder Spur von Leben;
At last grasps he the dear, sweet burden, cold, and without trace of life;
(At last he grasps the dear, sweet burden, cold, and without a sign of life;)

dɔx bə'gɪnt' laen 'laezəs 'beːbən 'hɛrt͡s lʊnt' 'buːzən jɛt͡st t͡su: 'heːbən,
doch beginnt ein leises Beben Herz und Busen jetzt zu heben,
yet begins a light trembling heart and bosom now to raise,
(nevertheless a light trembling now begins to stir her heart and lift her bosom,)

ʊnt dʊrç 'flamə, damp͡f lʊnt' gra̯os t^hrɛːk't' leːɐ̯ 'glyk'lɪç zi: hɪ'na̯os.
und durch Flamme, Dampf und Graus trägt er glücklich sie hinaus.
and through flame, steam and horror carries he successfully her out.
(and through flames, smoke, and horror he successfully carries her out of the burning castle.)

'p^hʊrp'ʊr k^heːɐ̯t' la̯of 'liːrə 'vaŋən, vo: deːɐ̯ 't'ra̯ot'ə zi: gə'k^hʏst^h.
Purpur kehrt auf ihre Wangen, wo der Traute sie geküsst.
Crimson returns to her cheeks, where the beloved one her (had) kissed.
(Crimson returns to her cheeds, where her beloved had kissed her.)

'jʏŋlɪŋ, 'zaːgə, veːɐ̯ du: bɪst^h, lɪç bə'ʃvøːrə dɪç, deːɐ̯ 'baŋən!
"Jüngling, sage, wer du bist, ich beschwöre dich, der Bangen!
"Young man, say who you are, I beseech you, to the anxious woman!
("Young man, tell this anxious woman who you are, I beseech you!)

hɛlt' laen 'lɛŋəl mɪç lʊm'faŋən,
hält ein Engel mich umfangen,
holds an angel me embraced,
(Does an angel hold me in his arms,)

deːɐ̯/deːr la̯of 'zaenəm 'leːɐ̯dənfluːk' 'maenəs 'liːbən 'bɪlt'nɪs t^hruːk?
der auf seinem Erdenflug meines Lieben Bildnis trug?"
who on his earth- flight my dear one's image bore?"
(an angel who assumed the image of my dear one for his flight to earth?")

[*Seeing the knight as they emerge from the fire, Adelwold and Emma are afraid of his reaction:*]

ʃt'ar t͡su'zamənʃrɪk't' deːɐ̯ 'bløːdə, dɛn deːɐ̯ 'rɪt'ɐ, nɔx lam t^hoːɐ̯,
Starr zusammenschrickt der Blöde, denn der Ritter, noch am Tor,
Motionlessly is terrified the shy man, for the knight, still at the gate,
(The shy young man suddenly freezes, terrified, for the knight, still at the gate,)

la̯oʃt' mɪt' 'hɪngəvant'əm loːɐ̯ 'jeːdəm la̯ot deːɐ̯ 'zyːsən 'reːdə.
lauscht mit hingewandtem Ohr jedem Laut der süssen Rede.
listens with hence-trurned ear to every sound of the sweet speech.
(is listening intently to every sound of that sweet speech.)

[*But the knight greets them warmly, with tears of joy:*]

dɔx den 't͡svaeflɐ t^hɛːt' lɛɐ̯'manən balt dɛs 'rɪt'ɐs gruːs lʊnt' k^hʊs,
Doch den Zweifler tät ermannen bald des Ritters Gruss und Kuss,
Yet the doubter [object] did embolden soon the knight's greeting and kiss,
(But the frightened doubter was soon emboldened by the greeting and kiss of the knight,)

de:m   Im   'zy:səst'ən gə'nʊs hɛl   de:ɐ̯ 'vɔnə   'tsɛːrən 'ranən.
dem   im   süssesten Genuss hell   der Wonne   Zähren rannen.
to whom in the sweetest pleasure brightly the rapture's tears   ran.
(whose tears of rapture ran brightly in sweetest gratification.)

du: ɛs, du:? zaːk' Ian,   fɔn 'vanən? vas dɪç kʰɔnt' fɔn miːɐ̯ fɛɐ̯'banən?
"Du es, du? sag an,   von wannen? was dich konnt' von mir verbannen?
"You it, you? Tell further, from whence? What you could from me exile?
("Is it you, you? Tell us where you have come from! What could have exiled you from me?)

vas dɪç—   'nɪmɐ loːn Içs diːɐ̯ —'ɛma 'viːdɐgaːp' ʊnt' miːɐ̯?
Was dich—   nimmer lohn' ich's dir— Emma   wiedergab und mir?"
What you [object]—never   repay I   it you— to Emma gave again and to me?"
(What has given you—I can never repay you for it!—again to Emma and to me?")

[Adelwold explains to the knight why he left:]

'daenəs fluːxs mɪç   tsu: Iɛnt'ˈlast'ən, vaːɐ̯/vaːr Ies pflɪçt, das Iɪç Iɛnt'ˈvɪç,
"Deines Fluchs mich zu entlasten, war   es Pflicht, dass ich entwich,
"Of your curse myself to unburden,   was   it duty,   that I disappeared,
("To unburden myself of your curse, it was my duty to disappear,)

'aelɪç, vɪlt' ʊnt' 'fʏrçt'ɐlɪç,   tʰriːp's mɪç 'zɔndɐ ru: ʊnt' 'rast'ən;
eilig, wild und fürchterlich, trieb's mich sonder Ruh und Rasten;
hastily, wildly and frightfully,   drove it me   without peace and rest;
(something drove me on, hastily, wildly and fearfully, without peace or rest;)

dɔrt' Im 'kʰloːst'ɐ, vo: zi: 'pʰrast'ən, 'laːp't'ən 'tʰrɛːnən mɪç ʊnt' 'fast'ən,
dort im Kloster, wo   sie prassten, labten Tränen mich und Fasten,
there in the monastery, where they feasted,   refreshed tears   me and fasting,
(there at the monastery, where the others were feasting, tears and fasting were my refreshment,)

bɪs de:ɐ̯ 'frɔmən 'pɪlgɐ ʃaːɐ̯ fɔl tsʊm tsu:k'   fɛɐ̯'zaməlt' vaːɐ̯;
bis der frommen Pilger Schar voll zum Zug   versammelt war;
until the pious   pilgrims' troop fully for the expedition assembled was;
(until the band of pious pilgrims was fully assembled for the expedition;)

[God brought Adelwold back to the castle when Emma was in danger.]

dɔx mɪt' 'ʊnzɪçt'baːrən 'kʰɛt'ən, tso:k' mɪç 'pʰlœtslɪç 'gɔt'əs hant'
doch mit unsichtbaren Ketten, zog   mich plötzlich Gottes Hand
but with invisible   chains drew me   suddenly God's hand
(but suddenly, with invisible chains, the hand of God drew me)

jɛtst tsu'rʏk' fɔn lant tsu: lant' heːɐ̯ tsu:ɐ̯ bʊrk', maen 'tʰɔøɐst'əs tsu: 'rɛt'ən!
jetzt zurück von Land zu Land her zur Burg, mein Teuerstes zu retten!
now back   from land to land hither to the castle, my dearest   to rescue!
(now from land to land back here to the castle to rescue my dearest!)

nɪm zi:, 'rɪt'ɐ, nɪm ʊnt' ʃp'rɪç das 'Iʊrt'ael 'Iy:bɐ mɪç!
Nimm sie, Ritter, nimm und sprich das Urteil   über mich!"
Take her, knight, take and speak the judgment over me!"
(Take her, knight, take her, and pass judgment on me!")

[Both Adelwold and Emma assume that the family-proud knight will disapprove of their love.]

ˈɛma hart‘, ɪn ˈdyːstʀəs ˈʃvaẹgən viː ɪn ˈmɪt‘ɐnaxt‘ gəˈhʏltʰ;
Emma harrt, in düstres Schweigen wie in Mitternacht gehüllt;
Emma waits, in dark silence as in midnight wrapped;
(Emma, wrapped in dark silence as in midnight, awaits her father's answer;)

ˈʃtarɐ dɛn ḷaẹn ˈmarmoːɐ̯bɪlt‘ ˈharən ˈfʊrçt‘lɛɐ̯fʏlt‘ə ˈtsɔɐ̯gən,
starrer denn ein Marmorbild harren furchterfüllte Zeugen,
more ridgid than a marble statue wait fear- filled witnesses,
(the frightened witnesses are waiting in suspense, more motionless than marble statues,)

dɛn ḷɛs ˈtsvaẹfəlt‘ən di ˈfaẹgən, ɔp‘ dɛn ˈrɪt‘ɐʃt‘ɔlts tsuː ˈbɔɐ̯gən
denn es zweifelten die Feigen, ob den Ritterstolz zu beugen
for it doubted the timid ones, whether the knightly pride to bend
(for the faint-hearted ones doubted whether ...)

jeː fɛɐ̯mœçt‘ ḷaẹn ˈhoːɐ muːt‘ ˈzɔndɐ ˈḷaːnənglants ʊnt‘ guːtʰ.
je vermöcht' ein hoher Mut sonder Ahnenglanz und Gut.
ever might be able a high courage without ancestral luster and possessions.
(sublime courage with neither ancestral luster nor possesstions might ever be able to bend knightly pride.)

[But the knight, filled with relief, gratitude, and admiration for Adelwold's courage, gives his blessing to their marriage:]

daẹn ḷɪst‘ ˈḷema! ˈḷeːvɪç daẹn! ḷɛŋst‘ ḷɛntˈʃaẹdən tʰɛːt deːɐ̯ ˈhɪməl,
"Dein ist Emma! ewig dein! Längst entscheiden tät der Himmel,
"Yours is· Emma! eternally yours! Long since decide did the heaven,
("Emma is yours, eternally yours! Heaven has long since decided,)

raẹn viː gɔlt‘ bɪst duː ˈfʊndən, ˈḷaːdəlvɔlt‘, groːs ɪn ˈḷeːdəlmuːt‘ ʊnt‘ ˈḷaẹdən,
rein wie Gold bist du funden, Adelwold, gross in Edelmut und Leiden,
pure as gold are you found, Adelwold, great in noble courage and suffering,
(you have been found to be as pure as gold, Adelwold, great in noble courage and in suffering;)

nɪm, ḷɪç ˈgeːbə ziː mɪt‘ ˈfrɔɐ̯dən, nɪm, deːɐ̯ ˈhɪməl tʰɛːt‘ ḷɛntˈʃaẹdən,
nimm, ich gebe sie mit Freuden, nimm, der Himmel tät entscheiden,
take, I give her with joys, take, the heaven did decide,
(take her, I give her to you with joy, take her! Heaven has decided,)

ˈnant‘ə zɛlpst‘ ḷɪm ˈdɔnɐ̯ḷaọt‘ ziː foːɐ̯/foːr ˈḷɛŋəln ˈdaẹnə braọtʰ.
nannte selbst im Donnerlaut sie vor Engeln deine Braut.
named itself in the thunder-sound her before angels your bride.
(heaven itself named her your bride in sounds of thunder, in the presence of the angels.)

nɪm ziː hɪn mɪt‘ ˈfaːt‘ɐ̯zeːgən! ḷiːn vɪrt‘ ˈneːbən ˈmaẹnə ʃult‘,
Nimm sie hin mit Vatersegen! Ihn wird neben meine Schuld,
Take her hence with father-blessing! Him will next to my guilt,
(Take her as your own with a father's blessing! Next to my guilt, ...)

ax mɪt‘ ˈḷaŋmuːt‘ ʊnt‘ gəˈdʊlt‘, deːɐ̯/deːr ḷaẹnst‘ kʰɔmt‘ gəˈrɪçt tsuː ˈheːgən,
ach mit Langmut und Geduld, der einst kommt Gericht zu hegen,
ah with forbearance and patience, He who one day comes judgment to pass,

(He who will one day come to pass judgment will, ah! with forbearance and patience,)

ˈlɑ͜of di ˈpʰryːfʊŋsvaːgə ˈleːgən, miːɐ̯ fɛɐ̯ˈt͡saen ʊm ˈlɔ͜ørətˈveːgən,
auf die Prüfungswaage legen, mir verzeihn um euretwegen,
onto the testing scales to lay, me forgive for your sake,
(place me on the testing scales, will forgive me for *your* sake,)

deːɐ̯, fɔn ˈlaet͜ˈləm ʃt͜ˈɔlt͡s bəˈflɛk͜ˈt͜, baet͜ˈ lɔ͜øç ʃiːɐ̯/ʃiːr lɪns grɑːp͜ˈ gəˈʃt͡rɛk͜ˈtʰ.
der, von eitlem Stolz befleckt, beid' euch schier ins Grab gestreckt.''
who, by idle pride stained, both you nearly into the grave stretched.''
(*me*—who, stained by idle pride, nearly sent you both to your grave.'')

fɛst͜ˈ lʊmˈʃlʊŋən jɛt͡st͜ˈ fɔn ˈliːnən blɪk͜ˈt deːɐ̯ graes t͡sʊm ˈhɪməl lɑ͜of:
Fest umschlungen jetzt von ihnen blickt der Greis zum Himmel auf:
Firmly embraced now by them looks the old man to the heaven up:
(Firmly embraced by them now, the old man looks up toward heaven:)

ˈfrøːlɪç ˈlɛndət͜ˈ zɪç maen lɑ͜of! ˈʃp͜ˈuːrən deːɐ̯ fɛɐ̯ˈkʰleːrʊŋ
''fröhlich endet sich mein Lauf!'' Spuren der Verklärung
''Joyfully ends itself my course!'' Traces of the transfiguration
(''Joyfully my life is ending!'' Traces of transfiguration)

ˈʃiːnən lɑ͜os dɛs ˈhoxlɛnt͜ˈt͡sʏk͜ˈt͜ˈən ˈmiːnən, lʊnt͜ˈ lɑ͜of ˈdampfəndən ru͜ˈiːnən
schienen aus des Hochentzückten Mienen, und auf dampfenden Ruinen
appeared from the sublimely enraptured mien(s), and on steaming ruins
(appeared in his sublimely enraptured expression; and on the smoking ruins)

fyːk͜ˈt͜ˈ leːɐ̯ ˈʃvaegənt͜ˈ ˈliːrə hant͜ˈ lɪn das ˈlaŋlɛɐ̯zeːnt͜ˈə bant͜ˈ.
fügt' er schweigend ihre Hand in das langersehnte Band.
joined he silently her hand into the long-desired bond.
(he silently joined their hands in the long-desired bond.)

[At twenty-six pages (two of them with repeat signs at either end) this may well be the longest song ever written; it is certainly Schubert's longest! The poem has forty verses of eight lines each; Schubert set it in 628 bars. Much of the music is mere illustration; but some of the lyrical sections are very beautiful.]

aˈdjø
Adieu
Farewell

(Edouard Bélanger)

vwasi lɛ̃stɑ̃ syˈprɛːmə, lɛ̃stɑ̃ də noˌzaˈdjø!
Voici l'instant suprême, l'instant de nos adieux!
Here is the instant supreme, the instant of our farewells!
(Here is the final moment, the moment of our farewells!)

o twa! sœl bjæ̃ kə ʒɛːmə! sɑ̃ mwa rəturˌ ˌno sjø!
O toi! seul bien que j'aime! sans moi retourne aux cieux!
O you! only good that I love! without me return to the heavens!
(O you, only good that I love, return to heaven without me!)

38

la moː‿ rɛ‿ ty‿ naˈmiːə ki rɑ̃ la libɛrˈte;
La mort est une amie qui rend la liberté;
The death is a friend who gives back the freedom;
(Death is a friend who gives back freedom;)

o sjɛl rəswa la ˈviːe / e puːr letɛrniˈte!
au Ciel reçois la vie et pour l'éternité!
in the sky receive the life and for the eternity!
(receive life in heaven, and for eternity!)

adjø, ty va maˈtɑ̃ːdrə : bjæ̃to ʒə dwa parˈtiːr.
Adieu, tu vas m'attendre: bientôt je dois partir.
Farewell, you are going me to await: soon I must depart.
(Farewell, you are going to wait for me: soon I must depart.)

mõ cœːr fidɛː le ˈtɑ̃ːdrə tə gar‿ dœ̃ suvəˈniːr.
Mon coeur fidèle et tendre te garde un souvenir.
My heart faithful and tender for you keeps a memory.
(My faithful, tender heart keeps a memory for you.)

adjø ʒyska loˈrɔːrə dy ʒuː‿ rɑ̃ ki ʒe fwɑ,
Adieu jusqu'à l'aurore du jour en qui j'ai foi,
Farewell until the dawn of the day in which I have faith,

dy ʒuːr ki dwa‿ tɑ̃ˈkɔːrə mə reyniː‿ ra twa.
du jour qui doit encore me réunir à toi.
of the day which must again me reunite to you.
(of the day which must reunite me again with you.)

[This song, mistakenly attributed to Schubert by a publisher in Berlin in 1843 and included in Peters' volume VI, is not by Schubert at all. The actual composer was August Heinrich von Weyrauch. The song was first published in 1824 (during Schubert's lifetime) with a German text by Gottlob Wetzel.]

aˈlɪndə
Alinde

Op. 81, No. 1 [1827] (Johann Friedrich von Rochlitz)

di ˈzɔnə zɪŋkˈtˈ ɪns ˈtʰiːfə meːɐ̯, daː ˈvɔltˈə ziː ˈkʰɔmən.
Die Sonne sinkt ins tiefe Meer, da wollte sie kommen.
The sun sinks into the deep sea, there wanted she to come.
(The sun is sinking into the deep sea; this is the time she said she would come.)

gəˈruːɪç tʰraːpˈtˈ deːɐ̯ ˈʃnɪtˈɐ laen̩ˈheːɐ̯, miːɐ̯/miːr lɪsts bəˈkʰlɔmən.
Geruhig trabt der Schnitter einher, mir ist's beklommen.
Calmly trots the reaper along, to me is it uneasy.
(The reaper trots calmly on his way; I feel uneasy.)

hast, ˈʃnɪtˈɐ, maen ˈliːpˈçən nɪçtˈ gəˈzeːn̩? aˈlɪndə, laˈlɪndə!
Hast, Schnitter, mein Liebchen nicht gesehn? Alinde, Alinde!
Have (you), reaper, my sweetheart not seen? Alinda, Alinda!
(Reaper, have you not seen my sweetheart? Alinda, Alinda!)

ʦuː vaɛpˈ lʊntˈ ˈkʰɪndɐn mʊs lɪç geːn, kʰan nɪçtˈ naːx ˈandɐn ˈdɪrnən zeːn;
"Zu Weib und Kindern muss ich gehn, kann nicht nach andern Dirnen sehn;
"To wife and children must I go, can not after other girls look:
("To my wife and my children I must go; I can not look after other girls;)
        [When this poem was written, "*Dirne*" meant simply "girl"; today it means "prostitute."]

ziː ˈvartˈən maen ˈlʊntˈɐ deːɐ̯ ˈlɪndə.
sie warten mein unter der Linde."
they wait for me under the linden tree."
(they—my wife and children—are waiting for me under the linden tree.")

deːɐ̯ moːntˈ bəˈtʰrɪt di ˈhɪməlsbaːn, nɔx vɪl ziː nɪçtˈ ˈkʰɔmən.
Der Mond betritt die Himmelsbahn, noch will sie nicht kommen.
The moon enters the orbit, still wants she not to come.
(The moon rises in its orbit; still she does not come.)

dɔrtˈ leːkˈtˈ laen ˈfɪʃɐ das ˈfaːɐ̯ʦɔøkˈ lan, miːɐ̯/miːr lɪsʦ bəˈkʰlɔmən.
Dort legt ein Fischer das Fahrzeug an, mir ist's beklommen.
There docks a fisherman the vessel ... , to me is it uneasy.
(There a fisherman is docking his vessel; I feel uneasy.)

hast, ˈfɪʃɐ, maen ˈliːpˈçən nɪçtˈ gəˈzeːn? aˈlɪndə, laˈlɪndə!
Hast, Fischer, mein Liebchen nicht gesehn? Alinde, Alinde!
Have (you), fisherman, my sweetheart not seen? Alinda, Alinda!
(Fisherman, have you not seen my sweetheart? Alinda, Alinda!)

mʊs ˈzuːxən, viː miːɐ̯ di ˈrɔøzən ʃtˈeːn,
"Muss suchen, wie mir die Reusen stehn,
"Must look, how for me the basket-traps are,
("I must look and see how my basket-traps are doing,)

haːpˈ ˈnɪmɐ ʦaetˈ naːx ˈjʊŋfɐn ʦuː geːn,
hab nimmer Zeit nach Jungfern zu gehn,
have never time after young girls to go,
(I never have time to go looking after young girls;)

ʃao, vɛlç ˈlaenən faŋ lɪç ˈfɪndə.
schau, welch einen Fang ich finde."
look what a catch I find."

di ˈlɪçtˈən ʃtˈɛrnə ʦiːn hɛˈraof, nɔx vɪl ziː nɪçtˈ ˈkʰɔmən.
Die lichten Sterne ziehn herauf, noch will sie nicht kommen.
The light stars draw on, still wants she not to come.
(The bright stars are gathering; still she does not come.)

dɔrtˈ laelt deːɐ̯ ˈjɛːgɐ(r) lɪn ˈrʏstˈɪgəm laof, miːɐ̯/miːr lɪsʦ bəˈkʰlɔmən.
Dort eilt der Jäger in rüstigem Lauf, mir ist's beklommen.
There hurries the huntsman in vigorous pace, for me is it uneasy.
(There comes the huntsman, hurrying at a vigorous pace; I feel uneasy.)

hast, ˈjɛːgɐ, maen ˈliːpˈçən nɪçtˈ gəˈzeːn? aˈlɪndə, laˈlɪndə!
Hast, Jäger, mein Liebchen nicht gesehn? Alinde, Alinde!
Have (you), huntsman, my sweetheart not seen? Alinda, Alinda!
(Huntsman, have you not seen my sweetheart? Alinda, Alinda!)

mus naːx dem ˈbrɔønlɪçən ˈreːbɔk geːn, haːpˈ ˈnɪmɐ lʊstˈ naːx mɛːdəln tsuː zeːn;
Muss nach dem bräunlichen Rehbock gehn, hab nimmer Lust nach Mädeln zu sehn;
"Must after the brownish roebuck go, have never desire after girls to look;
("I have to go in search of the brown roebuck; I have never felt the inclination to look for girls;)

dɔrtˈ ʃlaeçtˈ leːɐ̯/leːr ɪm ˈlaːbəntˈvɪndə.
dort schleicht er im Abendwinde."
there sneaks it (the buck) in the evening wind."
(there it is, moving stealthily in the evening wind.")

ɪn ˈʃvartsɐ naxtˈ ʃtˈeːtˈ hiːɐ̯ deːɐ̯ haen, nɔx vɪl ziː nɪçtˈ ˈkʰɔmən.
In schwarzer Nacht steht hier der Hain, noch will sie nicht kommen.
In black night stands here the grove, still wants she not to come.
(The grove here is submerged in dark night; still she does not come.)

fɔn ˈlalən leːˈbəntˈgən ɪr ɪç laˈlaen, baŋ ʊntˈ bɛˈkʰlɔmən.
Von allen Lebend'gen irr ich allein, bang und beklommen. [*poem:* allem]
From all living (creatures) go astray I alone, fearful and uneasy.
(I go wandering aimlessly away from all living creatures, alone, fearful, and uneasy.)

diːɐ̯/diːr ˈlɛço darf lɪç maen laetˈ gəˈʃtˈeːn : aˈlɪndə, laˈlɪndə!
Dir Echo darf ich mein Leid gestehn: Alinde, Alinde!
To you, Echo, may I my sorrow confess: Alinda, Alinda!
(To you, Echo, I may confess my sorrow: Alinda, Alinda!)

aˈlɪndə liːs ˈlɛço ˈlaezə hɛˈryːbɐveːn; daː zaː lɪç ziː miːɐ̯ tsur ˈzaetˈə ʃtˈeːn :
"Alinde" liess Echo leise herüberwehn; da sah ich sie mir zur Seite stehn:
"Alinde" · let Echo softly hither waft; then saw I her to me at the side stand:
(Echo let the name "Alinda" softly waft back to me; then I saw *her* standing at my side:)

duː ˈzuːxtˈəstˈ zoː tʰrɔø, nuːn ˈfɪndə!
"Du suchtest so treu, nun finde!"
"You searched so faithfully, now find!"

[The impatient lover is waiting for his sweetheart to meet him. She is late and he is uneasy. He asks the reaper, the fisherman, and the huntsman if they have seen her. They are too busy with their own affairs. Finally he calls out her name. Echo sends it back to him; and when he turns around — there is his Alinda, saying: "You looked for me so faithfully, now you've found me."]

ˈaləs lʊm ˈliːbə
Alles um Liebe
Everything For Love

Posthumously published [composed 1815] (poem by Ludwig Kosegarten)

vas lɪstˈ lɛs, das di ˈzeːlə fʏltʰ? lax, ˈliːbə fʏlt ziː, ˈliːbə!
Was ist es, das die Seele füllt? Ach, Liebe füllt sie, Liebe!
What is it, that the soul fills? Ah, love fills it, love!
(What is it that fills the soul? Ah, love fills it, love!)

zi: fʏlt' nɪçt' gɔlt', nɔx 'gɔldəsˌveːɐ̯t', nɪçt' vas di 'ʃnøːdə vɛlt' bə'geːɐ̯tʰ,
Sie füllt nicht Gold, noch Goldeswert, nicht was die schnöde Welt begehrt,
It fills not gold, nor gold's worth, not what the base world covets,
(It is filled not by gold, nor by what gold can buy, nor by that which the base world covets;)

zi: fʏlt' nuːɐ̯ 'liːbə, 'liːbə! vas ɪst' ɛs, das di 'zeːnzʊxt' ʃt'ɪltʰ?
sie füllt nur Liebe, Liebe! Was ist es, das die Sehnsucht stillt?
it fills only love, love! What is it, that the yearning stills?
(it is filled only by love, by love! What is it that stills yearning?)

lax, 'liːbə ʃt'ɪlt' ziː, 'liːbə! zi: ʃt'ɪlt' nɪçt' 'tʰiːt'əl, ʃt'ant' nɔx raŋ,
Ach, Liebe stillt sie, Liebe! Sie stillt nicht Titel, Stand noch Rang,
Ah, love stills it, love! It stills not title, station nor rank,
(Ah, love stills it, love! It is not stilled by a title, high station or rank,)

lʊnt' nɪçt' dɛs 'ruːməs 'ʃɛlənkʰlaŋ; zi: ʃt'ɪlt' nuːɐ̯ 'liːbə, 'liːbə!
und nicht des Ruhmes Schellenklang; sie stillt nur Liebe, Liebe!
and not the fame's tinkling sound; it stills only love, love!
(nor by the tinkling sound of fame; it is stilled only by love, by love!)

vas ɪsts, vo'naːx das hɛrts tsɛɐ̯'lɛçtstʰ? ɛs 'lɛçtsət', lax, naːx 'liːbə!
Was ist's, wonach das Herz zerlechzt? Es lechzet, ach, nach Liebe!
What is it, for which the heart is languishing away? It thirsts, ah, for love!

ɛs 'ʃmaxt'ət' nɪçt' naːx drʊk' lʊnt' kʰʊs,
Es schmachtet nicht nach Druck und Kuss,
It languishes not for squeeze and kiss,
(It does not languish for hugs and kisses)

nɪçt' naːx deːɐ̯ 'vɔlʊst' 'fɔlgənʊs; ɛs 'ʃmaxt'ət' nuːɐ̯ naːx 'liːbə.
nicht nach der Wollust Vollgenuss; es schmachtet nur nach Liebe.
not for the sensual pleasures' full enjoyment; it languishes only for love.
(nor for the unrestrained enjoyment of sensual pleasures; it languishes only for love.)

gɛrn geːb ɪç, vas lɪç haːp' lʊnt' bɪn, gɛrn geːb ɪçs hɪn lʊm 'liːbə.
Gern geb' ich, was ich hab und bin, gern geb' ich's hin um Liebe.
gladly give I what I have and am, gladly give I it away for love.
(I would gladly give whatever I have, whatever I am, I would gladly give it away for love.)

dɛs 'raeçt'uːms 'bʊnt'ɐ 'zaefənʃaom, deːɐ̯ 'vɔlʊst' raoʃ,
Des Reichtums bunter Seifenschaum, der Wollust Rausch,
The wealth's bright lather ["soap-foam"], the voluptuousness's intoxication,
(The bright soap-bubbles of wealth, the intoxication of voluptuousness,)

dɛs 'ruːməs tʰraom, vas frɔmt' lɛs 'loːnə 'liːbə!
des Ruhmes Traum, was frommt es ohne Liebe!
the fame's dream, what avails it without love!
(the dream of fame, what use are they without love?)

fiːl 'zyːsɐ lɪsts, gə'rɪŋ lʊnt' larm lan 'tʰrɔøɐ brʊst' fɛɐ̯'ʃmaxt'ən,
Viel süsser ist's, gering und arm an treuer Brust verschmachten,
Much sweeter is it, modest and poor at faithful breast to languish,
(It is much sweeter to languish upon a loving and loyal breast, humble and poor,)

als ˈʊŋəliːpˈtˈ ʊntˈ ˈliːbəloːs den tʰaːkˈ fɛɐˈpʰrasən,
als ungeliebt und liebelos den Tag verprassen,
than unloved and loveless the day to waste in riotous living,
(than to waste one's days in riotous living, unloved and loveless,)

ʊntˈ ɪm ʃoːs deːɐ ˈvɔlʊstˈ lyːbəˈnaxtˈən.
und im Schoss der Wollust übernachten.
and in the lap of the lust to pass the night.
(and to pass one's nights in the lap of lust.)

liːpˈtˈ ˈhɛrtslɪç mɪç, liːpˈtˈ ˈʃmɛrtslɪç mɪç di ˈlaenə, diː lɪç ˈmaenə —
Liebt herzlich mich, liebt schmerzlich mich die Eine, die ich meine —
loves sincerely me, loves painfully me the one, whom I love—
(If the one whom I love loves me sincerely, even though it be in pain and sorrow, —)

["*meinen*" = to mean (usual); to love (poetical)]

nɪm ˈlaləs, ˈlaləs hɪn, gəˈʃɪkʰ, nɪm ruː ʊntˈ ruːm ʊntˈ ˈleːbənsglʏkʰ;
nimm alles, alles hin, Geschick, nimm Ruh und Ruhm und Lebensglück;
take all, all away, Fate, take peace and fame and life's happiness;

miːɐ gnyːkˈtˈ, miːɐ gnyːkˈt di ˈlaenə.
mir gnügt, mir gnügt die Eine.
for me suffices, for me suffices the one.
(the one I love is all I need.)

ʊntˈ zɔltˈ lɪç fɛrn fɔn liːɐ, fɔn liːɐ daˈhɪn maen ˈleːbən ˈtʰraoɐn,
Und sollt' ich fern von Ihr, von Ihr dahin mein Leben trauern,
And should I far from her, from her away my life grieve,
(And should I grieve my life away, far from her, from *her*,)

ʊntˈ ˈvʏstˈə nuːɐ, das duː mɪç liːpstˈ, das duː miːɐ, ˈhɛrtsgəˌliːpˈtˈə, bliːpstʰ,
und wüsste nur, dass Du mich liebst, dass Du mir, Herzgeliebte, bliebst,
and knew (I) only, that you me love, that you to me, heart's beloved, remain,
(and if I knew only that you love me, that you remain to me, beloved of my heart,)

veːɐ ˈdʏrftˈə mɪç bəˈdaoɐn? ʊntˈ vɛːɐ/vɛːr lɪç ɪn deːɐ skˈlaːvəˈrae,
wer dürfte mich bedauern? Und wär' ich in der Sklaverei,
who could me be sorry for? And were I in the slavery,
(who could be sorry for me? And even if I were a slave)

ɪn ˈfrɔødəloːzɐ ˈvɪltˈnɪs, ʊntˈ ˈvɛːrə daen, nuːɐ daen gəˈvɪs, [*poem:* **freundenloser**]
in freudeloser Wildnis, und wäre Dein, nur Dein gewiss,
in joyless wilderness, and were of you, only of you sure,
(in some joyless wilderness, and were sure of you, only sure of you,)

zoː ˈvɛːrə skˈlaːvəˈrae miːɐ zyːs, ʊntˈ pˈaraˈdiːs di ˈvɪltˈnɪs.
so wäre Sklaverei mir süss, und Paradies die Wildnis.
so would be slavery to me sweet, and paradise the wilderness.
(then slavery would be sweet to me, and the wilderness would be paradise.)

ʊntˈ ˈhʏltˈə ˈtʰoːdəsˌfɪnstˈɐnɪs dɪç, ˈmaenəs ˈleːbəns ˈzɔnə,
Und hüllte Todesfinsternis Dich, meines Lebens Sonne,
And veiled death-darkness you, my life's sun,
(And if the darkness of death veiled you, sun of my life [he is addressing his own source of life])

ʊntʻ ʃtʻʏrpʻ   lɪç nuːɐ̯ fɔn liːɐ̯ gəˈmaɛntʻ, fɔn liːɐ̯ bəˈkʰlaːkʻtʻ, fɔn liːɐ̯ bəˈvaɛntʰ,
und stürb'   ich nur von Ihr gemeint, von Ihr beklagt, von Ihr beweint,
and would die I   only by her loved, by her lamented, by her bewept,
(and if I would die only loved by her, only lamented by her, only bewept by her,)

zoː ʃtʻʏrpʻ   lɪç voːl   mɪtʻ ˈvɔnə.   [vɛːɐ̯ deːɐ̯ tʰoːtʻ miːɐ̯]
so stürb'   ich wohl   mit Wonne.   [*poem:* so wär' der Tod mir   Wonne]
so would die I   probably with rapture.   [then were the death for me rapture]
(then dying would probably be a kind of rapture for me.)

fiːl ˈbɛsɐ lɪsts̝, jʊŋ, ˈkʰrɛftʻɪç, kʰyːn lɪm larm deːɐ̯ ˈliːbə ʃtʻɛrbən,
Viel besser ist's, jung, kräftig, kühn im Arm der Liebe sterben,
Much better is it young, strong, bold in the arm of the love to die
(It is much better to die young, strong, and bold in the arms of love)

als ˈlʊŋgəliːpʻtʻ lʊntʻ ˈliːbəloːs
als ungeliebt und liebelos
than unloved   and loveless

ɪn ˈdʊmpfɐ ˈfrɔʏdən ˈmatʻəm ʃoːs   fɛɐ̯ˈlaltʻən/fɛrˈlaltʻən lʊntʻ fɛɐ̯ˈdɛrbən.
in dumpfer Freuden mattem Schoss veralten   und verderben.
in dull   joys' feeble lap   to grow old   and to decay
(to grow old and decay in the feeble lap of dull pleasures.)

[The words are a bit extravagant—and there are too many of them—but the music is pretty.]

als lɪç ziː lɛɐ̯ˈrøːtʻən zaː
Als ich sie erröten sah
When I Saw Her Blush

Published posthumously [composed 1815] (Bernhard A. Ehrlich)

al maɛn ˈvɪrkʻən, lal maɛn ˈleːbən ʃtʻreːpʻtʻ naːx   diːɐ̯, vɛɐ̯ˈleːɐ̯tʻə/vɛrˈleːɐ̯tʻə, hɪn!
All mein Wirken, all mein Leben strebt nach dir, Verehrte,   hin!
All my   activity, all my life strives toward you, revered one,   onward!
(All my activity, all my life strives onward toward you, revered woman!)

ˈalə ˈmaɛnə ˈzɪnə ˈveːbən miːɐ̯ daɛn bɪltʻ, loː ˈtsaɔbərɪn!
alle meine Sinne weben mir   dein Bild, o Zauberin!
All my   senses weave for me your image, O sorceress!

duː lɛntʻˈflaməstʻ ˈmaɛnən ˈbuːzən tsu deːɐ̯ ˈlaɛɐ harmoˈniː,
Du entflammest meinen Busen zu der Leier Harmonie,
You inflame   my   bosom to the lyre's harmony,

duː bəˈgaɛstʻɐstʻ meːr lals   ˈmuːzən   lʊntʻ lɛntʻˈtsʏkʻəstʻ meːr lals ziː!
du begeisterst mehr als   Musen   und entzückest mehr als sie!
you inspire   more than (the) Muses (do,) and charm   more than they!

ax daɛn ˈblaɔəs ˈlaɔgə ˈʃtʻraːlət dʊrç den ʃtʻʊrm deːɐ̯ ˈzeːlə mɪltʻ,
Ach, dein blaues Auge strahlet durch den Sturm der Seele mild,
Ah, your blue   eye beams through the storm of the soul gently,

44

ʊnt daen 'zyːsəs 'lɛçəln   'maːlət 'roːzɪç miːɐ   deːɐ 'tsuːkʰʊnft' bɪlt'.
und dein süsses Lächeln malet rosig mir   der Zukunft   Bild.
and your sweet smile   paints rosy for me the future's   image.
(and your sweet smile paints a rosy image of the future for me.)

'hɛrlɪç ʃmʏk't dɛs 'hɪməls 'grɛntsən tsvaːr |ɑoˈroːras 'pʰʊrp'ʊrlɪçtʰ,
Herrlich schmückt des Himmels Grenzen zwar   Auroras Purpurlicht,
Gloriously adorns   the heaven's borders to be sure Aurora's crimson light,
(Aurora's crimson light adorns heaven's borders gloriously, to be sure;)

aːbɐ 'liːp'lɪçərəs 'glɛntsən lyːbɐ'dɛk't   daen 'langəzɪçtʰ,
aber lieblicheres Glänzen überdeckt   dein Angesicht,
but (a) lovelier   radiance spreads across your face

vɛn mɪt' 'vɔnətʰrʊŋk'nən   'blɪk'ən, ax! |ʊnt' |ʊnlɑosˈʃp'rɛçlɪç ʃøːn
wenn mit wonnetrunknen   Blicken, ach! und unaussprechlich schön
when with rapture-intoxicated glances, ah! and inexpressibly   beautifully

'maenə 'lɑogən fɔl |ɛnt'tsʏk'ən 'pʰʊrp'ʊrn dɪç |ɛɐ'røːt'ən zeːn.
meine Augen voll Entzücken purpurn dich erröten   sehn.
my   eyes full of delight   purple you blush   see.
(my eyes, filled with delight, see you blush purple.)

[Because of the high *tessitura*, this lovely early song is a daunting technical challenge to the singer. Aurora is the goddess of the dawn.]

'alt'ə 'liːbə 'rɔst'ət' niː
Alte Liebe rostet nie
Old Love Never Rusts

Posthumously published [composed 1816] (poem by Johann Mayrhofer)

'alt'ə 'liːbə 'rɔst'ət' niː,   høːɐt' lɪç |ɔft di 'mʊt'ɐ 'zaːgən;
Alte Liebe rostet nie,   hört' ich oft   die Mutter sagen;
Old love rusts   never, heard I   often the mother say;
("Old love never rusts," I often heard my mother say;)
                              [*poem:* **rostet nicht** (nɪçt', not), *each time, including the title*]

'alt'ə 'liːbə 'rɔst'ət' niː,   mʊs lɪç nuːn |ɛɐ'faːrənt' 'kʰlaːgən.
alte Liebe rostet nie,   muss ich nun erfahrend   klagen.
old love rusts   never, must I   now experiencing lament.
("Old love never rusts," I must now lament out of my own experience.)

viː di lʊft' |ʊmˈgiːp't' ziː mɪç,   diː   lɪç |aenst di 'maenə 'nant'ə,
Wie die Luft umgibt   sie mich,   die   ich einst die Meine nannte,
Like the air   surrounds she me, (she) whom I once the mine   called,
(She surrounds me like the air, she whom once I called my own,)
                              [*poem:* **mein** (maen, my) **eigen** ('|aegən, own) **nannte**]

di: lıç 'li:p't'ə 'rıt'ɐlıç,   di: mıç ın di 'fɛrnə   'zant'ə.
die   ich liebte ritterlich,   die mich in die Ferne   sandte.
whom I   loved   chivalrously, who me   into the distance sent.
(she whom I loved as a knight loves his lady, she who sent me away.)

[de:ɐ̯   lıç 'le:p't'ə...   'vae̯t'ə]
[*poem:* **der   ich lebte... in die Weite sandte**]
[for whom I   lived...   distance]

zae̯t di 'həldə   lıç fɛɐ̯'lo:ɐ̯, ha:b ıç me:r ʊnt' lant' gə'ze:ən, —
Seit die Holde   ich verlor, hab' ich Meer und Land gesehen, —
Since the lovely one I lost,   have I sea   and land seen, —
(Since I lost my lovely one I have seen many things on sea and land;)

fo:ɐ̯ de:ɐ̯ 'ʃø:nst'ən   'frao̯ən flo:ɐ̯ dʊrft' lıç ʊnlɛɐ̯'ʃʏt't'ɐt' 'ʃt'e:ən.
vor   der schönsten   Frauen Flor durft' ich unerschüttert stehen.
before the most beautiful women's bevy could I   unshaken   stand.
(before a bevy of the most beautiful women I could stand unmoved.) ·

[*poem:* **vor dem (dem) schönsten Frauenflor**]

dɛn lao̯s mi:r li:ɐ̯ 'bılt'nıs t'ʰra:t   'tsʏrnənt' vi: tsʊm kʰampf mıt' 'li:nən,
Denn aus   mir ihr Bildnis trat   zürnend wie zum Kampf mit ihnen,
For   out of me her image stepped angrily as if to the battle with them,
(For her image strode out of me furiously, as if to do battle with them,)

[bılt']   [fo:ɐ̯ den gae̯st,]   [halp' ʊnt' halp' fɔl 'mıldə,]
[*poem:* **Denn ihr Bild trat   vor   den Geist, zürnend halb und halb voll Milde,**]
[For   her image stepped before the spirit, angry   half, and half full of mildness,]
[(For her image appeared before my spirit, half angry and half gentle,—)]

mıt dem 'tsao̯bɐ,   den si: hat', 'mʊst'ə zi: das ʃp'i:l gə'vınən.
mit dem Zauber, den sie hat, musste sie das Spiel gewinnen.
with the magic,   that she has, had to she the game win.
(with the magic that she has, she *had* to win the game.)

[ʊnt' vas 'ırgənt 'tsao̯bɐ hae̯st', vıç   bə'ʃe:mt dem 'li:bən 'bıldə.]
[*poem:* **und was irgend Zauber heisst, wich   beschämt dem lieben Bilde.**]
[and what ever   magic is called, yielded shamed   to the dear   image.]
[(and whatever magic other women had, yielded, shamed, to her dear image.]

da: de:ɐ̯ 'gart'ən, dɔrt das hao̯s, vo: lıç ɔft' zo: 't'ʰrao̯lıç 'kʰo:st'ən!
Da   der Garten, dort das Haus, wo   ich oft   so traulich   kosten!
There (is) the garden, there the house, where I   often so intimately talked of love!

[*poem:* **Hier** (hi:ɐ̯, here) **der Garten... wo ich einst** (lae̯nst', once)]

ze: lıç rɛçtʰʔ zi: ʃve:p't' hɛ'rao̯s -- vırt di 'alt'ə 'li:bə 'rɔst'ən?
Seh' ich recht? Sie schwebt heraus -- wird die alte Liebe rosten?
See I   right? She floats   out --   will the old   love rust?
(Do I see what I think I see? She is coming out of the house.... Will old love ever rust?)

[The title suggests humor; but the poet has been hurt. He cannot forget his first love, much as he has tried to. Schubert's charming, simple strophic setting is in the style of a folksong.]

aˈmaːli̯a
Amalia

Op. 173, No. 1 [1815] (Friedrich von Schiller)

ʃøːn viː ˈlɛŋəl, fɔl valˈhalas ˈvɔnə, ʃøːn   foːɐ̯/foːr ˈalən jʏŋlɪŋən   vaːɐ̯/vaːr leːɐ̯!
Schön wie Engel, voll Walhallas Wonne, schön vor   allen Jünglingen war   er!
Fair   as angels, full of Valhalla's rapture, beautiful before all   young men was   he!

ˈhɪmlɪʃ   mɪlt zaen blɪk, viː ˈmae̯ənzɔnə rʏkgəˈʃtˈraːlt fɔm   ˈblɑo̯ən ˈʃpˈiːgəlmeːɐ̯.
himmlisch mild sein Blick, wie Maiensonne rückgestrahlt vom   blauen Spiegelmeer.
heavenly gentle his look, like May sun   reflected   from the blue   mirror-sea.
(His look was celestially gentle, like May sunshine reflected from the blue mirror of the sea.)

ˈzaenə ˈkʰʏsə paraˈdiːzɪʃ   ˈfyːlən! viː t͡svae ˈflamən   zɪç   lɛɐ̯ˈgraefən,
Seine Küsse paradiesisch fühlen! wie zwei Flammen sich   ergreifen,
His   kisses paradisaical feel!   as two flames themselves seize,
(his kisses feel like Paradise! As two flames join together,)
                    [*Peters:* **Seine Lippen** (ˈlɪpˈən, lips); *poem:* **zwo** (t͡svoː, two) **Flammen**]

viː ˈharfəntʰøːnə ɪn lae̯ˈnandɐ ˈʃpˈiːlən, t͡su deːɐ̯ ˈhɪməlfɔlən   harmoˈniː
wie Harfentöne in   einander spielen, zu der himmelvollen Harmonie
as harp   tones into each other play,   to the heaven- full   harmony
(as the tones of the harp mingle with each other, to the heavenly harmony...)

ˈʃtˈʏrt͡stˈən, ˈfloːgən, ˈʃmɔlt͡sən   gaestˈ ɪn gaest t͡suˈzamən,
stürzten,   flogen, schmolzen Geist in Geist zusammen,
tumbled,   flew,   melted   spirit into spirit together,
(one spirit tumbled, flew, melted into the other,)   [*poem:* **Geist und** (ʊntˈ, and) **Geist**]

ˈlɪpˈən,   ˈvaŋən   ˈbrantˈən, ˈt͡sɪtˈɐtˈən, ˈzeːlə ran   ɪn ˈzeːlə;
Lippen, Wangen brannten, zitterten, Seele rann in   Seele;
lips,   cheeks burned,   trembled, soul ran   into soul;

eːɐ̯tˈ ʊntˈ ˈhɪməl ˈʃvamən,   viː t͡sɛɐ̯ˈrɔnən ʊm   diː ˈliːbəndən!
Erd' und Himmel schwammen, wie zerronnen um   die Liebenden!
earth and heaven swam,   as if dissolved   around the loving ones!

eːɐ̯/eːr lɪstˈ hɪn! fɛɐ̯ˈgeːbəns, ax, fɛɐ̯ˈgeːbəns ˈʃtˈøːnət liːm   deːɐ̯ ˈbaŋə   ˈzɔøft͡sɐ naːx!
Er   ist hin! vergebens, ach, vergebens stöhnet ihm   der bange Seufzer nach!
He   is gone! In vain,   ah, in vain   moans for him the anxious sigh   after!
(He is gone! In vain, ah, in vain the mournful sigh moans after him!)

eːɐ̯/eːr lɪstˈ hɪn, ʊntˈ ˈlalə lʊst   dɛs ˈleːbəns ˈrɪnət hɪn ɪn lae̯n vɛɐ̯ˈloːrnəs ax!
Er   ist hin, und alle Lust   des Lebens rinnet hin in ein verlornes Ach!
He   is gone, and all pleasure of the life   runs away in a   lost   "Ah!"
(He is gone, and all joy in living runs away in a lost cry of pain!)
                    [*poem:* **wimmert** (ˈvɪmɐtˈ, whimpers) **hin**]

[Amalia is the heroine of Schiller's play, *Die Räuber* (*The Robbers*). She sings this song, as she thinks of her banished lover Karl. Schubert treats the middle section as a dramatic recitative.]

am bax lɪm ˈfryːlɪŋ
Am Bach im Frühling
By the Brook in the Springtime

Op. 109, No. 1 [1816] (Franz von Schober)

duː braːxstˈ ziː nuːn, di ˈkʰaltˈə ˈrɪndə, lʊntˈ ˈriːzəlst froː   lʊntˈ fra͜e daˈhɪn,
Du brachst sie nun, die kalte   Rinde, und   rieselst froh   und frei   dahin,
You broke   it now, the cold   rind,   and   ripple   happily and freely forth,

di ˈlʏftˈə ˈveːən ˈviːdɐ ˈlɪndə, lʊntˈ moːs lʊntˈ graːs vɪrtˈ   nɔ͜ø lʊntˈ gryːn.
die Lüfte   wehen wieder linde, und   Moos und Gras wird   neu und grün.
the breezes blow   again   gently, and   moss and   grass become new and   green.

[*poem:* **wird frisch** (frɪʃ, fresh) **und grün**]

aˈla͜en, mɪt   ˈtʰra͜ʊrɪgəm gəˈmyːtˈə tʰreːtˈ lɪç vi: zɔnst ͡tsuː ˈda͜enɐ fluːtʰ,
Allein, mit   traurigem Gemüte   tret ich wie sonst zu   deiner Flut,
Alone, with (a) sorrowful   spirit   step I   as usual to   your   flood,
(But with a sorrowful spirit I come as usual to your waters,)

[*poem:* **Doch ich** (dɔx lɪç, but I) — **mit traurigem Gemüte**]

deːɐ/deːr ˈleːɐdə ˈlalgəma͜enə ˈblyːtˈə   kʰɔmtˈ ˈma͜enəm ˈhɛr͡tsən nɪçt ͡tsuː guːtʰ.
der   Erde   allgemeine Blüte   kommt meinem Herzen nicht zu gut.
the   earth's general   blossoming comes to my   heart   not   as   benefit.
(the general blossoming of the earth brings no benefit to my heart.)

hiːɐ ˈtʰra͜ebən ˈlimɐ   ˈgla͜eçə ˈvɪndə, kʰa͜en ˈhɔfən kʰɔmtˈ lɪn ˈma͜enən zɪn, lals
Hier treiben immer   gleiche Winde, kein   Hoffen kommt in   meinen Sinn, als
Here drift   always (the) same   winds, no   hoping comes into my   mind, than
(Here in my heart the same winds are always blowing; no hope comes to my mind, other than)

das lɪç hiːɐ/hiːr la͜en ˈblyːmçən   ˈfɪndə, bla͜ʊ, vi: zi: deːɐ/deːr lɛɐˈlɪnrʊŋ/lɛrˈlɪnrʊŋ blyːn.
dass ich hier   ein Blümchen finde, blau, wie sie der   Erinnrung   blühn.
that I   here   a   little flower find, blue, as   those of the   memory   bloom.
(that I may find a little flower here, blue like forget-me-nots, the flowers of memory.)

[The words are addressed by an unhappy lover to the brook, which has just burst its covering of ice. This song lies lower than most of Schubert's songs in their original keys. The opening section is repeated da capo, after the contrasting "recitative" in which the composer set the last four lines of the poem.]

an ˈeːɐstˈən ˈma͜eˌmɔrgən
Am ersten Maimorgen
On the First May Morning

Privately published by Reinhard van Hoorickx [composed 1816?] (poem by Matthias Claudius)

ˈhɔ͜øtˈə vɪl lɪç ˈfrøːlɪç, ˈfrøːlɪç za͜en,
Heute will ich fröhlich, fröhlich sein,
Today want I   merry,   merry   to be,
(Today I want to be merry, merry;)

48

'kʰaenə vaes   lʊntʰ 'kʰaenə 'zɪtʰə   'hø:rən;
keine Weis'   und keine Sitte   hören;
no   wise advice and no   proper behavior to hear;
(I want to hear no wise advice and no talk of proper behavior;)

vɪl   mɪç   'vɛltsən,   lʊntʰ fy:ɐ̯ 'frɔ͡ødə ʃrae̯n,
will mich wälzen,   und für Freude schrein,
want myself to wallow and for   joy   shout,
(I want to wallow in cheer and shout for joy,)

lʊnt de:ɐ̯ 'kʰø:nɪç zɔl   mi:ɐ̯ das nɪçtʰ 've:rən.
und der König soll mir   das nicht wehren.
and the   king   shall to me that not   forbid.
(and not even the king can stop me.)

[Schubert wrote this little song for the album of his sweetheart Therese Grob. It was not included in either of the "complete" collections, but has been edited and privately published by Reinhard van Hoorickx.]

Am Feierabend see *Die schöne Müllerin*

am 'fɛnstʰɐ
Am Fenster
At the Window

Op. 105, No. 3 [1826] (Johann Gabriel Seidl)

i:ɐ̯ 'li:bən 'mao̯ɐn hɔltʰ lʊnt tʰrao̯t, di   li:ɐ̯ mɪç kʰy:l lʊm'ʃli:st,
Ihr lieben Mauern hold und traut, die   ihr mich kühl umschliesst,
You dear   walls,   lovely and familiar, which you me   coolly surround,
(You dear walls, lovely and familiar, you that coolly surround me)
                                    [*poem:* **sanft** (zanftʰ, gentle) **und traut**]

ʊntʰ 'zɪlbɐglɛntsənt 'ni:dɐʃao̯tʰ,   vɛn 'dro:bən 'fɔlmo:nt lɪst :
und silberglänzend niederschaut, wenn droben   Vollmond ist:
and   silver-gleaming down   look,   when up above full moon is:
(and look down, gleaming like silver, when a full moon is up above,)
                                    [*poem:* **silberglänzig** ('zɪlbɐglɛntsɪç, silver-gleamy)]

i:ɐ̯ za:t mɪç lae̯nst zo: 'tʰrao̯rɪç da:,   mae̯n hao̯pʰtʰ lao̯f 'ʃlafɐ   hantʰ,
Ihr saht mich einst so traurig da,   mein Haupt auf schlaffer Hand,
you saw me   once so   sad   there, my   head   on   limp   hand,
(you saw me so sad here once before, my head leaning on my limp hand,)

als   lɪç lɪn mi:ɐ̯/mi:r la'lae̯n mɪç   za:, lʊntʰ 'kʰae̯nɐ mɪç fɛɐ̯'ʃtʰantʰ.
als   ich in mir   allein mich sah, und keiner mich verstand.
when I   in me   alone myself saw, and no one me   understood.
(when I saw myself alone in me, and no one understood me.)

jɛtstʰ bra:x   lae̯n 'landɐ lɪçtʰ he'ran: di 'tʰrao̯ɐtsae̯tʰ   lɪstʰ lʊm :
Jetzt brach ein ander Licht heran: die Trauerzeit   ist um:
Now dawned an   other   light ... :   the time of mourning is   over:
(Now another light has dawned: the time of mourning is over;)   [*"heranbrechen"* = to dawn]

ʊnt' 'manʧə ʦiːn mɪt' miːɐ̯ diː baːn dʊrçs   'leːbənshae̯lɪçt'uːm.
und manche ziehn mit mir die Bahn durchs   Lebensheiligtum.
and many   travel with me   the road   through the sacred shrine of life.
(and many people have joined me on my path through this sacred gift called life.)

ziː rao̯p't deːɐ̯ 'ʦuːfal 'leːvɪç niː   ao̯s 'mae̯nəm 't'rɔø̯ən zɪn :
Sie raubt der Zufall ewig nie   aus meinem treuen Sinn:
Them robs the chance ever never out of my   faithful mind:
(Chance will never ever steal them from my faithful heart:)

ɪn 't'iːfst'ɐ 'zeːlə t'raːk' lɪç ziː, daː rae̯çt' k'ae̯n 'ʦuːfal hɪn.
in tiefster Seele trag ich sie, da   reicht kein Zufall hin.
in deepest soul carry I   them, there reaches no   chance thither.
(I carry them in the deepest part of my soul, where chance cannot reach them.)

duː 'mao̯ɐ vɛːnst' mɪç t'ryːp', viː ae̯nstʰ,   das lɪst di ʃt'ɪlə frɔø̯t';
Du Mauer wähnst mich trüb,   wie einst,   das ist die stille Freud';
You wall   imagine me   troubled, as once before: that is the quiet joy;
(You, wall, imagine me to be troubled, as I was before; the mood you see is one of quiet joy;)

vɛn duː fɔm   'moːnt'lɪçt' viːdɐ ʃae̯nst', vɪrt'   miːɐ̯ di brʊst' zoː vae̯tʰ.
wenn du vom   Mondlicht wieder scheinst, wird   mir die Brust so weit.
when you from the moonlight again shine,   becomes to me the breast so wide.
(when you are shining again from the moonlight, my breast becomes so full.)

an 'jeːdəm 'fɛnst'ɐ vɛːn   lɪç dan lae̯n 'frɔø̯ndəshao̯p't', gə'zɛŋk'tʰ,
An jedem Fenster wähn' ich dann ein Freundeshaupt, gesenkt,
At every   window imagine I   then a   friend's head, bent down,
(At every window I imagine then a friend's head, looking down,)

                                        [*GA:* **wähnt'** (vɛːnt', would imagine)]

das ao̯x zoː ʃao̯t ʦum 'hɪməl an, das ao̯x zoː 'mae̯nɐ dɛŋk'tʰ!
das auch so schaut zum Himmel an, das auch so meiner denkt!
that also so looks to the sky   at, that also so of me   thinks!
(that also looks at the sky, as I do, and that also is thinking of me!)

                                        [*poem:* **und** (ʊnt', and) **auch so meiner denkt**]

[The poet stands in the familiar courtyard and looks up at the windows, gleaming in the moonlight. Content and happy now, he remembers a time when he used to be depressed and sad. Everything has since changed for him: spiritual light has come into his life, and others have joined him on his path, friends who are forever secure in his heart. He addresses the walls themselves, then one particular wall, where he can picture friendly faces looking out and thinking kindly thoughts of him as they look up at the sky.]

am 'flʊsə
Am Flusse
To the River

Posthumously published [composed 1815 and 1822] (poem by Johann Wolfgang von Goethe)

fɛɐ̯'fliːsət', 'fiːlgəliːp't'ə 'liːdɐ, ʦum 'meːrə deːɐ̯ fɛɐ̯'gɛsənhae̯tʰ!
Verfliesset, vielgeliebte Lieder, zum Meere der   Vergessenheit!
Flow away, much-loved songs, to the sea   of the oblivion!
(Flow away, much-loved songs, to the sea of oblivion!)

kʰaen ˈkʰnaːbə zɪŋ   lɛntˈtsʏkˈtʰ lɔøç ˈviːdɐ,   kʰaen ˈmɛːtˈçən ɪn deːɐ̯ ˈblyːtˈəntsa̯etʰ.
kein Knabe sing' entzückt euch wieder, kein Mädchen in der Blütenzeit.
No   boy   sing delighted you again, no   girl   in the blossom-time.
(May no boy sing you again, delighted, nor any girl in the time of blossoms.)

iːɐ̯ ˈzaŋətˈ nuːɐ̯ fɔn ˈmaenɐ ˈliːbən;   nuːn ʃpˈrɪçtˈ ziː ˈmaenɐ ˈtʰrɔøə   hoːn.
Ihr sanget nur von meiner Lieben;   nun spricht sie meiner Treue   Hohn.
You sang   only of   my   dear one; now speaks she to my   faithfulness scorn.
(You, my songs, sang only of my dear one; now she defies and scorns my faithfulness.)

iːɐ̯ vartˈ ɪns   ˈvasɐ ˈlaengəʃriːbən;   zoː fliːst dɛn lɑɔx mɪtˈ liːm daˈfɔn.
Ihr wart ins   Wasser eingeschrieben; so fliesst denn auch mit ihm davon.
You were into the water   written;   so flow   then too with it   away.
(You were written on water; so flow away then with it too.)

[Schubert composed two settings of this short poem. The first, from 1815, is more dramatic, more emotional; the second, from 1822, simpler, more philosophical.]

am ˈɡraːbə lanˈzɛlmos
Am Grabe Anselmos
At Anselmo's Grave

Op. 6, No. 3 [1816] (Matthias Claudius)

das lɪç dɪç fɛɐ̯ˈloːrən ˈhaːbə, das duː nɪçtˈ meːɐ̯   bɪstʰ,
Dass ich dich verloren habe, dass du nicht mehr   bist,
That I   you lost   have, that you not   any more are,
(That I have lost you, that you are no more,)

lax! das hiːr ɪn ˈdiːzəm ˈɡraːbə maen lanˈzɛlmo lɪstʰ, das lɪstˈ maen ʃmɛrts!
ach! dass hier in diesem Grabe mein Anselmo ist, das ist   mein Schmerz!
ah! that here in this   grave my   Anselmo is, that is   my   pain!
(ah! that my Anselmo is here in this grave, that is   my   pain!)

zeːtˈ, viː ˈliːpˈtˈən viːɐ̯/viːr lʊns ˈbaedə, lʊntˈ, zoː laŋ lɪç bɪn, kʰɔmtˈ ˈfrɔødə
Seht, wie liebten wir   uns beide, und, so lang' ich bin, kommt Freude
See, how loved   we   us   both, and, so long I   am, comes joy
(See how we both loved each other, and, as long as I live, joy will come)
        [*poem:* **Seht, wir liebten uns, wir beide** (See, we loved each other, we two)]

ˈniːmaːls ˈviːdɐ(r) ɪn maen hɛrts.
niemals wieder in mein Herz.
never   again   into my   heart.

[The poet has lost a dear friend. The shock of death's finality makes him feel that he will never again be happy. Schubert's music expresses overwhelming pain at the loss of someone who died too young. The singer is reminded to stress only those syllables that call for emphasis, no matter on which beat of the bar they happen to fall (not "*dass*" or "*ist*," for example).]

Am Meer / Das Meer erglänzte weit hinaus see *Schwanengesang*

'amənliːt'
Ammenlied
Nurse's Song

Posthumously published [composed 1814] (poem by Michael Lubi)

am   'hoːən, 'hoːən tʰʊrm, daː   veːt' lạen 'kʰalt'ɐ ʃt'ʊrm:
Am   hohen, hohen Turm, da   weht ein   kalter Sturm:
At the high,   high   tower, there blows a   cold   storm:

gə'dʊlt'! di 'glœk'lạen 'lɔɸt'ən,   di 'zɔnə blɪŋk't' fɔn 'vaet'ən.
Geduld! die Glöcklein läuten,   die Sonne blinkt von weiten.
Patience! The little bells are ringing, the sun   gleams from afar.

ɪm   'tʰiːfən, 'tʰiːfən tʰaːl, daː   rạoʃt' lạen 'vasɐfal:
Im   tiefen, tiefen Tal,   da   rauscht ein   Wasserfall:
In the deep,   deep   valley, there roars   a   waterfall:

gə'dʊlt'! lạen 'bɪsçən   'vaet'ɐ, daː   rɪnt   das 'bɛçlạen 'haet'ɐ.
Geduld! ein Bisschen weiter, da   rinnt das Bächlein heiter.
Patience! A   bit   farther, there trickles the brooklet serenely.

[poem: **dann** (dan, then) **rinnt]**

am   'kʰaːlən, 'kʰaːlən bạom, dɛk't' zɪç lạen 'tʰɔɸçən   kʰạom:
Am   kahlen, kahlen Baum, deckt sich ein Täubchen kaum:
On the bare,   bare   tree,   covers itself a   little dove scarcely:
(On the bare, leafless tree a little dove can scarcely find shelter:)

gə'dʊlt'! balt' blyːn di 'lạoən,   dan vɪrts   zạen 'nɛst'çən 'bạoən.
Geduld! bald blühn die Auen,   dann wird's sein Nestchen bauen.
Patience! Soon bloom the meadows, then will   it its   little nest build.
(Patience! Soon the meadows will bloom; then it will build its little nest.)

dɪç friːɐt',   mạen 'tœçt'ɐlạen! kʰạen frɔɸnt' zaːk't': kʰɔm he'rạen!
Dich friert,   mein Töchterlein! Kein Freund sagt: Komm' herein!
You are freezing, my   little daughter! No   friend   says: "Come   in!"

las 'lʊnzɐ 'ʃt'ʏnt'çən 'ʃlaːgən, dan 'veːɐdəns 'lɛnlạen   'zaːgən.
Lass unser Stündchen schlagen, dann werden's Englein   sagen.
Let   our   little hour strike,   then will   it little angels say.
(Let our last little hour strike: then little angels will say it.)

das 'bɛst'ə 'ʃt'yːp'çən giːp't' gɔt' 'jeːnəm,   den   leːɐ liːp'tʰ.
Das beste Stübchen gibt Gott jenem,   den   er liebt.
The best   little room gives God to that one whom He loves.
(God gives the best little room to the one whom He loves.)

[A nurse is singing to a little girl in a simple, folksong style.]

52

amfiˈaːrą͜ɔs [amfj̩aˈraːɔs] *
Amphiaraos
Amphiaraus

Posthumously published [composed 1815] (poem by Theodor Körner)

foːɐ̯   ˈtʰeːbəns ˈziːbənfax ˈgɛːnəndən ˈtʰoːrən
Vor   Thebens siebenfach gähnenden Toren
In front of Thebes' sevenfold   yawning   gates

laːkˈ ın ˈfʊrçtbaːrən ˈbryːdɐ̯ʃtˈrą͜et das heːɐ̯ deːɐ̯ ˈfʏrstˈən t͜sʊm ˈʃlaːgən bəˈrą͜etʰ,
lag in furchtbaren Brüderstreit das Heer der   Fürsten zum Schlagen bereit,
lay in frightful   fraternal strife the army of the princes to the fighting   ready,
(the army of the princes lay ready to fight in a frightful fraternal strife,)

ım   ˈhą͜elıgən ˈlą͜edə t͜sʊm ˈmɔrdə fɛɐ̯ˈʃvoːrən.
im   heiligen Eide zum Morde verschworen.
in the sacred   oath   to the murder sworn.
(by a sacred oath committed to murder.)

ʊntˈ mıt dɛs ˈpant͜se̯s ˈblɛndəndəm lıçtˈ
Und mit des Panzers blendendem Licht
And with the armor's blinding   light

gəˈrʏstˈətʰ, ˌals gɛltˈ   ɛs, di vɛlt t͜suː bəˈkʰriːgən,
gerüstet, als gält'   es, die Welt zu bekriegen,
armed,   as if were intended it   the world to make war upon,
(armed, as if it were intended that they make war upon the whole world,)

ˈtʰrɔ͜ømən ziː   ˈjɑ͜ɔxt͜səntˈ   fɔn ˈkʰɛmpfən lʊntˈ ˈziːgən,
träumen sie   jauchzend von Kämpfen und Siegen,
dream   they exulting   of battling   and winning,
(exulting, they dream of fighting and winning,)

nuːɐ̯/nuːr ˌamfiˈaːrą͜ɔs, deːɐ̯ ˈhɛrlıçə,   nıçtʰ.
nur   Amphiaraos, der Herrliche, nicht.
only   Amphiaraus, the glorious one, not.
(all except Amphiaraus, the glorious one.)

dɛn   ˌeːɐ̯ liːstˈ ın dem ˈeːvıgən ˈkʰrą͜ezə deːɐ̯ ˈʃtˈɛrnə,
Denn er liest in dem ewigen Kreise der   Sterne,
For   he reads in the eternal circle   of the stars

veːn   diː ˈkʰɔməndən ˈʃtˈʊndən ˈfą͜entˈlıç bəˈdroːn. dɛs ˈzɔnənleŋkˈe̯s gəˈvaltˈıgɐ̯ zoːn
wen die kommenden Stunden feindlich bedrohn. Des Sonnenlenkers gewaltiger Sohn
whom the coming   hours   inimically threaten. The sun-   ruler's powerful   son

ziːtˈ   kʰlaːɐ̯/kʰlaːr ın deːɐ̯ t͜suːkˈʊnftˈ ˈneːbəlndə ˈfɛrnə.
sieht klar   in   der Zukunft   nebelnde Ferne.
sees   clearly   into the future's   misting   distance.

eːɐ̯ kʰɛnt dɛs ˈʃɪkˈzaːls fɛɐ̯ˈdɛrpˈlɪçən bʊntˈ,
Er kennt des Schicksals verderblichen Bund,
He knows the destiny's fatal bond,
(He knows the fatal bonds of destiny,)

eːɐ̯ vaes, viː di ˈvʏrfəl, di ˈlae̯zɐrnən, ˈfalən,
er weiss, wie die Würfel, die eisernen, fallen,
he knows how the dice, the iron ones, fall,

leːɐ̯ ziːt di mœˈira* mɪtˈ ˈbluːtˈɪɡən ˈkʰralən;
er sieht die Möira mit blutigen Krallen; [*poem:* **Moira** (ˈmɔ/ra)]
he sees the Fates with bloody claws;

dɔx di ˈhɛldən fɛɐ̯ˈʃmɛːən den ˈhae̯lɪɡən mʊntˈ.
doch die Helden verschmähen den heiligen Mund.
but the heroes scorn the sacred mouth (the god-inspired words from his mouth).

eːɐ̯ zaː dɛs ˈmɔrdəs ɡəˈvaltˈzaːmə ˈtʰaːtˈən,
Er sah des Mordes gewaltsame Taten,
He saw the murder's violent deeds,
(He foresaw violent deeds of murder,)

eːɐ̯ ˈvʊstˈə, vas liːm di ˈpartsə ʃpan. zoː ɡɪŋ leːɐ̯ tsʊm kʰampf, lae̯n fɛɐ̯ˈloːrnɐ man,
er wusste, was ihm die Parze spann. So ging er zum Kampf, ein verlorner Mann,
he knew what for him the Fate spun. Thus went he to the battle, a lost man,
(he knew what one of the three Fates was spinning for him. Thus he went to battle, a lost man,)

fɔn dem ˈlae̯ɡnən ˈvae̯bə ˈʃmɛːlɪç fɛɐ̯ˈraːtˈən.
von dem eignen Weibe schmählich verraten.
by the own wife shamefully betrayed.
(shamefully betrayed by his own wife [who had been bribed to persuade him to join the battle].)

eːɐ̯ vaːɐ̯ zɪç deːɐ̯ ˈhɪmlɪʃən ˈflamə bəˈvʊstʰ,
Er war sich der himmlischen Flamme bewusst,
He was himself of the heavenly flame aware,
(He was aware of the heavenly flame)   [*"sich* (dative) *bewusst sein"* = to be aware]

diː hae̯s di ˈkʰrɛftˈɪɡə ˈzeːlə dʊrçˈɡlyːtˈə;
die heiss die kräftige Seele durchglühte;
which hotly the powerful soul through-glowed;
(which glowed hot through the powerful soul;)

deːɐ̯ ˈʃtˈɔltsə ˈnantˈə zɪç lapɔloˈiːdə,
der Stolze nannte sich Apolloide,
the proud man called himself a son of Apollo,

ɛs ˈʃluːkˈ liːm lae̯n ˈɡœtˈlɪçəs hɛrts̩ lɪn deːɐ̯ brʊstʰ.
es schlug ihm ein göttliches Herz in der Brust.
there beat for him a divine heart in the breast.
(the heart of a god was beating in his breast.)

viːʔ lɪç, tsu deːm di ˈɡœtˈɐ ɡəˈreːdətʰ,
"Wie? ich, zu dem die Götter geredet,
"Who? I, to whom the gods have spoken,

54

deːn deːɐ̯ 'vaːɐ̯haet' 'haeligə 'dʏft'ə   lʊm'weːn, lɪç zɔl lɪn gə'maenɐ ʃlaxt' fɛɐ̯'geːn,
den der Wahrheit heilige Düfte   umwehn, ich soll in gemeiner Schlacht vergehn,
whom the truth's   holy   fragrances waft about, I   shall in common battle   perish,
(I, who am enveloped with the holy fragrance of truth, should perish in the common slaughter,)

                   [*poem:* **den der Weissheit** ('vaeshaet', wisdom's) **heilige Düfte umwehn]**

fɔn peri'kʰlyːmenɔs hant' gə'tʰøːt'ətʰ? fɛɐ̯'dɛrbən vɪl   lɪç dʊrç   'laegənə mact',
von Periklymenos Hand getötet?   Verderben will ich durch   eigene Macht,
by Periclymenus's hand killed?   To perish   want I   through own   strength,
(killed by the hand of Periclymenus? I want to die through my own strength,)

lʊnt' ʃt'aonənt'   fɛɐ̯'neːm lɛs di 'kʰɔmənfə 'ʃt'ʊndə
und staunend   vernehm' es die kommende Stunde
and in amazement may hear it the coming   hour
(and may some hour yet to come hear about it)

laos 'kʰʏnft'ɪgɐ 'zɛŋɐ gə'haelɪçt'əm 'mʊndə,
aus künftiger Sänger geheiligtem Munde,
from future   singers' sanctified   mouths,
(from the sanctified mouths of future singers,)

viː lɪç kʰyːn mɪç   gə'ʃt'ʏrtst' lɪn di 'leːvɪgə naxtʰ.
wie ich kühn mich gestürzt   in die ewige Nacht."
how I   boldly myself plunged   into the eternal night."
(how I boldly plunged myself into the eternal night.")

ʊnt' lals   deːɐ̯ 'bluːt'ɪgə kʰampf bə'gɔnən lʊnt di 'leːbnə fɔm   'mɔrt'gəʃrae viːdɐ'haltʰ,
Und als   der blutige Kampf begonnen und die Eb'ne vom   Mordgeschrei wiederhallt,
And when the   bloody battle   has begun and the plain   from the murder-shrieks echoes,
(And when the bloody battle has begun and the plain is echoing with the shrieks of death,)

zoː ruːft' leːɐ̯ fɛɐ̯'tsvaefəlnt':
so ruft er verzweifelnd:
so calls he despairing:
(he cries out in despair:)

 lɛs naːt'   mɪt' gə'valt', vas   miːɐ̯ di lʊn'tʰryːk'lɪçə 'partsə gə'ʃp'ɔnən.
"Es naht   mit Gewalt, was mir   die untrügliche Parze gesponnen.
"It   draws near with power,   what for me the infallible   Fate has spun,
("That which the infallible spinner of my destiny has spun is drawing near inexorably,)

dɔx voːk't' lɪn deːɐ̯ brʊst' miːr laen 'gœt'lɪçəs bluːt',
Doch wogt in der Brust mir ein göttliches Blut,
But   surges in the breast to me a   divine   blood,
(But the blood of a god is surging in my breast,)

drʊm   vɪl lɪç laox veːɐ̯t' des   lɛɐ̯'tsɔøgɐs fɛɐ̯'dɛrbən.
drum   will ich auch wert des   Erzeugers verderben."
therefore want I   also worthy of the begetter   perish."
(therefore I want to perish in a way that is worthy of my father.")

ʊnt'   'vant'ə di 'rɔsə laof   'leːbən lʊnt' 'ʃt'ɛrbən,
Und   wandte die Rosse auf   Leben und Sterben,
And (he) turned the horses toward life   and death,

ʊnt' jaːk't ʦuː dɛs 'ʃt'roːməs hoːx'brɑozəndɐ fluːt'.
und jagt zu des Stromes hochbrausender Flut.
and chases to the river's high- raging flood.
(and races to the high, rushing river.)

vɪlt' 'ʃnɑobən di 'rɔsə, lɑot' 'rasəlt deːɐ 'vaːgən,
Wild schnauben die Rosse, laut rasselt der Wagen,
Wildly snort the horses, loudly rattles the chariot,
(The horses are wildly snorting, the chariot rattles loudly,)

[*poem:* **die Hengste** ('hɛŋst'ə, stallions)]

das 'ʃt'ampfən deːɐ 'huːfə ʦɛɐ'malmət di baːn.
das Stampfen der Hufe zermalmet die Bahn.
the pounding of the hooves pulverizes the road.

ʊnt' 'ʃnɛlɐ ʊnt' 'ʃnɛlɐ nɔx raːst' ɛs hɛ'ran,
Und schneller und schneller noch rast es heran,
And faster and faster still speeds it onwards,
(And faster and still faster rider and chariot go racing onwards,)

als gɛlt' ɛs di 'flʏçt'ɪgə ʦaet ʦuː ɛɐ'jaːgən.
als gält' es die flüchtige Zeit zu erjagen.
as if were intended it the fleeting time to chase.
(as if they were trying to overtake fleeting time itself.)

viː vɛn leːɐ di 'lɔɸçt'ə dɛs 'hɪməls gə'rɑop't',
Wie wenn er die Leuchte des Himmels geraubt,
As if he the light of the heaven stolen,
(As if he had stolen the light of heaven,)

kʰɔmt' leːr lɪn 'vɪrbəln deːɐ 'vɪnʦbrɑot' gə'floːgən;
kommt er in Wirbeln der Windsbraut geflogen;
came he in swirls of the whirlwind flown;
(he came flying with the rush of the whirlwind;)

ɛɐ'ʃrɔk'ən 'heːbən di 'gœt'ɐ deːɐ 'voːgən
erschrocken heben die Götter der Wogen
alarmed raise the gods of the waves
(alarmed, the gods of the waters raise)

lɑos 'ʃɔɸməndən 'fluːt'ən das 'ʃɪlfɪçt'ə hɑop't'.
aus schäumenden Fluten das schilfichte Haupt.
out of foaming torrents the reeded head.
(their reed-crowned heads out of the foaming torrents.)

ʊnt' 'pʰlœʦlɪç, lals vɛn deːɐ 'hɪməl lɛɐ'glyːt'ə,
Und plötzlich, als wenn der Himmel erglühte, [*poem:* **Doch** (dɔx, but) **plötzlich**]
And suddenly, as if the sky were glowing,

ʃt'ʏrʦt' laen blɪʦ lɑos deːɐ 'haet'ɐn lʊft',
stürzt ein Blitz aus der heitern Luft,
plunges a lightning out of the serene air,
(a lightning flash streaks through the cloudless air,)

56

lʊnt di ˈleːɐ̯də ˈts̬eɐ̯ˈraɛst‘ zɪç ts̬uːɐ̯ ˈfʊrçt‘baːrən kʰlʊftʰ;
und die Erde zerreisst sich zur furchtbaren Kluft;
and the earth tears open itself to the fearful cleft;
(and the earth tears itself open to form a fearful cleft;)

daː riːf lɑot‘ ˈjɑɔxts̬ənt deːɐ̯ lap‘ɔloˈiːdə:
da rief laut jauchzend der Apolloide:
there called loudly rejoicing the son of Apollo:
(thereupon the son of Apollo, loudly rejoicing, cried out:)

daŋk‘ diːɐ̯, gəˈvalt‘ɪɡɐ! fɛst‘ ʃt‘eːt‘ miːɐ̯ deːɐ̯ bʊnt‘.
"Dank dir, Gewaltiger! fest steht mir der Bund.
"Thanks to you, powerful one! firmly stands for me the covenant.
("Thank you, Powerful One! My covenant holds firm.)

daɛn blɪts̬ lɪst‘ miːɐ̯ deːɐ̯/deːr lʊnˈʃt‘ɛrp‘lɪçkʰaet‘ ˈziːɡəl; ɪç ˈfɔlɡə diːɐ̯, ts̬ɔøs!
Dein Blitz ist mir der Unsterblichkeit Siegel; ich folge dir, Zeus!"
Your lightning is to me the immortality's seal; I follow you, Zeus!"
(Your lightning is my seal of immortality; I follow you, Zeus!")

ʊnt‘ leːɐ̯ ˈfast‘ə di ˈts̬yːɡəl lʊnt‘ ˈjaːk‘t‘ə di ˈrɔsə hɪˈnap‘ ɪn den ʃlʊnt‘.
Und er fasste die Zügel und jagte die Rosse hinab in den Schlund.
And he grasped the reins and drove the horses down into the abyss.

[* Schubert sets the name Amphiaraos with the stress on the second "a"; modern mythographers accent the third. Similarly, *Möira*, set by Schubert with a stress on the [i], is now spelled in German without the *Umlaut* and pronounced "ˈmɔøra,"with the accent on the first syllable. The English version is Mœræ, and, like "the Parcæ" (German "*Parzen*"), it refers to the Fates, the three sisters who spun the thread of each individual destiny. Amphiaraus, son of Apollo, was a seer from Argos, one of the Argonauts, and one of the "Seven against Thebes." He had been reluctant to join the warriors arrayed against Thebes, having foreseen that all but one would die defeated, no matter how bravely they fought. As he was fleeing in his chariot to avoid an ignominious death in the general slaughter, a thunderbolt from Zeus opened up the earth under him and he disappeared, descending alive to the realm of the dead. Schubert noted on his manuscript that he had composed this highly dramatic, unusually long song in just five hours!]

am zeː / ɪn dɛs zeːs ˈvoːɡənʃp‘iːlə
Am See / In des Sees Wogenspiele
By the Lake / In the Play of Waves on the Lake

Posthumously published [composed in 1823] (Franz von Bruchmann)

ɪn dɛs zeːs ˈvoːɡənʃp‘iːlə ˈfalən dʊrç den ˈzɔnənʃaen
In des Sees Wogenspiele fallen durch den Sonnenschein
In the lake's wave- plays fall through the sunshine
(In the play of waves on the lake through the sunshine there fall ...)

ˈʃt‘ɛrnə, ax, gaːɐ̯ ˈfiːlə, ˈfiːlə, ˈflamənt‘ ˈlɔøçt‘ənt‘ ʃt‘eːts̬ hɪˈnaen.
Sterne, ach, gar viele, viele, flammend leuchtend stets hinein.
stars, ah, very many, many, flamingly radiant continually in.
(continually into the lake very many, many stars, flamingly radiantly.)

ven de:ɐ menʃ   tsʊm ze: gə'vɔrdən, ɪn de:ɐ 'ze:lə 'vo:gənʃp'i:lə
Wenn der Mensch   zum See   geworden, in der Seele Wogenspiele
When the human being to the lake (has) become, in the soul's wave- plays
(When the human being has become like the lake, then into the play of waves in the soul ...)

'falən lɑos dɛs 'hɪməls   'pfɔrt'ən 'ʃt'ɛrnə, ax, ga:ɐ 'fi:lə, 'fi:lə.
fallen aus des Himmels Pforten Sterne, ach, gar viele, viele.
fall out of the heaven's portals stars, ah, very many, many.
(very many, many stars fall out of heaven's portals.)

[To the poet, watching the waves on the lake as they sparkle in the sunshine, it seems as if the stars have fallen out of the sky into the water and are shining up at him from the dancing ripples. He reflects that, when the consciousness of a human being becomes like a lake, many, many stars will come out of heaven to sparkle in the soul. This idea is reminiscent of the teaching of Eastern mystics that in meditation the mind becomes like a deep and quiet pond in which transcendent intuitions can emerge, like stars of light reflected in water. Schubert's accompaniment suggests the rise and fall of the waves, and the repetitions and rests near the end of the song can be interpreted as conveying an ecstatic spiritual insight arising from meditation.]

am ze: / zɪts lɪç lɪm gra:s
Am See / Sitz ich im Gras
By the Lake / When I Sit in the Grass

Posthumously published [composed 1814]
(1st stanza by Johann Mayrhofer, 2nd by Max Kalbeck)

zɪts lɪç lɪm   gra:s lam 'glat'ən ze:, bɛ'ʃlaeçt   di 'se:lə 'baŋəs ve:,
Sitz ich im   Gras am   glatten See, beschleicht die Seele banges Weh,
Sit I   in the grass by the smooth lake, steals upon the soul anxious pain,
(When I sit in the grass by the smooth lake, an anxious pain steals into my soul;)

vi: 'le:ɔlsharfən   kʰlɪŋt' mɪç lan   laen 'lʊnnɛnba:rɐ 'tsɑobɐva:n. [*poem:* **mit Äolsharfen**]
wie Äolsharfen   klingt mich an   ein unnennbarer Zauberwahn.
like Aeolian harps sounds me to — a nameless   magic- illusion.
(A nameless magical illusion comes to me as if in the sounds of Aeolian harps.)

[*Peters variant:*]

[mɪt' 'gaest'ɐr(r)larmən ry:rt   mɪç lan gə'haemnɪsfɔlɐ 'tsɑobɐban.]
[mit Geisterarmen   rührt   mich an geheimnisvoller Zauberbann.]
[with ghostly arms   touches me ... mysterious   magic spell.][*"anrühren"*= to touch]
[(a mysterious magic spell holds me, as if ghostly arms were touching me.)]

das 'ʃɪlfro:ɐ   'naegət' 'zɔøftsənt' zɪç, di 'lu:fɐblu:mən 'gry:sən mɪç,
Das Schilfrohr neiget   seufzend sich, die Uferblumen grüssen mich,
The reed   bends   sighingly itself, the bank-flowers greet   me,
(The reeds bend down as if sighing; the flowers on the bank greet me,)

de:ɐ 'fo:gəl kʰla:k't, di 'lʏft'ə ve:n, fo:ɐ 'ʃmɛrtsəslʊst'   mœçt'   lɪç fɐɐ'ge:n!
der Vogel klagt, die Lüfte wehn, vor Schmerzeslust   möcht   ich vergehn!
the bird   laments, the breezes blow, from pain-   pleasure would like I   to die!
(the bird laments, the breezes blow, I would like to die from the savoring of pain!)
[*Peters:* **Schmerzenslust**]

58

[*Continuation, as found in the* Gesamtausgabe:]

viː miːɐ̯ das ˈleːbən ˈkʰrɛftˈɪç kʰvɪltʰ ʊntˈ zɪç ɪn ˈraʃən ˈʃtˈrøːmən ʃpˈiːltʰ.
Wie mir das Leben kräftig quillt und sich in raschen Strömen spielt.
How to me the life   powerfully gushes up and itself in rapid   streams   plays.
(How powerfully life gushes up in me and plays about in rapid streams!)

viːs baltˈ ɪn ˈtʰryːbən ˈmasən geːɐ̯tʰ ʊntˈ balt ʦʊm ˈʃpˈiːɡəl zɪç fɛɐ̯ˈkʰleːɐ̯tʰ.
Wie's bald in trüben Massen gärt und bald zum Spiegel sich verklärt.
How it now in dark   masses seethes and now to the mirror itself transfigures.
(How the water one moment is seething in dark masses, and the next has changed into a mirror!)

[*"bald...bald"* = now...now]

bəˈvʊstˈzaen ˈmaenɐ ˈtʰiːfstˈən kʰraftʰ, laen ˈvɔnəmeːɐ̯/-meːr ɪn miːɐ̯/miːr lɛɐ̯ˈʃaftʰ.
Bewusstsein meiner tiefsten Kraft, ein Wonnemeer in mir   erschafft.
Consciousness of my   deepest strength a   rapture-sea in me   creates.
(Consciousness of my deepest inner strength creates a joyful sea in me.)

[*poem:* **meiner innern** (ˈɪnɐn, inner) **Kraft**]

ɪç ˈʃtˈʏrʦə kʰyːn ɪn ˈzaenə fluːtʰ ʊntˈ ˈrɪŋə lʊm das ˈhøːçstˈə guːtʰ.
Ich stürze kühn in seine Flut und ringe um das höchste Gut.
I   plunge boldly into its   waters and struggle for the highest good.

[*poem:* **Ich stürze mich** (mɪç, myself) **in seine Flut**]

oː ˈleːbən, bɪstˈ zoː ˈhɪmlɪʃ ʃøːn, ɪn ˈdaenən ˈtʰiːfən, ɪn ˈdaenən høːn!
O Leben, bist so himmlisch schön,   in deinen Tiefen, in deinen Höh'n!
O life, (you) are so celestially beautiful, in your   depths, in your   heights!

[*poem:* **in deinen Tiefen, deinen Höh'n**]

daen ˈfrɔøntˈlɪç lɪçtˈ zɔl lɪç nɪçtˈ zeːn, den ˈfɪnstˈɐn pfaːt dɛs ˈlɔrkˈʊs geːn?
dein freundlich Licht soll ich nicht sehn, den finstern Pfad des Orkus gehn?
your friendly   light shall I not see, the dark   path of the Orcus walk?
(Shall I no longer see your friendly light, must I walk the dark path of Orcus, god of death?)

[*poem:* **den düstern** (ˈdyːstˈɐn, dark) **Gang** (ɡaŋ, path) **zum** (ʦʊm, to) **Orkus**]

dɔx bɪst duː miːɐ̯ das ˈhøːçstˈə nɪçt, drum lɔpf- -rɪç ˈfrɔødɪç dɪç deːɐ̯ pflɪçtʰ;
Doch bist du mir das Höchste nicht, drum opfr' ich freudig dich der Pflicht;
But are you to me the highest not, therefore sacrifice I gladly you to the duty;
(But to me, life, you are not the highest good; therefore I gladly sacrifice you to duty;)

[ˈɑox]   [lɪç ˈlɔp frə ˈhaetˈɐ]
[*poem:* **Auch du bist mir das Höchste nicht: ich opfre heiter dich der Pflicht**]
[Also]   [serenely]

aen ˈʃtˈraːlənbɪltˈ ʃveːpˈtˈ miːɐ̯ foˈran, lʊntˈ ˈmuːtˈɪç vaːg ɪç s ˈleːbən dran!
ein Strahlenbild schwebt mir voran, und mutig wag' ich's Leben dran!
a   radiant image hovers for me ahead, and bravely risk I   the life   on it!
(a radiant image hovers ahead of me, and I bravely risk my life for its sake!)

[*poem:* **und mutig wag' ich Alles** (ˈlaləs, everything) **dran.**]

das ˈʃtˈraːlənbɪltˈ lɪstˈ lɔftˈ bəˈtʰrɛːntʰ, vɛn lɛs dʊrç ˈmaenən ˈbuːzən brɛntʰ.
Das Strahlenbild ist oft betränt, wenn es durch meinen Busen brennt. [*GA:*,]
The radiant image is often tear-stained, when it through my   breast burns.
(That radiant image is often stained by my tears as it burns through my breast.)

[*poem:* **wie** (viː as) **es durch meinen Busen brennt.** (original punctuation)]

di ꞌtʰreːnən vɛkꞌ fɔm   ꞌvaŋənroːtʰ, ʊnt dan ɪn ꞌtʰɑozəntꞌfaxən tʰoːtꞌ!
Die Tränen weg vom   Wangenrot, und dann in   tausendfachen Tod!
The tears   away from the cheek- red, and then into thousandfold   death!
(Away from my red cheeks, tears! And then into a thousandfold death!)

duː vaːʁstꞌ zoː ꞌmɛnʃlıç,   vaːʁstꞌ zoː hɔltꞌ,   loː ꞌgroːsɐ ꞌdɔøtʃɐ   ꞌleːopʰoltꞌ,
Du warst so menschlich, warst so hold,   o grosser deutscher Leopold,
You were so humane,   were so gracious, O great   German Leopold,
          [*poem:* **und** (ʊntꞌ, and) **so hold, und gut** (guːtꞌ, good) **, o deutscher Leopold**]

di ꞌmɛnʃhaetꞌ ꞌfyːltꞌə dıç zoː gants   ʊntꞌ ꞌraeçtꞌə diːɐ̯ den ꞌlɔpfɛkʰrants.
die Menschheit fühlte dich so ganz   und reichte dir   den Opferkranz.
the mankind   felt   you so completely and handed to you the sacrificial wreath.
(mankind felt you to be so, completely, and conferred upon you the sacrificial wreath.)
          [*poem:* **die Menschheit** *füllte* (ꞌfʏltə) **dich so ganz** = (your) humanity *filled* you so fully]

[*the version in the published poem makes much more sense; "fühlte" may have been a copying error; his own humane feelings filled him so fully that they earned him the "sacrificial wreath."*]

ʊntꞌ heːɐ̯   gəꞌʃmʏkꞌtꞌ ʃpꞌraŋst duː hıꞌnapꞌ, fyːɐ̯ ꞌmɛnʃən ın das ꞌvɛləngraːpꞌ.
Und hehr   geschmückt sprangst du hinab, für Menschen in   das Wellengrab.
And sublimely adorned   sprang you down, for humans   into the wave- grave.
(And thus sublimely adorned you sprang down into the watery grave for the sake of others.)
          [*poem:* **ein Retter** (laen ꞌrɛtꞌɐ, a rescuer) **in das Wellengrab**]

foːɐ̯ diːɐ̯/diːr lɛɐ̯ꞌblaeçtʰ, loː ꞌfʏrstꞌənzoːn, tʰɛrmoːpʰylɛ ʊntꞌ ꞌmaːratʰɔn.
Vor dir   erbleicht, o Fürstensohn, Thermopylae und Marathon.
Before you   pales,   O son of princes, Thermopylae and Marathon.
(The heroes of Thermopylae and Marathon pale before you, O son of princes!)
          [*poem:* **Vor dir erblichen** (lɛɐ̯ꞌblıçən, paled), **Fürstensohn**]

das ꞌʃılfroːɐ̯ ꞌnaegətꞌ zɔøftsəntꞌ zıç, di ꞌluːfɐbluːmən ꞌgryːsən mıç,
Das Schilfrohr neiget   seufzend sich, die Uferblumen grüssen mich,
The reed   bends   sighingly itself, the bank-flowers greet   me,
(The reeds bend down as if sighing; the flowers on the bank greet me,)

deːɐ̯ ꞌfoːgəl kʰlaːkꞌt, di ꞌlʏftꞌə veːn, foːɐ̯ ꞌʃmɛrtsəslʊstꞌ   mœçtꞌ   lıç fɛɐ̯ꞌgeːn!
der Vogel klagt,   die Lüfte wehn, vor Schmerzeslust   möcht   ich vergehn!
the bird laments, the breezes blow, from pain-   pleasure would like I   to die!
(the bird laments, the breezes blow, I would like to die from the savoring of pain!)

[*Verses by Max Kalbeck, added to the original Peters edition after the words "*vor Schmerzenslust möcht' ich vergehn", *falsifying the song:*]

[voːl vaes lıç, vas das ꞌʃılfroːɐ̯ zaːkꞌtꞌ, ʊntꞌ vas das liːt dɛs   ꞌfoːgəls kʰlaːkꞌtʰ,
[Wohl weiss ich, was das Schilfrohr sagt,   und was das Lied des   Vogels klagt,
[Well know I   what the reed   says   and what the song of the bird   laments,
[(Well I know what the reeds are saying and what the song of the bird is lamenting;)

ax, lʊftꞌ ʊntꞌ fluːtꞌ ʊntꞌ fɛltꞌ ʊnt haen zıntꞌ lal lɛɐ̯ꞌfʏltꞌ fɔn ꞌglaeçɐ pʰaen!
ach, Luft und Flut   und Feld und Hain sind all erfüllt von gleicher Pein!
ah, air and stream and field and grove are all filled   with similar pain!

60

tsuː ˈfɔlgən vɛːnt‘ | ɪç diːɐ̯, naˈtuːɐ̯, lʊnt‘ | geː lɑof | ˈlaɛk‘nɐ ˈlaɛdən | ʃp‘uːɐ̯,
Zu folgen wähnt | ich dir, Natur, und | geh auf | eigner Leiden | Spur,
To follow imagined I | you, Nature, and (I) go | on (my) own | sufferings' track,
(I imagined I was following you, Nature; and yet I merely follow the track of my own suffering;)

ɛs | kʰɔmt di naxt‘ mɪt‘ ˈlaɛzəm ʃrɪt‘ | lʊnt‘ nɪmt‘ | lʊns ˈlalə, ˈlalə mɪtʰ.]
es | kommt die Nacht mit leisem Schritt und nimmt uns Alle, Alle mit.]
there comes the night with quiet step | and takes | us all, all with.]
(Night comes with a quiet step and takes all of us away with her.)]

[The Peters edition presents a drastically truncated and falsified version of Schubert's song, using only the first twenty bars (of 107!), and an altered form of the first two verses of Mayrhofer's poem, followed by two verses by Max Kolbeck that have nothing to do with the intention of the original poet. Schubert's complete song, as reproduced in the *Gesamtausgabe* is faithful to the sense of Mayrhofer's ideas, although some lines are different from the published poem, as indicated above. Schubert composed directly from the poet's manuscript; so perhaps it is the poet himself who may have made the changes in revising his work for publication. The poem was inspired by the heroism of Duke Leopold of Brunswick, who drowned in the icy waters of the Oder River while attempting to rescue victims of a flood. Mayrhofer was preoccupied with death and eventually committed suicide. Here he meditates upon a heroic death for the sake of others. The singer of the song must ascend to two heroic high B flats.]

am ˈʃt‘roːmə
Am Strome
By the Broad River

Op. 8, No. 4 [1817] (Johann Mayrhofer)

ɪst‘ miːɐ̯s dɔx, | lals zaɛ maɛn ˈleːbən lan den ˈʃøːnən ʃt‘roːm gəˈbʊndən.
Ist mir's doch, | als sei mein Leben an den schönen Strom gebunden.
Is to me it, after all, | as if be my life to the beautiful river linked.
(It seems to me, after all, as if my life is linked to the beautiful river.)

haːb ɪç ˈfroːəs | nɪçt‘ lan ˈzaɛnəm ˈluːfɐ(r) lʊnt‘ bəˈtryːp‘t‘əs hiːɐ̯/hiːr lɛmˈpfʊndən?
Hab ich Frohes | nicht an seinem Ufer und Betrübtes hier empfunden?
Have I glad feeling | not on its bank and sad feeling here felt?
(Have I not experienced both glad and sad feelings on its bank?)

[poem: **Hab' ich Frohes nicht am** (lam, on the) **Ufer]**

jaː, duː ˈglaɛçəst ˈmaɛnɐ ˈzeːlə; ˈmançmaːl gryːn lʊnt‘ glat‘ gəˈʃt‘alt‘ətʰ,
Ja, du gleichest meiner Seele; manchmal grün und glatt gestaltet,
Yes, you resemble my soul; sometimes green and smooth formed,
(Yes, you resemble my soul: sometimes green and smooth in form,)

lʊnt tsuː ˈtsaɛt‘ən ˈhɛrʃən ˈʃt‘ʏrmə ˈʃɔ̃ømənt‘, ˈlʊnruːfɔl, gəfalt‘ətʰ!
und zu Zeiten herrschen Stürme schäumend, unruhvoll, gefaltet!
and at times prevail storms foaming, restless, ruffled!
(and at other times storms prevail, the water foaming, turbulent, the surface ruffled!)

[poem: **herrschen Winde** (ˈvɪndə, winds)]

'fliːsəst tsuː dem 'fɛrnən 'meːrə, darfst'   lal'daː nɪçt' 'haemɪʃ 've:ɐdən.
Fliessest zu   dem fernen Meere, darfst   allda nicht heimisch werden.
(You) flow to   the distant sea, (you) are allowed there not   homelike to become.
(You flow to the distant sea; there you are not allowed to feel at home.)

                          [*poem:* **Fliessest fort zum** (fɔrt tsʊm, forth to the) **fernen Meere**]

mɪç drɛŋts   laox lɪn 'mɪldrə 'landə, 'fɪndə nɪçt das glʏk'   laof 'le:ɐdən.
Mich drängt's auch in   mildre Lande, finde nicht das Glück   auf Erden.
Me   urges it also into milder land, (I) find not   the happiness on earth.
(Something also urges me onward to a milder land; yet I shall not find happiness on earth.)

[Mayrhofer, the melancholy author of this poem, was frustrated by the conflict between his duties as a clerk in the censorship office and his desire to be a free spirit expressing itself in poetry. Schubert, with whom he shared a humble lodging for two years, composed forty-seven songs to his verses.]

an 'kʰloːən / bae deːɐ 'liːbə 'raenst'ən 'flamən
An Chloen / Bei der Liebe reinsten Flammen
To Chloe / Love's Purest Flames

Posthumously published [composed 1816] (poem by Johann Georg Jacobi)

bae deːɐ 'liːbə 'raenst'ən 'flamən   glɛntst das 'larmə 'hʏt'əndax:
Bei der Liebe reinsten Flammen glänzt das arme Hüttendach:
At the love's purest   flames   gleams the poor cottage-roof:
(The roof of our poor cottage gleams when our love ignites its purest flames:)

'liːp'çən! 'leːvɪç nuːn bae'zamən! 'liːp'çən! 'tʰrɔømənt' 'loːdɐ vax!
Liebchen! ewig   nun beisammen! Liebchen! träumend oder wach!
Darling! Forever now together! Darling! Dreaming or   awake!

                          [*poem:* **schlafend** ('ʃlaːfənt', sleeping) **oder wach**]

'zyːsəs, 'tsɛrt'lɪçəs lʊm'faŋən, vɛn deːɐ tʰaːk' lam 'hɪməl graot:
Süsses, zärtliches Umfangen, wenn der Tag   am   Himmel graut:
Sweet. tender   embracing when the day in the sky   becomes grey:
(Sweet, tender embraces when the day begins to dawn:)

'haemlɪç 'kʰlɔpfəndəs fɛɐ'laŋən, vɛn   deːɐ/deːr 'laːbənt' 'niːdɐtʰaoth!
heimlich klopfendes Verlangen, wenn der   Abend niedertaut!
secretly throbbing desiring,   when the   evening is dewing down!
(secretly throbbing desire when the evening dew is falling!)

'vɔnə   dɔrt' laof 'alən 'huːgəln, vɔn   lɪm tʰaːl, lʊnt' 'juːbəl hiːɐ!
Wonne dort auf allen Hügeln, Wonn' im   Tal,   und Jubel   hier!
Rapture there on all   hills,   rapture in the valley, and jubilation here!
(Rapture out there on all the hillsides, rapture in the valley, and jubilation in here!)

'fɔlə 'fraehaet, tsuː fɛɐ'riːgəln 'lʊnzrə 'kʰlaenə 'hʏt'əntʰyːɐ!
Volle Freiheit, zu verriegeln unsre kleine Hüttentür!
Full freedom, to bolt   our   little   cottage door!
(Full freedom to bolt the little door of our cottage!)

62

'loːp‚gəzaŋ   ɪn 'fɪnst‚ɐnɪsən,   voː   kʰaen 'naedɐ zɪç   feɐ̯'ʃt‚ɛk‚tʰ;
Lobgesang   in Finsternissen, wo   kein   Neider sich   versteckt;
Song of praise in dark places,   where no   envier   himself hides;
(A song of praise in dark places where no envious person is hiding;)

voː   nɪçt‚ meːɐ̯/meːr ɪn'deːm viːɐ̯ 'kʰysən, 'jeːdəs 'lʏft‚çən   ʊns ɛɐ̯'ʃrɛk‚tʰ!
wo   nicht mehr,   indem wir küssen, jedes Lüftchen   uns erschreckt!
where no   more,   while we kiss,   every little breeze us   frightens!)
(where no more, while we are kissing, every little breeze frightens us!)

ʊnt‚ viːɐ̯ 'tʰaelən 'alə 'frɔødən, zɔn   ʊnt‚ moːnt‚ ʊnt‚ 'ʃt‚ɛrnənglants;
Und wir teilen   alle Freuden, Sonn' und Mond und Sternenglanz;
And we share   all joys,   sun   and moon and stars- radiance;
(And we share all our joys, the sun and the moon and the radiance of the stars;)

'alən 'zeːgən,   'aləs 'laedən,   'arbaet‚ ʊnt‚ gə'beːt‚ ʊnt tʰants.
allen Segen,   alles Leiden,   Arbeit und Gebet und Tanz.
every blessing,   every suffering, work   and   prayer and dance.

zoː,   bae 'raenɐ 'liːbə 'flamən,   'ɛndət‚ zɪç deːɐ̯ 'ʃøːnə   laof;
So,   bei reiner Liebe Flammen, endet   sich der   schöne   Lauf;
Thus, at   pure   love's flames,   ends   itself the   beautiful course;
(Thus, when we keep alight the flames of pure love, will end the beautiful course of our life;)

'ruːɪç   'ʃveːbən viːɐ̯ tsu'zamən, 'liːp‚çən! 'liːp‚çən! 'hɪməl laof.
ruhig   schweben wir zusammen, Liebchen! Liebchen! Himmel auf.
peacefully soar   we   together,   darling!   darling!   heaven   towards.
(peacefully, darling, we shall soar together toward heaven.)

[Daphnis and Chloe were lovers in a Greek romance from the fourth or fifth century A.D. Their names were revived during the eighteenth century in rococo pastoral poetry and used by later poets, as a deliberate archaism, to evoke an idyllic Arcadia.]

an 'kʰloːən / di 'munt‚ɐkʰaet‚ ɪst‚ 'maenən 'vaŋən
An Chloen / Die Munterkeit ist meinen Wangen
To Chloe / Cheerfulness has fled my cheeks

Completed (first five bars were missing) and privately printed by Reinhold van Hoorickx
[composed 1816?] (poem by Johann Peter Uz)

di 'munt‚ɐkʰaet‚ ɪst‚   'maenən 'vaŋən,   den 'laogən gluːt‚ ʊnt‚ ʃp'raːx lɛnt‚'gaŋən;
Die Munterkeit ist   meinen Wangen,   den Augen Glut und Sprach entgangen;
The cheerfulness is (from) my   cheeks, (from) the eyes   fire   and   speech escaped;
(Cheerfulness has fled from my cheeks, fire and speech have left my eyes;)

deːɐ̯ munt‚ vɪl   kʰaom laen 'lɛçəln 'vaːgən; kʰaom vɪl   deːɐ̯ 'vɛlk‚ə   laep‚ zɪç 'tʰraːgən,
der Mund will   kaum ein Lächeln wagen; kaum will   der welke   Leib sich tragen,
the mouth wants hardly a   smile   to risk; hardly wants the   withered body itself to carry,
(my mouth will hardly risk a smile; my withered body can hardly bear itself upright,)

deːɐ̯ 'bluːmən lam 'mɪtʰaːgə glaeçt‚,   van 'floːra lɛçtst‚   ʊnt 'tseːfyːɐ̯ vaeçtʰ.
der   Blumen am Mittage gleicht,   wann Flora lechzt   und Zephyr weicht.
which flowers at the midday   resembles, when Flora is parched and Zephyr retreats.
(my body, which resembles flowers in the noon sun, when Flora is parched and Zephyr retreats.)

dɔx mɛrkʻ lɪç, van zɪç   ˈkʰloːə ˈtsaegətʰ, das maen lɛntʻˈflamtʻɐ blɪkʻ
Doch merk' ich, wann sich   Chloe zeiget,   dass mein entflammter Blick
But notice I,   when herself Chloe shows, that my   inflamed   gaze
(But I notice that whenever Chloe shows herself my inflamed gaze)

nɪçtʻ ˈʃvaegətʰ, lʊntʻ ˈzṵaːda   naːx den ˈlɪpʻən ˈfliːgətʰ; laen ˈglyːəntʻ roːtʻ
nicht schweiget, und Suada   nach den Lippen flieget; ein glühend Rot
not is silent,   and eloquent verbosity to the lips   flies; a   glowing red
(is not silent, and eloquent verbosity flies up to my lips; a glowing red)

lɪm ˈlantʻlɪts   ˈliːgətʰ, lʊntʻ ˈlaləs zɪç lan miːɐ fɛɐˈjʏŋtʻ,   viː ˈbluːmən,
im Antlitz   lieget, und alles sich an mir verjüngt, wie Blumen,
in the countenance lies,   and all   itself in me rejuvenates, like flowers,
(is in my face, and everything in me is rejuvenated, like flowers)

diː   deːɐ tʰao dʊrçˈdrɪŋtʰ. lɪç zeː laof ziː mɪtʻ ˈbaŋəm ˈzeːnən,
die   der Tau durchdringt. Ich seh auf sie mit bangem Sehnen,
which the dew penetrates. I   look at her with anxious longing,

ʊntʻ kʰan den blɪkʻ nɪçtʻ ˈvɛkɡəvøːnən: di ˈlanmuːt, diː   lɪm   ˈlaoɡə ˈvaxətʻ
und kann den Blick nicht weggewöhnen: die Anmut, die   im   Auge wachet
and can the gaze not   away-accustom: the grace, which in the eye is awake
(and cannot accustom my gaze to move away: the grace that is awake in her eyes)

ʊntʻ lʊm di ˈjʊŋən ˈvaŋən   ˈlaxət, t͡siːtʻ ˈmaenən ˈvɛkɡəvɪçnən   blɪkʻ
und um   die jungen Wangen lachet, zieht meinen weggewichnen Blick
and about the young cheeks   laughs, draws my   away-withdrawn glance
(and smiles around her young cheeks draws my withdrawn glance)

mɪtʻ ˈɡʏldnən ˈbandən ʃtʻeːts   t͡suˈrʏkʰ. maen bluːtʻ ʃtʻrøːmtʻ mɪtʻ ɡəˈʃvindɛn
mit güldnen Banden stets   zurück. Mein Blut strömt mit geschwindern
with golden bonds continually back.   My   blood streams with faster
(continually back, with bonds of gold. My blood flows with faster)

ˈɡʏsən; lɪç brɛn, lɪç ˈt͡sɪtʻrə, ziː t͡suː ˈkʰʏsən; lɪç ˈzuːxə ziː mɪtʻ ˈvɪldən ˈblɪkʻən,
Güssen; ich brenn', ich zittre, sie zu küssen; ich suche sie mit wilden Blicken,
gushes; I burn,   I   tremble her to kiss;   I   seek her with wild   glances,
(surges; I am burning, trembling to kiss her; I look about for her with wild glances,)

ʊntʻ ˈlʊnɡədʊltʻ vɪl   mɪç lɛɐˈʃtʻɪkʻən, lɪnˈdeːm lɪç ˈlɪmɐ ˈzeːnzʊxt͡sfɔl
und Ungeduld will   mich ersticken, indem ich immer sehnsuchtsvoll
and impatience wants me   to suffocate, since   I   always full of longing
(and feel as if impatience will suffocate me, since always, full of longing, I)

ziː zeːn lʊntʻ nɪçtʻ lʊmˈlarmən zɔl.
Sie sehn und nicht umarmen soll.
her see and not   to embrace am supposed.
(see her and am not supposed to embrace her.)

[The beginning of the manuscript was cut away, probably by Schubert's step-brother Andreas, who may have assumed that it was an extra copy of a different song with the same title. What was left is considered by Dietrich Fischer-Dieskau to be Schubert's most beautiful setting of a poem by Uz. Flora is the goddess of flowers, Zephyr is the soft west wind breeze, personified.]

an den 'fry:lɪŋ
An den Frühling
To the Spring

First version: Op. 172, N0. 5 [1815] (Friedrich von Schiller)
Second version [also composed in 1815] published posthumously

vɪl'kʰɔmən,   'ʃøːnɐ   'jʏŋlɪŋ!   du: 'vɔnə   deːɐ̯   na'tuːɐ̯!
Willkommen, schöner Jüngling! du Wonne der   Natur!
Welcome,   beautiful youth!   you delight of the Nature!
(Welcome, beautiful youth, you delight of Nature!)

mɪt 'daɛnəm 'bluːmənkʰœrp'çən vɪl'kʰɔmən   laʊf deːɐ̯ fluːɐ̯!
Mit deinem Blumenkörbchen willkommen auf der Flur!
With your   flower basket   welcome   on   the meadow!

aɛ, laɛ! daː   bɪst' jaː   'viːdɐ,   lʊnt'   bɪst' zoː liːp' lʊnt' ʃøːn!
Ei, ei! da   bist ja   wieder, und   bist so lieb und schön!
Ah, ah! there (you) are really again, and (you) are so dear and beautiful!
(Ah! There you are again, and you are so dear and beautiful!)

                                                              [*first version:* **da bist du** (duː, you) **wieder**]

ʊnt' frɔʏn viːɐ̯/viːr lʊns   zoː 'hertslɪç,, lɛnt''geːɡən diːɐ̯ tsuː geːn.
und freun wir   uns   so herzlich, entgegen dir zu gehn.
and gladden we   ourselves so heartily, toward   you to go.
(and we rejoice so heartily to go to meet you.)

dɛŋk'st'   laʊx nɔx lan maɛn 'mɛːt'çən? laɛ, 'liːbɐ,   dɛŋk'ə dɔx!
Denkst   auch noch an   mein Mädchen? Ei, Lieber, denke doch!
Think (you) also still about my   girl?   Ah, dear one, think   by all means!
(Are you too still thinking about my girl? Ah, dear one, do think about her!)

dɔrt' 'liːp't'ə mɪç das 'mɛːt'çən, lʊnt' 'smɛːt'çən liːp't' mɪç nɔx!
Dort liebte mich das Mädchen, und s'Mädchen liebt mich noch!
There loved me   the girl,   and the girl   loves me   still!
(The girl loved me over there, and the girl still loves me!)

fyːɐ̯s 'mɛːt'çən 'mançəs 'blyːmçən lɛɐ̯'baːt' lɪç m‌iːɐ̯   fɔn diːɐ̯,
Fürs Mädchen manches Blümchen erbat   ich mir   von dir,
For the girl   many a   little flower requested I   for myself from you,
(I requested from you many a little flower for me to give to my girl,)

ɪç kʰɔm lʊnt' 'bɪt'ə 'viːdɐ(r), lʊnt du:? du: giːp'st' lɛs miːɐ̯.
ich komm und bitte wieder, und du? du gibst   es mir.
I   come and ask   again;   and you? You give   it to me.

[Many composers set this poem to music; Schubert's second version is the most familiar of them. He himself also composed a setting for male chorus. His first version is in the style of a simple folksong, with a delightful short "*Ländler*" tune in the piano part, between verses.]

ˈandɛŋkˈən
Andenken
Remembrance

Posthumously published [composed 1814] (poem by Friedrich von Matthisson)

ɪç ˈdɛŋkˈə da͜en, vɛn dʊrç den ha͜en deːɐ̯ ˈnaxtˈɪgalən laˈkʰɔrdə ˈʃalən!
Ich denke dein, wenn durch den Hain der Nachtigallen Akkorde schallen!
I think of you when through the grove the nightingales' chords resound!

van dɛŋkst duː ma͜en?
Wann denkst du mein? [*poem:* **Wenn** (vɛn, when) **denkst du mein?**]
When think you of me?
(When do you think of me?)

ɪç ˈdɛŋkˈə da͜en ɪm ˈdɛmɐʃa͜en deːɐ̯/deːr ˈlaːbəntˈhɛlə lam ˈʃatˈənkʰvɛlə!
Ich denke dein im Dämmerschein der Abendhelle am Schattenquelle!
I think of you in the twilight gleam of the sunset at the shady spring!

voː dɛŋkst duː ma͜en?
Wo denkst du mein?
Where think you of me?
(Where do you think of me?)

ɪç ˈdɛŋkˈə da͜en mɪtˈ ˈzyːsɐ pʰa͜en, mɪtˈ ˈbaŋəm ˈzeːnən lʊntˈ ˈha͜esən ˈtʰrɛːnən!
Ich denke dein mit süsser Pein, mit bangem Sehnen und heissen Tränen!
I think of you with sweet pain, with anxious longing and hot tears!

viː dɛŋkst duː ma͜en?
Wie denkst du mein?
How think you of me?
(How do you think of me?)

oː ˈdɛŋkˈə ma͜en, bɪs ͡tsʊm fɛɐ̯ˈla͜en/fɛrˈla͜en la͜of ˈbɛsɐm ˈʃtˈɛrnə!
O denke mein, bis zum Verein auf besserm Sterne!
Oh think of me, until to the union on better star!
(Oh think of me until we are united on a better star!)

ɪn ˈjeːdɐ ˈfɛrnə dɛŋkˈ lɪç nuːɐ̯ da͜en!
In jeder Ferne denk' ich nur dein!
In every distant place think I only of you!
(In every distant place I think only of you!)

[This charming, graceful setting of a poem that was also set by Beethoven and Schumann should not be confused with "*Nähe des Geliebten,*" which also starts with the words "*ich denke dein.*"]

an den moːnt' / 'fʏləst' 'viːdɐ buʃ lʊnt tʰaːl
An den Mond / Füllest wieder Busch und Tal
To the Moon / You Fill Again Bush and Valley

Published posthumously [both versions composed in 1815] (Johann Wolfgang von Goethe)

'fʏləst' 'viːdɐ buʃ   lʊnt tʰaːl   ʃt'ɪl   mɪt' 'neːbəlglants,
Füllest   wieder Busch und Tal   still   mit Nebelglanz,
(You) fill again   bush   and valley quietly with misty radiance,

'løːzəst'   'lɛnt'lɪç lɑox lɑen'maːl 'mɑenə 'zeːlə gants.
lösest   endlich auch einmal   meine Seele ganz.
(you) set free at last   also once   my   soul   completely.
(you also set my soul completely free at last.)

'brɑet'əst'   'lyːbɐ mɑen gə'fɪlt' 'lɪndɐnt   'dɑenən blɪkʰ,
Breitest   über mein Gefild lindernd deinen Blick,
(You) extend over my   fields soothingly your   glance,
(You extend your glance soothingly over my fields,)

viː dɛs 'frɔʏndəs 'lɑogə mɪlt' 'lyːbɐ mɑen gə'ʃɪkʰ.
wie des Freundes Auge mild über mein Geschick.
as   the friend's   eye   gently over my   fate.
(as my friend's eyes gently extend their influence over my fate.)

'jeːdən 'naːxkʰlaŋ fyːlt' mɑen hɛrts   froː   lʊnt 'tʰryːbɐ tsaetʰ,
Jeden Nachklang fühlt mein Herz   froh' und trüber Zeit,
Each   echo   feels my   heart (of) happy and sad   time,
(My heart feels each echo of happy and sad times,)

'vandlə   'tsvɪʃən frɔʏt' lʊnt' ʃmɛrts   lɪn deːɐ/deːr 'lɑenzaːmkʰaetʰ.
wandle   zwischen Freud und Schmerz in der   Einsamkeit.
(I) wander between joy   and pain   in the   solitude.
(I wander in solitude between joy and pain.)

fliːsə, fliːsə, 'liːbɐ flʊs! 'nɪmɐ   veːɐd ɪç froː;
Fliesse, fliesse, lieber Fluss! nimmer werd' ich froh;
Flow,   flow,   dear river! Never   will I   happy (be);
(Flow, flow, dear river! Never will I be happy;)

zoː vɛɐ'rɑoʃt'ə ʃerts   lʊnt' kʰʊs lʊnt di 'tʰrɔʏə   zoː.
so verrauschte Scherz und Kuss, und die Treue   so.
thus died away   jest   and kiss and the faithfulness so.
(jests and kisses flowed away as the river flows, and so did faithfulness.)

ɪç bə'zaːs   lɛs dɔx   lɑen'maːl, vas zoː 'kʰœst'lɪç lɪstʰ!
Ich besass   es doch   einmal,   was so köstlich ist!
I   possessed it   though once,   what so precious is!
(I once possessed it, though, that which is so precious)

das man dɔx   tsuː 'zɑenɐ kʰvaːl 'nɪmɐ/nɪmɐr lɛs fɛɐ'gɪstʰ!
dass man doch zu seiner Qual   nimmer   es vergisst!
that one surely to one's torment never   it forgets!
(that one—to one's torment!—surely never forgets it!)

ˈrɑ͜oʃə, flʊs, das tʰaːl ɛntˈlaŋ, ˈloːnə rast' ʊnt' ˈloːnə ruː,
Rausche, Fluss, das Tal entlang, ohne Rast und ohne Ruh,
Rush, river, the valley along, without rest and without peace,
(Rush, river, down the valley, without rest and without peace,) [*poem:* **ohne Rast und Ruh**]

ˈrɑ͜oʃə, ˈflʏst'rə ˈmaenəm zaŋ meloˈdiːən t͜suː,
rausche, flüstre meinem Sang Melodien zu, [*"meinem,"* not *"meinen,"* as sometimes printed]
murmur, whisper my song melodies to,
(murmur, whisper melodies to my song,)

vɛn duː ɪn deːɐ̯ ˈvɪnt'ɐnaxt' ˈvyːt'ənt' ˈlyːbɐʃvɪlstʰ,
wenn du in der Winternacht wütend überschwillst,
when you in the winter night furiously overflow,
(when you furiously overflow your banks on a winter's night,)

ˈoːdɐ/oːdɐ ʊm di ˈfryːlɪŋspʰraxt' ˈjʊŋɐ ˈkʰnɔsp'ən kʰvɪlstʰ.
oder um die Frühlingspracht junger Knospen quillst.
or for the spring splendor of young buds well up.
(or well up for the spring splendor of young buds.)

ˈzeːlɪç, veːɐ̯ zɪç foːɐ̯ deːɐ̯ vɛlt' ˈloːnə has fɛɐ̯ˈʃliːstʰ,
Selig, wer sich vor der Welt ohne Hass verschliesst,
Blest, whoever himself from the world without hate shuts away,
(Blest is he who shuts himself away from the world without hatred,)

ˈaenən frɔ͜ønt' lam ˈbuːzən hɛlt' ʊnt' mɪt deːm gəˈniːstʰ,
einen Freund am Busen hält und mit dem geniesst,
a friend to the breast holds and with him enjoys
(holds a friend to his breast, and with him enjoys)

vas, fɔn ˈmɛnʃən nɪçt' gəˈvʊst', loːdɐ nɪçt' bəˈdaxtʰ,
was, von Menschen nicht gewusst, oder nicht bedacht,
what, by human beings not known or not thought of,
(that which—not known or thought of by human beings—)

dʊrç das ˈlabyˈrɪnt deːɐ̯ brʊst' ˈvandəlt' lɪn deːɐ̯ naxtʰ.
durch das Labyrinth der Brust wandelt in der Nacht.
through the labyrinth of the breast wanders in the night.
(wanders throught the labyrinth of the breast in the night.)

[Goethe wrote this deeply felt poem after a young woman, Christel von Lassberg, unhappy in love, had drowned herself in the Ilm River near his cottage in Weimar. The poet, moved by the melancholy beauty of a moonlit night as he walks beside the river, longs to communicate feelings of love and loss with a sympathetic friend. Schubert's second setting is considered to be one of his masterpieces. The German text can be sung by a man or by a woman, since the pronouns are unspecific as to gender.]

an den moːnt' / gɔøs, 'liːbɐ moːnt'
An den Mond / Geuss, lieber Mond
To the Moon / Pour, Dear Moon

Op. 57, No. 3 [1815 and 1816] (Ludwig Henirich Hölty)

gɔøs, 'liːbɐ moːnt', gɔøs 'daenə 'zɪlbɐflɪmɐ   dʊrç   'diːzəs 'buːxəngryːn,
Geuss, lieber Mond, geuss deine Silberflimmer durch dieses Buchengrün,
Pour,   dear   moon,   pour   your   silver-glimmer   through   this   beech-tree-green,
(Pour, dear moon, pour your silver glimmer through the green of this beech tree,)

voː   fant'a'ziːən   lʊnt 'traomgə'ʃt'alt'ən 'lɪmɐ   foːɐ   miːɐ fo'ryːbɐ fliːn!
wo   Phantasien und Traumgestalten immer vor   mir vorüber fliehn!
where fantasies   and dream-figures   always in front of me past   fly!
(where fantasies and dream-images always fly past before me!)

ɛnt''hylə dɪç,   das lɪç di 'ʃt'ɛt'ə 'fɪndə, voː   lɔft' maen 'mɛːt'çən zaːs,
Enthülle dich,   dass ich die Stätte finde, wo   oft mein Mädchen sass,
Unveil   yourself, that I   the place   find, where often my   girl   sat,
(Unveil yourself, that I may find the place where my girl often used to sit,)

ʊnt' lɔft', lɪm veːn   dɛs   'buːxbaoms lʊnt deːɐ 'lɪndə, deːɐ 'gɔldnən ʃt'at' fɛɐ'gaːs!
und oft, im Wehn   des   Buchbaums und der Linde, der goldnen Stadt vergass!
and often, in the fluttering of the beech tree   and the   linden, the   golden   city   forgot!
(and often, in the fluttering of the beech and linden trees, forgot the golden city!)

ɛnt''hylə dɪç,   das lɪç dɛs ʃt'raoxs mɪç 'frɔøə, deːɐ 'khyːlʊng liːɐ gə'raoʃt',
Enthülle dich,   dass ich des Strauchs mich freue, der Kühlung ihr gerauscht,
Unveil   yourself, that I   of the shrub   myself gladden, which cooling   to her rustled,
(Unveil yourself, that I may find delight in the shrub that cooled her as it rustled in the breeze,)

ʊnt' 'laenən khrants laof 'jeːdən 'laŋɐ   'ʃt'rɔøə, voː   ziː den bax bɛ'laoʃt'.
und einen Kranz auf jeden Anger   streue, wo   sie den Bach belauscht.
and a   wreath onto every   meadow scatter   where she the   brook listened to.
(and that I may scatter a wreath onto every meadow where she used to listen to the brook.)

dan, 'liːbɐ moːnt', dan nɪm den 'ʃlaeɐ 'viːdɐ, lʊnt traor lʊm 'daenən frɔønt',
Dann, lieber Mond, dann nimm den Schleier wieder, und traur' um deinen Freund,
Then, dear   moon,   then take   the veil   again,   and mourn for   your   friend,

ʊnt' 'vaenə dʊrç   den 'vɔlk''ənfloːɐ hɛɐ'niːdɐ, viː daen fɛɐ'lasnɐ   vaenth!
und weine durch   den Wolkenflor hernieder, wie dein Verlassner weint!
and weep   through the cloud- crape down,   as   your forsaken one weeps!
(and look down, weeping through your crape of clouds as your forsaken friend is weeping!)

[The prelude of this exquisite song reminds one of Beethoven's "Moonlight Sonata. The pianist's right hand portrays the moon gleaming through passing clouds; the bass line suggests the darkness of the night. The vocal melody seems to float like the moon in the sky. The middle section is in a contrasting rhythm, as the moon illumines the scenes where love was won and lost.]

an den moːnt‘ / vas ‘ʃɑ̯ɔəst duː zoː hɛl lʊnt‘ kʰlaːɐ̯
An den Mond / Was schauest du so hell und klar
To the Moon / Why do you look so brightly and clearly

Posthumously published [composed 1816] (poem by Ludwig Heinrich Christoph Hölty)

vas ‘ʃɑ̯ɔəst   duː zoː hɛl   lʊnt‘ kʰlaːɐ̯ dʊrç   ‘diːzə ‘lapfəlbɔ̯øməˌ
Was schauest du so hell   und klar durch diese Apfelbäume,
Why look   you so brightly and clearly through these apple-trees,
(Why do you look so brightly and clearly through these apple-trees)

voː   lae̯nst dae̯n frɔ̯ønt‘ zoː ‘zeːlɪç   vaːɐ̯ lʊnt ‘tʰrɔ̯ømt‘ə ‘zyːsə ‘tʰrɔ̯ømə?
wo   einst dein Freund so selig   war und träumte süsse Träume?
where once   your friend so blissful was and dreamed sweet dreams?
(where once your friend was so blissfully happy and dreamed sweet dreams?)

fɛɐ̯‘hylə ‘dae̯nən ‘zɪlbɐglants̬,   lʊnt‘ ‘ʃɪmrə,   viː duː ‘ʃɪmɐst‘,
Verhülle deinen Silberglanz,   und schimmre, wie du schimmerst,
Veil   your   silver-radiance, and shimmer, as you shimmer,
(Veil your silvery radiance and shimmer more dimly, as you shimmer)

vɛn duː den ‘fryːən   ‘tʰoːt‘ənkʰrants̬ deːɐ̯ ‘jʊŋən   brɑ̯ɔt‘ bə‘flɪmɐstʰ!
wenn du den frühen Totenkranz   der   jungen Braut beflimmerst!
when you the early   funeral wreath of the young bride beglimmer!
(when you glimmer upon the early funeral wreath of the young bride!)

duː ‘blɪk‘st‘ lʊm‘zɔnst‘ zoː hɛl   lʊnt‘ kʰlaːɐ̯ lɪn ‘diːzə ‘lɑ̯ɔbə ‘niːdɐ;
Du blickst umsonst so hell   und klar in   diese Laube nieder;
You look   in vain   so brightly and clearly into this arbor down;
(In vain do you look down into this arbor so brightly and clearly;)

niː ‘fɪndəst duː das ‘froːə pʰaːɐ̯/pʰaːr lɪn ‘liːrəm ‘ʃat‘ən   ‘viːdɐ!
nie   findest du das frohe Paar   in ihrem Schatten wieder!
never find   you the happy pair   in its   shadow   again!
(never again will you find the happy pair in its shadow!)

ae̯n ‘ʃvarts̬əs ‘fae̯nt‘lɪçəs gə‘ʃɪk‘   lɛnt‘rɪs miːɐ̯   ‘mae̯nə ‘ʃøːnə!
Ein schwarzes feindliches Geschick entriss mir   meine Schöne!
A   black,   hostile   fate   tore   from me my   beautiful one!

kʰae̯n ‘zɔ̯øftsɐ ‘ts̬ɑ̯ɔbɐt‘ ziː ts̬u‘rʏk‘, lʊnt‘ ‘kʰae̯nə ‘zeːnzʊxts̬tʰreːnə!
Kein Seufzer zaubert sie zurück, und keine Sehnsuchtsträne!
No   sigh   conjures her back, and no   yearning- tear!
(No sigh can conjure her back again, and no tear of yearning!)

oː ‘vandəlt‘ ziː hɪn‘fɔrt‘   ‘lae̯nmaːl lan ‘mae̯nɐ ‘ruːəʃt‘ɛlə,
O wandelt sie hinfort   einmal   an meiner Ruhestelle,
Oh wanders she in the future sometime at my   resting place,
(Oh, if she should wander near my resting place sometime in the future,)

dan ‘maxə flʊks mɪt ‘tʰryːbəm   ʃt‘raːl dɛs ‘graːbəs ‘bluːmən ‘hɛlə!
dann mache flugs mit trübem   Strahl des Grabes Blumen helle!
then make at once with melancholy beam the grave’s flowers bright!
(then at once illumine the flowers on the grave with one of your melancholy beams!)

zi: 'zɛtsə 'vaenənt' zıç lɑofs graːp', voː 'roːzən 'niːdɐhaŋən,
Sie setze weinend sich aufs Grab, wo Rosen niederhangen,
She may set weeping herself onto the grave, where roses hang down,
(May she sit down weeping on my grave, where roses are are drooping,)

ʊnt' 'pflʏk'ə zıç laen 'blyːmçən lap', lʊnt drʏk' lɛs lan di 'vaŋən.
und pflücke sich ein Blümchen ab, und drück' es an die Wangen.
and pluck herself a little flower off, and press it to the cheeks.
(and pick herself a little flower, and press it against her cheek.)

[Schubert found a simple, graceful melody, with an effective change of key in the middle, for his strophic setting of this melancholy poem.]

an den moːnt' lın 'laenɐ 'hɛrp'st'naxt^h
An den Mond in einer Herbstnacht
To the Moon on an Autumn Night

Posthumously published [composed 1818] (poem by Aloys Wilhelm Schreiber)

'frɔønt'lıç lıst daen 'lant'lits, zoːn dɛs 'hıməls, 'frɔønt'lıç!
Freundlich ist dein Antlitz, Sohn des Himmels, freundlich!
Friendly is your countenance, son of the sky, friendly!
[*the moon*, der Mond, *is masculine in German, feminine in Latin languages*]

laes zınt 'daenə 't^hrıt'ə dʊrç dɛs 'lɛːtɐs 'vyːst'ə, 'holdɐ 'naxt'gəfɛːɐt'ə.
Leis sind deine Tritte durch des Äthers Wüste, holder Nachtgefährte.
Soft are your steps through the ether's wilderness, lovely night-companion.

daen 'ʃımɐ lıst zanft' lʊnt' lɛɐ'k^hvık'ənt', viː das vɔrt dɛs 't^hroːst'əs
Dein Schimmer ist sanft und erquickend, wie das Wort des Trostes
Your shimmer is gentle and refreshing, like the word of the comfort
(Your shimmer is gentle and refreshing, like a word of comfort)

fɔn dɛs 'frɔøndəs 'lıp'ə, ven laen 'ʃrɛk'lıçɐ 'gaeɐ(r) lan deːɐ 'zeːlə naːk't^h.
von des Freundes Lippe, wenn ein schrecklicher Geier an der Seele nagt.
from the friend's lip, when a frightful vulture at the soul gnaws.
(from the lips of a friend when a frightful vulture is gnawing at one's soul.)

'mançə 't^hrɛːnə ziːst duː, ziːst' zoː 'mançəs 'lɛçəln,
Manche Träne siehst du, siehst so manches Lächeln,
Many a tear see you, (you) see so many a smile,
(Many a tear you see, you see many a smile,)

høːɐst deːɐ 'liːbə 't^hrɑolıçəs gə'flʏst'ɐ, 'lɔøçt'əst liːɐ/liːr lɑof 'ʃt'ıləm 'pfaːdə,
hörst der Liebe trauliches Geflüster, leuchtest ihr auf stillem Pfade,
(you) hear the love's cozy whispering, shine for it on quiet pathway,
(you hear the cozy whispers of love, you shine down upon the quiet pathway, for love's sake,)

'hɔfnʊŋ ʃveːp't' lɑof 'daenəm 'ʃt'raːlə he'rap', he'rap' tsʊm 'ʃt'ılən 'dʊldɐ,
Hoffnung schwebt auf deinem Strahle herab, herab zum stillen Dulder,
hope hovers on your beam downwards, down to the quiet endurer,
(hope hovers downwards with your rays, down to the one who quietly suffers,)

deːɐ̯ fɛɐ̯ˈlasən geːtʼ lɑ̯of bəˈdɔrntʼəm veːkʼ. duː ziːstʼ lɑ̯ox ˈmae̯nə ˈfrɔ̯øndə,
der verlassen geht auf bedorntem Weg. Du siehst auch meine Freunde,
who forsaken goes on thorny way. You see also my friends,
(who, forsaken, goes his thorn-infested way. You also see my friends,)

tsɛɐ̯ˈʃtʼrɔ̯øtʼ lɪn ˈfɛrnən ˈlandən; duːˈgiːsəst ˈdae̯nən ˈʃɪmɐ lɑ̯ox
zerstreut in fernen Landen; du giessest deinen Schimmer auch
scattered in distant lands; you pour your shimmer also

lɑ̯of di ˈfroːən ˈhyːgəl, voː lɪç lɔftʼ lals ˈkʰnaːbə ˈhypftʼə, [*poem:* **wo ich als Knabe hüpfte**]
auf die frohen Hügel, wo ich oft als Knabe hüpfte,
onto the happy hills, where I often as boy hopped,
(onto the happy hills where as a boy I often used to leap about,)

voː lɔftʼ bae̯ ˈdae̯nəm ˈlɛçəln lae̯n ˈlʊnbəkʰantʼəs ˈzeːnən mae̯n ˈjʊŋəs hɛrts lɛɐ̯ˈgrɪf.
wo oft bei deinem Lächeln ein unbekanntes Sehnen mein junges Herz ergriff.
where often at your smile an unknown yearning my young heart gripped.
(where a yearning, unknown before, often gripped my young heart when you were smiling.)

duː blɪkʼstʼ lɑ̯ox lɑ̯of di ˈʃtʼɛtʼə, voː ˈmae̯nə ˈliːbən ruːn, [*poem:* **ruhen** (ˈruːən, rest)]
Du blickst auch auf die Stätte, wo meine Lieben ruhn,
You look also upon the place where my dear ones rest,

voː deːɐ̯ tʰɑ̯o fɛltʼ lɑ̯of liːɐ̯ graːpʼ, lʊnt di ˈgrɛːzɐ ˈdryːbɐ veːn, lɪn dem ˈlaːbəntʼhɑ̯oxə.
wo der Tau fällt auf ihr Grab, und die Gräser drüber wehn, in dem Abendhauche.
where the dew falls upon their grave, and the grasses over it flutter in the evening breeze.
(where the dew falls upon their graves, and the grass ripples over them in the evening breeze.)
[*poem:* **wehen** (ˈveːən)]

dɔx dae̯n ˈʃɪmɐ drɪŋtʼ nɪçtʼ lɪn di ˈdʊŋkʼlə ˈkʰamɐ,
Doch dein Schimmer dringt nicht in die dunkle Kammer,
But your shimmer penetrates not into the dark chamber,
(But your shimmer does not penetrate into the dark chamber)

voː ziː ˈruːən fɔn dɛsˈleːbəns ˈmyːn, voː lɑ̯ox lɪç baltʼ ˈruːən ˈveːɐ̯də!
wo sie ruhen von des Lebens Mühn, wo auch ich bald ruhen werde!
where they rest from the life's cares, where also I soon rest will!
(where they rest from the cares of life, where soon I too shall rest!) [*poem:* **Mühe** (ˈmyːə, care)]

duː vɪrstʼ geːn lʊnt ˈviːdɐkʰeːrən, duː vɪrst zeːn nɔx ˈmançəs ˈlɛçəln;
Du wirst gehn und wiederkehren, du wirst sehn noch manches Lächeln;
You will go and come back again, you will see still many a smile;
(You will go and come back again; you will still see many a smile;) [*poem:* **und sehn noch...**]

dan veːɐ̯d ɪç nɪçtʼ meːɐ̯ ˈlɛçəln, dan veːɐ̯d ɪç nɪçtʼ meːɐ̯ ˈvae̯nən,
dann werd' ich nicht mehr lächeln, dann werd' ich nicht mehr weinen,
then will I not more smile, then will I not more weep,
(then I shall not smile any more, then I shall not weep any more,)

mae̯n vɪrtʼ man nɪçtʼ meːɐ̯ gəˈdɛŋkʼən lɑ̯of ˈdiːzɐ ˈʃɔ̯ønən ˈleːɐ̯də!
mein wird man nicht mehr gedenken auf dieser schönen Erde!
of me will one not more think on this beautiful earth!
(no one will think of me any more on this beautiful earth!)
[*poem:* **mein wird man dann** (dan, then) **nicht mehr gedenken**]

72

[*An den Mond in einer Herbstnacht*, a lovely song, would be more popular if it were not so long. The singer must be careful not to stress syllables that would not be stressed in speaking the lines, even though the music may appear to give unjustified prominence to certain words, such as "*ist*" in the first line, or "*an*" in the phrase: "*wenn ein schrecklicher Geier an der Seele nagt.*"]

an den ʃlaːf
An den Schlaf
To Sleep

Posthumously published [composed 1816] (poem by Johann Peter Uz?)

kʰɔm,   ʊnt' 'zɛŋk'ə di ʊmˈfloːɐ̯t'ən   'ʃvɪŋən,
Komm, und senke die umflorten   Schwingen,
Come, and sink   the crape-covered wings,
(Come, and sink your dark wings,)

'zyːsɐ 'ʃlʊmɐ, |ɑ̯of den 'myːdən blɪkʰ! 'zeːgnɐ,   frɔ̯ønt'!
süsser Schlummer, auf den müden Blick! Segner,   Freund!
sweet slumber,   onto the weary look! Bringer of blessings, friend!
(sweet slumber, onto my weary eyes! Bringer of blessings, friend!)

|ɪn 'dɑ̯enən 'armən 'drɪŋən   tʰroːst' ʊnt' 'balzaːm |ɑ̯ofs   fɛɐ̯'loːɐ̯nə glʏkʰ.
in deinen Armen dringen Trost   und Balsam aufs   verlorne Glück.
in your   arms   rush   comfort and balm   onto the lost   happiness.
(In your arms comfort and balm rush to assuage lost happiness.)

[This very simple song is one of Schubert's shortest. A copy identifies the poet as Johann Peter Uz, but this poem is not included in any of his published works.]

an den tʰoːt'
An den Tod
To Death

Posthumously published [composed 1817] (Christian Daniel Schubart)

tʰoːt', du: 'ʃrɛk'ən   deːɐ̯ na'tʰuːɐ̯, 'ɪmɐ   'riːzəlt 'dɑ̯enə luːɐ̯,
Tod, du Schrecken der Natur, immer rieselt deine Uhr,
Death, you terror   of the nature, ever   trickles your clock,
(Death, you terror of Nature, the sand in your hour-glass is always trickling down,)

di gə'ʃvʊŋnə   'zɛnzə blɪŋk't'ʰ, graːs ʊnt' halm ʊnt' 'bluːmə zɪŋk't'ʰ.
die geschwungne Sense blinkt, Gras und halm und Blume sinkt.
the swung   scythe flashes, grass and stalk and flower sinks.
(the swung scythe flashes, grass and stalk and flower fall.)

'mɛːə nɪçt' |oːn   'ʊnt'ɐʃiːt' 'diːzəs 'blyːmçən, das leːɐ̯st' blyːtʰ;
Mähe nicht ohn   Unterschied dieses Blümchen, das erst   blüht;
Mow not   without distinction this   little flower that just blooms;
(Do not mow down indiscriminately this little flower that just started to bloom,)

'di:zəs 'rø:sçən le:ɐ̯st' halp' ro:tʰ, zae̯ barm'hɛrtsɪç, 'li:bə tʰo:t'!
dieses Röschen erst halb rot, sei barmherzig, lieber Tod!
this little rose just half red, be merciful, dear death!
(this little rose, not yet fully red; be merciful, dear Death!)

A second verse, found in some editions:

[tʰo:t', van kʰɔmst du:, 'mae̯nə lʊstʰ? tsi:st den dɔlç lao̯s 'mae̯nɐ brʊst?
[Tod, wann kommst du, meine Lust? ziehst den Dolch aus meiner Brust?
[Death, when come you, my delight? draw the dagger out of my breast?
[(Death, when will you come, my delight? When will you draw the dagger out of my breast?)

ʃt'rae̯fst di 'fɛsəl fɔn de:ɐ̯ hant'? lax, van dɛk'st du: mɪç mɪt' zant'?
streifst die Fessel von der Hand? ach, wann deckst du mich mit Sand?
strip off the fetters from the hand? ah, when cover you me with sand?
(When will you strip off the fetters from my hands? Ah, when will you cover me with sand?)

kʰɔm, lo: tʰo:t', vɛns di:ɐ̯ gə'fɛltʰ, ho:l gə'faŋnə lao̯s de:ɐ̯ vɛltʰ :
Komm, o Tod, wenn's dir gefällt, hol Gefangne aus der Welt:
Come, O Death, if it to you is pleasing, fetch prisoners out of the world:
(Come, O Death, if it please you, and take prisoners away with you out of the world:)
          [*poem:* **Drum** (drʊm, therefore), **o Tod, wenn dir's** (vɛn di:ɐ̯s, if to you it) **gefällt**]

kʰɔm, fɔl'lɛndə 'mae̯nə no:tʰ; zae̯ barm'hɛrtsɪç, 'li:bə tʰo:t'!]
komm, vollende meine Not; sei barmherzig, lieber Tod!]
come, put an end to my distress; be merciful, dear Death!]
          [*poem:* **Komm, vollende ihre** ('li:rə, their) **Not**]

[The first verse (the only one printed in the Peters collection) is a plea to Death to spare the budding flower that has barely begun to live. Some other publishers have included a second verse (above, not recommended), in which a prisoner calls upon Death to release him from his chains. The original poem contained sixteen quatrains; if all were to be sung, Schubert's setting would need six more verses!]

an di 'lɛpfəlbɔ̯ø̯mə, vo: lɪç 'ju:li̯ən lɛɐ̯'blɪk't'ə
An die Äpfelbäume, wo ich Julien erblickte
To the Appletrees, where I caught a glimpse of Julia

Posthumously published [composed 1815] (Ludwig Heinrich Christoph Hölty)

ae̯n 'hae̯lɪç 'zɔø̯zəln lʊnt' lae̯n gə'zaŋəstʰo:n dʊrçtsɪt'rə 'dae̯nə 'vɪpfəl,
Ein heilig Säuseln und ein Gesangeston durchzittre deine Wipfel,
A holy rustling and a song- tone through-tremble your tree-tops,
(A holy rustling and a songlike tone tremble through your tree-tops,)

o: 'ʃat'əngaŋ, vo: baŋ lʊnt' vɪlt' de:r 'le:ɐ̯st'ən li:bə 'ze:lɪgə 'tʰao̯məl
o Schattengang, wo bang und wild der ersten Liebe selige Taumel
O shadow- walk, where fearful and wild the first love's blissful delirium
(O shady walk, where fearfully and wildly the blissful delirium of first love)

mae̯n hɛrts bə'rao̯ʃt'ən. di 'la:bənt'zɔnə 'be:p't'ə vi: 'lɪçt'əs gɔlt'
mein Herz berauschten. Die Abendsonne bebte wie lichtes Gold
my heart intoxicated. The setting sun quivered like light gold
(intoxicated my heart. The light of the setting sun quivered like pale gold)

durç 'pʰʊrp'ʊrblyːt'ən, 'beːp't'ə viː 'lɪçt'əs gɔlt' ʊm 'iːrəs 'buːzəns 'zɪlbəʃlaeɐ,
durch Purpurblüten, bebte wie lichtes Gold um ihres Busens Silberschleier,
through purple blossoms, trembled like light gold around her bosom's silver veil,

ʊnt' lɪç zɛɐ'flɔs ɪn lɛnt'tsʏk'ʊŋsʃaoɐ. naːx 'laŋɐ 'tʰrɛnʊŋ
und ich zerfloss in Entzückungsschauer. Nach langer Trennung
and I melted in rapture- shivers. After long separation
(and I melted away in shivers of rapture. After a long separation)

kʰʏsə mɪt' 'lɛŋəlskʰʊs laen 'tʰrɔøɐ 'jʏŋlɪŋ hiːɐ das gə'liːp't'ə vaep', [*GA:*Engelkuss]
küsse mit Engelskuss ein treuer Jüngling hier das geliebte Weib,
may kiss with angel- kiss a faithful youth here the beloved woman,
(may a faithful youth kiss his beloved woman here with an angel-kiss,)

ʊnt' ʃvøːr ɪn 'diːzəm 'blyːt'əndʊŋk'əl 'leːvgə 'tʰrɔøə deːr 'aosɛɐkʰoːrnən!
und schwör in diesem Blütendunkel ewge Treue der Auserkornen!
and swear in this blossom-darkness eternal faithfulness to the chosen one!

aen 'blyːmçən 'ʃp'rɔsə, vɛn viːɐ gə'ʃt'ɔrbən zɪnt', laos 'jeːdəm 'raːzən, [*GA:* wann (van)]
Ein Blümchen sprosse, wenn wir gestorben sind, aus jedem Rasen,
A little flower may sprout, when we dead are, out of every lawn,
(May a little flower, when we are dead, sprout out of every plot of grass)

'vɛlçən liːɐ fuːs bə'ryːɐt', ʊnt tʰraik' laof 'jeːdəm 'zaenɐ 'blɛt'ɐ
welchen ihr Fuss berührt, und trag auf jedem seiner Blätter
which her foot touched, and bear on each of its petals
(which her foot has touched, and may each of its petals bear)

'maenəs fɛɐ'hɛrlɪçt'ən 'meːt'çəns 'naːmən.
meines verherrlichten Mädchens Namen.
my glorified girl's name.
(the name of my glorified girl!)

[The attractive melody is varied each time it recurs, and the character of the accompaniment is totally different the last time.]

an di lɛnt''fɛrnt'ə
An die Entfernte
To the Distant One

Posthumously published [composed 1822] (poem by Johann Wolfgang von Goethe)

zoː haːb ɪç 'vɪrk'lɪç dɪç fɛɐ'loːrən? bɪst duː, oː 'ʃøːnə, miːɐ/miːr lɛnt''floːn?
So hab ich wirklich dich verloren? bist du, o Schöne, mir entflohn?
So have I really you lost? Are you, O lovely one, from me fled?
(So have I really lost you? Have you, O lovely one, fled from me?)

nɔx kʰlɪŋt' ɪn den gə'voːnt'ən 'loːrən laen 'jeːdəs vɔrt', laen 'jeːdɐ tʰoːn.
Noch klingt in den gewohnten Ohren ein jedes Wort, ein jeder Ton.
Still sounds in the accustomed ears an every word, an every tone.
(Every word, every tone is still sounding in my ears, which are by now accustomed to that.)

zoː viː dɛs 'vandrɐs blɪk' lam 'mɔrgən fɛɐ̯'geːbəns lɪn di 'lʏft'ə drɪŋtʰ,
So wie des Wandrers Blick am Morgen vergebens in die Lüfte dringt,
Just as the wanderer's gaze in the morning in vain into the airs penetrates,
(Just as, in the morning, the wanderer's gaze searches through the air in vain,)

vɛn, lɪn dem 'blaɔən raɔm fɛɐ̯'bɔrgən, hoːx 'lyːbɐ(r) liːm di 'lɛrçə zɪŋtʰ :
wenn, in dem blauen Raum verborgen, hoch über ihm die Lerche singt:
when, in the blue space hidden, high above him the lark sings:
(when, hidden in blue space, high above him the lark is singing:)

zoː drɪŋət 'lɛŋst'lɪç hɪn lʊnt' 'viːdɐ dʊrç fɛlt' lʊnt' bʊʃ lʊnt' valt' maɛn blɪkʰ;
so dringet ängstlich hin und wieder durch Feld und Busch und Wald mein Blick;
thus pierces anxiously now and again through field and bush and forest my gaze;
(thus my gaze repeatedly and anxiously pierces through field and bush and forest:)

dɪç 'ruːfən 'lalə, 'lalə 'maɛnə 'liːdɐ; oː kʰɔm, gə'liːp't'ə, miːɐ̯ ʦu'rʏkʰ!
dich rufen alle, alle meine Lieder; o komm, Geliebte, mir zurück!
you [object] call all, all my songs [subject]; O come, beloved, to me back!
(all, all my songs call you; oh, beloved, come back to me!) [Goethe's poem: only one *"alle"*]

[This fine song has been unjustly neglected. Goethe wrote the poem in 1789, thinking of his absent beloved, Charlotte von Stein, the inspiration for the lovely Charlotte in *The Sorrows of Young Werther*, his famous novel.]

an di 'frɔʏdə
An die Freude
To Joy

Op. 111, No. 1 [1815] (Friedrich von Schiller)

'frɔʏdə, 'ʃøːnɐ 'gœt'ɐfʊŋk'ən, 't'ɔxt'ɐ(r) laɔs le'lyːziʊm.
Freude, schöner Götterfunken, Tochter aus Elysium,
Joy, beautiful divine spark, daughter from Elysium,

viːɐ̯ bə't'reːt'ən 'fɔʏɐt'rʊŋk'ən, 'hɪmlɪʃə, daɛn 'haɛlɪçt'uːm!
wir betreten feuertrunken, Himmlische, dein Heiligtum!
we enter, drunk with fire, heavenly one, your sanctuary!

'daɛnə 'ʦaɔbɐ 'bɪndən 'viːdɐ, vas di 'moːdə ʃt'rɛŋ gə't'aɛltʰ:
Deine Zauber binden wieder, was die Mode streng geteilt:
Your magics bind again what the fashion strictly separates:
(Your magic powers bind together again what fashion rigorously separates:)

'lalə 'mɛnʃən 'veːɐ̯dən 'bryːdɐ, voː daɛn 'zanft'ɐ 'flyːgəl vaɛltʰ.
alle Menschen werden Brüder, wo dein sanfter Flügel weilt.
all human beings become brothers, where your soft wing lingers.

zaɛt' lʊm'ʃlʊŋən, mɪli'oːnən! 'diːzən kʰʊs deːɐ̯ 'gantsən vɛltʰ!
Seid umschlungen, Millionen! diesen Kuss der ganzen Welt!
Be embraced, you millions! This kiss for the whole world!

'bry:dɐ(r), 'ly:bɐm 'ʃt'ɛrnəntsɛltʰ mʊs ɪ̯aɛn 'gu:t'ɐ 'fa:t'ɐ 'vo:nən!
Brüder, überm Sternenzelt muss ein guter Vater wohnen!
Brothers, above the starry tent must a good father dwell!
(Brothers, above the canopy of stars a good father must be dwelling!)

ve:m de:ɐ̯ 'gro:sə vʊrf gə'lʊŋən, 'ɪ̯aɛnəs 'frɔɟndəs frɔɟnt tsu: zaɛn,
Wem der grosse Wurf gelungen, eines Freundes Freund zu sein,
He for whom the great throw has succeeded, a friend's friend to be,
(He for whom the great endeavor to be a friend to a friend has been successful,)

ve:ɐ̯/ve:r ɪ̯aɛn 'hɔldəs vaɛp' lɛɐ̯'rʊŋən, 'mɪʃə 'saɛnən 'ju:bəl ɪ̯aɛn!
wer ein holdes Weib errungen, mische seinen Jubel ein!
he who a lovely woman has won, mingle his jubilation in!
(he who has won a lovely woman, let him mingle his jubilation with ours!)

ja: — ve:ɐ̯/ve:r ɪ̯aɒx nu:ɐ̯/nu:r 'ɪ̯aɛnə 'ze:lə zaɛn nɛnt' ɪ̯aɒf de:m 'le:ɐ̯dənrʊnt'!
Ja — wer auch nur eine Seele sein nennt auf dem Erdenrund!
Yes — whoever even only one soul his names on the earth- globe!
(Yes, whoever can name even one single soul his own on this globe of earth!)

ʊnt' ve:ɐ̯s ni: gə'kʰɔnt, de:ɐ̯ 'ʃt'e:lə 'vaɛnənt' zɪç ɪ̯aɒs 'di:zəm bʊnt'!
und wer's nie gekonnt, der stehle weinend sich aus diesem Bund!
and he who it never could, he may steal weeping himself out of this alliance!
(and he who never could do that, may he slink away weeping from this alliance!)

vas den 'gro:sən rɪŋ bə'vo:nət', 'hʊldɪgə de:ɐ̯ zymp'a'tʰi:!
Was den grossen Ring bewohnet, huldige der Sympathie!
That which the great ring inhabits, do homage to fellow-feeling!
(That which inhabits the great ring should do homage to fellow-feeling!)

tsu: den 'ʃt'ɛrnən 'laɛt'ət' zi:, vo: de:r 'ʊnbəkʰant'ə 'tʰro:nətʰ.
zu den Sternen leitet sie, wo der Unbekannte thronet.
to the stars leads it, where the Unknown is throned.
(It leads to the stars, where the Unknown is throned.)

'frɔɟdə 'tʰrɪŋk'ən 'alə 've:zən ɪ̯an den 'bryst'ən de:ɐ̯ na'tu:ɐ̯;
Freude trinken alle Wesen an den Brüsten der Natur;
Joy drink all being at the breasts of the Nature;
(All beings drink joy at the breasts of Nature;)

'alə 'gu:t'ən, 'alə 'bø:zən 'fɔlgən 'li:rɐ 'ro:zənʃp'u:ɐ̯.
alle Guten, alle Bösen folgen ihrer Rosenspur.
all good creatures, all bad ones follow her rose- track.
(all good creatures and all bad ones follow her rose-covered track.)

kʰysə ga:p' zi: ʊns ʊnt' 're:bən, 'ɪ̯aɛnən frɔɟnt', gə'pʰry:ft' ɪm tʰo:t';
Küsse gab sie uns und Reben, einen Freund, geprüft im Tod;
Kisses gave she to us, and grape-vines, a friend, tested in the death;
(She gave us kisses and wine, friendship that lasts beyond death;)

'vɔlʊst' vart' dem vʊrm gə'ge:bən, ʊnt de:ɐ̯ 'çe:rʊp' ʃt'e:t' fo:ɐ̯ gɔtʰ.
Wollust ward dem Wurm gegeben, und der Cherub steht vor Gott.
lust was to the worm given, and the cherub stands before God.
(lust was given to the worm, and the cherub stands before God.)

iː̯ ʃtˈʏrt̯st̯ˈ ˈniːdɐ, mɪliˈoːnən? ˈlaːnəst duː den ˈʃœpˈfɐ, vɛltʰ?
Ihr stürzt nieder, Millionen? Ahnest du den Schöpfer, Welt?
You sink down, millions? Surmise you the Creator, world?
(Do you sink down, you millions? Can you imagine the Creator, world?)

zuːx liːn ˈlyːbɐm ˈʃtˈɛrnənt͜sɛltʰ! ˈlyːbɐ ˈʃtˈɛrnən mʊs leː̯ɐ̯ ˈvoːnən!
Such ihn überm Sternenzelt! über Sternen muss er wohnen!
Seek Him above the starry tent! above stars must He dwell!
(Seek Him above the canopy of stars! He must dwell above the stars!)

ˈfrɔ͜ødə h͜aest diː ˈʃtˈarkˈə ˈfeːdɐ lɪn deː̯ɐ̯/deːr ˈleːvɪɡən naˈtʰuː̯ɐ̯.
Freude heisst die starke Feder in der ewigen Natur.
Joy is the name of the strong spring in the eternal Nature.
(Joy is the name of the main-spring in eternal Nature.)

ˈfrɔ͜ødə, ˈfrɔ͜ødə tʰr͜aepˈt di ˈrɛːdɐ(r) lɪn deː̯ɐ̯ ˈɡroːsən ˈvɛltˈənluː̯ɐ̯.
Freude, Freude treibt die Räder in der grossen Weltenuhr.
Joy, joy drives the wheels in the great cosmic clock.

ˈbluːmən lɔkˈtˈ ziː l͜aos deːn ˈkʰ͜aemən, ˈzɔnən l͜aos deːm fɪrmaˈmɛntʰ,
Blumen lockt sie aus den Keimen, Sonnen aus dem Firmament,
Flowers lures she out of the buds, suns out of the firmament,
(She lures flowers out of their buds, suns out of the firmament,)

ˈsfɛːrən rɔltˈ ziː lɪn den ˈrɔ͜ømən, diː dɛs ˈseːɐs roː̯ɐ̯ nɪçtˈ kʰɛntʰ.
Sphären rollt sie in den Räumen, die des Sehers Rohr nicht kennt.
spheres rolls she in the spaces which the star-gazer's telescope not knows.
(she rolls spheres in space which are unknown to the star-gazer's telescope.)

froː, viː ˈz͜aenə ˈzɔnən ˈfliːɡən dʊrç dɛs ˈhɪməls ˈpʰrɛçtˈɡən pʰlaːn,
Froh, wie seine Sonnen fliegen durch des Himmels prächtgen Plan,
Happily, as its suns fly through the heaven's magnificent plain,
(Happily, as heaven's suns fly through its magnificent plain,)

ˈl͜aofət, ˈbryːdɐ, ˈlɔ͜ørə baːn, ˈfrɔ͜ødɪç viː l͜aen hɛlt t̯sʊm ˈziːɡən!
laufet, Brüder, eure Bahn, freudig wie ein Held zum Siegen!
run, brothers, your course, joyously as a hero to the victory!
(run your course, brothers, as joyously as a hero runs toward victory!)

͜aos deː̯ɐ̯ ˈvaː̯ɐ̯h͜aetˈ/vaːrh͜aetˈ ˈfɔ͜øɐʃpˈiːɡəl ˈlɛçəltˈ ziː deːn ˈfɔrʃɐ(r) lan;
Aus der Wahrheit Feuerspiegel lächelt sie den Forscher an;
Out of the truth's fire- mirror smiles she the investigator at;
(Out of Truth's fiery mirror she smiles at the seeker;)

t̯suː deː̯ɐ̯ ˈtʰuːɡəntˈ ˈʃtˈ͜aeləm ˈhyːɡəl ˈl͜aetˈ ət ˈ ziː dɛs ˈdʊldɐs baːn.
zu der Tugend steilem Hügel leitet sie des Dulders Bahn.
to the Virtue's steep hill guides she the patient endurer's course.
(she guides the course of him who patiently endures to the steep hill of Virtue.)

͜aof dɛs ˈɡl͜aobəns ˈzɔnənbɛrɡə ziːt man ˈliːrə ˈfaːnən veːn,
Auf des Glaubens Sonnenberge sieht man ihre Fahnen wehn,
On the Faith's sun- mountain sees one her banners wave,
(One can see her banners waving on top of the sun-illuminated mountain of Faith,)

dʊrç den rɪs gəʃpˈrɛŋtʻɐ ˈzɛrgə ziː ‖ɪm kʰoːɐ deːr ˈɛŋəl ʃtʻeːn.
durch den Riss gesprengter Särge sie im Chor der Engel stehn.
through the crack of burst coffins her in the choir of the angels stand.
(through the cracks of burst coffins one can see her standing in the angel's choir.)

ˈdʊldətʻ ˈmuːtɪç, mɪliˈoːnən! ˈdʊldətʻ fyːɐ di ˈbɛsrə vɛltʰ!
Duldet mutig, Millionen! duldet für die bessre Welt!
Endure bravely, millions! Endure for the better world!
(Endure bravely, you millions! Endure for the better world that is to come!)

ˈdroːbən ˈyːbɐm ʃtʻɛrnəntsɛltʰ vɪrtʻ ‖aen ˈɡroːsə ɡɔtʻ bəˈloːnən.
Droben überm Sternenzelt wird ein grosser Gott belohnen.
Up there above the starry tent will a great god reward.
(Up there above the canopy of stars a great god will reward your patience and courage.)

ˈɡœtʻɐn kʰan man nɪçtʻ fɛɐˈɡɛltʻən; ʃøːn ‖ɪsts, ˈiːnən ɡlaeç tsuː zaen.
Göttern kann man nicht vergelten; schön ist's, ihnen gleich zu sein.
Gods can one not repay; beautiful is it, to them similar to be.
(One cannot repay gods; it is beautiful to be like them.)

ɡraːm ‖ʊntʻ ˈ‖armuːtʻ zɔl zɪç ˈmɛldən, mɪt den ˈfroːən zɪç ‖ɛɐˈfrøøn.
Gram und Armut soll sich melden, mit den Frohen sich erfreun.
Affliction and Poverty shall themselves announce, with the happy ones themselves rejoice.
(Affliction and Poverty shall come forward and rejoice with the Happy Ones.)

ɡrɔl ‖ʊntʻ ˈraxə zae fɛɐˈɡɛsən, ‖ʊnzɛm ˈtʰoːtʻfaentʻ zae fɛɐˈtsiːn,
Groll und Rache sei vergessen, unserm Todfeind sei verziehn,
Rancor and revenge be forgotten, our deadly enemy be forgiven,

ˈkʰaenə ˈtʰrɛːnə zɔl ‖iːn ˈpʰrɛsən, ˈkʰaenə ˈrɔøə ˈnaːɡə ‖iːn!
keine Träne soll ihn pressen, keine Reue nage ihn!
no tear shall him depress, no remorse gnaw him!
(no tear shall depress him, no remorse gnaw him!)

ˈ‖ʊnzɐ ˈʃʊltʻbuːx zae fɛɐˈnɪçtʻətʻ! ‖aosɡəzøːnt di ˈɡantsə vɛltʰ!
Unser Schuldbuch sei vernichtet! ausgesöhnt die ganze Welt!
Our account-book be annihilated, reconciled the entire world!
(Let our old scores be wiped out, let the whole world be reconciled!)

ˈbryːdɐ(r), ˈyːbɐm ˈʃtʻɛrnəntsɛlt ˈrɪçtʻətʻ ɡɔtʻ, viː viːɐ ɡəˈrɪçtʻətʰ.
Brüder, überm Sternenzelt richtet Gott, wie wir gerichtet.
Brothers, above the starry tent, judges God, as we (have) judged.
(Brothers, above the canopy of stars God judges us as we have judged.)

ˈfrɔødə ʃpʻˈruːdəltʻ ‖ɪn pʰoˈkʰaːlən; ‖ɪn deːɐ ˈtʰraobə ˈɡɔldnəm bluːtʰ
Freude sprudelt in Pokalen; in der Traube goldnem Blut
Joy effervesces in goblets; in the grape's golden blood

ˈtʰrɪŋkʻən ˈzanftʻmuːtʻ ˈkʰaniˈbaːlən, di fɛɐˈtsvaeflʊŋ ˈhɛldənmuːtʰ —
trinken Sanftmut Kannibalen, die Verzweiflung Heldenmut —
drink gentleness cannibals, the despair heroic courage —
(cannibals drink gentleness, despair imbibes heroic courage —)

ˈbryːdɐ, fliːkˈtˈ fɔn ˈlɔʏrən ˈzɪtsən, vɛn deːɐ̯ ˈfɔlə ˈrøːmɐ kʰraestʰ,
Brüder, fliegt von euren Sitzen, wenn der volle Römer kreist,
Brothers, fly from your seats when the full goblet circles,   ["*Römer*"= large glass]

last den ʃaom tsʊm ˈhɪməl ʃpˈrɪtsən: ˈdiːzəs glaːs dem ˈguːtˈən gaestʰ!
lasst den Schaum zum Himmel spritzen: dieses Glas dem guten Geist!
let the foam to the heaven splash: this glass to the good spirit!
(let the foam splash up to heaven: raise this glass to the Good Spirit!)

deːn deːɐ̯ ˈʃtˈɛrnə ˈvɪrbəl ˈloːbən, deːn dɛs ˈzeːrafs ˈhymnə pʰraestʰ,
Den der Sterne Wirbel loben, den des Seraphs Hymne preist,
Whom the stars' vortices extol, whom the seraph's hymn praises,

ˈdiːzəs glaːs dem ˈguːtˈən gaestˈ ˈlyːbɐm ˈʃtˈɛrnəntsɛlt dɔrtˈ ˈloːbən!
dieses Glas dem guten Geist überm Sternenzelt dort oben!
this glass to the Good Spirit over the starry tent there above!
(this glass to the Good Spirit up there above the canopy of stars!)

ˈfɛstˈən muːtˈ ɪn ˈʃveːrəm ˈlaedən, ˈhylfə, voː diː ˈʊnʃʊltˈ vaentʰ,
Festen Mut in schwerem Leiden, Hülfe, wo die Unschuld weint, [*Peters:* **schweren**]
Firm courage in heavy suffering, help where the innocence weeps,
(Firm courage in grievous suffering, help wherever Innocence is weeping,)

ˈeːvɪçkʰaetˈ gəˈʃvoːrnən ˈlaedən, ˈvaːrhaetˈ/ˈvaːɐ̯haetˈ ˈgeːgən frɔʏntˈ ʊntˈ faentˈ,
Ewigkeit geschwornen Eiden, Wahrheit gegen Freund und Feind,
eternity sworn oaths, truth against friend and foe,
(Oaths sworn and kept for eternity, the truth toward friend and foe alike,)

ˈmɛnɐʃtˈɔlts foːɐ̯ ˈkʰøːnɪkˈsˌtʰroːnən, ˈbryːdɐ, gɛltˈ ɛs guːtˈ ʊntˈ bluːtʰ:
Männerstolz vor Königsthronen, Brüder, gält es Gut und Blut:
manly pride before kings' thrones, brothers, concerns it property and blood:
(manly pride before the thrones of kings, brothers, when life and property are at stake;)

deːm fɛɐ̯ˈdiːnstˈə ˈzaenə ˈkʰroːnən, ˈʊntˈɐgaŋ deːɐ̯ ˈlyːgənbruːtʰ!
dem Verdienste seine Kronen, Untergang der Lügenbrut!
to the merit its crowns, downfall to the lie-telling brood!
(to merit its rewards, downfall to the breed of liars!)

ʃliːst den ˈhaelgən ˈtsɪrkˈəl ˈdɪçtˈɐ, ʃvøːɐ̯tˈ bae ˈdiːzəm ˈgɔldnən vaen,
Schliesst den heilgen Zirkel dichter, schwört bei diesem goldnen Wein,
Close the holy circle more tightly, swear by this golden wine

deːm gəˈlypˈdə tʰrɔʏ tsuː zaen, ʃvøːɐ̯tˈ ɛs bae dem ˈʃtˈɛrnənrɪçtˈɐ!
dem Gelübde treu zu sein, schwört es bei dem Sternenrichter!
to that vow true to be, swear it by the starry judge!
(to be true to that vow, swear it by the starry judge!)

[The famous *finale* of Beethoven's Ninth Symphony uses parts of this same poem as its text (all of the first verse and "chorus," as designated in Schubert's version, the second and third verses, the third and fourth choruses).]

80

an di ˈfrɔøndə
An die Freunde
To My Friends

Posthumously published [composed 1819] (poem by Johann Mayrhofer)

ɪm   valt‘,   ɪm   valt   daː   graːpˈtʻ mɪç   ɭaen, gants ˈʃtʻɪlə   ˈloːnə   kʰrɔøts ɭʊntʻ ʃtʻaen,
Im   Wald, im   Wald da   grabt mich ein, ganz stille ohne   Kreuz und Stein,
In the woods, in the woods there bury   me   ... ,   quite   quietly without cross   and   stone,

dɛn   vas   liːɐ̯ ˈtʰʏrmət, ˈyːbɐʃnaetʻ ɭʊntʻ ˈyːbɐrɪndətʻ ˈvɪntʻɐstsaetʰ.
denn was   ihr türmet, überschneit und   überrindet Winterszeit.
since what you pile up, over-snows and over-crusts wintertime.
(since winter will cover over with snow and crust with frost whatever you raise up.)

ʊntʻ van   diː ˈleːɐ̯də zɪç fɛɐ̯ˈjʏŋtʻ   ɭʊntʻ ˈbluːmən ˈmaenəm ˈhyːgəl brɪŋtʰ,
Und wann die Erde sich verjüngt   und Blumen meinem Hügel bringt,
And when the earth itself rejuvenates and flowers to my   mound brings,
(And when the earth is rejuvenated and brings flowers to my grave,)
                                        [*poem:* sie (ziː, it) **Veilchen** (ˈfaelçən, violets) **meinem Hügel bringt**]

das frɔøtʻ   lɔøç, [liːɐ̯] ˈguːtʻən,   ˈfrɔøət lɔøç,   diːs ˈlaləs lɪst dem ˈtʰoːtʻən glaeç;
das freut   euch, [ihr] Guten,   freuet   euch,   dies Alles ist dem Toten gleich;
that gladdens you, [you] good ones, gladden yourselves; that all   is to the dead   the same;
(that makes you glad; good friends, be pleased; it is all the same to the dead;)
              [*poem:* **Das freut euch, Gute** (ˈguːtʻə, good ones)**... ist Alles doch** (dɔx, though) **dem...**]

dɔx naen, dɛn ˈlɔørə ˈliːbə ʃpʻant di ˈlɛstʻə   ɭɪn das ˈgaestʻɐlantʻ,
doch nein, denn eure Liebe spannt die Äste   in das Geisterland,
but   no,   for   your love spreads the branches into the spirit- land,
(but no! — for your love spreads out its branches into the spirit world,)

ʊnt diː   lɔøç fyːɐ̯t tsuː ˈmaenəm graːpʻ, tsiːtʻ mɪç gəˈvaltʻɪgɐ   hɛˈrapʻ.
und die   euch führt zu meinem Grab, zieht mich gewaltiger   herab.
and that [love] which you leads to my   grave draws me   more powerfully down.
(and the love that leads you to my grave draws me more powerfully near to you.)

[This song foreshadows the poet's suicide, which took place in 1836. The music starts like a
ghostly funeral march, first with single notes in the bass, then with bare and desolate octaves.
The *Gesamtausgabe* follows Schubert's manuscript, in A minor; the Peters version is based on
the first edition, in F minor, with some variants.]

an di gəˈliːpʻtʻə
An die Geliebte
To the Beloved

Posthumously published [composed in 1815] (poem by Josef Ludwig Stoll)

oː das lɪç diːɐ̯   fɔm   ˈʃtʻɪlən ˈlaogə ɭɪn ˈzaenəm ˈliːbəfɔlən ʃaen
O dass ich dir   vom   stillen Auge in seinem liebevollen Schein
Oh that I   to you from the quiet eye in its   love-full   shine
(Oh, that I might suck from your cheek the tear that fell from your silent eye in its loving luster,)

di 'tʰreːnə fɔn deːɐ̯ 'vaŋə 'zɑo̯gə, leː   ziː di 'leːɐ̯də 'tʰrɪŋk'ət' ɑe̯n!
die Träne von der Wange sauge, eh   sie die Erde   trinket ein!
the tear   from the   cheek   suck, before it the earth   drinks   up!
(before the earth drinks it up!)

voːl   hɛlt' ziː 'ts̪øːgɐnt' ɑo̯f deːɐ̯ 'vaŋə
Wohl   hält sie zögernd auf der Wange
No doubt stops it hesitantly on the cheek
(No doubt it stops hesitantly on your cheek)

ʊnt' vɪl   zɪç hɑe̯s   deːɐ̯ 'tʰrɔø̯ə   vɑe̯n;
und will   sich heiss   der Treue   weihn;
and wants itself fervently to the faithfulness consecrate;
(and wants to consecrate itself fervently to faithfulness;)

nuːn   lɪç ziː zoː lɪm   kʰʊs lɛm'pfaŋə, nuːn zɪnt' lɑo̯x 'dɑe̯nə 'ʃmɛrts̪ən   mɑe̯n.
nun   ich sie   so im   Kuss empfange, nun sind auch deine Schmerzen mein.
now that I   them so in the kiss   receive,   now are also   your   sorrows   mine.
(now that I receive them like that in my kiss, now your sorrows are also mine.)

[*An die Geliebte* was composed on the name day of Schubert's first love, Therese Grob.]

An die Harmonie see *Gesang an die Harmonie*

an di 'lɑo̯t'ə
An die Laute
To the Lute

Op. 81, No. 2 [1827] (Johann Friedrich von Rochlitz)

'lɑe̯zɐ,   'lɑe̯zɐ,   'kʰlɑe̯nə 'lɑo̯t'ə, 'flʏst'rə, vas lɪç diːɐ̯ fɛɐ̯'tʰrɑo̯t'ə,
Leiser,   leiser,   kleine Laute, flüstre, was ich dir   vertraute,
More softly, more softly, little   lute,   whisper what I   to you confided
(Whisper more softly, little lute, what I confided to you)

dɔrt' ts̪uː 'jeːnəm 'fɛnst'ɐ hɪn!   viː di 'vɛlən 'zanft'ɐ 'lʏft'ə,
dort zu jenem Fenster hin!   Wie die Wellen sanfter Lüfte,
there to   that   window hence! Like the waves of gentle breezes,
(up to that window there! Like the undulations of gentle breezes,)

'moːndənglants̪ ʊnt' 'bluːməndʏft'ə,   zɛnd lɛs deːɐ̯ gə'biːt'ərɪn!
Mondenglanz und Blumendüfte,   send' es der   Gebieterin!
moon-radiance and flower-fragrances, send it   to the mistress!
(like moonlight and the fragrance of flowers, send it to the lady who rules my heart!)
["*Gebieterin*" = a woman with the power to command, a ruler]

'nɑe̯dɪʃ   zɪnt dɛs 'naxbaːrs/naxbaːɐ̯s 'zøːnə, ʊnt' lɪm   'fɛnst'ɐ 'jeːnɐ 'ʃøːnə
Neidisch sind des Nachbars   Söhne, und im   Fenster jener Schöne
Envious are the neighbor's   sons, and in the window of that beautiful woman
(The neighbor's sons are envious; and in the window of that beautiful woman)

82

'flɪmɐt' nɔx ḁen 'ḁenzaːm lɪçtʰ. drʊm nɔx 'laezɐ, 'kʰlḁenə 'laot'ə :
flimmert noch ein einsam Licht. Drum noch leiser, kleine Laute:
glimmers still a lonely light. Therefore still more softly, little lute:
(a lonely light is still glimmering. Therefore still more softly, little lute:)

dɪç̩ fɛɐ̯'neːmə di fɛɐ̯'tʰraot'ə, 'naxbaːrn/naxbaːɐ̯n 'laːbɐ — 'naxbaːrn/naxbaːɐ̯n nɪçtʰ!
dich vernehme die Vertraute, Nachbarn aber— Nachbarn nicht!
you hear the intimate friend, neighbors however—neighbors not!
(let my lady hear you, but not the neighbors!)

[A delightfully mischievous little serenade, in which the piano imitates the lute.]

an di 'laeɐ
An die Leier
To the Lyre

Op. 56, No. 2 [1822] (Franz von Bruchmann, after the Greek poet Anacreon)

ɪç vɪl fɔn 'aːt'rɔɵs 'zøːnən, fɔn 'kʰat'mʊs vɪl ɪç 'zɪŋən!
Ich will von Atreus' Söhnen, von Kadmus will ich singen!
I want of Atreus's sons, of Cadmus want I to sing!
(I want to sing about the sons of Atreus and about the hero Cadmus!)

dɔx 'maenə 'zaet'ən 'tʰøːnən nuːɐ̯ 'liːbə ɪm lɛɐ̯'kʰlɪŋən.
Doch meine Saiten tönen nur Liebe im Erklingen.
Yet my strings sound only love in the resounding.
(Yet the strings of my lyre sound only tones of love.)

ɪç 'tʰaoʃə ʊm di 'zaet'ən, di 'laeɐ mœçt' ɪç 'tʰaoʃən!
Ich tausche um die Saiten, die Leier möcht ich tauschen!
I exchange the strings, the lyre would like I to exchange!
(I change the strings, I would like to exchange the lyre!)

al'tsiːdəns 'ziːgəs'ʃraet'ən zɔlt' 'liːrɐ maxt' ɛnt'raoʃən!
Alcidens Siegesschreiten sollt' ihrer Macht entrauschen!
Alcides' triumph-strides should their power thunder forth!
(Their power should thunder forth the triumphant strides of Alcides [Heracles/Hercules]!)

dɔx 'maenə 'zaet'ən 'tʰøːnən nuːɐ̯ 'liːbə ɪm lɛɐ̯'kʰlɪŋən!
Doch meine Saiten tönen nur Liebe im Erklingen!
Yet my strings sound only love in the resounding!
(Yet the strings of my lyre sound only tones of love!)

zoː leːpt dɛn voːl, he'roːən! dɛn 'maenə 'zaet'ən 'tʰøːnən,
So lebt denn wohl, Heroen! denn meine Saiten tönen,
So fare then well, heroes! for my strings sound,
(So farewell then, heroes! For my strings sound,)

ʃt'at' 'hɛldənzaŋ tsuː 'droːən, nuːɐ̯ 'liːbə ɪm lɛɐ̯'kʰlɪŋən.
statt Heldensang zu drohen, nur Liebe im Erklingen.
instead of heroic song to threaten, only love in the resounding.
(instead of threatening a song about heroes, only tones of love.)

[Atreus was a king of Mycenae; his sons were Agamemnon and Menelaus, famous for their part in the Trojan War and in many an ancient Greek drama. Cadmus, brother of Europa, founded the Grecian city of Thebes. Alcides was one of the names of Heracles (Hercules), the son of Zeus by Alcmene, a mortal woman; he was said to be the strongest man on earth. The Greek poet Anacreon celebrated the joys of life and youth. In this poem he pretends to want to sing of heroic warriors; but his insubordinate lyre insists on singing of love. Schubert's song emphasizes the conflict by alternating heroic declamation with a suavely lyrical, legato melody.]

an di muˈzikʰ
An die Musik
To Music

Op. 88, No. 4 [1817] (Franz von Schober)

duː ˈhɔldə kʰʊnstʰ, ɪn ˈviːfiːl ˈɡrɑɔən ˈʃtʼʊndən,
Du holde Kunst, in wieviel grauen Stunden,
You lovely art , in how many grey hours,

voː mɪç dɛs ˈleːbəns ˈvɪldɐ kʰraes ʊmˈʃtrɪkʼtʰ,
wo mich des Lebens wilder Kreis umstrickt,
where me the life's wild circle entangles,
(when life's wild vortex ensnares me,)

hast duː maen hɛrts tsuː ˈvarmɐ liːpʼ lɛntʼtsʊndən,
hast du mein Herz zu warmer Lieb entzunden,
have you my heart to warmer love ignited,
(you have ignited my heart to warmer love,)

hastʼ mɪç ɪn lˈaenə ˈbɛsrə vɛltʼ lɛntʼrʏkʼtʰ!
hast mich in eine bessre Welt entrückt!
have me into a better world carried away!
(have carried me away into a better world!)

ɔftʼ hatʼ laen ˈzɔøftsɐ, daenɐ harf lɛntʼflɔssən,,
Oft hat ein Seufzer, deiner Harf entflossen,
Often has a sigh, from your harp flowed forth,
(Often a sigh, that from your harp flowed forth,)

aen ˈzʏːsɐ, ˈhaelɪɡɐ(r) laˈkʰɔrtʼ fɔn diːɐ̯
ein süsser, heiliger Akkord von dir
a sweet, holy chord from you

den ˈhɪməl ˈbɛsrɐ ˈtsaetʼʼən miːɐ̯/miːr lɛɐ̯ˈʃlɔsən, —
den Himmel bessrer Zeiten mir erschlossen, —
the heaven of better times to me opened, —
(has opened the heaven of better times to me, —)

duː ˈhɔldə kʰʊnstʼ, lɪç ˈdaŋkʼə diːɐ̯ daˈfyːɐ̯, duː ˈhɔldə kʰʊnstʼ, lɪç ˈdaŋkʼə diːɐ̯!
du holde Kunst, ich danke dir dafür, du holde Kunst, ich danke dir!
you lovely art, I thank you for that, you lovely art, I thank you!

[This song is Schubert's hymn of gratitude to the art of music, his solace in times of sorrow and his window into heaven.]

84

an di 'naxt'ıgal / eːɐ̯ liːk't' ʊnt' ʃleːft' ʲan 'maenəm 'hɛrt͜sən
An die Nachtigall / Er liegt und schläft an meinem Herzen
To the Nightingale / He Lies and Sleeps at my Heart

Op. 98, No. 1 [1816] (Matthias Claudius)

eːɐ̯ liːk't' ʊnt' ʃleːft' ʲan 'maenəm 'hɛrt͜sən, maen 'guːt'ɐ 'ʃut͜sgaest'   zaŋ liːn laen,
Er liegt und schläft an meinem Herzen, mein guter Schutzgeist   sang ihn ein,
He lies and sleeps at my   heart,   my   good guardian spirit sang him to sleep,

ʊnt' lıç kʰan 'frøːlıç   zaen ʊnt' 'ʃert͜sən,
und ich kann fröhlich sein und scherzen,
and I   can merry   be   and joke,
(and I can be merry and joke,)

kʰan 'jeːdɐ   bluːm ʊnt' 'jeːdəs   blat͜s mıç   frɔøn.
kann jeder   Blum' und jedes   Blatts mich   freun.
can of every flower and of every leaf   myself gladden.
 (I can take delight in every flower and every leaf.)

'naxt'ıgal,   ax! zıŋ miːɐ̯ den 'laːmoːɐ̯ nıçt' vax!
Nachtigall, ach! sing mir den Amor   nicht wach!
Nightingale, ah! sing me the Cupid not   awake!
(Oh nightingale! Don't wake up Cupid!)

[The poet, in this miniature gem, is glad that love is dormant for the moment; he can enjoy nature and feel at ease without the distraction of desire. But at any moment an amorous nightingale might stir Cupid into action again.]

an di 'naxt'ıgal / gɔøs nıçt' zoː laǫt
An die Nachtigall / Geuss nicht so laut
To the Nightingale / Do not Pour so Loudly

Op. 172, No. 3 [1815] (Ludwig Heinrich Christoph Hölty)

gɔøs   nıçt' zoː laǫt   deːɐ̯ 'liːp'lɛntflamt'ən 'liːdɐ 'tʰoːnraeçən ʃal
Geuss nicht so laut   der   liebentflammten Lieder tonreichen Schall
Pour   not   so loudly of the love-inflamed   songs tone-rich   sound
(Do not pour so loudly the rich tones of love-inflamed songs)

fɔm   'blyːt'ənlast   dɛs   'lapfəlbaǫms hɛɐ̯'niːdɐ(r), loː 'naxt'ıgal!
vom   Blütenast   des   Apfelbaums hernieder, o Nachtigall!
from   the blossom-bough of the apple-tree   down,   O nightingale!
(down from the blossoming bough of the apple-tree, O nightingale!)

duː 'tʰøːnəst' miːɐ̯ mıt 'daenɐ 'zyːsən 'kʰeːlə di 'liːbə vax;
Du tönest   mir   mit deiner süssen Kehle die Liebe wach;
You sound   in me with your   sweet throat the love awake;
(With your sweet throat you sing love awake in me;)

dɛn ʃoːn dʊrçbeːp't   di 'tʰiːfə 'maenɐ 'zeːlə daen 'ʃmɛlt͜sənt' lax!
denn schon durchbebt   die Tiefe meiner Seele dein schmelzend Ach!
for   already through-trembles the depths of my soul your melting   "Ah"!
(for already your melting sigh is trembling through the depths of my soul!)

dan fliːt deːɐ̯ ʃlaːf fɔn 'nɔɔ̯əm 'diːzəs 'laːgɐ(r), lɪç 'ʃt'arə dan
Dann flieht der Schlaf von neuem dieses Lager, ich starre dann
Then flees the sleep from new from this couch, I stare then
(Then sleep flees anew from this couch, I stare then)

mɪt' 'nasəm blɪkʰ, lʊnt tʰoːt'ənblaɛ̯ç lʊnt' 'haːgɐ, den 'hɪməl lan.
mit nassem Blick, und totenbleich und hager, den Himmel an.
with moist glance, and dead-pale and haggard, the heaven at.
(with moist eyes, and deathly pale and haggard, at heaven.)

flɔɔ̯ç, 'naxt'ɪgal, lɪn 'gryːnə 'fɪnst'ɐnɪsə, lɪns 'haɛ̯ngəʃt'rɔɔ̯ç, ['hoːnɪçʃt'rɔɔ̯ç]
Fleuch, Nachtigall, in grüne Finsternisse, ins Haingesträuch, [*Peters:* Honigsträuch]
Fly, nightingale, into green darknesses, into the grove-bushes [honey-bush]
(Fly, nightingale, into the green darkness, into the bushes of the grove,)

ʊnt' ʃp'ɛnt' lɪm nɛst deːɐ̯ 't'rɔɔ̯ən 'gat'ɪn 'kʰysə, lɛnt'flɔɔ̯ç, lɛnt''flɔɔ̯ç!
und spend im Nest der treuen Gattin Küsse, entfleuch, entfleuch!
and dispense in the nest of the faithful wife kisses, fly away, fly away!
(and dispense kisses in the nest of your faithful mate! Fly away, fly away!)

[Johannes Brahms' setting of this poem is much more famous than Schubert's version, lovely as this is. The *Gesamtausgabe* gives G sharp as the singer's last note in the second bar, the Peters edition prints an F sharp. There is also a word in the Peters version, indicated above, that does not appear in either the original poem or in the first published version, considerably altered by the editor, Johann Voss, which was the basis of Schubert's song.]

an di na't'ʰuːɐ̯
An die Natur
To Nature

Posthumously published [composed 1816] (poem by Friedrich Leopold, Graf zu Stolberg)

'zyːsə, 'haɛ̯lɪgə na't'ʰuːɐ̯, las mɪç geːn lɑɔf 'daɛ̯nɐ ʃp'uːɐ̯,
Süsse, heilige Natur, lass mich gehn auf deiner Spur,
Sweet, holy Nature, let me walk in your footsteps,

'laɛ̯t'ə mɪç lan 'daɛ̯nɐ hant', viː lae̯n kʰɪnt' lam 'gɛŋəlbant'!
leite mich an deiner Hand, wie ein Kind am Gängelband!
lead me by your hand, like a child on the leading-string!

vɛn lɪç dan lɛɐ̯'myːdət' bɪn, zɪŋk' lɪç diːɐ̯/diːr lam 'buːzən hɪn,
Wenn ich dann ermüdet bin, sink' ich dir am Busen hin,
When I then tired am, sink I to you on the bosom down,
(Then, when I am tired, I shall sink down against your bosom,)

'aːt'mə 'zyːsə 'hɪməlslʊst' 'haŋənt' lan deːɐ̯ 'mʊt'ɐbrʊstʰ.
atme süsse Himmelslust hangend an der Mutterbrust.
breathe sweet heaven- pleasure clinging to the mother-breast.
(and breathe sweet heavenly pleasure, clinging to our mother's breast.)

ax! viː voːl lɪst' miːɐ̯ baɛ̯ diːɐ̯! vɪl dɪç 'liːbən fyːɐ̯/fyːr lʊnt' fyːɐ̯;
Ach! wie wohl ist mir bei dir! will dich lieben für und für;
Ah! How well is to me with you! (I) will you love for(ever) and for(ever);
(Ah, how well I feel with you! I shall love you forever and ever;)

86

las mɪç geːn ḷɑof ˈdɑenɐ ʃpˈuːɐ̯, ˈzyːsə, ˈhɑelɪgə naˈtʰuːɐ̯!
lass mich gehn auf deiner Spur,   süsse, heilige Natur!
let me walk in   your footsteps, sweet, holy   Nature!

[Count Stolberg wrote this poem after visiting the Rhine Falls in Switzerland. Schubert's simple strophic setting seems to expresses the poet's images of childhood. This was the first of his songs that Therese Grob, the sweetheart of his youth, had seen, and he transposed it upwards to accommodate her high voice.]

an di ˈzɔnə / ˈkʰøːnɪkˈlɪçə ˈmɔrgənzɔnə
An die Sonne / Königliche Morgensonne
To the Sun / Majestic Morning Sun

Posthumously published [composed 1815] (poem by Christoph August Tiedge)

ˈkʰøːnɪkˈlɪçə ˈmɔrgənzɔnə,   zɑe gəˈgryːstˈ ɪn ˈdɑenɐ ˈvɔnə,
Königliche Morgensonne, sei gegrüsst in deiner Wonne,
Majestic   morning sun, be greeted in your   rapture,

hoːx   gəˈgryːstˈ ɪn ˈdɑenɐ pʰraxtʰ!
hoch gegrüsst in deiner Pracht!
highly greeted in your   splendor!

gɔldən fliːstˈ ʃoːn   ḷʊm   di ˈhyːgəl dɑen gəˈvantˈ, ḷʊnt das gəˈflyːgəl
Golden fliesst schon um   die Hügel dein Gewand, und das Geflügel
Golden flows already around the hills   your garment, and the feathered flock
(Already your garment flows like gold about the hills, and the birds)

ˈɑenəs ˈjeːdən ˈvaldəs vaxtʰ.
eines jeden Waldes wacht.
of an every forest   is awake.
(of every forest are awake.)

[ˈaləs ˈfyːlət ˈdɑenən ˈzeːgən; ˈfluːrən   ˈzɪŋən diːɐ̯/diːr ḷɛntˈˈgeːgən,
[Alles fühlet deinen Segen; Fluren   singen dir   entgegen,
[All feels your   blessing; meadows sing   to you to meet,
[(All things feel your blessing; meadows sing to greet you,)

ˈaləs vɪrt   t͡suˈzamənkʰlaŋː ḷʊnt duː ˈhøːrəstˈ gɛrn   di ˈkʰøːrə
alles wird   Zusammenklang: und du hörest gern   die Chöre
all becomes together- sound: and you hear   gladly the choirs
(all becomes harmony: and you gladly listen to the choirs)

ˈfroːɐ   ˈvɛldɐ(r), loː zoː ˈhøːrə, høːɐ̯/høːr ḷɑox ˈmɑenən ˈloːpˈgəzaŋ.
froher Wälder, o so höre, hör'   auch meinen Lobgesang.
of happy forests,   oh, then hear, hear   also   my   song of praise.

ˈhoːɐ ˈgœtˈɪn, ḷɪç ɛmˈpfaŋə mɪtˈ froˈlɔkˈəndəm gəˈzaŋə
Hohe Göttin, ich empfange mit frohlockendem Gesange
High goddess, I   receive   with rejoicing   song

hiːɐ̯/hiːr ɪn ˈmaenɐ ˈʃtˈɪlə dɪç! ˈdaenɐ ˈleːɐ̯stˈə ˈlɔkˈɐroːzə
hier in meiner Stille dich! Deine erste Lockerrose
here in my quiet you! Your first loose- rose
(here in my quiet place—you! Your first light-hearted rosy light)

ˈʃtˈraːltˈə varm ɪns ˈliːpˈgəkˈhoːzə ˈmaenɐ tˈhrɔ͡øm lʊntˈ ˈvɛkˈtˈə mɪç.
strahlte warm ins Liebgekose meiner Träum' und weckte mich.
beamed warmly into the love-caress of my dreams and wakened me.

mɪtˈ bəˈʃtˈraːltˈəm ˈlangəzɪçtˈə ʃtˈeː ɪç daː ɪn ˈdaenəm ˈlɪçtˈə;
Mit bestrahltem Angesichte steh' ich da in deinem Lichte;
With irradiated face stand I here in your light;
(I stand here in your light with an irradiated face;)

ˈlalɐɐ̯vɛrməntˈ ˈlɛçəlst duː viː di ˈgɔtˈhaetˌ ˈdaenə ˈkˈhlaːɐ̯haetʰ
allerwärmend lächelst du wie die Gottheit, deine Klarheit
all-warmingly smile you like the godhead, your clarity
(you smile like the godhead, warming all; your brightness)

hiːɐ̯ dem vaːn lʊnt dɔrt deːɐ̯ ˈvaːɐ̯haetˌ ˈdʊldəndɐ(r) lals ˈmɛnʃən tsuː.
hier dem Wahn und dort der Wahrheit, duldender als Menschen zu.
here to the illusion and there to the truth, more tolerantly than humans at.
(smiles now upon illusion and now upon truth, more tolerant than humans are.)

["*zulächeln*" (with dative) = smile at, smile on]

duː lɛɐ̯ˈhaetˈɐstˈ mɪt deːɐ̯ ˈfʏlə ˈdaenɐ ˈgɔtˈhaetˈ ˈmaenə ˈʃtˈɪlə,
Du erheiterst mit der Fülle deiner Gottheit meine Stille,
You cheer with the fullness of your divinity my quietness,
(Your divine light brightens my quiet room)

viː den pˈhɔmpˈ dɛs ˈfʏrstˈənzaːls. zae gəˈzʊŋən! ˈhoːxgəzʊŋən!
wie den Pomp des Fürstensaals. Sei gesungen! Hochgesungen!
like the pomp of the princely hall. Be sung! High-sung!
(with the splendor of a princely hall. Be praised in song, hymned,)

ˈhoːxgəpˈhriːzən fɔn den ˈtsʊŋən ˈjeːdəs ˈhyːgəls, ˈjeːdəs tˈhaːls.]
Hochgepriesen von den Zungen jedes Hügels, jedes Tals.]
High-praised by the tongues of every hill, of every valley.]
(exalted by the tongues of every hill and of every valley!)]

[This poem was formerly erroneously attributed to Gabriele von Baumberg. Schubert copied out only the first verse, enclosed in repeat marks. His setting, though brief, is impressively majestic. The other four verses are in brackets, above.]

an di ˈzɔnə / ˈzɪŋkˈə, ˈliːbə ˈzɔnə
An die Sonne / Sinke, liebe Sonne
To the Sun / Set, Dear Sun

Op. 118, No. 5 [1815] (Gabriele von Baumberg)

ˈzɪŋkˈə, ˈliːbə ˈzɔnə, ˈzɪŋkˈə! ˈlɛndə ˈdaenən tˈhryːbən lɑ͡of,
Sinke, liebe Sonne, sinke! Ende deinen trüben Lauf,
Set, dear sun, set! End your dreary course,

88

ʊnt' lan 'daenə 'ʃt'ɛlə 'vɪŋk'ə balt den moːnt' hɛ'rɑ̯ɔf.
und an deine Stelle winke bald den Mond herauf.
and into your place beckon soon the moon up.
(and summon soon the moon up into your place.)

'hɛrlɪçɐ(r) ʊnt' 'ʃøːnɐ 'drɪŋə 'aːbɐ 'mɔrgən dan hɛɐ̯'fyːɐ̯,
Herrlicher und schöner dringe aber morgen dann herfür,
More gloriously and more beautifully surge however tomorrow then forth,
(Tomorrow, however, surge forth more gloriously and more beautifully,)

["*herfür*" = a poetical variant of "*hervor*"]

'liːbə zɔn! ʊnt' mɪt' diːɐ̯ 'brɪŋə 'maenən 'liːbən miːɐ̯.
liebe Sonn'! und mit dir bringe meinen Lieben mir.
dear sun! And with you bring my beloved man to me.

[Gabriele von Baumberg (1786-1839), whose poetry was praised by Goethe, was hailed as a Viennese "Sappho." Schubert set five of her poems to music, all in 1815. The full title of this poem is *Als ich einen Freund des nächsten Morgens auf dem Lande zum Besuche erwartete* (As I was waiting in the country for the visit of a friend on the next morning).]

An die Türen will ich schleichen see *Harfenspieler II*

an di 'ʊnt'ɐgeːəndə 'zɔnə
An die untergehende Sonne
To the Setting Sun

Op. 44 [1816] (Ludwig Kosegarten)

'zɔnə, duː zɪŋk'stʰ! zɪŋk' ɪn 'friːdən, loː 'zɔnə! ʃt'ɪl ʊnt' 'ruːɪç
Sonne, du sinkst! Sink in Frieden, o Sonne! Still und ruhig
Sun, you are setting! Set in peace, O sun! Quiet and peaceful

ɪst 'daenəs 'ʃaedəns gaŋ, 'ryːrənt' ʊnt' 'faeɐlɪç 'daenəs 'ʃaedəns 'ʃvaegən.
ist deines Scheidens Gang, rührend und feierlich deines Scheidens Schweigen.
is your parting's progress, touching and solemn your parting's silence.

'veːmuːt' 'lɛçəlt daen 'frɔɪnt'lɪçəs 'ɑ̯ogə, 'tʰrɛːnən ɛnt'tʰrɔɪ̯fəln den 'gɔldənən 'vɪmp'ɐn;
Wehmut lächelt dein freundliches Auge, Tränen enträufeln den goldenen Wimpern;
Melancholy smiles your friendly eye, tears drip from the golden eyelashes;
(Your friendly eye is smiling melancholy, tears drip from the golden eyelashes;)

'zeːgnʊŋən ʃt'røːmst duː deːɐ̯ 'dʊft'əndən 'eːɐ̯də.
Segnungen strömst du der duftenden Erde.
Blessings stream you to the fragrant earth.
(you stream blessings down to the fragrant earth.)

'ɪmɐ 'tʰiːfɐ, 'ɪmɐ 'laezɐ, 'ɪmɐ 'ɛrnst'ɐ, 'faeɐlɪçɐ
Immer tiefer, immer leiser, immer ernster, feierlicher
Ever more deeply, ever more quietly, ever more seriously, more solemnly

[*poem:* **immer ernster *und*** (ʊnt', and) **feierlicher**]

'zɪŋk'əst duː den 'lɛːt'ɐ hɪ'nap'. 'zɔnə, duː zɪŋk'stʰ.....
sinkest du den Äther hinab. Sonne, du sinkst..... [usw.]
sink you to the ether downwards. Sun, you are setting.... [etc.]
(you descend through the ether. Sun, you are setting.... [etc.])

[*poem:* **sinkst du den Azur** (laˈtsuːɐ̯, azure) **hinab**]

ɛs 'zeːgnən di 'fœlk'ɐ(r), ɛs 'zɔɸzəln di 'lʏft'ə,
Es segnen die Völker, es säuseln die Lüfte,
There bless the nations, there murmur the breezes,
(The people of the world give their blessing, the breezes are murmuring,)

ɛs 'rɔɸçɐn di 'dampfəndən 'viːzən diːɐ̯ naːx,
es räuchern die dampfenden Wiesen dir nach,
there smoke the steaming meadows you after,
(the steaming meadows send their smoke after you,)

'vɪndə dʊrçˈriːzəln daɛ̯n 'lɔk'ɪɡəs haːɐ̯/haːr; 'voːɡən 'kʰyːlən di 'brɛnəndə 'vaŋə;
Winde durchrieseln dein lockiges Haar; Wogen kühlen die brennende Wange;
winds through-ripple your curly hair; waves cool the burning cheek;
(winds ripple your curly hair; waves cool your burning cheek;)

vaɛ̯t' la̯ɔf tʰuːt' zɪç daɛ̯n 'vasɐbɛtʰ. ruː lɪn 'friːdən! ruː lɪn 'vɔnə!
weit auf tut sich dein Wasserbett. Ruh in Frieden! ruh in Wonne!
wide open makes itself your water- bed. Rest in peace! rest in bliss!
(your watery bed opens wide to receive you. Rest in peace! Rest in bliss!)

di 'naxt'ɪɡal 'fløːt'ət diːɐ̯ 'ʃlʊmɐɡəzaŋ. 'zɔnə, duː zɪŋk'stʰ....
die Nachtigall flötet dir Schlummergesang. Sonne, du sinkst.... [usw.]
the nightingale warbles to you slumber- song. Sun, you are sinking.... [etc.]
(the nightingale warbles a lullaby to you. Sun, you are singing.... [etc.])

[Ludwig Kosegarten (1758-1818) was a country clergyman from northern Germany. Schubert left out nearly half of the verses from this poem. What was left he set in rondo form, with the opening lines recurring in the middle and at the end.]

an 'la̯ɛnə 'kʰvɛlə
An eine Quelle
To a Spring

Op. 109, No. 3 [1816] (Matthias Claudius)

duː 'kʰla̯ɛnə 'ɡryːnl̥ʊmvaksnə 'kʰvɛlə, lan deːɐ̯/deːr lɪç 'dafnə jʏŋst' ɡə'zeːn!
Du kleine grünumwachs'ne Quelle, an der ich Daphne jüngst gesehn!
You little green-overgrown spring, at which I Daphne lately [have] seen!
(You little spring, overgrown with greenery, at which I lately saw Daphne,)

daɛ̯n 'vasɐ vaːɐ̯ zoː ʃt'ɪl lʊnt' 'hɛlə! lʊnt 'dafnəs bɪlt daˈrɪn zoː ʃøːn!
dein Wasser war so still und helle! und Daphnes Bild darin so schön!
your water was so still and clear, and Daphne's image in it so beautiful!

[*poem:* **Dein Wasser war so still! so helle!**]

90

oː vɛn ziː zɪç ˈnoxmaːl lam ˈluːfɐ ˈzeːən lɛstʰ,
o wenn sie sich nochmal am Ufer sehen lässt,
oh if she herself once again on the bank see lets,
(Oh, if she lets herself be seen once again on the bank,)

zoː ˈhaltə duː liːɐ̯ ˈʃøːnəs bɪlt dɔx fɛstʰ;
so halte du ihr schönes Bild doch fest;
then hold you her lovely image surely firmly;
(then do hold fast her lovely image;)

ɪç ˈʃlaɛ̯çə ˈhaɛ̯mlɪçˈ dan mɪtˈ ˈnasən ˈlaɔ̯gən hɪn,   [*poem:* **denn** (dɛn, then)]
ich schleiche heimlich dann mit nassen Augen hin,
I sneak secretly then with moist eyes hence,
(I shall then sneak away to you secretly, with moist eyes,)

dem bɪltˈ ˈmaɛ̯nə noːt tsuː ˈkʰlaːgən; dɛn, vɛn lɪç baɛ̯ liːɐ̯ ˈzɛlbɐ bɪn, [*poem:* **Bilde**]
dem Bild meine Not zu klagen; denn, wenn ich bei ihr selber bin,
to the image my distress to lament; for, when I with her herself am,
(to lament my distress to the image; for when I am with her in person)

dan, lax, dan kʰan lɪç liːɐ̯ nɪçts ˈzaːgən.   [*poem:* **denn, ach! denn**]
dann, ach, dann kann ich ihr nichts sagen.
then, ah, then can I to her nothing say.
(then, ah, then I am speechless and can say nothing to her.)

[Daphne was a nymph loved by the god Apollo in Greek mythology. Her name became a popular one for nymphs and shepherdesses in eighteenth-century pastoral poetry.]

an ˈlɛma / ɛma
An Emma / Emma
To Emma / Emma

Op. 58, No. 2 [1814] (Friedrich von Schiller)

vaɛ̯tˈ lɪn ˈneːbəlɡraɔ̯ɐ ˈfɛrnə liːkˈtˈ miːɐ̯ das fɛɐ̯ˈɡaŋnə ɡlʏkʰ,
Weit in nebelgrauer Ferne liegt mir das vergangne Glück,
Far away in mist- gray distance lies for me the past happiness,
(My past happiness lies far away from me in the mist-gray distance;)

nuːɐ̯/nuːr lan ˈlaɛ̯nəm ˈʃøːnən ˈʃtˈɛrnə vaɛ̯ltˈ mɪtˈ ˈliːbə nox deːɐ̯ blɪkʰ;
nur an einem schönen Sterne weilt mit Liebe noch der Blick;
only on a beautiful star lingers with love still the look;
(only on a beautiful star does my gaze linger with love;)

aːbɐ viː dɛs ˈʃtˈɛrnəs pʰraxtˈ, lɪstˈ lɛs nuːɐ̯/nuːr laɛ̯n ʃaɛ̯n deːɐ̯ naxtʰ.
aber wie des Sternes Pracht, ist es nur ein Schein der Nacht.
but, like the star's splendor, is it only an appearance of the night.
(but, like the star's splendor, it is only an apparition of the night.)

ˈdɛkˈtˈə diːɐ̯ deːɐ̯ ˈlaŋə ˈʃlʊmɐ, diːɐ̯ deːɐ̯ tʰoːt di ˈlaɔ̯gən tsuː,
Deckte dir der lange Schlummer, dir der Tod die Augen zu,
Covered to you the long slumber, to you the death the eyes up,
(If the long sleep, if death covered up your eyes,)   ["*zudecken*" = to cover up, conceal]

dıç   bə'zɛːsə   dɔx maɛn 'kʰʊmɐ,   'maɛnəm 'hɛrt͡sən 'leːp't'əst duː.
dich   besässe   doch mein Kummer,   meinem Herzen lebtest du.
you [object] would possess yet   my   grief [subject], for my   heart   lived   you.
(my grief would yet possess you, you would be living in my heart.)

aːbɐ(r) lax! duː leːp'st' ɪm   lɪçtʰ, 'maɛnɐ 'liːbə leːp'st duː nɪçtʰ.
Aber ach! du lebst im   Licht, meiner Liebe lebst du nicht.
But   ah! you live   in the light; for my love   live   you not.
(But--ah!--you live in the light, you are alive; you do not live for my love.)

kʰan deːɐ 'liːbə zyːs fɛɐ'laŋən, 'ɛma, kʰans fɛɐ'gɛŋlɪç zaɛn?
Kann der Liebe süss Verlangen, Emma, kann's vergänglich sein?
Can the love's sweet longing,   Emma, can   it transient   be?
(Can love's sweet longing be transient, Emma?)

vas da'hın lɪst' ʊnt' fɛɐ'gaŋən, 'ɛma, kʰans di liːbə zaɛn?
Was dahin ist und vergangen, Emma, kann's die Liebe sein?
What gone is   and past,   Emma, can   it the love be?
(What is over and gone, Emma, can that be love?)

'iːrɐ 'flamə 'hɪməlsgluːtʰ,   ʃt'ɪrp't' ziː viː laɛn 'ɪrdɪʃ   guːtʰ?
Ihrer Flamme Himmelsglut,   stirbt sie wie ein irdisch Gut?
Its   flame's heaven- incandescence, dies   it like an earthly commodity?
(The heavenly incandescence of love's flame--can that perish like some earthly commodity?)

[This was the first of Schubert's songs to be published as sheet-music, some others having been printed earlier in magazines. Schubert made several attempts to capture this poem in music.]

An Franz Schubert see *Geheimnis*

an 'laora, lals ziː 'kʰlɔp'ʃt'ɔks 'laoflɛɐʃt'eːʊŋsliːt' zaŋ
An Laura, als sie Klopstocks Auferstehungslied sang
To Laura, as She Sang Klopstock's Song of Resurrection

Posthumously published [composed in 1814] (poem by Friedrich von Matthisson)

'hɛrt͡sən, diː   geːn 'hɪməl zɪç   lɛɐ'heːbən,
Herzen, die   gen Himmel sich   erheben,
Hearts, which toward heaven themselves lift,
(Hearts which lift themselves toward heaven,)

'tʰreːnən, diː dem   'laogə ʃt'ɪl lɛnt'ˈbeːbən,
Tränen, die dem   Auge still entbeben,
tears,   which [from] the eye   quietly tremble out,
(Tears which come trembling from one's eyes,)

'zɔøft͡sɐ. diː   den   'lɪp'ən laes lɛnt'ˈfliːn,
Seufzer, die den   Lippen leis entfliehn,
sighs,   which [from] the lips   softly escape,
(sighs which softly escape from the lips,)

'vaŋən, diː mɪt' 'landaxˌtsɡluːt' zɪç 'maːlən,
Wangen, die mit Andachtsglut sich malen,
cheeks, which with devotion's fire themselves paint,
(cheeks which are flushed with the fervor of religious devotion,)

'trʊŋk'nə 'blɪk'ə, di lɛnt'tsʏk'ʊŋ 'ʃt'raːlən, 'daŋk'ən diːɐ, loː 'haɛlfɛɐk'ʰʏndərɪn!
trunkne Blicke, die Entzückung strahlen, danken dir, o Heilverkünderin!
intoxicated glances, which rapture radiate, thank you, O salvation-annunciatress!
(intoxicated glances, which radiate rapture, express thanks to you, O messenger of salvation!)

'lɑora! 'lɑora! 'hɔrçənt 'diːzən 'tʰøːnən, 'mʏsən 'lɛŋəlzeːlən zɪç fɛɐ'ʃøːnən,
Laura! Laura! horchend diesen Tönen, müssen Engelseelen sich verschönen,
Laura! Laura! listening to these tones, must angel-souls themselves make beautiful,
(Laura! Laura! Listening to those tones, angelic souls must become even more beautiful,)

'haɛlɪɡə den 'hɪməl 'lɔfən zeːn, 'ʃveːɐmuːtsfɔlə 'tsvaɛflɐ 'zanft'ɐ 'kʰlaːɡən,
Heilige den Himmel offen sehn, schwermutsvolle Zweifler sanfter klagen,
saints the heaven open see, melancholy doubters more mildly lament,
(saints must see the heavens open up, melancholy doubters must lament less bitterly,)

'kʰalt'ə 'freːflɐ lan di brʊst' zɪç 'ʃlaːɡən, lʊnt' viː 'zeːraf abba'doːna fleːn!
kalte Frevler an die Brust sich schlagen, und wie Seraph Abbadona flehn!
cold criminals on the breast themselves beat, and like Seraph Abbadona entreat!
(cold criminals beat their breast and plead like the fallen angel Abbadona!)

mɪt den tʰøːnən dɛs tri'ʊmfɡçəzaŋəs tʰraŋk' lɪç 'foːɐɡəfyːl dɛs 'lyːbɐɡaŋəs
Mit den Tönen des Triumphgesanges trank ich Vorgefühl des Überganges
With the tones of the triumph- song drank I presentiment of the transition
(With the tones of the song of triumph I drank a presentiment of the transition)

fɔn deːɐ 'graːp'naxt tsʊm fɛɐ'kʰlɛːrʊŋsɡlants!
von der Grabnacht zum Verklärungsglanz!
from the grave-night to the transfiguration-radiance!
(from the night of the grave to the radiance of transfiguration!)

als fɛɐ'neːm lɪç 'sfɛːrənmeloˌdiːən, vɛːnt' lɪç diːɐ/diːr, loː 'leːɐdə, tsuː lɛnt''fliːən,
als vernähm ich Sphärenmelodien, wähnt ich dir, o Erde, zu entfliehen,
as if were perceiving I sphere- melodies, imagined I from you, O earth, to flee,
(as if I were hearing the music of the spheres, I imagined that I fled from you, O earth,)

zaː ʃoːn 'lʊnt'ɐ miːɐ deːɐ 'ʃt'ɛrnə tʰants!
sah schon unter mir der Sterne Tanz!
saw already below me the stars' dance!
(I saw the dance of the stars already below me!)

ʃoːn lʊm'laːt't'mət'ə mɪç dɛs 'hɪməls 'mɪldə,
Schon umatmete mich des Himmels Milde, [*poem:* **umatmete mich Himmelsmilde**]
Already breathed around me the heaven's mildness,
(Already the mild atmosphere of heaven breathed all around me,)

ʃoːn bə'ɡryːst' lɪç 'jɑoxtsənt di ɡə'fɪldə,
schon begrüsst ich jauchzend die Gefilde,
Already greeted I exultantly the fields
(Already I greeted exultantly the fields)

voː   dɛs ˈleːbəns ʃtˈroːm dʊrç   ˈpalmən   flɔøstʰ;
wo   des Lebens Strom durch Palmen   fleusst;   [*"fleusst"* = *"fliesst"* = flows]
where the life's   stream through palm-trees flows;
(where the river of life flows through palm groves;)

ˈglɛntsənt' fɔn deːɐ̯ ˈneːɐn   ˈgɔtˈhaet'   ʃtˈraːlə
glänzend von der nähern Gottheit Strahle
shining   from the nearer   divinity's rays
(shining from the rays of the nearer Divinity,)

ˈvandəlt'ə dʊrç   pʰaraˈdiːzəstʰaːlə, ˈvɔnəʃɑoɐnt'   maen lɛnt'ʃveːp't'ɐ gaestʰ!
wandelte durch Paradiesestale,   wonneschauernd mein   entschwebter Geist!
wandered through Paradise-valleys, rapture-shivering my   floated away   spirit!
(my spirit, shivering with rapture as it floated away away from earth, wandered through the valleys of Paradise!)

[The poet was moved to write this poem after he heard a young lady named Laura sing a musical setting of Klopstock's poem, *"Die Auferstehung"* ("The Resurrection"). Her rendition was for him an ecstatic spritual illumination. "Seraph Abbadona" plays an important role in Klopstock's *"Messias"* ("Messiah"). One of the fallen angels who rebelled with Lucifer against the supremacy of God, he is portrayed as deeply repentent and remorseful, and in book XIX he is forgiven and re-admitted into heaven.]

an maen hɛrts
An mein Herz
To My Heart

Posthumously published [composed in 1825] (poem by Ernst Schulze)

oː hɛrts, zae ˈlɛnt'lɪç ˈʃt'ɪlə! vas ʃleːk'st duː zoː ˈʊnruːfɔl?
O Herz, sei   endlich stille! was schlägst du so   unruhvoll?
O heart, be at last   still! Why beat   you so unrestfully?
(O my heart, be still at last! Why are you beating so restlessly?)

ɛs lɪst' jaː   dɛs ˈhɪməls   ˈvɪlə,   das lɪç ziː ˈlasən zɔl!
es ist ja   des Himmels Wille, dass ich sie lassen soll!
It is   surely the heaven's will   that I   her leave should!
(It is surely heaven's will that I should leave her!)

ʊnt' gaːp' lɑox daen ˈjʊŋəs ˈleːbən diːɐ̯ nɪçts   lals vaːn   lʊnt' pʰaen,
Und gab   auch dein junges Leben dir nichts   als Wahn   und Pein,
And gave also your young   life to you nothing but delusion and pain,
(And even if your young life gave you nothing but delusion and pain,)

hats liːɐ̯   nuːɐ̯ ˈfrɔødə gəˈgeːbən, zoː maːks fɛɐ̯ˈloːrən zaen!
hat's ihr   nur Freude gegeben, so mag's verloren sein!
has it to her only joy   given,   so may it lost   be!
(it has given her only joy; so let it be lost!)

ʊnt' vɛn ziː lɑox niː   daen ˈliːbən lʊnt' niː   daen ˈliːbə fɛɐ̯ʃt'ant',
Und wenn sie auch nie   dein Lieben und nie   dein' Liebe verstand,
And if   she also never your loving and never your love   understood,
(And even if she never understood your loving or your love,)

[*poem:* **und nie dein Leiden** (ˈlaedən, suffering) **verstend**]

94

zoː bɪst duː dɔx tʰrɔ̮ø gəˈbliːbən, lʊntʼ gɔtʼ hats ˈdroːbən lɛɐ̯ˈkʰantʰ.
so bist du doch treu geblieben, und Gott hat's droben erkannt.
so are you nevertheless faithful remained, and God has it up above perceived.
(you have nevertheless remained faithful, and God has perceived that up above.)

viːɐ̯ ˈvɔlən lɛs ˈmuːtɪç lɛɐ̯ˈtʰraːgən, zoː laŋ nuːɐ̯ diː ˈtʰrɛːnə nɔx rɪntʰ,
Wir wollen es mutig ertragen, so lang nur die Träne noch rinnt,
We want it bravely to bear, so long only the tear still runs,
(Let us bear it bravely as long, at least, as tears are still streaming,)

ʊntʼ ˈtʰrɔ̮ømən fɔn ˈʃøːnərən ˈtʰaːgən, diː ˈlaŋə foˈryːbɐ zɪntʼ.
und träumen von schöneren Tagen, die lange vorüber sind.
and to dream of more beautiful days, which long past are.
(and dream of more beautiful days which are long past.)

ʊntʼ ziːst duː di ˈblyːtʼən lɛɐ̯ˈʃaenən, lʊntʼ ˈzɪŋən di ˈføːgəl lʊmˈheːɐ̯,
Und siehst du die Blüten erscheinen, und singen die Vögel umher,
And see you the blossoms appear, and sing the birds all around,
(And if you see the blossoms appearing and birds are singing all around,)

zoː maːkʼst duː voːl ˈhaemlɪç ˈvaenən, dɔx ˈkʰlaːgən zɔlst duː nɪçtʼ meːɐ̯.
so magst du wohl heimlich weinen, doch klagen sollst du nicht mehr.
so may you well secretly weep, but lament shall you not more.
(then you well may secretly weep; but you shall not complain any more.)

geːn dɔx di ˈleːvɪgən ˈʃtʼɛrnə dɔrtʼ ˈloːbən mɪtʼ ˈgɔldənəm lɪçtʰ
Gehn doch die ewigen Sterne dort oben mit goldenem Licht
Move after all the eternal stars there up above with golden light
(After all, the eternal stars up above move by with golden light)

ʊntʼ ˈlɛçəln zoː ˈfrɔ̮øntʼlɪç fɔn ˈfɛɐ̯nə, lʊnt ˈdɛŋkʼən dɔx ˈlʊnzɐ nɪçtʰ.
und lächeln so freundlich von ferne, und denken doch unser nicht.
and smile so friendlily from afar, and think nevertheless of us not.
(and smile at us from afar in such a friendly way, and yet they do not think about us.)

[The words are all addressed to the poet's heart, and its agitation is powerfully expressed in Schubert's accompaniment. The title of the poem is *"Am 23sten Januar 1816."*]

an maen kʰlaˈviːɐ̯
An mein Klavier
To My Piano

Posthumously published [composed in 1816] (poem by Christian Daniel Schubart)

ˈzanftʼəs ˈkʰlaˈviːɐ̯! ˈvɛlçə lɛntˈtsʏkʼʊŋən ˈʃafəst duː miːɐ̯!
Sanftes Klavier! welche Entzückungen schaffest du mir!
Gentle piano! what delights create you for me!
(Gentle piano, what delights you create for me!) [*poem:* **schaffst du in mir!** (*in* me)]

vɛn zɪç di ˈʃøːnən ˈtʰɛndəlntʼ fɛɐ̯ˈvøːnən,
Wenn sich die Schönen tändelnd verwöhnen,
When themselves the beautiful ones triflingly pamper,
(When the beautiful ones are triflingly pampering themselves,)

vae̯   lɪç mɪç diːɐ̯,   'liːbəs kʰla'viːɐ̯!
weih   ich mich dir,   liebes Klavier!
consecrate I   myself to you, dear   piano!
(I consecrate myself to you, dear piano!)

bɪn lɪç la'laen, haox lɪç diːɐ̯   'maenə lɛm'pfɪndʊŋən laen, 'hɪmlɪʃ   lʊntˈ raen.
Bin ich allein, hauch ich dir   meine Empfindungen ein, himmlisch und rein.
Am I   alone, breathe I   to you my   feelings   into, heavenly   and pure.
(When I am alone I beathe into you my feelings, heavenly and pure.)

'lʊnʃʊltˈ lɪm   'ʃpˈiːlə, 'tʰuːgəntˈgəˌfyːlə 'ʃpˈrɛçən laos diːɐ̯, 'tʰraotˈəs kʰla'viːɐ̯!
Unschuld im   Spiele, Tugendgefühle sprechen aus   dir, trautes Klavier!
Innocence in the play,   virtue- feelings speak   out of you, dear   piano!
(Innocence at play, feelings of virtue speak out of you, dear piano!)

zɪŋ lɪç da'tsuː, 'goldənɐ 'flyːgəl, vɛlç 'hɪmlɪʃə   ruː   'lɪspˈəlstˈ miːɐ̯ duː!
Sing ich dazu,   goldener Flügel, welch himmlische Ruh lispelst mir   du!
Sing I   to it,   golden   wing, what heavenly   peace whisper to me you!
(When I sing to your accompaniment, golden wing,* what heavenly peace you whisper to me!)

'tʰrɛːnən deːɐ̯ 'frɔødə 'nɛtsən di 'zaetˈə! 'zɪlbɐnɐ   kʰlaŋ tʰrɛːkˈt den gə'zaŋ.
Tränen der   Freude netzen die Saite!   silberner Klang trägt   den Gesang.
Tears   of the joy   moisten the string! Silver   sound carries the song.
(Tears of joy moisten the strings! Silver sound carries the song.)

'goldnəs kʰla'viːɐ̯! vɛn mɪç lɪm   'leːbən 'zɔrgən lʊm'ʃveːbən,
Goldnes Klavier! Wenn mich im   Leben Sorgen umschweben,
Golden   piano!   When me   in the life   cares   hover around,
(Golden piano! When cares hover around me in life,)

'tʰøːnə duː miːɐ̯, 'tʰraotˈəs kʰla'viːɐ̯!
töne   du mir,   trautes Klavier!
resound you for me, dear   piano!
(resound for me, dear piano!)

[* *Flügel* means "wing," literally; it also is the German term for "grand piano"; *Klavier* (or *Clavier*, as it was spelled in the original poem) can refer to any one of various keyboard instruments, depending upon the period. It is now the generic word for piano, the specific word for an upright piano. The original title of the poem was *Serafina an ihr Clavier*; there is reason to believe that the poet was referring to the soft tones of a clavichord. Schubert, who felt the sentiments of the poem very personally, left out Serafina and two stanzas, one of which implied that the speaker was a woman, so that this song could become an expression of his own feelings].

an min'jõ
An Mignon
To Mignon

Op. 19, No. 2 [1815] (Johann Wolfgang von Goethe)

'yːbɐ tʰaːl lʊntˈ flʊs gə'tʰraːgən, 'tsiːətˈ raen deːɐ̯ 'zɔnə 'vaːgən.
Über Tal   und Fluss getragen,   ziehet rein der   Sonne Wagen.
Over valley and river   borne,   passes purely the sun's   chariot.
(Borne over valley and river, the chariot of the sun passes in its purity.)

ax! zi: re:k't' ɪn 'li:rəm lɑọf, zo: vi: 'dɑẹnə, 'mɑẹnə 'ʃmɛrtsən,
Ach! sie regt in ihrem Lauf, so wie deine, meine Schmerzen,
Ah! It stirs in its course, as like yours, my pains,
(Ah! In its course it stirs up my pains, just as it does yours,)

tʰi:f ɪm 'hɛrtsən, 'ɪmɐ 'mɔrgəns 'vi:dɐ(r) lɑọf.
tief im Herzen, immer morgens wieder auf.
deep in the heart, always in the morning again up.
(deep inside my heart, every morning anew.)

kʰɑọm vɪl mi:ɐ di naxt' nɔx 'frɔmən,
Kaum will mir die Nacht noch frommen,
Scarcely will to me the night still be of use,
(The night will scarcely be a benefit to me any more,)

dɛn di 'tʰrɔ̨ø̈mə 'zɛlbɐ 'kʰɔmən nu:n ɪn 'tʰrɑọrɪgɐ gə'ʃt'alt';
denn die Träume selber kommen nun in trauriger Gestalt;
for the dreams themselves come now in sorrowful form;
(for the dreams themselves come now in sorrowful form;)

ʊnt' lɪç 'fy:lə 'di:zɐ 'ʃmɛrtsən ʃt'ɪl ɪm 'hɛrtsən 'hɑẹmlɪç 'bɪldəndə gə'valtʰ.
und ich fühle dieser Schmerzen still im Herzen heimlich bildende Gewalt.
and I feel these pains' quietly in the heart secretly shaping power.
(and I feel the secretly shaping power of these pains quietly at work in my heart.)

ʃo:n zɑẹt' 'mançən 'ʃø:nən 'ja:rən ze: lɪç 'ʊnt'ən 'ʃifə 'fa:rən,
Schon seit manchen schönen Jahren seh ich unten Schiffe fahren,
Already since many beautiful years see I down below ships sail,
(For many beautiful years, now, I have seen ships sailing down there on the water,)

'je:dəs kʰɔmt' lan 'zɑẹnən lɔrtʰ; 'la:bɐ(r) lax! di 'ʃt'e:t'ən 'ʃmɛrtsən,
jedes kommt an seinen Ort; aber ach! die steten Schmerzen,
each comes to its place; but ah! the constant pains,
(each arrives at its destination; but ah! the constant pains,)

fɛst' lɪm 'hɛrtsən, 'ʃvɪmən nɪçt' lɪm 'ʃt'ro:mə fɔrtʰ.
fest im Herzen, schwimmen nicht im Strome fort.
firmly fixed in the heart, swim not in the stream away.
(firmly fixed in my heart, do not swim away in the river.)

ʃø:n lɪn 'kʰlɑẹdɐn mʊs lɪç 'kʰɔmən, lɑọs dem ʃraŋk' zɪnt' zi: gə'nɔmən,
Schön in Kleidern muss ich kommen, aus dem Schrank sind sie genommen,
Handsome in clothes must I come, out of the wardrobe are they taken,
(I have to make myself look good in clothes taken out of the wardrobe cabinet,)

vɑẹl lɛs 'hɔ̨ø̈t'ə 'fɛstʰa:k' lɪstʰ; 'ni:mant' 'la:nət das fɔn 'ʃmɛrtsən
weil es heute Festtag ist; niemand ahnet, dass von Schmerzen
because it today holiday is; no one suspects that from pains
(because today is a holiday; no one suspects that from pain...)

hɛrts lɪm 'hɛrtsən 'grɪmɪç mi:ɐ tsɛɐ'rɪsən lɪstʰ.
Herz im Herzen grimmig mir zerrissen ist.
heart in the heart fiercely for me torn apart is.
(...my inner heart is fiercely torn apart.)

ˈhaemlɪç mʊs lɪç ˈlɪmɐ ˈvaenən, ˈlaːbɐ ˈfrɔɞ̯ntˈlɪç kʰan lɪç ˈʃaenən,
Heimlich muss ich immer weinen, aber freundlich kann ich scheinen,
Secretly must I always weep, but friendly can I appear,
(I always have to weep secretly, but I can appear friendly,)

ʊntˈ zoˈgaːɐ̯ gəˈzʊntˈ lʊntˈ roːtʰ; ˈveːrən ˈtʰøːtˈlɪç ˈdiːzə ˈʃmɛrtsən ˈmaenəm ˈhɛrtsən,
und sogar gesund und rot; wären tödlich diese Schmerzen meinem Herzen,
and even healthy and ruddy; were fatal these pains to my heart,
(and even healthy and ruddy; if these pains were fatal to my heart,)

ax! ʃoːn ˈlaŋə vɛːɐ̯/veːr lɪç tʰoːtʰ.
ach! schon lange wär ich tot.
ah! already long were I dead.
(ah! I would already be long dead!)

[Mignon is a famous waif in Goethe's novel *Wilhelm Meisters Lehr- und Wanderjahre*, but this poem is not from the novel. Schubert's song is one of several that he dedicated to the famous poet without ever receiving a note of thanks or any acknowledgement, although Goethe noted receipt of some of the songs in his diary. (The *Gesamtausgabe* includes versions in two keys.)]

an ˈroːza — laens
An Rosa (I)
To Rosa (I)

Posthumously published [composed 1815] (poem by Ludwig Kosegarten)

vaˈrʊm bɪst duː nɪçtˈ hiːɐ̯, ˈmaenə gəˈliːpˈtˈəstˈə,
Warum bist du nicht hier, meine Geliebteste,
Why are you not here, my most beloved one,

das mɪç ˈgʏrtˈə daen larm, das mɪç daen ˈhɛndədrʊkˈ ˈlaːbə,
dass mich gürte dein Arm, dass mich dein Händedruck labe,
that me encircle your arm, that me your hand- clasp comfort,
(so that your arm might encircle me, so that the clasp of your hand might comfort me,)

das duː mɪç ˈprɛsəstˈ lan daen ˈʃlaːgəndəs ˈʃvɛstˈɐhɛrts.
dass du mich pressest an dein schlagendes Schwesterherz.
that you me press to your beating sister- heart.
(so that you might press me to your beating heart, which is a sister to my own.)

ˈroːza, bɪst duː miːɐ̯ hɔltˈ? ˈroːza, zoː hɔltˈ, viː lɪç, vaːɐ̯ diːɐ̯ ˈkʰaenɐ,
Rosa, bist du mir hold? Rosa, so hold, wie ich, war dir keiner,
Rosa, are you to me loving? Rosa, as loving as I (am) was to you no man,
[to be "*hold*" (lovely) to someone = to love someone]
(Rosa, do you love me? Rosa, no other man has loved you as much as I do,)

ʊntˈ vɪrtˈ ˈkʰaenɐ diːɐ̯ ˈviːdɐ zaen fɔn den ˈzøːnən deːɐ̯/deːr ˈleːɐ̯də.
und wird keiner dir wieder sein von den Söhnen der Erde,
and will no man to you again be of the sons of the earth,
(and no other man from among the sons of the earth will love you again as I do,)

fɔn den 'zø:nən |e'ly:ziʊms.
von den Söhnen Elysiums.
of   the   sons   of Elysium.
(nor from among the sons of paradise.)

'vɛrmɐ,   'ro:za, fy:ɐ̯'va:ɐ̯, 'vɛrmɐ(r) |ʊnt 'tsɛrt'lɪçɐ
Wärmer,   Rosa, fürwahr, wärmer   und zärtlicher
More warmly, Rosa, truly,   more warmly and more tenderly --

'kʰœnt'ə 'nɪmɐ   fy:ɐ̯ dɪç 'ʃla:gən   maen 'fy:lənt' hɛrts,
könnte nimmer für dich schlagen mein fühlend Herz,
could   never   for you beat   my   feeling heart,
(my sensitive heart could never beat for you more warmly, more tenderly,)

hɛt' |aen ʃo:s |ʊns gə'bo:rən, hɛt' |ʊns 'laenɐlae   brʊst' gə'zɔøk't'.
hätt' ein Schoss uns geboren, hätt' uns einerlei   Brust gesäugt.
had   one womb   us born,   had   us one and the same breast suckled.
(even if one womb had born us both, or one and the same breast had suckled us.)

'mat'ə   'la:bət   de:ɐ̯ kʰvɛl, 'my:də   de:ɐ̯/de:r 'la:bənt' ʃt'ɛrn,
Matte   labet   der Quell, Müde   der   Abendstern,
Faint ones refreshes the spring, weary one the   evening star,
(The spring refreshes those who are faint with thirst, the evening star is a comfort to the weary,)
            [*poem:* **Lecher**—misprint for "**Lechzer**" ('lɛçtsɐ, parched ones)?—**labet der Quell**]

'ɪrə 'vandrɐ   de:ɐ̯ mo:nt', 'kʰraŋk'ə   das 'mɔrgənro:tʰ;
irre Wandrer der Mond, Kranke   das Morgenrot;
lost wanderer the   moon, sick people the dawn;
(the moon is a comfort to the lost wanderer, the dawn to those who are ill;)

mɪç |ɛɐ̯'la:bət, gə'li:p't'ə,   daen |ʊm'faŋən |am 'kʰrɛft'ɪkst'ən.
mich erlabet, Geliebte,   dein Umfangen am   kräftigsten.
me   refreshes, beloved one, your embrace   to the most powerful (degree).
(your embrace, my beloved, refreshes me most powerfully.)
            [*poem:* **am labendsten** ('la:bəntst'ən, most refreshingly)]

va'rʊm bɪst du: nɪçt' hi:ɐ̯, 'maenə fɛɐ̯'tʰraot'əst'ə,
Warum bist du nicht hier, meine Vertrauteste,
Why   are you not   here, my   most dear friend,

das dɪç 'gʏrt'ə maen |arm, das |ɪç di:ɐ̯ 'zy:sən gru:s   'lɪsp'(l),
dass dich gürte   mein Arm, dass ich dir   süssen Gruss lispl',
that you encircle my   arm, that I   to you sweet greeting whisper,
(so that my arm might encircle you, so that I might whisper to you a sweet greeting,)

(l)ʊnt' 'fɔørɪç   dɪç 'drʏk'ə |an maen 'ʃla:gəndəs   'bru:dɐhɛrts.
und   feurig   dich drücke an mein schlagendes Bruderherz.
and   passionately you press   to my   beating   brother-heart.
(and passionately press you to my beating heart, which is the brother to yours.)
            [*poem:* **dich presse** ('pʰrɛsə, press)]

[Schubert's graceful melody sets the first verse of the poem; but the other verses do not fit the vocal line without some distortion of the natural accentuation of certain words.]

an 'roːza — t͜svae
An Rosa (II)
To Rosa (II)

Posthumously published [composed 1815] (poem by Ludwig Kosegarten)

'roːza, dɛŋkst duː lan mıç? 'ınıç gə'dɛŋk' lıç daen.
Rosa, denkst du an mich? Innig gedenk' ich dein.
Rosa, think you of me? Sincerely think I of you.
(Rosa, are you thinking of me? Sincerely I am thinking of you.)

dʊrç den 'gryːnlıçən valt' 'ʃımɐt das 'laːbənt'roːtʰ,
Durch den grünlichen Wald schimmert das Abendrot,
Through the greenish woods shimmers the sunset-red,
(The red blaze of sunset is shimmering through the green woods,)

ʊnt di 'vıp͜fəl deːɐ 'tʰanən reːkt das 'zɔøzəln dɛs 'leːvıgən.
und die Wipfel der Tannen regt das Säuseln des Ewigen.
and the tops of the fir-trees stirs the murmur of the Eternal.
(and the murmuring breath of the Eternal One stirs the tops of the fir-trees.)
        [*poem:* **Auf** (lɑof, on) **den Wipfeln der Tannen rinnt** (rınt, flows) **das Säuseln...**]

'roːza, 'veːrəst duː hiːɐ, zeː lıç lıns 'laːbənt'roːtʰ 'daenə 'vaŋən gə'tʰɑoxtʰ,
Rosa, wärest du hier, säh' ich ins Abendrot deine Wangen getaucht,
Rosa, were you here, would see I in the sunset-red your cheeks immersed,
(Rosa, if you were here I would see your cheeks immersed in the redness of the sunset,)
        [veːɐst duː bae miːɐ]   [das]   [bə'glyːn]
        [*poem:* **wärst du bei mir, säh' ich das Abendrot deine Wangen beglühn**]
        [were you with me, would see I the sunset your cheeks make glow]
        [[(if you were with me I would see the sunset make your cheeks glow)]]

zeː lıç fɔm 'laːbənt'hɑox 'daenə 'lɔk'ən gə'rıŋəltʰ—'leːdlə 'zeːlə, miːɐ 'veːrə voːl!
säh' ich vom Abendhauch deine Locken geringelt—edle Seele, mir wäre wohl!
would see I from the evening breeze your locks ringed— noble soul, to me were well!
(I would see your curls spun by the evening breeze — noble soul, that would make me happy!)
        [*poem:* **deine Locken durchrieseln** (dʊrç'riːzəln, rippled through)
                — **edle Seele, so wär'** (zoː veːɐ, so were) **mir wohl**]

'liːbɐ leːn lıç lan diːɐ/diːr, lals lan deːɐ/deːr 'laenzaːmkʰaet 'tʰrɑot'əm 'buːzən.
Lieber lehn' ich an dir, als an der Einsamkeit Trautem Busen.
More gladly lean I on you, than on the solitude's beloved bosom.
(I lean on you more gladly than on the bosom of my beloved solitude.)

miːɐ kʰlıŋt' 'zyːsɐ deːɐ 'fløːt'əntʰoːn 'daenɐ 'kʰlaːgəndən 'ʃt'ımə,
Mir klingt süsser der Flötenton deiner klagenden Stimme,
To me sounds sweeter the flute- tone of your lamenting voice,
(The flute-like tone of your lamenting voice sounds sweeter)

als das 'zɔøzəln lım 'tʰanənhaen.
als das Säuseln im Tannenhain.
than the rustling in the fir-tree grove.

ɔft‘ lʊmˈfɪŋəst duː mɪç, ˈmaenə hɔltʻˈzeːlɪgə, mɪt‘ fɛɐ̯ˈtʰraolɪçəm larm,
Oft umfingest du mich, meine Holdselige, mit vertraulichem Arm,
Often embraced you me, my most lovely one, with intimate arm,
(Often you embraced me intimately in your arms, my most lovely one,)
[*poem:* **umfingst** (lʊmˈfɪŋst)]

vɛn lɪç lan ˈdaenɐ brʊst‘
wenn ich an deiner Brust
when I at your breast
(when at your breast I,)

melaŋˈkʰoːlɪʃən ˈfriːdən, ˈʃvɛrmənsmyːdə, mɪç ˈrɛt‘ət‘ə.
melancholischen Frieden, schwärmensmüde, mich rettete.
melancholy peace, weary of revelling, for myself rescued.
(weary of revelling, salvaged for myself a melancholy peace.)

ˈjeːdəs ˈlaezərə veː, ˈjeːdəs fɛɐ̯ˈʃviːgnə lax, das den ˈbuːzən miːɐ̯ pʰrɛstʰ,
Jedes leisere Weh’, jedes verschwieg’ne Ach, das den Busen mir presst,
Every rather quiet cry of pain, every silent sigh that the breast for me presses,
(Every quiet cry of pain, every silent sigh that oppresses my breast,)

haoxt‘ lɪç diːɐ̯/diːr ˈlœft‘ɐ(r) laos, ˈʃœpft‘ə ˈfraeərən ˈloːdəm,
haucht’ ich dir öfter aus, schöpfte freieren Odem,
exhaled I to you rather often out, drew freer breath,
(I so often exhaled to you, drew a freer fresh breath,)

kʰlɔm heˈroːɪʃɐ ˈfɛlzənˌlan.
klomm heroischer felsenan.
climbed more heroically cliff-upwards.
(and then could climb more courageously the cliffs that rise before me.)

niː zɔl ˈdaːrʊm laen frɔønt‘ ˈmaenɐ hɔltʻˈzeːlɪgən ˈroːza ˈmaŋəln,
Nie soll darum ein Freund meiner holdseligen Rosa mangeln,
Never shall for that reason a friend for my most lovely Rosa be lacking,
(For that reason my lovely Rosa shall never lack a friend,)
[*poem:* **Rosa ermangeln** (lɛɐ̯ˈmaŋəln)]

ʊnt‘ niː ˈmɪldərʊŋ ˈliːrəm graːm!
und nie Milderung ihrem Gram! [*poem:* **Mild’rung** (ˈmɪldrʊŋ)]
and never alleviation for her grief!
(and shall never lack alleviation in her grief!)

niː zae ˈtʰroːst‘loːs liːɐ̯ ˈlaedən, ˈliːrə ˈlʊrnə niː ˈbluːmənleːɐ̯!
Nie sei trostlos ihr Leiden, ihre Urne nie blumenleer!
Never be comfortless her sorrows, her urn never flower- bare!
(May her sorrows never be without comfort, and may her urn never lack flowers!)

[Schubert left two versions of this song, the second written on the back of *An Rosa I.*.]

an 'ʃvaːgɐ 'kʰroːnɔs
An Schwager Kronos
To Coachman Cronus

Op. 19, No. 1 [1816] (Johann Wolfgang von Goethe)

ʃpʻuːtʻə dɪç,   'kʰroːnɔs! fɔrt   den 'rasəlndən   tʰrɔtʰ! bɛrkʻlapʻ 'glaetʻət deːɐ veːkʻ;
Spute   dich,   Kronos! fort   den rasselnden Trott! Bergab   gleitet   der Weg;
Hurry   yourself, Cronus! Onward the rattling   trot! Downhill glides   the   way;
(Hurry up, Coachman Time! Onward the rattling trot! The way is gliding downhill;)

'eːkʻləs   'ʃvɪndəln   'tsøːgɐtʻ miːɐ foːɐ   di 'ʃtʻɪrnə daen 'tsɑodɐn / 'hɑodɐn.
ekles   Schwindeln   zögert   mir   vor   die Stirne   dein Zaudern / Haudern*.
nauseating dizziness [object] delays   for me in front of the forehead your   dawdling [subject].
(your dawdling in front of my forehead delays nauseating dizziness = the sight of your dawdling,
you seated just in front of my forehead, keeps me nauseatingly dizzy.)

    [*Most editions print "*Zaudern*"; the word used in the original poem is "*Haudern*," which
    originally meant to drive for hire, hence to move at a jog-trot, to amble or mosey along.]

frɪʃ,   'hɔlpʻetʻ lɛs glaeç, 'yːbɐ ʃtʻɔkʻ lʊntʻ 'ʃtʻaenə den tʰrɔtʻ raʃ lɪns   'leːbən hɪ'naen!
Frisch, holpert es gleich, über Stock und Steine den Trott rasch ins   Leben hinein!
Briskly, jolts   it at once, over stick and stones the trott fast into the life (into)!
                ["*über Stock und Stein*" = an idiom similar to "up hill and down dale"]
(Quick! even if there are lots of jolts, speed up the trot, up hill and down dale, right into life!)

nuːn ʃoːn 'viːdɐ den lɛr'laːtʻməndən ʃrɪtʰ, nuːn ʃoːn 'viːdɐ 'myːzaːm bɛrkʻhɪ'nɑof!
Nun schon wieder den eratmenden   Schritt, nun schon wieder mühsam   berghinauf!
Now already again the lung-filling   step,   now already again   laboriously uphill!
        [*poem:* **nun schon wieder den eratmenden Schritt mühsam Berg hinauf!**]]

ɑof dɛn, nɪçt tʰrɛːgə dɛn, 'ʃtʻreːbəntʻ lʊntʻ 'hɔfəntʻ hɪ'nan!
Auf denn, nicht träge denn, strebend und hoffend hinan!
Up then, not sluggish then, striving   and hoping onward!
(Come on, then! Don't be sluggish, then! Striving and hoping, move onward!)

vaetʰ, hoːx, 'hɛrlɪç rɪŋs   den blɪkʻ lɪns   'leːbən hɪ'naen,
Weit, hoch, herrlich rings   den Blick ins   Leben hinein,   [*poem:* **herrlich der Blick**]
Far,   high, glorious all around the gaze into the life (into),
(High up, I cast my gaze into life, spread out in the distance so gloriously!)

fɔm   gə'bɪrkʻ   tsʊm gə'bɪrkʻ
vom   Gebirg   zum Gebirg
from the mountain range to the mountain range
(From one mountain range to another)

'ʃveːbət   deːr 'leːvɪgɐ gaestʰ, 'leːvɪgən 'leːbəns 'laːndəfɔl.
schwebet der ewige Geist, ewigen Lebens ahndevoll. *
soars   the eternal spirit, of eternal life   presentiment-full.
    [*"*ahndevoll*" = "*ahnungsvoll*," in this sense; "*Ahndung*" is an obsolete form of "*Ahnung*"]
(soars the eternal spirit, full of intimations of eternal life.)

'zaet'verts dɛs 'ly:bɐdaxs 'ʃat'ən tsiːt dɪç lan,
Seitwärts des Überdachs Schatten zieht dich an,
Sideways the roof's shadow draws you onwards,
(The shadow of the top of your coach, cast sideways and somewhat in front of you, gives the impression of drawing you onwards,)

ʊnt' laen 'frɪʃʊŋ fɛɐ'haesəndɐ blɪkʰ laof deːɐ 'ʃvɛlə dɛs 'mɛːt'çəns daː.
und ein Frischung verheissender Blick auf der Schwelle des Mädchens da.
and a regeneration-promising glance on the threshold of the girl there.
(and a glance that promises regeneration from the girl standing there on her threshold.)

'laːbə dɪç! miːɐ/miːr laox, 'mɛːt'çən, 'diːzən 'ʃɔøməndən tʰraŋkʰ,
Labe dich! Mir auch, Mädchen, diesen schäumenden Trank,
Refresh yourself! For me too, girl, that foaming drink,

'diːzən 'frɪʃən gə'zʊnt'haetsbkɪkʰ! lap' dɛn, 'raʃɐ hɪ'nap'! ziː, di 'zɔnə zɪŋk'tʰ!
diesen frischen Gesundheitsblick! Ab denn, rascher hinab! Sieh, die Sonne sinkt!
that fresh health- look! Down then, faster downwards! See, the sun sinks!
(that fresh look of health! Down then, faster downwards! See, the sun is sinking!)

eː ziː zɪŋk'tʰ, leː mɪç 'graezən lɛɐ'graeft' lɪm 'moːrə 'neːbəldʊftʰ,
Eh sie sinkt, eh mich Greisen ergreift im Moore Nebelduft,
Before it sets, before me old man seizes in the swamp mist- exhalation,
(Before it sets, before an exhalation of mist in the swamp seizes me as an old man,)

lɛnt'tsaːnt'ə 'kʰiːfɐ 'ʃnat'ən lʊnt das 'ʃlɔt'ɐndə gə'baen. 'tʰrʊŋk'nən
entzahnte Kiefer schnattern und das schlotternde Gebein. Trunknen
toothless jaws cackle and the wobbling bones. Drunk
(before toothless jaws and wobbling bones chatter and rattle.)

fɔm 'lɛtst'ən ʃt'raːl raes mɪç, laen 'foøemeːɐ miːɐ/miːr lɪm 'ʃɔøməndən 'laokʰ,
vom letzten Strahl reiss mich, ein Feuermeer mir im schäumenden Aug,
from the last ray tear me, a fire- sea me in the foaming eye,
(Drag me, drunk from the last ray of the setting sun, a sea of fire before my foaming eyes,)

mɪç gə'blɛndət'ən 'tʰaoməlndən lɪn deːɐ 'hœlə 'nɛçt'lɪçəs tʰoːɐ!
mich geblendeten Taumelnden in der Hölle nächtliches Tor!
me dazzled staggering one into the hell's nocturnal gate!
(drag me, dazzled and staggering, through the nocturnal gate of hell!)

tʰøːnə, 'ʃvaːgɐ(r), lɪns hɔrn, 'raslə den 'ʃaləndən tʰraːp',
Töne, Schwager, ins Horn, rassle den schallenden Trab,
Sound, coachman, into the horn, rattle the ringing trot,
(Sound your horn, coachman! Let the trotting hooves and the carriage rattle and ring,)

das deːɐ/deːr 'lɔrkʊs fɛɐ'neːmə: viːɐ 'kʰɔmən,
dass der Orkus vernehme: wir kommen,
so that the Orcus may hear: we are coming,
(so that Orcus, the god of death, may hear that we are coming,)

das glaeç lan deːɐ tʰyːɐ deːɐ vɪrt' lʊns 'froønt'lɪç lɛm'pfaŋə. [*poem:* **Türe** ('tʰyːrə)]
dass gleich an der Tür der Wirt uns freundlich empfange.
so that right away at the door the host us friendly receive.
(so that the host may receive us right away at the door in a friendly way.)

[*An Schwager Kronos* is one of Goethe's most famous poems, and Schubert's powerful setting has captured every nuance. Goethe wrote the first version of the poem in 1774 while traveling in a mail-coach during his time of youthful "storm and stress." Schubert used a later revision (different in several respects) in which, during the printing, "*Zaudern*" was erroneously substituted for "*Haudern*." The piano part begins by expressing the "rattling trot"; Schubert marks the tempo "not too fast," to remind us that the young poet considers the horses to be moving with less speed than he wishes. He is longing to plunge headlong into life's experiences, come what may. Better to die young--so he thinks at the time--than to rot away toothless and staggering! Note the *subito piano* at the mention of the "mist in the swamp." In Goethe's time "*Schwager*," which usually means "brother-in-law," was the nickname for a coachman. Cronus, the Greek god who devours his own children, is our "Father Time." Orcus is a deity of the dead.]

an ziː
An Sie
To Her

Posthumously published [composed 1815] (poem by Friedrich Gottlieb Klopstock)

ʦaet', fɛɐ̯'kʰʏndərɪn deːɐ̯ 'bɛst'ən 'frɔødən, 'naːə 'zeːlɪgə ʦaetʰ,
Zeit, Verkünderin der besten Freuden, nahe selige Zeit,
Time, annunciator of the best joys, near blessed Time,

dɪç ɪn deːɐ̯ 'fɛrnə 'ɑostsufɔrʃən, fɛɐ̯'gɔs ɪç 'tʰryːbəndɐ 'tʰrɛːnən ʦuː fiːl.
dich in der Ferne auszuforschen, vergoss ich trübender Tränen zu viel'.
you in the distance out to search, shed I of troubled tears too many.
(searching for you in far-off lands, I shed too many troubled tears.)

ʊnt dɔx kʰɔmst duː! loː, dɪç, jaː, 'ɛŋəl 'zɛndən, 'ɛŋəl 'zɛndən dɪç miːɐ̯,
Und doch kommst du! O, dich, ja, Engel senden, Engel senden dich mir,
And yet come you! Oh, you, yes, angels send, angels send you to me,
(And yet you come! Oh yes, angels send you to me,)

diː 'mɛnʃən 'vaːrən, glaeç miːɐ̯ 'liːp't'ən, nuːn 'liːbən, viː aen ʊn'ʃt'ɛrplɪçɐ liːp'tʰ.
die Menschen waren, gleich mir liebten, nun lieben, wie ein Unsterblicher liebt.
who human beings were, like me loved, now love, as an immortal loves.
(who once were humans who loved as I do, and who now love as an immortal loves.)

ɑof den 'flyːgəln deːɐ̯ ruː, ɪn 'mɔrgənlʏft'ən, hɛl fɔm 'tʰɑoə des tʰaːks,
Auf den Flügeln der Ruh, in Morgenlüften, hell vom Taue des Tags,
On the wings of the peace, in morning breezes, bright from the dew of the day,
(On the wings of peace, in the morning breezes, bright from the dew of the dawning day,)

deːɐ̯ 'høːɐ 'lɛçəlt', mɪt dem 'leːvɪgən 'fryːlɪŋ kʰɔmst duː den 'hɪməl hɛ'rap'.
der höher lächelt, mit dem ewigen Frühling kommst du den Himmel herab.
which more sublimely smiles, with the eternal springtime come you the heaven down.
(which smiles more sublimely, with the eternal springtime you come down from heaven.)

dɛn ziː 'fyːlət' zɪç ganʦ ʊnt' giːst' ɛnt'ʦʏk'ʊŋ ɪn dem 'hɛrʦən ɛm'poːɐ̯, di 'fɔlə 'zeːlə,
Denn sie fühlet sich ganz und giesst Entzückung in dem Herzen empor, die volle Seele,
For it feels itself whole and pours rapture in the heart upwards, the full soul,
(For the full soul feels itself whole, and fills the heart with lofty rapture,)

vɛn ziː, das ziː gə'liːp'tʼ vɪrtʼ, 'tʰrʊŋkʼən fɔn 'liːbə, zɪçs dɛŋkʼtʰ!
wenn sie, dass sie geliebt wird, trunken von Liebe, sich's denkt!
when it, that it loved is, drunk from love, itself it thinks (realizes)!
(when it realizes, drunk with love, that it is loved!)

[The poet dedicated this poem to the woman who became his first wife. The verses themselves are addressed not to her directly but to "Time," to "blessed Time" that—after long searching and waiting—finally brought him someone to love who loved him in return.]

an 'zɪlvi̯a [gə'zaŋː an 'zɪlvi̯a]
An Sylvia [Gesang: An Sylvia]
To Sylvia [Song: To Sylvia]
(from William Shakespeare's *Two Gentlemen from Verona*)

Op. 106, No. 4 [1826] (German rhythmical translation by Eduard von Bauernfeld)

vas ɪstʼ 'zɪlvi̯a, 'zaːgətʼ lan, das ziː di 'vae̯tə fluːɐ̯ pʰrae̯stʰ?
Was ist Sylvia, saget an, dass sie die weite Flur preist?
What is Sylvia, announce, that her the wide common praises?
(What is Sylvia—announce it!—that everyone on the wide common praises her?)

["*ansagen*" = to announce; to notify]

ʃøːn lʊnt tsaːɐ̯tʼ zeː lɪç ziː naːn,
Schön und zart seh ich sie nahn,
Beautiful and delicate see I her come near,
(I see her coming near, beautiful and delicate;)

lae̯f 'hɪməls gʊnstʼ lʊnt 'ʃpʼuːɐ̯ vae̯stʰ, das liːɐ̯/liːr 'laləs 'lʊntʼetʰaːn.
auf Himmels Gunst und Spur weist, dass ihr alles untertan.
to heaven's favor and trace points that to her everything (is) subject.
(that everything is subject to her indicates heaven's favor and mark.)

ɪstʼ ziː ʃøːn lʊntʼ guːt da'tsuː? rae̯ts laːpʼtʼ viː 'mɪldə 'kʰɪntʼhae̯tʰ;
Ist sie schön und gut dazu? Reiz labt wie milde Kindheit;
Is she beautiful and kind as well? Charm refreshes like gentle childhood;

'iːrəm lae̯kʼ lae̯ltʼ 'laːmoːɐ̯ tsuː, dɔrtʼ hae̯ltʼ leːɐ̯ 'zae̯nə 'blɪntʼhae̯tʰ,
ihrem Aug eilt Amor zu, dort heilt er seine Blindheit,
to her eye hurries Cupid to, there heals he his blindness,
(Cupid hurries to her eyes, he heals his blindness there)

lʊntʼ fɛɐ̯'vae̯ltʼ lɪn 'zyːsɐ ruː.
und verweilt in süsser Ruh.
and lingers in sweet rest.

'daːrʊm 'zɪlvi̯a, tʰøːn, oː zaŋ, deːɐ̯ 'hɔldən 'zɪlvi̯a 'leːrən;
Darum Sylvia, tön, o Sang, der holden Sylvia Ehren;
Therefore (to) Sylvia, sound, O song, to the lovely Sylvia honors;
(Therefore, O song, sound honors to Sylvia, to the lovely Sylvia;)

'jeːdən rae̯ts bə'ziːkʼtʼ ziː laŋ, den 'leːɐ̯də kʰan gə'veːrən:
jeden Reiz besiegt sie lang, den Erde kann gewähren:
every charm won she long since, that earth can grant:
(she has long since won every charm that earth can grant:)

'kʰrɛnt̮sə liːɐ̯/liːr lʊntʼ 'zae̯tʼənkʰlaŋ!
Kränze ihr und Saitenklang!
wreaths to her and strings-sound!
(wreathe her head and strike the harp!)

[Since Schubert's friend Eduard von Bauernfeld, who translated Shakespeare's poem (from Act IV, scene 2, of the play), kept a compatible rhythm, the song can be sung with the original English words:

Who is Sylvia? What is she,	Is she kind as she is fair?
That all our swains commend her?	For beauty lives with kindness.
Holy, fair, and wise is she;	Love doth to her eyes repair,
The heavens such grace did lend her,	To help him of his blindness,
That she might admired be.	And being helped, inhabits there

Then to Sylvia let us sing,
That Sylvia is excelling:
She excels each mortal thing
Upon this dull earth dwelling:
To her let us garlands bring.]

anˈtʰiːgone lʊntʼ ˈløːdipʰ
Antigone und Oedip
Antigone and Œdipus

Op. 6, No. 2 [1817] (Johann Mayrhofer)

ANTIGONE:

iːɐ̯ ˈhoːən ˈhɪmlɪʃən, lɛɐ̯ˈhøːrət deːɐ̯ ˈtʰɔxtʼɐ ˈhɛrt̮slɛntʼ ʃtʼrøːmtʼəs ˈfleːən:
Ihr hohen Himmlischen, erhöret der Tochter herzentströmtes Flehen:
You high heavenly ones, hear the daughter's heart-streamed supplication:
(You high heavenly beings, hear the supplication that streams from a daughter's heart:)
[*poem:* **Flehn** (fleːn)]

lastʼ ˈlae̯nən ˈkʰyːlən hao̯x des ˈtʰroːstʼəs ɪn des ˈfaːtʼɐs ˈgroːsə ˈzeːlə veːn.
Lasst einen kühlen Hauch des Trostes in des Vaters grosse Seele wehn.
let a cool breath of the comfort into the father's great soul blow.
(let a cool breath of comfort blow into my father's great soul.)
[*poem:* **in Oedips** (ˈøːdips) **grosse Seele wehn**]

gəˈnyːgətʰ, ˈlɔɐ̯rən t̮sɔrn t̮su: ˈzyːnən, diːs ˈjʊŋə ˈleːbən,—neːmtʼ ɛs hɪn,
Genüget, euren Zorn zu sühnen, dies junge Leben,—nehmt es hin,
Suffices, your anger to propitiate, this young life, — take it hence,
(If this young life suffices to propitiate your anger, then take it,)

ʊntʼ ˈlɔɐ̯ɐ ˈraxəʃtʼraːl fɛɐ̯ˈnɪçtʼə di tʰiːf bəˈtʰryːpʼtʼə ˈdʊldərɪn.
und euer Rachestrahl vernichte die tief betrübte Dulderin.
and your revenge-ray annihilate the deeply troubled patiently enduring woman.
(and may a ray of your revenge annihilate this deeply troubled one, who will patiently endure it.)
[*poem:* **und eurer** (ˈlɔɐ̯ɐ) **Rache Strahl**]

'deːmyːt'ɪç 'falt'ə lɪç di 'hɛndə, — das 'fɪrmamɛnt' blaep't' glat' lʊnt' raen,
Demütig falte ich die Hände, — das Firmament bleibt glatt und rein,
Humbly fold I the hands, — the firmament remains smooth and clear,
(I humbly fold my hands; the sky remains cloudless and clear,)

ʊnt' 'ʃt'ɪlə lɪsts, nuːɐ̯ 'laǫə 'lʏft'ə dʊrç'ʃaǫɐn nɔx den 'alt'ən haen.
und stille ist's, nur laue Lüfte durchschauern noch den alten Hain.
and still is it, only mild breezes through-shiver still the old grove.
(and the air is still; only mild breezes still shiver through the old grove.)

vas zɔøftst' lʊnt' ʃt'øːnt deːɐ̯ 'blaeçə 'faːt'ɐ? lɪç laːns, —
Was seufzt und stöhnt der bleiche Vater? ich ahn's, —
Why sighs and moans the pale father? I surmise it, —
(Why does my pale father sigh and moan? I think I know:)

aen 'fʊrçt'baːrəs gə'zɪçt' fɛɐ̯'ʃɔøçt' fɔn liːm den 'laeçt'ən 'ʃlʊmɐ;
ein furchtbares Gesicht verscheucht von ihm den leichten Schlummer;
a frightful apparition chases away from him the light slumber;

eːɐ̯ ʃp'rɪŋt' fɔm 'raːzən laǫf, leːɐ̯ ʃp'rɪçtʰ:
er springt vom Rasen auf, er spricht:
he jumps from the turf up, he speaks:
(he jumps up from the turf, he speaks:)

OEDIP (Œdipus):

ɪç 'tʰrɔømə 'laenən 'ʃveːrən 'tʰraǫm. ʃvaŋ nɪçt den 'ʦɛp't'ɐ 'diːzə 'rɛçt'ə?
Ich träume einen schweren Traum. Schwang nicht den Zepter diese Rechte?
I am dreaming an oppressive dream. Swung not the scepter this right hand?
(I am dreaming an oppressive dream. Did not this right hand swing the scepter?)

[*poem:* **Ich träumte** ('tʰrɔømt'ə, dreamed)]

dɔx 'hoːhaet' 'løːst'ən 'ʃt'ark'ə 'mɛçt'ə diːɐ̯/diːr laǫf, loː graes, lɪn 'nɪçt'gən ʃaǫm.
Doch Hoheit lösten starke Mächte dir auf, o Greis, in nichtgen Schaum.
Yet high position dissolved mighty powers to you ... , O old man, into empty foam.
(Yet mighty powers dissolved your high position, O old man, into empty foam.)

["*auflösen*" = to dissolve]

tʰraŋk' lɪç lɪn 'ʃøːnən 'tʰaːgən nɪçtʰ lɪn 'maenɐ 'groːsən 'feːt'ɐ 'halə,
Trank ich in schönen Tagen nicht in meiner grossen Väter Halle,
Drank I in beautiful days not in my great ancestors' hall,
(In beautiful days did I not drink, in the hall of my great ancestors,)

baem 'hɛldənzaŋ lʊnt' 'hœrnɐʃalə, loː 'heːlios, daen 'gɔldən lɪçtʰ,
beim Heldensang und Hörnerschalle, o Helios, dein golden Licht,
amidst the heroic song and horn- sound, O Helios, your golden light,
(while singers sang of heroes to the sounding of horns, your golden light, O Helios,)

das lɪç nuːn 'nɪmɐ 'ʃaǫən kʰan? 'ʦɛɐ̯'ʃt'øːrʊŋ ruːftʰ fɔn 'alən 'zaet'ən:
das ich nun nimmer schauen kann? Zerstörung ruft von allen Seiten:
which I now never see can? Destruction calls from all sides:
(which I now can never see again? Destruction calls from all sides:)

ʦʊm ˈtʰoːdə zɔlst duː dɪç   bəˈraɛtˈən; daɛn ˈɪrdɪʃ   vɛrkˈ lɪstˈ ˈʔapˈɡətʰaːn.
"Zum Tode sollst du dich   bereiten; dein irdisch Werk ist abgetan."
"To the death shall you yourself prepare; your earthly work is finished."
("You shall prepare yourself for death; your earthly work is finished.")

[This scene for dramatic soprano and bass was inspired by one of Sophocles' plays, *Œdipus at Colonos*, the second in a trilogy. Œdipus was a king of Grecian Thebes; Antigone was one of his beloved daughters. In the first of the three plays, Œdipus learned to his horror that—without knowing who they were—he had killed his father and married his mother. To atone for his inadvertent sin, he blinded himself. Antigone has accompanied her father into exile. She offers her own life to the gods in return for his; but the sky is clear: no lightning comes to strike her down. Œdipus moans in his sleep. When he awakens, he recalls—in present helplessness—his former glory as a powerful king, when he could still rejoice in the light of Helios, the sun god. Now he is blind and homeless. He must prepare for death.]

Aria dell' angelo see *Quell' innocente figlio*

ˈaria di aˈbramo
Aria di Abramo
Abraham's Aria

Unpublished until 1940 [composed 1812] (text from *Isaac*, oratorio by Pietro Metastasio)

ˈentra ˈlwoːmo aˈlːloːr ke ˈnːnaʃːʃe   in   un maːr di ˈtːtante ˈpeːne,
Entra l'uomo allor che nasce   in un mar di tante   pene,
Enters the man when that he is born into a sea of so many pains,
(From the moment of his birth man enters into a sea of so much pain,)

ke si   aˈvːvetːʦa ˈdalːle ˈfaʃːʃe   ˈɔɲːɲi aˈfːfanːno a sosteˈneːr.
che si   avvezza   dalle   fasce   ogni affanno a sostener.
that himself he accustoms from the swaddling clothes every affliction to endure.
(that, from the cradle onwards, he is accustomed to enduring every affliction.)

ma per ˈluːi si ˈraːro ɛ il ˈbeːne, ma la ˈdʒɔːja ɛ koˈsi ˈraːra,
Ma per lui si raro è il bene, ma la gioia è così rara,
But for him so rare is the good, but the joy is so rare,
(But for him a sense of well-being and good fortune are so rare, and joy is so rare,)

ke a sːsoˈfːfriːr ˈmai non imˈpaːra le sorˈpreːse del pjaˈtʃeːr.
che a soffrir   mai non impara le sorprese del   piacer.
that to suffer   never not he learns the surprises of the pleasure.
(that he never learns how to react to the surprise of pleasure.)

[Under the supervision of his teacher, Antonio Salieri, Schubert made several settings of this text, only one for solo voice. It has been edited by Reinhard van Hoorickx, privately printed in 1965, and recorded (DG 1981007).]

'aːrįə lᵾos metaˈstaːzįos diˈdoːne: 'vedi 'kwanto aˈdoːro
Arie aus Metastasio's "Didone": Vedi quanto adoro
Aria from Metastasio's *Didone* ("Dido"): Vedi quanto adoro

Posthumously published [composed 1816] (poem by Pietro Metastasio)

'veːdi kwanto aˈdoːro anˈkoːra, inˈgraːto! kon 'uno 'zgwardo 'soːlo
Vedi quanto adoro ancora, ingrato! Con uno sguardo solo
See how much I adore still, ungrateful man! With one glance alone
(See how much I still adore you, ungrateful man! With one glance only)

mi 'toʎːʎi 'oɲːɲi diˈfeːsa e mːmi diˈzarmi.
mi togli ogni difesa e mi disarmi.
from me you take away every defence and me you disarm.
(you take away from me every defence and you disarm me.)

ed 'ai kɔːr di traˈdirmi? e pwɔi laˈʃːʃarmi?
Ed hai cor di tradirmi? e puoi lasciarmi?
And have you heart to betray me? and can you leave me?
(And have you the heart to betray me? And can you leave me?)

aː! non laˈʃːʃarmi, nɔ, bɛlːl 'iːdol 'mioː di kːki mi fːfideˈrɔ, se tːtu minˈganːni?
Ah! non lasciarmi, no, bell' idol mio: di chi mi fiderò, se tu m'inganni?
Ah! not leave me, no, beautiful idol mine: in whom myself shall I trust, if you me deceive?
(Ah! Do not leave me, no, my beautiful idol! In whom shall I trust, if *you* deceive me?)

di 'vːviːta maŋkeˈrɛi nel 'dirti aˈdːdio;
Di vita mancherei nel dirti addio;
Of life I would lack in the tell you farewell;
(I would die in saying farewell to you;)

ke 'vːviver non poˈtrɛi fra 'tːtanti aˈfːfanːni.
che viver non potrei fra tanti affanni.
since to live not I would be able among so many sorrows.
(since I would not be able to live with so many sorrows.)

[Pietro Metastasio set the style for baroque opera, and many of his librettos were set by numerous different composers, while the poetry of individual arias was frequently used out of context for concert arias. Queen Dido of Carthage was deserted by her Trojan lover, Aeneas, who left her to fulfill his destiny by founding Rome. She—along with Ariadne—became an archetypal symbol of the woman abandoned by her lover.]

Ariette der Claudine see *Liebe schwärmt auf allen Wegen*

Ariette der Lucinde see *Hin und wieder fliegen Pfeile*

'aːt'ʏs
Atys
Attis (or Attys)

Posthumously published [composed 1817] (poem by Johann Mayrhofer)

deːɐ̯ 'kʰnaːbə zɔøftst' 'lyːbɐs 'gryːnə meːɐ̯; fɔm 'fɛrnəndən 'luːfɐ kʰaːm leːɐ̯ heːɐ̯.
Der Knabe seufzt übers grüne Meer; vom fernenden Ufer kam er her.
The boy sighs over the green sea; from the far-becoming shore came he hither.
(The boy sighs over the green sea; he came this far from the ever-more-distant shore.)

[*poem:* **am dämmernden** (ɑm 'dɛmɐndən, on the growing dark) **Ufer**]

eːɐ̯ vʏnʃt' zɪç 'mɛçt'ɪgə 'ʃvɪŋən, diː 'zɔlt'ən liːn t͡sʊm 'haɛmɪʃən lant',
Er wünscht sich mächtige Schwingen, die sollten ihn zum heimischen Land,
He wishes himself mighty wings, which should him to the homelike land,
(He wishes he had mighty wings, which should take him to his homeland,)

[*GA:* **ins** (ɪns, into the) **heimische Land**]

vo'ran liːn 'leːvɪgə 'zeːnzʊxt' maːnt', ɪm 'raʊʃəndən 'fluːgə 'brɪŋən.
woran ihn ewige Sehnsucht mahnt, im rauschenden Fluge bringen.
of which him eternal yearning reminds, in the rushing flight bring.
(of which eternal yearning reminds him, in their rushing flight.)

oː 'haɛmveː! ʊnlɐɐ̯'grʏnt'lɪçɐ ʃmɛrt͡s, vas 'fɔlt'ɐst duː das 'jʊŋə hɛrt͡s?
"O Heimweh! unergründlicher Schmerz, was folterst du das junge Herz?
"O homesichness! Unfathomable pain, why torture you the young heart?
("O homesickness, unfathomable pain, why do you torture my young heart?)

kʰan 'liːbə dɪç nɪçt' fɐɐ̯'drɛŋən? duː vɪlst di frʊxt, diː 'hɛrlɪç raɛft',
Kann Liebe dich nicht verdrängen? du willst die Frucht, die herrlich reift,
Can love you not supplant? You want the fruit, which gloriously ripens,
(Can love not supplant you? Do you want to singe the fruit that is so gloriously ripening,)

[*GA:* **So** (zoː, so) **willst du die Frucht** ("*willst du*" = dotted eighth, sixteenth)]

diː gɔlt' ʊnt' 'flʏsɪgɐ 'pʰʊrp'ʊr ʃt'raɛft', mɪt 'tøːt'lɪçəm 'fɔøɐ fɐɐ̯'zɛŋən?
die Gold und flüssiger Purpur streift, mit tötlichem Feuer versengen?
which gold and liquid purple streaks, with deadly fire singe?
(that is streaked with gold and liquid purple,—do you want to singe it with deadly fire?)

ɪç 'liːbə ʊnt' 'raːzə, — lɪç haːp' ziː gə'zeːn.
Ich liebe und rase, — ich hab sie gesehn. [*GA:* **Ich liebe, ich rase,**]
I love and am delirious,—I have her seen.
(I am in love and delirious: I have seen her.)

di 'lʏft'ə dʊrç'ʃnɪt' ziː lɪm 'ʃt'ʊrməsveːn lɑɔf 'løːvəngət͡soːgənəm 'vaːgən.
Die Lüfte durchschnitt sie im Sturmeswehn auf löwengezogenem Wagen.
The airs traversed she in the storm- blowing on lion- drawn chariot.
(She traversed the air in a gale, on a chariot drawn by lions.)

ɪç 'mʊst'ə 'fleːən: oː nɪm mɪç mɪtʰ!
Ich musste flehen: o nimm mich mit! [*GA:* **flehn** (fleːn)]
I had to implore: oh take me with!
(I had to plead: "Oh, take me with you!")

110

maen 'leːbən ɪst 'dyːst'ɐ(r) ʊnt' 'lap'gəblyːtʰ.   vɪrst duː 'maenə 'bɪt'ə   fɛɐ'zaːgən?
Mein Leben ist düster   und abgeblüht.   Wirst du meine Bitte   versagen?
My   life   is   mournful and finished blooming. Will you my   request refuse?
(My life is sad; it's bloom has faded. Will you refuse my request?)

ziː 'ʃɑ͡ot'ə   mɪt' 'gyːt'ɪgəm 'lɛçəln   mɪç ʔan;
Sie schaute mit gütigem Lächeln mich an;
She looked with kindly   smile   me   at;
(She looked at me with a kindly smile;)

        [*Schubert's MS:* **mit gütige*n* Lächeln zurück** (ʦu'rʏkʰ,) looked *back* with kindly smile*s*]

naːx   'tʰraːʦiən tʰruːk' ʊns das 'løːvəngəʃp'an,   [*GA:* **zog** (ʦoːk', drew) **uns**]
nach Thrazien trug   uns das Löwengespann,
toward Thrace   carried us   the lion-drawn chariot,
(the lion-drawn chariot carried us to Thrace;)

daː diːn ʔɪç ʔals 'p'riːst'ɐ, liːɐ/liːr 'ʔaegən. den 'raːzəndən   kʰrɛnʦt' ʔaen 'zeːlɪgəs glʏkʰ:
da   dien ich als Priester, ihr   eigen. Den Rasenden   kränzt ein seliges Glück:
there serve I   as   priest, her   own. The delirious one crowned a   blissful happiness:
(there I serve her as priest of her own cult. A blissful happiness crowned me in my delirium;)

                                      [*poem:* **kränzet** ('kʰrɛnʦət')]

deːɐ/deːr 'lɑ͡ofgəvaxt'ə 'ʃɑ͡odɐt' ʦu'rʏkʰ, kʰaen gɔt' vɪl zɪç 'hɪlfraeç lɛɐ'ʦaegən.
Der   Aufgewachte schaudert zurück, kein Gott will sich hilfreich erzeigen.
the   awakened one shudders back,   no   god wants himself helpful to show.
(when I came to, I recoiled in horror; no god will show me any mercy.)

dɔrtʰ, dɔrt' 'hɪnt'ɐ den 'bɛrgən,   ʔɪm 'ʃaedəndən ʃt'raːl dɛs   'laːbənʦ
Dort, dort hinter den Bergen,   im   scheidenden Strahl des   Abends
There, there behind the mountains, in the parting   ray   of the evening
                                [*poem:* **hinter Gebirgen** (gə'bɪrgən, mountains)]

ɛnt'ʃlʊmɐt'   maen 'fɛːt'ɐlɪç tʰaːl: oː vɛːɐ/vɛːr ʔɪç 'jeːnzaeʦ deːɐ 'velən!
entschlummert mein väterlich Tal: O wär   ich jenseits   der Wellen!"
falls asleep   my   paternal valley: Oh were I   on the far side of the waves!"
(my ancestral valley falls asleep: Oh if only I were on the far side of the waves!")

zɔ͡øfʦət deːɐ kʰnaːbə, loː vɛːɐ/vɛːr ʔɪç 'jeːnzaeʦ   deːɐ 'velən!
seufzet der Knabe, "o wär   ich jenseits   der Wellen!"
sighed the boy,   "Oh were I   on the far side of the waves!"
(sighed the boy, "Oh if only I were on the far side of the waves!")

        [*poem:* **so** (zoː, so) **seufzet der Knabe** ("*o wär ich...Wellen*" is not repeated)]

dɔx 'ʦʏmbəlgətʰøːn   fɛɐ'kʰʏndət di 'gœt'ɪn, ["*Cymbel*" = in modern German: "*Zimbel*"]
Doch Cymbelgetön   verkündet die Göttin,
But   cymbal-sounding announced the goddess,
(but a clashing of cymbals announced the approach of the goddess;)

eːɐ ʃt'ʏrʦt' fɔn høːn   ʦu 'grʏndən ʊnt' valdɪgən 'ʃt'elən.
er stürtzt von Höhn zu Gründen und waldigen Stellen.
he plunged from heights to grounds and wooded   places.
(he plunged headlong from the heights down onto a wooded place far below.)

        [*poem:* **von den Höhn** (from *the* heights)... *GA:* **in** (ʔɪn, into) **Gründe und waldige Stellen**]

[There are various versions of the myth of Cybele, a Phrygian earth goddess, and Attis (or Attys), her young lover. According to this interpretation, he had seen her flying through the air in her chariot drawn by a pair of lions. In amorous madness he had begged her to take him with her, and she had carried him away to Thrace, where he then became a priest of her cult. Now, awakening from his first infatuation, he realizes that his love for the goddess is overshadowed by his intense longing for his distant homeland beyond the sea. Cybele is offended. She hurls him down to his destruction. In the myth, the goddess finds him unfaithful, casts him into a state of madness in which he castrates himself and bleeds to death under a fir-tree. In art, Cybele is often depicted with a crown of towers. Her priests, called corybantes, worshipped her with the clashing of cymbals. After his death, Attis was venerated as a fertility god. (Where there are differences, the Peters edition is closer to the wording of the poem, the *Gesamtausgabe* to Schubert's MS.)]

Auf dem Flusse see *Winterreise*

ɑof dem zeː
Auf dem See
On the Lake

Op. 92, No. 2 [1817] (Johann Wolfgang von Goethe)

ʊntʼ ˈfrɪʃə ˈnaːrʊŋ, ˈnɔøəs bluːtʰ zaʊkʼ ɪç lɑos ˈfraɐ vɛltʰ;
Und frische Nahrung, neues Blut saug ich aus freier Welt;
And fresh nourishment, new blood imbibe I out of free world;
(And I imbibe fresh nourishment, new blood, from the air of this free world;)

viː lɪstʼ naˈtʰuːɐ̯ zoː hɔltʼ ʊntʼ guːtʰ, diː mɪç lam ˈbuːzən hɛltʰ!
wie ist Natur so hold und gut, die mich am Busen hält!
how is nature so lovely and kind, which me at the breast holds!
(how lovely and kind Nature is, who holds me at her breast!)

di ˈvɛlə ˈviːgət ˈlʊnzən kʰaːn lɪm ˈruːdɐtʰakʼtʼ hɪˈnɑof,
Die Welle wieget unsern Kahn im Rudertakt hinauf,
The wave rocks our boat in the oar- rhythm up,
(The waves rock our boat upwards to the rhythm of the oars,)

ʊntʼ ˈbɛrgə, ˈvɔlkʼɪç ˈhɪməlˌlan bəˈgeːgnən ˈlʊnzəm lɑof.
und Berge, wolkig himmelan, begegnen unserm Lauf.
and mountains, cloudy heavenwards, meet our course.

ɑokʼ, maen lɑokʼ, vas zɪŋkst duː ˈniːdɐ? ˈgɔldnə ˈtʰrɔømə, kʰɔmtʼ liːɐ ˈviːdɐ?
Aug, mein Aug, was sinkst du nieder? Goldne Träume, kommt ihr wieder?
Eye, my eye, why sink you down? Golden dreams, come you again?
(Why do you look downwards, my eyes? Golden dreams, will you come back again?)

vɛkʼ, duː tʰrɑom! zoː gɔlt duː bɪstʰ; hiːɐ̯/hiːr lɑox liːpʼ lʊntʼ ˈleːbən lɪstʰ.
Weg, du Traum! so Gold du bist; hier auch Lieb und Leben ist.
Away, you dream! as gold [as] you are; here too love and life is.
(Away, you dream, however golden you are! Here too there is love and life.)

ɑof deːɐ̯ ˈvɛlə ˈblɪŋkʼən ˈtʰɑozəntʼ ˈʃveːbəndə ˈʃtʼɛrnə;
Auf der Welle blinken tausend schwebende Sterne;
On the wave sparkle thousand floating stars;
(On the waves a thousand floating stars are sparkling;)

112

'vae̯çə 'neːbəl 'tʰrɪŋk'ən rɪŋs   di 'tʰʏrməndə 'fɛrnə;
weiche Nebel trinken rings   die türmende Ferne;
soft   mists drink   all around the towering   distance;
(all around, soft mists drink up the towering distance;)

'mɔrgənvɪnt' ʊmˈflyːgəlt di bəˈʃat'ət'ə bʊxtʰ,
Morgenwind umflügelt   die beschattete Bucht,
morning-wind about-wings the shadowed   bay,
(the morning breeze wings about the shadowed bay,)

ʊnt' ɪm   zeː bəˈʃp'iːgəlt' zɪç di 'rae̯fəndə frʊxtʰ.
und im   See bespiegelt sich die reifende Frucht.
and in the lake mirrors   itself the ripening fruit.
(and in the lake the ripening fruit is mirrored.)

[Goethe wrote this poem on Lake Zurich in Switzerland, during the summer of 1775, as he was recovering from a love affair (a "golden dream"). The "free world" of the first line may refer to Switzerland, a small island of democracy in Goethe's Europe; or it may simply be nature itself and the great outdoors. In the first part of the song Schubert suggests the rhythm of the oars; at the change of meter we can imagine the morning breeze rippling the water, breaking sunlight into "a thousand floating stars."]

ɑo̯f dem ʃt'roːm
Auf dem Strom
On the Current

Op. 119 [1828] (Ludwig Rellstab)

nɪm   di 'lɛt̯st'ən 'lapʃiːt̯skʰʏsə,   ʊnt di 'veːəndən, di 'gryːsə,
Nimm die letzten Abschiedsküsse, und die wehenden, die Grüsse,
Take the last   farewell- kisses, and the blowing,   the greetings,
(Take the last kisses of farewell, and these blown greetings)

diː   ɪç nɔx lans 'luːfɐ 'zɛndə, leː   dae̯n fuːs zɪç 'ʃae̯dənt' 'vɛndə!
die   ich noch ans Ufer sende, eh   dein Fuss sich scheidend wende!
which I   still to the bank send, before your foot itself parting   turn!
(which I am still sending to the shore, before your feet turn away in parting!)

ʃoːn   vɪrt'   fɔn dɛs 'ʃt'roːməs 'voːgən raʃ   deːɐ̯ 'naxən 'fɔrt'gətsoːgən,
Schon wird   von des Stromes Wogen rasch der Nachen fortgezogen,
Already becomes by the current's waves swiftly the skiff   carried away,
(Already the skiff is being swiftly carried away by the waves of the current;)

[*Peters:* **des** *Sturmes* ('ʃt'ʊrməs, storm's) **Wogen**]

dɔx den 'trɛːnəndʊŋk'lən blɪk'   t̯siːt di 'zeːnzʊxt' ʃt'eːt̯s   t̯suˈrʏkʰ.
doch den tränendunklen Blick zieht die Sehnsucht stets   zurück.
but the tear- dark   glance draws the yearning   constantly back.
(but yearning constantly draws the tear-darkened glance back toward the place of parting.)

ʊnt' zoː tʰrɛːk't'   mɪç dɛn di 'vɛlə fɔrt' mɪt' 'ʊnleɐ̯ˌfleːt'ɐ ʃnɛlə.
Und so trägt   mich denn die Welle fort mit unerflehter Schnelle.
And so carries me   then the wave away with unentreated swiftness.
(And so the waves carry me away, then, with unasked-for swiftness.)

ax, ʃoːn ˈɪst di fluːɐ̯ fɛɐ̯ˈʃvʊndən, voː ˈlɪç ˈzeːlɪç ziː gəˈfʊndən!
Ach, schon ist die Flur verschwunden, wo ich selig sie gefunden!
Ah, already is the meadow disappeared, where I blissfully her found!
(Ah, already the meadow where I blissfully found her has disappeared!)

[*poem:* **entschwunden** (ɛntˈʃvʊndə)]

ˈeːvɪç hɪn, liːɐ̯ ˈvɔnətʰaːgə! ˈhɔfnʊŋsleːɐ̯ fɛɐ̯ˈhalt di ˈkʰlaːgə
Ewig hin, ihr Wonnetage! Hoffnungsleer verhallt die Klage
Eternally gone, you rapture-days! Hope- empty dies away the lament
(Eternally gone, you days of rapture! Empty of hope, the lament dies away)

[*poem:* **verschallt** (fɛɐ̯ˈʃalt)]

ʊm das ˈʃøːnə ˈhaemaːtˈlant, voː lɪç ˈliːrə ˈliːbə fant.
um das schöne Heimatland, wo ich ihre Liebe fand.
for the beautiful homeland, where I her love found.
(for my beautiful homeland, where I found her love.)

ziː, viː fliːt deːɐ̯ ʃtˈrant foˈryːbɐ(r) ʊnt viː drɛŋkt ˈles mɪç hɪˈnyːbɐ,
Sieh, wie flieht der Strand vorüber und wie drängt es mich hinüber,
See, how flies the shore past and how urges it me over there,
(See how the shore flies by; and how something inside of me is urging me to be there,)

ʦiːt mɪt ˈlʊnnɛnbaːrən ˈbandən lan deːɐ̯ ˈhytə dɔrt ʦuː ˈlandən,
zieht mit unnennbaren Banden an der Hütte dort zu landen, [*Peters:* **die** (di) **Hütte**]
draws with inexpressible bonds at the cottage there to land,
(is drawing me with inexpressible bonds to land at the cottage there,)

ɪn deːɐ̯ ˈlao̯bə dɔrt ʦuː ˈvae̯lən; dɔx dɛs ˈʃtˈroːməs ˈvɛlən ˈlae̯lən
in der Laube dort zu weilen; doch des Stromes Wellen eilen
in the arbor there to linger; but the current's waves hurry
(to linger in the arbor there; but the waves of the current hurry)

ˈvae̯tɐ(r) ˈloːnə rastˈ lʊnt ruː, ˈfyːrən mɪç dem ˈvɛltˈmeːɐ̯ ʦuː.
weiter ohne Rast und Ruh, führen mich dem Weltmeer zu.
farther without rest and peace, lead me to the ocean to.
(farther without rest or pause, lead me toward the ocean.)

ax, foːɐ̯ ˈjeːnɐ ˈdʊŋkˈlən ˈvyːstə, fɛrn fɔn ˈjeːdɐ ˈhae̯tˈɐn ˈkʰystˈə,
Ach, vor jener dunklen Wüste, fern von jeder heitern Küste,
Ah, before that dark wilderness, far from any cheerful coast,
(Ah, confronting that dark wilderness, far from any cheerful coast,)

voː ˈkʰae̯n ˈlae̯lant ʦuː lɛɐ̯ˈʃao̯ən; loː viː fastˈ mɪç ˈʦɪtˈɐntˈ ˈgrao̯ən!
wo kein Eiland zu erschauen; o, wie fasst mich zitternd Grauen!
where no island to be seen; oh, how seizes me tremblingly horror!
(where no island can be seen; oh, how horror seizes me and makes me tremble!)

ˈveːmuːʦtʰrɛːnən zanft ʦuː ˈbrɪŋən, kʰan kʰae̯n ˈliːt fɔm ˈluːfɐ ˈdrɪŋən;
Wehmutstränen sanft zu bringen, kann kein Lied vom Ufer dringen;
Melancholy-tears gently to bring, can no song from the shore force a way;
(No song from the shore can penetrate the distance, gently to bring tears of melancholy;)

[*Peters:* **zum** (ʦʊm, to the) **Ufer** (no song can reach *to* the shore...)]

114

nuːɐ̯ deːɐ̯ ʃtʰʊrm veːtʰ kʰalt daˈheːɐ̯ dʊrç   das gra̯oɡəˈhoːbnə meːɐ̯!
nur der Sturm weht kalt daher durch das graugehobne Meer!
only the storm blows coldly thence through the grey-raised   sea!
(only the storm-wind blows coldly toward me through the grey and heaving sea!)

kʰan dɛs ˈla̯oɡəs ˈzeːnəntʰ ˈʃva̯efən   ˈkʰa̯enə ˈluːfɐ meːɐ̯/meːr lɛɐ̯ˈɡra̯efən,
Kann des Auges sehnend Schweifen keine Ufer mehr   ergreifen,
Can   the eye's yearning sweep   no   shore any more apprehend,
(When the yearning sweep of my eyes can no longer discern any shore,)

nuːn zoː ʃa̯o   lɪç tsuː den ʃtʰɛrnən la̯of lɪn ˈjeːnən ˈha̯elɡən ˈfɛrnən!
nun so schau ich zu den Sternen auf in jenen heilgen Fernen!
now so look I   to the stars   up in those holy   distances!
(then I look up at the stars in their holy remoteness!)
                    [*poem + Peters:* **nun so blick' (blɪkʰ) ich zu den Sternen dort** (dɔrtʰ, there)**...**]

ax! ba̯e ˈliːrəm ˈmɪldən ˈʃa̯enə   nantʰ lɪç ziː tsuˈleːɐ̯st di ˈma̯enə;
Ach! bei ihrem milden Scheine nannt ich sie zuerst   die Meine;
Ah! by their gentle light   called I her first   the mine;
(Ah! by their gentle light I first called her mine;)

[(*in the song the last lines are repeated with this variation:*)]
[ba̯e deːɐ̯ ˈʃtʰɛrnə ˈmɪldəm ˈʃa̯enə]
[Bei der Sterne mildem Scheine...]   [*Peters:* **milden** (ungrammatical error)]
[By the   stars' gentle   light...]

dɔrtʰ fiˈla̯eçtʰ, loː ˈtʰrøːstʰəntʰ ɡlʏkʰ, dɔrtʰ bəˈɡeːɡ......nɪç ˈliːrəm   blɪkʰ!
dort vielleicht, o tröstend Glück, dort begegn' ich i h re m Blick!
there perhaps,   oh comforting chance, there encounter I *her*   glance!
(there perhaps, oh comforting thought, there among the stars I may again encounter *her* glance!)

[This piece was composed especially for a concert, in which it was sung in the key of E major (a
third higher than the Peters edition) with a horn obbligato. It can also be performed with cello.
Where there are variants, the *Gesamtausgabe* is generally more faithful to the original text of the
poem and to Schubert's MS., though Peters follows the wording of the poem in the final stanza.]

                    a̯of dem ˈvasɐ tsuː ˈzɪŋən
                    Auf dem Wasser zu singen
                    To be Sung on the Water

                Op. 72 [1823] (Leopold Graf von Stollberg)

ˈmɪtʰən lɪm   ˈʃɪmɐ   deːɐ̯ ˈʃpʰiːɡəlndən ˈvɛlən
Mitten im   Schimmer der   spiegelnden Wellen
Middle in the shimmer   of the reflecting   waves
(In the midst of the shimmer of the reflecting waves)

ˈɡla̯etʰətʰ, viː ˈʃvɛːnə,   deːɐ̯ ˈvaŋkʰəndə kʰaːn;
gleitet,   wie Schwäne, der wankende Kahn;
glides,   like swans,   the wavering boat;
(the swaying boat glides like a swan;)

115

ax, lɑof deːɐ̯ ˈfrɔødə ˈzanftˈʃɪmɐndən   ˈvɛlən
ach, auf der Freude sanftschimmernden Wellen
ah, on the joy's soft-shimmering waves
(ah, on the softly shimmering waves of joy)

ˈglaetˈət di ˈzeːlə daˈhɪn viː deːɐ̯ kʰaːn;
gleitet die Seele dahin wie der Kahn;
glides the soul along like the boat;
(the soul glides along like the boat;)

dɛn fɔn dem ˈhɪməl hɛˈrapˈ lɑof di ˈvɛlən
denn von dem Himmel herab auf die Wellen
for from the heaven downwards onto the waves
(for from heaven down onto the waves)

ˈtʰanʦət das ˈlaːbəntˈroːtˈ rʊntˈ lʊm den kʰaːn.
tanzet das Abendrot rund um den Kahn.
dances the sunset round about the boat.
(the red glow of sunset dances all around the boat.)

ˈyːbɐ den ˈvɪpfəln dɛs ˈvɛstˈlɪçən ˈhaenəs ˈvɪŋkˈət lʊns ˈfrɔøntˈlɪç deːɐ̯ ˈrøːtˈlɪçə ʃaen;
Über den Wipfeln des westlichen Haines winket uns freundlich der rötliche Schein;
Over the treetops of the western grove waves to us friendly the reddish gleam;
(Over the treetops of the western grove the reddish gleam beckons to us in a friendly way;)

ʊntˈɐ den ˈʦvaegən dɛs ˈlœstˈlɪçən ˈhaenəs ˈzɔøzəlt deːɐ̯ ˈkʰalmʊs lɪm ˈrøːtˈlɪçən ʃaen;
unter den zweigen des östlichen Haines säuselt der Kalmus im rötlichen Schein;
under the branches of the eastern grove murmurs the calamus in the reddish light;
(under the branches of the eastern grove the reeds murmur in the reddish light;)

ˈfrɔødə dɛs ˈhɪməls lʊntˈ ˈruːə dɛs ˈhaenəs ˈlaetˈmət di ˈzeːl lɪm lɛɐ̯ˈrøːtʰəndən ʃaen.
Freude des Himmels und Ruhe des Haines atmet die Seel im errötenden Schein.
Joy of the heaven and peace of the grove breathes the soul in the reddening light.
(the soul breathes the joy of heaven and the peace of the grove in the reddening light.)

ax, lɛs lɛntˈʃvɪndətˈ mɪt ˈtʰɑoɪgəm ˈflyːgəl miːɐ̯/miːr lɑof den ˈviːgəndən ˈvɛlən di ʦaetʰ.
Ach, es entschwindet mit tauigem Flügel mir auf den wiegenden Wellen die Zeit.
Ah, it vanishes with dewy wing for me on the rocking waves the time.
(Ah, for me on the rocking waves time flies away on dewy wings.)

ˈmɔrgən lɛntˈʃvɪndə mɪtˈ ˈʃɪmɐndəm ˈflyːgəl
Morgen entschwinde mit schimmerndem Flügel
Tomorrow vanish with shimmering wing
(May time vanish again tomorrow on shimmering wings)
                    [*poem:* **schimmernden** (ˈʃɪmɐndən) **Flügel** (wing*s*)]

ˈviːdɐ viː ˈgɛstˈɐn lʊntˈ ˈhɔøtˈə di ʦaetʰ,
wieder wie gestern und heute die Zeit,
again as yesterday and today the time,
(as it has vanished yesterday and today,)

116

bıs lıç ları 'høːərəm 'ʃtraːləndən 'flyːgəl 'zɛlbɐ(r) lɛnt''ʃvɪndə deːɐ̯ 'vɛkzəlndən ʦaetʰ.
bis ich auf höherem strahlenden Flügel selber entschwinde der wechselnde Zeit.
until I on higher radiant wing myself vanish to the changing time.
(until I myself on higher radiant wings vanish to changing time.)

[The accompaniment realistically mirrors the rippling of the water; the harmony, as it shifts from minor to major, floods the scene each time anew with a burst of sunset glow. The poet's soul, mirroring the nature all around him, joyfully breathes in the beauty and tranquillity, as its voyage parallels that of the little boat.]

ların den ziːk' deːɐ̯ 'dɔøtʃən
Auf den Sieg der Deutschen
On the Victory of the Germans

Posthumously published [composed 1813] (author unknown)

fɛɐ̯'ʃvʊndən zɪnt di 'ʃmɛrʦən,
Verschwunden sind die Schmerzen,
Disappeared are the pains,
(The pains have disappeared,)

vael ları bə'kʰlɛmt'ən 'hɛrʦən kʰaen 'zɔøfʦɐ 'viːdɐhaltʰ. drʊm 'juːbəlt' hoːx,
weil aus beklemmten Herzen kein Seufzer widerhallt. Drum jubelt hoch,
because out of oppressed hearts no sigh echoes. Therefore rejoice highly,
(because no sigh is echoing any more out of oppressed hearts. Therefore rejoice greatly,)

liːɐ̯ 'dɔøtʃə, dɛn di fɛɐ̯'ruːxt'ə 'pʰaetʃə hat' 'lɛnt'lıç 'ларsgə'kʰnaltʰ.
ihr Deutsche, denn die verruchte Peitsche hat endlich ausgeknallt.
you Germans, for the infamous whip has finally cracked out.
(you Germans, for the infamous whip has finally cracked its last.)

zeːt' 'fraŋk'raeçs kʰrea'tʰuːrən, ziː 'maxt'ən 'dɔøtʃlanʦ 'fluːrən
Seht Frankreichs Kreaturen, sie machten Deutschlands Fluren
See France's creatures, they made Germany's meadows

ʦʊm 'bluːt'ıgən lal'tʰaːɐ̯! di 'giːrıgə hyˈɛːnə fras 'hɛrmans 'leːdlə 'zøːnə
zum blutigen Altar! Die gierige Hyäne frass Hermanns edle Söhne
to the bloody altar! The greedy hyena devoured Hermann's noble sons
(into a bloody altar! The greedy hyena has devoured Germany's noble sons)

dʊrç meːɐ̯/meːr lals 'ʦvanʦıç jaːɐ̯..
durch mehr als zwanzig Jahr.
through more than twenty year.
(throughout more than twenty years.)

ɛs 'vʊrdən mɪli'oːnən fɔm 'dɔnɐ deːɐ̯ kʰa'noːnən ʦʊm 'jamɐ(r) 'ларgəʃrɛk'tʰ,
Es wurden Millionen vom Donner der Kanonen zum Jammer aufgeschreckt,
There were millions from the thunder of the cannons to the misery up-frightened,
(Millions were awakened to misery, terrified by the thunder of the cannon,)

ɛs   laːkʼ lɑɔf ʃtʼɛːtʼ lʊntʼ ˈflɛkʼən fɛɐ̯ˈvyːstʼʊŋ, ˈtʰoːdəsʃrɛkʼən,
Es   lag   auf Städt' und Flecken Verwüstung, Todesschrecken,
There lay   upon towns and villages devastation, death-terror,
(On towns and villages there lay devastation and the terror of death,)

fɔm ˈzaːtʼan ˈlɑɔsgəhɛkʼtʰ. lɛs   varf diːs ˈlʊngəhɔʏɐ
vom Satan ausgeheckt. Es   warf dies Ungeheuer
by Satan devised.   There threw this monster
(devised by Satan. That monster—Napoleon Bonaparte—cast,)

dʊrç ˈmɛnʃənmɔrtʼ   lʊntʼ ˈfɔʏɐ fɛɐ̯ˈtsvaeflʊŋ lʊm   zɪç   heːɐ̯;
durch Menschenmord und Feuer Verzweiflung um   sich her;
through humans- murder and fire   despair   around himself hither;
(through murder and fire,—cast despair all around himself here, wherever he went;)

ɛs ʃiːn   lals lɛːkʼ lɑɔf ˈkʰroːnən zoː viː lɑɔf natsiˈoːnən di ˈraxə   ˈgɔtʼəs ʃveːɐ̯.
es schien als läg' auf Kronen so wie auf Nationen die Rache   Gottes schwer.
it seemed as if lay upon crowns so as upon nations   the vengeance of God heavily.
(it seemed as if God's vengeance lay heavily upon crowned heads as upon entire nations.)

di ˈmɛnʃhaet tsuː lɛɐ̯ˈrɛtʼən fɔn ˈliːrən ˈskʼlaːvənkʰɛtʼən lɛntʼˈʃtʼant das ˈbruːdɐbantʼ,
Die Menschheit zu   erretten von ihren Sklavenketten entstand das Bruderband,
The humanity   to   rescue   from their slave- chains was formed the brother-bond,
(To rescue humanity from the chains of slavery an alliance of brother nations was formed,)

frants, ˈvɪlhɛlm, lalɛˈksandɐ ˈvɛtʼlaefən mɪt laeˈnandɐ tsʊm voːl   fyːɐ̯s ˈfaːtʼɐlantʼ.
Franz, Wilhelm, Alexander wetteifern mit einander   zum Wohl fürs Vaterland.
Franz, Wilhelm, Alexander vied   with one another to the welfare for the fatherland.
(Franz, Wilhelm, and Alexander vied with one another for the welfare of the fatherland.)

dɔx ˈløːstraeçs ˈguːtʼɐ ˈkʰaezɐ ʃluːkʼ   fyːɐ̯ di ˈziːgəsraezɐ di ˈfriːdənpʰalmə foːɐ̯.
Doch Östreichs guter Kaiser schlug für die Siegesreiser die Friedenspalme vor.
But Austria's good   emperor proposed for the victory-sprigs the peace- palm (...)
(But Austria's good emperor proposed the palm-branch of peace instead of the sprigs of victory.)
                              [*"schlug vor"* (infinitive: *vorschlagen*) = proposed, suggested, offered]

ʃtʼatʼ   froː di hant tsuː ˈbiːtʼən
Statt   froh die Hand zu bieten
Instead of happily the hand to offer,
(Instead of happily offering to shake hands,)

bliːpʼ   fyːɐ̯ gəˈvynʃtʼən ˈfriːdən tʰɑɔpʼ dɛs tʰyˈranən loːɐ̯.
blieb   für gewünschten Frieden taub des Tyrannen Ohr.
remained for wished-for   peace   deaf the tyrant's ear.
(the tyrant remained deaf to the plea for peace.)

ziː tsiːn lɑɔs ˈliːrən ˈʃtʼaːtʼən lals ˈrɛçɐ   ˈbøːzɐ ˈtʰaːtʼən,
Sie ziehn aus   ihren Staaten als Rächer böser Taten,
They come out of their states   as avengers of evil deeds,

tsuː ˈbyrgən ˈdɔʏtʃlants ruː. ziː tsiːn tsʊm kʰampf, ziː ˈziːgən,
zu bürgen Deutschlands Ruh. Sie ziehn zum Kampf, sie siegen,
to guarantee Germany's   peace.They go   to the battle, they are victorious,
(to guarantee peace in German lands. They go into battle, they are victorious)

118

ʊnt' 'fraŋk'raẹçs 'rɛst'ə   'fliːgən bə'ziːk't   deːɐ̯ 'haẹmaːt tsuː.
und Frankreichs Reste   fliegen besiegt   der Heimat   zu.
and France's   remnants fly   conquered the homeland to.
(and the remnants of France's troops fly back to their homeland, conquered.)

deːɐ̯ kʰampf lɪst' nuːn lɛnt'ʃiːdən.   balt', balt' lɛɐ̯'ʃaẹnt deːɐ̯ 'friːdən
Der Kampf ist nun entschieden. Bald, bald erscheint der Frieden
The battle is   now decided.   Soon, soon appears the peace
(The battle has now been decided. Soon, soon peace will appear)

ɪn 'hɪmlɪɐ̯   gə'ʃt'altʰ. drʊm   'juːbəlt' hoːx,   liːɐ̯ 'dɔʏtʃə,
in himmlischer   Gestalt. Drum   jubelt hoch, ihr Deutsche,
in heavenly   form.   Therefore rejoice greatly, you Germans,

dɛn di fɛɐ̯'ruːxt'ə 'pʰaẹtʃə hat' 'laẹnmaːl 'lọosgək'ʰnaltʰ.
denn die verruchte Peitsche hat einmal   ausgeknallt.
for   the infamous whip   has finally   cracked its last.

[This early song celebrates the defeat of Napoleon by Austrian and Prussian forces at the battle of Leipzig, fought between the sixteenth and nineteenth of October 1813, a major turning point in European history. Emperor Franz of Austria, King Wilhelm of Prussia, and Czar Alexander of Russia were allies. The accompaniment is for two violins and cello, most probably intended for Schubert himself (then sixteen years old), his brother (violin), and his father (easy cello part).]

ạof den tʰoːt' laẹnɐ 'naxt'ɪgal
Auf den Tot einer Nachtigall
On the Death of a Nightingale

Posthumously published [1815 (incomplete), 1816] (Ludwig Heinrich Christoph Hölty)

ziː lɪst da'hɪn,   diː 'maẹənliːdɐ 'tʰøːnt'ə, di 'zɛŋərɪn,
Sie ist dahin,   die Maienlieder tönte,   die Sängerin,
She is gone, (she) who May- songs sounded, the singer,
(She is gone, she who sounded songs of May, the singer) [*"Nachtigall"* is feminine in German.]

diː dʊrç liːɐ̯ liːt den 'gantsən haẹn fɛɐ̯'ʃøːnt'ə, ziː lɪst da'hɪn!
die durch ihr Lied den ganzen Hain verschönte, sie ist dahin!
who through her song the entire grove beautified, she is gone!
(who through her song beautified the entire grove, she is gone!)

ziː, 'deːrən tʰoːn miːɐ̯/miːr ɪn di 'zeːlə 'halt'ə,   vɛn lɪç lam bax,
Sie, deren Ton mir   in die Seele hallte,   wenn ich am   Bach,
She, whose tone to me   in the soul resounded, when I   by the brook,
(She, whose tone resounded in my soul when, by the brook)

deːɐ̯ dʊrç gə'byʃ lɪm 'laːbənt'gɔldə 'valt'ə,   lạof 'bluːmən laːk'!
der durch Gebüsch im Abendgolde wallte,   auf Blumen lag!
which through bushes in the evening-gold wandered, on flowers lay!
(which meandered among the bushes in the gold of evening, I lay bedded on flowers!)

ziː 'gʊrgəlt'ə, tʰiːf lạos deːɐ̯ 'fɔlən 'kʰeːlə, den 'zɪlbɐʃlaːk':
Sie gurgelte, tief aus der vollen Kehle, den Silberschlag:
She gargled,   deep out of the full   throat, the silver-birdsong*:
(She brought her silver song from out of the depths of a full throat:)

deːɐ̯ 'viːdɐhal ɪn 'zaᴇnɐ 'fɛlzənhøːlə ʃluːk' laᴇs liːn   naːx.
der Wiederhall in seiner Felsenhöhle schlug leis' ihn   nach.
the echo   in its   rocky cave sang* softly it (the song) after.
(the echo in its rocky cave sang it softly after her.)

di 'lɛnt'lɪçən gə'zɛŋ ʊnt' 'fɛlt'ʃalmaᴇən lɛɐ̯'kʰlaŋən draᴇn;
Die ländlichen Gesäng' und Feldschalmeien erklangen drein;
The rustic   songs   and field-shawms   sounded   into it;
(Rustic songs and the sound of shepherds' pipes mingled with her melody;)

ɛs 'tʰantsət'ən di 'jʊŋfraᴏn 'liːrə 'raᴇən   ɪm 'laːbənt'ʃaᴇn.
es   tanzeten   die Jungfraun ihre Reihen   im Abendschein.
there danced   the maidens   their round dances in the evening-glow.
(young girls danced their rounds in the glow of sunset.)

aᴏf 'moːzə hɔrçt' laᴇn 'jʏŋlɪŋ   mɪt' lɛnt'tsʏk'ən dem 'hɔldən laᴏtʰ,
Auf Moose horcht' ein Jüngling mit Entzücken dem holden Laut,
On moss   listened a   youth   with delight   to the lovely sound,
(Reclining on moss, a young man listened with delight to the lovely sound,)

ʊnt' 'ʃmaxt'ənt' hɪŋ lan 'liːrəs 'liːp'lɪŋs 'blɪk'ən di 'jʊŋə braᴏtʰ:
und schmachtend hing an ihres Lieblings Blicken die junge Braut:
and languishingly hung on her   darling's glances the young bride:
(and the young bride hung languishingly on her darling's every glance:)

ziː 'drʏk't'ən zɪç   baᴇ 'jeːdɐ 'daᴇnɐ 'fuːgən di hant' laᴇn'maːl,
sie drückten sich   bei jeder deiner Fugen die Hand einmal,
they squeezed themselves at   each   of your fugues the hand once,
(they squeezed one another's hand once at each of your musical flights,)

ʊnt' 'høːɐ̯t'ən nɪçt', vɛn 'daᴇnə ʃvɛst'ɐn   'ʃluːgən, loː 'naxt'ɪgal!
und hörten   nicht, wenn deine Schwestern schlugen, o Nachtigall!
and heard   not,   when your sisters   sang,*   O nightingale!
(and did not hear when your sister birds sang, O nightingale!)

ziː 'hɔrçt'ən diːɐ̯, bɪs dʊmpf di 'laːbənt'glɔk'ə dɛs 'dɔrfəs kʰlaŋ,
Sie horchten dir, bis dumpf die Abendglocke des   Dorfes klang,
They listened to you, until dully   the evening bell   of the village rang,

ʊnt' 'hɛsp'erʊs, glaᴇç 'laᴇnɐ 'gɔldnən 'flɔk'ə laᴏs 'vɔlk'ən draŋ;
und Hesperus, gleich einer goldnen Flocke aus Wolken drang;
and Hesperus, like   a   golden flake   out of clouds broke through;
(and Hesperus, like a golden snowflake, broke through the clouds;)

ʊnt'   'gɪŋən dan ɪm vɛn deːɐ̯ 'maᴇənkʰyːlə, deːɐ̯ 'hʏt'ə tsuː,
und   gingen dann im Wehn der Maienkühle, der Hütte zu,
and (they) went   then in the blowing of the May- coolness, the cottage to,
(and the lovers then went to their cottage, as the cool breeze of the May night began to blow,)

mɪt' 'laᴇnɐ brʊst' fɔl 'tsɛːɐ̯t'lɪçɐ gə'fyːlə, fɔl 'zyːsɐ ruː.
mit einer Brust voll   zärtlicher Gefühle, voll   süsser Ruh'.
with a   breast full of tender   feelings, full of sweet peace.

120

[*"*Schlag*" (therefore "*schlagen, schlug(en)*" too) can refer to birdsong, among other meanings. Hesperus is one of the names of the evening star. Schubert's first setting of this poem was left incomplete, lacking the last three notes.]

ɑof deːɐ̯ brʊkʰ
Auf der Bruck
On the Bruck (a wooded hilltop resort near Göttingen)

Op. 93, No. 2 [1825] (Ernst Schulze)

frɪʃ 'tʰraːbɐ 'zɔndɐ ruː lʊntˈ rastˈ, mɑen 'guːtˈəs rɔs, dʊrç naxtˈ lʊntˈ 'reːgən!
Frisch trabe sonder Ruh und Rast, mein gutes Ross, durch Nacht und Regen!
Briskly trot   without peace and rest, my   good   horse, through night and rain!
(Trot lively, my good horse, without stopping or resting, through the night and the rain!)

vas ʃɔøst du: dɪç   foːɐ̯ bʊʃ lʊntˈ lastˈ lʊntˈ 'ʃtˈrɑoxəlstˈ lɑof den 'vɪldən 'veːgən?
Was scheust du dich   vor Busch und Ast   und strauchelst auf den wilden Wegen?
Why shy   you yourself at bush   and branch and stumble   on the wild   pathways?
(Why do you shy at bushes and branches and stumble on the wild pathways?)

deːntˈ   lɑox deːɐ̯ valtˈ zɪç tʰiːf lʊnt dɪçtˈ, dɔx mʊs leːɐ̯/leːɪr 'lentˈlɪç zɪç lɛɐ̯'ʃliːsən;
Dehnt   auch der Wald sich tief und dicht, doch muss er   endlich sich erschliessen;
Stretches even the   forest itself deep and thick, yet   must it   finally itself finish;
(Even though the forest stretches out deep and thick, it still must finally come to an end;)

ʊntˈ 'frɔøntˈlɪç vɪrtˈ lɑen 'fɛrnəs lɪçtˈ lʊns lɑos dem 'dʊŋkˈəln 'tʰaːlə 'gryːsən.
und freundlich wird ein fernes Licht uns aus   dem dunkeln Tale grüssen.
and friendlily   will a   distant light us out of the dark   valley greet.
(and a distant light will greet us like a friend from out of the dark valley.)

voːl   kʰœntˈ lɪç 'lyːbɐ bɛrkˈ   lʊntˈ fɛltˈ lɑof 'dɑenəm 'ʃlaŋkˈən 'rʏkˈən 'fliːgən
Wohl   könnt ich über Berg   und Feld auf deinem schlanken Rücken fliegen
No doubt could I   over mountain and field on your   slender   back   fly
(No doubt I could fly over mountain and field on your slender back)

ʊntˈ mɪç lam 'bʊntˈən ʃpˈiːl deːɐ̯ vɛltˈ, lan 'hɔldən 'bɪldɐn mɪç fɛɐ̯'gnyːgən;
und mich am   bunten Spiel der   Welt, an holden Bildern mich vergnügen;
and myself at the colorful game of the world, at lovely images myself amuse;
(and amuse myself at the world's colorful game, with lovely images;)

manç   'lɑogə laxtˈ miːɐ̯ 'tʰrɑolɪç tsuː lʊntˈ bɔøtˈ miːɐ̯ 'friːdən, liːpˈ lʊntˈ 'frɔødə,
manch Auge lacht mir traulich zu und beut mir Frieden, Lieb und Freude,
many an eye   laughs me cordially at and offers me peace,   love, and joy,
(many an eye smiles at me invitingly and offers me peace, love, and joy;)

ʊnt 'dɛnox   lɑel lɪç 'loːnə ruː tsu'rʏkˈ, tsu'rʏkˈ tsuː 'mɑenəm 'lɑedə.
und dennoch   eil ich ohne Ruh zurück, zurück zu meinem Leide.
and nevertheless hurry I without rest back, back to my   sorrow.
(and yet, without stopping to rest, I hurry back, back to my sorrow.)

den ʃoːn drɑe 'tʰaːgə vaːɐ̯/vaːr lɪç fɛrn fɔn liːɐ̯, di: 'leːvɪç mɪç   gə'bʊndən;
Denn schon drei Tage war   ich fern von ihr, die ewig   mich gebunden;
For already three days was   I   far from her, who eternally me (has) bound;
(For it is already three days that I have been far from her, who has bound me to her eternally;)

draͤe ˈtʰaːgə ˈvaːrən zɔn ʊntˈ ʃtˈɛrn ʊntˈ leːɐ̯tˈ ʊntˈ ˈhɪməl fɛɐ̯ˈʃvʊndən.
drei Tage waren Sonn und Stern' und Erd und Himmel verschwunden.
three days were sun and stars and earth and heaven disappeared.
(for three days the sun and stars and earth and heaven had disappeared.)

fɔn lʊstˈ ʊntˈ ˈlaͤedən, diː maͤen hɛrts baͤe liːɐ̯ baltˈ ˈhaͤeltˈən, baltˈ tsɛɐ̯ˈrɪsən,
Von Lust und Leiden, die mein Herz bei ihr bald heilten, bald zerrissen,
Of pleasure and suffering, which my heart with her now healed, now tore apart,
(Of pleasure and pain, which—near her—would one moment heal my heart, the next tear it apart,)

fyːltˈ ɪç draͤe ˈtʰaːgə nuːɐ̯ den ʃmɛrts, ʊntˈ lax! di ˈfrɔøde mʊstˈ ɪç ˈmɪsən!
fühlt' ich drei Tage nur den Schmerz, und ach! die Freude musst ich missen!
felt I three days only the pain, and ah! the joy had I to miss!
(I felt for three days only the pain, and—ah!—I had to miss the joy!)

vaͤetˈ zeːn viːɐ̯/viːr ˈlyːbe lantˈ ʊntˈ zeː tsʊr ˈvɛrmən fluːɐ̯ den ˈfoːgəl ˈfliːgən;
Weit sehn wir über Land und See zur wärmern Flur den Vogel fliegen;
Far see we over land and sea to the warmer meadow the bird fly;
(We see birds fly far over land and sea to a warmer meadow;)

viː ˈzɔltˈə den di ˈliːbə jeː ɪn ˈiːrəm ˈpfaːdə zɪç bəˈtʰryːgən?
wie sollte denn die Liebe je in ihrem Pfade sich betrügen?
how should then the love ever in its path itself deceive?
(how then should love ever deceive itself about its path?)

drʊm ˈtʰraːbə ˈmuːtˈɪç dʊrç di naxtʰ! ʊntˈ ˈʃvɪndən laͤox di ˈdʊŋkˈəln ˈbaːnən,
Drum trabe mutig durch die Nacht! und schwinden auch die dunkeln Bahnen,
Therefore trot bravely through the night! and disappear even the dark pathways,
(Therefore trot bravely through the night! And even if the dark pathways disappear,)

deːɐ̯ ˈzeːnzʊxtˈ ˈhɛləs ˈlaͤogə vaxtʰ, ʊntˈ ˈzɪçe fyːɐ̯tˈ mɪç ˈzyːsəs ˈlaːnən.
der Sehnsucht helles Auge wacht, und sicher führt mich süsses Ahnen.
the longing's bright eye is awake, and safely leads me sweet surmise.
(the bright eye of longing is awake, and sweet anticipation leads me safely.)

[The lover has been away from his beloved for three days; full of impatient longing for her, he hurries back to her on horseback through a dark and rainy night. The title has nothing to do with a bridge ("*Brücke*"); it refers, rather, to a wooded hilltop, a holiday resort near Göttingen. Schubert rearranged the lines of the last stanza; in the poem the sentence starting "*Weit sehn wir über Land und See*" comes after "*und sicher führt mich süsses Ahnen.*"]

aͤof deːɐ̯ ˈdoːnaͤo
Auf der Donau
On the Danube

Op. 21, No. 1 [1817] (Johann Mayrhofer)

aͤof deːɐ̯ ˈvɛlən ˈʃpˈiːgəl ʃvɪmt deːɐ̯ kʰaːn, ˈlaltˈə ˈbʊrgən ˈraːgən ˈhɪməllan;
Auf der Wellen Spiegel schwimmt der Kahn. Alte Burgen ragen himmelan;
On the waves' mirror swims the boat. Old castles rear up toward heaven;
(The boat swims upon the mirror of the waves. Old castles rear up toward heaven;)

'tʰanənvɛldɐ 'rɑoʃən 'gaest'ɐglaeç, lʊnt das hɛrts̬ lɪm 'buːzən vɪrt' lʊns waeç.
Tannenwälder rauschen geistergleich, und das Herz im Busen wird uns weich.
Fir-tree forests murmur like ghosts, and the heart in the bosom becomes for us weak.
(Fir-tree forests murmur like ghosts, and our hearts become weak in our bosoms.)

dɛn deːɐ̯ 'mɛnʃən 'vɛrk'ə 'zɪŋk'ən lal: voː lɪst tʰʊrm, voː 'pfɔrt'ə, voː deːɐ̯ val,
Denn der Menschen Werke sinken all: wo ist Turm, wo Pforte, wo der Wall,
For the humans' works sink all: where is tower, where gates, where the rampart,
(For all the works of human beings fall into ruin: where are tower, gates, and ramparts?)

[*poem:* **wo ist Turm** *und* **Pforte,**]

voː ziː zɛlpstʰ, di 'ʃt'ark'ən, 'leːɐ̯tsgəʃɪrmt,
wo sie selbst, die Starken, erzgeschirmt,
where they themselves, the strong ones, metal-shielded,
(where are they themselves, the strong men, armored with metal,)

diː lɪn kʰriːk' lʊnt' 'jaːk'dən 'hɪngəʃt'ʏrmtʰ? voː? voː?
die in Krieg und Jagden hingestürmt? Wo? Wo?
who in war and hunts stormed forth? Where? Where?
(who stormed forth to war and to the hunt? Where are they? Where?)

'tʰrɑorɪgəs gə'ʃt'ʁʏp'ə 'vʊxɐt' fɔrtʰ, 'veːrənt' 'frɔmɐ 'zaːgə kʰraft' fɛɐ̯'dɔrtʰ.
Trauriges Gestrüppe wuchert fort, während frommer Sage Kraft verdorrt.
Sad undergrowths spread rankly forth, while pious legend's power withers.
(Dismal undergrowth continues to spread rankly, while the power of pious legend withers away.)

ʊnt' lɪm 'kʰlaenən 'kʰaːnə vɪrt' lʊns baŋ,
Und im kleinen Kahne wird uns bang,
And in the little boat becomes for us uneasy,
(And in the little boat we begin to feel uneasy:)

'velən droːn, viː tsaet'ən, 'lʊnt'ɐgaŋ, 'lʊnt'ɐgaŋ, 'lʊnt'ɐgaŋ.
Wellen drohn, wie Zeiten, Untergang, Untergang, Untergang.
waves threaten, like times, decline, downfall, ruin.
(the waves, like time itself, threaten "decline, downfall, ruin.")

[The river flows ever onwards, like time itself, indifferent to the works of man, the ancient castles on its banks that are falling into ruin. The song, with its descent to the low F sharp, was intended to be sung by a bass, and the vocal part was originally written in the bass clef.]

ɑof deːɐ̯ 'riːzənkʰɔp'ə
Auf der Riesenkoppe
On the Riesenkoppe ("Giant-Summit," a mountain)

Posthumously published [composed 1818] (poem by Karl Theodor Körner)

hoːx lɑof dem 'gɪpfəl 'daenɐ gə'bɪrgə ʃt'eː lɪç lʊnt' ʃt'ɑon lɪç!
Hoch auf dem Gipfel deiner Gebirge steh ich und staun ich!
High upon the summit of your mountain range stand I and am astonished I!
(High up upon the summit of your mountain range I stand and look about with astonishment,)

'glyːənt' bə'gaest'ɐt', 'haelɪgə 'kʰɔp'ə, 'hɪməlslanʃt'ʏrmərin!
glühend begeistert, heilige Koppe, Himmelanstürmerin!
fervently enraptured, holy summit, heaven- stormer! ["*Koppe*" = "*Kuppe*" = summit]

vaet' ɪn di 'fɛrnə 'ʃvaefən di 'tʰrʊŋk'nən, 'frɔɵdɪɡən 'blɪk'ə;
Weit in die Ferne schweifen die trunknen, freudigen Blicke;
Far into the distance sweep the intoxicated, joyful glances;
(My intoxicated, joyful gaze sweeps far into the distance;)

'yːbɐlal 'leːbən, 'ʏp'ɪɡəs 'ʃt'reːbən, 'yːbɐlal 'zɔnənʃaen!
überall Leben, üppiges Streben, überall Sonnenschein!
everywhere life, abundant aspiration, everywhere sunshine!
(everywhere I look I see life, abundant aspiration, sunshine!)

'blyːəndə 'fluːrən, 'ʃɪmɐndə 'ʃt'ɛːt'ə, 'draɐ 'kʰøːnɪɡə 'ɡlʏk'lɪçə 'lɛndɐ
Blühende Fluren, schimmernde Städte, dreier Könige glückliche Länder
blooming meadows, shimmering cities, of three kings happy lands
(Blooming meadows, shimmering cities, the happy lands of three kings)

ʃao lɪç bə'ɡaest'ɐt', ʃao lɪç mɪt' 'hoːɐ, mɪt' 'lɪnɪɡɐ lʊstʰ.
schau ich begeistert, schau ich mit hoher, mit inniger Lust.
see I enraptured, see I with high, with heartfelt delight.
(I see, enraptured, I see with sublime, with heartfelt delight.)

aox 'maenəs 'faːt'ɐlants 'ɡrɛntsə lɛɐ'blɪk' lɪç,
Auch meines Vaterlands Grenze erblick ich,
Also my fatherland's border see I,
(I also see the border of my fatherland,)

voː mɪç das 'leːbən 'frɔɵnt'lɪç bə'ɡryːst'ə,
wo mich das Leben freundlich begrüsste,
where me the life friendlily greeted,
(where life first gave me its friendly greeting,)

voː mɪç deːɐ 'liːbə 'haelɪɡə 'zeːnzʊxt' 'ɡlyːənt' lɛɐ'ɡrɪf.
wo mich der Liebe heilige Sehnsucht glühend ergriff.
where me the love's holy yearning fervently seized.
(where love's holy yearning fervently seized me.)

zae miːɐ ɡə'zeːɡnət' hiːɐ/hiːr lɪn deːɐ 'fɛrnə, 'liːp'lɪçə 'haemaːtʰ!
Sei mir gesegnet hier in der Ferne, liebliche Heimat!
Be by me blessed here in the distance, lovely homeland!
(I send you my blessing from here in the distance, lovely homeland!)

zae miːɐ ɡə'zeːɡnət', lant' 'maenɐ 'tʰrɔɵmə, kʰraes 'maenɐ 'liːbən, zae miːɐ ɡə'ɡryːstʰ!
Sei mir gesegnet, Land meiner Träume, Kreis meiner Lieben, sei mir gegrüsst!
Be by me blessed, land of my dreams, circle of my dear ones, be by me greeted!
(I send you my blessing, land of my dreams, I send you my greeting, home of my dear ones!)

[To this poem that hymns the exalted feelings aroused by the spacious view from a mountain-top, Schubert adds a pair of pianistic yodels in the interlude after *"inniger Lust"* and a postlude that is typical of popular "mountain music" in the alpine regions of Europe. The poet's home city was Dresden; the "Giant Summit" (*Riesenkoppe*) is a peak in the Riesengebirge mountain-range from which Germany, Poland, and Bohemia—*"dreier Könige Länder"*—could be seen.]

124

ɑɔf 'laenən/aenəm 'kʰɪrçhoːf
Auf einen Kirchhof / Auf einem Kirchhof
Onto a Churchyard / At a Churchyard

Posthumously published [composed 1815] (Baron Franz Xaver von Schlechta)

zae gə'gryːstʻ, gə'vaetʻə 'ʃtʻɪlə, diː miːɐ̯ 'zanftʻə 'tʰrɑɔɐ vɛkʻtʰ,
Sei gegrüsst, geweihte Stille, die mir sanfte Trauer weckt,
Be greeted, consecrated stillness, which in me gentle mourning awakens,
(I greet you, consecrated stillness, which awakens a gentle mourning in me,)

voː na'tʰuːɐ̯ di 'bʊntʻə 'hʏlə 'frɔ̨øntʻlɪç 'yːbɐ 'greːbɐ dɛkʻtʰ.
wo Natur die bunte Hülle freundlich über Gräber deckt.
where Nature the colorful cloak kindly over graves spreads.
(where kindly Nature spreads a colorful cloak over the graves.)

laeçtʻ fɔn 'vɔlkʻəndʊftʻ gə'tʰraːgən zɛŋkʻt di 'zɔnə 'liːrən lɑɔf,
Leicht von Wolkenduft getragen senkt die Sonne ihren Lauf,
Lightly by cloud- vapor borne sinks the sun its course,
(Lightly borne by cloud-vapor, the sun is setting in its course,)

ɑɔs deːɐ̯ 'fɪnstʻɐn 'eːɐ̯də 'ʃlaːgən 'glyːənt 'roːtʻə 'flamən lɑɔf!
aus der finstern Erde schlagen glühend rote Flammen auf!
out of the dark earth spring glowingly red flames up!
(out of the darkening earth glowing red flames spring up!) [*"aufschlagen"* (here) = to spring up]

ax, lɑɔx liːɐ̯/liːr, lɛɐ̯'ʃtʻartʻə 'bryːdɐ, 'haːbətʻ 'zɪŋkʻəntʻ liːn fɔl'braxtʰ;
Ach, auch ihr, erstarrte Brüder, habet sinkend ihn vollbracht; ["*ihn*" = *den Lauf*]
Ah, also you, torpid brothers, have sinking it completed;
(Ah, you too, torpid brothers, have finished your declining course;)

zaŋkʻtʻ liːɐ̯ lɑɔx zoː 'hɛrlɪç 'niːdɐ lɪn dɛs 'graːbəs 'ʃɑɔɐnaxtʰ?
sankt ihr auch so herrlich nieder in des Grabes Schauernacht?
sank you too so gloriously down into the grave's terror- night?
(did you too descend so gloriously into the terrifying night of the grave?)

'ʃlʊmɐtʻ zanftʻ, liːɐ̯ 'kʰaltʻən 'hɛrtsən, lɪn deːɐ̯ 'dyːstʻɐn 'laŋən ruː,
Schlummert sanft, ihr kalten Herzen, in der düstern langen Ruh,
Slumber gently, you cold hearts, in the dark long rest,

'ɔ̨ørə 'vʊndən, 'lɔ̨ørə 'ʃmɛrtsən 'dɛkʻətʻ mɪlt di 'eːɐ̯də tsuː!
eure Wunden, eure Schmerzen decket mild die Erde zu!
your wounds, your pains covers gently the earth up!
(the earth gently covers up your wounds, your pains!)

nɔ̨ø tsɛɐ̯'ʃtʻøːrən, nɔ̨ø lɛɐ̯'ʃafən 'tʰraepʻt das raːt deːɐ̯ 'vɛltʻənluːɐ̯,
Neu zerstören, neu erschaffen treibt das Rad der Weltenuhr,
Newly destroy, newly create drives the wheel of the world- clock,
(Destruction and creation anew--that drives the wheel of the cosmic clock,)

'kʰrɛftʻə, diː lɪm fɛls lɛɐ̯'ʃlafən, 'blyːən 'viːdɐ(r) lɑɔf deːɐ̯ fluːɐ̯!
Kräfte, die im Fels erschlaffen, blühen wieder auf der Flur!
Powers, which in the rock slacken, bloom again on the meadow!
(Powers that slacken in the rock bloom again on the meadow!)

ʊnt' ˈlɑox duː, gəˈliːp't'ə ˈhʏlə, ˈzɪŋk'əst ˈt͡sʊk'ənt'   ˈlɑenst' hɪˈnap',
Und auch du, geliebte Hülle, sinkest zuckend   einst   hinab,
And also   you, beloved shell, sink   convulsively someday downwards,
(And you too, dear outer shell, will one day sink down convulsively,)

ʊnt' lɛɐ̯ˈblyːst' lɪn ˈʃøːnst'ɐ ˈfʏlə   nɔø, lɑen ˈblyːmçən lɑof dem graːp'.
und erblühst in schönster Fülle   neu, ein Blümchen auf dem Grab.
and bloom   in loveliest fullness anew, a   little flower on the grave.

vaŋkst',   lɑen ˈflɛmçən, dʊrç di ˈgryft'ə, ˈlɪrəst' ˈflɪmɐnt dʊrç   den moːɐ̯,
Wankst,   ein Flämmchen, durch die Grüfte, irrest   flimmernd durch den Moor,
[You] waver, a   little flame,   through the tombs,   meander flickeringly through the fen,
(You waver, a little flame, through tombs, meander—flickering—through the fen,)

ʃvɪŋst',   lɑen ʃt'raːl, dɪç   lɪn di ˈlʏft'ə, ˈkʰlɪŋəst' hɛl,   lɑen tʰoːn, lɛmˈpʰoːɐ̯!
schwingst, ein Strahl, dich   in die Lüfte, klingest hell,   ein Ton, empor!
swing,   a   ray,   yourself into the airs, sound   brightly, a   tone, upwards!
(soar upwards into the air, a ray of light, ring brightly, a tone!)

ˈaːbɐ duː, das   lɪn miːɐ̯ ˈleːbət', vɪrst' lɑox duː des ˈvʊrməs rɑop'?
Aber du, das   in mir lebet, wirst   auch du des Wurmes Raub?
But   you, that which in me   lives,   become also you the worm's   prey?
(But you, who are that which lives inside me, will you too become a prey of the worm?)

vas   lɛnt'ˈt͡sʏk'ənt' mɪç lɛɐ̯ˈheːbət', bɪst' lɑox duː nuːɐ̯/nuːr ˈlɑetəl ʃt'ɑop'?
Was   entzückend mich erhebet, bist auch du nur   eitel Staub?
[That] which rapturously me lifts up,   are also you only   empty dust?
(You who lift me up so rapturously, are you too only empty dust?)

nɑen! vas   lɪç lɪm ˈlɪnɐn ˈfyːlə, vas   lɛnt'ˈt͡sʏk'ənt' mɪç lɛɐ̯ˈheːp'tʰ,
Nein! was   ich im Innern fühle, was   entzückend mich erhebt,
No!   That which I   in the inside feel,   that which rapturously me lifts up,
(No! What I am feeling inside of me, that which rapturously lifts me up,)

ɪst deːɐ̯ ˈgɔt'haet' ˈraenə ˈhʏlə,   lɪst' liːɐ̯ hɑox, deːɐ̯/deːr lɪn miːɐ̯ leːp'tʰ.
ist der Gottheit reine Hülle,   ist ihr Hauch, der   in mir lebt.
is the divinity's pure raiment, is   its breath, which   in me lives.
(is the pure raiment of divinity, it is a trace of the breath of God that lives on in me.)

[The poet meditates on death. The body will turn to dust; but—out of that dust—life will renew itself in other forms. It may be that a wraith will wander about, earthbound, for a while after death, before it moves on to other, higher spheres. But is there not also within us a part that will neither turn to dust nor haunt a graveyard, an immortal soul, a link to God that will never break? The form of Schubert's song was obviously influenced by Italian opera, with its recitatives and exuberant ending. The poet's title was *Im Kirchhofe* ("*In* the Churchyard"); Schubert, who used a version that differs from the published poem, headed his setting *Auf einen Kirchhof*, a grammatically unusual formulation, which the Peters Edition changed to *Auf eine*m *Kirchhof.*]

Aufenthalt see *Schwanengesang*

126

'ɑoflǿːzʊŋ
Auflösung
Dissolving — Loosening — Resolving a Discord

Posthumously published [composed 1824] (poem by Johann Mayrhofer)

fɛɐ̯'bɪrk' dɪç,   'zɔnə,   dɛn di 'gluːt'ən deːɐ̯ 'vɔnə fɛɐ̯'zɛŋən maen gə'baen;
Verbirg dich,   Sonne, denn die Gluten der   Wonne versengen mein Gebein;
Hide   yourself, sun,   for   the fires   of the bliss singe   my bones;
(Hide yourself, sun, for the fires of bliss are singeing my bones;)

fɛɐ̯'ʃt'ʊmət 't'ǿːnə, 'fryːlɪŋs   'ʃǿːnə   'flʏçt'ə   dɪç   ʊnt' las mɪç la'laen!
verstummet, Töne, Frühlings Schöne,   flüchte   dich   und lass mich allein!
be silent,   tones; spring's   loveliness, take to flight yourself and leave me   alone!
(be silent, tones; loveliness of spring, flee and leave me alone!)

'kʰvɪlən dɔx   ɑos   'alən 'falt'ən 'maenɐ 'zeːlə 'liːp'lɪçə gə'valt'ən,
Quillen doch aus   allen Falten meiner Seele liebliche Gewalten,
Spring   after all out of all   folds of my   soul lovely   forces,
(Lovely forces, after all, are springing forth out of all the folds of my soul,)

diː   mɪç ʊm'ʃlɪŋən, 'hɪmlɪʃ   'zɪŋən; — geː 'ʊnt'ɐ, vɛltʰ,
die   mich umschlingen, himmlisch singen; — geh unter, Welt,
which me   embrace,   celestially sing; —   go down, world,
(which embrace me, which sing celestially; — perish, world,)   ["*untergehen*" = founder, perish]

ʊnt' 'ʃt'ǿːrə 'nɪmɐ   di 'zyːsən ɛ't'eːrɪʃən 'kʰǿːrə! geː 'ʊnt'ɐ, vɛlt', geː 'ʊnt'ɐ!
und störe   nimmer die süssen ätherischen Chöre! geh unter, Welt, geh unter!
and disturb never   the sweet ethereal   choirs! Go down, world, go down!
(and never disturb the sweet ethereal choirs! Disappear, world! Disappear!)

[The suicidal poet longs ecstatically for death, for release from the world; the musician, however, feels the call of a different and more beautiful world—not death, but rather ethereal realms of art, into which his spirit is free to soar on the wings of inspiration. Let the material world disappear!]

'ɑogənliːt'
Augenlied
Eyes Song

Posthumously published [composed 1815] (poem by Johann Mayrhofer)

'zyːsə 'ɑogən, 'kʰlaːrə 'brɔnən, 'maenə kʰvaːl ʊnt' 'zeːlɪçkʰaetʰ
Süsse Augen, klare Bronnen, meine Qual   und Seligkeit
Sweet eyes,   clear   fountains, my   torment and bliss

ɪst'   fyːɐ̯'vaːr ɑos lɔɸç gə'rɔnən ʊnt' maen 'dɪçt'ən   lɔɸç   gə'vaetʰ.
ist   fürwahr aus   euch geronnen und mein Dichten   euch   geweiht.
is (has) truly   out of you   run   and my   poetry-writing to you (is) dedicated.
(have truly come flowing out of you, and my poetry is dedicated to you.)
                                                    [*GA:* **aus euch gewonnen** (gə'vɔnən, won)]
                                              [*Peters:* **mein Dichten euch entflohn** (lɔɸç lɛnt''floːn, escaped from you)]

voː lɪç ˈvaelə, voː lɪç ˈlaelə, ˈliːbənt ˈʃtˈraːlət liːɐ̯ mɪç lan,
Wo ich weile, wo ich eile, liebend strahlet ihr mich an,
Where I linger, where I hurry, lovingly beam you me at,
(Wherever I may linger, to wherever I may hurry, lovingly you beam at me,)

iːr lɛɐ̯ˈlɔøçtˈətʰ, liːɐ̯ bəˈfɔøçtˈətˈ miːɐ̯ mɪt ˈtʰrɛːnən ˈmaenə baːn.
ihr erleuchtet, ihr befeuchtet mir mit Tränen meine Bahn.
you illumine, you moisten for me with tears my path.
(you illumine my path, you moisten it with tears.)

ˈtʰrɔøə ˈʃtˈɛrnə, ˈʃvɪndət ˈnɪmɐ, ˈlaetˈət mɪç tsʊm ˈlaxerɔn!
Treue Sterne, schwindet nimmer, leitet mich zum Acheron!
Faithful stars, disappear never, lead me to the Acheron!
(Faithful stars, never disappear! Lead me to the Acheron! [i.e.: Be my guide until I die.])

ʊntˈ mɪtˈ lɔørəm ˈlɛtstˈən ˈʃɪmɐ zae maen ˈleːbən laox lɛntˈˈfloːn.
Und mit eurem letzten Schimmer sei mein Leben auch entflohn.
And with your last glimmer be my life also fled.
(And with your last glimmer may my life also end.)

[In Greek mythology, the Acheron is one of the tributaries of the river Styx in the underworld realm of the dead. Through this song the distinguished baritone Michael Vogl (1768-1840), who soon became one of the composer's best friends and champions, first became acquainted with Schubert and his lieder.]

aos ˈdie̯ːgo manaˈsares
Aus "Diego Manazares"
From *Diego Manazares*

Posthumously published [composed 1816] (poem by Franz Xaver von Schlechta)

voː lɪrst duː dʊrç ˈlaenzaːmə ˈʃatˈən deːɐ̯ naxtʰ,
Wo irrst du durch einsame Schatten der Nacht,
Where wander you through lonely shadows of the night,
(Where are you wandering through lonely shadows of the night,)
                    [*poem:* **durch einsame Schluchten** (ˈʃlʊxtˈən, ravines) **der Nacht**]

voː bɪst duː, maen ˈleːbən, maen glʏkʰ?
wo bist du, mein Leben, mein Glück?
where are you, my life, my happiness?

ʃoːn zɪnt di gəˈʃtˈɪrnə deːɐ̯ naxtˈ laos ˈtʰaoəndən ˈvɔlkˈən lɛɐ̯ˈvaxtʰ,
Schon sind die Gestirne der Nacht aus tauenden Wolken erwacht,
Already are the stars of the night out of dew-dropping clouds awakened,
(Already the stars of the night have been awakened out of dew-dropping clouds,)
                    [*poem:* **aus tauendem** (ˈtʰaoəndəm) **Dunkel** (ˈdʊŋkˈəl, darkness) **erwacht**]

ʊntˈ lax, deːɐ̯ gəˈliːpˈtˈə kʰeːɐ̯tˈ nɔx nɪçtˈ tsuˈrʏkʰ.
und ach, der Geliebte kehrt noch nicht zurück.
and ah, the beloved returns yet not back.
(and ah, my beloved has not yet come back.)

[*Diego Manazares* is the title of a play in which Ilmerine, the heroine, sang this appealing song, which does not appear in the Peters collection.]

128

ɑɔs heˈli̯oːpˈolɪs (la̯ɛns)
Aus Heliopolis (I)
From "Heliopolis" (I)

Op. 65, No. 3 [1822] (Johann Mayrhofer)

ɪm ˈkʰalt‛ən, ˈrɑ̯ɔən ˈnɔrdən lɪst‛ ˈkʰʊndə miːɐ̯ gəˈvɔrdən
Im kalten, rauhen Norden ist Kunde mir geworden
In the cold, rugged North is information to me become
(In the cold, rugged North tidings reached me)

fɔn ˈa̯ɛnɐ ʃt‛at, deːɐ̯ ˈzɔnənʃt‛atʰ. voː va̯ɛlt das ʃif, voː lɪst deːɐ̯ pfaːt‛,
von einer Stadt, der Sonnenstadt. Wo weilt das Schiff, wo ist der Pfad,
of a city, of the sun-city. Where lingers the ship, where is the path,
(of a city, of the city of the sun. Where is the ship, where is the path)
[*published poem:* **von einer Sonnenstadt... wo winkt** (vɪŋt, beckons) **der Pfad**]

diː mɪç tsu ˈjeːnən ˈhalən ˈt‛raːgən? fɔn ˈmɛnʃən kʰɔnt‛ lɪç nɪçts lɛɐ̯ˈfraːgən,
die mich zu jenen Hallen tragen? Von Menschen konnt ich nichts erfragen,
which me to those halls convey? From people could I nothing ascertain,
(which might convey me to those halls? From people I could ascertain nothing;)
[*poem:* **zu ihren** (ˈliːrən, its) **Hallen**]

ɪm ˈtsviːʃp‛alt‛ ˈvaːrən ziː fɛɐ̯ˈvɔrən, tsur ˈbluːmə, diː zɪç ˈheːli̯ɔs lɛɐ̯ˈkʰoːrən,
im Zwiespalt waren sie verworren. Zur Blume, die sich Helios erkoren,
in the dissension were they confused. To the flower which for himself Helios chosen,
(they were confused with dissension. To the flower which Helios has chosen for his own,)
[*published poem:* **in** (ɪn) **Zwiespalt waren sie verloren** (fɛɐ̯ˈloːrən, lost)]

diː ˈleːvɪç lɪn za̯ɛn ˈlant‛lɪts blɪk‛t‛, vant‛ lɪç mɪç nuːn, lʊnt‛ vart‛ lɛnt‛tsʏk‛t‛ʰː
die ewig in sein Antlitz blickt, wandt ich mich nun, und ward entzückt:
which eternally into his face looks, turned I myself now, and was enchanted:
(which eternally looks into his face, I now turned, and was enchanted:)

ˈvɛndə, zoː viː lɪç, tsur ˈzɔnə ˈda̯ɛnə ˈlɑ̯ɔgən! dɔrt‛ lɪst‛ ˈvɔnə, dɔrt‛ lɪst‛ ˈleːbən;
"Wende, so wie ich, zur Sonne deine Augen! dort ist Wonne, dort ist Leben;
"Turn, just as I, to the sun your eyes! There is rapture, there is life;
("Turn your eyes, as I do, to the sun! Rapture is there, life is there;)
[*poem:* **deine Blicke** (ˈblɪk‛ə, glances)]

t‛rɔ̯ø lɛɐ̯ˈgeːbən, ˈp‛ɪlgrə tsuː lʊnt ˈtsva̯ɛflə nɪçt‛: ˈruːə ˈfɪndəst duː lɪm lɪçt‛ʰ.
treu ergeben, pilgre zu und zweifle nicht: Ruhe findest du im Licht.
faithfully devoted, go on a pilgrimage and doubt not: peace find you in the light.
(faithfully devoted one, go on a pilgrimage and do not doubt: you shall find peace in the light.)

lɪçt‛ lɛɐ̯ˈtsɔ̯øgət‛ ˈlalə ˈgluːt‛ən, ˈhɔfnʊŋspflantsən, ˈt‛aːt‛ənfluːt‛ən!
Licht erzeuget alle Gluten, Hoffnungspflanzen, Tatenfluten!"
Light engenders all fires, hope's plants, deeds-floods!"
(Light engenders all fires, it gives life to the plants of hope and begets a flood of deeds!")

[Heliopolis means "City of the Sun." Helios (or Helius) is the Greek sun god. The sunflower was once a nymph in love with him; she always turned her face toward the sun as she followed his course through the sky. Schubert copied the words from Mayrhofer's MS, changing only one word ("*ihren*" became "*jenen*"); the published poem had other changes, indicated above.]

ɑos heˈlïoːpˈolɪs (t͡svɑe̯) / heˈlïoːpˈolɪs
Aus "Heliopolis" (II) / Heliopolis
From "Heliopolis" (II) / Heliopolis (Schubert's title)

Posthumously published [composed 1822] (poem by Johann Mayrhofer)

fɛls   lɑof ˈfɛlzən ˈhɪŋgəvɛlt͡sət', ˈfɛst'ɐ grʊnt' lʊnt ˈt'ʰrɔøɐ   halt'ʰ;
Fels   auf Felsen hingewälzet, fester Grund und treuer   Halt;
Rock on rocks hence rolled, firm   ground and trustworthy footing;
(Rocks piled onto rocks, firm ground and a secure footing;)

ˈvasɐfɛlə,   ˈvɪndəsˌʃɑoɐ(r), ˈlʊnbəgrɪfənə   gəˈvalt'ʰ —
Wasserfälle, Windesschauer, unbegriffene   Gewalt —
waterfalls,   wind- showers, uncomprehended power —

ˈɑenzaːm lɑof gəˈbɪrgəs   ˈt͡sɪnə, ˈkʰloːst'ɐ viː lɑox ˈbʊrkˈruˌiːnə:
Einsam auf Gebirges   Zinne, Kloster- wie auch Burgruine:
alone   on mountain range's pinnacle, monastery- as also castle-ruins:
(alone on the pinnacle of a mountain range, among the ruins of a monastery and a castle:)

graːp' ziː deːɐ/deːr lɛrˈlɪnrʊŋ/lɛɐ̯ˈlɪnrʊŋ lɑen! dɛn deːɐ ˈdɪçt'ɐ leːp't' fɔm   zɑen.
grab' sie der   Erinn'rung   ein! Denn der Dichter lebt vom   Sein.
engrave them the   memory   in! For the poet lives from the being.
(engrave those things in your memory! For the poet lives in the experience of Being.)

ˈaːt'mə du: den ˈhɑelgən ˈleːt'ɐ, ʃlɪŋ   di ˈlarmə lʊm   di vɛlt'ʰ;
Atme du den heil'gen Äther, schling' die Arme um   die Welt;
Breathe you the holy   ether, wind   the arms around the world;
(Inhale the holy ether, wind your arms around the world;)

nuːɐ dem ˈvʏrdɪgən,   dem ˈgroːsən ˈblɑebə ˈmuːt'ɪç   t͡sugəˈzɛlt'ʰ!
nur dem Würdigen,   dem Grossen bleibe mutig   zugesellt!
only to the worthy ones, to the great ones remain courageously joined!
(remain courageously associated only with great and worthy souls!)

[*poem:* **und** (lʊnt, and) **dem Würdigen...**]

las di ˈlɑedənʃaft'ən ˈzɑozən lɪm   meˈt'ʰalənən laˈkʰort'ʰ;
Lass die Leidenschaften sausen im   metallenen Akkord;
Let the passions   roar   in the metallic   chord;
(Let your passions roar in a ringing chord;)

vɛn   di ˈʃt'arkˈən ˈʃt'ʏrmə ˈbrɑozən, ˈfɪndəst duː das ˈrɛçt'ə vɔrt'ʰ.
wenn die starken Stürme brausen, findest du das rechte Wort.
when the strong   storms rage,   find   you the right word.
(when powerful storms are raging you will find the right words.)

[Mayrhofer and Schubert shared lodgings for a while. Their temperaments were very different: the poet unsmiling and aloof, the musician gregarious and friendly; yet they remained good friends until separated by Mayrhofer's tragic suicide. In this poem from his larger work entitled "Heliopolis" Mayrhofer expresses the exhilaration of standing on a mountain top alone with the elements and giving free vent to one's passions, an experience of being that will inspire the poet to find winged words. He seems to be encouraging his friend to find himself in the same way.]

'aːve maˈriːa / ˈɛləns ˈdrɪtˈɐ gəˈzaŋ
Ave Maria / Ellens dritter Gesang
Ave Maria / Ellen's Third Song
("Hymn to the Virgin" from Sir Walter Scott's *The Lady of the Lake*)

Op. 52, No. 4 [1825] (German translation by P. A. Storck)

'aːve maˈriːa!　　　ˈjʊŋfraʊ mɪltˈ, lɛɐ̯ˈhøːrə ˈaenɐ ˈjʊŋfraʊ ˈfleːən,
Ave Maria!　　Jungfrau mild, erhöre einer Jungfrau flehen,
Ave Maria (Hail Mary)! Virgin　mild,　hear　a　virgin's supplication,
(Hail Mary! Gentle Virgin, hear a virgin's supplication,)

laʊs ˈdiːzəm ˈfɛlzən　　ʃtˈar lʊntˈ vɪltˈ　zɔl maen gəˈbeːt tsuː diːɐ̯ ˈhɪnveːən.
aus　diesem Felsen　　starr und wild　soll mein Gebet zu dir hinwehen.
out of this　rocky place, stark and wild,　shall my　prayer　to　you waft away.
(may my prayer waft up to you from out of this stark, wild chasm.)

viːɐ ˈʃlaːfən ˈzɪçɐ bɪs tsʊm ˈmɔrgən, lɔpˈ ˈmɛnʃən　　nɔx zoː ˈgraʊzaːm zɪntˈ.
Wir schlafen sicher bis zum Morgen, ob　Menschen　　noch so grausam sind.
We sleep　safe　until to the morning,　whether human beings still　so　cruel　are.
(We shall sleep safe until the morning, no matter how cruel human beings may be.)

oː ˈjʊŋfraʊ, ziː deːɐ̯ ˈjʊŋfraʊ ˈzɔrgən,　loː ˈmʊtˈɐ, høːɐ̯/høːr laen ˈbɪtˈəntˈ kʰɪntˈ!
O Jungfrau, sieh der Jungfrau Sorgen,　o Mutter, hör　ein bittend Kind!
O Virgin,　see the virgin's anxieties, O Mother, hear　a　pleading child!

aːve maˈriːa! lʊnbəflɛkˈtʰ!　vɛn　viːɐ̯/viːr laʊf ˈdiːzən fɛls ˈhɪnzɪŋkˈən
Ave Maria! unbefleckt! Wenn wir　auf diesen Fels hinsinken
Ave Maria! immaculate! When we　upon this　rock sink down
(Ave Maria! immaculate! When we sink down upon this rock)

tsʊm ʃlaːf, lʊntˈ lʊns daen ʃuts　bəˈdɛkˈtʰ. vɪrtˈ vaeç deːɐ̯ ˈhartˈə fɛls lʊns ˈdʏŋkˈən.
zum Schlaf, und uns dein Schutz　bedeckt, wird weich der　harte Fels uns dünken.
to the sleep, and us　your protection covers,　will soft　the　hard rock to us seem.
(to sleep, and your protection covers us, the hard stone will seem soft to us.)

du ˈlɛçəlstˈ, ˈroːzəndʏftˈə　ˈveːən lɪn ˈdiːzɐ ˈdʊmpfən ˈfɛlzənkʰlʊftʰ.
Du lächelst, Rosendüfte　wehen in dieser dumpfen Felsenkluft.
You smile,　rose-fragrances waft　in this　gloomy　ravine.
(You smile, and the fragrance of roses wafts through this gloomy ravine.)

oː ˈmʊtˈɐ, ˈhøːrə ˈkʰɪndəs ˈfleːən,　　oː ˈjʊŋfraʊ, ˈlaenə ˈjʊŋfraʊ ruːftʰ!
O Mutter, höre Kindes Flehen,　　o Jungfrau, eine Jungfrau ruft!
O Mother, hear child's supplication, O Virgin,　a　virgin　calls!
(O Mother, hear the supplication of your child, O Virgin, a virgin is calling to you!)

aːve maˈriːa! ˈraenə maːkˈtˈ!　deːɐ̯/deːr ˈleːɐ̯də lʊntˈ deːɐ̯ lʊft dɛˈmoːnən.
Ave Maria! Reine Magd!　Der　Erde und der Luft Dämonen,
Ave Maria! Pure　maiden! The　earth's and the air's demons,
(Ave Maria! Pure maiden! The demons of the earth and of the air,)

fɔn ˈdaenəs ˈlaogəs hʊlt‘ fɛɐ̯ˈjaːk‘tʰ, ziː ˈkʰœnən hiːɐ̯ nɪçt‘ bae lʊns ˈvoːnən.
von deines Auges Huld verjagt, sie können hier nicht bei uns wohnen.
by your eye's graciousness chased away, they can here not with us dwell.
(driven away by the graciousness of your eyes, they cannot dwell with us here.)

viːɐ̯ vɔln lʊns ʃt‘ɪl dem ˈʃik‘zaːl ˈbɔɶ̯gən, daː lʊns daen ˈhaelgɐ tʰroːst‘ ˈlanveːtʰ ;
Wir wolln uns still dem Schicksal beugen, da uns dein heilger Trost anweht;
We want ourselves quietly to the destiny to bow, since us your holy comfort wafts to;
(We want quietly to submit to destiny, since your holy comfort is wafting toward us;)

deːɐ̯ ˈjʊɲfrao ˈvɔlə hɔlt dɪç ˈnaegən,
der Jungfrau wolle hold dich neigen,
to the virgin be willing graciously yourself to incline,
(may you be willing graciously to incline your ear to a virgin,)

dem kʰɪnt, das fyːɐ̯ den ˈfaːt‘ɐ fleːtʰ! ˈaːve maˈriːa!
dem Kind, das für den Vater fleht! Ave Maria!
to the child, who for the father pleads! Ave Maria!
(to a child who is pleading for her father! Ave Maria!)

[It may come as a surprise to many that this song is *not* a setting of the famous Latin prayer, although those words have often been twisted and stretched to fit this famous melody. Here are the original words from *The Lady of the Lake* by Sir Walter Scott:

Ave Maria! maiden mild! / Listen to a maiden's prayer!
Thou canst hear though from the wild, / Thou canst save amid despair.
Safe may we sleep beneath thy care, / Though banish'd, outcast, and reviled--
Maiden! hear a maiden's prayer; / Mother, hear a suppliant child!
Ave Maria!

Ave Maria! undefiled! / The flinty couch we now must share
Shall seem with down of eider piled, / If thy protection hover there.
The murky cavern's heavy air / Shall breathe of balm if thou hast smiled;
Then, Maiden! hear a maiden's prayer; / Mother, list a suppliant child!
Ave Maria!

Ave Maria! stainless styled! / Foul demons of the earth and air,
From this their wonted haunt exiled, / Shall flee before thy presence fair.
We bow us to our lot of care, / Beneath thy guidance reconciled;
Hear for a maid a maiden's prayer, / And for a father hear a child!
Ave Maria!

Ellen's father, Lord Douglas, has been banished by the king. They have taken refuge in a cave in the mountains near Loch Katrine. Her "Hymn to the Virgin" is preceded by these lines:

But hark! what mingles in the strain? / It is the harp of Allan-bane,
That wakes its measure slow and high, / Attuned to sacred minstrelsy.
What melting voice attends the strings? / 'Tis Ellen, or an angel, sings.
(from Canto III, XXVIII)]

baˈlaːdə / aen ˈfrɔølaen ʃɑot fɔm ˈhoːən tʰʊrm
Ballade / "Ein Fräulein schaut vom hohen Turm"
Ballad / "A Damsel Looks Out from the High Tower"

Op. 126 [1825] (Joseph Kenner)

aen ˈfrɔølaen ʃɑot fɔm   ˈhoːən tʰʊrm   das ˈvaetˈɐ meːɐ̯ zoː baŋ;
Ein Fräulein schaut vom   hohen Turm   das weite Meer so bang;
A damsel looks from the high tower (at) the broad sea so anxiously;
(A damsel is looking out so anxiously at the broad sea from the high tower;)

tsʊm ˈtʰrɑoɐ̯ʃveːrən   ˈtsɪtˈɐʃlaːkˈ halt   ˈdyːstˈɐ(r)   liːɐ̯ gəˈzaŋ :
zum trauerschweren Zitherschlag hallt   düster   ihr Gesang:
to the grief- heavy   zither-beat   resounds mournfully her song:
(her song resounds mournfully to the accompaniment of the zither:)

mɪç ˈhaltˈən ʃlɔs   lʊntˈ ˈriːgəl fɛstʰ, maen ˈrɛtˈɐ vaeltˈ zoː laŋ.
"Mich halten Schloss und Riegel fest, mein Retter weilt so lang."
"Me hold lock   and bolt fast, my rescuer tarries so long."
("I am held captive under lock and bolt; my rescuer tarries so long!")

zae voːl gəˈtʰroːst, duː ˈleːdlə maetˈ ! ʃɑo, ˈhɪntɐm ˈkʰraedənʃtˈaen
Sei wohl getrost,   du edle Maid! Schau, hinterm Kreidenstein
Be well comforted, you noble maiden! Look, behind the chalk- stone

tʰraeptˈ ɪn deːɐ̯ ˈbʊxtˈʊŋ   ˈdʊŋkˈəlhaetˈ laen ˈkʰriːksboːtˈ hɛˈraen :
treibt in der Buchtung Dunkelheit ein Kriegsboot herein:
drifts in the bay's   darkness   a warship   into:
(a warship is drifting into the darkness of the bay:)

deːɐ̯/deːr ˈlaːrənbʊʃ,   deːɐ̯ ˈroːzənʃɪltˈ—   das lɪst deːɐ̯ ˈrɛtˈɐ daen!
der   Aarenbusch, der Rosenschild —   das ist der Retter dein!
the   eagle- crest, the rose- escutcheon — that is the rescuer yours!
(the eagle-crest, the roses on the coat of arms — that is your rescuer!)

ʃoːn   ruːft dɛs ˈhuːnən hɔrn tsʊm ʃtˈraetˈ hɪˈnapˈ tsʊm ˈmʊʃəlraen.
Schon   ruft des Hunen Horn zum Streit hinab zum Muschelrain.
Already calls the giant's horn to the fight   down to the shell- border
["*Hune*" = archaic form of *Hüne* = giant; "*Muschelrain*" = line of shells washed up by the sea]
(Already the giant's horn sounds the summons to a fight down by the sea.)

vɪlˈkʰɔmən,   ˈʃmʊkˈɐ   ˈkʰnaːbə, miːɐ̯, bɪst duː tsu: ˈʃtˈɛlə ˈkʰɔmən?   [ˈkʰʊmən]
"Willkommen, schmucker Knabe, mir, bist du zu Stelle kommen?   [*GA:* kummen]
"Welcome,   pretty   boy,   to me; are you to place come?   [come]
("Welcome, pretty boy! Have you come to take a stand here?)

[*poem:* **zur** (tsʊr) **Stelle kummen**]

gaːɐ̯ baltˈ fɔm   ˈʃvartsən ˈʃɪldə diːɐ̯   hɑo lɪç di ˈgɔldnən ˈbluːmən.
Gar bald vom   schwarzen Schilde dir   hau' ich die goldnen Blumen.
Very soon from the black   shield for you hew I   the golden flowers.
(Very soon I shall hack those golden flowers off your black shield.)

di ˈaxtseːn ˈbluːmən, ˈbluːtˈbətʰaɔtˈ, leːs ˈdaenə ˈkʰøːnɪkˈlɪçə braɔtˈ laɔf
Die achtzehn Blumen, blutbetaut, les' deine königliche Braut auf
The eighteen flowers, blood-bedewed, gather your royal bride up
(Let your royal bride gather up the eighteen flowers, bedewed with blood,)

laɔs dem zant deːɐ̯ ˈvoːgən, nuːɐ̯ flɪŋkˈ di veːɐ̯ gəˈtsoːgən!
aus dem Sand der Wogen, nur flink die Wehr gezogen!"
out of the sand of the waves, only quickly the weapon drawn!"
(out of the sand of the waves; but let your weapon be drawn quickly and nimbly!")

tsom tʰʊrm laɔf ʃalt das ˈʃveːɐ̯tˈgəkʰlɪr! viː hart di braɔtˈ zoː baŋ!
Zum Turm auf schallt das Schwertgeklirr! wie harrt die Braut so bang!
To the tower up resounds the sword- clanging! How waits the bride so anxiously!
(The clanging of swords resounds up to the tower! How anxiously the bride is waiting!)

deːɐ̯ kʰampf drøːntˈ laɔt dʊrçs ˈvaltˈreˌviːɐ̯, zoː ˈheftˈɪç ʊntˈ zoː laŋ.
der Kampf dröhnt laut durchs Waldrevier, so heftig und so lang.
The battle roars loudly through the forest preserve, so fiercely and so long.

ʊntˈ ˈɛntˈlɪç, ˈɛntˈlɪç dɔø̯çtˈ les liːɐ̯/liːr, lɛɐ̯ˈʃtˈɪrptˈ deːɐ̯ ˈhiːbə kʰlaŋ.
Und endlich, endlich däucht es ihr, erstirbt der Hiebe Klang.
And finally, finally seemed it to her, died away the blows' sound.
(And finally, finally it seemed to her that the sound of the blows had died away.)

ɛs kʰraxt das ʃlɔs, di tʰyːɐ̯ kʰlaftˈ laɔf, diː ˈliːrən ziːtˈ ziː ˈviːdɐ —
Es kracht das Schloss, die Tür klafft auf, die Ihren sieht sie wieder —
It makes a loud noise the lock, the door flies open, the hers sees she again —
(The lock makes a loud noise, the door flies open, she sees her own people again —)

ziː laeltˈ ɪm ˈlaːtˈəmloːzən laɔf tsom ˈmʊʃəlplaːnə ˈniːdɐ,
sie eilt im atemlosen Lauf zum Muschelplane nieder.
she rushes in the breathless run to the shell- plain down.
(she runs in breathless haste down to the battlefield among the shells.)

daː liːktˈ deːɐ̯ ˈpʰaenɪgɐ tsɛɐ̯ˈʃɛltʰ. — dɔx veː, dɪçtˈ ˈneːbən ˈniːdɐ,
Da liegt der Peiniger zerschellt. — doch weh, dicht neben nieder,
There lies the tormentor shattered. — But woe! close beside down,
(There lies the tormentor, dead. — But—alas!—close beside him on the ground)

ax! ˈdɛkˈən s ˈbluːtˈbəʃpˈrɪtstˈə fɛlt dɛs ˈretˈɐs ˈblasə ˈgliːdɐ.
ach! decken 's blutbespritzte Feld des Retters blasse Glieder.
ah! cover the blood-sprinkled field the rescuer's pale limbs.
(ah! the rescuer's pale limbs cover the blood-sprinkled field.)

ʃtˈɪl ˈzaməltˈ ziː di ˈroːzən laɔf lɪn ˈliːrən ˈkʰɔøʃən ʃoːs
Still sammelt sie die Rosen auf in ihren keuschen Schoss
Quietly gathers she the roses up into her chaste lap
(Quietly she gathers the roses up onto her chaste lap)

ʊntˈ ˈbɛtˈətˈ ˈliːrən ˈliːbən draɔf; laen ˈtʰrɛːnçən ʃtˈiːltˈ zɪç loːs,
und bettet ihren Lieben drauf; ein Tränchen stiehlt sich los,
and beds her love upon it; a little tear steals itself free,
(and makes a bed for her love upon it; a little tear steals away from her eyelid,)

ʊnt tʰɑot di ˈbrɑetʰən ˈvʊndən lan, lʊntʰ zaːkʰtʰ : lɪç, lɪç haːpʰ das gəˈtʰaːn!
und taut   die breiten Wunden an, und sagt: ich, ich hab das getan!
and bedews the broad   wounds ... , and says: I, I   have that done!
(and bedews the gaping wounds, and says: "I, I have done this!")

daː fras   lɛs ˈlaenən ˈʃantʰgəzɛl des ˈrɑobəs lɪm gəˈmyːtʰ,   [ˈlaenəm]
Da frass   es einen Schandgesell des Raubes im Gemüt, [*poem:* einem]
Then ate [as animals do] it a   shame- partner of the robbery in the mind,
(Then the thought ate into the mind of one of the infamous partners in the robbery)

das diː, diː ˈzaenən hɛrn fɛɐ̯ˈdarpʰ, frae naːx deːɐ̯ ˈhaemaːt tsiːtʰ.
dass die, die seinen Herrn verdarb, frei nach der Heimat   zieht.
that she, who his   lord   ruined,   freely toward the homeland goes.
(that she who brought ruin to his lord is free to return to her homeland.)

fɔm bʊʃ, voː   leːɐ̯ fɛɐ̯ˈkʰrɔxən laːkʰ lɪn ˈvɪldɐ ˈtʰoːdəslʊstʰ,
Vom   Busch, wo   er verkrochen lag in wilder Todeslust,
From the bush   where he hidden   lay in wild   death- lust,
(From the bush where he lay hidden, in a wild lust for blood,)

pfaeftʰ ʃnɛl   zaen ˈbɔltsən   dʊrç di lʊftʰ, lɪn ˈliːrə ˈkʰɔ̈øʃə brʊstʰ.
pfeift   schnell sein Bolzen   durch die Luft, in ihre keusche Brust.
whistles quickly his   crossbow arrow through the air   into her chaste   breast.
(an arrow from his crossbow whistles quickly through the air into her chaste breast.)

daː vartʰ liːɐ̯ voːl lɪm ˈbrɑotʰgəˌmax, lɪm ˈkʰiːsgrʊntʰ, ʃtʰɪl lʊntʰ kʰlaen;
Da ward ihr wohl im Brautgemach, im   Kiesgrund, still und klein;
Then became for her surely in the bridal chamber, in the gravelly soil, quiet and small;
(Then all surely became quiet and small for her in her bridal chamber in the gravelly soil;)

ziː ˈzɛŋkʰtʰən ziː dem ˈliːbən naːx,   dɔrtʰ ˈlʊntɐ(r) ˈlaenəm ʃtʰaen,   [ˈlaenən]
sie senkten sie dem Lieben nach,   dort unter   einem Stein,   [*GA:* einen]
they lowered her the dear one following, there under   one   stone,
(they buried her beside her dear one, there, under one stone,)

deːn liːɐ̯ fɔn ˈdɪstʰəln ˈlyːbɐveːtʰ,   nɔx neːçst des ˈtʰʊrməs ˈtʰrʏmɐn   zeːtʰ.
den ihr von Disteln überweht,   noch nächst des Turmes Trümmern seht.
which you by thistles over-fluttered still next to the tower's ruins   see.
(which you can still see next to the ruins of the tower, with thistles fluttering over it.)

[The Breitkopf & Härtel edition gives the song the title "Ballade"; the Peters edition identifies the song by its first line.]

bae dem ˈgraːbə ˈmaenəs ˈfaːtʰɐs
Bei dem Grabe meines Vaters
At My Father's Grave

Posthumously published [composed 1816] (poem by Matthias Claudius)

ˈfriːdə zae lʊm   ˈdiːzən ˈgraːpʰ ʃtʰaen heːɐ̯!   ˈzanftʰɐ ˈfriːdə ˈgɔtʰəs!
Friede sei um   diesen Grabstein her!   sanfter Friede Gottes!
Peace be around this   gravestone on all sides! gentle peace of God!
(Peace be all around this gravestone, the gentle peace of God!)

ax, zi: 'ha:bən 'laenən 'gu:t'ən man bə'gra:bən, ʊnt' mi:ɐ̯ va:ɐ̯/va:r le:ɐ̯ me:ɐ̯;
Ach, sie haben einen guten Mann begraben, und mir war   er mehr;
Ah, they have a   good man buried,   and to me was   he more;
(Ah, they have buried a good man, and to me he was even more than that;)

'tʰrɔøft'ə mi:ɐ̯ fɔn 'se:gən, 'di:zɐ man, vi: laen ʃt'ɛrn lɑos 'bɛsɐn 'vɛlt'ən!
träufte mir   von Segen,   dieser Mann, wie ein Stern aus bessern Welten!
dripped for me with blessings, this man, like a star from better   worlds!
(that man showered me with blessings, like a star from another, better world!)

[poem: wie ein milder ('mɪldɐ, gentle) Stern]

ʊnt' lɪç kʰans li:m   nɪçt' fɛɐ̯'gɛlt'ən, vas le:ɐ̯ mi:ɐ̯   gə'tʰa:n.
und ich kann's ihm   nicht vergelten, was er mir   getan.
and I can it to him not repay,   what he for me (has) done.
(And I cannot repay him for that which he has done for me.)

e:ɐ̯/e:r lɛnt''ʃli:f;   zi: 'gru:bən li:n hi:ɐ̯/hi:r laen. 'laezɐ, 'zy:sɐ tʰro:st' fɔn gɔtʰ,
Er   entschlief; sie gruben ihn hier ein. Leiser, süsser Trost   von Gott,
He   passed away; they buried him here in. Quiet, sweet comfort from God,
(He passed away; they buried him here. Quiet, sweet comfort from God,)

[poem: von Gott gegeben (gə'ge:bən, given)]

ʊnt' laen 'la:ndən   fɔn dem 'e:vgən 'le:bən dyft'   lʊm zaen gə'baen!
und ein Ahnden   von dem ew'gen Leben düft'   um sein Gebein!
and a   presentiment of the eternal life be fragrant about his bones!

bɪs li:n 'je:zʊs 'kʰrɪstʊs, gro:s lʊnt' he:ɐ̯, 'frɔøntlɪç vɪrt' lɛɐ̯'vɛk'ən, lax, zi: 'ha:bən
Bis ihn Jesus Christus, gross und hehr,   freundlich wird erwecken, ach, sie haben
Until him Jesus Christ,   great and exalted, friendlily will awaken,   ah, they have
(Until Jesus Christ, great and exalted, will awaken him with kindliness, ah, they have)

li:n bə'gra:bən! 'laenən 'gu:t'ən man bə'gra:bən, lʊnt' mi:ɐ̯ va:ɐ̯/va:r le:ɐ̯ me:ɐ̯.
ihn begraben! einen guten Mann begraben, und mir war   er mehr.
him buried!   a   good   man buried,   and to me was   he more.
(buried him, a good man! And to me he was even more than that.)

[poem: without "ihn begraben!"]

[Matthias Claudius (1740-1815) strove to use simple, natural language in his poetry, in reaction
against the flowery style of some of his contemporaries. Schubert set eleven of his poems to
music, several of them expressing the poet's heartfelt religious sentiments.]

bae di:ɐ̯ la'laen / bae di:ɐ̯!
Bei dir allein / Bei Dir!
With You Alone / With You!

Op. 95, No. 2 [1826] (Johann Gabriel Seidl)

bae di:ɐ̯/di:r la'laen lɛm'pfɪnt' lɪç, das lɪç 'le:bə, das 'ju:gənt'mu:t'   mɪç ʃvɛltʰ,
Bei dir   allein empfind ich, dass ich lebe, dass Jugendmut   mich schwellt,
With you   alone feel   I   that I live,   that youth- courage me swells,
(Only with you do I feel that I am alive, that the courage of youth is swelling my breast,)

das ˈlaenə ˈhaetˈrə vɛlt deːɐ̯ ˈliːbə mɪç dʊrçˈbeːbə;
dass eine heitre Welt der Liebe mich durchbebe;
that a serene world of the love me through-tremble;
(that a serene world of love may tremble through me;)

mɪç frɔøtˈ maen zaen bae diːɐ̯/diːr laˈlaen! bae diːɐ̯/diːr laˈlaen
mich freut mein Sein bei dir allein! Bei dir allein
me gladdens my being with you alone! With you alone
(my existence makes me glad only when I am with you! Only with you)

veːtˈ miːɐ̯ di lʊftˈ zoː ˈlaːbəntʰ, dʏŋkˈtˈ mɪç di fluːɐ̯ zoː gryːn,
weht mir die Luft so labend, dünkt mich die Flur so grün,
blows for me the air so soothingly, seems (to) me the meadow so green,
(does the air blow so soothingly, does the meadow seem so green,)

zoː mɪlt dɛs ˈlɛntsəs blyːn, zoː ˈbalzaːmraeç deːɐ̯/deːr ˈlaːbəntˈ,
so mild des Lenzes Blühn, so balsamreich der Abend,
so mild the spring's blooming, so balm- rich the evening,
(The bloom of spring so mild, the evening so balmy,)

zoː kʰyːl deːɐ̯ haen, bae diːɐ̯/diːr laˈlaen! bae diːɐ̯/diːr laˈlaen
so kühl der Hain, bei dir allein! Bei dir allein
so cool the grove, with you alone! With you alone
(the grove so cool, only with you! Only with you)

fɛɐ̯ˈliːɐ̯t deːɐ̯ ʃmɛrts zaen ˈhɛrbəs, gəˈvɪnt di frɔøtˈ lan lʊst!
verliert der Schmerz sein Herbes, gewinnt die Freud' an Lust!
loses the pain its bitterness, gains the joy in pleasure!
(does pain lose its bitterness and joy gain in pleasure!)

duː ˈzɪçɐ̯stˈ ˈmaenə brʊst dɛs ˈlangəʃtˈamtˈən ˈlɛrbəs;
Du sicherst meine Brust des angestammten Erbes;
You guarantee my breast of the innate inheritance;
(You guarantee my breast its innate inheritance;)

lɪç fyːl mɪç maen bae diːɐ̯/diːr laˈlaen!
ich fühl mich mein bei dir allein!
I feel myself mine with you alone!
(I feel myself mine only with you!)

[An exuberant, heartfelt declaration of love! The Breitkopf & Härtel title is given first, above.]

baem ˈvɪndə
Beim Winde
When the Wind Blows

Posthumously published [composed 1819] (poem by Johann Mayrhofer)

ɛs ˈtʰrɔømən di ˈvɔlkˈən, di ˈʃtˈɛrnə, deːɐ̯ moːntˈ,
Es träumen die Wolken, die Sterne, der Mond,
There dream the clouds, the stars, the moon,
(The clouds, the stars, the moon are dreaming,)

di ˈbɔømə, di ˈføːɡəl, di ˈbluːmən, deːɐ̯ ʃtˈroːm.
die Bäume, die Vögel, die Blumen, Der Strom.
the trees,   the birds,   the flowers,   the river.
(the trees, the birds, the flowers, the river are dreaming.)

zi: ˈviːɡən lʊntˈ ʃmiːɡən zɪç   tʰiːfɐ   tsuˈrʏkʰ,
Sie wiegen und schmiegen sich   tiefer   zurück,
They lull   and nestle down themselves more deeply back,
(They lull themselves to sleep and nestle down more deeply,)

tsuːɐ̯ ˈruːɡən ˈʃtˈɛtˈə, tsʊm ˈtʰɑɔɪɡən ˈbɛtˈə, tsʊm ˈhaemlɪçən ɡlʏkʰ.
zur ruhigen Stätte, zum tauigen Bette, zum   heimlichen Glück.
to the quiet   place,   to the dewy   bed,   to the secret   happiness.
(having gone back to their quiet place, to their dewy bed, to their secret happiness.)

[*poem:* **zum tauigen Better, zur ruhigen Stätte**]

dɔx ˈblɛtˈɐɡəzɔøzəl lʊntˈ ˈvɛləngəkʰrɔøzəl fɛɐ̯kʰʏndən lɛɐ̯vaxən.
Doch Blättergesäusel und Wellengekräusel verkünden Erwachen.
But leave- rustling and wave-   ruffling announce   awakening.
(But the rustling of the leaves and the ruffling of the waves announce an awakening.)

dɛn ˈleːvɪç   ɡəˈʃvɪndə,   ˈlʊnruːɡə ˈvɪndə, zi: ˈʃtˈøːrən, zi: ˈfaxən.   [ˈʃtˈøːnən]
Denn ewig   geschwinde, unruhige Winde, sie   stören, sie   fachen. [*GA:* **sie stöhnen**]
For   eternally fast,   restless   winds, they disturb, they fan.   [moan]

[*poem:* **sie stören und** (lʊntˈ, and) **fachen**]

eːɐ̯stˈ ˈʃmaeçəlndə ˈreːɡʊŋ,   dan ˈvɪldə bəˈveːɡʊŋ;
Erst schmeichelnde Regung, dann wilde Bewegung;
First flattering   stirring,   then wild   motion;
(First a pleasant stirring, then a wild agitation;)

ʊnt ˈdeːnəndə ˈrɔømə fɛɐ̯ˈʃlɪŋən   di ˈtʰrɔømə.
und dehnende Räume verschlingen die Träume.
and expanding spaces swallow up   the dreams.

ɪm ˈbuːzən, ɪm   ˈraenən,   bəˈvaːrə di daenən; lɛs ˈʃtˈrøːmə daen bluːtʰ:
Im   Busen, im   reinen,   bewahre die deinen; es ströme dein blut:
In the bosom, in the pure one, preserve the yours;   it   stream   your blood:
(Preserve your dreams in your pure bosom; may your blood rush through your veins)

foːɐ̯ ˈraːzəndən ˈʃtˈʏrmən bəˈzɔnən tsuː ˈʃɪrmən   di ˈhaelɪɡə gluːtʰ.
vor rasenden Stürmen besonnen zu   schirmen die heilige Glut.
from raging   storms   prudently to   shield   the holy   fire.
(prudently to shield the sacred fire from raging storms.)

[Schubert repeats the four opening lines at the end of the song, in a music that more than once recalls the next to last song in *Die schöne Müllerin*. The singer must be careful to tie the word "*besonnen*" meaningfully—and expressively—to the rest of the line, past the *fermata,* the rest, and the double bar.]

138

'bɛrt'as liːt' ɪn deːɐ̯ naxtʰ
Berthas Lied in der Nacht
Bertha's Song in the Night

Posthumously published [composed 1819] (poem by Franz Grillparzer)

naxt' ʊmˈhʏlt' mɪt' ˈveːəndəm ˈflyːɡəl ˈtʰɛːlɐ(r) ʊnt' ˈhyːɡəl ˈlaːdənt t͡suːɐ̯ ruː.
Nacht umhüllt mit wehendem Flügel Täler   und Hügel ladend   zur Ruh.
Night veils   with fluttering   wing   valleys and   hills   invitingly to the rest.
(With fluttering wings Night veils the valleys and the hills, inviting them to their rest.)
                    [*in Schubert's repetition:* **umhüllet die** (ʊmˈhʏlət di, veils the) **Täler**]

ʊnt dem ˈʃlʊmɐ,   dem ˈliːp'lɪçən ˈkʰɪndə, ˈlaɛzə ʊnt' ˈlɪndə ˈflʏst'ɐt' ziː t͡suː:
Und dem Schlummer, dem lieblichen Kinde, leise und linde flüstert sie zu:
And to the sleep,   to the lovely   child,   softly and gently whispers she to:
(And to Sleep, that lovely child, she softly and gently whispers:)

vaɛst du: laɛn ˈlaʊɡə ˈvaxənt' ɪm ˈkʰʊmɐ, ˈliːp'lɪçɐ ˈʃlʊmɐ,
"Weisst du ein Auge wachend im   Kummer, lieblicher Schlummer,
 "Know   you an   eye   waking   in the worry,   lovely   Sleep,
("If you know of eyes that are awake with worry, dear Sleep,)

ˈdrʏk'ə miːɐ̯s t͡suː.   fyːlst du: zaɛn ˈnaːən, ˈlaːnəst du: ruː?
drücke mir's   zu."   Fühlst du sein Nahen, ahnest du Ruh?
press   for me it closed." Feel   you his   nearing, surmise you rest?
(close them for me." Do you feel Sleep nearing? Do you have a presentiment of rest?)

ˈaləs,   ˈlaləs   dɛk't deːɐ̯ ˈʃlʊmɐ, ˈʃlʊmrə, zo: ˈʃlʊmrə laox du:.
Alles,   alles   deckt der Schlummer, schlummre, so schlummre auch du.
Everything, everything covers the sleep,   sleep,   so sleep   also you.
(Sleep covers everything, everything; so sleep, you too, so sleep.)
                    [*poem:* **Alles deckt Schlummer, schlummre auch du.**]

[Grillparzer is considered the greatest Austrian poet of his era. He was one of Schubert's
friends, but this is Schubert's only setting of a Grillparzer poem. It seems to have been intended
for inclusion in a play, *Die Ahnfrau* ("The Ancestress"), but was not printed with the script.]

'blaŋk'a (das ˈmɛːt'çən)
Blanka (Das Mädchen)
Blanka (The Girl)

Posthumously published [composed 1818] (poem by Friedrich von Schlegel)

vɛn mɪç ˈlaɛnzaːm ˈlʏft'ə ˈfɛçəln, mʊs lɪç ˈlɛçəln,
Wenn mich einsam   Lüfte   fächeln, muss ich lächeln,
If   me lonesomely breezes fan,   must I smile,
(If, when I am lonesome, breezes fan me, I have to smile,)

viː lɪç ˈkʰɪndɪʃ ˈtɛndəlnt' ˈkʰoːzə mɪt deːɐ̯ ˈroːzə.
wie ich kindisch   tändelnd kose mit der Rose.
as I   childlikely dallying fondle with the rose.
(as I, childlike, play with the rose, dallying, caressing it.)

'vɛːrən nɪçt di 'nɔ͜øən 'ʃmɛrtsən, mœçt‘ lɪç 'ʃɛrtsən;
Wären nicht die neuen Schmerzen, möcht   ich scherzen;
Were not the new pains,   would like I to jest;
(Were it not for the new pains I am feeling, I would like to have fun;)

kʰœnt‘ lɪç, vas lɪç 'laːndə, 'zaːgən, vʏrd ɪç 'kʰlaːgən, [*"ahnden"* (in obsolete sense) = *"ahnen"*]
könnt ich, was ich ahnde, sagen, würd ich klagen,
could I, what I sense, say,   would I complain,
(If I could say what I am sensing I would complain)

ʊnt‘ lɑͨox 'baŋə 'hɔfənt‘ 'fraːgən: vas fɛ͜ɐ̯'kʰʏndən 'mɑ͜enə 'loːzə?
und auch bange hoffend fragen: Was verkünden meine Loose?   [*Schubert & P.:* **auch**]
and also anxious hopingly ask: "What foretell   my   fortunes?"
(and, anxiously hoping, ask: "What does my fortune foretell?")
     [*GA & poem:* **und euch** (lɔ͜øç, you) **bange hoffend fragen** (and, anxiously hoping, ask you:)]

'tʰɛndlɪç glɑ͜eç   mɪt‘ ʃɛrts lʊnt‘ 'roːzə, mʊs lɪç 'lɛçəlnt 'dɛnɔx   'kʰlaːgən.
Tändl' ich gleich   mit Scherz und Rose, muss ich lächelnd dennoch   klagen.
Dally I right now with jest and rose, must I smilingly nevertheless complain.
(Though I may dally right now with jests and roses, I nevertheless, smiling, must complain.)

[Schubert's very young girl hovers charmingly between jests and complaints in lovely,
alternating major and minor harmonies.]

blõ'dɛl t͜su: ma'riːən
Blondel zu Marien
Blondel to Mary

Posthumously published [composed 1818] (poet unknown)

ɪn 'dyːst‘rɐ naxt‘, vɛn graːm mɑ͜en 'fyːlənt‘ hɛrts lʊm't͜siːət͹,
In düstrer Nacht, wenn Gram mein fühlend Herz umziehet,
In gloomy night, when grief my   feeling   heart envelops,
(In gloomy nights, when grief envelops my sensitive heart,)

dɛs 'glʏk‘əs   'zɔnə miːɐ̯/miːr lɛnt‘'vɑ͜eçt‘ lʊnt‘ 'liːrə praxt͹;   [lɛnt‘'fliːət‘]
des Glückes   Sonne mir   entweicht und ihre Pracht;   [*poem:* **mir   entfliehet**]
the happiness's sun   for me   vanishes and its splendor;   [from me flees]
(the sun of happiness and its splendor vanish for me;)

da: 'lɔ͜øçt‘ət‘ fɛrn   lɪn 'fɔ͜ørɪç 'vɔnɪk‘lɪçəm 'glantsə
da leuchtet fern   in feurig wonniglichem Glanze
then shines in the distance in fiery wondrous   luster
(then, in the distance, in fiery wondrous luster, there shines)

viː lɪn deːɐ̯ 'liːbə 'ʃt‘raːlənkʰrant͜sə lɑ͜en 'hɔldɐ ʃtɛrn.
wie in der Liebe Strahlenkranze ein holder Stern.
as in the love's rays- wreath a   lovely star.
(a lovely star, as if wreathed with rays of love.)

ʊnt‘ 'leːvɪç   rɑ͜en leːp‘t‘ 'lʊnt‘ɐ 'vɔnə, 'lʊnt‘ɐ 'ʃmɛrtsən,
Und ewig   rein lebt   unter Wonne, unter Schmerzen,
And eternally pure lives under rapture, under pains,
(And, whether I am subject to rapture or to pain, its reflection, eternally pure, lives)

ɪm   'fraeən 'liːbəfɔlən 'hɛrtsən zaen 'viːdɐʃaen,   ['tʰrɔɸən]
im   freien liebevollen Herzen sein Wiederschein, [*poem:* **im treuen liebevollen Herzen**]
in the free love-full heart its reflection,   [faithful]
(in the free, loving heart, its reflection,)   [*poem:* **sein Wiederschein.** (period)]

zoː hɔlt' ʊnt' mɪlt'; vɪrt' 'ʊnt'ɐ 'tʰrøːst'əndən gə'ʃt'alt'ən
so hold und mild; wird unter tröstenden Gestalten [*poem:* **So hold und mild wird...**]
so lovely and mild; will under comforting forms
(so lovely and mild; in comforting forms,)

aox ɪn deːɐ 'fɛrnə mɪç ʊm'valt'ən   daen 'tsaobɐbɪlt'.
auch in der Ferne mich umwalten   dein Zauberbild.
even in the distance me around-hold sway your magic image.
(even in foreign lands, your magical image will hold sway all around me.)

[In one of the many legends that surround King Richard I of England, "the Lionhearted," Blondel de Nesle, a troubadour, went from castle to castle in search of his captured king, singing under tower windows the beginning of a song they both knew well and hoping to hear his friend's voice finish the melody. It is sometimes assumed that the embellishments of the vocal line of Schubert's song, uncharacteristic of his serious style, were added—or recommended to him—by the singer Michael Vogl, who befriended the composer and helped to popularize his songs.]

'bluːmənliːt'
Blumenlied
Flower Song

Posthumously published [composed 1816] (poem by Ludwig Hölty)

ɛs ɪst' aen 'halbəs 'hɪməlraeç,   vɛn, pʰara'diːzəsbluːmən glaeç,
Es ist ein halbes Himmelreich,   wenn, Paradiesesblumen gleich,
It is a half heavenly kingdom, when, Paradise- flowers like,
(It is like seeing half of heaven when, like flowers from Paradise,)

aos kʰleː di 'bluːmən 'drɪŋən; ʊnt' vɛn di 'føːgəl
aus Klee die Blumen dringen; und wenn die Vögel
out of clover the flowers press; and when the birds
(the flowers spring up from the clover; and when the birds)

'zɪlbɐhɛl ɪm 'gart'ən hiːɐ/hiːr, ʊnt dort' lam kʰvɛl, aof 'blyːt'ənbɔɸmən 'zɪŋən.
silberhell im Garten hier, und dort am Quell, auf Blütenbäumen singen.
silver-bright in the garden here, and there at the spring, on blossom-trees sing.
(sing silver-brightly in the garden here, or there by the spring, on blossoming trees.)

dɔx 'holdɐ blyːt' aen 'leːdləs vaep', fɔn 'zeːlə guːt', ʊnt' ʃøːn fɔn laep',
Doch holder blüht ein edles Weib, von Seele gut, und schön von Leib,
But lovlier blooms a noble woman, of soul good, and beautiful of body,
(But lovelier still blooms a noble woman, good of soul and beautiful of body)

ɪn 'frɪʃɐ 'juːgənt',blyːt'ə. viːɐ 'lasən 'alə 'bluːmən ʃt'eːn,
in frischer Jugendblüte. Wir lassen alle Blumen stehn,
in fresh youth- blossom. We let all flowers stand,
(in the fresh blossom of youth. We leave all the flowers alone)

das 'liːbə 'vae̯pˈçən   ˈlantsuzeːn, ˈʊntˈ frɔ́øn ˈʊns   ˈliːrɐ 'gyːtˈə.
das liebe Weibchen   anzusehn, und freun uns   ihrer Güte.
the dear little woman to look at, and gladden ourselves in her goodness.
(to look at the dear young woman and delight in her goodness.)

[Hölty's poem was based on a love song by the medieval *Minnesänger* Walter von der Vogelweide. Schubert set it in a Mozartean vein.]

'bʊndəsliːtˈ
Bundeslied
Song of Solidarity

Posthumously published [composed 1815] (poem by Johann Wolfgang von Goethe)

ɪn 'lalən 'guːtˈən 'ʃtˈʊndən, lɛɐ̯ˈhǿːtˈ fɔn liːpˈ ˈʊntˈ vae̯n,
In allen guten Stunden, erhöht von Lieb' und Wein,
In all   good   hours,   exalted by love and wine,

zɔl 'diːzəs liːtˈ fɛɐ̯ˈbʊndən fɔn ˈʊns gə'zʊŋən zae̯n!
soll dieses Lied verbunden von uns gesungen sein!
shall this   song united   by us sung   be!
(shall this song be sung by us united!)

ʊns hɛlt deːɐ̯ gɔt tsu'zamən, deːɐ̯/deːr lʊns hiːɐ̯ˈheːɐ̯ gə'braxtʰ.
Uns hält der Gott zusammen, der   uns hierher gebracht.
Us holds the god together,   who   us hither   brought.
(The god who brought us to this place holds us together.)

ɛɐ̯ˈnɔ́øtˈ ˈlʊnzrə 'flamən,   leːɐ̯ hatˈ ziː 'langəfaxtʰ.
Erneuert unsre Flammen, er hat sie   angefacht.
Renew   our flames,   he has them ignited.
(Renew our flames, for it is he who ignited them.)

zoː 'glyːətˈ 'frǿːlɪç 'hɔ́øtˈə, zae̯tˈ rɛçtˈ fɔn 'hɛrtsən lae̯ns!
So glühet fröhlich heute, seid recht von Herzen eins!
So glow   merrily today, be   right from hearts one!
(So glow merrily today, be as one, right from your hearts!)

ɑo̯f, tʰrɪŋkˈtˈ lɛɐ̯ˈnɔ́øtˈɐ 'frɔ́ødə diːs glaːs des 'lɛçtˈən   vae̯ns!
Auf, trinkt erneuter Freude dies Glas des   echten   Weins!
Up, drink with renewed joy   this glass of the unadulterated wine!
(Come! Drink with renewed joy this glass of unadulterated wine!)

ɑo̯f, ɪn deːɐ̯ 'hɔldən 'ʃtˈʊndə ʃtˈoːstˈ lan, ˈʊntˈ 'kʰʏsət tʰrɔ́ø,
Auf, in der holden Stunde stosst an, und küsset treu,
Up, in the friendly hour clink to, and kiss   loyally,
(Come! In this friendly hour clink glasses together and kiss each other in loyalty,)

bae̯ 'jeːdəm 'nɔ́øən 'bʊndə, di 'laltˈən   'viːdɐ nɔ́ø!
bei jedem neuen Bunde, die alten   wieder neu!
at each   new bonding, the old (bonds) again new!
(at each new bonding the old bonds are renewed!)

veːɐ̯ leːpˀtˀ ɪn ˈlʊnzɐm ˈkʰraͤzə, lʊntˀ leːpˀtˀ nɪçtˀ ˈzeːlɪç drɪn?
Wer lebt in unserm Kreise, und lebt nicht selig drin?
Who lives in our circle, and lives not happily therein?
(Who lives in our circle and does not live happily in it?)

gəˈniːst di ˈfraͤə ˈvaͤzə lʊntˀ ˈtʰrɔ̝ø̯ən ˈbruːdəzɪn!
Geniesst die freie Weise und treuen Brudersinn!
Enjoy the free way and loyal fraternal feeling!
(Enjoy the free and easy ways of our group and the loyal fraternal feelings that unite us!)

zoː blaͤpˀtˀ dʊrç ˈlalə ˈt͡saͤtˀən hɛrt͡s ˈhɛrt͡sən ˈt͡suːɡəkʰeːɐ̯tʰ;
So bleibt durch alle Zeiten Herz Herzen zugekehrt;
So remains through all times heart to hearts turned to;
(So each heart remains open to the other hearts through all times, good or bad;)

fɔn ˈkʰaͤnən ˈkʰlaͤnɪçkʰaͤtˀən vɪrtˀ ˈlʊnzɐ bʊntˀ gəˈʃtˀøːɐ̯tʰ.
von keinen Kleinigkeiten wird unser Bund gestört.
by no trifles will be our bond disturbed.
(our bond will not be disturbed by any trifles.)

ʊns hatˀ laͤn gɔtˀ gəˈzeːgnətˀ mɪtˀ ˈfraͤəm ˈleːbənsblɪkʰ,
Uns hat ein Gott gesegnet mit freiem Lebensblick,
Us has a god blessed with free life- view,
(A god has blessed us with a liberated view of life,)

ʊntˀ ˈlaləs vas bəˈgeːgnətˀ, lɛɐ̯ˈnɔ̝ø̯ətˀ ˈlʊnzɐ glʏkʰ.
und alles, was begegnet, erneuert unser Glück.
and everything that encounters (us) renews our happiness.
(and everything that comes our way renews our happiness.)

dʊrç ˈgrɪlən nɪçtˀ gəˈdrɛŋətˀ, fɛɐ̯ˈkʰnɪkˀtˀ zɪç ˈkʰaͤnə lʊstʰ;
Durch Grillen nicht gedränget, verknickt sich keine Lust;
Through melancholy thoughts not constrained, breaks itself no pleasure;
(Unconstrained by any melancholy thoughts, no pleasure is spoiled;)

dʊrç ˈt͡siːrən nɪçtˀ gəˈɛŋətˀ, ʃleːkˀtˀ ˈfraͤɐ(r) ˈlʊnzrə brʊstʰ.
durch Zieren nicht geenget, schlägt freier unsre Brust.
through false politeness not constricted, beats more freely our breast.
(Unconstricted by false politeness, our hearts beat more freely.)
["*Zieren*" = to put on airs, to be affected, to refuse something out of false politeness]

mɪtˀ ˈjeːdəm ʃrɪtˀ vɪrtˀ ˈvaͤtˀɐ di ˈraʃə ˈleːbənsbaːn,
Mit jedem Schritt wird weiter die rasche Lebensbahn,
With every step becomes wider the swift life- course,
(With every step the swift course of life broadens out before us,)

ʊntˀ ˈhaͤtˀɐ(r), ˈlɪmɐ ˈhaͤtˀɐ ʃtˀaͤkˀtˀ ˈlʊnzɐ blɪkˀ hɪˈnan.
und heiter, immer heiter steigt unser Blick hinan.
and serenely, always serenely climbs our gaze upwards.
(and serenely, always serenely our gaze ascends toward heaven.)

ʊns vɪrtʻ lɛs ˈnɪmɐ ˈbaŋə, vɛn ˈlaləs ʃtʻa͜ekʻtʻ lʊntʻ fɛltʰ,
Uns wird es nimmer bange, wenn alles steigt und fällt,
Us becomes it never fearful, when all rises and falls,
(We never become fearful, though all things rise and fall,)

ʊntʻ ˈbla͜ebən ˈlaŋə, ˈlaŋə! la͜of ˈleːvɪç zoː gəˈzɛltʰ.
und bleiben lange, lange! auf ewig so gesellt.
and remain long, long! for ever so allied.
(and may we remain allied like this for a long, long time!--forever!)

[*Bundeslied* starts out in the style of a hearty drinking-song for young German males to sing together over wine or beer at some student-tavern; but Goethe characteristically introduces a more sophisticated tone than one expects to find in songs of that type.]

Canzone see *Vier Canzonen*

kʰavaˈtʰiːnə fyːɐ ˈla͜enə bas ˈʃtʻɪmə la͜os deːɐ ˈloːpʻɐː lalˈfɔnso lʊntʻ lɛsˈtrɛla
Cavatine für eine Bassstimme aus der Oper: Alfonso und Estrella
Cavatina "for a Bass Voice," from the Opera *Alfonso and Estrella*

Posthumously published [composed 1821-1822] (text by Franz von Schober)

vɛn lɪç dɪç, ˈhɔldə, ˈzeːə, zoː gla͜opʻ lɪç ˈkʰa͜enən ʃmɛrt͜s,
Wenn ich dich, Holde, sehe, so glaub' ich keinen Schmerz,
When I you, lovely one, see, then believe I no pain,
(When I see you, lovely one, then I do not believe in pain,)

ʃoːn ˈda͜enə ˈbloːsə ˈnɛːə bəˈzeːlɪçt ˈdiːzəs hɛrt͜s.
schon deine blosse Nähe beseligt dieses Herz.
already your mere nearness makes blissful this heart.
(already your mere nearness makes this heart of mine blissful.)

di ˈla͜edən zɪnt t͜sɛɐˈrɔnən, diː zɔnst di brʊstʻ gəˈkʰvɛːltʰ,
Die Leiden sind zerronnen, die sonst die Brust gequält,
The sufferings are melted away, which otherwise the breast tormented,
(The suffering that formerly tormented my breast has melted away,)

ɛs ˈlɔ͜øçtʻən ˈtʰa͜ozəntʻ ˈzɔnən deːɐ ˈlʊstʻlɛntʻbrantʻən vɛltʰ.
es leuchten tausend Sonnen der Lustentbrannten Welt.
there shine a thousand suns for the pleasure-inflamed world.
(a thousand suns are shining upon a world inflamed with pleasure.)

ʊntʻ ˈnɔ͜øə ˈkʰrɛftʻə ˈblɪt͜sən lɪns ˈtʰrʊŋkʻnə hɛrt͜s hɪˈna͜en,
Und neue Kräfte blitzen ins trunkne Herz hinein,
And new powers strike lightning into the intoxicated heart into,
(And new powers penetrate my intoxicated heart like flashes of lightning,)

ja, lɪç vɪl dɪç bəˈʃʏt͜sən, lɪç vɪl da͜en ˈdiːnɐ za͜en.
ja, ich will dich beschützen, ich will dein Diener sein.
yes, I want you to protect, I want your servant to be.
(yes, I want to protect you, I want to be your servant.)

144

[The title printed in the Peters edition is misleading: the aria belongs to the leading *tenor* (Alfonso) in the opera, and was for some reason transposed by the editor a major sixth downwards (from C to E flat major). Schubert had no luck with any of his several operas; none of them was a success. Alfonso, a king's son, finds Estrella in a forest and falls in love with her.]

'kʰoːra lan di zɔnə
Cora an die Sonne
Cora to the Sun

Posthumously published [composed 1815] (poem by Gabriele von Baumberg)

naːx zoː 'fiːlən 'tʰryːbən 'tʰaːgən zɛntʼ lʊns 'viːdərʊm lae̯n'maːl,
Nach so vielen trüben Tagen send' uns wiederum einmal,
After so many dreary days send us again once,
(After so many dreary days, send us once again,)

'mɪtʼlae̯tsfɔl fyːɐ̯/fyːr 'lʊnzrə 'kʰlaːgən, 'lae̯nən 'zanftʼən 'mɪldən ʃtʼraːl!
mitleidsvoll für unsre Klagen, einen sanften milden Strahl!
sympathy-full for our laments, one soft, gentle ray!
(with sympathy for our laments, one soft, gentle ray!)

'liːbə 'zɔnə! tʰrɪŋkʼ den 'reːgən, deːɐ̯ hɛ'rapʼ tsuː 'ʃtʼʏrtsən drɔɪ̯tʰ;
Liebe Sonne! trink' den Regen, der herab zu stürzen dräut;
Dear sun! drink the rain, which down to pour threatens;
(Dear sun, drink up the rain, which threatens to come pouring down;)

'dae̯nə 'ʃtʼraːlən zɪntʼ lʊns 'zeːgən, 'dae̯nə 'blɪkʼə 'zeːlɪçkʰae̯tʰ.
deine Strahlen sind uns Segen, deine Blicke Seligkeit.
your rays are to us blessing, your glances bliss.
(your rays are a blessing to us, your glances are bliss.)

ʃae̯n, lax, 'ʃae̯nə, 'liːbə 'zɔnə! 'jeːdə 'frɔɪ̯də daŋkʼ lɪç diːɐ̯,
Schein', ach, scheine, liebe Sonne! Jede Freude dank' ich dir,
Shine, ah, shine, dear sun! Every joy thank I to you,
(Shine, ah, shine, dear sun! Every joy I owe to you,)

'alə gae̯sts lʊntʼ 'hɛrtsənsvɔnə, lɪçtʼ lʊntʼ 'vɛrmə kʰɔmtʼ fɔn diːɐ̯.   [gae̯stʼ]
alle Geists- und Herzenswonne, Licht und Wärme kommt von dir.   [*Peters:* **Geist-**]
all spirit- and heart- rapture, light and warmth comes from you.
(all rapture of the heart and spirit, all light and warmth comes from you.)

[The short piano introduction printed in the Peters edition is not by Schubert and should be omitted. Gabriele von Baumberg was "the Viennese Sappho."]

'kʰrɔnan / 'ɔsi̯ans gə'zɛŋə 'nʊmɐ ts̬vaɛ
Cronnan / Ossian's Gesänge, Nº 2
Cronnan / Ossian's Songs, No. 2

Posthumously published [composed 1815] (poem by James Macpherson—"Ossian")
From the prose poem *Carric-Thura* (German translation by Edmund von Harold)

SHILRIK:

ıç zıts̬ baɛ de:ɐ̯ 'mo:zıçt'ən   (mo:zıgən) 'kʰvɛlə, ˌam 'gıpfəl des 'ʃt'ʏrmıʃən 'hy:gəls;
Ich sitz' bei der moosigten   (moosigen)*Quelle, am Gipfel des stürmischen Hügels;
I   sit   by the moss-covered (mossy)   spring, at the summit of the stormy   hill;
(*Original poem:* I sit by the mossy fountain; on the top of the hill of the winds.)

'y:bɐ mi:ɐ̯ braɔst'   laɛn baɔm; (ʃt'ro:m,) 'dʊŋk'lə 'vɛlən 'rɔlən 'ly:bɐ di 'haɛdə.
über mir braust   ein Baum; (Strom,) dunkle Wellen rollen über die Heide.
over me roars (rustles) a   tree; (stream,) dark   waves roll over the heath.
(One tree is rustling above me. Dark waves roll over the heath.)

di ze: lıst' ʃt'ʏrmıʃ da'rʊnt'ɐ.   (di ze: tʰo:p't' laɔt' lan de:ɐ̯ 'brandʊŋ.)
Die See ist stürmisch darunter.   (Die See tobt laut an der Brandung.)
The Sea is stormy   down below. (The sea rages loudly in the surf.)
(The lake is troubled below.)

di 'hırʃə 'ʃt'aɛgən ('ts̬i:ən) fɔm   'hy:gəl hɛ'rap'.
Die Hirsche steigen (ziehen) vom   Hügel herab.
The deer   climb (move) from the hill   down.
(The deer descend from the hill.)

kʰaɛn 'jɛ:gɐ vırt' lın de:ɐ̯ 'fɛrnə gə'ze:n. (kʰaɛn 'jɛ:gɐ fɛɐ̯'fɔlgət' 'li:rə ʃp'u:ɐ̯.)
Kein Jäger wird in der Ferne   gesehn. (Kein Jäger verfolgt ihre Spur.)
No   hunter is in the distance seen. (No   hunter pursues their trace.)
(No hunter at a distance is seen.)

lɛs lıst' 'mıt'a:k', 'la:bɐ 'laləs lıst' ʃt'ıl. (dɔx hɛrʃt 'ti:fəs 'ʃvaɛgən,)
Es ist Mittag, aber alles ist still. (doch herrscht tiefes Schweigen,)
It is midday, but all is still. (but reigns deep silence,)
(It is midday; but all is silent.)

'tʰraɔrıç zınt' 'maɛnə 'laɛnza:mən gə'daŋk'ən. ('ʃve:ɐ̯mu:t' hɛlt' 'maɛnə 'ze:lə gə'fɛsəltʰ.)
Traurig sind meine einsamen Gedanken. (Schwermut hält meine Seele gefesselt.)
Sad   are my lonely   thoughts. (melancholy holds my   soul enchained.)
(Sad are my thoughts alone.)

ɛɐ̯'ʃi:nst du: 'la:bɐ(r), lo: 'maɛnə gə'li:p't'ə,
Erschienst du aber,   o meine Geliebte, [*Harold:* **Erschienst du aber, meine Geliebte**]
Appeared you however, O my   beloved,
(Didst thou but appear, O my love!)

vi: laɛn 'vandrɐ(r) laɔf de:ɐ̯ 'haɛdə, ('ʃve:bənt' 'ly:bɐ di 'dʊft'əndə 'haɛdə,)
wie ein Wandrer auf der Heide, (schwebend über die duftende Heide,)
like a   wanderer on the heath, (hovering   above the fragrant heath,)
(a wanderer on the heath!)

da̯en haːɐ̯ ˈfliːgənt‘ lɪm ˈvɪndə, da̯en ˈbuːzən hoːx lɑ͜ofˈvalənt‘,
dein Haar fliegend im Winde, dein Busen hoch aufwallend,
your hair flying in the wind, your bosom highly agitated,
(Thy hair floating on the wind behind thee; thy bosom heaving on the sight;)
[*Harold:* **dein Busen, sichtbar** (ˈzɪçt‘baːɐ̯, visible)**, aufwallend!]**

ˈda̯enə ˈlɑ͜ogən fɔl ˈtʰrɛːnən, fyːɐ̯ ˈda̯enə ˈfrɔ͜ʏndə,
deine Augen voll Tränen, für deine Freunde,
your eyes full of tears for your friends,
(thine eyes full of tears for thy friends,)

diː deːɐ̯ ˈneːbəl dɛs ˈhyːgəl (lam ˈhyːgəl) fɛɐ̯ˈbark‘!
die der Nebel des Hügels (am Hügel) verbarg!
whom the mist of the hill (on the hill) concealed!
(whom the mist of the hill had concealed!)

dɪç vɔlt‘ lɪç ˈtʰrøːst‘ən, loː ˈma̯enə gəˈliːp‘t‘ə,
Dich wollt' ich trösten, o meine Geliebte, [*H:* **Dich wollt' ich trösten, meine Geliebte]**
You wanted I to comfort, O my beloved,
(Thee I would comfort, my love,)

dɪç vɔlt‘ lɪç ˈfyːrən t͜sʊm ˈhɑ͜ozə ˈma̯enəs ˈfaːt‘ɐs!
dich wollt' ich führen zum Hause meines Vaters!
you wanted I to lead to the house of my father!
(and bring thee to thy father's house!) [*note:* English: "*thy* father's," German: "*my* father's"]

ˈaːbɐ(r) lɪst‘ ziː lɛs, diː dɔrt‘ viː la̯en ʃt‘raːl dɛs lɪçt͜s lɑ͜of deːɐ̯ ˈha̯edə lɛɐ̯ˈʃa̯entʰ?
Aber ist sie es, die dort wie ein Strahl des Lichts auf der Heide erscheint?
But is she it, who there like a beam of the light on the heath apears?
(But is it she that there appears, there like a beam of light on the heath?)

kʰɔmst duː, loː ˈmɛːt‘çən, ˈlyːbɐ ˈfɛlzən, ˈlyːbɐ ˈbɛrgə t͜suː miːɐ̯,
Kommst du, o Mädchen, über Felsen, über Berge zu mir,
Come you, O maiden, over rocks, over mountains to me,
(Comest thou, O maid, over rocks, over mountains, to me,)

ˈʃɪmɐnt‘ viː lɪm ˈhɛrpst‘ə deːɐ̯ moːnt‘, viː di zɔn lɪn deːɐ̯ gluːt dɛs ˈzɔmɐs?
schimmernd wie im Herbste der Mond, wie die Sonn' in der Glut des Sommers?
shimmering as in the autumn the moon, as the sun in the heat of the sommer?
(bright as the moon in autumn, as the sun in a summer storm?)
[*Harold:* **wie die Sonne in einem Sturme** (ˈla̯enəm ˈʃt‘ʊrmə, a storm) **des Sommers]**

ziː ʃp‘rɪçtʰ; ˈlaːbɐ viː ʃvax lɪst‘ ˈliːrə ˈʃt‘ɪmə,
Sie spricht; aber wie schwach ist ihre Stimme,
She speaks; but how weak is her voice,
(She speaks: but how weak her voice!)

viː das ˈlʏft‘çən lɪm ˈʃilfə deːɐ̯ zeː. (dɛs zeːs.)
wie das Lüftchen im Schilfe der See. (des Sees.)
like the breeze in the reeds of the sea! (of the lake.)
(like the breeze in the reeds of the lake!)

VINVELA:

kʰeːʁst duː fɔm   ˈkʰriːɡə ˈʃaːtˈloːs   (ˈʊnbəˈʃɛːdɪçt)   ʦuˈrʏkʰ?
"Kehrst du vom   Kriege schadlos   (unbeschädigt) zurück? [*Harold:* **unbeschädigt**]
"Return you from the war   without harm (unharmed)   back?
("Returnest thou safe from the war?)

voː   zɪnt ˈdaenə ˈfrɔøndə, maen ɡəˈliːpˈtˈɐ?
Wo   sind deine Freunde, mein Geliebter?
Where are   your   friends,   my   beloved?
(Where are thy friends, my love?)

lɪç fɛʁˈnaːm ˈdaenən tʰoːtˈ lɑof dem ˈhyːɡəl; ɪç fɛʁˈnaːm liːn lʊntˈ bəˈvaentˈə dɪç!
Ich vernahm deinen Tod   auf dem Hügel; ich vernahm ihn und beweinte dich!"
I   heard of your   death on   the   hill;   I   heard of it   and wept for   you!"
(I heard of thy death on the hill; I heard and mourned thee, Shilric!")
          [*Harold:* **ich vernahm ihn, und betrauerte** (bəˈtʰrɑoɐtˈə, mourned) **dich, Shilrik!**]

SHILRIK:

jaː, ˈmaenə ˈʃøːnstˈə,   (ˈtʰɔørəs ˈmɛːtˈçən,) lɪç ˈkʰeːrə (ˈkʰeːʁtˈə) ʦuˈrʏkʰ,
Ja,   meine Schönste,   (teures Mädchen,) ich kehre (kehrte) zurück,
Yes, my   most beautiful one, (dear   maiden,) I   come (came)   back,
(Yes, my fair, I return;)

ˈlaːbɐ(r) laˈlaen fɔn ˈmaenəm ɡəˈʃlɛçtʰ.
aber   allein von meinem Geschlecht.
but   alone of my   race.
(but I alone of my race.)

ˈjeːnə zɔlst duː nɪçtˈ meːʁ/meːr lɛʁˈblɪkˈən, (duː zɔlstˈ ˈjeːnə ˈnɪmɐ(r) lɛʁˈblɪkˈən,)
Jene sollst du nicht mehr   erblicken, (Du sollst jene nimmer erblicken,)
Them shall you not   any more   see,   (You shall   them never   see,)
(Thou shalt see them no more:)   [*Harold:* **Du sollst jene nicht mehr erblicken**]

lɪç haːpˈ ˈliːrə ˈɡrɛːbɐ(r) lɑof deːʁ ˈflɛçə lɛʁˈrɪçtˈətʰ.
ich hab' ihre Gräber   auf der Fläche errichtet.
I   have their graves   on   the plain   raised.
(their graves I raised on the plain.)

ˈaːbɐ vaˈrʊm bɪst duː lam   ˈhyːɡəl deːʁ ˈvyːstˈə?
Aber warum bist du am   Hügel der   Wüste?
But   why   are   you on the hill   of the desert?
(But why art thou on the desert hill?)

vaˈrʊm laˈlaen lɑof deːʁ ˈhaedə? (lɑof dem ˈhyːɡəl?)
warum allein auf der Heide? (auf dem Hügel?)
why   alone on the heath? (on the   hill?)
(Why on the heath alone?)

VINVELA:

oː ˈʃɪlrɪkˈ, lɪç bɪn laˈlaen, laˈlaen lɪn deːʁ ˈvɪntɐbəˌhɑozʊŋ.
"O Shilrik, ich bin allein, allein in der   Winterbehausung.
"O Shilrik, I   am alone, alone in the   winter-house.
("Alone I am, O Shilrik, alone in the winterhouse.)

148

ɪç ʃt'arp' foːɐ̯ ʃmɛrts 've:gən diːɐ̯. 'ʃɪlrɪkʰ, lɪç liːk' lɛɐ̯'blast' ɪn dem graːp'.
Ich starb vor Schmerz wegen dir. Shilrik, ich lieg' erblasst in dem Grab."
I died of grief because of you. Shilrik, I lie pale in the grave."
(With grief for thee I fell, Shilrik; I am pale in the tomb.")

[_Harold:_ **Ich starb für** (fyːɐ̯, for) **Schmerz**]

SHILRIK:

ziː 'glaɛt'ətʰ, ziː dʊrç'ze:gəlt di lʊft' (ziː lɛɐ̯'he:p't' zɪç, ziː lɛnt'ʃve:p't dʊrç di lʊft')
Sie gleitet, sie durchsegelt die Luft (Sie erhebt sich, sie entschwebt durch die Luft)
She glides, she sails through the air (she lifts herself, she hovers away through the air)
(She fleets, she sails away;)

viː 'ne:bəl foːɐ̯m vɪnt'. (foːɐ̯ dem 'vɪndə.)
wie Nebel vorm Wind. (vor dem Winde.)
like mist before the wind. (before the wind.)
(as mist before the wind!)

ʊnt' vɪlst duː nɪçt' 'blaɛbən? blaɛp',('vaɛlə!) lʊnt' ʃɑo (ziː) 'maɛnə 't'reːnən!
Und willst du nicht bleiben? Bleib', (Weile!) und schau' (Sieh') meine Tränen!
And will you not stay? Stay, (Stay!) and see (See) my tears!
(and wilt thou not stay, Vinvela! Stay and behold my tears!)

[_H:_ **Und willst du nicht bleiben, Vinvela? Bleib, und beschau** (bə'ʃɑo) **meine Tränen!**]

'tsiːɐ̯lɪç lɛɐ̯'ʃaɛnst duː, (lɛɐ̯'ʃiːnst duː,)   [_Harold:_ **zierlich erscheinst du, Vinvela!**]
Zierlich erscheinst du, (erschienst du,)
Graceful appear you, (appeared you,)
(fair thou appearest, Vinvela!)

lɪm 'le:bən vaːɐ̯st duː ʃøːn. (zo: ʃøːn, viː lɪm 'le:bən duː vaːɐ̯stʰ.)
im Leben warst du schön. (so schön, wie im Leben du warst.)
in the life were you beautiful. (so beautiful, as in the life you were.)
(fair thou wast; when alive!)

ɪç vɪl 'zɪtsən baɛ deːɐ̯ 'moːzɪçt'ən ('moːzɪgən) 'kʰvɛlə,
Ich will sitzen bei der moosigten (moosigen) Quelle,
I will sit by the moss-covered (mossy) spring,
(By the mossy fountain I will sit;)

lam 'gɪpfəl dɛs 'ʃt'ʏrmɪʃən 'hy:gəls. (dɛs 'hy:gəls.)
am Gipfel des stürmischen Hügels. (des Hügels.)
at the summit of the stormy hill. (of the hill.)
(on the top of the hill of winds.)

vɛn 'laləs lɪm 'mɪt'aːk' he'rʊm ʃvaɛk't, (vɛn 'laləs lʊm mɪç lɪm 'mɪtaːk' ʃvaɛk't',)
Wenn Alles im Mittag herum schweigt, (wenn Alles um mich im Mittag schweigt,)
When all in the midday around is silent, (when all around me in the midday is silent,)
(When midday is silent around!)   [_Harold:_ **Wenn alles um** (lʊm, at) **Mittag...**]

dan ʃp'rɪç mɪt' miːɐ̯/miːr, lo: 'vɪnvela!
dann sprich mit mir, o Vinvela!
then speak with me, O Vinvela!
(O talk with me, Vinvela!)

kʰɔm lɑ̯of dem lae̯çt' bə'fly:gəlt'ən 'hɑ̯oxə! lɑ̯of dem 'lʏft'çən de:ɐ̯/de:r 'lae̯nlø:də kʰɔm!
Komm auf dem leicht beflügelten Hauche! Auf dem Lüftchen der   Einöde komm!
Come on the lightly-winged   breeze! On the breeze of the   desert come!
(Come on thy light-winged gale! on the breeze of the desert, come!)

las mɪç, vɛn du: fo:ɐ̯'bae̯ge:st, 'dae̯nə 'ʃt'ɪmə fɛɐ̯'ne:mən,
Lass mich, wenn du vorbeigehst, deine Stimme vernehmen,
Let me,   when you go by,   your   voice   hear,
(Let me hear thy voice as thou passest,)

vɛn 'laləs lɪm 'mɪt'a:k' he'rom ʃvae̯k't ʰ. (vɛn 'laləs lɪm 'mɪt'a:k' lʊm   mɪç ʃvae̯k't ʰ.)
wenn Alles im   Mittag herum schweigt. (wenn Alles im   Mittag um   mich schweigt.)
when all   in the midday around is silent. (when all   in the midday around me   is silent.)
(when midday is silent around!)   [*Harold:* **wenn alles um Mittag schweigt!**]

[*There are two widely-differing published versions of the text. The *Gesamtausgabe* (Breitkopf & Härtel) prints the text as Schubert set it. The version that is printed in the well-known Peters collection is based upon the first published edition, by Diabelli in 1830, and those variants are indicated above in parentheses. The title refers to the name of an ancient (and fictitious) Caledonian bard, who is asked to "raise the song of Shilrik; when he returned to his hills, and Vinvela was no more. He leaned on her grey mossy stone; he thought Vinvela lived. He saw her fair-moving on the plain, but the bright form lasted not: the sunbeam fled from the field, and she was seen no more. Hear the song of Shilrik, it is soft but sad." James Macpherson's work was passed off as a genuine antiquity, supposedly by "Ossian," a third-century Irish bard. It aroused great interest and enthusiasm, especially in German-speaking lands, during the late eighteenth century and well into the nineteenth.]

Danksagung an den Bach see *Die schöne Müllerin*

'dafnə lam bax
Daphne am Bach
Daphne at the Brook

Posthumously published [composed 1816] (poem by Friedrich Leopold, Graf zu Stollbert)

ɪç ha:p' lae̯n 'bɛçlae̯n 'fondən fɔm   'ʃt'ɛ:t'çən 'tsi:mlɪç vae̯t ʰ,
Ich hab' ein Bächlein funden vom   Städchen ziemlich weit,
I   have a   brooklet found from the town   rather   far,
(I have found a brooklet rather far from the town,)

da: bɪn lɪç 'mançə 'ʃt'ondən lɪn 'ʃt'ɪlɐ(r) 'lae̯nza:mkʰae̯t ʰ.
da   bin ich manche Stunden in stiller   Einsamkeit.
there am I many   hours   in quiet   solitude.
(there I spend many hours in quiet solitude.)

ɪç tʰe:t' mi:ɐ̯   glae̯ç lɛɐ̯'kʰi:zən lae̯n 'pʰlɛtsçən 'kʰy:ləs mo:s;
Ich tät mir   gleich erkiesen ein Plätzchen kühles Moos;
I   did for myself right away choose   a   little place of cool moss;
(Right away I choose for myself a little spot of cool moss:)

da: zɪts lɪç, lont da: 'fli:sən mi:ɐ̯ 'tʰrɛ:nən lɪn den ʃo:s.
da   sitz' ich, und da   fliessen mir Tränen in den Schoss.
there sit I,   and there flow   for me tears   into the lap.
(there I sit, and there tears flow down onto my lap.)

150

fyːɐ̯ dɪç, fyːɐ̯ dɪç nuːɐ̯ ˈvalət' ma̯en ˈjuːɡənt'lɪçəs bluːtʰ;
Für dich, für dich nur wallet mein jugendliches Blut;
For you, for you only seethes my youthful blood;
(My young blood throbs for you, only for you;)

dɔx ˈla̯ezə nuːɐ̯/nuːr lɛɐ̯ˈʃalət' da̯en naːm lan ˈdiːzɐ fluːtʰ.
doch leise nur erschallet dein Nam' an dieser Flut.
but softly only sounds your name at this stream.
(but your name is only softly sounded at this stream.)

ɪç ˈfyrçt'ə, das mɪç 't'hɔ̸ʃə la̯en ˈla̯oʃɐ(r) la̯os deːɐ̯ ʃt'atʰ;
Ich fürchte, dass mich täusche ein Lauscher aus der Stadt;
I fear that me may deceive an eavesdropper out of the town;
(I fear that an eavesdropper from the town may deceive me;)

ɛs ʃrɛk't' mɪç das ɡəˈrɔ̸ʃə fɔn ˈjeːdəm ˈphap'əlblatʰ.
es schreckt mich das Geräusche von jedem Pappelblatt.
it frightens me the noise of every poplar-leaf.
(the rustle of every poplar tree leaf frightens me.)

ɪç ˈvynʃə miːɐ̯ t͡suˈrʏk'ə den ˈflʏçt'ɪçst'ən ɡəˈnʊs;
Ich wünsche mir zurücke den flüchtigsten Genuss;
I wish for myself back the most fleeting enjoyment;
(I wish a certain all-too-fleeting enjoyment would come back to me;)

ɪn ˈjeːdəm ˈla̯oɡənblɪk'ə fyːl lɪç den ˈlap'ʃiːt͡skʰʊs.
in jedem Augenblicke fühl' ich den Abschiedskuss.
in every moment feel I the farewell kiss.
(every moment I feel that parting kiss.)

ɛs vart miːɐ̯ voːl lʊnt' ˈbaŋə, lals mɪç da̯en larm lʊmˈʃlɔs,
Es ward mir wohl und bange, als mich dein Arm umschloss,
It became for me well and fearful, when me your arm embraced,
(I felt both happy and fearful when your arm embraced me,)

als nɔx la̯of ˈma̯enə ˈvaŋə da̯en ˈlɛt͡st'əs 'tʰrɛːnçən flɔs!
als noch auf meine Wange dein letztes Tränchen floss!
when still onto my cheek your last little tear flowed!
(when your last teardrop fell onto my cheek!)

fɔn ˈma̯enəm ˈbluːmənhyːɡəl zaː lɪç diːɐ̯ ˈlaŋə naːx;
Von meinem Blumenhügel sah ich dir lange nach;
From my flower-hill saw I you for a long time after;
(From my flower-covered hill I followed you with my eyes for a long time;)

ɪç ˈvynʃə miːɐ̯ di ˈflyːɡəl deːɐ̯ 'tʰɔ̸p'çən la̯of dem dax;
ich wünsche mir die Flügel der Täubchen auf dem Dach;
I wish for myself the wings of the doves on the roof;
(I wish I had the wings of the doves on the roof;)

nuːn ɡla̯ob ɪç t͡suː fɛɐ̯ˈɡeːən mɪt' ˈjeːdəm ˈla̯oɡənblɪkʰ.
nun glaub' ich zu vergehen mit jedem Augenblick.
now believe I to die with every moment.
(now I believe I am dying at every moment.)

vɪlst duː dae̮n ˈliːpˈçən ˈzeːən, zoː ˈkʰɔmə balt ʦuˈrʏkʰ!
Willst du dein Liebchen sehen, so komme bald zurück!
Want you your sweetheart to see, then come soon back!
(If you want to see your sweetheart again, then come back soon!)

[The Daphne of the title is just a simple girl in love, not the mythological nymph. The opening melody of this strophic song suggests the later, greater *"Wohin?"* from *Die schöne Müllerin*.]

das ˈlaːbəntˈroːtʰ
Das Abendrot
The Sunset

Posthumously published [composed 1818] (poem by Aloys Wilhelm Schreiber)

duː ˈhae̮lɪç, ˈɡlyːəntˈ ˈlaːbəntˈroːtˈ, deːɐ̯ ˈhɪməl vɪl ɪn ɡlanʦ ʦɛɐ̯ˈrɪnən;
Du heilig, glühend Abendrot, der Himmel will in Glanz zerrinnen;
You holy, glowing sunset, the sky wants into splendor to melt;
(You holy, glowing sunset, the sky wants to melt into splendor;)

zoː ˈʃae̮dən ˈmɛrtˈyrɐ fɔn ˈhɪnən, hɔltˈ ˈlɛçəltˈ ɪn dem ˈliːbəstʰoːtˈ.
so scheiden Märtyrer von hinnen, hold lächelnd in dem Liebestod.
thus depart martyrs from hence, graciously smiling in the love- death.
(thus martyrs leave this life, graciously smiling as they die for their love.)

dɛs ˈlao̮fɡaŋs ˈbɛrɡə ʃtˈɪl lʊntˈ ɡrao̮! lam ɡraːpˈ dɛs tʰaːks di ˈhɛlən ˈɡluːtˈən!
Des Aufgangs Berge still und grau! am Grab des Tags die hellen Gluten!
The dawn's mountains quiet and grey! at the grave of the day the bright fires!
(The mountains of the dawn quiet and grey! The bright fires at the dying of the day!)

[*poem:* **steil** (ʃtˈae̮l, steep) **und grau**]

deːɐ̯ ʃvaːn lao̮f ˈpʰʊrpˈʊrroːtˈən ˈfluːtˈən, lʊntˈ ˈjeːdə halm lɪm ˈzɪlbɐtʰao̮!
der Schwan auf purpurroten Fluten, und jeder Halm im Silbertau!
the swan on crimson streams, and every blade in the silver dew!
(The swan floating on crimson waters, and every blade shining with silver dew!)

oː ˈzɔnə, ˈɡɔtˈəsʃtˈraːl, duː bɪstˈ niː ˈhɛrlɪçɐ(r) lals lɪm lɛntˈˈfliːn! [lɛntˈˈfliːən]
O Sonne, Gottesstrahl, du bist nie herrlicher als im Entfliehn! [*poem:* **Entfliehen**]
O sun, God's ray, you are never more glorious than in the fleeing!
(O sun, ray of God's light, you are never more glorious than in your going!)

duː vɪlstˈ lʊns ɡɛrn hɪˈnyːbɐʦiːn, voː ˈdae̮nəs ˈɡlanʦəs ˈlʊrkʰvɛl lɪstʰ.
Du willst uns gern hinüberziehn, wo deines Glanzes Urquell ist.
You want us [object] gladly to draw over, where your splendor's primal source is.
(You would gladly draw us to the other world, where the primal source of your splendor reigns.)

[*poem:* **hinüberziehen** (hɪˈnyːbɐʦiːən)]

[This majestic song, though notated in the treble cleff in the Peters edition, is intended for a bass voice with a sonorous low E natural.]

152

das bɪltʻ
Das Bild
The Image

Posthumously published [composed 1815] (poet unknown)

a̯en ˈmɛːtʻçən lɪsts, das fryː lʊntʻ ʃpʻɛːtʻ miːɐ̯ foːɐ̯   deːɐ̯ ˈzeːlə ˈʃveːbətʻ,
Ein Mädchen ist's, das früh und spät   mir   vor   der Seele schwebet,
A girl   is it, that early and late   to me before the soul hovers,
(It is a girl that hovers before my soul, day and night,)

a̯en ˈmɛːtʻçən, viː lɛs ʃtʻeːtʻ lʊntʻ geːtʻ, la̯os ˈhɪməlsra̯ets   gəˈveːbətʻ.
ein Mädchen, wie es steht und geht, aus Himmelsreiz   gewebet.
a   girl,   as she stands and walks, out of heaven's charm woven.
(a girl, as she stands and walks, woven out of heaven's charms.)

ɪç zeːs,   vɛn lɪn ma̯en ˈfɛnstʻɐ mɪltʻ deːɐ̯ ˈjʊŋə ˈmɔrgən ˈblɪŋkʻətʻ,
Ich seh's, wenn in   mein Fenster mild der junge Morgen blinket,
I see her when into my   window mildly the young morning gleams,
(I see her when the young morning is gleaming gently through my window,)

ɪç zeːs,   vɛn ˈliːpʻlɪç viː das bɪltʻ, deːɐ̯/deːr ˈla̯ebəntʻ ʃtʻɛrn miːɐ̯ ˈvɪŋkʻətʻ.
ich seh's, wenn lieblich wie das Bild, der   Abendstern mir winket.
I see her when lovely   as the image, the   evening star to me beckons.
(I see her when, lovely as her image, the evening star beckons to me.)

miːɐ̯ fɔlkʻts, la̯en ˈtʻrɔɶɐ ˈveːkgənɔs,   tsʊr ruː lʊntʻ lɪns   gəˈtʻʏməl,
Mir folgt's, ein treuer Weggenoss',   zur Ruh und ins   Getümmel,
Me follows it, a   faithful way-companion, to the rest and into the tumult,
(Her image follows me, a faithful companion on my way, to rest or into the tumult of the day,)

ɪç fɛntʻ   lɛs lɪn deːɐ̯/deːr ˈleːɐ̯də ʃoːs, lɪç fɛntʻ   lɛs zɛlpstʻ lɪm ˈhɪməl,
ich fänd'   es in der   Erde Schoss, ich fänd'   es selbst im   Himmel.
I would find it in the   earth's bosom, I would find it even   in the sky.
(I would find it in the depths of the earth, I would find it even in the sky.)

ɛs ʃveːpʻtʻ foːɐ̯ miːɐ̯/miːr lɪn fɛltʻ lʊntʻ valtʻ, pʻraŋkʻtʻ   ˈlyːbɐm   ˈbluːmənbeːtʻə,
Es schwebt vor   mir   in Feld und Wald, prangt   überm   Blumenbeete,
It hovers   before me   in field and forest, is resplendent above the flower- beds,

ʊntʻ glɛntstʻ lɪn ˈzeːrafiːms gəˈʃtʻaltʻ lam laltʻaːɐ̯, voː lɪç ˈbeːtʻə.
und glänzt in Seraphims Gestalt am Altar, wo ich bete.
and gleams   in seraph's   form   at the altar   where I pray.
(and gleams in the form of a seraph at the altar where I pray.)

aˈla̯en das bɪlt,   das ʃpʻɛːtʻ lʊntʻ fryː miːɐ̯ foːɐ̯   deːɐ̯ ˈzeːlə ˈʃveːbətʻ,
Allein das Bild, das spät und früh mir vor   der Seele schwebet,
But   the image, that late   and early to me before the soul hovers,
(But the image that hovers before my soul night and day,)

ɪsts nuːɐ̯ gəˈʃɶpf deːɐ̯ fantʻaˈziː,   la̯os lʊftʻ lʊnt tʻra̯om gəˈveːbətʻ?
ist's nur Geschöpf der Phantasie, aus Luft und Traum gewebet?
Is it only creature of the imagination, out of air and dream woven?
(Is it only a creature of my imagination, woven out of air and dreams?)

oː naɛn, zoː   varm lǫox 'liːbə miːɐ̯ das 'lɛŋəlbɪltʰnɪs 'maːlət,   [lɛŋəlsbɪltʰnɪs]
O nein, so   warm auch Liebe mir   das Engelbildnis malet, [*Peters:* Engelsbildnis]
Oh no,   however warmly ...   love   for me the angelic image paints,
                                      ["*so warm auch*" = however warm(ly)]
(Oh no! However warmly love paints that angelic image for me,)

ɪsts̩ dɔx nuːɐ̯ 'ʃatʰən   fɔn deːɐ̯ tsiːɐ̯, diː   lan dem 'mɛːtʰçən 'ʃtʰraːlətʰ.
ist's doch nur Schatten von der Zier, die   an dem Mädchen strahlet.
is it yet only shadow   of the beauty, which from the girl   radiates.
(it is still only a shadow of the beauty that radiates from the girl.)

[This strophic song has some original and effective touches, especially at the ends of the verses.
The first bar of the accompaniment was added by an editor when the song was published.]

das 'lɛço
Das Echo
The Echo

Posthumously published [composition date unknown; 1826-28?] (poem by Ignaz Franz Castelli)

hɛrts̩'liːbə,, 'guːtʰə 'mʊtʰɐ̯(r), loː 'grɔlə   nɪçtʰ mɪtʰ miːɐ̯,
Herzliebe, gute Mutter, o grolle   nicht mit mir,
heart-dear. good Mother, O be angry not   with me,
(Dear, kind Mother, oh, don't be angry with me!)

duː zaːst den hans mɪç 'kʰʏsən, dɔx lɪç kʰan   nɪçts̩   da'fyːɐ̯;
du sahst den Hans mich küssen, doch ich kann   nichts dafür;
you saw the Hans me   kiss,   but I   can (do) nothing for that;
(You saw Hans kiss me; but I can't help that.)

ɪç vɪl   diːɐ̯/diːr 'laləs   'zaːgən, dɔx 'haːbə nuːɐ̯ gə'dʊltʰ:
ich will dir   alles   sagen, doch habe nur Geduld:
I   want to you everything tell,   but   have only patience:
(I want to tell you everything, but you must only have patience.)

das 'lɛço drǫos lam   'hyːgəl, bạem 'byːgəl, das lɪstʰ lan 'laləm ʃʊltʰ.
das Echo drauss' am   Hügel, beim Bügel, das ist an allem schuld.
the echo outside on the hill,   by the bow, that is for all to blame.
(the echo outside on the hill, by the bow,—that is to blame for everything.)

ɪç zaːs dɔrt lǫof deːɐ̯ 'viːzə,   daː hatʰ leːɐ̯ mɪç gə'zeːn,
Ich sass dort auf der Wiese,   da   hat er mich gesehn,
I   sat there on the meadow, there has he me   seen,
(I was sitting there on the meadow; he saw me there,)

dɔx bliːpʰ   leːɐ̯/eːr 'leːɐ̯lɛɐ̯giːbɪç/leːrlɛɐ̯giːbɪç hypʃ lɪn deːɐ̯ 'fɛrnə ʃtʰeːn,
doch blieb er   ehrerbietig   hübsch in der Ferne stehn,
yet remained he   respectfully   nicely in the distance stand(ing),
(yet he remained standing respectfully at a decent distance,)

ʊntʰ ʃpʰraːx: gɛrn tʰrɛːtʰ   lɪç 'neːɐ̯, nɛːmst duːs nɪçtʰ 'lyːbəl lǫof:
und sprach: "Gern trät   ich näher, nähmst du's nicht übel auf:
and spoke: "Gladly would step I   nearer, would take you it not ill   up:
(and he said: "I'd like to come nearer, if you wouldn't take it ill:)

154

za:k‘, bɪn lɪç di:ɐ̯ vɪl'kʰɔmən? 'kʰɔmən! ri:f ʃnɛl das 'lɛço drɑof!
sag, bin ich dir willkommen?” “Kommen!” rief schnell das Echo drauf!
say, am I to you welcome?” “Come!” called quickly the echo upon that!
(say, am I welcome?” At that, the echo quickly called: “Come!”)

dan kʰa:m le:ɐ̯/le:r lɑof di 'vi:zə, tsu: mi:ɐ̯ hɪn zɛtst‘ le:ɐ̯ zɪç,
Dann kam er auf die Wiese, zu mir hin setzt’ er sich,
Then came he onto the meadow, to me hence set he himself,
(Then he came onto the meadow and sat down by me,)

hi:s mɪç di 'ʃø:nə 'li:zə lʊnt‘ ʃlaŋ den larm lʊm mɪç,
hiess mich die schöne Liese und schlang den Arm um mich,
called me the beautiful Lisa and coiled the arm around me,
(he called me “beautiful Lisa” and coiled his arm around me,)

lʊnt‘ ba:t‘, lɪç mœçt‘ li:m 'za:gən, lɔp‘ lɪç li:m gu:t‘ kʰan zaen?
und bat, ich möcht ihm sagen, ob ich ihm gut kann sein?
and begged. I might to him say, whether I to him good can be?
(and begged me to tell him whether I could love him.) [*“jemandem gut sein”* = to love someone]

das ve:ɐ̯/ve:r li:m ze:ɐ̯/ze:r lɛɐ̯'frɔ̘ølɪç; 'fraelɪç! ri:f ʃnɛl das 'lɛço draen.
das wär’ ihm sehr erfreulich; “Freilich!” rief schnell das Echo drein.
that would be to him very gratifying; “Of course!” called quickly the echo therein.
(that would be very gratifying to him, of course. “Of course!” the echo quickly interrupted.)

[fɛɐ̯'gny:k‘t‘ za:k‘t‘ le:ɐ̯ mi:ɐ̯ 'vaet‘ɐ(r): le:ɐ̯ 've:rə mi:ɐ̯ ʃo:n lɔft‘ gə'fɔlk‘t‘ fɔn fɛrn
[Vergnügt sagt’ er mir weiter: er wäre mir schon oft gefolgt von fern
[Pleased, said he to me further: he had me already often followed from afar
[(Pleased, he told me further that he had already often followed me at a distance)

lʊnt‘ 'ha:bə tsu: 'ʃp‘reçən mɪç gə'hɔft‘ʰ; dɔx 'frʊxt‘lo:s va:ɐ̯/va:r lɛs 'lɪmɐ,
und habe zu sprechen mich gehofft; doch fruchtlos war es immer,
and has to speak (to) me hoped; but fruitless was it always,
(and hoped to speak to me; but it was always fruitless,)

dɛn maxt‘ le:ɐ̯s nɔx zo: faen, bə'mɛrk‘t‘ hɛt‘ lɪç li:n 'nɪmɐ;
denn macht’ er’s noch so fein, bemerkt hätt’ ich ihn nimmer;
for did he it ever so fine, noticed would have I him never;
(for no matter how expertly he did it, I would *never* have noticed him;)

'ɪmɐ! fi:l ʃnɛl das 'lɛço laen.]
“Immer!” fiel schnell das Echo ein.]
“Ever!” chimed quickly the echo in.] [*“einfallen”* (in this case) = to interrupt, to chime in]
(“Ever!” the echo quickly interrupted.)]

di:s hø:ɐ̯t‘ le:ɐ̯/le:r, lʊnt‘ hat‘ 'nɛːɐ tsu: 'rʏk‘ən mi:ɐ̯ gə'va:k‘t‘ʰ, ['hø:rənt‘]
Dies hört’ er, und hat näher zu rücken mir gewagt, [*poem* Dies hörend hat er...]
This heard he, and has nearer to move to me dared, [hearing]
(He heard that, and dared to move nearer to me,)

e:ɐ̯ 'glɑop‘t‘ə vo:l, lɪç 'hɛt‘ə das 'laləs li:m gə'za:k‘t‘ʰ;
er glaubte wohl, ich hätte das alles ihm gesagt;
he believed no doubt I had that all to him said;
(he no doubt believed that *I* had said all that to him;)

ɛɐ̯ˈlaopst duː,   ʃpˈraːx leːɐ̯ ˈt͡seːɐ̯tˈlɪç,
"Erlaubst du," sprach er zärtlich,
"Allow   you," spoke he tenderly,
("Will you allow me," he said tenderly,)

das lɪç lals ˈmaenə braotʰ dɪç rɛçtˈ fɔn ˈhɛrt͡sən ˈkʰʏsə?
"dass ich als meine Braut dich recht von Herzen küsse?"
"that I   as my   bride you right from heart kiss?"
("to kiss you as my bride, right from the heart?")   [*poem:* **vom** (fɔm, from the) **Herzen**]

ˈkʰʏsə! ʃriː jɛt͡st das ˈlɛço laotʰ.
"Küsse!" schrie jetzt das Echo laut.
"Kiss!" cried now the echo loudly.
("Kiss!" the echo now loudly cried.)

nuːn ziː, zoː lɪst͡s gəˈkʰɔmən, das hans miːɐ̯ gaˈpˈ den kʰʊs,—
Nun sieh, so ist's gekommen, dass Hans mir   gab den Kuss,—
Now see, thus is it come,   that Hans to me gave the kiss,—
(Now you see, that's how it happened that Hans gave me the kiss,—)

das ˈbøːzə, ˈbøːzə ˈlɛço, lɛs maxtˈ miːɐ̯ fiːl fɛɐ̯ˈdrʊs; [*poem:* **das** (das, that) **macht mir**]
das böse, böse Echo, es macht mir   viel Verdruss;
the wicked, wicked echo, it makes for me much annoyance;
(the wicked, wicked echo, it causes me a lot of trouble;)

ʊntˈ ˈjɛt͡so vɪrtˈ leːɐ̯ ˈkʰɔmən, vɪrstˈ ˈzeːən ˈzɪçɐ̯lɪç,
und jetzo wird er kommen, wirst   sehen sicherlich,
and now will he come,   you will see surely
(and now he will be coming, you will surely see,)

ʊntˈ vɪrtˈ fɔn diːɐ̯ bəˈgeːrən lɪn ˈleːrən   t͡suː ˈzaenəm ˈvaebə mɪç.
und wird von dir begehren in Ehren   zu seinem Weibe mich.
and will from you ask   with with due deference as his   wife me.
(and will with due deference ask you for me as his wife.)   ["in Ehren" = with due deference]

ɪst diːɐ̯   deːɐ̯ hans, liːpˈ ˈmʊtˈɐ, nɪçtˈ rɛçt t͡suː ˈmaenəm man,
Ist dir   der Hans, lieb Mutter, nicht recht zu meinem Mann,
Is for you the Hans, dear Mother, not   right as my   husband,
(If Hans isn't right for you as my husband, dear Mother,)

zoː zaːkˈ, das liːm   das ˈlɛço den ˈbøːzən ʃtˈraeç gəˈtʰaːn;
so sag, dass ihm   das Echo den bösen Streich getan;
then say, that for him the echo the wicked trick   (had) done;
(then tell him that the echo played a wicked trick on him;)
            [*poem:* **so sage** (ˈzaːgə), **dass das Echo ihm diesen** (ˈdiːzən, this) **Streich getan**]

dɔx glaopst duː, das viːɐ̯ ˈpʰasən t͡suː ˈlaenəm ˈleːɐ̯pʰaːɐ̯,
doch glaubst du, dass wir passen zu einem Ehepaar,
but believe you, that we are suited as a   married couple,
(but if you believe that we are suited to be a married couple,)

156

dan mʊst duː liːn nɪçt‘ ‘kʰrɛŋk‘ən, maːkst ‘dɛŋk‘ən, das lɪç das ‘lɛço vaːɐ̯!
dann musst du ihn nicht kränken, magst denken, dass ich das Echo war!
then must you him not offend, you may think, that I the echo was!
(then you must not offend him; you may think that *I* was the echo!)

[*poem:* **mag** (maːk‘) **denken** (he may think = let him think that I was the echo)]

[This is Schubert's only setting of a poem by Castelli, who wrote the libretto for Schubert's one-act opera *Die Verschworenen*, a version of *Lysistrata*, later revised as *Der häusliche Krieg*, after the censors had refused to approve the original text. Neither version was produced during Schubert's lifetime. *Das Echo* was probably written to satisfy a publisher's demand for something of a "merry, comic nature." Schubert omitted the fourth verse, in brackets above, but it is included in the *Gesamtausgabe*. The echo effect appears in each verse of this strophic song, as in the interludes.]

das ‘fɪndən
Das Finden
The Find

Posthumously published [composed 1815] (poem by Ludwig Kosegarten)

ɪç haːp‘ laen ‘mɛːt‘çən ‘fʊndən, zanft‘, ‘leːdəl, dɔ͜ʏtʃ lʊnt‘ guːtʰ,   [‘mɛːk‘t‘laen]
Ich hab' ein Mädchen funden, sanft, edel, deutsch und gut, [*poem:* **Mägdlein**]
I have a girl found, gentle, noble, German and good,
(I have found a girl who is gentle, noble, German, and good;)

iːɐ̯ blɪk‘ lɪst‘ mɪlt‘ lʊnt‘ ‘glɛntsənt‘, viː ‘laːbənt‘zonəngluːtʰ,   [‘frɔ͜ʏnt‘lɪç]
ihr Blick ist mild und glänzend, wie Abendsonnenglut, [*poem:* **mild und freundlich**]
her look is mild and radiant, like sunset- fire,   [friendly]

iːɐ̯ haːɐ̯ viː ‘zɔmɐveːbən, liːɐ̯/iːr ‘lɑ͜ʊɡə ‘faelçənblɑ͜ʊ;
ihr Haar wie Sommerweben, ihr Auge veilchenblau;
her hair like gossamer, her eye violet- blue;

dem ‘roːzənkʰɛlç deːɐ̯ ‘lɪp‘ən lɛnt‘kʰvɪlt‘ ɡə‘zaŋ viː tʰɑ͜ʊ.
dem Rosenkelch der Lippen entquillt Gesang wie Tau.
from the rose- chalice of the lips springs song like dew.
(from the rosy chalice of her lips song springs forth like dew.)

iːɐ̯ bɑ͜ʊ lɪst‘ hoːx lʊnt‘ ‘hɛrlɪç. liːɐ̯ vʊx viː
Ihr Bau ist hoch und herrlich. Ihr Wuchs wie
Her build is tall and splendid. Her figure like
(Her body is tall and splendid. Her figure is like)

tʰiːf lɪm haen deːɐ̯ ‘bɪrk‘ə ‘ʃlaŋk‘ə ‘ʃøːnhaet‘, liːɐ̯ ‘buːzən ‘ʃvaːnənraen.
tief im Hain der Birke schlanke Schönheit, ihr Busen Schwanenrein.
deep in the grove the birch's slender beauty, her bosom swan- pure.
(the slender beauty of the birch-tree deep in the grove, her bosom is white as a swan's.)

[deːɐ̯ ‘buːxən ʃlaŋkst‘ lʊnt‘ ‘ʃøːnst‘ə;]
[*poem:* **der Buchen schlankst' und schönste;**]
[(the slimmest and loveliest of the beech-trees;)]

ɪm ˈhoːən ˈʃvaːnənbuːzən kʰlɔpft˺ liːɐ̯/liːr ɪaen ˈleːdəl hɛrts,
Im hohen Schwanenbusen klopft ihr ein edel Herz,
In the high swan- bosom beats in her a noble heart,
(In her high swan-like bosom a noble heart is beating,)

    [iːɐ̯ ʃlɛːkt˺ ɪaen hɛrts ɪm ˈbuːzən zoː ˈkɪnt˺lɪç lʊnt˺ zoː tʰrɔ̸,]
    [*poem:* **Ihr schlägt ein Herz im Busen so kindlich und so treu,**]
    [(The heart that beats in her bosom is so childlike and so faithful,)]

das kʰɛnt˺ nɪçt˺ t͡svaŋ nɔx ˈlaonən, nɪçt˺ ˈfrɛçə lʊst˺ nɔx ʃmɛrt͡s.
das kennt nicht Zwang noch Launen, nicht freche Lust noch Schmerz.
that knows not compulsion nor whims, not shameless pleasure nor pain.
(that does not know compulsion or whims, that knows neither shameless pleasure nor pain.)

    [frɛmt˺ ˈalɐ tʰʏk˺ lʊnt˺ ˈlaonə, fɛrn ˈalɐ ˈt͡siːrəraɐ̯.]
    [*poem:* **fremd aller Tück' und Laune, fern aller Ziererei.**]
    [(a stranger to all malice and caprice, far from all affectation.)]

ɪn ˈduːstras ˈgryːnɐ ˈvɪlt˺nɪs, lam ˈkʰlaːrən ˈrɪnval-flʊs,
In Dustras grüner Wildnis, am klaren Rinval-Fluss,
In Dustra's green wilderness, by the clear Rinval River,

    [vɪst˺ liːɐ̯, voː dʊrç di ˈviːzən di ˈluːt˺a ˈblɪt͡sənt˺ laelth?]
    [*poem:* **Wisst ihr, wo durch die Wiesen die Lutha blitzend eilt?**]
    [(Do you know where the Lutha hurries through the meadows as fast as lightning?)]

valt˺ ˈlaenzaːm lʊnt˺ fɛɐ̯ˈloːrən dɛs ˈhɔldən ˈmɛːt˺çəns fuːs.
wallt einsam und verloren des holden Mädchens Fuss.
wanders lonely and lost the lovely girl's foot.
(the lovely girl is wandering, alone and lost.)

    [dɔrt˺ lɪst͡s, voː lɪm fɛɐ̯ˈbɔrgnən das ˈleːdlə ˈmɛːk˺t˺laen vaelth.]
    [*poem:* **Dort ist's, wo im Verborgnen das edle Mägdlein weilt.**]
    [(There it is that the noble girl lingers, unnoticed.)]

ziː ʃveːp˺t˺ daˈhɪn. laen ˈkʰrɛnt͡sçən ʃmʏk˺t˺ liːɐ̯ das haːɐ̯.   [dɔrt˺ ˈvandəlt˺ ziː.]
Sie schwebt dahin. Ein Kränzchen schmückt ihr das Haar. [*poem:* **Dort wandelt sie.**]
She floats along. A little wreath adorns for her the hair.   [There wanders she.]
(She seems to float when she walks. A little wreath adorns her hair.)   [(There she wanders.)]

lɛs ʃmʏk˺t˺ laen ʃt˺raos den ˈhoːən ˈbuːzən, deːn ziː lɪm tʰao gəˈpflʏk˺tʰ.
Es schmückt ein Strauss den hohen Busen, den sie im Tau gepflückt.
There adorns a bouquet the high bosom, which she in the dew (has) plucked.
(Her high bosom is adorned with a bouquet that she has plucked in the dew.)

    [liːɐ̯ ʃmʏk˺t di brʊst˺ laen ʃt˺raos deːɐ̯ ˈbluːmən, di ziː...]
    [*poem:* **Ihr schmückt die Brust ein Strauss der Blumen, die sie...**]
    [(Her breast is adorned with a bouquet of the flowers that she plucked in the dew.)]

das ˈmɛːt˺çən haːb ɪç ˈfʊndən. lɪm ˈkʰɔ̸ʃən ˈfryːgəvant˺
Das Mädchen hab' ich funden. Im keuschen Frühgewand
The girl have I found. In the chaste morning-garment
(I have found the girl. In a modest morning garment)

    [ˈalzo haːb ɪç ziː ˈfʊndən. voːl lan deːɐ̯ ˈluːt˺a ʃt˺rant˺]
    [*poem:* **Also hab' ich sie funden. Wohl an der Lutha Strand**]
    [(Thus have I found her. Probably on the shore of the Lutha]

158

gɪŋ zi: lɪm dʊft deːɐ̯ 'fryːə lan 'rɪnvals 'bluːmənrant'.
ging sie im Duft der Frühe an Rinvals Blumenrand.
walked she in the fragrance of the early morning along Rinval's flower- border.
(she was walking along the Rinval's border of flowers in the fragrance of the early morning.)

[za: lɪç zi: 'laenzaːm 'vandəln lɪm 'laeçt'ən 'fryːgəvant'.]
[*poem:* **sah' ich sie einsam wandeln im leichten Frühgewand.**]
[(I saw her wandering alone in a light morning garment.)]

aen 'laezəs 'lʏft'çən 'rɪŋəlt' liːɐ̯ 'vɛlənʃt'røːmənd haːɐ̯,
Ein leises Lüftchen ringelt' ihr wellenströmend Haar,
A light little breeze ruffled her wavy flowing hair,

ʊnt dʊrç di 'ɛrlən 'halt'ə liːɐ̯ 'liːt'çən zyːs lʊnt' kʰlaːɐ̯.
und durch die Erlen hallte ihr Liedchen süss und klar.
and through the alders echoed her little song sweet and clear.
(and her little song reverberated among the alder-trees, sweet and clear.)

[ʊnt dʊrç di 'pʰap'əln 'fløːt'ət' liːɐ̯ 'liːt'çən hɛl lʊnt' kʰlaːɐ̯.]
[*poem:* **und durch die Pappeln flötet' ihr Liedchen hell und klar.**]
[(and her little song fluted through the poplar-trees, bright and clear.)]

ɪç laːk' lɪn 'kʰleːgədʏft'ən lam 'blaobəblyːmt'ən bax;
Ich lag in Kleegedüften am blaubeblümten Bach;
I lay in clover-scents by the blue-flowered brook;
(I had been lying by the brook among the blue flowers and the fragrance of clover;)

ɪç beːp't' lɛmpʰoːɐ̯/lɛmpʰoːr, lʊnt' 'ʃaot'ə dem 'leːdlən 'mɛːt'çən naːx.
ich bebt' empor, und schaute dem edlen Mädchen nach.
I trembled up, and looked the noble girl after.
(I stood up, trembling, and gazed after the noble girl.) [*poem:* **ich fuhr** (fuːɐ̯) **empor** (I jumped up)]

fɛɐ̯'tsɔøç, fɛɐ̯'tsɔøç, du: 'hɔldə! daen blɪk' lɪst' liːp' lʊnt' guːtʰ.
Verzeuch, verzeuch, du Holde! Dein Blick ist lieb und gut.
Delay, delay, you lovely one! Your glance is dear and kind.
(Don't go away, lovely one! Your glance is sweet and kind.)

["*verzeuch*" (poetic) = "*verziehe*" = (obsolete use) delay, hesitate]
[*poem:* **du siehst so** (du: ziːst' zoː, you look so) **lieb und gut**]

aox lɪç bɪn dɔøtʃ lʊnt' 'leːdəl, laen 'jʏŋlɪŋ frɔm lʊnt' guːtʰ.
Auch ich bin deutsch und edel, ein Jüngling fromm und gut.
Also I am German and noble, a young man devout and good.
(I too am German and well-born, a devout, good young man.)

zi: 'vant'ə zɪç, zi: 'zɔømt'ə, zi: 'vɪŋk't'ə 'frɔønt'lɪç miːɐ̯;
Sie wandte sich, sie säumte, sie winkte freundlich mir;
She turned herself, she lingered, she waved friendlily to me;
(She turned, she lingered, she waved to me in a friendly way;)

froː 'liːrəs blɪks lʊnt' 'vɪŋk'əs, floːk' lɪç lɛnt't'sʏk't' tsu: liːɐ̯.
froh ihres Blicks und Winkes, flog ich entzückt zu ihr.
glad of her look and wave, flew I enraptured to her.
(happy about the way she looked at me and waved, I flew to her, enraptured.)

ɛɐ̯'haːbən ʃt'ant' ʊnt' 'haɛl̯ɪç foːɐ̯ miːɐ̯ das 'hoːə vaɛp'.
Erhaben stand und heilig vor mir das hohe Weib.
Exalted stood and holy before me the sublime woman.
(Exalted and holy, that sublime woman was standing before me.)

ɪç 'laːbɐ ʃlaŋ fɛɐ̯'tʰrɑol̯ɪç den l̯arm l̯ʊm 'liːrən l̯aɛp'.
Ich aber schlang vertraulich den Arm um ihren Leib.
I though wound familiarly the arm around her body.
(I, though, wound my arm familiarly around her body.)

ɪç haːp' das 'leːdlə 'mɛːt'çən l̯an 'maɛnɐ hant' gə'fyːɐ̯tʰ;
Ich hab' das edle Mädchen an meiner Hand geführt;
I have the noble girl by my hand led;
(I have taken the noble girl by the hand;)

ɪç bɪn mɪt' liːɐ̯/iːr l̯am 'ʃt'aːdən dɛs baxs hɪ'nap'ʃp'atsiːɐ̯tʰ. ['l̯uːfɐ]
ich bin mit ihr am Staden des Bachs hinabspaziert. [*Peters:* **am Ufer**]
I am (have) with her by the river-side walk of the brook down walked [bank]
(I have walked with her down to the path by the brook.) ["*Staden*" is dialect]

ɪç haːp' zi: 'liːp'gəvɔnən, l̯ɪç vaɛs, zi: l̯ɪst' miːɐ̯ guːtʰ.
Ich hab' sie liebgewonnen, ich weiss, sie ist mir gut.
I have her grown fond of, I know she is to me good. [idiom: = she loves me]
(I have grown fond of her, I know that she loves me.)

drʊm zaɛ maɛn liːt' liːɐ̯/iːr 'l̯aegən, liːɐ̯/iːr 'l̯aɛgən guːt' l̯ʊnt' bluːtʰ.
Drum sei mein Lied ihr eigen, ihr eigen Gut und Blut.
Therefore be my song her own, her own property and blood.
(Therefore may my song be hers, her own possession and her own flesh and blood.)

["*Gut und Blut*" = life and property]

[Schubert's setting of this poem that is one moment artfully naïve, the next somewhat pretentious, is marked "*etwas langsam, unschuldig*" (somewhat slowly, *innocently*), and, though it is a trifle, eighteen bars long (not counting the many repetitions), it has typical Schubertean charm. He copied out only one verse, with a notation that there were six more. The Peters edition offers the first and last verses, the *Gesamtausgabe* all seven, but with many variants from the published poem (apparently Schubert worked from a different version, no longer available).]

Das Fischermädchen see *Schwanengesang*

das gə'haɛmnɪs
Das Geheimnis
The Secret

Posthumously published [composed 1815 and 1823] (poem by Friedrich von Schiller)

zi: 'kʰɔnt'ə miːɐ̯ kʰaen 'vœrt'çən 'zaːgən, 'tsu: 'fiːlə 'l̯ɑoʃɐ 'vaːrən vax;
Sie konnte mir kein Wörtchen sagen, zu viele Lauscher waren wach;
She could to me no little word say, too many eavesdroppers were awake;
(She couldn't say a single word to me: too many eavesdroppers were on the alert;)

den blɪk‿ nuːɐ̯ dʊrft‿ ɪç ˈʃʏçt‿ɐn ˈfraːɡən, ʊnt‿ voːl fɛɐ̯ˈʃt‿ant‿ ɪç, vas ɛːɐ̯ ʃpraːx.
den Blick nur durft' ich schüchtern fragen, und wohl verstand ich, was er sprach.
the look only could I shyly question, and well understood I, what it spoke.
(only her look could I shyly question, and well did I understand what it spoke.)

laɛs kʰɔm ɪç heːɐ̯/heːr ɪn ˈdaɛnɐ ˈʃt‿ɪlə, duː ʃøːn bəˈlɑop‿t‿əs ˈbuːxənts̪ɛltʰ,
Leis' komm' ich her in deine Stille, du schön belaubtes Buchenzelt,
Softly come I hither into your stillness, you beautifully foliated beech- tent,
(Softly I come into your stillness, you beech-grove so beautifully canopied with foliage,)

fɛɐ̯ˈbɪrk‿ ɪn ˈdaɛnɐ ˈɡryːnən ˈhʏlə di ˈliːbəndən dem lɑok‿ deːɐ̯ vɛltʰ!
verbirg in deiner grünen Hülle die Liebenden dem Aug' der Welt!
hide in your green covering the loving ones to the eye of the world!
(hide the lovers from the eyes of the world under your cover of green!)

fɔn ˈfɛrnə mɪt‿ fɛɐ̯ˈvɔrnəm ˈz̪ɑozən ˈlarbaɛt‿ət deːɐ̯ ɡəˈʃɛft‿ɡə tʰaːk‿,
Von Ferne mit verworrnem Sausen arbeitet der geschäftge Tag,
From afar with confused buzzing works the busy day,
(From afar one can hear the confused sounds of the busy working day,)

ʊnt dʊrç deːɐ̯ ˈʃt‿ɪmən ˈhoːləs ˈbrɑozən lɛɐ̯ˈkʰɛn ɪç ˈʃveːrɐ ˈhɛmɐ ʃlaːk‿.
und durch der Stimmen hohles Brausen erkenn' ich schwerer Hämmer Schlag.
and through the voices' hollow roar recognize I heavy hammers' blow.
(and, through the hollow roar of many voices, I recognize the crash of heavy hammers.)

zoː ˈz̪ɑoɐ rɪŋt di ˈkʰarɡən ˈloːzə deːɐ̯ mɛnʃ dem ˈhart‿ən ˈhɪməl lap‿;
So sauer ringt die kargen Lose der Mensch dem harten Himmel ab;
So sourly wrests the meager allotment the human being the hard heaven from;
(So sourly must the laborer wrest from hard heaven his meager allotment;)

dɔx laɛçt‿ lɛɐ̯ˈvɔrbən, lɑos dem ˈʃoːsə deːɐ̯ ˈɡœt‿ɐ fɛlt das ɡlʏk‿ hɛˈrap‿.
doch leicht erworben, aus dem Schosse der Götter fällt das Glück herab.
yet easily won, out of the lap of the gods falls the happiness down.
(yet happiness falls down to us, easily won, from the lap of the gods.)

das jaː di ˈmɛnʃən niː lɛs ˈhøːrən, viː ˈtʰrɔø̯ə liːp‿ lʊns ʃt‿ɪl bəˈɡlʏk‿tʰ!
Dass ja die Menschen nie es hören, wie treue Lieb' uns still beglückt!
That by all means the people never it hear, how faithful love us quietly makes happy!
(May other people never hear how quietly faithful love makes us happy!

ziː ˈkʰœnən nuːɐ̯ di ˈfrɔø̯də ˈʃt‿øːrən, va̯ɛl ˈfrɔø̯də niː ziː zɛlpst‿ lɛnt‿ˈts̪ʏk‿tʰ.
Sie können nur die Freude stören, weil Freude nie sie selbst entzückt.
Them could only the joy disturb, because joy never them themselves delighted.
(Our joy would only disturb them, since they themselves have never known such joy.)

di vɛlt‿ vɪrt‿ niː das ɡlʏk‿ lɛɐ̯ˈlɑobən, lals ˈbɔø̯t‿ə nuːɐ̯ vɪrt‿ lɛs ɡəˈhaʃtʰ;
Die Welt wird nie das Glück erlauben, als Beute nur wird es gehascht;
The world will never the happiness allow, as booty only will be it snatched;
(The world will never freely allow happiness; only as booty can it be snatched;)

[*first version (and poem):* **als Beute wird es nur gehascht**]

ɛntˈvɛndən mʊst duːs ˈloːdɐ ˈrɑ̯ɔbən, leː   dɪç di ˈmɪsgʊnst ˈlyːbɐraʃtʰ.
entwenden musst du's oder rauben, eh'   dich die Missgunst überrascht.
pilfer   must you it or   steal, before you the envy   surprises.
(you must pilfer it or steal it before envy takes you by surprise.)

lae̯s lɑ̯ɔf den ˈt͡seːən kʰɔmt͡s gəˈʃlɪçən,   di ˈʃtˈɪlə   liːpˈtˈ lɛs lʊnt di naxtʰ;
Leis' auf den Zehen kommt's geschlichen, die Stille   liebt es und die Nacht;
Softly on the tiptoes comes it sneaked,   the stillness loves it and the night;
(Softly on tiptoes it comes sneaking; it loves stillness and the night;)

mɪtˈ ˈʃnɛlən   ˈfyːsən lɪst͡s lɛntˈvɪçən, voː   dɛs fɛɐ̯ˈreːtˈɐs ˈlɑ̯ɔgə vaxtʰ.
mit schnellen Füssen ist's entwichen, wo   des Verräters Auge wacht.
with fast   feet   is it escaped,   where the betrayer's eye is awake.
(it escapes on fast feet wherever the betrayer's eye is alert.)

oː ˈʃlɪŋə   dɪç,   du ˈzanftˈə ˈkʰvɛlə, lae̯n ˈbrae̯tˈɐ ʃtˈroːm lʊm   lʊns hɛˈrʊm,
O schlinge dich,   du sanfte Quelle, ein breiter Strom um   uns herum,
Oh coil   yourself, you gentle spring, a   broad stream around us   around,
(Oh coil yourself all around us, gentle spring, like a broad stream,)

ʊnt ˈdroːəntˈ   mɪtˈ lɛmˈpʰøːɐ̯tˈə ˈvɛlə fɛɐ̯ˈtʰae̯dɪgə diːs ˈhae̯lɪçtʰuːm!
und drohend   mit empörter Welle verteidige dies Heiligtum!
and threatening with indignant wave defend   this sanctuary!
(and, threatening with angry waves, defend this sanctuary!)

[Schubert composed two different settings of the poem: the first, in simple strophic form, from 1815, expresses shyness and delicacy, the second, more elaborate version of 1823 is more faithful to the varying images in the poem. Both share a similar tiptoe figure in part of the accompaniment and both deserve to be known.]

das gəˈʃtˈøːɐ̯tˈə glʏkʰ
Das gestörte Glück
Interrupted Happiness

Posthumously published [composed 1815] (poem by Theodor Körner)

ɪç haːpˈ lae̯n ˈhae̯səs ˈjʊŋəs bluːtˈ, viː liːɐ̯ voːl   ˈlalə vɪstʰ,
Ich hab ein heisses junges Blut, wie ihr wohl   alle wisst,
I   have a   hot   young blood, as you probably all   know,
(I am young and hot-blooded, as you probably all know;)

ɪç bɪn dem ˈkʰʏsən gaːɐ̯ t͡su guːtˈ,   lʊntˈ haːpˈ nɔx niː gəˈkʰʏstʰ;
ich bin dem Küssen gar zu gut,   und hab noch nie geküsst;
I   am to the kissing entirely too favorably disposed, and have still never kissed;
(I am only too favorably disposed to kissing, and yet till now have never kissed;)

den lɪstˈ miːɐ̯/miːr lɑ̯ɔx mae̯n ˈliːpˈçən   hɔltˈ, s vaːɐ̯ dɔx lals vɛns nɪçtˈ ˈveːɐ̯dən zɔltʰ:
denn ist mir   auch mein Liebchen hold, 's war doch als wenn's nicht werden sollt':
for   is to me   even my sweetheart kind, it was yet as if   it not become should:
(for even though my sweetheart is kind to me, it seemed as if it should never happen:)

tʰrɔts ˈalɐ myː lʊntˈ ˈalɐ lɪstˈ, haːb ɪç dɔx ˈniːmaːls nɔx gəˈkʰʏstʰ.
trotz aller Müh und aller List, hab ich doch niemals noch geküsst.
in spite of all effort and all cunning, have I yet never still kissed.
(in spite of all my effort and all my cunning, I have nevertheless still never kissed.)

dɛs ˈnaxbaːɐ̯s ˈrøːsçən lɪstˈ miːɐ̯ guːtˈ; ziː gɪŋ tsuːɐ̯ ˈviːzə fryː,
Des Nachbars Röschen ist mir gut; sie ging zur Wiese früh,
The neighbor's Rosie is to me favorably disposed; she went to the meadow early,
(My neighbor's daughter Rosie likes me; she went to the meadow early in the morning,)

ɪç liːf liːɐ̯ naːx lʊntˈ ˈfastˈə muːtˈ, lʊntˈ ʃlaŋ den larm lʊm ziː:
ich lief ihr nach und fasste Mut, und schlang den Arm um sie:
I ran her after and seized courage, and wound the arm around her:
(I ran after her, plucked up my courage, and wound my arm around her:)

daː ʃtˈax lɪç lan dem ˈmiːdɐbantˈ miːɐ̯/miːr ˈlae̯nə ˈnaːdəl lɪn di hantˈ;
da stach ich an dem Miederband mir eine Nadel in die Hand;
there stuck I at the bodice-ribbon to me a pin into the hand;
(at that moment I stuck a pin from her bodice into my hand;)

das bluːtˈ liːf ʃtˈarkˈ, lɪç ʃpˈraŋ naːx hao̯s, lʊntˈ mɪt dem ˈkʰʏsən vaːɐ̯/vaːr lɛs lao̯s.
das Blut lief stark, ich sprang nach Haus, und mit dem Küssen war es aus.
the blood ran strong, I sprang toward house, and with the kissing was it over.
(my blood flowed profusely, I ran home, and that was the end of my chance for a kiss.)

jʏŋstˈ gɪŋ lɪç zoː tsʊm ˈtsae̯tˈfɐɐ̯tʰrae̯pˈ, lʊntˈ tʰraːf ziː dɔrtˈ lam flʊs,
Jüngst ging ich so zum Zeitvertreib, und traf sie dort am Fluss,
Recently went I just to the pastime, and met her there at the river,
(Recently I went for a walk more or less to pass the time, and happened to meet her by the river,)

ɪç ʃlaŋ den larm lʊm ˈliːrən lae̯pˈ, lʊntˈ baːtˈ lʊm ˈlae̯nən kʰʊs;
ich schlang den Arm um ihren Leib, und bat um einen Kuss;
I wound the arm around her body, and asked for a kiss;
(I wound my arm around her body and asked for a kiss;)

ziː ˈʃpˈɪtstˈə ʃoːn den ˈroːzənmʊntˈ, daː kʰaːm deːr ˈlaltˈə ˈkʰɛtˈənhʊntˈ,
sie spitzte schon den Rosenmund, da kam der alte Kettenhund,
she puckered already the rose- mouth, there came the old watch-dog,
(she was already puckering her rosy lips; at that moment the old watch-dog came)

lʊntˈ bɪs mɪç ˈvyːtˈəntˈ lɪn das bae̯n! daː liːs lɪç voːl das ˈkʰʏsən zae̯n.
und biss mich wütend in das Bein! Da liess ich wohl das Küssen sein.
and bit me furiously in the leg! There let I surely the kissing be.
(and bit me furiously on the leg! At that moment, you can be sure, I let the kissing be.)

drao̯f zaːs lɪç lae̯nstˈ foːɐ̯/foːr ˈliːrə tʰyːɐ̯/tʰyːr lɪn ˈʃtˈɪlə frɔɪ̯tˈ lʊntˈ lʊstʰ,
Drauf sass ich einst vor ihrer Tür in stiller Freud' und Lust,
Thereupon sat I once in front of her door in quiet joy and pleasure,
(After that, I once was sitting in front of her door in quiet joy and pleasure;)

ziː gaːpˈ liːɐ̯ ˈliːbəs ˈhɛntˈçən miːɐ̯/miːr, lɪç tsoːkˈ ziː lan di brʊstʰ:
sie gab ihr liebes Händchen mir, ich zog sie an die Brust:
she gave her dear little hand to me, I drew her to the breast:
(she gave me her dear little hand, I drew her to my breast:)

daː ʃpˈraŋ deːɐ̯ ˈfaːtˈɐ ˈhɪntˈɐm tˈoːɐ̯, voː leːɐ̯/leːr ʊns lɛŋstˈ bəˈlaʊ̯ʃtˈ, hɛɐ̯ˈfoːɐ̯,
da sprang der Vater hinterm Tor, wo er uns längst belauscht', hervor,
there sprang the father behind the gate, where he us long since eavesdropped, out,
(At that moment her father jumped out from behind the gate, where he had been spying on us for some time already,)

ʊntˈ viː ɡəˈvøːnlɪç vaːɐ̯ deːɐ̯ ʃlʊsː lɪç kʰaːm laʊ̯x lʊm den ˈdrɪtˈən kʰʊs.
und wie gewöhlich war der Schluss: ich kam auch um den dritten Kuss.
and as usual was the ending: I came (away) also without the third kiss.
(and the ending was as usual: I lost the third kiss too.) ["*um etwas kommen*" = to lose something]

eːɐ̯stˈ ˈɡɛstˈɐn tʰraːf lɪç ziː lam haʊ̯s, ziː riːf mɪç laɛ̯s heˈraɛ̯n:
Erst gestern traf ich sie am Haus, sie rief mich leis' herein:
Just yesterday met I her at the house, she called me softly inside:
(Just yesterday I met her at her house; she called me softly to come inside:

maɛ̯n ˈfɛnstˈɐ ɡeːtˈ lɪn n hoːf hɪˈnaʊ̯s, hɔ̜ø̯tˈ ˈlaːbənt vartˈ lɪç daɛ̯n.
"Mein Fenster geht in 'n Hof hinaus, heut' Abend wart ich dein."
"My window goes into the courtyard out, today evening wait I for you."
("My window looks out into the courtyard; this evening I shall be waiting for you.")
[" *'n* " = *den* = the]

daː kʰaːm lɪç dɛn lɪn ˈliːbəsvaːn, lʊntˈ ˈleːktˈə ˈmaɛ̯nə ˈlaɛ̯tˈɐ(r) lan;
Da kam ich denn in Liebeswahn, und legte meine Leiter an;
There came I then in love- madness, and laid my ladder against;
(I came there then in a delirium of love and laid my ladder against her wall;)

dɔx ˈlʊntˈɐ miːɐ̯ braːx ziː lɛntˈtsvaɛ̯, lʊntˈ mɪt dem ˈkʰʏsən vaːɐ̯s foːɐ̯ˈbaɛ̯.
doch unter mir brach sie entzwei, und mit dem Küssen war's vorbei.
but under me broke it in two, and with the kissing was it over.
(but it broke in two under me and that was the end of kissing.)

ʊntˈ ˈlaləmaːl ɡeːtˈ miːɐ̯s nuːn zoː; loː! das lɪçs ˈlaɛ̯dən mʊs!
Und allemal geht mir's nun so; o! dass ich's leiden muss!
And all the time goes for me it now so; oh! that I it endure must!
(And that's the way it goes for me all the time; oh! that I should have to endure it!)

maɛ̯n ˈleːptˈaːkˈ veːɐ̯d lç ˈnɪmɐ froː, kʰriːɡ lç nɪçtˈ baltˈ nən kʰʊs.
Mein Lebtag werd' ich nimmer froh, krieg' ich nicht bald 'nen Kuss.
My life-day will be I never happy, get I not soon a kiss.
(As long as I live I shall never be happy if I don't soon get a kiss.)
["*mein Lebtag*" = in all my life; "*'nen*" = "*einen*" = a]

das ɡlʏkˈ ziːtˈ mɪç zoː ˈfɪnstˈɐ(r) lan, vas haːb lç ˈlarmɐ vɪçtˈ ɡəˈtʰaːn?
Das Glück sieht mich so finster an, was hab ich armer Wicht getan?
The luck looks me so ominously at, what have I poor wretch done?
(Luck looks at me so ominously! What have I done, poor wretch?)

drʊm, veːɐ̯/veːr lɛs høːɐ̯tˈ, lɛɐ̯ˈbarmə zɪç, lʊntˈ zaɛ̯ zoː ɡuːtˈ lʊntˈ ˈkʰʏsə mɪç.
Drum, wer es hört, erbarme sich, und sei so gut und küsse mich.
Therefore, whoever it hears, have pity herself, and be so kind and kiss me.
(Therefore, whoever hears this song, have pity and be so kind and kiss me.)
["*sich erbarmen*" = to have pity]

[This delightful song has charmingly humorous words and should be fun to sing.]

164

das graːpʼ
Das Grab
The Grave

Posthumously published [composed 1815-1819] (poem by Johann Gaudenz von Salis-Seewis)

das graːpʼ ˈɪst tʰiːf ˈlʊntʼ ˈʃtʼɪlə, ˈlʊntʼ ˈʃaodɐhaftʼ zaen rantʼ,
Das Grab ist tief und stille, und schauderhaft sein Rand,
The grave is deep and still, and horrifying (is) its   brink,

ɛs dɛkʼtʼ mɪtʼ ˈʃvartsɐ ˈhʏlə laen ˈlʊnbəkʰantʼəs lantʼ.
es deckt mit schwarzer Hülle ein unbekanntes Land.
it covers with black   veiling an   unknown   land.

das liːt deːɐ ˈnaxtʼɪɡalən tʰøːntʼ nɪçtʼ lɪn ˈzaenəm ʃoːs.
Das Lied der Nachtigallen tönt nicht in seinem Schoss.
The song of the nightingales sounds not in its   bosom.
(The song of the nightingales is not heard from its depths.)

deːɐ ˈfrɔøntʼʃaftʼ ˈroːzən ˈfalən nuːɐ/nuːr laof dɛs ˈhyːɡəls moːs.
Der Freundschaft Rosen fallen nur   auf des Hügels Moos.
The friendship's roses fall only   onto the mound's moss.
(The roses of friendship fall only onto the moss of the little mound of earth.)

fɛɐˈlasnə ˈbrɔøtʼə ˈrɪŋən lʊmˈzɔnst di ˈhɛndə vʊntʼ;
Verlassne Bräute ringen umsonst die Hände wund;
Forsaken brides wring in vain the hands sore;
(Forsaken brides wring their hands sore in vain;)

deːɐ ˈvaezə ˈkʰlaːɡən ˈdrɪŋən nɪçtʼ lɪn deːɐ ˈtʰiːfə grʊntʼ.
der Waise Klagen dringen nicht in der Tiefe Grund.
the orphan's laments penetrate not into the depths' bottom.
(the orphan's laments do not penetrate to the bottom of its depths.)

dɔx zɔnstʼ lan ˈkʰaenəm ˈlɔrtʼə voːnt di lɛɐˈzeːntʼə ruː;
Doch sonst   an keinem Orte wohnt die ersehnte Ruh;
But otherwise at no   place dwells the longed-for peace;
(But the peace we long for can be found at no other place;)

nuːɐ dʊrç di ˈdʊŋkʼlə ˈpfɔrtʼə geːtʼ man deːɐ ˈhaemaːt tsuː.
nur durch die dunkle Pforte geht man der Heimat zu.
only through the dark gate goes one to the homeland to.
(only through that dark gate do we go back to our original and ultimate home.)

das ˈlarmə hɛrts, hiːˈniːdən   fɔn ˈmançəm ʃtʼʊrm bəˈveːkʼtʰ,
Das arme Herz, hienieden   von manchem Sturm bewegt,
The poor heart, here on earth by many a   storm stirred,
(The poor heart, tossed about by many a storm here on earth,)

ɛɐˈlaŋt den ˈvaːrən ˈfriːdən nuːɐ,   voː lɛs nɪçtʼ meːɐ ʃleːkʼtʰ.
erlangt den wahren Frieden nur,   wo es nicht mehr schlägt.
attains the true peace only (there) where it no longer beats.
(attains true peace only there where it no longer beats.)

[Schubert made five attempts to set this *Das Grab*, the last four of them completed, all for mixed or male chorus. It is not a solo *Lied* at all; but the *Gesamtausgabe* published three versions among the lieder, and another was more recently discovered in an Austrian monastery.]

das ˈgroːsə haleˈluːja
Das grosse Halleluja
The Great Hallelujah

Posthumously published [composed 1816] (poem by Friedrich Gottlieb Klopstock)

ˈeːrə zae dem ˈhoːxlɐɡˌhaːbnən, dem ˈleːɐ̯stʰən,
Ehre sei dem Hocherhabnen, dem Ersten,
Honor be to the High-exalted,   to the First,

dem ˈfaːtʰɐ deːɐ̯ ˈʃœpfʊŋ,   dem   ˈʊnzrə ˈpsalmən ˈʃtʰaməln,
dem Vater der   Schöpfung, dem   unsre Psalmen stammeln,
to the Father of the Creation,   to whom our   psalms   stammer,
(to the Father of Creation, to whom we stammer our psalms,)

ɔpˈɡlaeç deːɐ̯ ˈvʊndəbaːrə   leːɐ̯/leːr ʊnlaosˈʃpˈreçlɪç ʊntʰ ʊnˈdɛŋkˈbaːɐ̯/-baːr ɪstʰ!
obgleich der   wunderbare Er   unaussprechlich und undenkbar   ist!
although the   wondrous He   ineffable   and inconceivable   is!
(although that wondrous He is ineffable and inconceivable to us!)

ˈaenə ˈflamə   fɔn dem lalˈtʰaːɐ̯/lalˈtʰaːr lan dem tʰroːn lʲstʰ lɪn ˈʊnzrə ˈzeːlə ɡəˈʃtʰrøːmtʰ.
Eine Flamme von dem Altar   an dem Thron ist in unsre Seele geströmt.
A   flame   from the altar   at the throne is   into our   soul   streamed.
(A flame from the altar at His throne has streamed into our soul.)   [*poem:* **unsere** (ˈʊnzərə)]

viːɐ̯ frɔøn lʊns   ˈhɪməlsfrɔødən,   das viːɐ̯ zɪntʰ lʊntʰ ˈlyːbɐ liːn lɛɐ̯ˈʃtʰaonən ˈkʰœnən!
Wir freun uns   Himmelsfreuden, dass wir sind und über ihn erstaunen   können!
We gladden ourselves of heaven-joys,   that we exist and over Him marvel   can!
(We revel in the joys of heaven, realizing that we exist and can marvel at Him!)
                                                                [*poem:* **freuen** (ˈfrɔøən)]

ˈeːrə zae liːm   laox fɔn lʊns lan den ˈɡrɛːbən hiːɐ̯,
Ehre sei ihm   auch von uns an den Gräbern hier,
Honor be to Him also from us at the graves   here,
(Honor be to Him from us, too, whose earthly lives end at the grave,)

ɔpˈvoːl lan ˈzaenəs ˈtʰroːnəs ˈletstʰən ˈʃtʰuːfən dɛs ˈlɛrtslenəls ˈniːdɐɡəvɔrfnə   ˈkʰroːnə
obwohl an seines Thrones letzten Stufen des Erzengels niedergeworfne Krone
although at His   throne's last   steps   the archangel's down- thrown   crown
(although on the last step of His throne the archangel's crown has been cast down in obeisance)

lʊntʰ ˈzaenəs ˈpʰraesɡəzaŋs ˈvɔnə   tʰøːntʰ!
und seines Preisgesangs Wonne tönt!
and his   praise- song's rapture sounds!
(and the rapture of his song of praise is sounding!)

ˈeːrə zae lʊnt daŋkʰ lʊntʰ pʰraes dem ˈhoːxlɐɡˌhaːbnən, dem ˈleːɐ̯stʰən,
Ehre sei und Dank und Preis dem Hocherhabnen, dem Ersten,
Honor be and thanks and praise to the High-exalted,   to the First,
(Honor and thanks and praise be to the High-exalted, to the First,)

deːɐ̯ nɪçt‘ bə'gan ʊnt‘ nɪçt‘ 'ḁofhøːrən vɪrt‘,
der nicht begann und nicht aufhören wird,
who not began and not end will,
(who is without beginning and without end,)

deːɐ̯ zo'gaːɐ̯ dɛs ʃt‘ḁops bə'voːnɐn gaːp‘, nɪçt‘ 'ḁoftsuhøːrən! [*poem:* **Staubes** ('ʃt‘ḁobəs)]
der sogar des Staubs Bewohnern gab, nicht aufzuhören!
who even the dust's dwellers gave, not to end!
(who gave everlasting life even to those who dwell in the dust!)

[*Schubert cut four lines of poetry here.*]

'eːrə diːɐ̯, 'hoːxlɐ̯ḥaːbnɐ, 'leːɐ̯st‘ɐ, 'faːt‘ɐ deːɐ̯ 'ʃœpfʊŋ,
Ehre dir, Hocherhabner, Erster, Vater der Schöpfung,
Honor to Thee, High-exalted One, First, Father of the Creation,
(Honor to Thee, High-exalted One, First, Father of Creation,)

'ʊnḁos,ʃp‘reçlɪçɐ, loː 'ʊndɛŋk‘baːrɐ!
Unaussprechlicher, o Undenkbarer!
Ineffable One, O Inconceivable One!

[Although included in the Breitkopf & Härtel collection of Schubert's solo songs, this piece is liturgical in musical style and clearly not a typical *Lied*. It is written in two staves, with the words inserted between them, three-part chords above, a "walking bass" below, and was originally published as a trio for female voices. (The casting down of the archangel's crown refers to an oriental gesture of reverent submission.)]

das 'haᴇmveː / ɑx, deːɐ̯ gə'bɪrkszoːn
Das Heimweh / Ach, der Gebirgssohn
Homesickness / Ah, the Son of the Mountains

Op. 79, No. 1 [1825] (Johann Ladislaus Pyrker)

ɑx, deːɐ̯ gə'bɪrkszoːn hɛŋt‘ mɪt‘ 'kʰɪnt‘lɪçɐ liːp‘ lan deːɐ̯ 'haᴇmaːtʰ!
Ach, der Gebirgssohn hängt mit kindlicher Lieb' an der Heimat!
Ah, the son of the mountains is attached with childlike love to the homeland!

viː, den 'lalp‘ən gə'rḁop‘t‘, hɪn'vɛlk‘ət di 'bluːmə,
Wie, den Alpen geraubt, hinwelket die Blume,
As, from the Alps stolen, withers away the flower,
(As the alpine flower, stolen from the Alps, withers away,)

zoː vɛlk‘t‘ leːɐ̯, liːɐ̯/iːr lɛnt‘'rɪsən, da'hɪn.
so welkt er, ihr entrissen, dahin.
so withers he, from it torn, away.
(so does he wither away, torn from his mountain homeland.)

ʃt‘eːts ziːt‘ leːɐ̯ di 't‘rḁolɪçə 'hʏt‘ə, diː liːn gə'baːɐ̯,
Stets sieht er die trauliche Hütte, die ihn gebar,
Constantly sees he the cozy cottage which him bore,
(Constantly he sees the cozy cottage where he was born,)

ɪm 'hɛlən gryːn lʊm'dʊft‘əndɐ 'mat‘ən,
im hellen Grün umduftender Matten,
in the bright green of fragrant meadows,

ziːt das ˈdʊŋkˈələ ˈføːrəngəˈhœlt̯s, di ˈraːgəndə ˈfɛlsvantˈ ˈyːbɐ(r) liːm,
sieht das dunkele Föhrengehölz, die ragende Felswand über ihm,
sees the dark pinewoods, the towering cliff above him,

ʊntˈ nɔx bɛrkˈ ˈḁ̯ɔf bɛrkˈ ɪn lɛɐ̯ˈʃʏtˈɐndɐ ˈhoːhaet̯ ˈḁ̯ɔfgətʰʏrmtʰ,
und noch Berg auf Berg in erschütternder Hoheit aufgetürmt,
and still mountain after mountain in unnerving height piled up,
(and still mountain after mountain, towering up to terrifying heights,)

[*poem:* **Berg' auf Berg'** (plural: mountains upon mountains)]

ʊntˈ ˈglyːəntˈ ɪm ˈroːzənʃɪmɐ des ˈlaːbənt̯s.
und glühend im Rosenschimmer des Abends.
and glowing in the rosy shimmer of the evening.

ˈɪmɐ ʃveːpˈtˈ ɛs liːm foːɐ̯. fɛɐ̯ˈdʊŋkˈəltˈ ɪstˈ ˈalas ˈlʊm liːn heːɐ̯.
Immer schwebt es ihm vor. Verdunkelt ist alles um ihn her.
Always hovers it him before. Obscured is everything around him hither.
(The image always hovers before him. Everything else around him is obscured.)

ˈɛŋstˈlɪç hɔrçtˈ leːɐ̯; liːm dɔ̯øçtˈ, leːɐ̯ ˈhøːrə das ˈmuːən deːɐ̯ ˈkʰyːə
Ängstlich horcht er; ihm deucht, er höre das Muhen der Kühe
Anxiously listens he; to him seems, he hears the mooing of the cows
(He listens anxiously; it seems to him that he can hear the mooing of the cows)

fɔm ˈnaːən gəˈhœlt̯s, ˈlʊntˈ hoːx fɔn den ˈlalpˈən heˈrʊntˈɐ ˈglœkˈlḁ̯ɛn ˈkʰlɪŋən,
vom nahen Gehölz, und hoch von den Alpen herunter Glöcklein klingen,
from the near-by woods, and high from the Alps downward little bells ring,
(from the near-by woods, and the sound of little bells ringing comes down from the high Alps,)

[*poem:* **von dem** (fɔn dem) **nahen Gehölz**]

iːm dɔ̯øçtˈ, leːɐ̯ ˈhøːrə das ˈruːfən deːɐ̯ ˈhɪrtˈən,
ihm deucht, er höre das Rufen der Hirten,
to him seems, he hears the calling of the shepherdess,
(it seems to him that he can hear the call of the shepherdess,)

ˈoːdɐ(r) lḁ̯ɛn liːt deːɐ̯ ˈzɛnərɪn, di: mɪtˈ ˈlʊmˈʃlaːgəndɐ ˈʃtˈɪmə
oder ein Lied der Sennerin, die mit umschlagender Stimme
or a song of the alpine dairy-maid, who with yodelling voice

ˈfrɔ̯øːdɪç t̯sʊm ˈviːdɐhal ˈḁ̯ɔfjḁ̯ɔxt̯stˈ meloˈdiːən des ˈlalpˈlant̯s:
freudig zum Widerhall aufjauchzt Melodien des Alplands:
joyously to the echo shouts for joy melodies of the Alpland:
(joyously shouts to the echo melodies of the Alpland:)

ˈɪmɐ tʰøːntˈ ɛs liːm naːx. liːn ˈfɛsəlt deːɐ̯ ˈlaxəndən ˈleːbnən ˈlanmuːtˈ nɪçtʰ,
immer tönt es ihm nach. Ihn fesselt der lachenden Eb'nen Anmut nicht,
always sounds it to him after. Him shackles the laughing plain's grace not,
(that song always rings in his ears. The grace of the smiling plain does not hold him captive,)

eːɐ̯ ˈfliːət deːɐ̯ ʃtˈɛːtˈ ˈlḁ̯ɛnlɛŋəndə ˈmḁ̯ɔɐn, ˈlḁ̯ɛnzaːm,
er fliehet der Städt' einengende Mauern, einsam,
he flees the cities' confining walls, lonesome,
(he flees from the confining walls of the cities, all alone,)

ʊnt‘ ʃɑοt‘ ‘lɑοfvaenənt‘ fɔm   ‘hyːgəl di ‘haemɪʃən ‘bɛrgə;
und schaut aufweinend vom   Hügel die heimischen Berge;
and looks weeping   from the hill (at) the native   mountains;
(and, weeping, looks from the hill towards his native mountains:)

ax, lɛs tsiːt‘ liːn da‘hɪn mɪt‘ ‘ʊnviːdəʃt‘eːlɪçɐ   ‘zeːnzʊxtʰ!
ach, es zieht ihn dahin mit unwiderstehlicher Sehnsucht!
ah, it draws him thither with irresistible   longing!
(ah, he is drawn there with irresistible longing!)

[The author of this poem was an archbishop and the patriarch of Venice. Schubert met him in 1825, at Bad Gastein, and set two of his poems to music. This rather long song captures a feeling for the alpine setting as well as the emotion of the young man who grew up in the mountains.]

das ‘haemveː / ɔft‘ lɪn ‘laenzaːm ‘ʃt‘lən ‘ʃt‘ʊndən
Das Heimweh / Oft in einsam stillen Stunden
The Longing for Home / Often in Lonely Quiet Hours

Posthumously published [composed 1816] (poem by Theodor Hell, Max Kalbeck*)

ɔft‘ lɪn ‘laenzaːm ‘ʃt‘ɪlən ‘ʃt‘ʊndən haːb ɪç laen gə‘fyːl lɛm‘pfʊndən,
Oft in einsam   stillen Stunden hab’ ich ein Gefühl empfunden,
Often in lonely   quiet hours   have I an   emotion felt,
(Often in lonely quiet hours I have felt an emotion,)

ʊnlɛɐ‘kʰleːɐbaːɐ, ‘vʊndɐbaːɐ, das   viː ‘zeːnzʊxt‘ naːx deːɐ ‘fɛrnə,
unerklärbar,   wunderbar, das   wie Sehnsucht nach der Ferne,
inexplicable,   wonderful, which, like yearning for   the distance,

hoːx hɪ‘nɑοf lɪn ‘bɛsrə ‘ʃt‘ɛrnə, viː laen ‘laezəs ‘laːnən   vaːɐ.
hoch hinauf in   bessre Sterne, wie ein leises Ahnen   war.
high upwards into better stars, like a   soft   presentiment was.
(high upwards toward better stars, was like a soft presentiment.)

[voːl   di ‘lalt‘ən ‘bɔʷømə ‘viːdɐ ‘naegən ‘liːrə ‘vɪpfəl ‘niːdɐ
[Wohl   die alten Bäume wieder neigen ihre Wipfel nieder
[No doubt the old   trees   again bend   their tops   down

lɑοf das hɑοs lam ‘valdəsrant‘.   ‘ʃt‘ɪlə, ‘ʃt‘ɪlə! las mɪç ‘lɑοʃən!
auf das Haus am   Waldesrand.   Stille, stille! Lass mich lauschen!
onto the house at the edge of the woods. Quiet, quiet! Let me   listen!

‘fɛrnheːɐ tʰøːnt‘ laen ‘laezəs ‘rɑοʃən: kʰɔm tsu‘rʏk‘ lɪns ‘haemaːtlant‘!
Fernher tönt   ein leises Rauschen: komm zurück ins   Heimatland!
From afar sounds a   soft   murmur: “come back   to the homeland!”

veːɐ zɔl ‘maenɐ ‘liːbə ‘loːnən? dɔrt, voː   ‘frɛmdə ‘mɛnʃən ‘voːnən
Wer soll meiner Liebe lohnen? Dort, wo   fremde Menschen wohnen,
Who shall my   love reward? There, where strange people   live,
(Who shall reward my love? There, where strangers live,)

ge: lıç nıçt' me:ɐ̯/me:r laen lʊnt' laǫs. 'dro:bən ıln de:ɐ̯ 'ʃt'ɛrnənrɔ̨ømən
geh ich nicht mehr   ein und aus. Droben in der Sternenräumen
go I   no   longer   in and out. Up above in the starry   spaces
(I no longer am at home. Up above among the stars)

lʊnt'ɐ 'gɔldnən 'hımǝlsbɔ̨ømən   'vart'ət' mǎen das 'fa:t'ɐhǫos.]
unter   goldnen Himmelsbäumen wartet mein das Vaterhaus.]
beneath golden heaven- trees   waits for me the father house.]
(Beneath the golden trees of heaven my home is waiting for me.)]

jɛtst', vo: fɔn de:ɐ̯ 'haema:t'   'fri:dən lıç zo: laŋ ʃo:n   'lap'gǝʃi:dən
Jetzt, wo   von der Heimat   Frieden ich so lang schon abgeschieden
Now, when from the homeland's peace I   so long already separated
(Now, when I have already been separated so long from the peace of my homeland)

lʊnt' ıln 'vǎet'ɐ 'frɛmdǝ   bın, fy:lt' laen 'lɛŋst'lıç 'haesǝs 'ze:nǝn,
und in weiter Fremde   bin, fühlt ein ängstlich heisses Sehnen,
and in far-off foreign land am, feels a n anxious hot   longing,
(and am in a far-off foreign land, my inner mind feels an anxious, passionate longing,)

lʊnt'ɐ 'zanft'ǝn 've:mu:tstʰrɛ:nǝn,   't'ʰi:fbǝ've:k't' mǎen 'lınrɐ zın.
unter sanften Wehmutstränen,   tiefbewegt   mein innrer Sinn.
beneath gentle tears of melancholy, deeply moved, my   inner mind.

'di:zǝs, vǎes lıç tsu: lɛɐ̯'kʰlɛ:rǝn, lıst' laen 'lınıgǝs bǝ'ge:rǝn
Dieses, weiss ich zu erklären, ist ein   inniges Begehren
This, know I to   explain, is a   hearfelt craving
(This—I know how to explain it—is a heartfelt craving)

na:x dem 'frɔ̨øndǝ, 'li:bǝnt' mıç, ıln di 'lalt'ǝn, 'zy:sǝn 'bandǝ,
nach dem Freunde, liebend mich, in die alten, süssen Bande,
for the friend, loving me, in the old,   sweet band,
(for my friend, who loves me, in the old, sweet group of friends,)

na:x dem 't'ʰɔ̨ørǝn 'fa:t'ɐlandǝ, lʊnt das 'haemve: nɛnt' lɛs zıç.
nach dem teuren Vaterlande, und das Heimweh   nennt es sich.
for the dear   fatherland, and the homesickness calls it itself.
(for my dear fatherland, and it is called homesickness.)

vi:, vɛn 'je:nǝs lʊnlɛɐ̯'kʰlɛ:ɐ̯t'ǝ, 'dɛsǝn 'haelgǝ glu:t' lıç 'nɛ:ɐ̯t'ǝ
Wie, wenn jenes Unerklärte,   dessen heilge Glut ich nährte
As if   that inexplicable,   whose holy fire I nourished
(As if that inexplicable feeling, whose sacred fire I nourished)

ʃt'e:ts   lım 'ʃt'ılǝn 'hɛrtsǝnsrǫom, vɛn lɛs lǫox laen 'haemve: 've:rǝ
stets   im stillen Herzensraum, wenn es auch ein Heimweh   wäre
constantly in the still heart- space, if it even a   homesickness were
(constantly in the quiet depths of my heart, as if it even might be a homesickness)

na:x de:ɐ̯ 'hø:ɐn, 'bɛsǝn 'sfɛ:rǝ, lʊnt' laen 'la:nʊŋsfɔlɐ t'ʰrǫom!
nach der höhern, bessern Sphäre, und ein ahnungsvoller Traum!
for the higher, better sphere, and a   presentiment-full dream!
(for a higher, better sphere, and a dream full of presentiment!)

170

vɛn ɪn ˈʃtʼʊndən ˈzeːlgɐ ˈvae̯ə
Wenn in Stunden selger Weihe
if in hours of blissful consecration
(As if, in hours of blissful consecration,)

zɪç deːɐ ˈfryːɐn ˈvɔnən ˈrae̯ə ˈdʊŋkʼəl veːɐ mae̯n gae̯stʼ bəˈvʊstʰ,
sich der frühern Wonnen Reihe dunkel wär' mein Geist bewusst,
itself of the earlier raptures' series darkly were my spirit aware,
(my spirit were darkly aware of a series of earlier joys,)

vɛn zɪç ˈnɔø̯ə ˈzɪnə ˈfɛndən,
wenn sich neue Sinne fänden,
if themselves new senses found,
(as if new senses were found,)

diː das ˈhøːərə fɛɐˈʃtʼɛndən ɪn deːɐ ˈtʼiːfbəveːkʼtʼən brʊstʰ!
die das Höhere verständen in der tiefbewegten Brust!
which the higher understood in the deeply-moved breast!
(which understood in my deeply-moved breast a more sublime reality!)

jaː, zoː ɪsts! dɛs ˈhae̯mveːs ˈʃmɛrtsən ˈtsae̯gən ˈmae̯nəm ˈtʼrɔø̯ən ˈhɛrtsən
Ja, so ist's! Des Heimwehs Schmerzen zeigen meinem treuen Herzen
Yes, so is it! The homesickness's pains show to my faithful heart
(Yes, it is so! The pains of homesickness reveal to my faithful heart)

ˈae̯nəs ˈfaːtʼɐlandəs glʏkʰ; ʊntʼ vas niː deːɐ mʊntʼ nɔx ˈnantʼə,
eines Vaterlandes Glück; und was nie der Mund noch nannte,
a fatherland's happiness; and what never the mouth yet named,
(the happiness of a fatherland; and what my mouth has never yet named)

ɪstʼ ae̯os ˈfryːɐm ˈfaːtʼɐlandə ae̯n bəˈzeːltʼɐ ˈzɔnənblɪkʰ.
ist aus früherm Vaterlande ein beseelter Sonnenblick.
is out of earlier fatherland a soul-stirring sunny-glance.
(is a soul-stirring, sunny glance from an earlier fatherland.)

[*The original poem by "Theodor Hell" (pen-name of Karl Gottfried Winkler) has six verses and is printed in the *Gesamtausgabe* (Breitkopf & Härtels). Schubert wrote out only the first verse, but marked a repeat sign at the end. For the Peters edition a second and a third verse were commissioned from Max Kalbeck, omitting all of Theodor Hell's verses except the first, and it is *that* version that one is more likely to hear. Both versions are included above, the verses by Max Kalbeck in brackets.]

das liːtʼ ɪm ˈgryːnən
Das Lied im Grünen
The Song in the Greenery

Op. 115, No. 1 [1827] (Friedrich Reil)

ɪns ˈgryːnə, ɪns ˈgryːnə, daː lɔkʼtʼ ʊns deːɐ ˈfryːlɪŋ, deːɐ ˈliːpʼlɪçə ˈkʰnaːbə,
Ins Grüne, ins Grüne, da lockt uns der Frühling, der liebliche Knabe,
Into the green, into the green, there lures us the spring, the lovely boy,
(Into the green, into the green, there the spring, that lovely boy, is luring us,)

ʊnt' fy:ɐ̯rt' ɪʊns ɪam   'blu:mənlʊmˌvʊndənən 'ʃt'a:bə
und führt uns am   blumenumwundenen Stabe
and leads us by the flower- entwined   staff
(and leads us with his flower-entwined staff)

hɪ'naɔs, vo: di 'lɛrçən ɪʊnt' 'amzəln zo: vax,
hinaus, wo   die Lerchen und Amseln   so wach,
out,   where the larks   and blackbirds so astir,
(out there, where the larks and blackbirds are so astir,)

ɪn 'vɛldɐ(r), ɪaɔf 'fɛldɐ(r), ɪaɔf 'hy:gəl, t͡sʊm bax, ɪns   'gry:nə, ɪns   'gry:nə.
in Wälder, auf Felder, auf Hügel, zum Bach, ins   Grüne, ins   Grüne.
in woods, on   fields,   onto hills, to the brook, into the green, into the green.

ɪm   'gry:nən, ɪlm 'gry:nən, da: le:p't' ɪɛs zɪç 'vɔnɪç,   da: 'vandəln vi:ɐ̯ 'gɛrnə
Im   Grünen, im   Grünen, da lebt es sich wonnig, da   wandeln wir gerne
In the green,   in the green,   there lives it itself blissfully, there wander we gladly
(In the green, in the green, there one can live blissfully, there we like to wander)

ɪʊnt' 'hɛft'ən di 'ɪaɔgən da'hɪn ʃo:n   fɔn 'fɛrnə,
und heften die Augen dahin schon von ferne,
and fix   the eyes   thither already from afar,
(and fix our eyes on it even from afar,)

ʊnt vi: vi:ɐ̯ zo: 'vandəln mɪt' 'haɛtərɐ brʊstʰ,
und wie wir so wandeln mit heiterer Brust,
and as we so wander with cheerful breast,
(and as we wander like that with cheerful hearts,)

ɪʊm'valət'   ɪʊns 'ɪmɐ di 'kʰɪnt'lɪçə lʊst', ɪlm 'gry:nən, ɪlm 'gry:nən.
umwallet   uns immer die kindliche Lust,   im Grünen, im Grünen.
around-undulates us always the childlike pleasure, in the green, in the green.
(a childlike pleasure always undulates in and around us, in the green, in the green.)

ɪm   'gry:nən, ɪlm 'gry:nən, da: ru:t' man zo: vo:l, ɪɛm'pfɪndət' zo: 'ʃø:nəs,
Im   Grünen, im   Grünen, da   ruht man so wohl, empfindet so   Schönes,
In the green,   in the green,   there rests one so well, senses   so much beautiful,
(In the green, in the green, there one rests so well, one senses so much that is beautiful,)

[poem: **und** (ɪʊnt', and) **empfindet]**

ʊnt 'dɛŋk'ət' bə'ha:k'lɪç ɪan 'di:zəs ɪʊnt' 'je:nəs,
und denket behaglich an dieses und jenes,
and thinks   comfortably of this   and that,
(and thinks, unhurried and at ease, of this and that,)

ʊnt 't͡saɔbɐt' fɔn 'hɪnən,   ɪax, vas   ɪʊns bə'drʏk't',
und zaubert von hinnen,   ach, was   uns bedrückt,
and conjures from here away, ah, whatever us oppresses,
(and conjures away, ah, whatever may be oppressing us,)

ʊnt' 'ɪaləs   hɛɐ̯'baɛ, ɪʊnt' 'ɪaləs   hɛɐ̯'baɛ, vas den 'bu:zən ɪɛnt't͡sʏk't' ɪlm   'gry:nən.
und alles   herbei, und alles   herbei, was den Busen entzückt im   Grünen.
and everything hither, and everything hither, which the bosom delights in the green.
(and conjures up everything that delights the heart, in the green.)

172

ɪm   ˈgryːnən, daː ˈveɐ̯dən di ʃtˈɛrnə zoː kʰlaːɐ̯,
Im   Grünen, da   werden die Sterne so klar,
In the green,   there become the stars   so clear,
(In the green, there the stars become so bright,)

diː   di ˈvae̯zən deːɐ̯ ˈfoːɐ̯vɛlt   ͡tsʊr ˈlae̯tʊŋ dɛs ˈleːbəns ʊns ˈpʰrae̯zən,
die die Weisen der Vorwelt   zur Leitung des Lebens uns preisen,
which the wise men of the ancient world for the guidance of the life   to us praise,
(the stars, which the wise men of antiquity recommend to us as guidance in our lives,)

daː ˈʃtˈrae̯çən di ˈvœlkˈçən zoː ͡tsaːɐ̯t   ʊns daˈhɪn,
da   streichen die Wölkchen so zart   uns dahin,
there pass   the little clouds so delicately us by,
(there the little clouds pass over our heads so lightly,)

daː ˈhae̯tˈɐn di ˈhɛr͡tsən, daː kʰleːɐ̯tˈ ͡zɪç deːɐ̯ zɪn, ɪm ˈgryːnən.
da heitern die Herzen, da   klärt sich der Sinn, im   Grünen.
there cheer up the hearts,   there clears itself the mind, in the green.
(there hearts cheer up, there the mind becomes clear, in the green.)

ɪm   ˈgryːnən, daː ˈvʊrdə manç ˈpʰleːnçən ʊo̯f ˈflyːgəln gəˈtʰraːgən,
Im   Grünen, da   wurde manch Plänchen auf Flügeln getragen,
In the green,   there was   many a little plan on wings borne,
(In the green, there many a little plan took flight,)

di ˈ͡tsuːkʰʊnft deːɐ̯ ˈgreːmlɪçən ˈlanzɪçtˈ ɛntˈʃlaːgən,   [*Schubert's MS:* **Aussicht** (ˈʊo̯szɪçtˈ)]
die Zukunft der grämlichen Ansicht entschlagen,
the future   of the morose   aspect divested,
(the future was divested of its morose aspect,)

daː ʃtˈɛrkˈtˈ ͡zɪç das ˈʊo̯gə, daː laːpˈtˈ ͡zɪç deːɐ̯ blɪkʰ,
da   stärkt sich das Auge, da   labt   sich der Blick,
there refreshes itself the eye,   there refreshes itself the look,
(there the eye is refreshed, there the look is refreshed,)   [*"sich stärken"* = to take refreshment]

zanftˈ ˈviːgən di ˈvʏnʃə ͡zɪç   hɪn ʊnt ͡tsuˈrʏkˈ ɪm   ˈgryːnən.
sanft wiegen die Wünsche sich   hin und zurück im   Grünen.
gently rock   the wishes   themselves to and fro   in the green.
(our wishes gently rock to and fro in the green.)
       [*poem:* **da tändeln** (daː ˈtʰɛndəln, there dally) **die Wünsche dahin** (daˈhɪn) **und zurück**]
                   [lae̯çt ˈtʰɛndəlt di ˈzeːnzʊxt daˈhɪn ʊnt ͡tsuˈrʏk]
             [*Schubert:* **leicht tändelt die Sehnsucht dahin und zurück**]
                   [lightly dallies the longing   to   and fro...   ]
                       [(longing dallies lightly to and fro)]

ɪm   ˈgryːnən lam ˈmɔrgən, lam ˈlaːbəntˈ ɪn ˈtʰrʊo̯lɪçɐ ˈʃtɪlə
Im   Grünen am   Morgen, am   Abend in traulicher Stille
In the green   in the morning, in the evening in intimate   stillness,
       [The Peters edition prints *"treulicher"* (faithful) instead of *"traulicher"* (intimate).]

ɛntˈkʰae̯mətˈ manç ˈliːtˈçən   ʊntˈ ˈmançə liˈdʏlə,
entkeimet   manch Liedchen und manche Idylle,
germinates   many a little song and many an idyll,
(many a little song and many an idyll germinates,)
                   [*poem:* **da wurde** (daː ˈvʊrdə, there was) **manch Liedchen**]

ʊnt' 'hyːmən lɔft' kʰrɛntst den pʰo'eːt'ɪʃən ʃɛrts,
und Hymen oft   kränzt den poetischen Scherz,
and Hymen often crowns the poetical   pleasantry, [Hymen was the Greek god of marriage.]

[gə'dɪçt'ət', gə'ʃp'iːlt', ɪn 'zeːnzʊxt' ʊnt' ʃɛrts.]
[*poem:* **gedichtet, gespielt, in Sehnsucht und Scherz.**]
[written,   played,   in longing   and jest.   ]

[mɪt' fɛɐ̯'gnyːgən ʊnt' ʃmɛrts,]
[*Schubert:* **gedichtet, gespielt, mit Vergnügen und Schmerz,**]
[with pleasure   and pain,   ]

dɛn laeçt' lɪst di 'lɔk'ʊŋ,   lɛm'pfɛŋlɪç das hɛrts lɪm 'gryːnən.
denn leicht ist die Lockung, empfänglich das Herz im   Grünen.
for   easy is the enticement, susceptible the heart in the green.
(for enticement is easy and the heart is susceptible in the green.)

[oː 'gɛrnə lɪm 'gryːnən bɪn lɪç ʃoːn lals 'kʰnaːbə lʊnt' 'jʏŋlɪŋ   gə'veːzən
[O gerne im   Günen bin ich schon als Knabe und Jüngling gewesen
[Oh gladly in the green have I   already as boy   and youth   been
[(Oh, already as a boy and as an adolescent I was glad to be out in the green)

ʊnt' 'haːbə gə'lɛrnt' lʊnt' gə'ʃriːbən,   gə'leːzən lɪm   ho'raːts lʊnt' 'pʰlaːt' o,
und habe gelernt und geschrieben, gelesen im   Horaz und Plato,
and have learned and written,   read   in the Horace and Plato,
(and have studied and written, read in Horace and Plato,)

dan 'viːlant' lʊnt' kʰant', lʊnt' 'glyːəndən 'hɛrtsəns mɪç 'zeːlɪç gə'nant', lɪm 'gryːnən.]
dann Wieland und Kant, und glühenden Herzens mich selig   genannt, im   Grünen.]
then Wieland and Kant, and with glowing heart   myself blissful called, in the green.]
(then Wieland and Kant, and with a glowing heart considered myself blissful, in the green.)]

[*GA & Peters (less grammatical):* **glühendes Herzens**]

ɪns   'gryːnə last' 'haet'ɐ(r) lʊns 'fɔlgən dem 'frɔɪ̯nt'lɪçən 'kʰnaːbən!
Ins   Grüne lasst heiter   uns folgen dem freundlichen Knaben!
Into the green let   merrily   us follow the friendly   boy!
(Let us merrily follow the friendly boy—the spring—into the green!)

gryːnt' laenst' lʊns das 'leːbən nɪçt' 'fœrdɐ,
Grünt einst   uns   das Leben nicht förder,
Greens one day for us the life   not further,
(If life one day no longer blossoms for us,)

[*poem:* **nicht mehr, ei!** (nɪçt' meːɐ̯, lae! no more, ah!**); *P & Schubert:* **förder;** *GA:* **fürder**]

zoː 'haːbən viːɐ̯ 'kʰlyːk'lɪç di 'gryːnəndə tsaet' nɪçt' fɛɐ̯'zɔɪ̯mtʰ,
so haben wir klüglich die grünende Zeit   nicht versäumt,
then have we wisely   the verdant time   not missed,
(then we shall wisely not have missed the verdant time,)

ʊnt' van lɛs gə'gɔlt'ən, dɔx 'glʏk'lɪç gə'tʰrɔɪ̯mt',   lɪm 'gryːnən.
und wann es gegolten, doch glücklich geträumt,   im   Grünen.
and when it was valid, yet happily (have) dreamed, in the green.
(and when it was there, yet happily have dreamed in the greenery.)

[*poem:* **und, seit** (zaet', since) **es gegolten,**]

[The verse in brackets above was not set by Schubert, but was added when the song was first
published, using repeat signs. The song is an acknowledged masterpiece.]

das liːtʻ fɔm ˈrae̯fən
Das Lied vom Reifen
The Song about the Hoar-Frost

Posthumously published [composed 1817] (poem by Matthias Claudius)

zeːtʻ ˈmae̯nə ˈliːbən ˈbɔ̈ɸmə lan, viː ziː zoː ˈhɛrlɩç ʃtʻeːn,
Seht meine lieben Bäume an, wie sie so herrlich stehn,
Look my   dear trees at, how they so gloriously stand,
(Look at my beloved trees, how gloriously they stand there,)

ɑo̯f ˈlalən ˈtsvae̯gən ˈlangətʰaːn mɩtʻ ˈrae̯fən   ˈvʊndɐʃɸ̈ːn!
auf allen Zweigen angetan mit Reifen   wunderschön!
on all   branches clad   with hoar-frost exquisitely!
(every branch exquisitely dressed in hoar-frost!)

fɔn ˈlʊntən lan   bɩs ˈloːbən nɑo̯s   lɑo̯f ˈlalən ˈtsvae̯gəlae̯n
Von unten an   bis oben 'naus   auf allen Zweigelein
from below starting till above outwards on all   little twigs
(starting at the bottom and spreading outwards to the top, from every little twig)

hɛŋts   vae̯s lʊnt tsiːɐ̯lɩç, tsaːɐ̯tʻ lʊntʻ kʰrɑo̯s, lʊntʻ kʰan nɩçtʻ ˈʃɸ̈nɐ   zae̯n.
hängt's weiss und zierlich, zart   und kraus, und kann nicht schöner   sein.
hangs it white and graceful, delicate and crisp, and can not   more beautiful be.
(it hangs, white and graceful, delicate and crisp, and it could not be more beautiful.)

ʊntʻ ˈlalə ˈbɔ̈ɸmə rʊntʻ ˈlʊmheːɐ̯, lal ˈlalə vae̯tʻ lʊntʻ brae̯tʰ
Und alle Bäume rund umher, all' alle weit und breit
And all trees   round about, all, all far   and wide

ʃtʻeːn daː,   gəˈʃmʏkʻtʻ mɩtʻ ˈglae̯çɐ(r) leːɐ̯, lɩn ˈglae̯çɐ ˈhɛrlɩçkʰae̯tʰ.
stehn da,   geschmückt mit gleicher Ehr', in gleicher Herrlichkeit.
stand there, adorned   with similar   honor, in similar   glory.

ʊntʻ ziː   bəˈlɔ̈ɸgəln lʊnt bəˈzeːn kʰan ˈjeːdɐ ˈbɑo̯ɐsman,
Und sie   beäugeln und besehn kann jeder Bauersmann,
And them ogle   and inspect can every farmer,
(And any farmer can ogle and inspect them,)

kʰan hɩn lʊntʻ heːɐ̯ daˈrʊntɐ   geːn lʊntʻ ˈfrɔ̈ɸən zɩç   daˈran.
kann hin und her darunter   gehn und freuen sich   daran.
can to and fro under them walk and gladden himself at it.
(can walk to and fro under them and take pleasure in the sight.)

ɑo̯x hoːltʻ leːɐ̯ vae̯pʻ lʊntʻ ˈkʰɩndɐlae̯n   fɔm   ˈkʰlae̯nən ˈfɔ̈ɸɐheːɐ̯tʻ,
Auch holt   er Weib und Kinderlein   vom   kleinen Feuerherd,
Also fetches he wife and little children from the little   fire- hearth,
(He also fetches his wife and children from their little hearth,)

ʊntʻ marʃ   mɩtʻ lɩn den valtʻ hɩˈnae̯n! lʊnt das lɩstʻ voːl vas   veːɐ̯tʰ.
und Marsch mit in den Wald hinein! Und das ist wohl was   wert.
and march   with into the woods into! And that is   well something worth.
(and says: "March with me into the woods and you'll see something well worth looking at!")

'aenfɛltɪgɐ naˈtʰuːɐ̯-gəˈnʊs loːn laˈlfants drʊm ʊnt dran
Einfältiger Natur- Genuss ohn' Alfanz drum und dran
Simple nature- enjoyment without tomfoolery around it and at it
(The simple enjoyment of nature without a lot of fuss)

ɪstˈ ˈliːpˈlɪç, viː ḷaen ˈliːbəskʰʊs fɔn ˈḷaenəm ˈfrɔmən man.
ist lieblich, wie ein Liebeskuss von einem frommen Mann.
is lovely, like a love- kiss from a good man.

iːɐ̯ ˈʃtˈɛːtˈɐ haːpˈtˈ fiːl ˈʃøːnəs dɪŋ, fiːl ˈʃøːnəs ˈyːbɐ(r)ˈlal,
Ihr Städter habt viel schönes Ding, viel Schönes überall,
You city people have many a beautiful thing, much beautiful everywhere,
(You city people have many fine things, much that is beautiful, everywhere,)

kʰreˈdiːtˈ ʊntˈ gɛltˈ ʊntˈ ˈgɔldnən rɪŋ, ʊntˈ baŋkˈ ʊntˈ ˈbœrzənzaːl;
Kredit und Geld und goldnen Ring, und Bank und Börsensaal;
Credit and money and gold ring, and bank and stock exchange;

dɔx ˈḷɛrlə, ˈḷaeçə, vaetˈ ʊntˈ fɪçtˈ ḷɪm ˈraefən naː ʊntˈ fɛrn—
doch Erle, Eiche, Weid' und Ficht' im Reifen nah und fern—
but alder, oak, willow and fir in the hoar-frost near and far—

zoː guːtˈ vɪrts lɔøç nuːn ˈḷaenmaːl nɪçtˈ, liːɐ̯ ˈliːbən ˈraeçən hɛrn!
so gut wird's euch nun einmal nicht, ihr lieben reichen Herrn!
that well becomes it for you now once not, you dear rich gentlemen!
(it simply will not go that well for you, you dear rich gentlemen!)

das hatˈ naˈtʰuːɐ̯, naːx ˈliːrɐ/liːrɐr lartˈ gaːɐ̯/gaːr ˈḷaegnən gaŋ tsuː geːn,
Das hat Natur, nach ihrer Art gar eignen Gang zu gehn,
That has nature, according to her way entirely own way to go,
(That has Nature, in accordance with her way of going entirely in her own course,)

ʊns ˈbaoɐslɔøtˈən ˈḷaofgəʃpˈaːɐ̯tˈ, diː ˈlandɐs nɪçts fɛɐ̯ˈʃtˈeːn.
uns Bauersleuten aufgespart, die anders nichts verstehn.
for us farmer-folk saved, who otherwise nothing understand.
(saved for us farmer-folk, who understand nothing in any *other* way.)

fiːl ʃøːn, fiːl ʃøːn ḷɪstˈ ˈḷʊnzɐ valtˈ! dɔrtˈ ˈneːbəl ˈyːbɐ(r)ˈlal,
Viel schön, viel schön ist unser Wald! Dort Nebel überall,
Very beautiful, very beautiful is our woods! There mist everywhere,

hiːɐ̯/hiːr ˈḷaenə ˈvaesə ˈbaomgəˌʃtˈalt ḷɪm ˈfɔlən ˈzɔnənʃtˈraːl
hier eine weisse Baumgestalt im vollen Sonnenstrahl
here a white tree- shape in the full sunbeam
(here the white shape of a tree in full sunshine)

lɪçtˈhɛl, ʃtˈɪl, ˈleːdəl, raen ʊntˈ frae, ʊntˈ ˈyːbɐ(r) ˈlaləs faen!
lichthell, still, edel, rein und frei, und über alles fein!
light-bright, quiet, noble, pure and free, and above all delicate!

oː ˈlalɐ ˈmɛnʃən ˈzeːlə zae zoː ˈlɪçtˈhɛl ʊntˈ zoː raen!
O aller Menschen Seele sei so lichthell und so rein!
Oh all human beings' soul be so light-bright and so pure!
(Oh might the souls of all human beings be so bright and so pure!)

176

viː̱ɐ zeːn das lan lʊnt 'dɛŋkˈən nɔx 'laenfɛltɪkˈlɪç daˈbae:
Wir sehn das an und denken noch einfältiglich dabei:
We look that at and think still in our simple way thereat:
(We look at that and think still in our simple way at the same time:)

voˈheːɐ deːɐ raef lʊntˈ viː leːɐ dɔx tsuˈʃtˈandə ˈkʰɔmən zaeʔ
woher der Reif und wie er doch zustande kommen sei?
whence the frost and how it after all into being come might be?
(where did the frost come from, and how might it have come into being?)

den 'gɛstˈɐn 'laːbənt, ˌtsvaekˈlaen raen! kʰaen 'raefən ln deːɐ tʰaːtʰ!—
Denn gestern Abend, Zweiglein rein! Kein Reifen in der Tat!—
For yesterday evening, twigs clean! No hoar-frost in the deed!—
(For yesterday evening the twigs were clean! There was indeed no frost on them!—)

mʊs 'laenɐ dɔx gəˈveːzən zaen, deːɐ/deːr liːn gəˈʃtrɔɸətˈ hatʰ.
muss einer doch gewesen sein, der ihn gestreuet hat.
must someone after all been have, who it sprinkled has.
(there must have been someone who sprinkled it.)

aen 'lɛŋəl 'gɔtˈəs geːtˈ bae naxtˈ, ʃtˈrɔɸtˈ 'haemlɪç hiːɐ/hiːr lʊnt dɔrtʰ,
Ein Engel Gottes geht bei Nacht, streut heimlich hier und dort,
An angel of God walks by night, sprinkles secretly here and there,

ʊntˈ vɛn deːɐ 'baoɐsman lɛɐ'vaxtˈ, lɪstˈ leːɐ ʃoːn 'viːdɐ fɔrtʰ.
und wenn der Bauersmann erwacht, ist er schon wieder fort.
and when the farmer awakes, is he already again away.
(and when the farmer wakes up, the angel is already gone again.)

duː 'lɛŋəl, deːɐ zoː 'gyːtˈɪç lɪstˈ, viːɐ 'zaːgən daŋkˈ lʊntˈ pʰraes,
Du Engel, der so gütig ist, wir sagen Dank und Preis,
You angel, who so kind is, we say thanks and praise,
(You angel, you who are so kind, we thank you and praise you,—)

oː max lʊns dɔx tsʊm 'haelgən kʰrɪst di 'bɔɸmə 'viːdɐ vaes!
o mach uns doch zum heilgen Christ die Bäume wieder weiss!
oh make us, do, at the holy Christ the trees again white!
(oh, for Christmas *do* make us the trees all white again!) ["*zum heiligen Christ*" = at Christmas]

[Hoar-frost forms on trees, bushes, and grass when mist freezes, edging every twig, leaf, or blade with silvery-white crystal lace. Schubert apparently expected only the first three of the fifteen verses to be sung (ending with "*in gleicher Herrlichkeit*").]

Das Mädchen (Wenn mich einsam Lüfte fächeln) see *Blanka*

177

das ˈmɛːtˈçən / viː zoː ˈlɪnɪç, mœçtˈ lɪç ˈzaːgən
Das Mädchen / Wie so innig, möcht' ich sagen
The Girl / How Ardently, I would Like to Say

Posthumously published [composed 1819] (poem by Friedrich von Schlegel)

viː   zoː ˈlɪnɪç,   mœçtˈ   lɪç ˈzaːgən, zɪç   deːɐ̯ ˈmaɛ̯nə miːɐ̯/miːr lɛɐ̯ˈgiːpˈtʰ,
Wie so innig, möcht' ich sagen, sich der Meine mir ergibt,
How so ardently, would like I   to say, himself the mine   to me   devotes,
(I would like to say how ardently my lover devotes himself to me)

ʊm   tsuː ˈlɪndən ˈmaɛ̯nə ˈkʰlaːgən,   das leːɐ̯ nɪçtˈ zoː ˈlɪnɪç   liːpˈtʰ.
um   zu lindern meine Klagen,   dass er nicht so innig   liebt.
in order to   alleviate my   complaints, that he   not   so sincerely loves.
(in order to alleviate my complaints that he does not love me as sincerely as I wish.)

vɪl   lɪçs ˈzaːgən, zoː lɛntˈˈʃveːpˈtˈ lɛs; ˈvɛːrən ˈtʰøːnə miːɐ̯   gəˈliːən   [fɛɐ̯ˈliːən]
Will ich's sagen, so entschwebt es; wären Töne mir   geliehen, [variant: verliehen]
Want I   it to say, so floats away it;   were   tones to me lent,   [lent]
(If I try to say it, the words float away; if musical tones were lent to me,)
                                         [*Schubert & Peters:* **geliehen;** *GA & poem:* **verliehen**]

flœs   lɛs hɪn   lɪn harmoˈniːɐ̯n, dɛn   lɪn ˈjeːnən ˈtʰøːnən leːpˈtˈ lɛs;
flöss'   es hin   in Harmonien, denn in   jenen Tönen lebt   es;
would flow it thither in harmonies,   for   in those tones   lives   it;
(it would flow out of me in harmonies, for it lives in those tones;)

nuːɐ̯ di ˈnaxtˈɪgal kʰan ˈzaːgən, viː leːɐ̯/leːr ˈlɪnɪç   zɪç   miːɐ̯ giːpˈtʰ,
nur die Nachtigall kann sagen, wie er   innig   sich   mir gibt,
only the nightingale can   say,   how he   ardently himself to me gives,
(only the nightingale can say how ardently he gives himself to me,)

ʊm   tsuː ˈlɪndən ˈmaɛ̯nə ˈkʰlaːgən,   das leːɐ̯ nɪçtˈ zoː ˈlɪnɪç   liːpˈtʰ.
um   zu lindern meine Klagen,   dass er nicht so innig   liebt.
in order to   alleviate my   complaints, that he   not   so sincerely loves.
(in order to alleviate my complaints that he does not love me as sincerely as I wish.)

[That charming song fluctuates between major and minor as the girl expresses hopes or fears.]

das ˈmɛːtˈçən laͅos deːɐ̯ ˈfrɛmdə
Das Mädchen aus der Fremde
The Maiden from Another Land

Posthumously published [two versions, 1814, 1815] (poem by Friedrich von Schiller)

ɪn ˈlaɛ̯nəm tʰaːl baͅe   ˈlarmən ˈhɪrtˈən   lɛɐ̯ˈʃiːn   mɪtˈ ˈjeːdəm ˈjʊŋən jaːɐ̯,
In einem Tal bei   armen Hirten   erschien mit jedem jungen Jahr,
In a   valley among poor   shepherds appeared with each   young   year,
(To poor shepherds in a valley there appeared with every springtime,)

zoˈbalt   di ˈleːɐ̯stˈən ˈlɛrçən ˈʃvɪrtˈən,   laͅen ˈmɛːtˈçən ʃøːn   lʊntˈ ˈvʊndɐbaːɐ̯.
sobald   die ersten Lerchen schwirrten,   ein Mädchen schön   und wunderbar.
as soon as the first   larks   were whirring, a   maiden beautiful and wondrous.
(as soon as the first larks were whirring in the air, a beautiful and wondrous maiden.)

zi: vaːɐ̯ nɪçt‘ ‖ɪn dem tʰaːl gəˈboːrən, man ˈvʊstə nɪçt‘, voˈheːɐ̯ zi: kʰaːm;
Sie war nicht in dem Tal geboren, man wusste nicht, woher sie kam;
She was not in the valley born, one knew not whence she came;
(She was not born in the valley, no one knew where she came from;)

dɔx ʃnɛl vaːɐ̯/vaːr ˈliːrə ʃpˈuːɐ̯ fɛɐ̯ˈloːrən, zoˈbalt das ˈmɛːtˈçən ˈlapˈʃiːt‘ naːm.
doch schnell war ihre Spur verloren, sobald das Mädchen Abschied nahm.
but quickly was her trace lost, as soon as the maiden leave took.
(but all trace of her was quickly lost, as soon as the maiden took her leave.) [*poem:* **und schnell**]

bəˈzeːlɪgənt‘ vaːɐ̯/vaːr ˈliːrə ˈnɛːə, ‖ʊnt‘ ˈlalə ˈhɛrt͡sən ˈvʊrdən ˈvaet‘ʰ;
Beseligend war ihre Nähe, und alle Herzen wurden weit;
blissful was her nearness, and all hearts became open;
(Her presence was blissful, and all hearts were opened to her;)

dɔx ˈlaenə ˈvʏrdə, ˈlaenə ˈhøːə ‖ɛntˈfɛrntə di fɛɐ̯tʰˈraolɪçkʰaetʰ.
doch eine Würde, eine Höhe entfernte die Vertraulichkeit.
yet a dignity, a loftiness kept at a distance the familiarity.
(yet a certain dignity, a loftiness discouraged familiarity.)

zi: ˈbraxt‘ə ˈbluːmən mɪt‘ ‖ʊnt‘ ˈfrʏçt‘ə, gəˈraeft‘ ‖aof ˈlaenɐ(r) ˈlandɐn fluːɐ̯,
Sie brachte Blumen mit und Früchte, gereift auf einer andern Flur,
She brought flowers with and fruits, ripened on an other meadow,
(She brought flowers and fruits with her that had ripened on other meadows,)

ɪn ˈlaenəm ˈlandɐn ˈzɔnənlɪçt‘ə, ‖ɪn ˈlaenɐ ˈglʏkˈlɪçən naˈtʰuːɐ̯.
in einem andern Sonnenlichte, in einer glücklichern Natur.
in an other sun- light, in a more fortunate nature.
(in a different sunlight, in a more fortunate nature.)

ʊnt ˈtʰaelt‘ə ˈjeːdəm ˈlaenə ˈgaːbə, dem ˈfrʏçt‘ə, ˈjeːnəm ˈbluːmən ‖aos;
Und teilte Jedem eine Gabe, dem Früchte, jenem Blumen aus;
And handed to each a gift, to this one fruits, to that one flowers out;
(And she distributed to each a gift, to this one fruit, to that one flowers;)

deːɐ̯ ˈjʏŋlɪŋ ‖ʊnt deːɐ̯ graes ‖am ˈʃt‘aːbə, ‖aen ˈjeːdɐ gɪŋ bəˈʃɛŋkˈt‘ naːx ‖aos.
der Jüngling und der Greis am Stabe, ein Jeder ging beschenkt nach Haus.
the youth and the old man with the cane, an each went enriched toward home.
(the youth and the old man with a cane, each went home enriched.)

vɪlˈkʰɔmən ˈvaːrən ‖alə ˈgɛst‘ə; dɔx ˈnaːt‘ə zɪç ‖aen ˈliːbənt‘ pʰaːɐ̯,
Willkommen waren alle Gäste; doch nahte sich ein liebend Paar,
Welcome were all guests; but approached itself a loving pair,
(All guests were welcome; but if a loving pair approached,) [“nahte sich” = approached]

deːm ˈraeçt‘ə zi: deːɐ̯ ˈgaːbən ˈbɛst‘ə, deːɐ̯ ˈbluːmən ‖alɐˈʃøːnst‘ə daːɐ̯.
dem reichte sie der Gaben beste, der Blumen allerschönste dar.
to it presented she the gifts’ best, the flowers’ loveliest of all ... .
(to them she presented the best of the gifts, the very loveliest of the flowers.)

[“*darreichen*” = to offer, to proffer, to present]

[Schubert wrote his first setting of this allegorical poem for his youthful sweetheart Therese Grob during the night after she had just sung the first performance of his Mass in F Major.]

das 'meːt‿çən fɔn ǀɪnɪs'tʰoːrə / a̯os dem gə'zaŋ: 'fɪŋgal / 'ɔsi̯ans gə'zɛŋə, 'nʊmɐ 'ziːbən
Das Mädchen von Inistore / aus dem Gesang: Fingal / Ossian's Gesänge, N⁰ 7
The Maid of Inistore / from the song: Fingal / Ossian's Songs, No. 7

Posthumously published [composed 1815] (prose poem by James Macpherson—"Ossian")
(German translation by Edmund von Harold)

'meːt‿çən ǀɪnɪs'tʰoːrəs, va̯en ǀa̯of dem 'fɛlzən deːɐ̯ 'ʃt‿ʏrmɪʃən 'vɪndə,
Mädchen Inistores, wein'* auf dem Felsen der stürmischen Winde,
Maid of Inistore, weep on the rock of the stormy winds,
(*Macpherson:* Weep on the rocks of roaring winds, O maid of Inistore!)
　　　　　　　　[*Harold:* **der heulenden** ('hɔ‿øləndən, howling) **Winde;** *Peters:* ***weit** (an error)]

na̯ek‿' 'lyːbɐ 'vɛlən da̯en 'tsiːɐ̯lɪçəs ha̯op‿'tʰ,
neig' über Wellen dein zierliches Haupt, [*Harold:* **über die** (diː, the) **Wellen**]
bend over (the) waves your fair head,
(Bend thy fair head over the waves,)

duː, deːm ǀan 'liːp‿'ra̯ets deːɐ̯ ga̯est deːɐ̯ 'hyːgəl va̯eçtʰ,
du, dem an Liebreiz der Geist der Hügel weicht,
you, to whom in loveliness the ghost of the hill yields, (you, to whose loveliness...)
(thou lovelier than the ghosts of the hills;)

vɛn leːɐ̯/leːr ǀɪn 'a̯enəm 'zɔnənʃt‿'raːl des 'mɪt‿'aːks 'lyːbɐ 'mɔrvəns 'ʃva̯egən hɪn'gla̯et‿'ətʰ.
wenn er in einem* Sonnenstrahl des Mittags über Morvens Schweigen hingleitet.
when it in a sun- beam of the noon over Morven's silence glides hence.
(when it glides away in a sunbeam at noon over the silence of Morven.)
　　　　　　　　　　　　　　　[*Peters:* ***reinem** (an error)]

eːɐ̯/leːr ǀɪst‿' gə'falən, deːɐ̯ 'jʏŋlɪŋ, lɛɐ̯'liːk‿'t', bla̯eç 'ʊnt‿'ɐ deːɐ̯ 'kʰlɪŋə ku'tʰʊlɪns!
Er ist gefallen, der Jüngling, erliegt,* bleich unter der Klinge Cuthullins!*
He is fallen, the youth, defeated, pale beneath the sword of Cuthullin!
(He is fallen! thy youth is low! Pale beneath the sword of Cuthullin!)
　　　　　　　　　　[*Peters:* ***er liegt** (he lies), **Euthullins** (errors)]

nɪçt‿' meːɐ̯ vɪrt deːɐ̯ muːt 'da̯enən 'liːbən lɛɐ̯'heːbən, dem bluːt deːɐ̯ gə'biːt‿'ɐ tsuː 'gla̯eçən.
Nicht mehr wird der Mut deinen Lieben* erheben, dem Blut der Gebieter zu gleichen.
No more shall the valor thy love raise the blood of rulers to match.
(No more shall valor raise thy love to match the blood of kings.)
　　　　　[*Harold:* ***Geliebten** (gə'liːp‿'t‿'ən, beloved), *Peters:* **Geist** (ghost, an error)]

ɔ: 'meːt‿çən ǀɪnɪs'tʰoːrəs, 'tʰreːnar, deːɐ̯ 'tsiːɐ̯lɪçə 'tʰreːnar ǀɪst tʰoːtʰ.
O Mädchen Inistores, Trenar, der zierliche Trenar ist tot.
O maid of Inistore, Trenar, the graceful Trenar is dead.
(Trenar, graceful Trenar died, O maid of Inistore!)

ɪn 'za̯enɐ 'ha̯emaːt‿' 'hɔ‿ølən 'za̯enə 'dɔgən, ziː zeːn 'za̯enən 'gla̯et‿'əndən ga̯estʰ.
In seiner Heimat heulen seine Doggen, sie seh'n seinen gleitenden Geist.
In his homeland howl his dogs, they see his gliding ghost.
(His grey dogs are howling at home! they see his passing ghost.)
　　　　　　　[**seine grauen** ('gra̯o‿ən, grey) **Doggen; sie sehen** ('zeːən)...]

180

ɪn ˈzaᶒɛnɐ ˈhalə liːkˈtˈ zaᶒɛn ˈboːgən ˈʊngəʃpˈantʰ,
In seiner Halle liegt sein Bogen ungespannt, [*Harold:* **ist** (ɪstˈ, is) **sein Bogen ungespannt**]
In his   hall lies his bow   unstrung,
(His bow is in the hall unstrung.)

man høːɐ̯tˈ lᶏof dem ˈhyːgəl ˈzaᶒɛnɐ ˈhɪrʃə ˈkʰaᶒɛnən ʃal,
man hört auf dem Hügel seiner Hirsche keinen Schall,
one hears on the hill   of his deer no   sound,
(No sound is in the hills of his hinds.)

man høːɐ̯tˈ lᶏof dem ˈhyːgəl nuːn ˈkʰaᶒɛnən ʃal!
man hört auf dem Hügel nun keinen Schall!
one hears on the hill now no   sound!

[*As noted above, there are several errors in the Peters collection, all derived from misprints or mistakes in the first edition of the song by the publisher Diabelli: "*weit*" for "*wein*'"; "*reinem*" for "*einem*"; "Euthullins" for "Cuthullins"; "*Geist*" for "*Lieben*." Inistore is the Celtic name for the Orkney Islands. For a discussion of "Ossian" and Macpherson, see the song "Cronnan."]

das maˈriːənbɪltˈ
Das Marienbild
The Picture of the Virgin Mary

Posthumously published [composed 1818] (poem by Aloys Wilhelm Schreiber)

zaᶒɛ gəˈgryːst, duː frᶏo deːɐ̯ hʊltˈ, ʊnt deːɐ̯ ˈraᶒɛnən, ˈʃøːnən ˈmɪnə,
Sei gegrüsst, du Frau der Huld, und der   reinen, schönen Minne,
Be greeted,   you Lady of the Grace, and of the pure,   beautiful love,
(Hail, Lady of Grace and of pure, beautiful love,)

ˈoːnə ˈmaːkˈəl, ˈoːnə ʃultˈ ʊntˈ fɔn ˈdeːmuːtsfɔləm ˈzɪnə!
ohne Makel, ohne   Schuld und von demutsvollem Sinne!
without blemish, without guilt, and of humble   mind!

ˈfrɔmə ˈlaᶒɛnfaltˈ ˈvœlpˈtˈə diːɐ̯ ˈdiːzə ˈɛrmlɪçə kʰaˈpʰɛlə
Fromme Einfalt wölbte dir   diese ärmliche Kapelle
Pious   simplicity vaulted for you this lowly   chapel

ɪn den ʃtˈam deːɐ̯/deːr ˈlaᶒɛçə hiːɐ̯, ˈoːnə ˈzɔᶏølən, ˈoːnə ˈʃvɛlə.
in den Stamm der   Eiche hier, ohne   Säulen, ohne   Schwelle.
in the trunk of the   oak-tree here, without columns, without threshold.

ˈføːgəlaᶒɛn lᶏof ˈjeːdəm lastˈ ˈzɪŋən ˈdaᶒɛnəm ˈkʰɪntˈlaᶒɛn ˈliːdə,
Vögelein auf jedem Ast   singen deinem Kindlein Lieder,
Little birds on every bough sing to your baby   songs,

dʊrçs   gəˈtsvaᶒɛkˈ lɪm ˈgɔldnən glastˈ ˈʃtˈaᶒɛgən ˈɛŋəl lᶏof ʊntˈ ˈniːdɐ.
durchs   Gezweig im goldnen Glast   steigen Engel auf und nieder.
through the branches in the golden radiance climb   angels up and down.
(through the branches angels soar up and down in golden radiance.)

ʊnt dem ˈhɛrtsən vɪrt‘   zoː laeçt‘, veːɐ̯/veːr lɛs lɑox fɔn graːm lʊmˈʃp‘ɔnən,
Und dem Herzen wird   so leicht, wär'   es auch von Gram umsponnen,
And to the heart   becomes so light, were   it even by grief enmeshed,
(And the heart grows so light, even if it were enmeshed in grief,)

ʊnt dem ˈp‘ɪlgɐ vɪrt‘ gəˈraeçt‘ ˈlaːbʊŋ   lɑos dem ˈgnaːdənbrɔnən.
und dem Pilger wird gereicht Labung   aus dem Gnadenbronnen.
and to the pilgrim is   given   refreshment from the fountain of Grace.

voːl   laen ˈhyt‘laen bɑot‘   lɪç gɛrn hiːɐ̯/hiːr lɪm   ˈʃt‘ɪlən ˈvaldəsgrʊndə,
Wohl ein   Hüttlein baut'   ich gern hier   im   stillen Waldesgrunde,
Indeed a   little hut would build I   gladly here   in the quiet forest depths,
(Indeed I would like to build a little hut here in the quiet depths of the forest,)

das   miːɐ̯ ˈdiːzɐ ˈmeːrəsʃt‘ɛrn ˈlɔøçt‘ə   nuːn lʊm ˈjeːdə ˈʃt‘ʊndə;
dass mir   dieser Meeresstern leuchte   nun um jede Stunde;
so that for me this   star of the sea might shine now at   every hour;
                                                     [*poem:* **nun und** (lʊnt‘, and) **jede Stunde**]

das   lɪn ˈdiːzəm ˈk‘laenən rɑom miːɐ̯ deːɐ̯ ˈhɪməl   ˈlangəhøːrə,
dass in diesem kleinen Raum mir der Himmel angehöre,
so that in this   little   space to me the heaven might belong,
(so that in this little space heaven might belong to me,)

das   k‘aen ˈbaŋɐ, ˈbøːzɐ t‘rɑom ˈmaenən ˈlɛtst‘ən ˈʃlʊmɐ   ˈʃt‘øːrə.
dass kein banger, böser Traum meinen letzten Schlummer störe.
so that no   anxious, bad dream my   last   slumber   may disturb.
(so that no anxious bad dream may disturb my final slumber.)

[In Germany and Austria there are many little roadside shrines with statues or paintings of the Virgin Mary, often with the Christchild in her arms, as lovingly indicated in the poem above.]

das ˈroːzənbant‘
Das Rosenband
The Rosy Ribbon

Posthumously published [composed 1815] (poem by Friedrich Gottlieb Klopstock)

ɪm   ˈfryːlɪŋsgartən   fant‘ lɪç ziː;   [ˈfryːlɪŋsʃat‘ən]
Im   Frühlingsgarten fand ich sie; [*poem, Peters:* **Frühlingsschatten**]
In the spring   garden found I her;   [spring   shadow]
(I found her in the spring garden;)

daː   bant‘ lɪç ziː mɪt‘ ˈroːzənbɛndɐn: ziː fyːlt‘ lɛs nɪçt‘ lʊnt‘ ˈʃlʊmɐt‘ə.
da   band ich sie mit Rosenbändern: sie fühlt' es nicht und schlummerte.
there bound I   her with rosy ribbons: she felt   it not   and slumbered.
(there I bound her with rosy ribbons: she did not feel it and slumbered on.)

lɪç zaː   ziː lan; maen ˈleːbən hɪŋ mɪt‘ ˈdiːzəm blɪk‘ lan ˈliːrəm ˈleːbən;
Ich sah   sie an; mein Leben hing mit diesem Blick an ihrem Leben;
I   looked her at; my   life   hung with that   look from her   life;
(I looked at her; with that look my life became bound to her life;)

ıç fyːlt' lɛs voːl lʊnt' vʊst' lɛs nıçtʰ. dɔx 'lıspˈəlt' lıç liːɐ̯ 'laezə tsuː
ich fühlt' es wohl und wusst' es nicht. Doch lispelt' ich ihr leise zu
I felt it indeed and knew it not. Yet whispered I to her softly to
(I felt it, indeed, but did not *know* it. Yet I whispered softly to her)
        [poem, Peters: **Doch lispelt' ich ihr sprachlos** ('ʃpˈraːxloːs, speechlessly) **zu]**

ʊnt' 'raoʃt'ə mıt den 'roːzənbɛnɐn: daː 'vaxt'ə ziː fɔm 'ʃlʊmɐ(r) laof.
und rauschte mit den Rosenbändern: da wachte sie vom Schlummer auf.
and rustled with the rosy ribbons: thereupon woke she from the slumber up.
(and rustled the rosy ribbons: at that she woke up from her sleep.)

ziː zaː mıç lan; liːɐ̯ 'leːbən hıŋ mıt 'diːzəm blık' lan 'maenəm 'leːbən,
Sie sah mich an; ihr Leben hing mit diesem Blick an meinem Leben,
She looked me at; her life hung with that look from my life,
(She looked at me; with that look her life became bound to my life,)

ʊnt' lʊm lʊns vart' leˈlyːziʊm. [varts]
und um uns ward Elysium. [*poem:* **und um uns ward's Elysium**]
and around us became Elysium. [became it (it became)]
(and Paradise was all around us.)

[That tender song is one of Schubert's gems. Klopstock wrote the poem for his beloved wife.]

das 'zeːnən
Das Sehnen
Longing

Op. 172, No. 4 [1815] (poem by Ludwig Kosegarten)

'veːmuːt, diː mıç hylt', 'vɛlçə 'gɔt'haet' ʃt'ılt' maen lʊnˈlɛnt'lıç 'zeːnən?
Wehmut, die mich hüllt, welche Gottheit stillt mein unendlich Sehnen?
Melancholy, that me envelops, what divinity stills my endless longing?
(Melancholy that envelops me, what god can still my endless longing?)

diː liːɐ̯ 'maenə 'vımp'ɐn nɛst', 'naːmənloːzən graːm lɛnt'ˈpʰrɛstʰ, 'fliːsət', 'fliːsət, 'tʰrɛːnən.
Die ihr meine Wimpern nässt, namenlosen Gram entpresst, fliesset, fliesset, Tränen.
Who you my eyelashes wet, nameless griefs wrung from, flow, flow, tears.
(You who wet my eyelashes, you who were wrung from nameless griefs, flow, flow, my tears.)
        [*GA:* **Wimper** ('vımp'ɐ, eyelash), *poem (singular grief):* **namenlosem** ('naːmənloːzəm)]

moːnt, deːɐ̯ liːp' lʊnt' tʰraot' lın maen 'fɛnst'ɐ ʃaot', 'zaːgə, vas miːɐ̯ 'feːlə!
Mond, der lieb und traut in mein Fenster schaut, sage, was mir fehle!
Moon, that lovingly and intimately in my window looks, say, what to me is lacking!
(Moon, who look lovingly and intimately through my window, tell me what I am lacking!)

'ʃt'ɛrnə, diː liːɐ̯ 'droːbən blıŋk't', 'hɔldən gruːs miːɐ̯ 'frɔønt'lıç vıŋk'tʰ,
Sterne, die ihr droben blinkt, holden Gruss mir freundlich winkt,
Stars, who you above twinkle, gracious greeting to me friendlily wave,
(Stars, you who twinkle up above and give me a gracious and friendly greeting,)

nɛnt' miːɐ̯, vas mıç 'kʰveːlə. 'laezə 'ʃaoɐ veːn,
nennt mir, was mich quäle. Leise Schauer wehn,
name for me what me torments. Soft shivers flutter,
(tell me what is tormenting me. The air is quivering softly,)

ˈzyːsəs ˈliːbəsfleːn   gɪrt' lʊm   mɪç lɪm   ˈdyːst'ɐn.   [vɪrt']
süsses Liebesflehn   girrt um   mich im   Düstern. [*poem:* **wirrt um mich**]
sweet love- entreaty coos around me   in the dusk.   [jumbles]
(the sweet entreaty of love coos around me in the dusk.)

ˈroːzən lʊnt' viˈoːlənduft'   ˈvʏrtsən rɪŋs   di ˈtsaɔbəlʊft^h, ˈhɔldə ˈʃt'ɪmən ˈflʏst'ɐn.
Rosen- und Violenduft   würzen rings   die Zauberluft, holde Stimmen flüstern.
Rose and violet-fragrance spice   all around the magic air , lovely voices   whisper.
(The fragrance of roses and violets spices the enchanted air all around, lovely voices whisper.)

ɪn di ˈfɛrnə   ʃt'reːp't', viː lɑof ˈflyːgəln ʃveːp't'   maen lɛɐ̯ˈhøːt'əs ˈveːzən.
In die Ferne   strebt,   wie auf Flügeln schwebt mein erhöhtes Wesen.
Into the distance strives,   as if on wings   soars   my   uplifted   being.
(My uplifted being strives into the distance, soars as if on wings.)

                    [*Peters:* **in der** (deːɐ̯) **Ferne** (*in* the distance)]

ˈfrɛmdɐ t͡suːk,   gəˈhaemə k^hraft', ˈnaːmənloːzə ˈlaedənʃaft^h,   las, lax las gəˈneːzən!
Fremder Zug,   geheime Kraft,   namenlose Leidenschaft, lass, ach lass genesen!
Strange impulse, secret   power,   nameless   passion,   let, ah let recover!
(Strange impulse, secret power, nameless passion, let, oh let me be healed!)

ˈɛŋst'əndɐ   bəˈk^hlɛmt' mɪç di ˈveːmuːt',   hɛmt' ˈlaːt'əm miːɐ̯/miːr lʊnt' ˈreːdə.
Ängstender   beklemmt mich die Wehmut,   hemmt Atem mir   und Rede.
More alarmingly oppresses me   the melancholy, stifles   breath to me   and speech.
(Melancholy oppresses me more alarmingly, stifles my breath and my speech.)

ˈaenzaːm ˈʃmaxt'ən,   loː deːɐ̯ p^haen! loː dɛs graːms, laˈlaen t͡suː zaen lɪn dɛs ˈleːbəns ˈløːdə!
Einsam schmachten, o der Pein! O des Grams, allein zu sein in des Lebens Öde!
Lonely   to languish,   oh the pain! Oh the grief,   alone to be   in the life's   desert!
(To languish in solitude—oh the pain! Oh the grief, to be alone in the desert of life!)

ɪst dɛn, lax, k^haen larm, deːɐ̯/deːr lɪn frɔøt'   lʊnt' harm ˈliːbənt' mɪç lʊmˈʃlœsə?
Ist denn, ach, kein Arm, der   in Freud' und Harm liebend mich umschlösse?
Is then, ah, no   arm, which   in joy   and sorrow lovingly me   might embrace?
(Is there then, ah, no arm, which might embrace me lovingly in joy and sorrow?)

ɪst dɛn, lax, k^haen ˈfyːlənt' hɛrt͡s, ˈk^haenəs,
Ist denn, ach, kein fühlend Herz, keines,
Is then, ah, no   feeling heart, none,
(Is there then, ah, no feeling heart, none,)

drɪn lɪn lʊst'   lʊnt' ʃmɛrt͡s ˈmaenəs zɪç lɛɐ̯ˈgœsə?
drin in Lust   und Schmerz meines sich ergösse?
in which in pleasure and pain   mine   itself might pour?
(into which mine might pour itself out in pleasure and pain?)

diː liːɐ̯/liːr ˈlaenzaːm   k^hlaːk't', ˈlaenzaːm vɛn lɛs t^haːk't', ˈlaenzaːm vɛn lɛs ˈnaxt'ət^h,
Die ihr einsam   klagt, einsam wenn es tagt, einsam wenn es nachtet,
Who you lonesomely lament, lonely   when it dawns, lonely   when it becomes night,
(You who lament in solitude, lonely when day dawns, lonely when night falls,)

184

ʊngəˈtʰrøːstˈətˈ, lax, fɛɐ̯ˈlɛçtˈstˈ/fɛrˈlɛçtˈstˈ liːɐ̯ das ˈhɔldə ˈdaːzae̯n,
ungetröstet, ach, verächzt ihr das holde Dasein,
uncomforted, ah, bemoan you the fair existence,
(uncomforted, ah, you bemoan this fair existence,)

lɛçtˈstˈ, ˈʃmaxtˈətˈ ʊntˈ fɛɐ̯ˈʃmaxtˈətʰ.
lechzt, schmachtet und verschmachtet.
are parched with thirst, languish, and pine away.

[The poet was a village priest. His title for this poem was "*Sehnsucht.*" Schubert's strophic setting, marked "*etwas geschwind*" ("rather fast") flows along more briskly than one might expect from the melancholy mood of the poem.]

das ziː hiːɐ̯ gəˈveːzən!
Dass sie hier gewesen!
That She Has Been Here!

Op. 59, No. 2 [1822 (?)] (Friedrich Rückert)

das deːɐ̯/deːr ˈɔstˈvɪntˈ ˈdʏftˈə ˈhao̯xətˈ ɪn di ˈlʏftˈə,
Dass der Ostwind Düfte hauchet in die Lüfte,
That the east wind fragrances breathes into the airs,
(That the east wind breathes fragrance into the air,)

ˈdaːdʊrç tʰuːtˈ leːɐ̯ kʰʊntˈ, das duː hiːɐ̯ gəˈveːzən.
dadurch tut er kund, dass du hier gewesen.
through that does he make known that you here (have) been.
(through *that* it makes known that you have been here.)

das hiːɐ̯ ˈtʰrɛːnən ˈrɪnən, ˈdaːdʊrç vɪrst duː ˈɪnən,
Dass hier Tränen rinnen, dadurch wirst du innen,
That here tears are flowing, through that become you aware,
(That tears are flowing here, through *that* you become aware,)

                              [*poem:* **Weil** (vae̯l, because) **hier Tränen rinnen,**]

vɛːɐ̯s diːɐ̯ zɔnstˈ nɪçtˈ kʰʊntˈ, das ɪç hiːɐ̯ gəˈveːzən.
wär's dir sonst nicht kund, dass ich hier gewesen.
were it to you otherwise not known, that I here (have) been.
(if it were otherwise not known to you, that I have been here.)

ˈʃøːnhae̯tˈ ˈloːdɐ ˈliːbə, ˈɔpˈ fɛɐ̯ˈʃtˈɛkˈtˈ ziː ˈbliːbə?
Schönheit oder Liebe, ob versteckt sie bliebe?
Beauty or love, whether concealed it may remain?
(Beauty or love—can either remain concealed?)

ˈdʏftˈə tʰuːn lɛs ʊnt ˈtʰrɛːnən kʰʊntˈ, das ziː hiːɐ̯ gəˈveːzən.
Düfte tun es und Tränen kund, dass sie hier gewesen.
Fragrances do it—and tears— make known, that she here (has) been.
(Fragrance and tears reveal that she has been here.)

[The haunting harmonies, suspended in the air like the fragrance they describe, anticipate Wagner's *Tristan und Isolde*! The key is elusive until the words "*dass du hier gewesen*" bring tonal clarity. A beautiful song!]

Das Wandern see *Die schöne Müllerin*

das vaːɐ̯ lɪç
Das war ich
That Was I

Posthumously published [composed 1815] (poem by Theodor Körner)

jʏŋst   ˈtʰrɔ̸mtˈə miːɐ̯/miːr, lɪç zaː lɑ̯of ˈlɪçtˈən ˈhø̸ːən lae̯n ˈmɛːtˈçən
Jüngst träumte mir,   ich sah auf lichten Höhen ein Mädchen
Recently dreamed to me,   I   saw on light   heights a   girl
(Recently I dreamed that I saw a girl on sunlit heights)

zɪç   lɪm   ˈjʊŋən tʰaːkˈ lɛɐ̯ˈgeːən, zoː hɔltˈ, zoː zyːs, das lɛs diːɐ̯ ˈfœlɪç glɪç.
sich im   jungen Tag ergehen, so hold, so süss, dass es dir   völlig glich.
herself in the young day stroll,   so lovely, so sweet, that she to you fully resembled.
(strolling in the early morning, so lovely, so sweet, that she fully resembled you.)

ʊntˈ foːɐ̯/foːr liːɐ̯ laːkˈ lae̯n ˈjʏŋlɪŋ   lɑ̯of den ˈkʰniːən,
Und vor   ihr lag ein Jüngling auf den Knien,
And in front of her lay a   young man on the knees,
(And in front of her a young man was on his knees,)

eːɐ̯ ʃiːn   ziː zanftˈ lan ˈzae̯nə brʊst t͡suː ˈt͡siːən, lʊnt das, lʊnt das vaːɐ̯/vaːr lɪç.
er schien sie sanft an seine Brust zu ziehen, und das, und das war   ich.
he seemed her gently to his   breast to draw,   and that, and that was   I.
(he seemed to be drawing her gently close to his breast, and that, and that was I.)

dɔx   baltˈ fɛɐ̯ˈlɛndətˈ ˈhatˈə zɪç di ˈst͡seːnə. lɪn ˈtʰiːfən ˈfluːtˈən zaː lɪç jɛt͡st di ˈʃø̸ːnə,
Doch bald verändert hatte sich die Szene. In tiefen Fluten sah ich jetzt die Schöne,
But soon changed   had itself the scene. In deep   waters saw I   now the lovely one,
(But the scene soon had changed. I now saw the lovely one in deep waters,)

viː liːɐ̯   di ˈlɛt͡stˈə, ˈʃvaxə kʰraftˈ lɛntˈˈvɪç.
wie ihr   die letzte, schwache Kraft   entwich.
as for her the last,   weak   strength vanished.
(as her last, weak strength was ebbing away.)

daː   kʰaːm lae̯n ˈjʏŋlɪŋ ˈhʏlfrae̯ç liːɐ̯ gəˈfloːgən, leːɐ̯ ʃpˈraŋ liːɐ̯ naːx,
Da   kam ein Jüngling hülfreich ihr   geflogen, er sprang ihr nach,
At that moment came a   young man helpfully to her flown,   he jumped her after,
(At that moment a young man came rushing to help her; he jumped in after her,)

ʊnt tʰruːkˈ ziː lɑ̯os den ˈvoːgən, lʊnt das, lʊnt das vaːɐ̯/vaːr lɪç.
und trug   sie aus den Wogen, und das, und das war   ich.
and carried her out of the waves, and that, and that was   I.

zoː ˈmaːltˈə zɪç deːɐ̯ tʰrɑ̯om lɪn ˈbʊntˈən ˈt͡syːgən,
So malte sich der Traum in bunten Zügen,
Thus painted itself the dream in colorful traits,
(Thus the dream was painted in bright colors,)

ʊnt' 'lyːbɐ(r)|al   zaː |ıç di 'liːbə 'ziːɡən,
und überall   sah ich die Liebe siegen,
and everywhere saw I   the love   triumph,
(and everywhere I saw love triumph,)

ʊnt' 'laləs, 'laləs 'dreːt'ə   zıç |ʊm   dıç! duː floːkst' foˈran |ın 'ʊnɡəbʊndnɐ 'fraeə,
und alles, alles drehte   sich um   dich! Du flogst   voran in ungebund'ner Freie,
and all,   all   revolved itself around you! You flew   ahead in unfettered   freedom,
(and everything, everything revolved around you! You flew ahead in unfettered freedom,)

deːɐ 'jʏŋlıŋ   tsoːk'   diːɐ naːx mıt' 'ʃt'ılɐ 'tʰrɔøə, |ʊnt das, |ʊnt das vaːɐ/vaːr |ıç.
der Jüngling   zog   dir nach mit stiller Treue, und das, und das war   ich.
the   young man followed you after with quiet   loyalty, and that, and that was   I.
(the young man followed after you in quiet loyalty, and that, and that was I.)

ʊnt' |als |ıç 'lent'lıç |aos dem tʰraom |ɐɡ'vaxt'ə,
Und als   ich endlich aus dem Traum erwachte,
And when I   finally from the dream awoke,
(And when I finally awoke from the dream,)

deːɐ 'nɔøə tʰaːk' di 'nɔøə 'zeːnzʊxt' 'braxt'ə,
der neue Tag   die neue Sehnsucht brachte,
the new day   the new longing   brought,
(the new day brought new longing,)

daː bliːp'   daen 'liːbəs, 'zyːsəs bılt' |ʊm   mıç.
da blieb   dein liebes, süsses Bild um   mich.
there remained your dear,   sweet image around me.
(for your dear, sweet image was still all around me.)

ıç zaː dıç fɔn deːɐ 'kʰʏsə gluːt' |ɐɡ'varmən,
Ich sah dich von der Küsse Glut erwarmen,
I   saw you from the kisses' fire   become warm,
(I saw you becoming warm from the fire of kisses,)

|ıç zaː dıç 'zeːlıç |ın dɛs 'jʏŋlıŋs |armən, |ʊnt das, |ʊnt das vaːɐ/vaːr |ıç.
ich sah dich selig   in des Jünglings   Armen, und das, und das war   ich.
I   saw you blissful in the young man's arms,   and that, and that was   I.

[The poem has six verses, but the Peters edition printed only the first four. Here are the last two:]

daː   tʰraːtst   duː 'lent'lıç |aof dɛs 'leːbəns 'veːɡən
Da   tratst   Du endlich auf des Lebens Wegen
There advanced you at last   on   the life's   pathways
(There you came at last on life's pathway)

mıt' 'hɔldɐ(r) 'lanmuːt 'frɔønt'lıç   miːɐ/miːr |ent'ɡeːɡən,
mit holder Anmut freundlich mir   entgegen,
with lovely   grace   friendlily to me   towards,
(towards me, with lovely grace and in a friendly way,)

ʊnt 'tʰiːfə, 'haesə 'zeːnzʊxt' 'fast'ə mıç.
und tiefe, heisse Sehnsucht fasste mich.
and deep, hot   longing   seized me.

zaːst duː den ˈjʏŋlɪŋ   nɪçt‘ mɪt‘ ˈtʰrʊŋk‘nən ˈblɪk‘ən?
Sahst Du den Jüngling   nicht mit trunknen Blicken?
Saw you the young man not   with intoxicated glances?
(Did you not see the young man with the intoxicated glances?)

ɛs ʃluːk‘ zaen herts ɪm   ˈzeːligən ɛnt‘tsʏk‘ən! ʊnt‘ das vaːɐ̯/vaːr lɪç!
Es schlug sein Herz im   seligen Entzücken! Und das war   ich!
It beat   his heart in the blissful delight!   And that was   I!
(His heart was beating in blissful delight! And that was I!)

duː tsoːkst‘ mɪç ɪn den kʰraes des   ˈhøːɐn   ˈleːbəns,
Du zogst   mich in den Kreis des   Höhern Lebens,
You drew   me   into the sphere of the higher   life,
(You drew me into the sphere of a nobler way of life,)

ɪn diːɐ̯ fɛɐ̯ˈmeːlt‘ zɪç ˈalə kʰraft‘ des   ˈʃt‘reːbəns, ʊnt‘ ˈalə ˈmaenə ˈvʏnʃə   ˈruːfən dɪç.
in Dir vermählt sich alle Kraft des   Strebens, und alle meine Wünsche rufen Dich.
in you marries   itself all power of the striving,   and all my   wishes   call   you.
(in you are united all the powers of aspiration, and all my wishes are calling for you.)

hat‘ ˈlaenɐ(r) laenst daen herts daˈfɔn gəˈt‘raːgən,
Hat Einer   einst Dein Herz davon getragen,
Has someone once your heart away carried,
(If someone, one day, has won your heart,)

dʏrft‘   lɪç nuːɐ̯ dan mɪt‘ ˈlaot‘əm ˈmʊndə ˈzaːgən: jaː, das vaːɐ̯/vaːr lɪç!
dürft’   ich nur dann mit lautem Munde sagen: ja, das war   ich!
would be allowed I   only then with loud   mouth to say: yes, that was   I!
(then, and only then, I would be allowed to say loudly: yes, that was I!)

[Besides this utterly charming finished song, Schubert left a six-bar fragment, with a different melody. It is not recommended that all six verses, above, should be sung; four are sufficient.]

das ˈvaenən
Das Weinen
Weeping

Op. 106, No. 2 [1827] (Karl Gottfried von Leitner)

gaːɐ̯ ˈt‘røːst‘lɪç   kʰɔmt‘ gəˈrɔnən deːɐ̯ ˈt‘reːnən ˈhaelgɐ kʰvɛl,
Gar tröstlich   kommt geronnen der Tränen heilger Quell,
Very comfortingly comes flowing the tears’   sacred spring,
(The sacred spring of tears flows very comfortingly,)

reçt‘ viː laen ˈhaelʊŋsbrɔnən,   zoː ˈbɪt‘ɐ, haes ʊnt‘ hɛl.
recht wie ein Heilungsbronnen, so bitter, heiss und hell.
just like a   healing fountain, so bitter, hot,   and clear.

daˈrʊm   duː brʊst‘ fɔl   ˈvʊndən, fɔl   graːm ʊnt‘ ˈʃt‘ɪlɐ pʰaen,
Darum   du Brust voll Wunden, voll Gram und stiller Pein,
Therefore, you breast full of wounds, full of grief and quiet pain,

ʊntʼ vɪlst duː baltʼ gəˈzʊndən,   zoː ˈtʰɑ̯ɔxə daː hɪˈnae̯n.
und willst du bald gesunden, so tauche da   hinein.
and want you soon to be healed, then plunge there into.
(if you want to be healed soon, then immerse yourself therein.)

ɛs   voːntʼ ɪn ˈdiːzən ˈvɛlən gəˈhae̯mə ˈvʊndɐkʰraftʰ,
Es   wohnt in diesen Wellen geheime Wunderkraft,
There dwells in those waves secret   miraculous power,
(In those waters there dwells a secret, miraculous power,)

diː   ɪstʼ fyːɐ̯ ˈveːə ˈʃtʼɛlən ḁe̯n ˈlɪndɐ ˈbalzaːmzaftʰ.
die   ist für wehe Stellen ein   linder Balsamsaft.
which is for sore places a   gentle balm- juice.
(which is a gentle balm for sore places.)

diː vɛkstʼ   mɪt ˈdae̯nən ˈʃmɛrtsən, ʊntʼ ˈfasətʼ, heːpʼtʼ ʊntʼ rɔltʼ
Die wächst mit deinen Schmerzen, und fasset, hebt   und rollt
That increases with your   pains,   and seizes, lifts, and rolls
(That power increases with your suffering, and it seizes, lifts up, and rolls away)

den ˈbøːzən ʃtʼae̯n fɔm   ˈhɛrtsən, deːɐ̯ dɪç tsɛɐ̯ˈdrʏkʼən vɔltʰ.
den bösen Stein vom   Herzen, der dich zerdrücken wollt'.
the evil   stone from the heart,   that you to crush   wanted.
(from your heart the evil stone that would crush you.)

das haːb ɪç zɛlpstʼ ḽɛmˈpfʊndən hiːɐ̯/hiːr ɪn dem ˈtʰrɑ̯ɔɐlantʼ,
Das hab' ich selbst empfunden hier   in dem Trauerland,
That have I   myself felt   here   in the land of mourning,
(I myself have felt that, here in the land of mourning,)

vɛn ɪç, fɔm   floːɐ̯/floːr ḽʊmˈvʊndən, ḽan ˈliːbən ˈgrɛːbɐn ʃtʼantʼ.
wenn ich, vom Flor   umwunden, an lieben Gräbern stand.
when I,   by the crêpe   swathed,   at dear   graves stood.
(when, swathed in crêpe, I stood beside the graves of loved ones.)

daː   ʃaltʼ   ɪn ˈḽɪrəm ˈveːnən ḽɪç zɛlpstʼ ḽɑ̯ɔf ˈmae̯nən gɔtʰ,
Da   schalt   in irrem Wähnen ich selbst auf   meinen Gott,
There inveighed in confused imagining I   even   against my God,
(There, in my confused mind, I even inveighed against my God,)

ɛs ˈhiːltʼən nuːɐ̯ di ˈtʰrɛːnən deːɐ̯ ˈhɔfnʊŋ ˈʃifçən floːtʰ.   [miːɐ̯ di ˈtʰrɛːnən]
es hielten nur die Tränen der   Hoffnung Schiffchen flott. [*Peters:* **mir   die Tränen...]**
it held   only the tears of the hope's   little boat afloat.   [for me the tears]
(only tears kept the little boat of hope afloat.) [(tears kept the little boat of hope afloat for me.)]

drʊm,   hɛlt dɪç ḽɑ̯ɔx ḽʊmˈfaŋən deːɐ̯ ˈʃveːɐ̯muːt ˈtʰryːpstʼə naxtʰ,
Drum,   hält dich auch umfangen der Schwermut trübste Nacht,
Therefore, holds you too encircled the sorrow's darkest night,
(Therefore, if you too are engulfed in the darkest night of sorrow,)

fɛɐ̯ˈtʰrɑ̯ɔ ɪn ˈḽaləm ˈbaŋən deːɐ̯ ˈtʰrɛːnən ˈtsɑ̯ɔbɐmaxtʰ.
vertrau in allem Bangen der Tränen Zaubermacht.
trust   in all   anxiety the tears' magic power.
(in the midst of all your anxiety put your trust in the magic power of tears.)

balt', vɛn fɔm 'haesən 'vaenən diːɐ̯ roːt das 'l̦ɑo̯gə glyːtʰ,
Bald, wenn vom heissen Weinen dir rot das Auge glüht,
Soon, when from the hot weeping for you red the eye glows,
(Soon, when your eyes glow red from burning tears,)

vɪrt' nɔø deːɐ̯ tʰaːk' lɛɐ̯'ʃaenən, vael ʃoːn deːɐ̯ 'mɔrgən blyːtʰ.
wird neu der Tag erscheinen, weil schon der Morgen blüht.
will new the day appear, because already the morning blooms.
(a new day will appear, for already the morning is becoming bright.)

[The four stanzas of the poem are set to identical, hymn-like music in this song in praise of the healing power of tears, composed at a time when Schubert was experiencing revived symptoms of his illness.]

Das Wirtshaus see *Winterreise*

das 'tsyːgənglœk'laen
Das Zügenglöcklein
The Passing Bell

Op. 80, No. 2 [1826?] (Johann Gabriel Seidl)

kʰlɪŋ di naxt dʊrç, 'kʰlɪŋə, 'zyːsən 'friːdən 'brɪŋə deːm, fyːɐ̯ deːn duː tʰøːnstʰ!
Kling' die Nacht durch, klinge, süssen Frieden bringe dem, für den du tönst!
Ring the night through, ring, sweet peace bring to him for whom you sound!
(Ring, ring the night through, bring sweet peace to him for whom you are sounding!)

kʰlɪŋ ɪn 'vaet'ə 'fɛrnə, zoː duː 'pʰɪlgɐ 'gɛrnə mɪt deːɐ̯ vɛlt' fɛɐ̯'zøːnstʰ!
kling' in weite Ferne, so du Pilger gerne mit der Welt versöhnst!
Ring into far distance, so you pilgrims gladly with the world reconcile!
(Ring out into the far distance, for thus you gladly reconcile pilgrims with the world!)
 [*poem:* **Kling' in stille** ('ʃt'ɪlə) **Ferne** (ring out into the quiet distance)]

'laːbɐ veːɐ̯ vɪl 'vandɛn tsuː den 'liːbən 'landɛn, diː fo'rɑo̯sgəvaltʰ?
Aber wer will wandern zu den lieben Andern, die vorausgewallt?
But who wants to wander to the dear others, who have gone on before?
(But who wants to journey to the dear ones who have gone on before?)

tsoːk' leːɐ̯ gɛrn diː 'ʃelə? beːp't' leːɐ̯/leːr lan deːɐ̯ 'ʃvɛlə, van he'raen lɛɐ̯'ʃaltʰ?
Zog er gern die Schelle? bebt er an der Schwelle, wann "Herein" erschallt?
Pulled he gladly the bell? Trembles he on the threshold when "Come in" sounds?
(Did he gladly pull on the bell-rope? Does he tremble on the threshold when "Come in" sounds?)

gɪlts dem 'bøːzən 'zoːnə, deːɐ̯ nɔx fluːxt dem 'tʰøːnə, vael leːɐ̯ 'haelɪç lɪstʰ?
Gilt's dem bösen Sohne, der noch flucht dem Tone, weil er heilig ist?
Is meant it for the wicked son, who still curses the tone because it sacred is?
(Is it meant for the wicked son who still curses the tone because it is sacred?),

naen, lɛs kʰlɪŋt' zoː 'l̦ɑot'ɐ, vi: laen 'gɔt'fɛɐ̯tʰrɑot'ɐ 'zaenə 'l̦ɑo̯fbaːn ʃliːstʰ!
Nein, es klingt so lauter, wie ein Gottvertrauter seine Laufbahn schliesst!
No, it tolls so pure as a God-confidant his career closes!
(No, it tolls with so pure a sound when a man who is close to God ends his earthly journey!)

ˈlaːbɐ(r) ˈɪsts ˌaen ˈmyːdɐ, deːn fɛɐ̯ˈvaest di ˈbryːdɐ, deːm ˌaen ˈtʰrɔɠøəs tʰiːɐ
Aber   ist's ein Müder,   den   verwaist   die Brüder, dem   ein   treues Tier
But   is   it a   weary one, whom deserted (have) the brothers, for whom a   faithful animal
(But is it a weary soul, whom his kin have deserted, for whom only a faithful animal)

ˈaentsɪç liːs den ˈɡlaobən ˌan di vɛltˈ nɪçtˈ ˈraobən, ruːf liːn, ɡɔt, tsuː diːɐ̯!
einzig   liess den Glauben an die Welt nicht rauben,   ruf' ihn, Gott, zu dir!
only   let the faith   in the world not   be stolen, call him, God, to Thee!
(kept his faith in the world from being stolen from him,—call him, O God, to Thee!)

> [*GA:* **ruft** (ruːftˈ, calls—Schubert's error?); *poem, Peters:* **ruf'**]

ɪsts deːɐ̯ ˈfroːən   ˈaenɐ, deːɐ̯ di ˈfrɔ̈ødən ˈraenɐ liːpˈ ˌʊntˈ ˈfrɔ̈øntˈʃaft tʰaeltʰ,
Ist's der   Frohen   Einer, der die Freuden reiner Lieb' und Freundschaft teilt,
Is   it of the happy ones one,   who the joys   of pure love and friendship   shares,
(If it is one of the happy ones who shares the joys of pure love and friendship,)

ɡœn liːm nɔx di ˈvɔnən ˈʊntˈɐ ˈdiːzɐ ˈzɔnən, voː   leːɐ̯ ˈɡɛrnə vaeltʰ!
gönn' ihm noch die Wonnen unter   dieser Sonnen, wo   er   gerne weilt!
grant him still the delights beneath this   sun,   where he gladly lingers!
(grant him still the delights of life beneath this sun, where he would be glad to linger!)

[The title of this lovely song refers to the little bell that tolls in Austrian churches when someone is dying in the parish. For whom this time? The bell sounds repeatedly in octaves in every bar, and none of the five stanzas is exactly like any of the others. There is compassion, and a sense of the beauty as well as the sadness of the world. The loyal dog is a touching moment in the poem.]

dɛlˈfiːnə / tsvae ˈstseːnən
Delphine / Zwei Szenen
Delphine / "Two Scenes" (title in the *Gesamtausgabe*, with "Florio")

Op. 124, No. 1 [1825] (from the play *Lacrimas* by Christian Wilhelm von Schütz)

ax, vas zɔl ˌɪç bəˈɡɪnən foːɐ̯ ˈliːbə?
Ach, was soll ich beginnen vor Liebe?
Ah, what shall I   do   for love?

ax, viː zi: ˈɪnɪç   dʊrçˈdrɪŋətˈ maen ˈɪnrəs!
ach, wie sie innig   durchdringet mein Inn'res!
Ah, how it   intimately penetrates   my   innermost being!
(Ah, how intimately it penetrates my innermost being!)

ˈziːə, ˈjʏŋlɪŋ,   das ˈkʰlaenstˈə fɔm   ˈʃaetˈəl bɪs tszur zoːl
Siehe, Jüngling, das Kleinste vom   Scheitel bis zur Sohl'
See,   young man, the smallest   from the crown   till to the sole
(See, young man, the smallest part of me from the top of my head to the soles of my feet)

ˌɪst diːɐ̯/diːr ˈaentsɪç ɡəˈvaeətʰ.
ist dir   einzig geweihet.
is to you   alone consecrated.
(is consecrated to you alone.)

oː ˈbluːnən! ˈbluːmən! fɛɐ̯ˈvɛlkʼətʰ, lɔøç ˈpfleːɡətʼ nuːɐ̯, bɪs ziː liːpʼ lɛɐ̯ˈkʰɛnət, di ˈzeːlə!
O Blumen! Blumen! verwelket, euch pfleget nur, bis sie Lieb' erkennet, die Seele!
Oh flowers! flowers! fade, you tends only, until it love recognizes, the soul!
(Oh flowers, fade! The soul only cultivates you until it recognizes love!)

nɪçts vɪl lɪç tʰuːn, ˈvɪsən lʊntʼ ˈhaːbən,
Nichts will ich tun, wissen und haben,
Nothing want I to do, to know and to have,
(I want to do nothing, to know and to have nothing,)

ɡəˈdaŋkʼən deːɐ̯ ˈliːbə, di ˈmɛçtʼɪç mɪç ˈfastʼə, ɡəˈdaŋkʼən deːɐ̯ ˈliːbə nuːɐ̯ ˈtʰraːɡən.
Gedanken der Liebe, die mächtig mich fasste, Gedanken der Liebe nur tragen.
thoughts of the love, which mightily me seized, thoughts of the love only carry.
(except only to sustain thoughts of love, which seized me powerfully.)

[*poem:* **Gedanken der Liebe, die mächtig mich fasste** (refers to "*Liebe*"), **nur tragen.**]

[*Peters:* **fassen** (ˈfasən, seize—refers to "*Gedanken*")]

ˈɪmɐ zɪn lɪç, vas lɪç lɑ̯os ˈɪnbrʊnstʼ voːl ˈkʰœnə tʰuːn,
Immer sinn' ich, was ich aus Inbrunst wohl könne tun,
Always wonder I what I out of ardor possibly might be able to do,
(I am forever wondering what I might be able to do in my ardor,)

dɔx tsu zeːɐ̯ hɛltʼ mɪç ˈliːbə lɪm drʊkʰ, nɪçts, nɪçts lɛstʼ ziː tsuː. [lɪn]
doch zu sehr hält mich Liebe im Druck, nichts, nichts lässt sie zu. [P: in Druck]
but too much holds me love in the pressure, nothing, nothing allows it ... . [in]
(but love holds me too tightly, and it allows me to do nothing else, it concedes me nothing.)

["*lässt zu*" from "*zulassen*" (infinitive) = to allow, to concede]

jɛtst, daː lɪç ˈliːbə, mœçtʼ lɪç ˈleːɐ̯stʼ ˈleːbən, lʊntʼ ˈʃtʼɛrbə.
Jetzt, da ich liebe, möcht' ich erst leben, und sterbe.
Now, when I love, would like I for the first time to live, and (I) die.
(Now that I am in love, for the first time I would like to *live* fully—and here I am dying of love!)

[*poem:* **mögt'** (møːkʼtʼ—old form) **ich erst leben**]

jɛtst, daː lɪç ˈliːbə, mœçtʼ lɪç hɛl ˈbrɛnən, lʊntʼ ˈvɛlkʼə.
Jetzt, da ich liebe, möcht' ich hell brennen, und welke.
Now, when I love, would like I brightly to burn, and (I) wither.
(Now that I am in love I would like to burn with a bright flame—and I find myself withering!)

[*GA:* **möcht' ich erst** (leːɐ̯stʼ, for the first time) **brennen**]

voˈtsuː lɑ̯ox ˈbluːmən ˈrae̯ən lʊntʼ ˈvɛsən? lɛntʼˈblɛtʼɐtʰ!
Wozu auch Blumen reihen und wässern? Entblättert!
For what purpose, also, flowers arrange in rows and water? Petals shed!
(What is the use of arranging flowers in rows and watering them? Their petals soon will fall!)

zoː ziːtʼ, viː ˈliːbə mɪç lɛntʼˈkʰrɛftʼətʼ, zae̯n ˈʃpʼɛːən.
so sieht, wie Liebe mich entkräftet, sein Spähen. [*poem:* **wie mich Liebe**]
So sees, how love me weakens, his watching.
(Thus his watchful eyes can see how love is weakening me.)

deːɐ̯ ˈroːzə ˈvaŋə vɪl ˈblae̯çən, lɑ̯ox ˈmae̯nə,
Der Rose Wange will bleichen, auch meine,
The rose's cheek will fade, also mine,
(The cheeks of the rose will fade, as will mine as well,)

192

iːɐ̯ ʃmʊkʼ   ͡tsɛɐ̯ˈfɛltʼ, viː fɛɐ̯ˈʃaenən di ˈkʰlaedɐ.
ihr Schmuck zerfällt, wie verscheinen die Kleider.
her adornment decays,   as become worn the clothes.
(her adornment decays, just as clothes become worn.)

ax, ˈjʏŋlɪŋ,   daː duː mɪç ʾɛɐ̯ˈfrɔʁəst dʊrç ˈtʰrɔʏ̯ə,
Ach, Jüngling, da   du mich erfreuest durch Treue,
Ah, young man, since you me   delight   through faithfulness,
(Ah, young man, since you delight me with your faithfulness,)
                [*GA & Peters (in the repetitions):* **mit** (mɪtʼ, with) **Treue** (*poem:* **durch**)]

viː kʰan mɪç mɪtʼ ʃmɛr͡ts zoː bəˈʃtʼrɔʏ̯ən di ˈfrɔʏ̯də?
wie kann mich mit Schmerz so bestreuen die Freude?
how can me   with pain   so bestrew   the joy?
(how can joy bestrew me so with pain?)   [*End of the poem*]

ax, vas zɔl lɪç bəˈɡɪnən foːɐ̯ ˈliːbə?
Ach, was soll ich beginnen vor Liebe?
Ah, what shall I   do   for love?
(Ah, what can I do when I am in love?)   [*A repeat of the opening lines*]

[The lady is perplexed by the mystery of love. Her joy in it is mingled with pain: she never wanted more eagerly to be alive, yet love seems to enervate her and she feels as if she is dying; she never wanted more urgently to be beautiful, yet love and its uncertainties seem to be undermining her beauty. The poem comes from a play, from Act IV of *Lacrimas*; Schubert's song is like an operatic aria, with a long high B flat at the first *fortissimo* climax and then at the end a crowning high C!]

dem ʊnˈʔɛntʼlɪçən
Dem Unendlichen
To the Infinite One

Posthumously published [composed 1815] (poem by Friedrich Gottlieb Klopstock)

viː ʾɛɐ̯ˈheːpʼtʼ zɪç das hɛr͡ts, vɛn ʾɛs   dɪç, ʊnˈʔɛntʼlɪçɐ, dɛŋkʼtʰ!
Wie erhebt   sich das Herz, wenn es   dich, Unendlicher, denkt!
How lifts   itself the heart, when it (of) you, Infinite One, thinks!
(How the heart is lifted up, when it thinks of you, Infinite One!)

viː zɪŋkʼtʼ ʾɛs, vɛn ʾɛs ʾaof zɪç hɛˈrʊntʼɐʃaotʰ!—   [vɛns]
wie sinkt es, wenn es auf sich herunterschaut!— [*poem:* **wenn's auf sich...]**
how sinks it,   when it upon itself gazes down!—
(How it sinks, when it gazes down upon itself!

ˈeːləntʼ ʃaot͡s   ˈveːkʰlaːɡənt dan ʊntʼ naxtʼ ʊnt tʰoːtʼ!
Elend schaut's wehklagend dann und Nacht und Tod!
Misery beholds it lamenting   then and night and death!
(Lamenting, it beholds then only misery, night, and death!)

aˈlaen duː ruːfstʼ mɪç ʾaos ˈmaenɐ naxt,
Allein du rufst mich aus   meiner Nacht,
But   you call   me   out of my   night,

deːɐ̯/deːr ɪm ˈleːlənt, deːɐ̯/deːr ɪm ˈtʰoːdə hɪlftʰ!   [tʰoːtʼ]
der   im   Elend, der   im   Tode hilft!   [poem: im Tod]
who   in the misery, who   in the death help!
(you who help in misery, who help in death!)

dan dɛŋkʼ lɪç lɛs gants, da   duː ˈleːvɪç mɪç ʃuːfstʼ,
dann denk' ich es ganz, dass du ewig   mich schufst,
then think I   it   fully, that   you eternal me   created,
(Then I contemplate fully the thought that you created my soul to be eternal,)

ˈhɛrlɪçɐ!   deːn   kʰaen pʰraes, ˈlʊntʼən lam graːpʼ, ˈloːbən lam tʰroːn, hɛr, gɔtʰ!
Herrlicher! den   kein Preis, unten am   Grab, oben am   Thron, Herr, Gott!
Glorious One! whom no   praise, below   at the grave,   above at the throne, Lord,   God!
(Glorious One, whom no praise, here below by the grave or above near your throne, Lord, God,)
                         [poem: **Herr, Herr Gott** (Lord, Lord God)]

deːn, ˈdaŋkʼəntʼ lɛntʼˈflamtʼ, kʰaen ˈjuːbəl   gəˈnuːkʼ bəˈzɪŋtʰ!
den,   dankend entflammt, kein Jubel   genug besingt!
whom, thankingly inflamed,   no   jubilation enough extolls!
(whom no jubilation, however fervent with gratitude, ever sufficiently extolls!)

veːtʼ, ˈbɔ͡ømə dɛs ˈleːbəns, lɪns   ˈharfəngətʰøːn!
Weht, Bäume des   Lebens, ins   Harfengetön!
Blow, trees   of the life,   into the harp-   tones!
(Rustle, trees of life, with the tones of the harps!)

ˈrɑ͡oʃə mɪtʼ ˈliːnən lɪns   ˈharfəngəˈtʰøːn, kʰrɪstʼalne ʃtʼroːm!
rausche mit ihnen ins   Harfengetön, kristallner Strom!
murmur with them   into the harp-   tones, crystal   stream!
(Let your murmur mingle with theirs in the music of the harps, crystal stream!)

iːɐ̯ ˈlɪspʼəltʼ lʊntʼ rɑ͡oʃtʼ, lʊntʼ, ˈharfən, liːɐ̯ tʰøːntʼ niː   lɛs gants!
ihr lispelt und rauscht, und, Harfen, ihr tönt   nie   es ganz!
You whisper and murmur, and, harps,   you sound never it fully!
(You whisper and murmur, and, harps, you never sound the message fully!)

gɔtʼ lɪstʼ lɛs, gɔtʼ lɪstʼ lɛs, deːn   liːɐ̯ pʰraestʰ! ˈvɛltʼən, ˈdɔnɐtʼ, lɪm ˈfae̯ɐlɪçən gaŋ,
Gott ist es, *Gott ist es*, den   ihr preist! Welten, donnert, im   feierlichen Gang,
God is it, God is   it, whom you praise! Worlds, thunder, in the solemn   movement,
(It is God, it is *God* whom you praise! Worlds, thunder forth in your solemn movement,)
               [poem: **Donnert, Welten in feierlichem Gang, in der Posaunen Chor!**]

ˈvɛltʼən, ˈdɔnɐtʼ lɪn deːɐ̯ pʰoˈzɑ͡onən kʰoːɐ̯!
Welten, donnert in der Posaunen   Chor!
worlds, thunder in the trombones's choir!   [in German the "last trump" is a trombone]
(worlds, add your thunder to the choir of trumpets!)
                         [duː loˈriːɔn, ˈvaːgə, duː lɑ͡ox!]
               [line omitted by Schubert: **Du Orion, Wage, du auch!**]
                         [you, Orion, Libra, you too!]

tʰøːntʼ, lal liːɐ̯ ˈzɔnən lɑ͡of deːɐ̯ ˈʃtʼraːsə   fɔl glants, lɪn deːɐ̯ pʰoˈzɑ͡onən kʰoːɐ̯!
tönt,   all' ihr Sonnen auf der Strasse   voll Glanz,   in der Posaunen Chor!
Sound, all   you suns   on the thoroughfare full of splendor, in the trombones' choir!
(Sing, all you suns in your radiant orbits, sing with the choir of trumpets!)

194

 iːɐ̯ 'vɛltʰən, liːɐ̯ 'dɔnɐt,   duː, deːɐ̯ pʰoˈzɑ͜onən kʰoːɐ̯, 'haləstʰ niː   lɛs gants!
Ihr Welten, ihr donnert, du, der Posaunen Chor, hallest nie   es ganz!
You worlds, you thunder, you, the trombones' choir, sound never it fully!
(You heavenly spheres, you thunder forth, you, choir of trumpets, you never sound it fully!)

> [*poem:* **Ihr Welten donnert und du, der Posaunen Chor, hallest nie es ganz,**]

gɔtʰ'! gɔtʰ'! gɔtʰ' lɪstʰ' lɛs, deːn   liːɐ̯ pʰrɑ͜estʰ!
Gott! *Gott*! **Gott ist es, den   ihr preist!**
God! God! God is   it, whom you praise!
(God! God! It is God, whom you praise!)

[*Dem Unendlichen*, a magnificent song, begins with a powerful recitative that builds to an exultant climax on the word "*Jubel*"; then comes a broadly flowing melody that suggests the music of the spheres, the majestic harmonies of the universe that are unheard by human ears. Schubert left three versions, all of which are printed in the *Gesamtausgabe*; the major difference is that in the third the recitative is a whole tone higher. Peters prints the familiar second version.]

deːɐ̯ 'laːbənt' / deːɐ̯ 'laːbət' blyːtʰ
Der Abend / Der Abend blüht
The Evening / The Evening Is Blossoming

Op. 118, No. 2 [1815] (Ludwig Kosegarten)

deːɐ̯/deːr 'laːbənt' blyːtʰ,   tʰeˈmoːra glyːtʰ' lɪm glants deːɐ̯ 'tʰiːfgəzʊŋk'nən 'zɔnə.
Der   Abend blüht,   Temora glüht im Glanz der   tiefgesunknen Sonne.
The   evening is blossoming, Temora glows in the radiance of the deep- sunk   sun.

> [*poem:* **Arkona** (larˈkʰoːna) **glüht**]

ɛs kʰʏst di zeː di 'zɪŋk'əndə, fɔn 'leːɐ̯fʊrçt' 'ʃɑ͜odənt'   lʊnt' fɔn 'vɔnə.
Es küsst die See die Sinkende, von Ehrfurcht schaudernd und von Wonne.
It kisses the sea, the sinking one, with reverence shivering   and with rapture.
(The sinking sun kisses the sea, shivering with reverence and with rapture.)

> [*poem:* **schauernd** ('ʃɑ͜oɐnt', shivering)]

ɑen 'grɑ͜oɐ dʊftʰ dʊrçˈveːp't   di lʊftʰ, lʊmˈʃlaɐt 'dɑ͜oras 'gʏldnə 'lɑ͜oən.
Ein grauer Duft durchwebt   die Luft, umschleiert Daura's güld'ne Auen.
A grey   vapor weaves through the air, veils   Daura's golden meadows.
(A grey vapor weaves through the air, veiling Daura's golden meadows.)

ɛs   rɑ͜oʃt' lʊmheːɐ̯ das 'dyːstʰrə meːɐ̯, lʊnt' rɪŋs hɛrʃt' 'laːnʊŋsraeçəs 'grɑ͜oən.
Es   rauscht umher   das düstre Meer, und rings herrscht ahnungsreiches Grauen.
There murmurs all around the dark sea,   and around reigns   presentiment-rich greying.
(The dark sea is murmuring on all sides, and all around reigns twilight, rich in presentiment.)

> [variant: "*ahndungsreiches*"; "*Ahndung*," obsolete in the sense intended here, = "*Ahnung*"]

oː 'tʰrɑ͜otʰ'əs lantʰ'! oː 'haelgɐ ʃt'rant'! loː fluːɐ̯, diː jeːdə   fluːɐ̯ fɛɐ̯ˈdʊŋk'əltʰ.
O trautes Land! o heil'ger Strand! O Flur,   die jede   Flur verdunkelt.
O beloved land! O sacred shore! O meadow, which every (other) meadow darkens.
(O beloved land! O sacred shore! O meadow, which puts every other meadow in the shade!)

fluːɐ̯, 'deːrən ʃoːs di bluːm lɛntʰ'ʃp'rɔs, diː 'lalə   'bluːmən lyːbɐ'fʊŋk'əltʰ.
Flur,   deren Schoss die Blum' entspross, die alle   Blumen überfunkelt.
Meadow, from whose womb the flower sprang   which all (other) flowers outsparkles.
(Meadow, from whose womb that flower sprang that outshines all other flowers.)

pʰaːɐ̯tʰ nɪçt den ʃneː deːɐ̯ 'liːlɪə di 'hɔldə   mɪt deːɐ̯ gluːtʰ deːɐ̯ 'roːzən?
Paart nicht den Schnee der   Lilie die Holde   mit der Glut der   Rosen?
Pairs not   the snow   of the lily the lovely one with the fire of the roses?
(Does not that lovely one combine the snowy whiteness of the lily with the red fire of the rose?)

di lɑo,   lɑen kranʦ fɔl   dʊftʰ   ʊntʰ glanʦ,
Die Au,   ein Kranz voll Duft   und Glanz,
The meadow, a   garland full of fragrance and splendor,

rɑeçtʰ liːɐ̯   den pʰrɑes, deːɐ̯ 'tʰaːdəlloːzən.
reicht ihr   den Preis, der Tadellosen.
awards to her the prize,   the flawless one.
(awards the prize to *her*, the flawless one.)

iːɐ̯/iːr 'lambradʊft   dʊrçveːt   di lʊftʰ, ʊntʰ 'vʏrʦətʰ rɪŋs   di neː ʊntʰ 'fɛrnə.
Ihr Ambraduft   durchweht   die Luft, und würzet   rings   die Näh' und Ferne.
Her amber fragrance wafts through the air,   and spices   all around the near and far.
(Her amber fragrance wafts through the air and spices everything near or far, all around.)

ʊntʰ ʃtʰɪrptʰ das lɪçt   des   'liːdəs nɪçtʰ, zoː rɑeçtʰ liːɐ̯ naːm lɑenstʰ lan di 'ʃtʰɛrnə.
Und stirbt das Licht des   Liedes nicht, so   reicht ihr Nam' einst   an die Sterne.
And dies   the light of the song   not, then reaches her name one day to the stars.
(And if the light of song does not fade, then one day her name will reach the stars.)

oː 'tʰrɑotʰəs lantʰ, oː 'heːrɐ   ʃtʰrantʰ, zɑe ʃtʰɔlʦ lɑof 'dɑenɐ 'bluːmən 'bluːmə.
O trautes Land, o hehrer Strand, sei stolz   auf deiner Blumen Blume.
O beloved land, O sublime shore, be proud of   your   flowers' flower.
(O beloved land, O sublime shore, be proud of the fairest of your flowers.)

das 'hɑelgə meːɐ̯/meːr ʊntʰ rɪŋs ʊm'heːɐ̯ di 'lɪnzəln 'hʊldgən   'dɑenəm 'ruːmə.
Das heil'ge Meer   und rings umher die Inseln huld'gen   deinem Ruhme.
The sacred sea   and, round about,   the islands pay homage to your glory.

naxtʰ hʏltʰ den ʃtʰrantʰ, tʰe'moːra ʃvantʰ.   fɛɐ̯'loːdɐtʰ zɪntʰ dɛs 'ʃpʰɛːtʰroːʦ 'gluːtʰən.
Nacht hüllt den Strand, Temora schwand. Verlodert sind des Spätrots   Gluten.
Night veils the shore,   Temora vanished. Burned out are the late-red's fires.
(Night veils the shore; Temora has vanished. The sunset's last fires have burned out.)

                                                                      [*poem:* **Arkona schwand**]

das 'vɛltʰmeːɐ̯ grɔltʰ, ʊntʰ 'gluːtʰroːtʰ rɔlt deːɐ̯ 'fɔlmoːntʰ lɑos den 'dyːstʰɐn 'fluːtʰən.
Das Weltmeer grollt, und glutrot   rollt der Vollmond aus   den düstern Fluten.
The ocean   roars, and fire-red   rolls the full moon out of the dark   waters.
(The ocean roars, and the full moon rises red as fire out of the dark waters.)

                                       [*poem:* **und blutrot** ('bluːtʰroːtʰ, blood-red) **rollt**]

[Is it actually a flower—or a lovely girl—that inspired this poem? In any case, the poet was writing about Rügen, his favorite island in the Baltic Sea, where the amber trees are found. "Temora" was Schubert's whim: the name in Kosegarten's poem was "Arkona." Schubert evidently made the change under the influence of his enthusiasm for the Ossianic poems, in which Temora is the castle of ancient Irish kings. The song is strophic, in seven identical verses.]

deːɐ̯ ˈlaːbənt‘ / ˈpʰʊrp‘ʊr maːlt di ˈtʰanənhyːɡəl
Der Abend / Purpur malt die Tannenhügel
The Evening / The Pine-covered Hills are Painted Purple

Posthumously published [composed 1814] (poem by Friedrich von Matthisson)

ˈpʰʊrp‘ʊr maːlt di ˈtʰanənhyːɡəl   naːx deːɐ̯ ˈzɔnə ˈʃae̯dəblɪkʰ,
Purpur malt die Tannenhügel   nach der Sonne Scheideblick,
Purple   paints the pine-covered hills after the sun's parting glance,
(The pine-covered hills are painted purple after the sun's parting glance,)

ˈliːp‘lɪç   ʃt‘raːlt dɛs ˈbaxəs ˈʃp‘iːɡəl ˈhɛsp‘ɐs ˈfak‘əlɡlants tsuˈrʏkʰ.
lieblich   strahlt des Baches Spiegel Hespers Fackelglanz zurück.
charmingly beams the brook's mirror Hesperus's torch- gleam back.
(the mirror of the brook charmingly beams back the gleam of Hesperus's torch.)
                  [Hesperus is the evening star, as personified in Greek mythology]

viː ɪn ˈtʰoːt‘ənhalən ˈdyːst‘ɐ vɪrts ɪm ˈpʰap‘əlvae̯dənhae̯n,
Wie in Totenhallen düster wird's im Pappelweidenhain,
As in halls of the dead dark grows it in the poplar-meadow-grove,
(It is growing as dark in the poplar-grove of the meadow as in the halls of the dead,)

ˈʊnt‘ɐ ˈlae̯zəm ˈblat‘ɡəflʏst‘ɐ ˈʃlʊmɐn ˈalə ˈføːɡəl ˈae̯n.
unter leisem Blattgeflüster schlummern alle Vögel ein.
beneath soft   leaf- whispering fall asleep   all   birds ... . [*"einschlummern"* = to fall asleep]
(beneath softly whispering leaves all the birds are falling asleep.)

nuːɐ̯ dae̯n ˈlaːbənt‘liːt‘,   loː ˈɡrɪlə, tʰøːnt‘ nɔx ɑo̯s bəˈtʰɑot‘əm ɡrʏn,
Nur dein Abendlied, o Grille, tönt noch aus betautem Grün,
Only your evening song, O cricket, sounds still out of bedewed   green,
(Only your evening song, O cricket, is still sounding out of the dew-covered greenery,)

dʊrç deːɐ̯ ˈdɛmrʊŋ ˈtsɑobɐhʏlə ˈzyːsə ˈtʰrɑo̯ɐmeloˈdiːən.
durch der Dämmrung Zauberhülle süsse Trauermelodien.
through the twilight's   magic veil, sweet mournful melodies.

tʰøːnst du: ˈlae̯nst‘ ɪm ˈlaːbənt‘hɑoxə, ˈɡrɪlçən,   ɑof mae̯n ˈfryːəs ɡraːp‘
Tönst du einst im Abendhauche, Grillchen, auf mein frühes Grab
Sound you one day in the evening breath, little cricket, upon my   early   grave
(If one day you sing in the evening breeze, little cricket, on my early grave)

ɑos deːɐ̯ ˈfrɔøntˈʃaft‘ ˈroːzənʃt‘rɑoxə, ˈdae̯nən ˈkʰlaːkɡəzaŋ hɛˈrap‘:
aus der Freundschaft Rosenstrauche, deinen Klaggesang herab:
out of the friendship's rosebush,   your   lament-song down:
(your song of lamentation from out of the rosebush planted by my friends:)

vɪrt‘ nɔx ʃt‘eːts   mae̯n ɡae̯st diːɐ̯ ˈlɑoʃən, ˈhɔrçənt‘, viː leːɐ̯ jɛtst diːɐ̯   ˈlɑoʃtʰ,
wird noch stets   mein Geist dir lauschen, horchend, wie er jetzt dir   lauscht,
will still constantly my   spirit to you listen,   hearkening, as it now to you listens,
(my spirit will still constantly listen to you, as it listens to you now,)
                  [*poem:* **wird mein Geist noch stets dir lauschen**]

dʊrç   dɛs 'hyːgəls 'bluːmənrɑosən,   viː diːs 'zɔmɐlʏftʼçən   rɑoʃtʰ.
durch   des Hügels Blumenrauschen, wie dies Sommerlüftchen rauscht.
through the hill's   flower- rustling,   as this summer breeze murmurs.
(through the rustling of the flowers on the hill, as this summer breeze is murmuring.)
                    [des Hügels Blumen rauschen (rustling through the flowers on the hill)]

[After three identical verses there are several bars of recitative before the final verse.]

deːɐ 'alpʼənjɛːgɐ / ɑof 'hoːəm 'bɛrgəsrʏkʼən
Der Alpenjäger / Auf hohem Bergesrücken
The Alpine Huntsman / On a High Mountain Ridge

Op. 13, No. 3 [1817] (Johann Mayrhofer)

ɑof 'hoːəm 'bɛrgəsrʏkʼən,   voː   'frɪʃɐ   'aləs gryːntʰ,
Auf hohem Bergesrücken, wo   frischer alles grünt,
On high   mountain ridge, where fresher all   grows,
(On a high mountain ridge, where everything grows fresher,)

ɪns   lantʼ hɪ'napʼtsublɪkʼən, das 'neːbəllaeçt tsɛɐ'rɪntʰ, lɛɐ'frɔøt den 'alpʼənjɛːgɐ.
ins   Land hinabzublicken, das nebelleicht zerrinnt, erfreut den Alpenjäger.
into the land down to gaze,   that mist- light dissolves, gladdens the alpine huntsman.
(it gladdens the alpine huntsman to gaze down at the lowland, as it disappears in a light haze.)

jeː 'ʃtʼaelɐ(r)   lʊntʼ jeː 'ʃrɛːgɐ   di 'pfaːdə zɪç   fɛɐ'ʃvɪndən,
Je steiler   und je schräger   die Pfade sich   verwinden,
The more steeply and the more slopingly the paths themselves wind about,
(The more steeply and the more slopingly the paths wind about,)

jeː meːɐ gə'faːɐ/gə'faːr lɑos 'ʃlʏndən,   zoː 'fraeɐ   ʃleːkʼt di brʊstʰ.
je mehr Gefahr   aus Schlünden, so freier   schlägt die Brust.
the more danger   from abysses, the more freely beats the breast.

eːɐ/eːr lɪst deːɐ 'fɛrnən 'liːbən,   diː liːm   da'haem gə'bliːbən, zɪç 'zeːlɪgɐ   bə'vʊstʰ.
Er   ist der fernen Lieben,   die ihm   daheim geblieben, sich seliger   bewusst.
He   ist of the distant dear one, who for him at home stayed,   self more blissfully aware.
(He is more blissfully aware of the distant dear one who is waiting at home for him.)

ʊntʼ lɪstʼ leːɐ nuːn lam 'tsiːlə, zoː drɛŋtʼ zɪç lɪn deːɐ 'ʃtʼɪlə laen 'zyːsəs bɪltʼ liːm foːɐ;
Und ist er nun am Ziele, so drängt sich in der Stille ein süsses Bild ihm vor;
And is he now at the goal, then urges itself in the stillness a sweet image him before;
(And if he is now at his goal, then a sweet image comes before him in the stillness;)
                    [*poem:* **ein süsses Bildnis** ('bɪltʼnɪs, image) **vor**]

deːɐ 'zɔnə 'gɔldnə 'ʃtʼraːlən,
der Sonne goldne Strahlen,
the sun's golden rays,

ziː 'veːbən lʊntʼ ziː 'maːlən, diː   leːɐ/leːr lɪm   tʰaːl lɛɐ'kʰoːɐ.
sie weben und sie malen, die   er   im   Tal erkor.
they weave and they paint her whom he   in the valley chose.
(weave and paint a portrait of the one whom he has chosen, down in the valley.)

198

[The jaunty song above is in three parts, the middle section a different melody, somewhat slower, and the last part a repeat of the first, with the same words.]

deːɐ̯ ˈalpˈənjɛːgɐ / vɪlst duː nɪçt das ˈlɛmlae̯n ˈhyːtˈən?
Der Alpenjäger / Willst du nicht das Lämmlein hüten?
The Alpine Huntsman / Will You Not Tend the Lamb?

Op. 37, No. 2 [1817] (Friedrich von Schiller)

vɪlst duː nɪçt das ˈlɛmlae̯n ˈhyːtˈən? ˈlɛmlae̯n lɪstˈ zoː frɔm lʊntˈ zanftʰ,
Willst du nicht das Lämmlein hüten? Lämmlein ist so fromm und sanft,
Will you not the little lamb tend?   Little lamb is so meek and gentle,
(Will you not tend the lamb? The lamb is so meek and gentle,)

nɛːɐ̯tˈ zɪç fɔn dɛs ˈgraːzəs ˈblyːtˈən, ʃpˈiːləntˈ lan dɛs ˈbaxəs ranftʰ.
nährt sich von des Grases Blüten,   spielend an des Baches Ranft.
feeds itself from the grass's blossoms, playing at the brook's edge.
(it feeds upon the blossoms in the grass, playing by the edge of the brook.)

ˈmʊtˈɐ, ˈmʊtˈɐ, las mɪç ˈgeːən, ˈjaːgən naːx dɛs ˈbɛrgəs ˈhøːən!   [høːn]
"Mutter, Mutter, lass mich gehen, jagen nach des Berges Höhen!" [(repeat:)] **Höh'n**
"Mother, Mother, let me go,   hunt toward the mountain's heights!"
("Mother, Mother, let me go hunting to the high part of the mountain!")

vɪlst duː nɪçt di ˈheːɐ̯də ˈlɔkˈən mit dɛs ˈhɔrnəs ˈmʊntˈɐm kʰlaŋ?
Willst du nicht die Herde locken mit des Hornes munterm Klang?
Will you not the herd   call with the horn's cheerful sound?
(Will you not call the herd with the cheerful sound of the horn?)

ˈliːpˈlɪç tʰøːnt deːɐ̯ ʃal deːɐ̯ ˈglɔkˈən lɪn dɛs ˈvaldəs ˈlʊstˈgəzaŋ.
lieblich tönt   der Schall der Glocken in des Waldes Lustgesang.
Lovely sounds the clang of the bells   in the forest's pleasure-song.
(The clanging of the bells sounds lovely, mingled with the happy song of the forest.)

ˈmʊtˈɐ, ˈmʊtˈɐ, las mɪç ˈgeːən, ˈʃvae̯fən lɑo̯f den ˈvɪldən ˈhøːən!   [naːx]
"Mutter, Mutter, lass mich gehen, schweifen auf den wilden Höhen!" [*Peters:* **nach den...**]
"Mother, Mother, let me go,   rove   on the wild   heights!"   [towards]
("Mother, Mother, let me go roving about on the wild heights!")

vɪlst duː nɪçt deːɐ̯ ˈblyːmlae̯n ˈvartˈən, diː lɪm ˈbeːtˈə ˈfrɔø̯ntˈlɪç ʃtˈeːn?
Willst du nicht der Blümlein warten, die im Beete freundlich stehn?
Will you not the flowers   tend, which in the bed friendlily   stand?
(Will you not tend the flowers, that look so friendly in their bed?)

ˈdrɑo̯sən ˈlaːdət dɪç kʰae̯n ˈgartˈən; vɪltˈ lɪsts lɑo̯f den ˈvɪldən høːn.
draussen ladet dich kein Garten; wild ist's auf den wilden Höh'n.
Out there invites you no   garden; wild is it on the wild   heights.
(Out there no garden invites you; it is rugged on those wild heights.)

las di ˈblyːmlae̯n, las ziː ˈblyːən! ˈmʊtˈɐ, ˈmʊtˈɐ, las mɪç ˈtsiːən!   [tsiːn]
"Lass die Blümlein,   lass sie   blühen! Mutter, Mutter, lass mich ziehen!" [**zieh'n**]
"Leave the little flowers, let them bloom! Mother, Mother, let me   go!"

ʊnt deːɐ̯ ˈkʰnaːbə gɪŋ ʦuː ˈjaːgən, lʊntˈ lɛs tʰraep̚tˈ lʊntˈ raestˈ liːn fɔrtʰ,
Und der Knabe ging zu jagen, und es treibt und reisst ihn fort,
And the boy went to hunt, and it drives and pulls him onwards,
(And the boy went hunting, and something drives and pulls him onwards,)

ˈrastˈloːs fɔrtˈ mɪtˈ ˈblɪndəm ˈvaːgən lan dɛs ˈbɛrgəs ˈfɪnstˈen lɔrtʰ;
rastlos fort mit blindem Wagen an des Berges finstern Ort;
restlessly onwards with blind daring to the mountains's dark place;

foːɐ̯/foːr liːm heːɐ̯ mɪtˈ ˈvɪndəsʃnɛlə fliːk̚t di ˈʦɪtˈɐndə gaˈʦɛlə.
vor ihm her mit Windesschnelle fliegt die zitternde Gazelle.
before him hither with wind- swiftness flies the trembling gazelle.
(before him the trembling gazelle flies with the swiftness of the wind.)

ɑof deːɐ̯ ˈfɛlzən ˈnakˈtˈə ˈrɪpˈən ˈkʰlɛtˈɐt ziː mɪtˈ ˈlaeçˈtˈəm ʃvʊŋ;
Auf der Felsen nackte Rippen klettert sie mit leichtem Schwung;
Onto the cliff's naked ribs clambers it with light bound;
(It climbs onto the naked ribs of the cliff with a light bound;)

dʊrç den rɪs gəˈbɔrstˈnɐ ˈkʰlɪpˈən tʰrɛːk̚tˈ ziː deːɐ̯ gəˈvaːk̚tˈə ʃpˈrʊŋ;
durch den Riss geborst'ner Klippen trägt sie der gewagte Sprung;
through the fissure of ruptured crags carries it the daring leap;
(the daring leap carries it across the fissure of ruptured crags;)

[gəˈʃpˈaltˈnɐ kʰlɪpˈən]
[*GA:* **gespalt'ner Klippen**]
[split crags]

ˈlaːbɐ ˈhɪntˈɐ(r) liːɐ̯ fɛɐ̯ˈvoːgən fɔlkˈtˈ leːɐ̯ mɪt dem ˈtʰoːdəsboːgən.
aber hinter ihr verwogen folgt er mit dem Todesbogen.
but behind it boldly follows he with the death- bow.
(but behind the gazelle he is following boldly with the deadly bow.)

[*"verwogen"* (archaic) = *"verwegen"* = bold, boldly]

ˈjɛʦo lɑof den ˈʃrɔfən ˈʦɪŋkˈən hɛŋtˈ ziː, lɑof dem ˈhøːçstˈən graːtʰ,
Jetzo auf den schroffen Zinken hängt sie, auf dem höchsten Grat,
Now onto the steepest spikes hangs it, on the highest ridge,
(Now it is hanging onto the steepest spikes of rock on the highest ridge,)

voː di ˈfɛlzən jɛː fɛɐ̯ˈzɪŋkˈən, lʊntˈ fɛɐ̯ˈʃvʊndən lɪst deːɐ̯ pfaːtˈ.
wo die Felsen jäh versinken, und verschwunden ist der Pfad.
where the cliffs abruptly sink, and disappeared is the path.
(where the cliffs drop down abruptly and the path has disappeared.)

ˈʊntˈɐ zɪç di ˈʃtˈaelə ˈhøːə, ˈhɪntˈɐ zɪç dɛs ˈfaendəs ˈnɛːə.
Unter sich die steile Höhe, hinter sich des Feindes Nähe.
Below oneself the steep heights, behind oneself the enemy's nearness.
(Below the gazelle the steep precipice, behind it the nearness of the enemy.)

mɪt dɛs ˈjamɐs ˈʃtˈʊmən ˈblɪkˈən fleːtˈ ziː ʦuː dem ˈhartˈən man,
Mit des Jammers stummen Blicken fleht sie zu dem harten Mann,
With the distress's silent looks prays it to the hardhearted man,
(With silent looks of distress the gazelle implores the hardhearted man,)

200

fle:t'   lʊm'zɔnst, dɛn 'lo:stsu̯ˌdrʏk'ən, le:k't' le:ɐ̯ ʃo:n   den 'bo:gən lan;
fleht   umsonst, denn loszudrücken, legt   er   schon   den Bogen an;
implores in vain,   for   to shoot,   aims   he   already the   bow   ... ;
(implores in vain, for already he is aiming the bow to shoot;)   [*"anlegen"* = to take aim]

'pʰlœtslɪç lɑos   de:ɐ̯ 'fɛlzənʃp'alt'ə tʰrɪt   de:ɐ̯ gaestʰ, de:ɐ̯ 'bɛrgəslalt'ə.
plötzlich aus   der Felsenspalte tritt der Geist, der Bergesalte.
suddenly out of the   rock- cleft   steps the spirit,   the   old man of the mountain.
(suddenly a spirit, the old man of the mountain, steps out of a cleft in the rock.)

ʊnt' mɪt' 'zaenən 'gœt'ɐhɛndən ʃytst'   le:ɐ̯ das gə'kʰvɛ:lt'ə tʰi:ɐ̯.
Und mit   seinen Götterhänden schützt er   das gequälte   Tier.
And with his   god- hands   protects he the   tormented   animal.
(And with his godlike hands he protects the tormented animal.)

mʊst du: tʰo:t' lʊnt' 'jamɐ   'zɛndən, ru:ft' le:ɐ̯, bɪs he'rɑof tsu: mi:ɐ̯?
"Musst du Tod   und Jammer senden," ruft er, "bis herauf zu   mir?
"Must   you death and   distress   send,"   calls   he, "till up here to   me?"
("Must you send death and distress," he calls, "all the way up to me?")

rɑom fy:ɐ̯/fy:r 'lalə hat di   'le:ɐ̯də; vas fɛɐ̯'fɔlkst du: 'maenə 'he:ɐ̯də?
Raum für   Alle hat die Erde; was verfolgst du   meine   Herde?"
Room for   all   has the earth; why persecute you my   herd?"
(The earth has room for all; why must you persecute my herd?")

[This is a song for those animal lovers who are opposed to the cruel "sport" of hunting!]

Der Atlas see *Schwanengesang*

de:ɐ̯ 'blɪndə 'kʰna:bə
Der blinde Knabe
The Blind Boy

Op. 101, No. 2 [1825] (Colley Cibber, translated by Jacob Nicolaus von Craigher de Jachelutta)

o: za:k't', li:ɐ̯ 'li:bən,   mi:ɐ̯/mi:r laen'ma:l, vɛlç dɪŋ lɪsts, lɪçt' gə'nantʰ?
O sagt,   ihr Lieben,   mir   einmal,   welch Ding ist's, Licht genannt?
Oh say,   you dear people, to me   once,   what   thing is it, light called?
(Oh tell me, dear people, what is this thing called "light"?)

vas   zɪnt dɛs 'ze:əns 'frɔɪ̯dən lal, di: 'ni:ma:ls lɪç gə'kʰantʰ?
Was sind des Sehens Freuden all', die   niemals ich gekannt?
What are the   seeing's joys   all, which never   I   (have) known?
(What are all the joys of seeing, which I have never known?)

di 'zɔnə, di: zo: hɛl   li:ɐ̯ ze:t', mi:ɐ̯/mi:r 'larmən   ʃaent' zi: ni:;
Die Sonne, die   so hell   ihr seht, mir   Armen   scheint sie nie;
The sun,   which so bright you see,   for me,   poor one, shines   it   never;
(The sun that you see shining so bright, for me, poor fellow, it never shines;)

iːɐ̯ zaːk'tʼ, ziː lɑof lʊntʼ 'niːdɐgeːtʼ, lɪç vaes nɪçtʼ van, nɔx viː.
ihr sagt,   sie auf- und niedergeht, ich weiss nicht wann, noch wie.
you say,   it up and down goes, I   know not when, nor how.
(you say that it rises and sets; I do not know when, nor how.)

ɪç max   miːɐ̯ zɛlpstʼ zoː tʰaːkʼ viː naxtʰ, diˈvael lɪç ʃlaːf lʊntʼ ʃpʼiːl;   [ʊntʼ naxtʼ]
Ich mach' mir   selbst so Tag   wie Nacht, dieweil ich schlaf' und spiel'; [*GA:* und Nacht]
I   make for me self   so day   as night, while I   sleep and play;   [and night]
(I make day as well as night for myself, depending on whether I am sleeping or playing;)

maen 'lɪnrəs 'leːbən ʃøːn miːɐ̯ laxtʰ, lɪç haːpʼ deːɐ̯ 'frɔødən viːl.
mein inn'res Leben schön mir   lacht, ich hab' der Freuden viel.
my   inner life   nicely for me laughs, I   have of the joys   many.
(my inner life smiles nicely for me, I have many joys.)

tsvaːɐ̯   kʰen lɪç nɪçtʼ, vas lɔøç leɐ̯ˈfrɔøt, dɔx dryk'tʼ   mɪç 'kʰaenə ʃʊltʼ,
Zwar   kenn' ich nicht, was euch erfreut, doch drückt   mich keine Schuld,
Admitedly know I   not   what you gladdens, but oppresses me no   guilt,
(Admitedly I do not know what makes you glad; but at least I am not plagued by any guilt,)

drʊm   frɔø lɪç mɪç ɪn 'maenəm laetʼ   lʊnt tʰraːkʼ lɛs mɪtʼ gəˈdʊltʼ.
drum   freu' ich mich in meinem Leid   und trag' es mit Geduld.
therefore gladden I   myself in my   affliction and bear it with patience.
(therefore I am happy in my affliction, and bear it with patience.)

ɪç bɪn zoː 'glʏk'lɪç, bɪn zoː raeç mɪt deːm, vas   gɔtʼ miːɐ̯ gaːp,
Ich bin so glücklich, bin so reich mit dem, was   Gott mir gab,
I   am so happy,   am so rich with that which God to me gave,
(I am so happy, am so rich with all that God has given me,)

bɪn viː laen 'kʰøːnɪç froː, lɔp'ˈglaeç laen 'larmɐ 'blɪndɐ kʰnaːpʼ.
bin wie ein König froh, obgleich ein armer blinder Knab'.
am as a   king happy, although a   poor blind boy.
(I am happy as a king, although I am a poor blind boy.)

[The repeated figure in the accompaniment may be interpreted as portraying the blind boy's way of feeling around in front of him cautiously as he moves. The poem, by the Shakespearean actor Colley Cibber, has been criticized for putting into the mouth of a blind person feelings that the sighted author, with little genuine empathy, would sentimentally like to imagine there. The translator was asked by Schubert to keep the original rhythms intact, so that both the German and the English words could be printed with the music. Here is the original English poem:

O say! what is that thing called Light, / Which I must ne'er enjoy;
What are the blessings of the sight, / O tell your poor blind boy!
You talk of wondrous things you see, / You say the sun shines bright;
I feel him warm, but how can he / Or make it day or night?
My day or night myself I make / Whene'er I sleep or play;
And could I ever keep awake / With me 'twere always day.
With heavy sighs I often hear / You mourn my hapless woe;
But sure with patience I can bear / A loss I ne'er can know.
Then let not what I cannot have / My cheer of mind destroy:
Whilst thus I sing, I am a king, / Although a poor blind boy.]

202

de:ɐ̯ ˈbluːmənbriːf
Der Blumenbrief
The Letter in Flowers

Posthumously published [composed 1818] (Aloys Wilhelm Schreiber)

ɔø̯ç ˈblyːmlae̯n vɪl lɪç ˈzɛndən t͡sʊr ˈʃøːnən ˈjʊŋfrao̯ dɔrtʰ,
Euch Blümlein   will ich senden zur   schönen Jungfrau dort,
You   little flowers want I   to send to the beautiful virgin   there,
(I want to send you little flowers to that beautiful virgin there,)

fleːtʰ ziː, mae̯n lae̯t t͡suː ˈlɛndən mɪtʰ ˈlae̯nəm ˈguːtʰən vɔrtʰ.
fleht sie, mein Leid zu enden mit einem guten Wort.
entreat her, my   sorrow to end   with a   kind   word.
(entreat her to end my sorrow with a kind word.)

duː, ˈroːzə, kʰanstʰ liːɐ̯ ˈzaːgən, viː lɪç lɪn liːpʰ lɛɐ̯ˈglyː,
Du, Rose, kannst ihr   sagen, wie ich in Lieb erglüh,
You, rose, can   to her say,   how I in love glow,
(You, rose, can tell her how I am glowing with love,)

viː lɪç lʊm ziː mʊs ˈkʰlaːgən lʊntʰ ˈvae̯nən ʃpʰɛːtʰ lʊntʰ fryː.
wie ich um sie muss klagen und weinen spät   und früh.
how I   for her must lament and weep   late   and early.
(how I must lament for her and weep night and day.)

[Schubert left out one verse, addressed to the violet.]

duː, ˈmʏrtʰə, ˈflʏstʰrə ˈlae̯zə liːɐ̯ ˈmae̯nə ˈhɔfnʊŋ t͡suː,
Du, Myrte, flüstre leise ihr   meine Hoffnung zu,
You, myrtle, whisper softly to her my   hope   to,
(You, myrtle, softly whisper to her my hope,)

zaːkʰ lao̯f dɛs ˈleːbəns ˈrae̯zə glɛnt͡stʰ liːm kʰae̯n ʃtʰɛrn lals duː.
sag': "auf des Lebens Reise glänzt ihm   kein Stern als du."
say: "on the life's   journey shines for him no   star but you."
(say: "On the journey of life no star is shining for him but you.")

duː, ˈrɪŋəlbluːmə, ˈdɔø̯tʰə liːɐ̯ deːɐ̯ fɛɐ̯ˈt͡svae̯flʊŋ ʃmɛrt͡s,
Du, Ringelblume, deute ihr   der Verzweiflung Schmerz,
You, marigold,   explain to her the despair's   pain,
(You, marigold, explain to her the pain of despair,)

zaːkʰ liːɐ̯ dɛs ˈgraːbəs ˈbɔø̯tʰə vɪrtʰ ˈloːnə dɪç zae̯n hɛrt͡s.
sag' ihr: "des Grabes Beute wird   ohne   dich sein Herz."
say to her: "the grave's prey becomes without you his   heart."
(say to her: "Without you his heart will become a prey to death.")

[This lovable song shows that the lover's lamentations, his weeping night and day, and his talk of death are not to be taken seriously.]

deːɐ̯ ˈbluːmən ʃmɛrts̬
Der Blumen Schmerz
The Flower's Pain

Op. 173, No. 4 [1821] (Johann, Count Majláth)

viː tʰøːnt' lɛs miːɐ̯ zoː ˈʃɑorɪç dɛs ˈlɛntsəs ˈleːɐ̯st'əs veːn,   [lɪst']
Wie tönt es mir so schaurig des Lenzes erstes Weh'n, [*poem:* **wie ist es mir**]
How sounds it to me so horrible the spring's first   blowing,   [is]
(How horrible the first breeze of spring sounds to me,)

viː dʏŋk't' lɛs miːɐ̯ zoː 'tʰrɑorɪç, das 'bluːmən 'lɑoflɛɐ̯'ʃt'eːn!
wie dünkt es mir so traurig, dass Blumen auferstehn!
how seems it to me so sad,   that flowers rise up from the dead!
(how sad it seems to me that flowers rise up again!)

ɪn 'liːrɐ 'mʊt'ɐ(r) 'larmən, daː 'ruːt'ən ziː zoː ʃt'ɪl!
In ihrer Mutter Armen, da   ruhten sie so still!
In their mother's arms,   there rested they so quietly!
(In the arms of their mother they rested so quietly!)

nuːn 'mʏsən, lax, di 'larmən   hɛɐ̯'foːɐ̯ lans   'vɛlt'gəvyːl!   [lɪns]
nun müssen, ach, die Armen   hervor   ans   Weltgewühl! [*poem:* **ins Weltgewühl**]
now must,   ah,   the poor things (come) out into the world-tumult!   [into the]
(now, alas, the poor things must come out into the tumult of the world!)

di 'ts̬aːɐ̯t'ən 'kʰɪndɐ 'heːbən di 'hɔøp't'ɐ ʃɔø lɛm'pʰoːɐ̯:
Die zarten   Kinder heben die Häupter scheu empor:
The delicate children lift   the heads   shyly up:
(The delicate children shyly lift up their heads:)

veːɐ̯ 'ruːfət' lʊns lɪns   'leːbən lɑos 'ʃt'ɪlɐ naxt' hɛɐ̯'foːɐ̯?   [lɑos 'tʰiːfɐ naxt'...]
"Wer rufet uns ins   Leben aus   stiller Nacht hervor?" [*Peters:* **"aus   tiefer Nacht?"**]
"Who calls us   into the life   out of quiet night forth?"   ["...out of deep night?"]
("Who calls us into life out of the quiet night?")   [("...out of the deep night?")]

deːɐ̯ lɛnts̬ mɪt 'ts̬ɑobɐvɔrt'ən, mɪt' 'hɑoxən 'zyːsɐ lʊstʰ,
Der Lenz mit Zauberworten, mit Hauchen süsser Lust,
The spring with magic words,   with breathing of sweet pleasure,
(Spring, with magic words, breathing sweet pleasure,)

lɔk't' lɑos den 'dʊŋk'lən 'pfɔrt'ən ziː fɔn deːɐ̯ 'mʊt'ɐ brʊstʰ.
lockt aus   den dunklen Pforten sie von der Mutter Brust.
lures out of the dark   portals them from the mother's breast.
(lures them out of the dark portals, away from their mother's breast.)

ɪn 'brɔøt'lɪç 'helɐ 'fɑeɐ   lɛɐ̯'ʃɑent deːɐ̯ 'bluːmən pʰraxtʰ:
In bräutlich heller Feier   erscheint der Blumen Pracht:
In bridal   bright celebration appears   the flowers' splendor:
(The splendor of the flowers appears in a bright bridal celebration:)

204

dɔx fɛrn ʃoːn ɪst deːɐ̯ 'fraɛ̯ɐ̯, vɪlt‘ glyːt deːɐ̯ 'zɔnə maxtʰ;
Doch fern   schon ist der Freier, wild   glüht der Sonne Macht;
But far away already is the wooer, fiercely glows the sun's might;
(But the wooer is already far away, and the sun's might glows fiercely;)

nuːn 'kʰʏndən 'liːrə 'dʏft‘ə,   das ziː fɔl 'zeːnzʊxt‘ zɪnt‘,
nun künden ihre Düfte,   dass sie voll Sehnsucht sind,
now announce their fragrances, that they full of longing   are,
(now their fragrances announce that they are full of longing,)

vas   'laːbənt‘ vʏrt͡st di 'lʏft‘ə, lɛs lɪst deːɐ̯ 'ʃmɛrt͡sən kʰɪnt‘!
was   labend   würzt die Lüfte, es ist der Schmerzen Kind!
that which refreshingly spices the breezes, it is the pains'   child!
(that which refreshingly spices the breezes is the child of pain!)

di 'kʰɛlçə 'zɪŋk‘ən 'niːdɐ, ziː 'ʃɑo̯ən 'leːɐ̯dənvɛrt͡s.
Die Kelche sinken   nieder, sie schauen erdenwärts.
The chalices sink   down, they look   earthwards.
(Their chalices droop, they look downwards at the earth.)

oː 'mʊt‘ɐ! nɪm   lʊns 'viːdə,   das 'leːbən giːp‘t‘ nuːɐ̯ ʃmɛrt͡s!
"O Mutter! nimm uns wieder, das Leben gibt   nur Schmerz!"
"Oh Mother! take us   again,   the life   gives only pain!"
("Oh Mother, take us back again, life gives only pain!")

[di 'vɛlk‘ən 'blɛt‘ɐ 'falən, mɪlt dɛk‘t deːɐ̯ ʃneː ziː t͡suː—
[Die welken Blätter fallen, mild deckt der Schnee sie zu—
[The withered leaves fall,   gently covers the snow   them up—
[The withered leaves fall, the snow gently covers them up—]

ax gɔt‘! zoː geːt͡s mɪt‘ 'lalən, lɪm 'graːbə nuːɐ̯/nuːr lɪst‘ ruː.]
Ach Gott! So   geht's mit allen, im   Grabe nur   ist Ruh.]
Ah God! Thus goes it with all,   in the grave only   is   peace.]
(Ah, God! Thus it is for all of us: only in the grave can peace be found.)]

[There are two versions of this song; the last verse (in brackets, above) is not in the Peters edition, which is also different in other details from the one printed in the *Gesamtausgabe*. The pessimistic poet, who had been a part of Schubert's circle in Vienna, eventually drowned himself in Starnberg Lake. His sentimental, gloomy words, with their unconventionally negative view of spring, inspired Schubert to a lovely and expressive song.]

Der Doppelgänger see *Schwanengesang*

deːɐ̯ 'draetse:nt'ə psalm
Der VIII. Psalm
Psalm XIII

Fragment published in 1928 [composed 1819] (German translation by Moses Mendelssohn)
(Song completed and published by Reinhard van Hoorickx in The Music Review, 1977)

ax, hɛr, viː 'laŋə vɪlst duː maen zoː gants fɛɐ̯'ɡɛsən?
Ach, Herr, wie lange willst du mein so ganz vergessen?
Ah, Lord, how long wilt Thou of me so completely forget?
(Ah, Lord, how long wilt Thou forget me so completely?)

viː 'laŋə nɔx daen 'lant'lɪts miːɐ̯ fɛɐ̯'bɛrɡən? viː 'laŋə mʊs lɪç
Wie lange noch dein Antlitz mir verbergen? Wie lange muss ich
How long still Thy countenance from me hide? How long must I
(How long still wilt Thou hide Thy countenance from me? How long must I)

'maenən ɡaest' mɪt' 'zɪnən, maen hɛrts mɪt' 'zɔrɡən 'tʰɛːk'lɪç 'kʰvɛːlən?
meinen Geist mit Sinnen, mein Herz mit Sorgen täglich quälen?
my spirit with brooding, my heart with cares daily torment?
(daily torment my spirit with brooding, my heart with cares?)

viː 'laŋə nɔx maen faent' ɔp'ziːɡən? ʃɑo hɛ'rap', ɛɐ̯'høːrə mɪç,
Wie lange noch mein Feind obsiegen? Schau herab, erhöre mich,
How long still my enemy to be victorious? Look down, hear me,
(How long still shall my enemy be victorious? Look down, hear me,)

ax, 'leːvɪɐ̯, maen ɡɔtʰ, lɛɐ̯'lɔøçt'ə 'maenə 'lɑoɡən 'viːdɐ,
ach, Ewiger, mein Gott, erleuchte meine Augen wieder,
ah, Eternal One, my God, illumine my eyes again,

das lɪç dɛs 'tʰoːdəs nɪçt' lɛnt'ʃlaːfə. zɔnst' ʃp'rɪçt' maen faent':
dass ich des Todes nicht entschlafe. Sonst spricht mein Feind:
so that I of the death not fall asleep. Otherwise speaks my enemy:
(so that I may not fall asleep the prey of death. Otherwise my enemy will say:)

den lyːbɐ'vant' lɪç! fro'lɔk'ən 'viːdɐzaxɐ 'maenəs 'faləs.
"Den überwand ich!" Frohlocken Widersacher meines Falles.
"Him overcame I!" Rejoice adversaries of my fall.
("I conquered him!" My adversaries will rejoice at my fall.)

dɔx lɪç fɛɐ̯'tʰrɑoə 'daenɐ 'ɡyːt'ə, maen hɛrts fro'lɔk'ət' lɔp' 'daenɐ 'hʏlfə. [ax]
Doch ich vertraue deiner Güte, mein Herz frohlockt ob deiner Hülfe. [Ach, ich...]
But I am confident of Thy kindness, my heart rejoices in Thy help. [Ah]

dem 'leːvɪɡən 'zɪŋə lɪç, dɛn leːɐ̯ tʰaːt' miːɐ̯ voːl!
Dem Ewigen singe ich, denn er tat mir wohl! [*original text:* **dem Ewigen singe;**]
To the Eternal One sing I, for He did to me good!
(To the Eternal One I sing, for He has been good to me!)

[Schubert gave this song the title Psalm XII, presumably because in the old Latin Vulgate it was so numbered, even though it is entitled Psalm XIII in Mendelssohn's translation. The last few bars of Schubert's setting are missing; Reinhard van Hoorickx created a new five-bar ending, which can be found, along with the entire song, in The Music Review, 1977, pages 289-292.]

206

de:ɐ̯ ˈlae̯nza:mə
Der Einsame
The Solitary One

Op. 41 [1825?] (Karl Lappe)

vɛn ˈmae̯nə ˈgrɪlən ˈʃvɪrən, bae̯ naxt', lam ʃp'ɛːt' lɛɐ̯'vɛrmt'ən heːɐ̯t', [van]
Wenn meine Grillen schwirren, bei Nacht, am spät erwärmten Herd, [GA: **wann***]
When my crickets buzz, at night, by the late warmed hearth, [when]

dan zɪts lɪç, mɪt' fɛɐ̯'gnyːk't'əm zɪn, fɛɐ̯'tʰrao̯lɪç tsu: de:ɐ̯ ˈflamə hɪn,
dann sitz' ich, mit vergnügtem Sinn, vertraulich zu der Flamme hin,
then sit I, with contented mind, privately by the flame down,
(then I sit down privately by the fire, with a contented mind,)

zo: lae̯çt', zo: lunbə'ʃveːɐ̯tʰ.
so leicht, so unbeschwert. [*Schubert himself substituted "wenn" for the original "wann."*]
so easy, so untroubled.
(so at ease, so untroubled.)

ae̯n 'tʰrao̯t'əs 'ʃt'ɪləs 'ʃt'ʏnt'çən blae̯p't' man nɔx gɛrn lam ˈfɔ̯øɐ vax.
Ein trautes stilles Stündchen bleibt man noch gern am Feuer wach.
A cozy quiet little hour stays one still gladly by the fire awake.
(One gladly stays awake still for a cozy, quiet little hour by the fire.)

man ʃyːɐ̯tʰ, vɛn zɪç di 'lo:ə zɛnk't', di 'funk'ən lao̯f, lunt' zɪntʰ, lunt' dɛŋk'tʰ:
Man schürt, wenn sich die Lohe senkt, die Funken auf, und sinnt, und denkt: [wann]
One pokes, when itself the fire sinks, the sparks up, and muses, and thinks:
(When the fire dies down a bit, one pokes the sparks up, and muses, and thinks:)

nuːn 'la:bəma:l lae̯n tʰa:k'!
"Nun abermal ein Tag!"
"Now once more a day!"
("Another day gone by!")

vas 'li:bəs 'lo:də 'lae̯dəs zae̯n lao̯f fy:ɐ̯/fy:r luns da'he:ɐ̯gəbraxtʰ,
Was Liebes oder Leides sein Lauf für uns dahergebracht,
Whatever good or bad its course for us hither brought,
(Whatever good or bad its course may have brought us)

ɛs ge:t' nɔx 'lae̯nma:l durç den zɪn; la'lae̯n das 'bøːzə vɪrft' man hɪn,
es geht noch einmal durch den Sinn; allein das Böse wirft man hin,
it goes still once through the mind; but the bad throws one away,
(passes once again through the mind; but one throws the bad away,)

ɛs 'ʃt'øːrə nɪçt di naxtʰ.
es störe nicht die Nacht.
it may disturb not the night.
(it must not disturb the night.)

tsu: 'lae̯nəm 'fro:ən 'tʰrao̯mə bə'rae̯t'ət' man gə'max zɪç tsuː,
Zu einem frohen Traume bereitet man gemach sich zu,
For a happy dream prepares one unhurriedly oneself ... , ["*zubereiten*" = to prepare]
(One calmly prepares oneself for a pleasant dream,)

vɛn 'zɔrgəloːs l̯aen 'hɔldəs bɪlt' mɪt' 'zanft'ɐ lʊst di 'zeːlə fʏlt,
wenn sorgelos ein holdes Bild mit sanfter Lust die Seele füllt, [wann]
when carefree a lovely image with gentle pleasure the soul fills,
(when a lovely image fills the carefree soul with gentle pleasure,)

ɛɐ̯'giːp't' man zɪç deːɐ̯ ruː. oː viː l̯ɪç miːɐ̯ gə'falə l̯ɪn 'maenɐ 'ʃt'ɪlən 'lɛnt'lɪçᵏ̪haet̯ʰ!
ergibt man sich der Ruh. O wie ich mir gefalle in meiner stillen Ländlichkeit!
yields one oneself to the rest. Oh how I myself please in my quiet rusticity!
(one yields to rest. Oh how I please myself in my quiet rusticity!)

vas l̯ɪn dem ʃvarm deːɐ̯ 'l̯aot'ən vɛlt das 'l̯ɪrə hɛrt̯s gə'fɛsəlt' hɛltʰ,
Was in dem Schwarm der lauten Welt das irre Herz gefesselt hält,
What in the swarm of the noisy world the confused heart shackled holds,
(That which holds the confused heart shackled in the tumult of the noisy world)

giːp't' nɪçt t̯su'friːdənhaet̯ʰ.
gibt nicht Zufriedenheit.
gives not contentment.
(does not bring contentment.)

t̯sɪrp't' 'l̯ɪmɐ, 'liːbə 'haemçən, l̯ɪn 'maenɐ 'ᵏ̪hlaozə, l̯ɛŋ l̯ʊnt' ᵏ̪hlaen.
Zirpt immer, liebe Heimchen, in meiner Klause, eng und klein.
Chirp ever, dear crickets, in my cell, narrow and small.
(Keep chirping, dear crickets, in my narrow little cell.)

l̯ɪç dʊlt' l̯ɔʏ̯ç gɛrn̪ː liːɐ̯ ʃt'øːɐ̯t' mɪç nɪçtʰ, vɛn 'l̯ɔʏ̯ɐ liːt das 'ʃvaegən brɪçtʰ,
Ich duld' euch gern: ihr stört mich nicht, wenn euer Lied das Schweigen bricht,
I put up with you gladly: you disturb me not, when your song the silence breaks,
(I put up with you gladly: you do not disturb me; when your song breaks the silence) [wann]

bɪn l̯ɪç nɪçt' gant̯s l̯a'l̯aen.
bin ich nicht ganz allein.
am I not completely alone.
(I am not completely alone.)

[The accompaniment can suggest the raking of the coals or the chirping of the cricket, whichever is needed at the moment (although when the motif moves into the treble it clearly belongs to the cricket!). In this song about the joys of a solitary life there is an obvious sense of comfort and contentment on the surface, but Dietrich Fischer-Dieskau detects an undercurrent of wistfulness in Schubert's music, no doubt inspired by the last line of the poem. The high G's near the end were an afterthought, absent from an earlier version. The poet was a schoolmaster and a recluse.]

deːɐ̯ lɛnt'ˈfɛrnt'ən
Der Entfernten
To the Distant One

Posthumously published [composed 1816?] (poem by Johann Gaudenz von Salis-Seewis)

voːl dɛŋk' l̯ɪç 'l̯alɛnt'ˈhalbən, l̯oː duː lɛnt'ˈfɛrnt'ə, daen!
Wohl denk' ich allenthalben, o du Entfernte, dein!
Well think I everywhere, O you distant one, of you!
(I may well think of you everywhere, O my distant beloved!)

fry:, vɛn di 'vɔlkʻən 'falbən,   lʊntʻ ʃpʻɛːtʻ ιm   'ʃtʻɛrnənʃaen.
früh, wenn die Wolken falben,   und spät   im   Sternenschein.
early, when the clouds turn yellow, and late,   in the star-shine.
(early, at dawn, when the clouds turn yellow, and late, at night, by starlight.)

ιm   grʊnt dɛs 'mɔrgəngɔldəs, lιm 'roːtʻən 'laːbəntʻlιçtʰ,
Im   Grund des Morgengoldes, im   roten Abendlicht,
In the depths of the morning-gold, in the red   evening-light,
(In the golden depths of the dawn sky, in the red light of sunset,)

ʊm'ʃveːpst du: mιç, loː 'hɔldəs, gə'liːpʻtʻəs 'tʰraomgə'zιçtʰ!
umschwebst du mich, o holdes, geliebtes Traumgesicht!
around hover you me,   O lovely, beloved   dream-vision!
(you hover around me, O lovely, beloved dream-vision!)

[ɛs   fɔlkʻtʻ lιn 'lalə 'vaetʻə daen 'tʰraotʻəs bιltʻ miːɐ̯ naːx,
[Es   folgt in alle Weite   dein trautes Bild mir nach,
[There follows into all   distance your dear   image me after,
[(Your dear image follows after me into any distance,)

ɛs valtʻ miːɐ̯ ʃtʻeːts tsʊr 'zaetʻə, lιn 'tʰrɔ̸mən 'loːdɐ vax;   [lιm]
es wallt mir   stets   zur   Seite, in Träumen oder wach; [*poem:* **im   Träumen**]
it walks for me always at the side, in dreams   or   awake;   [in the dreaming]
(it always walks beside me, in my dreams or when I am awake;)

vɛn 'lyftʻə   zanftʻ bə'ʃtʻraeçən deːɐ̯ zeː bə'ʃιlftʻən ʃtʻrantʻ,
wenn Lüfte   sanft bestreichen der See beschilften Strand,
when breezes gently graze   the sea's reeded   shore,
(when breezes are gently grazing the reeds by the seashore,)

lʊm'flystʻən   miːɐ̯ di 'ʃlaefən fɔn 'zaenəm   'buːzənbantʻ.
umflüstern   mir die Schleifen von seinem   Busenband.
whisper around me the bows   of   its (the image's) bosom-ribbon.
(the bows of the ribbons at your bosom seem to whisper around me.)

aen 'lapʻglants 'zaenəs 'ʃlaeɐs ʃaentʻ laof di zaːtʻ   gə'veːpʻtʰ;
Ein Abglanz   seines Schleiers scheint auf die Saat   gewebt;
A   reflection of its   veil   seems on the standing corn woven;
(A reflection of your veil seems to be woven on the field of corn;)

zaen haox, vas dɛs gə'mɔ̸ɐs bə'veːkʻtʻən 'lɛpʻιç heːpʻtʰ;
sein Hauch, was des Gemäuers bewegten Eppich hebt;
its   breath, what the masonry's stirred   ivy   lifts;
(your breath is what stirs and lifts the ivy on the masonry;)

deːɐ̯ 'kʰlaedʊŋ 'vaeçə 'faltʻən, gə'fɔrmtʻ laos glants lʊnt dʊftʰ,
der Kleidung weiche Falten, geformt aus Glanz   und Duft,
the garments' soft   folds,   formed   out of splendor and fragrance,
(the soft folds of your garments, formed of splendor and fragrance,)

lɛntʻʻʃvιndən   lιn den 'ʃpʻaltʻən deːɐ̯/deːr 'ɸ̸ːdən 'fɛlzənkʰlʊftʰ.]
entschwinden in den Spalten der   öden Felsenkluft.]
disappear   in the clefts   of the   bleak rocky chasm.]

voː 'rɑɔʃəndɐ   ʊnt 'tʰryːbɐ deːɐ̯ ʃtʰroːm gə'bɪrgə   tʰrɛntʰ,
Wo   rauschender und trüber der Strom Gebirge   trennt,
Where noisier   and darker the   river   mountains cleaves,
(There where the river, darker and thunderng more loudly, cleaves the mountains,)

veːtʰ lɔftʰ zaen lɑɔtʰ hɛ'ryːbɐ, deːn 'maenə 'zeːlə kʰɛntʰ;
weht oft   sein Laut herüber, den   meine Seele kennt;
wafts often its   sound over here, which my   soul   knows;
(its sound, which my soul knows so well, often wafts over here to me;)

vɛn lɪç den fɛls lɛɐ̯'kʰlɪmə, deːn nɔx kʰaen fuːs lɛɐ̯'raeçtʰ,
wenn ich den Fels erklimme, den   noch kein Fuss erreicht,
when I   the rock climb   which yet no   foot (has) reached,
(when I climb up to the rock that as yet no other foot has reached,)

lɑɔʃ lɪç, lɑɔʃ lɪç naːx 'jeːnɐ 'ʃtʰɪmə; dɔx 'lɛço ʃvaektʰ.
lausch' ich, lausch' ich nach jener Stimme; doch Echo schweigt.
listen I, listen I for   that   voice;   but echo is mute.
(I listen for that voice; but the echo is mute.)
      [*poem:* **lausch' ich nach jener Stimme; doch Kluft** (kʰlʊftʰ, chasm) **und Echo schweigt.**]

voː dʊrç di naxt deːɐ̯ 'fɪçtʰən laen 'dɛmrʊŋsflɪmɐ   valtʰ,
Wo   durch die Nacht der   Fichten ein Dämmrungsflimmer wallt,
Where through the night of the fir-trees a   twilight-   glimmer flutters,
(There where a glimmer of twilight sifts through the darkness of the fir-trees,)

zeː lɪç dɪç 'tsøːgɛntʰ 'flʏçtʰən, gə'liːpʰtʰə 'lʊftʰgəʃtʰaltʰ!
seh' ich dich zögernd flüchten, geliebte   Luftgestalt!
see I   you hesitantly fleeing,   beloved   air- form!
(I see you hesitantly fleeing, beloved ethereal apparition!)

vɛn, zanft diːɐ̯ 'naːxtsulaŋən,   deːɐ̯ 'zeːnzʊxtʰ larm zɪç heːpʰtʰ,
Wenn, sanft dir   nachzulangen,   der Sehnsucht Arm sich hebt,
When, gently to you towards to reach, the   longing's   arm   itself raises,
(Then, when my arm is gently raised to reach toward you in longing,)

ɪst daen fan'tʰoːm tsɛɐ̯'gaŋən vi: 'tʰɑɔgədʏftʰ fɛɐ̯'ʃveːpʰtʰ.
ist dein Phantom zergangen, wie Taugedüft verschwebt.
is your phantom dissolved   like dew-vapor floated away.
(your phantom has dissolved, has floated away like a vapor of dew.)

[This simple, attractive melody is better known in Germany in a version for male chorus. The Peters edition prints verses one, four, and five, which seems to have been Schubert's final choice; the *Gesamtausgabe* places the first and second verses with the vocal line, and prints the third, fourth, and fifth separately at the end, ignoring Schubert's change in the text of the fourth verse. The second and third verses, missing from the Peters edition, are in brackets, above.]

210

deːɐ̯ lɛntˈˈzyːntˈə loˈrestʰ
Der entsühnte Orest
Orestes Absolved

Posthumously published [composed 1817?] (poem by Johann Mayrhofer)

ʦuː ˈmaenən ˈfyːsən brɪçst duː dɪç,   loː ˈhaemaːtlɪçəs meːɐ̯,
Zu meinen Füssen brichst du dich, o heimatliches Meer,
At my   feet   break you yourself, O native   sea,
(Your waves break at my feet, O my native sea,)   [*poem:* **wiegst** (viːkst, rock) **du dich**]

ʊntˈ   ˈmʊrməlstˈ zanftʰ. tʰriˈʊmf! tʰriˈʊmf! ɪç ˈʃvɪŋə ʃveːɐ̯tˈ ʊntˈ ʃpˈeːɐ̯.
und   murmelst sanft. Triumph! Triumph! ich schwinge Schwert und Speer.
and (you) murmur softly. Triumph! Triumph! I wield   sword   and spear.
(and you murmur softly. Triumph! I wield my sword and spear.)
        [ɪç ˈruːfə diːɐ̯]
     [*poem:* **Ich rufe dir: Triumph! Triumph! und** (ʊntˈ, and) **schwinge Schild und Speer.**]
     [I   call to you: ("Triumph!")]

myˈkeːnə leːɐ̯tˈ ʲals ˈkʰøːnɪç mɪç, bɔøtˈ ˈmaenəm ˈvɪrkˈən raʊm,
Mykene ehrt   als König mich, beut meinem Wirken Raum,
Mycenae honors as king   me,   offers to my   actions room,
(Mycenae honors me as their king and offers me freedom to act as I choose,)

ʊntˈ ˈlyːbɐ ˈmaenəm ˈʃaetˈəl zaʊst dɛs ˈleːbəns ˈɡɔldnɐ baʊm.
und über meinem Scheitel saust des Lebens goldner Baum.
and above my   head   rustles the life's   golden tree.
(and the golden tree of life is rustling above my head.)
     [*poem:* **und über meinen** (ˈmaenən) **Scheitel saust des Lebens reicher** (ˈraeçɐ, rich) **Baum**]

mɪtˈ ˈmɔrɡəntˈlɪçən ˈroːzən ʃmʏkˈt   deːɐ̯ ˈfryːlɪŋ ˈmaenə baːn,
Mit morgendlichen Rosen schmückt der Frühling meine Bahn,
With morning-fresh roses adorns   the spring   my   path,
(The spring adorns my path with morning-fresh roses,)

ʊntˈ laof deːɐ̯ ˈliːbə ˈvɛlən ʃveːpˈt daˈhɪn maen ˈlaeçtˈɐ kʰaːn.   [deːɐ̯ ˈlaeçtˈə]
und auf der Liebe Wellen schwebt dahin mein leichter Kahn. [*poem:* **der leichte Kahn**]
and on the   love's waves floats   thither my   light   boat.   [the]
(and my light boat is floating onward on waves of love.)

diˈaːna naːtˈ;   loː ˈrɛtˈərɪn, lɛɐ̯ˈhøːrə duː maen fleːn!
Diana naht;   o Retterin, erhöre du mein Fleh'n!
Diana approaches; O rescuer, hear   you my   entreating!
(Diana approaches; O rescuer, hear my entreaty!)

las mɪç, das ˈhøːçstˈə ˈvʊrdə   miːɐ̯, ʦuː ˈmaenən ˈfɛːtˈɐn geːn.
lass mich, das Höchste wurde   mir, zu meinen Vätern geh'n.
Let me,   the highest was (granted) to me, to my   fathers go.
(Since the highest prize, absolution, has already been granted to me, let me join my ancestors.)
                      [vartˈ miːɐ̯ jaː— nuːn ʦuː den]
       [*poem:* **lass mich—das Höchste ward mir ja—   nun zu den Vätern geh'n.**]
                [was   to me surely—now to   the]

[Orestes, in Greek mythology, was honor-bound to avenge the murder of his father Agamemnon, King of Mycenae; but one of the murderers was Queen Clytaemnestra, Orestes' own mother. He killed his mother and her paramour, and for the crime of matricide he was pursued by the Furies. But at his trial in Athens, the god Apollo spoke as his advocate, and Athena herself decided in his favor (not Diana, as suggested in the poem, although Diana-Artemis plays a role in some of the dramatizations of his story). Here, after a year of intense suffering and expiation in exile, Orestes returns to his homeland on the bay of Argos, absolved and purified through divine intervention, and, his goal achieved, wanting now only to die in peace.]

deːɐ̯ ˈfɪʃɐ
Der Fischer
The Fisherman

Op. 5, No. 3 [1815] (Johann Wofgang von Goethe)

das ˈvasɐ rɑ̯oʃt,   das ˈvasɐ   ʃvɔl,   ʼaen ˈfɪʃɐ   zaːs daˈran,
Das Wasser rauscht', das Wasser schwoll, ein Fischer   sass daran,
The water   mumured, the water   swelled, a   fisherman sat   at it,
(The water murmured, the water swelled, a fisherman sat on the bank,)

zaː   naːx deːɐ̯/deːr ˈʼaŋəl ˈruːəfɔl,   kʰyːl bɪs   ʼans hɛrts hɪˈnan.   [*P., modern Germ.]
sah   nach der*   Angel ruhevoll, kühl bis   ans   Herz hinan. [*P., modern Germ.]
watched after the   rod   calmly,   cool as far as to the heart upward.
(watched his rod calmly, his cool-bloodedness extending even as far as up to his heart.)
         [*GA & poem: **nach dem** (dem) **Angel** ("Angel" was masculine in the 18th century)]

ʊntʼ viː leːɐ̯ zɪtst ʼʊntʼ viː leːɐ̯ lɑ̯oʃt,   tʰaeltʼ zɪç di fluːtʼ ʼɛmˈpʰoːɐ̯:
Und wie er sitzt und wie er lauscht, teilt   sich die Flut empor:
And as   he   sits   and as   he   listens, parts   itself the water upwards:
(And as he sits there and listens, the waters are parted upwards:)

ɑ̯os   dem bəˈveːkʼtʼən ˈvasɐ   rɑ̯oʃtʼ   ʼaen ˈfɔ̝øçtʼəs vaepʼ   hɛɐ̯ˈfoːɐ̯.
aus   dem bewegten   Wasser rauscht ein feuchtes Weib   hervor.
out of the   stirred   water   swishes a   damp   woman forth.
(out of the stirred water a damp woman swishes out.)

ziː zaŋ tsu̯ liːm, ziː ʃpʼraːx tsu̯ liːmː vas lɔkst du: ˈmaenə bruːtʰ
Sie sang zu ihm, sie sprach zu ihm: "Was lockst du meine Brut
She sang to   him, she spoke   to   him: "Why entice you my   brood
(She sang to him, she spoke to him: "Why do you entice my brood)

mɪtʼ ˈmɛnʃənvɪts   ʼʊntʼ ˈmɛnʃənlɪstʼ   hɪˈnɑ̯of lɪn ˈtʰoːdəsgluːtʰʔ
mit Menschenwitz und Menschenlist hinauf in Todesglut?
with human   wit and human   guile up   into death-fire?
(with human wit and human guile up into deadly heat?)

ax ˈvʏstʼəst duː, viːs   ˈfɪʃlaen   lɪstʼ zoː ˈvoːlɪç lɑ̯of dem grʊntʼ,
Ach wüsstest du, wie's   Fischlein ist so wohlig auf dem Grund,
Ah, knew   you, how the little fish is   so happy in   the   depths,
(Ah, if you knew how happy the little fish is in the depths,)

212

du: ʃt'iːkst' he'rʊnt'ɐ, viː du: bɪst', ʊnt' 'vʏrdəst' leːɐst' ɡə'zʊnt'.
du stiegst herunter, wie du bist, und würdest erst gesund.
you would climb down, as you are, and would become for the first time well.
(you would come down, just as you are, and would feel truly well for the first time.)

laːp't' zɪç di 'liːbə 'zɔnə nɪçt, deːɐ moːnt' zɪç nɪçt' ɪm meːɐ?
Labt sich die liebe Sonne nicht, der Mond sich nicht im Meer?
Refreshes itself the well-loved sun not, the moon itself not in the sea?
(Do not the well-loved sun and moon refresh themselves in the sea?)

kʰeːɐt' 'vɛlənlaːt'mənt' liːɐ ɡə'zɪçt' nɪçt 'dɔp'əlt 'ʃøːnɐ heːɐ?
kehrt wellenatmend ihr Gesicht nicht doppelt schöner her?
Returns wave- breathing their face not doubly more beautiful hither?
(Do their faces not return to you doubly beautiful after breathing the waves?)

lɔk't dɪç deːɐ 'tʰiːfə 'hɪməl nɪçt, das 'fɔ͡øçt'fɛɐkʰleːɐt'ə blɑo?
Lockt dich der tiefe Himmel nicht, das feuchtverklärte Blau?
Entices you the deep heaven not, the moist- transfigured blue?
(Does this deep heaven not entice you, this water-transfigured blue?)

lɔk't dɪç dɑen 'lɑeɡən 'lanɡəzɪçt' nɪçt' heːɐ/heːr ɪn 'leːvɡən tʰɑo?
lockt dich dein eigen Angesicht nicht her in ewgen Tau?"
Entices you your own face not hither into eternal dew?"
(Does the reflection of your own face not entice you down into this eternal dew?")

das 'vasɐ rɑoʃt, das 'vasɐ ʃvɔl, nɛtst' liːm den 'nak't'ən fuːs,
Das Wasser rauscht', das Wasser schwoll, netzt' ihm den nackten Fuss,
The water murmured, the water swelled, wet him the naked foot,
(The water murmured, the water swelled, wet his naked foot,)

zɑen hɛrt͡s vʊːks liːm zoː 'zeːnzʊxt͡sfɔl, viː bɑe deːɐ 'liːpst'ən gruːs.
sein Herz wuchs ihm so sehnsuchtsvoll, wie bei der Liebsten Gruss.
his heart grew for him so longing- full, as at the beloved's greeting.
(his heart grew as full of longing as if his beloved had called.)

ziː ʃp'raːx t͡suː liːm, ziː zaŋ t͡suː liːm, daː vaːɐs ʊm liːn ɡə'ʃeːn;
Sie sprach zu ihm, sie sang zu ihm, da war's um ihn geschehn;
She spoke to him, she sang to him, there was it for him come to pass;
(She spoke to him, she sang to him: then he was done for;)

[idiom: "*um ihn geschehen*" = he was done for]

halp' t͡soːk' ziː liːn, halp' zaŋk' leːɐ hɪn, ʊnt' vart' nɪçt' meːɐ ɡə'zeːn.
halb zog sie ihn, halb sank er hin, und ward nicht mehr gesehn.
half pulled she him, half sank he hence, and was not more seen.
(she half pulled him down, he half sank down on his own and was never seen again.)

[Schubert set in simple strophic form this fanciful poem about the mysterious lure of the water.]

deːɐ̯ ˈflʏçtˈlɪŋ
Der Flüchtling
The Fugitive

Posthumously published [composed 1816] (poem by Friedrich von Schiller)

frɪʃ ˈlaːtˈmət dɛs ˈmɔrgəns leˈbəndɪɐ̯ haox;
Frisch atmet des Morgens lebendiger Hauch;
Fresh breathes the morning's lively breath;
(The lively morning breeze breathes out freshness;)

ˈpʰʊrpˈʊrɪʃ tsʊkˈt dʊrç ˈdyːstˈrɐ ˈtʰanən ˈrɪtsən das ˈjʊŋə lɪçtˈ
purpurisch zuckt durch düst'rer Tannen Ritzen das junge Licht
purplish quivers through dark pines' slits the young light
(the young light flashes streaks of purple through the slits among the pine branches)

ʊntˈ ˈlɔʏgəltˈ laos dem ʃtˈraox; ɪn ˈgɔldnən ˈflamən
und äugelt aus dem Strauch; in gold'nen Flammen
and ogles out from the bush; in golden flames

ˈblɪtsən deːɐ̯ ˈbɛrgə ˈvɔlkˈənʃpˈɪtsən. mɪtˈ ˈfrɔʏdɪç meˈloːdɪʃ gəˈvɪrbəltˈəm liːtˈ
blitzen der Berge Wolkenspitzen. Mit freudig melodisch gewirbeltem Lied
flash the mountains' cloud- peaks. With joyously melodiously warbled song
(the cloud-capped peaks of the mountains are flashing. With joyous, melodiously warbled song)

bəˈgryːsən lɛɐ̯ˈvaxəndə ˈlɛrçən di ˈzɔnə, diː ʃoːn ɪn ˈlaxəndɐ ˈvɔnə
begrüssen erwachende Lerchen die Sonne, die schon in lachender Wonne
greet awakening larks the sun, which already in laughing rapture
(awakening larks are greeting the sun, which already, in smiling rapture,)

ˈjuːgəntˈlɪç ʃøːn ɪn laoˈroːras lʊmˈlarmʊŋən glyːtʰ. zae, lɪçtˈ, miːɐ̯ gəˈzeːgnətʰ!
jugendlich schön in Auroras Umarmungen glüht. Sei, Licht, mir gesegnet!
youthfully beautiful in Aurora's embraces glows. Be, light, to me blessed!
(glows youthfully beautiful in the dawn's embraces. Light, I bless you!)

daen ˈʃtˈraːləngruːs ˈreːgnətˈ lɛɐ̯ˈvɛrmənt heɐ̯ˈnidɐ(r) laof ˈlaŋɐ(r) ʊntˈ lao.
Dein Strahlengruss regnet erwärmend hernieder auf Anger und Au.
Your ray- greeting rains warmingly down onto pasture and meadow.
(Your rays rain down a greeting, warming pasture and meadow.)

[*poem:* **Strahlenguss** (ˈʃtˈraːləngʊs, pouring out of rays)]

viː ˈflɪtˈɐn di ˈviːzən, viː ˈzɪlbɐfarpˈ ˈtsɪtˈen ˈtʰaozəntˈ ˈzɔnən ɪm ˈpʰɛrləndən tʰao!
Wie flittern die Wiesen, wie silberfarb zittern tausend Sonnen im perlenden Tau!
How sparkle the fields, how silver-color tremble a thousand suns in the pearling dew!
(How the fields sparkle, how a thousand silver suns are quivering in the pearly dew!)

[*poem:* **Wie silberfarb flittern die Wiesen, wie zittern Tausend Sonnen im perlenden Tau**]

ɪn ˈzɔʏzəlndɐ ˈkʰyːlə bəˈgɪnən di ˈʃpˈiːlə deːɐ̯ ˈjʊŋən naˈtʰuːɐ̯. di ˈtseːfyrə ˈkʰoːzən
In Säuselnder Kühle beginnen die Spiele der jungen Natur. Die Zephyre kosen
In rustling coolness begin the games of the young nature. The zephyrs caress
(In rustling coolness the games of young nature begin. The zephyrs caress)

214

lʊntʻ ʃmaeçəln lʊm ˈroːzən, lʊntʻ ˈdʏftʻə bəˈʃtʻrøːmən di ˈlaxəndə fluːɐ̯.
und schmeicheln um Rosen, und Düfte beströmen die lachende Flur.
and flatter around roses, and fragrances bestream the laughing meadow.
(and flatter the roses, and fragrances stream out over the smiling meadow.)

viː hoːx lɑ̯os den ˈʃtʻɛːtʻən di ˈrɑ̯oxvɔlkʻən ˈdampfən!
Wie hoch aus den Städten die Rauchwolken dampfen!
How high from the cities the smoke-clouds steam!
(How high the smoke clouds rise up from the cities!)

lɑ̯otʻ ˈviːɐn lʊntʻ ˈʃnɑ̯obən lʊntʻ ˈkʰnɪrʃən lʊntʻ ˈʃtʻrampfən di ˈrɔsə, di ˈfarən;
Laut wiehern und schnauben und knirschen und strampfen die Rosse, die Farren;
Loudly neigh and snort and gnash teeth and stamp the horses, the young bulls;
(Horses and young bulls are neighing, snorting, gnashing their teeth, and stamping;)
                    [*"strampfen"* (dialect) = *"stampfen"* (stamp) + *"strampeln"* (kick)]

di ˈvaːgən lɛɐ̯ˈkʰnarən lɪns ˈlɛçtsəndə tʰaːl.
die Wagen erknarren ins ächzende Tal.
the carts rattle and creak into the groaning valley.

di ˈvaldʊŋən ˈleːbən, lʊntʻ ˈlaːdlɐ(r) lʊntʻ ˈfalkʻən lʊntʻ ˈhaːbɪçtʻə ˈʃveːbən
Die Waldungen leben, und Adler und Falken und Habichte schweben
The woodlands are alive, and eagles and falcons and hawks are soaring

lʊntʻ ˈviːgən di ˈflyːgəl lɪm ˈblɛndəndən ʃtʻraːl.
und wiegen die Flügel im blendenden Strahl.
and rocking the wings in the dazzling ray.
(and flapping their wings in the dazzling light.)

den ˈfriːdən tsu ˈfɪndən, voˈhɪn zɔl lɪç ˈvɛndən lam ˈleːləndən ʃtʻaːpʻ?
Den Frieden zu finden, wohin soll ich wenden am elenden Stab?
The peace to find, whither shall I turn at the side of the wretched staff?
(To find peace which way shall I turn, my wretched walking staff at my side?)

di ˈlaxəndə ˈleːɐ̯də mɪtʻ ˈjʏŋlɪŋsgəˈbɛːɐ̯də, fyːɐ̯ mɪç nuːɐ̯/nuːr laen graːpʻ!
Die lachende Erde mit Jünglingsgebärde, für mich nur ein Grab!
The laughing earth with young man's bearing, for me only a grave!
(The smiling earth with its youthful bearing is for me only a grave!)

ʃtʻaek ̍ lɛmˈpʰoːɐ̯/lɛmˈpʰoːr, loː ˈmɔrgənroːtʻ,
Steig' empor, o Morgenrot,
Rise up, O dawn,

lʊntʻ ˈrøːtʻə mɪtʻ ˈpʰʊrpʻʊrnəm ˈkʰʊsə haen lʊntʻ fɛltʻ!
und röte mit purpurnem Kusse Hain und Feld!
and redden with crimson kiss grove and field!
(and make grove and field blush with your crimson kiss!)

ˈzɔ̯øzlə ˈniːdɐ(r), loː ˈlaːbəntʻroːtʻ, lʊntʻ ˈfløːtʻə lɪn ˈzanftʻən ˈʃlʊmɐ di ˈtʰoːtʻə vɛltʰ!
Säusle nieder, o Abendrot, und flöte in sanften Schlummer die tote Welt!
Rustle down, O sunset, and whistle into gentle slumber the dead world!
(Descend, O sunset, and with your rustling murmur lull the dead world into gentle sleep!)
                    [*"flöten"* = to make a gentle sound like that of the flute (*"Flöte"*)]

[zanft' ɪn]   [lɛɐ̯'ʃt'ɔrbnə]
[*poem:* **Säusle nieder, Abendrot, und flöte sanft in Schlummer die erstorbne Welt**]
[gently into]   [died away]

'mɔrgən, lax! du: 'rø:t'əst' 'la̯enə 't^ho:t'ənflu:ɐ̯;   lax! ʊnt du:, lo: 'la:bənt'ro:t^h!
Morgen, ach! du rötest eine Totenflur;   ach! und du, o Abendrot!
Morning, ah! you redden a   field of the dead; ah! and you, O sunset!

ʊm'flø:t'əst'   'ma̯enən 'laŋən 'ʃlʊmɐ   nu:ɐ̯.
umflötest   meinen langen Schlummer nur.
(you) whistle around my   long   slumber   merely.
(you merely surround my long sleep with the flute-like murmur of evening.)

[The poem starts with a rapturous paean on the beauty and freshness of dawn. After several
verses (and several pages of appropriate music in Schubert's song), the mood abruptly changes,
with a brief description of the noise and bustle of the town. Then comes the startlingly morose
ending, conventional enough in the era of "*Sturm und Drang,*" but rather jarring to a later age.]

de:ɐ̯ flu:k' de:ɐ̯ t͡saet^h
Der Flug der Zeit
The Flight of Time

Op. 7, No. 2 [1821?] (Ludwig von Széchényi)

ɛs flo: di t͡saet' ɪm 'vɪrbəlflu:gə   ʊnt t^hru:k' dɛs 'le:bəns p^hla:n mɪt' zɪç.
Es floh die Zeit im Wirbelfluge   und trug des Lebens Plan mit sich.
It fled the time in the whirlwind flight and carried the life's   plan with itself.
(Time fled by in a whirlwind flight, and carried with it the plan of life.)

vo:l   'ʃt'yrmɪʃ va:ɐ̯/va:r lɛs la̯of dem 't͡su:gə, bə'ʃve:ɐ̯lɪç   lɔft' ʊnt' 'vi:dəlɪç.
Wohl   stürmisch war   es auf dem Zuge, beschwerlich oft und widerlich.
To be sure, stormy   was   it on the flight, troublesome often and unsavory.
(To be sure, it was stormy on the way, often troublesome and unsavory.)

zo: gɪŋ lɛs fɔrt dʊrç 'lalə 't͡so:nən, dʊrç 'k^hɪndɐja:rə,   dʊrç 'ju:gənt'glʏk^h,
So ging es fort durch alle Zonen, durch Kinderjahre, durch Jugendglück,
So went it forth through all   zones,   through childhood years, through youth- happiness,
(So it went on, through all zones, through years of childhood, through the happiness of youth,)

dʊrç 't^hɛ:lɐ, vo: di 'frɔ̜ødən 'vo:nən, di: 'zɪnənt' zu:xt de:ɐ̯ 'ze:nzʊxt' blɪk^h,
durch Täler, wo die Freuden wohnen, die sinnend sucht der Sehnsucht Blick,
through valleys, where the joys   dwell,   which pensively seeks the longing's gaze,
(through valleys where pleasures dwell, which the gaze of longing pensively seeks,)

bɪs lan de:ɐ̯ 'frɔ̜ønt'ʃaft' 'lɪçt'əm 'hy:gəl di t͡saet' nu:n 'zanft'ɐ,   'ʃt'ɪlɐ   flo:k',
bis an der Freundschaft lichtem Hügel die Zeit nun sanfter,   stiller   flog,
till on the friendship's bright   hill   the time now more gently, more quietly flew,
(till, on the bright hill of friendship, time began to flow more gently, more quietly,)
[*Peters:* **lichten** ('lɪçt'ən, bright) **Hügel** ('hy:gəl, hills—plural)]

216

ʊnt‘ ˈlɛnt‘lɪç daː di ˈraʃən ˈflyːgəl ɪn ˈzyːsɐ ruː ʦuˈʦamən boːk‘.
und endlich da die raschen Flügel in süsser Ruh zusammen bog.
and at last there the swift wings in sweet rest together folded.
(and there at last folded its swift wings in sweet rest.)

[Schubert set this poem in a barcarolle rhythm, with fluctuations of harmony and mode that suggest the constant changes of life, the rather fast tempo slowing significantly at the last verse.]

deːɐ̯ flʊs
Der Fluss
The River

Posthumously published [composed 1820] (poem by Friedrich von Schlegel)

viː ræn gəˈzaŋ zɪç ˈvɪndət dʊrç ˈvʊndɐbaːrə ˈzaet‘ənʃp‘iːlə ˈrɑoʃən,
Wie rein Gesang sich windet durch wunderbarer Saitenspiele Rauschen,
As pure song itself coils through wondrous strings' murmuring,
(Just as pure song coils its way through the murmuring of wondrous strings,)

eːɐ̯ zɛlpst‘ zɪç ˈviːdɐfɪndət‘, viː ɑox di ˈvaezən ˈt‘ɑoʃən,
er selbst sich wiederfindet, wie auch die Weisen tauschen,
it itself itself again finds, how ever the melodies change,
(and finds itself again, however much the melodies change,)

das nɔ̄ø lɛnt‘ʦʏk‘t di ˈhøːrɐ(r) ˈeːvɪç ˈlɑoʃən.
dass neu entzückt die Hörer ewig lauschen.
so that newly delighted the hearers eternally listen,
(so that the hearers, delighted anew, cannot stop listening,)

zoː ˈfliːsət‘ miːɐ̯ gəˈdiːgən di ˈzɪlbɐmasə, ˈʃlaŋənglaeç gəˈvʊndən,
So fliesset mir gediegen die Silbermasse, schlangengleich gewunden,
thus flows to me pure the silver-mass, snake- like coiled,
(thus, to me, the silvery mass—the river—flows pure, in snake-like coils,)

dʊrç ˈbʏʃə, diː zɪç ˈviːgən, fɔm ˈʦɑobɐ zyːs gəˈbʊndən,
durch Büsche, die sich wiegen, vom Zauber süss gebunden,
through bushes, which themselves sway, from the magic sweetly bound,
(through bushes which sway to and fro, sweetly spellbound,)

vael ziː ɪm ˈʃp‘iːgəl nɔ̄ø zɪç zɛlpst‘ gəˈfʊndən.
weil sie im Spiegel neu sich selbst gefunden.
because they in the mirror newly themselves themselves (have) found,
(because they themselves have found themselves anew in the mirror of the river,)

voː ˈhyːgəl zɪç zoː ˈgɛrnə ʊnt‘ ˈhɛlə ˈvɔlk‘ən ˈlaezə ˈʃvaŋk‘ənt ˈʦaegən,
Wo Hügel sich so gerne und helle Wolken leise schwankend zeigen,
in which hills themselves so gladly and bright clouds gently wavering show,
(in which hills and bright clouds so gladly show themselves, gently wavering with the water,)

vɛn fɛrn ʃoːn ˈmat‘ə ˈʃt‘ɛrnə ɑos ˈblɑoɐ ˈt‘iːfə ˈʃt‘aegən,
wenn fern schon matte Sterne aus blauer Tiefe steigen,
when afar already faint stars out of blue depths climb,
(when in the distance faint stars are already rising out of the blue depths,)

deːɐ̯ ˈzɔnə ˈtʰrʊŋkˈnə ˈl̩ɑ̯ɡən ˈlapˈvɛrt̯s ˈnae̯ɡən.
der Sonne trunkne Augen abwärts neigen.
the sun's intoxicated eyes downwards bend.
(and the sun's intoxicated eyes are sinking downwards.)

zoː ˈʃimɐn ˈlalə ˈveːzən dem ˈl̩ʊmrɪs naːx l̩ɪm ˈkʰɪntˈlɪçən ɡəˈmyːtˈə, [den]
So schimmern alle Wesen dem* Umriss nach im kindlichen Gemüte, [**GA: den]**
Thus shimmer all beings, to the outline according, in the childlike mind,
(Thus all beings shimmer, according to their outline, in the childlike mind,)

das, t̯sʊr ˈʃøːnhae̯tˈ lɛɐ̯ˈleːzən, dʊrç ˈmɪldɐ ˈɡœtˈɐ ˈɡyːtˈə,
das, zur Schönheit erlesen, durch milder Götter Güte,
which, to the beauty chosen, through mild gods' kindness,
(which, chosen through the kindness of gentle gods to be beautiful,)

ɪn dem kʰrɪsˈtʰal bəˈvaːrt̯ di ˈflʏçtˈɡə ˈblyːtˈə.
in dem Kristall bewahrt die flücht'ge Blüte.
in the crystal preserves the fleeting blossom.
(preserves the fleeting blossom in the crystal water.)

[The poem takes a bit of puzzling over, but the music is very beautiful, in the style of an Italian aria from the romantic "*bel canto*" era. *According to the normal rules of German grammar, the words should read: "*dem Umriss nach*," not "*den*," as printed in the *Gesamtausgabe*.]

deːɐ̯ ˈɡae̯stˈɐtʰant̯s
Der Geistertanz
The Ghost Dance

Posthumously published [composed 1814] (poem by Friedrich von Matthisson)

di ˈbrɛtˈɐnə ˈkʰamɐ deːɐ̯ ˈtʰoːtˈən lɛɐ̯ˈbeːpˈtˈ,
Die bretterne Kammer der Toten erbebt,
The boarded chamber of the dead trembles
(The boards of the coffin tremble)

vɛn ˈt̯svœlfmaːl den ˈhamɐ di ˈmɪtˈɐnaxtˈ heːpˈtʰ.
wenn zwölfmal den Hammer die Mitternacht hebt.
when twelve times the hammer the midnight raises.
(when midnight raises the hammer twelve times.)

raʃ ˈtʰant̯sən l̩ʊm ˈɡreːbɐ(r) l̩ʊntˈ ˈmɔrʃəs ɡəˈbae̯n viːɐ̯ ˈlʊftˈɪɡən ˈʃveːbɐ
Rasch tanzen um Gräber und morsches Gebein wir luftigen Schweber
Quickly dance around graves and mouldering bones we airy hoverers
(We airy hovering creatures quickly dance around graves and mouldering bones)

den ˈzɑ̯ʊzəndən rae̯n. vas ˈvɪnzəln di ˈhʊndə bae̯m ˈʃlaːfəndən hɛrn?
den sausenden Reihn. Was winseln die Hunde beim schlafenden Herrn?
the whistling roundelay. Why whimper the dogs by the sleeping master?
(the whirling roundelay. Why do the dogs whimper by their sleeping master?)

ziː ˈvɪtˈɐn di ˈrʊndə deːɐ̯ ˈɡae̯stˈɐ fɔn fɛrn.
Sie wittern die Runde der Geister von fern.
They scent the round of the ghosts from afar.
(They scent the party of ghosts from afar.)

218

di ˈraːbən ˌɛntˈflatˈɐn deːɐ̯ ˈvyːstˈən ˌapˈtʰae̯,
Die Raben entflattern der   wüsten Abtei,
The ravens flutter out   of the deserted abbey,

ʊntˈ fliːn ˌan den ˈgatˈɐn dɛs ˈkʰɪrçhoːfs foɐ̯ˈbae̯.
und fliehn an den Gattern des   Kirchhofs vorbei.
and flee   by the fences   of the graveyard past.
(and fly past the fence around the graveyard.)

viːɐ̯ ˈgɑok'əln ʊntˈ ˈʃertsən hɪˈnap' ʊntˈ ˌɛmˈpʰoːɐ̯,
Wir gaukeln und scherzen hinab und empor, [*poem:* **Wir gaukeln , wir scherzen**]
We flit about and joke   down   and up,
(We joke and flit about, up and down,)

glae̯ç ˈɪrəndən ˈkʰertsən ɪm   ˈdʊnstˈɪgən moːɐ̯.
gleich irrenden Kerzen im   dunstigen Moor.
like   wandering candles in the misty   bog.
(like wandering candles—like will-o'-the-wisps—over the misty bog.)

oː hɛrts! ˈdɛsən ˈtsɑobɐ ˈtsʊr ˈmartˈɐ(r) ʊns vartˈ,
O Herz! dessen Zauber zur Marter   uns ward,
Oh heart! whose magic   to the torment to us became,
(Oh heart, whose magic became a torment to us,)

duː ruːstˈ nuːn ɪn ˈtʰɑobɐ fɛɐ̯ˈdʊmp͡fʊŋ, ɛɐ̯ˈʃtˈartʰ.
du ruhst nun in tauber Verdumpfung, erstarrt.
you rest   now in deaf   apathy,   benumbed.

tʰiːf barkst duː ɪm ˈdyːstˈɐn gəˈmaːx ˈʊnzɐ veː;
Tief bargst du im   düstern Gemach unser Weh;
Deep conceal you in the dark   chamber our   pain;
(You conceal our pain deep down inside the dark chamber;)

viːɐ̯ ˈglʏkˈlɪçən ˈflʏstˈɐn diːɐ̯ ˈfrøːlɪç: laˈdeː!
wir Glücklichen flüstern dir   fröhlich: Ade!
we   happy ones   whisper to you merrily: "Farewell!"

[Schubert made *four* settings of this would-be spooky Hallowe'en poem, the first two—both incomplete—when he was fifteen, a version for male quintet the following year. His last setting, written just three days before his early masterpiece, *Gretchen am Spinnrade*, is the best.]

Der getäuschte Verräter see *Il traditor deluso*

deːɐ̯ ˈgɔltˈʃmiːtsgəzɛl
Der Goldschmiedsgesell
The Goldsmith's Apprentice

Posthumously published [composed 1817] (poem by Johann Wolfgang von Goethe)

ɛs ˌɪst dɔx ˈmae̯nə ˈnaxbarɪn ˌae̯n ˈlalɐliːpstˈəs ˈmɛːtˈçən!
Es ist doch meine Nachbarin ein   allerliebstes Mädchen!
It is surely my   neighbor   a   most pretty girl!
(My neighbor is really a very pretty girl!)

vi: fry: lɪç lɪn deːɐ̯ 'vɛrk'ʃt'at' bɪn, blɪk' lɪç naːx   'liːrəm 'lɛːt'çən.
Wie früh ich in der Werkstatt bin, blick' ich nach   ihrem Lädchen.
As early I   in the workshop am, look I   towards her   little store.
(First thing in the morning, as soon as I am in the workshop, I look over at her little store.)

[tsu: rɪŋ   lʊnt' 'kʰɛt'ə   pʰɔx   lɪç dan di 'faɛnən 'gɔldnən 'dreːt'çən.
[Zu Ring und Kette   poch' ich dann die feinen goldnen Drähtchen.
[To ring and necklace hammer I   then the fine   gold   little threads.
[(After the ring and the necklace, I work on the fine little threads of gold.)

ax, deŋk' lɪç, van, lʊnt' 'viːdɐ, van lɪst' zɔlç laɛn rɪŋ   fyːɐ̯ 'kʰeːt'çən?
Ach, denk' ich, wann, und wieder, wann ist solch ein Ring für Käthchen?
Ah, think I,   when, and again,   when is   such a   ring for Katie?
(Ah, I think, when, and again, *when* will I have a ring like that to give Katie?)

ʊnt' tʰuːt' zi: leːɐ̯st di 'ʃalt'ɐn   lao̯f, da: kʰɔmt das 'gantsə 'ʃt'eːt'çən
Und tut   sie erst die Schaltern auf, da kommt das ganze Städtchen
And does she first the counters open, then comes the entire little town
(And as soon as she opens her counters, the entire town comes in)

ʊnt' faɛlʃt' lʊnt' vɪrp't' mɪt' 'hɛləm hao̯f lʊms 'lalɐlaɛ lɪm 'leːt'çən.]
und feilscht und wirbt mit hellem Hauf ums Allerlei im Lädchen.]
and bargains and solicits with bright crowd for the variety in the little store.]
(and bargains and competes in a huge crowd for the various things in her little store.)]

ɪç 'faɛlə; voːl   tsɛɐ̯'faɛl lɪç dan lao̯x 'mançəs 'gɔldnə dreːt'çən!
Ich feile; wohl   zerfeil' ich dann auch manches goldne Drähtchen!
I   file; probably misfile I   then also many a gold   thread!
(I file away; I probably overfile many a gold thread and ruin it!)

deːɐ̯ 'maɛst'ɐ brʊmt,   deːɐ̯ 'hart'ə   man! leːɐ̯ mɛrk't', les vaːɐ̯ das 'leːt'çən.
Der Meister brummt, der harte   Mann! Er merkt, es war das Lädchen.
The master grumbles, the hard-hearted man! He notices, it was the little store.

ʊnt' flʊks vi: nuːɐ̯ deːɐ̯ 'handəl ʃt'ɪl, glaɛç   graɛft' zi: naːx dem 'reːt'çən!
Und flugs wie nur der Handel still, gleich   greift sie nach dem Rädchen!
And quickly as only the business quiet, right away reaches she for   the little wheel!
(And quickly, whenever business quiets down, she right away goes to her spinning wheel!)

ɪç vaɛs voːl, vas zi: 'ʃp'ɪnən vɪl: lɛs hɔft das 'liːbə 'meːt'çən.
Ich weiss wohl, was sie spinnen will: es hofft das liebe Mädchen.
I   know well   what she to spin   wants: it hopes the dear girl.
(I know well what she intends to spin: the dear girl has hopes.)

das 'kʰlaɛnə 'fyːsçən tʰrɪt' lʊnt tʰrɪt; da: deŋk' lɪç miːɐ̯ das 'veːt'çə!
Das kleine Füsschen tritt   und tritt; da   denk' ich mir   das Wädchen!
The little   foot   treadles and treadles; thereupon think I   to myself the little calf!
(Her little foot moves the treadle up and down; that makes me think about her dainty calf!)

das 'ʃt'rʊmpfbant deŋk' lɪç lao̯x voːl   mɪt', lɪç ʃɛŋk'ts dem 'liːbən 'meːt'çə.
Das Strumpfband denk' ich auch wohl   mit, ich schenkt's dem lieben Mädchen.
The garter   think I   also probably with, I   gave   it to the dear girl.
(Along with the calf, I probably think about the garter, too, that I gave to the dear girl.)

220

ʊnt' naːx den 'lɪp'ən fyːɐ̯t deːɐ̯ ʃaʦ das lalɐˈfaɛnst'ə 'fɛːt'çən!
Und nach den Lippen führt der Schatz das allerfeinste Fädchen!
And to the lips guides the sweetheart the very finest thread!
(And my sweetheart takes the very finest thread to her lips!)

oː veːɐ̯/veːr lɪç dɔx lan 'zaɛnəm pʰlaʦ, viː kʰʏst' lɪç miːɐ̯ das 'mɛːt'çən!
O wär' ich doch an seinem Platz, wie küsst' ich mir das Mädchen!
Oh, were I only in its place, how would kiss I for myself the girl!
(Oh, if only I were in its place, how I would kiss the girl!)

[Schubert, in his light and charming strophic setting, omitted the second and third verses (in brackets above) of the seven printed in the *Gesamtausgabe*.]

deːɐ̯ gɔt' lʊnt di bajaˈdeːrə
Der Gott und die Bajadere
The God and the Temple Dancer

Posthumously published [composed 1815] (poem by Johann Wolfgang von Goethe)

mahaˈdøː, deːɐ̯ hɛr deːɐ̯/deːr 'leːɐ̯də, kʰɔmt' hɛˈrap' ʦʊm 'zɛçst'ən maːl,
Mahadöh, der Herr der Erde, kommt herab zum sechsten Mal,
Mahadeva, the lord of the earth, comes down for the sixth time,

das leːɐ̯/leːr 'lʊnzɐsglaɛçən 'veːɐ̯də, mɪt ʦu 'fyːlən frɔøt' lʊnt' kʰvaːl.
dass er unsersgleichen werde, mit zu fühlen Freud' und Qual.
that he our like might become, with to feel joy and suffering.
(that he might become like us, to feel joy and suffering with us.)

[*Peters:* **unsresgleichen** ('lʊnzrəsglaɛçən)]

eːɐ̯ bəˈkʰveːmt' zɪç, hiːɐ̯ ʦuː 'voːnən, lɛst' zɪç 'laləs zɛlpst' gəˈʃeːn.
Er bequemt sich, hier zu wohnen, lässt sich alles selbst geschehn.
He deigns himself here to dwell, lets to himself everything himself happen.
(He deigns to dwell here, and lets everything happen to him.)

zɔl leːɐ̯ 'ʃt'raːfən 'loːdɐ 'ʃoːnən, mʊs leːɐ̯ 'mɛnʃən 'mɛnʃlɪç zeːn.
Soll er strafen oder schonen, muss er Menschen menschlich sehn.
Shall he punish or spare, must he humans as a human see.
(If he is justly to punish or to spare, he must see human beings from a human point of view.)

ʊnt' hat' leːɐ̯ di ʃt'at' zɪç lals 'vandrɐ bə'tʰraxt'ət, di 'groːsən bə'lɑɒt',
Und hat er die Stadt sich als Wandrer betrachtet, die Grossen belauert,
And has he the city for himself as wanderer observed, the great ones spied on,
(And after he has observed the city for himself, as a traveler, spied on the great ones,)

lɑof 'kʰlaɛnə gə'laxt'ət, fɛɐ̯'lɛst' leːɐ̯ zi: 'laːbənʦ, lʊm 'vaet'ɐ ʦuː geːn.
auf Kleine geachtet, verlässt er sie Abends, um weiter zu gehn.
to little ones paid attention, leaves he them in the evening in order farther to go.
(paid attention to the little ones, he leaves them in the evening in order to go farther on his way.)

als leːɐ̯ nuːn hɪˈnɑosgəgaŋən, voː di 'lɛʦt'ən 'hɔøzɐ zɪnt',
Als er nun hinausgegangen, wo die letzten Häuser sind,
When he now (had) gone out, where the last houses are,
(When he had gone out to where the last houses are,)

ziːt‘ leːɐ̯, mɪt‘ gəˈmaːlt‘ən ˈvaŋən, laen fɛɐ̯ˈloːrnəs ˈʃøːnəs kʰɪnt‘.
sieht er, mit gemalten Wangen, ein verlornes schönes Kind.
sees he, with painted cheeks, a forlorn beautiful child.
(he sees a forlorn, beautiful child with painted cheeks.)

gryːs dɪç, ˈjʊŋfraʊ! —daŋk‘ deːɐ̯/deːr ˈleːrə! vart‘, lɪç kʰɔmə glaeç hɪˈnaʊs!
"Grüss' dich, Jungfrau!"—"Dank der Ehre! Wart', ich komme gleich hinaus!"
"Greet you, maiden!" —"Thanks for the honor! Wait, I come right away out!"
("Greetings to you, maiden!"—"Thank you for the honor! Wait, I shall come out right away!")

—ʊnt‘ veːɐ̯ bɪst duː? —bajaˈderə, lʊnt diːs lɪst deːɐ̯ ˈliːbə hɑos.
—"Und wer bist du?"—"Bajadere, und dies ist der Liebe Haus."
—"And who are you?"—"Temple dancer, and this is the love's house."
(—"And who are you?"—"A temple dancer, and this is the house of love.")

ziː ryːɐ̯t‘ zɪç, di ˈt͡sɪmbəln t͡sʊm ˈtʰant͡sə t͡suː ˈʃlaːgən;
Sie rührt sich, die Zimbeln zum Tanze zu schlagen;
She bestirred herself the cymbals to the dance to strike;
(She bestirred herself to strike the cymbals as accompaniment to her dance;)

ziː vaes zɪç zoː ˈliːp‘lɪç lɪm ˈkʰraezə t͡suː ˈtʰraːgən,
sie weiss sich so lieblich im Kreise zu tragen,
she knows how herself so charmingly in the circle to carry,
(she knows how to move so charmingly in a circle,)

ziː naek‘t‘ zɪç lʊnt‘ bɔøk‘t‘ zɪç, lʊnt‘ raeçt‘ liːm den ʃt‘rɑos.
sie neigt sich und biegt sich, und reicht ihm den Strauss.
she dips herself and bends herself, and hands him the bouquet.
(she dips and bends, and hands him a bouquet.)

ˈʃmaeçəlnt t͡siːt‘ ziː liːn t͡sʊr ˈʃvɛlə, ˈleːp‘haft‘ liːn lɪns hɑos hɪˈnaen.
Schmeichelnd zieht sie ihn zur Schwelle, lebhaft ihn ins Haus hinein.
Coaxingly draws she him to the threshold, vivaciously him into the house in.
(Coaxingly she draws him to the threshold, vivaciously she draws him into the house.)

ˈʃøːnɐ ˈfrɛmt‘lɪŋ, ˈlamp‘ənhɛlə zɔl zoˈglaeç di ˈhʏt‘ə zaen.
"Schöner Fremdling, lampenhelle soll sogleich die Hütte sein.
"Beautiful stranger, lamp- bright shall at once the cottage be.
("Beautiful stranger, the cottage shall at once be bright with lamplight.)

bɪst duː myːt‘, lɪç vɪl dɪç ˈlaːbən, ˈlɪndɛn ˈdaenɐ ˈfyːsə ʃmɛrt͡s.
Bist du müd', ich will dich laben, lindern deiner Füsse Schmerz.
Are you tired, I shall you refresh, soothe your feet's pain.
(If you are tired I shall refresh you, I shall soothe your sore feet.)

vas duː vɪlst, das zɔlst duː ˈhaːbən, ˈruːə, ˈfrɔødən ˈloːdɐ ʃɛrt͡s.
Was du willst, das sollst du haben, Ruhe, Freuden oder Scherz."
Whatever you want, that shall you have, rest, joy, or jest."
(You shall have whatever you want, be it rest, joy, or jest.")

ziː ˈlɪndɐt‘ gəˈʃɛft‘ɪç gəˈhɔøçəlt‘ə ˈlaedən. deːɐ̯ ˈgœt‘lɪçə ˈlɛçəlt‘;
Sie lindert geschäftig geheuchelte Leiden. Der Göttliche lächelt;
She soothes assiduously feigned pains. The divine one smiles;
(Assiduously she soothes his feigned pains. The divine being smiles;)

eːɐ̯ ˈziːət mɪt ˈfrɔɦdən, dʊrç ˈtʰiːfəs fɛɐ̯ˈdɛrbən, l̩aen ˈmɛnʃlɪçəs hɛrts̩.
er siehet mit Freuden, durch tiefes Verderben, ein menschliches Herz.
he sees with joys, through deep corruption, a human heart.
(through a deep layer of corruption he sees with joy a human heart.)

[ʊnt leːɐ̯ ˈfɔrdɐt ˈsklaːvəndiːnstˈə; ˈlɪmɐ ˈhaetˈrɐ vɪrt ziː nuːɐ̯,
[Und er fordert Sklavendienste; immer heitrer wird sie nur,
[And he demands slave-services; ever more cheerful becomes she only,
[(And he demands that she serve him like a slave; she only becomes more and more cheerful,)

ʊnt dɛs ˈmɛːtˈçəns ˈfryːə ˈkʰʏnstˈə ˈveːɐ̯dən naːx ʊnt naːx naˈtʰuːɐ̯.
und des Mädchens frühe Künste werden nach und nach Natur.
and the girl's early artifices become little by little nature.
(and what the girl had first begun to do with artifice became more and more natural.)

ʊnt zoː ˈʃtˈɛlət laof di ˈblyːtə balt ʊnt balt di frʊxt zɪç l̩aen;
Und so stellet auf die Blüte bald und bald die Frucht sich ein;
And thus presents after the blossom soon and soon the fruit itself ... ;
(And thus, after the blossom, little by little the fruit soon appears;)

["*sich einstellen*" = to appear, to present itself]

ɪst ɡəˈhoːɐ̯zaːm lɪm ɡəˈmyːtˈə, vɪrt nɪçt fɛrn di ˈliːbə zaen.
ist Gehorsam im Gemüte, wird nicht fern die Liebe sein.
is obedience in the disposition, will not far away the love be.
(if there is obedience in one's disposition, love will not be far away.)

ˈlaːbɐ, ziː ˈʃɛrfɐ(r) lʊnt ˈʃɛrfɐ ts̩u ˈpʰryːfən,
Aber, sie schärfer und schärfer zu prüfen,
However, her more sharply and more sharply to test,
(However, to test her more and more sharply,)

ˈvɛːlət deːɐ̯ ˈkʰɛnɐ deːɐ̯ ˈhøːən ʊnt ˈtʰiːfən lʊst lʊnt lɛntˈzɛts̩ən lʊnt ˈɡrɪmɪɡə pʰaen.
wählet der Kenner der Höhen und Tiefen Lust und Entsetzen und grimmige Pein.
chooses the knower of the heights and depths pleasure and horror and cruel pain.
(the one who knows both the heights and depths chooses pleasure and horror and cruel pain.)

ʊnt leːɐ̯ kʰʏst di ˈbʊntˈən ˈvaŋən, lʊnt ziː fyːlt deːɐ̯ ˈliːbə kʰvaːl,
Und er küsst die bunten Wangen, und sie fühlt der Liebe Qual,
And he kisses the brightly-colored cheeks, and she feels the love's anguish,
(And he kisses her brightly-colored cheeks, and she feels the anguish of love,)

ʊnt das ˈmɛːtˈçən ʃtˈeːt ɡəˈfaŋən, lʊnt ziː vaent ts̩ʊm leːɐ̯stˈənˈmaːl;
und das Mädchen steht gefangen, und sie weint zum erstenmal;
and the girl stands captive, and she weeps for the first time;

zɪŋkˈt ts̩uː ˈzaenən ˈfyːsən ˈniːdɐ, nɪçt lʊm ˈvɔlʊst nɔx ɡəˈvɪnstʰ,
sinkt zu seinen Füssen nieder, nicht um Wollust noch Gewinst,
(she) sinks at his feet down, not for lust nor gain,
(she sinks down at his feet, not for sensual pleasure nor for gain,)

ax! lʊnt di ɡəˈlɛŋkˈən ˈɡliːdɐ, ziː fɛɐ̯ˈzaːɡən ˈlalən diːnstʰ.
ach! und die gelenken Glieder, sie versagen allen Dienst.
ah! and the supple limbs, they deny all service.

ʊnt‘ zoː tsuː dɛs ˈlaːgɐs fɛɐ̯ˈgnyːk‘lɪçɐ ˈfaɐɐ̯ bəˈraɛt‘ən den ˈdʊŋk‘lən
Und so zu des Lagers vergnüglicher Feier bereiten den dunklen
And thus for the bed's pleasurable ceremony prepare the dark
(And thus, for the pleasurable ceremony of the bed, the hours of the night prepare the dark,)

bəˈhaːk‘lɪçən ˈʃlaɐɐ̯ di ˈnɛçt‘lɪçən ˈʃt‘ʊndən, das ˈʃøːnə gəˈʃp‘ɪnstʰ.]
behaglichen Schleier die nächtlichen Stunden, das schöne Gespinst.]
comfortable veil the nocturnal hours, the lovely gossamer.]
(comforting veil, the lovely gossamer veil of night.)]]

ʃp‘eːt‘ ɛnt‘ˈʃlʊmɐt‘ ˈʊnt‘ɐ ˈʃɛrtsən, fryː lɛɐ̯ˈvaxt‘ naːx ˈkʰʊrtsɐ rastʰ,
Spät entschlummert unter Scherzen, früh erwacht nach kurzer Rast,
Late fallen asleep among pleasantries, early awakened after brief rest,
(Having fallen asleep late during pleasantries, and awakening early after a brief rest,)

ˈfɪndət‘ ziː lan ˈliːrəm ˈhɛrtsən tʰoːt‘ den ˈfiːlgəliːp‘t‘ən gastʰ.
findet sie an ihrem Herzen tot den vielgeliebten Gast.
finds she at her heart dead the much-loved guest.
(she finds her much-loved guest lying dead at her breast.)

ˈʃraɛənt‘ ˈʃt‘ʏrtst‘ ziː lɑof liːn ˈniːdɐ(r); ˈlaːbɐ nɪçt‘ lɛɐ̯ˈvɛk‘t‘ ziː liːn,
Schreiend stürzt sie auf ihn nieder; aber nicht erweckt sie ihn,
Screaming falls violently she upon him down; but not wakes she him,
(Screaming, she throws herself upon his body; but she cannot waken him,)

ʊnt‘ man tʰrɛːk‘t di ˈʃtarən ˈgliːdɐ balt tsʊr ˈflaməngruːbə hɪn.
und man trägt die starren Glieder bald zur Flammengrube hin.
and one carries the rigid limbs soon to the flame- pit hence.
(and soon his rigid limbs are carried to the funeral pyre.)

ziː ˈhøːrət di ˈpʰriːst‘ɐ, di ˈtʰoːt‘əngəzɛŋə, ziː ˈraːzət‘ lʊnt‘ ˈrɛnət‘
Sie höret die Priester, die Totengesänge, sie raset und rennet
She hears the priests, the funeral songs; she is delirious and runs

ʊnt tʰaɛlət di ˈmɛŋə. veːɐ̯ bɪst duː? vas drɛŋst tsu deːɐ̯ ˈgruːbə dɪç hɪn?
und teilet die Menge. "Wer bist du? was drängst zu der Grube dich hin?"
and separates the crowd. "Who are you? What drives to the grave you hence?"
(and pushes through the crowd. "Who are you? What drives you to this grave?")

baɛ deːɐ̯ ˈbaːrə ʃt‘ʏrtst‘ ziː ˈniːdɐ(r), liːɐ̯ gəˈʃraɛ dʊrçˈdrɪŋt di lʊftʰ:
Bei der Bahre stürzt sie nieder, ihr Geschrei durchdringt die Luft:
By the bier falls violently she down, her cries penetrate the air:
(She throws herself down by the bier, her cries penetrate the air:)

ˈmaɛnən ˈgat‘ən vɪl lɪç ˈviːdɐ(r)! lʊnt‘ lɪç zuːx liːn lɪn deːɐ̯ grʊftʰ.
"Meinen Gatten will ich wieder! und ich such' ihn in der Gruft.
"My husband want I again! and I seek him in the tomb.
("I want my husband back! And I seek him in the tomb.)

zɔl tsuː ˈlaʃə miːɐ̯ tsɛɐ̯ˈfalən ˈdiːzɐ ˈgliːdɐ ˈgœt‘ɐpʰraxtʰ? [tsʊr ˈlaʃə]
Soll zu Asche mir zerfallen dieser Glieder Götterpracht? [GA: zur Asche]
Shall into ash for me disintegrate these limbs' godlike magnificence? [into the ash]
(Shall the godlike magnificence of these limbs disintegrate into ashes before my eyes?)

224

mǽn! leːɐ̯ vaːɐ̯/vaːr ɛs, mǽn foːɐ̯/foːr 'alən! lax nuːɐ̯/nuːr 'aenə 'zyːsə naxtʰ!
Mein! er war es, mein vor allen! Ach nur eine süsse Nacht!"
Mine! he was it, mine before all! Ah, only one sweet night!"
(Mine! He was mine, mine before all others! Ah, but only for one sweet night!")

ɛs 'zıŋən di 'pʰriːstʼɐ: viːɐ̯ 'tʰraːgən di 'altʼən, naːx 'laŋəm lɛɐ̯'matʼən
Es singen die Priester: "Wir tragen die Alten, nach langem Ermatten
There sing the priests: "We bear (away) the old, after long exhausting
(The priests chant: "We bear away the old after a long period of waning strength)

ʊntʼ ʃpʼɛːtʼəm lɛɐ̯'kʰaltʼən, viːɐ̯ 'tʰraːgən di 'juːgəntʼ, nɔx leː ziːs gə'daxtʰ.
und spätem Erkalten, wir tragen die Jugend, noch eh' sie's gedacht."
and late growing cold, we bear (away) the youth, even before they it thought."
(and then, later, a growing coldness; we bear away the young sooner than they expect.")

['høːrə 'daenɐ 'pʰriːstʼɐ 'leːrə: 'diːzɐ vaːɐ̯ daen 'gatʼə nıçtʰ.
["Höre deiner Priester Lehre: dieser war dein Gatte nicht.
["Hear your priest's teaching: this one was your husband not.
[("Hear the teaching of your priests: this man was not your husband.)

leːpst duː dɔx lals baja'deːrə, ʊntʼ zoː hast duː 'kʰaenə pflıçtʰ.
Lebst du doch als Bajadere, und so hast du keine Pflicht.
Live you after all as temple dancer, and thus have you no duty.
(You live, after all, as a temple dancer; and thus you have no duty as a wife.)

nuːɐ̯ dem 'kʰœrpʼɐ fɔlkʼt deːɐ̯ 'ʃatʼən lın das 'ʃtʼılə 'tʰoːtʼənraeç;
Nur dem Körper folgt der Schatten in das stille Totenreich;
Only (after) the body follows the shadow (subject) into the silent realm of the dead;
(Only the shadow follows the body into the silent realm of the dead;)

nuːɐ̯ di 'gatʼın fɔlkʼt dem 'gatʼən: das lıstʼ pflıçtʼ lʊntʼ ruːm tsu'glaeç.
nur die Gattin folgt dem Gatten: das ist Pflicht und Ruhm zugleich.
only the wife follows the husband: that is duty and glory at the same time.
(only the wife follows the husband: that is her duty and at the same time her glory.)

ɛɐ̯'tʰøːnə, drɔ'meːtʼə, tsuː 'haelıgɐ 'kʰlaːgə! loː, 'neːmətʼ, liːɐ̯ 'gœtʼɐ!
Ertöne, Drommete, zu heiliger Klage! O, nehmet, ihr Götter!
Sound, trumpet, to sacred lament! Oh take, you gods!
(Sound, trumpet, a sacred lamentation! Oh take, you gods,)

di 'tsiːɐ̯də deːɐ̯ 'tʰaːgə, loː 'neːmət den 'jyŋlıŋ lın 'flamən tsuː lɔøç!]
die Zierde der Tage, o nehmet den Jüngling in Flammen zu euch!"]
the ornament of the days, oh take the youth in flames to you!"]
(this ornament of his days, oh take the youth to you in flames!")]

zoː das kʰoːɐ̯, das loːn lɛɐ̯'barmən 'meːrətʼ 'liːrəs 'hertsəns noːtʰ;
So das Chor, das ohn' Erbarmen mehret ihres Herzens Not;
So the choir, which without mercy increases her heart's distress;
(Thus chants the choir, which without mercy increases her heart's distress;)

ʊntʼ mıtʼ 'laosgəʃtʼrɛkʼtʼən 'larmən ʃpʼrıŋtʼ ziː lın den 'haesən tʰoːtʼ.
und mit ausgestreckten Armen springt sie in den heissen Tod.
and with outstretched arms leaps she into the hot death.
(and with outstretched arms she leaps into the fiery death.)

dɔx deː̯ɐ̯ 'gœt'ɐ- 'jʏŋlɪŋ   'heːbət' l̥ɔos deːɐ̯ 'flamə zɪç   lɛm'pʰoːɐ̯,
Doch der Götter-Jüngling hebet aus   der Flamme sich   empor,
But the divine youth   raises out of the flame   himself up,
(But the divine youth rises up out of the flames,)

ʊnt' l̥ɪn 'zae̯nən l̥armən 'ʃveːbət   di gə'liːp't'ə mɪt' hɛɐ̯'foːɐ̯.
und in seinen Armen schwebet die Geliebte mit hervor.
and in his   arms   soars   the beloved with forth.
(and, in his arms, his beloved soars forth with him.)

ɛs   frɔø̯t'   zɪç di 'gɔt'hae̯t deːɐ̯ 'rɔø̯ɪgən 'zʏndɐ(r); l̥ʊn'ʃt'ɛrp'lɪçə 'heːbən
Es   freut   sich die Gottheit der   reuigen Sünder; Unsterbliche heben
There gladdens itself the divinity of the repentant sinners; immortals   raise
(Divinity rejoices in repentant sinners; immortals raise)

fɛɐ̯'loːrənə 'kʰɪndɐ mɪt' 'fɔø̯rɪgən l̥armən t͡sʊm 'hɪməl   lɛm'pʰoːɐ̯.
verlorene Kinder mit feurigen Armen zum Himmel empor.
lost   children with fiery   arms   to the heaven   aloft.
(lost children up to heaven with arms of fire.)

[The poem is too long, and too interesting in its details, for Schubert's simple, strophic setting to a melody that is reminiscent of a church hymn and has no trace of the exotic, the erotic, or the sublime in it. The Peters edition omits three verses, in brackets above.]

deːɐ̯ graːf fɔn 'haːpsbʊrk'
Der Graf von Habsburg
The Count of Habsburg

Published by Schubert's brother Ferdinand as his *own* work in 1853
later privately published by Reinhard van Hoorickx in 1968
[composed 1818?] (poem by Friedrich von Schiller)

t͡su: 'laːxən l̥ɪn 'zae̯nɐ 'kʰae̯zɐpʰraxtʰ   l̥ɪm 'l̥altˈɐtʰyːmlɪçən 'zaːlə
Zu Aachen in seiner Kaiserpracht   im altertümlichen Saale
At Aachen, in his   imperial splendor in the ancient   hall

zaːs 'kʰøːnɪç 'ruːdɔlfs   'hae̯lɪgə maxtʰ bae̯m 'fɛst'lɪçən 'kʰrøːnʊŋsmaːlə.
sass König Rudolphs* heilige Macht beim festlichen Krönungsmahle.*
sat King   Rudolph's holy   might at the festive   coronation meal.
(sat his anointed majesty King Rudolph at his festive coronation banquet.)
     [*Schubert (errors in copying):* **sass Königs** ('kʰøːnɪks) **Rudolphs... Königsmahle**]

di 'ʃp'ae̯zən tʰruːk' deːɐ̯ 'pfalt͡sgraːf   dɛs   rae̯ns, l̥ɛs 'ʃɛŋk't'ə deːɐ̯ 'bøːmə
Die Speisen trug   der Pfalzgraf   des   Rheins, es   schenkte der Böhme
The foods   carried the Count Palatine of the Rhine; there poured   the Bohemian
(The Count Palatine of the Rhine brought in the food, the Lord of Bohemia poured)

dɛs 'pʰɛrləndən vae̯ns, l̥ʊnt' l̥alə di 'vɛːlɐ, di 'ziːbən,   [den]   [vae̯n]
des   perlenden Weins,* und alle die Wähler, die Sieben, [*Sch.:* den perlenden Wein]
of the sparkling wine,   and all the electors, the seven,   [the]
(the sparkling wine, and all seven of the electors,)

viː deːɐ̯ ˈʃtʼɛrnə kʰoːɐ̯/kʰoːr ʊm   di ˈzɔnə zɪç   ʃtʼɛltʰ, ʊmˈʃtʼandən ɡəˈʃɛftʼɪç
wie der Sterne Chor   um   die Sonne sich stellt, umstanden geschäftig
as the stars' choir   around the sun itself places, surrounded busily
(like a choir of stars positioned around the sun, busily hovered about)

den ˈhɛrʃɐ   deːɐ̯ vɛltʰ, di ˈvʏrdə dɛs   ˈlamtʼəs tsuː ˈlyːbən.   [ˈheːrən]
den Herrscher* der   Welt, die Würde des   Amtes zu üben. [*S.:* **den Herren der Welt**]
the ruler   of the world, the dignity of the office to exercise.   [lord]
(the ruler of the world, to exercise the dignity of their high office.)

ʊntʼ rɪŋs   lɛɐ̯ˈfʏltʼə den ˈhoːən balˈkʰoːn das fɔlkʼ ɪn ˈfrɔødɡəm ɡəˈdrɛŋə,
Und rings   erfüllte den hohen Balkon das Volk in freudgem Gedränge,
And all around filled   the high balcony the people in joyful   crowding,
(And the ordinary people filled the high balcony all around in a joyful throng,)

lɑɔtʼ ˈmɪʃtʼə zɪç ɪn deːɐ̯ pʰoˈzɑɔnən tʰoːn das ˈjɑɔxtsəndə ˈruːfən deːɐ̯ ˈmɛŋə.
laut mischte sich in der Posaunen Ton das jauchzende Rufen der   Menge.
loudly mingled itself in the trombones' tone the exultant   shouts of the crowd.
(the exultant shouts of the crowd were loudly mingled with the sound of trumpets.)

den ɡəˈlɛndɪçtʼ naːx ˈlaŋəm fɛɐ̯ˈdɛrpʼlɪçən ʃtʼrɑɛtʰ
Denn geendigt nach langem verderblichen Streit
For ended,   after long, ruinous   conflict,

vaːɐ̯ di ˈkʰɑɛzɛloːzə, di ˈʃrɛkʼlɪçə   tsɑɛtʰ, ʊntʼ lɑɛn ˈrɪçtʼɐ vaːɐ̯ ˈviːdɐ(r) lɑɔf ˈleːɐ̯dən.
war die kaiserlose, die schreckliche Zeit, und ein Richter war wieder auf Erden.
was the emperorless, the terrible   time; and a judge   was again   on earth.
(was the terrible time without an emperor; and there was again a judge here on earth.)

nɪçtʼ blɪntʼ   meːɐ̯ ˈvaltʼət deːɐ̯/deːr ˈlɑɛzɐnə ʃpʼeːɐ̯, nɪçtʼ ˈfʏrçtʼət deːɐ̯ ˈʃvaxə,
Nicht blind   mehr waltet der   eiserne Speer, nicht fürchtet der Schwache,
Not   blindly (any) more ruled the   iron   spear, not feared   the weak man,
(The iron spear no longer ruled blindly; the weak were no longer afraid,)

deːɐ̯ ˈfriːtʼlɪçə meːɐ̯, dɛs ˈmɛçtʼɪɡən   ˈbɔøtʼə tsuː ˈveːɐ̯dən.
der Friedliche mehr,   des Mächtigen   Beute zu werden.
the peaceful one no longer, the powerful one's prey   to become.
(nor the peace-loving, of becoming the prey of the powerful.)

ʊnt deːɐ̯ ˈkʰɑɛzɐ(r) lɛɐ̯ˈɡrɑɛft den ˈɡɔldnən pʰoˈkʰaːl, ʊntʼ ʃpʼrɪçtʼ mɪt tsuˈfriːdənən ˈblɪkʼən:
Und der Kaiser   ergreift den goldnen Pokal,   und spricht mit zufriedenen Blicken:
And the emperor   grasps   the golden goblet,   and speaks with contented   glances:

voːl ˈɡlɛntsət das fɛstʰ, voːl ˈpʰraŋət   das maːl
wohl glänzet das Fest, wohl pranget   das Mahl
Indeed gleams the feast, indeed is resplendent the meal
("The feast is outstanding, to be sure, and the banquet is certainly resplendent)

mɑɛn ˈkʰøːnɪkʼlɪç hɛrts tsuː lɛntʼtsʏkʼən; dɔx den ˈzɛŋɐ fɛɐ̯ˈmɪs lɪç, den ˈbrɪŋɐ deːɐ̯ lʊstʰ,
mein königlich Herz zu entzücken doch den Sänger vermiss ich, den Bringer der   Lust,
my   royal   heart to delight;   but the singer miss   I,   the bringer of the joy,
(to delight my royal heart; but I miss the singer, the bringer of pleasure,)

deːɐ̯ mɪt ˈzyːsəm kʰlaŋ miːɐ̯ bəˈveːɡə di brust ʊnt mɪt ˈɡœtlɪç lɛɐ̯ˈhaːbənən ˈleːrən.
der mit süssem Klang mir bewege die Brust und mit göttlich erhabenen Lehren.
who with sweet sound to me may move the breast and with divinely lofty teaching.
(who with sweet sounds and with divinely lofty teaching moves my heart.)

zoː haːb ɪçs ɡəˈhalt ən fɔn ˈjuːɡənt lan, ʊnt vas lɪç lalsˈrɪt ɐ ɡəˈpfleːk t ʊnt ɡəˈtʰaːn,
So hab' ich's gehalten von Jugend an, und was ich als Ritter gepflegt und getan,
Thus have I it held from youth on, and what I as knight (have)cultivated and done,
(I have held to that since I was young, and what I have cultivated and done as a knight)

nɪçt vɪl lɪçs lalsˈkʰaezɐ(r) lɛntˈbeːrən. ʊnt ziː! lɪn deːɐ̯ ˈfyrst ən lʊmˈɡeːbəndən kʰraes
nicht will ich's als Kaiser entbehren. Und sieh! in der Fürsten umgebenden Kreis
not want I it as emperor to do without. And look! Into the princes' surrounding circle
(I do not want to do without as emperor. And look! Into the surrounding circle of princes)

tʰraːt deːɐ̯ ˈzɛŋɐ lɪm ˈlaŋən tʰaˈlaːrə, liːm ˈɡlɛntstə di ˈlɔkə ˈzɪlbɐvaes,
trat der Sänger im langen Talare, ihm glänzte die Locke silberweiss,
stepped the singer in the long robe, for him gleamed the curl silver-white,
(stepped the singer in his long robe; his hair gleamed silver-white,)

ɡəˈblaeçt fɔn deːɐ̯ ˈfylə deːɐ̯ ˈjaːrə. ˈzyːsɐ ˈvoːllaot ʃleːft lɪn deːɐ̯ ˈzaet ən ɡɔlt,
gebleicht von der Fülle der Jahre. "Süsser Wohllaut schläft in der Saiten Gold,
bleached by the fullness of the years. "Sweet harmony sleeps in the strings' gold,
(bleached by the fullness of years. "Sweet harmony sleeps in the gold of the strings,)

deːɐ̯ ˈzɛŋɐ zɪŋt fɔn deːɐ̯ ˈmɪnə zɔlt, leːɐ̯ ˈpʰraezət das ˈhøːçstə, das ˈbɛstə,
der Sänger singt von der Minne Sold, er preisset das Höchste, das Beste,
the singer sings of the love's reward, he praises the highest, the best,
(a singer sings of love's rewards, he praises the highest, the best,)

vas das hɛrts̬ zɪç vynʃt, vas deːɐ̯ zɪn bəˈɡeːɐ̯t, dɔx ˈzaːɡə, vas lɪst
was das Herz sich wünscht, was der Sinn begehrt, doch sage, was ist
what the heart for itself wishes, what the mind desires, but say, what is
(what the heart wishes for itself, what the mind desires; but say, what is)

dɛs ˈkʰaezɐs veːɐ̯t lan ˈzaenəm ˈhɛrlɪçst ən ˈfɛst ə? — nɪçt ɡəˈbiːt ən veːɐ̯d lç
des Kaisers wert an seinem herrlichsten Feste?" —"Nicht gebieten werd' ich
of the emperor worthy at his most glorious feast?" —"Not command shall I
(worthy of the emperor at his most glorious feast?" —"I shall not command)

dem ˈzɛŋɐ, ʃpˈrɪçt deːɐ̯ ˈhɛrʃɐ mɪt ˈlɛçəlndəm ˈmʊndə, leːɐ̯ ʃtˈeːt
dem Sänger," spricht der Herrscher mit lächelndem Munde, "er steht
the singer," speaks the ruler with smiling mouth, "he stands
(the singer," said the ruler with a smile on his lips, "he is)

lɪn dɛs ˈɡrøːsərən ˈhɛrən pflɪçt, leːɐ̯ ɡəˈhɔrçt deːɐ̯ ɡəˈbiːt əndən ˈʃtʊndə.
in des grösseren Herren Pflicht, er gehorcht der gebietenden Stunde.
in the greater lord's duty, he obeys the commanding hour.
(subject to a greater lord: he obeys the command of time.) ["*in Pflicht stehen*" = to be subject to]

viː lɪn den ˈlyft ən deːɐ̯ ˈʃtˈʊrmvɪnt zao̯st, man vaes nɪçt, fɔn ˈvanən
Wie in den Lüften der Sturmwind saust, man weiss nicht, von wannen
As in the airs the storm wind howls, one knows not, from whence
(When the storm wind howls through the air, no one knows from whence)

leːɐ̯ kʰɔmt' ʊnt' braost', viː deːɐ̯ kʰvɛl laos fɛɐ̯'bɔrɡənən 'tʰiːfən,
er kommt und braust, wie der Quell aus verborgenen Tiefen,
it comes and rages; like the spring from hidden depths,
(it comes and rages; like a spring that gushes up from hidden depths,)

zoː dɛs 'zɛŋɐs liːt' laos dem 'ɪnɐn ʃalt' ʊnt' 'vɛk'ət
so des Sängers Lied aus dem Innern schallt und wecket
thus the singer's song out of the inner being sounds and awakens
(thus the singer's song sounds out of his inner being, and awakens)

deːɐ̯ 'dʊŋk'əln ɡə'fyːlə ɡə'valt', diː ɪm 'hɛrtsən 'vʊndɐbaːɐ̯ 'ʃliːfən."
der dunkeln Gefühle Gewalt, die im Herzen wunderbar schliefen."
the dark feelings' force, which in the heart wondrously sleep."
(the force of unconscious, mysterious feelings that wondrously sleep in the heart.")

ʊnt deːɐ̯ 'zɛŋɐ raʃ ɪn di 'zaet'ən fɛlt' ʊnt' bə'ɡɪnt' ziː 'mɛçt'ɪç tsuː 'ʃlaːɡən:
Und der Sänger rasch in die Saiten fällt und beginnt sie mächtig zu schlagen:
And the singer quickly into the strings falls and begins them powerfully to strike:
(And the singer quickly attacks the strings and begins to strike them powerfully:)

aofs 'vaet'vɛrk' hɪ'naos rɪt' laen 'leːdlɐ hɛlt', den 'flʏçt'ɪɡən 'ɡɛmsbɔk' tsuː 'jaːɡən.
"Aufs Waidwerk hinaus ritt ein edler Held, den flüchtigen Gemsbock zu jagen.
"To the hunt out rode a noble hero, the fleeing chamois-buck to chase.
("A noble hero rode out to the hunt, to chase the fleeing chamois-buck.)

iːm 'fɔlk't'ə deːɐ̯ kʰnap' mɪt dem 'jɛːɡɐɡəʃɔs, ʊnt' lals leːɐ̯/leːr laof 'zaenəm 'ʃt'at'lɪçən
Ihm folgte der Knapp mit dem Jägergeschoss, und als er auf seinem stattlichen
Him followed the squire with the hunter-weapons, and as he on his stately
(His squire followed him with his hunting weapons, and as he, the nobleman, on his stately)

rɔs ɪn 'laenə lao kʰɔmt' ɡə'rɪt'ən, laen 'ɡlœk'laen hø:ɐ̯t' leːɐ̯/leːr lɛɐ̯'kʰlɪŋən fɛrn,
Ross in eine Au kommt geritten, ein Glöcklein hört er erklingen fern,
horse into a meadow comes ridden, a little bell heard he ringing far away,
(horse came riding onto a meadow, he heard a little bell ringing in the distance:)

laen 'pʰriːst'ɐ vaːɐ̯s mɪt dem laep' dɛs hɛrn, fo'ran kʰaːm deːɐ̯ 'mɛsnɐ ɡə'ʃrɪt'ən.
ein Priester war's mit dem Leib des Herrn, voran kam der Mesner geschritten.
a priest was it with the body of the Lord, ahead came the sacristan walking.
(it was a priest with the consecrated host, the body of the Lord, and a sacristan preceding him.)

ʊnt deːɐ̯ ɡraːf tsʊr 'leːɐ̯də zɪç 'naeɡət' hɪn das haop't' mɪt 'deːmuːt' lɛnt''blø:sət',
Und der Graf zur Erde sich neiget hin das Haupt mit Demut entblösset,
And the count to the earth himself bows down the head with humility uncovered,
(And the count bows his head, uncovered in humility, down toward the earth,)

tsuː fɛɐ̯'leːrən/fɛr'leːrən mɪt' 'ɡlaobɪɡəm 'kʰrɪst'ənzɪn vas 'lalə 'mɛnʃən lɛɐ̯'lø:zətʰ.
zu verehren mit glaubigem Christensinn was alle Menschen erlöset.
to honor with devout Christian-mind what all humans redeems.
(to honor with devout Christian feelings that which redeems all human souls.)

["*glaubigem*" = "*gläubigem*" in modern German]

aen 'bɛçlaen 'laːbɐ 'raoʃt'ə dʊrçs fɛlt',
Ein Bächlein aber rauschte durchs Feld,
A little brook, however, roared through the field,

fɔn dɛs ˈgiːsbaxs   ˈraesəndən ˈfluːtˈən gəˈʃvɛltˈ,   das ˈhɛmtˈə deːɐ̯ ˈvandərɐ ˈtʰrɪtˈə,
von des Giessbachs   reissenden Fluten geschwellt, das hemmte der Wanderer Tritte,
by the mountain torrent's rushing   waters swollen,   that hindered the wanderers' steps,
(swollen by the rushing waters of a mountain torrent; that blocked the wanderers' way,)

ʊntˈ baeˈzaetˈ leːkˈtˈ ˈjeːnɐ   das zakˈraˈmɛntˈ, fɔn den ˈfyːsən tsiːtˈ leːɐ̯ di ˈʃuːə   bəˈhɛntˈ,
und beiseit' legt jener das Sakrament, von den Füssen zieht er die Schuhe behend,
and aside   laid   that one the sacrament, from the feet   took he the shoes   nimbly,
(so the priest laid aside the sacrament and nimbly took the shoes off his feet,)

daˈmɪtˈ leːɐ̯ das ˈbɛçlaen dʊrçˈʃrɪtˈə.   vas ʃafst   duːʔ ˈreːdət deːɐ̯ graːf liːn   lan,
damit er das Bächlein durchschritte. 'Was schaffst du?' redet der Graf ihn an,
so that he the brooklet might cross.   'What are doing you?' says the count to him to,
(so that he might cross the brook. 'What are you doing?' asks the count,)   ["*anreden*" = address]

deːɐ̯/deːr liːn fɛɐ̯ˈvʊndətˈ bəˈtʰraxtˈətʰ. hɛr, lɪç ˈvalə tsuː ˈlaenəm ˈʃtˈɛrbəndən man,
der   ihn verwundert betrachtet. 'Herr, ich walle zu einem   sterbenden Mann,
who   him astonished observes.   'Sire, I go to a   dying   man,
(who observes him in astonishment. 'Sire, I am going to a dying man,)

deːɐ̯ naːx deːɐ̯ ˈhɪməlskʰɔstˈ ˈʃmaxtˈətʰ.   ʊnt daː   lɪç mɪç ˈnaːə dɛs ˈbaxəs ˈʃtˈeːkˈ,
der nach der Himmelskost schmachtet. Und da   ich mich nahe des Baches Steg,
who for   the   heaven- food pines.   And when I   myself near the brook's footbridge,
(who is pining for the celestial food. And just as I am nearing the footbridge to cross the brook,)

daː hatˈ liːn deːɐ̯ ˈʃtˈrøːməndə ˈgiːsbax hɪnˈvɛkˈ lɪm ˈʃtˈruːdəl deːɐ̯ ˈvɛlən gəˈrɪsən.
da hat ihn der strömende Giessbach hinweg im   Strudel der Wellen gerissen.
then has it the rushing   torrent   away   in the whirlpool of the waves torn.
(at that moment the rushing mountain torrent tore it away in the whirlpool of the waves.)

drʊm   das dem ˈlɛçtsəndən ˈveːɐ̯də zaen hael,   zoː vil lɪç
Drum   dass dem Lechzenden werde   sein Heil,   so will ich
Therefore, that to the parched one may come his   salvation, so want I
(Therefore, so that his salvation may be brought to the parched one, I want)

das ˈvɛsɐlaen   jɛtstˈ lɪn lael dʊrçvaːtˈən mɪtˈ ˈnakˈəndən ˈfyːsən.
das Wässerlein jetzt in Eil   durchwaten mit nackenden Füssen.'
the little water   now in haste through-wade with naked   feet.'
(to wade with naked feet through that little stream now in haste.')

daː   zɛtstˈ liːm deːɐ̯ graːf laof zaen ˈrɪtˈɐlɪç pfeːɐ̯tˈ, ʊntˈ raeçtˈ liːm
Da   setzt ihn der Graf auf sein ritterlich Pferd, und reicht ihm
Thereupon sets him the count on his   knightly horse, and hands him
(Thereupon the count sets the priest on his noble horse, and hands him)

di ˈpʰrɛçtˈɪgən ˈtsɔømə, das leːɐ̯ ˈlaːbə   den ˈkʰraŋkˈən, deːɐ̯ zaen bəˈgeːɐ̯tˈ,
die prächtigen Zäume, dass er labe   den Kranken, der sein   begehrt,
the magnificent reins,   that he may comfort the sick man, who of him desires,
(the magnificent reins, so that he may comfort the sick man who has need of him,)

ʊntˈ di ˈhaelɪgə pflɪçtˈ nɪçtˈ fɛɐ̯ˈzɔømə. ʊntˈ leːɐ̯ ˈzɛlbɐ(r) laof ˈzaenəs ˈkʰnapˈən tʰiːɐ̯
und die heilige Pflicht nicht versäume. Und er   selber auf seines Knappen Tier
and the holy   duty   not neglect.   And he himself on his   squire's animal
(and not be too late for his holy duty. And the count himself, on his squire's mount)

fɛɐ̯'gnyːk'ət' nɔx 'vaet'ɐ dɛs 'jaːgəns bə'giːɐ̯,　　de:ɐ̯/de:r 'landrə di 'raezə fɔl'fuːrət^h;

vegnüget　noch weiter des Jagens Begier,　der　andre die Reise vollführet;

gratifies　still further the hunt's keen desire, the　other one the journey carries out;

(goes on to gratify further his keen desire for the hunt, while the priest continues on his journey;)

ʊnt' lam　'neːçst'ən 'mɔrgən mɪt 'daŋk'əndəm blɪk'

und am　nächsten Morgen mit dankendem Blick

and on the next　morning with thanking　look

(and the next morning, with a look of gratitude,)

daː brɪŋt' le:ɐ̯ dem 'graːfən zaen rɔs tsu'rʏk', bə'ʃaedən lɪm　'tsyːgəl gə'fyːrət^h.

da　bringt er dem Grafen sein Ross zurück, bescheiden im　Zügel geführet.

there brings he to the count　his horse back,　modestly　by the bridle led.

(there he is, bringing the count back his horse, modestly led by the bridle.)

nɪçt' 'vɔlə　das gɔt', riːf mɪt 'deːmuːtszɪn de:ɐ̯ graːf, das tsʊm 'ʃt'raet'ən

'Nicht wolle　das Gott,' rief mit Demutssinn der Graf, 'dass zum Streiten

'Not　may want that God,' cried with humility-mind the　count, 'that to the fighting

('God will surely not want,' cried the count with feelings of humility, 'that to warfare)

lʊnt' 'jaːgən das rɔs　lɪç bə'ʃrɪt'ə　'fʏrdɛhɪn, das 'maenən 'ʃœpfɐ　gə'tʰraːgən!

und Jagen das Ross ich beschritte　fürderhin, das meinen Schöpfer　getragen!

and hunting the horse I　would bestride henceforth, that my　Creator (has) carried!

(and to the hunt I would mount the horse ever again that has carried my Creator!)

ʊnt' maːkst duːs nɪçt' 'haːbən tsu: 'laegnəm gə'vɪnst', zo: blaep'　lɛs gə'vɪt'mət

Und magst du's nicht haben zu eignem Gewinnst, so bleib'　es gewidmet

And wish　you it not to have for own　gain,　then may remain it dedicated

(And if you do not wish to have it for your own personal gain, then may it remain dedicated)

dem 'gœt'lɪçən diːnst', dɛn lɪç haːp' lɛs deːm ja:　gə'geːbən, fɔn deːm lɪç 'leːrə

dem göttlichen Dienst, denn ich hab' es d e m　ja　gegeben, von dem ich Ehre

to the divine　service, for I　have it to *Him* of course given,　from whom I　honor

(to the service of God; for I have of course given it to *Him*, from whom I hold in fee my honor)

lʊnt' 'lɪrdɪʃəs　guːt tsu: 'leːən 'tʰraːgə lʊnt' laep' lʊnt' bluːt' lʊnt' 'zeːlə lʊnt' 'laːt'əm lʊnt' '

und irdisches Gut　zu Lehen trage und Leib und Blut und Seele und Atem und

and earthly　goods in fee　hold and body and blood and soul and breath and

(and earthly possessions, as well as body and blood and soul and breath and)

leːbən. zo: mø:k' lɑoç gɔt, de:ɐ̯/de:r lal'mɛçt'ɪgə hɔrt,　de:ɐ̯

Leben.' So mög' auch Gott, der　allmächtige Hort,　der

life.'　So may　also God, the　almighty　treasure, who

(life.' Then may God, our all-powerful Treasure, who)

das 'fleːən de:ɐ̯ 'ʃvaxən lɛɐ̯'hø:rət', tsu: 'leːrən lɔøç 'brɪŋən hi:ɐ̯/hi:r lʊnt dɔrt',

das Flehen der　Schwachen erhöret, zu Ehren euch bringen hier　und dort,

the pleading of the weak　hears,　to honors you bring　here　and there,

(hears the pleas of the weak, also bring you into honors here, on earth, and there, in heaven,)

zo: vi: li:ɐ̯ jɛtst' li:n　gə'leːrət^h. li:ɐ̯ zaet' laen 'mɛçt'ɪgə graːf, bə'kʰant dʊrç

so wie ihr jetzt ihn　geehret. Ihr seid ein mächtiger Graf, bekannt　durch

just as you now Him (have) honored. You are a　powerful count, well-known through

(as you have now honored Him. You are a powerful count, well-known for your)

'rɪt'əlɪç 'valt'ən ɪm 'ʃvaetsɐlant', lɔøç bly:n zɛks 'li:p'lɪçə 't'œçt'ɐ.
ritterlich Walten im Schweizerland, euch blühn sechs liebliche Töchter.
chivalrous rule in the Switzerland, for you bloom six lovely daughters.
(chivalrous rule in Switzerland; you have six lovely daughters, blooming like flowers.)

zo: 'mø:gən zi:, ri:f le:ɐ bə'gaest'ɐt' laos, zɛks 'k'ro:nən lɔøç 'brɪŋən lɪn 'lɔøɐ haos
So mögen sie," rief er begeistert aus, "sechs Kronen euch bringen in euer Haus
So may they," cried he inspired out, "six crowns to you bring into your house
(So may they," he cried out, inspired by prophetic vision, "bring you six crowns into your house)

lʊnt' 'glɛntsən di 'ʃp'ɛ:tst'ən gə'ʃlɛçt'ɐ! lʊnt' mɪt' 'zɪnəndəm haop't'
und glänzen die spät'sten Geschlechter!" Und mit sinnendem Haupt
and (may) gleam the latest generations!" And with pensive head
(and may your posterity be glorious down to the last generations!" And with a pensive mind)

za:s de:ɐ 'k'aezɐ da:, lals dɛçt' le:ɐ fɐ'gaŋənɐ 'tsaet'ən, jɛtst, da: le:ɐ
sass der Kaiser da, als dächt' er vergangener Zeiten, jetzt, da er
sat the emperor there, as if thought he of past times, now, when he
(the emperor sat there, as if he might be thinking of times gone by; now, when he)

dem 'zɛŋɐ(r) lɪns 'laogə za:, da: lɐ'graeft' li:n de:ɐ 'vɔrt'ə bə'dɔøt'ən. di 'tsy:gə
dem Sänger ins Auge sah, da ergreift ihn der Worte Bedeuten. Die Züge
to the singer into the eye looked, then seized him the words' significance. The features
(looked the singer in the eye, the significance of the words struck him. The features)

dɛs 'p'ri:st'ɐs lɐ'k'ɛnt' le:ɐ ʃnɛl, lʊnt' fɐ'bɪrk't de:ɐ 't'rɛ:nən 'ʃt'ʏrtsəndən k'vɛl
des Priesters erkennt er schnell, und verbirgt der Tränen stürzenden Quell
of the priest recognizes he quickly, and hides the tears' gushing fountain
(of the priest he quickly recognizes, and he hides the gushing fountain of tears)

lɪn dɛs 'mant'əls 'p'ʊrp'ʊrnən 'falt'ən. lʊnt' 'laləs 'blɪk't'ə den 'k'aezɐ(r) lan, lʊnt'
in des Mantels purpurnen Falten. Und alles blickte den Kaiser an, und
in the cloak's purple folds. And all looked the emperor at, and
(in the purple folds of his cloak. And everyone looked at the emperor and)

lɐ'k'ant'ə den 'gra:fən, de:ɐ das gə't'a:n, lʊnt' fɐ'le:ɐt'ə das 'gœt'lɪçə 'valt'ən.
erkannte den Grafen, der das getan, und verehrte das göttliche Walten.
recognized the count who that (had) done, and venerated the divine governance.
(recognized the count who had done that deed, and all venerated the governance of God.)

[*Schubert made several errors in copying the poem: "*Königs Rudolf*" instead of "*König Rudolphs*," "*Königsmahle*" for "*Krönungsmahle*," "*den perlenden Wein*" instead of "*des perlenden Weins*" (spoiling the rhyme), and "*Herren*" instead of "*Herscher*." He only copied the first verse, but indicated that more should be sung by adding repeat marks. Rudolph of Hapsburg, whose ancient family seat, Habsburg Castle, can still be visited in Switzerland, was the founder of the royal and imperial house of Austria, and, as Rudolph I, was made Holy Roman Emperor in 1273. His daughters married into six royal houses, as predicted by the priest in Schiller's ballad.]

Der greise Kopf see *Winterreise*

232

de:ɐ̯ 'guːt'ə 'hɪrt'ə
Der gute Hirte
The Good Shepherd

Posthumously published [composed 1816] (poem by Johann Peter Uz)

vas 'zɔrgəst   duː? zae̯ 'ʃt'ɪlə, 'mae̯nə 'zeːlə! dɛn gɔt' lɪst' lae̯n 'guːt'ɐ hɪrtʰ,
Was sorgest   du? Sei stille, meine Seele! denn Gott ist ein guter Hirt,
Why are troubled you? Be still, my   soul! for God is a   good shepherd,
(Why are you troubled? Be still, my soul, for God is a good shepherd,)

                                         [*poem:* **denn Gott ist ein getreuer** (gə'tʰrɔ͜øɐ, faithful) **Hirt**]

deːɐ̯ miːɐ̯, l̩ɑox vɛn lɪç mɪç   nɪçt' 'kʰveːlə, nɪçts 'maŋəln 'lasən vɪrt'.
der mir,   auch wenn ich mich nicht quäle, nichts mangeln lassen wird.
who for me, even if   I   myself not   torment, nothing lack   let   will.
(who will let nothing be lacking for me, even if I am not suffering.)

eːɐ̯ 'vae̯dət' mɪç l̩ɑof 'bluːmənrae̯çɐ(r) l̩ɑo͜ə,   leːɐ̯ fyːɐ̯t' mɪç 'frɪʃən 'vasɐn   tsuː,
Er weidet mich auf blumenreicher Aue,   er führt mich frischen Wassern zu,
He feeds me   on flower- rich   pastures, he leads me fresh   waters   to,
(He feeds me on flower-covered pastures, he leads me to fresh waters,)

                    [*poem:* **und** (lʊnt', and) **führt mich frischen Wassern zu**]

ʊnt' 'brɪŋət' mɪç lɪm 'kʰyːlən 'tʰɑo͜ə tsʊr 'zɪçɐn 'laːbənt'ruː.
und bringet mich im   kühlen Taue zur sichern Abendruh'.
and brings me in the cool dew to the safe   evening rest.
(and brings me in the cool dew to a safe rest at evening.)

eːɐ̯ hø̈ːɐ̯t' nɪçt' l̩ɑof, mɪç 'liːp'rae̯ç tsu: bə'ʃɪrmən, lɪm ʃat'ən   foːɐ̯ dɛs 'tʰaːɡəs gluːtʰ,
Er hört nicht auf, mich liebreich zu beschirmen, im   Schatten vor des Tages Glut,
He stops not ... , me lovingly to shelter,   in the shade   before the day's heat,
(He does not cease to shelter me lovingly, in the shade from the heat of the day,)

                                  [*"hört auf"* from *"aufhören"* = to stop, to cease]

ɪn 'zae̯nəm 'ʃoːsə   foːɐ̯ den 'ʃt'ʏrmən lʊnt' 'ʃvartsɐ 'boːshae̯t vuːtʰ.
in seinem Schosse vor   den Stürmen und schwarzer Bosheit Wut.
in His   bosom   before the storms and black   malice's fury.
(in His bosom from storms and from the fury of dark malice.)

ɑox vɛn leːɐ̯ mɪç dʊrç 'fɪnst'rə 'tʰeːlə 'lae̯t'ən, mɪç dʊrç di 'vyːst'ə 'fyːrən vɪrt',
Auch wenn er mich durch finstre Täler leiten, mich durch die Wüste führen wird,
Even if   He me   through dark   valleys lead,   me through the desert guide will,
(Even if He will lead me through dark valleys, will guide me through the desert,)

vɪl lɪç nɪçts 'fʏrçt'ən; miːɐ̯ tsʊr 'zae̯t'ən geːt' 'diːzɐ 'tʰrɔ͜øə hɪrtʰ.
will ich nichts fürchten; mir   zur Seiten geht dieser treue Hirt.
shall I   nothing fear;   for me by the side   walks this   faithful shepherd.
(I shall fear nothing; by my side this faithful shepherd is walking.)

ɪç 'laːbɐ   vɪl liːn 'pʰrae̯zən lʊnt' liːm 'daŋk'ən! lɪç halt' lan 'mae̯nəm 'hɪrt'ən festʰ;
Ich aber   will ihn preisen und ihm danken! Ich halt' an meinem Hirten   fest;
I   however will him praise   and him thank! I   cling to my   shepherd firmly;
(But I will praise him and thank him! I shall cling firmly to my shepherd;)

ʊnt' mæen fɛɐ̯'tʰraɔ̯ən zɔl nɪçt' 'vaŋk'ən, vɛn 'aləs   mɪç fɛɐ̯'lɛstʰ.
und mein Vertrauen soll nicht wanken, wenn Alles   mich verlässt.
and my trust   shall not waver, when everything me forsakes.
(and my faith shall not waver, when all else forsakes me.)

[The poem is, obviously, a loose paraphrase of the 23rd psalm. Schubert omitted eight lines of poetry (a paraphrase of "He prepareth a table before me..."). He made a more famous setting of the psalm for chorus (in 1820), but this version is also quite lovely and expressive.]

deːɐ̯ 'hɛrpst'la:bənt'
Der Herbstabend
The Autumn Evening

Posthumously published [composed 1816] (poem by Johann Gaudenz von Salis-Seewis)

'a:bənt'glɔk'ənhalə 'tsɪt'ɐn dʊmpf dʊrç 'moːɐ̯gədyft'ə hɪn;
Abendglockenhalle zittern dumpf durch Moorgedüfte hin;
Evening bells' clangs vibrate dully   through marsh vapors hence;
(The clang of evening churchbells vibrates dully through the vapors that rise from the marsh;)

'hɪnt'ɐ 'je:nəs 'kʰɪrçhoːfs   'gɪt'ɐn blast dɛs 'dɛmɐlɪçts   kʰar'mi:n.
hinter jenes Kirchhofs   Gittern blasst des Dämmerlichts Karmin.
behind that churchyard's railings pales the twilight's   carmine.
(behind the railings of that churchyard the crimson glow of twilight is fading.)

aɔ̯s lʊm'ʃt'ʏrmt'ən 'lɪndəntsvae̯gən 'ri:zəlt' 'vɛlk'əs laɔ̯p' hɛ'rap',
Aus umstürmten Lindenzweigen rieselt welkes Laub herab,
From storm-stirred linden branches drizzles withered foliage down,
(From the storm-stirred linden branches withered leaves are fluttering down,)

ʊnt' gə'blae̯çt'ə 'gre:zɐ 'bɔøgən zɪç   laɔ̯f li:ɐ bə'ʃt'ɪmt'əs gra:p'.
und gebleichte Gräser beugen sich   auf ihr bestimmtes Grab.
and faded   grasses bend themselves on their allotted   graves.
(and faded grasses bend down over their allotted graves.)

'frɔøndɪn! vaŋk't', ɪm 'la:bənt'vɪndə, balt' laɔ̯x gra:s laɔ̯f 'maenɐ grʊftʰ,
Freundin! wankt, im   Abendwinde, bald auch Gras auf meiner Gruft,
Lady friend! sways, in the evening wind, soon also grass on my   grave,
(Dear friend, soon the grass will be swaying in the evening breeze over my grave too,)

ʃvɛrmt das laɔ̯p' lʊm 'li:rə 'lɪndə 'ru:əloːs ɪn 'fɔøçt'ɐ lʊftʰ,
schwärmt das Laub um   ihre Linde ruhelos in feuchter Luft,
swirls   the foliage around their linden restlessly in moist   air,
(the leaves will be swirling restlessly around the linden-tree in the moist air,)

vɛn ʃoːn 'maenə 'ra:zənʃt'ɛlə nuːɐ daen 'vɛlk'ɐ kʰrants nɔx tsiːɐtʰ,   [van]
wenn schon meine Rasenstelle nur dein welker Kranz noch ziert, [*poem:* wann schon]
when already my   plot of grass only your withered wreath still adorns,
(when already only your withered wreath still adorns my plot of grass,)

ʊnt' laɔ̯f 'le:t'əs 'laezɐ 'vɛlə zɪç maen 'ne:bəlbɪlt' fɛɐ̯'li:ɐtʰ:
und auf Lethes leiser Welle sich mein Nebelbild verliert:
and on Lethe's quiet wave itself my mist- image loses:
(and my misty image is disappearing on Lethe's* quiet waves:)

234

'laͻʃə dan! ɪm 'bly:t'ənʃɑͻɐ vɪrt' lɛs di:ɐ fɛɐ'ne:mlɪç ve:n:
lausche dann! Im Blütenschauer wird es dir vernehmlich wehn:
listen then! In the blossom-shower will it to you perceptibly waft:
(listen then! This thought will perceptibly waft into your mind in the shower of blossoms:)

[*poem:* **Blätterschauer** ('blɛt'ɐʃɑͻɐ, petal-shower)]

'je:nzaets 'ʃvɪndət' 'je:də t'rɑͻɐ; t'rɔøə vɪrt' zɪç 'vi:dɐze:n!
jenseits schwindet jede Trauer; Treue wird sich wiedersehn!
on the other side vanishes every grief; constancy will itself see again!
(every sorrow vanishes in the other world and constant lovers will see each other again!)

[*Lethe, "forgetfulness," was one of the rivers of the underworld land of the dead in Greek mythology. In the romantic era it was quite in fashion to imagine one's own deserted grave.]

de:ɐ hɪrt^h
Der Hirt
The Shepherd

Posthumously published [composed 1816] (poem by Johann Mayrhofer)

du: t^hʊrm! ʦu 'maenəm 'laedə ra:kst du: zo: ho:x lɛm'p^ho:ɐ,
Du Turm! zu meinem Leide ragst du so hoch empor,
You tower! To my pain rise you so high up,
(You, bell-tower! To my pain you rise up so high,)

ʊnt' 'ma:nest' 'grɑͻza:m 'lɪmɐ(r) lan das, vas lɪç fɛɐ'lo:ɐ. [zi:, di:]
und mahnest grausam immer an das, was ich verlor. [*poem:* **an sie, die ich verlor**]
and remind cruelly always of that which I lost. [her, whom]
(and cruelly always remind me of that which I have lost.) [(...of her whom I have lost.)]

zi: hɛŋt' lan 'laenəm 'landɐn, lʊnt' vo:nt' lɪm 'vaelɐ dɔrt^h.
Sie hängt an einem Andern, und wohnt im Weiler dort.
She is devoted to an other, and lives in the hamlet there.
(She is devoted to someone else, and lives in the hamlet there.)

maen 'larməs hɛrʦ fɛɐ'blu:t'ət', fɔm 'ʃɛrfst'ən pfael dʊrç'bo:ɐt^h.
Mein armes Herz verblutet, vom schärfsten Pfeil durchbohrt.
My poor heart is bleeding to death, by the sharpest arrow bored through.
(My poor heart is bleeding to death, bored through by the sharpest arrow.)

ɪn 'li:rən 'ʃø:nən 'lɑͻgən va:ɐ 'k^haenɐ(r) 'lʊnt^hrɔø ʃp'u:ɐ; ['brɑͻnən]
In ihren schönen Augen war keiner Untreu Spur; [*poem:* **In ihren braunen Augen**]
in her beautiful eyes was no infidelilty's trace; [brown]
(in her beautiful eyes there was no trace of infidelity;)

ɪç za: de:ɐ 'li:bə 'hɪməl, de:ɐ/de:r 'lanmu:t' ʃp'i:gəl nu:ɐ.
ich sah der Liebe Himmel, der Anmut Spiegel nur.
I saw the love's heaven, the grace's mirror only.
(I saw there only a heaven of love, a mirror of grace.)

[ɑͻs 'li:nən ʃp'ra:xən 'li:bə lʊnt' 'hɔldə 'lanmu:t' nu:ɐ.]
[*poem:* **aus ihnen sprachen Liebe und holde Anmut nur.**]
[out of them spoke love and lovely grace only.]

vo'hɪn lɪç mɪç nuːn 'vɛndə— deːɐ̯ tʰʊrm, leːɐ̯ 'fɔlgət' miːɐ̯;
Wohin ich mich nun wende—der Turm, er folget mir;
Wherever I myself now turn— the tower, it follows me;
(Wherever I turn now that bell-tower follows me;)   [*poem:* **wohin ich nun mich wende**]

oː zaːk't' leːɐ̯, ʃt'at deːɐ̯ 'ʃt'ʊndən, vas mɪç fɛɐ̯'nɪçt'ət', liːɐ̯!
o sagt' er, statt der Stunden, was mich vernichtet, ihr!
Oh would tell it, instead of the hours, what me is destroying, to her!
(Oh, if only, instead of telling the hours, it would tell her what is destroying me!)

[This simple, plaintive little song with four musically identical verses is the lament of a lovelorn shepherd. The bell-tower that rises above this country hamlet reminds him, visually and with its chime at every quarter hour, that his sweetheart who lives there is in love with another man.]

deːɐ̯ hɪrt' lɑ̯of dem 'fɛlzən
Der Hirt auf dem Felsen
The Shepherd on the Rock

Op. 129 [1828] (Wilhelm Müller, Helmina von Chézy)

vɛn lɑ̯of dem 'høːçst'ən fɛls lɪç ʃt'eː, lɪns 'tʰiːfə tʰaːl hɛɐ̯'niːdɐzeː, lʊnt' 'zɪŋə,
Wenn auf dem höchsten Fels ich steh', ins tiefe Tal herniederseh', und singe,
When on the highest rock I stand, into the deep valley look down, and sing,
(When I stand on the highest rock, look down into the deep valley, and sing,)

fɛrn lɑ̯os dem 'tʰiːfən 'dʊŋk'əln tʰaːl ʃvɪŋt' zɪç lɛm'pʰoːɐ̯ deːɐ̯ 'viːdɐhal deːɐ̯ 'kʰlʏft'ə.
fern aus dem tiefen dunkeln Tal schwingt sich empor der Widerhall der Klüfte.
far out of the deep dark valley soars itself up the echo of the ravines.
(far out of the deep, dark valley the echo from the ravines comes soaring up.)

jeː 'vaet'ɐ 'maenə 'ʃt'ɪmə drɪŋtʰ, jeː 'hɛlɐ zi: miːɐ̯ 'viːdɐ kʰlɪŋtʰ fɔn 'lʊnt'ən.
Je weiter meine Stimme dringt, je heller sie mir wieder klingt von unten.
The farther my voice penetrates, the clearer it to me again sounds from below.
(The farther my voice carries, the clearer it comes back to me from down below.)

maen 'liːp'çən voːnt' zoː vaet' fɔn miːɐ̯,
Mein Liebchen wohnt so weit von mir,
My sweetheart lives so far from me,

drʊm zeːn lɪç mɪç zoː haes naːx liːɐ̯ hɪ'nyːbɐ!
drum sehn' ich mich so heiss nach ihr hinüber!
therefor long I myself so ardently for her over there!
(for that reason I am so ardently longing for her over there!)

[ɪn 'tʰiːfəm graːm fɛɐ̯'tseːɐ̯/fɛɐ̯'tseːr lɪç mɪç, miːɐ̯/miːr lɪst di 'frɔødə hɪn,
[In tiefem Gram verzehr' ich mich, mir ist die Freude hin,
[In deep grief consume I myself, for me is the joy gone,
[(I am consumed by deep grief; for me all joy is gone,)

ɑ̯of 'leːɐ̯dən miːɐ̯ di 'hɔfnʊŋ vɪç, lɪç hiːɐ̯ zoː 'laenzaːm bɪn.
auf Erden mir die Hoffnung wich, ich hier so einsam bin.
on earth for me the hope retreated, I here so lonesome am.
(for me all hope on this earth has retreated; I am so lonesome here.)

236

zoː ˈzeːnənt‘ kʰlaŋ ɪm valt das liːt‘, zoː ˈzeːnənt‘ kʰlaŋ ɛs dʊrç di naxtʰ,
So sehnend klang im Wald das Lied, so sehnend klang es durch die Nacht,
So longingly rang in the woods the song, so longingly rang it through the night,
(So full of longing did the song ring out in the woods and through the night,)

di ˈhɛrtsən lɛs tsʊm ˈhɪməl ˈtsiːtʰ mɪt‘ ˈvʊndɐbaːrɐ maxtʰ.]
die Herzen es zum Himmel zieht mit wunderbarer Macht.]
the hearts it to the heaven draws with wondrous power.]
(that it draws hearts toward heaven with wondrous power.]

deːɐ̯ ˈfryːlɪŋ vɪl ˈkʰɔmən, deːɐ̯ ˈfryːlɪŋ ˈmaenə frɔøt‘,
Der Fühling will kommen, der Frühling meine Freud',
The spring will come, the spring, my joy;

nuːn max lɪç mɪç ˈfɛrt‘ɪç, tsʊm ˈvandɐn bəˈraetʰ.
nun mach' ich mich fertig, zum Wandern bereit.
now make I myself ready, to the wandering prepared.
(now I shall make myself ready, prepared to go wandering again.)

[This beautiful and famous song was composed as a showpiece with clarinet obbligato (*not* 'cello, as in some editions) for the soprano Anna Milder-Hauptmann, Beethoven's first Leonore/Fidelio. The words were derived from two different poems by Wilhelm Müller (*Der Berghirt*—"The Mountain Shepherd"—for the beginning, and *Liebesgedanken*—"Thoughts of Love"—for the end), with a middle section (in brackets above) attributed to Helmina von Chézy—a middle section with words that seem rather too sad to fit the cheerful tone of the outer verses, but which inspired Schubert to write some glorious music! This song, composed in October 1828, *may* have been Schubert's very last. He did not live to hear it performed.]

Der Jäger see *Die schöne Müllerin*

deːɐ̯ ˈjʏŋlɪŋ am ˈbaxə
Der Jüngling am Bache
The Youth by the Brook

Op. 87, No. 3 [third version, 1819] (poem by Friedrich von Schiller)

an deːɐ̯ ˈkʰvɛlə zaːs deːɐ̯ ˈkʰnaːbə, ˈbluːmən vant‘ leːɐ̯ zɪç tsʊm kʰrants,
An der Quelle sass der Knabe, Blumen wand er sich zum Kranz,
By the spring sat the boy, flowers twined he for himself to the wreath,
(The boy sat beside the spring, he twined flowers into a wreath,)

ʊnt‘ leːɐ̯ zaː ziː, ˈfɔrtgərɪsən, ˈtʰraebən lɪn deːɐ̯ ˈvɛlən tʰants.
und er sah sie, fortgerissen, treiben in der Wellen Tanz.
and he saw them, torn away, drifting in the waves' dance.
(and he saw them, torn away from him, drifting in the dance of the waves.)

ʊnt‘ zoː ˈfliːən ˈmaenə ˈtʰaːgə, viː di ˈkʰvɛlə, ˈrast‘loːs hɪn!
Und so fliehen meine Tage, wie die Quelle, rastlos hin!
And thus flee my days, like the spring, restlessly hence!
(And thus my days rush by, restlessly, like the spring!)

ʊnt' zoː 'blaeçət' 'maenə 'juːgənt', viː di 'kʰrɛntsə ʃnɛl fɛɐ̯'blyːn.
und so bleichet meine Jugend, wie die Kränze schnell verblühn.
and so fades my youth, like the wreaths quickly wilted.
(and thus my youth is fading away, quickly wilted like the wreaths.)

'fraːgət' nɪçt', va'rʊm lɪç 'tʰraorə lɪn dɛs 'leːbəns 'blyːt'əntsaetʰ.
Fraget nicht, warum ich traure in des Lebens Blütenzeit.
Ask not, why I mourn in the life's blossom time.
(Do not ask me why I mourn in the blossom time of life.)

'aləs 'frɔɤ̯ət' zɪç lʊnt' 'hɔfət', vɛn deːɐ̯ 'fryːlɪŋ zɪç lɛɐ̯'nɔɤ̯tʰ.
Alles freuet sich und hoffet, wenn der Frühling sich erneut.
All gladdens itself and hopes, when the springtime itself renews.
(All things rejoice and hope, when springtime returns.)

'aːbɐ diːzə 'tʰaozənt' 'ʃt'ɪmən deːɐ̯/deːr lɛɐ̯'vaxəndən na'tʰuːɐ̯
Aber diese tausend Stimmen der erwachenden Natur
But these thousand voices of the awakening nature
(But these thousand voices of awakening nature) ["*diese*" is missing in Schubert's first version.]

'vɛk'ən lɪn dem 'tʰiːfən 'buːzən miːɐ̯ den 'ʃveːrən 'kʰʊmɐ nuːɐ̯.
wecken in dem tiefen Busen mir den schweren Kummer nur.
waken in the deep bosom to me the heavy sorrow only.
(waken only heavy sorrow in the depths of my heart.)

vas zɔl miːɐ̯ di 'frɔɤ̯də 'frɔmən, diː deːɐ̯ 'ʃøːnə lɛnts miːɐ̯ bɔɤ̯tʰ?
Was soll mir die Freude frommen, die der schöne Lenz mir beut?
What shall to me the joy be of use, which the beautiful spring to me offers?
(What use to me is the joy that the beautiful spring offers me?)

'aenə nuːɐ̯/nuːr lɪsts, diː lɪç 'zuːxə, ziː lɪst' naː lʊnt' 'leːvɪç vaetʰ.
Eine nur ist's, die ich suche, sie ist nah und ewig weit.
One only is it, whom I seek, she is near and eternally far.
(There is only one whom I am seeking; she is near and yet forever far.)

'zeːnənt' braet' lɪç 'maenə 'larmə naːx dem 'tʰɔɤ̯rən 'ʃat'ənbɪlt',
Sehnend breit ich meine Arme nach dem teuren Schattenbild,
Longingly spread I my arms toward the dear shadow- image,
(With longing I stretch out my arms toward that beloved shadowy image,)

ax! lɪç kʰan lɛs nɪçt' lɛɐ̯'raeçən, lʊnt das hɛrts blaep't' lʊngə'ʃt'ɪltʰ! [lɪst']
ach! ich kann es nicht erreichen, und das Herz bleibt ungestillt! [*1812:* **ist ungestillt**]
ah! I can it not reach, and the heart remains unstilled! [is]
(ah! I cannot reach it, and my heart remains unstilled!)

kʰɔm hɛ'rap', duː 'ʃøːnə 'hɔldə, lʊnt fɛɐ̯'las daen 'ʃt'ɔltsəs ʃlɔs!
Komm herab, du schöne Holde, und verlass dein stolzes Schloss!
Come down, you beautiful lovely one, and leave your proud castle!
(Come down, you beautiful, lovely woman, and leave your proud castle!)

'bluːmən, diː deːɐ̯ lɛnts gə'boːrən, ʃt'rɔɤ̯ lɪç diːɐ̯/diːr lɪn 'daenən ʃoːs.
Blumen, die der Lenz geboren, streu ich dir in deinen Schoss.
Flowers, which the spring bore, strew I to you into your lap.
(I shall scatter flowers born of the spring into your lap.)

hɔrç,   deːɐ̯ haen lɛɐ̯ˈʃalt' fɔn 'liːdɐn,   lʊnt di 'kʰvɛlə 'riːzəlt' kʰlaːɐ̯!
Horch, der Hain erschallt von Liedern, und die Quelle rieselt klar!
Listen! The grove resounds with songs,   and the spring ripples limpidly!

rɑ̯om   lɪst' lɪn deːɐ̯ 'kʰlaenst'ən 'hʏt'ə   fyːɐ̯/fyːr laen 'glʏk'lɪç 'liːbənt' pʰaːɐ̯.
Raum ist in der kleinsten Hütte für   ein glücklich liebend Paar.
Room is   in the smallest   hut   for   a   happily loving   couple.
(There is room in the smallest hut for a happily loving couple.)

[Schubert first set this poem in 1812, when he was fifteen and a student of Antonio Salieri. Two and a half years later, he attempted a second version, in the minor mode throughout. The third, the best known of the three, was the only one to be published during his lifetime. All three are printed in the *Gesamtausgabe*, and all three are beautiful, the first, possibly, the loveliest of all.]

deːɐ̯ 'jʏŋlɪŋ lan deːɐ̯ 'kʰvɛlə
Der Jüngling an der Quelle
The Youth by the Spring

Posthumously published [composed in 1821?] (poem by Johann Gaudenz von Salis-Seewis)

'laezə 'riːzəlndɐ   kʰvɛl! liːɐ̯ 'valəndən 'flɪsp'ɐndən 'pʰap'əln,
Leise rieselnder Quell! ihr wallenden flispernden Pappeln,
Softly rippling   spring! You swaying,   whispering poplars,

'ɔøɐ 'ʃlʊmɐgərɔøʃ   'vɛk'ət di 'liːbə nuːɐ̯/nuːr lɑ̯of.
euer Schlummergeräusch wecket die Liebe nur   auf.
your slumber- noises   wake the love only   up.
(your sleepy murmuring only awakens love.)

'lɪndərʊŋ   zuːxt' lɪç bae lɔøç, lʊnt' zi: tsu: fɛɐ̯ˈgɛsən, di 'ʃp'røːdə,
Linderung sucht' ich bei euch, und sie zu vergessen, die Spröde,
Relief   sought I by you, and her to forget,   the obstinate one,
(I came to you looking for relief, and to forget her, that obstinate girl,)

ax, lʊnt' 'blɛt'ɐ(r) lʊnt' bax 'zɔøftsən, luˈiːzə, diːɐ̯   naːx,   luˈiːzə! luˈiːzə!
ach, und Blätter und Bach seufzen, Louise, dir   nach, Louise! Louise!
ah,   and leaves   and brook sigh,   Louise, for you after: "Louise! Louise!"
(ah, and the leaves and the brook are sighing for you, Louise!)

[This is surely one of Schubert's most enchanting songs, a perfect gem. He changed the final words, and the name of the girl, from "*Elisa, mir zu!*" (to me) to "*Louise, dir nach!*" (for you).]

deːɐ̯ 'jʏŋlɪŋ lɑ̯of dem 'hyːgəl
Der Jüngling auf dem Hügel
The Youth on the Hill

Op. 8, No. 1 [1820] (Heinrich Hüttenbrenner)

aen 'jʏŋlɪŋ   lɑ̯of dem 'hyːgəl mɪt' 'zaenəm 'kʰomɐ   zaːs;
Ein Jüngling auf dem Hügel mit seinem Kummer sass;
A   youth   on the hill with his   sorrow   sat;
(A youth was sitting on the hill with his sorrow;)

voːl vart deːɐ̯/deːr ˈɑ̯ogən ˈʃpˈiːɡəl liːm ˈtʰryːpˈ lʊnt ˈtʰreːnənnas.
wohl ward der Augen Spiegel ihm trüb und tränennass.
indeed became the eyes' mirror for him dim and wet with tears.
(indeed, the mirror of his eyes had become dim and wet with tears.)

zaː ˈfroːə ˈlɛmɐ ˈʃpˈiːlən lam ˈɡryːnən ˈfɛlzənhaŋ,
Sah frohe Lämmer spielen am grünen Felsenhang,
(He) saw happy lambs play on the green rocky slope,
(He saw happy lambs gambolling on the green hillside,)

zaː ˈfroːə ˈbeçlae̯n ˈkʰvɪlən das ˈbʊntˈə tʰaːl lɛntˈˈlaŋ;
sah frohe Bächlein quillen das bunte Tal entlang;
saw happy brooklets gush the bright-colored valley along;
(saw merry brooklets gushing through the bright-colored valley;)

di ˈʃmɛtˈɐlɪŋə ˈzoːɡən lam ˈroːtˈən ˈblyːtˈənmʊntˈ,
die Schmetterlinge sogen am roten Blütenmund,
the butterflies sucked at the red blossom-mouth,
(the butterflies were sipping at the red mouths of the flowers,)

viː ˈmɔrɡəntʰrɔ̯ømə ˈfloːɡən di ˈvɔlkˈən lɪn dem rʊntˈ,
wie Morgenträume flogen die Wolken in dem Rund,
like morning dreams flew the clouds in the circle,
(the clouds were circling in the sky like morning dreams,)

ʊntˈ ˈlaləs vaːɐ̯ zoː ˈmʊntˈɐ... ʊntˈ ˈlaləs ʃvam lɪn ɡlʏkʰ,
und alles war so munter... und alles schwamm in Glück,
and everything was so cheerful... and everything swam in happiness,

nuːɐ̯/nuːr lɪn zae̯n hɛrts̩ hɪˈnʊntˈɐ zaː nɪçt deːɐ̯ ˈfrɔ̯ødə blɪkʰ.
nur in sein Herz hinunter sah nicht der Freude Blick.
only into his heart down looked not the joy's gaze.
(but the light of joy did not shine down into his heart.)

ax! ˈdʊmpfəs ˈɡraːpˈɡəlɔ̯øtˈə lɪm ˈdɔrfə nuːn lɛɐ̯ˈkʰlaŋ,
Ach! dumpfes Grabgeläute im Dorfe nun erklang,
Ah! muffled death-tolling in the village now sounded,
(Ah! A muffled death-knell was now tolling in the village,)

ʃoːn ˈtʰøːntˈə lɑ̯os deːɐ̯ ˈvae̯tˈə lae̯n ˈkʰlaːɡəndɐ ɡəˈzaŋ;
schon tönte aus der Weite ein klagender Gesang;
already sounds from the distance a lamenting song;
(already a song of lamentation is sounding from the distance;)

zaː nuːn di ˈlɪçtˈɐ ˈʃae̯nən, den ˈʃvartsən ˈlae̯çəntsuːkˈ,
sah nun die Lichter scheinen, den schwarzen Leichenzug,
(he) saw now the lights shine, the black funeral procession,
(now he saw the gleam of candles and torches, the funeral procession all in black,)

fɪŋ ˈbɪtˈɐ(r) lan tsuː ˈvae̯nən, vae̯l man zae̯n ˈrøːsçən tʰruːkˈ.
fing bitter an zu weinen, weil man sein Röschen trug.
(he) started bitterly ... to weep, because one his Rosie bore. ["*fing an*" = started]
(and he started to weep bitterly, because they were bearing away his Rosie.)

jetst' liːs den zark' man 'niːdɐ, deːɐ̯ 'tʰoːt'əngrɛːbɐ kʰaːm,
Jetzt liess den Sarg   man nieder, der Totengräber kam,
Now let   the coffin one down, the   gravedigger came,
(Now they lowered the coffin; the gravedigger came,)

ʊnt' gaːp' deːɐ̯/deːr 'leːɐ̯də 'viːdɐ, vas gɔt' lɑos 'zɛlbɐ naːm.
und gab der   Erde wieder, was Gott aus   selber nahm.
and gave to the   earth again, what God out of same took.
(and gave back to the earth that which God had once formed from it.)

daː   ʃviːk'   dɛs 'jʏŋlɪŋs 'kʰlaːgə, ʊnt' 'beːt'ənt' vart'   zaen blɪkʰ,
Da   schwieg   des Jünglings Klage, und betend ward   sein Blick,
Thereupon became silent the youth's   lament, and praying became his   look,
(Thereupon the youth silenced his lamenting, and his look became prayerful;)

zaː   ʃoːn lam ʃøːnɐn   'tʰaːgə dɛs 'viːdɐzeːəns   glʏkʰ.
sah   schon am   schönern   Tage des Wiedersehens Glück.
(he) saw already on the more beautiful day the reunion's   happiness.
(he foresaw already the happiness of reunion on the more beautiful day that was to come.)

ʊnt' viː di 'ʃt'ɛrnə 'kʰaːmən, deːɐ̯ moːnt' hɛ'rɑofgəʃɪft',
Und wie die Sterne kamen, der Mond heraufgeschifft,
And as the stars   came,   the moon upward sailed,
(And as the stars came out and the moon was sailing higher,)

daː laːs leːɐ̯/leːr lɪn den 'ʃt'ɛrnən deːɐ̯ 'hɔfnʊŋ   'hoːə ʃrɪftʰ.
da las er   in den Sternen der Hoffnung hohe Schrift.
then read he   in the stars   the hope's   high writing.
(he read the sublime message of hope, written in the stars.)

[The poet was the younger brother of two of Schubert's close friends, Anselm and Josef Hüttenbrenner. No doubt he set the rather conventionally sentimental poem to please them, without any special inspiration, except for the music associated with the funeral procession, and the touching moment when the vocal line breaks with emotion at the words "*weil man...*".]

deːɐ̯ 'jʏŋlɪŋ lʊnt deːɐ̯ tʰoːt'
Der Jüngling und der Tod
The Youth and Death

Posthumously published [composed 1817] (poem by Josef von Spaun)

(Der Jüngling / The Youth)

di 'zɔnə zɪŋk't', loː kʰœnt' lɪç, loː kʰœnt' lɪç mɪt' liːɐ̯ 'ʃaedən,
Die Sonne sinkt, o könnt' ich, o könnt' ich mit ihr scheiden,
The sun   sinks, O could I, O could I   with it depart,
(The sun is sinking; oh if only I could depart with it,)

mɪt' 'liːrəm 'lɛtst'ən ʃt'raːl lɛnt''fliːən, lax 'diːzə 'naːmənloːzən 'kʰvaːlən 'maedən,
mit ihrem letzten Strahl entfliehen, ach diese namenlosen Qualen meiden,
with its   last   ray   to flee,   ah, these nameless   torments to flee from,
(to flee with its last ray, ah, to flee from these nameless torments,)

ʊntʽ vaetʽ ɪn ˈʃøːnrə ˈvɛltʽən ʦiːn! loː ˈkʰɔmə, tʰoːtʽ, lʊntʽ ˈløːzə ˈdiːzə ˈbandə!
und weit in schön're Welten zieh'n! O komme, Tod, und löse diese Bande!
and far away into more beautiful worlds move! O come, death, and loosen these bonds!
(and drift far away into more beautiful worlds! Oh come, death, and loosen these bonds!)

ɪç ˈlɛçlə diːɐ̯/diːr, loː ˈkʰnɔxənman, lɛntʽˈfyːrə mɪç laɛçtʽ ɪn gəˈtʰrɔ̯ømtʽə ˈlandə,
Ich lächle dir, o Knochenmann, entführe mich leicht in geträumte Lande,
I smile at you, O bone-man, abduct me lightly into dreamed-of lands,
(I am smiling at you, skeleton; carry me away lightly into lands I have dreamed of,)

oː kʰɔm lʊntʽ ˈryːrə mɪç dɔx lan, loː kʰɔm!
o komm und rühre mich doch an, o komm!
oh come and touch me do ... , oh come! ["*rühre ... an*" from "*anrühren*" = to touch]
(oh come and touch me, *do* touch me! Oh come!)

(Der Tod / Death)

ɛs ruːtʽ zɪç kʰyːl lʊntʽ zanftʽ ɪn ˈmaenən ˈlarmən,
Es ruht sich kühl und sanft in meinen Armen,
It rests itself coolly and gently in my arms,
(One rests coolly and gently in my arms;)

duː ruːfstʰ! lɪç vɪl mɪç ˈdaenɐ kʰvaːl lɛɐ̯ˈbarmən.
du rufst! Ich will mich deiner Qual erbarmen.
you call! I shall myself of your torment take pity. ["*sich erbarmen*" (reflexive) = to take pity]
(you call me! I shall take pity on your suffering.)

[This poem was obviously inspired by the success of *Der Tod und das Mädchen*, composed the month before, with clear references to the text of that earlier song, and with a similar motif to herald the words of Death. In contrast to the "maiden," the young man is *yearning* for death. This is Schubert's only setting of a poem by his close friend Josef von Spaun. Poem and song were indeed written during a time when suicide was alarmingly common among the young generation, many of whom were depressed by the reactionary suppression of new freedoms that marked the era of Metternich. Though not quite as memorable as the more famous song, this one is both beautiful and moving. Schubert left two versions of death's speech, the second transposed upwards, to match the *tessitura* of the youth's part.]

deːɐ̯ kʰampf
Der Kampf
The Battle

Op. 110 [1817] (Friedrich von Schiller)

naen! ˈlɛŋɐ veːɐ̯d ɪç ˈdiːzən kʰampf nɪçtʽ ˈkʰɛmpfən, den ˈriːzənkʰampf deːɐ̯ pflɪçtʰ.
Nein! länger werd' ich diesen Kampf nicht kämpfen, den Riesenkampf der Pflicht.
No! longer will I this battle not fight, the giant battle of the duty.
(No! I will no longer fight this battle, this gigantic battle of duty.)

kʰanst duː des ˈhɛrʦəns ˈflaməntʰriːpʽ nɪçt ˈdɛmpfən,
Kannst du des Herzens Flammentrieb nicht dämpfen,
Can you the heart's flame- instinct not suppress,
(If you cannot suppress the fiery instinct of the heart,)

zo: 'fɔrdrə, 'tʰuːgənt', 'diːzəs 'lɔpfɐ   nɪçtʰ! gə'ʃvoːrən haːb ɪçs,   ['foːdrə]
so fordre, Tugend, dieses Opfer   nicht! Geschworen hab' ich's, [*poem:* fodre (obs.)]
then demand, virtue, this   sacrifice not! Sworn   have I   it,   [demand]
(then, Virtue, do not demand this sacrifice! I took a vow, once,)

jaː, ɪç haːps gə'ʃvoːrən,   mɪç zɛlpst tsu: 'bɛndɪgən. hiːɐ̯/hiːr lɪst daen kʰrants,
ja, ich hab's geschworen, mich selbst zu bändigen. Hier   ist dein Kranz,
yes, I   have it sworn,   me   myself to restrain. Here   is your wreath,
(yes, I admit that I swore that I would restrain myself. Here is your wreath back,)

eːɐ̯ zae laof 'leːvɪç miːɐ̯ fɛɐ̯'loːrən! nɪm   liːn tsu'rʏkʰ, lʊnt' las mɪç 'zʏndɪgən!
er sei auf ewig mir   verloren! Nimm ihn zurück, und lass mich sündigen!
it be for ever to me lost!   Take it back,   and let me sin!
(let it be lost to me forever! Take it back, and let me sin!)

tsɛɐ̯'rɪsən zae, vas viːɐ̯ bə'dʊŋən 'haːbən! ziː liːp't' mɪç, 'daenə 'kʰroːnə zae fɛɐ̯'ʃɛrtstʰ!
Zerrissen sei, was wir bedungen haben! Sie liebt mich, deine Krone sei verscherzt!
Torn up   be what we agreed to have! She loves me, your crown be forfeited!
(Let our compact be torn up! She loves me, your crown shall be forfeit!)

glʏk''zeːlɪç, veːɐ̯/veːr lɪn 'vɔnətʰrʊŋk'ənhaet' bə'graːbən, zoː laeçt' vi: lɪç
Glückselig, wer   in Wonnetrunkenheit begraben, so leicht wie ich
Blissful,   (he) who in ecstasy-intoxication buried,   as lightly as I
(Blissful is he who, submerged in the intoxication of ecstasy, as lightly as I)

den 'tʰiːfən fal fɛɐ̯'ʃmɛrtstʰ! ziː ziːt den vʊrm lan 'maenɐ 'juːgənt' 'bluːmə 'naːgən,
den tiefen Fall verschmerzt! Sie sieht den Wurm an meiner Jugend Blume nagen,
the deep   fall puts up with! She sees the worm at my   youth's flower gnawing,
(puts up with the precipitous fall! She sees the worm gnawing at the flower of my youth,)

ʊnt' 'maenən lɛnts lɛnt''floːn, bə'vʊndɐt' ʃt'ɪl   maen 'hɛldənmyːt'ɪgəs lɛnt''zaːgən,
und meinen Lenz entflohn, bewundert still   mein heldenmütiges Entsagen,
and my   spring fled,   admires   quietly my   heroic brave   renunciation,
(she sees that my springtime is over, she quietly admires my heroic renunciation,)
                                                                    [*P:* **entflohen** (lɛnt''floːən)]
ʊnt' 'groːsmuːtsfɔl bə'ʃliːst' ziː 'maenən loːn.   mɪs'tʰrɑoə, 'ʃøːnə   'zeːlə,
und grossmutsvoll beschliesst sie meinen Lohn. Misstraue, schöne   Seele,
and magnanimously determines she my   reward. Mistrust,   beautiful soul,
(and magnanimously she determines my reward. Mistrust, beautiful soul,)

'diːzɐ(r) 'lɛŋəlgyːt'ə!   daen 'mɪt'laet' 'vafnət tsʊm fɛɐ̯'brɛçən mɪç.
dieser Engelgüte!   Dein Mitleid waffnet zum Verbrechen mich.
this   angel-kindness! Your sympathy arms   for the crime   me.
(this angelic kindness of yours! Your sympathy arms me for the crime.)

giːp't's lɪn des 'leːbəns 'lʊnlɛɐ̯mɛslɪçəm gə'biːt'ə, giːp't's 'laenən 'landɐn,
Gibt's in des Lebens unermesslichem Gebiete, gibt's einen andern,
Is there in the life's immeasurable   domain, is there an   other,
(Is there in life's immeasurable domain another,) ["*gibt es*" (idiom) = is there]

'ʃøːnɐn   loːn, lals dɪç? lals das fɛɐ̯'brɛçən, das lɪç 'leːvɪç 'fliːən 'vɔlt'ə?
schönern Lohn, als dich? Als das Verbrechen, das ich ewig   fliehen wollte?
lovelier   reward than you? Than the crime   that I forever to flee wanted?
(lovelier reward than you? Than the crime that I wanted forever to avoid?)

tyˈranɪʃəs   gəˈʃɪkʼ!   deːɐ̯/deːr ˈlaen̯t͡sgə loːn,   deːɐ̯ ˈmaenə ˈtʰuːgənt ˈkʰrøːnən ˈzɔltʼə,
Tyrannisches Geschick! Der   einz'ge Lohn, der meine Tugend krönen sollte,
Tyrannical   fate!   The   only   reward that my   virtue   crown   should,
(Tyrannical fate! The only reward that should be my virtue's crown)

ɪstʼ ˈmaenɐ ˈtʰuːgəntʼ ˈlɛt͡stʼɐ(r) ˈlaogənblɪkʰ!
ist meiner Tugend letzter   Augenblick!
is   my   virtue's final   moment.
(will mark the very end of my virtue.)

[This exuberantly dramatic song, with its ironic verbal paradox, was specifically intended for the bass voice (and includes an optional low D at the end). First "Virtue" itself is addressed; then the kind lady. The conflict—the "battle"—is between passion and virtuous restraint, and passion is on the point of winning, thanks to the lady's love, that was won, paradoxically, by the man's former "heroic" renunciation of love for virtue's sake.]

deːɐ̯ ˈkʰnaːbə
Der Knabe
The Boy

Posthumously published [composed 1820] (poem by Friedrich von Schlegel)

vɛn   lɪç nuːɐ̯/nuːr laen ˈføːglaen ˈvɛːrə, lax, viː vɔltʼ lɪç ˈlʊstʼɪç ˈfliːgən,
Wenn ich nur   ein Vöglein wäre, ach, wie wollt' ich lustig fliegen,
If   I   only   a   little bird were, ah, how would I   merrily fly,
(If only I were a little bird! Ah, how merrily I would fly,)

ˈalə ˈføːgəl vaetʼ bəˈziːgən. vɛn   lɪç zoː laen ˈfoːgəl bɪn, darf lɪç ˈaləs, ˈaləs ˈhaʃən,
alle Vögel weit besiegen. Wenn ich so   ein Vogel bin, darf ich alles, alles haschen,
all birds far conquer. When I   such a   bird am, may I all, all snatch,
(I'd beat all the other birds in flying by far. When I am such a bird, I may snatch everything,)

ʊnt di ˈhøçstʼən ˈkʰɪrʃən ˈnaʃən; ˈfliːgə dan t͡suːr ˈmʊtɐ hɪn.
und die höchsten Kirschen naschen; fliege dann zur   Mutter hin.
and the highest cherries nibble; fly then to the mother hence.
(and nibble the highest cherries; then I would fly back to Mother.)

ɪstʼ ziː bøːs lɪn ˈliːrəm zɪn, kʰan lɪç liːpʼ mɪç lan ziː ˈʃmiːgən,
Ist sie bös' in ihrem Sinn, kann ich lieb   mich an   sie schmiegen,
Is she angry in her   mind, can I   sweetly myself against her nestle,
(If she happens to be angry in her mind, I can sweetly nestle against her,)

ˈiːrən lɛrnstʼ   gaːɐ̯ baltʼ bəˈziːgən. ˈbʊntʼə   ˈfeːdɐn, ˈlaeçtʼə ˈflyːgəl,
ihren Ernst   gar bald besiegen. Bunte   Federn, leichte Flügel,
her   seriousness very soon overcome. Bright-colored feathers, light wings,
(and overcome her seriousness very soon. Brightly colored feathers and light wings)

dyrftʼ lɪç lɪn deːɐ̯ ˈzɔnə ˈʃvɪŋən,   das di ˈlʏftʼə laotʼ lɛɐ̯ˈkʰlɪŋən,
dürft' ich in der Sonne schwingen, dass die Lüfte laut erklingen,
might I in the sun flourish,   so that the airs loudly ring out,
(I could flap in the sunlight so that the air would ring out loudly,)

vaes nıçts̯ meːɐ̯ fɔn bant' lʊnt 'tˢyːgəl. vɛːɐ̯/vɛːr lıç lyːbɐ 'jeːnə 'hyːgəl,
weiss nichts mehr von Band und Zügel. Wär' ich über jene Hügel,
know nothing more of strap and bridle. Were I above that hill,
(I would know nothing more of curb or bridle. If I were high above that hill,)

ax, dan vɔlt' lıç 'lʊst'ıç 'fliːgən, 'alə 'føːgəl vaet̯ bə'ziːgən.
ach, dann wollt' ich lustig fliegen, alle Vögel weit besiegen.
ah, then would I merrily fly, all birds far conquer.
(ah, then I would fly merrily and beat all the other birds by far.)

[Schubert has created an endearing little masterpiece here.]

deːɐ̯ 'kʰnaːbə lın deːɐ̯ 'viːgə
Der Knabe in der Wiege
The Baby Boy in the Cradle

Posthumously published [composed 1817] (poem by Anton Ottenwalt)

eːɐ̯ ʃleːft' zoː zyːs, deːɐ̯ 'mʊt'ɐ 'blık'ə 'haŋən lan 'liːrəs 'liːp'lıŋs 'laezəm 'laːt'əmtˢuːk',
Er schläft so süss, der Mutter Blicke hangen an ihres Lieblings leisem Atemzug,
He sleeps so sweetly, the mother's glances hang on her darling's soft breath,
(He sleeps so sweetly; his mother's glances hang on the soft breathing of her darling,)

deːn ziː mıt' 'ʃt'ıləm 'zeːnzʊxtˢfɔləm 'baŋən zoː 'laŋə 'ʊnt'ɐm 'hertsən tʰruːk'.
den sie mit stillem sehnsuchtsvollem Bangen so lange unterm Herzen trug.
whom she with quiet yearning- full anxiety so long under the heart carried.
(whom she carried with quiet, yearning anxiousness so long beneath her heart.)

ziː ziːt' zoː froː di 'vɔlən 'vaŋən 'glyːən lın 'gɛlbə 'rıŋəllɔk'ən halp' fɛɐ̯'ʃt'ɛk't',
Sie sieht so froh die vollen Wangen glühen in gelbe Ringellocken halb versteckt,
She sees so gladly the full cheeks glow in yellow ringlet-curls half hidden,
(She is so glad to see his full cheeks glowing, half-hidden in yellow curls.)

ʊnt' vıl das 'ɛrmçən zanft' hɛ'rʊnt'ɐ 'tˢiːən, das zıç lım 'ʃlʊmɐ(r) 'l‌ɑosgəʃt'rɛk't'.
und will das Ärmchen sanft herunter ziehen, das sich im Schlummer ausgestreckt.
and wants the little arm gently under to pull, that itself in the sleep stretched out.
(and tries gently to tuck under the covers his little arm that he had stretched out in his sleep.)

ʊnt' laes lʊnt' 'laezɐ 'ʃɑok'əlt' ziː di 'viːgə lʊnt' zıŋt den 'kʰlaenən 'ʃleːfɐ laes lın ruː;
Und leis' und leiser schaukelt sie die Wiege und singt den kleinen Schläfer leis' in Ruh;
and soft and softer rocks she the cradle and sings the little sleeper soft in rest;
(and more and more softly she rocks the cradle and sings the little sleeper softly to sleep;)

aen 'lɛçəln 'ʃp'iːlət' lʊm di 'hɔldən 'tˢyːgə, dɔx blaep't das 'l‌ɑogə 'friːt'lıç tˢuː.
ein Lächeln spielet um die holden Züge, doch bleibt das Auge friedlich zu.
a smile plays about the lovely features, but stays the eye peacefully closed.
(a smile plays about the lovely features, but his eyes stay peacefully closed.)

ɛɐ̯'vaxst duː, 'kʰlaenɐ, loː zoː 'lɛçlə 'viːdɐ(r), lʊnt' ʃɑo liːɐ hɛl lıns 'mʊt'ɐlaŋgəzıçt':
Erwachst du, Kleiner, o so lächle wieder, und schau ihr hell ins Mutterangesicht:
Awake you, little one, oh then smile again, and look her brightly in the mother-face:
(When you wake up, little one, oh, then smile again, and look brightly into your mother's face:)

zoː ˈlɑ͜oțˈɐ ˈliːbə ʃɑ͜oțˈ lɛs lɑ͜of dɪç ˈniːdɐ, nɔx ˈkʰɛnəst duː di ˈliːbə nɪçtʰ.
so lauter Liebe schaut es auf dich nieder, noch kennest du die Liebe nicht.
such pure love looks it at you down, still know you the love not.
(it looks down at you with such pure love, though you still do not know what love means.)

balțˈ ˈlaːbɐ lɛrnst duː ziː lɑ͜os ˈliːrən ˈblɪkˈən, lɑ͜os ˈliːrəm ˈhɛrtsən, vɛn lɛs zanfțˈ bəˈveːkˈtʰ
Bald aber lernst du sie aus ihren Blicken, aus ihrem Herzen, wenn es sanft bewegt
Soon though learn you it from her glances, from her heart, when it, gently moved
(Soon, though, you will learn it from her glances, from her heart, when it, gently moved)

fɔn ˈmʏțˈɐlɪçəm ˈfɔlərən lɛnˈțsʏkˈən lan ˈda͜enəm ˈkʰla͜enən ˈhɛrtsən ʃleːkˈtʰ.
von mütterlichem volleren Entzücken an   deinem kleinen Herzen schlägt.
by motherly fuller delight, against your little heart beats.
(by fuller motherly delight, beats against your little heart.)

ʊnțˈ ˈlɛrnəsțˈ   ˈʃpˈraːxə țsuː dɛs ˈhɛrtsəns ˈtʰriːbə,
Und lernest   Sprache zu des Herzens Triebe,
And (you) learn speech to the heart's instinct,
(And you learn speech according to the instinct of the heart,)

țsuˈleːɐ̯sțˈ mɪțˈ ˈʃțˈaməln nuːɐ̯ den ˈmʊțˈɐlɑ͜otʰ,
zuerst mit Stammeln nur den Mutterlaut,
first with stammering only the mother-sound,
(at first by stammering only the sounds your mother makes,)

ʊnțˈ balțˈ nɔx ˈmançəs ˈzyːsə vɔrt deːɐ̯ ˈliːbə, lʊnțˈ vɪrst den ˈda͜enən zoː fɛɐ̯ˈtʰrɑ͜otʰ.
und bald noch manches süsse Wort der Liebe, und wirst den Deinen so vertraut.
and soon yet many a sweet word of the love, and become to the yours so familiar.
(and soon many another sweet word of love, and you will become so familiar with your words.)

ʊnțˈ lɛrnst den ˈtʰɔ͜øgrən ˈfaːțˈɐ(r) lɑ͜ox lɛɐ̯ˈkʰɛnən,
Und lernst   den teuren Vater   auch erkennen,
And (you) learn the dear father also to recognize,
(And you learn to recognize your dear father,)

lʊnțˈ ˈla͜elsțˈ liːm țsuː fɔn ˈda͜enɐ ˈmʊțˈɐ brʊstʰ,
und eilst ihm zu von deiner Mutter Brust,
and hurry to him to from your mother's breast,
(and hurry to him from your mother's breast,)

ʊnțˈ lɛrnst di ˈdɪŋə ˈʃa͜edən   lʊnțˈ bəˈnɛnən, lʊnțˈ fyːlst dɛs ˈdɛŋkˈəns ˈnɔ͜øə lʊstʰ.
und lernst die Dinge scheiden   und benennen, und fühlst des Denkens neue Lust.
and learn the things to distinguish and name,   and feel the thinking's new pleasure.
(and learn to distinguish various things and name them, and feel the new pleasure of thinking.)

ʊnțˈ ˈlɛrnəsțˈ ˈbeːțˈən lɑ͜os deːɐ̯ ˈmʊțˈɐ ˈmʊndə naːx ˈliːrəs ˈhɛrtsəns ˈkʰɪnțˈlɪç ˈfrɔmən zɪn,
Und lernest beten aus der Mutter Munde nach ihres Herzens kindlich frommen Sinn,
And learn to pray from the mother's mouth after her heart's childlike pious sense,
(And learn to pray from your mother's mouth, according to her heart's childlike, pious sense;)

ɛs ˈva͜ezət diːɐ̯/diːr lɪn ʃțˈɪlɐ(r) ˈlaːbənțˈʃțʊndə deːɐ̯ ˈfaːțˈɐ naːx den ˈʃțˈɛrnən hɪn;
es weiset dir in stiller Abendstunde der Vater nach den Sternen hin;
there points for you in quiet evening hour the father toward the stars hence;
(in a quiet evening hour your father will point out the stars to you,)

dɔrtʼ, voː deːɐ̯ ˈfaːtʼɐ(r) ˈlalɐ ˈmɛnʃən ˈvoːnətʰ,
dort, wo der Vater aller Menschen wohnet,
there, where the father of all people dwells,
(up there, where the father of all people lives,)

deːɐ̯ dɪç, lʊntʼ ˈlalə ˈzaɛ̯nə ˈkʰɪndɐ liːpʼtʰ,
der dich, und alle seine Kinder liebt,
who you, and all his children loves,
(a father who loves you and all of his children,)

deːɐ̯/deːr ˈlaləs ˈguːtʼə ˈfɛːtʼɐlɪç bəˈloːnətʰ, lʊntʼ ˈjeːdəm ˈzaɛ̯nə ˈfrɔɐ̯də giːpʼtʰ.
der alles Gute väterlich belohnet, und jedem seine Freude gibt.
who all good paternally rewards, and to each his joy gives.
(who paternally rewards all good deeds, and who gives to everyone his or her joy.)

da ˈvandəlst duː zoː raɛ̯n lʊntʼ froː lɑɔ̯f ˈleːɐ̯dən,
Da wandelst du so rein und froh auf Erden,
Then wander you so pure and happy on earth,
(Then you will live on earth so pure and happy,)

daɛ̯n hɛrts zoː ˈglɔɐ̯bɪç lʊntʼ zoː guːtʼ lʊntʼ vaɛ̯ç! zoː ˈblaɛ̯bə, ˈhɔldɐ,
dein Herz so gläubig und so gut und weich! So bleibe, Holder,
your heart so faithful and so good and tender! Thus stay, lovely one,
(your heart so faithful and so good and tender! Stay like that, lovely one,)

vɪlst duː ˈglʏkʼlɪç ˈveːɐ̯dən, dɛn ˈzɔlçɐ(r) lɪst das ˈhɪməlraɛ̯ç.
willst du glücklich werden, denn solcher ist das Himmelreich.
want you happy to become, for of such is the heavenly kingdom.
(if you want to be happy, for of such is the kingdom of heaven.)

[All nine verses of this pretty lullaby might put the audience to sleep along with the baby. Because of the rests on the last page of the music, none of the verses after the second, except for the sixth ("*und lernst den teuren Vater*"), fits the musical phrases without some alteration of the notation. Schubert provided repeat signs, but did not indicate how many verses should be sung.]

deːɐ̯ ˈkʰøːnɪç lɪn ˈtʰuːlə
Der König in Thule
The King of Thule

Op. 5, No. 5 [1816] (from *Faust* by Johann Wolfgang von Goethe)

ɛs vaːɐ̯/vaːr laɛ̯n ˈkʰøːnɪç lɪn ˈtʰuːlə gaːɐ̯ tʰrɔɐ̯ bɪs lan das graːpʼ,
Es war ein König in Thule gar treu bis an das Grab,
There was a king in Thule utterly faithful until to the grave,
(There was a king in Thule who was utterly faithful even to the grave,)

dem ˈʃtʼɛrbəntʼ ˈzaɛ̯nə ˈbuːlə ˈlaɛ̯nən ˈgɔldnən ˈbɛçɐ gaːpʼ.
dem sterbend seine Buhle einen goldnen Becher gab.
to whom dying his mistress a golden goblet gave.
(to whom his dying mistress gave a golden goblet.)

εs   gɪŋ |i:m   nɪçts   da'ry:bɐ, |e:ɐ̯ le:ɐ̯t' |i:n 'je:dən ʃmɑos;
Es   ging ihm   nichts darüber, er leert' ihn jeden Schmaus;
There went for him nothing above that, he drained it   every feast;
(For him nothing was more highly prized; he drained it at every feast;)

di 'lɑogən 'gɪŋən |i:m   'ly:bɐ, zo: lɔft' |e:ɐ̯ tʰraŋk' da'rɑos.
die Augen gingen ihm   über, so oft   er trank daraus.
the eyes   went   for him over, as often as he drank from it.
(his eyes overflowed with tears as often as he drank from it.)

ʊnt' |als |e:ɐ̯ kʰa:m tsu 'ʃt'ɛrbən, tse:lt' |e:ɐ̯ 'zaenə ʃt'ɛ:t' |ɪm   raeç,
Und als   er kam zu sterben, zählt'   er seine Städt' im   Reich,
And when he came to   die,   counted he his   towns in the kingdom,
(And when he came to die, he counted the towns in his kingdom,)

gœnt' |aləs   'zaenən 'lɛrbən, den 'bɛçɐ nɪçt tsu'glaeç.   ['zaenəm 'lɛrbən]
gönnt' alles   seinen Erben, den Becher nicht zugleich. [GA: seinem Erben*]
granted everything to his   heirs, the goblet not   along with it. [to his   heir (singular)]
(he granted everything to his heirs, except for that goblet.)

e:ɐ̯ za:s baem 'kʰø:nɪçsma:lə, di 'rɪt'ɐ(r) |ʊm |i:n he:ɐ̯,
Er sass beim Königsmahle, die Ritter um   ihn her,
He sat at the royal banquet, the knights around him about,
(He sat at the royal banquet, his knights all around him,)

ɑof 'ho:əm 'fɛ:t'ɐza:lə,   dɔrt' |ɑof dem ʃlɔs |am   me:ɐ̯.
auf hohem Vätersaale,   dort auf dem Schloss am   Meer.
in   lofty   ancestral hall, there in the castle   by the sea.
(in the lofty ancestral hall, there in his castle by the sea.)

dɔrt' ʃt'ant de:ɐ̯/de:r |alt'ə 'tseçɐ,   tʰraŋk' 'lɛtst'ə 'le:bənsglu:tʰ,
Dort stand der   alte Zecher, trank letzte Lebensglut,
There stood the   old drinker, drank last   life's fire,
(There stood the old drinker, drank the last flame of life,)

ʊnt' varf den 'haelgən 'bɛçɐ hɪ'nʊnt'ɐ/hɪ'nʊnt'ɐr |ɪn di flu:tʰ.
und warf den heil'gen Becher hinunter   in   die Flut.
and threw the sacred   goblet down   into the flood.
(and threw the sacred goblet down into the waves below.)

e:ɐ̯ za: |i:n 'ʃt'ʏrtsən, tʰrɪŋk'ən |ʊnt' 'zɪŋk'ən tʰi:f |ɪns   me:ɐ̯,
Er sah   ihn stürzen, trinken und sinken tief ins   Meer,
He watched it fall,   drink   and sink   deep into the sea,
(He watched it fall, fill, and sink deep into the sea,)

di 'lɑogən 'tʰe:t'ən |i:m 'zɪŋk'ən; tʰraŋk' ni: 'laenən 'tʰrɔpfən me:ɐ̯.
die Augen täten   ihm sinken; trank nie   einen Tropfen mehr.
the eyes   did   him sink;   drank never a   drop   more.
(his eyelids lowered; he never drank another drop.)

[This haunting ballad is sung by Margarete, "Gretchen," in Part I of Goethe's *Faust*; she has just
met a handsome stranger, and she softly sings a song to herself while she is thinking about him.
Thule (pronounced 'θju:li in English) is a legendary island, originally imagined to be where the
sun sets, later in the farthest northern seas; the Romans, sailing around Britain, gave the name to

248

the largest of the Shetland Islands; later is was thought to be Iceland. *Both "*seinem*" and "*seinen*" are authentic; the first is found in the *Ur-Faust*, the latter in most later versions.]

deːɐ̯ ˈkʰrɔ͡øt͡st͡suːk̚
Der Kreuzzug
The Crusade

Posthumously published [composed 1827] (poem by Karl Gottfried von Leitner)

ae̯n ˈmyːnɪç ʃtˈeːt̚ ɪn ˈzae̯nɐ t͡sɛl lam ˈfɛnstˈɐɡɪtˈɐ ɡrao̯,
Ein Münich steht in seiner Zell am Fenstergitter grau,
A monk stands in his cell at the window grating grey,
(A monk stands in his cell at the grey window grating,)
      ["*Münich*" is medieval German for "monk" (in modern German: "*Mönch*")]

fiːl ˈrɪtˈɐslɔø̯t̚ ɪn ˈvafən hɛl, diː ˈrae̯tˈən dʊrç di lao̯.
viel Rittersleut in Waffen hell, die reiten durch die Au.
many knight-people in weapons bright, they ride through the meadow.
(many knights in bright armor are riding through the meadow.)

ziː ˈzɪŋən ˈliːdɐ ˈfrɔmɐ(r) lart̚ ɪn ˈʃøːnəm ˈlɛrnstˈəm kʰoːɐ̯, [lɪm ˈʃøːnən, ˈlɛrnstˈən]
Sie singen Lieder frommer Art in schönem ernstem Chor, [*GA:* im schönen, ernsten]
They sing songs of devout nature in beautiful, solemn chorus, [in the]
(They sing songs of a devout nature in beautiful, solemn chorus,)

lɪnˈmɪtˈən fliːk̚tˈ, fɔn ˈzae̯də t͡saːɐ̯t, di ˈkʰrɔø̯t͡səsfaːn lɛmˈpʰoːɐ̯.
inmitten fliegt, von Seide zart, die Kreuzesfahn' empor.
in their midst flies, of silk delicate, the cross- flag aloft.
(in their midst the crusaders' flag, made of delicate silk, flies aloft.)

ziː ˈʃtˈae̯ɡən lan dem ˈzeːɡəʃtˈaːt̚ das ˈhoːə ʃif hɪˈnan.
Sie steigen an dem Seegestad' das hohe Schiff hinan.
They climb at the seashore the tall ship up to.
(At the edge of the sea thy climb aboard the tall ship.)

ɛs lɔø̯ftˈ hɪnˈvɛkˈ lao̯f ˈɡryːnəm pfaːt̚, lɪst̚ balt̚ nuːɐ̯ viː lae̯n ʃvaːn.
Es läuft hinweg auf grünem Pfad, ist bald nur wie ein Schwan.
It moves away on green path, is soon only like a swan.
(It sails away on its green pathway, and soon it seems as small as a swan.)

deːɐ̯ ˈmyːnɪç ʃtˈeːt̚ lam ˈfɛnstˈɐ nɔx, ʃao̯tˈ ˈliːnən naːx hɪˈnao̯s:
Der Münich steht am Fenster noch, schaut ihnen nach hinaus:
The monk stands at the window still, looks them after out:
(The monk is still standing at the window, looking out after them:)

lɪç bɪn, viː liːɐ̯/liːr, lan ˈpʰɪlɡɐ dɔx, lʊntˈ blae̯pˈlɪç ɡlae̯ç t͡suː hao̯s.
"Ich bin, wie ihr, ein Pilger doch, und bleib ich gleich zu Haus.
"I am, like you, a pilgrim after all, and stay I though at home.
("I am, like you, a pilgrim, after all, even though I stay at home.)

dɛs ˈleːbəns faːɐ̯t̚ dʊrç ˈvɛləntʰruːk̚ lʊntˈ ˈhae̯sən ˈvyːstˈənzant̚,
Des Lebens Fahrt durch Wellentrug und heissen Wüstensand,
The life's journey through waves-treachery and hot desert sand,
(Life's journey through treacherous waves and burning desert sand,)

ɛs lɪstʻ jaː lɑox laen ˈkʰrɔøtsəstsuːkʻ lɪn das gəˈloːpʻtʻə lantʻ.
es ist ja   auch ein Kreuzeszug   in das gelobte Land.''
it is after all also a   crusade   into the promised land.''

[The song was written in D major; a publisher had it transposed into E major, as in the Peters edition. There are echoes of more than one song from *Winterreise*, in various phrases.]

deːɐ̯ ˈlaedəndə
Der Leidende
The Sufferer

Posthumously published [composed 1816] (author unknown*)

ˈnɪmɐ tʰraːkʻ lɪç ˈlɛŋɐ ˈdiːzɐ ˈlaedən lastʰ, nɪm den ˈmyːdən ˈpʰɪlgɐ
Nimmer trag' ich länger dieser Leiden   Last, nimm den müden Pilger
Never   bear I longer these sufferings' burden, take the weary pilgrim
(No longer can I bear the burden of this suffering; take the weary pilgrim)

baltʻ hɪˈnɑof tsu diːɐ̯. ˈlɪmɐ(r), ˈlɪmɐ(r) ˈlɛŋɐ   vɪrts   lɪn ˈmaenəm ˈbuːzən,
bald hinauf zu dir. Immer, immer enger   wird's   in meinem Busen,
soon up to you. Ever, ever   narrower becomes it in my   bosom,
(soon up to you. My heart feels more and more constricted,)

ˈlɪmɐ(r), ˈlɪmɐ(r) ˈtʰryːbɐ vɪrt   deːɐ̯/deːr ˈlɑogən blɪkʰ. ˈnɪmɐ   tʰraːkʻ lɪç ˈlɛŋɐ
immer, immer trüber wird   der   Augen Blick. Nimmer trag' ich länger
ever, ever   dimmer becomes the   eyes' gaze. Never   bear I longer
(dimmer and dimmer grows the gaze of my eyes. No longer can I bear)

ˈdiːzɐ ˈlaedən lastʰ. ˈlœfnə miːɐ̯ den ˈhɪməl, ˈmɪldɐ, ˈgyːtʻgɐ gɔtʰ!
dieser Leiden   Last. Öffne mir den Himmel, milder, güt'ger Gott!!
these sufferings' burden. Open to me the heaven, mild, kindly God!
(the burden of this suffering. Open heaven to me, merciful, kindly God!)

las mɪç ˈmaenə ˈʃmɛrtsən ˈzɛŋkʻən lɪn das graːpʻ. ˈlaltsufiːlə ˈkʰvaːlən
lass mich meine Schmerzen senken in das Grab. Allzuviele   Qualen
let me my   sorrows   sink into the grave. All too many torments
(Let me sink my sorrows into the grave. All too many torments)

vyːtʻən miːɐ̯/miːr lɪm ˈlinən.   [ˈlɪnrən] hɪn lɪstʻ ˈjeːdə ˈhɔfnʊŋ,
wüten mir   im   Innern. [*Peters:* Inn'ren] Hin ist jede Hoffnung,
rage for me   in the inside.   Gone is every hope,
(rage within me. Gone is every hope,)

hɪn dɛs ˈhɛrtsəns gluːtʰ. ˈlœfnə miːɐ̯ den ˈhɪməl, ˈmɪldɐ, ˈgyːtʻgɐ gɔtʰ!
hin des Herzens Glut. Öffne mir den Himmel, milder, güt'ger Gott!
gone the heart's fire. Open to me the heaven, mild, kindly God!
(gone is the ardor of my heart. Open heaven to me, merciful, kindly God!)

[In both the Gesamtausgabe and Peters the poem is attributed to Ludwig Hölty; but it has not been found in any of his published works. Schubert left two versions; the second has a different melody to nearly the same accompaniment. It is the first version—probably the more beautiful one—that is printed in the Peters edition. It appeared with the title *Klage* (Complaint) in the songbook of Therese Grob, Schubert's first love; the melody reappeared in the play *Rosamunde*.]

Der Leiermann see *Winterreise*

deːɐ̯ ˈliːbəndə
Der Liebende
The Lover

Posthumously published [composed 1815] (poem by Ludwig Hölty)

bəˈglʏkˈtˈ, bəˈglʏkˈtˈ, veːɐ̯ dɪç lɛɐ̯ˈblɪkˈtˈ, lʊnt ˈdaenən ˈhɪməl ˈtʰrɪŋkˈətʰ,
Beglückt, beglückt, wer dich erblickt, und deinen Himmel trinket,
Blessed, blessed, he who you sees, and your heaven drinks,
(Blessed, blessed is he who sees you, and drinks your heaven, the heaven that you are,)

vɛn daen gəˈzɪçtˈ fɔl ˈlɛŋəllɪçt den gruːs des ˈfriːdəns ˈvɪŋkˈətʰ. [veːm]
wenn dein Gesicht voll Engellicht den Gruss des Friedens winket. [*poem:* wem dein...]
when your face full of angel-light the greeting of the peace nods. [(he) to whom]
(when your face, full of angelic light, nods the greeting of peace.)

aen ˈzyːsɐ blɪkˈ, laen vɪŋkˈ, laen nɪkˈ, glɛntstˈ miːɐ̯ viː ˈfryːlɪŋszɔnən;
Ein süsser Blick, ein Wink, ein Nick, glänzt mir wie Frühlingssonnen;
A sweet glance, a sign, a nod, shines for me like spring suns;
(A sweet glance, a sign, a nod, for me they are like the sun shining in spring;)

den ˈgantsən tʰaːkˈ zɪn lɪç liːm naːx, lʊntˈ ʃveːpˈ lɪn ˈhɪməlsvɔnən.
den ganzen Tag sinn' ich ihm nach, und schweb' in Himmelswonnen.
the whole day think I it after, and float in heaven- raptures.
(the whole day I keep thinking about it, and float in heavenly bliss.)

daen ˈhɔldəs bɪltˈ fyːɐ̯tˈ mɪç zoː mɪltˈ lan ˈzanftˈɐ ˈbluːmənkʰɛtˈə;
Dein holdes Bild führt mich so mild an sanfter Blumenkette;
Your lovely image leads me so gently by soft flower- chain;
(Your lovely image leads me so gently by a soft chain made of flowers;)

ɪn ˈmaenəm larm lɛɐ̯vaxtˈ lɛs varm, lʊntˈ geːtˈ mɪtˈ miːɐ̯ tsuː ˈbɛtˈə.
in meinem Arm erwacht es warm, und geht mit mir zu Bette.
in my arm awakes it warm, and goes with me to bed.
(it wakes up warm in my arms, and goes to bed with me.)

bəˈglʏkˈtˈ, bəˈglʏkˈtˈ, veːɐ̯ dɪç lɛɐ̯ˈblɪkˈtˈ, lʊnt ˈdaenən ˈhɪməl ˈtʰrɪŋkˈətʰ,
Beglückt, beglückt, wer dich erblickt, und deinen Himmel trinket;
Blessed, blessed, he who you sees, and your heaven drinks,
(Blessed, blessed is he who sees you, and drinks your heaven, the heaven that you are,)

veːm ˈzyːsɐ blɪkˈ lʊntˈ vɪŋkˈ lʊntˈ nɪkˈ tsʊm ˈzyːsɐn ˈkʰʏsə ˈvɪŋkətʰ. [veːn]
wem süsser Blick und Wink und Nick zum süssern Küsse winket. [*poem:* wen]
to whom sweet glance and sign and nod to the sweeter kisses signals. [(he) whom]
(he to whom the sweet glance and sign and nod are a signal for even sweeter kisses.)

[A delightful, energetic little song of joy at the sweet look of forgiveness that signals the return of peace after a lovers' quarrel.]

deːɐ̯ 'liːp'lɪçə ʃt'ɛrn
Der liebliche Stern
The Lovely Star

Posthumously published [composed 1825] (poem by Ernst Schulze)

iːɐ̯ 'ʃt'ɛrnlaen, ʃt'ɪl ɪn deːɐ̯ 'høːə,   iːɐ̯ 'ʃt'ɛrnlaen, 'ʃp'iːlənt' ɪm   meːɐ̯,
Ihr Sternlein, still in der Höhe, ihr Sternlein, spielend im   Meer,
You little stars, quiet in the heights, you little stars, playing   in the sea,

vɛn lɪç fɔn 'fɛrnə da'heːɐ̯ zoː 'frɔønt'lɪç lɔøç 'lɔøçtz'ən 'zeːə,
wenn ich von ferne daher so freundlich euch leuchten   sehe,
when I   from afar hither so friendly   you gleam(ing) see,
(when I see you gleaming at me from afar in such a friendly way,)

zoː vɪrt' miːɐ̯ fɔn voːl lʊnt' fɔn 'veːə deːɐ̯ 'buːzən zoː baŋ   lʊnt' zoː ʃveːɐ̯.
so wird mir   von Wohl und von Wehe der Busen so bang   und so schwer.
then grows in me for weal and for woe   the bosom so anxious and so heavy.
(then, for weal and woe, my heart grows so anxious and so heavy.)

[*poem:* **mein** (maen, my) **Busen**]

ɛs 'tsɪt'ɐt' fɔn 'fryːlɪŋsvɪndən deːɐ̯ 'hɪməl lɪm 'flʏsɪɡən gryːn;
Es   zittert von Frühlingswinden der Himmel im   flüssigen Grün;
There quivers from spring   winds the sky   in the liquid   green;
(The sky is quivering in the liquid green, ruffled by the spring winds;)

manç 'ʃt'ɛrnlaen zaː lɪç lɛnt'blyːn, manç 'ʃt'ɛrnlaen zaː lɪç lɛnt'ʃvɪndən;
manch' Sternlein sah ich entblüh'n, manch' Sternlein sah ich entschwinden;
many a little star saw I   blossom out, many a little star saw I   disappear;
(I saw many a little star blossom, I saw many a little star disappear;)

dɔx kʰan lɪç das 'ʃøːnst'ə nɪçt' 'fɪndən, das 'fryːɐ̯ dem 'liːbəndən ʃiːn.
doch kann ich das schönste nicht finden, das früher dem Liebenden schien.
but can I   the loveliest not find,   that formerly for the loving one shone.
(but I cannot find the loveliest one, that formerly shone for this loving man.)

nɪçt' kʰan lɪç tsʊm 'hɪməl mɪç 'ʃvɪŋən, tsuː 'zuːxən den 'frɔønt'lɪçən ʃt'ɛrn;
Nicht kann ich zum Himmel mich schwingen, zu suchen   den freundlichen Stern;
Not can I   to the sky   myself soar,   to search for the friendly   star;
(I cannot soar up to the sky to search for the friendly star;)

ʃt'eːts hɛlt' liːn di 'vɔlk'ə miːɐ̯ fɛrn! tʰiːf 'lʊnt'ən, daː mœçt' lɛs ɡə'lɪŋən,
stets   hält ihn die Wolke mir   fern! Tief unten, da   möcht' es gelingen,
constantly holds it   the cloud from me far! Deep below, there might it succeed,
(the clouds keep it constantly far from me! Down there in the deep water, there I might succeed)

das 'friːt'lɪçə tsiːl tsuː lɛɐ̯'rɪŋən! tʰiːf 'lʊnt'ən, daː ruːt' lɪç zoː ɡɛrn!
das friedliche Ziel zu erringen! Tief unten, da   ruht' ich so gern!
the peaceful   goal to achieve! Deep below, there rested I   so gladly!
(in achieving my peaceful goal! Down there in the depths I would so gladly rest!)

vas viːkˈtˈ liːɐ̯/liːr lɪm ˈlɑ̯ʊlɪçən   ˈʃpˈiːlə, liːɐ̯ ˈlʏftˈçən, den ˈʃvaŋkˈəndən kʰaːn?
Was wiegt ihr   im   laulichen   Spiele, ihr Lüftchen, den schwankenden Kahn?
Why lull   you   in the half-hearted play,   you breezes,   the rocking   boat?
(Why do you lull the gently rocking boat in such half-hearted play, you breezes?)

[*Schubert's MS:* **den wogenden** (ˈvoːɡəndən, rocking) **Kahn**]

oː tʰrɑ̯ɛpˈtˈ liːn lɑ̯ʊf ˈrɑ̯ʊərɐ baːn hɛɐ̯ˈniːdɐ(r) lɪns   ˈvoːɡəngəvyːlə!
O   treibt   ihn auf rauherer Bahn hernieder ins   Wogengewühle!
Oh, drive   it   on rougher   course down   into the waves-tumult!
(Oh, drive it along a rougher course into the tumult of the waves!)

last tʰiːf lɪn deːɐ̯ ˈvaləndən ˈkʰyːlə   dem ˈliːpˈlɪçən ˈʃtˈɛrnə mɪç naːn!
Lasst tief in der wallenden Kühle   dem lieblichen Sterne mich nah'n!
Let   deep in the   undulating coolness to the lovely   star   me   draw near!
(In the undulating coolness of the depths let me draw near to that lovely star!)

[The poem seems to say that the beloved has died and that her heart-broken lover is picturing her as a star in heaven; seeing the stars reflected in the sea, he imagines what it would be like to drown and join at least her reflection. But the music does not match the tragic implication. Perhaps it is only a fantasy on the part of the poet (nevertheless, he lost his sweetheart when she was barely eighteen years old, and died himself while still in his twenties). The accompaniment mirrors the smooth rocking of the boat, with only now and then a passing dissonance.]

deːɐ̯ ˈliːdlɐ
Der Liedler
The Minstrel

Op. 38 [1815?] (Josef Kenner)

giːpˈ, ˈʃvɛstˈɐ,   miːɐ̯ di harf hɛˈrapˈ, giːpˈ miːɐ̯ biˈrɛtˈ lʊntˈ ˈvandɐʃtˈaːpˈ,
"Gib, Schwester, mir   die Harf' herab, gib   mir   Birett und Wanderstab,
"Give, sister,   to me the harp   down,   give to me biretta and   walking stick,
("Sister, take down and hand me my harp, give me my cap and my staff,)

["*Birett*" = "*Barett*" = biretta, a kind of flat-topped cap]

kʰan hiːɐ̯ nɪçtˈ ˈfʏrdɐ ˈvɑ̯ɛlən! bɪn ˈlaːnənloːs,   bɪn nuːɐ̯/nuːr lɑ̯ɛn kʰnɛçtˈ,
kann hier nicht fürder weilen! Bin ahnenlos,   bin nur   ein Knecht,
can   here not   further linger! Am without ancestors, am only   a   vassal,
(I cannot linger here any longer! I am without noble ancestors, I am only a vassal,)

bɪn fyːɐ̯ di ˈleːdlə mɑ̯ɛt ʦuː ʃlɛçtʰ,   mʊs ʃtˈraks fɔn ˈhɪnən ˈlɑ̯ɛlən.
bin für die edle Maid   zu schlecht, muss stracks vo   hinnen eilen.
am for   the noble maiden too bad,   must at once from here   hurry (away).
(I am not good enough for the noble maiden, I must hurry away from here at once.)

ʃtˈɪl, ˈʃvɛstˈɐ,   bɪstˈ   ɡɔtˈloːpˈ nuːn brɑ̯ʊtʰ, vɪrstˈ ˈmɔrgən   ˈvɪlhɛlm ˈlaŋɡətʰrɑ̯ʊtʰ,
Still   Schwester, bist   Gottlob   nun Braut, wirst morgen   Wilhelm angetraut,
(Be) still, sister,   you are, praise God, now bride, will   tomorrow to Wilhelm (be) wed,
(Be still, sister! You are, God be praised, now a bride; tomorrow you will be married to Wilhelm,)

zɔl mɪç nɪçʦ   ˈvɑ̯ɛtˈɐ ˈhaltˈən! nuːn ˈkʰʏsə mɪç, leːpˈ, ˈtʰruːdə, voːl!
soll mich nichts   weiter halten! Nun küsse mich, leb', Trude, wohl!
shall me   nothing further hold!   Now kiss me,   fare, Trude, well!
(nothing shall hold me here longer! Now kiss me, Trude, farewell!)

di:s 'hɛrtsə, ʃmɛrts lʊnt' 'li:bəfɔl, las gɔt den hɛrn bə'valt'ən.
dies Herze, schmerz- und liebevoll, lass Gott den Herrn bewalten."
this heart, pain-   and love-full, let God the Lord   govern."
(Let the Lord God guide this heart, so full of pain and love.")

de:ɐ 'li:dlɐ tso:k' dʊrç 'mançəs lant', lam 'lalt'ən ʁaen lʊnt 'do:nɑoʃt'rant',
Der Liedler zog   durch manches Land, am   alten Rhein- und Donaustrand,
The minstrel traveled through many a land, on the old   Rhine and Danube bank,
(The minstrel traveled through many a land, on the old banks of the Rhine and the Danube,)

vo:l 'ly:bɐ bɛrk' lʊnt' 'flysə. vi: vaet' le:ɐ fli:t^h, vo:hın le:ɐ tsi:t^h,
wohl über Berg   und Flüsse. Wie weit er flieht, wohin er zieht,
surely over mountain and rivers. How far he flees, whither he goes,
(over mountains and rivers. However far he flees, wherever he goes,)

e:ɐ t^hre:k't den vʊrm lım 'hɛrtsən mıt', lʊnt' zıŋt' nu:ɐ zi:, di 'zy:sə.
er trägt   den Wurm im   Herzen mit, und singt nur Sie, die Süsse.
he carries the worm in the heart   with, and sings only Her, the sweet one.
(he carries with him a worm in his heart, and sings only of Her, his sweet lady.)

ʊnt' le:ɐs nıçt' 'lɛŋɐ, nıçt' 'lɛŋɐ 't^hra:gən k^han,
Und er's nicht länger, nicht länger tragen kann,
And he it no longer, no   longer bear   can,
(And when he can no longer bear it,)

t^he:t' zıç mıt' ʃve:ɐt' lʊnt' 'p^hantsɐ(r) lan, den t^ho:t' zıç tsu: lɛɐ'ʃt'raet'ən,
tät sich   mit Schwert und Panzer   an, den Tod sich   zu erstreiten,
puts himself with sword and armor   on, the death for himself to win in battle,
(he puts on his sword and armor, to seek his death in battle,)

ım t^ho:t' lıst' ru:, lım gra:p' lıst' ru:, das gra:p' dɛk't' hɛrts lʊnt' 'vynʃə tsu:;
im Tod ist Ruh', im   Grab ist Ruh', das Grab deckt Herz und Wünsche zu;
in the death is peace, in the grave is peace, the grave covers heart and wishes   up;
(in death is peace, in the grave is peace, the grave covers up the heart and its desires;)

ɑen gra:p' vıl le:ɐ/le:r lɛɐ'raet'ən. de:ɐ t^ho:t' li:n flo:, lʊnt' ru: li:n flo:!
ein Grab will er   erreiten. Der Tod ihn floh, und Ruh' ihn floh!
a   grave wants he   to ride to. The death him fled, and peace him fled!
(he wants to ride to his grave. But death fled before him, and peace fled before him!)

[The minstrel has joined the troops of the Duke; they are maneuvering near his homeland:]

dɛs 'hɛrtso:ks 'banɐ 'flat'ɐt' fro: de:ɐ 'haema:t' gru:s lɛnt''ge:gən,
Des Herzogs Banner flattert froh   der Heimat   Gruss   entgegen,
The duke's   banner flutters happily the homeland's greeting toward,
(The duke's banner flutters happily toward the homeland's greeting,)

ɛnt''ge:gən valt', lɛnt''ge:gən ʃalt de:ɐ 'frɔøndə gru:s dʊrç za:t' lʊnt' valt'
entgegen wallt, entgegen schallt der Freunde Gruss durch Saat   und Wald
toward   comes, toward   resounds the friends' greeting through green crops and forest
(through green crops and forests the greeting of friends comes resounding towards them)

ɑof ˈlalən veːkˈ lʊntˈ ˈʃtˈeːɡən.   daː vartˈ   liːm   ˈlʊntˈɐm ˈpʰantsɐ veː!
auf allen Weg' und Stegen.   Da ward   ihm   unterm Panzer weh!
on all   roads and foot-bridges. Then became for him beneath armor   painful!
(on every road and foot-bridge. Then beneath his armor his heart felt pain!)

ɪm   ˈfryːroːtˈ ɡlyːt   deːɐ̯ ˈfɛrnə ʃneː   deːɐ̯ ˈhaemɪʃən ɡəˈbɪrɡə;
Im Frührot glüht' der ferne Schnee der   heimischen Gebirge;
In the dawn   gleamed the distant snow of the native   mountains;
(The distant snow of his native mountains was gleaming in the dawn light;)

iːm   vaːɐ̯/vaːr, lals tsøːks   mɪtˈ ˈhyːnənkʰraft daˈhɪn zaen hɛrts, deːɐ̯   brʊstˈ lɛntˈraftʰ,
ihm war,   als zög's mit Hünenkraft dahin sein Herz, der   Brust entrafft,
to him was,   as if drew it with giant- power thither his   heart, from the breast wrenched,
(it seemed to him as if, with gigantic power, something were drawing his heart,
                wrenched from his breast, toward his homeland,)

als lɔps liːn hiːɐ̯/hiːr lɛɐ̯ˈvʏrɡə.   daː kʰɔntˈ leːɐ̯s ˈfʏrdɐ nɪçtˈ bəˈʃtˈeːn:
als ob's ihn hier   erwürge.   Da konnt' er's fürder nicht bestehn:
as if it him here   would suffocate. Then could he it further not   endure:
(as if he were suffocating here. Then he could not endure it any longer:)

mʊs   ˈmaenə ˈhaemaːtˈ ˈviːdɐzeːn,   mʊs ziː nɔx ˈlaenmaːl ˈʃɑoən!
"Muss meine Heimat wiedersehn, muss Sie noch einmal   schauen!
"(I) must my   homeland see again,   must Her still once   see!
("I must see my homeland again! I must see Her one more time,)

diː mɪt deːɐ̯ ˈmɪnə ˈroːzənhantˈ laen hɛrts lan ˈjeːnə ˈbɛrɡə   bantˈ,
die mit der Minne Rosenhand ein Herz an jene Berge   band,
who with the love's rose- hand a   heart to those mountains tied,
(who with the rose-like hand of love tied a heart to those mountains,)

diː ˈhɛrlɪçən,   diː ˈblɑoən!   daː   varf leːɐ̯ veːɐ̯/veːr   lʊntˈ ˈvafə vɛkˈ,
die herrlichen,   die blauen!"* Da   warf er Wehr   und Waffe weg,
the glorious ones, the blue ones!" Thereupon threw he military gear and weapon away,
(those glorious mountains, blue in the distance!" Thereupon he threw away all his weapons,)

[*GA does not indicate where the quotation ends; Peters' indication is in error.]

zaen ˈrʏsttsɔøkˈ vɛkˈ lɪns   ˈdɔrnɡəheːkˈ; di ˈliːdɐraeçən   ˈzaetˈən, di ˈharfə nuːɐ̯,
sein Rüstzeug weg ins   Dorngeheg; die liederreichen Saiten, die Harfe nur,
his armor   away into the thorn-thicket; the song-rich   strings, the harp only,
(he threw his armor into a bramble thicket; only the harp, with its strings so rich in songs)

deːɐ̯ ˈzyːsən   ruːm, zaen ˈkʰlaːɡəpsalm, zaen ˈhaelɪçtʰuːm, zɔl liːn tsuˈrʏkˈ bəˈɡlaetˈən.
der Süssen   Ruhm, sein Klagepsalm, sein Heiligtum,   soll ihn zurück begleiten.
the sweet one's glory, his   lament-psalm, his   sacred object, shall him back   accompany.
(to glorify his sweet love, to hymn his lament, his most sacred possession, shall accompany him.)

ʊntˈ lals deːɐ̯ ˈvɪntɐ tʰraːtˈ   lɪns   lantˈ, deːɐ̯ frɔstˈ lɪm lɑof di ˈʃtˈrøːmə bantˈ,
Und als der Winter trat   ins   Land, der Frost im Lauf' die Ströme band,
And as the winter stepped into the land, the frost in the course the streams bound,
(And as the winter came to the land, and the frost stopped the rivers in their courses,)

bə'tʰraːt' leːɐ̯ 'zaɛnə 'bɛrgə, daː laːks, laɛn 'laɛçəntʰuːx fɔn laɛs,
betrat er seine Berge, da lag's, ein Leichentuch von Eis,
set foot he (upon) his mountains, there lay it, a shroud of ice,
(he set foot again upon his mountains; there it lay, his land, a shroud of ice,)

laːks fɔrn lʊnt' 'neːbən 'tʰoːt'ənvaɛs, viː 'tʰɑ̯ozənt' 'hyːnənzɛrgə,
lag's vorn und neben totenweiss, wie tausend Hünensärge,
lay it in front and beside dead-white, like a thousand giant coffins,
(it lay in front of him and next to him, deathly white, the mountains like a thousand giant coffins,)

laːks 'lʊnt'ɐ/lʊnt'ɐr liːm, zaɛn 'mʊt'ɐtʰaːl, das 'grɛːflɪç ʃlɔs lɪm 'laːbənt' ʃt'raːl,
lag's unter ihm, sein Muttertal, das gräflich Schloss im Abendstrahl,
lay it below him, his mother-valley, the count's castle in the sunset ray,
(below him lay his native valley, the count's castle glowing in the last rays of the sunset,)

voː 'mɪla drɪn gə'bɔrgən. glʏk' lɑ̯of! deːɐ̯/deːr 'lalp'ə 'pʰɪlgɐruː
wo Milla drin geborgen. Glück auf! der Alpe Pilgerruh'
where Milla within (was) sheltered. Luck up! the Alp's pilgrim-rest
(in which Milla was sheltered. Good luck! The alpine hostel for pilgrims)

vɪŋk't' 'hɔɤ̯t'ə ruː diːɐ̯/diːr 'lɛrmst'ɐ tsuː; tsor 'fɛst'ə, 'liːdlɐ, 'mɔrgən!
winkt heute Ruh' dir Ärmster zu; zur Feste, Liedler, morgen!
beckons today rest for you poorest one to; to the fortress, minstrel, tomorrow!
(beckons you to rest today, poor tired fellow; tomorrow, minstrel, to the castle!)

ɪç haːp' nɪçt' rast', lɪç haːp' nɪçt' ruː, mʊs 'hɔɤ̯t'ə nɔc deːɐ̯ 'fɛst'ə tsuː,
Ich hab' nicht Rast, ich hab' nicht Ruh', muss heute noch der Feste zu,
I have not rest, I have not peace, must today still to the fortress to,
("I shall have no rest, I shall have no peace, I must reach the castle this very day,)

voː 'mɪla drɪn gə'bɔrgən. bɪst' ʃt'ar, bɪst' blas; bɪn 'tʰoːt'ənkʰraŋkʰ,
wo Milla drin geborgen. "Bist starr, bist blass;" bin totenkrank,
where Milla within (is) sheltered. "(you) are rigid, are pale." (I) am deathly ill,
(where Milla is sheltered."—"You are stiff with cold, you are pale."—"I am deathly ill;)

hɔɤ̯t' lɪst' nɔx maɛn! tʰoːt', gɔt' zae daŋkʰ, tʰoːt' fɪnt' mɪç voːl deːɐ̯ mɔrgən.
heut' ist noch mein! tot, Gott sei Dank, tot find't mich wohl der Morgen.
today is still mine! Dead, God be thanks, dead finds me probably the morrow.
(today is still mine! Thanks be to God, tomorrow will probably find me dead.")

hɔrç 'mɑ̯olgətʰraːp', hɔrç 'ʃɛlənkʰlaŋ, fɔm ʃlɔs he'rap'
Horch Maulgetrab, horch Schellenklang, vom Schloss herab
Hark mule-trotting, hark little bells-sound, from the castle down
(Listen to the sound of mules' hooves, the jingling of little bells; down from the castle)

deːɐ̯/deːr lalp' lɛnt''laŋ tsoːks 'lʊnt'ɐ 'fak'əlhɛlə.
der Alp' entlang zog's unter Fackelhelle.
the alp alongside moves it under torch- brightness.
(along the mountainside comes a torchlit procession.)

laɛn 'rɪt'ɐ fyːɐ̯t', liːm 'langətʰrɑ̯otʰ, fyːɐ̯t' 'mɪla haɛm lals 'zaɛnə brɑ̯otʰ.
Ein Ritter führt, ihm angetraut, führt Milla heim als seine Braut.
A knight leads, to him married, leads Milla home as his bride.
(A knight is leading Milla, now married to him, to his home as his bride.)

bɪstʻ   ˈliːdlɐ   ʃoːn   tsʊr   ˈʃtʻɛlə!   deːɐ̯ ˈliːdlɐ   ʃaʊtʻ,   ʊntʻ zaŋkʻ ɪn zɪç.
Bist   Liedler   schon   zur   Stelle!   Der Liedler   schaut',   und sank in sich.
(You) are, minstrel, already at the place!   The minstrel watched,   and sank into himself.
(Minstrel, you are already there! The minstrel watched, and his spirits sank.) [*"zur Stelle"* = here]

daː   brɪçtʻ   ʊntʻ   ˈʃnɑobətʻ   ˈvyːtʻɪkʻlɪç laen   ˈveːɐ̯vɔlf dʊrçs   gəˈheːgə,
Da   bricht und   schnaubet wütiglich ein   Werwolf durchs   Gehege,
Then breaks and   snorts   furiously a   werewolf through the hunting-ground,
(Then a werewolf breaks through the hunting-ground, snorting furiously,)

di ˈmɑolə fliːn,   kʰaen zɑom zi: tsvɪŋt,   deːɐ̯ ˈʃɛkʻə   ʃtʻʏrtstʰ. veː,   veː!
die Maule fliehn, kein Saum sie   zwingt, der Schecke   stürzt. Weh, weh!
the mules flee,   no   burden them forces,   the   dappled horse falls.   Alas, alas!
(the mules flee, casting off their burdens, the dappled horse falls to the ground. Alas, alas!—)

ˈmɪla zɪŋkʻtʻ loːnˈmɛçtʻɪç* hɪn   lɪm   ˈveːgə. daː   rɪs leːɐ̯ zɪç,   laen blɪts   lɛmˈpʰoːɐ̯,
Milla sinkt ohnmächtig hin   im   Wege. Da   riss er sich,   ein Blitz   empor,
Milla sinks   unconscious down   on the road.   Then tore he   himself, a   lightning up,
(Milla sinks down onto the road, unconscious. Thereupon the minstrel leaped up like lightning,)

[*Schubert's setting accents the second syllable; the first is usually stressed]

[*Peters:* **am** (am, by the) **Wege**]

tsʊm hɔrt   deːɐ̯   ˈhaesgəmɪntʻən   foːɐ̯,   hoːx lɑof des ˈlʊntʰiːɐ̯s   ˈnakʻən
zum Hort   der   Heissgeminnten vor,   hoch auf des Untiers   Nacken
to the protection of the ardently loved one forward, high onto the   monster's neck
(leaping forward to protect the one he ardently loved; high onto the monster's neck)

ʃvaŋ   leːɐ̯ zaen ˈtʰɔørəs ˈharfənʃpʻiːl, das   lɛs tsɛɐ̯ˈʃpʻlɪtʻɐtʻ   ˈniːdefiːl,
schwang er   sein teures Harfenspiel, dass   es zersplittert   niederfiel,
swung   he his   precious harp,   so that it   shattered   fell down,
(he swung his precious harp, so that it shattered,)

lʊntʻ nɪkʻ lʊntʻ ˈraxən   ˈkʰnakʻən. lʊntʻ vɛn   leːɐ̯ ʃtʻarkʻ vi: ˈzɪmzɔn vɛːɐ̯,
und Nick und Rachen knacken. Und wenn er   stark wie Simson wär',
and neck and throat   cracked. And if   he strong as Samson were,
(and injured the neck and throat of the beast. And if he were as strong as Samson,)

ɛɐ̯ˈʃœpftʻ maːkʻ leːɐ̯/leːr lʊntʻ ˈzɔndɐ veːɐ̯   den ˈgrɪmən   nɪçtʻ bəˈʃtʻeːən,
erschöpft mag er   und sonder Wehr   den Grimmen   nicht bestehen,
exhausted may he   and without weapon the enraged one not   overcome,
(exhausted and without weapons he still could not overcome the enraged animal;)

fɔm   ˈbuːzən, fɔm   tsɛɐ̯ˈflaeʃtʻən larm kʰvɪlts   ˈhɛrtsbluːtʻ   ˈniːdɐ,
vom   Busen, vom   zerfleischten Arm quillt's   Herzblut   nieder,
from the breast, from the lacerated   arm gushes the heart's blood down,
(from his breast, from his lacerated arm his heart's blood gushes down,)

ˈliːbəvarm,   ʃiːɐ̯   dɛŋkʻtʻ leːɐ̯ tsuː fɛɐ̯ˈgeːən. laen blɪkʻ lɑof ziː,
liebewarm, schier denkt er   zu vergehen. Ein Blick auf Sie,
love-warm, sheer thinks he   to die.   A   glance at Her,
(warm with love; he clearly thinks he is going to die. One glance at Her, though,)

ʊnt' 'lalə kʰraft' mɪt' 'la̯enmaːl leːɐ̯ tsu'zamənraftʰ, diː nɔx fɛɐ̯'bɔrgən 'ʃliːfə!
und alle Kraft mit einmal er zusammenrafft, die noch verborgen schliefe!
and all strength at once he summons up, which still hidden slept!
(and at once he summons up all the strength that was still left hidden and asleep in him!)

rɪŋt' ʊm den 've̯ːɐ̯vɔlf larm ʊnt' hant', ʊnt' ʃt'ʏrtst' zɪç fɔn deːɐ̯ 'fɛlzənvant'
Ringt um den Werwolf Arm und Hand, und stürzt sich von der Felsenwand
Winds around the werewolf arm and hand, and plunges himself from the cliff
(He winds his arms and hands around the werewolf and plunges from the cliff)

mɪt' liːm ɪn 'ʃvɪndlə 't̪ʰiːfə. faːɐ̯, 'liːdlɐ, faːɐ̯/faːr lɑo̯f 'le̯ːvəç voːl,
mit ihm in schwindle Tiefe. Fahr', Liedler, fahr' auf ewig wohl,
with it into dizzy depths. Fare, minstrel, fare for ever well,
(with the monster into dizzying depths. Farewell, minstrell, farewell forever,)

da̯en 'hɛrtsə ʃmɛrts ʊnt' 'liːbəfɔl, hat' ruː ɪm graːp' gə'fʊndən;
dein Herze schmerz- und liebevoll, hat Ruh' im Grab gefunden;
your heart pain- and love-full, has peace in the grave found;
(your heart so full of pain and of love, has at last found peace in the grave;)

das graːp' lɪst' 'lalɐ 'pʰɪlgɐ ruː, das graːp' dɛk't' hɛrts ʊnt' 'vʏnʃə tsuː,
das Grab ist aller Pilger Ruh', das Grab deckt Herz und Wünsche zu,
the grave is all pilgrims' rest, the grave covers heart and wishes up,
(the grave offers rest to all pilgrims, the grave covers up the heart and its wishes,)

maxt' 'laləs la̯et' gə'zʊndən.
macht alles Leid gesunden.
makes all sorrow healed.
(and heals all sorrow.)

[Schubert's friend, the painter Moritz von Schwind, was inspired by this quasi-operatic ballad to make a series of illustrations. The poet was a fellow student at the Imperial *Stadtkonvikt*, a training school for the Court Chapel Choir, where Schubert made numerous lasting friendships.]

Der Lindenbaum see *Winterreise*

deːɐ̯ 'moːnt'la̯ːbənt'
Der Mondabend
The Moonlit Evening

Op. 131, No. 1 [1815] (Johann Gottfried Kumpf, pseudonym "Ermin")

ra̯en ʊnt' 'frɔ̯ønt'lɪç laxt deːɐ̯ 'hɪməl 'niːdɐ(r) lɑo̯f di 'dʊŋk'lə 'le̯ːɐ̯də;
Rein und freundlich lacht der Himmel nieder auf die dunkle Erde;
Pure and friendly laughs the sky down at the dark earth;
(The sky, pure and friendly, smiles down at the dark earth;)

't̪ʰɑo̯zənt' 'gɔldnə 'lɑo̯gən 'blɪŋk'ən 'liːp'lɪç ɪn di brʊst deːɐ̯ 'mɛnʃən,
tausend goldne Augen blinken lieblich in die Brust der Menschen,
a thousand golden eyes shine charmingly into the breast of the humans,
(a thousand golden eyes shine charmingly into the hearts of human beings,)

ʊnt dɛs ˈmoːndəs ˈlɪçt‘ə ˈʃa͜ebə ˈzeːgəlt‘ ˈha͜et‘ɐ dʊrç di ˈblɔ͜ø͜ə.
und des Mondes lichte Scheibe segelt heiter durch die Bläue.
and the moon's light disk sails serenely through the blue.

a͜of den ˈgɔldnən ˈʃt‘raːlən ˈts͜ɪt‘ɐn ˈzyːsɐ ˈveːmuːt‘ ˈzɪlbɐtʰrɔpf͜ən,
Auf den goldnen Strahlen zittern süsser Wehmut Silbertropfen,
On the golden rays tremble sweet melancholy's silver drops,
(On the golden rays the silver drops of sweet melancholy tremble,)

ˈdrɪŋən zanft‘ mɪt‘ ˈla͜ezəm ˈha͜oxə ǀɪn das ˈʃt‘ɪlə hɛrt͜s fɔl ˈliːbə,
dringen sanft mit leisem Hauche in das stille Herz voll Liebe,
penetrate gently with light breath into the quiet heart full of love,

ʊnt‘ bəˈfɔ͜ø͜çt‘ən miːɐ̯ das ˈǀa͜ogə mɪt deːɐ̯ ˈzeːnzʊxt ˈt͜saːɐ̯t‘əm ˈtʰa͜o͜ə.
und befeuchten mir das Auge mit der Sehnsucht zartem Taue.
and moisten to me the eye with the longing's delicate dew.
(and moisten my eyes with the delicate dew of longing.)

ˈfʊŋk‘əlnt‘ pʰraŋt deːɐ̯ ʃt‘ɛrn dɛs ˈǀaːbənt͜s ǀɪn den ˈlɪçt‘bəzɛːt‘ən ˈrɔ͜ømən,
Funkelnd prangt der Stern des Abends in den lichtbesä'ten Räumen,
Sparkling is resplendent the star of the evening in the light-strewn spaces,
(The evening star sparkles resplendently in the light-strewn expanses,)

ʃp‘iːlt‘ mɪt‘ ˈza͜enəm ˈdeːmant‘blɪt͜sən dʊrç deːɐ̯ ˈlɪçt‘ə ˈdʊft‘gəˈveːbə,
spielt mit seinem Demantblitzen durch der Lichte Duftgewebe,
plays with its diamond flashes through the candles' vapor-web,
(plays with its diamond flashes through the vapor-web of the candles,)
[note: the normal plural of "*Licht*" (Light) = "*Lichter*"; "*Lichte*" = candles]

ʊnt‘ fiːl ˈhɔldə ˈǀɛŋəlskʰnaːbən ˈʃt‘rɔ͜øən ˈliːl͜jən ǀʊm di ˈʃt‘ɛrnə.
und viel holde Engelsknaben streuen Lilien um die Sterne.
and many charming angel-boys scatter lilies around the stars.
(and many charming cherubs scatter lilies around the stars.)

ʃøːn ǀʊnt‘ heːɐ̯/heːr ǀɪst‘ voːl deːɐ̯ ˈhɪməl ǀɪn dɛs ˈǀaːbənt͜s ˈvʊndɐglant͜sə,
Schön und hehr ist wohl der Himmel in des Abends Wunderglanze,
Beautiful and sublime is, to be sure, the sky in the evening's woundrous radiance,
(To be sure, the sky is beautiful and sublime in the wondrous radiance of evening,)

ˈaːbɐ ˈma͜enəs ˈleːbəns ˈʃt‘ɛrnə ˈvoːnən ǀɪn dem ˈkʰla͜enst‘ən ˈkʰra͜ezəː
aber meines Lebens Sterne wohnen in dem kleinsten Kreise:
but my life's stars dwell within the smallest circle:
(but the stars of my life dwell within the smallest circle:)

ɪn das ˈǀa͜ogə ˈma͜enɐ ˈzɪli zɪnt‘ ziː ˈǀalə hɪngəˈt͜sa͜obɐtʰ. [ˈzʏli]
in das Auge meiner Silli sind sie alle hingezaubert. [*GA:* Sylli]
in the eye of my Silli are they all thither conjured.
(they have all been conjured into the eyes of my Silli.)

[Schubert has made a simple, attractive stophic song out of this poem to a girl whose name may have been Silvia (or Sylvia).]

deːɐ̯ ˈmɔrgənkʰʊs
Der Morgenkuss
The Morning Kiss

Posthumously published [composed 1815] (poem by Gabriele von Baumberg)

dʊrç ˈlaɛnə ˈgantsə naxt‘ zɪç naː tsuː zaen, [ˈnaːə]
Durch eine ganze Nacht sich nah zu sein, [*poem:* **sich nahe sein**]
Through an entire night each other near to be, [near to be]
(To be near to each other throughout an entire night,)

zoː hant‘ lɪn hant‘, zoː larm lɪm ˈlarmə ˈvaelən,
so Hand in Hand, so Arm im Arme weilen,
so hand in hand, so arm in the arm to linger,
(to linger so, hand in hand, arm in arm,)

zoː fiːl lɛmˈpfɪndən, ˈloːnə ˈmɪttsutʰaelən, lɪst‘ ˈlaenə ˈvɔnəfɔlə pʰaen.
so viel empfinden, ohne mitzuteilen, ist eine wonnevolle Pein.
so much to feel, without communicating, is a blissful pain.
(to feel so much without putting it into words, that is a blissful pain.)

zoː ˈlɪmɐ ˈzeːlənblɪk‘ lɪm ˈzeːlənblɪk‘
So immer Seelenblick im Seelenblick
So always soul- look in the soul- look
(Thus always each soul gazing into the other)

lɑox den gəˈhaemst‘ən vʊnʃ dɛs ˈhɛrtsəns ˈzeːən,
auch den geheimsten Wunsch des Herzens sehen,
even the most secret wish of the heart to see,
(to see even the most secret wish of the heart;)

zoː ˈveːnɪç ˈʃp‘rɛçən lʊnt‘ zɪç dɔx fɛɐ̯ˈʃt‘eːən, lɪst‘ ˈhoːəs ˈmartəfɔləs glʏkʰ.
so wenig sprechen und sich doch verstehen, ist hohes martervolles Glück.
so little to speak and each other yet to understand, is high torture-full happiness.
(to speak so little, and yet to understand each other, that is a sublime agony of happiness.)

tsʊm loːn fyːɐ̯ di lɪm tsvaŋ fɛɐ̯ˈʃvʊndnə tsaet, dan bae dem ˈmɔrgənʃt‘raːl,
Zum Lohn für die im Zwang verschwund'ne Zeit, dann bei dem Morgenstrahl,
As the reward for the in the constraint vanished time, then at the morning-ray,
(Then, in the light of dawn, as compensation for the time that had perforce to vanish,)

varm, mɪt‘ lɛnt‘tsʏk‘ən, zɪç mʊnt‘ lan mʊnt‘ lʊnt‘ hɛrts lan hɛrts tsuː ˈdrʏk‘ən,
warm, mit Entzücken, sich Mund an Mund und Herz an Herz zu drücken,
warm, with rapture, each other mouth to mouth and heart to heart to press,
(warm, with rapture to press mouth to mouth and heart to heart,—)

oː diːs lɪst‘ ˈlɛŋəlzeːlɪçkʰaetʰ!
o dies ist Engelseligkeit!
oh, this is angelic bliss!

[The original song is printed in the *Gesamtausgabe*; the Peters edition reproduces the first *published* version, from 1850, which was transposed down a minor third, with note values doubled and a shorter prelude. The erotic poem is by "the Sappho of Vienna"; its full title is *"Der Morgenkuss nach einem Ball"* (The Morning Kiss After a Ball).]

260

deːɐ̯ ˈmɔrgənʃtˈɛrn
Der Morgenstern
The Morning Star

Fragment [composed 1815] (poem by Theodor Körner)

ʃtˈɛrn deːɐ̯   ˈliːbə,   ˈglantsɡəbɪldə,   ˈɡlyːənt'   viː di ˈhɪməlsbrɑ̯ɔtʰ
Stern der   Liebe, Glanzgebilde,   glühend wie die Himmelsbraut
Star   of the love,   radiance-creature,   glowing like the heaven- bride
(Star of love, radiant creature, glowing like a heavenly bride) [*"Himmelsbraut"* also = nun]

ˈvandɐst   dʊrç   di ˈlɪçtˈɡəfɪldə,   ˈkʰyndənt,   das deːɐ̯ ˈmɔrgən ɡrɑ̯ɔtʰ.
wanderst   durch die Lichtgefilde, kündend,   dass der Morgen graut.
(you) wander through the light-fields,   announcing that the   morning breaks [*literally* grays].
(you wander through the fields of light, announcing that day is breaking.)

ˈfrɔɪ̯ntˈlɪç   kʰɔmst   duː ˈanɡətsoːɡən,   ˈfrɔɪ̯ntˈlɪç   ʃveːpst   duː ˈhɪməlvɛrts,
Freundlich kommst du angezogen,   freundlich schwebst du himmelwärts,
Friendly   come   you approached,   friendly   soar   you heavenwards,
(You rise with your friendly light, and you soar higher as you fade in the growing daylight,)

ˈɡlɪtsɐnt   dʊrç   dɛs ˈɛːtʰɐs ˈvoːɡən,   ʃtˈraːlst duː ˈhɔfnʊŋ   ɪn das hɛrts.
glitzernd durch   des Äthers Wogen, strahlst du Hoffnung in   das Herz.
glittering through the ether's waves,   beam   you hope   into the heart.
(glittering through the waves of ether, you beam hope into our hearts.)

viː   ɪn ˈʃɔɪ̯məndən   pʰoˈkʰaːlən 'tʰrɑ̯ɔbənpʰʊrpʊr 'muːtˈɪç ʃvɛltʰ,
Wie in schäumenden Pokalen   Traubenpurpur mutig schwellt,
As in foaming   goblets   grape- purple bravely swells,
(As the purple wine rises bravely in foaming goblets,)

zoː dʊrçˈlɔɪ̯çtˈən   ˈdaɛ̯nə ʃtˈraːlən di lɛɐ̯ˈvaxtˈə ˈfryːlɪŋsvɛltʰ.
so   durchleuchten deine Strahlen die erwachte Frühlingswelt.
thus through-radiate your   beams   the awakened spring-   world.
(thus do your beams radiate through the awakened world of spring.)

viː   ɪm   ˈhɛrlɪçən   ɡəˈʃiːbə   zɪç dɛs ˈɡɔldəs pʰraxtˈ fɛɐ̯ˈʃliːstʰ,
Wie im   herrlichen Geschiebe sich des Goldes Pracht verschliesst,
As in the glorious   detritus   itself the gold's splendor locks up,
(As the splendor of gold is locked inside the glorious detritus in the bed of a mountain stream,)

zoː lɛɐ̯ˈɡlɛntstst duː,   ʃtˈɛrn deːɐ̯   ˈliːbə,   deːɐ̯ den ˈmɔrgən   ʃtˈɪl   bəˈɡryːstʰ.
so erglänzt'st du, Stern der   Liebe, der den Morgen   still   begrüsst.
so gleam   you, star   of the love,   who the   morning [object] quietly greets.
(so do you gleam, star of love, who quietly greet the morning.)

ʊntˈ ɛs tʰraɛ̯ptˈ dɪç naːx den ˈʃtˈɛrnən, hɛl   ɪm   ˈdʊŋkˈəl tsuː lɛɐ̯ˈɡlyːn.
Und es   treibt   dich nach den Sternen, hell   im   Dunkel zu   erglühn.
And it drives   you after the stars   brightly in the dark   to   glow.
(And it is your task to glow brightly in the dark after the fixed stars have faded.)

'y:bɐ 'bɛrgə,   'ly:bɐ 'fɛrnən   mœçt'   lɪç 'laenmːl   mɪt diːɐ̯ tsiːn.
Über Berge,   über Fernen   möcht'   ich e i n m a l mit dir ziehn.
Over mountains, over distances would like I   *once*   with you to drift.
(Oh, I would like just *once* to drift with you over mountains and over vast distances!)

fast' mɪç, fast' mɪç, 'haelgə ʃt'raːlən, ʃlɪŋt'   lʊm   mɪç das 'gɔldnə bant',
Fasst mich, fasst mich, heil'ge Strahlen, schlingt um   mich das goldne Band,
Seize me,   hold me,   holy   rays,   loop   about me   the golden ribbon,
(Take hold of me, holy rays! Loop about me your golden ribbon of light,)

das   lɪç laos den 'leːɐ̯dənkʰvaːlən 'fliːə   lɪn laen 'glʏk'lɪç   lant'!
dass ich aus den Erdenqualen   fliehe in ein glücklich Land!
so that I   from the earth- torments escape into a   happy   land!
(so that I may escape from earthly torments into a happy land!)

dɔx   lɪç kʰan dɪç nɪçt' lɛɐ̯'fasən, nɪçt' lɛɐ̯'raeçən — ʃt'eːst' zoː fɛrn!
Doch ich kann dich nicht erfassen, nicht erreichen — stehst so fern!
But I   can   you not   grasp,   not   reach — (you) stand   so far away!
(But I cannot grasp you, cannot reach you: you are so far away!)

kʰan lɪç fɔn deːɐ̯ 'zeːnzʊxt' 'lasən? darf lɪçs, 'haelgɐ 'hɪməlsʃt'ɛrn?
Kann ich von der Sehnsucht lassen? Darf ich's, heil'ger Himmelsstern?
Can I   from the   longing   refrain? May I   it, holy   heaven-star?
(Can I refrain from this longing? *May* I, holy star of heaven?)

[A fragment, five and a half bars long, seems to have been the beginning of a fair copy of a lost original, since both melody and accompaniment are complete as far as they go. By using other music by Schubert and adding an accompaniment for the last few bars, Reinhard van Hoorickx has created a performing edition, privately printed in October, 1972.]

Der Müller und der Bach see *Die schöne Müllerin*

deːɐ̯ 'muːzənzoːn
Der Musensohn
The Son of the Muses

Op. 92, No. 1 [1822] (Johann Wolfgang von Goethe)

dʊrç   fɛlt' lʊnt' valt tsuː 'ʃvaefən,   maen 'liːt'çən vɛk' tsuː 'pfaefən,
Durch Feld und Wald zu schweifen, mein Liedchen weg zu pfeifen,
Through field and forest to roam,   my   little song away to   whistle,
(Through field and forest to roam, to whistle away my little song,)

zoː geːts fɔn lɔrt tsuː lɔrtʰ!
so geht's von Ort zu Ort!
thus goes it from place to place!
(that's how it goes from place to place!)

lʊnt' naːx dem 'tʰak't'ə 'reːgət', lʊnt' naːx dem maːs   bə'veːgət' zɪç 'laləs lan miːɐ̯ fɔrtʰ.
Und nach dem Takte   reget, und nach dem Mass   beweget sich alles an mir fort.
And to   the beat   stirs, and to   the   measure moves   itself all   by me forth.
(And everything starts to move to my beat, and continues moving to my measure.)

ıç kʰan ziː kʰɑom lɛɐ̯'vartʻən, di 'leːɐ̯stʻə bluːm lım 'gartʻən,
Ich kann sie kaum erwarten, die erste Blum' im Garten,
I can them hardly wait for, the first flower in the garden,
(I can hardly wait for them, the first flower in the garden,)

de 'leːɐ̯stʻə blyːtʻ lam bɑom. ziː 'gryːsən 'maenə 'liːdɐ,
die erste Blüt' am Baum. Sie grüssen meine Lieder,
the first blossom on the tree. They greet my songs,

lʊntʻ kʰɔmt deːɐ̯ 'vıntʻɐ 'viːdɐ, zıŋ lıç nɔx 'jeːnən tʰrɑom.
und kommt der Winter wieder, sing ich noch jenen Traum.
and comes the winter again, sing I still that dream.
(and when the winter comes again I still am singing that dream of them.)

ıç zıŋ liːn lın deːɐ̯ 'vaetʻə, lɑof 'laezəs lɛŋ lʊntʻ 'braetʻə,
Ich sing ihn in der Weite, auf Eises Läng' und Breite,
I sing it in the distance, on ice's length and breadth,
(I sing it in distant places, from one end of the icy landscape to the other,)

daː blyːt deːɐ̯ 'vıntʻɐ ʃøːn! lɑox 'diːzə 'blyːtʻə 'ʃvındətʻ,
da blüht der Winter schön! Auch diese Blüte schwindet,
then blooms the winter beautifully! Also this blossom disappears,
(then the winter blooms, becomes beautiful! This blossom too disappears,)

lʊntʻ 'nɔøə 'frɔødə 'fındətʻ zıç lɑof bə'bɑotʻən høːn.
und neue Freude findet sich auf bebauten Höhn.
and new joy finds itself on cultivated heights.
(and new joy is found on cultivated hillsides.)

dɛn viː lıç bae deːɐ̯ 'lındə das 'jʊŋə 'fœlkʻçən 'fındə,
Denn wie ich bei der Linde das junge Völkchen finde,
Then as I by the linden tree the young folk find,
(Then, when I find young folk by the linden tree,)

zo'glaeç lɛɐ̯'reːg ıç ziː. deːɐ̯ 'ʃtʻʊmpfə 'bʊrʃə bleːtʻ zıç,
sogleich erreg' ich sie. Der stumpfe Bursche bläht sich,
at once excite I them. The dull fellow puffs up himself,
(I at once excite them. The dull fellow puffs himself up,)

das 'ʃtʻaefə 'mɛːtʻçən dreːtʻ zıç naːx 'maenɐ melo'diː.
das steife Mädchen dreht sich nach meiner Melodie.
the stiff girl turns herself to my melody.
(the awkward girl starts to dance to my melody.)

iːɐ̯ geːpʻt den 'zoːlən 'flyːgəl
Ihr gebt den Sohlen Flügel
You give the soles wings
(You give wings to one's feet)

lʊntʻ tʰraepʻt dʊrç tʰaːl lʊntʻ 'hyːgəl den 'liːpʻlıŋ vaet fɔn hɑos.
und treibt durch Tal und Hügel den Liebling weit von Haus.
and drive through dale and hill the darling far from home.
(and drive your darling far from home, over hill and dale.)

liːɐ̯ 'liːbən, 'hɔldən 'muːzən,
Ihr lieben, holden Musen,
You dear,   gracious Muses,

van ruː lɪç liːɐ̯/liːr lam   'buːzən lɑ̯ox 'lɛntʰlɪç 'viːdɐ(r) lɑ̯os?
wann ruh' ich ihr   am   Busen auch endlich wieder aus?
when rest I   to her on the bosom also at last   again   out?
(when shall I at last again be able also to rest on her bosom?)

                    ["*ausruhen*" = to rest (particularly after strenuous activity)]

[In the last lines Goethe playfully asks the immortal muses to give him a little rest so that he can enjoy his less ethereal lady love a little, before he is off again on the eternal wanderings his career as a poet demands. This famous song also never rests. Schubert too, like Goethe, was kept constantly busy by the muses (but with little love to distract him from the tasks they imposed).]

Der Neugierige see *Die schöne Müllerin*

deːɐ̯ 'pʰɪlɡrɪm
Der Pilgrim
The Pilgrim

Op. 37, No. 1 [1823] (Friedrich von Schiller)

nɔx lɪn 'mae̯nəs 'leːbəns 'lɛntsə   vaːɐ̯/vaːr lɪç, lʊntʰ lɪç 'vandɐtʰ lɑ̯os,
Noch in meines Lebens Lenze   war   ich, und ich wandert' aus,
Still in   my   life's springtime was   I,   and I   wandered out,
(I was still in the springtime of my life, and I wandered forth,)

ʊnt deːɐ̯ 'juːɡəntʰ 'froːə 'tʰɛntsə liːs   lɪç lɪn dɛs 'faːtʰɐs hɑ̯os.
und der Jugend frohe Tänze liess ich in des Vaters Haus.
and the youth's happy dances left I   in the father's house.
(and I left behind in my father's house the happy dances of youth.)

al mae̯n 'lɛrpʰtʰae̯l, 'mae̯nə 'haːbə   varf lɪç 'frøːlɪç   'ɡlɑ̯obəntʰ hɪn,
All mein Erbteil,   meine Habe   warf ich fröhlich glaubend hin,
All my   inheritance, my   possessions tossed I   cheerfully believing away,
(In cheerful faith I tossed away all my inheritance and all my possessions,)

lʊntʰ lam   'lae̯çtʰən 'pʰɪlɡɐʃtʰaːbə tsoːkʰ lɪç fɔrtʰ mɪtʰ 'kʰɪndəzɪn.
und am   leichten Pilgerstabe   zog ich fort mit Kindersinn.
and with the light   pilgrim's staff set   I   forth with childlike mind.
(and, with a childlike mind, set forth with a light pilgrim's staff.)

dɛn mɪç tʰriːpʰ lae̯n 'mɛçtʰɪç 'hɔfən lʊntʰ lae̯n 'dʊŋkʰləs 'ɡlɑ̯obənsvɔrtʰ,
Denn mich trieb ein mächtig Hoffen und ein   dunkles Glaubenswort,
For   me   drove a   mighty hoping and a   dark   faith-   word,
(For a mighty hope drove me on, and a mysterious word of faith:)

'vandlə, riːfs,   deːɐ̯ veːkʰ lɪstʰ 'lɔfən, 'lɪmɐ naːx dem 'lɑ̯ofɡaŋ fɔrtʰ,
"Wandle," rief's, "der Weg ist offen, immer nach dem Aufgang fort,
"Wander," called it, "the way is open, always toward the sunrise   forth,
("Wander," it called, "the way is open, always head toward the rising sun,)

bɪs tsu: 'laenɐ 'gɔldnən 'pfɔrt'ən du: gə'laŋst, da: geːst du: laen,
bis zu einer goldnen Pforten du gelangst, da gehst du ein,
until at a golden gate you reach, there go you in,
(until you reach a golden gate; there you will enter,)

dɛn das 'ɪrdɪʃə vɪrt 'dɔrtən 'hɪmlɪʃ lʊnˈfɛɐ̯ˈgɛŋlɪç zaen. ['leːvɪç]
denn das Irdische wird dorten himmlisch unvergänglich sein." [*Peters:* **ewig unvergänglich**]
for the earthly will there celestially imperishable be." [eternally]
(for there that which is earthly will become eternally imperishable.")

'laːbənt' varts lʊnt' 'vʊrdə 'mɔrgən, 'nɪmɐ, 'nɪmɐ ʃt'ant' lɪç ʃt'ɪl;
Abend ward's und wurde Morgen, nimmer, nimmer stand ich still;
Evening became it and became morning, never, never stood I still;
(Evening would come and morning would follow; never, never did I stand still;)

'laːbɐ(r) 'lɪmɐ bliːps fɛɐ̯ˈbɔrgən, vas lɪç 'zuːxə, vas lɪç vɪl.
aber immer blieb's verborgen, was ich suche, was ich will.
but always remained it hidden, what I seek, what I want.
(but always it remained hidden, what I am looking for, what I want.)

'bɛrgə 'laːgən miːɐ̯/miːr lɪm 'veːgə, 'ʃt'røːmə 'hɛmt'ən 'maenən fuːs,
Berge lagen mir im Wege, Ströme hemmten meinen Fuss,
Mountains lay for me in the way, rivers obstructed my foot,
(Mountains lay in my way, rivers obstructed my step,)

'lyːbɐ 'ʃlʏndə baot' lɪç 'ʃt'eːgə, 'brʏk'ən dʊrç den 'vɪldən flʊs.
über Schlünde baut ich Stege, Brücken durch den wilden Fluss.
over chasms built I foot-bridges, bridges across the wild river.
(I built bridges over chasms and across the wild river.)

ʊnt tsu: 'laenəs ʃt'roːms gəˈʃt'aːdən kʰaːm lɪç, deːɐ̯ naːx 'mɔrgən flɔs;
Und zu eines Stroms Gestaden kam ich, der nach Morgen floss;
And to a river's banks came I, which toward morning flowed;
(And I came to the banks of a river that flowed toward the east;)

froː fɛɐ̯ˈtʰrɑɔənt' 'zaenəm 'faːdən, varf lɪç mɪç lɪn 'zaenən ʃoːs.
froh vertrauend seinem Faden, warf ich mich in seinen Schoss.
joyfully trusting to its thread, threw I myself into its bosom.
(joyfully trusting in its current—Ariadne's thread to me—I threw myself upon its bosom.)

hɪn tsu: 'laenəm 'groːsən 'meːrə tʰriːp' mɪç 'zaenɐ 'vɛlən ʃp'iːl:
Hin zu einem grossen Meere trieb mich seiner Wellen Spiel:
Away to a great sea drove me its waves' play:
(The play of its waves carried me to a great sea:)

foːɐ̯ miːɐ̯ liːk'ts lɪn 'vaet'ɐ 'leːrə, 'nɛːɐ bɪn lɪç nɪçt dem tsiːl.
vor mir liegt's in weiter Leere, näher bin ich nicht dem Ziel.
before me lies it in vast emptiness, nearer am I not to the goal.
(it lies before me in its vast emptiness; I am no nearer to my goal.)

ax, kʰaen veːk' vɪl 'daːhɪn 'fyːrən, lax, deːɐ̯ 'hɪməl 'lyːbɐ miːɐ̯ [ʃt'eːk']
Ach, kein Weg will dahin führen, ach, der Himmel über mir [*Schiller:* **kein Steg**]
Ah, no way will thither lead, ah, the heaven above me [foot-bridge]
(Ah, no way will lead me there; heaven, up above me,)

vɪl di 'leːɐ̯də nɪçt' bə'ryːrən, ʊnt das dɔrt' ɪst' 'niːmaːls hiːɐ!
will die Erde nicht berühren, und das Dort ist niemals Hier!
will the earth not touch, and the There is never Here!
(will not touch the earth, and the There is never Here!)

[The poem marvelously suggests the inscrutably mysterious relationship between earth and heaven, the quest that for the poet had no end other than a confrontation with a vast void. For the most part Schubert's pilgrim plods along, until the impressive moment when his journey ends on the shore of that shipless sea. The *ff* final chords, after an awed hush, suggest violent frustration.]

deːɐ̯ 'rat'ənfɛŋɐ
Der Rattenfänger
The Rat-catcher

Posthumously published [composed 1815] (poem by Johann Wolfgang von Goethe)

ɪç bɪn deːɐ̯ 'voːlbəkʰant'ə 'zɛŋɐ, deːɐ̯ 'fiːlgəra̯est'ə 'rat'ənfɛŋɐ,
Ich bin der wohlbekannte Sänger, der vielgereiste Rattenfänger,
I am the well-known singer, the much-traveled rat- catcher,

deːn 'diːzə 'alt'bəryːmt'ə ʃt'at' gə'vɪs bə'zɔndɐs 'nøːt'ɪç hatʰ.
den diese altberühmte Stadt gewiss besonders nötig hat.
whom this old-famed town certainly especially necessary has.
(of whom this famous old town certainly has special need.)

ʊnt' 'vɛːrəns 'rat'ən nɔx zoː 'fiːlə, ʊnt' 'vɛːrən 'viːzəl mɪt' ɪm 'ʃp'iːlə,
Und wären's Ratten noch so viele, und wären Wiesel mit im Spiele,
And were there rats ever so many, and were weasels with in the game,
(And however many rats there may be, and even if weasels are also in the game,)

fɔn 'lalən 'zɔɥb- rɪç 'diːzən lɔrtʰ, ziː 'mʏsən mɪt' la̯e'nandɐ fɔrtʰ.
von allen säubr' ich diesen Ort, sie müssen mit einander fort.
of all rid I this place, they must with one another away.
(I shall rid this place of all of them, they must all disappear together.)

dan lɪst deːɐ̯ guːt' gə'la͡͡ont'ə 'zɛŋɐ mɪt''ʊnt'ɐ(r) la͡͡ox la̯en 'kʰɪndɐfɛŋɐ,
Dann ist der gut gelaunte Sänger mitunter auch ein Kinderfänger,
Then is the good-humored singer at times also a children-catcher,
(Then, besides, the good-humored singer is also at times a child-catcher,)

deːɐ̯ zɛlpst di 'vɪldəst'ən bə't͡svɪŋt', vɛn leːɐ̯ di 'gɔldnən 'mɛːɐ̯çən zɪŋtʰ.
der selbst die wildesten bezwingt, wenn er die goldnen Märchen singt.
who even the wildest tames, when he the golden tales sings.
(who can tame even the wildest ones when he sings his golden tales.)

ʊnt' 'vɛːrən 'kʰaːbən nɔx zoː 'tʰrʊt͡sɪç, ʊnt' 'vɛːrən 'mɛːt'çən nɔx zoː 'ʃt'ʊt͡sɪç,
Und wären Knaben noch so trutzig, und wären Mädchen noch so stutzig,
And were boys ever so defiant, and were girls ever so perplexed,
(And however defiant the boys may be, and however perplexed the girls,)

ɪn 'me̯nə 'za͡et'ən gra̯ef ɪç la̯en, ziː 'mʏsən 'lalə hɪnt'ɐ'dra͡en.
in meine Saiten greif' ich ein, sie müssen alle hinterdrein.
in my strings grasp I into, they must all (follow) behind.
(when I pluck my strings, they all must follow me.)

dan ɪst deːɐ̯ ˈfiːlgəvantʼə ˈzɛŋɐ ɡəˈleːɡəntʼlɪç l̯aen ˈmɛːtʼçənfɛŋɐ: [nɪçtʼ ˈzɛltʼən l̯aox]
Dann ist der vielgewandte Sänger gelegentlich ein Mädchenfänger: [nicht selten auch]*
Then is the very versatile singer occasionally a girl- catcher: [not seldom also]
(Then, too, this very versatile singer is occasionally also a girl-catcher:)

> [*GA and Goethe's poem:* gelegentlich; *Peters:* nicht selten auch]

ɪn ˈkʰaenəm ˈʃtʼɛːtʼçən l̯aŋtʼ leːɐ̯/leːr l̯an, voː leːɐ̯s nɪçtʼ ˈmançɐ(r) l̯aŋəˈtʰaːn.
in keinem Städtchen langt er an, wo er's nicht mancher angetan.
in no little town arrives he at, where he it not to many a one (has) charmed.
(he never comes to any town where he does not charm quite a few of them.)

ʊntʼ ˈvɛːrən ˈmɛːtʼçən nɔx zoː ˈbløːdə, l̯ʊntʼ ˈvɛːrən ˈvaebɐ nɔx zoː ˈʃpʼrøːdə,
Und wären Mädchen noch so blöde, und wären Weiber noch so spröde,
And were girls ever so bashful, and were women ever so prudish,
(And however bashful the girls, however prudish the women may be,)]

> [*variant, in the Peters edition (Goethe's original poem as in* Gesamtausgabe):
> ʊntʼ ˈvɛːrən ˈfraoən nɔx zoː ˈʃpʼrøːdə, l̯ʊntʼ ˈvɛːrən ˈmɛːtʼçən nɔx zoː ˈbløːdə,
> **Und wären Frauen noch so spröde, und wären Mädchen noch so blöde,**
> And were women ever so prudish, and were girls ever so bashful,
> (And however prudish the women, however bashful the girls may be,)]

dɔx ˈl̯alən vɪrtʼ zoː ˈliːbəbaŋ, bae ˈtsaobɐzaetʼən l̯ʊntʼ ɡəˈzaŋ.
doch allen wird so liebebang, bei Zaubersaiten und Gesang.
still to all becomes so lovesick, at magic strings and song.
(still they all become so lovesick at the sound of my magic strings and my song.)

[Goethe's version of the "Pied Piper" story, which gives the "piper" a harp instead, was also set by Hugo Wolf. Schubert's version is much simpler, jaunty and "good-humored" (as the singer describes himself), with no sinister hints in the music, except perhaps those *acciaccature* in the accompaniment which in other contexts have sometimes suggested a devilish humor. Schubert originally wrote the song in G major; the first publisher transposed it one tone higher, as in the Peters edition, adding a four-bar introduction, which may or may not have been Schubert's idea.]

deːɐ̯ ˈzɛŋɐ
Der Sänger
The Singer

Op. 117 [1815] (Johann Wolfgang von Goethe)

vas høːɐ̯/høːr l̯ıç ˈdraosən foːɐ̯ dem tʰoːɐ̯, vas l̯aof deːɐ̯ ˈbrʏkʼə ˈʃalən?
"Was hör' ich draussen vor dem Tor, was auf der Brücke shallen?
"What hear I outside before the gate, what on the bridge sound(ing)?
("What do I hear outside the gate, what do I hear sounding on the bridge?)

las den ɡəˈzaŋ foːɐ̯/foːr l̯ʊnzɐm l̯oːɐ̯/loːr l̯ım ˈzaːlə ˈviːdɐhalən!
Lass den Gesang vor unserm Ohr im Saale widerhallen!"
Let the song before our ear in the hall echo!"
(Let the song echo in our ears through the hall!")

deːɐ̯ ˈkʰøːnɪç ʃpʻraːxs, deːɐ̯ ˈpʰaːʒə liːf, deːɐ̯ ˈpʰaːʒə kʰaːm, deːɐ̯ ˈkʰøːnɪç riːf:
Der König sprach's, der Page lief, der Page kam, der König rief:
The king spoke it, the page ran; the page came, the king called:
(Thus spoke the king, the page ran out; the page came back, the king cried:)
[*poem:* **der Knabe** (ˈkʰnaːbə, boy) **kam**]

lastʻ miːɐ̯ hɛˈraen den ˈlaltʻən! gəˈgryːsətʻ zaetʻ miːɐ̯/miːr, ˈleːdlə hɛrn,
"Lasst mir herein den Alten!"— "Gegrüsset seid mir, edle Herrn,
"Let to me in the old one!"—"Greeted be to me, noble lords,
("Let the old man enter!"—"I greet you, noble lords,)

gəˈgryːstʻ liːɐ̯ ˈʃøːnən ˈdaːmən! vɛlç ˈraeçɐ ˈhɪməl! ʃtʻɛrn bae ʃtʻɛrn!
gegrüsst ihr schönen Damen! Welch' reicher Himmel! Stern bei Stern!
greeted you lovely ladies! What rich heaven! Star upon star!
(I greet you, lovely ladies! What a rich heaven! Star upon star!)
[*poem:* **gegrüsst ihr, schöne** (ˈʃøːnə) **Damen!**]

veːɐ̯ ˈkʰɛnətʻ ˈliːrə ˈnaːmən? lɪm zaːl fɔl pʰraxtʻ lʊntʻ ˈhɛrlɪçkʰaetʻ
Wer kennet ihre Namen? Im Saal voll Pracht und Herrlichkeit
Who knows their names? In the hall full of splendor and glory
(Who can name them all? In this hall full of splendor and glory)

ʃliːstʻ, ˈlaogən, lɔøç, hiːɐ̯/hiːr lɪstʻ nɪçt tsaetʻ, zɪç ˈʃtaonənt tsuː lɛɐ̯ˈgœtsən.
schliesst, Augen, euch, hier ist nicht Zeit, sich staunend zu ergötzen."
close, eyes, yourselves, here is not time, oneself marveling to enjoy."
(close, my eyes; now is not the time to enjoy oneself in marveling.")

deːɐ̯ ˈzɛŋɐ drʏkʻt di ˈlaogən laen, lʊntʻ ʃluːkʻ lɪn ˈvɔlən ˈtʰøːnən;
Der Sänger drückt' die Augen ein, und schlug in vollen Tönen;
The singer pressed the eyes closed, and sang in full tones;
(The singer pressed his eyes closed, and sang in full tones;) ["*schlagen*" (here) = to sing (birds)]

di ˈrɪtʻɐ ˈʃaotʻən ˈmuːtʻɪç draen, lʊntʻ lɪn den ʃoːs di ˈʃøːnən.
die Ritter schauten mutig drein, und in den Schoss die Schönen.
the knights looked valiantly on, and in the lap the lovely ones.
(the knights watched him gallantly, and the lovely ladies looked modestly down at their laps.)

deːɐ̯ ˈkʰøːnɪç, deːm lɛs voːl gəˈfiːl, [deːm das liːtʻ gəˈfiːl]
Der König, dem es wohl gefiel, [*GA:* **dem das Lied gefiel** (Goethe's later version)]
The king, whom it well pleased [whom the song pleased]
(The king, whom the song well pleased,)

liːs, liːn tsuː ˈleːrən fyːɐ̯ zaen ʃpʻiːl, [liːs, liːn tsuː ˈloːnən]
liess, ihn zu ehren für sein Spiel, [*GA:* **liess, ihn zu lohnen** (Goethe wrote *ehren*)]
let, him to honor for his playing, [let, him to reward]
(to honor [reward] him for his playing, had)

ˈlaenə ˈgɔldnə ˈkʰɛtʻə ˈhoːlən. di ˈgɔldnə ˈkʰɛtʻə giːpʻ miːɐ̯ nɪçtʰ,
eine goldne Kette holen. "Die goldne Kette gib mir nicht,
a gold chain (be) brought. "The gold chain give me not,
(a gold chain be brought. "Do not give me the gold chain;)

268

di ˈkʰɛtˈə giːpˈ den ˈrɪtˈɐn, foːɐ̯ ˈdeːrən ˈkʰyːnəm ˈlangəzɪçt
die Kette gib den Rittern, vor deren kühnem Angesicht
the chain give to the knights, before whose bold countenance
(give the chain to the knights, before whose bold countenance)

deːɐ̯ ˈfaɛndə ˈlantsən ˈʃpˈlɪtˈɐn; giːpˈ ziː dem ˈkʰantslɐ, deːn duː hastʰ,
der Feinde Lanzen splittern; gib sie dem Kanzler, den du hast,
the enemies' lances shatter; give it to the chancellor, whom you have,
(the lances of your enemies shatter; give it to your chancellor,)

ʊntˈ las liːn nɔx di ˈgɔldnə last tsu ˈlandɐn ˈlastˈən ˈtʰraːgən.
und lass ihn noch die goldne Last zu andern Lasten tragen.
and let him still the golden burden to other burdens bear.
(and let him bear that golden burden along with his other burdens.)

ɪç ˈzɪŋə, viː deːɐ̯ ˈfoːgəl zɪŋt, deːɐ̯/deːr lɪn den ˈtsvaɛgən ˈvoːnətʰ:
Ich singe, wie der Vogel singt, der in den Zweigen wohnet:
I sing as the bird sings, who in the branches lives:
(I sing as the bird sings, who lives among the branches:)

das liːt, das lɑos deːɐ̯ ˈkʰeːlə drɪŋtˈ, lɪstˈ loːn, deːɐ̯ ˈraɛçlɪç ˈloːnətʰ.
das Lied, das aus der Kehle dringt, ist Lohn, der reichlich lohnet.
the song that out of the throat surges is reward which richly rewards.
(the song that surges from my throat is a reward that richly repays.)

dɔx darf lɪç ˈbɪtˈən, bɪtˈ lɪç laɛns: las miːɐ̯ den ˈbɛstˈən ˈbɛçɐ vaens
Doch darf ich bitten, bitt' ich eins: Lass mir den besten Becher Weins
But may I ask, ask I one (thing): let to me the best beaker of wine
(But if I may ask, I shall ask for one thing: let your best wine)

lɪn ˈpʰuːrəm ˈgɔldə ˈraɛçən. leːɐ̯ zɛtstˈ liːn lan, leːɐ̯ tʰraŋkˈ liːn lɑos:
in purem Golde reichen." Er setzt' ihn an, er trank ihn aus:
in pure gold (be) offered." He put it to (his lips), he drank it out:
(be offered to me in a beaker of pure gold." He put the beaker to his lips and drained it:)

oː tʰraŋkˈ fɔl ˈzyːsɐ ˈlaːbə! loː, voːl dem ˈhoxbəglʏkˈtˈən hɑos,
"O Trank voll süsser Labe! O, wohl dem hochbeglückten Haus,
"O drink full of sweet refreshment! Oh, happy the highly blessed house,

voː das lɪstˈ ˈkʰlaɛnə ˈgaːbə! lɛɐ̯ˈgeːts lɔøç voːl, zoː dɛŋkˈtˈ lan mɪç
wo das ist kleine Gabe! Ergeht's euch wohl, so denkt an mich
where that is small gift! Fares it with you well, then think of me
(where such is considered a trifling gift! If you are prospering, then think of me)

ʊntˈ ˈdaŋkˈətˈ gɔtˈ zoː varm, lals lɪç fyːɐ̯ ˈdiːzən tʰrʊŋkˈ lɔøç ˈdaŋkˈə.
und danket Gott so warm, als ich für diesen Trunk euch danke."
and thank God as warmly as I for this drink you thank."
(and thank God as warmly as I thank you for this drink.")

[Goethe's ballad, which was also set by Loewe, Schumann, and Hugo Wolf, implies that singing is its own reward, and that the recitalist should be satisfied with a glass of good wine afterwards. Not every professional musician would agree. Mozart's father complained that royalty too often rewarded with snuff-boxes when a generous fee in negotiable cash would have been far more welcome. The ballad is from the *Wilhelm Meister* novels. Schubert's music is deliberately old-fashioned, but suggests a rococo salon rather than a medieval castle.]

deːɐ̯ ˈzɛŋɐ lam ˈfɛlzən
Der Sänger am Felsen
The Singer on the Rock

Posthumously published [composed 1816] (poem by Karoline Pichler)

ˈkʰlaːgə, ˈmaɛnə ˈfløːtʼə, ˈkʰlaːgə di lɛntʼʃvʊndnən ˈʃøːnən ˈtʰaːgə,
Klage, meine Flöte, klage die entschwundnen schönen Tage,
Mourn, my   flute, mourn the vanished   beautiful days,

    [*poem (each time):* **Klag', o** (kʰlaːkʼ, loː) **meine Flöte,**]

lʊnt dɛs ˈfryːlɪŋs ˈʃnɛlə   flʊxtʼ, hiːɐ̯/hiːr lɑ̯of den fɛɐ̯ˈvɛlkʼtʼən ˈfluːrən,
und des Frühlings schnelle Flucht, hier   auf den verwelkten   Fluren,
and the spring's   rapid   flight, here   on the withered   meadows,

voː   maɛn gaɛstʼ lʊmˈzɔnst di ˈʃpʼuːrən ˈzyːsgəvoːntʼɐ   ˈfrɔɘ̯dən zuːxtʰ.
wo   mein Geist umsonst die Spuren süssgewohnter   Freuden sucht.
where my   spirit in vain the traces of sweet-accustomed joys   seeks.
(where my spirit seeks in vain the traces of sweet, accustomed joys.)

ˈkʰlaːgə, ˈmaɛnə ˈfløːtʼə, ˈkʰlaːgə! lˈaɛnzaːm ˈruːfəst duː dem ˈtʰaːgə,
Klage, meine Flöte, klage! Einsam   rufest du dem Tage,
Mourn, my   flute, mourn! Lonely   cry   you to the day,
(Mourn, my flute, mourn! Lonely, you cry out to the day,)

deːɐ̯ dem ʃmɛrts ts̯u ʃpʼɛːtʼ lɛɐ̯ˈvaxtʰ. lˈaɛnzaːm ˈʃalən   ˈmaɛnə ˈliːdɐ;
der dem Schmerz zu spät erwacht. Einsam   schallen meine Lieder;
which to the pain   too late awakes. Lonely sound   my   songs;
(which too late awakes to pain. My lonely songs resound;)

nuːɐ̯ das lˈeço haltʼ ziː ˈviːdɐ dʊrç di ˈʃatʼən ˈʃtʼɪlɐ naxtʰ.
nur das Echo hallt sie wieder durch die Schatten stiller Nacht.
only the echo sounds them back   through the shadows of quiet night.

ˈkʰlaːgə, ˈmaɛnə ˈfløːtʼə, ˈkʰlaːgə di lɛntʼfloːnən ˈʃøːnən ˈtʰaːgə,
Klage, meine Flöte, klage die entflohnen schönen Tage,
Mourn, my   flute, mourn the vanished   beautiful days,

voː   laɛn hɛrts̯, das miːɐ̯ nuːɐ̯ ʃluːkʼ, ˈdaɛnən ˈzanftʼən ˈliːdɐn ˈlɑ̯oʃtʼə,
wo   ein Herz, das mir   nur schlug, deinen sanften Liedern lauschte,
in which a   heart, that for me only beat, your   gentle   songs   listened to,
(in which a heart that only beat for me listened to your gentle songs,)

ˈts̯yrnəntʼ,   vɛn laɛn ˈts̯eːfyːɐ̯ ˈrɑ̯oʃtʼə,   lʊnt den ˈkʰlaɛnstʼən lɑ̯otʼ fɛɐ̯ˈtʰruːkʼ.
zürnend,   wenn ein Zephyr rauschte, und den kleinsten   Laut vertrug.
being annoyed, if   a   zephyr murmured, and the smallest   sound carried off.
(annoyed if a zephyr murmured and carried off, unheard, the slightest sound.)

'kʰlaːgə, 'ma̯enə 'fløːtʻə, 'kʰlaːgə! 'nɪmɐ 'kʰeːrən 'diːzə 'tʰaːgə!
Klage, meine Flöte, klage! Nimmer kehren diese Tage!
Mourn, my   flute, mourn! Never   return   these days!
(Mourn, my flute, mourn! Never will those days return!)

'ʊngəryːɐ̯tʻ høːɐ̯t 'deːli̯a 'ma̯enɐ 'liːdɐ 'baŋəs 'zeːnən,
Ungerührt hört Delia meiner Lieder banges Sehnen,
Unmoved hears Delia   my   songs' anxious longing,
(Unmoved, Delia hears the anxious longing of my songs,)

ziː, diː   lɪç ba̯e 'da̯enən 'tʰøːnən lɔftʻ ɪn lʊstʻ   fɛɐ̯'loːrən zaː!
sie, die   ich bei deinen Tönen oft   in Lust   verloren sah!
she, whom I   at   your   tones often in pleasure lost   saw!
(she, whom I often saw lost in pleasure at your tones!)

'kʰlaːgə, 'ma̯enə 'fløːtʻə, 'kʰlaːgə!
Klage, meine Flöte, klage!
Mourn, my   flute, mourn!

kʰyrtst   den 'faːdən 'ma̯enɐ 'tʰaːgə balt deːɐ̯ 'ʃtʻrɛŋən 'pʰartsə ʃtʻaːl:
Kürzt   den Faden meiner Tage bald der strengen Parze Stahl:
Shortens the thread of my days soon the stern   Fate's steel:
(If the shears of the stern spinner of fate soon cut short the thread of my days:)

loː dan zɪŋ   la̯of 'leːtʻəs 'matʻən   ['kʰlaːgə dan]
o dann sing' auf Lethes Matten [*poem:* **klage   dann auf Lethes Matten**]
oh, then sing on Lethe's meads   [mourn then]
      [Lethe is the river of oblivion in the realm of the dead]

'ɪrgəntʻ 'la̯enəm 'guːtʻən 'ʃatʻən   'ma̯enə liːpʻ lʊntʻ 'ma̯enə kʰvaːl!
irgend einem guten Schatten meine Lieb' und meine Qual!
to some one   kind shade   my   love and my   torment!
(to some kindly wraith my love and my torment!)

[This is an exquisite song, unjustly neglected. Schubert indicated that the melody of the introduction to each verse, and the postlude, should be played on the flute. The five verses that he chose are part of a much longer "*Idyll*." The first two verses would suffice. Karoline Pichler, prolific author of novels and dramas, was noted for her literary salon in Vienna.]

deːɐ̯ 'ʃɛːfɐ lʊnt deːɐ̯ 'ra̯etʻɐ
Der Schäfer und der Reiter
The Shepherd and the Horseman

Op. 13, No. 1 [1817] (Friedrich de la Motte Fouqué)

a̯en 'ʃɛːfɐ   zaːs lɪm 'gryːnən, za̯en 'liːpʻçən zyːs lɪm larm;
Ein Schäfer sass im   Grünen, sein Liebchen süss im   Arm;
A   shepherd sat in the greenery, his   sweetheart sweet in the arm;
(A shepherd sat amid the greenery, his sweetheart in his arms;)

dʊrç 'buːxənvɪpfəl 'ʃiːnən deːɐ̯ 'zɔnə 'ʃtʻraːlən varm.
durch Buchenwipfel schienen der Sonne Strahlen warm.
through beech-tree tops shone   the sun's rays   warm.
(the warm rays of the sun shone through the tops of the beech-trees.)

zi: ˈkʰoːstʰən   froː lʊntʰ ˈhaetʰɐ fɔn ˈliːbəstʰɛndəlae;   [lɛs ˈkʰoːstʰə]
Sie kosten   froh und heiter von Liebeständelei; [*poem:* **es koste**]
They talked intimately, happy and cheerful with love- dalliance;   [it talked (idiom)]
(They were talking intimately, happy and cheerful in the dalliance of love;)

daː rɪtʰ, bəˈveːɐ̯tʰ, laen ˈraetʰɐ   den ˈɡlʏkʰˈlɪçən foːɐ̯ˈbae.
da ritt, bewehrt, ein Reiter   den Glücklichen vorbei.
then rode, armed,   a   horseman the happy ones past.
(then an armed horseman rode past the happy lovers.)

zɪts lapʰ lʊntʰ ˈzuːxə ˈkʰyːlə,   riːf liːm deːɐ̯ ˈʃɛːfɐ tsuː,
"Sitz ab und suche Kühle,"   rief ihm der Schäfer zu,
"Dismount and seek coolness," called to him the shepherd to,
("Dismount and come into the cool shade," the shepherd called to him,)

dɛs ˈmɪtʰaːks ˈnaːə ˈʃvyːlə   ɡəˈbiːtʰətʰ ˈʃtʰɪlə ruː.
"des Mittags   nahe Schwüle gebietet   stille Ruh'.
"the noonday's near sultriness commands quiet rest.
("The sultry heat of noonday is near, and bids you to rest quietly.")

nɔx laxtʰ lɪm ˈmɔrɡənɡlantsə zoː   ʃtʰrɑ͜ox lals ˈbluːmə hiːɐ̯,
Noch lacht im Morgenglanze so   Strauch als Blume hier,
Still laughs in the morning radiance as well bush   as flower here,
(Here bush as well as flower still smiles in the radiance of the morning,)

lʊntʰ ˈliːpʰçən pflʏkʰtʰ tsʊm ˈkʰrantsə di ˈʃøːnstʰən ˈblyːtʰən diːɐ̯.   [ˈfrɪʃən]
und Liebchen pflückt zum Kranze die schönsten Blüten   dir." [*poem:* **die frischen**]
and sweetheart plucks for the garland the loveliest blossoms for you."   [fresh]
(and my sweetheart will pluck the loveliest blossoms to make you a garland.")

daː ʃpʰraːx deːɐ̯ ˈfɪnstʰrə ˈraetʰɐː   niː hɛltʰ mɪç valtʰ lʊntʰ fluːɐ̯;   [hiːltʰ]
Da sprach der finstre Reiter: "Nie   hält mich Wald und Flur; [*poem:* **nie hielt**]
Then spoke the gloomy horseman: "Never holds me woods and meadow;   [held]
(Then the gloomy horseman spoke: "Woods and meadows never keep me;)

mɪç tʰraepʰtʰ maen ˈʃɪkʰzaːl ˈvaetʰɐ(r) lʊntʰ lax, maen ˈlɛrnstʰɐ ʃvuːɐ̯!
mich treibt mein Schicksal weiter   und ach, mein ernster Schwur!
me drives my destiny farther   and ah, my   solemn vow!
(my destiny and—ah!—my solemn vow drive me onwards!)

lç ɡaːpʰ maen ˈjʊŋəs ˈleːbən daˈhɪn lʊm ˈʃnøːdən zɔltʰ;   [laen ˈfrɪʃəs]
Ich gab mein junges Leben dahin um schnöden Sold; [*poem:* **Ich gab ein frisches**]
I gave my young life away for vile   money;   [a fresh (life)]
(I gave my young life away for vile money;)

ɡlʏk kʰan lɪç nɪçtʰ lɛɐ̯ˈʃtʰreːbən, nuːɐ̯ ˈhøːçstʰəns ruːm lʊntʰ ɡɔltʰ.
Glück kann ich nicht erstreben, nur höchstens Ruhm und Gold.
Happiness can I not strive for, only at the most glory and gold.
(I cannot strive for happiness, only, at the most, for glory and gold.)

drʊm ʃnɛl, maen rɔs, lʊnt ˈtʰraːbə foːɐ̯ˈbae, voː ˈbluːmən blyːn!
Drum schnell, mein Ross, und trabe vorbei, wo Blumen blühn!
Therefore quickly, my steed, and trott past, where flowers bloom!
(Therefore make haste, my steed, and trott past where the flowers bloom!)

aenstˀ loːntˀ voːl ruː lɪm ˈgraːbə dɛs ˈkʰɛmpfəndən bəˈmyːn!
Einst lohnt wohl Ruh' im Grabe des kämpfenden Bemühn!"
One day rewards perhaps peace in the grave the fighting man's efforts!"
(One day the peace of the grave may reward the fighting man's efforts!")

[The song contrasts the happiness of the peaceful lovers in harmony with nature, on the one hand, and, on the other, the driven grimness of the man who has sold his soul in the search for power and glory. The poet is best known as the author of *Undine*, his tale of a water sprite.]

deːɐ̯ ˈʃatsgrɛːbɐ
Der Schatzgräber
The Treasure-seeker

Posthumously published [composed 1815] (poem by Johann Wolfgang von Goethe)

arm lam ˈbɔ͜øtˀəl, kʰraŋkˀ lam ˈhɛrt͡sən, ʃlɛpˀtˀ lɪç ˈmae̯nə ˈlaŋən ˈtʰaːgə.
Arm am Beutel, krank am Herzen, schleppt' ich meine langen Tage.
Poor in the purse, sick at the heart, dragged I my long days.
(Poor in purse, sick at heart, I dragged out my long days.)

ˈarmuːtˀ lɪst di ˈgrøːstˀə ˈpʰlaːgə, ˈrae̯çtˀuːm lɪst das ˈhøːçstˀə guːtʰ!
Armut ist die grösste Plage, Reichtum ist das höchste Gut!
Poverty is the greatest plague, wealth is the highest good!
[*Peters:* **Armut ist die höchste** (ˈhøːçstˀə, highest) **Plage** (Goethe's poem: *grösste Plage*)]

ʊnt, t͡su: ˈlɛndən ˈmae̯nə ˈʃmɛrt͡sən, gɪŋ lɪç ˈlae̯nən ʃats t͡su: ˈgraːbən.
Und, zu enden meine Schmerzen, ging ich einen Schatz zu graben.
And, to end my pains, went I a treasure to dig for.
(And, to put an end to my pain, I went to dig for treasure.)

ˈmae̯nə ˈzeːlə zɔlst du: ˈhaːbən! ʃriːpˀ lɪç hɪn mɪtˀ ˈlae̯gnəm bluːtʰ.
"Meine Seele sollst du haben!" schrieb ich hin mit eignem Blut.
"My soul shall you have!" wrote I hence with own blood.
("You shall have my soul!" I wrote in my own blood.)

ʊntˀ zo: t͡soːkˀ lɪç kʰrae̯s lʊm ˈkʰrae̯zə, ˈʃtˀɛltˀə ˈvʊndɐbaːrə ˈflamən,
Und so zog ich Kreis um Kreise, stellte wunderbare Flammen,
And so drew I circle around circles, placed marvelous flames,
(And so I drew a circle around other circles and placed together inside them marvelous flames,)

kʰrɑo̯tˀ lʊntˀ ˈkʰnɔxənvɛrkˀ t͡suˈzamən: di bəˈʃvøːrʊŋ vaːɐ̯ fɔlˈbraxtʰ.
Kraut und Knochenwerk zusammen: die Beschwörung war vollbracht.
herb and bone- work together: the incantation was complete.
(herbs, and bones: the incantation was complete.)

ʊntˀ lɑo̯f di gəˈlɛrntˀə ˈvae̯zə gruːpˀ lɪç naːx dem ˈlaltˀən ˈʃat͡sə
Und auf die gelernte Weise grub ich nach dem alten Schatze
And in the learned way dug I for the old treasure
(And, in the way I learned from the magic spell, I dug for the old treasure)

ɑo̯f dem ˈlaŋəˈt͡sae̯kˀtˀən ˈpʰlat͡sə. ʃvart͡s lʊntˀ ˈʃtˀʏrmɪʃ vaːɐ̯ di naxtʰ.
auf dem angezeigten Platze. Schwarz und stürmisch war die Nacht.
at the indicated place. Black and stormy was the night.
(at the indicated place. The night was black and stormy.)

ʊnt' lɪç za: lae̯n lɪçt' fɔn 'vae̯t'ən, lʊnt' lɛs kʰa:m, glae̯ç 'lae̯nəm 'ʃt'ɛrnə
Und ich sah ein Licht von weiten, und es kam, gleich einem Sterne
And I saw a light from afar,   and it came, like a   star

'hɪnt'ən lao̯s de:ɐ̯ 'fɛrnst'ən 'fɛrnə, 'le:bən lals lɛs 'tsvœlfə ʃlu:k'.
hinten aus der fernsten Ferne, eben als es Zwölfe schlug.
behind out of the farthest distance, just as it twelve struck.
(from beyond the farthest distance, just as the clock struck twelve.)

ʊnt da: galt' kʰae̯n 'foɐ̯bərae̯t'ən: 'hɛlɐ varts mɪt' 'lae̯nəm 'ma:lə
Und da galt   kein Vorbereiten: Heller ward's mit einem Male
And then was valid no preparing: brighter became it with one time
(And then there was no chance to prepare myself: all at once it became brighter)

fɔn dem glants de:ɐ̯ 'fɔlən 'ʃa:lə, di: lae̯n 'ʃø:nɐ 'kʰna:bə tʰru:k'.
von dem Glanz der vollen Schale, die ein schöner Knabe trug.
from the radiance of the full cup, which a handsome boy carried.

'hɔldə 'lao̯ogən za: lɪç 'blɪŋk'ən 'lʊnt'ɐ 'dɪçt'əm 'blu:mənkʰrantsə:
Holde Augen sah ich blinken unter dichtem Blumenkranze:
Gracious eyes saw I sparkle beneath thick flower- wreath:
(I saw gracious eyes sparkling beneath a thick wreath of flowers:)

ɪn dɛs 'tʰraŋk'əs 'hɪməlsglantsə tʰra:t' le:ɐ̯/le:r lɪn den kʰrae̯s he'rae̯n.
In des Trankes Himmelsglanze trat er   in den Kreis herein.
In the drink's heavenly radiance stepped he   into the circle into.
(In the drink's heavenly radiance, he stepped into the circle I had drawn.)

ʊnt' le:ɐ̯ hi:s mɪç 'frɔø̯nt'lɪç 'tʰrɪŋk'ən; lʊnt' lɪç daxt':
Und er hiess mich freundlich trinken; und ich dacht':
And he bid me kindly   drink;   and I thought:

lɛs kʰan de:ɐ̯ 'kʰna:bə mɪt de:ɐ̯ 'ʃø:nən 'lɪçt'ən 'ga:bə
Es kann der Knabe mit der schönen lichten Gabe
It can the boy with the beautiful light gift
(that boy with the beautiful glowing gift can)

'va:ɐ̯lɪç nɪçt de:ɐ̯ 'bø:zə zae̯n. 'tʰrɪŋk'ə mu:t dɛs 'rae̯nən 'le:bəns!
wahrlich nicht der Böse   sein. "Trinke Mut des reinen Lebens!
truly   not the evil one be. "Drink courage of the pure life!
(truly not be the Devil. "Drink the courage to live a pure life!)

dan fɛɐ̯'ʃte:st du: di bə'le:rʊŋ, kʰɔmst' mɪt' 'lɛŋst'lɪçɐ bə'ʃvø:rʊŋ
Dann verstehst du die Belehrung, kommst mit ängstlicher Beschwörung
Then understand you the advice,   come with anxious   incantation
(Then you will understand my advice and not come with anxious incantations)

nɪçt tsu'rʏk' lan 'di:zən lɔrtʰ. 'gra:bə hi:ɐ̯ nɪçt' me:ɐ̯ fɛɐ̯'ge:bəns.
nicht zurück an diesen Ort. Grabe hier nicht mehr vergebens.
not back to this place. Dig here not more in vain.
(back to this place. Do not dig here in vain any more.)

274

'tʰaːɡəs 'larbaet'! 'laːbənts 'ɡɛst'ə! 'zao̯rə 'vɔxən! 'froːə 'fɛstə!
Tages Arbeit! Abends Gäste! Saure Wochen! Frohe Feste!
In the day work! In the evening guests! Sour weeks! Happy holidays!
(Work hard by day! In the evening enjoy company! Hard weekdays, happy holidays!)

zae daen 'kʰynft'ɪç 'tsao̯bɐvɔrtʰ.
Sei dein künftig Zauberwort."
Be your future magic- word."
(Let that be your magic incantation in the future.")

[There is a hint of Goethe's own Faust in this poem: the discouraged man turns to witchcraft to
find a treasure, offers to sell his soul; but, instead of a devil, an angelic being shows him the
path—if not to redemption—at least to a more productive and happy life.]

deːɐ 'ʃɪfɐ / 'friːt'lɪç liːk' lɪç 'hɪngəɡɔsən
Der Schiffer / Friedlich lieg' ich hingegossen
The Boatman / I Lie Peacefully Sprawled

Posthumously published [composed 1820] (poem by Friedrich von Schlegel)

'friːt'lɪç liːɡ ɪç 'hɪngəɡɔsən, 'lɛŋk'ə hɪn lʊnt' heːɐ das 'ruːdɐ,
Friedlich lieg' ich hingegossen, lenke hin und her das Ruder,
Peacefully lie I poured out, steer to and fro the rudder,
(I lie peacefully sprawled out, steering the rudder this way and that,)

'aːt'mə kʰyːl lɪm lɪçt dɛs 'moːndəs, 'tʰrɔ͡ømə zyːs lɪm 'ʃt'ɪlən 'muːt'ə;
atme kühl im Licht des Mondes, träume süss im stillen Mute;
breathe cool in the light of the moon, dream sweetly in the quiet mood;
(breathing cool air in the moonlight, dreaming sweet dreams in a quiet mood;)

'glae̯t'ən las lɪç lao̯x den kʰaːn, 'ʃao̯ə lɪn di 'blaŋk'ən 'fluːt'ən,
gleiten lass ich auch den Kahn, schaue in die blanken Fluten,
glide let I also the boat, (I) look in the shining waters,
(I even let the boat drift as I look into the shining waters,)

voː di 'ʃt'ɛrnə 'liːp'lɪç 'ʃɪmɐn, 'ʃp'iːlə 'viːdɐ mɪt dem 'ruːdɐ.
wo die Sterne lieblich schimmern, spiele wieder mit dem Ruder.
where the stars delightfully shimmer, (I) play again with the rudder.
(where the stars shimmer delightfully; then I play with the rudder again.)

'zɛːsə dɔx das 'blɔndə 'mɛːk't'laen foːɐ miːɐ/miːr lao̯f dem 'bɛŋk'çən 'ruːənt',
Sässe doch das blonde Mägdlein vor mir auf dem Bänkchen ruhend,
Would sit only the blond girl before me on the thwart resting,
(If only a certain blond girl would be sitting in front of me, resting on the thwart,)

'zɛŋə 'ʃmaxt'ənt 'tsaːɐt'ə 'liːdɐ. 'hɪmlɪʃ vɛːɐ miːɐ dan tsu 'muːt'ə,
sänge schmachtend zarte Lieder. Himmlisch wär' mir dann zu Mute,
would sing languishing delicate songs. Heavenly would be for me then in mood,
(languishingly singing tender songs! That would put me into a heavenly mood,)

liːs mɪç 'nɛk'ən fɔn dem 'kʰɪndə, 'viːdɐ 'tʰɛndəlnt' mɪt deːɐ 'guːt'ən.
liess mich necken von dem Kinde, wieder tändelnd mit der Guten.
let myself be teased by the child, again flirting with the good one.
(I would let myself be teased by the child, flirting again with the good-natured girl.)

ˈfriːtˈlɪç   liːg ɪç ˈhɪngəgɔsən, ˈtʰrɔ̜ømə zyːs   lɪm   ˈʃtˈɪlən ˈmuːtˈə;
Friedlich lieg' ich hingegossen, träume süss   im   stillen Mute,
Peacefully lie I   poured out, dream   sweetly in the quiet   mood;
(I lie peacefully sprawled out, dreaming sweet dreams in a quiet mood;)

ˈaːtˈmə kʰyːl lɪm   lɪçt dɛs ˈmoːndəs, ˈfyːrə hɪn lʊntˈ heːɐ̯ das ˈruːdɐ,
atme   kühl im   Licht des Mondes, führe hin und her das Ruder.
breathe cool in the light of the moon,   guide to and fro the rudder,
(breathing cool air in the moonlight, guiding the rudder this way and that,)

[This appealing song calls for a wide range, nearly two octaves (from low A to high G sharp in
the original key), and the ability to sing very softly in all parts of that range. Twice the singer
may hum, or wordlessly vocalize, a one-bar phrase, an effect that is unique in Schubert's songs.]

deːɐ̯ ˈʃɪfɐ / ɪm ˈvɪndə, lɪm ˈʃtˈʊrmə
Der Schiffer / Im Winde, im Sturme
The Boatman / In the Wind, in the Storm

Op. 21, No. 2 [1817?] (Johann Mayrhofer)

ɪm   ˈvɪndə, lɪm   ˈʃtˈʊrmə bəˈfaːr ɪç den flʊs,
Im   Winde, im   Sturme befahr' ich den Fluss,
In the wind,   in the storm   travel I   the river,
(In the wind, in the storm I travel the river,)

di ˈkʰlaedɐ dʊrçˈvae̯çət   deːɐ̯ ˈreːgən lɪm   gʊs;
die Kleider durchweichet der Regen im   Guss;
the clothes through-soaks the   rain   in the downpour;
(the pouring rain soaks through my clothes;)

ɪç ˈpʰae̯tʃə di ˈvɛlən   mɪtˈ ˈmɛçtˈɪgəm ʃlaːkˈ, lɛɐ̯ˈhɔfəntˈ miːɐ̯ ˈhae̯tˈərən tʰaːkˈ.
ich peitsche die Wellen mit   mächtigem Schlag, erhoffend mir   heiteren Tag.
I   lash   the waves with powerful   stroke hoping for for me bright   day.
(I lash the waves with powerful strokes, hoping for a bright day.)
     [*poem:* **ich lenke** (lɪç ˈlɛŋkˈə, I steer) — **ich peitsche mit mächtigen Schlag die Wellen,**]

di ˈvɛlən, ziː ˈjaːgən das ˈlɛçtsəndə ʃif,   lɛs ˈdroːət   deːɐ̯ ˈʃtˈruːdəl,
Die Wellen, sie   jagen das ächzende Schiff, es   drohet   der Strudel,
The waves, they chase the creaking   boat, there threatens the whirlpool,
(The waves chase the creaking boat, the whirlpool is one danger,)
     [*poem:* **Die Fluten** (ˈfluːtˈən, waters), **sie jagen das schwankende** (ˈʃvaŋkˈəndə, rocking)]

lɛs ˈdroːət   das rɪf, gəˈʃtˈae̯nə lɛntˈˈkʰɔlɐn   den ˈfɛlzɪgən høːn,
es   drohet   das* Riff, Gesteine   entkollern   den felsigen Höhn,
there threatens the   reef, stones   rumble down from the rocky   heights,
(the reef is another, big stones come rumbling down from the rocky heights,)

ʊnt ˈtʰanən lɛɐ̯ˈzɔ̜øftsən viː ˈgae̯stˈɐgəʃtˈøːn. zoː ˈmʊstˈə lɛs ˈkʰomən,
und Tannen erseufzen   wie Geistergestöhn. So musste es kommen,
and fir-trees sigh   like ghost- moaning. So had   it to come,
(and fir-trees sigh like moaning ghosts. It had to come like this,)
     [*poem:* **und Fichten** (ˈfɪçtˈən, firs) **sie sausen** (ziː ˈzɑ̜ozən, they roar) **wie Geistergestöhn**]

lıç haːpˈ lɛs gəˈvɔltʰ, lıç ˈhasə das ˈleːbən bəˈhaːkˈlıç lɛntˈrɔltʰ;
ich hab' es gewollt, ich hasse das Leben behaglich entrollt;
I have it wanted, I hate the life comfortably unfurled;
(I wanted it, I hate a life that unfolds comfortably;)

ʊntˈ ˈʃlɛŋən di ˈvɛlən den ˈlɛçtsəndən kʰaːn, lıç ˈpʰra͜ezə dɔx ˈlımɐ
und schlängen die Wellen den ächzenden Kahn, ich preise doch immer
and would swallow the waves the creaking boat, I praise still always
(and even if the waves swallow up the creaking boat, I shall still always praise)
   [*poem:* **und schlängen die Fluten** (ˈfluːtˈən, waters) **den dröhnenden** (ˈdrøːnəndən, rumbling)]

di ˈla͜egənə baːn. drʊm ˈtʰoːzə dɛs ˈvasɐs lɔːnˈmɛçtˈıgɐ tsɔrn, [lɛs]
die eigene Bahn. Drum tose des Wassers ohnmächtiger Zorn, [*poem:* **Es tose**]
the own way. Therefore let rage the water's impotent fury, [There (idiom)]
(following one's own way. Therefore let the water's impotent fury rage,)

dem ˈhɛrtsən lɛntˈkʰvılətˈ la͜en ˈzeːlıgɐ bɔrn, di ˈnɛrfən lɛɐ̯ˈfrıʃəntˈ;
dem Herzen entquillet ein seliger Born, die Nerven erfrischend;
from the heart springs a blissful fountain, the nerves refreshing;
(a fountain of bliss springs up from the heart, refreshing my nerves;)

loː ˈhımlıʃə lʊstʰ, dem ˈʃtˈʊrmə tsu ˈtʰrɔtsən mıtˈ ˈmɛnlıçɐ brʊstʰ!
o himmlische Lust, dem Sturme zu trotzen mit männlicher Brust!
oh heavenly pleasure, the storm to defy with manly breast!
(oh heavenly pleasure, to brave the storm with a manly heart!)
   [*poem:* **dem Sturme gebieten** (gəˈbiːtˈən, to command)]

[The boatman exults in his strength as he braves the forces of nature. The voice part in this invigorating, virile song was notated by Schubert in the treble cleff, as in Peters, but was first published in the bass cleff, as in the *Gesamtausgabe*. *GA & poem:* **der Riff** (masculine); in modern German *Riff* is neuter; ***das* Riff** is correct (except when referring to a "riff" in jazz).]

deːɐ̯ ˈʃmɛtˈɐlıŋ
Der Schmetterling
The Butterfly

Op. 57, No. 1 [1820?] (Friedrich von Schlegel)

viː zɔl lıç nıçt ˈtʰantsən? lɛs maxtˈ ˈkʰa͜enə ˈmyːə, ʊntˈ ˈra͜etsəndə ˈfarbən
Wie soll ich nicht tanzen? es macht keine Mühe, und reizende Farben
Why should I not dance? It makes no effort, and charming colors
(Why should I not dance? It costs me no effort, and charming colors)

ˈʃımɐn hiːɐ̯/hiːr lım ˈgryːnən. ˈlımɐ ˈʃøːnɐ ˈglɛntsən ˈma͜enə ˈbʊntˈən ˈflyːgəl,
schimmern hier im Grünen. Immer schöner glänzen meine bunten Flügel,
shimmer here in the greenery. Ever more beautiful gleam my bright wings,

ˈlımɐ ˈzyːsɐ ˈha͜oxən ˈlalə ˈkʰla͜enən ˈblyːtˈən. lıç ˈnaʃə di ˈblyːtˈən,
immer süsser hauchen alle kleinen Blüten. Ich nasche die Blüten,
Ever sweeter breathe all little blossoms. I nibble the blossoms,
(Ever sweeter is the scent of all the little blossoms. I nibble at the blossoms,)

liːɐ̯ kʰœntˈ ziː nɪçtˈ ˈhyːtˈən. viː groːs lɪst di ˈfrɔ̯ødə, zaes ʃpˈɛːtˈ ˈloːdɐ ˈfryːə,
ihr könnt sie nicht hüten. Wie gross ist die Freude, sei's spät oder frühe,
you can them not protect. How great is the joy, be it late or early,
(you cannot protect them. How great is my joy, be it late or early,)

ˈlae̯çtˈzɪnɪç ʦu: ˈʃveːbən ˈlyːbɐ tʰaːl lʊntˈ ˈhyːɡəl! vɛn deːɐ̯/deːr ˈlaːbəntˈ ˈzɔ̯øzəltˈ,
leichtsinnig zu schweben über Tal und Hügel! Wenn der Abend säuselt,
thoughtlessly to float over valley and hill! When the evening rustles,

zeːtˈ liːɐ̯ ˈvɔlkˈən ˈɡlyːɐ̯n; vɛn di ˈlʏftˈə ˈɡɔldən, ʃae̯nt di ˈviːzə ˈɡryːnɐ.
seht ihr Wolken glühen; wenn die Lüfte golden, scheint die Wiese grüner.
see you clouds glow; when the airs golden, appears the meadow greener.
(you see the clouds glowing; when the air is golden, the meadow appears even greener.)

lɪç ˈnaʃə di ˈblyːtˈən, liːɐ̯ kʰœntˈ ziː nɪçtˈ ˈhyːtˈən.
Ich nasche die Blüten, ihr könnt sie nicht hüten.
I nibble the blossoms, you can them not protect.
(I nibble the blossoms, you cannot protect them.)

[The butterfly flutters in the airy introduction, a drone bass provides a rustic accompaniment to the happy-go-lucky melody.]

deːɐ̯ ziːkˈ
Der Sieg
The Victory

Posthumously published [composed 1824] (poem by Johann Mayrhofer)

oː ˈlʊnbəvœlkˈtˈəs ˈleːbən! zoː raen lʊnt tʰiːf lʊntˈ kʰlaːɐ̯!
O unbewölktes Leben! so rein und tief und klar!
O unclouded life, so pure and deep and clear!

ˈluːɐ̯altˈə/luːrlaltˈə ˈtʰrɔ̯ømə ˈʃveːbən lɑof ˈbluːmən ˈvʊndɐbaːɐ̯.
Uralte Träume schweben auf Blumen wunderbar.
Age-old dreams float on flowers wondrously.

deːɐ̯ ɡaest ʦɛɐ̯ˈbraːx di ˈʃraŋkˈən, dɛs ˈkʰœrpˈɐs ˈtʰrɛːɡəs blae̯;
Der Geist zerbrach die Schranken, des Körpers träges Blei;
The spirit shattered the bounds, the body's inert lead;

eːɐ̯ ˈvaltˈətˈ groːs lʊntˈ frae̯. lɛs ˈlaːbən di ɡəˈdaŋkˈən lan ˈleːdəns ˈfrʏçtˈən zɪç;
er waltet gross und frei. Es laben die Gedanken an Edens Früchten sich;
it controls, great and free. There refresh the thoughts with Eden's fruits themselves;
(the spirit is in control, great and free. Thoughts refresh themselves with the fruits of Eden;)

deːɐ̯/deːr ˈlaltˈə fluːx lɛntˈˈvɪç. vas lɪç lɑox je: ɡəˈlɪtˈən, di ˈpʰalmə lɪstˈ lɛɐ̯ˈʃtˈrɪtˈən,
der alte Fluch entwich. Was ich auch je gelitten, die Palme ist erstritten,
the old curse vanished. What I also ever (have) suffered, the palm is won,
(the old curse has vanished. Whatever I may have suffered, now the palm of victory is won,)

ɡəˈʃtˈɪlətˈ maen fɛɐ̯ˈlaŋən. di ˈmuːzən ˈzɛlbɐ ˈzaŋən di ʃlaŋ lɪn ˈtʰoːdəsʃlaːf,
gestillet mein Verlangen. Die Musen selber sangen die Schlang'* in Todesschlaf,
stilled (is) my desire. The Muses themselves sang the serpent into death-sleep,
(my desire is appeased. The Muses themselves sang the serpent* to the sleep of death,)

ʊnt‘ 'maenə hant‘, zi: tʰra:f. lo: 'lʊnbəvœlk‘t‘əs 'le:bən! zo: raen lʊnt tʰi:f lʊnt‘ kʰla:ɐ.
und meine Hand, sie traf. O unbewölktes Leben! so rein und tief und klar.
and my hand, it struck. O unclouded life! So pure and deep and clear!
(and my hand then struck the blow that killed it. O unclouded life! So pure and deep and clear!)

'lu:ɐlalt‘ə/'lu:rlalt‘ə 'tʰrɔø̯mə 'ʃve:bən laof 'blu:mən 'vʊndɐba:ɐ.
Uralte Träume schweben auf Blumen wunderbar.
Age-old dreams float on flowers wondrously.

[*The poet wrote "*Schlang*'" (serpent); for some reason the *Gesamtausgabe* changed the word to "*Sphinx*" (pronounced *sfɪŋks*), the name of a monster from Greek mythology that does not belong in Eden. The song was intended for the bass voice. The victory is a spiritual one, that of the spirit over the "leaden" flesh. The poet, who later committed suicide, saw "the unclouded life" as a *release* from earthly life; Schubert, less mystically pessimistic, seems to have interpreted the lines as referring to an inner spiritual realm, accessible to the living.]

de:ɐ ʃt‘ro:m
Der Strom
The River

Posthumously published [composed 1817?] (poet unknown)

maen 'le:bən vɛltst‘ zɪç 'mʊrənt‘ fɔrtʰ, lɛs ʃt‘aek‘t‘ lʊnt‘ fɛlt‘ lɪn 'kʰraozən 'vo:gən,
Mein Leben wälzt sich murrend fort, es steigt und fällt in krausen Wogen,
My life rolls itself grumbling onwards, it climbs and falls in curling waves,
(My life rolls grumbling onwards, it climbs and falls in curling waves,)

hi:ɐ bɔø̯mt‘ lɛs zɪç, ja:k‘t‘ 'ni:dɐ dɔrtʰ lɪn 'vɪldən 'tsy:gən, 'ho:ən 'bo:gən.
hier bäumt es sich, jagt nieder dort in wilden Zügen, hohen Bogen.
here rears up it itself, races down there in wild impulses, high arcs.
(here it rears up, there it races downwards, in wild spurts, high arcs.)

das 'ʃt‘ɪlə tʰa:l, das 'gry:nə fɛlt dʊrç'raoʃt‘ lɛs nu:n mɪt‘ 'laezəm 'be:bən,
Das stille Tal, das grüne Feld durchrauscht es nun mit leisem Beben,
The quiet valley, the green field through-ripples it now with soft quivering,
(Now it ripples through the quiet valley and the green field with a soft quivering;)

zɪç ru: lɛɐ'ze:nənt‘, 'ru:ɪgə vɛlt‘, lɛɐ'gœtst‘ lɛs zɪç lam 'ru:ɪgən 'le:bən.
sich Ruh' ersehnend, ruhige* Welt, ergötzt es sich am ruhigen Leben.
itself rest yearning for, peaceful world, delights it itself in the tranquil life.
(yearning for rest, for a peaceful world, it delights in the tranquil life.)

[**Peters:* **ruh'ge, ruh'gen]**

dɔx 'nɪmɐ 'fɪndənt‘, vas lɛs zu:xtʰ, lʊnt‘ 'lɪmɐ 'ze:nənt‘ tʰo:st‘ lɛs 'vaet‘ɐ,
Doch nimmer findend, was es sucht, und immer sehnend tost es weiter,
But never finding what it seeks, and always yearning rages it further,
(But, never finding what it seeks and always yearning, it rages onwards,)

lʊn'mu:t‘ɪç** rɔlts laof 'ʃt‘e:t‘ɐ flʊxt‘, vɪrt‘ 'nɪmɐ fro:, vɪrt‘ 'nɪmɐ 'haet‘ɐ.
unmutig rollt's auf steter Flucht, wird nimmer froh, wird nimmer heiter.
displeased rolls it in constant flight, becomes never happy, becomes never serene.
(unsatisfied, it rolls on in a constant flight, never happy, never serene.)

[**Schubert's music accents the second syllable; the first is normally stressed]

[Schubert dedicated *Der Strom* to Albert Stadler, one of his earliest friends, when Stadler—who may or may not have been the author—had to leave Vienna; the tone is one of passionate despair. The *Gesamtausgabe* prints the song in the bass clef (but in the same key as Peters.)]

Der stürmische Morgen see *Winterreise*

deːɐ ˈtʰɑoxɐ
Der Taucher
The Diver

Posthumously published [composed 1813, 1814] (poem by Friedrich von Schiller)

veːɐ vaːkˈtˈ ɛs, ˈrɪtˈɐsman ˈloːdɐ kʰnapʰ, ʦuː ˈtʰɑoxən ɪn ˈdiːzən ʃlʊntˈʔ
"Wer wagt es, Rittersmann oder Knapp', zu tauchen in diesen Schlund?
"Who dares it, knight or squire, to dive into this abyss?
("Who will dare, knight or squire, to dive into this abyss?)

ˈaenən ˈɡɔldnən ˈbɛçɐ vɛrf ɪç hɪˈnapˈ, fɛɐˈʃlʊŋən ʃoːn hatˈ liːn deːɐ ˈʃvarʦə mʊntˈ.
Einen goldnen Becher werf' ich hinab, verschlungen schon hat ihn der schwarze Mund.
A golden goblet throw I down, swallowed already has it the black mouth.
(I throw a golden goblet down to it; the black mouth has already swallowed it.)

veːɐ miːɐ den ˈbɛçɐ kʰan ˈviːdɐ ˈʦaegən, leːɐ maːkˈ liːn bəˈhaltˈən,
Wer mir den Becher kann wieder zeigen, er mag ihn behalten,
Whoever to me the goblet can again show, he may it keep,
(Whoever can show the goblet to me again may keep it;)

eːɐ/eːr lɪstˈ zaen ˈlaegən. deːɐ ˈkʰøːnɪç ʃpˈrɪçtˈ lɛs lʊntˈ vɪrftˈ fɔn deːɐ høː deːɐ ˈkʰlɪpˈə,
er ist sein eigen." Der König spricht es und wirft von der Höh' der Klippe,
it is his own." The king speaks it and throws from the height of the cliff,
(it is his." The king speaks, and throws from the top of the cliff,)

diː ʃrɔf lʊntˈ ʃtˈael hɪˈnɑoshɛŋtˈ lɪn di lʊnˈlɛntˈlɪçə zeː, den ˈbɛçɐ
die schroff und steil hinaushängt in die unendliche See, den Becher
which precipitous and steep hangs out into the infinite sea, the goblet
(which juts out, precipitous and steep, into the infinite sea, the goblet)

ɪn deːɐ çaˈrʏpˈdə ɡəˈhɔøl. veːɐ/veːr lɪst deːɐ bəˈhɛrtstˈə, lɪç ˈfraːɡə ˈviːdɐ, ʦuː ˈtʰɑoxən
in der Charybde Geheul. "Wer ist der Beherzte, ich frage wieder, zu tauchen
into the Charybdis's howling. "Who is the brave heart, I ask again, to dive
(into the howling of Charybdis. "Who is the brave-hearted man, I ask again, who will dive)

[Charybdis, in Homer's *Odyssey*, was a horrifying whirlpool that swallowed many ships.]

ɪn ˈdiːzə ˈtʰiːfə ˈniːdɐ? lʊntˈ di ˈrɪtˈɐ(r) lʊntˈ ˈkʰnapˈən lʊm liːn heːɐ fɛɐˈneːməns
in diese Tiefe nieder?" Und die Ritter und Knappen um ihn her vernehmen's
into those depths down?" And the knights and squires around him hither hear it
(down into those depths?" And the knights and squires around him hear that)

[*Peters (as in Schiller):* **Ritter, *die* Knappen**]

lʊntˈ ˈʃvaegən ʃtˈɪl, ˈzeːən hɪˈnapˈ lɪn das ˈvɪldə meːɐ, lʊntˈ ˈkʰaenɐ [zeːn]
und schweigen still, sehen hinab in das wilde Meer, und keiner [*2nd version:* seh'n]
and keep silent quietly, look down into the wild sea, and no one
(and keep silent; they look down into the wild sea, and no one)

280

den 'bɛçɐ gə'vɪnən vɪl. ʊnt deːɐ̯ 'kʰøːnɪç t͡sʊm 'drɪt'ən maːl 'viːdɐ 'fraːgətʰ:
den Becher gewinnen will. Und der König zum dritten Mal wieder fraget:
the goblet to win wants. And the king for the third time again asks:
(wants to win the goblet. And the king asks again for the third time:)

ɪst' 'kʰae̯nɐ, deːɐ̯ zɪç hɪ'nʊnt'ɐ 'vaːgətʰ? dɔx 'aləs nɔx ʃt'ʊm blae̯p't', vi: t͡su'foːɐ̯,
"Ist keiner, der sich hinunter waget?" Doch alles noch stumm bleibt, wie zuvor,
"Is no one, who himself downwards dares?" But all still silent stays, as before,
("Is there no one who dares to dive down?" But all remain silent, as before,)
                                        [*first version:* **Und** (ʊnt', and) **alles** (*Schiller:* **Doch alles**)]

ʊnt' 'lae̯n 'leːdəlkʰnɛçtʰ, zanft' ʊnt' kʰɛkʰ, tʰrɪt' 'lao̯s deːɐ̯ 'kʰnap'ən 't͡saːgəndəm kʰoːɐ̯,
und ein Edelknecht, sanft und keck, tritt aus der Knappen zagendem Chor,
and a noble squire, gentle and bold, steps out of the squires' faint-hearted chorus,
(and a noble squire, gentle and bold, steps out from the ranks of the other squires,)

ʊnt den 'gyrt'əl vɪrft' leːɐ̯, den 'mant'əl vɛk', ʊnt 'lalə di 'mɛnɐ(r) lʊm'heːɐ̯(r) ʊnt' 'frao̯ən
und den Gürtel wirft er, den Mantel weg, und alle die Männer umher und Frauen
and the belt throws he, the cloak away, and all the men around and women
(and he throws off his belt and his cloak, and all the men and women around him)

ao̯f den 'hɛrlɪçən 'jʏŋlɪŋ fɛɐ̯'vʊndət' ʃao̯n. ʊnt' vi: leːɐ̯ tʰrɪt' lan des 'fɛlzən haŋ
auf den herrlichen Jüngling verwundert schau'n. Und wie er tritt an des Felsen Hang
at the glorious youth amazed look. And as he steps to the cliff's overhang
(look at the glorious youth in astonishment. And as he steps to the edge of the cliff)
                                        [*Schiller:* **schauen** ('ʃao̯ən)]

ʊnt' blɪk't' lɪn den ʃlʊnt' hɪ'nap', di 'vasɐ, di: zi: hɪ'nʊnt'ɐʃlaŋ, di ça'rʏp'də
und blickt in den Schlund hinab, die Wasser, die sie hinunterschlang, die Charybde
and looks into the abyss down, the waters, which she swallowed down, the Charybdis
(and looks down into the abyss, the waters which Charybdis had swallowed down,)

jɛt͡st' 'brʏlənt' 'viːdəgaːp', ʊnt' vi: mɪt des 'dɔnɐs 'fɛrnəm gə'tʰoːzə lɛnt'ʃt'ʏrt͡sən zi:
jetzt brüllend wiedergab, und wie mit des Donners fernem Getose entstürzen sie
now roaring gave back, and as if with the thunder's distant rumble rush up they
(now she regurgitated, and, as if with the distant rumble of thunder, they rush up)
        [*Peters (and Schiller):* **des fernen** ('fɛrnən) **Donners Getose**, the distant thunder's rumble]

'ʃɔ̯ømənt dem 'fɪnst'ɐn 'ʃoːsə. ʊnt' les 'valət' ʊnt' 'ziːdət' ʊnt' 'brao̯zət' lʊnt t͡sɪʃt',
schäumend dem finstern Schosse. Und es wallet und siedet und brauset und zischt,
foaming from the dark womb. And it boils and seethes and roars and hisses,

vi: vɛn 'vasɐ mɪt' 'fɔ̯ør zɪç mɛŋtʰ, bɪs t͡sʊm 'hɪməl 'ʃp'rɪt͡sət deːɐ̯ 'dampfəndə
wie wenn Wasser mit Feuer sich mengt, bis zum Himmel spritzet der dampfende
as when water with fire itself mixes, till to the sky sprays the steaming
(as when water mixes with fire, till the steaming foam sprays up to the sky,)

gɪʃt', lʊnt' fluːt' lao̯f fluːt' zɪç loːn 'lɛndə drɛŋt', lʊnt' vɪl zɪç 'nɪmɐ(r)
Gischt, und Flut auf Flut sich ohn' Ende drängt, und will sich nimmer
foam, and flood upon flood itself without end surges, and wants itself never
(and flood upon flood surges up without end and never seems)

 lɛɐ̯ˈʃœpfən lʊntˈ ˈleːrən, lals ˈvɔltˈə das meːɐ̯ nɔx laen meːɐ̯ gəˈbɛːrən.　　dɔx
erschöpfen und leeren, als wollte das Meer noch ein Meer gebären.　　Doch
to exhaust and　empty,　as if wanted the sea　yet　a　sea　to give birth to. But
(to exhaust itself and empty itself, as if the sea wanted to give birth to yet another sea. But,)

ˈlɛntˈlɪç, daː leːkˈtˈ　zɪç　di ˈvɪldə gəˈvaltʰ, lʊntˈ ʃvarts　laos　dem ˈvaesən ʃɑom
endlich, da legt　sich die wilde Gewalt, und schwarz aus　dem weissen Schaum
finally,　then subsided itself the wild　force,　and　black　out of the　white　foam
(finally, the wild force subsided, and black, out of the white foam,)

kʰlaftˈ hɪˈnʊntˈɐ(r) laen ˈgeːnəndə　ʃpˈaltʰ, ˈgrʊntˈloːs, lals gɪŋs　lɪn　den ˈhœlənrɑom,
klafft hinunter　ein gähnender Spalt, grundlos, als ging's　in　den Höllenraum,
gapes downwards a　yawning　cleft,　bottomless, as if went it into the hell- space,
(a yawning cleft gapes open downwards, bottomless, as if it went down into the realm of hell,)

ʊntˈ ˈraesəntˈ　ziːtˈ　man di ˈbrandəndən ˈvoːgən
und reissend　sieht man die brandenden Wogen
and rapaciously sees one the breaking　waves
(and one sees the breaking waves rapaciously)

hɪˈnapˈ lɪn den ˈʃtˈruːdəlndən ˈtʰrɪçtˈɐ gəˈtsoːgən. jɛtstˈ ʃnɛl,　leː　di ˈbrandʊŋ
hinab in　den strudelnden Trichter gezogen. Jetzt schnell, eh'　die Brandung
down　into the swirling　funnel　drawn.　Now quickly, before the surge
(drawn down into the swirling funnel. Now quickly, before the surge)

ˈviːdɐkʰeːrətʰ, deːɐ̯ ˈjʏŋlɪŋ zɪç　gɔtˈ bəˈfiːltʰ,　lʊntˈ—laen ʃrae des　lɛntˈˈzɛtsəns
wiederkehret, der Jüngling sich Gott befiehlt,　und— ein Schrei des　Entsetzens
returns,　the youth　himself to God commends, and—　a　cry　of the horror
(returns, the youth commends himself to God, and—a cry of horror)　　[*Schiller:* **wiederkehrt**]

vɪrtˈ rɪŋs　gəˈhøːrətʰ, lʊntˈ ʃoːn hatˈ liːn deːɐ̯ ˈvɪrbəl　hɪnˈvɛkgəʃpˈyːltʰ, lʊntˈ
wird rings　gehöret, und schon hat ihn der Wirbel　hinweggespült, und
is　all around heard,　and already has him the whirlpool away- washed,　and
(is heard all around, and already the whirlpool has washed him away, and)　　[*Schiller:* **gehört**]

gəˈhaemnɪsfɔl ˈlyːbɐ dem ˈkʰyːnən ˈʃvɪmɐ　ʃliːstˈ　zɪç deːɐ̯ ˈraxən;
geheimnisvoll über dem kühnen Schwimmer schliesst sich der Rachen;
mysteriously over the bold　swimmer　closes　itself the yawning abyss;
(the yawning abyss mysteriously closes over the bold swimmer;)

eːɐ̯ tsaekˈtˈ zɪç　ˈnɪmɐ.　lʊntˈ ˈʃtˈɪlə vɪrts　ˈlyːbɐ dem ˈvasɐʃlʊntˈ,
er zeigt　sich　nimmer. Und stille wird's　über dem Wasserschlund,
he shows　himself never.　And quiet becomes it over the　water- gullet,
(he is no longer seen. And quiet descend over the watery gullet,)

ɪn deːɐ̯ ˈtʰiːfə　nuːɐ̯ ˈbrɑozətˈ lɛs hoːl,　lʊntˈ ˈbeːbəntˈ høːɐ̯tˈ man fɔn mʊnt tsuː mʊntˈ:
in der Tiefe　nur brauset es hohl,　und bebend hört man von Mund zu Mund:
in the　depths only roars　it hollowly, and trembling hears one from mouth to mouth:
(only a hollow roar is heard from the depths, and, trembling, one hears from mouth to mouth:)

ˈhoːxhɛrtsɪgɐ ˈjʏŋlɪŋ, ˈfaːrə voːl! ʊntˈ ˈhoːlɐ(r) lʊntˈ ˈhoːlɐ　høːɐ̯tˈ mans ˈhɔʏlən,
"Hochherziger Jüngling, fahre wohl!" Und hohler　und hohler　hört man's heulen,
"Noble-hearted youth,　fare well!" And hollower and hollower hears one it howl,
("Noble-hearted youth, farewell!" And more and more hollowly one hears Charybdis howling,)

282

ʊnt‘ ɛs hart‘ nɔx mɪt‘ 'baŋəm, mɪt‘ 'ʃrɛk‘lɪçəm 'vae̯lən. ʊnt‘ verfst duː
und es harrt noch mit bangem, mit schrecklichem Weilen. Und wärfst du
and it waits still with anxious, with frightful lingering. And threw you
(and everyone is still waiting in anxious, frightful suspense. And if you threw)

[*Peters:* **würfst** (vʏrfst)]

di 'kʰroːnə 'zɛlbɐ hɪ'nae̯n ʊnt‘ ʃp‘'rɛːçstʰ: veːɐ̯ miːɐ̯ 'brɪŋət di kʰroːn, leːɐ̯ zɔl ziː 'tʰraːgən
die Krone selber hinein und sprächst: wer mir bringet die Kron', er soll sie tragen
the crown itself in and would say: who to me brings the crown, he shall it wear
(in the crown itself, and said: "whoever brings me back the crown shall wear it)

ʊnt‘ 'kʰøːnɪç zae̯n! mɪç gə'lʏst‘ət‘ə nɪçt‘ naːx dem 'tʰɔɣrən loːn. vas di 'hɔɣləndə
und König sein! mich gelüstete nicht nach dem teuren Lohn. Was die heulende
and king be! me lusted not after the precious reward. What the howling
(and be king!" I would not covet the precious reward. What the howling)

'tʰiːfə daː 'ʊnt‘ən fɐɣ'heːlə, das lɛɐ̯'tseːlt‘ 'kʰae̯nə 'leːbəndə 'glʏk‘lɪçə 'zeːlə.
Tiefe da unten verhehle, das erzählt keine lebende glückliche Seele.
depths there below may hide, that tells no living happy soul.
(depths may conceal, down there, no living, happy soul will ever tell.)

voːl 'mançəs 'faːɐ̯tsɔɣk‘, fɔm 'ʃt‘ruːdəl lɛɐ̯'fastʰ, ʃɔs gɛː lɪn di 'tʰiːfə hɪ'nap‘;
Wohl manches Fahrzeug, vom Strudel erfasst, schoss gäh in die Tiefe hinab;
Surely many a vessel, by the whirlpool seized, shot suddenly into the depths down;
(Surely many a vessel, seized by the whirlpool, has suddenly shot down into the depths;)

[*Peters (as in Schiller):* **gefasst** (gə'fastʰ); "*gäh*" = "*jäh*" = suddenly]

dɔx tsɛɐ̯'ʃmɛt‘ɐt‘ nuːɐ̯ 'raŋən zɪç kʰiːl ʊnt‘ mast‘ hɛɐ̯'foːɐ̯
doch zerschmettert nur rangen sich Kiel und Mast hervor
but shattered only wrest themselves keel and mast forth
(but only in a shattered state do keel and mast wrest themselves free)

ɑos dem 'laləs fɐɣ'ʃlɪŋəndən graːp‘. ʊnt‘ 'hɛlɐ(r) ʊnt‘ 'hɛlɐ, viː 'ʃt‘ʊrməs 'zɑozən,
aus dem alles verschlingenden Grab. Und heller und heller, wie Sturmes Sausen,
from the all devouring grave. And clearer and clearer, like storm's roaring,
(from the all-devouring grave. And more and more clearly, like the raging of a storm,)

høːɐ̯t‘ mans 'neːɐ(r) ʊnt‘ 'lmɐ 'neːɐ 'brɑozən. ʊnt‘ ɛs 'valət‘ ʊnt‘ 'ziːdət‘ ʊnt‘ 'brɑozət‘
hört man's näher und immer näher brausen. Und es wallet und siedet und brauset
hears one it nearer and ever nearer roaring. And it boils and seethes and roars
(one hears it roaring, nearer and ever nearer. And it boils and seethes and roars)

ʊnt tsɪʃt‘, viː vɛn 'vasɐ mɪt‘ 'fɔɣɐ zɪç mɛŋtʰ, bɪs tsʊm 'hɪməl 'ʃp‘rɪtsət
und zischt, wie wenn Wasser mit Feuer sich mengt, bis zum Himmel spritzet
and hisses, as when water with fire itself mixes, till to the sky sprays
(and hisses, as when water mixes with fire, till up to the sky sprays)

deːɐ̯ 'dampfəndə gɪʃt‘, ʊnt‘ fluːt‘ lɑof fluːt‘ zɪç loːn 'lɛndə drɛŋt‘, ʊnt‘ viː mɪt
der dampfende Gischt, und Flut auf Flut sich ohn' Ende drängt, und wie mit
the steaming foam, and flood upon flood itself without end surges, and as if with
(the steaming foam, and flood upon flood surges up without end, as if with

[*Peters (as in Schiller):* **und Well' auf Well'** (vɛl)]

dɛs ˈdɔnɐs   ˈfɛrnəm gəˈtʰoːzə lɛntˈʃˈʏrt̩st̩ ɛs ˈbrʏlənt dem   ˈfɪnstˈɐn ˈʃoːsə.
des Donners fernem Getose entstürzt es brüllend dem   finstern Schosse.
the thunder's distant rumble rushes up   it roaring out of the dark   womb.
(the distant rumble of thunder, it rushes up, roaring, out of the dark womb.)

[Schiller, Peters, 1st version: **mit des fernen Donners Getose**]

ʊntˈ ziː! ˈ|ɑos dem ˈfɪnstˈɐ ˈfluːtˈəndən ʃoːs daː ˈheːbət zɪçs ˈʃvaːnənvɑes,
Und sieh! aus dem finster flutenden Schoss da   hebet sich's schwanenweiss,
And look! out of the dark   flooding   womb there lifts itself it swan-   white,
(And look! Out of the darkly flooding womb something as white as a swan is rising,)

ʊntˈ |ɑen |arm, |ʊntˈ |ɑen ˈglɛntsəndɐ ˈnakˈən vɪrtˈ   bloːs, |ʊntˈ |ɛs ˈruːdɐtˈ mɪtˈ kʰraftʰ
und ein Arm, und ein glänzender Nacken wird   bloss, und es rudert mit Kraft
and an arm, and a   shining   nape   becomes bare, and it paddles with strength
(and an arm and the shining nape of a neck become bared, and the arm is paddling with strength)

ʊntˈ mɪtˈ ˈ|ɛmzɪgəm flɑes, |ʊntˈ |eːɐ/|eːr |ɪsts, |ʊntˈ hoːx |ɪn ˈzɑenɐ ˈlɪŋkˈən ʃvɪŋtˈ |eːɐ
und mit emsigem Fleiss,   und er   ist's, und hoch in seiner Linken schwingt er
and with energetic diligence, and he   is it, and high in his   left hand brandishes he
(and with energetic diligence, and it is he, and high in his left hand he brandishes)

den ˈbɛçɐ   mɪtˈ ˈfrɔødɪgəm ˈvɪŋkˈən. ʊntˈ ˈ|aːtˈmətˈə laŋ |ʊntˈ ˈ|aːtˈmətˈə tʰiːf,
den Becher mit freudigem Winken. Und atmete   lang und atmete   tief,
the goblet with joyous   waving. And breathed long and breathed deeply,
(the goblet, waving it joyously. And he was breathling long, deep breaths,)

ʊntˈ bəˈgryːstˈə das ˈhɪmlɪʃə   lɪçtʰ. mɪtˈ froˈlɔkˈən |ɛs ˈ|ɑenɐ dem ˈ|andɐn riːf:
und begrüsste das himmlische Licht. Mit Frohlocken es einer dem andern rief:
and greeted   the heavenly   light. With jubilation it one   to the other cried:
(and he greeted the heavenly light. With jubilation the onlookers called to one another:)

|eːɐ leːpˈtˈ! |eːɐ/|eːr |ɪst daː! |ɛs bəˈhiːltˈ |iːn nɪçtʰ! |ɑos dem graːpˈ, |ɑos deːɐ ˈʃtˈruːdəlndən
"Er lebt! Er   ist da! Es behielt ihn nicht! Aus dem Grab, aus der strudelnden
"He lives! He   is there! It held   him not! From the grave, from the swirling
("He is alive! He is here! Charybdis did not hold him! Out of the grave, out of the swirling)

ˈvasɐhøːlə   hat deːɐ ˈbraːfə   gəˈrɛtˈət di ˈleːbəndə ˈzeːlə. ʊntˈ |eːɐ kʰɔmtʰ,
Wasserhöhle hat der Brave   gerettet die lebende Seele." Und er kommt,
water- cave   has the brave man rescued the living   soul." And he comes,
(water-cavern the brave man has rescued his living soul." And he comes forward,)

ɛs |ʊmˈrɪŋtˈ |iːn di ˈjuːbəlndə ʃaːɐ! tsuː dɛs ˈkʰøːnɪçs ˈfyːsən |eːɐ zɪŋtʰ,
es   umringt ihn die jubelnde Schar! zu des Königs Füssen er sinkt,
there surrounds him the rejoicing throng! At the king's feet   he sinks,
(surrounded by the rejoicing throng! At the king's feet he sinks down)

den ˈbɛçɐ rɑeçtˈ |eːɐ/|eːr |iːm ˈkʰniːənt daːɐ, |ʊnt deːɐ ˈkʰøːnɪç
den Becher reicht er   ihm knieend dar, und der König
the goblet presents he   to him kneeling ... , and the king
(and, kneeling, presents the goblet to him; and the king)   ["darreichen" = to present]

deːɐ̯ ˈliːpˈliçən ˈtʰɔxtˈɐ vɪŋkˈtʰ, diː fʏltˈ liːn mɪtˈ ˈfʊŋkˈəlndəm vaen bɪs ʦʊm ˈrandə;
der lieblichen Tochter winkt, die füllt ihn mit funkelndem Wein bis zum Rande;
to the lovely daughter beckons, who fills it with sparkling wine until to the rim;
(beckons his lovely daughter, who fills it with sparkling wine up to the rim:)

ʊnt deːɐ̯ ˈjʏŋlɪŋ zɪç ˈlalzo ʦʊm ˈkʰøːnɪç ˈvantˈə: ˈlaŋə ˈleːbə deːɐ̯ ˈkʰøːnɪç!
und der Jüngling sich also zum König wandte: "Lange lebe der König!
and the youth himself thus to the king turned: "Long live the king!
(and the youth turned to the king: "Long live the king!) [*Schiller:* **lang'** (laŋ) **lebe der König**]

ɛs ˈfrɔøə zɪç, veːɐ̯ da: ˈlaːtˈmətˈ lɪm ˈroːzɪçtˈən lɪçtʰ! ˈaːbə(r) da: lʊntˈən
Es freue sich, wer da atmet im rosigten Licht! Aber da unten
There gladden himself, who there breathes in the rose-colored light! But there down
(Let him be glad who breathes here in the rosy light! But down there)
[*Peters:* **rosigen** (ˈroːzɪɡən); *Schiller:* **Da unten aber**]

lɪsʦ ˈfʏrçtˈəlɪç, lʊnt deːɐ̯ mɛnʃ fɛɐ̯ˈzuːxə di ˈɡœtˈɐ nɪçtˈ,
ist's fürchterlich, und der Mensch versuche die Götter nicht,
is it frightful, and the human being (should) tempt the gods not,
(it is frightful, and man should not tempt the gods,)

lʊntˈ bəˈɡeːrə ˈnɪmɐ(r) lʊntˈ ˈnɪmɐ ʦuː ˈʃaoən, vas ziː ˈɡnɛːdɪç bəˈdɛkˈən
und begehre nimmer und nimmer zu schauen, was sie gnädig bedecken
and desire never and never to behold, what they graciously cover
(and should never, never desire to behold that which they graciously cover)

mɪtˈ naxtˈ lʊntˈ ˈɡraoən. lɛs rɪs mɪç hɪˈnʊntˈɐ ˈblɪʦəsʃnɛl,
mit Nacht und Grauen. Es riss mich hinunter blitzesschnell,
with night and horror. It tore me downwards, lightning-fast,
(with night and horror. It tore me downwards, as fast as lightning,)

da: ʃtˈʏrʦtˈ miːɐ̯/miːr laos ˈfɛlzɪɡəm ʃaxtˈ lɛntˈˈɡeːɡən laen ˈraesəndɐ kʰvɛl;
da stürzt' mir aus felsigem Schacht entgegen ein reissender Quell;
then shot to me out of rocky shaft toward a ravening jet of water;
(then a ravening jet of water shot toward me out of a rocky shaft;)
[*Schiller:* **wildflutend** (wildly flooding) **entgegen**]

mɪç ˈpʰakˈtˈə dɛs ˈdɔpˈəlʃtˈroːms ˈvyːtˈəndə maxtʰ, lʊntˈ viː ˈlaenən ˈkʰraezəl
mich packte des Doppelstroms wütende Macht, und wie einen Kreisel
me seized the double-stream's raging power, and like a spinning top
(the raging power of the double stream seized me, and like a spinning top)

mɪtˈ ˈʃvɪndəlndəm ˈdreːən tʰriːpˈ mɪçs lʊm, lɪç ˈkʰɔntˈə nɪçtˈ ˈviːdɐʃteːn.
mit schwindelndem Drehen trieb mich's um, ich konnte nicht widerstehn.
with dizzying twirling drove me it around, I could not resist.
(it hurled me around with its dizzying twirling; I could not resist.) [*Schiller:* **widerstehen**]

da: ˈʦaekˈtˈə miːɐ̯ ɡɔt, ʦuː deːm lɪç riːf, lɪn deːɐ̯ ˈhøːçstˈən, ˈʃrɛkˈlɪçən noːtʰ,
Da zeigte mir Gott, zu dem ich rief, in der höchsten, schrecklichen Not,
Thereupon showed to me God, to whom I called in the highest, most horrible need,
(Thereupon God, to whom I cried out in my moment of highest, most horrible need, showed me)

ɑos deːɐ̯ ˈtʰiːfə ˈraːgənt˺ l̯a͜en ˈfɛlzənrɪf;   das lɛɐ̯ˈfast˺ lɪç bəˈhɛnt˺ l̯ʊnt˺ lɛntˈran dem tʰoːt˺.
aus der Tiefe ragend ein Felsenriff; das erfasst' ich behend und entrann dem Tod.
from the depths jutting a   rock- reef; that seized I   nimbly and escaped the   death.
(a rocky reef jutting up out of the depths; I seized that nimbly, and escaped from death.)

[GA (1st version): **aus der Tiefe ein ragend Felsenriff]**

[GA (2nd version): **emporragend** (lɛmˈpʰoːɐ̯raːgənt˺, jutting up) **ein Felsenfiff]**

ʊnt daː hɪŋ l̯ɑ͜ox deːɐ̯ ˈbɛçɐ l̯an ˈʃpˈt̯sən kʰoˈralən,
Und da   hing auch der Becher an spitzen Korallen,
And there hung also the   goblet   on pointed corals,
(And there the goblet was also hanging on a pointed piece of coral,)

zɔnst˺ vɛːɐ̯/vɛːr leːɐ̯/leːr lɪns   ˈboːdənloːzə gəˈfalən. dɛn ˈl̯ʊntˈɐ miːɐ̯ laːks nɔx
sonst wär'   er   ins   Bodenlose gefallen. Denn unter mir lag's noch
else   were   it   into the bottomless fallen. For   under me lay it still
(otherwise it would have fallen into the bottomless pit. For beneath me that still lay)

ˈbɛrgətʰiːf   ɪn ˈpʰʊrpˈʊrnɐ ˈfɪnstˈɐnɪs daː,   l̯ʊnt˺ l̯ɔps hiːɐ̯ dem ˈloːrə gl̯a͜eç
bergetief   in purpurner Finsternis da,   und ob's hier dem   Ohre gleich
mountain-deep in purple   dimness   there, and al- it here to the ear   -though
(there, enormously deep, in purple dimness, and although here to the ear it)

ˈleːvɪç ʃliːf,   das ˈl̯ɑ͜ogə mɪt˺ ˈʃɑ͜odɐn   hɪˈnʊntˈɐ zaː,
ewig   schlief, das Auge mit Schaudern hinunter sah,
eternally slept,   the eye   with shuddering down   saw,
(seemed to be eternally asleep, the eye, looking down, saw with a shudder)

viːs fɔn zalaˈmandɐn l̯ʊnt˺ ˈmɔlçən l̯ʊnt ˈdraxən zɪç ˈreːkˈt̯ə   *[Schiller:* **sich regt']**
wie's von Salamandern und Molchen und Drachen sich regte
how it with salamanders   and   monsters and dragons itself stirred
(how it was teeming with salamanders and monsters and dragons)

lɪn dem ˈfʊrçtˈbaːrən ˈhœlənraxən.   ʃvarts ˈvɪməltˈən   daː,   lɪn ˈgrɑ͜ozəm gəˈmɪʃ,
in dem furchtbaren Höllenrachen.   Schwarz wimmelten da,   in grausem Gemisch,
in the fearful   hell- yawning abyss. Black   swarmed   there, in gruesome mixture,
(in that fearful yawning abyss of hell. Black, in a gruesome brew, there were swarming there,)

[GA (2nd version): **im grausen** (lɪm ˈgrɑ͜ozən, in the gruesome) **Gemisch]**

t̯su: ˈʃɔ͜øslɪçən   ˈkʰlʊmpˈən gəˈbalt̊,   deːɐ̯ ʃtˈaxlɪçtˈə ˈrɔxə,   deːɐ̯ ˈkʰlɪpˈənfɪʃ,
zu scheusslichen Klumpen geballt,   der stachlichte Roche, der Klippenfisch,
into hideous   clumps   clustered, the stinging   ray,   the klipfish,
(clustered into hideous clumps, the sting ray, the klipfish,)   *[Schiller:* **der stachligte]**

dɛs ˈhamɐs   ˈgrɔ͜ølɪçə ˈl̯ʊngəʃtˈalt̊,   ʊnt ˈdrɔ͜øənt˺
des Hammers   greuliche Ungestalt,   und dräuend
the hammer-head's horrible misshapen form, and, threateningly,

viːs miːɐ̯ di ˈgrɪmɪgən t̯sɛːnə deːɐ̯/deːr lɛntˈˈzɛt̯slɪçə hae̯, dɛs ˈmeːrəs hyˈɛːnə.
wies   mir die grimmigen Zähne der   entsetzliche Hai, des Meeres Hyäne.
showed me the   fierce   teeth   the   horrifying shark, the sea's   hyena.
(the horrifying shark, the hyena of the sea, showed me its fierce teeth.)

ʊnt daː hɪŋ lɪç ʊnt' vaːɐ̯s miːɐ̯ mɪt' 'grɑozən bə'vʊst', fɔn deːɐ̯ 'mɛnʃlɪçən 'hɪlfə
Und da **hing ich und war's mir** **mit Grausen bewusst, von der menschlichen Hilfe**
And there hung I and was it to me with horror aware from the human help
(And there I hung, and I was aware with horror that I was far from any human help,)

     [*GA (both versions):* **und war mir's** (vaːɐ̯ miːɐ̯s), *Schiller* **war's mir**; *Peters:* **Hülfe** ('hʏlfə)]

zoː vaɛt', 'ʊnt'ɐ 'larfən di 'laɛntsɪgə 'fyːləndə brʊst', la'laɛn lɪn deːɐ̯ 'grɛslɪçən
so weit, unter Larven die einzige fühlende Brust, allein in der grässlichen
so far, among specters the only feeling breast, alone in the horrible

'laɛnzaːmkʰaet', t'iːf 'ʊnt'ɐ dem ʃal deːɐ̯ 'mɛnʃlɪçən 're:də baɛ den lʊŋə'hɔøɐn
Einsamkeit, tief unter dem Schall der menschlichen Rede bei den Ungeheuern
solitude, deep beneath the sound of the human speech, among the monsters
(solitude, deep beneath the sound of human speech, among the monsters)

deːɐ̯ 't'rɑorɪgən 'løːdə. lʊnt' 'ʃɑodɐnt daxt' lɪçs, daː kʰrɔxs he'ran,
der traurigen Öde. Und schaudernd dacht ich's, da kroch's heran,
of the dismal wasteland. And shuddering thought I it, there crept it near,
(of that dismal wasteland. And with a shudder I thought that something was creeping nearer,)

're:kt'ə 'hʊndɐt' gə'leŋkə tsu'glaɛç, vɪl 'ʃnap'ən naːx miːɐ̯; lɪn des 'ʃrɛk'əns vaːn
regte hundert Gelenke zugleich, will schnappen nach mir; in des Schreckens Wahn
stirred a hundred joints at once, wants to snap at me; in the terror's madness
(moving a hundred limbs at once, wanting to snap at me; in the madness of my terror)

las lɪç loːs deːɐ̯ kʰo'ralə lʊm'kʰlamɐt'ən tsvaɛk'; glaɛç fast' mɪç deːɐ̯ 'ʃt'ruːdəl
lass' ich los der Koralle umklammerten Zweig; gleich fasst mich der Strudel
let I loose the coral's clutched branch; at once seized me the whirlpool
(I let go of the coral branch I had been clutching; at once the whirlpool seized me)

mɪt' 'raːzəndəm 't'oːbən, dɔx lɛs vaːɐ̯ miːɐ̯ tsʊm haɛl, leːɐ̯ rɪs mɪç naːx 'loːbən.
mit rasendem Toben, doch es war mir zum Heil, er riss mich nach oben."
with raging wildness, but it was for me to the salvation, it tore me toward above."
(with raging wildness, but for me it was salvation, for it pulled me upward.")

deːɐ̯ 'kʰøːnɪç da'rɔp' zɪç fɛɐ̯'vʊndɐt' ʃiːɐ̯ lʊnt' ʃp'rɪçtʰ: deːɐ̯ 'bɛçɐ(r) lɪst daɛn,
Der König darob sich verwundert schier und spricht: "Der Becher ist dein,
The king on that account himself astonishes sheerly and speaks: "The goblet is yours,
(The king is very astonished and says: "The goblet is yours,)

ʊnt 'diːzən rɪŋ nɔx bə'ʃt'ɪm lɪç diːɐ̯, gə'ʃmʏk't' mɪt dem 'kʰœst'lɪçst'ən
und diesen Ring noch bestimm' ich dir, geschmückt mit dem köstlichsten
and this ring besides destine I for you, adorned with the most precious
(and, in addition, I shall give to you this ring, adorned with the most precious)

'leːdəlgəʃt'aɛn, fɛɐ̯'zuːxst duːs nɔx 'laɛnmaːl lʊnt' brɪŋst' miːɐ̯ 'kʰʊndə, vas duː zaːstʰ
Edelgestein, versuchst du's noch einmal und bringst mir Kunde, was du sahst
jewels, (if) attempt you it still once more and bring me tidings what you saw
(jewels, if you will make the attempt once more and bring me tidings of what you have seen)

ɑof des meːɐ̯s t'iːfʊnt'ɐst'əm 'grʊndə. das 'høːɐ̯t'ə di 't'ɔxt'ɐ mɪt' 'vaeçəm
auf des Meers tiefunterstem Grunde." Das hörte die Tochter mit weichem
on the sea's deep-lowest floor." That heard the daughter with soft
(at the very bottom of the sea." The king's daughter heard that with tender)

gə'fy:l, lʊnt' mɪt' 'ʃmaeçəlndəm 'mʊndə zi: fle:tʰ: last', 'fa:t'ɐ,
Gefühl, und mit schmeichelndem Munde sie fleht: "Lasst, Vater,
feeling, and with coaxing mouth she implores: "Let, Father,
(emotion, and with coaxing words she implores: "Father, let)

    [*GA, Peters:* **lass** (Schubert's error? The king should be addressed in the second person plural)]

gə'nu:k' zaen das 'graoza:mə ʃp'i:l! le:ɐ hat' lɔφç bə'ʃt'andən, vas 'kʰaenɐ bə'ʃt'e:tʰ,
genug sein das grausame Spiel! Er hat euch bestanden, was keiner besteht,
enough be the cruel game! He has for you endured what no one endures,
(that be enough of the cruel game! He has endured for you what no other man can endure,)

ʊnt' kʰœnt' li:ɐ dɛs 'hɛrtsəns gə'lyst'ə nɪçt 'tse:mən, zo: 'møːgən di 'rɪt'ɐ
und könnt ihr des Herzens Gelüste nicht zähmen, so mögen die Ritter
and can you the heart's desires not tame, then may the knights
(and if you cannot tame the desires of your heart, then let the knights)

den 'kʰnap'ən bə'ʃɛ:mən. draof de:ɐ 'kʰø:nɪç graeft' na:x dem 'bɛçɐ ʃnɛl,
den Knappen beschämen." Drauf der König greift nach dem Becher schnell,
the squire put to shame." At that the king grasps for the goblet quickly,
(put the squire to shame." At that the king quickly grasps the goblet,)

ɪn den 'ʃt'ru:dəl li:n 'ʃlɔφdɛt' hɪ'naen: lʊnt' ʃafst du: den 'bɛçɐ mi:ɐ 'vi:dɐ
in den Strudel ihn schleudert hinein: "Und schaffst du den Becher mir wieder
into the whirlpool it flings into: "And procure you the goblet for me again
(and flings it into the whirlpool: "And if you procure the goblet for me again)

tsʊr ʃt'ɛl, zo: zɔlst du: de:ɐ 'tʰrɛflɪçst'ə 'rɪt'ɐ mi:ɐ zaen, lʊnt' zɔlst'
zur Stell', so sollst du der trefflichste Ritter mir sein, und sollst
at the place, then shall you the most excellent knight for me be, and shall
(here, then you shall be my most excellent knight, and you shall)   ["*zur Stelle*" = here]

zi: lals 'le:gəma:l hɔφt' nɔx lʊm'larmən, di: jɛtst' fy:ɐ dɪç 'bɪt'ət mɪt 'tsa:ɐt'əm
sie als Ehgemahl heut noch umarmen, die jetzt für dich bittet mit zartem
her as husband today yet embrace, who now for you pleads with tender
(embrace her as her husband yet today, my daughter who is now pleading for you with tender)

lɐ'barmən. da: lɐ'graefts li:m di 'ze:lə mɪt' 'hɪməlsgəvalt', lʊnt' lɛs blɪtst'
Erbarmen." Da ergreift's ihm die Seele mit Himmelsgewalt, und es blitzt
pity." Thereupon seized it for him the soul with heaven- force, and it flashes
(pity." Thereupon the squire's soul is seized with heavenly power, and it flashes)

laos den 'laogən li:m kʰy:n, lʊnt' le:ɐ 'zi:ət lɐ'rø:t'ən di 'ʃø:nə gə'ʃt'altʰ,
aus den Augen ihm kühn, und er siehet erröten die schöne Gestalt,
out of the eyes of him boldly, and he sees blush the lovely form,
(boldly out of his eyes, and he sees the lovely creature blushing,)

ʊnt' zi:t' zi: lɐ'blaeçən di 'ʃø:nə gə'ʃt'alt' lʊnt' 'zɪŋk'ən hɪn — da: tʰraep'ts li:n,
und sieht sie erbleichen die schöne Gestalt* und sinken hin — da treibt's ihn,
and sees her pale, the lovely form, and sink away — there drives it him,
(and sees her grow pale and swoon — that impels him)

    [**Schiller & GA (2nd version):* **und sieht sie erbleichen und sinken hin**]

den 'kʰœst‘lɪçən pʰraes tsu: lɛɐ̯'vɛrbən, ʊnt‘ ʃt‘ʏrtst‘   hɪ'nʊnt‘ɐ(r) lɑof 'le:bən ʊnt‘ 'ʃt‘ɛrbən.
den köstlichen Preis zu erwerben, und stürzt   hinunter   auf Leben und Sterben.
the precious   prize to gain,   and (he) plunges down   on to live and to die.
(to strive for the precious prize, and he dives down to life or death.)

vo:l   hø:ɐ̯t‘ man di 'brandʊŋ,   vo:l   kʰe:ɐ̯t‘ zi: tsu'rʏkʰ,
Wohl hört man die Brandung, wohl kehrt sie zurück,
Indeed hears one the surf,   indeed returns it   back,
(The roar of the surf is heard, the surge is coming back,)

zi: fɛɐ̯'kʰʏndɪçt de:ɐ̯ 'dɔnɐndə ʃal; da: bʏk‘t‘ zɪçs   hɪ'nʊnt‘ɐ
sie verkündigt der donnernde Schall; da   bückt sich 's   hinunter
it announces   the thundering sound; thereupon bends herself she down
(the thundering sound announces it; thereupon the girl bends down)
                                        [*GA (1st version):* **da bückt's sich** (da: bʏk‘ts zɪç)]

mɪt‘ 'li:bəndəm blɪkʰ: ɛs 'kʰɔmən di 'vasɐ(r) lal, zi: 'rɑoʃən   hɛ'rɑof,
mit liebendem Blick: es   kommen die Wasser all', sie rauschen herauf,
with loving   look: there come   the waters all, they rush   upwards,
(with a loving gaze: the waves all come rushing upwards,)

zi: 'rɑoʃən   'ni:dɐ, dɔx den 'jʏŋlɪŋ   brɪŋt‘ 'kʰaenəs 'vi:dɐ.   [*Schiller without* "doch"]
sie rauschen nieder, doch den Jüngling bringt keines wieder.
they rush   down,   but the youth   brings none   back again.
(then they rush down again; but none brings back the youth.)

[This powerful setting of a magnificent long ballad is a music drama in miniature. In general, where the *Gesamtausgabe* and Peters have printed different words, those in the former are more likely to be what Schubert copied onto his music and those in the latter are more faithful to Schiller's original poem. There are three different options to choose from: the *Gesamtausgabe* offers two quite differing versions, both by Schubert; the Peters edition combines elements from both, creating a third possibility.]

de:ɐ̯ tʰo:t‘ 'lɔsk‘ars
Der Tod Oscars
The Death of Oscar

Posthumously published [composed 1816] (prose poem by James Macpherson—"Ossian")
(German translation by Edmund von Harold)

va'rʊm 'lœfnəst du: 'vi:dɐ(r), lɛɐ̯'tsɔøk‘t‘ɐ fɔn lal'pʰi:n, di 'kʰvɛlə 'maenɐ 've:mu:tʰ,
Warum öffnest du wieder, Erzeugter von Alpin, die Quelle meiner Wehmut,
Why   open   you again, begotten   of Alpin, the spring of my   melancholy,
(*Macpherson:* Why openest thou afresh the spring of my grief, O son of Alpin,)

da: du: mɪç fra:kst‘, vi: 'lɔsk‘ar lɛɐ̯'la:k‘? 'maenə 'lɑogən zɪnt‘ fɔn 'tʰre:nən lɛɐ̯'blɪndətʰ,
da   du mich fragst, wie Oscar erlag?   Meine Augen sind von Tränen erblindet,
in that you me ask,   how Oscar died?   My   eyes   are by   tears   blinded,
(inquiring how Oscar fell? My eyes are blind with tears,)

ˈaːbɐ(r) lɛɐ̯(r)ˈlinərʊŋ ʃtˈraːlt‘ lɑos ˈmaenəm ˈhɛrtsən.. viː kʰan lɪç den ˈtʰrɑorɪgən fal
aber Erinnerung strahlt aus meinem Herzen. Wie kann ich den traurigen Fall
but memory beams from my heart. How can I the sad fall
(but memory streams from my heart. How can I relate the mournful death)

   [*Harold:* **an** (an, at) **meinem Herzen** (*Macpherson:* but memory beams on my heart)]

      [*Peters:* **Wie soll ich** (viː zɔl lɪç), how shall I]

dɛs ˈfyːrɐs deːɐ̯ ˈkʰriːgɐ(r) lɛɐ̯ˈtsɛːlən? ˈfyːrɐ deːɐ̯ ˈhɛldən, loː ˈlɔskˈar, maen zoːn,
des Führers der Krieger erzählen? Führer der Helden, o Oscar, mein Sohn,
of the leader of the warriors relate? Leader of the heroes, O Oscar, my son,
(of the head of the people? Chief of the warriors, Oscar, my son,)

zɔl lɪç dɪç nɪçt‘ meːɐ̯/meːr lɛɐ̯ˈblɪkˈən? leːɐ̯ fiːl, viː deːɐ̯ moːnt‘ lɪn ˈlaenəm ʃtˈʊrm,
soll ich dich nicht mehr erblicken? Er fiel, wie der Mond in einem Sturm,
shall I you not more see? He fell, as the moon in a storm,
(shall I see thee no more? He fell, as the moon in a storm,) [*Peters:* **dich nimmer** (nɪmɐ), never]

viː di ˈzɔnə lɪn deːɐ̯ ˈmɪtˈə ˈliːrəs lɑofs; vɛn ˈvɔlkˈən fɔm ˈʃoːsə deːɐ̯ ˈ voːgən
wie die Sonne in der Mitte ihres Laufs; wenn Wolken vom Schosse der Wogen
as the sun in the midst of its course; when clouds from the bosom of the waves
(as the sun from the midst of his course, when clouds rise from the waste of the waves,)

    [*Peters:* **wenn Wellen** (= waves; an error: "clouds" in Macpherson)]

zɪç ˈheːbən, vɛn das ˈdʊŋkˈəl dɛs ʃtˈʊrms larˈdanɪdɛs ˈfɛlzən ˈlaenhʏltʰ.
sich heben, wenn das Dunkel des Sturms Ardanniders Felsen einhüllt.
themselves raise, when the dark of the storm Ardannider's rocks wraps.
(when the blackness of the storm wraps the rocks of Ardannider.)

   [*Peters (error):* **Ardannidor's** (Ardannider is the name in Macpherson's poem]

viː ˈlaenə ˈlaltˈə ˈlaeçə fɔn ˈmɔrvən, fɛɐ̯ˈmoː- drɪç ˈlaenzaːm lɑof ˈmaenɐ ʃtˈɛlə.
Wie eine alte Eiche von Morven, vermodr' ich einsam auf meiner Stelle.
Like an old oak of Morven, moulder I lonely on my place.
(I, like an ancient oak on Morven, I moulder alone in my place.) [*Peters:* **an** (an) **meiner Stelle**]

deːɐ̯ ˈvɪntˈʃtˈoːs hatˈ miːɐ̯ ˈdi ˈlɛstˈə lɛntˈrɪsən; mɪç ˈʃrɛkˈən di ˈflyːgəl dɛs nɔrts.
Der Windstoss hat mir die Äste entrissen; mich schrecken die Flügel des Nords.
The wind-gust has from me the branches torn away; me frighten the wings of the north.
(The blast hath lopped my branches away; and I tremble at the wings of the north.)

deːɐ̯ hɛltˈ, loː lalˈpʰiːns lɛɐ̯ˈtsɔøkˈtˈɐ, fiːl nɪçtˈ ˈfriːtˈlɪç, viː graːs lɑof dem fɛltˈ;
Der Held, o Alpins Erzeugter, fiel nicht friedlich, wie Gras auf dem Feld;
The hero, O Alpin's begotten son, fell not peacefully, like grass on the field;
(But, son of Alpin, the hero fell not harmless as the grass on the field;)

deːɐ̯ ˈmɛçtˈɪgən bluːtˈ bəˈfɛrpˈtˈə zaen ʃveːɐ̯tʰ,
der Mächtigen Blut befärbte sein Schwert,
the mighty ones' blood stained his sword,
(the blood of the mighty was on his sword,)

    eːɐ̯ rɪs zɪç, mit tʰoːt, dʊrç di ˈraeən ˈliːrəs ʃtˈɔltsəs,
[*GA and Harold:*] **er riss sich, mit Tod, durch die Reihen ihres Stolzes,**
    he tore himself, with death, through the ranks of their pride,
    (and he travelled with death through the ranks of their pride.)

[eːɐ̯ ˈfyːɐ̯t'ə den tʰoːt' lɪn di ˈraeən ˈlʊnzrɐ faents;]
[*Peters:* **er führte den Tod in die Reihen unsrer Feinds;**]
[he led the death into the ranks of our enemies;]
[(he led death into the ranks of our enemies;)]

ˈaːbɐ(r) ˈlɔskˈar, lɛɐ̯ˈtsɔøkˈt'ɐ fɔn ˈkʰaːruːt, duː bɪst' lʊnˈryːmlɪç ɡəˈfalən,
aber Oscar, Erzeugter von Caruth, du bist unrühmlich gefallen,
but Oscar, begotten son of Caruth, you have unlaudably fallen,
(But Oscar, thou son of Caruth, thou hast fallen low!)

ˈdaenə ˈreçt'ə lɛɐ̯ˈʃluːk' ˈkʰaenən faent', ˈdaenən ʃp'eːɐ̯ bəˈflɛkt'ə das bluːt ˈdaenəs frɔønts.
deine Rechte erschlug keinen Feind, deinen Speer befleckte das Blut deines Freunds.
your right hand slew no enemy, your spear stained the blood of your friend.
(No enemy fell by thy hand. Thy spear was stained with the blood of thy friend.)

aens vaːɐ̯ ˈdermɪd lʊnt' ˈlɔskˈar; ziː ˈmeːt'ən di ˈʃlaxt'ən tsuˈzamən.
Eins war Dermid und Oscar; sie mähten die Schlachten zusammen.
As one were Dermid and Oscar; they mowed the battles together.
(Dermid and Oscar were one: they reaped the battle together.)

ˈiːrə ˈfrɔønt'ʃaft' vaːɐ̯ ʃt'ark', vi: liːɐ̯/liːr ˈlaezən, lʊnt' lɪm ˈfɛldə ˈvandəlt'ə deːɐ̯ tʰoːt'
Ihre Freundschaft war stark, wie ihr Eisen, und im Felde wandelte der Tod
Their friendship was strong as their iron, and in the field wandered the death
(Their friendship was strong as their steel; and death walked between them to the field.)

[*Peters:* **war fest** (fɛst') firm]

ˈtsvɪʃən ˈliːnən. zi: ˈfuːrən ˈɡeːɡən den faent', vi: tsvae ˈfɛlzən, di: fɔn ˈlardvəns
zwischen ihnen. Sie fuhren gegen den Feind, wie zwei Felsen, die von Ardvens
between them. They went against the foe like two rocks which from Ardven's
(They came on the foe like to rocks falling from the brows of Ardven.)

ˈʃt'ɪrnə zɪç ˈʃt'ʏrtsən. liːɐ̯ ˈʃveːɐ̯t' vaːɐ̯ fɔm ˈbluːt'ə deːɐ̯ ˈtʰapfen bəˈfɛrp't'ʰ.
Stirne sich stürzen. Ihr Schwert war vom Blute der Tapfern befärbt.
brow themselves hurl. Their sword was from the blood of the valiant stained.
(Their swords were stained with the blood of the valiant.)

ˈkʰriːɡɐ(r) lɛɐ̯ˈbeːp't'ən bae ˈliːrən ˈnaːmən! veːɐ̯ ɡlɪç ˈlɔskˈarn lals ˈdermɪd?
Krieger erbebten bei ihren Namen! Wer glich Oscarn als Dermid?
(warriors fainted at their names! Who was equal to Oscar, but Dermid?)

ʊnt' vːɐ ˈdermɪd lals ˈlɔskˈar? zi: lɛɐ̯ˈleːk't'ən den ˈmeçt'ɪɡən ˈdargo lɪm fɛlt',
Und wer Dermid als Oscar? Sie erlegten den mächtigen Dargo im Feld,
And who Dermid, but Oscar? They killed the mighty Dargo in the field,
(And who to Dermid, but Oscar? They killed mighty Dargo in the field,)

ˈdargo, deːɐ̯ ni: lɑos dem kʰampf lɛnt'ˈfloː. ˈzaenə ˈtʰoxt'ɐ vaːɐ̯ ʃøːn vi: deːɐ̯ ˈmɔrɡən,
Dargo, der nie aus dem Kampf entfloh. Seine Tochter war schön wie der Morgen,
Dargo, who never from the battle fled. His daughter was beautiful as the morning,
(Dargo, who never fled in war. His daughter was fair as the morn,)

zanft' vi: deːɐ̯ ʃt'raːl dɛs ˈlaːbənts. ˈliːrə ˈlɑoɡən ˈɡlɪçən tsvae ˈʃt'ɛrnən lɪm ˈreːɡən;
sanft wie der Strahl des Abends. Ihre Augen glichen zwei Sternen im Regen;
mild as the beam of the evening. Her eyes were like two stars in the rain;
(mild as the beam of night. Her eyes, like two stars in a shower:)

iːɐ/iːr ˈlaːtˈəm   dem ˈhɑ̯ɔxə dɛs   ˈfryːlɪŋs. liːɐ ˈbuːzən viː ˈnɔ̯øɡəfalnɐ ˈʃneː,
ihr Atem   dem Hauche des   Frühlings. Ihr Busen wie neugefallner Schnee,
her breath (like) the   breath of the spring.   Her bosom like new- fallen snow,
(her breath, the gale of spring: her breasts, as the new-fallen snow)

deːɐ/deːr lɑ̯ɔf deːɐ ˈviːɡəndən   ˈhɑ̯ɛdə zɪç vɛltstʰ. ziː vartˈ fɔn den ˈhɛldən ɡəˈzeːn,
der   auf der wiegenden   Haide sich wälzt. Sie ward von den Helden gesehn,
that   on the gently moving heath itself rolls. She was by the heroes seen,
(floating on the moving heath. The warriors saw her,)

              ʊntˈ ɡəˈliːpˈtʰ; ˈliːrə ˈzeːlən ˈvʊrdən lans ˈmɛːtˈçən ɡəˈhɛftˈətʰ.
[*GA & Harold*] **und geliebt; ihre Seelen wurden ans Mädchen geheftet.**
              and loved;   their souls were   to the girl   fastened.
              (and loved; their souls were fixed on the maid.)

                    [ʊntˈ ɡəˈliːpˈtʰ, ɪn ˈhɑ̯ɛsɐ ˈflamənɡluːtˈ lɛntˈˈbrantˈən ˈbɑ̯ɛdə.]
           [*Peters:* **und geliebt, in heisser Flammenglut entbrannten beide.**]
                    [and loved, in hot   flame- fire burned   both.]
                    [(and loved, both burned with an ardent flame.)]

ˈjeːdɐ ˈliːpˈtˈə ziː ɡlɑ̯ɛç ˈzɑ̯ɛnəm ruːm, ziː ˈvɔltˈə ˈjeːdɐ bəˈzɪtsən ˈloːdɐ ˈʃtˈɛrbən.
Jeder liebte sie gleich seinem Ruhm, sie wollte jeder besitzen oder sterben.
Each loved her like his   fame, her wanted each to possess or   to die.
(Each loved her as his fame; each must possess her or die.)

ˈaːbə(r) liːɐ hɛrts ˈveːltˈə ˈlɔskˈarn. ˈkʰaːruːts lɛɐˈtsɔ̯økˈtˈɐ vaːɐ deːɐ ˈjʏŋlɪŋ ˈliːrə ˈliːbə.
Aber   ihr Herz wählte Oscarn. Caruths Erzeugter   war der Jüngling ihrer Liebe.
But   her heart chose Oscar.   Caruth's begotten son was the young man of her love.
(But her soul was fixed on Oscar; the son of Caruth was the youth of her love)   [*Peters:* **Oscar**]

ziː fɛɐˈɡaːs das bluːtˈ ˈliːrəs ˈfaːtˈɐs, ʊntˈ ˈliːpˈtˈə di ˈrɛçtˈə,   di liːn lɛɐˈʃluːkˈ.
Sie vergass das Blut ihres Vaters, und liebte die Rechte,   die ihn erschlug.
She forgot the blood of her father, and loved the right (hand) that him slew.
(She forgot the blood of her father; and loved the hand that slew him.)

 ˈkʰaːruːts zoːn, ʃpˈraːx ˈdɛrmɪd, ɪç ˈliːbə, loː ˈlɔskˈar, ɪç ˈliːbə diːs ˈmɛːtˈçən.
"Caruths Sohn," sprach Dermid, "ich liebe, o Oscar, ich liebe dies Mädchen.
"Caruth's son,"   spoke Dermid, "I love, O Oscar, I love this girl.
("Son of Caruth," said Dermid, "I love; O Oscar, I love that maid.)

ˈaːbɐ(r) ˈliːrə ˈzeːlə hɛŋtˈ lan diːɐ, ʊntˈ nɪçts kʰan ˈdɛrmɪd ˈhɑ̯ɛlən. hiːɐ
Aber   ihre Seele hängt an dir, und nichts kann Dermid heilen. Hier
But   her soul clings to you, and nothing can Dermid heal.   Here
(But her soul cleaveth unto thee; and nothing can heal Dermid. Here,)

dʊrçˈdrɪŋ ˈdiːzən ˈbuːzən, loː ˈlɔskˈar, hɪlf ˈdɑ̯ɛnəm frɔ̯øntˈ mɪt ˈdɑ̯ɛnəm ˈʃveːɐtʰ!
durchdring' diesen Busen, o Oscar, hilf deinem Freund mit deinem Schwert!"
pierce   this   bosom, O Oscar, help your   friend with your   sword!"
(pierce this bosom, Oscar; relieve me, my friend, with thy sword.")

              [*Peters:* **durchstoss'** (dʊrçˈʃtˈoːs) = pierce]

[Oscar:]

niː zɔl maen ʃveːɐt, diˈarans zoːn, niː zɔl lɛs mɪt ˈdɛrmɪds ˈbluːtʼə bəˈflɛkˈtʼ zaen!
"Nie soll mein Schwert, Diarans Sohn, nie soll es mit Dermids Blute befleckt sein!"
"Never shall my sword, Diaran's son, never shall it with Dermid's blood stained be!"
("My sword, son of Diaran, shall never be stained with the blood of Dermid.")

[Dermid:]

veːɐ/veːr lɪst dan ˈvʏrdɪç mɪç ʦuː lɛɐˈleːgən? loː ˈlɔskʼar, ˈkʰaːruːʦ zoːn, las nɪçtʼ maen
"Wer ist dann würdig mich zu erlegen? o Oscar, Caruths Sohn, lass nicht mein
"Who is then worthy me to slay?   O Oscar, Caruth's son, let not my
("Who then is worthy to slay me, O Oscar son of Caruth? Let not my)

> [*Peters:* **mich zu fällen** (ˈfɛlən) to slay me]

ˈleːbən lʊnˈryːmlɪç fɛɐˈgeːən, las ˈniːmantʼ, lals ˈlɔskʼar mɪç ˈtʰøːtʼən.
Leben unrühmlich vergehen, lass niemand, als Oscar mich töten.
life ingloriously pass away, let no one   but Oscar me   kill.
(life pass away unknown. Let none but Oscar slay me.)

ʃikʼ   mɪç mɪtʼ ˈleːrə ʦʊm graːpʼ, lʊntʼ ruːm bəˈglaetʼə ˈmaenən tʰoːtʼ!
Schick' mich mit Ehre zum Grab, und Ruhm begleite   meinen Tod!"
Send me with honor to the grave, and fame accompany my death!"
(Send me with honor to the grave, and let my death be renowned.")

[Oscar:]

ˈdɛrmid, braox ˈdaenə ˈkʰlɪŋə, diˈarans lɛɐˈʦɔøkʼtʼɐ, ʃvɪŋ ˈdaenən ʃtʼaːl!
"Dermid, brauch' deine Klinge, Diarans Erzeugter, schwing' deinen Stahl!
"Dermid, use your blade, Diaran's begotten son, swing your steel!
("Dermid, make use of thy sword; son of Diaran, wield thy steel.)

> [*Peters:* **deine Waffe** (ˈdaenə ˈvafə, your weapon)]

oː, fiːl lɪç mɪt diːɐ, das maen tʰoːtʼ fɔn ˈdɛrmɪds ˈrɛçtʼən heːɐˈryːrə!
O, fiel' ich mit dir, dass mein Tod von Dermids Rechten herrühre!"
O, fell I with you, that my death from Dermid's right hand might proceed!"
(Would that I fell with thee! that my death came from the hand of Dermid!")

> [miːɐ ˈveːɐdə]
> [*Peters:* **von Dermids Rechten mir werde!"**]
> [to me become]
> [("that my death may come to me from Dermid's right hand!")]

ziː ˈfɔxtʼən baem ˈbaxə dɛs bɛrks, bae ˈbranos ʃtʼroːm. bluːtʼ ˈfɛrpʼtʼə
Sie fochten beim Bache des Bergs, bei Brannos Strom. Blut färbte
They fought by the brook of the mountain, by Branno's stream. Blood colored
(They fought by the brook of the mountain, by the streams of Branno. Blood tinged)

di ˈfliːsəndən ˈfluːtʼən lʊnt ran lʊm di bəˈmoːstʼən ˈʃtʼaenə.
die fliessenden Fluten und rann um die bemoosten Steine.
the flowing waters and ran around the moss-covered stones.
(the running water, and curled round the mossy stones.)

> [*Peters:* **die rinnenden** (ˈrɪnəndən) **Fluten**, the running waters]

ˈdɛrmid, deːɐ ˈʃtʼatʼlɪçə fiːl, leːɐ fiːl lʊntʼ ˈlɛçəltʼə lɪm tʰoːtʼ. —lʊntʼ fɛlst duː,
Dermid, der stattliche fiel, er fiel und lächelte im Tod. —"Und fällst du,
Dermid, the stately one fell, he fell and smiled in the death. —"And fall you,
(The stately Dermid fell; he fell, and smiled in death. —"And fallest thou,)

293

ˡɛɐ̯ˈtsɔɔ̯kˈtʼɐ diˈarans, fɛlst duː dʊrç di ˈrɛçtʼə fɔn ˈlɔskʼar! ˈdɛrmɪd, deːɐ̯
Erzeugter Diarans, fällst du durch die Rechte von Oscar! Dermid, der
begotten son of Diaran, fall you through the right hand of Oscar! Dermid, who
(son of Diaran, fallest thou by Oscar's hand! Dermid, who)

niː ɪm ˈkʰriːgə gəˈvɪçən, zeː ˡɪç dɪç ˈlalzo ɛɐ̯ˈliːgən? leːɐ̯ gɪŋ lʊntʼ ˈkʰeːɐ̯tʼə
nie im Kriege gewichen, seh' ich dich also erliegen?" Er ging und kehrte
never in the war yielded, see I you thus be defeated?" He went and returned
(never yielded in war, thus do I see thee fall!" He went, and returned)

tsʊm ˈmɛːtʼçən ˈzaɛnɐ ˈliːbə. leːɐ̯ ˈkʰeːɐ̯tʼə, ˈlaːbɐ ziː fɛɐ̯ˈnaːm ˈzaɛnən ˈjamɐ.
zum Mädchen seiner Liebe. Er kehrte, aber sie vernahm seinen Jammer.
to the maid of his love. He returned, but she perceived his grief.
(to the maid of his love. He returned, but she perceived his grief.)

vaˈrʊm diːs ˈdʊŋkʼəl, zoːn fɔn ˈkʰaːruːtʰ? vas ˡyːbɐˈʃatʼət ˈdaɛnə ˈmɛçtʼɪgə
Warum dies Dunkel, Sohn von Caruth? was überschattet deine mächtige
Why this darkness, son of Caruth? What overshadows your mighty
(Why this gloom, son of Caruth? What shades thy mighty)

ˈzeːlə? —ˡaɛnstʼ vaːɐ̯/vaːr ˡɪç, loː ˈmɛːtʼçən, ɪm ˈboːgən bəˈryːmtʰ, ˈlaːbɐ
Seele? —"Einst war ich, o Mädchen, im Bogen berühmt, aber
soul? —"Once was I, O maiden, for the bow famous, but
(soul? —"Though once renowned for the bow, O maid,)

ˈmaɛnən ruːm haːb ɪç ˈlɪtso fɛɐ̯ˈloːrən. lam baɔm, baɛm ˈbaxə dɛs ˈhyːgəls,
meinen Ruhm hab' ich itzo verloren. Am Baum, beim Bache des Hügels,
my fame have I now lost. On the tree, by the brook of the hill,
(I have lost my fame. Fixed on the tree by the brook of the hill,) [*Peters:* **ich jetzo** (ˈjɛtso, now)]

hɛŋt deːɐ̯ ʃilt dɛs ˈmuːtʼɪgən ˈgɔrmʊrs, deːn ˡɪç ɪm ˈkʰampfə ɛɐ̯ˈʃluːkʼ.
hängt der Schild des mutigen Gormurs, den ich im Kampfe erschlug.
hangs the shield of the valiant Gormur, whom I in the battle slew.
(is the shield of the valiant Gormur, whom I slew in battle.)

ɪç ˈhaːbə den tʰaːkʼ fɛɐ̯ˈgeːbəns fɛɐ̯ˈtseːɐ̯tʼ, lʊntʼ ˈkʰɔntʼə liːn nɪçtʼ mɪtʼ
Ich habe den Tag vergebens verzehrt, und konnte ihn nicht mit
I have the day in vain wasted, and could it not with
(I have wasted the day in vain, nor could) [*Peters:* **vergebens verbracht** (fɛɐ̯ˈbraxtʼ, spent)]

ˈmaɛnəm pfaɛl dʊrçˈdrɪŋən. —las mɪç, ɛɐ̯ˈtsɔɔ̯kʼtʼɐ fɔn ˈkʰaːruːt,
meinem Pfeil durchdringen." —"Lass mich, Erzeugter von Caruth,
my arrow pierce." —"Let me, begotten son of Caruth,
(my arrow pierce it." —"Let me try, son of Caruth,)

di kʰʊnst deːɐ̯ ˈtʰɔxtʼɐ fɔn ˈdargo fɛɐ̯ˈzuːxən. ˈmaɛnə ˈrɛçtʼə ˈlɛrntʼə
die Kunst der Tochter von Dargo versuchen. Meine Rechte lernte
the skill of the daughter of Dargo try. My right hand learned
(the skill of Dargo's daughter. My hands were taught)

den ˈboːgən tsuː ˈʃpʼanən, ɪn ˈmaɛnɐ kʰʊnstʼ froˈlɔkʼtʼə maɛn ˈfaːtʼɐ.
den Bogen zu spannen, in meiner Kunst frohlockte mein Vater."
the bow to bend, in my skill rejoiced my father."
(the bow: my father delighted in my skill.")

ziː gɪŋ; leːɐ̯ ʃtʼantʼ ˈhɪntʼɐ dem ʃiltʼ. ɛs ˈtsɪʃtʼə liːɐ̯ pfael, ɛs dʊrçˈdraŋ
Sie ging; er stand hinter dem Schild. Es zischte ihr Pfeil, es durchdrang
She went; he stood behind the shield. There hissed her arrow, it pierced
(She went. He stood behind the shield. Her arrow flew, and pierced)

ˈzaenə brʊstʰ. hael deːɐ̯ ˈʃneːvaesən ˈrɛçtʼən, ˈaox hael ˈdiːzəm ˈlaebənən ˈboːgən!
seine Brust. Heil der schneewiessen Rechten, auch Heil diesem eibenen Bogen!
his breast. Hail to the snow- white right hand, also hail to this yew bow!
(his breast. Blessed be that hand of snow; and blessed that bow of yew!)

veːɐ̯/veːr, lals ˈdargos ˈtʰɔxtʼɐ, vaːɐ̯ veːɐ̯tʼ, ˈkʰaːruːts lɛɐ̯ˈtsɔ̯ø̯ktʼən tsu: ˈtʰøːtʼən?
wer, als Dargos Tochter, war werth, Caruths Erzeugten zu töten?
who but Dargo's daughter was worthy, Caruth's begotten son to kill?
(Who but the daughter of Dargo was worthy to slay the son of Caruth?)

leːkʼ mɪç lɪns grːpʼ, ˈmaenə ˈʃøːnstʼə! leːkʼ mɪç lan ˈdɛrmɪds ˈzaetʼə!
"Leg' mich ins Grab, meine Schönste! Leg' mich an Dermids Seite!"
"Lay me in the grave, my fairest one! Lay me at Dermid's side!"
("Lay me in the earth, my fair one; lay me by the side of Dermid.")

[*Peters:* **Leg mich ins Grab, o Geliebte!** (loː gəˈliːpʼtʼə) O beloved]

— ˈlɔskʼar, fɛɐ̯ˈzɛtstʼə das ˈmɛːtʼçən, ˈmaenə zeːl lɪst di ˈzeːlə dɛs
—"Oscar," versetzte das Mädchen, "meine Seel' ist die Seele des
—"Oscar," replied the girl, "my soul is the soul of the
(—"Oscar!" the maid replied, "I have the soul of the)

ˈmɛçtʼɪgən ˈdargo. lɪç kʰan dem ˈtʰoːdə mɪtʼ ˈfrɔ̯ødə bəˈgeːgnən,
mächtigen Dargo. Ich kann dem Tode mit Freude begegnen,
mighty Dargo. I can the death with joy meet,
(mighty Dargo. Well pleased I can meet death.)

lç kʰan ˈmaenə ˈtʰraorɪçkʰaetʼ ˈlɛndən. zi: dʊrçˈʃtʼiːs ˈliːrən ˈvaesən ˈbuːzən
ich kann meine Traurigkeit enden." Sie durchstiess ihren weissen Busen
I can my sorrow end." She pierced her white bosom
(My sorrow I can end." She pierced her white bosom)

[*Peters:* **meine Trauer schnell** (ˈtʰraoɐ ʃnɛl) my sadness quickly]

mɪtʼ ʃtʼaːl, zi: fiːl, ˈbeːpʼtʼə, lʊnt ʃtʼarpʼ. ˈliːrə ˈgreːbɐ ˈliːgən baem ˈbaxə dɛs ˈhyːgəls,
mit Stahl, sie fiel, bebte, und starb. Ihre Gräber liegen beim Bache des Hügels,
with steel, she fell, trembled, and died. Their graves lie by the brook of the hill,
(with the steel. She fell; she trembled; and died. By the brook of the hill their graves are laid;)

[*Peters:* **sie sank** (zaŋkʰ) sank]

iːɐ̯ ˈgraːpʼmaːl bəˈdɛkʼt deːɐ̯/deːr ˈlʊnglaeçə ˈʃatʼən ˈlaenɐ ˈbɪrkʼə. lɔftʼ ˈgraːzən
ihr Grabmal bedeckt der ungleiche Schatten einer Birke. Oft grasen
their tomb covers the unequal shade of a birch. Often graze
(a birch's unequal shade covers their tomb. Often)

[*Peters:* **der zitternde** (ˈtsɪtʼɐndə, trembling) **Schatten**]

di ˈlastʼɪgən ˈzøːnə dɛs bɛrks lan ˈliːrən ˈgryːnəndən ˈgreːbən, vɛn deːɐ̯ ˈmɪtʼaːkʼ
die astigen Söhne des Bergs an ihren grünenden Gräbern, wenn der Mittag
the antlered sons of the mountain at their greening graves, when the midday
(on their green earthen tombs the branchy sons of the mountain feed, when midday)

'zaɛnə 'glyːəndən 'flamən ˈ|ɑosʃtʰˈrɔøtʰ, |ʊntʰ ˈʃvaɛgən ˈ|alə ˈhyːgəl bəˈhɛrʃtʰ.
seine glühenden Flammen ausstreut, und Schweigen alle Hügel beherrscht.
its burning flames spreads, and silence all hills rules.
(is all in flames, and silence over all the hills.)

[*Peters*: **und tiefes** ('tʰiːfəs, deep) **Schweigen die** (di, the) **Hügel beherrscht**]

[The original English text of this dramatic scene, which was translated into German quite faithfully, is in parentheses, above. The variants in brackets generally derive from the first published version, while the text printed in the *Gesamtausgabe* is closer to Harold's translation.]

deːɐ tʰoːtʰ |ʊntʰ das ˈmɛːtʰˈçən
Der Tod und das Mädchen
Death and the Maiden

Op. 7, No. 3 [1817] (Matthias Claudius)

(Das Mädchen / The Maiden)

foˈryːbɐ! |ax, foˈryːbɐ! geː ˈvɪldɐ ˈkʰnɔxənman!
Vorüber! ach, vorüber! geh, wilder Knochenmann!
Pass! ah, pass! go, wild bone-man! [*"vorübergehen"* = pass, go past]
(Pass me by! ah, go on your way, wild skeleton!)

|ɪç bɪn nɔx jʊŋ, geː ˈliːbɐ! |ʊntʰ ˈryːrə mɪç nɪçtʰ |an.
Ich bin noch jung, geh, Lieber! und rühre mich nicht an.
I am still young, go, dear one! and touch me not .... [*"anrühren"* = to touch]
(I am still young; go, dear one, and do not touch me.

(Der Tod / Death)

giːpʰ ˈdaɛnə hantʰ, duː ʃøːn |ʊntʰ tsaːɐtʰ gəˈbɪltʰ !
Gib deine Hand, du schön und zart Gebild!
Give your hand, you beautiful and delicate creature!
(Give me your hand, you beautiful and delicate creature!)

bɪn frɔøntʰ, |ʊntʰ ˈkʰɔmə nɪçt tsuː ˈʃtʰraːfən.
bin Freund, und komme nicht, zu strafen.
am friend, and come not to punish.
(I am a friend and do not come to punish.)

zaɛ ˈguːtʰəs muːts! |ɪç bɪn nɪçtʰ vɪltʰ, zɔlstʰ zanftʰ |ɪn ˈmaɛnən ˈlarmən ˈʃlaːfən!
Sei gutes Muts! ich bin nicht wild, sollst sanft in meinen Armen schlafen!
Be of good cheer! I am not wild, you shall gently in my arms sleep!
(Be of good cheer! I am not wild: you shall sleep gently in my arms!)

[In the piano prelude, death enters the sickroom of a young girl. Terrified, she begs him to spare her. In mysteriously soothing tones, death calmly reassures her that he comes as a friend; she will sleep gently in his arms. The near monotone of death's vocal line creates an uncanny effect.]

deːɐ̯ tʰrɑom
Der Traum
The Dream

Posthumously published [composed 1815] (poem by Ludwig Hölty)

miːɐ̯   tʰrɔømt', lɪç vaːɐ̯/vaːr laen 'føːɡəlaen, lʊnt' floːk' lɑof 'liːrəm ʃoːs,
Mir   träumt, ich war   ein Vögelein, und flog auf ihren Schoss,
To me dreamt, I   was   a   little bird, and flew onto her   lap,
(I dreamt I was a little bird and flew onto her lap,)

ʊnt tsʊpft' liːɐ̯/liːr, lʊm   nɪçt' las tsu: zaen, di 'buːzənənʃlaefən loːs;
und zupft' ihr,   um   nicht lass zu sein, die Busenschleifen los;
and pulled for her, so as not   lazy to be,   the bosom-bows   loose;
(and, so as not to be lazy, I pulled open the bows at her breast;)
          [*Peters:* **um nicht lapp** (lap', flabby) **zu sein, die Busenschleife** (-ʃlaefə, -bow) **los**]

ʊnt' floːk', mɪt' 'ɡɑok'əlhaft'əm fluːk', dan lɑof di 'vaesə hant',
und flog,   mit gaukelhaftem Flug, dann auf die weisse Hand,
and flew,   with juggler-like   flight, then onto the white hand,
(and then I flew onto her white hand, as fast as if I had been tossed by a nimble juggler,)

dan 'viːdɐ(r) lɑof das 'buːzəntʰuːx, lʊnt' pʰɪk't' lam 'roːt'ən bant'.
dann wieder auf das Busentuch, und pickt' am roten Band.
then again   onto the scarf,   and pecked at the red ribbon.

dan ʃveːp't' lɪç lɑof liːɐ̯ 'blɔndəs haːɐ̯/haːr, lʊnt 'tsvɪtʃɐt'ə   foːɐ̯ lʊstʰ,
Dann schwebt' ich auf ihr blondes Haar,   und zwitscherte vor Lust,
Then soared   I   onto her blond hair,   and twittered   with pleasure,
(Then I soared up onto her blond hair and twittered with pleasure,)

ʊnt' 'ruːt'ə, van   lɪç 'myːdə vaːɐ̯/vaːr, lan 'liːrɐ 'vaesən brʊstʰ.
und ruhte, wann ich müde war,   an ihrer weissen Brust.   [*poem:* **auf** (lɑof, on) **ihrer...**]
and rested, when I   tired was,   on her white   breast.
(and rested, when I was tired, on her white breast.)

kʰaen 'faelçənbɛt' lɪm   pʰaraˈdiːs geːt 'diːzəm 'laːɡɐ foːɐ̯.
Kein Veilchenbett im   Paradies geht diesem Lager vor.
No   violet- bed in the Paradise goes this   couch before.
(No bed of violets in Paradise excels this resting place.)   [*"vorgehen"* (in this case) = to excel]

vi: ʃliːf   zɪçs da: zo: zyːs,   zo: zyːs,   lan 'liːrəs 'buːzəns floːɐ̯!
Wie schlief   sich 's da so süss,   so süss,   an ihres Busens Flor!
How would sleep itself it there so sweetly, so sweetly, on her   bosom's gauze!
(How sweetly, how sweetly one would sleep there, on the soft gauze of her bosom!)

ziː 'ʃp'iːlt'ə, vi: lɪç 'tʰiːfɐ zaŋk', mɪt' 'laezəm 'fɪŋɐʃlaːk',
Sie spielte, wie ich tiefer sank, mit leisem Fingerschlag,
She played, as I deeper sank, with soft   finger- tap,
(Playfully, as I sank deeper, with a soft tap of her finger,)

deːɐ̯ miːɐ̯ dʊrç lae̯p‘ ʊnt‘ 'leːbən draŋ, mɪç 'froːən 'ʃlʊmrɐ vax;
der mir durch Leib und Leben drang, mich frohen Schlummrer wach;
which to me through body and life penetrated, me happy sleeper awake;
(which penetrated through my body and soul, she woke me, happy sleeper;)

zaː mɪç zoː 'vʊndɐfrɔɣ̃nt‘lɪç lan, ʊnt‘ boːt den mʊnt‘ miːɐ̯ daːɐ̯:
sah mich so wunderfreundlich an, und bot den Mund mir dar:
looked me so wondrous-friendly at, and offered the mouth to me ... : [*"darbieten"* = offer]
(she looked at me, and offered her mouth to me, in such a wonderfully friendly way,)

das lɪç les nɪçt‘ bə'ʃrae̯bən kʰan, viː froː, viː froː lɪç vaːɐ̯.
dass ich es nicht beschreiben kann, wie froh, wie froh ich war.
that I it not describe can, how happy, how happy I was.
(that I cannot describe how happy I was.)

daː 'tʰrɪp‘əlt‘ lɪç lao̯f 'lae̯nəm bae̯n, ʊnt‘ 'hat‘ə zoː mae̯n ʃp'iːl,
Da trippelt’ ich auf einem Bein, und hatte so mein Spiel,
Then tripped I on one leg, and had so my game,
(Then I hopped around on one leg, and made a game out of that,)

ʊnt‘ ʃp'iːlt‘ liːɐ̯ mɪt dem 'flyːgəlae̯n di 'roːt‘ə 'vaŋə kʰyːl.
und spielt’ ihr mit dem Flügelein die rote Wange kühl.
and played for her with the little wing the red cheek cool.
(and playfully cooled her red cheek with my little wing.)

dɔx lax! kʰae̯n 'leːɐ̯dəŋlʏk‘ bə'ʃt‘eːt, tʰaːk‘ zae̯ les 'loːdɐ naxtʰ!
Doch ach! kein Erdenglück besteht, Tag sei es oder Nacht!
But ah! no earthly happiness endures, day be it or night!
(But ah! no earthly happiness endures, whether it be day or night!)

ʃnɛl vaːɐ̯ mae̯n 'zyːsɐ tʰrao̯m fɛɐ̯'veːt‘, ʊnt‘ lɪç vaːɐ̯/vaːr 'lao̯fgəvaxtʰ.
Schnell war mein süsser Traum verweht, und ich war aufgewacht.
Quickly was my sweet dream blown away, and I was awakened.
(My sweet dream quickly vanished, and I woke up.)

[Schubert’s setting has charm, grace, and just the right light touch.]

deːɐ̯ 'ʊnglʏk‘'lɪçə
Der Unglückliche
The Unhappy One

Op. 87, No. 1 [1821] (Karoline Pichler)

di naxt‘ brɪçt‘ lan, mɪt‘ 'lae̯zən 'lʏft‘ən 'zɪŋk‘ət‘ ziː lao̯f di 'myːdən 'ʃt‘ɛrp‘lɪçən hɛ'rap‘;
Die Nacht bricht an, mit leisen Lüften sinket sie auf die müden Sterblichen herab;
The night breaks ... , with soft breezes sinks it upon the weary mortals down;
(Night is falling; with soft breezes it sinks down upon weary mortals;) [*"bricht an"* (here) = falls]

deːɐ̯ 'zanft‘ə ʃlaːf, dɛs 'tʰoːdəs 'bruːdɐ, 'vɪŋk‘ətʰ ʊnt‘ leːk‘t‘ ziː 'frɔɣ̃nt‘lɪç lɪn liːɐ̯ 'tʰɛːk‘lɪç
der sanfte Schlaf, des Todes Bruder, winket und legt sie freundlich in ihr täglich
the gentle sleep, the death’s brother, beckons and lays them friendlily into their daily
(gentle sleep, death’s brother, beckons and, in a kindly way, lays them down into their daily)

graːp'. jɛt͜st' 'vaxət'   l̩ɑof deːɐ̯ 'lɪçt'bərɑop't'ən 'leːɐ̯də fi'lɑeçt'   nuːɐ̯ nɔx di 'lark'lɪst'
Grab. Jetzt wachet auf der lichtberaubten Erde vielleicht nur noch die Arglist
grave. Now is awake on the light-bereft   earth perhaps only still the cunning
(grave. Now on the earth, bereft of light, perhaps only cunning is still awake)

l̩ʊnt deːɐ̯ ʃmɛrt͜s, l̩ʊnt' jɛt͜st, daː   l̩ɪç dʊrç nɪçt͜s gə'ʃt'øːrət' 'veːɐ̯də, las 'daenə 'vʊndən
und der Schmerz, und jetzt, da ich durch nichts gestöret werde, lass deine Wunden
and the pain,   and now, when I by   nothing disturbed am,   let your wounds
(and pain, and now, when I am not disturbed by anything, let your wounds)

'bluːt'ən, 'arməs hɛrt͜s! fɛɐ̯'zɛŋk'ə dɪç   l̩ɪn 'daenəs 'kʰʊmɐs   't'iːfən,
bluten, armes Herz! Versenke dich   in   deines Kummers Tiefen,
bleed, poor heart! Sink   yourself into your   sorrow's depths,
(bleed, poor heart! Sink down into the depths of your sorrow,)

ʊnt' vɛn   [van] fi'lɑeçt' l̩ɪn deːɐ̯ t͜sɛɐ̯'rɪsnən brʊst' halp' fɛɐ̯jɛːɐ̯t'ə 'laedən 'ʃliːfən,
und wenn [P.: wann] vielleicht in der zerrissnen Brust halb verjährte Leiden schliefen,
and if/when [when] perhaps   in the lacerated   breast half obsolete sorrows slept,
(and if perhaps half-forgotten sorrows have been sleeping in the lacerated breast,)

zoː 'vɛk'ə ziː   mɪt' 'grɑozaːm 'zyːsɐ lʊstʰ.   bə'rɛçnə di fɛɐ̯'loːrnən 'zeːlɪçkʰaet'ən,
so wecke sie   mit grausam süsser Lust.   Berechne die verlornen Seligkeiten,
then wake them with cruelly   sweet pleasure. Calculate the lost   blisses,

t͜seːl 'lalə 'bluːmən l̩ɪn dem pʰara'diːs, vo'rɑos   l̩ɪn 'daenɐ 'juːgənt' 'gɔldnən 't͜saet'ən
zähl' alle Blumen in dem Paradies, woraus   in deiner Jugend goldnen Zeiten
count all flowers in the paradise from which in your   youth's golden times
(count all the flowers in the paradise from which in the golden times of your youth)

di 'hart'ə hant dɛs 'ʃɪk'zaːls dɪç fɛɐ̯'ʃt'iːs! duː hast' gə'liːp'tʰ, duː hast
die harte Hand des Schicksals dich verstiess! Du hast geliebt, du hast
the hard hand of fate   you expelled! You have loved,   you have
(the hard hand of fate expelled you! You have loved, you have)

das glʏk'   l̩ɛm'pfʊndən, dem   'jeːdə 'zeːlɪçkʰaet deːɐ̯/deːr 'leːɐ̯də vaeçtʰ. duː hast'
das Glück   empfunden, dem   jede Seligkeit der   Erde weicht. Du hast
the happiness experienced, to which every bliss   of the   earth yields. You have
(experienced the happiness that surpasses every other earthly bliss. You)

l̩aen hɛrt͜s, das dɪç fɛɐ̯'ʃt'ant', gə'fʊndən, deːɐ̯ 'kʰyːnst'ən 'hɔfnʊŋ 'ʃøːnəs t͜siːl l̩ɛɐ̯'raeçtʰ.
ein Herz, das dich verstand, gefunden, der kühnsten Hoffnung schönes Ziel erreicht.
a   heart that you understood found,   the boldest hope's   beautiful goal reached.
(found a heart that understood you, you reached the beautiful goal of your boldest hope.)

daː 'ʃt'ʏrt͜st'ə dɪç l̩aen 'grɑozaːm 'maxt'vɔrt' 'niːdɐ, l̩ɑos 'daenən 'hɪməln 'niːdɐ,
Da stürzte dich ein grausam Machtwort nieder, aus deinen Himmeln nieder,
Then hurled   you a   cruel   power-word down, out of your   heavens down,
(Then a cruel peremptory order hurled you down, down out of your heavens,)

ʊnt daen 'ʃt'ɪləs glʏkʰ,   daen 'laltsuʃøːnəs 't'rɑombɪlt' 'kʰeːɐ̯t'ə 'viːdɐ
und dein stilles Glück,   dein allzuschönes Traumbild kehrte wieder
and your quiet happiness, your all-too-lovely vision   returned again

ʦuːɐ̯ ˈbɛsɐn vɛltʻ, lαos deːɐ/deːr lɛs kʰaːm, ʦuˈrʏkʰ. ˈʦɛɐ̯ˈrɪsən
zur bessern Welt, aus der es kam, zurück. Zerrissen
to the better world, from which it came, back. Torn asunder
(to the better world from which it came. Torn asunder)

zɪntʻ nuːn ˈlalə ˈzyːsən ˈbandə, miːɐ̯ ʃleːkʻtʻ kʰaen hɛrʦ meːɐ/meːr lαof deːɐ̯ ˈvaetʻən vɛltʰ.
sind nun alle süssen Bande, mir schlägt kein Herz mehr auf der weiten Welt.
are now all sweet bonds, for me beats no heart more in the wide world.
(are now all the sweet bonds; no heart beats for me any more in the whole wide world.)

[The poem is from *Olivier*, a novel by the prolific Karoline Pichler, who was noted iln Vienna for her literary salon. The song is one of the few for which Schubert wrote out a preliminary sketch. There is a story that when Schubert was shown the music, some time later, he failed to recognize it, saying: "Not bad! Who wrote it?"]

Der Unglückliche / Ich komme vom Gebirge her see *Der Wanderer*

deːɐ̯ ˈfaːtʻɐ mɪt dem ˈkʰɪndə
Der Vater mit dem Kinde
The Father with his Child

Posthumously published [composed 1827] (poem by Eduard von Bauernfeld)

dem ˈfaːtʻɐ liːkʻtʻ das kʰɪntʻ lɪm larm, lɛs ruːtʻ zoː voːl, lɛs ruːtʻ zoː varm,
Dem Vater liegt das Kind im Arm, es ruht so wohl, es ruht so warm,
For the father lies the child in the arm, it rests so well, it rests so warm,
(The child lies in its father's arm; it rests so well, it rests so warm,)

ɛs ˈlɛçəltʻ zyːs: liːpʻ ˈfaːtʻɐ maen—lʊntʻ mɪt dem ˈlɛçəln ʃleːft lɛs laen.
es lächelt süss: lieb' Vater mein— und mit dem Lächeln schläft es ein.
it smiles sweetly: "Dear father mine"—and with the smile falls it asleep.
(its sweet smile seems to say: "My dear father..."—and with that smile it falls asleep.)
["*schläft ... ein*": from *einschlafen* = to fall asleep]

deːɐ̯ ˈfaːtʻɐ bɔɡkʻtʻ zɪç, ˈlaːtʻmətʻ kʰαom, lʊnt lαoʃtʻ lαof ˈzaenəs ˈkʰɪndəs tʰrαom:
Der Vater beugt sich, atmet kaum, und lauscht auf seines Kindes Traum:
The father bends himself, breathes scarcely, and listens to his child's dream:
(The father bends down, scarcely breathing, and listens to his child's dream:)

eːɐ̯ dɛŋkʻtʻ lan di lɛntʻˈʃvʊndnə ʦaetʻ mɪtʻ ˈveːmuːʦfɔlɐ ˈzeːlɪçkʰaetʰ.
er denkt an die entschwund'ne Zeit mit wehmutsvoller Seligkeit.
he thinks of the vanished time with melancholy happiness.
(with melancholy happiness he thinks about time gone by.)

ʊntʻ ˈlaenə tʰreːn lαos ˈhɛrʦənsɡrʊntʻ fɛltʻ liːm lαof ˈzaenəs ˈkʰɪndəs mʊntʻ,—
Und eine Trän' aus Herzensgrund fällt ihm auf seines Kindes Mund,—
and a tear from heart's depths falls from him onto his child's mouth,—
(and a tear falls from the depths of his heart onto his child's mouth,—)

ʃnɛl kʰʏstʻ leːɐ̯/leːr liːm di ˈtʰreːnə lapʻ, lʊntʻ viːkʻtʻ lɛs ˈlaezə lαof lʊntʻ lapʻ.
schnell küsst' er ihm die Träne ab, und wiegt es leise auf und ab.
quickly kisses he for it the tear away, and rocks it softly to and fro.
(quickly he kisses away the tear, and rocks the child softly to and fro.)

um 'laenɐ 'gantsən vɛlt' gə'vɪn gɛːp' leːɐ das 'hɛrtsənskʰɪnt' nɪçt' hɪn. —
Um einer ganzen Welt Gewinn gäb' er das Herzenskind nicht hin.—
For a whole world's winning would give he the heart- child not up.—
(Not for the whole world would he give up that child of his heart.—)

duː 'zeːlɪgɐ ʃoːn ɪn deːɐ vɛltʰ, deːɐ zoː zaen glʏk' ɪn 'larmən hɛltʰ!
Du Seliger schon in der Welt, der so sein Glück in Armen hält!
You blessed even in the world, who thus his happiness in arms holds!
(You, who so can hold your happiness in your arms, feel the bliss of heaven even in this world!)

[A tender cradle song for a father is something of a rarity in the literature. This is Schubert's only song to a text by his intimate friend, who later left us a lively account of their adventures.]

deːɐ 'faɪt'ɐmœrdɐ
Der Vatermörder
The Parricide

Posthumously published [composed 1811] (poem by Gottlieb Conrad Pfeffel)

aen 'faːt'ɐ ʃt'arp' fɔn dɛs 'zoːnəs hant'. kʰaen vɔlf, kʰaen 't'iːgɐ, naen,
Ein Vater starb von des Sohnes Hand. Kein Wolf, kein Tiger, nein,
A father died from the son's hand. No wolf, no tiger, no,
(A father died by his own son's hand. No wolf, no tiger, no,)   [*poem:* **von Sohnes Hand**]

deːɐ mɛnʃ la'laen, deːɐ 'tʰiːrə fʏrst', lɛɐ'fant den 'faɪt'ɐmɔrt' la'laen.
der Mensch allein, der Tiere Fürst, erfand den Vatermord allein.
the human being alone, the beasts' prince, invented the parricide alone.
(man alone, the prince of beasts, invented parricide.) [*poem:* **der Mensch, der Tiere Fürst,..**]

deːɐ 'tʰɛːt'ɐ floː, lʊm dem gə'rɪçt' zaen 'ɔpfɐ tsuː lɛnt'tsiːn,
Der Täter floh, um dem Gericht sein Opfer zu entziehn,
The perpetrator fled, in order from the court of justice its victim to take away,
(The perpetrator fled, in order to deprive the court of justice of its victim,)

ɪn 'laenən valt'. dɔx kʰɔnt' leːɐ nɪçt' den 'lɪnɐn 'rɪçt'ɐ fliːn.
in einen Wald. Doch konnt er nicht den innern Richter fliehn.
into a forest. But could he not the inner judge escape.
(into a forest. But he could not escape the inner judge.)

fɛɐ'tseːɐt' lʊnt' 'haːgɐ, ʃt'ʊm lʊnt blaeç, mɪt' 'lʊmp'ən 'langət'aːn,   [fɛɐ'tsɛrt']
Verzehrt und hager, stumm und bleich, mit Lumpen angetan,   [*poem:* **Verzerrt**]
Consumed and haggard, silent and pale, with rags dressed,   [twisted]
(Consumed and haggard, silent and pale, dressed in rags,)

dem 'dɛːmɔn deːɐ fɛɐ'tsvaeflʊŋ glaeç, tʰraːf liːn laen 'hɛʃɐ(r) lan.
dem Dämon der Verzweiflung gleich, traf ihn ein Häscher an.
to the demon of the despair similar, met him a sheriff's officer ... .
(looking like the demon of despair, he was discovered by chance by a sheriff's officer.)
    ["*antreffen*" = to come across, to meet by chance]

fɔl grɪm tsɛɐ'ʃt'øːɐt'ə deːɐ bar'baːɐ(r) laen nɛst' mɪt' 'laenəm ʃt'aen
Voll Grimm zerstörte der Barbar ein Nest mit einem Stein
Full of fury destroyed the barbarian a nest with a stone
(Full of fury, the barbarian was destroying a nest with a stone)

ʊnt' 'mɔrdət'ə di 'kʰlaɛnə ʃaːɐ̯ deːɐ̯/deːr 'larmən 'føːgəlaɛn.
und mordete die kleine Schar der armen Vögelein.
and murdered the little brood of the poor fledglings.
(and murdering the little brood of poor fledglings.)

halt' lae̯n! riːf liːm deːɐ̯ 'ʃɛrgə ʦuː, fɛɐ̯'ruːxt'ɐ 'bøːzəvɪçtʰ,
"Halt ein!" rief ihm der Scherge zu, "Verruchter Bösewicht,
"Stop ...!" cried to him the constable to, "infamous villain, ["*halt ein!*" = Stop!]
("Stop!" shouted the constable, "You infamous villain,")
    [*poem:* **Verruchter Schadenfroh** ('ʃaːdənfroː, one who gloats over the misfortune of others)]

mɪt' 'vɛlçəm 'rɛçt'ə 'mart'ɐst duː di 'frɔmən 'tʰiːɐ̯çən zoː?
mit welchem Rechte marterst du die frommen Tierchen so?"
with what right torture you the innocent little creatures so?"
(what right do you have to torture the innocent little creatures like that?")

vas frɔm, ʃp'raːx 'je:nɐ, de:n di vuːt' kʰɑ̯ɔm 'høːɐ̯baːɐ̯ 'ʃt'aməln liːs,
"Was fromm," sprach jener, den die Wut kaum hörbar stammeln liess,
"What innocent," spoke the former, whom the rage barely audibly stammer let,
("What do you mean 'innocent'?" said the young man, stammering barely audibly in his rage,)

ɪç tʰaːt' lɛs, vae̯l di 'hœlənbruːt' mɪç 'faːt'ɐmœrdɐ hiːs.
"ich tat es, weil die Höllenbrut mich Vatermörder hiess."
"I did it, because the hellish brood me father-murderer called."
("I did it because this hellish brood called me a father-murderer.")

de:ɐ̯ man bə'ʃɑ̯ɔt' liːn, 'zae̯nə tʰaːt' fɛɐ̯'rɛːt' zae̯n 'lɪrɐ blɪkʰ.
Der Mann beschaut ihn, seine Tat verrät sein irrer Blick.
The man looked at him, his deed betrayed his crazed look.
(The older man looked at him: his crazed expression betrayed his deed.)

e:ɐ̯ fast den 'mœrdɐ(r), lʊnt das raːt' bə'ʃt'raːft das 'buːbənʃt'ʏkʰ.   [zae̯n]
Er fasst den Mörder, und das Rad bestraft das Bubenstück. [*poem:* **sein Bubenstück**]
He seized the murderer, and the wheel punished the piece of villainy.   [his]
(The constable seized the murderer, and the wheel punished the villainy.)

duː, 'hae̯lɪgəs gə'vɪsən, bɪst de:ɐ̯ 'tʰuːgənt' 'lɛtst'ɐ frɔø̯nt';
Du, heiliges Gewissen, bist der Tugend letzter Freund;
You, holy conscience, are the virtue's last friend;
(You, holy conscience, are virtue's last friend;)

ae̯n 'ʃrɛk'lɪçəs tʰri'ʊmfliːt' lɪst dae̯n 'dɔnɐ(r) 'liːrəm fae̯nt'.
ein schreckliches Triumphlied ist dein Donner ihrem Feind.
a fearful triumph-song is your thunder to her (virtue's) enemy.
(the thunder of your voice is a frightening song of triumph to virtue's enemy.)

[When he was fourteen years old, Schubert composed this far from merry song on the day after Christmas, all in one day, in a highly-charged operatic style, with several strenuous high B flats.]

302

de:ɐ̯ 'vaxt'əlʃlaːk'

Der Wachtelschlag

The Song of the Quail

Op. 68 [1822?] (Samuel Friedrich Sauter)

hɔrç, viː ʃalt͜s 'dɔrt'ən zoː 'liːp'lɪç hɛɐ̯'foːɐ̯:   [ax! miːɐ̯ ʃalt͜s 'dɔrt'ən]
Horch, wie schallt's dorten so lieblich hervor: **[GA: Ach! mir schallt's dorten...]**
Hark, how sounds it yonder so lovely forth: [Ah! To me sounds it yonder...]
(Listen! How lovely it sounds from yonder:)   ([Ah! To me it sounds...])
     [*first version of poem:* **Ach! wie schallt's dort so lieblich**; *later version:* **Horch, wie schallt's**]

'fʏrçt'ə gɔt'! 'fʏrçt'ə gɔtʰ! ruːft' miːɐ̯ di 'vaxt'əl ɪns loːɐ̯.
"Fürchte Gott! fürchte Gott!" ruft mir die Wachtel ins Ohr.
"Fear God! Fear God!" calls to me the quail into the ear.
("Fear God! Fear God!" the quail calls into my ear.)

'zɪtsənt' ɪm 'gryːnən, fɔn 'halmən ʊm'hʏltʰ,
Sitzend im Grünen, von Halmen umhüllt,
Sitting in the greenery, by stalks enveloped,
(Sitting amid the greenery, concealed by stalks,)

maːnt' ziː den 'hɔrçɐ ɪm 'zaːt'əngəfɪlt': 'liːbə gɔt'! 'liːbə gɔt'!   [lam]
mahnt sie den Horcher im Saatengefild: "Liebe Gott! liebe Gott! [*GA:* **am Saatengefild**]
reminds it the hearer in the cornfield: "Love God! Love God!   [at the]
(it reminds the listener in the cornfield: "Love God! Love God!)
     [*poem:* **im Schattengefild** ('ʃat'əngəfɪlt', shadowy field)]

leːɐ̯/leːr ɪst' zoː 'gyːt'ɪç, zoː mɪlt'. 'viːdɐ bə'dɔɡt'ət' liːɐ̯ 'hʏpfəndɐ ʃlaːk':
er ist so gütig, so mild." Wieder bedeutet ihr hüpfender Schlag:
He is so kind, so gentle." Again signifies its hopping call:
(He is so kind, so gentle!" Again its hopping call may mean:

'loːbə gɔt'! 'loːbə gɔtʰ! deːɐ̯ dɪç tsu 'loːnən fɛɐ̯'maːk'.
"Lobe Gott! lobe Gott! der dich zu lohnen vermag."
"Praise God! Praise God! who you to reward has the power."
("Praise God! Praise God, who has the power to reward you!")

ziːst du di 'hɛrlɪçən 'frʏçt'ə ɪm fɛlt'?   ['frʏçt'ən]
Siehst du die herrlichen Früchte im Feld? [*poem:* **Früchten** (no longer correct)]
See you the glorious fruits in the field?   [fruits]
(Do you see the glorious fruits of the field?)

nɪm ɛs tsuː 'hɛrtsən, bə'voːnɐ deːɐ̯ vɛlt': 'daŋk'ə gɔt'! 'daŋk'ə gɔt'!
Nimm es zu Herzen, Bewohner der Welt: "Danke Gott! danke Gott!"
Take it to heart, inhabitants of the world: "Thank God! Thank God,

deːɐ̯ dɪç ɛɐ̯'nɛːɐ̯t' ʊnt' ɛɐ̯'hɛltʰ. ʃrɛk't' dɪç ɪm 'vɛt'ɐ deːɐ̯ hɛr deːɐ̯ na'tʰuːɐ̯:
der dich ernährt und erhält. Schreckt dich im Wetter der Herr der Natur:
who you nourishes and sustains." Frightens you in the storm the Lord of Nature:
(who nourishes and sustains you!" If the Lord of Nature frightens you in a storm:)
     [*poem:* **Schreckt mich** (mɪç, me)]

'bɪt'ə   gɔt'! 'bɪt'ə   gɔt'! ruːft' ziː, leːɐ̯ 'ʃoːnət   di fluːɐ̯.
"Bitte   Gott! bitte   Gott!" ruft sie, er   schonet die Flur.
"Entreat God! Entreat God!" calls it, He   spares   the meadow.
("Entreat God! Entreat God!" it calls; He then spares the meadow.)

'maxən ɡə'faːrən deːɐ̯ 'kʰriːɡɐ diːɐ̯   baŋ: 'tʰrɑɔə ɡɔt'! 'tʰrɑɔə ɡɔtʰ!
Machen Gefahren der   Krieger dir   bang: "Traue Gott! traue Gott!"
Make   dangers   of the warriors to you fearful: "Trust God! Trust God!"
(When the dangers that soldiers are facing make you fearful: "Trust God! Trust God!")

> [*poem:* **Machen Gefahren des Krieges mir** (dɛs 'kʰriːɡəs miːɐ̯, of the war to me) **bang,**]
> [(When the dangers of war make me fearful,)]
> ['tʰrøːst'ət' mɪç 'viːdɐ   deːɐ̯ 'vaxt'əlɡəzaŋ]
> [*line omitted by Schubert:* **tröstet   mich wieder der Wachtelgesang**]
> [comforts me   again   the   quail's song]

ziː, leːɐ̯ fɛɐ̯'tsiːət' nɪçt' laŋ.
sieh, er verziehet nicht lang.
See, He delays   not   long.
(See! He will not tarry long.)

[The delightful music imitates the rhythm of the quail's call. In German folklore the quail is a particularly pious bird. The *Gesamtausgabe* variant is true to the version of the poem used by Schubert. The Peters edition, equally legitimate in this case, follows the first publication of the song by Diabelli. The various variants reflect later published versions of the poem. When Beethoven's setting of the poem was published, similar changes appeared between editions.]

deːɐ̯ 'valənʃt'aenɐ 'lantskʰnɛçt' baem tʰrʊŋkʰ
Der Wallensteiner Lanzknecht beim Trunk
Wallenstein's Lancer Drinking

Posthumously published [composed 1827] (poem by Karl Gottfried von Leitner)

heː! 'ʃɛŋk'ət' miːɐ̯/miːr ɪm 'hɛlmə laen, deːɐ̯/deːr ɪst dɛs 'kʰnap'ən 'bɛçɐ,
He! schenket mir   im Helme ein, der   ist des Knappen Becher,
Hey! pour   for me in the helmet into, that   is the squire's   cup,
(Hey! Pour it into my helmet, that is the squire's cup;)

eːɐ̯/eːr ɪst' nɪçt' zaeçt' ʊnt tʰrɑɔn   nɪçt kʰlaen, das frɔøt   den 'vak'ɐn 'tseçɐ.
er   ist nicht seicht und traun   nicht klein, das freut   den wackern Zecher.
it   is not shallow and, God knows, not small; that gladdens the valiant   drinker.

eːɐ̯ 'ʃytst'ə mɪç tsuː 'tʰɑɔzənt'maːl   foːɐ̯ 'kʰɔlbən, ʃveːɐ̯t'   ʊnt 'ʃp'iːsən,
Er schützte mich zu   tausendmal   vor Kolben, Schwert und Spiessen,
It protected me up to a thousand times from maces,   sword(s), and   pikes;

eːɐ̯ diːnt' miːɐ̯ jɛtst' lals 'tʰrɪŋk'pʰoˌkʰaːl ʊnt' ɪn deːɐ̯ naxt' lals 'kʰɪsən.
er dient mir jetzt als Trinkpokal   und in der Nacht als   Kissen.
it serves me   now as (a) drinking goblet, and in the night as (a) pillow.

foːɐ̯ 'lytsən tʰraːf liːn jʏŋst' laen ʃp'eːɐ̯; bɪn fast' lɪns   graːs ɡə'zʊŋk'ən,
Vor Lützen traf ihn jüngst ein Speer; bin fast ins   Gras gesunken,
At Lützen struck it   recently a   spear; am nearly into the grass sunk,
(At the Battle of Lützen recently a spear struck it; I nearly sank to the grass,)

jaː! veːɐ̯/veːr leːɐ̯ dʊrç, hɛt'   'nɪmɐmeːɐ̯(r) laen 'tʰrœpfəlçən gə'tʰrʊŋk'ən.
ja! wär' er durch, hätt'   nimmermehr ein Tröpfchen getrunken.
yes, were it through, would have nevermore a little drop drunk.
(yes, had it gone through, I would nevermore have drunk another little drop.)

dɔx kʰaːms nɪçt' zoː. lɪç 'daŋk'ə diːɐ̯, du: 'braːfə/braːvə 'pʰɪk'əlhaobə!   [dɔxs   kʰaːm]
Doch kam's nicht so. Ich danke dir, du brave   Pickelhaube! [*poem:* **Doch's kam**]
But came it not so. I thank you, you good spiked helmet!   [But it came]
(But it didn't come to that. I thank you, you trusty spiked helmet!)

deːɐ̯ 'ʃveːdə   'byːst'ə balt da'fyːɐ̯/da'fyːr lʊnt' 'rœçəlt'ə   lɪm   'ʃt'aobə.
der Schwede büsste bald dafür   und röchelte   im   Staube.
The Swede atoned soon for that   and death-rattled in the dust.
(The Swede soon atoned for that, and gave the death-rattle in the dust.)

nuː, tʰrøːst' liːn gɔt'! ʃɛŋk't' laen, ʃɛŋk't' laen! maen kʰruːk' hat 'tʰiːfə 'vʊndən,
Nu, tröst' ihn Gott! Schenkt ein, schenkt ein! mein Krug hat tiefe Wunden,
Well, comfort him God! Pour into, pour into! my mug has deep wounds,
(Well, God comfort him! Pour away, pour away! My mug here has deep wounds,)

dɔx hɛlt' leːɐ̯ nɔx den 'dɔøtʃən   vaen, lʊnt' zɔl miːɐ̯/miːr lɔft' nɔx 'mʊndən.
doch hält er noch den deutschen Wein, und soll mir   oft noch munden.
but holds it still the German wine, and shall to me   often still be appetizing.
(but it can still hold German wine, and I shall still often relish it.)

[Schubert caught the lusty, soldierly humor of the poem, with a touch of archaic harmony to suggest the period of Wallenstein's campaigns.]

deːɐ̯ 'vandərɐ / ɪç 'kʰɔmə fɔm gə'bɪrgə heːɐ̯
Der Wanderer / Ich komme vom Gebirge her
The Wanderer / I Come Here from the Mountains

Op. 4, No. 1 [1816] (Georg Philipp Schmidt von Lübeck)

ɪç 'kʰɔmə fɔm   gə'bɪrgə heːɐ̯, lɛs dampft das tʰaːl, lɛs braost das meːɐ̯.
Ich komme vom   Gebirge her, es dampft das Tal, es braust das Meer.
I come from the mountains hither, it steams the valley, it roars the sea.
(I come here from the mountains; the valley steams, the sea is roaring.)
       [*version of poem used by Schubert:* **es rauscht** (raoʃt, murmurs) **das Meer**]

ɪç 'vandlə ʃt'ɪl,   bɪn 'veːnɪç froː, lʊnt' 'lɪmɐ fraːk't deːɐ̯ 'zɔøftsɐ : voː?   'lɪmɐ voː ?
Ich wandle still,   bin wenig froh, und immer fragt der Seufzer: wo?   immer wo?
I wander quietly, am little glad, and always asks the sigh: where? always where?
(I wander quietly, am seldom happy, and always my sigh is asking: where? always where?)
       [*version of poem used by Schubert:* **frägt** (frɛːk't), an older form of the verb]

di 'zɔnə dyŋk't' mɪç hiːɐ̯ zoː kʰalt', di 'blyːt'ə vɛlk',   das 'leːbən lalt ʰ,
Die Sonne dünkt mich hier so kalt, die Blüte welk,   das Leben alt,
The sun seems me here so cold, the blossom withered, the life old,
(The sun here seems to me so cold, the blossoms seem withered, life seems old,)

ʊnt' vas ziː 'reːdən, 'leːɐ ʃal,   lɪç bɪn ḁen 'frɛmt'lɪŋ 'lyːbɐ(r)lal.
und was sie reden, leerer Schall, ich bin ein Fremdling überall.
and what they speak, empty sound, I   am a   stranger   everywhere.
(and the language that they speak seems to me meaningless sound: I am a stranger everywhere.)

voː   bɪst duː, maḁen gə'liːp't'əs lant'? gə'zuːxt',   gə'laːnt', ʊnt' niː ge'kʰantʰ!
Wo bist du, mein geliebtes Land? gesucht,   geahnt, und nie gekannt!
Where are you, my   beloved   land? searched for, imagined, and never known!

das lant, das lant' zoː 'hɔfnʊŋsgryːn, das lant' voː   'maḁenə 'roːzən blyːn,
Das Land, das Land so hoffnungsgrün, das Land wo   meine Rosen blühn,
The land, the land so hope-green,   the land where my   roses bloom,
(The land, the land so green with hope, the land where *my* roses bloom,)

voː 'maḁenə 'frɔɸndə 'vandəlnt' geːn, voː   'maḁenə 'tʰoːt'ən 'ḁooflɛɐʃt'eːn,
wo   meine Freunde wandelnd gehn, wo   meine Toten   auferstehn,
where my   friends wandering go, where my   dead   are resurrected,
(where my friends go wandering, where my dead are resurrected,) [*poem:* **wandeln** ('vandəln)]

das lant, das 'maḁenə 'ʃp'raːxə ʃprɪçt', loː lant', voː   bɪst duː?
das Land, das meine Sprache spricht,* o Land, wo   bist du?
the land, that my   language speaks,   O land, where are you?
(the land that speaks my language, O land, where are you?)

                                        [ʊnt' 'laləs hat', vas miːɐ gə'brɪçtʰ]
                        [**line omitted by Schubert: und alles hat, was mir gebricht]
                            [and all   has that to me is lacking]
                            [(and has everything that I now lack)]

ɪç 'vandlə ʃt'ɪl,   bɪn 'veːnɪç froː, ʊnt' 'ɪmɐ   fraːk't deːɐ 'zɔɸftsɐ : voː?   'ɪmɐ voː ?
Ich wandle still,   bin wenig froh, und immer fragt der Seufzer: wo?   immer wo?
I   wander quietly, am little glad, and always asks   the sigh: where? always where?
(I wander quietly, am seldom happy, and always my sigh is asking: where? always where?)

ɪm   'gaḁest'ɐhḁoox tʰɸːnts   miːɐ tsu'rʏkʰ :   [tʰɸːnt' miːɐs]
Im   Geisterhauch tönt's   mir zurück: [version of poem S. used: tönt mir 's zurück]
In the spirit-breath   sounds it to me back: [sounds to me it]
(The answer comes back to me in a ghostly whisper:)

 dɔrt', voː   du nɪçt' bɪst', dɔrt' lɪst das glʏkʰ!
"Dort, wo   du nicht bist, dort ist das Glück!"
"There where you not   are,   there is the happiness!"
("There where you are *not, there* is happiness!")
            [*version of the poem used by Schubert:* **D o rt, wo du nicht bist, ist das Glück!**]

[This traveler feels himself an alien wherever he goes; no matter how far he wanders, the land
that he is seeking forever eludes him. Here the people speak a language that is not his. Where is
the land where he will find his friends again, where his beloved dead will rise again? A ghostly
voice whispers: "Happiness is there where you are *not*." The *Gesamtausgabe* prints two versions
of this justly famous song: the first bears the title "*Der Unglückliche*" ("The Unhappy One"),
which is the title of the published version of the poem set by Schubert. That first version
erroneously gives the name of the poet as "Werner." Schubert himself chose "*Der Wanderer*" as
the title of the later, definitive version. The words are identical; the musical differences are
slight, mainly details in dynamic markings, except for a somewhat shorter postlude in the second

printed version, which is correctly attributed to Schmidt von Lübeck, whose poem was originally titled "*Des Fremdlings Abendlied*" ("The Strangers Evening Song") and exists in several forms.]

deːɐ̯ 'vandərɐ / viː 'dɔɥt'lɪç dɛs 'moːndəs lɪçt^h
Der Wanderer / Wie deutlich des Mondes Licht
The Wanderer / How Clearly the Moon's Light

Op. 65, No. 2 [1819] (Friedrich Schlegel)

viː 'dɔɥt'lɪç dɛs 'moːndəs lɪçt   t͡su miːɐ̯ ʃp'rɪçt^h, mɪç bə'zeːlənt t͡su deːɐ̯ 'raezə:
Wie deutlich des Mondes Licht zu mir spricht, mich beseelend zu der Reise:
How clearly the moon's light to me speaks, me inspiriting to the journey:
(How clearly the moon's light speaks to me, strengthening my spirit for the journey:)

'fɔlɡə tʰrɔɥ   dem 'lalt'ən glaezə, 'veːlə 'kʰaenə 'haemaːt' nɪçt^h.
"Folge treu   dem alten Gleise, wähle keine Heimat nicht.
"Follow faithfully the old   track, choose no   homeland not.
("Follow faithfully the old track, choose no land as your home.)

'leːvɡə 'pʰlaːɡə 'brɪŋən zɔnst   di 'ʃveːrən 'tʰaːɡə.
Ew'ge Plage bringen sonst   die schweren Tage.
Eternal trouble bring   otherwise the hard   days.
(Otherwise hard days will bring eternal trouble.)

fɔrt t͡su 'landɐn zɔlst duː 'vɛksəln, zɔlst duː vandɐn,
Fort zu andern sollst du wechseln, sollst du wandern,
On to others shall you change,   shall you wander,
(You shall change countries, you shall move on to other lands,)

laeçt' lɛnt'fliːənt' 'jeːdɐ 'kʰlaːɡə.   'zanft'ə lɛp' lʊnt' 'hoːə fluːt tʰiːf lɪm muːt',
leicht entfliehend jeder Klage."   Sanfte Ebb' und hohe Flut tief im Mut,
lightly fleeing from every complaint." Gentle ebb and high flood deep in the spirit,
(lightly fleeing from every complaint." With gentle ebb and high flood tides deep in my spirit,)

'van- drɪç zoː lɪm 'dʊŋk'əln 'vaet'ɐ, 'ʃt'aeɡə 'muːt'ɪç, 'zɪŋə 'haet'ɐ,   ['dʊŋk'əl]
wandr' ich so im Dunkeln weiter, steige mutig, singe heiter, [*poem:* Dunkel]
wander I   thus in the darkening onward, climb bravely, sing cheerfully,   [dark]
(thus I wander onward in the dark, climb bravely, sing cheerfully,)

lʊnt di velt' lɛɐ̯'ʃaent' miːɐ̯ guːt^h. 'laləs   'raenə zeː lɪç mɪlt' lɪm 'viːdɐʃaenə,
und die Welt erscheint mir gut. Alles   Reine seh' ich mild im Wiederscheine,
and the world seems   to me good. Everything pure see I   mild in the reflection,
(and the world seems good to me. In the mild reflected light I see everything pure,)

nɪçt͡s fɛɐ̯'vɔrən lɪn dɛs 'tʰaːɡəs gluːt' fɛɐ̯'dɔrən: froː lʊm'ɡeːbən, dɔx la'laenə.
nichts verworren in des Tages Glut verdorren: froh umgeben, doch alleine.
nothing confused in the day's heat withered: happily environed, yet alone.
(nothing confused, or withered as in the heat of the day; I am happily environed, though alone.)

[Schubert hauntingly suggests the solitariness of the nocturnal wanderer who takes his cue from the moon, who prefers to keep moving on, who sees the world in mild reflected light, rather than in the harsh and withering heat of the sun, who sings to cheer himself and accepts his aloneness.]

deː ̯ɐ 'vandəʀɐ lan den moːnt'
Der Wanderer an den Mond
The Wanderer to the Moon

Op. 80 [1826] (Johann Gabriel Seidl)

ɪç lɑ̯of deːɐ̯/deːr leːɐ̯t', lam 'hɪməl   duː, viːɐ̯ 'vandɐn 'bɑ̯edə 'ʀyst'ɪç tsuː:
Ich auf der   Erd', am Himmel du, wir wandern beide rüstig zu:
I   on the   earth, in the sky   you, we wander both briskly on:
(I on earth, you in the sky,—we both wander briskly on;)

ɪç lɛrnst' lʊnt' t^hryːp', duː mɪlt' lʊnt' rɑ̯en, vas maːk' deːɐ̯/deːr 'lʊnt'ɐʃiːt'   voːl   zɑ̯en?
ich ernst und trüb,   du mild und rein, was mag   der   Unterschied wohl   sein?
I serious and gloomy, you mild and pure, what may the   difference   perhaps be?
(I serious and glum, you mild and pure,—what might the difference between us be?)

ɪç 'vandrə fʀɛmt'   fɔn lant tsuː lant', zoː 'hɑ̯emaːt'loːs, zoː 'lʊnbək^hant^h;
Ich wandre fremd   von Land zu Land, so heimatlos,   so unbekannt;
I   wander as a stranger from land to land, so homeless,   so unknown;

bɛrk'   lɑ̯of, bɛrk'   lap', valt' lɑ̯en, valt' lɑ̯os, dɔx bɪn lɪç 'nɪrgənt', lax! tsuː hɑ̯os.
Berg   auf, Berg   ab,   Wald ein, Wald aus, doch bin ich nirgend, ach! zu Haus.
Mountain up, mountain down, woods in, woods out, but am I   nowhere, ah, at home.
(Uphill, downhill, into and out of the woods, but nowhere am I at home.)

                                            [*poem:* **doch nirgend bin ich ach! zu Haus**]

duː 'laːbɐ 'vandɐst' lɑ̯of lʊnt' lap' lɑ̯os 'lɔst'əns   viːk' lɪn 'vɛst'əns   graːp',
Du aber   wanderst auf und ab   aus Ostens   Wieg' in Westens   Grab,*
You however wander   up   and down from (the) east's cradle into (the) west's grave,

valst' 'lɛndɐ(r) lɑ̯en lʊnt' 'lɛndɐ(r) lɑ̯os, lʊnt' bɪst dɔx, voː   duː bɪst, tsuː hɑ̯os.
wallst Länder ein und Länder aus, und bist doch, wo   du bist, zu Haus.
travel lands in   and land   out, and are yet, wherever you are, at home.
(travel into and out of different lands, and are nevertheless, wherever you are, at home.)

deːɐ̯ 'hɪməl, 'lɛnt'loːs 'lɑ̯osgəʃp'ant', lɪst dɑ̯en gə'liːp't'əs 'hɑ̯emaːt'lant':
Der Himmel, endlos   ausgespannt, ist dein geliebtes Heimatland:
The sky,   endlessly spread out,   is your beloved   homeland:

oː 'glʏk'lɪç veːɐ̯, vo'hɪn   leːɐ̯ geːt, dɔx lɑ̯of deːɐ̯ 'hɑ̯emaːt' 'boːdən ʃt'eːt^h!
o glücklich, wer, wohin   er geht, doch auf der Heimat   Boden steht!
oh, happy   he who, wherever he goes, still on the homeland's soil   stands!
(oh, happy is he who, wherever he goes, still stands on his native soil!)

[*The Peters edition is astronomically unsound here, having the moon rise in the west and set in the east! Schubert's wanderer strums a guitar as he walks along, gazing up at the moon.]

Der Wegweiser see *Winterreise*

deːɐ̯ ˈvae̯bɐfrɔø̯nt'
Der Weiberfreund
The Philanderer

Posthumously published [composed 1828] (poem by Abraham Cowley)
(German translation by Josef Franz von Ratschky)

nɔx fant' fɔn ˈleːfəns ˈtʰœçt'ɐʃaːrən   lɪç ˈkʰae̯nə, diː miːɐ̯ nɪçt' gəˈfiːl;
Noch fand von Evens Töchterscharen   ich keine, die mir nicht gefiel;
Yet found of Eve's little daughter-troops I   none, who to me not   pleased;
(I have never yet found among Eve's troops of little daughters any who did not please me;)

fɔn ˈfynftseːn bɪs tsuː ˈfynftsɪç ˈjaːrən lɪst' ˈjeːdə ˈmae̯nɐ ˈvynʃə   tsiːl.
von fünfzehn bis zu fünfzig Jahren ist   jede meiner Wünsche Ziel.
from fifteen   till to fifty   years   is   each my   wishes'   goal.
(from fifteen up to fifty years old, each is the goal of my desires.)

dʊrç farp' lʊnt' fɔrm, dʊrç vɪts lʊnt' ˈgyːt'ə, dʊrç ˈlaləs fyːl lɪç mɪç lɛnt'ˈtsʏk't'ʰ;
Durch Farb' und Form, durch Witz und Güte,   durch alles fühl ich mich entzückt;
Through color and shape, through wit and kindness, through all   feel I   myself delighted;
(By color and shape, by wit and kindness, I feel delighted by everything about them;)

ae̯n ˈleːbənbɪlt deːɐ̯/deːr lafroˈdiːtə lɪst' ˈjeːdə, diː mae̯n lɑo̯k' lɛɐ̯ˈblɪk't'ʰ.
ein Ebenbild der   Aphrodite ist   jede, die mein Aug' erblickt.
a   likeness of the   Aphrodite is   each, that my   eye beholds.
(each one that my eye beholds is an image of Aphrodite, the goddess of love.)

zɛlpst diː fɛɐ̯ˈmaːk' mae̯n hɛrts tsuː ˈlaŋəln, bae̯ deːɐ̯   man ˈjeːdən rae̯ts fɛɐ̯ˈmɪstʰ:
Selbst die vermag   mein Herz zu angeln, bei der   man jeden Reiz vermisst:
Even   she has power my   heart to fish for, in   whom one   every   charm misses:
(Even she in whom every charm is missing has the power to fish for my heart:)

maːk' ˈlɪmɐhɪn liːɐ̯/liːr ˈlaləs ˈmaŋəln, vɛns   nuːɐ̯/nuːr lae̯n ˈvae̯p'lɪç ˈveːzən lɪstʰ!
mag immerhin ihr   alles mangeln, wenn's nur   ein weiblich Wesen ist!
may   for all that in her all   be lacking, if   it just   a   female   being is!
(let everything else be lacking in her, so long as she is a female!)

bae̯ ˈblɔndən, ˈrʊndən dẽdɔˈnɛt'ən pʰrae̯z ɪç diː ˈfʏlə   deːɐ̯ naˈtʰuːɐ̯:
Bei Blonden, runden Dindonetten preis' ich die Fülle   der Natur:
With blond,   round   little turkeys praise I   the fullness of the nature;
(With blond, plump little geese I praise the abundance of nature;)
        ["*dindon*" in French = turkey, also used in a derogatory sense similar to our "silly goose"]

an ˈhaːgɐn ˈʃmɛçt'ɪgən bryˈnɛt'ən rae̯tst' mɪç fɛɐ̯ˈliːp't'ɐ ˈzeːnzʊxt' ʃp'uːɐ̯.
an hagern schmächtigen Brünetten reizt   mich verliebter Sehnsucht Spur.
in haggard, slender   brunettes excites me   amorous   longing's trace.
(in lean and slender brunettes any trace of amorous longing excites me.)

bəˈtsɑo̯bɛnt' lɪst diː ˈʃlaŋk'ə ˈʃøːnə; dɔx lɑox deːɐ̯ ˈkʰrʊmən   ˈhʊldɪk   lɪç;
Bezaubernd ist die schlanke Schöne; doch auch der Krummen huldig'   ich;
Enchanting is the slim   beauty; but also the crooked one pay homage to I;
(The slender beauty is enchanting; but I also pay homage to the crooked;)

an 'laːmoːɐ̯s pf̣ael lɛɐ̯(r)'lɪnɐt' 'jeːnə,   lʊnt diː   lan 'zaɛnən 'boːgən mɪç.
an Amors Pfeil erinnert jene,   und die   an seinen Bogen mich.
of Cupid's arrow reminds   that one (the former), and this (the latter) of his   bow   me.
(the former reminds me of Cupid's arrow, and the latter of his bow.)

zoː flatʰ- rɪç 'rast'loːs,   glạe̯ç den 'biːnən, dʊrç 'laːmoːɐ̯s 'lʊst'gəfɪldə   hɪn,
So flattr' ich rastlos,   gleich den Bienen, durch Amors Lustgefilde   hin,
So flutter I   without rest, like the bees,   through Cupid's pleasure-fields on,
(So I flutter on tirelessly, like the bees, through Cupid's fields of pleasure,)

ʊnt' zɛlpst das 'lʊnkʰrạot' mʊs miːɐ̯ 'diːnən, lʊm   'zyːsən 'hoːnɪç drạos   tsuː tsiːn.
und selbst das Unkraut muss mir dienen, um   süssen Honig draus   zu ziehn.
and even the weed   must me serve   in order sweet honey from them to draw.
(and even the weeds serve me when I am gathering sweet honey out of those fields.)

[This chauvinistic little number is a translation of a seventeenth-century English poem called "The Inconstant." Schubert copied out the first verse only (all are printed above), and placed a repeat sign at the end. The English poem had seven stanzas. Schubert's setting is very charming.]

deːɐ̯ 'vɪnt'ɐlaːbənt'
Der Winterabend
The Winter Evening

Posthumously published [composed 1828] (poem by Karl Gottfried von Leitner)

ɛs lɪst' zoː ʃt'ɪl, zoː 'haɛmlɪç lʊm   mɪç, di zɔn lɪst' 'lʊnt'ɐ, deːɐ̯ tʰaːk' lɛnt'vɪç
Es ist so still, so heimlich um   mich, die Sonn' ist unter, der Tag entwich.
It is   so still, so secluded around me, the sun is   down, the day vanished.
        [*poem:* **so still und** (lʊnt', and) **heimlich** ; *Peters:* **die Sonn' ist unten** ('lʊnt'ən)]

viː ʃnɛl nuːn heˈran   deːɐ̯/deːr 'laːbənt' grạotʰ!   miːɐ̯/miːr lɪst' lɛs reçtʰ,
Wie schnell nun heran   der   Abend graut!   Mir   ist es recht,
How fast   now hitherward the   evening grows grey! For me   is it right,
(How quickly the evening is now growing grey! For me that is quite right,)

zɔnst' lɪst' miːɐ̯s   tsuː lạotʰ. jɛtst' 'laːbɐ(r) lɪsts 'ruːɪç, lɛs 'hɛmɐt' kʰaen ʃmiːt',
sonst   ist mir's   zu laut. Jetzt aber   ist's ruhig, es   hämmert kein Schmied,
otherwise is   for me it too loud. Now   however is it calm, there hammers no   smith,
(otherwise it's too loud for me. Now however all is calm; no smith is hammering,)

kʰaen 'kʰlɛmp'nɐ, das fɔlk' fɐɐ̯'liːf   lʊnt' lɪst' myːt'; lʊnt' zɛlpst,
kein Klempner, das Volk   verlief   und ist müd'; und selbst,
no   plumber,   the people dispersed and is tired; and even,
(nor any plumber; the people have dispersed and are tired; and even,)

das nɪçt' 'raslə deːɐ̯ 'vaːgən lạof, tsoːk' 'dɛk'ən deːɐ̯ ʃneː   dʊrç di 'gasən lạof.
dass nicht rass'le der Wagen Lauf, zog Decken der Schnee durch die Gassen auf.
so that not   rattle   the carts' course, pulled covers the snow   through the alleys up.
(so that the carts will not rattle as they pass, the snow has pulled the covers up over the streets.)

310

vi: tʰuːtʽ miːɐ̯ zoː voːl deːɐ̯ 'zeːlɪɡə 'friːdən! daː zɪts lɪç lɪm 'dʊŋkʽəl,
Wie tut mir so wohl der selige Frieden! Da sitz' ich im Dunkel,
How makes me so well the blessed peace! There sit I in the dark,
(How well this blessed peace makes me feel! There I sit in the dark,)

> [*GA:* **im Dunkeln** ('dʊŋkʽəln), in the darkening]

gants 'lapʽɡəʃiːdən, zoː gants fyːɐ̯ mɪç; nuːɐ̯ deːɐ̯ 'moːndənʃaen kʰɔmtʽ 'laezə
ganz abgeschieden, so ganz für mich; nur der Mondenschein kommt leise
totally solitary, so completely for myself; only the moonlight comes quietly

tsuː miːɐ̯/miːr lɪns ɡə'max. leːɐ̯ kʰentʽ mɪç ʃoːn, lʊntʽ lɛstʽ mɪç 'ʃvaeɡən, nɪmtʽ
zu mir ins Gemach.* Er kennt mich schon, und lässt mich schweigen, nimmt
to me into the room. It knows me already, and lets me be silent, takes
(into the room to me. It knows me already, and lets me be silent, takes up)

> [*poem:* **ins Gemach herein** (hɪ'naen, into).]

nuːɐ̯ 'zaenə 'larbaet, di 'ʃpʽɪndəl, das ɡɔltʽ, lʊntʽ 'ʃpʽɪnətʽ 'ʃtʽɪlə, veːpʽtʽ lʊntʽ 'leçəltʽ hɔltʽ,
nur seine Arbeit, die Spindel, das Gold, und spinnet stille, webt und lächelt hold,
only its work, the spindle, the gold, and spins quietly, weaves and smiles sweetly,

ʊntʽ hentʽ dan zaen 'ʃɪmɐndəs 'ʃlaeɐtʰuːx rɪŋs'lʊm lan ɡə'reːtʽ lʊntʽ 'vendən laos.
und hängt dann sein schimmerndes Schleiertuch ringsum an Gerät und Wänden aus.
and hangs then its shimmering veil- cloth all around on gear and walls out.
(and then spreads out its shimmering veil all around over the furniture and the walls.)

ɪstʽ ɡaːɐ̯/ɡaːr laen 'ʃtʽɪlɐ(r), laen 'liːbə bə'zuːx, maxtʽ miːɐ̯ ɡaːɐ̯ 'kʰaenə 'lʊnruː lɪm haos;
Ist gar ein stiller, ein lieber Besuch, macht mir gar keine Unruh' im Haus;
Is quite a quiet, a dear visitor, makes me at all no unrest in the house;
(It is quite a quiet, dear visitor, and makes no commotion at all in the house;)

> [*poem:* **Ist gar ein stiller, lieber Besuch**]

vɪl leːɐ̯ 'blaebən, zoː hatʽ leːɐ̯/leːr lɔrtʰ, frɔøts lɪːn 'nɪmɐ, zoː ɡeːtʽ leːɐ̯ fɔrtʰ.
will er bleiben, so hat er Ort, freut's ihn nimmer, so geht er fort.
wants it to stay, so has it room, pleases it it no more, so goes it away.
(if it wants to stay, there's plenty of room; if it doesn't feel like it any more, then it goes away.)

ɪç 'zɪtsə dan ʃtʽʊm lɪm 'fenstʽɐ gern, lʊntʽ 'ʃaoə hɪ'naof lɪn ɡə'vœlkʽ lʊntʽ ʃtʽern,
Ich sitze dann stumm im Fenster gern, und schaue hinauf in Gewölk und Stern,
I sit then silently at the window gladly, and look up into clouds and star,
(Then I like to sit silently at the window and look up at the clouds and the stars,)

'deŋkʽə tsu'rʏkʽ, lax vaetʽ, ɡaːɐ̯ vaetʽ, lɪn 'laenə 'ʃøːnə, fɐ'ʃvʊndnə tsaetʰ.
denke zurück, ach weit, gar weit, in eine schöne, verschwundne Zeit.
think back, ah far, very far, into a lovely, vanished time.

deŋkʽ lan ziː, lan das ɡlʏkʽ deːɐ̯ 'mɪnə, 'zɔøftsə ʃtʽɪl lʊntʽ 'zɪnə, lʊntʽ 'zɪnə.
Denk' an Sie, an das Glück der Minne, seufze still und sinne, und sinne.
Think of Her, of the happiness of the love, sigh softly and think, and think.
(I think of Her, of the happiness of love; I sigh softly and think and think.)

[In this lovely, rather long song there is charm, humor, and wistful nostalgia at the end; the man lost his beloved, long ago, but has made his peace with the world, as long as it is not too loud.
*Schubert omitted three lines at the point indicated: "*Brauche mich aber nicht zu genieren,/ nicht*

311

zu spielen, zu konversieren,/ oder mich sonst attent zu zeigen" (I don't need to trouble myself, however, nor to play games, to make conversation, or otherwise to pay any special attention) .]

deːɐ̯ tsuˈfriːdənə
Der Zufriedene
The Contented Man

Posthumously published [composed 1815] (poem by Christian Ludwig Reissig)

tsvaːɐ̯   ʃuːf   das glʏkˈ hiːˈniːdən   mɪç ˈveːdɐ raɑeç nɔx groːs,
Zwar   schuf das Glück hienieden   mich weder reich noch gross,
I admit that created the fortune here on earth me   neither rich nor great,
(I admit that fortune here on earth has created me neither rich nor great;)

aˈlaen   lɪç bɪn tsuˈfriːdən, viː mɪt dem ˈʃøːnstˈən loːs.
allein   ich bin zufrieden, wie mit dem schönsten Los.
nevertheless I   am content,   as if with the   finest   lot.

zoː gants naːx ˈmaenəm ˈhɛrtsən vartˈ miːɐ̯/miːr laen frɔøntˈ fɛɐ̯ˈɡœntʰ,   [ɡəˈɡœntʰ]
So ganz nach meinem Herzen ward mir   ein Freund vergönnt, [*variant:* **gegönnt**]
So totally after my   heart   was to me   a   friend   granted,
(A friend was granted to me so totally after my own heart,)

dɛn ˈkʰʏsən, ˈtʰrɪŋkˈən, ˈʃertsən   lɪstˈ laɑx zaen leleˈmɛntʰ.
denn Küssen, Trinken, Scherzen ist auch sein Element.
for to kiss, to drink, to joke   is also his   element.
(for he too is also in his element kissing, drinking, and joking.)

mɪtˈ liːm vɪrtˈ froː   lʊntˈ ˈvaezə manç ˈflɛʃçən   ˈlaɑsɡələːɐ̯tʰ;
Mit ihm wird froh   und weise manch Fläschchen ausgeleert;
With him is   happily and wisely many a little bottle emptied;
(With him, happily and wisely, many a bottle is emptied;)

dɛn laɑf deːɐ̯ ˈleːbənsraɑezə   lɪstˈ vaen das ˈbɛstˈə pfeːɐ̯tˈ.
denn auf der Lebensreise   ist Wein das beste Pferd.
for on the life-   journey is wine the best   horse.
(for on life's journey wine is the best horse.)

vɛn   miːɐ̯ bae ˈdiːzəm ˈloːzə nuːn laɑx laen ˈtʰryːbrəs fɛltʰ,
Wenn mir bei diesem Lose nun auch ein trüb'res fällt,
If   to me in this   lot now also a   gloomier falls,
(If in this lot of mine a gloomier one should also fall to me,)

zoː dɛŋkˈ lɪçː ˈkʰaenə ˈroːzə blyːt ˈdɔrnloːs lɪn deːɐ̯ vɛltʰ.
so denk' ich: keine Rose blüht dornlos in der Welt.
then think I: no   rose blooms thornless in the world.
(then I think: no rose in this world blooms without thorns.)

[This is one of several poems that were set by both Beethoven and Schubert, in this case in the same key and with strikingly similar triplets in the interludes (a guzzling motif?). Neither setting is melodically catchy enough to become the happy-go-lucky drinking song that the words imply.]

deːɐ̯ ˈtsʏrnəndə ˈbardə
Der zürnende Barde
The Angry Bard

Posthumously published [composed 1823] (poem by Franz von Bruchmann)

veːɐ̯ vaːkˈts, veːɐ̯ vaːkˈts, veːɐ̯ vaːkˈts, veːɐ̯ vɪl   miːɐ̯ di ˈlaeɐ tseɐ̯ˈbreçən?
Wer wagt's, wer wagt's, wer wagt's, wer will   mir   die Leier zerbrechen?
Who dares it, who dares it, who dares it, who wants to me the lyre   to shatter?
(Who dares, who dares, who dares, who wants to shatter my lyre?)

nɔx tʰaːkˈts, nɔx tʰaːkˈts, nɔx tʰaːkˈts, nɔx ˈglyːət di kʰraftˈ, mɪç   tsuː ˈreçən.
Noch tagt's, noch tagt's, noch tagt's, noch glühet die Kraft, mich   zu   rächen.
Still dawns it, still dawns it, still dawns it, still burns the strength myself to   avenge.
(It is still early in the day, and the strength to avenge myself is still burning.)

hɛˈran,   hɛˈran,   liːɐ̯/liːr ˈalə, veːɐ̯/veːr ˈɪmɐ zɪç   lɛɐ̯ˈkʰyːntʰ,
Heran, heran, ihr   alle, wer   immer sich   erkühnt,
Come on, come on, you   all, who   ever himself makes bold,
(Come on, step forward, all of you, whoever is bold enough;)

aos ˈdʊŋkˈlɐ ˈfɛlzənhalə ɪstˈ miːɐ̯ di ˈlaeɐ gəˈgryːntʰ.   [lɛɐ̯ˈgryːntʰ]
aus dunkler Felsenhalle ist mir   die Leier gegrünt.   [variant: ergrünt]
out of dark   cliff- hall has for me the lyre   sprouted.
(my lyre has sprouted out of a dark hall in the rocky cliff.)

ɪç ˈhaːbə das hɔlts gəˈʃpˈaltən ɪaos ˈriːzɪgəm ˈlaeçənbaom,
Ich habe das Holz gespalten aus riesigem Eichenbaum,
I   have the wood split   from gigantic oak- tree,
(I split the wood from a giant oak-tree,)

voˈrʊntˈɐ(r) ɪaenst di ˈaltˈən ɪʊmˈtʰantstˈən ˈvoːdans zaom.
worunter   einst die Alten   umtanzten   Wodans Saum.
under which once the ancients danced around Wodan's hem.
(under which our forebears danced around the hem of Wodan's cloak.)

di ˈzaetˈən raopˈtˈ ɪɪç deːɐ̯   ˈzɔnə, den ˈpʰʊrp'ʊrnən, ˈglyːəndən ʃtˈraːl,
Die Saiten raubt' ich der   Sonne, den purpurnen, glühenden Strahl,
The strings stole I   from the sun,   the crimson,   glowing   ray,
(I stole the strings from the sun, I stole its crimson, glowing rays,)

als ɪaenstˈ ziː ɪɪn ˈzeːlɪgɐ ˈvɔnə fɛɐ̯ˈzaŋkˈ ɪɪn das ˈblyːəndə tʰaːl.
als einst sie in seliger Wonne versank in   das blühende Tal.
as once   it in blissful rapture sank   into the flowering valley.
(as once it was sinking in blissful rapture into the flowering valley.)

aos ˈlaltˈɐ(r) ˈlaːnən   ˈlaeçən, ɪaos ˈroːtˈəm ˈlaːbəntˈgɔltˈ,
Aus alter   Ahnen   Eichen, aus   rotem   Abendgold,
Out of old   ancestors' oaks, out of red   sunset gold,
(Made of ancient ancestral oak and the red gold of sunset,)

vɪrst', 'laeɐ, du: 'nɪmɐ 'vaeçən, zo: laŋ di 'gœt'ɐ miːɐ̯ hɔlt'!
wirst, Leier, du nimmer weichen, so lang' die Götter mir hold!
will, lyre, you never retreat, as long as the gods to me (are) gracious!
(you will never retreat, my lyre, as long as the gods continue to be gracious to me!)

[The poet defies the repressive censors, critics, and politicians of the Metternich era in this manifesto of artistic freedom. Schubert wrote the voice part in the bass cleff, but it was printed in the treble by the first publisher; the song was clearly intended for a powerful baritone or bass. Wodan was the chief god of the Germanic tribes, the name altered to Wotan in Wagner's *Ring*.]

deːɐ̯ 'tsʏrnəndən 'di̯aːna
Der zürnenden Diana
To Angry Diana

Op. 36, No. 1 [1820] (Johann Mayrhofer)

jaː, 'ʃp'anə nuːɐ̯ den 'boːɡən mɪç tsuː 't'ø:t'ən, du: 'hɪmlɪʃ vaep'!
Ja, spanne nur den Bogen mich zu töten, du himmlisch Weib!
Yes, draw just the bow me to kill, you celestial woman!
(Yes, go ahead and draw your bow to kill me, divine woman,)

ɪm 'tsʏrnəndən lɛɐ̯'røːt'ən nɔx 'raetsəndɐ. lɪç veːɐ̯t' lɛs niː bə'rɔ̷øən,
im zürnenden Erröten noch reizender. Ich werd' es nie bereuen,
in the angering flush still more bewitching. I shall it never regret,
(even more bewitching in the flush of anger. I shall never regret it,)
[*poem:* **Im zornigen** ('tsɔrnɪɡən, angry) **Erröten**]

das lɪç dɪç zaː lam 'blyːəndən ɡə'ʃt'aːdə di 'nʏmfən lyːbə'raːɡən lɪn dem 'baːdə,
dass ich dich sah am blühenden Gestade die Nymphen überragen in dem Bade,
that I you saw on the blossoming bank the nymphs surpass(ing) in the bath,
(that I saw you on the flowery bank, outshining the nymphs at your bath,)
[*Peters and poem:* **am buschigen** ('buʃɪɡən, bushy) **Gestade**]

deːɐ̯ 'ʃøːnhaet' 'fuŋk'ən lɪn di 'vɪlt'nɪs 'ʃt'rɔ̷øən. niː veːɐ̯t' lɪç lɛs bə'rɔ̷øən.
der Schönheit Funken in die Wildnis streuen. Nie werd' ich es bereuen.
the beauty's sparks into the wilderness scattering. Never shall I it regret.
(radiating sparks of beauty into the wilderness. Never shall I regret it.)

den 'ʃt'ɛrbəndən vɪrt' nɔx daen bɪlt' lɛɐ̯'frɔ̷øən, leːɐ̯ 'laːt'mət' 'raenɐ,
Den Sterbenden wird noch dein Bild erfreuen, er atmet reiner,
The dying one [obj.] will still your image [subj.] delight, he breathes purer,
(Your image will still delight the dying man; he breathes more purely,)

leːɐ̯ 'laːt'mət' 'fraeɐ, veːm du: ɡə'ʃt'raːlət' 'loːnə 'ʃlaeɐ. daen pfael, leːɐ̯ t'raːf—
er atmet freier, wem du gestrahlet ohne Schleier. Dein Pfeil, er traf—
he breathes freer, on whom you beamed without veil. Your arrow, it struck—
(he breathes more freely, he upon whom your unveiled beauty shone. Your arrow, it struck—)
[*poem:* **atmet freier** (without **er**)]

dɔx 'lɪndə 'rɪnən di 'varmən 'vɛlən laos deːɐ̯ 'vundə;
doch linde rinnen die warmen Wellen aus der Wunde;
but gently flow the warm waves from the wound;
(but the warm waves flow gently from the wound;)

314

nɔx ˈtsɪtˈɐtˈ foːɐ̯   den ˈmatˈən ˈzɪnən dɛs ˈʃɑo̯əns ˈzyːsə ˈlɛtstˈə ˈʃtˈʊndə.
noch zittert vor   den matten Sinnen des Schauens süsse letzte   Stunde.
still trembles before the dull   senses the seeing's sweet last   hour.
(my last sweet hour of vision still vibrates before my failing senses.)

[One day, by chance, the huntsman Actaeon came upon the naked goddess Diana, bathing with her nymphs in a forest spring. He was bewitched by her divine beauty. When she noticed that a mortal was gazing at her nakedness, the outraged huntress with the silver bow transformed him into a stag and killed him with his own hunting dogs. In Mayrhofer's poem, the dying man rejoices that his last moments of life were blessed with a vision of ultimate loveliness. Schubert's somewhat operatic song is appropriately beautiful and deserves to be better known.]

deːɐ̯ tsvɛrkˈ
Der Zwerg
The Dwarf

Op. 22, No. 1 [1822?] (Matthäus von Collin)

ɪm   ˈtʰryːbən lɪçtˈ fɛɐ̯ˈʃvɪndən   ʃoːn di ˈbɛrgə,   ɛs   ʃveːɐ̯tˈ das ʃɪf
Im   trüben Licht verschwinden schon die Berge,   es   schwebt das Schiff
In the dim   light disappear   already the mountains, there floats   the ship
(In the dim light the mountains are already disappearing; the ship is floating)

ɑo̯f ˈglatˈən ˈmeːrəsvoːgən, voˈrɑo̯f di ˈkʰøːnɪgɪn mɪtˈ ˈliːrəm ˈtsvɛrgə.
auf glatten Meereswogen, worauf die Königin mit ihrem Zwerge.
on   smooth sea-   waves, on which the queen   with her   dwarf.
(on the smooth swell of the sea, on board the queen with her dwarf.)

[*poem:* **worin** (voˈrɪn, in which) **die Königin**]

ziː ʃɑo̯tˈ ɛmˈpʰoːɐ̯ tsʊm ˈhoːxgəvœlpˈtˈən ˈboːgən,
Sie schaut empor   zum hochgewölbten Bogen,
She looks   up   to the high- vaulted   arch,
(She looks up at the high-vaulted arch of heaven,)

hɪˈnɑo̯f tsuːɐ̯ ˈlɪçtdʊrçvɪrkˈtˈən   ˈblɑo̯ən ˈfɛrnə,
hinauf zur   lichtdurchwirkten blauen Ferne,
up   at the light-interwoven   blue   distance,
(at the blue distance, interwoven with light,)

diː   mɪt deːɐ̯ mɪlç dɛs ˈhɪməls blas dʊrçtsoːgən.
die   mit der Milch des Himmels blass durchzogen.
which with the milk of the sky   palely (is) traversed.
(which is traversed by the pale milky way.)

niː,   niː haːpˈtˈ liːɐ̯ mɪːɐ̯ gəˈloːgən nɔx, liːɐ̯ ˈʃtˈɛrnə, zoː ruːftˈ ziː ɑo̯s,
"Nie,   nie habt ihr mir gelogen noch, ihr Sterne," so   ruft sie aus,
"Never, never have you to me lied   yet, you stars,"   thus cries she out,
("Never, never yet have you lied to me, you stars," thus she cries out,)

[*poem:* **"Ihr habt mir nie gelogen noch, ihr Sterne,"**]

baltˈ veːɐ̯d ɪç nuːn ɛntˈʃvɪndən, liːɐ̯ zaːkˈtˈ ɛs miːɐ̯; dɔx ʃtˈɛrb ɪç ˈvaːɐ̯lɪç ˈgɛrnə.
"bald werd' ich nun entschwinden, ihr sagt es mir;   doch sterb' ich wahrlich gerne."
"soon shall I   now disappear,   you say   it to me; but die   I   truly   gladly."
("soon I shall be no more, you tell me that; but, truly, I shall die gladly.")

daː   tʰrɪt   deːɐ̯ tsvɛrk‘ tsur ˈkøːnɪgɪn, maːk‘ ˈbɪndən lʊm   ˈliːrən hals
Da tritt   der Zwerg zur Königin, mag binden um   ihren Hals
Then stepped the   dwarf to the queen,   may   bind   around her   neck
(Then the dwarf comes up to the queen, prepared to bind around her neck)

[*poem:* **Da geht** (geːt, goes) **der Zwerg zur Königin**]

di ʃnuːɐ̯   fɔn ˈroːt‘ɐ ˈzaedə, lʊnt‘ vaentʰ, lals vɔlt‘   leːɐ̯ ʃnɛl   foːɐ̯ graːm lɛɐ̯ˈblɪndən.
die Schnur von roter Seide, und weint, als wollt’ er schnell vor Gram erblinden.
the cord   of   red   silk,   and weeps as if wanted he   quickly   for sorrow to become blind.
(the cord of red silk, and he weeps as if he wanted quickly to become blind with sorrow.)

[*poem:* **als wollt’ vor Gram er schnell erblinden**]

eːɐ̯ ʃp‘rɪçtʰ: du: zɛlpst‘   bɪst‘ ʃult‘   lan ˈdiːzəm ˈlaedə,   vael   lʊm den ˈkʰøːnɪç
Er spricht: “Du selbst   bist schuld an diesem Leide,   weil   um den König
He speaks: “You yourself are   to blame for this   suffering, because for   the   king

du: mɪç   hast‘ fɛɐ̯ˈlasən;   jɛtst‘ vɛk‘t daen ˈʃt‘ɛrbən ˈlaentsɪç miːɐ̯   nɔx   ˈfrɔɐdøə.
du mich hast verlassen; jetzt weckt dein Sterben einzig mir   noch Freude.
you me   have forsaken;   now   wakes your dying   only   for me still   joy.
(you have forsaken me; now only your dying can reawaken joy in me.)

[*poem:* **nun macht** (nuːn maxt, now makes) **dein Sterben einzig mir nur** (nuːɐ̯, only) **Freude**]

tsvaːɐ̯   veːɐ̯d ɪç ˈleːvɪk‘lɪç mɪç ˈzɛlbɐ ˈhasən, deːɐ̯ diːɐ̯   mɪt ˈdiːzɐ hant‘
Zwar   werd’ ich ewiglich mich selber hassen, der dir   mit dieser Hand
Of course shall I   eternally me   self   hate,   who to you with this   hand
(Of course I shall eternally hate myself, who with this hand)

[*poem:* **Mich selber werd’ ich ewiglich wohl** (voːl, probably) **hassen**]

den tʰoːt‘ gəˈgeːbən, dɔx mʊst tsʊm ˈfryːən graːp‘ du: nuːn lɛɐ̯ˈblasən.
den Tod   gegeben, doch musst zum frühen Grab du nun erblassen,”
the death gave,   but   must to the early   grave you now grow pale.”
(gave you death; but you must now grow pale with death in an early grave.”)

zi: leːk‘t di hant‘ laɔfs hɛrts fɔl   ˈjʊŋəm ˈleːbən, lʊnt‘ laɔs dem laok‘
Sie legt die Hand aufs Herz voll   jungem Leben, und aus dem Aug’
She lays the hand on the heart full of young   life,   and from the   eye
(She lays her hand on her heart, so full of young life, and from her eyes)

di ˈʃveːrən ˈtʰreːnən ˈrɪnən,   das zi: tsʊm ˈhɪməl ˈbeːt‘ənt‘ vɪl   lɛɐ̯ˈheːbən.
die schweren Tränen rinnen,   das sie zum Himmel betend will   erheben.
the heavy   tears   run, (the eye) which she to the heaven   praying wants to raise.
(the heavy teardrops flow, from her eyes which she would raise to heaven in prayer.)

møːkst du: nɪçt‘ ʃmɛrts dʊrç ˈmaenən tʰoːt‘ gəˈvɪnən! zi: zak‘ts;
“Mögst du nicht Schmerz durch meinen Tod gewinnen!” Sie sagt’s;
“May   you not   pain   through my   death gain!”   She says it;
(“May you reap no pain from my death!” she says;)

[*poem:* **“O möchtest** (oː ˈmœçt‘əst, Oh might) **du nicht Schmerz**]

daː kʰʏst deːɐ̯ tsvɛrk‘ di ˈblaeçən ˈvaŋən, draɔf lalzoˈbalt‘ fɛɐ̯ˈgeːən liːɐ̯   di ˈzɪnən.
da küsst der Zwerg die bleichen Wangen, drauf alsobald vergehen ihr   die Sinnen.
then kisses the   dwarf the pale   cheeks,   thereat forthwith vanish   to her the senses.
(then the dwarf kisses her pale cheeks, whereupon her senses immediately slip away.)

[*poem:* **und** (lʊnt‘, and) **alsobald**]

deːɐ̯ tsvɛrk‘ ʃɑ̯ot‘ lan di frɑ̯o fɔm tʰoːt‘ bə'faŋən, leːɐ̯ zɛŋk‘t‘ ziː tʰiːf lɪns   meːɐ̯
Der Zwerg schaut an die Frau vom Tod befangen, er senkt sie tief ins   Meer
The dwarf looks at the woman by the death overcome, he lowers her deep into the sea
(The dwarf looks at the woman overcome by death; then he lowers her deep into the sea)

mɪt‘ 'lɑ̯egnən 'hendən, liːm brɛnt‘ naːx liːɐ̯ das hɛrts zoː fɔl fɛɐ̯'laŋən.
mit eignen Händen, ihm brennt nach ihr das Herz so voll Verlangen.
with own hands, in him burns for her the heart so full of desire.
(with his own hands; his heart is burning so full of desire for her.)

[*poem:* **das Herze** ('hɛrtsə) **voll Verlangen**]

an 'kʰɑ̯enɐ 'kʰʏst‘ə vɪrt‘ leːɐ̯ jeː meːɐ̯ 'landən.
An keiner Küste wird er je mehr landen.
On no shore will he ever again land.
(He will never again land on any shore.)

[The song captures the mystery and the sinister erotic undertones of the poem. It is said that Schubert composed it almost automatically, while carrying on a conversation with a friend. The original title of the poem was *Treubruch* ("Breach of Faith"). The interpreter has the challenge of three voices to be differentiated, the narrator, the queen, and the passionately anguished dwarf.]

Des Baches Wiegenlied see *Die schöne Müllerin*

dɛs 'fɪʃɐs 'liːbəsglʏkʰ
Des Fischers Liebesglück
The Fisherman's Luck in Love

Posthumously published [composed 1827] (poem by Karl Gottfried von Leitner)

dɔrt‘ 'blɪŋk‘ət dʊrç 'vɑ̯edən lʊnt‘ 'vɪŋk‘ət lɑ̯en 'ʃɪmɐ
Dort blinket durch Weiden und winket ein Schimmer
There gleams through willows and beckons a shimmer
(A shimmer is gleaming through the willow trees and beckoning)

'blasʃt‘raːlɪç fɔm 'tsɪmɐ deːɐ̯ 'hɔldən miːɐ̯ tsuː.
blassstrahlig vom Zimmer der Holden mir zu.
pale-rayed from the room of the lovely one to me to.
(to me with its pale rays from the room of my lovely one.)

lɛs 'gɑ̯ok‘əlt‘ viː 'lɪrlɪçt‘, lʊnt‘ 'ʃɑ̯ok‘əlt‘ zɪç 'lɑ̯ezə zɑ̯en 'lap‘glants
Es gaukelt wie Irrlicht, und schaukelt sich leise sein Abglanz
There flits about like will-o'-the-wisp, and rocks itself softly its reflection
(Its reflection flits about like the will-o'-the'wisp, and rocks softly)

lɪm 'kʰrɑ̯ezə dɛs 'ʃvaŋk‘əndən zeːs. lç 'ʃɑ̯oə mɪt‘ 'zeːnən
im Kreise des schwankenden Sees. Ich schaue mit Sehnen
in the circle of the undulating lake. I look with longing

lɪns 'blɑ̯oə deːɐ̯ 'vɛlən lʊnt‘ 'gryːsə den 'hɛlən, gə'ʃp‘iːgəlt‘ən ʃt‘raːl.
ins Blaue der Wellen und grüsse den hellen, gespiegelten Strahl.
into the blue of the waves and greet the bright, reflected beam.

ʊnt' 'ʃp'rɪŋə t̪sʊm 'ruːdɐ(r) lʊnt' 'ʃvɪŋə   den 'naxən
Und   springe zum Ruder   und   schwinge den Nachen
And (I) leap   to the rudder   and   swing   the boat

da'hɪn lɑof dem 'flaxən,   kʰrɪs'tʰalənən veːk'.   faen'liːp'çən ʃlaeçt   'tʰrɑolɪç
dahin auf dem flachen, kristallenen Weg.   Feinliebchen schleicht traulich
away on the smooth crystalline   course. Sweetheart   sneaks   confidentially
(away on its smooth crystalline course. My sweetheart sneaks quietly)

          [*Peters:* **dahin auf den** (lɑof den, onto the) **flachen**]

fɔm   'ʃt'yːp'çən he'rʊnt'ɐ(r) lʊnt' 'ʃp'uːt'ət' zɪç   'mʊnt'ɐ   t̪suː miːɐ̯/miːr lɪn das boːtʰ.
vom   Stübchen herunter   und   sputet   sich   munter   zu mir   in das Boot.
from the little room down   and   hurries   herself cheerfully to me   in   the   boat.
(down from her little room, and cheerfully hurries over to join me in the boat.)

gə'lɪndə dan 'tʰraebən di 'vɪndə lʊns 'viːdɐ   zeːr'laenvert̪s
Gelinde dann treiben die Winde uns wieder see-einwärts
Gently then drive   the winds us   again   lake-inwards
(The winds then gently blow us out onto the lake again)

fɔm   'fliːdɐ des   'luːfɐs hɪn'dan.   di 'blasən naxt'neːbəl*
vom   Flieder des   Ufers hindann. Die blassen Nachtnebel
from the lilac   of the shore away.   The pale   night- mist
(away from the lilacs by the shore. The pale evening mists)

     [*Schubert's setting accents the second syllable; the first would normally be stressed.]

lʊm'fasən mɪt' 'hylən foːɐ̯   'ʃp'ɛːɐn   den 'ʃt'ɪlən, lʊn'ʃʊldɪgən* ʃert̪s.
umfassen mit Hüllen vor   Spähern   den stillen, unschuldigen Scherz.
envelop   with veils   before prying eyes the quiet, innocent   jest.
(shields with its veils the quiet, innocent play from prying eyes.)

ʊnt 'tʰɑoʃən viːɐ̯ 'kʰʏsə, zoː 'rɑoʃən   di 'vɛlən lɪm   'zɪŋk'ən lʊnt' 'ʃvɛlən,
Und tauschen wir Küsse, so   rauschen die Wellen im   Sinken und Schwellen,
And exchange we kisses, then murmur the waves in the sinking and   swelling,
(And if we exchange kisses, then the waves murmur in their falling and rising,)

den 'hɔrçən   t̪sʊm tʰrɔt̪s,   nuːɐ̯ 'ʃt'ɛrnə bə'lɑoʃən lʊns 'fɛrnə,
den Horchern   zum Trotz.   Nur Sterne belauschen uns ferne,
the eavesdroppers to the defiance (of). Only stars   listen to   us (from) afar,
(to defy the eavesdroppers. Only the stars listen to us from afar,)

lʊnt' 'baːdən tʰiːf 'lʊnt'ɐ   den 'pfaːdən dɛs   'glaet'əndən kʰaːns.
und baden tief unter   den Pfaden des   gleitenden Kahns.
and bathe deep beneath the paths   of the gliding   boat.

zoː 'ʃveːbən viːɐ̯ 'zeːlɪç,   lʊm'geːbən fɔm   'dʊŋk'əl, hoːx 'yːbɐm   gə'fʊŋk'əl
So   schweben wir selig,   umgeben vom   Dunkel, hoch überm   Gefunkel
Thus float   we blissfully, surrounded by the darkness, high above the twinkling
(We are floating along blissfully in that way, surrounded by darkness, high above the twinkling)

deːɐ̯ 'ʃt'ɛrnə laen'heːɐ̯. lʊnt' 'vaenən   lʊnt' 'leçəln, lʊnt' 'maenən,
der Sterne einher. Und weinen   und lächeln, und meinen,
of the stars   along.   And (we) weep and smile,   and imagine
(of the stars. And we weep and smile, and imagine)   [*"einherschweben"* = to float along]

lɛnt'hoːbən deːɐ̯/deːr 'leːɐ̯də, ʃoːn 'loːbən, ʃoːn 'dryːbən tsuː zaen.
enthoben der Erde, schon oben, schon drüben zu sein.
removed from the earth, already above, already beyond to be.
(that we are removed from the earth and already up above, already in the realm beyond.)

[Schubert set this happy poem to a barcarolle rhythm, with languidly rippling sixteenths for the movement of the water, a minor key opening to suggest the friendly darkness, and an occasional upward leap in the voice part, at appropriate moments, to express enthusiasm, the airy fragrance of lilacs, or the sensation of soaring up to heaven.]

des 'mɛːt'çəns 'kʰlaːgə
Des Mädchens Klage
The Maiden's Lament

Op. 58, No. 3 (*second version of three*) [1815] (Friedrich von Schiller)

deːɐ̯/deːr 'laeçvalt' braost, di 'vɔlk'ən tsiːn, das 'mɛːk't'laen zitst' lan 'luːfɐs gryːn,
Der Eichwald braust, die Wolken ziehn, das Mägdlein sitzt an Ufers Grün,
The oak forest roars, the clouds scud, the girl sits on shore's green,
(The oak forest roars, the clouds scud by, the girl is sitting on the green shore,)
 [*1st version and poem:* **brauset** ('braozət'); *1st version:* **ziehen** ('tsiːən); *poem:* **sitzet** ('zitsət')]

ɛs briçt' ziç di 'velə mit' maxtʰ, lʊnt' ziː zɔøftst' hinaos lin di 'finst'rə naxt,
es bricht sich die Welle mit Macht, und sie seufzt hinaus in die finstre Nacht,
there breaks itself the wave with might, and she sighs out into the dark night,
(the waves break with mighty force, and she sighs into the dark night,)
 [*poem and song:* **mit Macht, mit Macht,**]

das 'laogə fɔm 'vaenən gə'tʰryːbətʰ! [gə'tʰryːp'tʰ] das herts list' gə'ʃt'ɔrbən,
das Auge vom Weinen getrübet! [*1st version:* **getrübt**] **"Das Herz ist gestorben,**
the eye from the weeping dimmed! "The heart has died,
(her eyes dimmed from weeping! "My heart is dead,) [*poem & 3rd version:* **von** (fɔn) **Weinen**]

di velt' list' leːɐ̯/leːr, lʊnt' 'vaet'ɐ giːp't' ziː dem 'vʊnʃə niçts meːɐ̯.
die Welt ist leer, und weiter gibt sie dem Wunsche nichts mehr.
the world is empty, and further gives it to the wish nothing more,
(the world is empty, and it offers nothing further to my desire,)

duː 'haeligə, 'ruːfə [ruːf] daen kʰint tsu'rʏkʰ, liç 'haːbə gə'nɔsən das 'lirdiʃə glʏkʰ,
Du Heilige, rufe [ruf'] dein Kind zurück, ich habe genossen das irdische Glück,
You holy one, call your child back, I have enjoyed the earthly happiness,
(Holy One, call back your child! I have enjoyed earthly happiness,)

iç 'haːbə gə'leːp't' lʊnt' gə'liːbətʰ! lɛs 'rinət deːɐ̯ 'tʰreːnən feɐ̯'geːp'liçɐ laof,
ich habe gelebt und geliebet!" Es rinnet der Tränen vergeblicher Lauf,
I have lived and loved!" There runs the tears' vain course,
(I have lived and loved!" —"Your tears run their vain course,)

di 'kʰlaːgə, ziː 'vɛk'ət di 'tʰoːt'ən niçt' laof; dɔx 'nenə, vas 'tʰrøːst'ət'
die Klage, sie wecket die Toten nicht auf; doch nenne, was tröstet
the lament, it wakes the dead not up; but name what comforts
(your lament will not bring the dead back to life; but say what might comfort)

lʊnt‘ 'ha͜elət di brʊst‘ nax deːɐ̯ 'zyːsən 'liːbə fɛɐ̯'ʃvʊndənɐ lʊsth,
und heilet die Brust nach der süssen Liebe verschwundener Lust,
and heals the breast after the sweet love's lost pleasure,
(and heal your heart after the lost pleasure of sweet love;)

ıç, di 'hımlıʃə, vıls nıçt‘ fɛɐ̯'zaːgən. las 'rınən deːɐ̯ 'thrɛːnən
ich, die Himmlische, will's nicht versagen. "Lass rinnen der Tränen
I, the heavenly one, will it not refuse. "Let run the tears'
(I, the Queen of Heaven, shall not withhold it." —"Let my tears run)

fɛɐ̯'geːp‘lıçən l͜aͦof, lɛs 'vɛk‘ə di 'khlaːgə den 'thoːt‘ən nıçt‘ l͜aͦof!
vergeblichen Lauf, es wecke die Klage den Toten nicht auf!
vain course, it wake the lament the dead not up!
(their vain course, let my lament not awaken the dead!)
        [*1st version:* **es wecket** ('vɛk‘ət) **die Klage die** (di, the—*plural*) **Toten nicht auf;**]

das 'zyːsəst‘ə glͦʏk‘ fyːɐ̯ di 'thr͜aͦoəndə brʊst‘, nax deːɐ̯ 'ʃøːnən 'liːbə
Das süsseste Glück für die trauernde Brust, nach der schönen Liebe
The sweetest happiness for the mourning breast, after the beautiful love's
(The sweetest happiness for the mourning heart after beautiful love's)
        [*1st version:* **traurende** ('thr͜aͦorəndə)]

fɛɐ̯'ʃvʊndənɐ lʊst‘, zınt deːɐ̯ 'liːbə 'ʃmɛrtsən lʊnt‘ 'khlaːgən.
verschwundener Lust, sind der Liebe Schmerzen und Klagen."
vanished pleasure, are the love's pains and laments."
(vanished pleasure are the pains and laments of love.")

[The poem comes from Act III of Schiller's play *The Piccolomini*, where it is meant to be sung with guitar accompaniment. Schubert made three settings, the first probably in 1811 at age fourteen, the second (best known, and the only one to be published during his lifetime) in 1815, and the third, the only one with an accompaniment that might suggest the guitar, in 1816.]

Des Müllers Blumen see *Die schöne Müllerin*

dɛs 'zɛŋɐs 'haːbə
Des Sängers Habe
The Minstrel's Possessions

Posthumously published [composed 1825] (poem by Franz Xaver von Schlechta)

ʃlaːk‘t‘ ma͜en 'gantsəs glͦʏk‘ lın 'ʃp‘lıt‘ɐ, neːmt‘ miːɐ̯/miːr 'lalə 'haːbə gla͜eç,
Schlagt mein ganzes Glück in Splitter, nehmt mir alle Habe gleich,
Strike my entire happiness into splinters, take from me all possessions at once,
(Shatter my entire happiness, take all my possessions, right now,)

'lasət‘ miːɐ̯ nuːɐ̯ 'ma͜enə 'tsıt‘ɐ, lʊnt‘ lıç 'bla͜ebə froː lʊnt‘ ra͜eç.
lasset mir nur meine Zither, und ich bleibe froh und reich.
leave me only my zither, and I remain happy and rich.
(leave me only my zither, and I shall remain happy and rich.)

320

[The following stanza does not appear in the published poem:]

vɛn dɛs ˈgraːməs ˈvɔlkˈən ˈtsiːən, hɑ̯oxtˈ ziː tʰroːstˈ ɪn ˈmae̯nə brʊstʰ,
Wenn des Grames Wolken ziehen, haucht sie Trost in meine Brust,
When the sorrow's clouds gather, breathes it comfort into my breast,
(When clouds of sorrow gather, it breathes comfort into my heart,)

ʊntˈ ɑ̯os ˈˈiːrəm ˈgɔldə ˈblyːən ˈalə ˈbluːmən ˈmae̯nɐ lʊstʰ.
und aus ihrem Golde blühen alle Blumen meiner Lust.
and out of its gold bloom all flowers of my pleasure.
(and all the flowers of my pleasure bloom out of that golden source.)

vɪl di ˈliːbə nɪçtˈ gəˈveːrən, ˈfrɔø̯ntˈʃaftˈ ˈbrɛçən ˈiːrə pflɪçtʰ,
Will die Liebe nicht gewähren, Freundschaft brechen ihre Pflicht,
Wants the love not to grant, friendship to break its duty,
(If love does not want to grant its blessing, if friendship wants to break its duty,)
     [*poem:* **bricht mir Freundschaft Treu und Pflicht** (if friendship's loyalty and duty break)]

kʰan lɪç ˈbae̯də ʃtˈɔlts lɛntˈˈbeːrən, ˈaːbɐ ˈmae̯nə ˈtsɪtˈɐ nɪçtʰ.
kann ich beide stolz entbehren, aber meine Zither nicht.
can I both proudly do without, but my zither not.
(I can proudly do without both of them, but not without my zither.)

ˈrae̯sətˈ ˈmae̯nəs ˈleːbəns ˈzeːnə, vɪrtˈ ziː miːɐ̯/miːr lae̯n ˈkʰɪsən zae̯n,
Reisset meines Lebens Sehne, wird sie mir ein Kissen sein,
Tears my life's sinew, will it for me a pillow be,
(If the sinews of my life are torn asunder, it will be my pillow,)
     [*poem:* **In des Scheidens schwerer Stunde soll sie mir ein Kissen sein**]
          [(In the hard hour of parting it shall be my pillow)]

ˈlʊlən mɪç di ˈzyːsən ˈtʰøːnə ɪn den ˈlɛtstˈən ˈʃlʊmɐ(r) lae̯n.
lullen mich die süssen Töne in den letzten Schlummer ein.
lull me the sweet tones into the last sleep into.
(the sweet tones will lull me into my last sleep.)
     [*poem:* **Singe sie mit süssem Munde in den letzten Schlaf mir ein.**]
          [(sing me sweetly to my last sleep.)]

ɪn den grʊnt dɛs ˈtʰanənhae̯nəs zɛŋkˈtˈ mɪç ˈlae̯zə dan hɪˈnapˈ;
In den Grund des Tannenhaines senkt mich leise dann hinab;
Into the ground of the fir-tree grove lower me softly then down;
(Then lower me softly down into the ground in the fir-tree grove;)
     [*poem:* **Senkt dann in den Grund des Haines den Entschlummerten hinab**]
          [(Then lower the sleeper down into the ground of the grove)]

ʊntˈ ʃtˈatˈ ˈae̯nəs ˈlae̯çənʃtˈae̯nəs, ʃtˈɛlt di ˈtsɪtˈɐ(r) ɑ̯of mae̯n graːpˈ;
und statt eines Leichensteines, stellt die Zither auf mein Grab;
and instead of a tombstone, place the zither on my grave;
          [*poem:* **auf sein** (his) **Grab**]

das lɪç, vɛn tsʊm ˈʃtˈɪlən ˈrae̯gən, ɑ̯os dɛs ˈtʰoːdəs ˈdʊŋkˈləm ban,
dass ich, wenn zum stillen Reigen, aus des Todes dunklem Bann,
so that I, when to the silent round-dance, out of the death's dark spell,
(so that I, when, out of death's dark spell, to dance their silent round,)
     [*poem:* **dass er, wenn zum Nebelreigen** (so that he, when to the misty round-dance)]

'mɪt'ɐnaxts di 'gaest'ɐ 'ʃt'aegən, 'liːrə 'zaet'ən 'ryːrən kʰan.
Mitternachts die Geister steigen, ihre Saiten rühren kann.
at midnight   the ghosts   rise up,   its   strings   touch   can.
(the ghosts rise up at midnight,—so that I can touch its strings.)

[*poem:* **Mitternachts die Schatten** (shades) **steigen**]

[Schubert felt the poem very personally and made—or asked his friend to make—extensive changes, including a totally new second stanza that replaced the second and third of the poem. In the last two stanzas he changed "*sein*" to "*mein*" and "*er*" to "*ich*," to make the effect even more personal. The zither here is a symbol of his art; when all else is taken from him, that must remain. Those lines—or parts of lines—that are different in the published poem are given above in brackets; the two stanzas that are not found in Schubert's version are as follows: *Sie horcht freundlich jeder Klage / Und hat einen Trost dafür, / Weiss was ich im Herzen trage / Und spricht gern davon mit mir. / Wenn die schlichten Saiten klingen, / Lichtet sich des Lebens Nacht / Und auf unsichtbaren Schwingen / Naht ein Gott in stiller Nacht* (It listens like a friend to every lament and has a consolation ready; it knows what I have in my heart and is glad to speak with me about it. Whenever the unpretentious strings are sounding, the darkness of life is lighted, and on invisible wings God draws near in the quiet night).]

Didone abbandonata see *Arie*

di 'lap'gəblyːt'ə 'lɪndə
Die abgeblühte Linde
The Faded Linden Tree

Op. 7, No. 1 [1821?] (Ludwig von Széchényi)

vɪrst du: 'halt'ən, vas du: ʃvuːɐ̯stʰ, vɛn miːɐ̯ di tsaet di 'lɔk'ən blaeçtʰ?
Wirst du halten, was du schwurst, wenn mir die Zeit die Locken bleicht?
Will you keep what you swore when for me the time the curls bleaches?
(Will you keep the vow you swore when time has turned my hair white?)

vi: du: 'lyːbɐ 'bɛrgə fuːɐ̯st', laelt das 'viːdɐzeːn nɪçt' laeçtʰ.
Wie du über Berge fuhrst, eilt das Wiedersehn nicht leicht.
As you over mountains went, hastens the reunion not easily.
(Since you went away over the mountains, our reunion in not coming easily.)

'ɛndruŋ lɪst das kʰɪnt deːɐ̯ tsaetʰ, vo'mɪt 'tʰrɛnuŋ luns bə'droːtʰ,
Ändrung ist das Kind der Zeit, womit Trennung uns bedroht,
Change is the child of the time, with which parting us threatens,
(Change is the child of time, and parting threatens us with change,)

unt' vas di 'tsuːkʰunft' bɔøt', lɪst' laen 'blɛsɐs 'leːbənsroːtʰ.
und was die Zukunft beut, ist ein blässers Lebensrot.
and what the future offers is a paler life- red.
(and what the future offers is a paler vital color.)

zi:, di 'lɪndə 'blyːət' nɔx, lals du: 'hɔøt'ə fɔn liːɐ̯ geːstʰ;
Sieh, die Linde blühet noch, als du heute von ihr gehst;
See, the linden tree blooms still, as you today from it go;
(See, the linden tree is still blooming as you leave it today;)

vɪrst‘   ziː ˈviːdɐ   ˈfɪndən, dɔx   ˈliːrə ˈblyːt‘ən   ʃt‘iːlt deːɐ̯ vɛst‘.
wirst   sie wieder finden, doch ihre Blüten   stiehlt der West.
(you) will it   again   find,   but   its   blossoms steals the   west (wind).
(you will find it again; but the west wind steals its blossoms.)

ˈaᴇnzaːm ʃt‘eːt‘ ziː dan,   foːɐ̯ˈbaᴇ geːt‘ man kʰaltʰ, bəˈmɛrk‘t‘ ziː kʰaᴏm.
Einsam steht sie dann, vorbei   geht man kalt,   bemerkt   sie kaum.
Solitary stands it then,   past   goes one cold, notices   it scarcely.
(It will stand alone then; people will pass by, indifferent, scarcely noticing it.)

nuːɐ̯ deːɐ̯ ˈgɛrt‘nɐ blaᴇp‘t‘ liːɐ̯ tʰrɔ̞ø, dᴇn leːɐ̯ liːp‘t‘ ɪn liːɐ̯ den baᴏm.
Nur der Gärtner bleibt ihr treu,   denn er liebt in ihr den Baum.
Only the   gardener remains to it true, for   he loves in it   the tree.
(Only the gardener will remain true to it, for he loves the tree for itself.)

[The poet was a Hungarian count, two of whose poems Schubert set to music. The form of this song is recitative and *arioso*.]

di ˈʔalmaxtʰ
Die Allmacht
Omnipotence

Op. 79, No. 2 [1825] (Johann Ladislaus Pyrker)

groːs ɪst‘ jeˈhoːva, deːɐ̯ hᴇr, dᴇn ˈhɪməl   ʊnt‘ ˈleːɐ̯də fᴇɐ̯ˈkʰyndən ˈzaᴇnə maxtʰ.
Gross is   Jehova, der Herr, denn Himmel und Erde verkünden seine Macht.
Great is   Jehovah, the Lord, for   heaven and earth proclaim   his   might.

duː høːɐ̯st‘ ziː ɪm ˈbraᴏzəndən ʃt‘ʊrm, ɪn dᴇs ˈvalt‘ʃt‘roːms laᴏt ˈʔaᴏfraᴏʃəndəm ruːf;
Du hörst sie im   brausenden Sturm, in des Waldstroms laut aufrauschendem Ruf;
You hear   it in the roaring   storm, in the forest stream's loudly rushing   cry;

duː høːɐ̯st‘ ziː ɪn dᴇs ˈgryːnəndən ˈvaldəs gəˈzɔ̞øzəl, ziːst‘ ziː ɪn ˈvoːgəndɐ ˈzaːt‘ən gɔlt‘,
du hörst   sie in des grünenden Waldes Gesäusel, siehst sie in wogender Saaten Gold,
you hear   it in the greening   forest's murmur, see   it in waving   corns' gold,
(you hear it in the murmur of the greening forest, see it in the gold of waving corn,)
                                                                    [*poem:* without the repeat of "*du hörst sie*"]

ɪn ˈliːp‘lɪçɐ ˈbluːmən ˈglyːəndəm ʃmɛlts, ɪm   glants dᴇs ˈʃt‘ᴇrnəbəzᴇːət‘ən ˈhɪməls.
in lieblicher Blumen glühendem Schmelz, im   Glanz   des sternebesäeten Himmels.
in lovely   flowers' glowing   glaze,   in the radiance of the star-   sown   heaven.
                                 [*later version of poem:* **des stern-umfunkelten** (star-sparked) **Himmels**]

ˈfʊrçt‘baːɐ̯ tʰø̞ːnt‘ ziː ɪm   ˈdɔnɐgərɔl,
Furchtbar tönt   sie im   Donnergeroll,
Fearful   sounds it in the thunder-roll,
(It resounds fearfully in the rolling thunder,)

ʊnt‘ flamt‘ ɪn dᴇs ˈblɪtsəs   ʃnᴇl hɪnˈtsʊk‘əndəm fluːk‘,
und flammt in des Blitzes   schnell hinzuckendem Flug,
and flames in the lightning's fast   hence-quivering flight,
(and flames in the fast, quivering flight of the lightning,)

dɔx ˈkʰʏndət   das ˈpʰɔxəndə hɛrts diːɐ̯ ˈfyːlbaːrɐ   nɔx jeˈhoːvas maxt,
doch kündet   das pochende Herz dir   fühlbarer   noch Jehovas Macht,
but   announces the throbbing heart to you more palpably still Jehovah's might,
(but your throbbing heart makes Jehovah's might known to you still more palpably,)

dɛs ˈleːvɪɡən ˈɡɔtˈəs, blɪkst duː ˈfleːənt ˈ ɛmˈpʰoːɐ̯(r) lʊntˈ hɔfstˈ l ̥aof hʊltˈ lʊntˈ lɛɐ̯ˈbarmən.
des ewigen Gottes, blickst du flehend empor   und hoffst auf Huld und Erbarmen.
the eternal God's, look   you praying up   and hope for grace and mercy.
(the might of the eternal God, if you look up in prayer and hope for grace and mercy.)
    [*first version of poem:* **des unendlichen Gottes... und hoffst der Erbarmungen Fülle!**]
        [(of the infinite God...and hope for the abundance of mercies!)]
    [*second version of poem:* **und hoffst von ihm** (from Him)) **Huld und Erbarmen!**]

[This truly magnificent song, celebrating the majesty of God as reflected in nature, was written at Bad Gastein, where the mountains, the forests, and the famous falls must have been a powerful inspiration to the composer. The song calls for a dramatic voice with a wide range, expressiveness in *pianissimo* as well as *fortissimo*, and the fervor to communicate a thrilling, sublime exultation. The poet was a churchman of high rank, and Schubert considered their meeting at Bad Gastein to have been one of the happiest encounters of his life.]

Die Art ein Weib zu nehmen see *Il modo di prender moglie*

di bəˈfraɛɐ lɔøˈroːpˈas ɪn pʰaˈriːs
Die Befreier Europas in Paris
The Liberators of Europe in Paris

Posthumously published [composed 1814] (poem by Johann Christian Mikan)

ziː zɪntˈ ɪn pʰaˈriːs! di ˈhɛldən, lɔøˈroːpˈas bəˈfraɛɐ! deːɐ̯ ˈfaːtˈɐ fɔn ˈløːstˈraɛç,
Sie sind in Paris! Die Helden, Europas   Befreier! Der Vater von Östreich,
They are in Paris! The heroes, Europe's liberators! The father of Austria,

deːɐ̯ ˈhɛrʃɐ   deːɐ̯ ˈrɔøsən, deːɐ̯ ˈviːdɐ(r)lɛɐ̯vɛkˈɐ deːɐ̯ ˈtʰapfərən ˈpʰrɔøsən!
der Herrscher der   Reussen, der Wiedererwecker der   tapferen Preussen!
the ruler   of the Russians, the reawakener   of the valiant Prussians!

das ɡlʏkˈ   ˈliːrɐ ˈfœlkˈɐ(r), lɛs vaːɐ̯/vaːr ˈliːnən ˈtʰɔøɐ, ziː zɪntˈ ɪn pʰaˈriːs!
Das Glück   ihrer   Völker, es war   ihnen teuer,   sie sind in Paris!
The happiness of their peoples, it was   to them precious, they are in Paris!
(The happiness of their peoples was precious to them. They are in Paris!)

nuːn lɪstˈ lʊns deːɐ̯ ˈfriːdə ɡəˈvɪs!
Nun ist uns der Friede gewiss!
Now is for us the peace certain!
(Now peace is assured for us!)

[The seventeen-year-old Schubert celebrated the defeat of Napoleon in this patriotic song. There were seven more verses to the poem, but he wrote out only the first, and that is how the song is printed in the *Gesamtausgabe*.]

di ˈbɛrɡə
Die Berge
The Mountains

Op. 57, No. 2 [1820?] (Friedrich von Schlegel)

ziːtˈ lʊns deːɐ̯ blɪkˈ ɡəˈhoːbən, zoː ɡlaopˈt das hɛrts di ˈʃveːrə ʦuː bəˈziːɡən,
Sieht uns der Blick gehoben, so glaubt das Herz die Schwere zu besiegen,
Sees us the gaze uplifted, so believes the heart the gravity to overcome,
(When the gaze of man looks up at us, then his heart believes that it is overcoming gravity,)

ʦuː den ˈhɪmlɪʃən ˈloːbən vɪl lɛs ˈdrɪŋən lʊntˈ ˈfliːɡən. deːɐ̯ mɛnʃ
zu den Himmlischen oben will es dringen und fliegen. Der Mensch
to the heavenly ones above wants it to penetrate and fly. The human being
(it wants to penetrate heaven and fly up to the gods above. The human being,)

lɛmˈpʰoːɐ̯ ɡəˈʃvʊŋən, ɡlaopˈtˈ ʃoːn, leːɐ̯ zae dʊrç di ˈvɔlkˈən ɡəˈdrʊŋən.
empor geschwungen, glaubt schon, er sei durch die Wolken gedrungen.
on high swung, believes already, he be through the clouds penetrated.
(soaring aloft, believes that he has already pierced the clouds.)

baltˈ mʊs leːɐ̯ ˈʃtˈaonəntˈ ˈmɛrkˈən, vi ˈleːvɪç fɛstˈ viːɐ̯/viːr laof lʊns zɛlpstˈ bəˈɡryndətʰ.
Bald muss er staunend merken, wie ewig fest wir auf uns selbst begründet.
Soon must he marveling note how eternally firm we on us self grounded.
(Soon he must notice, marveling, how firmly we are eternally grounded upon ourselves.)

dan ʃtˈreːpˈtˈ lɪn ˈzɪçɐn ˈvɛrkən zaen ˈɡantsəs tʰuːn, fɛɐ̯ˈbyndətʰ,
Dann strebt in sichern Werken sein ganzes Tun, verbündet,
Then strives in secure works his entire doing, allied,
(Then his entire activity, all his capacities allied, strives in securely-founded undertakings)

fɔm ˈɡrʊndə ni ʦuː ˈvaŋkˈən, lʊntˈ baotˈ vi ˈfɛlzən den bao deːɐ̯ ɡəˈdaŋkˈən.
vom Grunde nie zu wanken, und baut wie Felsen den Bau der Gedanken.
from the ground never to waver, and builds like rock the edifice of the thoughts.
(never to waver from a firm foundation, and builds a rock-solid edifice of thoughts.)

ʊnt dan lɪn ˈnɔøən ˈfrɔødən ziːtˈ leːɐ̯ di ˈkʰyːnən ˈkʰlɪpˈən ˈʃpˈɔtˈəntˈ ˈhaŋən;
Und dann in neuen Freuden sieht er die kühnen Klippen spottend hangen;
And then in new joys sees he the bold cliffs mockingly hang;
(And then with new joy he sees the bold cliffs hanging mockingly;)

fɛɐ̯ˈɡesəntˈ ˈlalɐ ˈlaedən, fyːltˈ leːɐ̯/leːr ˈlaentsɪç fɛɐ̯ˈlaŋən, lan dem ˈlapˈɡrʊnt ʦuː ˈʃertsən,
vergessend aller Leiden, fühlt er einzig Verlangen, an dem Abgrund zu scherzen,
forgetting all sufferings, feels he single desire, at the abyss to jest,
(forgetting all his suffering, he feels one single desire, to jest at the edge of the abyss,)

dɛn ˈhoːɐ̯ muːtˈ ʃvɪltˈ liːm lɪn ˈhoːəm ˈhɛrtsən.
denn hoher Mut schwillt ihm in hohem Herzen.
for high courage swells for him in high heart.
(for high courage swells in his noble heart.)

[This is the voice of the mountains calling to venturesome mankind: the "*uns*" in the first line, like the "*wir*" a little later, is the mountains' reference to themselves, a point overlooked by more than one translator.]

di ˈbeːtˀəndə
Die Betende
The Young Woman Praying

Posthumously published [composed 1814] (poem by Friedrich von Matthisson)

ˈlɑɔra ˈbeːtˀətˀ! ˈlɛŋəlharfən ˈhalən ˈfriːdən ˈgɔtˀəs lɪn liːɐ̯ ˈkʰraŋkˀəs hɛrts̟,
Laura betet! Engelharfen hallen Frieden Gottes in ihr krankes Herz,
Laura prays! Angel harps sound peace of God into her sick heart,
(Laura is praying! Angel harps sound the peace of God in her afflicted heart,)

ʊntˀ, viː ˈlaːbəls ˈlɔpfˌedyftˀə, ˈvalən ˈliːrə ˈzɔøftsɐ ˈhiməlverts̟.
und, wie Abels Opferdüfte, wallen ihre Seufzer himmelwärts.
and, like Abel's sacrifice-vapors, waft her sighs heavenward.
(and, like the smoke from Abel's sacrifice, her sighs waft straight up to heaven.)

viː ziː kʰniːtˀ, lɪn ˈlandaxtˀ ˈhɪŋəgɔsən, ʃøːn, viː ˈraːfael di ˈlʊnʃʊltˀ maːltʰ;
Wie sie kniet, in Andacht hingegossen, schön, wie Raphael die Unschuld malt;
As she kneels, in devotion poured away, beautiful, as Raphael the innocence paints;
(As she kneels, lost in devotion, she is as beautiful as innocence painted by Raphael;)

fɔm fɛɐ̯ˈkʰlɛːrʊŋsglantsə ʃoːn lʊmˈflɔsən, deːɐ̯/deːr lʊm ˈhiməlsvoːnɐ ʃtˀraːltʰ.
vom Verklärungsglanze schon umflossen, der um Himmelswohner strahlt.
by the transfiguration-gleam already bathed, which around heaven's inhabitants beams.
(already bathed in the glow of transfiguration that radiates around the inhabitants of heaven.)

oː ziː fyːltˀ, lɪm ˈlazən, ˈlɪndən ˈveːən, froː dɛs ˈhoːxlɛ̯ɡhaːbnən ˈgeːgənvartʰ,
O sie fühlt, im leisen, linden Wehen, froh des Hocherhab'nen Gegenwart,
Oh, she feels, in the soft, gentle flutter of air, happily the high-sublime one's presence,
(Oh, happily she feels, in the soft, gentle flutter of the air, the presence of the All-highest,)

ziːtˀ lɪm ˈgaestˀə ʃoːn di ˈpʰalmənhøːən, voː deːɐ̯ ˈlɪçtˀkʰrants ˈliːrə hartʰ!
sieht im Geiste schon die Palmenhöhen, wo der Lichtkranz ihrer harrt!
sees in the spirit already the palm-heights, where the light-wreath for her waits!
(she sees already in spirit the palm-covered heights where a wreath of light is waiting for her!)

zoː fɔn ˈlandaxtˀ, zoː fɔn ˈgɔtˀfɛɐ̯tʰrɑɔən ˈliːrə ˈlɛŋəlraenə brʊstˀ gəˈʃvɛltʰ,
So von Andacht, so von Gottvertrauen ihre engelreine Brust geschwellt,
Thus from devotion, thus from God-trust her angel-pure breast swollen,
(Thus, her angel-pure bosom swelling with devotion and trust in God,)

ˈbeːtˀənt ˈdiːzə ˈhaelɪgə tsuː ˈʃɑɔən, lɪstˀ laen blɪkˀ lɪn ˈjeːnə vɛltʰ.
betend diese Heilige zu schauen, ist ein Blick in jene Welt.
praying this saintly being to behold, is a glimpse into that world.
(to behold this saintly being at prayer is to be granted a glimpse into that other world.)

[Schubert clothes the poet's love and admiration for an angelic woman in hymnlike harmonies.]

326

di ˈbluːmənʃpˈraːxə
Die Blumensprache
The Language of Flowers

Op. 173, No. 5 [1817] (Anton Platner)

ɛs   ˈdɔɸtˈən di ˈbluːmən dɛs ˈhɛrt͡səns ɡəˈfyːlə, ziː ˈʃpˈrɛçən manç ˈha͜emlɪçəs vɔrtʰ;
Es   deuten die Blumen des Herzens Gefühle, sie   sprechen manch' heimliches Wort;
There interpret the flowers the heart's feelings, they speak   many a secret   word;
(Flowers interpret the feelings of the heart; they speak many a secret word;)

ziː ˈna͜eɡən zɪç   ˈtʰra͜olɪç   lam ˈʃvaŋkˈəndən   ˈʃtˈiːlə,
sie neigen sich   traulich   am   schwankenden Stiele,
they bend   themselves confidingly on the swaying   stem,
(they bend confidingly on their swaying stems,)

lals ˈt͡søːɡə di ˈliːbə ziː   fɔrtʰ. ziː ˈbɛrɡən fɛɐ̯ˈʃeːmtˈ zɪç   lɪm ˈdɛkˈəndən ˈla͜obə,
als zöge die Liebe sie fort. Sie bergen verschämt sich   im   deckenden Laube,
as if drew the love them forth. They hide   shyly   themselves in the covering   foliage,
(as if love were drawing them forth. They shyly hide in the covering foliage,)

lals ˈhɛtˈə fɛɐ̯ˈraːtˈən deːɐ̯ vʊnʃ ziː   dem ˈra͜obə.
als hätte verraten der Wunsch sie   dem Raube.
as if had   betrayed the wish   them to the rapine.
(as if desire had betrayed them to the ravisher.)

ziː ˈdɔɸtˈən lɪm   ˈla͜ezə bəˈt͡sa͜obɛndən ˈbɪldə deːɐ̯ ˈfra͜oən,   deːɐ̯ ˈmeːtˈçən zɪn;
Sie deuten im   leise bezaubernden Bilde der Frauen,   der Mädchen Sinn;
They interpret in the softly enchanting   image the women's, the girls'   mind;
(They interpret the minds of women and girls in a softly enchanting image;)
                                                          [*poem:* **der Mägdelein** (ˈmeːkˈdəla͜en) **Sinn**]

ziː ˈdɔɸtˈən das ˈʃøːnə,   di ˈlanmuːt, di ˈmɪldə,   ziː ˈdɔɸtˈən dɛs ˈleːbəns ɡəˈvɪn,
sie deuten   das Schöne, die Anmut, die Milde,   sie deuten   des Lebens Gewinn,
they interpret the beautiful, the grace, the gentleness, they interpret the life's   rewards,
(they interpret beauty, grace, gentleness, they interpret life's rewards;)

ɛs   hatˈ mɪt deːɐ̯ ˈkʰnɔspˈə, zoː ˈha͜emlɪç fɛɐ̯ˈʃlʊŋən,
es   hat mit der Knospe, so heimlich verschlungen,
there has with the bud,   so secretly   entwined,
(with the bud, secretly entwined,)

deːɐ̯ ˈjʏŋlɪŋ   di ˈpɛrlə deːɐ̯ ˈhɔfnʊŋ ɡəˈfʊndən.   [lɛɐ̯ˈrʊŋən]
der Jüngling   die Perle der Hoffnung gefunden.   [*poem:* errungen]
the young man the pearl of the hope   found.   [achieved]
(the young man has found the pearl of hope.)

ziː ˈveːbən deːɐ̯ ˈzeːnzʊxt, dɛs ˈharməs ɡəˈdaŋkˈən la͜os ˈfarbən lɪns ˈdʊftˈɪɡə kʰla͜etˈ,
Sie weben der Sehnsucht, des Harmes Gedanken aus Farben ins   duftige Kleid,
They weave the   longing's, the sorrow's thoughts out of colors into the fragrant dress,
(Out of colors they weave thoughts of longing and of sorrow into their fragrant dress;)

nɪçts̩ 'frɔmən deːɐ̯ 'tʰrɛnʊŋ gə'hɛsɪgə 'ʃraŋk'ən, di 'bluːmən
nichts frommen der Trennung gehässige Schranken, die Blumen
nothing avail the separation's hateful barriers, the flowers
(the hateful barriers of separation are unavailing, for flowers)

fɛɐ̯'kʰʏndən das laet̚'. vas lɑ̯ot̚' nɪçt deːɐ̯ mʊnt, deːɐ̯ bə'vaxt'ə, darf 'zaːgən,
verkünden das Leid. Was laut nicht der Mund, der bewachte, darf sagen,
proclaim the suffering. What aloud not the mouth, the guarded, may say,
(can proclaim our suffering. What the guarded mouth may not say aloud)

das 'vaːgət di hʊlt̚' zɪç ɪn 'bluːmən t͡su: 'kʰlaːgən!
das waget die Huld sich in Blumen zu klagen!
that dares the favor itself in flowers to lament!
(favor dares to lament through flowers!)

[The lover says it with flowers in this delightful song, blossoming with Viennese charm. Schubert omitted the last stanza: *Sie winken in lieblich gewundenen Kränzen / Die Freude zum festlichen Kreis, / Wenn flatternd das ringelnde Haar sie umglänzen, / Dem Bacchus, der Venus zum Preis; / Denn arm sind der Götter erfreuende Gaben, / Wenn Leier und Blumen das Herz nicht erlaben* (In charmingly wound garlands they summon joy to grace a festive company, when they gleam and flutter about curly hair to the glory of Bacchus and Venus; for poor are gifts— that might, otherwise, delight the gods—if music and flowers are not there to refresh the heart).]

Die böse Farbe see *Die schöne Müllerin*

di 'bʏrk' ʃaftʰ
Die Bürgschaft
The Surety

Posthumously published [composed 1815] (poem by Friedrich von Schiller)

t͡su: dio'nyːs, dem tʰy'ranən, ʃlɪç 'møːrɔs, den dɔlç ɪm gə'vandə;
Zu Dionys, dem Tyrannen, schlich Möros, den Dolch im Gewande;
To Dionysius, the tyrant, crept Moeros, the dagger in the garment;
(Moeros, his dagger concealed in his clothes, stealthily approached Dionysius, the tyrant;)

iːn 'ʃluːgən di 'hɛʃɐ(r) ɪn 'bandə. vas 'vɔlt'əst du: mɪt dem 'dɔlçə? ʃp'rɪç!
ihn schlugen die Häscher in Bande. "Was wolltest du mit dem Dolche? sprich!"
him struck the henchmen into bonds. "What wanted you with the dagger? Speak!"
(the henchmen put him in chains. "What did you intend with that dagger? Speak!")

ɛnt'geːgnət' liːm 'fɪnst'ɐ deːɐ̯ 'vyːt'ərɪç. — di ʃt'at' fɔm tʰy'ranən bə'fraeən!
entgegnet ihm finster der Wüterich. —"Die Stadt vom Tyrannen befreien!"
countered him darkly the ruthless tyrant. —"The city from the tyrant to free!"
(the ruthless tyrant asked him ominously. —"To free the city from the tyrant!")

— das sɔlst du: lam 'kʰrɔ̯øt͡sə bə'rɔ̯øən! — lɪç bɪn, ʃp'rɪçt' 'jeːnɐ,
—"Das sollst du am Kreuze bereuen!" —"Ich bin," spricht jener,
—"That shall you on the cross regret!" —"I am," says that one (= the other),
(—"You shall regret that on the cross!" —"I am," says the prisoner,)

tsu: ˈʃtˈɛrbən bəˈraet' lʊnt' ˈbɪtˈə nɪçt' lʊm maen ˈleːbən; dɔx vɪlst duː
"zu sterben bereit   und bitte nicht um mein Leben; doch willst du
"to die   prepared and ask not for my   life;   but want you
("prepared to die and I do not ask for my life; but if it be your will)

ˈgnaːdə miːɐ̯ ˈgeːbən, lɪç ˈfleːə dɪç lʊm drae ˈtʰaːgə tsaetʰ, bɪs lɪç
Gnade   mir geben, ich flehe dich um drei Tage Zeit, bis ich
clemency to me to give, I   entreat you for three days time, until I
(to show me clemency, I entreat you to give me three days' time, until I)

di ˈʃvɛstˈɐ   dem ˈgatˈən gəˈfraetʰ;   lɪç ˈlasə den frɔɸnt diːɐ̯/diːr lals ˈbʏrgən,
die Schwester dem Gatten gefreit;   ich lasse den Freund dir   als Bürgen,
the sister   to the husband to give in marriage; I   leave the friend for you as surety,
(can give my sister in marriage to her bridegroom; I shall leave my friend with you as surety;)

iːn maːkst duː, lɛntˈrɪn lɪç, lɛɐ̯ˈvʏrgən. daː   ˈlɛçəlt deːɐ̯ ˈkʰøːnɪç mɪtˈ ˈlargɐ lɪstʰ
ihn magst du, entrinn' ich, erwürgen." Da   lächelt der König mit arger List
him may   you, run away I,   strangle." Thereupon smiles the king   with wicked cunning
(if I run away you may put him to death." At that, the king smiles with wicked cunning)

ʊntˈ ʃpˈrɪçtˈ naːx ˈkʰʊrtsəm bəˈdɛŋkˈən: drae ˈtʰaːgə vɪl lɪç diːɐ̯ ˈʃɛŋkˈən;
und spricht nach kurzem Bedenken: "Drei Tage will ich dir schenken;
and speaks after short   reflection: "Three days will I to you grant;
(and, after a moment of reflection, says: "I shall give you three days;)

dɔx ˈvɪsə! vɛn ziː fɛɐ̯ʃtˈrɪçən, di frɪstʰ,   leː   duː tsuˈrʏkˈ miːɐ̯ gəˈgeːbən bɪstˈ,
doch wisse! wenn sie verstrichen, die Frist,   eh' du zurück mir   gegeben bist,
but know! if   it (is) expired, the grace period, before you back to me given   are,
(but know this: if the grace period has expired before you are returned to me,)

zoː mʊs leːɐ̯ ʃtˈat ˈdaenɐ(r) lɛɐ̯ˈblasən, dɔx diːɐ̯/diːr lɪst di ˈʃtraːfə   lɛɐ̯ˈlasən.
so muss er statt deiner   erblassen, doch dir   ist die Strafe   erlassen."
then must he instead of you grow pale, but to you   is the punishment remitted."
(then he must die instead of you; but *your* punishment will be remitted.")

ʊntˈ leːɐ̯ kʰɔmt tsum ˈfrɔɸndə: deːɐ̯ ˈkʰøːnɪç gəˈbɔɸt, das lɪç
Und er kommt zum Freunde: "Der König gebeut,   dass ich
And he comes to the friend: "The king   commands that I
(And Moeros goes to his friend, saying: "The king commands that I)

["*gebeut*"(obs.) = "*gebietet*" = commands]

lam kʰrɔɸts mɪt dem ˈleːbən bəˈtsaːlə das ˈfreːfəlndə ʃtˈreːbən; dɔx vɪl leːɐ̯
am   Kreuz mit dem Leben bezahle das frevelnde Streben; doch will er
on the cross with the life   pay for the criminal   endeavor; but will he
(pay on the cross with my life for my criminal attempt; but he will)

miːɐ̯ ˈgœnən drae ˈtʰaːgə tsaetˈ, bɪs lɪç di ˈʃvɛstˈɐ   dem ˈgatˈən gəˈfraetʰ;
mir gönnen drei Tage Zeit, bis ich die Schwester   dem Gatten gefreit;
to me grant   three days time, till I the sister   to the husband give in marriage;
(grant me three days' time, so that I may give my sister in marriage to her husband-to-be;)

zoː ˈbla̯ɛbə duː dem ˈkʰøːnɪç t͜sʊm ˈp̯fandə, bɪs lɪç ˈkʰɔmə, t͜su ˈløːzən di ˈbandə.
so bleibe du dem König zum Pfande, bis ich komme, zu lösen die Bande."
so remain you for the king as the security, till I come to loosen the bonds."
(so you will stay with the king as security until I come back to loosen your bonds.")

poem: **bleib'** (blaɛp')]

ʊntʰ ˈʃvaɛ̯gəntʰ lʊmˈlarmtʰ liːn deːɐ̯ ˈt͜hrɔ̯øə frɔ̯øntʰ lʊntʰ ˈliːfɛt zɪç la̯os
Und schweigend umarmt ihn der treue Freund und liefert sich aus
And without speaking embraces him the true friend and delivers himself up
(And without speaking his faithful friend embraces him and hands himself over)

dem tʰyˈranən; deːɐ̯/deːr ˈlandrə t͜siːtʰ fɔn ˈdanən. lʊntʰ leː nɔx das ˈdrɪtʰə ˈmɔrgənroːtʰ
dem Tyrannen; der And're zieht von dannen. Und eh' noch das dritte Morgenrot
to the tyrant; the other goes from thence. And before still the third dawn
(to the tyrant; Moeros goes his way. And even before the third dawn)

poem: **der Andere** (ˈlandərə) **ziehet** (ˈt͜siːət); **Und ehe** (ˈleːə) **das dritte Morgenrot**]

lɛɐ̯ˈʃaɛ̯ntʰ, hatʰ leːɐ̯ ʃnɛl mɪt dem ˈgatʰən di ˈʃvɛstʰɐ fɛɐ̯ˈlaɛ̯ntʰ/fɛrˈlaɛ̯ntʰ, [ˈʃaɛ̯ntʰ]
erscheint, hat er schnell mit dem Gatten die Schwester vereint, [*poem:* **scheint**]
appears, has he quickly with the husband the sister united, [appears]
(has appeared, he has quickly united his sister with her husband,)

aɛ̯ltʰ haɛm mɪtʰ ˈzɔrgəndɐ ˈzeːlə, daˈmɪtʰ leːɐ̯ di frɪstʰ nɪçtʰ fɛɐ̯ˈfeːlə.
eilt heim mit sorgender Seele, damit er die Frist nicht verfehle.
hurries home with troubled soul, so that he the deadline not miss.
(and he is hurrying home with a concerned soul, anxious not to miss the end of the grace period.)

daː giːstʰ lʊnˈlɛntʰlɪçɐ ˈreːgən hɛˈrapʰ, fɔn den ˈbɛrgən ˈʃtʰʏrt͜sən di ˈkʰvɛlən hɛˈrapʰ,
Da giesst unendlicher Regen herab, von den Bergen stürzen die Quellen herab,
Then pours unending rain down, from the mountains plunge the springs down,
(Then rain starts to pour down ceaselessly, down from the mountains streams are plunging,)

poem without 2nd "herab"]

ʊnt di ˈbɛçə, di ˈʃtʰrøːmə ˈʃvɛlən. lʊntʰ leːɐ̯ kʰɔmtʰ lans luːfɐ
und die Bäche, die Ströme schwellen. Und er kommt ans Ufer
and the brooks, the rivers swell. And he comes to the bank
(and the brooks and rivers swell. And he comes to the bank of a river)

mɪtʰ ˈvandɐndəm ʃtʰaːpʰ, daː ˈraɛ̯sət di ˈbrʏkʰə deːɐ̯ ˈʃtʰruːdəl hɪˈnapʰ,
mit wanderndem Stab, da reisset die Brücke der Strudel hinab,
with wandering staff, thereupon tears the bridge [obj.] the whirlpool [subj.] down,
(with his wanderer's staff; at that moment the whirling waters tear down the bridge,)

ʊnt ˈdɔnɐntʰ ˈʃpʰrɛŋən di ˈvoːgən dɛs gəˈvœlbəs ˈkʰrxəndən ˈboːgən.
und donnernd sprengen die Wogen des Gewölbes krachenden Bogen.
and thunderingly burst the waves the vault's crashing arches.
(and, thundering, the waves burst the crashing arches of the vault that had supported the bridge.)

ʊnt ˈt͜hroːstʰloːs lɪrtʰ leːɐ̯/leːr lan ˈluːfɐs rantʰ, viː vaɛ̯tʰ leːɐ̯/leːr laɔx ʃpʰˈɛːɐt lʊntʰ ˈblɪkʰətʰ,
Und trostlos irrt er an Ufers Rand, wie weit er auch spähet und blicket,
And desperately strays he at bank's edge, how far he also scouts and looks,
(And he wanders about in despair at the edge of the bank; however far he searches and looks,)

lʊnt di ʃt'ɪmə, di 'ruːfəndə, ʃik't^h— daː ʃt'øːst' kʰaɛn 'naxən
und die Stimme, die rufende, schickt— da stösst kein Nachen
and the voice, the calling, sends— there shoves off no boat
(However far he sends his calling voice, no boat shoves off there)   [*poem:* **schicket** ('ʃik'ət^h)]

fɔm 'zɪçɐn ʃt'rant, deːɐ/deːr liːn 'zɛtsə lan das gə'vynʃt'ə lant',
vom sichern Strand, der ihn setze an das gewünschte Land,
from the safe shore, which him might set upon the longed-for land,
(from the safety of the shore, none that might set him on the opposite bank he longs to reach,)

kʰaɛn 'ʃifɐ 'leŋk'ət di 'feːrə, lʊnt deːɐ 'vɪldə ʃt'roːm vɪrt tsʊm 'meːrə.
kein Schiffer lenket die Fähre, und der wilde Strom wird zum Meere.
no boatman steers the ferry, and the wild river becomes to the sea.
(no boatman will steer his ferry, and the wild river is becoming a sea.)

daː zɪŋk't' leːɐ/leːr lans 'luːfɐ(r) lʊnt' vaɛnt' lʊnt' fleːt, di 'hɛndə tsʊm tsɔøs lɛɐ'hoːbən:
Da sinkt er ans Ufer und weint und fleht, die Hände zum Zeus erhoben:
Then sinks he onto the bank and weeps and pleads, the hands to the Zeus raised:
(Then he sinks down at the bank and weeps and pleads, his hands raised up to Zeus:)

oː 'hɛmə dɛs 'ʃt'roːməs 't^hoːbən! lɛs 'laɛlən di 'ʃt'ʊndən, lɪm 'mɪt'aːk' ʃt'eːt di 'zɔnə,
"O hemme des Stromes Toben! Es eilen die Stunden, im Mittag steht die Sonne,
"O curb the river's raging! There hurry the hours, at the noon stands the sun,
("Oh curb the raging of the river! The hours are hurrying by, the sun has reached midday,)

ʊnt' vɛn ziː 'niːdɐgeːt', lʊnt' lɪç kʰan di ʃt'at' nɪçt' lɛɐ'raeçən,
und wenn sie niedergeht, und ich kann die Stadt nicht erreichen,
and if it goes down, and I can the city not reach,
(and it it sets before I can reach the city,)

zoː mʊs deːɐ frɔønt' miːɐ/miːr lɛɐ'blaeəən. dɔx 'vaksənt'
so muss der Freund mir erbleichen." Doch wachsend
then must the friend for me grow pale." But increasingly
(then my friend must die." But increasingly)

lɛɐ'nɔøt' zɪç dɛs 'ʃt'roːməs 't^hoːbən, lʊnt' 'velə laof 'velə tsɛɐ'rɪnət',
erneut sich des Stromes Toben, und Welle auf Welle zerrinnet,
renews itself the river's raging, and wave upon wave dissolves,
(the raging of the river is renewed, and one wave flows into the next,)
                                        [*poem:* **des Stromes Wut** (vuːt', fury)]

lʊnt' 'ʃt'ʊndə lan 'ʃt'ʊndə lɛnt''rɪnət^h; daː t^hraep't' liːn di laŋst',
und Stunde an Stunde entrinnet; da treibt ihn die Angst,
and hour on hour runs away; then drives him the fear,
(and hour after hour slips by; then fear impels him)

daː fast' leːɐ zɪç muːt' lʊnt' vɪrft' zɪç hɪ'naen lɪn di 'braozəndə fluːt',
da fasst er sich Mut und wirft sich hinein in die brausende Flut,
then seizes he for himself courage and throws himself in into the foaming torrent,
(to seize his courage and throw himself into the foaming torrent,)

ʊnt tʰa͜elt‘ mɪt‘ gəˈvaltʻɪgən ˈlarmən den ʃt‘roːm, ʊnt‘ la͜en gɔt‘ hat‘ lɛɐ̯ˈbarmən.
und teilt mit gewaltigen Armen den Strom, und ein Gott hat Erbarmen.
and cleaves with powerful arms the stream, and a god has mercy.
(and he cleaves the waters with powerful arms, and a god shows mercy.)

ʊnt‘ gəˈvɪnt das ˈluːfɐ(r) ʊnt‘ ˈla͜elət‘ fɔrt‘ ʊnt ˈdaŋk‘ət dem ˈrɛt‘əndən ˈgɔt‘ə;
Und gewinnt das Ufer und eilet fort und danket dem rettenden Gotte;
And gains the shore and hurries on and gives thanks to the rescuing god;
(And he gains the shore and hurries on and gives thanks to the rescuing god:)

daː ˈʃt‘ʏrt͜sət di ˈra͜obəndə ˈrɔt‘ə hɛɐ̯ˈfoːɐ̯/hɛɐ̯ˈfoːr la͜os dɛs ˈvaldəs ˈnɛçt‘lɪçəm lɔrtʰ,
da stürzet die raubende Rotte hervor aus des Waldes nächtlichem Ort,
then rushes the robbing band out from the forest's night-dark place,
(then a band of robbers rushes out from their dark hiding place in the forest,)

den p͜faːt‘ liːm ˈʃp‘ɛrənt‘, ʊnt‘ ˈʃna͜obət‘ mɔrt‘, ʊnt‘ ˈhɛmət dɛs ˈvandərɐs ˈla͜elə,
den Pfad ihm sperrend, und schnaubet Mord, und hemmet des Wanderers Eile,
the path to him blocking, and snorts murder, and hinders the wanderer's haste,
(blocking his path, and snorts murder, and hinders the wanderer's haste)

mɪt ˈdroːənt‘ gəˈʃvʊŋənɐ ˈkʰɔ͜ølə. vas vɔlt‘ liːɐ̯? ruːft‘ leːɐ̯,
mit drohend geschwungener Keule. "Was wollt ihr?" ruft er,
with menacingly swung club. "What want you?" calls he,
(with menacingly swung clubs. "What do you want?" he calls,)

foːɐ̯ ˈʃrɛk‘ən bla͜eç, lɪç ˈhaːbə nɪçt͜s, lals ma͜en ˈleːbən, das mʊs lɪç
vor Schrecken bleich, "ich habe nichts, als mein Leben, das muss ich
with fright pale, "I have nothing but my life; that must I
(pale with fright, "I have nothing but my life, and that I must) [*poem:* **für** (fyːɐ̯) **Schrecken**]

dem ˈkʰøːnɪgə ˈgeːbən! lʊnt‘ lɛnt‘ˈra͜est di ˈkʰɔ͜ølə dem ˈnɛːçst‘ən gla͜eç:
dem Könige geben!" Und entreisst die Keule dem Nächsten gleich:
to the king give!" And (he) snatches away the club from the nearest one instantly:
(give to the king!" And instantly he snatches a club away from the nearest of the robbers:)

lʊm dɛs ˈfrɔ͜øndəs ˈvɪlən lɛɐ̯ˈbarmt‘ lɔ͜øç!
"Um des Freundes willen erbarmt euch!" [*poem:* **erbarmet** (lɛɐ̯ˈbarmət‘)]
"For the friend's sake to pity move yourselves!"
("For my friend's sake have pity!")

ʊnt dra͜e, mɪt‘ gəˈvalt‘ɪgən ˈʃt‘ra͜eçən, lɛɐ̯ˈleːk‘t‘ leːɐ̯, di ˈlandɐn lɛnt‘ˈva͜eçən.
Und drei, mit gewaltigen Streichen, erlegt er, die andern entweichen.
And three, with powerful blows, kills he; the others disappear.
(And he kills three of them with powerful blows; the others run away.)

ʊnt di ˈzɔnə fɛɐ̯ˈzɛndət‘ ˈglyːəndən brant‘, lʊnt‘
Und die Sonne versendet glühenden Brand, und
And the sun sends out burning fire, and,

fɔn deːɐ̯/deːr lʊnˈlɛnt‘lɪçən ˈmyːə lɛɐ̯ˈmat‘ət‘, ˈzɪŋk‘ən di ˈkʰniː. oː hast duː
von der unendlichen Mühe ermattet, sinken die Knie. "O hast du
from the ceaseless effort exhausted, sink the knees. "O have you
(exhausted from the ceaseless effort, his knees give way. "Oh, have you) [*poem:* **Kniee** (ˈkʰniːə)]

mıç ˈgnɛːdıç lɑos ˈrɔʏbɐhantˈ, lɑos dem ʃtˈroːm mıç gəˈrɛtˈətˈ lans ˈhaɛlıgə lantˈ,
mich gnädig aus Räuberhand, aus dem Strom mich gerettet ans heilige Land,
me mercifully from robber-hand, from the torrent me rescued to the holy land,
(mercifully rescued me from the hand of robbers and out of the torrent onto sacred dry land,)

lontˈ zɔl hiːɐ fɛɐˈʃmaxtˈəntˈ fɛɐˈdɛrbən, lontˈ deːɐ frɔʏntˈ
und soll hier verschmachtend verderben, und der Freund
and shall here (I) fainting from thirst perish, and the friend
(and shall I perish here from thirst, and shall my friend,)

miːɐ, deːɐ ˈliːbəndə, ˈʃtˈɛrbən! lontˈ hɔrç! daː ˈʃpˈruːdəltˈ lɛs ˈzɪlbɐhɛl, gant͜s ˈnaːə,
mir, der liebende, sterben!" Und horch! da sprudelt es silberhell, ganz nahe,
for me, the loving one, die!" And hark! there bubbles up it silver-bright, very near,
(my loving friend, die for me!" And hark! There is a bubbling, silver-bright sound, very near,)

viː ˈriːzəlndəs ˈrɑoʃən, lontˈ ˈʃtˈɪlə hɛltˈ leːɐ, tsuː ˈlɑoʃən; lontˈ ziː, lɑos dem ˈfɛlzən,
wie riselndes Rauschen, und stille hält er, zu lauschen; und sieh', aus dem Felsen,
like rippling murmuring, and still holds he to listen; and lo, from the rock,
(like the murmur of rippling water, and he holds still to listen; and lo, out of the rock,)

gəˈʃvɛt͜sıç, ʃnɛl, ʃpˈrɪŋtˈ ˈmʊrməlntˈ hɛɐˈfoːɐ/hɛɐˈfoːr laen leˈbɛndıgɐ kʰvɛl,
geschwätzig, schnell, springt murmelnd hervor ein lebendiger Quell,
babbling, quick, springs murmuring forth a living spring,
(babbling, quick, murmuring, a living spring is gushing forth,)

ʊntˈ ˈfrɔʏdıç bʏkˈtˈ leːɐ zıç ˈniːdɐ(r) lontˈ lɛɐˈfrɪʃət di ˈbrɛnəndən ˈgliːdɐ.
und freudig bückt er sich nieder und erfrischet die brennenden Glieder.
and joyfully bends he himself down and refreshes the burning limbs.
(and he joyfully bends down and refreshes his burning body.)

ʊnt di ˈzɔnə blɪkˈt dʊrç deːɐ ˈt͜svaegə gryːn lontˈ maːlt lɑof ˈglɛnt͜səndən ˈmatˈən
Und die Sonne blickt durch der Zweige Grün und malt auf glänzenden Matten
And the sun looks through the branches' green and paints on gleaming meadows
(And the sun looks through the green of the branches and paints on gleaming meadows)

[*poem:* **auf den** (den, the) **glänzenden Matten**]

deːɐ ˈbɔʏmə gıˈgantˈıʃə ˈʃatˈən. lont t͜svae ˈvandrɐ ziːtˈ leːɐ di ˈʃtˈraːsə t͜siːn,
der Bäume gigantische Schatten. Und zwei Wand'rer sieht er die Strasse ziehn,
the trees' gigantic shadows. And two wanderers sees he the street coming down,
(the gigantic shadows of the trees. And he sees two wanderers coming down the road,)

[*poem:* **Wanderer** (ˈvandərɐ)]

vıl ˈlaeləndən ˈlɑofəs foˈryːbɐ fliːn, daː høːɐtˈ leːɐ di ˈvɔrtˈə ziː ˈzaːgən: jɛt͜stˈ
will eilenden Laufes vorüber fliehn, da hört er die Worte sie sagen: "Jetzt
wants in hurrying run past to flee, then hears he the words them say: "Now
(wants to flee past them, running hastily; then he hears them saying these words: "Right now)

vırtˈ leːɐ/leːr lans kʰrɔʏt͜s gəˈʃlaːgən! lontˈ di laŋstˈ bəˈflyːgəlt den ˈlaeləndən fuːs,
wird er ans Kreuz geschlagen!" Und die Angst beflügelt den eilenden Fuss,
is being he to the cross nailed!" And the fear winged the hurrying foot,
(he is being nailed to the cross!" And fear gave wings to his hurrying feet,)

liːn ˈjaːgən deːɐ̯ ˈzɔrgə ˈkʰvaːlən;
ihn jagen der Sorge Qualen;   [*Peters:* **Sorgen** (ˈzɔrgən, cares'—plural)]
him chase the anxiety's torments;
(the torments of anxiety chase him onwards;)   [*poem:* **und** (ʊnt', and) **ihn jagen**]

daː ˈʃɪmɐn lɪn ˈlaːbənt'roːts ˈʃt'raːlən fɔn ˈfɛrnə di ˈtsɪnən fɔn zyraˈkʰuːs,
da schimmern in Abendrots Strahlen von ferne die Zinnen von Syracus,
there shimmer in sunset's rays from afar the battlements of Syracuse,
(there are the battlements of Syracuse, shimmering from afar in the rays of the setting sun,)

ʊnt' lɛnt''geːgən kʰɔmt' liːm fiˈlɔst'rat'ʊs, dɛs ˈhaʊozəs ˈreːt'lɪçɐ ˈhyːt'ɐ, deːɐ̯/deːr
und entgegen kommt ihm Philostratus, des Hauses redlicher Hüter, der
and toward comes to him Philostratus, the house's honest custodian, who
(and coming toward him is Philostratus, the honest custodian of his household, who)

lɛɐ̯ˈkʰɛnət' lɛnt''zɛt̯st den gəˈbiːt'ɐ: tsuˈrʏk'! du ˈrɛt'əst den fr̮ɔ̯ɔnt' nɪçt' meːɐ̯, zoː
erkennet entsetzt den Gebieter: "Zurück! du rettest den Freund nicht mehr, so
recognizes horrified the master: "Back! you rescue the friend not more, so
(recognizes his master with horror: "Go back! You can rescue your friend no longer, so)

ˈrɛt'ə das ˈlaegənə ˈleːbən! den tʰoːt' lɛɐ̯ˈlaedət' leːɐ̯/leːr ˈleːbən. fɔn ˈʃt'ʊndə tsuː ˈʃt'ʊndə
rette das eigene Leben! den Tod erleidet er eben. Von Stunde zu Stunde
save the own life! The death suffers he right now. From hour to hour
(save your *own* life! He is meeting death right now. From hour to hour)

gəˈvart'ət' leːɐ̯ mɪt' ˈhɔfəndɐ ˈzeːlə deːɐ̯ ˈviːdɐkʰeːɐ̯,
gewartet' er mit hoffender Seele der Wiederkehr,
waited he with hoping soul for the return,
(he awaited your return with a hopeful soul,)

iːm ˈkʰɔnt'ə den ˈmuːt'ɪgən ˈglaoɒbən deːɐ̯ hoːn dɛs tʰyˈranən nɪçt' ˈraoɒbən. — ʊnt'
ihm konnte den mutigen Glauben der Hohn des Tyrannen nicht rauben."—"Und
from him could the brave faith the derision of the tyrant not rob." —"And
(the tyrant's derision could not rob from him his brave faith." —"And)

lɪst' lɛs tsuː ʃp'eːt', lʊnt' kʰan lɪç liːm nɪçt' laen ˈrɛt'ɐ vɪlˈkʰɔmən lɛɐ̯ˈʃaenən,
ist es zu spät, und kann ich ihm nicht ein Retter willkommen erscheinen,
is it too late, and can I to him not a rescuer welcome appear,
(if it is too late, and if I cannot appear before him as a welcome rescuer,)

zoː zɔl mɪç deːɐ̯ tʰoːt' mɪt' liːm fɛɐ̯ˈlaenən/fɛrˈlaenən.
so soll mich der Tod mit ihm vereinen.   [*poem without* "ihm"]
then shall me the death with him unite.
(then death shall unite me with him.)

dɛs ˈryːmə deːɐ̯ ˈbluːt'gə tʰyˈran zɪç nɪçt, das deːɐ̯ frɔ̯ɔ̯ønt
Dess rühme der blut'ge Tyrann sich nicht, dass der Freund
Of that boast the bloody tyrant himself not, that the friend
(Let the bloody tyrant not boast that one friend)

dem ˈfrɔ̯ɔ̯øndə gəˈbrɔxən di pflɪçt', leːɐ̯ ˈʃlaxt'ə deːɐ̯/deːr ˈlɔpfɐ ˈtsvaeə
dem Freunde gebrochen die Pflicht, er schlachte der Opfer zweie
to the friend (has) broken the obligation, he may slaughter of the sacrifices two
(has broken his obligation to the other; let him slaughter *two* sacrifices)

334

|ʊnt‘ ˈglɑobə |an liːp‘ |ʊnt ˈtʰrɔøə! |ʊnt di ˈzɔnə geːt‘ ˈʊnt‘ɐ,
und glaube an Lieb' und Treue!"   Und die Sonne geht unter,
and believe in love and faithfulness!" And the sun goes down,
(and learn to believe in love and faithfulness!" And the sun sets,)   [*poem:* **Liebe** (ˈliːbə)]

daː ʃt‘eːt‘ leːɐ̯/leːr |am tʰoːɐ̯ |ʊnt‘ ziːt das kʰrɔøts ʃoːn |ɛɐ̯ˈhøːtʰ, das di ˈmɛŋə
da steht er   am Tor und sieht das Kreuz schon erhöh't, das   die Menge
then stands he   at the gate and sees the cross already raised,   which the crowd
(then he stands at the gate and sees the cross already raised, which the crowd)   [*poem:* **erhöhet** (|ɛɐ̯ˈhøːətʰ)]

ˈgafənt‘ |ʊmˈʃt‘eːstʰ; |ʊnt‘ |an dem ˈzaelə ʃoːn tsiːt‘ man den frɔønt‘ |ɛmˈpʰoːɐ̯, daː
gaffend umstehet;   und an   dem Seile schon zieht man den Freund empor,   da
gawking around-stands; and with the   rope already pulls one the friend on high,   then
(stands around, gawking; and his friend is already being pulled up to the cross with a rope, then)   [*poem without* "und"]

tsɛɐ̯ˈtʰrɛnt‘ leːɐ̯ gəˈvalt‘ɪç den ˈdɪçt‘ən kʰoːɐ̯: mɪç, ˈhɛŋk‘ɐ! ruːft‘ leːɐ̯/leːr |ɛɐ̯ˈvyrgətʰ!
zertrennt er gewaltig   den dichten Chor: "Mich, Henker!"   ruft er,   "erwürget!
parts   he powerfully the thick   throng: "Me, executioner!" calls he,   "strangle!"
(he forces his way through the thick mob: "Kill me, executioner!" he calls,)

daː bɪn |ɪç, fyːɐ̯ deːn leːɐ̯ gəˈbyrgətʰ! |ʊnt‘ |ɛɐ̯ˈʃt‘aonən |ɛɐ̯ˈgraeft das fɔlk‘ |ʊmˈheːɐ̯,
da bin ich, für den   er gebürget!"   Und Erstaunen   ergreift das Volk   umher,
here am I,   for whom he stands surety!" And astonishment seizes   the people all around,
("here I am, for whom he stands surety!" And astonishment seizes the people all around,)   [*poem:* **ergreifet** (|ɛɐ̯ˈgraefət)]

|ɪn den ˈarmən ˈliːgən zɪç   ˈbaedə |ʊnt‘ ˈvaenən foːɐ̯ ˈʃmɛrtsən |ʊnt‘ ˈfrɔødə.
in den Armen liegen sich   Beide und weinen vor Schmerzen und Freude.
in the arms   lie   of each other both and weep for pains   and joy.
(the two friends are in each other's arms and weep for sorrow and joy.)   [*poem:* **für** (fyːɐ̯) **Schmerzen**]

daː ziːt‘ man kʰaen ˈlɑogə ˈtʰrɛːnənleːɐ̯, |ʊnt tsʊm ˈkʰøːnɪç brɪnt‘ man di ˈvʊndɐmeːɐ̯;
Da sieht man kein Auge tränenleer, und zum König bringt man die Wundermär;
Then sees one no   eye   tear- empty, and to the king   brings one the wonder-tidings;
(Then one can not see a single eye without a tear, and news of the marvel is brought to the king;)   [*poem:* **zum Könige** (ˈkʰøːnɪgə)]

deːɐ̯ fyːlt‘ |aen ˈmɛnʃlɪç ˈryːrən, lɛst‘ ʃnɛl foːɐ̯ den tʰroːn ziː ˈfyːrən.
der fühlt ein   menschlich Rühren, lässt schnell vor   den Thron sie   führen.
he feels a   human   stirring, lets quickly before the   throne them be led.
(he is stirred by a human feeling and quickly has them led before his throne.)   [*poem:* **menschliches** ˈmɛnʃlɪçəs)]

|ʊnt‘ blɪk‘t‘ ziː ˈlaŋə fɛɐ̯ˈvʊndɐt‘ |an. drɑof ʃp‘rɪçt‘ leːɐ̯: |ɛs lɪst‘ lɔøç gəˈlʊŋən,
Und blickt sie   lange verwundert an. Drauf   spricht er: "Es ist   euch gelungen,
And looks them long astonished at. Thereupon speaks he: "It is to you succeeded,
(And he looks at them for a long time, astonished. Then he speaks: "You have succeeded;)   [*poem:* **blicket** (ˈblɪk‘ət‘)]

liːɐ̯ haːp‿t das hɛrts miːɐ̯ bə'tsvʊŋən; lʊnt di 'tʰrɔø̯ə lɪst dɔx kʰaen 'leːrɐ vaːn;
ihr habt das Herz mir bezwungen; und die Treue ist doch kein leerer Wahn;
you have the heart of me overcome; and the faithfulness is after all no empty illusion;
(you have overcome my heart; and I see that faithfulness is not an empty illusion after all;)

[*poem:* **und die Treue, sie** (ziː) **ist doch** (it is after all...)]

zoː neːmt‿ lαox mɪç tsʊm gə'nɔsən lan! lɪç zae̯, gə'veːɐ̯t‿ miːɐ̯ di 'bɪt‿ə,
so nehmt auch mich zum Genossen an! Ich sei, gewährt mir die Bitte,
so accept also me as the comrade ... ! I be, grant to me the request,
(so accept me too as a comrade! Let me be—if you grant me this request—)

[*poem:* **nehmet** ('neːmət‿); *"annehmen"* = to accept]

ɪn 'lɔø̯rəm 'bʊndə deːɐ̯ 'drɪt‿ə.
in eurem Bunde der Dritte."
in your fellowship the third."
(the third in your fellowship.")

[This miniature opera for solo singer and accompanist is full of vivid tone-painting, expressive recitative, and effective melody. If the ending is somehow unconvincing, that is the fault of the poet, not of the musician. The story is derived from the ancient tale of Damon and Pythias, the classic paragons of faithful, self-sacrificing friendship, and Dionysius I, tyrant of Syracuse.]

di drae̯ 'zɛŋɐ
Die drei Sänger
The Three Singers

Published (incomplete) in 1895 [composed in 1815] (poem by Friedrich Bobrik)

deːɐ̯ 'kʰøːnɪç zaːs bae̯m 'froːən 'maːlə, di frαon lʊnt‿ 'rɪt‿ɐ(r) lʊm liːn [zɪç] heːɐ̯;
Der König sass beim frohen Mahle, die Frau'n und Ritter um ihn* [sich] her;
The king sat at the happy meal, the ladies and knights around him [himself] hither;
(The king sat at the happy feast, the ladies and knights gathered all around him;) [**GA variant*]

ɛs 'kʰrae̯st‿ən 'frøːlɪç ['fɛst‿lɪç] di pʰo'kʰaːlə, lʊnt‿ 'mançəs 'bɛk‿ən tʰraŋk‿ man leːɐ̯;
es kreisten fröhlich* [festlich] die Pokale, und manches Becken trank man leer;
there circled merrily [festively] the goblets, and many a bowl drank one empty;
(the goblets were circulated merrily, and many a bowl was drained;) [**GA variant*]

daː 'tʰøːnt‿ə kʰlaŋ fɔn 'gɔldnən 'zae̯t‿ən, deːɐ̯ 'zyːsɐ laːp‿t‿ lals 'gɔldnɐ vae̯n,
da tönte Klang von goldnen Saiten, der süsser labt als goldner Wein,
then resounded sound of golden strings, which sweeter refreshes than golden wine,
(then the sound of golden strings was heard, which refreshes more sweetly than golden wine,)

ʊnt‿ ziː! — drae̯ 'frɛmdə 'zɛŋɐ 'ʃrae̯t‿ən, zɪç 'nae̯gənt‿, lɪn den zaːl hi'nae̯n.
und sieh! — drei fremde Sänger schreiten, sich neigend, in den Saal hinein.
and look! — three strange minstrels stride, themselves bowing, into the hall into.
(and look! — three strange minstrels stride, bowing, into the hall.)

zae̯t‿ miːɐ̯ gə'gryːst‿, liːɐ̯ 'liːdɐzøːnə! bə'gɪnt deːɐ̯ 'kʰøːnɪç 'voːlgəmuːtʰ,
"Seid mir gegrüsst, ihr Liedersöhne!" beginnt der König wohlgemut,
"Be to me greeted, you songs-sons!" begins the king cheerfully,
("I greet you, sons of song!" the king cheerfully begins,)

ɪn 'deːrən brʊst das rɑ̯ęç deːɐ̯ 'tʰøːnə, ʊnt dɛs gə'zaŋs gə'haęmnɪs ruːtʰ!
"in deren Brust das Reich der Töne, und des Gesangs Geheimnis ruht!
"in whose breast the realm of the tones and the song's mystery rests!
("in whose hearts the realm of tones and the mystery of song are at rest!)

vɔlt' liːɐ̯ den 'leːdlən 'vɛt'ʃt'rɑ̯et' 'vaːgən, zoː zɔl lɛs 'høːçlɪç lʊns lɛɐ̯'frɔ̯øn,
Wollt ihr den edlen Wettstreit wagen, so soll es höchlich uns erfreun,
Want you the noble contest to venture, then shall it highly us delight,
(If you want to venture a noble contest, then we shall be highly delighted,)

lʊnt' veːɐ̯ den ziːk' da'fɔŋgətʰraːgən, maːk' 'lʊnzrəs ['lʊnzɛs] 'hoːfəs 'tsiːɐ̯də zaęn!
und wer den Sieg davongetragen, mag unsres* [unsers] Hofes Zierde sein!"
and he who the victory carries off, may our court's ornament be!"
(and he who wins will become the ornament of our court!") [*GA variant]

eːɐ̯ ʃp'rɪçts — deːɐ̯/deːr 'leːɐ̯st'ə ryːɐ̯t di 'zaęt'ən, di 'foːɐ̯vɛlt 'lœfnət' leːɐ̯ dem
Er spricht's — der Erste rührt die Saiten, die Vorwelt öffnet er dem
He speaks it — the first touches the strings, the prehistoric world opens he to the
(He announces that. The first singer touches the strings; he opens up the prehistoric world to the)

blɪkʰ. tsʊm 'grɑ̯ɔən 'lanfaŋ 'lalɐ 'tsaęt'ən lɛŋk't' leːɐ̯ deːɐ̯ 'høːrə ʃaːɐ̯ tsu'rʏkʰ;
Blick. Zum grauen Anfang aller Zeiten lenkt er der Hörer Schar* zurück;
gaze. To the grey beginning of all times directs he the listener's host back;
(gaze. He directs the host of listeners back to the grey beginning of all time;) [*Schubert: **Blick**]

eːɐ̯ 'mɛldət': viː zɪç, nɔ̯ø gə'boːrən, di vɛlt dem 'kʰaːɔs laęnst' lɛnt''vant';
er meldet: wie sich, neu geboren, die Welt dem Chaos einst entwand;
he reports: how itself, new born, the world from the chaos once extricated;
(he reports how the world, new born, once extricated itself from the primordial chaos;)

zaęn liːt' bə'haːk't den 'faęnst'ən 'loːrən, lʊnt' 'vɪlɪç fɔlk't' liːm deːɐ̯ fɛɐ̯'ʃt'ant'.
sein Lied behagt den feinsten* Ohren, und willig folgt ihm der V e r s t a n d.
his song pleased the finest ears, and willingly followed it the *understanding*.
(his song was pleasing even to the most refined ears, and the *intellect* followed it willingly.)
[*Schubert: **meisten** ('maęst'ən), most]

drɑ̯ɔf meːɐ̯ di 'høːrə tsuː lɛɐ̯'gœtsən, lɛɐ̯'kʰlɪŋt dɛs 'tsvaęt'ən 'lʊst'gə meːɐ̯
Drauf mehr die Hörer zu ergötzen, erklingt des Zweiten lust'ge Mähr'
Next, more the listeners to amuse, resounds the second one's merry tale
(Next, more to amuse the listeners, rings out the second singer's merry tale)

fɔn 'gnoːmən, faęn [feːn*] lʊnt' 'liːrən 'ʃɛtsən, lʊnt' fɔn deːɐ̯ 'gryːnən 'tsvɛrgə heːɐ̯;
von Gnomen, Fei'n* und ihren Schätzen, und von der grünen Zwerge Heer;
about gnomes, fairies, and their treasures, and about the green dwarfs' army;
[*Schubert: **fein** ("fine," clearly an error); "Fei" is an old form of "Fee" = fairy]

eːɐ̯ zɪnt' fɔn 'mançən 'vʊndɐdɪŋən, fɔn 'mançəm 'ʃvaŋk'ə, ʃlɑ̯ɔ lɛɐ̯'daxtʰ;
er singt von manchen Wunderdingen, von manchem Schwanke, schlau erdacht;
he sings about many marvels, about many a prank, slyly devised;

daː reːk't' deːɐ̯ ʃɛrts di 'loːzən 'ʃvɪŋən, lʊnt' 'jeːdɐ mʊnt' lɪm 'zaːlə laxtʰ.
da regt der S c h e r z die losen Schwingen, und jeder Mund im Saale lacht.
then stirs the *fun* the loose wings, and every mouth in the hall laughs.
(*fun* spreads its free and easy wings then, and every mouth in the hall is laughing.)

ʊnt‘ lan den 'drɪt‘ən tʰrɪft di 'ʀaeə.   — lʊnt‘ zanft‘, laos tʰiːf bə've:k‘t‘ɐ brʊst‘
Und an den Dritten trifft* die Reihe.* — Und sanft, aus tief bewegter Brust,
And at the third strikes the turn.   — And gently, out of deeply moved breast,
(And now the third singer has his turn. And gently, out of his deeply moved heart,)

　　　　　　　[*Schubert: **kommt die Reih'** (kʰɔmt di ʀae): "kommt" is more idiomatic (with "an")]

haoxt‘ le:ɐ/le:r laen li:t‘ fɔn li:p‘ lʊnt‘ 'tʰʀɔøə   lʊnt‘ fɔn de:ɐ 'ze:nzʊxt ʃmɛrts lʊnt‘
haucht er ein Lied von Lieb' und Treue* und von der Sehnsucht Schmerz und
breathes he a song of love and faithfulness and of the longing's pain and
(he breathes out a song of love and faithfulness, and of longing's pain and)   [*Schubert: **Treu'**]

lʊstʰ.   lʊnt‘ kʰaom das 'zaenə 'zaet‘ən 'kʰlɪŋən, ʃaot‘ 'je:dəs 'lant‘lɪts... [lɪn den ʃoːs,
Lust. Und kaum dass seine Saiten klingen, schaut jedes Antlitz... [in den Schoss,
pleasure. And scarcely that his strings resound, looks each face.. . [in the lap,
(pleasure. And scarcely do his strings resound, when each listener lowers his head,)

lʊnt‘ 'tʰrɛːnən dɛs gə'fyːləs 'rɪŋən zɪç laos fɛɐ'kʰlɛːɐt‘ən 'laogən loːs.
und Tränen des G e f ü h l e s ringen sich aus verklärten Augen los.
and tears of the *emotion* wrest themselves out of transfigured eyes free.
(and tears of *emotion* struggle free out of transfigured eyes.)

ʊnt 'tʰiːfəs 'ʃvaegən hɛrʃt‘ lɪm 'zaːlə, lals 'zaenəs 'liːdəs tʰoːn lɛnt‘'ʃvant‘. —
Und tiefes Schweigen herrscht im Saale, als seines Liedes Ton entschwand. —
And deep silence reigns in the hall, when his song's tone died away. —
(And deep silence reigns in the hall when the last tones of his song have died away. —)

daː ʃt‘eːt deːɐ 'kʰøːnɪç laof fɔm 'maːlə, lʊnt‘ raeçt dem 'drɪt‘ən 'zaenə hant‘:
Da steht der König auf vom Mahle, und reicht dem D r i t t e n seine Hand:
Then stands the king up from the meal, and holds out to the *third* his hand:
(Then the king rises from his chair and offers his hand to the *third* singer, saying:)

 blaep‘ bae lʊns, frɔønt‘! diːɐ/diːr lɪsts gə'lʊŋən, duː bɪst‘ lɛs, deːm deːɐ pʰraes
"Bleib' bei uns, Freund! dir ist's gelungen, du bist es, dem der Preis
"Stay with us, friend! to you is it succeeded, you are it, to whom the prize
("Stay with us, friend! You have been successful, you are the one to whom the prize)

gə'byːɐtʰ; das 'ʃøːnst‘ə liːt‘ hat de:ɐ gə'zʊŋən,
gebührt; das schönste Lied hat der gesungen,
is due; the most beautiful song has he sung,
(is due; the most beautiful song has been sung by him)

de:ɐ/de:r 'lʊnzɐ hɛrts tsʊr 'veːmuːt‘ ryːɐtʰ.]
der unser Herz zur Wehmut rührt."]
who our heart to the melancholy moves."]
(who moves our hearts to melancholy.")]

[The last page of Schubert's manuscript is missing (after the words "*schaut jedes Antlitz*"). The *Gesammtausgabe* printed the song in its incomplete form (with some variants from the original poem). The piece has been completed and privately printed by Reinhard van Hoorickx. As indicated, Schubert made some errors in copying the poem, as well as some deliberate changes.]

di ḷa̤ɛnziːdə'ḷa̤e̥
Die Einsiedelei
The Hermitage

Posthumously published [composed 1816, 1817] (poem by Johann Gaudenz von Salis-Seewis)

ɛs   'riːzəlt‘ kʰlaːɐ̯/kʰlaːr ʊnt‘ 'veːənt‘ ḷa̤en kʰvɛl ɪm   'ḷa̤e̥çənvalt‘;
Es   rieselt klar   und wehend ein Quell im   Eichenwald;
There trickles clear   and rippling a   spring in the oak   forest;
(A clear, rippling spring bubbles up in the oak forest;)

daː   vɛːl   ɪç 'ḷa̤enzaːm 'geːənt‘, miːɐ̯ 'ma̤enən 'ḷa̤ofḷɛnt‘haltʰ.
da   wähl' ich einsam gehend, mir   meinen Aufenthalt.
there choose I   solitarily walking, for me my   place to stay.
(there, walking in solitude, I choose the place where I would like to stay.)

miːɐ̯   'diːnət tsʊr   kʰa'pʰɛlə ḷa̤en 'grœt‘çən, 'dʊft‘ɪç   frɪʃ,
Mir   dienet zur Kapelle ein Gröttchen, duftig   frisch,
For me serves as the chapel   a   little grotto, fragrantly fresh,
(A little grotto, fragrant and cool, will serve as my chapel,)
        [*poem (according to Schochow):* **luftigfrisch** ('lʊft‘ɪç-, airy fresh); *GA & P:* **duftig frisch**]

tsuː 'ma̤enɐ 'kʰḷa̤ozneṭsɛlə fɛɐ̯'ʃlʊŋənəs   gə'byʃ.
zu meiner Klausnerzelle verschlungenes Gebüsch.
as my   hermit's cell tangled   bushes.
(tangled bushes as my hermit's cell.)

[*In GA (both versions) but not in Peters:*]

tsvaːɐ̯   'dyːst‘ɐ(r) ɪst‘ ʊnt 'tʰryːbɐ di 'naːə vyːst‘ə'na̤e; a'ḷa̤en nuːɐ̯ 'dɛst‘o 'liːbɐ
Zwar   düster ist und trüber die nahe Wüstenei; allein nur desto lieber
Of course dark   is   and drearier the near wilderness; but   only all the dearer
(Of course the nearby wilderness is dark and drearier;)
                        [*1st version:* **die wahre** ('vaːrə, true) **Wüstenei**]

deːɐ̯ 'ʃt‘ɪlən fant‘a'za̤e. daː   ruː ḷɪç ḷɔft‘ ḷɪm   'dɪçt‘ən, bə'blyːmt‘ən 'ha̤edəkʰra̤otʰ;
der   stillen Phantasei. Da   ruh' ich oft im   dichten, beblümten Heidekraut;
to the quiet   phantasy.   There rest I   often in the thick,   flowered   heath-herb;
(to the quiet phantasy. There I often rest in the thick, flowering herbage of the heath;)

hoːx veːn di 'ʃvaŋk‘ən   'fɪçt‘ən, ḷʊnt‘ 'ʃt‘øːnən 'zɔ̥øftsɐḷa̤otʰ.
hoch wehn die schwanken Fichten, und   stöhnen Seufzerlaut.
high wave the supple   fir-trees, and   moan   sighing sound.
(high up the supple fir-trees wave, and moan their sighing sound.)

voː   fɔn va'xɔldɐʃt‘rɔ̥øçən   den 'kʰiːzəlʃt‘a̤ek‘   hɪ'nan   [-ʃt‘eːk‘]
Wo   von Wacholdersträuchen den Kieselsteig   hinan [*GA, 1st version:* **Kieselsteg**]
Where from juniper   bushes   the pebbled footpath upward   [footpath]
(Where, from juniper bushes, up the pebbled footpath)

fɛɐ̯'vɔrnə   'raŋk‘ən 'ʃḷa̤eçən,   daː brɛç ḷɪç miːɐ̯   di baːn;
Verworrne Ranken schleichen, da   brech' ich mir   die Bahn;
tangled   tendrils steal,   there break I   for myself the path;
(tangled tendrils are stealing, there I break a path for myself;)

dʊrç   dɛs   gə'haͻəs   'ʃt'ʊmp'ən,   voː   'vɪldə   'leːɐt'beːɐn   ʃt'eːn,
durch   des Gehaues Stumpen,   wo   wilde Erdbeern   stehn,
through the clearing's stumps,   where wild   strawberries stand,
(among the stumps of the clearing, where wild strawberries are growing,)

["*Stumpen*" (dialect) = "*Stumpfen*" = stumps]

kʰlɪm   ɪç   lɑͻf   'fɛlzənkʰlʊmp'ən, das lant'   ʊm'heːɐ   tsuː zeːn.
klimm ich auf Felsenklumpen, das Land   umher   zu sehn.
climb I   onto rock- clumps,   the countryside all around to see.
(I climb up onto clumps of rock to see the countryside all around.)

[According to the Peters edition in Schubert's first version (1816) only:]

nɪçts   lʊnt'ɐ'brɪçt das 'ʃvaͻegən   deːɐ   'vɪlt'nɪs   vaͻet' lʊnt' braͻetʰ,
Nichts   unterbricht das Schweigen der   Wildnis   weit und breit,
Nothing interrupts   the   silence   of the wilderness, far   and   wide,

als   vɛn   lɑͻf 'dyrən   'tsvaͻegən laͻen 'gryːnʃp'ɛçt'   hak't' lʊnt' ʃraͻetʰ,
als   wenn auf dürren Zweigen ein Grünspecht   hackt und schreit,
except when on   dry   branches a   green woodpecker pecks and   cries,

aͻen raːp'   lɑͻf 'hoːɐ   'ʃp'ɪtsə bə'moːst'ɐ   'tʰanən   kʰrɛçtstʰ,
ein Rab' auf hoher Spitze bemooster Tannen krächzt,
a   raven on high   point of mossy   fir-tree caws,
(a raven is cawing at the top of a tall, moss-covered fir-tree,)

ʊnt'   lɪn deːɐ 'fɛlzənrɪtsə   laͻen 'rɪŋəltʰͻøp'çən   lɛçtstʰ.
und in der Felsenritze   ein Ringeltäubchen ächzt.
and in the rock- crevice a   ring- dove   moans.
(and in a crevice of the rocks a ring-dove is moaning.)

viː   zɪç   das hɛrts lɛɐ'vaͻet'ɐt' lɪm   'lɛŋən, 'dɪçt'ən valt'!
Wie sich das Herz erweitert   im   engen, dichten Wald!
How itself the heart expands   in the close, dense   forest!
(How the heart expands in the close, dense forest!)

den 'lͻ:dən 'tʰryːp'zɪn   'haͻet'ɐt   deːɐ 'tʰrɑͻt'ə 'ʃat'ən   balt'.
den öden Trübsinn heitert   der traute Schatten bald.
the bleak depression cheers up the   cozy   shadow   soon.
(The cozy shade soon cheers away any bleak depression.)

kʰaͻen lyːbɐ'leːgnɐ   'ʃp'ɛːɐ(r)   lɛɐ'fɔrʃt'   hiːɐ 'maͻenə ʃp'uːɐ;
Kein überleg'ner Späher   erforscht   hier meine Spur;
No   superior   prying eye investigates here my   trace;
(The prying eye of no superior will be investigating my traces here;)

hiːɐ bɪn lɪç fraͻe lʊnt' 'neːɐ   deːɐ/deːr 'laͻenfalt' lʊnt' na'tʰuːɐ.
hier bin ich frei und   näher der   Einfalt   und Natur.   [*GA, 1st version:* **Ich bin hier**]
here am I   free   and   nearer to the   simplicity and   nature.
(here I am free, and nearer to simplicity and to nature.)

340

o: bli:p'   [ve:ɐ̯] lıç fɔn den 'kʰɛt'ən dɛs 'vɛlt'gəvırəs   fraͤ!
O blieb' [*Peters, 2nd version:* **wär**] **ich von den Ketten des Weltgewirres   frei!**
Oh, might remain   [were] I   from the chains of the world-confusion free!
(Oh, if only I might remain free from the chains of wordly confusion!)

kʰœnt' lıç tsu: di:ɐ̯ mıç   'rɛt'ən, du: 'tʰrɑot'ə   [gə'li:p't'ə] zi:də'laͤ!
könnt' ich zu dir mich retten, du traute [*Peters, 2nd:* **geliebte**] **Siedelei!**
Could I   to   you myself rescue, you dear   [beloved] hermitage!
(If I could only escape to you, my beloved hermitage!)   ["*sich retten*" = to escape]

fro:, das lıç dem   gə'kʰrɑozə   [gə'kʰrɑozə] dɛs 'mɛnʃənʃvarms   lɛnt''vıç,
froh, dass ich dem   Gebrause [*Peters, 1st:* **Gekrause**] **des Menschenschwarms entwich,**
glad, that I   from the roaring   [frizzling?] of the human   swarm   fled,
(Glad that I fled the noise of the human swarm,)

bɑot'   lıç hi:ɐ̯/hi:r 'laͤnə 'kʰlɑozə   fy:ɐ̯ 'li:p'çən   lʊnt' fy:ɐ̯ mıç.
baut'   ich hier   eine Klause   für Liebchen und für mich.
would build I   here   a   hermitage for sweetheart and for me.
(I would build here a hermitage for my sweetheart and for me.)

[Schubert wrote three different settings of this poem, the first as a quartet for male voices titled
"*Lob der Einsamkeit*" (In Praise of Solitude); in the Peters edition of the first version for *solo*
voice four of the original six verses of the poem are printed (the second and third are missing), of
the second version only three (the first, fifth, and sixth). The *Gesamtausgabe* includes all six.]

di lɛnt'tsʏk'ʊŋ lan 'lɑora
Die Entzückung an Laura
Delight in Laura

posthumously published [composed 1816, 1817] (poem by Friedrich von Schiller)

'lɑora, 'ly:bɐ 'di:zə vɛlt tsu: 'flʏçt'ən   vɛ:n   lıç
Laura, über diese Welt zu flüchten wähn' ich,
Laura, above this   world to   take flight imagine I
(Laura, I imagine that I am taking flight above this world,)

mıç   lın 'hıməlsmaͤənglants   tsu: 'lıçt'ən, vɛn daͤn blık' lın 'maͤnəm 'blık'ə flımtʰ;
mich in Himmelsmaienglanz   zu lichten, wenn dein Blick in meinem Blicke flimmt;
myself in heaven- May- radiance to   lighten, when your glance in   my   gaze   glistens;
(bathing myself in the heavenly radiance of May, when your glance glistens before my eyes;)

'ɛ:t'ɐlʏft'ə tʰrɔɪ̯m lıç, 'laͤntsuzɑogən, vɛn   maͤn bılt' lın 'daͤnɐ 'zanft'ən 'lɑogən
ätherlüfte träum' ich, einzusaugen,   wenn mein Bild in deiner sanften Augen
ethereal air dream I   to imbibe,   when my   image in your gentle eyes'
(I dream that I inhale ethereal air when my image is swimming in...)

'hıməlblɑoəm   'ʃp'i:gəl ʃvımtʰ.   'laͤɐkʰlaŋ lɑos pʰara'di:zəs 'fɛrnən,
himmelblauem Spiegel schwimmt. Leierklang aus Paradieses Fernen,
heaven-blue   mirror swims.   Lyre-sound from paradise's distances,
(the heavenly blue mirror of your gentle eyes. The sound of lyres from far-away paradise,)

ˈharfənʃvʊŋ lɑos ˈlangəneːmɐn ˈʃtˈɛrnən raːz ɪç, lɪn mɑen ˈtʰrʊŋkˈnəs loːɐ̯ ʦuː ʦiːn;
Harfenschwung aus angenehmern Sternen ras' ich, in mein trunknes Ohr zu ziehn;
harp- soaring from more agreeable stars rush I into my intoxicated ear to draw;
(the sound of soaring harps from more agreeable stars I rush to draw into my intoxicated ears;)

ˈmɑenə ˈmuːzə fyːlt di ˈʃɛːfəʃtˈʊndə, vɛn fɔn ˈdɑenəm ˈvɔlʊstˈhɑesən ˈmʊndə
meine Muse fühlt die Schäferstunde, wenn von deinem wollustheissen Munde
my muse feels the lovers' hour, when from your sensual-hot mouth
(my muse senses the hour for lovers when from your sensual, warm mouth)

ˈzɪlbɐtʰøːnə ˈlʊngɛrn fliːn. lamoˈrɛtˈən zeː lɪç ˈflyːgəl ˈʃvɪŋən,
Silbertöne ungern fliehn. Amoretten seh' ich Flügel schwingen,
silver tones reluctantly escape. Cupids see I wings flap,
(silvery tones reluctantly take flight. I see Cupids flap their wings,)

ˈhɪntˈɐ diːɐ̯ di ˈtʰrʊŋkˈnən ˈfɪçtˈən ˈʃpˈrɪŋən, viː fɔn ˈlɔrfəøs ˈzɑetˈənruːf bəˈleːpˈtʰ;
hinter dir die trunknen Fichten springen, wie von Orpheus' Saitenruf belebt;*
behind you the intoxicated fir-trees leap, as by Orpheus's strings-call animated;
(behind you I see the intoxicated fir-trees leap, as if brought to life by the call of Orpheus's lyre;)

ˈraʃɐ ˈrɔlən lʊm mɪç heːɐ̯ di ˈpʰoːlə, vɛn lɪm ˈvɪrbəltʰantsə ˈdɑenə ˈzoːlə
rascher rollen um mich her die Pole, wenn im Wirbeltanze deine Sohle
faster roll around me ... the poles, when in the whirling dance your sole
(the poles revolve around me more swiftly when, in the whirling dance, your sole)

ˈflyçtˈɪç, viː di ˈvɛlə, ˈʃveːpˈtʰ. ˈdɑenə ˈblɪkˈə, vɛn ziː ˈliːbə ˈlɛçəln,
flüchtig, wie die Welle, schwebt. Deine Blicke, wenn sie Liebe lächeln,
fleetingly, as the wave, hovers. Your glances, when they love smile,
(hovers as fleetingly as a wave. Your glances, when they smile love,)

ˈkʰœntˈən ˈleːbən dʊrç den ˈmarmoːɐ̯ ˈfɛçəln, ˈfɛlzənlaːdən ˈpʰʊlzə lɑen;
könnten Leben durch den Marmor fächeln, felsenadern Pulse leihn;
could life through the marble fan, rock- veins pulses lend;
(could fan life into inanimate marble, could lend a pulse to the veins in rock;)

ˈtʰrɔ͜ømə ˈveːɐ̯dən lʊm mɪç heːɐ̯ ʦuː ˈveːzən, kʰan lɪç nuːɐ̯/nuːr lɪn ˈdɑenən ˈlɑogən ˈleːzən,
Träume werden um mich her zu Wesen, kann ich nur in deinen Augen lesen,
dreams become around me ... to being, can I only in your eyes read,
(dreams become reality all around me, if I can just read in your eyes:)

ˈlɑora, ˈlɑora, mɑen!
Laura, Laura, mein!
Laura, Laura, mine!

[*Orpheus, son of Apollo, had the power to move trees and stones with his singing and the sound of his lyre. This beautiful, rapturous (and high-lying!) song was written in 1816; in the following year Schubert attempted to illustrate the various ideas in the poem with greater specificity, but he gave up after two incomplete fragments (which are printed in the *Gesamtausgabe*).]

342

di ˈleːɐ̯də
Die Erde
The Earth

Posthumously published [composed 1817] (poem by Friedrich von Matthisson)

vɛn   zanftˈ lɛntˈtsʏkˈtˈ maen ˈɑogə ziːtˈ, viː ʃøːn   ɪm   lɛnts di ˈleːɐ̯də blyːtʰ;
Wenn sanft entzückt mein Auge sieht, wie schön   im   Lenz die Erde blüht;
When gently enraptured my   eye   sees how beautiful in the spring the earth blossoms;
(When my eyes, gently enraptured, see how beautifully the earth blossoms in the spring;)

viː ˈjeːdəs ˈveːzən ˈangəʃmiːkˈtˈ lan ˈliːrən ˈzeːgənsbrʏstˈən liːkˈtʰ;
wie jedes Wesen angeschmiegt an ihren Segensbrüsten liegt;
how every being   nestled   at her   blessings-breast lies;
(how every created thing lies nestled at her bountiful breast;)

ʊntˈ viː ziː ˈjeːdən ˈzɔøkˈlɪŋ liːpˈtˈ, liːm gɛrn di ˈmɪldə ˈnaːrʊŋ   giːpˈtʰ,
und wie sie jeden Säugling liebt, ihm gern die milde Nahrung   gibt,
and how she each   infant   loves, to it gladly the gentle nourishment gives,
(and how she loves each of her infants and gladly gives it gentle nourishment,)

ʊntˈ zoː ɪn ˈʃtˈeːtˈɐ ˈjuːgəntˈkʰraftˈ hɛrfoːɐ̯brɪŋtˈ, nɛːɐ̯tˈ ʊntˈ ˈvakstˈuːm ʃaftʰ:
und so in steter Jugendkraft hervorbringt, nährt und Wachstum schafft:
and thus in constant youth- strength forth brings, feeds and growth   creates:
(and thus, in constant youthful strength, brings forth, feeds, and creates growth:)

dan fyːl lɪç ˈhoːən ˈbuːzəndraŋ, tsuː ˈryːmən deːn mɪt tʰaːtˈ ʊntˈ zaŋ,
dann fühl' ich hohen Busendrang, zu rühmen den mit Tat und Sang,
then feel I   high bosom-urge to praise Him with deed and song,
(then I feel a great urge in my heart to praise Him with deed and song,)

dɛs ˈvʊndɐfɔl   ˈlalmaxtsruːf   di ˈvaetˈə vɛltˈ zoː ʃøːn   lɛɐ̯ˈʃuːf.
dess wundervoller Allmachtsruf   die weite Welt so schön   erschuf.
whose marvelous   Omnipotence-call the wide world so beautiful created.
(whose miraculous omnipotent word created this vast and so beautiful world.)

[This long-lost song, except for a fragment which itself was lost in 1906, was not discovered until 1969. It was then published in 1970 by Bärenreiter. It is missing, of course, from both the *Gesamtausgabe* and the Peters edition. The poem exists in two very differing versions; the first was titled *Die schöne Erde*; the second, of which Schubert set the first three of five verses, was published under the title *Die Erde*, Schubert's title for the song.]

di lɛɐ̯ˈʃaenʊŋ (ɛɐ̯ˈlɪnərʊŋ)
Die Erscheinung (Erinnerung)
The Apparition (Remembrance)

Op. 108, No. 3 [1815] (Ludwig Kosegarten)

ɪç laːkˈ lɑof ˈgryːnən ˈmatˈən,   lan ˈkʰlaːrɐ ˈkʰvɛlən rantˈ.
Ich lag auf grünen Matten,   an klarer Quellen Rand.
I   lay on green   meadows, at clear   springs' edge.
(I lay in green meadows, at the edge of clear springs.)

miːɐ̯ ˈkʰyːltʼən ˈɛrlənʃatʼən deːɐ̯ ˈvaŋən ˈhae̯sən brantʼ.
Mir kühlten Erlenschatten der Wangen heissen Brand.
Me cooled   alder shadows the   cheeks' hot   burning.
(The shade of alders cooled the hot fire of my cheeks.)

ɪç ˈdaxtʼə   diːs ʊntʼ ˈje̠ːnəs, ʊntʼ ˈtʰrɔɸmtʼə, zanftʼ bəˈtʰryːpʼtʰ,
Ich dachte   dies und jenes, und träumte, sanft betrübt,
I   thought (of) this and that,   and dreamed, gently troubled,

fiːl ˈguːtʼəs ʊntʼ fiːl ˈʃɸːnəs, das ˈdiːzə vɛltʼ nɪçtʼ giːpʼtʰ.
viel Gutes und viel   Schönes, das diese Welt nicht gibt.
much good   and   much beautiful that this   world not   gives.
(of many good and beautiful things that this world does not give.)
        [*poem:* **viel Süsses** (ˈzyːsəs, sweet) **mir** (miːɐ̯, for myself) **und Schönes, was** (vas, which)]

ʊntʼ ziː, dem   hae̯n ɛntʼˈʃveːpʼtʼə lae̯n ˈmɛːkʼtʼlae̯n ˈzɔnənkʰlaːɐ̯.
Und sieh, dem   Hain entschwebte ein Mägdlein   sonnenklar.
And see, from the grove floated   a   maiden   sun- clear.
(And lo! From the grove a maiden came floating in the air, as clear as day.)

ae̯n ˈvae̯sɐ ˈʃlae̯ɐ ˈveːpʼtʼə lʊm liːɐ̯ nʊsˈbrɑo̯nəs haːɐ̯.
Ein weisser Schleier webte   um   ihr nussbraunes Haar.
A   white   veil   fluttered about her nut- brown   hair.

iːɐ̯/iːr ˈlɑo̯gə,   fɔɸçtʼ ʊntʼ ˈʃɪmɐntʼ,   lʊmˈflɔs lɛˈtʰeːrɪʃ blɑo̯.
Ihr Auge,   feucht und schimmernd, umfloss ätherisch Blau.
Her eye [obj.], moist and   shimmering, bathed ethereal   blue [subj.].
(Ethereal blueness bathed her moist and shimmering eyes.)

di ˈvɪmpʼɐn ˈnɛstʼə   ˈflɪmɐnt deːɐ̯ ˈveːmuːtʼ   ˈpʰɛrləntʰɑo̯.
Die Wimpern nässte   flimmernd der Wehmut   Perlentau.
The eyelashes moistened glisteningly the   melancholy's pearl- dew.
(The pearly dew of melancholy glisteningly moistened her eyelashes.)
        [*poem, according to Schochow:* **Die Wimper** (eyelash, singular)]

ae̯n ˈtʰrɑo̯ɐntʼ ˈlɛçəln ˈʃveːpʼtʼə lʊm ˈliːrən ˈzyːsən mʊntʼ.   [ae̯n ˈtʰrɑo̯rɪç ˈlɛçəln]
Ein trauernd Lächeln schwebte um   ihren süssen Mund. [*Peters:* **ein traurig lächeln**]
A   grieving smile   hovered about her   sweet mouth.   [a   sad   smile]
        [*poem, according to Schochow:* **Ein traurend** (ˈtʰrɑo̯rəntʼ) **Lächeln**]

ziː ˈʃɑo̯ɐtʼə,   ziː ˈbeːpʼtʼə. liːɐ̯/iːr ˈlɑo̯gə, ˈtʰreːnənvʊntʼ,
Sie schauerte, sie bebte.   Ihr   Auge, tränenwund,
She shuddered, she trembled. Her   eyes, sore from tears,

iːɐ̯ ˈhɪnʃɑo̯n ˈliːbəszeːnəntʼ, zoː vɛntʼ   lɪç, ˈzuːxtʼə   mɪç.
ihr Hinschaun liebesehnend, so wähnt' ich, suchte   mich.
her gazing,   lovelorn,   so imagined I,   searched for me.
(her lovelorn gaze, so I imagined, was searching for me.)

veːɐ̯ vaːɐ̯, viː lɪç, zoː ˈvɛːnəntʼ, zoː ˈzeːlɪç veːɐ̯, viː lɪç?
Wer war, wie ich, so wähnend, so selig   wer, wie ich?
Who was, as I,   so imagining, so blissful who, as   I?
(Who, imagining as I imagined, was ever as blissful as I?)

ɪç lao͡f, ziː t͡suː lʊmˈfasən! lʊntˈ lax! ziː tʰraːt t͡suˈrʏkʰ.
Ich auf, sie zu umfassen! Und ach! sie trat zurück.
I up, her to embrace! And ah! she stepped back.
(I stood up to embrace her! And, alas, she stepped back.)

ɪç zaː ziː ʃnɛl lɛɐ̯ˈblasən, lʊntˈ ˈtʰryːbɐ vartˈ liːɐ̯ blɪkʰ.
Ich sah sie schnell erblassen,* und trüber ward ihr Blick.
I saw her quickly grow pale, and more troubled became her gaze.
(I saw her quickly grow pale, and her gaze became more troubled.)

[**Peters:* **schneller blassen** (a misprint)]**

ziː zaː mɪç lan zoː ˈlɪnɪç, ziː viːs mɪtˈ ˈliːrə hantˈ
Sie sah mich an so innig, sie wies mit ihrer Hand
She looked me at so fervently, she pointed with her hand
(She looked at me so fervently! She pointed with her hand)

ɛɐ̯ˈhaːbən lʊnt tʰiːfˈzɪnɪç gɛn ˈhɪməl, lʊntˈ fɛɐ̯ˈʃvantˈ.
erhaben und tiefsinnig gen Himmel, und verschwand.
sublimely and thoughtfully toward heaven, and disappeared.

faːɐ̯ voːl, faːɐ̯ voːl, lɛɐ̯ˈʃaenʊŋ! faːɐ̯ voːl! dɪç kʰen lɪç voːl!
Fahr' wohl, fahr' wohl, Erscheinung! Fahr' wohl! Dich kenn' ich wohl!
Fare well, fare well, apparition! Fare well! You know I well!
(Farewell, farewell, apparition! Farewell! I know you well!)

ʊnt ˈdaenəs ˈvɪŋkˈəs ˈmaenʊŋ fɛɐ̯ˈʃtˈeː lɪç, viː lɪç zɔl!
Und deines Winkes Meinung versteh' ich, wie ich soll!
And your signal's meaning understand I, as I should!
(And I understand the meaning of your signal, as I should!)

voːl fyːɐ̯ di t͡saetˈ gəˈʃiːdən, laentˈ lʊns laen ˈʃøːnrəs bantˈ.
"Wohl für die Zeit geschieden, eint uns ein schönres Band.
"Indeed for the time separated, unites us a more beautiful bond.
("Though we are separated in the realm of time, a more beautiful bond unites us.)

hoːx ˈdroːbən, nɪçtˈ hiːˈniːdən, hatˈ liːpˈ liːɐ̯ ˈfaːtˈɐlantˈ. [hiːɐ̯ ˈniːdən]
Hoch droben, nicht hienieden, hat Lieb' ihr Vaterland." [*GA:* **hier nieden]**
High above, not here below, has love its homeland." [here below]
(Love has its home high above, not here below.") [*variant spelling:* **hinieden** (*poem*)]

[Schubert titled his first draft *Erinnerung: Die Erscheinung*, hence the variant titles. The apparition appears to tell the poet that ideal love is found not in this world but only in the next. The music is reminiscent of *Die Forelle*, though the two poems have nothing in common at all.]

di ˈleːɐ̯stˈə ˈliːbə
Die erste Liebe
First Love

Posthumously published [composed 1815] (poem by Johann Georg Fellinger)

di ˈleːɐ̯stˈə ˈliːbə fʏlt das hɛrt͡s mɪtˈ ˈzeːnən naːx ˈlaenəm ˈlʊnbəkʰantˈən ˈgaestˈɐlandə,
Die erste Liebe füllt das Herz mit Sehnen nach einem unbekannten Geisterlande,
The first love fills the heart with longing for an unknown spirit- land,
(First love fills the heart with longing for some unknown realm of the spirit,)

di 'zeːlə 'gɑɔkˈəltˈ ɑn dem 'leːbənsrandə, lʊntˈ 'zyːsə 'veːmuːtˈ 'lɛtsətˈ zɪç lɪn 'tʰrɛːnən:
die Seele gaukelt an dem Lebensrande, und süsse Wehmut letzet sich in Tränen:
the soul juggles at the edge of life, and sweet melancholy comforts itself in tears:

daː vaxtˈ lɛs lɑɔf, das 'foːɐɡəfyːl dɛs 'ʃøːnən, du: ʃɑɔst di 'gœtˈɪn
Da wacht es auf, das Vorgefühl des Schönen, du schaust die Göttin
Then wakes it up, the premonition of the beautiful, you see the goddess
(Then the premonition of beauty awakens; you see the goddess)

lɪn dem 'lɪçtˈgəvandə, gə'ʃlʊŋən zɪnt dɛs 'glɑɔbəns 'laɛzə 'bandə; lʊntˈ 'tʰaːgə
in dem Lichtgewande, geschlungen sind des Glaubens leise Bande; und Tage
in the dress of light, entwined are the faith's quiet bonds; and days
(in the dress of light; the quiet bonds of faith are tied; and days)

'riːzəln hɪn lɑɔf 'liːbəstˈøːnən. du: ziːstˈ nuːɐ zi: la'laɛn lɪm 'viːdɐʃaɛnə, di 'hɔldə,
rieseln hin auf Liebestönen. Du siehst nur sie allein im Widerscheine, die Holde,
trickle by on love- tones. You see only her alone in the reflection, the lovely one,
(trickle by to the tones of love. You see only her alone, reflected everywhere, the lovely one,)
[*Peters:* **Wiederscheine** (same pronunciation, same meaning, less usual)]

deːɐ du: gants dɪç 'hɪngəgeːbən, nuːɐ zi: dʊrçʃveːpˈt 'daɛnəs 'daːzaɛns 'rɔømə.
der du ganz dich hingegeben, nur sie durchschwebt deines Daseins Räume.
to whom you wholely yourself gave away, only she floats through your existence's spaces.
(to whom you have given yourself completely, only she floats through the spaces of your being.)
[*GA:* **durchwebt** (dʊrçveːpˈt, weaves through); *poem:* **durchschwebet** (dʊrçʃveːbət)]

zi: 'lɛçəlt diːɐ he'rapˈ fɔm 'gɔltˈgəzɔømə, vɛn 'ʃtˈɪlə 'lɪçtˈɐ(r)
Sie lächelt dir herab vom Goldgesäume, wenn stille Lichter
She smiles to you down from the gold-fringe, when quiet lights
(She smiles down to you from the golden fringes of heaven when quiet lights)

lan den 'hɪməl 'ʃveːbən, deːɐ/deːr 'leːɐdə 'juːbəlst du: : zi: lɪst di 'maɛnə!
an den Himmeln schweben, der Erde jubelst du: Sie ist die Meine!
in the heavens hover, to the earth cry out joyfully you: "She is the mine!"
(are hovering in the sky; you cry out joyfully to the earth: "She is mine!")

[The *Gesamtausgabe* prints the song in the original key of C; it was first published in B flat, the key of the Peters edition. Schubert's setting is through-composed and musically inventive.]

di lɛɐ̯'vartˈʊŋ
Die Erwartung
Anticipation

Op. 116 [1816] (Friedrich von Schiller)

høːr ɪç das 'pfœrtˈçən nɪçtˈ 'geːən? hatˈ nɪçt deːɐ 'riːgəl gə'kʰlɪrtʰ?
Hör' ich das Pförtchen nicht gehen? Hat nicht der Riegel geklirrt?
Hear I the little gate not move? Has not the bolt clanked?
(Don't I hear the little gate creak? Didn't the bolt just clank?) [*1st version:* **hört'** (høːɐtˈ) heard]

naen, lɛs vaːɐ̯ dɛs 'vɪndəs 'veːən, deːɐ̯ dʊrç di 'pʰapˈəln ʃvɪrtʰ.
Nein, es war des Windes Wehen, der durch die Pappeln schwirrt.
No, it was the wind's blowing, which through the poplars hums.
(No, it was wind blowing, humming through the poplars.)

[*1st version + poem:* **durch diese** ('diːzə, these) **Pappeln**]

o 'ʃmʏkˈə dɪç, duː 'gryːnbəlɑopˈtʰəs dax, duː zɔlst
O schmücke dich, du grünbelaubtes Dach, du sollst
Oh adorn yourself, you green-foliaged roof, you shall
(Adorn yourself, you green roof of leaves, you shall)

di 'lanmuːtˈʃtˈraːləndə lɛmˈpfaŋən! liːɐ̯ 'tsvaegə, bɑotˈ laen 'ʃatˈəndəs gə'max,
die Anmutstrahlende empfangen! Ihr Zweige, baut ein schattendes Gemach,
the grace- radiating one receive! You branches, build a shading room,
(receive the woman who radiates grace! You branches, build a shady room,)

mɪtˈ 'hɔldɐ naxtˈ ziː 'haemlɪç tsuː lʊm'faŋən! lʊntˈ lal liːɐ̯ 'ʃmaeçəllʏftˈə,
mit holder Nacht sie heimlich zu umfangen! und all ihr Schmeichellüfte,
with lovely night her secretly to encircle! And all you caressing breezes,
(to encircle her secretly with lovely night! And all you caressing breezes,)

'veːɐ̯dətˈ vax lʊntˈ ʃɛrtstˈ lʊntˈ ʃpˈiːltˈ lʊm 'liːrə 'roːzənvaŋən,
werdet wach und scherzt und spielt um ihre Rosenwangen,
become awake and have fun and play around her rose- cheeks,
(wake up, have fun, and play around her rosy cheeks)

vən 'zaenə 'ʃøːnə 'bʏrdə, laeçtˈ bə'veːkˈtʰ, deːɐ̯ 'tsaːɐ̯tˈə fuːs tsʊm zɪts deːɐ̯ 'liːbə tʰrɛːkˈtʰ.
wenn seine schöne Bürde, leicht bewegt, der zarte Fuss zum Sitz der Liebe trägt.
when its lovely burden, lightly moved, the delicate foot to the seat of love carries.
(when her delicate foot, lightly moving, carries its lovely burden to the seat of love.)

'ʃtˈɪlə! vas ʃlʏpft dʊrç di 'hɛkˈən 'raʃəlntˈ mɪtˈ 'laeləndəm lɑof?
Stille! was schlüpft durch die Hecken raschelnd mit eilendem Lauf?
Quiet! What slips through the hedge rustling with hurrying pace?
(Quiet! What is slipping through the hedge with a rustling sound and a hurried pace?)

naen, lɛs 'ʃɔøçtˈə nuːɐ̯ deːɐ̯ 'ʃrɛkˈən lɑos dem bʊʃ den 'foːgəl lɑof.
Nein, es scheuchte nur der Schrecken aus dem Busch den Vogel auf.
No, there scared just the fright out of the bush the bird up.
(No, a sudden fright just scared a bird out of the bush.)

oː 'lœʃə 'daenə 'fakˈəl, tʰaːkˈ! hɛɐ̯'foːɐ̯, duː 'gaestˈgə naxtʰ, mɪt 'daenəm
O lösche deine Fackel, Tag! hervor, du geist'ge Nacht, mit deinem
Oh extinguish your torch, day! Come forth, you spiritual night, with your

'hɔldən 'ʃvaegən! braetˈ lʊm lʊns heːɐ̯ den 'pʰʊrpˈʊrroːtˈən floːɐ̯,
holden Schweigen! breit' um uns her den purpurroten Flor,
lovely silence! Spread around us hither the purple gauze,
(lovely silence! Spread your purple veil all around us,)

ʊm'ʃpˈɪnə lʊns mɪtˈ gə'haemnɪsfɔlən 'tsvaegən! deːɐ̯ 'liːbə 'vɔnə
umspinne uns mit geheimnisvollen Zweigen! der Liebe Wonne
entwine us with secretive branches! The love's rapture
(entwine us with secretive branches! Love's rapture) [*poem:* **umspinn'**]

fliːt dɛs ˈlɑ͜oʃes loːɐ̯, ziː fliːt dɛs ˈʃtˈraːləs ˈʊnbəʃa͜ednən ˈtsɔʏ͜gən;
flieht des Lauschers Ohr, sie flieht des Strahles unbescheid'nen Zeugen;
flees the eavesdropper's ear, it flees the ray's immodest witness;
(flees from the eavesdropper's ear, it flees from a ray of light, that immodest witness;)

nuːɐ̯ ˈhɛspˈɐ, deːɐ̯ fɛɐ̯ˈʃviːgənə, laˈla͜en darf ʃtˈɪl heːɐ̯ˈblɪkˈəntˈ liːɐ̯ fɛɐ̯ˈtʰrɑ͜otˈɐ za͜en.
nur Hesper, der Verschwiegene, allein darf still herblickend ihr Vertrauter sein.
only Hesperus, the silent one, alone may quietly hither-looking its confidant be.
(only Hesperus alone, the silent evening star, may quietly look on and be its confidant.)

riːf lɛs fɔn ˈfɛrnə nɪçtˈ ˈla͜ezə, ˈflʏstˈəndən ˈʃtˈɪmən gla͜eç?
Rief es von ferne nicht leise, flüsternden Stimmen gleich?
Called it from afar not softly, whispering voices like?
(Was that not a soft call from afar, like whispering voices?)

na͜en, deːɐ̯ ʃvaːn lɪsts, deːɐ̯ di ˈkʰra͜ezə tsiːt dʊrç den ˈzɪlbɐtʰa͜eç.
Nein, der Schwan ist's, der die Kreise zieht durch den Silberteich.
No, the swan is it, that the circles traces through the silver pond.
(No, it is a swan, tracing circles over the silver pond.) [*poem:* **ziehet** (ˈtsiːət)]

ma͜en loːɐ̯/loːr lʊmˈtʰøːntˈ la͜en harmoˈniːənflʊs, deːɐ̯ ˈʃpˈrɪŋkʰvɛl fɛltˈ mɪtˈ
Mein Ohr umtönt ein Harmonienfluss, der Springquell fällt mit
My ear around-sounds a harmonies- river, the fountain falls with
(A stream of harmonies resounds around my ears, the jet of water in the fountain falls with)

ˈlangəneːməm ˈrɑ͜oʃən, di ˈbluːmə na͜ekˈtˈ zɪç ba͜e dɛs ˈvɛstˈəs kʰʊs,
angenehmem Rauschen, die Blume neigt sich bei des Westes Kuss,
pleasant murmuring, the flower bends itself at the west wind's kiss,
(a pleasant murmur, the flowers bend to the kiss of the west wind,)

ʊntˈ ˈlalə ˈveːzən zeː lɪç ˈvɔnə ˈtʰɑ͜oʃən, di ˈtʰrɑ͜obə vɪŋkˈtˈ,
und alle Wesen seh' ich Wonne tauschen, die Traube winkt,
and all living things see I joy exchange: the grape beckons
(and I see all living things sharing joy with each other: the grape beckons,)

di ˈpfɪrʃə tsʊm gəˈnʊs, diː ˈlʏpˈɪç ˈʃvɛləntˈ ˈhɪntˈɐ ˈblɛtˈən ˈlɑ͜oʃən,
die Pfirsche zum Genuss, die üppig schwellend hinter Blättern lauschen,
the peach to the enjoyment, which luxuriantly swelling behind leaves listen,
(inviting the peach to pleasure, both, luxuriantly swelling, listen behind leaves,)
[*"die Pfirsche"* (obs.) = *"der Pfirsich"* (deːɐ̯ ˈpfɪrzɪç) = the peach]

di lʊftˈ, gəˈtʰɑ͜oxtˈ lɪn deːɐ̯ gəˈvʏrtsə fluːt, ˈtʰrɪŋkˈtˈ fɔn deːɐ̯ ˈha͜esən ˈvaŋə miːɐ̯ di gluːtʰ.
die Luft, getaucht in der Gewürze Flut, trinkt von der heissen Wange mir die Glut.
the air, immersed in the spices' stream, drinks from the hot cheek of me the fire.
(the air, immersed in the stream of spicy scents, drinks the fire from my hot cheeks.)

høːr ɪç nɪçt ˈtʰrɪtˈə lɛɐ̯ˈʃalən? rɑ͜oʃts nɪçt den ˈlɑ͜opˈgaŋ daˈheːɐ̯? [na͜en]
Hör' ich nicht Tritte erschallen? Rauscht's nicht den Laubgang daher? [*poem:* **Nein,**]
Hear I not steps resounding? Rustles it not the foliage-walk from there? [No,]
(Don't I hear the sound of steps? Isn't something rustling the foliage that arches over the walk?)

di frʊxt‘ lɪst dɔrt‘ gəˈfalən, fɔn deːɐ̯/deːr ˈlaɛgnən ˈfʏlə ʃveːɐ̯.
Die Frucht ist dort gefallen, von der eig'nen Fülle schwer.
The fruit has there fallen, with the own fullness heavy.
(A fruit has fallen there, heavy with its own ripeness.) [*1st version:* **von ihrer** (ˈiːrɐ(r), its) **eignen**]

dɛs ˈtʰagəs ˈflamənlaʊ̯gə ˈzɛlbɐ brɪçt‘ lɪn ˈzyːsəm ˈtʰoːt‘, lʊnt‘ ˈzaɛnə ˈfarbən
Des Tages Flammenauge selber bricht in süssem Tod, und seine Farben
The day's flame- eye itself breaks in sweet death, and its colors
(The flaming eye of day itself is dimmed in sweet death, and its colors)

ˈblasən; kʰyːn ˈlœfnən zɪç lɪm ˈhɔldən ˈdɛmɐlɪçt di ˈkʰɛlçə ʃoːn,
blassen; kühn öffnen sich im holden Dämmerlicht die Kelche schon,
fade; boldly open themselves in the lovely twilight the chalices already,
(fade; already, in the lovely twilight, the flowers boldly open their chalices,)

diː ˈzaɛnə ˈgluːt‘ən ˈhasən. ʃt‘ɪl heːp‘t deːɐ̯ moːnt‘ zaɛn ˈʃt‘raːlənt‘ ˈlangəzɪçtʰ,
die seine Gluten hassen. Still hebt der Mond sein strahlend Angesicht,
which its fires hate. Quietly lifts the moon its beaming face,
(which hate the heat of the day. Quietly the moon lifts its beaming face,)

di vɛlt tsɛɐ̯ˈʃmɪltst‘ lɪn ˈruːɪç ˈgroːsə ˈmasən, deːɐ̯ ˈgʏrt‘əl lɪst‘
die Welt zerschmilzt in ruhig grosse Massen, der Gürtel ist
the world melts away into calmly big masses, the girdle is

fɔn ˈjeːdəm raɛts gəˈløːst‘, lʊnt‘ ˈlaləs ˈʃøːnə tsaɛk‘t‘ zɪç miːɐ̯/miːr lɛnt‘ˈbløːstʰ.
von jedem Reiz gelöst, und alles Schöne zeigt sich mir entblösst.
from every charm loosened, and everything beautiful shows itself to me naked.
(loosened from every charm, and everything beautiful reveals itself to me in its nakedness.)

zeː lɪç nɪçts ˈvaɛsəs dɔrt‘ ˈʃɪmɐn? glɛntsts nɪçt‘ viː ˈzaɛdnəs gəˈvant‘?
Seh' ich nichts Weisses dort schimmern? glänzt's nicht wie seid'nes Gewand?
See I nothing white there shimmering? Gleams it not like silken garment?
(Don't I see something white shimmering there? Doesn't it gleam like a silk garment?)

naɛn, lɛs lɪst deːɐ̯ ˈzɔ̷ɔlə ˈflɪmɐn lan deːɐ̯ ˈdʊŋk‘əln ˈtʰaksʊsvant‘. oː ˈzeːnənt‘ hɛrts,
Nein, es ist der Säule Flimmern an der dunkeln Taxuswand. O sehnend Herz,
No, it is the column's glimmering at the dark yew- wall. O yearning heart,
(No, it is the glimmer of the column against the dark wall of yew trees. O yearning heart,)

[*variant (Shochow):* **dunklen** (ˈdʊŋk‘lən)]

lɛɐ̯ˈgœtsə dɪç nɪçt‘ meːɐ̯, mɪt‘ ˈzyːsən ˈbɪldən ˈveːzənloːs tsuː ˈʃp‘iːlən! deːɐ̯/deːr larm,
ergötze dich nicht mehr, mit süssen Bildern wesenlos zu spielen! Der Arm,
amuse yourself not more with sweet images insubstantially to play! The arm,
(amuse yourself no longer by playing with sweet, insubstantial images! The arm)

deːɐ̯ ziː lʊmˈfasən vɪl, lɪst‘ leːɐ̯, kʰaɛn ˈʃat‘ənglʏk kʰan ˈdiːzən ˈbuːzən ˈkʰyːlən.
der sie umfassen will, ist leer, kein Schattenglück kann diesen Busen kühlen.
that her to embrace wants, is empty, no shadow- happiness can this bosom cool.
(that wants to embrace her is empty, and no mere *shadow* of happiness can cool this breast.)

oː ˈfyːrə miːɐ̯ di ˈleːbəndə daˈheːɐ̯, las ˈiːrə hant, di ˈtseːɐ̯t'lɪçə, mɪç ˈfyːlən!
O führe mir die Lebende daher, lass ihre Hand, die zärtliche, mich fühlen!
Oh lead to me the living one hither, let her hand, the delicate, me feel!
(Oh lead the living woman to me here, let me feel her delicate hand,)

[*Peters:* **die Liebende** (ˈliːbəndə, loving one) **daher**]

den ˈʃat'ən nuːɐ̯ fɔn ˈiːrəs ˈmant'əls zaͦom ʊnt' ɪn das ˈleːbən t'rɪt deːɐ̯ ˈhoːlə t'raͦom.
den Schatten nur von ihres Mantels Saum und in das Leben tritt der hohle Traum.
the shadow just of her cloak's hem, and into the life steps the hollow dream.
(let me feel just the shadow of the hem of her cloak — and the hollow dream will step into life.)

ʊnt' laes, viː laͦos ˈhɪmlɪʃən ˈhøːən, di ˈʃt'ʊndə des ˈɡlʏk'əs ɛɐ̯ˈʃaent',
Und leis', wie aus himmlischen Höhen, die Stunde des Glückes erscheint,
And softly, as from heavenly heights, the hour of the happiness appears,
(And softly, as if from heavenly heights, the hour of happiness arrives:)

zoː vaːɐ̯ ziː ɡəˈnaːt', ˈʊnɡəzeːən, ʊnt' ˈvɛk't'ə mɪt' ˈkʰʏsən den frɔͦønt'.
so war sie genaht, ungesehen, und weckte mit Küssen den Freund.
so had she approached, unseen, and awakened with kisses the friend.
(so she had come near, unseen, and she awakened her friend with kisses.)

[Schiller is waiting for his beloved, Charlotte von Lengefeld, in ecstatic anticipation; again and again he hears some tiny sound and imagines that she is coming, but each time he is mistaken. Finally he gives up and falls asleep. She awakens him with a kiss. Out of this long poem Schubert made a sort of cantata, in which recitative alternates with varied and quite lovely lyrical movements. Schubert revised this early work for publication near the end of his life; except for a longer ending, repeating the last four lines of the poem, the main modification was to transpose certain sections down a half or a whole tone, thus bringing the end of the cantata back to the key of its beginning (the original version has been published by Bärenreiter in *Ausgewählte Lieder*).]

di foˈrɛlə
Die Forelle
The Trout

Op. 32 [1817] (Christian Daniel Schubart)

ɪn ˈlaenəm ˈbɛçlaen ˈhɛlə, da ˈʃɔs ɪn ˈfroːɐ̯(r) laͦel
In einem Bächlein helle, da schoss in froher Eil
in a brooklet clear, there shot in happy haste
(In a clear little brook, in happy haste,..)

di ˈlaͦonɪʃə foˈrɛlə foˈryːbɐ viː laͦen pfaͦel. [*poem:* **die launige** (ˈlaͦonɪɡə, droll) **Forelle**]
die launische Forelle vorüber wie ein Pfeil.
the capricious trout past like an arrow.
(...the capricious trout shot past like an arrow.)

ɪç ʃt'ant' lan deːm ɡəˈʃt'aːdə ʊnt' zaː ɪn ˈzyːsɐ ruː
Ich stand an dem Gestade und sah in süsser Ruh
I stood on the bank and watched in sweet tranquillity

des ˈmʊnt'ɐn ˈfɪʃlaens ˈbaːdə ɪm ˈkʰlaːrən ˈbɛçlaen tsuː. [*poem:* **Fisches** (ˈfɪʃəs, fish's)]
des muntern Fischleins Bade im klaren Bächlein zu.
the cheerful little fish's bath in the clear brooklet. ["*sah...zu,*" (from *zusehen*) = watched]

aen 'fɪʃɐ   mɪt deːɐ̯/deːr 'ruːt'ə voːl   lan dem 'luːfɐ ʃt'ant',
Ein Fischer   mit der   Rute wohl   an dem Ufer stand,
A   fisherman with the   rod   to be sure on the   bank   stood,
(To be sure, a fisherman with his rod stood on the bank)

unt' zaː mɪt' 'kʰalt'əm 'bluːt'ə viː zɪç   das 'fɪʃlaen   vant'.
und sah mit kaltem   Blute wie sich das Fischlein wand.
and saw with cold   blood   how itself the little fish turned.
(and saw with cold blood how the little fish turned this way and that.)

zoː laŋ   dem 'vasɐ   'hɛlə,   zoː daxt' lɪç, nɪçt' gə'brɪçt',
So lang   dem Wasser Helle,   so dacht   ich, nicht gebricht,
As long as to the water   clearness, so thought I,   not   is lacking,
(As long as the water is not lacking in clearness , so I thought,)

                    ["*gebricht*" from "*gebrechen*" (with dative) = to lack, be wanting]

zoː fɛŋt'   leːɐ̯ di fo'rɛlə mɪt' 'zaenɐ(r) 'laŋəl   nɪçtʰ.
so fängt er die Forelle mit seiner   Angel   nicht.
so catches he the trout   with his   fishing tackle not.
(for so long he will not catch the trout with his fishing tackle.)

dɔx 'lɛnt'lɪç vart   dem 'diːbə di tsaet' tsuː laŋ.   leːɐ̯ maxt
Doch endlich ward dem Diebe die Zeit zu   lang. Er macht
But finally became for the thief the time too   long. He makes
(But finally the wait became too long for the thief. ...)

                    [*poem:* **Doch plötzlich war** ('pʰlœt̯slɪç vaːɐ̯, suddenly was) **dem Diebe**]

das 'bɛçlaen 't'ʏk'ɪʃ   't'ryːbə, lunt' leː   lɪç lɛs gə'daxtʰ,
das Bächlein tückisch   trübe, und eh   ich es gedacht,
the brooklet maliciously muddy, and before I   it thought,
(He maliciously makes the brooklet muddy, and, before I knew it,)

zoː 'tsʊk't'ə 'zaenə 'ruːt'ə, das 'fɪʃlaen   'tsap'əlt' dran,
so zuckte   seine Rute, das Fischlein zappelt   dran,
so   jerked   his   rod,   the little fish flapped   at (the end of) it,
(his rod gave a jerk and the little fish was soon flapping from the end of it;)

ʊnt' lɪç mɪt' 'reːgəm 'bluːt'ə zaː   di bə't'roːgnə   lan.
und ich mit regem Blute sah   die Betrogne   an.
and I   with agitated blood looked the deceived one at.
(and I with agitated blood looked at the cheated fish.)

[I was watching a trout having a good time in a clear stream. There was also a fisherman
watching and waiting. As long as the water stays clear, I thought, the clever fish will not be
fooled by the bait. But the impatient fisherman maliciously muddied up the stream. The next
thing I knew, the trout was flapping from the end of his fishing rod, and I, resenting the
unfairness, looked at the poor deceived fish with pity.... The accompaniment to Schubert's
famous song portrays the darting movements of the fish, as he flicks his tail to turn this way and
that. The original poem includes some lines not set to music by Schubert: a warning to young
girls to think of the trout when they are at "the golden spring of self-assured youth." They should
hurry away from the seductive bait before they come to grief like the unsuspecting trout.]

di ˈfrøːlɪçkʰaetʰ
Die Fröhlichkeit
Cheerfulness

Posthumously published [composed 1815] (poem by Martin Josef Prandstetter)

vɛs ˈlaːdɐn ˈlaeçtˈəs bluːt dʊrçʃpˈrɪŋt, deːɐ̯/deːr lɪstˈ laen ˈraeçɐ man;
Wess' Adern leichtes Blut durchspringt, der ist ein reicher Mann;
Whose veins light blood through-leaps, he is a rich man;
(The man through whose veins light blood is leaping is a rich man;)

ɑox ˈkʰaenə ˈgɔldnən ˈkʰɛtˈən tsvɪŋtˈ liːm fʊrçtˈ lʊntˈ ˈhɔfnʊŋ lan.
auch keine goldnen Ketten zwingt ihm Furcht und Hoffnung an.
also no gold chains [obj.] forces to him fear and hope [double subj.] on.
(also fear and hope do not force golden chains onto him.)

dɛn ˈfrøːlɪçkʰaetˈ gəˈlaetˈətˈ liːn bɪs lan laen ˈzanftˈəs graːpˈ
Denn Fröhlichkeit geleitet ihn bis an ein sanftes Grab
For cheerfulness leads him until to a gentle grave
(For cheerfulness leads him...)

voːl dʊrç laen ˈlaŋəs ˈleːbən hɪn lan ˈliːrəm ˈtsɑobɐʃtˈaːpˈ.
wohl durch ein langes Leben hin an ihrem Zauberstab.
probably through a long life hence at its magic wand.
(with its magic wand through a long life, probably, and eventually to a gentle death.)

mɪtˈ ˈlalən ˈmɛnʃən ˈlɑosgəzøːntˈ, liːpˈtˈ leːɐ̯/leːr lals ˈbryːdɐ ziː:
Mit allen Menschen ausgesöhnt, liebt er als Brüder sie:
With all human beings reconciled, loves he as brothers them:
(Reconciled with all human beings, he loves them as brothers:)

deːɐ̯ ˈraxə ˈhɛlə ˈflamə brɛntˈ lɪn ˈzaenəm ˈhɛrtsən niː.
der Rache helle Flamme brennt in seinem Herzen nie.
the revenge's bright flame burns in his heart never.
(the bright flame of revenge never burns in his heart.)

dɛn ˈfrɔøntˈʃaftˈ lɪsts, diː das lʊmflɪçtˈ mɪtˈ ˈlarmən ˈloːnə tsaːl:
Denn Freundschaft ist's, die das umflicht mit Armen ohne Zahl:
For friendship is it, which that (heart [obj.]) weaves about with arms without number:
(For it is friendship that embraces his heart with numberless arms:)

drʊm hastˈ leːɐ̯ ˈzaenə ˈfaendə nɪçtˈ lʊntˈ kʰɛntˈ ziː nɪçtˈ laenˈmaːl.
drum hasst er seine Feinde nicht und kennt sie nicht einmal.
therefore hates he his enemies not and knows them not even.
(therefore he does not hate his enemies, and does not even know them.)

voˈhɪn zaen ˈmʊntˈrɐ blɪkˈ zɪç kʰeːɐ̯tˈ, lɪstˈ ˈlaləs ʃøːn lʊntˈ guːtʰ,
Wohin sein muntrer Blick sich kehrt, ist alles schön und gut,
Wherever his cheerful gaze itself turns, is everything beautiful and good,
(Wherever he turns his cheerful gaze, everything is beautiful and good,)

ɪstˀ ˈlaləs haɛl ʊntˀ ˈliːbənsveːɐ̯tˀ ʊntˀ ˈfrøːlɪç viː zaɛn muːtʰ.
ist alles heil und liebenswert   und fröhlich wie sein Mut.
is all well and worthy of love and cheerful as his spirit.
(everything is well and worthy of love and as cheerful as his spirit.)

fyːɐ̯/fyːr liːn nuːɐ̯ vɪrtˀ   baɛ ˈzɔnənʃaɛn   di vɛlt ʦʊm pʰaraˈdiːs,
Für ihn nur wird   bei Sonnenschein die Welt zum Paradies,
For him only becomes by sunshine   the world to the paradise,
(Only for him does the world become a paradise when the sun is shining,)

ɪstˀ kʰlaːɐ̯ deːɐ̯ bax, di ˈkʰvɛlə raɛn, ʊntˀ liːɐ̯ gəˈmʊrməl zyːs.
ist klar der Bach, die Quelle rein, und ihr Gemurmel süss.
is clear the brook, the spring pure, and its murmur   sweet.
(only for him is the brook clear, the spring pure, or its murmur sweet.)

ɪn ˈleːvɪç ˈvɛksəlndɐ gəˈʃtˀaltˀ laːpˀtˀ liːn di ˈbluːmənfluːɐ̯,
In ewig wechselnder Gestalt labt   ihn die Blumenflur,
In eternally changing form   refreshes him the flower- meadow,
(The flower-covered meadow refreshes him in its eternally changing forms,)

ʊntˀ nuːɐ̯ fyːɐ̯/fyːr liːn vɪrtˀ ˈnɪmɐ(r) lalt di ˈhaɛligə naˈtʰuːɐ̯.
und nur für   ihn wird nimmer alt die heilige Natur.
and only for   him grows never old the holy   nature.
(and only for him does holy nature never grow old.)

drʊm   veːr ɪç raɛç, viː ˈkʰrøːzʊs vaːɐ̯/vaːr, ʊntˀ ˈmɛçtˀɪç ˈloːbənˈdraɛn,
Drum   wär' ich reich, wie Krösus war,   und mächtig obendrein,
Therefore, were I rich as Croesus was,   and powerful besides,

ʊntˀ ˈveːrən ˈkʰlʊmpˀən ˈgɔldəs gaːɐ̯, zoː groːs viː ˈbergə,   maɛn;
und wären Klumpen Goldes gar, so gross wie Berge,   mein;
and were nuggets of gold even, as big as mountains, mine;
(and if nuggets of gold, even, as big as mountains, were mine,)

ʊntˀ veːr ɪç nɔx   fɔn ˈlaləm hɛr vas   fɔn deːɐ̯ ˈnɔrtˀzeː lan
und wär' ich noch   von Allem Herr was   von der Nordsee an
and were I furthermore of all   lord which from the North Sea on
(and if I were furthermore the lord of all...)

bɪs tʰiːf hɪˈnapˀ lans ˈʃvarʦə meːɐ̯ je: ˈmɛnʃənlɑ̯ogən zaːn;
bis tief hinab ans   schwarze Meer je Menschenaugen sahn;
till deep down at the Black   Sea ever human   eyes saw;
(that human eyes have ever seen from the North Sea to deep down by the Black Sea,)

ʊntˀ ˈhɛtˀə ˈfroːəs ˈmuːtˀəs nɪçtˀ, zoː zɛŋkˀtˀ lɪç tʰryːpˀ den blɪkʰ;
und hätte frohes Mutes nicht, so senkt' ich trüb den Blick;
and had happy spirit not, then sank I sadly the gaze;
(and did not have a happy heart, then I would sadly lower my eyes,)

ɪç ˈdʏŋkˀtˀə   miːɐ̯/miːr laɛn ˈlarmɐ vɪçtˀ, ʊntˀ ˈʃpˀrɛːçə   ʦuː dem glʏkʰ:
ich dünkte   mir ein armer Wicht, und spräche   zu dem Glück:
I would think myself a   poor wretch, and would speak to the Fortune:
(I would think myself a poor wretch, and say to Fortune:)

oː 'gœt'ɪn, lɪst' maẹn voːl   diːɐ̯ liːp', zoː 'hø̞ːrə mɪç!
O Göttin, ist mein Wohl   dir lieb, so höre mich!
O goddess, is my   well-being to you dear, then hear me!
(O goddess, if you care about my well-being, then hear me!)

nɪm hiːɐ̯ ʦuˈrʏk' diːs 'laləs, 'laːbɐ giːp' miːɐ̯ 'laẹçt'əs bluːt daˈfyːɐ̯!
nimm hier zurück dies alles, aber gieb mir leichtes Blut dafür!
take here back this all, but give to me light blood for it!
(Take back all of this here, but give me in exchange light blood and a cheerful heart!)

dɛn 'frøːlɪçkʰaẹt' maxt' raẹç lʊnt' fraẹ, lʊnt' nuːɐ̯ deːɐ̯ 'zɛlt'nə man
Denn Fröhlichkeit macht reich und frei, und nur der seltne Mann
For cheerfulness makes rich and free, and only the rare man
(For cheerfulness makes you rich and free, and only the rare man)

ɪst' 'glʏk'lɪç, zaẹ leːɐ̯, veːɐ̯/veːr leːɐ̯ zaẹ,   deːɐ̯ ziː lɛɐ̯'halt'ən kʰan.
ist glücklich, sei er, wer er sei, der sie erhalten kann.
is happy, be he who he may be, who it preserve can.
(is happy, be he whoever he may be, who can preserve it.)

[Good advice! This cheerful little strophic song lies high and shoots up briefly to high B natural.]

di 'fryːə 'liːbə
Die frühe Liebe
Young Love

Posthumously published [composed 1816] (poem by Ludwig Heinrich Christoph Hölty)

ʃoːn lɪm 'bʊnt'ən   'kʰnaːbənkʰlaẹdə, 'pfleːk't'ən 'hʏpʃə 'mɛːk'dəlaẹn
Schon im bunten   Knabenkleide, pflegten hübsche Mägdelein
Already in bright-colored boy's clothes, tended pretty girls
(When I was still in knee pants, pretty girls tended)

'maẹnə 'liːpst'ə 'lɑogənvaẹdə,   meːɐ̯/meːr lals pʰʊp' lʊnt' bal ʦuː zaẹn.
meine liebste Augenweide,   mehr als Pupp' und Ball zu sein.
my favorite eye- pasture (= feast for the eyes), more than doll and ball to be.
(to be my favorite feast for the eyes, more than any doll or ball.)

ɪç fɛɐ̯'gaːs deːɐ̯ 'foːgəlnɛst'ɐ, varf maẹn 'ʃt'ɛk'ənpfeːɐ̯t' lɪns   graːs,
Ich vergass der Vogelnester, warf mein Steckenpferd ins   Gras,
I forgot the birds' nests, tossed my hobby-horse into the grass,

vɛn lam bɑom baẹ 'maẹnɐ 'ʃvɛst'ɐ(r) 'laẹnə 'ʃøːnə 'dɪrnə zaːs.
wenn am Baum bei meiner Schwester eine schöne Dirne sass.
when at the tree beside my sister a beautiful girl sat.
(when a beautiful girl was sitting beside my sister under a tree.)
        [note: "*Dirne*," once innocent, has acquired a negative connotation in modern German]

'frɔɣt'ə mɪç deːɐ̯ 'mʊnt'ɐn 'dɪrnə, 'liːrəs 'roːt'ən 'vaŋənpʰaːrs,
Freute mich der muntern Dirne, ihres roten Wangenpaars,
Delighted myself in the cheerful girl, in her red cheeks- pair,
(I delighted in the cheerful girl, in her red cheeks,)

'i:rəs 'mʊndəs, 'li:rɐ 'ʃt'ɪrnə, 'li:rəs 'blɔndən 'lɔk'ənha:ɐ̯s;
ihres Mundes, ihrer Stirne, ihres blonden Lockenhaars;
in her mouth,   in her brow,   in her blond   curly   hair;

blɪk't' lɑ̯ɔf 'bu:zəntʰu:x ʊnt' 'mi:dɐ, 'hɪnt'ɛvɛrts gə'le:nt' lam   bɑ̯ɔm;
blickt' auf Busentuch und Mieder, hinterwärts gelehnt am   Baum;
glanced at   bosom-scarf and bodice,   backwards   leaned   against the tree;
(I would glance at her bosom-scarf and bodice, as she leaned back against the tree;)

'ʃt'rɛk't'ə dan lɪns   gra:s mɪç 'ni:dɐ,   dɪç' lan 'li:rəs 'kʰlɑ̯ɛdəs zɑ̯ɔm.
streckte dann ins   Gras mich nieder, dicht an ihres Kleides Saum.
stretched then into the grass myself down, close to her   dress's   hem.
(then I would stretch out in the grass, close to the hem of her dress.)

[vas lɪç 'vɑ̯ɛlant tʰa:t' lals 'kʰna:bə, ve:ɐ̯d ɪç 'va:ɐ̯lɪç 'lɪmɐ tʰu:n,
[Was ich weiland tat   als Knabe, werd' ich wahrlich immer tun,
[What I   back then did   as boy,   shall I   truly   always do,
[(What I used to do back then as a boy I shall surely always be doing,)

bɪs lɪç ve:ɐ̯t' lɪm 'kʰy:lən 'gra:bə 'ne:bən 'mɑ̯ɛnən 'fɛt'ɐn   ru:n.]
bis ich werd' im   kühlen Grabe neben   meinen Vätern   ruhn.]
until I   shall in the cool   grave beside my   forefathers rest.]
(till I am resting beside my forefathers in a cool grave.)]

[The last verse of the poem, in brackets above, was not copied out by Schubert.]

di 'fry:ən 'grɛ:bɐ
Die frühen Gräber
The Early Graves

Posthumously published [composed 1815] (poem by Friedrich Gottlieb Klopstock)

vɪl'kʰɔmən,   lo: 'zɪlbɐnɐ mo:nt', 'ʃø:nɐ, 'ʃt'ɪlɐ gə'fɛ:ɐ̯t'ə de:ɐ̯ naxtʰ!   [gə'fɛ:ɐ̯t']
Willkommen, o   silberner Mond, schöner, stiller Gefährte der   Nacht! [*poem:* Gefährt]
Welcome,   O silver   moon, beautiful, silent companion of the night!

du: lɛnt'ˈfli:st'? 'lɑ̯ɛlə nɪçt', blɑ̯ɛp', gə'daŋk'ənfrɔ̯ɔnt'! 'ze:ət' le:ɐ̯ blɑ̯ɛp't',
Du entfliehst? Eile   nicht, bleib, Gedankenfreund! Sehet, er bleibt,
You flee?   Hasten not, stay, thoughts- friend! See, it stays,
(You flee? Do not hasten away, stay, friend of my meditations! See, it stays;)

das gə'vœlk' 'valt'ə nu:ɐ̯ hɪn.   dɛs 'mɑ̯ɛəs lɛɐ̯'vaxən lɪst' nu:ɐ̯ 'ʃø:nɐ   nɔx,
das Gewölk wallte nur hin.   Des Maies Erwachen ist nur schöner   noch,
the clouds   move only hence. The May's awakening is   only more beautiful still,
(it is only the clouds that are moving. May's awakening is only even more beautiful,)

vi: di 'zɔmɐnaxtʰ,   vɛn li:m   tʰɑ̯ɔ, hɛl vi: lɪçt', lɑ̯ɔs de:ɐ̯ 'lɔk'ə 'tʰrɔ̯øftʰ,
wie die Sommernacht, wenn ihm   Tau, hell   wie Licht, aus der Locke träuft,
like the summer night, when from him dew, bright as light, from the curls drips,
(like the summer night, when dew, bright as light, is dripping from his curls,)

ʊnt ʦuː dem ˈhyːgəl hɛˈrɑof ˈrøːtˈlɪç   leːɐ̯ kʰɔmtʰ.   [kʰœmtʰ]
und zu dem Hügel herauf rötlich er kommt. [*GA:* **kömmt,** *poem:* **kömt** (both dialect)]
and at the hill up reddishly he comes.
(and he rises red above the hill.)

iːɐ̯/iːr ˈleːdlərən,   lax! lɛs bəˈvɛkstʼ ˈlɔ̸ørə ˈmaːlə   ʃoːn ˈlɛrnstʼəs moːs!
Ihr Edleren, ach! es bewächst eure Male schon ernstes Moos!
You nobler ones, ah! there grows on your tombstones already solemn moss!
(You nobler ones, ah! there is already solemn moss growing on your tombstones!)

oː viː vaːɐ̯ ˈglʏkʼlɪç lɪç, lals lɪç nɔx mɪtʼ lɔ̸øç
O wie war glücklich ich, als ich noch mit euch
Oh how was happy I, when I still with you
(Oh how happy I was, when, still with you, I)

ˈzaːə zɪç ˈrøːtʼən den tʰaːkʼ, ˈʃɪmɐn   di naxtʰ!
sahe sich röten den Tag, schimmern die Nacht!
saw itself redden the day, shimmer the night!
(watched the day dawning, saw the night sky shimmering!)

[The publisher Diabelli transposed Schubert's original one whole tone higher, added a four-bar introduction, and changed a chord from major to minor (under the *fermata* in the voice part). His is the version printed in the Peters edition; the *Gesamtausgabe* is true to what Schubert wrote.]

di gəˈbʏʃə
Die Gebüsche
The Bushes

Posthumously published [composed 1819] (poem by Friedrich von Schlegel)

ɛs ˈveːət kʰyːl lʊntʼ ˈlaezə di lʊft dʊrç ˈdʊŋkʼlə ˈlɑoən,   lʊntʼ nuːɐ̯ deːɐ̯ ˈhɪməl
Es wehet kühl und leise die Luft durch dunkle Auen, und nur der Himmel
There blows cool and quiet the air through dark meadows, and only the sky
(The air wafts cool and quiet through dark meadows, and only the sky)

ˈlɛçəltʼ lɑos ˈtʰɑozəntʼ ˈhɛlən ˈlɑogən. ɛs   reːkʼtʼ nuːɐ̯/nuːr ˈlaenə ˈzeːlə zɪç
lächelt aus tausend hellen Augen. Es regt nur eine Seele sich
smiles from thousand bright eyes. There stirs only one soul itself
(is smiling out of a thousand bright eyes. Only one soul is stirring)

lɪn dɛs ˈmeːrəs ˈbrɑozən, lʊntʼ lɪn den ˈlaezən ˈvɔrtʼən, diː   dʊrç di ˈblɛtʼɐ ˈrɑoʃən.
in des Meeres Brausen, und in den leisen Worten, die durch die Blätter rauschen.
in the sea's roaring, and in the quiet words which through the leaves rustle.
(amid the roar of the sea, and in the quiet words that are rustling through the leaves.)
                    [*poem:* **in der Meere** (deːɐ̯ ˈmeːrə, the seas'—plural) **Brausen**]

zo tʰø̸ːntʼ lɪn ˈvɛlə ˈvɛlə, voː ˈgaestʼɐ ˈhaemlɪç ˈtʰrɑorən; zoː ˈfɔlgən ˈvɔrtʼə ˈvɔrtʼən,
So tönt in Welle Welle, wo Geister heimlich trauern; so folgen Worte Worten,
Thus sounds in wave wave, where spirits secretly mourn; thus follow words words,
(Thus wave echoes wave where spirits secretly mourn; thus words follow words)

voː ˈɡaest'ɐ ˈleːbən ˈhaoxən. dʊrç ˈalə ˈtʰøːnə ˈtʰøːnət' ɪm ˈbʊnt'ən ˈleːɐdəntʰraomə
wo Geister Leben hauchen. Durch alle Töne tönet im bunten Erdentraume
where spirits life breathe. Through all tones sounds in the motley earth- dream
(where spirits breathe life. Through all the tones that are sounding in earth's many-colored dream)

aen, nuːɐ/nuːr ‖aen ˈlaezɐ tʰoːn ɡəˈtsoːɡən, fyːɐ deːn, deːɐ ˈhaemlɪç ˈlaoʃətʰ.
ein, nur ein leiser Ton gezogen, für den, der heimlich lauschet.
one, just *one* soft tone (is) drawn, for him, who secretly listens.
(one, just *one* soft tone keeps sounding for him who secretly listens.)

[*poem:* **ein leiser Ton** ("nur e i n" *is Schubert's addition to the poem*)]

[This lovely song has a soaring, lyrical line supported by a flowing, harp-like accompaniment.]

di ɡəˈfaŋənən ˈzɛŋɐ
Die gefangenen Sänger
The Captive Singers

Posthumously published [composed 1821] (poem by August Wilhelm von Schlegel)

høːɐst duː fɔn den ˈnaxt'ɪɡalən di ɡəˈbyʃə ˈviːdɐhalən?
Hörst du von den Nachtigallen die Gebüsche widerhallen?
Hear you from the nightingales the bushes echoing?
(Do you hear the bushes echoing with the song of the nightingales?)

ziː, ‖ɛs kʰaːm deːɐ ˈhɔldə mae. ˈjeːdəs buːlt' ʊm ˈzaenə ˈtʰraot'ə,
Sieh, es kam der holde Mai. Jedes buhlt um seine Traute,
See, there came the lovely May. Each woos for its dear one,
(See, lovely May has come. Each one woos its sweetheart,)

ˈʃmɛltsənt' ˈzaːɡən ˈalə ˈlaot'ə, ˈvɛlçə vɔn ɪm ˈliːbən zae.
schmelzend sagen alle Laute, welche Wonn' im Lieben sei.
meltingly tell all sounds what rapture in the loving be.
(all the sounds tell meltingly what rapture there is in loving.)

ˈandrə, diː ɪm ˈkʰeːfɪç ˈleːbən, ˈhɪnt'ɐ(r) ˈiːrən ˈɡɪt'ɐʃt'ɛːbən,
Andre, die im Käfig leben, hinter ihren Gitterstäben,
Others, who in the cage live, behind their bars,
(Others, who live in cages, behind bars,)

ˈhøːrən ˈdraosən den ɡəˈzaŋ; ˈmœçt'ən ɪn di ˈfraehaet' ˈaelən,
hören draussen den Gesang; möchten in die Freiheit eilen,
hear outside the song, would like into the freedom to hurry,
(hear the song that comes from outside, and would like to hurry out into freedom,)

ˈfryːlɪŋslʊst' ʊnt' ˈliːbə ˈtʰaelən, ‖ax, daː hɛmt' ziː ˈlɛŋɐ tsvaŋ. ʊnt' nuːn
Frühlingslust und Liebe teilen, ach, da hemmt sie enger Zwang. Und nun
spring's joy and love to share; ah, there hems in them narrow constraint. And now
(to share in the joy of spring and love; ah, narrow constraint there hems them in. And now)

[*poem:* **Und es** (‖ɛs, there—literally "it")]

drɛŋt' zɪç ɪn di ˈkʰeːlə ‖aos deːɐ ˈɡraːmtsɐrɪsnən ˈzeːlə ˈʃmɛt'ɐnt' ˈiːrəs liːts ɡəˈvaltʰ,
drängt sich in die Kehle aus der gramzerrissnen Seele schmetternd ihres Lieds Gewalt,
urges itself into the throat from the grief-torn soul pealing their song's power,
(the power of their song surges out of their grief-torn souls, pealing, into their throats,)

vo: lɛs, ʃt'at' ım veːn deːɐ̯ 'haɛnə 'mıt̯t̯suvalən,
wo es, statt im Wehn der Haine mitzuwallen,
where it, instead of in the waving of the grove with to float,
(where, instead of floating with the others through the swaying grove, it)

lan deːɐ̯ 'ʃt'aɛnə 'hart'ən ba͜o t̯su'rʏk'ə pʰralt ʰ. zo: ım 'leːɐ̯dənt ʰaːl gə'faŋən,
an der Steine hartem Bau zurücke prallt. So, im Erdental gefangen,
against the stones' hard structure back rebounds. Thus, in the earth-valley imprisoned,
(strikes against the hard stone walls and rebounds back. Thus, imprisoned in this vale of earth,)

[poem & Peters: **von** (fɔn, from) **der Steine]**

hø:ɐ̯t deːɐ̯ 'mɛnʃən ga͜est' mıt' 'baŋən 'heːrɐ 'bryːdɐ melo'diː,
hört der Menschen Geist mit Bangen hehrer Brüder Melodie,
hears the humans' spirit with uneasiness sublime brothers' melody,
(the human spirit hears with uneasiness the melody of sublime brothers,)

[poem: **des Menschen** (dɛs 'mɛnʃən, the human's—singular) **Geist...**
hoher ('hoːɐ, exalted) **Brüder Harmonie** (harmo'niː, harmony)]

zuːxt' lom'zɔnst t̯su: 'hıməlsha͜et'ɐn 'diːzəs 'daːza͜en t̯su: lɛɐ̯'va͜et'ɐn, lont das
sucht umsonst zu Himmelsheitern dieses Dasein zu erweitern, und das
seeks in vain to heaven's brightening this existence to expand, and that
(seeks in vain to expand this existence toward heaven's serenity; and that effort)

[poem: **strebt** (ʃt'reːp't', strives) **umsonst]**

nɛnt' leːɐ̯ pʰoe'ziː. 'laːbɐ ʃa͜ent' leːɐ̯/leːr 'liːrə 'rʏt'mən 'juːbəlhymnən la͜ox t̯su: 'vıt'mən,
nennt er Poesie. Aber scheint er ihre Rythmen Jubelhymnen auch zu widmen,
calls he poetry. But seems he its rhythms to hymns of joy also to dedicate,
(he calls poetry. But if he seems to dedicate its rhythms also to hymns of rejoicing,)

[Peters: **ihren Rythmen Jubelhymnen** (hymns of joy to its rhythms)]

vi: la͜os 'leːbənstʰroŋk'ɐ brost ʰ, 'dɛnɔx 'fyːləns 't̯saːɐ̯t'ə/t̯saːrt'ə 'hɛrt̯sən,
wie aus lebenstrunkner Brust, dennoch fühlen's zarte Herzen,
as if from life- intoxicated breast, nevertheless feel it sensitive hearts,
(as if from a heart intoxicated with life, nevertheless sensitive hearts will feel)

a͜os deːɐ̯ vort̯səl 't ʰiːfɐ 'ʃmɛrt̯sən ʃt'amt di 'blyːt'ə 'za͜enɐ lost ʰ.
aus der Wurzel tiefer Schmerzen stammt die Blüte seiner Lust.
from the root of deep pains originates the blossom of his joy.
(that the blossom of his joy springs from the root of deep suffering.)

[This interesting and touching song perfectly reflects the moods and ideas of the poem, which, having been written in 1810, pre-dates the suppression of artistic freedom by Metternich in the aftermath of Napoleon's provocations and, instead of referring to that, as has sometimes been assumed, speaks more generally to the problem of the artist who feels stifled by mundane constraints and longs to fly freely in the empyrean of uncontaminated beauty, where "sublime brothers"—personifications of ideal human potential—are singing their mysterious melodies.]

358

di gəˈʃtˈɪrnə
Die Gestirne
The Constellations

Posthumously published [composed 1816] (poem by Friedrich Gottlieb Klopstock)

ɛs   ˈtʰøːnət ̍ zaᴇn loːpˈ fɛltˈ ͜ lʊntˈ valt,   tʰaːl   lʊntˈ gəˈbɪrkˈ,   das gəˈʃtaːtˈ ˈhalətˈ,
Es   tönet   sein Lob Feld und Wald, Tal   und Gebirg,   das Gestad' hallet,
There sounds His   praise field and woods, valley and mountains, the shore   resounds,
(The fields and woods, valleys and mountains sound His praise, the shore resounds,)

ǀɛs   ˈdɔnɐt   das meːᴇ̯ dʊmpf ˈbrɑ͜ozənt dɛs ͜ lʊnˈlɛntˈlɪçən loːpˈ,
es   donnert das Meer dumpf brausend des Unendlichen Lob,
there thunders the sea   dully   roaring   the Infinite One's praise,
(the sea thunders with a dull roar its praise of the Infinite One,)

ˈziːə, dɛs   ˈhɛrlɪçən,   ̍ʊnlɛᴇ̯ˌraᴇçtˈən fɔn dem ˈdaŋkˈliːt   deːᴇ̯   naˈtʰuːᴇ̯!
siehe, des   Herrlichen,   Unerreichten von dem Danklied   der   Natur!
see!   of the Glorious One, Unreached   by the   thanks-song of the nature!
(see!—of the Glorious One, whom nature's song of gratitude can never adequately apprehend!)

[ɛs   zɪŋt di naˈtʰuːᴇ̯ ˈdɛnɔx   deːm, ˈvɛlçᴇ zi: ʃuːf,   liːᴇ̯ gəˈtʰøːn ˈʃalətˈ
[Es   singt die Natur   dennoch   dem,   welcher sie schuf, ihr Getön   schallet
[There sings the nature   nevertheless to Him, that   it   created, its clamor   sounds
[(Nature sings, nevertheless, to Him who created it, and its clamor sounds)

fɔm   ˈhɪməl hɛˈrapˈ, ˈlɑ͜otˈpʰraᴇzəntˈ ǀɪn ͜ lʊmˈvœlkˈəndᴇ naxtˈ
vom   Himmel herab, lautpreisend in umwölkender Nacht
from   the heaven down, loudly praising in clouding-over night
(down from the sky; loudly praising, in clouding-over night,)

ˈruːfət dɛs ʃtˈraːls   gəˈfeːᴇ̯tˈ   fɔn den ˈvɪpfəln, ǀʊnt deːᴇ̯ bɛrkˈ   hɑ͜optˈ ǀɛs hɛˈrapˈ!]
rufet des Strahls   Gefährt'   von den Wipfeln, und der Berg'   Haupt es herab!]
calls the lightning's companion from the   tree-tops, and the mountains' head   it   down!]
(the thunder calls down from the tree-tops and from the top of the mountains!)]

ɛs   ˈrɑ͜oʃət   deːᴇ̯ haᴇn, ǀʊntˈ zaᴇn bax ˈlɪspˈəlt ǀɛs lɑ͜ox mɪtˈ ǀɛmˈpʰoːᴇ̯, ˈpʰraᴇzəntˈ,
Es   rauschet der Hain, und sein Bach lispelt   es auch mit empor,   preisend,
There murmurs the grove, and its   brook whispers it too with upwards, praising,
(The grove is murmuring, and its brook whispers with it, upwards to God, praising,)

ǀaᴇn ˈfaᴇrᴇ,   vi: leːᴇ̯! di lʊftˈ veːtˈ ǀɛs tsu: dem ˈboːgən mɪtˈ ǀɑ͜of!   [veːts]
ein Feirer,   wie er! die Luft weht es zu dem Bogen mit auf!   [poem: weht's]
a   celebrant, like it! The air   blows it to the   vault   with up!
(a celebrant, like the grove! The air, too, wafts the message up to the vault of heaven!)

hoːx ǀɪn deːᴇ̯ ˈvɔlkˈə vart deːᴇ̯/deːr ǀɛᴇ̯ˈhaltˈʊŋ   ǀʊntˈ deːᴇ̯ hʊltˈ   ˈboːgən gəˈzɛtstʰ.
Hoch in der Wolke ward der   Erhaltung   und der Huld   Bogen gesetzt.
High in the cloud was the   preservation's and the graciousness's bow set.
(The rainbow, symbol of Preservation and Grace, was set high up among the clouds.)

[ʊnt‘ ‘ʃvaͤegəst dɛn duː, ‘vɛlçən gɔt‘ ‘leːvɪç lɛɐ̯‘ʃuːf? ʊnt‘ fɛɐ̯ʃt‘ʊmst‘
[Und schweigest denn du, welchen Gott ewig   erschuf? Und verstummst
[And are silent   then you, whom   God eternal created? And are (you) struck dumb
[(And are you then silent, you whom God has created to be eternal? And are you struck dumb)

‘mɪt‘ən lɪm   pʰraͤes lʊm   dɪç heːɐ̯?   gɔt‘ ‘ha͟ʊxt‘ə diːɐ̯/diːr lʊn‘ʃt‘ɛrp‘lɪçkʰaͤet‘ laͤen!
mitten im   Preis’ um   dich her? Gott hauchte dir   Unsterblichkeit   ein!
midst   in the praise around you hither? God breathed to you   immortality   into!
(in the midst of the praise that is all around you? God breathed immortality into you!)

‘daŋk‘ə   dem ‘hɛrlɪçən!   ‘lʊnlɛɐ̯raͤeçt‘ blaͤep‘t‘ fɔn dem ‘la͟͟ʊfʃvʊŋ   dɛs   gə‘zaŋs
Danke   dem Herrlichen!   Unerreicht bleibt von dem Aufschwung des   Gesangs
Give thanks to the Glorious One! Unattained remains by the   upward flight of the song
(Give thanks to the Glorious One! Unattained by the upward flight of the song remains)

deːɐ̯ ‘geːbɐ(r); la‘laͤen ‘dɛnɔx   zɪŋ,   pʰraͤes liːn, loː duː, deːɐ̯/deːr lɛm‘pfɪŋ! ‘lɔͽçt‘əndəs
der Geber; allein dennoch   sing, preis’ ihn, o du, der   empfing! Leuchtendes
the Giver; but   nevertheless sing, praise Him, O you, who   received! Radiant
(the Giver; but you, who have *received*, sing and praise Him nevertheless! Radiant)

kʰoːɐ̯/kʰoːr lʊm   mɪç heːɐ̯/heːr, ‘lɛrnst‘ˌfrɔͽdɪç, duː lɛɐ̯heːbɐ dɛs   hɛrn, tʰreːt‘ lɪç hɛɐ̯tsuː,
Chor   um   mich her,   ernst-freudig, du Erheber des   Herrn, tret’ ich herzu,
choir   around me   here,   serious-joyful, you extoller of the Lord, step I   up,
(choir of stars all around me, serious and joyful, you extollers of the Lord, I step up to join you,)

lʊnt‘ zɪŋ   lɪn lɛnt‘tsʏk‘ʊŋ, loː duː kʰoːɐ̯, ‘psalmə mɪt diːɐ̯!]
und sing’ in Entzückung, o du Chor, Psalme mit dir!]
and sing in rapture,   O you choir, psalms with you!]
(and, in rapture, sing psalms with you, O choir!)]

deːɐ̯   ‘vɛlt‘ən lɛɐ̯‘ʃuːf, dɔrt dɛs tʰaːks ‘zɪŋk‘əndəs gɔlt‘, lʊnt den ʃt‘ɑ͟͟ʊp‘ hiːɐ̯
Der   Welten erschuf, dort des Tags sinkendes Gold, und den Staub hier
(He) who worlds created, there the day’s setting   gold, and the dust   here
(He who created worlds, that golden sun setting there, and here the earth, dust)

fɔl   gə‘vʏrməgəˌdrɛŋ,   veːɐ̯/veːr lɪst deːɐ̯? lɛs lɪst‘ gɔtʰ!   [‘vʏrməgədrɛŋ]
voll Gewürmegedräng, wer   ist der? Es ist Gott! [GA (doesn’t fit): Würmegedräng]
full of worm-   crowding, who   is that? It is   God!
(full of swarming worms, who is that? It is God!)

‘faːt‘ɐ! zoː ‘ruːfən viːɐ̯; lʊnt‘ lʊn‘tseːlbaːɐ̯, diː mɪt‘ lʊns ‘ruːfən, zaͤet‘ liːɐ̯!
Vater! so rufen wir; und unzählbar, die mit uns rufen, seid ihr!
Father! thus call we; and innumerable, who with us call,   are you (the callers)!
(“Father!” thus we cry out; and you who call with us, you are numberless!)

[deːɐ̯   ‘vɛlt‘ən lɛɐ̯‘ʃuːf, dɔrt den lɔͽn! ‘haͤesɐ(r) lɛɐ̯‘giːst‘ zɪç zaͤen hɛrts!
[Der   Welten erschuf, dort den Leun! Heisser ergiesst sich sein Herz!
[(He) who worlds created, there the lion! Hotter   pours out itself his heart!
[(He who created worlds, created Leo there, the lion! Regulus, his heart, shines more warmly!)

‘vɪdɐ(r), lʊnt dɪç, kʰap‘ri‘kʰɔrn, ‘pʰlaͤeonən, sk‘ɔrpʰiˈoːn, lʊnt den kʰreːps.
Widder, und dich, Capricorn, Pleionen, Skorpion, und den Krebs.
Ram,   and you, Capricorn, Pleiades, scorpion,   and the crab.
(He created Aries the ram, and you, Capricorn, the daughters of Pleione, Scorpio, and Cancer.)

'ʃt'aegəndɐ vɛːk'tʼ ziː dɔrt den bə'glaet'ɐ. mɪt dem pfael
Steigender wägt sie dort den Begleiter. Mit dem Pfeil
Rampant weighs she there the companion. With the arrow
(She there, Libra the scales, weighs her neighbor the lion in his rampant pose. With an arrow)

'tsiːlət' ʊnt' blɪtst deːɐ 'ʃytsə! viː tʰøːnt, dreːt' leːɐ zɪç, 'kʰœçɐ(r) ʊnt' pfael!
zielet und blitzt der Schütze! Wie tönt, dreht er sich, Köcher und Pfeil!
aims and sparkles the archer! How sounds, turns he himself, quiver and arrow!
(Sagittarius takes aim and sparkles! How they jingle when he turns, the quiver and arrows!)

viː fɛɐ'laent'/fɛr'laent' 'lɔøçt'ət' liːɐ, 'tsvɪlɪŋə, hɛ'rap'! ziː 'heːbən lɪm tʰri'ʊmfə
Wie vereint leuchtet ihr, Zwilling', herab! Sie heben im Triumphe
How unitedly shine you, twins, down! They raise in the triumph
(How unitedly you shine down, Gemini, the twins! They raise in the triumph)

des gaŋs 'frɔødɪç den 'ʃt'raːlənfuːs! ʊnt deːɐ fɪʃ 'ʃp'iːlət', ʊnt'
des Gangs freudig den Strahlenfuss! Und der Fisch spielet, und
of the procession joyfully the radiating foot! And the fish plays, and
(of the procession of stars so joyfully their radiant feet! And Pisces, the fish, play and)

blɛːst' 'ʃt'røːmə deːɐ gluːtʰ. di roːs lɪn dem kʰrants 'dʊft'ət' lɪçtʰ! 'kʰøːnɪk'lɪç
bläst Ströme der Glut. Die Ros' in dem Kranz duftet Licht! Königlich
blows streams of the fire. The rose in the wreath exhales light! Regally
(blow out streams of fiery light. The rose in Ariadne's Crown exhales light as perfume! Regally)

ʃveːp'tʼ, lɪn dem blɪk' 'flamə, deːɐ/deːr 'laːdlɐ, gə'bɔøt' gə'hoːɐzaːm
schwebt, in dem Blick Flamme, der Adler, gebeut Gehorsam
soars, in the look flame, the eagle, commands obedience ["*gebeut*" = "*gebietet*"]
(Aquila, the eagle, is soaring, with flame in his eyes, and commanding obedience)

den gə'fɛːɐt'ən lʊm zɪç! ʃt'ɔlts den gə'boːgnən hals, lʊnt deːɐ 'fɪt'ɪç
den Gefährten um sich! Stolz den gebognen Hals, und der Fittich
to the companions around himself! Proud the bent neck, and the wing
(from the companion stars around him! Its neck bent proudly, and its wings)

lɪn di høː, 'ʃvɪmət deːɐ ʃvaːn!] veːɐ gap' melo'diː, 'laeɐ, diːɐ?
in die Höh, schwimmet der Schwan!] Wer gab Melodie, Leier, dir?
in the heights, swims the swan!] Who gave melody, lyre, to you?
(raised on high, Cygnus, the swan, is swimming!] Who gave you melody, Lyra, heavenly lyre?)

tsoːk' das gə'tʰøːn lʊnt das gɔlt' 'hɪmlɪʃɐ 'zaet'ən diːɐ/diːr laof?
zog das Getön und das Gold himmlischer Saiten dir auf?
drew the tones and the gold of heavenly strings for you up?
(Who drew forth the tones and the gold of heavenly strings from you?)

duː 'ʃaləst tsuː dem 'kʰraezəndən tʰants, 'vɛlçən, bə'zeːlt' fɔn diːɐ, deːɐ pʰla'neːt'
Du schallest zu dem kreisenden Tanz, welchen, beseelt von dir, der Planet
You resound to the circling dance, which, inspirited by you, the planet
(You make music for the circling dance that, inspired by you, the planets)

hɛlt' lɪn deːɐ 'laofbaːn lʊm dɪç heːɐ. [lɪn 'fɛst'lɪçəm ʃmʊk' ʃveːp't',
hält in der Laufbahn um dich her. [In festlichem Schmuck schwebt,
holds in the orbit around you hither. [In festive adornment hovers,
(dance in their orbits around you. [In festive adornment hovers,)

lʊnt tʰrɛːkˈtˈ halm ɪn deːɐ hantˈ lʊnt dɛs vaɛns lɑop` di ɡəˈflyːɡəltˈə ˈjʊɳfrɑo!
und trägt Halm' in der Hand und des Weins Laub die geflügelte Jungfrau!
and carries stalks in the hand and the wine's foliage the winged virgin!
(carrying Spica, an ear of grain, in her hand, and vine leaves, Virgo, the winged virgin!)

lɪçtˈ ʃtˈʏrtstˈ lɑos deːɐ/deːr lʊrn leːɐ daˈhɪn! ˈlaːbɐ(r) loˈriːɔn ʃɑotˈ lɑof den ˈɡʏrtˈəl,
Licht stürzt aus der Urn' er dahin! Aber Orion schaut auf den Gürtel,
Light tumbles out of the urn he down! But Orion looks at the belt,
(Aquarius pours down light out of his urn! But Orion is looking at his belt;)

naːx deːɐ/deːr lʊrn ˈʃɑoətˈ leːɐ nɪçtʰ! lax, ˈɡœsə dɪç laɛnstˈ, ˈʃaːlə, ɡɔtˈ
nach der Urn' schauet er nicht! Ach, gösse dich einst, Schale, Gott
at the urn looks he not! Ah, might pour you once, bowl, God
(he does not look at the urn! Ah, if God would one day pour you out, Crater, heavenly bowl,)

lɑof den lalˈtʰaːɐ, zoː tsɛɐˈfiːl lɪn ˈtʰrʏmɐ di ˈʃœpfʊɳ!
auf den Altar, so zerfiel in Trümmer die Schöpfung!
onto the altar, then would fall into ruins the Creation!
(onto Ara the altar, then Creation would fall into ruin!)

lɛs breːç dɛs lɔøn hɛrts! lɛs fɛɐˈziːkˈtˈə di lʊrn!
es bräch' des Leun Herz! es versiegte die Urn'!
It would break the lion's heart! It would dry up the urn!

ˈhalətˈə ˈtʰoːdəstʰoːn lʊm di ˈlaɛɐ(r)! lʊntˈ ɡəˈvɛlkˈtˈ ˈzɛɳkˈə deːɐ kʰrantsˈ!
Hallete Todeston um die Leier! und gewelkt sänke der Kranz!
would sound death-tone around the lyre! and withered would sink the wreath!
(Tones of death would sound around the lyre, and Ariadne's wreath would sink down withered!)

dɔrtˈ ʃuːf ziː deːɐ hɛr! hiːɐ dem ʃtˈɑop` ˈneːɐ den moːntˈ,
Dort schuf sie der Herr! hier dem Staub näher den Mond,
There created them the Lord, *here*, to the dust nearer, the moon [accusative],
(The Lord created them to be there where they are, and the moon to be here, nearer to the earth,)

zoː, ɡəˈnɔs ˈʃvaɛɡəndɐ ˈkʰyːləndɐ naxtˈ, zanftˈ ˈʃɪmɐntˈ
so, Genoss schweigender kühlender Nacht, sanft schimmernd
thus, companion of silent, cooling night, gently shimmering
(thus the companion of the silent, cooling night, gently shimmering,)

di lɛɐˈdʊldɐ dɛs ʃtˈraːls ˈhaɛtˈɐtʰ! lɪn ˈjeːnɐ naxt deːɐ/deːr lɛntˈˈʃlaːfnən,
die Erdulder des Strahls heitert! in jener Nacht der Entschlafnen,
the sufferers of the ray soothes! In that night of the fallen asleep (passed away),
(soothes those who suffer from the rays of the sun! In that night of the dead,)

daː lʊmˈʃtˈraːltˈ laɛnstˈ ziː ɡəˈʃtˈɪrn!] lɪç ˈpʰraɛzə den hɛrn! ˈpʰraɛzə deːn, ˈvɛlçɐ
da umstrahlt einst sie Gestirn!] Ich preise den Herrn! preise den, welcher
then irradiates once them constellation!] I praise the Lord! praise Him who
(then constellations of stars will irradiate them one day!] I praise the Lord! I praise Him who)

dɛs moːnts lʊnt dɛs tʰoːts ˈkʰyːləndɐ, ˈhaɛlɪɡɐ naxt, tsuː ˈdɛmɐn lʊnt tsuːˈlɔøçtˈən ɡəˈboːtʰ.
des Monds und des Tods kühlender, heiliger Nacht, zu dämmern und zu leuchten gebot.
the moon's and the death's cooling, holy night, to grow dark and to shine ordered.
(commanded the cooling, holy night of the moon and of death to grow dark and yet to shine.)

362

'leːɐdə, duː graːpʻ, das ʃtʻeːts lɑof lʊns hartʻ, gɔtʻ hatʻ mɪtʻ 'bluːmən dɪç bə'ʃtʻrɔøtʰ!
Erde, du Grab, das stets auf uns harrt, Gott hat mit Blumen dich bestreut!
Earth, you grave, that ever for us waits, God has with flowers you strewn!
(Earth, you grave that is always waiting for us, God has strewn you with flowers!)

[nɔø 'ʃafəntʻ bə'veːkʻtʻ, ʃtʻeːtʻ leːɐ/leːr lɑof tsuː dem gə'rɪçt, das gə'baendɛkʻəndə graːpʻ,
[Neu schaffend bewegt, steht er auf zu dem Gericht, das gebeindeckende Grab,
[Newly creating moves, stands He up to the judgment, the bones-covering grave,
[(God, creating anew, agitates the bones-covering graves when He stands up to begin Judgment,)

das gə'fɪlt deːɐ zaːtʻ, gɔtʻ! lɛs lɛɐ'vaxətʻ, veːɐ ʃleːftʰ! [*GA:* leːɐ/leːr lɛɐ'vaxətʻ]
das Gefild der Saat, Gott! Es erwachet, wer Schläft! [*GA:* Er erwachet]
the fields of the seed, God! There awakes who sleeps! [He awakens]
(and stirs the fields of human seed! Those who were sleeping awake!)

'dɔnɐ(r) lɛntʻʃtʻʏrtst dem tʰroːn! tsʊm gə'rɪçtʻ halts, lʊnt das graːpʻ høːɐts,
Donner entstürzt dem Thron! Zum Gericht hallt's, und das Grab hört's,
Thunder crashes down from the throne! To the judgment sounds it, and the grave hears it,
(Thunder rumbles down from the throne! It sounds the call to judgment, and the grave hears it,)

lʊnt deːɐ tʰoːtʻ!]
und der Tod!]
and the death!]
(and so does death!)]

[The Peters edition has selected five of the fifteen verses; the *Gesamtausgabe* prints them all, but not under the voice part. Schubert wrote out only the first verse, followed with repeat marks. (The verses omitted by the Peters edition—those which most justify the title!—are in brackets, above. To fit them to the music minor adjustments need to be made in the vocal line.)]

di 'gœtʻɐ 'griːçənlants / fra'gmɛntʰ lɑos dem gə'dɪçtʻə / 'ʃøːnə vɛltʻ, voː bɪst duː?
Die Götter Griechenlands / Fragment aus dem Gedichte / Schöne Welt, wo bist du?
The Gods of Greece / A Fragment from the Poem / Beautiful World, Where Are You?

Posthumously published [composed 1819] (from a poem by Friedrich von Schiller)

'ʃøːnə vɛltʰ, voː bɪst duː? 'kʰeːrə 'viːdɐ, 'hɔldəs 'blyːtʻənlaltʻɐ deːɐ na'tʰuːɐ.
Schöne Welt, wo bist du? Kehre wieder, holdes Blütenalter der Natur.
Beautiful world, where are you? Return again, lovely blossom-age of the nature.
(Beautiful world, where are you? Come back again, lovely blossoming age of nature.)

ax, nuːɐ/nuːr lɪn dem 'feːənlant deːɐ 'liːdɐ leːpʻtʻ nɔx 'daenə 'faːbəlhaftʻə ʃpʻuːɐ.
Ach, nur in dem Feenland der Lieder lebt noch deine fabelhafte Spur.
Ah, only in the fairyland of the songs lives still your fabled trace.
(Ah, only in the fairyland of song does your fabled trace still survive.)

'ɑosgəʃtʻɔrbən 'tʰrɑoɐt das gə'fɪldə, 'kʰaenə 'gɔtʻhaet tsaekʻtʻ zɪç 'maenəm blɪkʰ.
Ausgestorben trauert das Gefilde, keine Gottheit zeigt sich meinem Blick.
Died out mourns the field, no divinity shows himself to my gaze.
(Quiet as the grave, the deserted fields are in mourning; no god reveals himself to my gaze.)

ax, fɔn ˈjeːnəm ˈleːbənvarmən ˈbɪldə bliːpʻ deːɐ̯ ˈʃatʻən nuːɐ̯ t͡suˈrʏkʰ.
Ach, von jenem lebenwarmen Bilde blieb der Schatten nur zurück.
Ah, of that life- warm image remained the shadow only back.
(Ah, only the shadow of that warm and living image has remained.)

[Schubert chose to set only the twelfth of the sixteen stanzas of Schiller's poem celebrating the golden age of ancient Greece and lamenting its loss. The song exists in two versions, both on the same manuscript, the second penciled in above the first. It is known by various titles, the most common given above. Bittersweet nostalgia is expressed with alternate major and minor modes.]

di ˈhɛrpstʻnaxtʰ / di ˈveːmuːtʰ
Die Herbstnacht / Die Wehmut
The Autumn Night / Melancholy

Posthumously published [composed 1816] (poem by Johann Gaudenz von Salis-Seewis)

mɪtʻ ˈla͜ezən ˈharfəntʰøːnən za͜e, ˈveːmuːtʻ, miːɐ̯ gəˈgryːstʰ! loː ˈnʏmfə,
Mit leisen Harfentönen sei, Wehmut, mir gegrüsst! O Nymphe,
With soft harp- tones be, melancholy, by me greeted! O nymph,
(I greet you, Melancholy, with the soft tones of the harp! O nymph,)

diː deːɐ̯ ˈtʰreːnən gəˈva͜etʻən kʰvɛl fɛɐ̯ˈʃliːstʰ!
die der Tränen geweihten Quell verschliesst!
who the tears' consecrated spring locks!
(who locks the consecrated spring of tears!)

mɪç veːtʻ lan ˈda͜enɐ ˈʃvɛlə la͜en ˈlɪndɐ ˈʃa͜oɐ(r) lan,
Mich weht an deiner Schwelle ein linder Schauer an,
me comes on your threshold a gentle shudder over, [*"anwehen"* (here) = comes over]
(On your threshold a gentle shudder comes over me,)

ʊnt ˈda͜enəs ˈt͡sviːlɪçt͡s ˈhɛlə glɪmtʻ la͜of dɛs ˈʃɪkʻzaːls baːn.
und deines Zwielichts Helle glimmt auf des Schicksals Bahn.
and your twilight's brightness glimmers on the destiny's path.
(and the glow of your twilight glimmers on the path of destiny.)

duː, zoː di ˈfrɔ͜ødə ˈva͜enən, di ˈʃveːɐ̯muːtʻ ˈlɛçəln ha͜estʰ,
Du, so die Freude weinen, die Schwermut lächeln heisst,
You, so the joy to weep, the sorrow to smile bid,
(You, in so far as you bid joy weep and sorrow smile,)

kʰan vɔn ʊntʻ ʃmɛrt͡s fɛɐ̯ˈla͜enən, das harm lɪn lʊstʻ fɛɐ̯ˈflɔ͜østʰ;
kann Wonn' und Schmerz vereinen, dass Harm in Lust verfleusst;
can rapture and pain unite, so that grief into pleasure flows away;
(can unite rapture and pain, so that grief flows away into pleasure;) [*"verfleusst"* = *"verfliesst"*]

duː hɛlstʻ bəˈvœlkʻtʻə ˈlʏftʻə mɪtʻ ˈlaːbəntʻzɔnənʃa͜en,
du hellst bewölkte Lüfte mit Abendsonnenschein,
you brighten clouded airs with evening sunshine,
(you brighten the clouded air with evening sunshine,)

heŋst‘ 'lamp‘ən ɪn di 'grʏft‘ə lʊnt‘ kʰrøːnst den 'laeçənʃt‘aen.
hängst Lampen in die Grüfte und krönst den Leichenstein.
hang lamps in the tombs and crown the gravestone.
(you hang lamps in tombs and crown gravestones.)

[duː naːst‘, vɛn ʃoːn di 'kʰlaːgə den 'buːzən 'zanft‘ɐ deːntʰ,
[Du nahst, wenn schon die Klage den Busen sanfter dehnt,
[You approach when already the lament the breast more softly expands,
[(You approach when lamentation is already swelling the breast more gently,)

deːɐ graːm lan zarko'faːgə di 'myːdə 'ʃlɛːfə leːntʰ;
der Gram an Sarkophage die müde Schläfe lehnt;
the grief at sarcophagi the weary temple leans;
(when grief leans her weary temple against sarcophagi;)

vɛn di gə'dʊlt‘ gə'lasən zɪç lan di 'hɔfnʊŋ ʃmiːk‘tʰ,
wenn die Geduld gelassen sich an die Hoffnung schmiegt,
when the patience calmly itself to the hope clings,
(when patience calmly clings to hope,)

deːɐ 'tsɛːrən tʰao lɪm 'nasən, 'ʃmɛrtsloːzən blɪk‘ fɐɐ'ziːk‘tʰ.
der Zähren Tau im nassen, schmerzlosen Blick versiegt.
the tears' dew in the wet, painless gaze dries up.
(when the dew of tears dries up in the moist gaze, devoid of pain.)

duː, di lɑof 'bluːmənlaeçən dɛs 't‘iːfzɪns 'vɪmp‘ɐ zeŋk‘tʰ,
Du, die auf Blumenleichen des Tiefsinns Wimper senkt,
You, who on flower- corpses the pensiveness's eyelash lowers,
(You who lower the eyelashes of pensiveness over dead flowers,)

bae 'blɛt‘ɐloːzən ʃt‘rɔøçən deːɐ 'blyːt‘əntsaet‘ gə'deŋk‘tʰ;
bei blätterlosen Sträuchen der Blütezeit gedenkt;
amid leafless bushes of the blossom-time thinks,
(who amid leafless shrubbery remember the blossoms,)

ɪn 'floːrəns 'bʊnt‘ə 'kʰroːnən laen 'dʊŋk‘ləs 'faelçən veːp‘tʰ,
in Florens bunte Kronen ein dunkles Veilchen webt,
in Flora's bright-colored crowns a dark violet weaves,
(who weave a dark violet in Flora's many-colored crown of flowers,)

ʊnt‘ ʃt‘ɪl, mɪt‘ laltsy'oːnən, lʊm 'ʃɪfbrʊxs,tʰrʏmɐ ʃveːp‘tʰ.
und still, mit Alcyonen, um Schiffbruchstrümmer schwebt.
and still, with Alcyone,* [al'saeɔni] about shipwreck- debris hovers.
(and who quietly hover with Alcyone about the debris after a shipwreck.)

oː duː, di zɪç zoː 'gɛrnə tsu'rʏk‘ tsʊr 'kʰɪnt‘haet tʰrɔømtʰ,
O du, die sich so gerne zurück zur Kindheit träumt,
O you, who yourself so gladly back to the childhood dreams,
(O you who like to dream yourself back to childhood,)

zelpst‘ liːɐ gə'vœlk‘ fɔn 'fɛrnə mɪt‘ 'zɔnəngɔlt‘ bə'zɔømtʰ:
selbst ihr Gewölk von ferne mit Sonnengold besäumt:
even its clouds from afar with sun- gold seam:
(who even seam its clouds with golden sunshine,)

vas ⎸ʊns ⎸ɛɐ̯'ɪnrʊŋ/ɛr'ɪnrʊŋ 'ʃɪldɐt' mɪt' ʃt'ɪləm glanʦ fɛɐ̯'brɛːmtʰ,
was uns Erinnrung schildert mit stillem Glanz verbrämt,
which for us memory depicts with quiet splendor embellished,
(childhood, which our memory depicts as embellished with quiet splendor;)

deːɐ̯ 'tʰrɛnʊŋ 'kʰvaːlən 'mɪldɐt' ⎸ʊnt di fɛɐ̯'ʦvaɛ̯flʊŋ ʦɛːmtʰ.
der Trennung Qualen mildert und die Verzweiflung zähmt.
the parting's torments alleviates and the despair tames.
(you alleviate the torments of parting and tame despair.)

deːɐ̯ 'laɛ̯dənʃaft'ən 'hɔrdən, deːɐ̯ 'zɔrgən 'raːbənʦuːk',
Der Leidenschaften Horden, der Sorgen Rabenzug,
The passions' hordes, the cares' raven-flight,
(The hordes of our passions, the raven-flight of black cares,)

ɛnt''fliːn foːɐ̯ den la'kʰɔrdən, diː 'daɛ̯nə 'harfə ʃluːk';
entfliehn vor den Akkorden, die deine Harfe schlug;
flee before the chords which your harp struck;
(vanish before the chords which you strike from your harp;)

du: 'ʦaɔ̯bɐst' ⎸'alp'ənzøːnən, fɛɐ̯bant' ⎸aɔ̯f 'flandɛns moːɐ̯,
du zauberst Alpensöhnen, verbannt auf Flanderns Moor,
you conjure up for sons of the Alps, banished to Flanders' bog,
(for sons of the Alps who are banished to the bogs of Flanders you conjure up)

mɪt' 'zɔnənraɛ̯gəntʰøːnən deːɐ̯ 'haɛ̯maːt' 'bɪldɐ foːɐ̯.
mit Sonnenreigentönen [sic] der Heimat Bilder vor. [*Schubert's error in copying?*]
with sun- roundelay-tones the homeland's images before (them).
(images of their homeland before their eyes, with musical tones from a sunny roundelay.)
 [*poem:* **mit Sennenreigentönen** ('zɛnənraɛ̯gəntʰøːnən, Alpine pasture roundelay tones)]

ɪn 'daɛ̯nən 'ʃat'ənhalən vaɛ̯st du: di 'zɛŋɐ(r) ⎸aɛ̯n;
In deinen Schattenhallen weihst du die Sänger ein;
In your shadow- halls ordain you the singers in;
(In your shadowy halls you ordain singers;)

leːɐ̯st' 'jʊŋə 'naxt'ɪgalən di 'tʰraɔ̯ɐmelo͜ˌdaɛ̯n;
lehrst junge Nachtigallen die Trauermelodein;
teach young nightingales the mournful melodies;
(you teach their mournful melodies to young nightingales;)

du: naɛ̯kst', vo: 'grɛːbɐ 'gryːnən, daɛ̯n ⎸oːɐ̯ ʦu: 'hœlt'is tʰoːn;
du neigst, wo Gräber grünen, dein Ohr zu Höltys Ton;
you bend, where graves are green, your ear to Hölty's tone;
(where graves are green, you bend your ear to Hölty's poetry,)

pflʏkst' moːs fɔn 'bʊrk'ru͜ˌiːnən mɪt' 'maɛ̯nəm 'mat'ɪsɔn.]
pflückst Moos von Burgruinen mit meinem Matthisson.]
pluck moss from castle ruins with my Matthisson.]

ryːɐ̯/ryːr ⎸'ʊntɐ 'tʰrɛːnənvaɛ̯dən nɔx ⎸ɔft' maɛ̯n 'zaɛ̯t'ənʃp'iːl;
Rühr' unter Tränenweiden noch oft mein Saitenspiel;
Touch under weeping willows still often my lyre;
(Touch my lyre still often, under weeping willows;)

feɐ̯'ʃmɪlts lɑox graːm ʊnt' 'lae̯dən ɪn 'zyːsəs 'naːxgəfyːl;
verschmilz auch Gram und Leiden in süsses Nachgefühl;
melt   also grief and suffering in sweet after-feeling;
(also melt grief and suffering into the sweet emotion that may come in their aftermath;)

giːp' 'ʃtɛrk'ʊŋ   dem lɛɐ̯'vae̯çt'ən!
gib Stärkung   dem Erweichten!
give strengthening to the weakened!

heːp' lɑos dem 't'rɑo̯ɐfloːɐ̯,   vɛn 'gɔt'əs 'ʃt'ɛrnə 'lɔ̷øçt'ən, den 'landaxtsblɪk' lɛm'p'hoːɐ̯!
Heb' aus   dem Trauerflor,   wenn Gottes Sterne leuchten, den Andachtsblick empor!
Lift out of the mourning crape, when God's stars shine,   the devotion- gaze upward!
(Lift upwards the gaze of devotion, away from mourning crape, when God's stars are shining!)

[*Alcyone, grief-stricken when her husband perished in a shipwreck, leaped into the sea and was transformed by the compassionate gods into a kingfisher, the bird once believed to nest on the waves just before and after the winter solstice (during the "halcyon days" when the sea was calm). **Ludwig Heinrich Christopher Hölty (1748-1776) and Friedrich von Matthisson (1761-1831) were poets, many of whose poems were set by Schubert. Schubert's own title for this song was "*Die Herbstnacht*"; the title of the original poem is "*Die Wehmut*," and that is how the song is listed in the *Gesamtausgabe* and in the Peters edition (which does not include the verses in brackets, above, or the second verse, which the *Gesamtausgabe* prints with the music).]

di 'jʊŋə 'nɔnə
Die junge Nonne
The Young Nun

Op. 43, No. 1 [1824 or 1825] (Jacob Nicolaus Craigher)

viː brɑo̯st dʊrç di 'vɪpfəl deːɐ̯ 'hɔ̷øləndə ʃt'ʊrm! lɛs   'k'hlɪrən di 'balk'ən,
Wie braust durch die Wipfel der heulende Sturm! Es   klirren die Balken,
How roars   through the treetops the howling storm! There rattle   the rafters,
(How the howling storm roars through the treetops! The rafters are rattling,)

lɛs 'tsɪt'ɐt   das hɑo̯s! lɛs   'rɔlət deːɐ̯ 'dɔnɐ(r), lɛs   'lɔ̷øçt'ət deːɐ̯ blɪts,
es   zittert   das Haus! Es   rollet der Donner, es   leuchtet der Blitz,
there trembles the house! There rolls the thunder, there flashes the lightning,
(the house is trembling! Thunder is rolling, lightning is flashing,)

ʊnt' 'fɪnst'ɐ di naxt'h viː das graːp'! 'lɪmɐhɪn,   'lɪmɐhɪn, zoː t'hoːp't' lɛs
und finster die Nacht wie das Grab! Immerhin,   immerhin, so tobt' es
and dark   the night as the grave! Be that as it may, as it may, thus raged it
(and the night is as dark as the grave! Be that as it may, thus a storm was raging)

lɑox jʏŋst' nɔx lɪn miːɐ̯! lɛs 'brɑo̯st'ə das 'leːbən, viː 'jɛtso deːɐ̯ ʃt'ʊrm,
auch jüngst noch in mir! Es   brauste das Leben, wie jetzo der Sturm,
also recently still in me! There roared the life,   as now the storm,
(still recently also in me! Life roared, as the storm roars now,)   [*poem:* **noch jüngst auch]**

ɛs 'beːp't'ən di 'gliːdɐ, viː 'jɛtso das hɑo̯s, lɛs 'flamt'ə di 'liːbə,
es   bebten   die Glieder, wie jetzo das Haus, es   flammte die Liebe,
there trembled the limbs,   as now the house, there flamed   the love,
(my limbs trembled as the house trembles now, love flamed)

vi: 'jɛʦo deːɐ̯ blɪʦ,   ᴜnt' 'fɪnst'ɐ di brʊstʰ vi: das graːp'.
wie jetzo der Blitz,   und finster die Brust wie das Grab.
as now the lightning, and dark   the breast as the grave.
(as the lightning now flames, and my heart was as dark as the grave.)

nuːn 'tʰoːbə, duː 'vɪldɐ, gə'valt'ɪgɐ ʃt'ʊrm, ɪm   'hɛrʦən lɪst' 'friːdə,
Nun tobe, du wilder, gewaltiger Sturm, im   Herzen ist Friede,
Now rage, you wild,   powerful   storm; in the heart is peace,
(Now rage, you wild, powerful storm; in my heart there is peace,)

ɪm   'hɛrʦən lɪst' ruː, dɛs 'brɔɣt'ɪgams 'harət di 'liːbəndə brɑɔtʰ,
im   Herzen ist Ruh', des   Bräutigams harret die liebende Braut,
in the heart   is calm, for the bridegroom waits the loving   bride,
(in my heart there is calm; the loving bride is waiting for her bridegroom,)

gə'raenɪçt' ɪn 'pʰryːfəndɐ gluːtʰ, deːɐ/deːr 'leːvɪgən 'liːbə gə'tʰrɑɔtʰ.
gereinigt in prüfender Glut, der   ewigen Liebe getraut.
purified in testing   fire, to the   eternal love wed.
(purified in the testing fire, wed to eternal love.)

ɪç 'harə, maen 'haelant', mɪt' 'zeːnəndəm blɪkʰ! kʰɔm, 'hɪmlɪʃɐ   'brɔɣt'ɪgam,
Ich harre, mein Heiland, mit sehnendem Blick! komm, himmlischer Bräutigam,
I wait, my Savior,   with yearning gaze! Come, heavenly   bridegroom,

'hoːlə di brɑɔtʰ, lɛɐ̯'løːzə di 'zeːlə fɔn 'ɪrdɪʃɐ   haftʰ!
hole die Braut, erlöse   die Seele von irdischer Haft!
fetch the bride, release the soul from earthly bonds!
(take your bride, release my soul from earthly bonds!)

hɔrç, 'friːt'lɪç lɛɐ̯'tʰøːnət das 'glœk'laen fɔm   tʰʊrm!
Horch, friedlich ertönet   das Glöcklein vom   Turm! [*poem:* **am** (lam, at the) **Turm**]
Hark, peacefully sounds the little bell from the tower!
(Listen, the little bell sounds peacefully from the tower!)

ɛs   lɔk't' mɪç das 'zyːsə gə'tʰøːn lal'mɛçtɪç   ʦu: 'leːvɪgən høːn. lale'luːja!
Es   lockt mich das süsse Getön allmächtig   zu ewigen Höhn. Alleluja!
There lures me the sweet pealing all-powerfully to eternal heights. Hallelujah!
(The sweet pealing lures me all-powerfully to the eternal heights. Hallelujah!)

[At first *pianissimo*, the storm outside rages in the accompaniment throughout the song, even as the young nun speaks about the peace she feels in her heart, and the sound of the distant tower bell is there from the beginning. Powerful emotions that once inflicted only pain, have now found their outlet in passionate longing for union with the heavenly bridegroom. A masterpiece.]

di ˈkʰnaːbəntsaetʰ
Die Knabenzeit
Boyhood

Posthumously published [composed 1816] (poem by Ludwig Hölty)

viː ˈɡlʏkˈlɪç, veːm das ˈkʰnaːbənkʰlaetˈ nɔx lʊm di ˈʃʊltˈɐ fliːkˈtʰ!
Wie glücklich, wem   das Knabenkleid   noch um   die Schultern fliegt!
How happy, (he) whom the boy- garb still around the shoulders flies!
(How happy is he from whose shoulders a boy's jacket is still flapping!)

niː ˈlɛstˈɐtˈ leːɐ deːɐ ˈbøːzən tsaetˈ, ʃteːts ˈmʊntˈɐ(r) lʊntˈ fɛɐˈɡnyːkˈtʰ.
Nie   lästert er der bösen Zeit, stets   munter und vergnügt.
Never reviles he the evil time, constantly lively and cheerful.
(He never reviles the evil time, as adults so often do, and he is constantly lively and cheerful.)

[*poem (the accusative case, more usual):* **die böse** (di ˈbøːzə) **Zeit**]

das ˈhœltsɐnə ˈhuˈzaːrənʃveːɐtˈ bəˈlʊstˈɪɡətˈ liːn lɪtstʰ,
Das hölzerne Husarenschwert belustiget ihn itzt,
The wooden hussar's sword amuses him now,

deːɐ ˈkʰraezəl lʊnt das ˈʃtˈɛkˈənpfeːɐtˈ, laof deːm leːɐ ˈhɛrɪʃ zɪtstʰ.
der Kreisel   und das Steckenpferd, auf dem er herrisch sitzt.
the spinning top and the hobby-horse, on which he masterfully sits.
(the spinning top and the hobby-horse, on which he sits masterfully.)

ʊntˈ ˈʃvɪŋətˈ leːɐ dʊrç ˈblaoə lʊft den ˈbʊntˈɡəʃtˈraeftˈən bal,
Und schwinget er durch blaue Luft den buntgestreiften Ball,
And swings he through blue air the brightly striped ball,
(And if he tosses his brightly striped ball up into the blue sky,)

zoː ˈlaxtˈətˈ leːɐ nɪçtˈ ˈblyːtˈəndʊftˈ, nɪçtˈ lɛrç lʊntˈ ˈnaxtˈɪgal.
so achtet   er nicht Blütenduft,   nicht Lerch' und Nachtigall.
then pays heed to he not blossom scent, not lark and nightingale.
(then he pays no heed to the scent of blossoms or to the lark and the nightingale.)

nɪçts tʰryːpˈtˈ liːm, nɪçts lɪn ˈvaetˈɐ vɛltˈ, zaen ˈhaetˈrəs ˈlangəzɪçtʰ,
Nichts trübt ihm,   nichts in weiter Welt, sein heitres Angesicht,
Nothing clouds for him, nothing in wide world, his cheerful face,
(Nothing clouds his cheerful face, nothing in the whole wide world,)

als vɛn zaen bal lɪns ˈvasɐ fɛltˈ, lals vɛn zaen ʃveːɐt tsɛɐˈbrɪçtʰ.
als   wenn sein Ball ins   Wasser fällt, als wenn sein Schwert zerbricht.
other than if his ball into the water falls, than if his sword breaks.
(unless his ball should happen to fall into the water, or his sword should break.)

oː ˈkʰnaːbə, ʃpˈiːl lʊntˈ ˈlaofə nuːɐ, den ˈliːbən ˈlaŋən tʰaːkˈ,
O Knabe, spiel' und laufe nur, den lieben langen Tag,
O boy, play and run only, the dear long day,
(Just play and run, boy, the livelong day,)

durç 'gart'ən ʊnt dʊrç 'gry:nə flu:ɐ̯ den 'ʃmɛt'ɐlɪŋən na:x.
durch Garten und durch grüne Flur den Schmetterlingen nach.
through garden and through green meadow the butterflies after.
(through the garden and over green meadows, chasing butterflies.)

balt' 'ʃvɪtsəst du:, nɪçt' 'ɪmɐ fro:, ɪm 'ɛŋən 'kʰɛmɐlaen,
Bald schwitzest du, nicht immer froh, im engen Kämmerlein,
Soon sweat you, not always glad, in the narrow little room
(Soon enough you will be sweating, and not always gladly, in your narrow little room)

ʊnt' lɛrnst fɔm 'dɪk'ən 'tsi:tsero fɛɐ̯'ʃɪmɛlt'əs la'tʰaen!
und lernst vom dicken Cicero verschimmeltes Latein!
and learn from the thick Cicero moldy Latin!
(and learning musty Latin from a thick volume of Cicero!)

[Schubert himself revised the first three bars of this entertaining song. In the first full bar the vocal part should be e″, g′ sharp; in the third full bar the pitches should be d″, f′ sharp, d″, b.]

Die Krähe see *Winterreise*

di 'laobə
Die Laube
The Arbor

Op. 172, No. 2 [1815] (Ludwig Hölty)

'nɪmɐ ve:ɐ̯d ɪç, 'nɪmɐ daen fɛɐ̯'gɛsən, 'kʰy:lə 'gry:nə 'dʊŋk'əlhaetʰ
Nimmer werd' ich, nimmer dein vergessen, kühle grüne Dunkelheit,
Never shall I, never of you forget, cool green darkness,
(Never, never shall I forget you, cool green darkness,) [*Peters:* **nimmer dich** (dɪç) **vergessen**]

vo: maen 'li:bəs 'mɛ:t'çən lɔft' gə'zɛsən, ʊnt des 'fry:lɪŋs zɪç gə'frɔøtʰ.
wo mein liebes Mädchen oft gesessen, und des Frühlings sich gefreut.
where my dear girl often (has) sat, and of the spring herself gladdened.
(where my dear girl often sat and delighted in the spring.)

'ʃaoɐ vɪrt dʊrç 'maenə 'nɛrfən 'be:bən, ve:ɐ̯d ɪç 'daenə 'bly:t'ən ze:n,
Schauer wird durch meine Nerven beben, werd' ich deine Blüten sehn,
Thrill will through my nerves quiver, shall I your blossoms see,
(A thrill quivers through my nerves when I see your blossoms,)

ʊnt' li:ɐ̯ 'bɪlt'nɪs mi:ɐ̯/mi:r ɛnt'ge:gənʃve:bən, 'li:rə 'gɔt'haet' mɪç ʊm've:n.
und ihr Bildnis mir entgegenschweben, ihre Gottheit mich umwehn.
and her image to me toward- hover, her divinity me about-waft.
(and see her image hover toward me, her divine being waft about me.)

'tʰrɛːnənfɔl, ve:ɐ̯d ɪç, baem 'mo:ndənlɪçt'ə, ɪn de:ɐ̯ 'gaest'ɐʃt'ʊndə graon,
Tränenvoll, werd' ich, beim Mondenlichte, in der Geisterstunde Graun,
Tearful, shall I, by the moonlight, in the ghosts- hour's dread,
(Full of tears, by moonlight, at the dread hour of the ghosts, I shall) [*Peters:* **Grauen** ('graoən)]

diːɐ̯/diːr lɛntˈgeːgəntsɪtˈɐn, lʊntˈ gəˈzɪçtˈə lao̯f gəˈzɪçtˈə veːɐ̯d ɪç ʃao̯n,
dir   entgegenzittern,   und Gesichte auf Gesichte werd' ich schaun,
to you   toward- tremble, and apparition upon apparition shall I   see,
(go toward you, trembling, and shall see apparition upon apparition,)

mɪç   lɪn ˈmançən ˈgœtˈɐtʰrao̯m fɛɐ̯ˈlɪrən/fɛrˈlɪrən, bɪs lɛntˈtsʏkˈʊn mɪç dʊrçˈbeːpˈtʰ,
mich in manchen Göttertraum verirren,   bis Entzückung mich durchbebt,
myself into many a   gods- dream stray,   till rapture   me   through-quivers,
(stray into many a celestial dream, until rapture quivers through me,)

ʊntˈ naːx ˈmae̯nəm ˈzyːsən ˈtʰɔ̯øpˈçən ˈgɪrən, ˈdɛsən ˈlapˈʃiːtˈ foːɐ̯ miːɐ̯ ʃveːpˈtʰ.
und nach meinem süssen Täubchen girren, dessen Abschied vor   mir schwebt.
and after my   sweet little dove coo, whose parting   before me hovers.
(and coo for my sweet little dove, whose parting hovers before me.)

vɛn   lɪç lao̯f deːɐ̯ baːn deːɐ̯ ˈtʰuːgəntˈ ˈvaŋkˈə, ˈvɛltˈfɛɐ̯gnyːgʊn mɪç bəˈʃtˈrɪkˈtʰ,
Wenn ich auf der Bahn der   Tugend wanke, Weltvergnügung mich bestrickt,
When I   on the path of the virtue   waver, world-pleasure me   ensnares,
(When I waver on the path of virtue, when worldly pleasure ensnares me,)   [*GA:* **Wann** (van)]

dan dʊrçˈglyːə   mɪç deːɐ̯ ˈfɔ̯øɐ̯gədaŋkˈə, vas lɪn diːɐ̯/diːr lɪç lae̯nstˈ lɛɐ̯ˈblɪkˈtʰ.
dann durchglühe mich der Feu'rgedanke, was in dir   ich einst erblickt.
then through-burn me the fire- thought, what in you   I   once   beheld.
(then may the fiery thought burn through me of what I once beheld in you.)

ʊntˈ, lals ʃtˈrøːmtˈ lao̯s ˈgɔtəs ˈlɔfnəm ˈhɪməl   ˈtʰuːgəntˈkʰraftˈ lao̯f mɪç heˈrapˈ,
Und, als   strömt' aus Gottes offnem Himmel Tugendkraft   auf mich herab,
And, as if streamed from God's open   heaven virtue- power onto me   down,
(And, as if virtue's power streamed down upon me from God's open heaven,)
                                                                        [*Peters:* **Offnen** (misprint?)]

veːɐ̯d ɪç ˈfliːən, lʊntˈ fɔm   ˈleːɐ̯tˈgəˈvɪməl ˈfɛrnən ˈmae̯nən ˈpʰɪlgɛʃtˈaːpˈ.
werd' ich fliehen, und vom   Erdgewimmel fernen meinen Pilgerstab.
shall I flee,   and from the earth-swarm distance my   pilgrim-staff.
(I shall flee, and remove my pilgrim's staff from the earthly swarm.)

[Graceful and expressive music, with a touch of Halloween in the second verse (which could be
omitted without major damage to the message).]

di ˈliːbə / ˈkʰlɛːrçəns liːtˈ / ˈfrɔ̯øtˈfɔl lʊntˈ ˈlae̯tˈfɔl
Die Liebe / Klärchens Lied / Freudvoll und leidvoll
Love / Clara's Song / Joyful and Sorrowful

Posthumously published [composed 1815] (poem by Johann Wolfgang von Goethe)

ˈfrɔ̯øtˈfɔl lʊntˈ ˈlae̯tˈfɔl,   gəˈdaŋkˈənfɔl zae̯n; ˈlaŋən lʊntˈ ˈbaŋən lɪn ˈʃveːbəndɐ pʰae̯n;
Freudvoll und leidvoll,   gedankenvoll sein; langen und bangen in schwebender Pein;
Joyful   and sorrowful, thoughtful   to be; to long and to fear in suspenseful   pain;
(To be joyful and sorrowful, lost in thought; to feel longing and fear in pain and suspense;)

ˈhɪməlhoːx ˈjao̯xtsənt, tsum ˈtʰoːdə bəˈtʰryːpˈtʰ; ˈglʏkˈlɪç laˈlae̯n lɪst di ˈzeːlə, diː liːpˈtʰ.
himmelhoch jauchzend, zum Tode betrübt;   glücklich allein ist die Seele, die liebt.
heaven-high exulting,   to the death depressed; happy   alone is the soul that loves.
(exulting up to heaven, depressed to death; only the soul that loves is truly happy.)

[The short poem is the text for a song in Act III Scene 2 of *Egmont*, and is sung by Clara (or Clärchen), Egmont's sweetheart and the victim of the notorious Duke of Alba. Beethoven wrote a famous overture and incidental music for the play, including a setting of this poem (lengthened by repetitions). Schubert created a masterpiece of expression in only twenty-one bars.]

di ˈliːbə / voː veːt deːɐ̯ ˈliːbə ˈhoːɐ̯ ga̯est^h?

Die Liebe / Wo weht der Liebe hoher Geist?

Love / Where Does Love's Noble Spirit Breathe?

Posthumously published [composed 1817] (poem by Gottlieb von Leon)

voː   veːt   deːɐ̯ ˈliːbə ˈhoːɐ̯   ga̯est^h? leːɐ̯ veːt'   ɪn bluːm lʊnt' ba̯om,
Wo   weht der Liebe hoher Geist? Er weht in Blum' und Baum,
Where blows the love's high   spirit? It blows in flower and tree,
(Where does love's noble spirit breathe? It breathes in flower and tree,)

ɪm   ˈva̯et'ən ˈleːɐ̯dənra̯om, leːɐ̯ veːt', voː   zɪç   di ˈkʰnɔsp'ən ˈʃp'alt'ən
im   weiten Erdenraum, er weht, wo   sich   die Knospen   spalten
in the wide   earth- space, it   blows where themselves the buds   burst
(in the wide world, it breathes where buds burst open)

ʊnt' voː   di ˈblyːmla̯en zɪç   lɛnt'ˈfalt'ən. voː   veːt deːɐ̯ ˈliːbə ˈhoːɐ̯ ga̯est^h?
und wo   die Blümlein sich   entfalten. Wo   weht der Liebe hoher Geist?
and where the flowerlets themselves unfold.   Where blows the love's high   spirit?
(and where little flowers unfold. Where does love's noble spirit breathe?)

eːɐ̯ veːt' ɪm   ˈaːbənt'glan̪ts,   leːɐ̯ veːt' ɪm   ˈʃt'ɛrnənkʰran̪ts, voː   biːn lʊnt'
Er weht im   Abendglanz,   er weht im   Sternenkranz, wo   Bien' und
It blows in the evening-splendor, it blows in the star-   wreath, where bee and
(It breathes in the splendor of a sunset, in the circling stars; it breathes where bees and)

ˈma̯eənkʰeːfɐ ˈʃvɪrən   lʊnt ʦa̯ːɐ̯t/ʦaːrt di ˈtʰʊrt'əltʰa̯obən ˈgɪrən. voː
Maienkäfer schwirren und zart   die Turteltauben   girren. Wo
cockchafers hum,   and delicately the turtledoves   coo.   Where
(beetles hum, and turtledoves softly coo. Where)

veːt   deːɐ̯ ˈliːbə ˈhoːɐ̯   ga̯est^h? eːɐ̯ veːt' ba̯e frɔ̯øt' lʊnt' ʃmɛrʦ ɪn ˈalɐ ˈmʏt'ɐ   hɛrʦ,
weht der Liebe hoher Geist? Er weht bei Freud' und Schmerz in aller Mütter Herz,
blows the love's high   spirit? It blows in joy   and pain   in all   mothers' heart,
(does love's noble spirit breathe? It breathes in joy and pain in the heart of every mother;)

leːɐ̯ veːt' ɪn ˈjʊŋən ˈnaxt'ɪgalən, vɛn ˈliːp'lɪç ˈliːrə ˈliːdɐ ˈʃalən.
er weht in jungen Nachtigallen, wenn lieblich ihre Lieder schallen.
it blows in young   nightingales, when lovely   their songs resound.
(it breathes in young nightingales, when their lovely songs are sounding.)

voː   veːt   deːɐ̯ ˈliːbə ˈhoːɐ̯ ga̯est^h? ɪn ˈvasɐ,   ˈfɔ̯øɐ, lʊft' lʊnt' ɪn dɛs ˈmɔrgəns dʊft^h,
Wo   weht der Liebe hoher Geist? In Wasser, Feuer, Luft und in des Morgens Duft,
Where blows the love's high   spirit? In water, fire,   air, and in the morning's scent,
(Where does love's noble spirit breathe? In water, fire, air, and in the fragrance of the morning,)

eːɐ̯ veːtʰ, voː   zɪç l̯aen 'leːbən 'reːgətʰ l̯ʊntʰ voː   zɪç nuːɐ̯/nuːr l̯aen hɛrts bə'veːgətʰ.
er weht, wo   sich ein Leben reget und wo   sich nur   ein Herz beweget.
it blows where itself one life   stirs and where itself only   one heart moves.
(it breathes wherever a single life is stirring, wherever a single heart is beating.)

[The most attractive feature of this graceful song is the feeling of two-four time near the end of a
piece in three-four.]

Die liebe Farbe see *Die schöne Müllerin*

di 'liːbə hatʰ gə'loːgən
Die Liebe hat gelogen
Love has Lied

Op. 23, No. 1 [1822] (August Graf von Platen-Hallermünde)

di 'liːbə hatʰ gə'loːgən, di 'zɔrgə 'lastʰətʰ ʃveːɐ̯,
Die Liebe hat gelogen, die Sorge lastet   schwer,
The love   has   lied,   the care   weighs heavy,
(Love has lied, care is a heavy burden,)

bə'tʰroːgən, l̯ax! bə'tʰroːgən hatʰ 'l̯aləs mɪç l̯ʊm'heːɐ̯!
betrogen, ach! betrogen hat   alles mich umher!
betrayed, ah! betrayed has all   me   around!
(everything around me has betrayed me!)

ɛs   'fliːsən 'haesə 'tʰrɔpfən di 'vaŋə ʃtʰeːts   he'rapʰ,
Es   fliessen heisse Tropfen die Wange stets   herab,   [*poem:* **Es rinnen** ('rɪnən, run)]
There flow   hot   drops   the cheek constantly down,
(Hot teardrops are constantly flowing down my cheek.)

las   l̯apʰ, m̯aen hɛrts, tsuː 'kʰlɔpfən, duː 'l̯arməs hɛrts, las   l̯apʰ!
lass ab,   mein Herz, zu klopfen, du armes Herz, lass ab!
leave off, my   heart, to beat,   you poor   heart, leave off!
(Stop beating, my heart, you poor heart, stop!)
                              [*poem:* **lass ab, lass ab zu klopfen, lass ab, mein Herz, lass ab.**]

[Schubert found a deeply moving musical expression for this terse, seemingly simple poem that
distills the pain of utter disillusionment into eight short lines. The Peters version follows the first
edition in ending bar eleven with a minor chord, where the *Gesamtausgabe* has opted for major,
in symmetry with earlier phrases. The original manuscript of this masterpiece has disappeared.]

di 'liːbəndə ʃr̯aepʰtʰ
Die Liebende schreibt
A Girl in Love is Writing

Op. 165, No. 1 [1819] (Johann Wolfgang von Goethe)

l̯aen blɪkʰ fɔn 'daenən 'l̯aogən l̯ɪn di 'maenən, l̯aen kʰʊs fɔn 'daenəm mʊntʰ
Ein Blick von deinen Augen in   die meinen, ein Kuss von deinem Mund
A   look from your   eyes   into the mine, a   kiss from your   mouth
(A look from your eyes into mine, a kiss from your mouth)

ˈᴜͻͻf ˈmaͤnəm ˈmᴜndə, veːͷ ˈdaːfͻn hat', viː lɪç, gəˈvɪsə ˈkʰᴜndə,
auf meinem Munde, wer davon hat, wie ich, gewisse Kunde,
on   my   mouth, who thereof has, as I,   certain knowledge,
(on my mouth—to one who has, as I have, a certain knowledge of that,)

maːk' deːm   vas   ˈlandes voːl   lɛͷˈfrͻͽlɪç ˈʃaͤnən?
mag dem   was   anders wohl   erfreulich scheinen?
may to that person anything else   possibly gratifying seem?
(can anything else possibly seem gratifying?)

ɛntˈfɛrnt' fͻn diːͷ, lɛntˈfrɛmdət' fͻn den ˈmaͤnən,
Entfernt von dir, entfremdet   von den Meinen,
Distanced from you, estranged   from the mine,
(Far from you, estranged from my family,)

fyːͷ/fyːr lɪç ʃt'eːts   di gəˈdaŋk'ən lɪn di ˈrᴜndə, lᴜnt' ˈimɐ
führ   ich stets   die Gedanken in die Runde, und immer
lead   I   constantly the thoughts   into the circle, and always
(I constantly let my thoughts circle about, and always)

ˈtʰrɛfən ziː lᴜͻf ˈjeːnə ˈʃt'ᴜndə, di ˈlaͤntsɪgə;   daː faŋ lɪç lan tsuː ˈvaͤnən.
treffen sie auf jene Stunde, die einzige;   da fang' ich an zu weinen.
strike they upon that hour,   the one and only one; then start I on to weep.
(they light upon that hour, that one and only hour; and then I start to weep.)

di ˈtʰrɛːnə ˈtʰrͻk'nət' ˈviːdɐ(r) lᴜnfɛͷˈzeːəns: leːͷ liːp't' jaː,   dɛŋk' lɪç,
Die Träne trocknet wieder unversehens: er liebt ja,   denk ich,
The tear   dries   again suddenly: he loves certainly, think I,
(The tears dry again in less than no time; I think to myself: "He certainly loves me,)

heːͷ/heːr lɪn ˈdiːzə ˈʃt'ɪlə, loː ˈzͻlt'əst duː nɪçt' lɪn di ˈfɛrnə ˈraͤçən?
her   in diese Stille, o solltest du nicht in die Ferne reichen?
hither   into this quiet, oh should you not into the distance reach?
(his love comes here to me in this quiet place; why then should I not reach out into the distance?")

fɛͷˈnɪm das ˈlɪsp'əln ˈdiːzəs ˈliːbəsveːəns: maͤn ˈlaͤntsɪç glʏk'   lᴜͻf ˈleːͷdən
Vernimm das Lispeln   dieses Liebeswehens: mein einzig Glück   auf Erden
Perceive the whispering of this love- blowing: my   only   happiness on earth
(Hear the whispering of this love blowing toward you: my only happiness on earth)

lɪst daͤn ˈvɪlə, daͤn ˈfrͻͽnt'lɪçɐ tsuː miːͷ; giːp' miːͷ/miːr laͤn ˈtsaͤçən!
ist dein Wille, dein freundlicher zu mir; gib mir   ein Zeichen!
is your will,   your friendly (will) to me; give me   a sign!
(is your will, your good will toward me; give me a sign!)

[The *Gesamtausgabe* and Peters print two somewhat different versions: the words of the last two lines are mated differently to the music, four bars have slight variants in the notes, and each is in a different key, duplicating one or the other of the first two published versions (1832 in B flat, 1863 in A major). The poem, a sonnet, dates from 1807, when Goethe was in love with Minna Herzlieb. The song is a lovely one; the tear that dries *"unversehens"* (in less than no time) is not a tragic one; the girl is in love, and she and her lover are—temporarily, we can assume,—apart.]

374

di ˈliːbəsgœtˤɐ
Die Liebesgötter
The Gods of Love

Posthumously published [composed 1816] (poem by Johann Peter Uz)

ˈtsyːpˤrɪs, ˈmaenɐ ˈfʏlɪs glɑ̯ɛç, zaːs fɔn ˈgraːtsi̯ən ʊmˈgeːbən;
Cypris, meiner Phyllis gleich, sass von Grazien umgeben;
Cypris, to my Phyllis like, sat by Graces surrounded;
(Cypris, who looked like my Phyllis, sat surrounded by Graces;)

dɛn lɪç zaː liːɐ ˈfroːəs rɑ̯ɛç; mɪç bəˈrɑ̯oʃtˤən ˈtsyːpˤɐns ˈreːbən.
denn ich sah ihr frohes Reich; mich berauschten Cyperns Reben.
for I saw her happy realm; me intoxicated Cyprian grapevines.
(for I saw her happy realm; Cyprian wine intoxicated me.)

ɑ̯ɛn gəˈvɑ̯etˤɐ ˈmʏrtˤənvaltˤ, den gəˈhɑ̯emə ˈʃatˤən ˈʃvɛrtstˤən,
Ein geweihter Myrtenwald, den geheime Schatten schwärzten,
A consecrated myrtle grove, which secret shadows darkened,
(A consecrated myrtle grove, darkened by mysterious shadows,)

vaːɐ deːɐ ˈgœtˤɪn ˈɑ̯oflɛntˤhaltʰ, voː di ˈliːbəsgœtˤɐ ˈʃertstˤən.
war der Göttin Aufenthalt, wo die Liebesgötter scherzten.
was the goddess's abode, where the Cupids were frolicking.

[ˈfiːlə ˈgɪŋən pʰaːɐ bɑ̯e pʰaːɐ: ˈlandrə ˈzaŋən, diː lɪç ˈkʰantˤə,
[Viele gingen Paar bei Paar: andre sangen, die ich kannte,
[Many went pair by pair; others sang, whom I knew,
[(Many were walking in couples; others, whom I recognized, were singing,)
                                    [*poem:* **andre sungen** (ˈzʊŋən, sang—archaic German)]

ˈdeːrən ˈlɑ̯ogə ˈʃalkˤhaftˤ vaːɐ/vaːr lʊntˤ fɔl ˈʃlɑ̯oɐ ˈvɔlʊstˤ ˈbrantˤə.
deren Auge schalkhaft war, und voll schlauer Wollust brannte.
whose eye roguish was, and full of sly lasciviousness burned.
(whose eyes were roguish, and burning, full of sly lasciviousness.)

ˈfiːlə ˈfloːgən ˈrʏstˤɪç lɑ̯os, mɪt dem ˈboːgən lɪn deːɐ ˈreçtˤən.
Viele flogen rüstig aus, mit dem Bogen in der Rechten.
Many flew briskly out, with the bow in the right hand.
(Many flew away on brisk excursions, with their bow in their right hands.)

ˈfiːlə ˈvaːrən nɪçt tsuː hɑ̯os, vɑ̯el ziː bɑ̯e lyˈɛːən ˈtseçtˤən.
Viele waren nicht zu Haus, weil sie bei Lyäen zechten.
Many were not at home, because they with Lyaeus were carousing.
(Many were not at home, because they were carousing with Lyaeus.)

deːɐ fɔl ˈbløːdɐ(r) ˈlʊnʃʊltˤ ʃiːn, hɛrʃtˤ lɑ̯of ˈʃtˤɪlən ˈʃɛːfɐ(r)lɑ̯oən.
Der voll blöder Unschuld schien, herrscht auf stillen Schäferauen.
Who full of bashful innocence seemed, rules on quiet shepherd-meadows.
(He, who seemed full of bashful innocence, is the ruler of quiet sheep meadows.)

ˈfɔøɐɐeç, fɛɐˈʃviːgən, kʰyːn zaː deːɐ ˈliːpˈlɪŋ ˈjʊŋɐ ˈfraͻən.
Feuerreich, verschwiegen, kühn sah der Liebling junger Frauen.
fire- rich, silent,   bold looked the favorite of young women.
(The favorite of young women looked fiery, silent, and bold.)

dͻx lɛɐˈmyːdət ˈhɪŋɡəkʰrymtʰ, ʃliːf deːɐ ˈliːbəsɡͻt deːɐ ˈeːən:
Doch ermüdet   hingekrümmt, schlief der Liebesgott der   Ehen:
But tired   crumpled,   slept the love- god of the marriages:
(But worn out, crumpled, the Cupid of marriages was sleeping:)

ʊntˈ tsyˈtʰeːrə, zeːɐ/zeːr lɛɐˈɡrɪmtʰ, hiːs liːn lͻͻx tsʊm ˈbaxʊs ˈɡeːən.]
und Cythere, sehr   ergrimmt, hiess ihn auch zum Bacchus gehen.]
and Cytherea, very   angry,   bade him also to the Bacchus go.]
(and Cytherea, very angry, ordered him to go also to Bacchus.)]

ˈʊntˈɐ ˈɡryːnɐ ˈbyʃə naxtʰ, ˈʊntˈɐ(r) ˈlapˈɡəleɡnən ˈʃtˈrͻøçən,
Unter   grüner Büsche Nacht, unter   abgelegnen   Sträuchen,
Beneath green bushes' night, beneath out-of-the-way bushes,
(In the darkness under green bushes, beneath out-of-the-way shrubbery,)

voː zoː ˈmançə ˈnymfə laxtʰ, zaː lɪç ziː lam ˈliːpˈstˈən   ˈʃlͻͻçən.
wo so manche Nymphe lacht, sah ich sie am   liebsten   schleichen.
where so many a nymph laughs, saw I them at the most preferredly sneaking.
(where so many a nymph is laughing, I saw them sneaking by preference.)

ˈfiːlə floːn mɪtˈ ˈlaͻçtˈəm fuːs ˈlalən tsvaŋ   bəˈtʰrɛntˈɐ   ˈkʰɛtˈən,
Viele flohn mit leichtem Fuss allen   Zwang   betränter   Ketten,
Many fled with light   foot from all constraint of tear-stained chains,
(Many lovers fled on light feet from the constraint of tear-stained chains,)

ˈflatˈɐtˈən fͻn kʰʊs tsuː kʰʊs lʊntˈ fͻn ˈblͻndən tsuː bryˈnɛtˈən.   [fuːs]
flatterten von Kuss zu Kuss und von Blonden zu Brünetten. [*Peters:* **von Fuss zu Fuss**]
flitted   from kiss to kiss, and from blondes to brunettes.   [foot]

[ˈkʰlaͻnə ˈɡœtˈɐ ˈfͻlɐ lɪstʰ,   ˈdeːrən pfaͻl kʰaͻn hɛrts fɛɐˈfeːlətʰ,
[Kleine Götter voller List,   deren Pfeil kein Herz verfehlet,
[Little gods   full of cunning, whose arrow no   heart misses,
[(Little gods full of cunning, whose arrow never fails to strike a heart,)

ʊntˈ fͻn ˈnɛkˈtˈar ˈtʰrʊŋkˈən lɪstʰ, ͻpˈ leːɐ ɡlaͻç di ˈtʰoːrən ˈkʰvɛːlətʰ:
und vom Nektar trunken ist, ob er gleich die Toren quälet:
and from the nectar drunk is, although it ... the fools torments:
(and is drunk with nectar, although it torments fools:)

                    [*"ob ... gleich"* (separable in older German) = *obgleich* = although]

blaͻptˈ, lax! blaͻptˈ nͻx ˈlaŋə tsaͻtʰ, ˈmaͻnə ˈjuːɡəntˈ froː tsuː ˈmaxən!
bleibt, ach! bleibt noch lange Zeit, meine Jugend froh zu machen!
stay,   ah,   stay   still long time, my   youth   happy to make!
(stay, ah, stay for a long time yet, to make my youth a happy one!)

van liːɐ/liːr laͻnstˈ lɛntˈˈvɪçən zaͻtˈ, vɪl lɪç baͻ lyˈɛːən ˈlaxən.]
Wann ihr   einst   entwichen seid, will ich bei Lyäen lachen.]
When you   one day vanished are,   want I   with Lyaeus to laugh.]
(When you have vanished one day, I shall want to laugh with Lyaeus.)]

376

[The Peters edition prints two of the five verses, the Gesamtausgabe all of them (those omitted in Peters are in brackets, above). Cypris and Cytherea are among the several names of Aphrodite, the Grecian goddess of love, who favored the island of Cyprus, and whose flower was the myrtle. Dionysus, the god of wine, was also variously known as Lyaeus and Bacchus. The gods in Schubert's charming song are figurines made of eighteenth-century Dresden china.]

Die Macht der Augen see *L'incanto degli occhi*

di maxt deːɐ̯ ˈliːbə
Die Macht der Liebe
The Power of Love

Posthumously published [composed 1815] (poem by Johann Nepomuk von Kalchberg)

ˈyːbɐ(r)lal voˈhɪn maen ˈlꭤꭤ̯ogə ˈblɪkʼətʼ, ˈhɛrʃətʼ ˈliːbə, fɪnd ɪç ˈliːrə ʃpʼuːɐ̯;
Überall wohin mein Auge blicket, herrschet Liebe, find' ich ihre Spur;
Everywhere where my eye looks, reigns love, find I its trace;
(Wherever I turn my eyes love is reigning, I find its trace;)
 [*poem:* **Ja** (jaː, yes/truly) **überall, wohin... gebietet** (gəˈbiːtʼətʼ, governs/commands) **Liebe**]

ˈjeːdəm ʃtʼrꭤꭤ̯ox lʊntʼ ˈblyːmçən lꭤꭤ̯of deːɐ̯ fluːɐ̯ hatʼ ziː tʰiːf liːɐ̯ ˈziːgəl ˈlaengədrʏkʼətʰ.
jedem Strauch und Blümchen auf der Flur hat sie tief ihr Siegel eingedrücket.
on every bush and flowerlet on the meadow has it deeply its seal imprinted.
(it has deeply imprinted its seal on every bush and flower in the meadow.)
 [*poem:* **selbst** (zɛlpstʼ, even) **jedem Strauch... hat sie ihr zartes** (ˈtsaːɐ̯tʼəs, delicate) **Siegel**]

ziː lɛɐ̯ˈfʏlt, dʊrçˈglyːtʼ, fɛɐ̯ˈjʏŋtʼ lʊntʼ ˈʃmʏkʼətʼ ˈlaləs ˈleːbəndə lɪn deːɐ̯ naˈtʰuːɐ̯;
Sie erfüllt, durchglüht, verjüngt und schmücket alles Lebende in der Natur;
It fills, inflames, rejuvenates, and adorns all living things in the nature;
(It fills, inflames, rejuvenates, and adorns all living things in nature:)
 [*poem:* **Ihr Geist** (liːɐ̯ gaestʼ, its spirit) **erfüllt... schmücket das All** (das lal, the all)
 der rastlos wirkenden (ˈrastʼloːs ˈvɪrkʼəndən, restlessly working) **Natur**]

eːɐ̯tʼ lʊntʼ ˈhɪməl, ˈjeːdə kʰreaˈtʰuːɐ̯, ˈleːbən nuːɐ̯ dʊrç ziː, fɔn liːɐ̯ bəˈglʏkʼətʰ.
Erd' und Himmel, jede Kreatur, leben nur durch sie, von ihr beglücket.
earth and heaven, every creature, live only through it, by it made happy.
(earth and heaven, all creatures live only through love, made happy by love.)
 [*poem:* **und** (lʊntʼ, and) **Erd'... sie** (ziː, they) **leben nur durch sie**]

[Schubert took the liberty of altering every line of the poetry when he set the first quatrain to music. Then he made a notation on the manuscript that one more stanza should be sung. That too required some drastic changes in the original wording. The rest of the poem simply will not fit. Here it is, for those who may be interested: *So muss denn, blinder Herrscher! Alles sich / Gehorsam unter deinem Bogen schmiegen? / Ja wohl, es atmet alles nur für dich! / Was lebt, das schlürft in taumelndem Vergnügen / Aus deinem Honigkelch in langen Zügen; / Doch Wermut hast du nur allein für mich!* (So must everything, blind ruler, obediently cringe beneath your bow? Yes indeed, eveything lives and breathes only for you! Whatever is alive quaffs in giddy pleasure long draughts from your cup of honey; but only wormwood have you reserved for me!)]

di ˈmae̯naxtʰ
Die Mainacht
The May Night

Posthumously published [composed 1815] (poem by Ludwig Hölty)

van deːɐ̯ ˈzɪlbɐnə moːnt dʊrç di gəˈʃtrɔ̯øçə blɪŋkˈtʰ, [*poem:* **Wenn** (vɛn, when/if)]
Wann der silberne Mond durch die Gesträuche blinkt,
When the   silvery   moon through the shrubbery   shines,
(When the silvery moon shines through the shrubbery,)

ʊntˈ zae̯n ˈʃlʊmɐndəs   lɪçtˈ ˈyːbɐ den ˈraːzən ʃtˈrɔ̯øtʰ,
und sein schlummerndes Licht über den Rasen streut,
and its   slumbering   light over the lawn   strews,
(and strews its slumbering light over the lawn,)

ʊnt di ˈnaxtˈɪgal ˈfløːtˈətʰ, ˈvand- lɪç ˈtʰrɑo̯rɪç fɔn bʊʃ   tsuː bʊʃ.
und die Nachtigall flötet,   wandl' ich traurig von Busch zu Busch.
and the nightingale warbles, wander I   sadly   from bush   to bush.
(and the nightingale is warbling, I wander sadly from bush to bush.)

ˈzeːlɪç pʰrae̯s lɪç dɪç dan, ˈfløːtˈəndə ˈnaxtˈɪgal,
Selig   preis'   ich dich dann, flötende Nachtigall,
Blessed consider I   you then, fluting   nightingale,
(Then I consider you blessed, fluting nightingale,)

vae̯l   dae̯n ˈvae̯pˈçən mɪt diːɐ̯ ˈvoːnətˈ ɪn ˈae̯nəm nɛstʰ,
weil   dein Weibchen mit dir wohnet in einem Nest,
because your little wife with you lives   in one   nest,
(because your little wife lives with you in one nest,)

ˈiːrəm ˈzɪŋəndən ˈgatˈən ˈtʰɑo̯zənt ˈtʰrɑo̯lɪçə ˈkʰʏsə giːpˈtʰ.
ihrem singenden Gatten   tausend   trauliche Küsse gibt.
to her singing   husband (a) thousand intimate   kisses gives.
(and gives her singing husband a thousand intimate kisses.)

ˈyːbɐhʏlətˈ   fɔn lɑo̯pˈ, ˈgɪrətˈ ae̯n ˈtʰɑo̯bənpʰaːɐ̯ zae̯n ɛntˈtsʏkˈʊŋ miːɐ̯ foːɐ̯;
Überhüllet   von Laub, girret ein Tauben paar sein Entzückung mir   vor;
Covered over with foliage, coos a   dove- pair its rapture   to me before;
(Concealed in the foliage, a pair of doves is cooing its rapture in front of me;)

ˈaːbɐ(r) lɪç ˈvɛndə mɪç, ˈzuːxə ˈdʊŋkˈlərə ˈʃatˈən,   ʊnt di ˈae̯nzaːmə ˈtʰrɛːnə rɪntʰ.
aber   ich wende mich, suche dunklere Schatten, und die einsame   Träne rinnt.
but   I   turn   myself, seek darker   shadows, and the solitary   tear   runs.
(but I turn away, seek darker shadows, and a solitary tear runs down my cheek.)

van, loː ˈlɛçəlndəs bɪltˈ, ˈvɛlçəs viː ˈmɔrgənroːt dʊrç di ˈzeːlə miːɐ̯ ʃtˈraːltʰ,
Wann, o lächelndes Bild, welches wie Morgenrot durch die Seele mir   strahlt,
When, O smiling   image, which   like dawn   through the soul to me beams,
(When, O smiling image, which beams through my soul like the dawn,)

fınd ıç laof 'leːɐ̯dən dıçʔ ˈ lʊnt di ˈlaɛnzaːmə ˈtʰrɛːnə beːpˈtʰ ˈ miːɐ̯ ˈhaɛsɐ di vaŋ heˈrapˈ.
find'ich auf Erden dich? Und die einsame Träne bebt mir heisser die Wang' herab.
find I on earth you? And the solitary tear trembles me hotter the cheek down.
(shall I find you on earth? And the solitary tear trembles down my cheek hotter than ever.)

[Three of the four verses of this poem were set most memorably by Johannes Brahms. Schubert's version, in a more conventional, strophic form, has a touching melancholy charm of its own.]

di ˈmɛnɐ zɪntˈ meˈʃantʰ
Die Männer sind méchant
Men Are Wicked

Op. 95, No. 3 [1828?] (Johann Gabriel Seidl)

duː ˈzaːkˈtˈəstˈ miːɐ̯/miːr lɛs, ˈmʊtˈɐ(r)ː leːɐ̯/leːr lıstˈ laen ˈʃpˈrɪŋınsfɛltˈ!
Du sagtest mir es, Mutter: Er ist ein Springinsfeld!
You told me it, Mother: he is an irresponsible young man!
(You told me so, Mother: he is an irresponsible young man!)

ıç vʏrd ɛs diːɐ̯ nıçtˈ ˈglaobən, bis lıç mıç kʰraŋk gəˈkʰveːltʰ!
Ich würd' es dir nicht glauben, bis ich mich krank gequält!
I would it from you not believe, until I myself sick (had) tormented!
(I would not believe you until I had tormented myself sick.)

jaː, jaː nuːn lıstˈ leːɐ̯s ˈvɪrkˈlıç; lıç hatˈ liːn nuːɐ̯ fɛɐ̯ˈkʰantʰ!
Ja, ja, nun ist er's wirklich; ich hatt' ihn nur verkannt!
Yes, yes, now is he it really; I had him only misjudged!
(Yes, yes, I now know that he really is what you said; I had only failed to see that!)

duː ˈzaːkˈtˈəstˈ miːɐ̯s, loː ˈmʊtˈɐ: di ˈmɛnɐ zıntˈ meˈʃantʰ!
Du sagtest mir's, o Mutter: "Die Männer sind méchant!"
You told me it, O Mother: "The men are wicked!"
(You told me, Mother: "Men are wicked!")

voːɐ̯m dɔrf, lım bʊʃ, lals ˈgɛstˈɐn di ˈʃtˈılə ˈdɛmrʊŋ zaŋkʰ,
Vor'm Dorf, im Busch, als gestern die stille Dämm'rung sank,
In front of the village, in the bush, as yesterday the quiet twilight sank,
(Yesterday, as twilight was falling quietly, in the bushes outside the village,)

daː raoʃtˈ lɛs ˈguːtˈən ˈlaːbəntˈ! daː raoʃtˈ lɛs ˈʃøːnən daŋkʰ!
da rauscht' es: "Guten Abend!" Da rauscht' es: "Schönen Dank!"
there murmered it: "Good evening!" Then murmured it: "Nice thanks!"
(someone murmured: "Good evening!" Someone else murmured: "Many thanks!")

ıç ʃlıç hınˈtsuː, lıç ˈhɔrçtˈə; lıç ʃtˈant viː ˈfɛstˈgəbantʰ:
Ich schlich hinzu, ich horchte; ich stand wie festgebannt:
I sneaked near, I listened; I stood as if spell-bound:

eːɐ̯ vaːɐ̯s mɪtˈ ˈlaenɐ(r) ˈlandɐn— di ˈmɛnɐ zıntˈ meˈʃantʰ!
er war's mit einer Andern— "Die Männer sind méchant!"
he was it with an other girl—"The men are wicked!"
(it was he, with another girl... "Men are wicked!")

oː ˈmʊtˌɐ, ˈvɛlçə ˈkʰvaːlən! lɛs mʊs heˈrɑos, lɛs mʊs!—
O Mutter, welche Qualen! Es muss heraus, es muss!—
Oh Mother, what torments! It must out, it must!—
(Oh Mother, what torments! It must come out, it must!—)

ɛs bliːpˈ nıçtˈ bloːs bɑem ˈrɑoʃən, lɛs bliːpˈ nıçtˈ bloːs bɑem gruːs!
Es blieb nicht bloss beim Rauschen, es blieb nicht bloss beim Gruss!
It remained not merely with the murmuring, it remained not merely with the greeting!
(It didn't just stop at murmuring, it didn't just stop at greeting!)

fɔm ˈgruːsə kʰaːms ʦʊm ˈkʰʊsə, fɔm kʰʊs ʦʊm drʊkˈ deːɐ hantˈ,
Vom Grusse kam's zum Kusse, vom Kuss zum Druck der Hand,
From the greeting came it to the kiss, from the kiss to the press of the hand,
(After the greeting it came to a kiss, after the kiss it came to holding hands,)

fɔm drʊkˈ, lax ˈliːbə ˈmʊtˌɐ!— di ˈmɛnɐ zıntˈ meˈʃantʰ!
vom Druck, ach liebe Mutter!— "Die Männer sind méchant!"
from the press, ah dear Mother!— "The men are wicked!"
(after that... Oh, dear Mother, men are really terrible!)

[The above delicious, humorous masterpiece belongs to the *genre* called "Refrain Songs." Sung by a soprano who has an engaging personality, charm, and comic flair it can be irresistible.]

di ˈmoːntˈnaxtʰ
Die Mondnacht
The Moonlit Night

Posthumously published [composed 1815] (poem by Ludwig Kosegarten)

ˈziːə, vi: di ˈmoːndəsʃtˈraːlən bʊʃ lʊntˈ fluːɐ/fluːr lın ˈzılbɐ ˈmaːlən!
Siehe, wie die Mondesstrahlen Busch und Flur in Silber malen!
See how the moonbeams bush and meadow in silver paint!
(See how the moonbeams paint bush and meadow silver!)
[*poem, according to Schochow:* **Mondenstrahlen** (ˈmoːndənʃtˈraːlən)]

vi: das ˈbɛçlɑen rɔltˈ lʊntˈ flımtʰ! ˈʃtˈraːlən ˈreːgnən, ˈfʊŋkˈən ˈʃmɛtˈɐn
Wie das Bächlein rollt und flimmt! Strahlen regnen, Funken schmettern
How the brooklet ripples and glistens! Rays rain down, sparks cascade

fɔn den zanftˈ gəˈreːkˈtˈən ˈblɛtˈɐn, lʊntˈ di ˈtʰɑofluːɐ glɛnʦtˈ lʊntˈ glımtʰ.
von den sanft geregten Blättern, und die Tauflur glänzt und glimmt.
from the gently stirred leaves, and the dew-meadow gleams and glimmers.
(from the gently stirred leaves, and the dew-covered meadow gleams and glimmers.)

ˈglɛnʦəntˈ lɛɐˈdɛmɐn deːɐ bɛrgə ˈgıpfəl, ˈglɛnʦəntˈ deːɐ ˈpʰapˈəln ˈvoːgəndə ˈvıpfəl.
Glänzend erdämmern der Berge Gipfel, glänzend der Pappeln wogende Wipfel.
Gleaming are dawning the mountains' peaks, gleaming the poplars' waving crowns.
(The mountain peaks gleam as if in dawning light; the crowns of the swaying poplars sparkle.)

dʊrç di ˈglanʦlʊmrɑoʃtˈən ˈrɔømə ˈflystˈɐn ˈʃtˈımən, ˈgɑokˈəln ˈtʰrɔømə,
Durch die glanzumrauschten Räume flüstern Stimmen, gaukeln Träume,
Through the splendor-all-around-intoxicated spaces whisper voices, beguile dreams,
(Through spaces intoxicated by surrounding splendor voices whisper, dreams beguile,)
[*poem:* **glanzberauschten** (ˈglanʦbərɑoʃtˈən, splendor-intoxicated)]

ˈʃpˈrɛçən miːɐ̯ fɛɐ̯ˈtʰrɑ͜ʊlıç ʦuː. ˈzeːlıçkʰa͜et, diː   mıç ɡəˈmaːnət‘, ˈhøːçstˈə lʊst,
sprechen mir   vertraulich zu. Seligkeit, die   mich gemahnet, höchste Lust,
speak   to me intimately to. Bliss,   which me   reminds,   highest pleasure,
(they speak to me intimately. Bliss, which stirs remembrance, keenest pleasure,)

diː   zyːs   mıç ˈʃvaːnət‘,   ʃpˈrıç, voː   blyːst‘, voː   ˈʦa͜et‘ıçst duː?
die süss   mich schwanet,   sprich, wo   blühst, wo   zeitigst du?
which sweetly me   fills with presentiment, speak, where bloom, where ripen   you?
(which fills me sweetly with presentiment, speak, where are you blooming, where ripening?)

ˈʃpˈrɛŋə di brʊst‘ nıçt‘, ˈmɛçt‘ıɡəs ˈzeːnən! ˈlœʃət   di ˈveːmuːt‘,   ˈlaːbəndə ˈtʰrɛːnən!
Sprenge die Brust nicht, mächtiges Sehnen! Löschet   die Wehmut,   labende Tränen!
Burst   the breast not,   powerful longing! Extinguish the melancholy, soothing tears!
(Do not burst my breast, powerful longing! Quench my melancholy, soothing tears!)
                               [*poem:* **mächtiges Dehnen!** (ˈdeːnən, expanding)]

viː,   lax, viː deːɐ̯   kʰva͜il ɡəˈneːzən? voː,   lax, voː   la͜en ˈliːbənt‘ ˈveːzən,
Wie, ach, wie der   Qual genesen? Wo,   ach, wo   ein liebend Wesen,
How, ah,   how from the torment recover? Where, ah, where a   loving   being,
(How, ah, how shall I recover from the torment? Where, ah, where shall I find a loving being)

das di ˈzyːsən ˈkʰvaːlən ʃt‘ıltʰ? la͜ens ıns   ˈlandrə ɡaːɐ̯   fɛɐ̯ˈzʊŋk‘ən,
das die süssen Qualen stillt? Eins ins   andre gar   versunken,
who the sweet   torments stills? One in the other utterly sunk,
(who will relieve the sweet torture? One utterly sunk into the other,)

ɡaːɐ̯   fɛɐ̯ˈloːrən, ɡaːɐ̯/ɡaːr lɛɐ̯ˈtʰrʊŋk‘ən, bıs   zıç ˈje͜idə ˈløːdə   fʏltʰ...
gar   verloren, gar   ertrunken, bis   sich jede Öde   füllt...
utterly lost,   utterly drowned,   until itself each emptiness fills...
(utterly lost, utterly drowned, until each emptiness is filled...)

ˈzɔlçəs, lax, vɛːn lıç, ˈkʰyːlt‘ə   das ˈzeːnən, ˈlœʃt‘ə   di ˈveːmuːt‘
Solches, ach, wähn’ ich, kühlte   das Sehnen, löschte   die Wehmut
Such,   ah, imagine I,   would cool the longing, would quench the melancholy
(Such a being, ah, I imagine, would cool my longing, would quench my melancholy)
                            [*poem, according to Schochow:* **wähnt’** (vɛːnt‘, would imagine) **ich**]

mıt‘ ˈkʰœst‘lıçən ˈtʰrɛːnən. ˈla͜enə   va͜es lıç, lax, nuːɐ̯/nuːr ˈla͜enə,
mit köstlichen Tränen. Eine   weiss ich, ach, nur   Eine,
with precious   tears.   One woman know I,   ah, only   one,
(with precious tears. I know one woman, ah, only one,)

dıç nuːɐ̯ va͜es lıç, dıç, loː ˈra͜enə,   diː dɛs ˈhɛrʦəns ˈveːmuːt‘   ma͜entʰ.
dich nur weiss ich, dich, o Reine,   die des Herzens Wehmut   meint.
you only know I,   you, O pure one, who the heart’s   melancholy understands/loves.
(I know only you, you, pure one, who understands and loves the melancholy of the heart.)
                                  [*poem:* **dich, du** (duː, you) **Reine**]

dıç lʊmˈrıŋənt‘, fɔn diːɐ̯/diːr lʊmˈrʊŋən, dıç lʊmˈʃlıŋənt‘,
Dich umringend, von dir   umrungen, dich umschlingend,
You encircling, by you   encircled, you embracing,
(Encircling you, encircled by you, embracing you,)

fɔn diːɐ̯/diːr ˌʊmˈʃlʊŋən, gaːɐ̯/gaːr ˌɪn ˌa͜ens mɪt diːɐ̯ fɛɐ̯ˈˌa͜entʰ/fɛrˈˌa͜entʰ... ʃøːn, ˌax
von dir umschlungen, gar in Eins mit dir vereint... Schon', ach
by you embraced, utterly in one with you united... Spare, ah
(embraced by you, utterly united with you as one being... Spare, ah)

ˈʃoːnə den ˈvɔnəfɛɐ̯zʊŋkʼnən! ˈhɪməl ˌʊntʼ ˈˌeːɐ̯də fɛɐ̯ˈʃvɪndən dem ˈtʰrʊŋkʼnən.
schone den Wonneversunk'nen! Himmel und Erde verschwinden dem Trunk'nen.
spare the rapture-sunken! Heaven and earth vanish to the intoxicated one.
(spare me, sunk in rapture! For me, intoxicated with bliss, heaven and earth vanish.)
[*poem:* **des** (dɛs, the—genitive, poetic/obsolete usage) **Wonneversunk'nen]**

[Schubert's lovely song captures the rhapsodic romanticism of the poem to perfection.]

di ˈmʊtʼɐ ˈˌeːɐ̯də / liːtʼ / dɛs ˈleːbəns tʰaːkʼ ˌɪstʼ ʃveːɐ̯
Die Mutter Erde / Lied / Des Lebens Tag ist schwer
Mother Earth / Song / Life's Day is Heavy

Posthumously published [composed 1823] (poem by Friedrich Leopold, Graf zu Stolberg)

dɛs ˈleːbəns tʰaːkʼ ˌɪstʼ ʃveːɐ̯/ʃveːr ˌʊntʼ ʃvyːl, dɛs ˈtʰoːdəs ˈˌaːtʼəm ˌa͜eçtʼ ˌʊntʼ kʰyːl;
Des Lebens Tag ist schwer und schwül, des Todes Atem leicht und kühl;
The life's day is heavy and sultry, the death's breath light and cool;
(Life's day is heavy and sultry, death's breath is light and cool;)
[*poem:* **des Todes Odem** (ˈˌoːdəm, breath—poetic/archaic)]

eːɐ̯ ˈveːətʼ ˈfrɔ͜øntʼlɪç ˌʊns hɪˈnapʼ, viː ˈvɛlkʼəs ˌa͜opʼ ˌɪns ˈʃtʼɪlə graːpʼ.
er wehet freundlich uns hinab, wie welkes Laub ins stille Grab.
it blows friendlily us down, like withered foliage into the quiet grave.
(friendly, it wafts us down like withered leaves into the quiet grave.)

ɛs ʃa͜ent deːɐ̯ moːntʼ, ˌɛs fɛlt deːɐ̯ tʰa͜o ˌa͜ofs graːpʼ viː ˌa͜of di ˈbluːmənˌa͜o;
Es scheint der Mond, es fällt der Tau aufs Grab wie auf die Blumenau;
There shines the moon, there falls the dew onto the grave as onto the flower- meadow;
(The moon shines, the dew falls on the grave as on the flowery meadow;)

ˌa͜ox fɛlt deːɐ̯ ˈfrɔ͜øndə tʰrɛːn hɪˈna͜en, ˌɛɐ̯ˈhɛltʼ fɔn ˈzanftʼɐ ˈhɔfnʊŋ ʃa͜en.
auch fällt der Freunde Trän' hinein, erhellt von sanfter Hoffnung Schein.
also falls the friends' tear into it, lit by gentle hope's gleam.
(the tears of friends also fall into the grave, lit by the gleam of a gentle hope.)
[*Peters & poem:* **doch** (dɔx, yet) **fällt]**

ʊns ˈzaməltʼ ˈˌalə, kʰla͜en ˌʊntʼ groːs, di ˈmʊtʼɐ(r) ˌeːɐ̯tʼ ˌɪn ˈˌiːrən ʃoːs;
Uns sammelt alle, klein und gross, die Mutter Erd' in ihren Schoss;
Us gathers all, small and great, the mother earth into her lap;
(Mother earth gathers all of us, great and small, into her lap;) [*poem:* **sammlet** (ˈzamlətʼ)]

oː zɛːn viːɐ/viːr ˌiːɐ/ˌiːr ˌɪns ˈˌangəzɪçtʰ, viːɐ̯ ˈʃɔ͜øtʼən ˈˌiːrən ˈbuːzən nɪçtʰ!
O sähn wir ihr ins Angesicht, wir scheuten ihren Busen nicht!
Oh, would see we her in the face, we would fear her bosom not!
(Oh, if we could look into her face we would not fear her bosom!)

[Schubert wrote this beautiful and moving song as he was undergoing a serious crisis in the illness that eventually took his life. Here he faces death with serenity. A magical moment is the

382

major harmony at the hint of a reunion after death. The title of the poem is simply "*Lied*"; the first publisher gave the song the title "*Die Mutter Erde*," as in the Peters edition.]

di naxtʰ / di naxtʻ lɪst ˈdʊmp̮fɪç lʊntʻ ˈfɪnstʻɐ
Die Nacht / Die Nacht ist dumpfig und finster
The Night / The Night is Dull and Dark

Posthumously published [composed 1817] (prose poem by James Macpherson—"Ossian")
From *Croma* (German translation by Edmund von Harold)

ˈbardə
BARDE ("FIRST BARD"—five bards are passing the night in the house of a chief):

di naxtʻ lɪst ˈdʊmp̮fɪç lʊntʻ ˈfɪnstʻɐ. lan den ˈhyːgəln ruːn di ˈvɔlkən.
Die Nacht ist dumpfig und finster. An den Hügeln ruhn die Wolken.
The night is dull and dark. On the hills rest the clouds.
([Macpherson's words:] The night is dull and dark. The clouds rest on the hills.)

kʰa͜en ʃtʻɛrn mɪtʻ ˈgryːntsɪtʻɐndəm ʃtʻraːl; kʰa͜en moːntʻ ʃa͜ot dʊrç di lʊftʰ.
Kein Stern mit grünzitterndem Strahl; kein Mond schaut durch die Luft.
No star with green-trembling beam; no moon looks through the air.
(No star with green trembling beam; no moon looks from the sky.)
                    [ˈʃɪmɐ,   kʰa͜en ˈmoːntʻʃtʻraːl lɛɐˈhɛlət das tʰaːl.]
        [*GA & Peters:* **grünzitterndem Schimmer, kein Mondstrahl erhellet das Tal.**]
                    [shimmer,   no   moonbeam   brightens the valley.]

ɪm ˈvaldə høːr ɪç den ha͜ox; ˈlaːbɐ(r) lɪç høːɐ/høːr liːn va͜et lɪn deːɐ ˈfɛrnə.
Im Walde hör' ich den Hauch; aber ich hör' ihn weit in der Ferne.
In the woods hear I the breath; but I hear it far in the distance.
(I hear the blast in the wood; but I hear it distant far.)

deːɐ ʃtʻroːm dɛs tʰaːls lɛɐˈbra͜ostʻ; ˈlaːbɐ za͜en ˈbra͜ozən lɪstʻ ˈʃtʻʏrmɪʃ lʊnt tʰryːpʻ.
Der Strom des Tals erbraust; aber sein Brausen ist stürmisch und trüb.
The stream of the valley roars; but its roaring is stormy and sad.
(The stream of the valley murmurs; but its murmur is sullen and sad.)
                    [*GA & P:* **Der Strom des Bergs** (bɛrks, mountain)...]
                    [(*Harold:*) **ist *störrisch*** (ˈʃtʻœrɪʃ, stubborn) **und trüb.**]

fɔm ba͜om ba͜em ˈgraːbə deːɐ ˈtʰoːtʻən, høːɐtʻ man laŋ di ˈkʰrɛçt͜səndə lɔøl.
Vom Baum beim Grabe der Toten, hört man lang die krächzende Eul'.
From the tree at the grave of the dead hears one long the croaking owl.
(From the tree at the grave of the dead the long-howling owl is heard.)
            [tʰøːnt deːɐ/deːr ˈlɔølə ˈkʰlaːgəndɐ zaŋ.]
  [*GA & P:* **tönt der Eule klagender Sang.** (*Harold:*) **hört man *die lang* krächzende...**]
            [sounds the owl's lamenting song.]

an deːɐ/deːr ˈleːbnə lɛɐˈblɪkʻ lɪç ˈla͜enə ˈdɛmɐndə ˈbɪldʊŋ! lɛs lɪstʻ la͜en ga͜estʰ!
An der Ebne erblick ich eine dämmernde Bildung! es ist ein Geist!
On the plain see I a dim form! It is a ghost!
(I see a dim form on the plain! It is a ghost!)
                    [a͜of deːɐ ˈha͜edə... ˈla͜enən ˈdɛmɐndən ˈʃatʻən,]
                    [*GA & P:* **Auf der Heide... einen dämmernden Schatten,**]
                    [On the heath... a dim shadow,]

eːɐ̯ ˈʃvɪndət*, leːɐ̯ fliːt*. dʊrç ˈdiːzən veːk* vɪrt* ˈlae̯nə ˈlae̯çə ɡəˈtʰraːɡən:
er schwindet, er flieht. Durch diesen Weg wird eine Leiche getragen:
It disappears, it flees. Through this way will a corpse be carried:
(It fades, it flies. Some funeral shall pass this way:) ["*Leiche*" in dialect = funeral]

ˈiːrən pfaːt* bəˈt͡sae̯çnət das ˈlʊft*ˈbɪlt*. di ˈfɛrnərə ˈdɔɡə hɔ͡ølt*
ihren Pfad bezeichnet das Luftbild. Die fernere Dogge heult
its path indicates the air-image. The more distant dog howls
(the meteor marks the path. The distant dog is howling) ["meteor" = any phenomenon in the air]
[(*Harold:*) **Der fernere Dogge** ("*Dogge*" is a feminine noun in modern German)]

fɔn deːɐ̯ ˈhʏt*ə dɛs ˈhyːɡəls, deːɐ̯ hɪrʃ liːk*t* ɪm ˈmoːzə dɛs bɛrks:
von der Hütte des Hügels. Der Hirsch liegt im Moose des Bergs:
from the hut of the hill. The stag lies in the moss of the mountain:
(from the hut of the hill. The stag lies on the mountain moss:)
[*GA & P.:* **Moose des Tannigs** (ˈtʰanɪks, more usually "*Tannichs*"or "*Tannichts,*"fir thicket),]

ˈneːbən liːm ruːt di ˈhɪndɪn. ɪn ˈt͡sae̯nəm ˈlast*ɪçt*ən ɡəˈvae̯ə hø͡ːɐ̯t* ziː den vɪnt*,
neben ihm ruht die Hindin. In seinem astigten Geweihe hört sie den Wind,
beside him rests the hind. In his branched antlers hears she the wind,
(the hind is at his side. She hears the wind in his branchy horns.)
[*GA & P:* **astigen** (ˈlast*ɪɡən); *Schubert (in error):* **Hündinn** ("*Hündin*" = bitch, female dog)]

fɛːɐ̯t* la͡of ʊnt* leːk*t* zɪç t͡sʊr ˈruːə ˈviːdɐ ˈniːdɐ.
fährt auf und legt sich zur Ruhe wieder nieder.
starts up and lays herself to the rest again down.
(She starts, but lies again.) [*At this point three sentences of the poem were cut by Schubert.*]
[(*Harold:*) **fährt auf, legt sich wieder zur Ruhe.**]

ˈdyːst*ɐ(r) ʊnt* ˈkʰɔ͡øçənt, t͡sɪt*ɐnt* ʊnt* ˈtʰra͡orɪç fɛɐ̯ˈloːɐ̯ deːɐ̯ ˈvandrɐ den veːk*.
Düster und keuchend, zitternd und traurig verlor der Wand'rer den Weg.
Dark and panting, trembling and sad lost the traveler the way.
(Dark, panting, trembling, sad, the traveler has lost his way.) [(*Harold:*) **Düster, keuchend,**]

eːɐ̯/eːr ɪrt dʊrç ɡəˈbʏʃə, dʊrç ˈdɔrnən lɛŋs deːɐ̯ ˈʃp*ruːdəlndən ˈkʰvɛlə.
Er irrt durch Gebüsche, durch Dornen längs der sprudelnden Quelle.
He strays through shrubs, throught thorns along the gurgling rill.
(Through shrubs, through thorns, he goes, along the gurgling rill.)

eːɐ̯ ˈfʏrçt*ət di ˈkʰlɪp*ə ʊnt den zʊmpf, leːɐ̯ ˈfʏrçt*ət den ɡae̯st deːɐ̯ naxt*.
Er fürchtet die Klippe und den Sumpf, er fürchtet den Geist der Nacht.
(He fears the rock and the fen, he fears the ghost of the night.)

deːɐ̯/deːr ˈalt*ə ba͡om ɛçt͡st t͡suː dem ˈvɪnt*ʃt*oːs; deːɐ̯ ˈfaləndə ˈlast* lɛɐ̯ˈʃalt*.
Der alte Baum ächzt zu dem Windstoss; der fallende Ast erschallt.
(The old tree groans to the blast; the falling branch resounds.)
[*GA & P:* **es kracht** (ɛs kʰraxt, there crashes) **der fallende Ast.**]

di fɛɐ̯ˈvɛlk*t*ə, t͡suˈzamən fɛɐ̯ˈvɔrənə ˈkʰlɛt*ə ˈtʰrae̯p*t deːɐ̯ vɪnt* ˈlyːbɐ das ɡras.
Die verwelkte, zusammen verworrene Klette treibt der Wind über das Gras.
The withered, together entangled bur(s) [obj.] drives the wind [subj.]over the grass.
(The wind drives the withered burs, clung together, along the grass.)
[*GA & P:* **zum Knäuel** (t͡sʊm ˈkʰnɔ͡øəl, to a ball) **verworrene Klette**]

384

ɛs lıst deːɐ̯ ˈlae̯çt'ə tʰrıt' ˈlae̯nəs ˈɡae̯st'əs! leːɐ̯ beːp't' lın deːɐ̯ ˈmıt'ə deːɐ̯ naxtʰ.
Es ist der leichte Tritt eines Geistes! er bebt in der Mitte der Nacht.
It is the light tread of a ghost! He trembles in the midst of the night.
(It is the light tread of a ghost! He trembles amidst the night.)
     [*GA & P:* **er bebt durch die Schauer** (dʊrç di ˈʃɑo̯ɐ̯, through the terror) **der Nacht.**]

di naxt' lıst 'dyːst'ɐ̯, 'dʊŋk'əl, lʊnt' 'hɔɸlənt'; 'vɔlk'ıçt', 'ʃt'ʏrmıʃ,
Die Nacht ist düster, dunkel, und heulend; wolkigt, stürmisch,
The night is gloomy, dark, and howling; clouded, stormy,
(Dark, dusty, howling is night, cloudy, windy,)   [*Peters:* **wolkig** ('vɔlk'ıç, cloudy)]
     [*GA & P:* **düster, dunkel und grau'nvoll** ('grɑo̯nfɔl, ghastly)]

ʊnt' 'ʃvaŋɐ̯ mıt' 'ɡae̯st'ɐn! di 'tʰoːt'ən 'ʃt'rae̯fən lʊm'heːɐ̯!
und schwanger mit Geistern! Die Toten streifen umher!
and pregnant with ghosts! The dead streak about!
(and full of ghosts! The dead are abroad!)
    [*GA & P:* **zu eigen den** (tsu: 'lae̯ɡən den, belonging to the) **Geistern.**]

ɛm'pfaŋt' mıç fɔn deːɐ̯ naxt', 'mae̯nə 'frɔɸndə.   [iːɐ̯]
Empfangt mich von der Nacht, meine Freunde. [*GA & P:* **ihr, meine Freunde!**]
Receive me from the night, my friends.   [you]
(My friends, receive me from the night.)

deːɐ̯ ɡə'biːt'ɐ   deːɐ̯ 'hɔɸp't'lıŋ
DER GEBIETER (THE MASTER): [*GA & P:* **DER HÄUPTLING** (THE CHIEF):]

las 'vɔlk'ən lan 'hyːɡəln ruːn; 'ɡae̯st'ɐ 'fliːɡən lʊnt' 'vandrɐ 'beːbən.
Lass Wolken an Hügeln ruhn; Geister fliegen und Wandrer beben.
Let clouds on hills rest, spirits fly and travelers tremble.
(Let clouds rest on the hills: spirits fly, and travelers fear.) [*GA & P:* **Geister irren** ('lırən, stray)]

las di 'vındə deːɐ̯ 'vɛldɐ zıç 'heːbən, 'brɑo̯zəndə 'ʃt'ʏrmə hɛ'rap'ʃt'ae̯ɡən.
Lass die Winde der Wälder sich heben, brausende Stürme herabsteigen.
Let the winds of the woods themselves raise, roaring storms descend.
(Let the winds of the woods arise, the sounding storms descend.)
   [*GA & P:* **Stürme das Tal durchweh'n** (das tʰaːl dʊrç'veːn, blow through the valley),]

'ʃt'røːmə 'brʏlən, 'fɛnst'ɐ 'kʰlırən, 'gryːnbəflyːɡəlt'ə 'dɛmpfə 'fliːɡən;
Ströme brüllen, Fenster klirren, grünbeflügelte Dämpfe fliegen;
Streams roar, windows clatter, green-winged vapors fly;
(Roar streams and windows flap, and green-winged meteors fly!) ["meteors"= airy apparitions]
  [(*Harold:*) **Fenster** *schmettern* ('ʃmɛt'ɐn, clang) , *GA & P:* **Dämpfe ziehen** ('tsiːən, move),]

den 'blae̯çən moːnt' zıç 'hınt'ɐ 'zae̯nən 'hyːɡəln lɛɐ̯'heːbən,
den bleichen Mond sich hinter seinen Hügeln erheben,
the pale moon itself (from) behind its hills raise,
(Rise the pale moon from behind her hills,)
     [*GA & P:* **hinter dunkeln** ('dʊŋk'əln, dark) **Hügeln**]
    [(*Harold:*) **der bleich**e **Mond** (deːɐ̯ 'blae̯çə— nominative case, new sentence;
    Schubert continues the sequence "*Lass...*", which calls for the accusative case)]

'loːdɐ zaen hɑop't' ɪn 'vɔlk'ən 'laenhylən; di naxt' gɪlt' miːɐ glaeç;
oder sein Haupt in Wolken einhüllen; die Nacht gilt mir gleich;
or its head in clouds cover; the night means to me (the) same;
(or enclose her head in clouds! Night is alike to me,) ["is alike to me"= is all the same to me]
                            [feɐ'hylən]   [ʃɔɸ lɪç nɪçt']
            [*GA & P:* **in Wolken verhüllen! Die Nacht scheu' ich nicht,**]
                            [conceal]   [dread I not (I do not dread the night)]

di lʊft' zae blɑo, 'ʃt'ʏrmɪʃ, 'loːdɐ 'dʊŋk'əl. di naxt' fliːt' [fliːk't'] foːɐm ʃt'raːl,
die Luft sei blau, stürmisch, oder dunkel. Die Nacht flieht [fliegt*] vorm Strahl,
the air be blue, stormy, or dark. The night flees [flies] before the (sun)beam,
(blue, stormy, or gloomy the sky. Night flies before the beam,) [**(Harold:)** *fliegt* **vorm Strahl**]
                    [kʰlaːɐ... ziː   lɛnt''fliːt' foːɐ dem ʃt'raːl]
            [*GA & P:* **die Luft sei klar... Sie entflieht vor dem Strahl,**]
                    [clear... It (night) flees before the beam]

vɛn leːɐ/leːr lam 'hyːgəl zɪç giːstʰ. deːɐ 'jʊŋə tʰaːk keːɐt' fɔn 'zaenən 'vɔlk'ən,
wenn er am Hügel sich giest. Der junge Tag kehrt von seinen Wolken,
when it at the hill itself pours. The young day returns from its clouds,
(when it is poured on the hill. The young day returns from his clouds,)
                    [di 'hyːgəl feɐ'gɔldətʰ... kʰeːɐt' fɔm   'fernən 'lɔst'ən]
            [*GA & P:* **wenn er die Hügel vergoldet... kehrt vom fernen Osten,**]
                    [the hills gilds... returns from the far east]

'aːbɐ viːɐ 'kʰeːrən 'nɪmɐ tsu'rʏkʰ.   [nɪçt' meːɐ]
aber wir kehren nimmer zurück.   [**(Harold:)** *nicht mehr* **zurück**]
but we return never back.   [no more]
(but we return no more.)

voː zɪnt' 'ʊnzrə 'fyːrɐ deːɐ 'foːɐvɛltʰ? voː zɪnt' 'ʊnzrə vaet' bə'ryːmt'ən gə'biːt'ɐ?
Wo sind unsre Führer der Vorwelt? wo sind unsre weit berühmten Gebieter?
Where are our leaders of the former ages? Where are our far famed rulers?
(Where are our chiefs of old? Where our kings of mighty name?)

'ʃvaegənt' zɪnt di 'fɛldɐ(r) 'liːrɐ 'ʃlaxt'ən. kʰɑom zɪnt' 'liːrə 'moːzɪçt'ən 'greːbɐ
Schweigend sind die Felder ihrer Schlachten. Kaum sind ihre moosigten Gräber
Silent are the fields of their battles. Scarcely are their moss-covered graves
(The fields of their battles are silent. Scarce their mossy tombs)
                    ['ʃvaegən dɛk't' di 'fɛldɐ]   ['moːzɪgən]
            [*GA & P:* **Schweigen deckt die Felder...** (*Peters:*) **moosigen**]
                    [Silence covers the fields]   [mossy]

nɔx 'lyːbrɪç. man vɪrt' lɑox 'ʊnzɐ feɐ'gɛsən.   [zoː vɪrt' man]
noch übrig. Man wird auch unser vergessen.   [*GA & P:* **So wird man auch unser**]
still remaining. One will also us forget.   [Thus will one]
(remain. We shall also be forgot.)

diːs lɛɐ'haːbənə gə'bɔɸ vɪrt tseɐ'falən.   ['diːzɐ 'mɛçt'ɪgə bɑo]
Dies erhabene Gebäu wird zerfallen.   [*GA & P:* **Dieser mächtige Bau**]
This lofty building will fall into ruin.   [This mighty building]
(This lofty house shall fall.)

'ʊnzrə 'zøːnə 'veːɐ̯dən di 'tʰrʏmɐ(r) ɪm 'graːzə nɪçt‘ lɛɐ̯'blɪk‘ən.
Unsre Söhne werden die Trümmer im Grase nicht erblicken.
Our sons will the ruins in the grass not behold.
(Our sons shall not behold the ruins in grass.)

['ʊnzrə 'lɛnk‘əl] [nuːɐ̯/nuːr]
[*GA & P:* **Unsre Enkel werden die Trümmer im Grase nur erblicken.**]
[Our grandchildren] [only]

zi: 'veːɐ̯dən di 'gra͜ezən bə'fraːgən: voː 'ʃt‘andən di 'ma͜oɐn 'ʊnzrə 'fɛːt‘ɐ?
Sie werden die Greisen befragen: "Wo standen die Mauern unsrer Väter?"
They will the old men ask: "Where stood the walls of our fathers?"
(They shall ask of the aged, "Where stood the walls of our fathers?")

[*GA & P:* **die Greise** (gra͜ezə)]

ɛɐ̯'tʰøːnət das liːt‘ lʊnt‘ 'ʃlaːgət di 'harfən;
Ertönet das Lied und schlaget die Harfen;
Sound the song and strike the harps;
(Raise the song, and strike the harp;)

[ʃt‘ɪmt‘ lan den gə'zaŋ, gra͜eft‘ raʃ ɪn di 'za͜et‘ən!]
[*GA & P:* **Stimmt an den Gesang, greift rasch in die Saiten!**]
[tune up the song, grasp quickly into the strings!]
["*anstimmen*" = begin to sing, tune up]

'zɛndət di 'frøːlɪçən 'mʊʃəln hɛ'rʊm.
sendet die fröhlichen Muscheln herum.
send the joyous (drink-)shells around.
(send round the shells of joy.)

['frøːlɪç lɛɐ̯'kʰlɪŋə deːɐ̯ 'bɛçɐ(r) ɪm kʰra͜es.]
[*GA & P:* **Fröhlich erklinge der Becher im Kreis.**]
[Joyously clink the cups in the circle.]

ʃt‘ɛlt‘ 'hʊndɐt‘ 'kʰɛrtsən ɪn di 'høːə. 'jʏŋlɪŋə, 'mɛːt‘çən bə'gɪnət den tʰant͜s.
Stellt hundert Kerzen in die Höhe. Jünglinge, Mädchen beginnet den Tanz.
Place a hundred candles into the height. Youths, maidens, begin the dance.
(Suspend a hundred tapers on high. Youth and maids begin the dance.)

[deːɐ̯ 'fak‘əln 'lɪçt‘glant͜s lɛɐ̯'lɔ͜øçt‘ə di 'halə.]
[*GA & P:* **Der Fackeln Lichtglanz erleuchte die Halle.**]
[(Let) the torches' light-splendor light up the hall.]

na: za͜e la͜en 'gra͜olɔk‘ɪgɐ 'bardə, miːɐ̯ di 'tʰaːt‘ən deːɐ̯ foːɐ̯'vɛlt t͜su: 'zɪŋən;
Nah sei ein graulockiger Barde, mir die Taten der Vorwelt zu singen;
Near be a grey-locked bard to me the deeds of the former times to sing;
(Let some grey bard be near me to tell the deeds of other times;)

[ruːft‘ miːɐ̯ den 'zaŋbəgaːp‘t‘ən 'bardən, lʊns di 'tʰaːt‘ən...]
[*GA & P:* **Ruft mir den sangbegabten Barden, uns die Taten...**]
[Call to me the song-gifted bard, to us the deeds...]

fɔn 'kʰøːnɪgən bə'ryːmt‘ ɪn 'lʊnzɛm lant‘, fɔn gə'biːt‘ɛn, di: viːɐ̯ nɪçt‘ meːɐ̯ zeːn.
von Königen berühmt in unserm Land, von Gebietern, die wir nicht mehr sehn.
of kings renowned in our land, of masters whom we no more see.)
(of kings renowned in our land, of chiefs we behold no more.)

[fɔn 'hɛldən, di: ʃ‘ɔn lɛŋst daˈhɪn.]
[*GA & P:* **von Helden, die schon längst dahin.**]
[of heroes who already long ago (have passed) away.]

las di naxt' 'lalzo fɐɐ'ge:ən, bɪs de:ɐ 'mɔrgən lɪn 'lunzən 'halən lɛɐ'ʃaenə.
Lass die Nacht also vergehen, bis der Morgen in unsern Hallen erscheine.
Let the night thus pass   until the morning in our   halls may appear.
(Thus let the night pass until morning shall appear in our halls.)
                    [last]   [lɪm tʰo:ɐ dɛs 'lɔst'ən]   ['lɔst'əns]
    [*GA & P:* **Lasst die Nacht... Morgen im Tor des Osten** (*Peters: Ostens*) **erscheinet.**]
                [let (2nd person plural)]   [in the gate of the east]

dan zaen nɪçt' 'fɛrnə de:ɐ 'bo:gən, di 'dɔgən, di 'jʏŋlɪŋə de:ɐ ja:k't'.
Dann sei'n nicht ferne der Bogen, die Doggen, die Jünglinge der Jagd.
Then be not far the bow, the dogs, the youths of the chase.
(Then let the bow be at hand, the dogs, the youths of the chase.)
                [dan 'rʏst'ət tsur 'ja:k't'lust den 'bo:gən, di 'dɔgən, das 'mu:t'ɪgə rɔs!]
    [*GA & P:* **Dann rüstet zur Jagdlust   den Bogen, die Doggen, das mutige Ross!**]
                [Then prepare for the hunt-pleasure the bow, the dogs, the valiant steed!]

vi:ɐ 've:ɐdən di 'hy:gəl mɪt dem 'mɔrgən bə'ʃt'aegən, lunt di 'hɪrʃə lɛɐ'vɛk'ən.
Wir werden die Hügel mit dem Morgen besteigen, und die Hirsche erwecken.
We shall the hills with the morning ascend,   and the stags awake.
(We shall ascend the hill with day, and awake the deer.)   [lɪm 'fry:ro:t']
                [*GA & P:* **Wir werden die Hügel im Frührot besteigen,**]
                                [in the dawn]

["JAGDLIED" (by Zacharias Werner, not part of Macpherson's poem or Schubert's song):

tʰra'ra:! tʰra'ra:! vi:ɐ 'tsi:ən hɪ'naos, luns 'lɔk'ət di 'bɔøt'ə de:ɐ ja:k't'!
Trarah! Trarah! Wir ziehen hinaus, uns locket die Beute der Jagd!
Trarah! Trarah! We go out, us lures the booty of the hunt!
(Trarah! We are going out, the booty of the hunt lures us!)

ɛs 'fli:ət di naxt', lɛs zi:k't de:ɐ 'zɔnə pʰraxtʰ; das lɪçt'
Es fliehet die Nacht, es siegt der Sonne Pracht; das Licht
There flees the night, there triumphs the sun's splendor; the light
(The night is fleeing, the sun's splendor triumphs; the light)

hat' 'ly:bɐ das 'dunk'əl maxtʰ! laof, laof, laof! de:ɐ 'junə tʰa:k' luns laxtʰ!
hat über das Dunkel Macht! Auf, auf, auf! Der junge Tag uns lacht!
has over the darkness power! Up, up, up! The young day for us laughs!
(has power over the darkness! Up, up, up! The young day is smiling on us!)

tʰra'ra:! das 'ja:k't'hɔrn lɛɐ'tʰø:nt', di 'hɪrʃə lɪns tʰa:l hɛ'rap' tsi:n.
Trarah! Das Jagdhorn ertönt, die Hirsche ins Tal herab zieh'n.
Trarah! The hunting horn sounds, the stags into the valley down come.
(Trarah! The hunting horn is calling, the stags are coming down into the valley.)

di 'ne:bəl lɛnt'fli:n, de:ɐ 'bɛrgə 'gɪpfəl gly:n, vi:ɐ 'ʃɔøən nɪçt
Die Nebel entflieh'n, der Berge   Gipfel glüh'n, wir scheuen nicht
The mist disappears, the mountains' summits glow, we shun not
(The mist disappears, the summits of the mountains gleam, we do not shun)

de:ɐ 'ja:k't'lust'   my:n. tʰra'ra:! laof! tsum 'valdə last' luns tsi:n!
der Jagdlust   Müh'n. Trarah! Auf! Zum Walde lasst uns zieh'n!
the hunting-pleasure's efforts. Trarah! Up! To the woods let us go!
(the exertions of the hunt. Trarah! Up! Let us go to the woods!)

388

[Schubert's manuscript was lost and unavailable to the editors of the *Gesamtausgabe* and the Peters edition, who had no choice but to reproduce the corrupt version originally published by Diabelli with many unwarranted changes in Schubert's text, with changes in the notation, and with a Hunting Chorus appended, that was not even by Macpherson (but rather by Zacharias Werner, from *Wanda, Königin der Sarmaten*). Schubert's original was discovered by Odd Udbye in the 1960s, in a library in Budapest. The main text, above, is based on that authentic version; the changes found in the published editions are given in brackets. Until the discovery of the manuscript, the horn fanfares in the postlude were assumed to be inauthentic; but it is now clear that they were in fact composed by Schubert. The ineffective ending is probably the reason why the piece is rarely performed, in spite of its musical interest. As for the prose poem, Macpherson claimed, in a footnote, that it had been written a thousand years after Ossian's era, the third century, but that it was the only later work in his style that was worthy of inclusion with the poetry of the ancient Irish bard (who turned out to be a fictitious creation of Macpherson himself). The Ossian myths were enormously popular in Schubert's day, especially in Germany.]

di naxtʰ / duː fɛɐ̯ˈʃtˈøːɐ̯stˈ lʊns nɪçtˈ, loː naxtʰ
Die Nacht / Du verstörst uns nicht, o Nacht
The Night / You Do Not Disturb Us, O Night

Posthumously published [composed 1816?] (poem by Johann Peter Uz)

duː fɛɐ̯ˈʃtˈøːɐ̯stˈ lʊns nɪçtˈ, loː naxtʰ! ziː, viːɐ̯ ˈtʰrɪŋkˈən lɪm gəˈbʏʃə,
Du verstörst uns nicht, o Nacht! Sieh, wir trinken im Gebüsche,
You disturb us not, O night! See, we drink in the bushes,
(You do not disturb us, night! See, we are drinking among the bushes,)

ʊntˈ laen ˈkʰyːlɐ vɪntˈ lɛɐ̯ˈvaxtʰ, das leːɐ̯/leːr ˈlʊnzɛn vaen lɛɐ̯ˈfrɪʃə.
und ein kühler Wind erwacht, dass er unsern Wein erfrische.
and a cool wind awakes, so that it our wine may refresh.
(and a refreshing breeze is stirring, to cool our wine.)

ˈmʊtˈɐ ˈhɔldɐ ˈdʊŋkˈəlhaetʰ, naxtˈ, fɛɐ̯ˈtʰraotˈə ˈzyːsɐ ˈzɔrgən,
Mutter holder Dunkelheit, Nacht, Vertraute süsser Sorgen,
Mother of gracious darkness, night, confidante of sweet cares,

diː bəˈtʰroːgnɐ ˈvaxzaːmkʰaetʰ ˈfiːlə ˈkʰʏsə ʃoːn fɛɐ̯ˈbɔrgən!
die betrog'ner Wachsamkeit viele Küsse schon verborgen!
who from cheated vigilance many kisses already (has) concealed!
(who has already concealed many kisses from cheated vigilance!)

diːɐ/diːr laˈlaen zae ˈmɪtˈbəvʊstʰ vɛlç fɛɐ̯ˈgnyːgən mɪç bəˈraoʃə
Dir allein sei mitbewusst welch Vergnügen mich berausche,
You* alone be with-aware what pleasure me may intoxicate [*subjunctive*]
(You alone be aware with me of what pleasure may intoxicate me)

[*"**bewusst**," in the sense of "aware" calls for the dative pronoun]

vɛn lɪç lan gəˈliːpˈtˈɐ brʊstʰ ˈlʊntˈɐ tʰao lʊntˈ ˈbluːmən ˈlaoʃə!
wenn ich an geliebter Brust unter Tau und Blumen lausche! [*poem:* **wann** (van, when)]
when I at beloved breast beneath dew and flowers listen!
(when, at the breast of my beloved, amid the dew and the flowers, I am listening!)

'mʊrməlt‘ liːɐ̯, vɛn 'laləs ruːtʰ,   'mʊrməlt‘, 'zanft‘bəveːk‘t‘ə 'bɔømə,
Murmelt ihr, wenn alles ruht,   murmelt, sanftbewegte   Bäume,
Murmur you, when all is at rest, murmur, gently stirred   trees,
(Murmur, you gently swaying trees, when all is at rest,)   *[poem:* **wann** (van, when)]

ba̯e dem 'ʃp‘ruːdəln 'haesɐ flu:tʰ, mɪç ɪn 'vɔlʊst‘fɔlə 't‘rɔømə!   ['haesrɐ]
bei dem Sprudeln heisser Flut, mich in wollustvolle Träume!   [*GA:* **heiss'rer***]
with the foaming of hot flood, me into voluptuous dreams!   [of hotter]
(as the hot flood foams, murmur me into voluptuous dreams!)

                 [*Peters:* **in anmutsvolle** ('anmuːt̯sfɔlə / graceful)**Träume]**
          [**poem:* **heischrer** ('haeʃrɐ, of hoarser—*"heischer"* (obs.) = *"heiser"* = hoarse)]

[Except for the harmonies under the word *"erfrische"* (later also *"verborgen," "lausche,"* and
"Träume"), this placid song is rather uneventful, with no hint of the lover's *"wollustvolle"*
dreams (bowdlerized by Peters' Victorian editor to "graceful" dreams).]

Die Nebensonnen see *Winterreise*

di 'nɔnə
Die Nonne
The Nun

Posthumously published [composed 1815] (poem by Ludwig Hölty)

ɛs liːp‘t‘ ɪn 'vɛlʃlant‘   'ɪrgənt‘voː laen 'ʃøːnɐ   'jʊŋɐ 'rɪt‘ɐ
Es   liebt' in Welschland   irgendwo ein schöner   junger Ritter
There loved in southern Europe somewhere a   handsome young   knight
(Somewhere in southern Europe a handsome young knight loved)

              [*"Welschland"* = Italy, France, or Spain]

aen 'mɛːt‘çən, das deːɐ̯   vɛlt‘ ɛnt‘'floː, t‘rɔts   'kʰloːst‘ɐt‘oːɐ̯/-t‘oːr lʊnt‘ 'gɪt‘ɐ;
ein Mädchen, das der   Welt entfloh, trotz   Klostertor   und Gitter;
a   girl   who from the world fled,   in spite of convent gate   and   grating;
(a girl who had fled the world to become a nun; no convent gate or bars could keep him out;)

ʃp‘raːx   fiːl fɔn 'zaenɐ 'liːbəspʰaen lʊnt‘ ʃvuːɐ̯/ʃvuːr laof 'zaenən 'kʰniːən,
sprach   viel von seiner Liebespein und schwur   auf seinen Knieen,
(he) spoke much about his   love- pain and swore   on his   knees
(he spoke much about his love and its pain, and swore on his knees)

zi: laos dem 'kʰɛrk‘ɐ tsuː bə'fraeən lʊnt‘ ʃt‘eːts fyːɐ̯ zi: tsuː 'glyːən   [bə'fraen]
sie aus dem Kerker zu befreien und stets   für sie zu glühen. [*poem:* **befrein]**
her out of the prison to free   and always for her to glow.
(to free her from her prison and always to love her ardently.)

ba̯e 'diːzəm 'mʊt‘ɐgɔt‘'əsbɪlt‘,   ba̯e 'diːzəm 'jeːzʊskʰɪndə,
"Bei diesem Muttergottesbild,   bei diesem Jesuskinde,
"By this   image of the Mother of God, by this   Jesus Child,

das 'liːrə 'mʊt‘ɐ(r)larmə fʏlt‘, ʃvøːɐ̯/ʃvøːr lɪçs diːɐ̯/diːr, loː be'lɪndə!
das ihre Mutterarme füllt, schwör' ich's dir,   o Belinde!
that her mother-arms fills, swear   I   it to you, O Belinda!
(that fills her motherly arms, I swear this to you, Belinda!)

diːɐ̯/diːr lɪstʻ ma͜en 'gant͜səs hɛrt͜s gə'va͜etʻ,   zoː laŋ   lɪç 'loːdəm 'haːbə!
Dir   ist   mein   ganzes   Herz   geweiht,   so   lang   ich   Odem   habe!
To you is   my   whole   heart consecrated, as   long (as) I   breath have!
(My whole heart is consecrated to you, as long as I draw breath!) [*"Odem"* = *"Atem"* = breath]

ba͜e 'ma͜enɐ 'zeːlən 'zeːlɪçkʰa͜et, dɪç liːb ɪç bɪs t͜sum 'graːbə!
Bei   meiner Seelen Seligkeit,   dich lieb' ich bis zum Grabe!"
By   my   soul's   bliss,   you love I   till to the grave!"
(By my soul's hope of bliss, I shall love you unto the grave!")

vas gla͜opʻtʻ la͜en 'larməs 'mɛːtʻçən nɪçt, t͜su'maːl   lɪn 'a͜enɐ 't͜sɛlə?
Was glaubt ein armes Mädchen nicht, zumal   in einer Zelle?
What believes a   poor   girl   not, especially in a   cell?
(What will a poor girl not believe, especially if she is confined in a convent cell?)

ax, ziː fɛɐ̯'gaːs deːɐ̯ 'nɔnənpflɪçt,   des 'hɪməls   lʊnt deːɐ̯ 'hœlə.
Ach, sie vergass der   Nonnenpflicht, des Himmels   und der Hölle.
Ah, she forgot the nun- duty,   the heaven   and the hell.
(Alas, she forgot her duty as a nun, forgot heaven and hell.) [*"vergessen"* formerly with genitive]

diː,   fɔn den 'ɛŋəln 'langəʃa͜otʻ, zɪç   'iːrəm 'jeːzu 'va͜etʻə,
Die,   von den Engeln angeschaut, sich   ihrem Jesu weihte,
(She) who, by the angels watched,   herself to her Jesus dedicated,
(She, who had dedicated herself to her Jesus with angels as witnesses,)

di 'ra͜enə 'ʃøːnə   'gɔtʻəsbra͜otʻ vartʻ   'a͜enəs 'freːflɛs   'bɔʏtʻə.
die reine schöne   Gottesbraut ward   eines Frevlers Beute.
the pure,   beautiful bride of God, became a   criminal's prey.
(she, the pure, beautiful bride of God, became the prey of a criminal.)

dra͜of 'vʊrdə,   viː di 'mɛnɐ   zɪntʻ, za͜en hɛrt͜s fɔn ʃtʊntʻ lan 'la͜oɐ;
Drauf wurde,   wie die Männer sind, sein Herz von Stund' an lauer;
Then became, as the men   are, his   heart from hour   on   more tepid;
(Then, as is the way of men, his heart became more and more tepid from that hour on;)

eːɐ̯/eːr lyːbʻliːs   das 'armə kʰɪntʻ la͜of 'eːvɪç 'iːrɐ 'tʻra͜oɐ,
er   überliess das arme Kind auf ewig ihrer Trauer,
he   abandoned the poor   child for   ever   to her   grief,

fɛɐ̯'gaːs deːɐ̯/deːr 'altʻən 't͜sɛːɐ̯tʻlɪçkʰa͜etʻ lʊntʻ 'alɐ 'za͜enɐ(r) 'a͜edə,
vergass der   alten Zärtlichkeit   und aller seiner   Eide,
forgot the   old   tenderness   and all   of his   vows,

ʊntʻ floːkʻ lɪm 'bʊntʻən   'galakʰla͜etʻ   naːx 'nɔʏɐ(r) 'a͜ogənva͜edə;   [floː]
und flog im   bunten   Galakleid   nach neuer Augenweide;   [*poem:* floh]
and flew in the brightly colored ceremonial dress toward new   feast for the eyes;   [fled]
(and flew, in his brightly colored ceremonial dress, toward some new feast for the eyes;)

bə'gan mɪtʻ 'landɐn 'va͜ebɐn ra͜en   lɪm 'kʰɛrt͜sənhɛlən 'zaːlə,
begann mit andern Weibern Reih'n   im   kerzenhellen Saale,
began with other   women   round dances in the candle-bright ballroom,
(he began to dance with other women in the candlelit ballroom,)

gaːpʻ ˈlandɛn ˈvaɛbɐn ʃmaeçəˈlaen baem ˈlaotʻən ˈtʰraobənmaːlə,
gab andern Weibern Schmeichelein beim lauten Traubenmahle,
gave to other women flatteries at the noisy grapes- meal,
(flattered other women at the noisy, wine-drenched dinner,)

ʊntʻ ˈryːmtʻə zɪç dɛs ˈmɪnəglʏks baeˈ ˈzaenɐ ˈʃøːnən ˈnɔnə,
und rühmte sich des Minneglücks bei seiner schönen Nonne,
and boasted himself of the luck in love with his beautiful nun,
(and bragged about his good luck in love with his beautiful nun,)

ʊntʻ ˈjeːdəs ˈkʰʊsəs, ˈjeːdəs blɪks, ʊntʻ ˈjeːdɐ(r) ˈlandɛn ˈvɔnə.
und jedes Kusses, jedes Blicks, und jeder andern Wonne.
and of every kiss, of every look, and of every other delight.
(bragging publicly about her every kiss, every look, and every other delight.)

di ˈnɔnə, fɔl fɔn ˈvɛlʃɐ vuːtʰ, ɛntˈglyːtʻ ɪn ˈliːrəm ˈmuːtʻə,
Die Nonne, voll von welscher Wut, entglüht' in ihrem Mute,
The nun, full of Southern fury, blazed up in her heart,

ʊntʻ zan laof nɪçts lals dɔlç ʊntʻ bluːtʻ, ʊnt ˈtʰrɔømtʻə nuːɐ fɔn ˈbluːtʻə.
und sann auf nichts als Dolch und Blut, und träumte nur von Blute.
and thought of nothing but dagger and blood, and dreamed only of blood.

ziː ˈdɪŋtʻə ˈpʰlœtsliç ˈlaenə ʃaːɐ fɔn ˈvɪldən ˈmɔøçəlmœrdɛn,
Sie dingte plötzlich eine Schar von wilden Meuchelmördern,
She hired suddenly a band of fierce assassins,

den man, deːɐ ˈtʰrɔøloːs ˈvɔrdən vaːɐ, lɪns ˈtʰoːtʻənraeç tsuː ˈfœrdɛn.
den Mann, der treulos worden war, ins Totenreich zu fördern.
the man, who faithless become had, into the realm of the dead to dispatch.
(to dispatch to the realm of the dead the man who had become unfaithful.)

diː ˈboːrən ˈmançəs ˈmœrdɐʃveːɐtʻ lɪn ˈzaenə ˈʃvartsə ˈzeːlə:
Die bohren manches Mörderschwert in seine schwarze Seele:
They plunge many a murderous sword into his black soul:

zaen ˈʃvartsɐ ˈfalʃɐ gaestʻ lɛntˈfɛːɐtʻ viː ˈʃveːfəldampf deːɐ ˈhøːlə.
sein schwarzer falscher Geist entfährt wie Schwefeldampf der Höhle.
his black false spirit slips out like sulphur- mist from the cave of his heart.
(his black, false spirit slips out from its den in his heart like a sulphurous mist.)
["*Höhle*" = cave, den, etc.; also a ventricle of the heart, here the seat of his soul]

eːɐ ˈvɪmɐt dʊrç di lʊftʻ, voː zaen laen ˈkʰraləntʰɔøfəl ˈharətʰ;
Er wimmert durch die Luft, wo sein ein Krallenteufel harret;
It whimpers through the air, where for it a clawed devil waits;
(It whimpers through the air, where a devil's claws are waiting to snatch it;)

draof vartʻ zaen ˈbluːtʻəndəs gəˈbaen lɪn ˈlaenə grʊftʻ fɛɐˈʃartʰ.   [fɛɐˈʃarətʰ]
drauf ward sein blutendes Gebein in eine Gruft verscharrt. [*poem:* **verscharret**]
then were his bleeding remains into a vault hastily buried.
(then his bleeding remains were hastily buried in a vault.)

di 'nɔnə floːk', viː naxt' bə'gan, tsʊr 'kʰlaɛnən 'dɔrfkʰaˌpʰɛlə,
Die Nonne flog, wie Nacht begann, zur kleinen Dorfkapelle,
The nun flew, as night began, to the little village chapel,

ʊnt' rɪs den 'vʊndən 'rɪt'ɛsman lɑos 'zaɛnɐ 'ruːəʃtɛlə,
und riss den wunden Rittersmann aus seiner Ruhestelle,
and tore the injured knight from his resting place,

rɪs liːm das 'buːbənhɛrts hɛ'rɑos, lʊnt' varfs, den tsɔrn tsuː 'byːsən,
riss ihm das Bubenherz heraus, und warf's, den Zorn zu büssen,
tore from him the knavish heart out, and threw it, the anger to satisfy,
(tore out his knavish heart, and threw it down, to satisfy her fury,)

das dʊmpf lɛɐ̯'ʃɔl das 'gɔt'əshɑos, lʊnt' tʰraːt lɛs mɪt den 'fyːsən.
dass dumpf erscholl das Gotteshaus, und trat es mit den Füssen.
so that dully resounded the house of God, and trampled it with the feet.
(so that the house of God rang with a dull sound, and trampled the heart underfoot.)

iːɐ̯ gaɛst' zɔl, viː di 'zaːgən geːn, ɪn 'diːzɐ 'kʰɪrçə 'vaɛlən,
Ihr Geist soll, wie die Sagen gehn, in dieser Kirche weilen,
Her ghost shall, as the legends go, in this church linger,
(Her ghost, so goes the legend, is supposed to linger in this church,)

ʊnt' bɪs lɪm dɔrf di 'hɛːnə kʰrɛːn, balt' 'vɪmɐn lʊnt' balt' 'hɔɸlən.
und, bis im Dorf die Hähne krähn, bald wimmern und bald heulen.
and, until in the village the cocks crow, now whimper and now howl.
(and, until the cocks crow in the village, is sometimes heard to whimper and sometimes to howl.)

zoˈbalt deːɐ̯ 'hamɐ 'tsvœlfə ʃlɛːk't', rɑoʃt' ziː lan 'graːp'ʃt'aɛnvɛndən
Sobald der Hammer zwölfe schlägt, rauscht sie an Grabsteinwänden
As soon as the hammer twelve stikes, rustles she at tombstone walls
(As soon as the clock strikes twelve, she rustles past tombstone-lined walls,)
[poem: **Sobald der Zeiger** ('tsaɛgɐ, pointer/hand of the clock)*]*

lɑos 'laɛnɐ grʊft' lɛm'pʰoːɐ̯/lɛm'pʰoːr, lʊnt' tʰrɛːk't' laɛn 'bluːt'ənt' hɛrts lɪn 'hɛndən.
aus einer Gruft empor, und trägt ein blutend Herz in Händen.
out of a vault up, and carries a bleeding heart in hands.
(up from a vault, and carries in her hands a bleeding heart.)

di 'tʰiːfən, 'hoːlən 'lɑogən ʃp'ryːn laɛn 'dyːst'ɐroːt'əs 'fɔɸɐ,
Die tiefen, hohlen Augen sprühn ein düsterrotes Feuer,
The deep, hollow eyes emit a dark red fire,

ʊnt' glyːn, viː 'ʃveːfəlflamən glyːn, dʊrç 'liːrən 'vaɛsən 'ʃlaɛɐ.
und glühn, wie Schwefelflammen glühn, durch ihren weissen Schleier.
and glow, as sulphur flames glow, through her white veil.

ziː gaft' lɑof das tsɛɐ̯'rɪsnə hɛrts mɪt' 'vɪldɐ 'raxgəbɛrdə
Sie gafft auf das zerrissne Herz mit wilder Rachgebärde
She stares at the mutilated heart with wild revenge-gesture/bearing
(She stares at the mutilated heart in an attitude of wild revenge)

ʊnt‘ heːp‘t‘ ɛs 'drae̯maːl 'hɪməlvɛrts̬ ʊnt‘ vɪrft‘ ɛs ḷao̯f di 'e̯eːɐ̯də.
und hebt es dreimal himmelwärts und wirft es auf die Erde.
and raises it three times toward heaven and hurls it onto the ground.

ʊnt‘ rɔlt di 'ḷao̯gən 'fɔlɐ vuːt, diː 'ae̯nə 'hœlə 'blɪk‘ən,
Und rollt die Augen voller Wut, die eine Hölle blicken,
And rolls the eyes full of fury, which a hell look,
(And she rolls her eyes, full of fury, which make visible an inner hell,)

ʊnt‘ 'ʃyt‘əlt‘ ḷao̯s dem 'ʃlae̯ɐ bluːt‘, ḷʊnt‘ ʃt‘ampft das hɛrts̬ ḷɪn 'ʃt‘ʏk‘ən.
und schüttelt aus dem Schleier Blut, und stampft das Herz in Stücken.
and shakes from the veil blood, and stamps the heart into pieces.
(and shakes blood from her veil, and tramples the heart to pieces.)

ae̯n 'blae̯çɐ 't‘oːt‘əflɪmɐ maxt‘ ḷɪn'dɛs di 'fɛnst‘ɐ 'hɛlə [ae̯n 'dʊŋk‘lɐ...]
Ein bleicher Totenflimmer macht indess die Fenster helle. [*poem:* **Ein dunkler...**]
A pale deathly glimmer makes meanwhile the windows light. [A dark...]
(A pale, ghostly glimmer meanwhile lights up the windows from inside.)

deːɐ̯ 'vɛçt‘ɐ, deːɐ̯ das dɔrf bə'vaxt‘, zaːs ḷɔft‘ ḷɪn deːɐ̯ kʰa'pʰɛlə.
Der Wächter, der das Dorf bewacht, sah's oft in der Kapelle.
The watchman, who the village guards, saw it often in the chapel.
(The watchman who guards the village has often seen it in the chapel.)

[Recommended for a Hallowe'en recital only.]

di 'pʰɛrlə
Die Perle
The Pearl

Posthumously published [composed 1816] (poem by Johann Georg Jacobi)

ɛs gɪŋ ḷae̯n man ts̬ʊr 'fryːlɪŋsts̬ae̯t‘ dʊrç bʊʃ ḷʊnt‘ fɛldɐ vae̯t‘ ḷʊnt‘ brae̯t‘
Es ging ein Mann zur Frühlingszeit durch Busch und Felder weit und breit
There went a man in the springtime through bush and fields far and wide
(A man wandered in the springtime through bush and field, far and wide,)

ʊm 'bɪrk‘ə, buːx ḷʊnt‘ 'ḷɛrlə;
um Birke, Buch' und Erle;
around birch, beech, and alder;

deːɐ̯ 'bɔø̯mə gryːn ḷɪm 'mae̯ənlɪçtʰ, di 'bluːmən 'drʊnt‘ɐ zaː leːɐ̯ nɪçt‘;
der Bäume Grün im Maienlicht, die Blumen drunter sah er nicht;
the trees' green in the May light, the flowers thereunder saw he not;
(he did not see the green trees in the May sunlight, nor the flowers beneath them;)

leːɐ̯ 'zuːxt‘ə 'zae̯nə 'pʰɛrlə. [di 'pʰɛrlə vaːɐ̯ zae̯n 'hø̯ːçst‘əs guːt‘,
er suchte seine Perle. [Die Perle war sein höchstes Gut,
he was looking for his pearl. [The pearl was his highest good,
(he was looking for his pearl. [The pearl was his most precious possession,)

leːɐ̯ hatʰ ʊm ziː dɛs ˈmeːrəs fluːt dʊrçˈʃɪftʰ, ʊntʰ fiːl gəˈlɪtʰən;
er hatt' um sie des Meeres Flut durchschifft, und viel gelitten;
he had for it the seas' waters through-sailed, and much suffered;
(for its sake he had sailed the seas and suffered much;)

fɔn liːɐ̯ dɛs ˈleːbəns tʰroːstʰ gəˈhɔftʰ, ɪm ˈbuːzən ziː bəˈvaːɐ̯tʰ,
von ihr des Lebens Trost gehofft, im Busen sie bewahrt,
from it the life's consolation hoped, in the bosom it guarded,
(he had hoped it would be his consolation in life, he had guarded it in his bosom,)

ʊntʰ ɔft dem ˈrɔøbɐ(r) ˈlapˈgəʃtʰrɪtʰən. diː zuːxtʰ leːɐ̯ nuːn mɪtʰ veː ʊntʰ lax:
und oft dem Räuber abgestritten. Die sucht' er nun mit Weh und Ach:
and often to the robber denied. It sought he now with moaning and groaning:
(and had often defended it from robbers. Now he was searching for it, moaning and groaning.)

daː viːs man liːm den ˈhɛlən bax, ʊntʰ drɪn di ˈgɔldnə ˈʃmɛrlə;
da wies man ihm den hellen Bach, und drin die goldne Schmerle;
thereupon showed one him the clear brook, and in it the golden loach;
(Thereupon someone showed him a clear brook in which a golden loach was swimming;)

nɪçts half deːɐ̯ bax ɪm ˈzɔnənglants, ɪm ˈbaxə nɪçts deːɐ̯ ˈʃmɛrlən ˈtʰants;
nichts half der Bach im Sonnenglanz, im Bache nichts der Schmerlen Tanz;
nothing helped the brook in the sun- gleam, in the brook nothing the loaches' dance;
(the brook in the sunlight and the dance of the loaches were no help to him;)

eːɐ̯ ˈzuːxtʰə ˈzaenə ˈpʰɛrlə. ʊntʰ ˈzuːxən vɪrtʰ leːɐ̯/leːr ˈlɪmɐ zoː, vɪrtʰ nɪçtʰ
er suchte seine Perle. Und suchen wird er immer so, wird nicht
he was searching for his pearl. And search will he always thus, will not
(he was searching for his pearl. And he will be always searching like that, will not)

dɛs ˈleːbəns ˈveːɐ̯dən froː, nɪçtʰ meːɐ̯ di ˈmɔrgənʃtʰʊndən lam ˈpʰʊrpˈʊrroːtʰən ˈhɪməl zeːn,
des Lebens werden froh, nicht mehr die Morgenstunden am purpurroten Himmel sehn,
of the life become glad, not more the morning hours in the crimson sky see,
(become glad to be alive, will no longer notice the dawn in the crimson sky,)

bɛrkʰ la͜ɔf ʊntʰ ˈniːdɐ mʊs leːɐ̯ gen, bɪs das leːɐ̯ ziː gəˈfʊndən.]
Berg auf und nieder muss er gehn, bis dass er sie gefunden.]
mountain up and down must he go, till that he it (has) found.]
(uphill and down he must go, until he has found it.])

deːɐ̯/deːr ˈlarmɐ ˈpʰɪlgɐ! zoː viː leːɐ̯, geː lɪç tsʊr ˈfryːlɪŋstsaetʰ lʊmˈheːɐ̯
Der arme Pilger! So wie er, geh' ich zur Frühlingszeit umher
The poor pilgrim! Just as he, go I in the springtime about
(The poor pilgrim! Just as he does, I go about in the springtime)

ʊm ˈbɪrkʰə, buːx ʊntʰ ˈlɛrlə; dɛs ˈma͜eəs ˈvʊndɐ zeː lɪç nɪçtʰ; [ˈma͜eən]
um Birke, Buch' und Erle; des Maies Wunder seh' ich nicht; [*poem:* **des Maien**]
around birch, beech, and alder; the May's marvels see I not;
(around birch, beech, and alder; I do not notice the marvels of May;)

vas ˈlaːbɐ(r), lax! vas mɪːɐ̯ gəˈbrɪçtʰ, lɪstʰ meːɐ̯/meːr lals ˈlaenə ˈpʰɛrlə. vas mɪːɐ̯ gəˈbrɪçtʰ
was aber, ach! was mir gebricht, ist mehr als eine Perle. Was mir gebricht,
what however, ah! what to me lacks, is more than a pearl. What to me lacks,
(that which I lack, however, is more than a pearl. What I lack)

vas lıç fɛɐ̯'loːɐ̯, vas lıç tsʊm 'høːçstʼən guːtʼ lɛɐ̯'kʰoːɐ̯, lıstʼ liːpʼ lım 'tʰrɔ͜øən 'hɛrtsən;
was ich verlor, was ich zum höchsten Gut erkor, ist Lieb' im treuen Herzen;
what I lost, what I to the highest good chose, is love in the faithful heart;
(what I lost, what I chose as my most precious possession, is the love of a faithful heart;)

[*poem:* **in treuem** (lın 'tʰrɔ͜øəm) **Herzen,** is love in (a) faithful heart]

fɛɐ̯'geːbəns val lıç lɑ͜of lʊntʼ lapʼ; dɔx fınd ıç lae̯nstʼ lae̯n 'kʰyːləs graːpʼ,
vergebens wall' ich auf und ab; doch find' ich einst ein kühles Grab,
In vain wander I up and down; but find I one day a cool grave,
(in vain I wander up and down; but when one day I find a cool grave,)

das 'lɛndətʼ 'lalə 'ʃmɛrtsən.
das endet alle Schmerzen.
that ends all pains.
(that will end all my suffering.)

[There are too many verses to this attractive song; those in brackets, above, may be omitted without too much damage. The accompaniment suggests the constant searching for the treasure.]

Die Post see *Winterreise*

di 'roːzə
Die Rose
The Rose

Op. 73 [1820?] (Friedrich von Schlegel)

ɛs 'lɔkʼtʼə 'ʃøːnə 'vɛrmə, mıç lan das lıçt tsuː 'vaːgən,
Es lockte schöne Wärme, mich an das Licht zu wagen,
There enticed lovely warmth me to the light to venture,
(Lovely warmth enticed me to venture into the light;)

daː 'brantʼən 'vıldə 'gluːtʼən; das mʊs lıç 'leːvıç 'kʰlaːgən.
da brannten wilde Gluten; das muss ich ewig klagen.
there burned fierce fires; that must I forever lament.
(fierce fires were burning there: that I must forever lament.)

ıç 'kʰɔntʼə 'laŋə 'blyːən lın 'mıldən 'hae̯tʼɐn 'tʰaːgən;
Ich konnte lange blühen in milden heitern Tagen;
I could long bloom in mild, serene days;
(I could bloom for a long time in mild, serene days;)

nuːn mʊs lıç 'fryːə 'vɛlkʼən, dem 'leːbən ʃoːn lɛntʼ'zaːgən.
nun muss ich frühe welken, dem Leben schon entsagen.
now must I early wither, to the life already renounce.
(now I must wither early, renounce life already.)

ɛs kʰaːm di 'mɔrgənrøːtʼə, daː liːs lıç 'laləs 'tsaːgən lʊntʼ 'lœfnətʼə di 'kʰnɔspʼə,
Es kam die Morgenröte, da liess ich alles Zagen und öffnete die Knospe,
There came the dawn, then left I all hesitating and opened the bud,
(Dawn came, I abandoned all hesitation and opened the bud,)

voː lal ˈra͜e̯tsə ˈlaːgən. lɪç ˈkʰɔnt'ə ˈfrɔ͡øntˈlɪç ˈdʊft'ən lʊnt' ˈma͜e̯nə ˈkʰroːnə ˈtʰraːgən,
wo all Reize lagen. Ich konnte freundlich duften und meine Krone tragen,
where all charms lay. I could obligingly be fragrant and my crown wear,
(where all my charms lay. I could spread my fragrance obligingly and wear my crown;)

daː vart t͡su he͜a̯s di ˈzɔnə, diː mʊs lɪç drʊm fɛɐ̯ˈkʰlaːgən.
da ward zu heiss die Sonne, die muss ich drum verklagen.
then became too hot the sun, it must I therefor accuse.
(then the sun became too hot, I must accuse it of that.)

vas zɔl deːɐ̯ ˈmɪldə ˈlaːbənt'? mʊs lɪç nuːn ˈtʰrɑo̯rɪç ˈfraːgən.
Was soll der milde Abend? muss ich nun traurig fragen.
What shall the mild evening? must I now sadly ask.
(What good is the mild evening to me, I must now sadly ask myself.)

eːɐ̯ kʰan mɪç nɪçt' meːɐ̯ ˈrɛt'ən, di ˈʃmɛrt͡sən nɪçt' fɛɐ̯ˈjaːgən.
Er kann mich nicht mehr retten, die Schmerzen nicht verjagen.
It can me not any more rescue, the pains not chase away.
(It can no longer rescue me or chase away my pain.)

di ˈrø̈ːt'ə lɪst' fɛɐ̯ˈblɪçən, balt' vɪrt' mɪç ˈkʰɛlt'ə ˈnaːgən.
Die Röte ist verblichen, bald wird mich Kälte nagen.
The redness is faded, soon will me coldness gnaw.
(The red glow of sunset has faded; soon the cold will gnaw at me.)

ma͜e̯n ˈkʰʊrt͡səs ˈjʊŋəs ˈleːbən vɔlt' lɪç nɔx ˈʃt'ɛrbənt' ˈzaːgən.
Mein kurzes junges Leben wollt' ich noch sterbend sagen.
My short young life wanted I still dying to tell.
(In dying I still wanted a chance to tell about my short young life.)

[The very first bar of the introduction paints a portrait of the delicate rose. As it begins to wilt, it sings its melody in the minor mode, but the very last phrase shifts philosophically back to major. The song was first published in F major; then, with Schubert's approval, in G, for light soprano.]

di ˈʃat'ən
Die Schatten
The Shades*

Posthumously published [composed 1813] (poem by Friedrich von Matthisson)

ˈfrɔ͡øndə, ˈdeːrən ˈgrʏft'ə zɪç ʃoːn bəˈmoːst'ən! van deːɐ̯ ˈfɔlmoːnt'
Freunde, deren Grüfte sich schon bemoosten! Wann der Vollmond
Friends, whose tombs themselves already (have) mossed over! When the full moon
(Friends, whose tombs are already moss-covered! When the full moon)

ˈlyːbɐ dem ˈvaldə ˈdɛmɐtʰ, ˈʃveːbən ˈlɔ͡ørə ˈʃat'ən lɛmˈpʰoːɐ̯
über dem Walde dämmert, schweben eure Schatten empor
over the forest dawns, float your shades* up
(dawns over the forest, your phantoms float up)

[*Schatten = shade = the spirit after its separation from the body, an ancient Greek concept]

fɔm ˈʃtˈɪlən ˈluːfɐ dɛs ˈleːtˈə. sa͜etˈ miːɐ̯/miːr, ˈʊnfɛɐ̯ˈgɛslɪçə, froː gəˈzeːgnətʰ!
vom stillen Ufer des Lethe. Seid mir, Unvergessliche, froh gesegnet!
from the quiet bank of the Lethe. Be by me, unforgettable ones, happily blessed!
(from the quiet banks of Lethe, river of oblivion. Unforgettable friends, I bless you with joy!)
[*poem:* **der** (deːɐ̯, the—genitive of the feminine article) **Lethe** (*more correct German*)]

duː foːɐ̯/foːr ˈlalən, ˈvɛlçɐ(r) ɪm buːx deːɐ̯ ˈmɛnʃha͜etʰ
Du vor allen, welcher im Buch der Menschheit
You before all, who in the book of the humanity
(You above all, who in the book of humanity)

miːɐ̯ deːɐ̯ hiͦeroˈglyːfən zoː fiːl gəˈdɔͦtˈətʰ, ˈreːtˈlɪçɐ ˈbɔnɛ!
mir der Hieroglyphen so viel gedeutet, redlicher Bonnet!
to me of the hieroglyphics so many interpreted, honest Bonnet!
(interpreted so many of the hieroglyphics to me, honest Bonnet!)

lɛŋstˈ fɛɐ̯ˈʃlʏrftˈ ɪm ˈʃtˈruːdəl deːɐ̯ ˈbrandʊŋ vɛːrə voːl ma͜en ˈfaːɐ̯tsɔͦkˈ,
Längst verschlürft im Strudel der Brandung wäre wohl mein Fahrzeug,
Long ago swallowed up in the vortex of the surf were probably my vessel,
(Long ago my vessel would probably have been swallowed up in the vortex of the surf,)

ˈoːdɐ(r) lam rɪf tsɛɐ̯ˈʃmɛtˈɐtʰ, ˈhɛtˈətˈ liːɐ̯ nɪçtʰ, ˈgeːniən gla͜eç,
oder am Riff zerschmettert, hättet ihr nicht, Genien gleich,
or on the reef shattered, had you not, genii like,
(or shattered on a reef, if you, my friends, had not, like genii,)

ɪm ˈʃtˈʊrmə ˈʃɪrməntˈ gəˈvaltˈətʰ. ˈviːdɐzeːn, ˈviːdɐzeːn deːɐ̯ ˈliːbəndən!
im Sturme schirmend gewaltet. Wiedersehn, Wiedersehn der Liebenden!
in the storm protectingly held sway. Reunion, reunion of the loving friends!
(guided me protectingly through the storm. Reunion of loving friends,)
[*poem:* only one "*wiedersehn*"]

voː deːɐ̯ ˈha͜emaːtˈ ˈgɔldnə ˈʃtˈɛrnə ˈlɔͦçtˈən, loː duː
Wo der Heimat goldne Sterne leuchten, o du
Where the homeland's golden stars shine, O you
(where the golden stars of our homeland are shining! Oh you)

deːɐ̯/deːr ˈlarmən ˈpsyːçə, diː gəˈbʊndən ɪm ˈgraːpˈtʰaːl ˈʃmaxtˈətʰ, ˈhɪmlɪʃə ˈzeːnzʊxtʰ!
der armen Psyche, die gebunden im Grabtal schmachtet, himmlische Sehnsucht!
of the poor Psyche, who bound in the grave-vale languishes, heavenly longing!
(heavenly longing of the poor soul, who is languishing here, bound to this valley of the grave!)
[*poem:* **heiligste** (ˈha͜elɪçstˈə, holiest) **Sehnsucht**]

[The long *cantabile* vocal line soars up to high B natural in this rather lovely early song, composed under the influence of Schubert's teacher, Antonio Salieri. The death of Charles Bonnet (1720-93), Swiss scientist and teacher, inspired this poem by his friend and disciple. Psyche is the personification of the soul, who is joined in marriage to the god of love. Lethe was the river of oblivion in the underworld realm of the dead, according to Greek cosmology.]

di ˈʃøːnə ˈmʏlərɪn
Die schöne Müllerin
The Beautiful Daughter of the Miller
Song Cycle, Op.25 [1823-1824] (Wilhelm Müller)

1.

das ˈvandɐn
Das Wandern
Wandering

das ˈvandɐn lɪst dɛs ˈmʏlɐs lʊst, das ˈvandɐn!
Das Wandern ist des Müllers Lust, das Wandern!
The wandering is the miller's pleasure, the wandering!
(Wandering is the miller's pleasure, wandering!)

das mʊs lɑ̯en ˈʃlɛçtˈɐ ˈmʏlɐ zɑ̯en, deːm ˈniːmaːls fiːl das ˈvandɐn lɑ̯en,
Das muss ein schlechter Müller sein, dem niemals fiel das Wandern ein,
That must a bad miller be, to whom never occurred the [idea of] wandering, --
(He who never thought of wandering must be a poor miller,) ["*fiel...ein*" (*einfallen*) = occured]

das ˈvandɐn. fɔm ˈvasɐ ˈhaːbən viːɐ̯s gəˈlɛrntʰ, fɔm ˈvasɐ!
das Wandern. Vom Wasser haben wir's gelernt, vom Wasser!
The wandering. From the water have we it learned, from the water!
(wandering, wandering. We have learned it from the water, from the water!)

das hatˈ nɪçtˈ rastˈ bɑ̯e tʰaːkˈ lʊntˈ naxtʰ, lɪstˈ ʃtˈeːts lɑ̯of ˈvandɐʃaftˈ bəˈdaxtʰ,
Das hat nicht Rast bei Tag und Nacht, ist stets auf Wanderschaft bedacht,
That has not rest by day and night, is constantly on wandering intent,
(That has no rest by day or by night, and is constantly intent on wandering,)

das ˈvasɐ. das zeːn viːɐ̯/viːr lɑ̯ox den ˈrɛːdɐn lapˈ, den ˈrɛːdɐn!
das Wasser. Das sehn wir auch den Rädern ab, den Rädern!
the water. That perceive we also the wheels from, the wheels!
(That we also learn from the wheels!) ["*sehen...ab*" = (in this particular case) look at and imitate]

diː garɐ̯ nɪçtˈ ˈgɛrnə ˈʃtˈɪlə ʃtˈeːn, diː zɪç mɑ̯en tʰaːkˈ nɪçtˈ ˈmyːdə dreːn,
Die gar nicht gerne stille stehn, die sich mein Tag nicht müde drehn,
Which at all not gladly still stand, which themselves my day not tired turn,
(Which do not like to stand still at all, which are not ever tired of turning,)
["*mein Tag*" (colloquial idiom) = in all my days = ever]

di ˈrɛːdɐ! di ˈʃtˈɑ̯enə zɛlpstˈ, zoː ʃveːɐ̯ ziː zɪntˈ, di ˈʃtɑ̯enə!
die Räder! Die Steine selbst, so schwer sie sind, die Steine!
the wheels! The stones themselves, as heavy they are, the stones!
(The stones themselves, heavy as they are, the stones!)

ziː ˈtʰanʦən mɪt den ˈmʊntˈɐn rɑ̯en lʊntˈ ˈvɔlən garɐ̯ nɔx ˈʃnɛlɐ zɑ̯en,
Sie tanzen mit den muntern Reihn und wollen gar noch schneller sein,
They dance with the cheerful roundelay and want even still faster to be,
(They dance along with the cheerful roundelay and want to be even still faster,)

di ʃtʼae̯nə. oː ˈvandɐn, ˈvandɐn, ˈmae̯nə lʊstʰ, oː ˈvandɐn!
die Steine. O Wandern, Wandern, meine Lust, o Wandern!
the stones. O wandering, wandering, my pleasure, O wandering!

hɛr ˈmae̯stʼɐ(r) lʊntʼ frao̯ ˈmae̯stʼərɪn, lastʼ mɪç ɪn ˈfriːdən ˈvae̯tʼɐ ˈt͡siːn
Herr Meister und Frau Meisterin, lasst mich in Frieden weiter ziehn
Sir master and madam mistress, let me in peace farther move on
(Master, sir, and mistress, ma'am, let me move on in peace)

lʊntʼ ˈvandɐn.
und wandern.
and wander.

[The song cycle, *Die schöne Müllerin*, tells the story of a young journeyman miller who finds work at a mill and falls in love with the daughter of his employer. In this, the first song of the cycle, he has just completed his apprenticeship and is leaving the master who has taught him his trade. He starts out on his search for a job, newly independent, full of energy and optimism, and ready for adventure. This strophic song offers a challenge to singer and accompanist to find subtle ways of varying each verse: the accompanist, for example, can play the verse about the water in a flowing legato, the verse about the mill-wheels with a staccato touch (to suggest the wooden clatter), and the verse about the millstones with a heavy emphasis on the bass and a slightly slower tempo. The original title of the poem is "*Wanderschaft*" (Traveling, Journey).]

2.
voˈhɪn?
Wohin?
Where To?

ɪç høːɐ̯t lae̯n ˈbɛçlae̯n ˈrao̯ʃən voːl lao̯s dem ˈfɛlzənkʰvɛl,
Ich hört' ein Bächlein rauschen wohl aus dem Felsenquel,
I heard a brooklet murmur probably out of the rock-spring,
(I heard a brooklet murmuring, probably coming out of a spring among the rocks,)

hɪˈnapʼ t͡sʊm ˈtʰaːlə ˈrao̯ʃən zoː frɪʃ lʊntʼ ˈvʊndɐhɛl.
hinab zum Tale rauschen so frisch und wunderhell.
downwards to the valley rush so fresh and wonder-clear.
(rushing down towards the valley, so fresh and wondrously clear.)

ɪç vae̯s nɪçtʼ viː miːɐ̯ ˈvʊrdə, nɪçtʼ veːɐ̯ den raːtʼ miːɐ̯ ɡaːpʼ,
Ich weiss nicht, wie mir wurde, nicht, wer den Rat mir gab,
I know not what to me became, not who the advice to me gave,
(I don't know what came over me, nor who told me to do it,)

ɪç ˈmʊstʼə lao̯x hɪˈnʊntʼɐ mɪtʼ ˈmae̯nəm ˈvandɐʃtʼaːpʼ.   [ɡlae̯ç]
ich musste auch hinunter mit meinem Wanderstab. [*poem:* **ich musste gleich hinunter**]
I had to also [go] down with my walking stick.   [right away]
(I too had to head downwards with my walking stick.)

hɪˈnʊntʼɐ(r) lʊntʼ lˈɪmɐ ˈvae̯tʼɐ(r), lʊntʼ lˈɪmɐ dem baxə naːx,
Hinunter und immer weiter, und immer dem Bache nach,
Downwards and ever farther, and ever the brook after,
(Downwards and ever farther, and always following the brook,)

ʊnt' ˡɪmɐ 'frɪʃɐ 'rɑ͜ʊʃt'ə lʊnt' ˡɪmɐ 'hɛlɐ deːɐ̯ bax.
und immer frischer rauschte und immer heller der Bach.
and ever fresher murmured and ever clearer the brook.
(and the brook was babbling more and more freshly and more and more brightly.)

ɪst das dɛn 'ma͜enə 'ʃtraːsə? oː 'bɛçla͜en, ʃprɪç, voˈhɪn?
Ist das denn meine Strasse? O Bächlein, sprich, wohin?
Is that then my road? Oh brooklet, speak, to where?

duː hast' mɪt da͜enəm 'rɑ͜ʊʃən miːɐ̯ gan͜ts bəˈrɑ͜ʊʃt den zɪn.
Du hast mit deinem Rauschen mir ganz berauscht den Sinn.
You have with your babbling me completely enchanted the mind.
(With your babbling you have completely enchanted my mind.)

vas zaːk' lɪç dɛn fɔm 'rɑ͜ʊʃən? das kʰan kʰa͜en 'rɑ͜ʊʃən za͜en:
Was sag' ich denn vom Rauschen? das kann kein Rauschen sein:
What say I then about the babbling? that can no babbling be:
(What am I saying about babbling? That can't be just babbling:)
[*poem:* **von** (fɔn, of/about) **Rauschen**]

ɛs 'zɪŋən voːl di 'nɪksən tʰiːf ˡʊnt'ən ˡliːrən ra͜en.
Es singen wohl die Nixen tief unten ihren Reihn.
There sing probably the water nymphs deep down below their roundelays.
(The water nymphs must be singing their roundelays down in the depths.)
[*poem:* **dort** (dɔrt', there) **unten:** down there, there below)]

las 'zɪŋən, gəˈzɛl, las 'rɑ͜ʊʃən, lʊnt' 'vandrə 'frølɪç naːx!
Lass singen, Gesell, lass rauschen, und wandre fröhlich nach!
Let sing, comrade, let murmur, and wander merrily after!
(Let them sing, friend, let the brook murmur and follow it merrily!)

ɛs geːn ja 'myːlənreːdɐ(r) lɪn 'jeːdəm 'kʰlaːrən bax.
Es gehn ja Mühlenräder in jedem klaren Bach.
There go after all millwheels in every clear brook.
(After all, there will be mill-wheels turning in every clear brook.)

[The young miller starts to follow a brook, reasoning that sooner or later it will bring him to a mill, where perhaps he may find employment. The murmur of the brook seems to be a siren song that leads him onward toward his destiny.]

3.

haltʰ!
Halt!
Halt!

'a͜enə 'myːlə zeː lɪç 'blɪŋk'ən lɑ͜ʊs den ˡɛrlən hɛ'rɑ͜ʊs, ['blɪk'ən]
Eine Mühle seh' ich blinken aus den Erlen heraus, [*poem:* **seh' ich blicken**]
A mill see I gleam out of the alder trees hither, [look]
(I see a mill gleaming through the alder trees,)

dʊrç 'rɑ͜ʊʃən lʊnt' 'zɪŋən brɪçt' 're:dɐgəbrɑ͜ʊs.
durch Rauschen und Singen bricht Rädergebraus.
through murmuring and singing breaks wheels-roaring.
(a roaring of wheels breaks through the murmur of the brook and the singing of the water sprites.)

ae̯ vɪl'kʰɔmən, |ae̯ vɪl'kʰɔmən, 'zyːsɐ 'myːləngəzaŋ!
Ei willkommen, ei willkommen, süsser Mühlengesang!
Ah! welcome! ah! welcome, sweet mill-song!

ʊnt das hao̯s, viː zoː 'tʰrao̯lɪç! |ʊnt di 'fɛnstɐ, viː blaŋkʰ!
Und das Haus, wie so traulich! und die Fenster, wie blank!
And the house, how so cosy! and the windows, how shiny!
(And the house, how cosy it is! And the windows, how shiny!)

ʊnt di 'zɔnə, viː 'hɛlə fɔm 'hɪməl zi: ʃae̯nt!
und die Sonne, wie helle vom Himmel sie scheint!
and the sun, how brightly from the heaven it shines!
(and the sun, how brightly it shines down from heaven!)

ae̯, 'bɛçlae̯n, 'liːbəs 'bɛçlae̯n, vaːɐ̯/vaːr lɛs 'lalzo gə'mae̯nt?
Ei, Bächlein, liebes Bächlein, war es also gemeint?
Ah, brooklet, dear brooklet, was it like this meant?
(Ah, brooklet, dear brooklet, was it meant to happen like this? Was this place meant for me?)

[The young miller comes upon a mill among the alder trees by the brook. The place looks inviting. Did the brook lead him here on purpose? Was he meant to find this mill?]

4.
'daŋk'zaːgʊŋ an den bax
Danksagung an den Bach
Saying Thanks to the Brook

vaːɐ̯/vaːr lɛs 'lalzo gə'mae̯nt, mae̯n 'rao̯ʃəndɐ frɔø̯ntʰ?
War es also gemeint, mein rauschender Freund?
Was it like this meant, my murmuring friend?
(Was it meant to happen like this, my murmuring friend?)

dae̯n 'zɪŋən, dae̯n 'kʰlɪŋən, vaːɐ̯/vaːr lɛs 'lalzo gə'mae̯ntʰ?
dein Singen, dein Klingen, war es also gemeint?
your singing, your tinkling, was it like this meant?
(Your singing, your babbling, is *this* what they meant?)

tsʊr 'mʏlərɪn hɪn! zoː 'lao̯tʰət deːɐ̯ zɪn.
Zur Müllerin hin! so lautet der Sinn.
To the miller's daughter away! so sounds the sense.
(Away to the miller's daughter! That was the sense of your singing.)

gɛltʰ, haːb ɪçs fɛɐ̯'ʃtʰandən? tsʊr 'mʏlərɪn hɪn!
Gelt, hab' ich's verstanden? zur Müllerin hin!
Right? have I it understood? to the miller's daughter away!
(Right? Have I understood it? Away to the miller's daughter!)

hatʰ zi: dɪç gə'ʃɪktʰ? 'loːdɐ hastʰ mɪç bə'rʏktʰ?
Hat sie dich geschickt? oder hast mich berückt?
Has she you sent? or have you me ensnared?
(Has *she* sent you? Or have you been fooling me?)

das mœçt‘ lıç nɔx ‘vısən, lɔp‘   zi: dıç gə‘ʃıktʰ.
das möcht’ ich noch wissen, ob   sie dich geschickt.
that would like I   still   to know, whether she you sent.
(I would still like to know that, whether *she* sent you.)

nuːn viːs lɑọx maːk‘ zaẹn, lıç ‘geːbə mıç   drạen:
Nun wie’s auch mag sein, ich gebe mich   drein:
Well, how it also may be,   I   give   myself into it:
(Well, however it may be, I go along with it:)   [“*wie auch*” = however]

vas lıç zuːx, haːb ıç ‘fʊndən, viːs   ‘ımɐ maːk‘ zaẹn.
was ich such’, hab ich funden, wie’s immer mag sein.
what I   seek   have I   found,   how it ever   may   be.
(I have found what I am looking for, however it may be.)

naːx ‘larbaẹt‘ lıç fruːk‘, nuːn haːb ıç gə‘nuːk‘,
Nach Arbeit ich frug, nun hab ich genug,
For work   I   asked, now have I   enough,
(I asked for work; now I have enough,)

fyːɐ̯ di ‘hɛndə, fyːɐ̯s ‘hɛrt͡sə fɔl‘lɑọf   gə‘nuːk‘!
für die Hände, fürs Herze vollauf   genug!
for the hands, for the heart   abundantly enough!
(more than enough for my hands and for my heart!)

[He has met the pretty daughter of the miller and is falling in love with her.]

5.
am ‘faẹɐ̯laːbn̩t‘
Am Feierabend
At the End of the Workday

hɛt‘ lıç ‘tʰɑọzənt‘ ‘larmə t͡su ‘ryːrən!   kʰœnt‘ lıç ‘brɑọzənt‘ di ‘reːdɐ ‘fyːrən!
Hätt ich tausend Arme zu rühren!   könnt ich brausend die Räder führen!
Had I   thousand arms to   set in motion! Could I   roaring   the wheels drive!
(If only I had a thousand arms to set in motion! If only I could set the mill-wheels roaring!)

kʰœnt‘ lıç ‘veːən dʊrç   ‘lalə ‘hạenə! kʰœnt‘ lıç ‘drẹən ‘lalə ‘ʃt‘ạenə!
könnt ich wehen durch   alle Haine! könnt ich drehen alle Steine!
Could I   blow   through all   groves! could I   turn   all   stones!
(If only I could blow like the wind through all the trees! If only I could turn every millstone!)

das   di ‘ʃøːnə ‘mʏlərın   ‘mɛrk‘t‘ə   ‘mạenən ‘tʰrɔ̨ø̃n zın!
dass   die schöne Müllerin   merkte   meinen treuen Sinn!
so that the beautiful daughter of the miller would notice my   faithful intention!

ax, viː lıst mạen larm zoː ʃvax!   vas lıç ‘heːbə, vas lıç ‘tʰraːgə,
Ach, wie ist mein Arm so schwach! Was ich hebe, was ich trage,
Ah, how is my   arm so weak!   What I   lift,   what I   carry,
(Ah, how weak my arm is! What I lift, what I carry,)

vas lıç 'ʃnaedə,   vas lıç 'ʃlaːgə, 'jeːdɐ 'kʰnapə   tʰuːt' miːɐs naːx.
was ich schneide, was   ich schlage, jeder Knappe   tut   mir's nach.
what I   cut,   what I   strike,   any   miller's apprentice does me it after.
(what I cut, what I strike, any miller's apprentice can do it after me just as well.)

[*poem:* jeder Knappe tut es (lɛs, it) nach]

ʊnt daː zıts lıç lın deːɐ 'groːsən 'rʊndə, lın deːɐ 'ʃt'ılən, 'kʰyːlən 'faeɐʃt'ʊndə,
Und da   sitz ich in der grossen Runde, in der stillen, kühlen Feierstunde,
And there sit I   in the big   circle, in the quiet, cool   leisure hour,
(And there I sit in the big circle with the others, in the quiet, cool hour after work is done,)

ʊnt deːɐ 'maestɐ ʃprıçt tsuː 'lalən: 'lɔøɐ vɛrk' hat' miːɐ gə'falən;
und der Meister spricht zu   allen: euer Werk hat mir gefallen;
and the master speaks to all: your work has me   pleased;
(and the master speaks to all: your work has pleased me;)

ʊnt das 'liːbə 'mɛːtçən zaːktʰ 'lalən 'laenə 'guːt'ə naxtʰ.
und das liebe Mädchen sagt   allen eine gute Nacht.
and the dear girl   says   to all a   good night.

[The young worker wishes he could impress the miller's daughter with his zeal and devotion. If
only he had a thousand arms! The master speaks with gravity, his daughter with sweetness.]

6.
deːɐ 'nɔøgiːrıgə
Der Neugierige
The Curious One

ıç 'fraːgə 'kʰaenə 'bluːmə, lıç 'fraːgə 'kʰaenən ʃt'ɛrn;
Ich frage   keine Blume, ich frage   keinen Stern;
I question no   flower, I question no   star;
(I do not ask the question of any flower, I do not ask the question of any star;)

ziː 'kʰœnən miːɐ/miːr 'lalə nıçt' 'zaːgən, vas lıç lɛɐ'fyːɐ   zoː gɛrn.
sie können mir   alle nicht sagen, was ich erführ   so gern.
they can   me   all not tell,   what I would find out so gladly.
(none of them can tell me what I so eagerly would like to know.)

ıç bın ja   laox kʰaen 'gɛrtnɐ. di 'ʃt'ɛrnə ʃt'eːn tsuː hoːx;
Ich bin ja   auch kein Gärtner, die Sterne stehn zu hoch;
I   am after all also no   gardener, the stars stand too high;
(Furthermore, I am not a gardener, after all, and the stars are too high to reach;)

maen 'bɛçlaen vıl lıç 'fraːgən,   lɔp' mıç maen hɛrts bə'loːk'.
mein Bächlein will ich fragen,   ob   mich mein Herz belog.
my   brooklet want I   to question, whether me   my   heart lied to.
(I want to ask my little brook whether my heart lied to me.)

oː 'bɛçlaen 'maenɐ 'liːbə, viː bıst duː hɔøt' zoː ʃt'ʊm!
O Bächlein meiner Liebe, wie bist du heut so stumm!
Oh brooklet of my love, how are you today so silent!
(Oh brooklet of my love, how silent you are today!)

404

vɪl   jaː   nuːr ˈlae̯nəs   ˈvɪsən,   lae̯n ˈvœrtçən   lʊm   lʊntˈlʊm.
Will   ja   nur eines   wissen,   ein Wörtchen um   und um.
[I] Want after all only one thing to know, one   little word around and around.
(I only want to know *one* thing, after all, one little word one way or the other.)

["*um und um*"= on (or from) all sides]

    jaː   hae̯st   das ˈlae̯nə ˈvœrtçən,   das ˈlandrə ˈhae̯sətˈ   nae̯n;
    "Ja,"   heisst   das eine   Wörtchen, das andre heisset: "Nein;"
    "Yes,"   is called the one   little word, the other   is called: "No";
    (The one little word is "Yes," the other is "No";)

di: ˈbae̯dən ˈvœrtçən   ˈʃliːsən   di: ˈgantsə vɛltˈˈ   miːɐ̯/miːr lae̯n.
die beiden Wörtchen schliessen die ganze Welt mir   ein.
the both   words   enclose   the whole world for me.   ... .   ["*einschliessen*"= enclose]
(those two words encompass the whole world for me.)

o: ˈbeçlae̯n ˈmae̯nɐ ˈliːbə, vas bɪst du ˈvʊndɐlɪç!
O Bächlein meiner Liebe, was bist du wunderlich!
Oh brooklet of my   love,   how are you strange!
(Oh brooklet of my love, how strange you are!)

vɪls   jaː   nɪçtˈ ˈvae̯tˈɐ   zaːgən, zaːkˈ, beçlae̯n, liːptˈ zi: mɪç?
Will's   ja   nicht weiter   sagen, sag, Bächlein, liebt sie mich?
[I] want it certainly not   farther (to others) to tell, say, brooklet, loves she me?
(I certainly won't repeat it to anyone, tell me, brooklet, -- does she love me?)

[In this tender song the shy young man asks his friend the brook to tell him if the miller's lovely
daughter loves him, yes or no. The brook is strangely silent.]

7.
ˈʊngədʊltˈ
Ungeduld
Impatience

ɪç ʃnɪtˈ   lɛs gɛrn lɪn ˈlalə ˈrɪndən lae̯n,
Ich schnitt   es gern in   alle Rinden ein,
I   would cut it gladly into all   barks   ... ,   ["*schnitt ein*" from "*einschneiden*" = cut into]
(I would like to carve it into every tree-trunk,)

ɪç gryːpˈ   lɛs gɛrn lɪn ˈjeːdən ˈkʰiːzəlʃtˈae̯n,
ich grüb   es gern in   jeden Kieselstein,
I   would engrave it gladly into every pebble,
(I would like to engrave it on every pebble,)

ɪç mœçtˈ   lɛs zeːn   lao̯f ˈjeːdəs ˈfrɪʃə   beːtʰ
ich möcht   es sä'n   auf jedes frische Beet
I   would like it to sow on every fresh   plot
(I would like to sow it on every fresh flower-bed)

mɪtˈ ˈkʰrɛsənzaːmən, deːɐ̯/deːr lɛs ʃnɛl   fɛɐ̯reːtʰ,
mit Kressensamen, der   es schnell verrät,
with cress-seed,   which   it quickly would betray,
(with cress-seed, which would quickly divulge it,)   [cress-seed is very quick to sprout!]

ɑof ˈjeːdən ˈvaesən ˈtsɛtˈəl   mœçtˈ   lɪçs ˈʃraebən:
auf jeden weissen Zettel   möcht   ich's schreiben:
on every white   scrap of paper would like I   it to write:
(I would like to write it on every scrap of white paper:)

daen lɪst maen hɛrts, lʊntˈ zɔl lɛs ˈleːvɪç   ˈblaebən.
dein ist mein Herz, und soll es ewig   bleiben.
yours is my   heart, and shall it eternally remain.
(yours is my heart, and it shall eternally remain yours.)

ɪç mœçtˈ   miːɐ̯ ˈtsiːən ˈlaenən ˈjʊŋən ʃtˈaːɐ̯/ʃtˈaːr,
Ich möcht   mir ziehen einen   jungen Star,
I would like me to train a   young   starling,
(I would like to train me a young starling,)

bɪs das leːɐ̯ ʃprɛːç   di ˈvɔrtˈe raen lʊntˈ klaːɐ̯/klaːr,
bis dass er spräch   die Worte rein   und klar,
until that he would speak the words cleanly and clearly,
(until he would speak the words cleanly and clearly,)

bɪs leːɐ̯ ziː ʃprɛːç   mɪtˈ ˈmaenəs ˈmʊndəs kʰlaŋ,
bis er sie spräch   mit meines Mundes klang,
until he them would speak with my   mouth's sound,
(until he would speak them with the sound of my voice,)

mɪtˈ ˈmaenəs ˈhɛrtsəns ˈfɔləm, ˈhaesəm draŋ;   [*Peters:* **vollem, heissen** (ˈhaesən) **Drang**]
mit meines Herzens vollem, heissem Drang;
with my   heart's   full,   ardent   urgency;
(with the full ardent urgency of my heart;)

dan zɛŋ   leːɐ̯ hɛl   dʊrç ˈliːrə ˈfɛnstˈɐʃaebən:
dann säng   er hell   durch ihre Fensterscheiben:
then would sing he brightly through her windowpanes:
(then he would brightly sing through her windowpanes:)

daen lɪstˈ maen hɛrts, lʊntˈ zɔl lɛs ˈleːvɪç   ˈblaebən.
dein ist mein Herz, und soll es ewig   bleiben.
yours is my   heart, and shall it eternally remain.
(yours is my heart, and it shall eternally remain yours.)

den ˈmɔrgənvɪndən mœçtˈ   lɪçs ˈhɑoxən laen,
Den Morgenwinden möcht   ich's hauchen ein,
To the morning winds would like I   it to breathe into,
(I would like to breathe it into the morning winds,)

ɪç mœçtˈ   lɛs ˈzɔøzəln dʊrç   den ˈreːgən haen;
ich möcht   es säuseln durch den regen Hain;
I would like it to whisper through the moving grove;
(I would like to whisper it through the swaying trees;)

oː ˈlɔøçtˈətˈ   lɛs lɑos ˈjeːdəm ˈbluːmənʃtˈɛrn!
o leuchtet'   es aus   jedem Blumenstern!
oh would shine it out of every flower-star!
(oh if it would only shine out of every starlike flower!)

tryːkʻ   lɛs deːɐ̯ dʊft   t͜suː iːɐ̯ fɔn naː ʊntʻ fɛrn!
trüg   es der Duft   zu ihr von nah und fern!
would carry it   the   fragrance to   her from near and far!
(if the fragrance would carry it to her from near and far!)

iːɐ̯ ˈvoːgən, kʰœntʻ liːɐ̯ nɪçt͜s   lals ˈreːdɐ ˈtʰrae̯bən?
Ihr Wogen, könnt ihr nichts als Räder treiben?
You waves,   can   you nothing but wheels drive?
(You waves, can you do nothing but drive mill-wheels?)

dae̯n lɪstʻ mae̯n hɛrt͜s, ʊntʻ zɔl lɛs ˈleːvɪç   ˈblae̯bən.
dein ist mein Herz, und soll es ewig   bleiben.
yours is   my   heart, and shall it eternally remain.
(yours is my heart, and it shall eternally remain yours.)

ɪç mae̯ntʻ,   lɛs mʏstʻ lɪn ˈmae̯nən ˈla̯o̯gən ʃtʻeːn,
Ich meint,   es müsst in meinen Augen stehn,
I   would think, it ought in my   eyes   to stand,
(I should think that it would have to be seen in my eyes,)

a̯o̯f ˈmae̯nən ˈvaŋən   mʏstʻ mans ˈbrɛnən zeːn,
auf meinen Wangen müsst man's brennen sehn,
on my   cheeks   ought one it burning to see,
(on my cheeks one ought to see it burning,)

t͜suː leːzən vɛːɐ̯s   la̯o̯f ˈmae̯nəm ˈʃtʻʊmən mʊntʻ,
zu lesen wär's   auf meinem stummen Mund,
to   read   would be it on my   silent   mouth,
(it should be readable on my silent mouth,)

ae̯n ˈjeːdɐ(r) ˈlaːtʰəmt͜suːkʻ gɛːps   la̯o̯tʻ liːɐ̯ kʰʊntʻ;
ein jeder Atemzug gäb's   laut ihr   kund;
an   every   breath   would give it loudly to her known;
(every breath should loudly make it known to her;)

ʊntʻ siː mɛrktʻ nɪçt͜s   fɔn lal dem ˈbaŋən ˈtʰrae̯bən:
und sie merkt nichts von all dem bangen Treiben:
and she notices nothing of   all the   anxious activity:

dae̯n lɪstʻ mae̯n hɛrt͜s, ʊntʻ zɔl lɛs ˈleːvɪç   ˈblae̯bən.
dein ist mein Herz, und soll es ewig   bleiben.
(yours is my heart, and it shall eternally remain yours.)

[The words tumble out of him in this exuberant song. He would like his love for her to be proclaimed everywhere; but the girl never seems to notice what must surely be very obvious.]

8.

'mɔrgəngruːs
Morgengruss
Morning Greeting

'guːt'ən 'mɔrgən, 'ʃøːnə 'mYlərɪn!   voː ʃt'ɛkst du glaeç   das 'kʰœpfçən hɪn,
Guten Morgen, schöne Müllerin!   **wo steckst du gleich**   **das Köpfchen hin,**
Good morning, lovely maid of the mill! where hide   you right now the little head ... ,
(Good morning, lovely maid of the mill! Where are you hiding your little head right now,)

lals veːɐ̯ diːɐ̯ vas   gə'ʃeːən? fɛɐ̯'driːst dɪç dɛn maen gruːs zoː ʃveːɐ̯?
als wär dir was   geschehen? Verdriesst dich denn mein Gruss so schwer?
as if were to you something happened? Annoys   you then my   greeting so gravely?
(as if something had happened to you? Does my greeting annoy you then so oppressively?)

fɛɐ̯'ʃt'øːɐ̯t dɪç dɛn maen blɪk' zoː zeːɐ̯? zoː mʊs lɪç 'viːdɐ 'geːən.
verstört dich denn mein Blick so sehr? So   muss ich wieder gehen.
disturbs you then my   look so much? Then must I   again go.
(Does my look disturb you then so very much? Then I must go away again.)

oː las mɪç nuːɐ̯ fɔn 'fɛrnə ʃt'eːn, naːx 'daenəm 'liːbən 'fɛnst'ɐ zeːn,
O lass mich nur von ferne stehn, nach   deinem lieben Fenster sehn,
Oh let me   only from afar stand, toward your   dear   window look,
(Oh, just let me stand at some distance away and look at your dear window,)

fɔn 'fɛrnə, gants fɔn 'fɛrnə! duː 'blɔndəs 'kʰœpfçən, kʰɔm hɛɐ̯'foːɐ̯!
von ferne, ganz   von ferne! Du blondes Köpfchen, komm hervor!
from afar,   entirely from afar!   You blond   little head, come forth!

hɛɐ̯'foːɐ̯/hɛɐ̯'foːr laos 'lɔøɾəm 'rʊndən tʰoːɐ̯/tʰoːr, liːɐ̯ 'blaoən 'mɔrgənʃt'ɛrnə!
hervor   aus eurem runden Tor,   ihr blauen Morgensterne!
forth   out of your round gate,   you blue   morning stars!

iːɐ̯ 'ʃlʊmɐ'tʰrʊŋknən 'lɔøgəlaen, liːɐ̯ 'tʰaobə'tʰryːpt'ən 'blyːməlaen,
Ihr schlummertrunknen Äugelein, ihr taubetrübten   Blümelein,
You slumber- drunk   little eyes, you dew-dimmed   little flowers,

vas 'ʃɔøət' liːɐ̯ di 'zɔnə? hat' lɛs di naxt' zoː guːt' gə'maentʰ,
was scheuet ihr die Sonne? Hat es die Nacht so gut gemeint,
why shun   you the sun?   Has it the night so well meant,
(why do you shun the sun? Was the night so good to you,)

das liːɐ̯/liːr lɔøç   ʃliːst' lʊnt' bYkt'   lʊnt' vaentʰ naːx 'liːrɐ 'ʃt'ɪlən 'vɔnə?
dass ihr euch   schliesst und bückt   und weint nach ihrer stillen Wonne?
that you yourselves close   and bow down and weep after its   quiet rapture?
(that you close, droop, and weep, longing to recapture its quiet bliss, your lovely dreams?)

nuːn 'ʃYt'əlt' lap' deːɐ̯ 'tʰrɔømə floːɐ̯, lʊnt' heːpt' lɔøç frɪʃ lʊnt' frae lɛm'poːɐ̯
Nun schüttelt ab der Träume Flor, und hebt euch   frisch und frei empor
Now shake off the dreams' gauze, and raise yourself fresh and free up
(Now shake off the veil of dreams and rise up, fresh and free,)

ɪn ˈgɔtˈəs ˈhɛlən ˈmɔrgən! di ˈlɛrçə ˈvɪrbəltˈ ɪn deːɐ̯ lʊftʰ,
in Gottes hellen Morgen! Die Lerche wirbelt in der Luft,
into God's bright morning! The lark warbles in the air,

ʊntˈ lɑos dem ˈtʰiːfən ˈhɛrtsən ruːft di ˈliːbə lae̯tˈ lʊntˈ ˈzɔrgən.
und aus dem tiefen Herzen ruft die Liebe Leid und Sorgen.
and out of the deep heart calls the love sorrow and cares.
(and love calls sorrow and care away from the depths of the heart.)

[The miller's daughter does not show her face at the window when the young man comes to give her his morning greeting. Should he perhaps stand farther away and watch her window from a distance? Were her dreams so lovely that she does not want to wake up? She should come out into God's bright morning: love will charm any unhappiness out of her heart!]

9.

des ˈmʏlɐs ˈbluːmən
Des Müllers Blumen
The Miller's Flowers

am ˈbax fiːl ˈkʰlae̯nə ˈbluːən ʃtˈeːn, lɑos ˈhɛlən, ˈblɑo̯ən ˈlɑo̯gən zeːn;
Am Bach viel kleine Blumen stehn, aus hellen, blauen Augen sehn;
By the brook many little flowers stand, out of bright blue eyes [they] look;
(Many little flowers grow by the brook and look up out of bright blue eyes;)

deːɐ̯ bax, deːɐ̯/deːr lɪst des ˈmʏlɐs frɔø̯ntˈ lʊntˈ ˈhɛlblɑo̯ ˈliːpçəns ˈlɑo̯gə ʃae̯ntʰ,
der Bach, der ist des Müllers Freund und hellblau Liebchens Auge scheint,
the brook, it is the miller's friend and bright blue sweetheart's eye shines,
(the brook is the miller's friend and my sweetheart's eyes are bright blue,)

drʊm zɪntˈ les ˈmae̯nə ˈbluːmən.
drum sind es meine Blumen.
therefore are it my flowers.
(therefore they are *my* flowers.)

dɪçtˈ lʊntˈɐ(r) ˈliːrəm ˈfɛnstˈɐlae̯n, daː vɪl lɪç ˈpflantsən di ˈbluːmən lae̯n;
Dicht unter ihrem Fensterlein, da will ich pflanzen die Blumen ein;
Close under her little window, there want I to plant the flowers ... ;
(Right under her little window, that's where I want to transplant the flowers;)

["*einpflanzen*" = plant, implant]

daː ruːftˈ liːɐ̯ tsuː, vɛn ˈlaləs ʃvae̯ktʰ, vɛn zɪç liːɐ̯ hɑo̯ptˈ tsʊm ˈʃlʊmɐ nae̯ktʰ,
da ruft ihr zu, wenn alles schweigt, wenn sich ihr Haupt zum Schlummer neigt,
then call her to, when all is still, when itself her head to the sleep bends,
(then, you flowers, call to her, when all is still, when her head is nodding with sleep,)

iːɐ̯ vɪstˈ ja, vas lɪç ˈmae̯nə.
ihr wisst ja, was ich meine.
you know surely what I mean.
(you know, don't you, what I want to say.)

ʊntˈ vɛn ziː tʰɛːt diː ˈlɔø̯klae̯n tsuː lʊntˈ ʃleːftˈ ɪn ˈzyːsɐ, ˈzyːsɐ ruː,
Und wenn sie tät die Äuglein zu und schläft in süsser, süsser Ruh,
And if she should close the little eyes ... and sleeps in sweet, sweet repose,
(And if she should close her little eyes and be sleeping in sweet, sweet repose,)

dan ˈlɪspˈəltˈ ˈals ˈaen ˈtʰrɑomgəzɪçtˈ liːɐ̯ tsuː ː fɛɐ̯ˈgɪs, fɛɐ̯ˈgɪs maen nɪçtʰ!
dann lispelt als ein Traumgesicht ihr zu: Vergiss, vergiss mein nicht!
then whisper as a dream-vision her to: Forget, forget mine [= me] not!
(then whisper to her in a dream-vision: "Do not forget me! Forget-me-not!")

das ˈɪstˈ ˈɛs vas ˈɪç ˈmaenə.
Das ist es, was ich meine.
That is it, what I mean.
(That is what I want to say.)

ʊntˈ ˈʃliːst ziː fryː di ˈlaːdən ˈɑof, dan ˈʃɑotˈ mɪtˈ ˈliːbəsblɪkˈ hɪˈnɑof;
Und schliesst sie früh die Laden auf, dann schaut mit Liebesblick hinauf;
And opens she early the shutters up, then look with love-glance upwards;
(And when she opens the shutters early in the morning, look up at her with glances of love;)

deːɐ̯ tʰɑo ˈɪn ˈɔøʀən ˈɔøgəlaen, das ˈzɔlən ˈmaenə ˈtʰreːnən zaen,
der Tau in euren Äugelein, das sollen meine Tränen sein,
the dew in your little eyes, that shall my tears be,
(the dew in your little eyes, that shall be my tears,)

diː vɪl ˈɪç ˈɑof ˈɔøç ˈvaenən.
die will ich auf euch weinen.
which want I on you weep.
(which I shall weep on you.).

[The little blue flowers that grow by the brook remind the young miller of his sweetheart's eyes; he would like to transplant them to a spot under her window, where they could give her his message: "Forget-me-not!"]

10.
ˈtʰreːnənˌreːgən
Tränenregen
Rain of Tears

viːɐ̯ ˈzaːsən zoː ˈtʰrɑolɪç baeˈzamən ˈɪm ˈkʰyːlən ˈɛrləndax,
Wir sassen so traulich beisammen im kühlen Erlendach,
We sat so cosily next to each other in the cool alder-tree roof,
(We were sitting next to each other so cosily in the cool shelter of alder-trees,)

viːɐ̯ ˈʃɑotˈən zoː ˈtʰrɑolɪç tsuˈzamen hɪˈnapˈ ˈɪn den ˈriːzəlndən bax.
wir schauten so traulich zusammen hinab in den rieselden Bach.
We looked so cosily together down into the rippling brook.
(So cosily together we were looking down into the rippling brook.)

deːɐ̯ moːntˈ vaːɐ̯/vaːr ˈɑox gəˈkʰɔmən, di ˈʃtˈɛrnlaen ˈhɪntˈɐdraen,
Der Mond war auch gekommen, die Sternlein hinterdrein,
The moon was also come, the little stars right after,
(The moon had also joined us, followed by the little stars,)

ʊntˈ ˈʃɑotˈən zoː ˈtʰrɑolɪç tsuˈzamən ˈɪn den ˈzɪlbɐnən ˈʃpˈiːgəl hɪˈnaen.
und schauten so traulich zusammen in den silbernen Spiegel hinein.
and [they] looked so cosily together into the silver mirror ... .
(and they were also looking into the silver mirror so cosily together.)

ɪç za: na:x ˈkʰaɛnəm ˈmoːndə, na:x ˈkʰaɛnəm ˈʃtˈɛrnənʃaen,
Ich sah   nach keinem Monde, nach keinem Sternenschein,
I looked at no   moon, at no   star-shine,
(I did not look at the moon, nor at the sparkling of the stars,)

ɪç ˈʃɑɔtˈə   na:x ˈliːrəm ˈbɪldə, na:x ˈliːrən ˈlɑɔgən laˈlaen.
ich schaute nach ihrem Bilde, nach ihren Augen allein.
I looked at her image, at her eyes alone.
(I looked at her reflection, into her eyes alone.)

ʊntˈ ˈza:ə   zi: ˈnɪkˈən lʊntˈ ˈblɪkˈən hɛˈrɑof lɑos dem ˈzeːlɪgən bax̯
Und sahe sie nicken und blicken herauf aus dem seligen Bach,
And [I] saw them nod   and look up   out of the blissful brook,
(And I saw them nodding and looking up out of the blissful brook,)

di: ˈblyːmlaen lam ˈluːfɐ, di ˈblɑoən, zi: ˈnɪkˈtˈən lʊntˈ ˈblɪkˈtˈən liːɐ̯ na:x,
die Blümlein   am Ufer, die blauen, sie nickten und blickten ihr nach.
the little flowers on the bank, the blue ones, they nodded and looked her after.
(the little blue flowers on the bank were nodding and looking just as she was.)

ʊntˈ lɪn den bax fɛɐ̯ˈzʊŋkˈən deːɐ̯ ˈgantsə ˈhɪməl   ʃiːn,
Und in den Bach versunken der ganze Himmel schien,
And into the brook sunken   the whole heaven seemed,
(And all of heaven seemed to have sunk into the brook,)

ʊntˈ ˈvɔltˈə mɪç mɪtˈ hɪˈnʊntˈɐ(r) lɪn ˈzaenə ˈtʰiːfə tsiːn.
und wollte mich mit hinunter in seine Tiefe ziehn.
and wanted me with down   into its depths to draw.
(and was trying to draw me too downwards into its depths.)

ʊntˈ ˈlyːbɐ den ˈvɔlkˈən lʊntˈ ˈʃtˈɛrnən, da: ˈriːzəltˈə ˈmʊntˈɐ deːɐ̯ bax
Und über den Wolken und Sternen, da rieselte munter der Bach
And over the clouds and stars,   there rippled cheerfully the brook
(And the brook was cheerfully rippling along there, over the clouds and stars,)

ʊntˈ ri:f mɪtˈ ˈzɪŋən lʊntˈ ˈklɪŋən : gəˈzɛlə. gəˈzɛlə, miːɐ̯ na:x!
und rief mit Singen und Klingen: Geselle, Geselle, mir nach!
and called with singing and tinkling: Comrade, comrade, me after!
(and in its singing and tinkling the brook was calling: "Comrade, comrade, follow me!")

da: ˈgɪŋən di ˈlɑɔgən miːɐ̯/miːr ˈlyːbɐ, da: vartˈ lɛs lɪm ˈʃpˈiːgəl zo: kʰrɑos;
Da   gingen die Augen mir   über, da   ward es im Spiegel so kraus;
Thereupon went the eyes for me over, thereupon became it in the mirror so ruffled;
(At that my eyes overflowed, and the falling tears ruffled the surface of the mirror;)

zi: ʃpra:x: lɛs kʰɔmtˈ laen ˈreːgən, laˈdeː!   lɪç geː na:x hɑos.
sie sprach: es kommt ein Regen, ade!   ich geh' nach Haus.
she spoke: it comes a rain, goodbye! I go to [my] house.
(she said: "it looks as if it's going to rain; goodbye! I'm going home.")

[The young miller sits next to his sweetheart by moonlight on the bank of the brook, gazing at her reflection in the water. The scene seems idyllic; but the brook calls to him: "Come away, my friend, and follow me!" Does he notice the warning? Or is it the beauty and happiness of the moment that move him so deeply? Tears fall from his eyes into the brook; as they ruffle the surface of the water, the unromantic girl, who lives in another, more everyday world, assumes that it is starting to rain, says goodbye, and runs home.]

11.

ˈmaen!
Mein!
Mine!

ˈbɛçlaen, las daen ˈraoʃən zaen! rɛːdɐ, ʃtʼɛltʼ lɔøɐ ˈbraozən laen!
Bächlein, lass dein Rauschen sein! Räder, stellt eur Brausen ein!
Brooklet, let your babbling be! Wheels, stop your roaring ... !
(Brooklet, stop your babbling! Mill-wheels, stop your roaring!)   [*"einstellen"* (here) = stop]

al liːɐ ˈmʊntʼɐn ˈvaltʼføːgəlaen, groːs ʊntʼ kʰlaen, ˈlɛndətʼ ˈlɔørə meloˈdaen!
all' ihr muntern Waldvögelein, gross und klein, endet eure Melodein!
all you cheerful little woodbirds, big and small, end your melodies!

dʊrç deːn haen laos ʊntʼ laen ˈʃalə hɔøtʼ laen raem laˈlaen :
Durch den Hain aus und ein schalle heut' ein Reim allein:
Through the grove out and in let sound today one rhyme alone:
(Through the grove, in and out, let only one rhyme resound today:)

di gəˈliːpʼtʼe ˈmʏlərɪn lɪstʼ maen!
die geliebte Müllerin ist mein!
the beloved miller-girl is mine!

ˈfryːlɪŋ, zɪnt das ˈlalə ˈdaenə ˈblyːməlaen? ˈzɔnə, hast duː ˈkʰaenən ˈhɛlɐn ʃaen?
Frühling, sind das alle deine Blümelein? Sonne, hast du keinen hellern Schein?
Spring, are those all your little flowers? Sun, have you no brighter shine?

ax! zoː mʊs lɪç gants laˈlaen, mɪt deːm ˈzeːlɪgən ˈvɔrtʼə maen,
Ach! so muss ich ganz allein, mit dem seligen Worte "m e i n,"
Ah! so must I all alone, with the blissful word *"mine,"*
(Ah! then I must, all by myself, with the blissful word "mine,")

ˈʊnfɛɐʃtʼandən lɪn deːɐ ˈvaetʼən ˈʃœpfʊŋ zaen!
unverstanden in der weiten Schöpfung sein!
un-understood in the broad creation be!
(be not understood in all of creation!)

[He shouts to the world that the miller's daughter has given him her heart: all of nature should appear transfigured! Why has nothing changed? The world seems to go on just as before. No matter! He is content to be all alone in his exuberant happiness.]

12.

ˈpʰaozə
Pause
Pause

ˈmaenə ˈlaotʼə haːb lç gəˈhɛŋtʼ lan di vantʼ,
Meine Laute hab' ich gehängt an die Wand,
My lute have I hung on the wall,
(I have hung up my lute on the wall,)

ha:p' zi: lʊm'ʃlʊŋən   mɪt' 'laenəm 'gry:nən bant' —
hab' sie umschlungen mit einem grünen Band —
have it around-wound with a   green ribbon —
(and have wound a green ribbon around it —)

ıç kʰan nıçtʰ me:ɐ̯ 'zıŋən, maen hɛrts lɪst ʦu: fɔl,
ich kann nicht mehr singen, mein Herz ist zu voll,
I can not   more sing,   my heart is too full,
(I cannot sing any more, my heart is too full,)

vaes nıçtʰ, vi: lıçs lın 'raemə 'ʦvıŋən zɔl.
weiss nicht, wie ich's in Reime zwingen soll.
know not, how I   it in rhyme force   shall.
(I do not know how to force it into rhyme.)

'maenɐ 'ze:nzʊxt' 'alɐ'haesəst'ən ʃmɛrts
Meiner Sehnsucht allerheissesten Schmerz
Of my yearning all- hottest   pain
(The most burning pain of my yearning)

dʊrft'   lıç 'lɑoshɑoxən lın 'li:dɐʃɛrts,
durft'   ich aushauchen in Liederscherz,
was permitted I   out to breathe in song- jest,
(I was able to breathe out in the pleasantries of song,)

ʊnt' vi: lıç 'kʰla:k't'ə zo: zy:s   lʊnt' faen,
und wie ich klagte   so süss   und fein,
and as I   lamented so sweetly and delicately,

glɑop't' lıç dɔx,   maen 'laedən ve:ɐ̯ nıçt' kʰlaen.   [maent']
glaubt' ich doch,   mein Leiden wär' nicht klein.   [_poem:_ meint' ich doch]
believed I nevertheless my   suffering were not small.   [thought]
(I nevertheless believed that my suffering was not small.)
                    ["believed" calls for the subjunctive form of the verb, i.e.: "_wär(e)_ "]

ae, vi: gro:s lıst' vo:l   'maenəs 'glʏk'əs   lastʰ,
Ei, wie gross ist wohl   meines Glückes   Last,
Oh, how big is presumably my   happiness's burden,
(Oh, how large is the burden of my happiness)

das kʰaen kʰlaŋ lɑof 'e:ɐ̯dən lɛs lın zıç   fastʰ?
dass kein Klang auf Erden es in sich fasst?
that no   sound on earth   it in itself contains?
(if no sound on earth can contain it?)

nu:n, 'li:bə 'lɑot'ə, ru: lan dem 'na:gəl hi:ɐ̯!
Nun, liebe Laute, ruh' an dem Nagel hier!
Well, dear lute,   rest on the   nail   here!

ʊnt' ve:t' laen 'lʏftçən   'ly:bɐ di 'zaet'ən di:ɐ̯,
und weht ein Lüftchen   über die Saiten dir,
and blows a   little breeze over the strings for you,
(and if a little breeze blows over your strings,)

ʊnt ʃtraeft 'laenə 'biːnə mɪt 'liːrən 'flyːgəln dɪç,
und streift eine Biene mit ihren Flügeln dich,
and grazes a bee with her wings you,
(and if a bee grazes you with its wings,)

daː vɪrt miːɐ̯ zoː 'baŋə, ʊnt lɛs dʊrç'ʃaoɐt mɪç! *[poem:* **da wird mir bange]**
da wird mir so bange, und es durchschauert mich!
then becomes to me so alarmed, and it shudders me!
(then I become so alarmed, and I shudder!)

va'rʊm liːs lɪç das bant laox 'hɛŋən zoː laŋ?
Warum liess ich das Band auch hängen so lang?
Why let I the ribbon also hang so long?
(Why did I let the ribbon hang down so low?)

ɔft fliːkts lʊm di 'zaet'ən mɪt 'zɔøftsəndəm kʰlaŋ.
Oft fliegt's um die Saiten mit seufzendem Klang.
Often flies it over the strings with sighing sound.
(Often it flutters over the strings with a sighing sound.)

ɪst lɛs deːɐ̯ 'naːxkʰlaŋ 'maenɐ 'liːbəsˈpʰaen?
Ist es der Nachklang meiner Liebespein?
Is it the after-sound of my love- pain?
(Is it the echo of the former pain of my love?)

zɔl lɛs das 'foːɐ̯ʃp'iːl 'nɔøɐ 'liːdɐ zaen?
Soll es das Vorspiel neuer Lieder sein?
Shall it the prelude of new songs be?
(Might it be the prelude to new songs?)

[When he was sad he found comfort in singing songs, accompanying himself on the lute. Now he is so happy that he feels no need of singing. He has hung up his lute on the wall, and wrapped a green ribbon around it. Music, for him, is associated with times of sorrow. Now and then a breeze stirs the strings, or a bee grazes them; when the end of the green ribbon brushes them, he hears a sighing sound come from the lute. It frightens him. Maybe it is only an echo from the songs he sang when he was sad. Or could it be an augury of more sad songs to come? Does Schubert's hopeful-sounding major chord on "*Vorspiel*" ("prelude") perhaps contradict the apparent sense of the poet's last line? The miller boy seems afraid that a sound from the lute might be an omen of sadness ahead. Perhaps the major chord is an attempt to drive away the uneasy premonition. In any case, the interpreter must be aware of the uncertainty.]

13.
mɪt dem 'gryːnən 'laot'ənbant
Mit dem grünen Lautenband
With the Lute's Green Ribbon

ʃaːt lʊm das 'ʃøːnə 'gryːnə bant, das lɛs fɛɐ̯'blaeçt hiːɐ̯/hiːr lan deːɐ̯ vant,
"Schad' um das schöne grüne Band, dass es verbleicht hier an der Wand,
"Too bad for the lovely green ribbon, that it fades here on the wall,
("It's a shame that that lovely green ribbon is fading here on the wall,)

414

ıç haːpʽ das gryːn zoː gɛrn!
ich hab' das Grün so gern!"
I   have the   green   so   fond!" ["*gern haben*" = to like, to be fond of]
(I am so fond of green!")

zoː ʃpʽraːxst du, ˈliːpçən, hɔɣt tsu miːɐ̯;
So sprachst du,   Liebchen, heut' zu   mir;
So spoke   you, dear one,   today to   me;
(that's what you said to me today, dearest;)

glaɛç   kʰnʏpf lıçs lapʽ lʊntʽ zɛnd ɛs diːɐ̯ :
gleich   knüpf' ich's ab   und   send' es dir:
right away untie   I   it ...   and   send   it to you: ["*abknüpfen*" = untie]
(I shall untie it right away and send it to you:)

nuːn haːpʽ das ˈgryːnə gɛrn!
Nun hab' das Grüne gern!
now   have the   green   fond!
(now be fond of green!)

ıst lɑox   daɛn ˈgantsɐ ˈliːpstʽɐ vaɛs, zɔl gryːn dɔx   ˈhaːbən ˈzaɛnən pʰraɛs,
Ist auch   dein ganzer Liebster weiss, soll Grün doch   haben seinen Preis,
Is   even if your whole   lover   white, shall green nevertheless have   its   praise,
(even if your whole lover is white—dressed in white, and covered with white flour—
                                                  green shall nevertheless have its due,)

ʊntʽ lıç lɑox haːb ɛs gɛrn. vaɛl   ˈlʊnzrə liːpʽ lıstʽ ˈlımɐ   gryːn,
und ich auch hab' es gern. Weil   unsre Lieb' ist   immer grün,
and   I   too have it fond. Because our   love   is   ever   green,
(and I too am fond of it. Because our love is forever green,)

vaɛl   gryːn deːɐ̯ ˈhɔfnʊŋ ˈfɛrnən blyːn, drʊm   ˈhaːbən viːɐ̯/viːr lɛs gɛrn.
weil   grün der Hoffnung Fernen   blühn, drum   haben wir   es gern.
because green the   hope's   distances bloom, therefore have   we   it fond.
(because hope is blooming green in the distance, for those reasons we are fond of it.)

nuːn ˈʃlıŋə   ın di ˈlɔkʽən daɛn das ˈgryːnə bantʽ gəˈfɛlıç   laɛn,
Nun schlinge in die Locken dein das grüne Band gefällig   ein,
Now twine   in   the curls   yours the green   ribbon pleasingly into,
(Now twine the green ribbon charmingly into your curls,)

du hast ja   s gryːn zoː gɛrn.
du hast ja   's Grün so gern.
you have after all the green so   fond.
(you are so fond of green, after all.)

dan vaɛs lıç voː di ˈhɔfnʊŋ   voːntʽ, dan vaɛs lıç voː di: ˈliːbə tʰroːntʰ,
Dann weiss ich, wo   die Hoffnung wohnt, dann weiss ich, wo   die Liebe thront,
Then know I   where the hope   dwells, then know I   where the love is enthroned,
(Then I shall know where hope makes its home, then I shall know where love is enthroned,)

dan ha:b ıç s gry:n le:ɐ̯st' gɛrn.
dann hab' ich's Grün erst gern.
then have I the green for the first time fond.
(then I shall be fond of green at last.)

[The young miller's sweetheart admires the green ribbon that is tied to his lute. Obligingly, he gives it to her, asks her to twine it into her hair. But there is something that disconcerts him about her preference for green, the traditional color of German huntsmen, whereas *white* is the mark of a miller.]

14.
de:ɐ̯ 'jɛ:gɐ
Der Jäger
The Huntsman

vas zu:xt dɛn de:ɐ̯ 'jɛ:gɐ(r) lam 'my:lbax hi:ɐ̯?
Was sucht denn der Jäger am Mühlbach hier?
What seeks then the huntsman at the mill-stream here?
(What is the huntsman looking for here by the mill-stream?)

blaɛp', 'tʰrɔtsɪgɐ 'jɛ:gɐ(r), lɪn 'daɛnəm re'vi:ɐ̯!
bleib', trotziger Jäger, in deinem Revier!
stay, defiant huntsman, in your hunting preserve!

hi:ɐ̯ gi:pt' lɛs kʰaɛn vɪlt tsu 'ja:gən fy:ɐ̯ dıç,
hier gibt es kein Wild zu jagen für dich,
here gives it no game to hunt for you,
(Here there is no game for you to hunt,) ["*es gibt*" = there is]

hi:ɐ̯ vo:nt' nu:ɐ̯/nu:r laɛn 're:laɛn, laɛn 'tsa:məs, fy:ɐ̯ mıç.
hier wohnt nur ein Rehlein, ein zahmes, für mich.
here dwells only a little doe, a tame one, for me.
(here there lives only a little doe, a tame one, for me.)

ʊnt' vɪlst du das 'tseɐ̯t'lıçə 're:laɛn ze:n, zo: la 'daɛnə 'bʏksən lɪm 'valdə ʃt'e:n,
Und willst du das zärtliche Rehlein sehn, So lass deine Büchsen im Walde stehn,
And want you the gentle little doe to see, then let your guns in the woods stand,
(And if you want to see the gentle doe, then leave your guns in the woods,)

ʊnt' las 'daɛnə 'kʰlafəndən 'hʊndə tsu haos,
und lass deine klaffenden Hunde zu Haus, [more usual: "*kläffenden*" = yelping, barking]
and leave your yelping dogs at home,

ʊnt' las laof dem 'hɔrnə den zaos lʊnt' braos,
und lass auf dem Horne den Saus und Braus,
and leave on the horn the racket and tumult,
(and leave off all that racket and holler on your horn,)

ʊnt' 'ʃe:rə fɔm 'kʰınə das 'ʃt'rʊp'ıgə ha:ɐ̯,
und schere vom Kinne das struppige Haar,
and shave from the chin the bristly hair,
(and shave off the bristly hair from your chin,)

416

zɔnst‘ ʃɔøt‘ zɪç ɪm ˈgart‘ən das ˈreːlaen fyɐ̯ˈvaːɐ̯.
sonst scheut sich im Garten das Rehlein fürwahr.
or else scares herself in the garden the little doe for sure.
(or else the little doe in the garden will be frightened for sure.)

dɔx ˈbɛsɐ, du ˈblaebəst‘ ɪm ˈvaldə daˈtsuː
Doch besser, du bleibest im Walde dazu
Still better, you stay in the forest in addition
(Better still, stay in the forest yourself)

ʊnt‘ ˈliːsəst di ˈmyːlən ʊnt‘ ˈmʏlɐ(r) ɪn ruː.
und liessest die Mühlen und Müller in Ruh’.
and leave the mills and millers in peace.
(and leave mills and millers in peace.)

vas ˈt‘ɑogən di ˈfiʃlaen ɪm ˈgryːnən gəˈtsvaek‘?
Was taugen die Fischlein im grünen Gezweig?
What use are the little fish in the green branches?
(What use are fish up in the trees?)

vas vɪl dɛn das ˈlaeçɔrn ɪm ˈblɔølɪçən t‘aeç?
was will denn das Eichhorn im bläulichen Teich?
what wants then the squirrel in the bluish pond?
(What would a squirrel be doing in the blue water of the pond?)

drʊm ˈblaebə, du ˈt‘rɔtsigɐ ˈjeːgɐ(r), ɪm haen,
drum bleibe, du trotziger Jäger, im Hain,
therefore stay, you defiant huntsman, in the grove,

ʊnt‘ las mɪç mɪt‘ ˈmaenən drae ˈreːdɐn laˈlaen;
und lass mich mit meinen drei Rädern allein;
and leave me with my three wheels alone;
(and leave me alone with my three mill-wheels;)

ʊnt‘ vɪlst ˈmaenəm ˈʃɛtsçən dɪç ˈmaxən bəˈliːp‘t‘,
und willst meinem Schätzchen dich machen beliebt,
and want [you] to my sweetheart yourself to make popular,
(and if you want to ingratiate yourself with my sweetheart,)

zoː ˈvɪsə, maen frɔønt‘, vas liːɐ̯ ˈhɛrtsçən bəˈt‘ryːp‘t‘ :
so wisse, mein Freund, was ihr Herzchen betrübt:
so know, my friend, what her heart troubles:
(then know, my friend, what is troubling her heart:)

di ˈleːbɐ, di ˈk‘ɔmən tsu naxt‘ ɑos dem haen
Die Eber, die kommen zu Nacht aus dem Hain
the boars, they come at night out of the grove
(the boars come out of the woods at night)

ʊnt‘ ˈbrɛçən ɪn ˈliːrən ˈk‘oːlˈgart‘ən laen, ʊnt‘ ˈt‘reːt‘ən ʊnt‘ ˈvyːlən heˈrʊm ɪn dem fɛlt‘;
und brechen in ihren Kohlgarten ein, und treten und wühlen herum in dem Feld;
and break into her cabbage garden into, and trample and root about in the field;
(and break into her cabbage patch, and trample and root about in the field;)

di ˈleːbɐ, diː ˈʃiːsə, duː ˈjeːgɐ hɛltʼ!
die Eber, die schiesse, du Jäger Held!
the boars, them shoot, you huntsman hero!
(shoot those boars, you hunter-hero!)

[A huntsman has come lurking around the mill, looking for human game. The miller's daughter smiles at him a bit too sweetly. He should go back to his woods and leave the mill alone!]

15.

ˈa͜efɐzʊxtʼ lʊntʼ ʃtʼɔlts
Eifersucht und Stolz
Jealousy and Pride

voˈhɪn zo ʃnɛl, zo kʰra͜os lʊntʼ vɪltʼ, ma͜en ˈliːbɐ bax?
Wohin so schnell, so kraus und wild, mein lieber Bach? [*poem:* **so kraus, so wild**]
Where to so fast, so ruffled and wild, my dear brook?

a͜elst duː fɔl tsɔrn dem ˈfrɛçən ˈbruːdɐ ˈjeːgɐ naːx?
eilst du voll Zorn dem frechen Bruder Jäger nach?
hurry you full of anger the fresh brother huntsman after?
(Are you hurrying full of anger after that insolent huntsman?)

kʰeːɐ/kʰeːr lʊm, kʰeːɐ/kʰeːr lʊm, lʊntʼ ʃiltʼ leːɐst ˈda͜enə ˈmʏlərin
Kehr' um, kehr' um, und schilt erst deine Müllerin
Turn around, turn back, and scold first your miller-girl

fyːɐ/fyːr ˈliːrən ˈla͜eçtʼən, ˈloːzən, kʰla͜enən ˈflatʼɐzin.
für ihren leichten, losen, kleinen Flattersinn.
for her frivolous, loose, little flighty mind.

zaːst duː ziː ˈgɛstʼɐn ˈlaːbənt nɪçtʼ lam ˈtʰoːrə ʃtʼeːn,
Sahst du sie gestern Abend nicht am Tore stehn,
Saw you her yesterday evening not at the gate stand,
(Didn't you see her yesterday evening standing at the gate,)

mɪtʼ ˈlaŋəm ˈhalzə naːx deːɐ ˈgroːsən ˈʃtʼraːsə zeːn?
mit langem Halse nach der grossen Strasse sehn?
with long neck toward the big road look?
(stretching her neck to watch the big road?)

vɛn fɔn dem faŋ deːɐ ˈjeːgɐ ˈlʊstʼɪç tsiːtʼ naːx ha͜os,
Wenn von dem Fang der Jäger lustig zieht nach Haus,
When from the catch the huntsman merrily comes homeward,

da ʃtʼɛkʼtʼ kʰa͜en ˈzɪtʼzaːm kʰɪnt den kʰɔpf tsʊm ˈfɛnstʼɐ na͜os.
da steckt kein sittsam Kind den Kopf zum Fenster 'naus.
then sticks no well brought up child the head to the window out.
(then no well brought up child sticks her head out the window.)

geː, ˈbɛçla͜en, hɪn lʊntʼ zaːkʼ liːɐ das; dɔx zaːkʼ liːɐ nɪçtʰ,
Geh', Bächlein, hin und sag' ihr das; doch sag' ihr nicht,
Go, brooklet, there [to her] and say to her that; but say to her not
(Go to her, brooklet, and tell her that; but don't tell her,)

hØːrst du, kʰa̯en vɔrt', fɔn 'ma̯enəm 'tʰrɑɔrɪgən gə'zɪçtʰ;
hörst du, kein Wort, von meinem traurigen Gesicht;
hear you, no word, of my sorrowful face;
(—not a word, do you hear?—about my sorrowful face;

zaːk' liːɐ̯ : leːɐ̯ ʃnɪt͜st' ba̯e miːɐ̯ zɪç 'a̯enə p̮fa̯ef lɑɔs roːɐ̯
sag' ihr: Er schnitzt bei mir sich eine Pfeif' aus Rohr
say to her: he cuts by me himself a pipe out of reed
(say to her: he is by my banks cutting himself a pipe out of a reed)

lʊnt' blɛːst den 'kʰɪndɐn 'ʃØːnə tʰɛnt͜s lʊnt' 'liːdɐ foːɐ̯.
und bläst den Kindern schöne Tänz' und Lieder vor.
and blows for the children lovely dances and songs ... .

[The young miller does not want his sweetheart to think that he is suffering because of her obvious interest in the huntsman. The brook should report to her that he is utterly indifferent, cheerfully entertaining some children with dance-tunes on a reed-pipe he has made.]

16.
di 'liːbə 'farbə
Die liebe Farbe
The Beloved Color

ɪn gryːn vɪl lɪç mɪç 'kʰla̯edən, lɪn 'gryːnə 'tʰrɛːnən'va̯edən :
In Grün will ich mich kleiden, in grüne Tränenweiden:
In green want I myself to dress, in green weeping willows:
(I want to dress in green, in green weeping willows:)

ma̯en ʃat͜s hat s gryːn zoː gɛrn.
mein Schatz hat's Grün so gern.
my sweetheart has the green so fond.
(my sweetheart is so fond of green.)

vɪl 'zuːxən 'a̯enən t͜sy'pʰrɛsən'ha̯en, 'a̯enə 'ha̯edə fɔn 'gryːnəm 'roːsmara̯en:
Will suchen einen Zypressenhain, eine Heide von grünem Rosmarein:
[I] want to seek out a cypress grove, a heath of green rosemary:

mein Schatz hat's Grün so gern. (my sweetheart is so fond of green.)

voːl'lɑɔf t͜sʊm 'frØːlɪçən 'jaːgən! voːl'lɑɔf dʊrç ha̯et' lʊnt' 'haːgən!
Wohlauf zum fröhlichen Jagen! wohlauf durch Heid' und Hagen!
Now then! to the jolly hunting! Come on! through heath and hedges!

mein Schatz hat's Grün so gern. (my sweetheart is so fond of green.)

das vɪlt, das lɪç 'jaːgə, das lɪst deːɐ̯ tʰoːt', di 'ha̯edə, di ha̯es lɪç di 'liːbəs'noːtʰ :
Das Wild, das ich jage, das ist der Tod, die Heide, die heiss ich die Liebesnot:
The quarry that I hunt, that is the death, the heath, that call I the love-distress:
(The quarry that I hunt, that is death; the heath—I call that "love's distress":)

mein Schatz hat's Grün so gern. (my sweetheart is so fond of green.)

graːpˈtˈ miːɐ̯/miːr laen graːpˈ lɪm 'vaːzən, dɛkˈtˈ mɪç mɪtˈ 'gryːnəm 'raːzən:
Grabt mir ein Grab im Wasen, deckt mich mit grünem Rasen:
Dig me a grave in the turf, cover me with green grass:

mein Schatz hat's Grün so gern. (my sweetheart is so fond of green.)

kʰaen 'kʰrɔ̯øtslaen ʃvarts̬, kʰaen 'blyːmlaen bʊntʰ,
Kein Kreuzlein schwarz, kein Blümlein bunt,
No little cross black, no little flowers colorful,
(No little black cross, no little colorful flowers,)

gryːn, 'aləs gryːn zoː rɪŋs lʊntˈ rʊntˈ:
grün, alles grün so rings und rund:
green, everything green so round and about:
(green, everything green all around and about:)

mein Schatz hat's Grün so gern. (my sweetheart is so fond of green.)

[A sad and bitter irony pervades this song, the first verse resigned, the second energetic, the third deeply melancholic.]

17.
di 'bøːzə 'farbə
Die böse Farbe
The evil color

ɪç 'mœçtˈə tsiːn lɪn di vɛltˈ hɪˈnaos, hɪˈnaos lɪn di 'vaetˈə vɛltʰ;
Ich möchte ziehn in die Welt hinaus, hinaus in die weite Welt;
I would like to go into the world out, out into the wide world;
(I would like to go out into the world, out into the wide world;)

vɛn s nuːɐ̯ zoː gryːn, zoː gryːn nɪçtˈ veːɐ̯ daː 'draosən lɪn valtˈ lʊntˈ fɛltˈ!
wenn's nur so grün, so grün nicht wär' da draussen in Wald und Feld!
if it only so green, so green not were there outside in forest and field!
(if only it were not so green, so green out there in forest and field!)

ɪç 'mœçtˈə di gryːnən 'blɛtˈɐ(r) lal 'pflʏkˈən fɔn 'jeːdəm tsvaekˈ,
Ich möchte die grünen Blätter all' pflücken von jedem Zweig,
I would like the green leaves all to pluck from every twig,
(I would like to pluck all the green leaves off every twig,)

ɪç 'mœçtˈə di gryːnən 'grɛːzɐ(r) lal 'vaenən gants̬ 'tʰoːtˈənˈblaeç.
ich möchte die grünen Gräser all' weinen ganz totenbleich.
I would like the green grasses all to weep entirely dead-pale.
(I would like to weep all the grass as pale as death.)

ax! gryːn, duː 'bøːzə 'farbə duː, vas ziːstˈ mɪç 'lɪmɐ(r) lan
Ach! Grün, du böse Farbe du, was siehst mich immer an
Ah! green, you evil color you, why look [you] me always at
(Ah! Green, you evil color, why do you always look at me)

zoː ʃtʼɔlts, zoː kʰɛkʼ, zoː ʃaːdənfroː, mɪç ˈarmən, ˈarmən ˈvaesən man?
so stolz, so keck, so schadenfroh, mich armen, armen weissen Mann?
so proudly, so boldly, so gloatingly, me poor, poor white man?
(so proudly, so boldly, so gloatingly, at me, a poor, poor white man?)

[*poem:* **mich armen weissen Mann**]

ɪç ˈmœçtʼə ˈliːgən foːɐ̯/foːr ˈiːrə tʰyːɐ̯/tʰyːr. ɪm ʃtʼʊrm ʊntʼ ˈreːgən ʊntʼ ʃneː,
Ich möchte liegen vor ihrer Tür, im Sturm und Regen und Schnee,
I would like to lie before her door, in the storm and rain and snow,
(I would like to lie before her door, in a storm, in rain and snow,) [*poem:* **in** (ɪn, in) **Sturm...**]

ʊntʼ ˈzɪŋən gants ˈlaezə bae tʰaːkʼ ʊntʼ naxt das ˈaenə ˈvœrtʼçən laˈdeː!
und singen ganz leise bei Tag und Nacht das eine Wörtchen Ade!
and sing very softly by day and night the single little word "Farewell!"

hɔrç, vɛn ɪm valtʼ laen ˈjaːkʼtʰɔrn ʃalt daː kʰlɪŋtʼ liːɐ̯ ˈfɛnstʼɐlaen;
Horch, wenn im Wald ein Jagdhorn schallt, da klingt ihr Fensterlein;
Hark, when in the woods a hunting horn rings, then sounds her little window;
(Listen! When a hunting horn sounds in the woods, then her little window can be heard opening;)

[*poem:* **ein Jagdhorn ruft** (ruːftʼ, calls)**, so** (zoː, so/then) **klingt**]

ʊntʼ ʃaotʼ ziː laox naːx miːɐ̯ nɪçtʼ laos, darf ɪç dɔx ˈʃaoən hɪˈnaen.
und schaut sie auch nach mir nicht aus, darf ich doch schauen hinein.
and looks she even for me not out, may I yet look in.
(and even though she is not looking out for me, still I may look in.)

oː ˈbɪndə fɔn deːɐ̯ ʃtʼɪrn diːɐ̯/diːr lapʼ das ˈgryːnə, ˈgryːnə bantʼ;
O binde von der Stirn dir ab das grüne, grüne Band;
Oh, bind from the forehead to you off the green, green ribbon; [*"abbinden"* = unbind]
(Oh, unbind from your forehead the green, green ribbon;)

laˈdeː, laˈdeː! ʊntʼ ˈraeçə miːɐ̯ tsʊm ˈlapʃiːtʼ ˈdaenə hantʼ!
ade, ade! und reiche mir zum Abschied deine Hand!
Goodbye, goodbye! and extend to me at the farewell your hand!
(Goodbye, goodbye! and give me your hand in farewell!)

[As in the previous song, the repeated notes of the hunter's horn keep sounding obsessively in the accompaniment.]

18.

ˈtʰrɔkʼnə ˈbluːmən
Trockne Blumen
Dry Flowers

iːɐ̯ ˈblyːmlaen ˈlalə, di ziː miːɐ̯ gaːpʼ, lɔøç zɔl man ˈleːgən mɪtʼ miːr lɪns graːpʼ.
Ihr Blümlein alle, die sie mir gab, euch soll man legen mit mir ins Grab.
You little flowers all, which she to me gave, you shall one lay with me in the grave.
(All you little flowers which she gave to me, you shall be laid with me in my grave.)

viː zeːtʼ liːr ˈlalə mɪç lan zoː veː, lals lɔpʼ liːɐ̯ ˈvʏstʼətʼ, viː miːɐ̯ gəˈʃeː?
Wie seht ihr alle mich an so weh, als ob ihr wüsstet, wie mir gescheh'?
How look you all me at so sadly, as if you knew what to me be happening?
(How sadly you all look at me, as if you knew what is happening to me!)

iːɐ̯ 'blyːmlaen 'lalə, viː vɛlkʼ, viː blasʔ liːɐ̯ 'blyːmlaen 'lalə, voˈfɔn zoː nasʔ
Ihr Blümlein alle, wie welk, wie blass? ihr Blümlein alle, wovon so nass?
You little flowers all, how withered, how pale? you little flowers all, from what so wet?
(All you little flowers, how withered, how pale! All you little flowers, what made you so wet?)

ax, 'tʰrɛːnən 'maxən nɪçtʼ 'maeənˈgryːn, 'maxən 'tʰoːtʼə 'liːbə nɪçtʼ 'viːdɐ blyːn,
Ach, Tränen machen nicht maiengrün, machen tote Liebe nicht wieder blühn,
Ah, tears make not May-green, make dead love not again bloom,
(Ah, tears cannot bring back the green of May nor make dead love bloom again,)

ʊntʼ lent͜s vɪrtʼ 'kʰɔmən, ʊntʼ 'vɪntʼɐ vɪrtʼ geːn,
und Lenz wird kommen, und Winter wird gehn,
and spring will come, and winter will go,

ʊntʼ 'blyːmlaen 'veːɐ̯dən ɪm 'graːzə ʃtʼeːn,
und Blümlein werden im Grase stehn,
and little flowers will in the grass stand,
(and little flowers will rise up in the grass,)

ʊntʼ 'blyːmlaen 'liːgən ɪn 'maenəm graːpʼ, di 'blyːmlaen 'lalə, di ziː miːɐ̯ gaːpʼ.
und Blümlein liegen in meinem Grab, die Blümlein alle, die sie mir gab.
and little flowers lie in my grave, the little flowers all, which she to me gave.
(and little flowers will be lying in my grave, all the little flowers that she gave to me.)

ʊntʼ vɛn ziː 'vandəltʼ lam 'hyːgəl foːɐ̯'bae
Und wenn sie wandelt am Hügel vorbei
And when she wanders at the mound past
(And when she wanders past that little mound of earth)

ʊnt deŋkʼtʼ lɪm 'hɛrt͜sən : deːɐ̯ maentʼ lɛs tʰrɔø!
und denkt im Herzen: der meint' es treu!
and thinks in the heart: *he* meant it faithfully!
(and thinks in her heart: "*He* was faithful to me!")

dan, 'blyːmlaen 'lalə, hɛ'ra͜os, hɛ'ra͜os! deːɐ̯ mae lɪstʼ 'kʰɔmən, deːɐ̯ 'vɪntʼ(ɐ) lɪstʼ la͜os.
dann, Blümlein alle, heraus, heraus! der Mai ist kommen, der Winter ist aus.
then, little flowers all, out, out! the May is come, the winter is over.
(then, all you little flowers, come out, come out! May has come, the winter is over!)

[If she happens to pause by his grave and think for a moment how much he loved her, then the faded flowers she had once given to him will revive and shoot up out of the earth, and he will know that the long winter is over.]

19.
deːɐ̯ 'mʏlɐ ʊnt deːɐ̯ bax
Der Müller und der Bach
The Miller and the Brook

(Der Müller / The Miller)

voː laen 'tʰrɔøəs 'hɛrt͜sə lɪn liːbə fɛɐ̯'geːtʰ. daː 'vɛlkʼən di 'liːljən la͜of 'jeːdəm beːtʰ;
Wo ein treues Herze in Liebe vergeht, da welken die Lilien auf jedem Beet;
When a faithful heart in love dies, then wither the lilies on every flower-bed;
(When a faithful heart dies in love, then the lilies wither in every flower-bed;)

422

daː mʊs ɪn di ˈvɔlkˈən deːɐ̯ ˈfɔlmoːntˈ geːn,
da muss in die Wolken der Vollmond gehn,
then must into the clouds the full moon go,
(then the full moon must hide in the clouds,)

daˈmɪtˈ ˈzaȇnə ˈtʰrɛːnən di ˈmɛnʃən nɪçtˈ zeːn;
damit seine Tränen die Menschen nicht sehn;
so that its tears the human beings not see;
(so that human beings will not see its tears;)

daː ˈhaltˈən di ˈlɛnlaȇn, di ˈlaȗgən zɪç tsuː
da halten die Englein die Augen sich zu
then hold the little angels the eyes themselves closed
(then the little angels close their eyes)

ʊntˈ ˈʃlʊxtsən lʊntˈ ˈzɪŋən di ˈzeːlə tsʊr ruː.
und schluchzen und singen die Seele zur Ruh'. [*poem:* **zu** (tsuː, to) **Ruh'**]
and sob and sing the soul to the rest.
(and sob and sing the soul to rest.)

(**Der Bach** / The Brook)

ʊntˈ vɛn zɪç di liːbə dem ʃmɛrts ɛntˈˈrɪŋtʰ,
Und wenn sich die Liebe dem Schmerz entringt,
And when itself the love [from] the pain wrests free,
(And when love *overcomes* pain,)

aȇn ˈʃtˈɛrnlaȇn, laȇn ˈnɔȍəs, lam ˈhɪməl lɛɐ̯ˈblɪŋkˈtʰ,
ein Sternlein, ein neues, am Himmel erblinkt,
a little star, a new one, in the sky twinkles,
(a little star, a new one, twinkles in the sky,)

daː ˈʃpˈrɪŋən draȇ ˈroːzən, halpˈ roːtˈ lʊntˈ halpˈ vaȇs,
da springen drei Rosen, halb rot und halb weiss, [*poem:* **halb rot, halb weiss**]
then spring three roses, half red and half white,
(then three roses, half red and half white,)

diː ˈvɛlkˈən nɪçtˈ ˈviːd(ɐ̯), laȗs ˈdɔrnənraȇs;
die welken nicht wieder, aus Dornenreis;
which wither not again, out of thorn-sprig;
(which will never wither, will spring out of a sprig of thorns;)

ʊnt di ˈlɛŋəlaȇn ˈʃnaȇdən di ˈflyːgəl zɪç lapˈ
und die Engelein schneiden die Flügel sich ab
and the little angels cut the wings themselves off
(and the little angels cut off their wings)

ʊntˈ geːn ˈlalə ˈmɔrgən tsʊr ˈleːɐ̯də heˈrapˈ.
und gehn alle Morgen zur Erde herab.
and go every morning to the earth down.
(and go down to earth every morning.)

(**Der Müller** / The Miller)

ax ˈbɛçla̤e̯n, ˈliːbəs ˈbɛçla̤e̯n, duː ma̤e̯nstˈ lɛs zoː guːtʰ;
Ach Bächlein, liebes Bächlein, du meinst es so gut;
Ah brooklet, dear brooklet, you mean it so well;
(Ah brooklet, dear brooklet, you mean so well;)

ax ˈbɛçla̤e̯n, ˈla̤ːbɐ va̤e̯st duː, viː ˈliːbə tʰuːtʰ?
ach Bächlein, aber weisst du, wie Liebe tut?
ah brooklet, but know you, how love does?
(ah brooklet, but do you know what love is like?)

ax ˈlʊntˈən, daː ˈlʊntˈən di ˈkʰyːlə ruː! lax ˈbɛçla̤e̯n, ˈliːbəs ˈbɛçla̤e̯n, zoː ˈzɪŋə nuːɐ̯ tsuː.
Ach unten, da unten die kühle Ruh'! ach Bächlein, liebes Bächlein, so singe nur zu.
Ah below, there below the cool peace! ah brooklet, dear brooklet, so sing only to.
(Ah down there, down there, the cool peace! Ah brooklet, dear brooklet, just sing me to sleep.)

[In this heart-breaking dialogue, the boy wants to die: it seems to him that all nature would weep for one who dies of love. The brook, in its ancient wisdom, tells him that nature would rather rejoice to see a brave soul *overcome* its pain. But the young miller gently suggests that his friend has never experienced the agony of rejected love; he yearns to find peace in the cool water at the bottom of the brook and asks only that the brook shall sing him to sleep.]

20.
dɛs ˈbaxəs ˈviːgənliːtˈ
Des Baches Wiegenlied
The Brook's Lullaby

ˈguːtˈə ruː, ˈguːtˈə ruː! tʰuː di ˈla̤o̯gən tsuː! ˈvandrɐ, duː ˈmyːdɐ, du bɪst tsuː ha̤o̯s.
Gute Ruh, gute Ruh'! tu' die Augen zu! Wandrer, du müder, du bist zu Haus.
Good rest , good rest! close the eyes ... ! Wanderer, you weary one, you are at home.
(Good rest, good rest! Close your eyes! Wanderer, you weary one, you are at home.)

[*"tu'… zu"*: from *"zutun"* = to close]

di tʰrɔø lɪstˈ hiːɐ̯, zɔlstˈ ˈliːgən ba̤e̯ miːɐ̯,
Die Treu' ist hier, sollst liegen bei mir,
The faithfulness is here, [you] shall lie with me
(Faithfulness is here; you will lie with me)

bɪs das meːɐ̯ vɪl ˈtʰrɪŋkˈən di ˈbɛçla̤e̯n la̤o̯s.
bis das Meer will trinken die Bächlein aus.
until the sea will drink the brooklets out.
(until the sea drinks up all brooklets.)

vɪl ˈbɛtˈən dɪç kʰyːl la̤o̯f ˈva̤e̯çən pfyːl lɪn deːm ˈbla̤o̯ən kʰrɪstˈalənən ˈkʰɛmɐla̤e̯n.
Will betten dich kühl auf weichen Pfühl in dem blauen kristallenen Kämmerlein.
[I] will bed you cooly onto soft pillow in the blue crystal little chamber.
(I shall bed you down cooly on a soft pillow in a little blue crystal chamber.)

[*poem:* **auf weichem** (ˈva̤e̯çəm) **Pfühl**, on soft pillow]

hɛˈran, hɛˈran, vas ˈviːgən kʰan,
Heran, heran, was wiegen kann,
Come hither, come hither whatever lull can,
(Come hither, come hither, whatever call lull!)

'vo:gət' lʊnt' 'vi:gət den 'kʰna:bən mi:ɐ̯/mi:r la͜en!
woget und wieget den Knaben mir ein!
undulate and rock the boy for me to sleep! ["*einwiegen*" = rock to sleep]
(Undulate, and rock the boy to sleep for me!)

vɛn la͜en 'ja:k't'hɔrn ʃalt' la͜os dem 'gry:nən valt',
Wenn ein Jagdhorn schallt aus dem grünen Wald,
When a hunting horn sounds out of the green forest,

vɪl lɪç 'za͜ozən lʊnt' 'bra͜ozən vo:l lʊm dɪç he:ɐ̯.
will ich sausen und brausen wohl um dich her.
will I rush and roar indeed around you .... ["*um ... her*" = all around]
(I shall indeed rush and roar all around you [to drown out the sound of the horn].)

blɪk't' nɪçt' hɛ'ra͜en, 'bla͜oə 'bly:məla͜en!
Blickt nicht herein, blaue Blümelein!
Look not inside, blue little flowers!
(Do not look in, little blue flowers!)

i:ɐ̯ maxt' 'ma͜enəm 'ʃlɛ:fɐ di 'tʰrɔ͜ømə zo: ʃve:ɐ̯.
ihr macht meinem Schläfer die Träume so schwer.
you make for my sleeper the dreams so heavy.
(You would give my sleeper such bad dreams.)

hɪn'vɛk', hin'vɛk' fɔn dem 'my:lənʃt'e:k', hin'vɛk', hin'vɛk', 'bø:zəs 'mɛ:k'dəla͜en,
Hinweg, hinweg von dem Mühlensteg, hinweg, hinweg, böses Mägdelein,
Away, away from the mill-path, away, away, wicked girl,
[*poem:* **von dem Mühlensteg, böses Mägdlein** ('mɛ:k't'la͜en)]

das li:n da͜en 'ʃat'ən, da͜en 'ʃat'ən nɪçt' vɛk'tʰ!
dass ihn dein Schatten, dein Schatten nicht weckt!
so that him your shadow, your shadow not wakes!
(so that your shadow may not wake him!)
[*poem:* **dass ihn dein Schatten nicht weckt!**]

vɪrf mi:ɐ̯ hɛ'ra͜en da͜en 'tʰy:la͜en fa͜en, das lɪç di 'la͜ogən li:m 'halt'ə bə'dɛk'tʰ!
Wirf mir herein dein Tüchlein fein, dass ich die Augen ihm halte bedeckt!
Toss me in your little kerchief fine, so that I the eyes for him hold covered!
(Toss in to me your fine little kerchief, so that I may keep his eyes covered!)

'gu:t'ə naxt', 'gu:t'ə naxt'! bɪs 'laləs vaxtʰ,
Gute Nacht, gute Nacht! bis alles wacht,
Good night, good night! until *all* awakes,

ʃla:f la͜os 'da͜enə 'frɔ͜ødə, ʃla:f la͜os da͜en la͜et'!
schlaf' aus deine Freude, schlaf' aus dein Leid!
sleep out your joy, sleep out your sorrow!

de:ɐ̯ 'fɔlmo:nt' ʃt'a͜ek'tʰ, de:ɐ̯ 'ne:bəl va͜eçtʰ,
Der Vollmond steigt, der Nebel weicht,
The full moon rises, the mist retreats,

ʊnt deːɐ̯ ˈhɪməl daː ˈloːbən, viː ɪstˈ leːɐ̯ zoː vaˌeˑtʰ!
und der Himmel da oben, wie ist er so weit!
and the sky there above, how is it so wide!
(and the sky up above, how vast it is!)

[The brook, like a loving mother, sings a lullaby to the unhappy boy who lies in its depths, where he will sleep until all souls are summoned. With its murmuring, the brook will drown out the sound of the hunter's horn. The full moon and the starry canopy above him will beautify his death, and surely heaven will understand and forgive him.]

di ˈzɔmɐnaxtʰ
Die Sommernacht
The Summer Night

Posthumously published [composed 1815] (poem by Friedrich Gottlieb Klopstock)

vɛn deːɐ̯ ˈʃɪmɐ fɔn dem moːndə nuːn hɛˈrapˈ lɑ͜of di ˈvɛldɐ zɪç lɛɐ̯ˈgiːstʰ,
Wenn der Schimmer von dem Monde nun herab auf die Wälder sich ergiesst,
When the shimmer of the moon now down onto the woods itself pours,
(When the shimmering light of the moon pours down onto the woods now,)
[*poem & 2nd version:* **in die Wälder,** into the woods]

ʊntˈ gəˈryçə mɪt den ˈdʏftˈən fɔn deːɐ̯ ˈlɪndə ɪn den ˈkʰyːlʊŋən veːn:
und Gerüche mit den Düften von der Linde in den Kühlungen wehn:
and aromas with the fragrances of the linden in the cool breezes waft:
(and various aromas are wafting in the cool breezes along with the fragrance of the linden-tree:)

zoː ʊmˈʃatˈən mɪç gəˈdaŋkˈən lan das graːpˈ ˈmaͤenɐ gəˈliːpˈtˈən,
so umschatten mich Gedanken an das Grab meiner Geliebten,
so shadow me thoughts of the grave of my beloved,
(then thoughts of my beloved's grave come over me like a dark shadow,)
[*poem:* **an das Grab der** (deːɐ̯, of the) **Geliebten]**

ʊntˈ lɪç zeː lɪm ˈvaldə nuːɐ̯/nuːr lɛs ˈdɛmɐn,
und ich seh' im Walde nur es dämmern, [*poem:* **in dem** (ɪn dem, in the) **Walde]**
and I see in the woods only it growing dark,
(and I only see that it is growing dark in the woods,)

ʊntˈ lɛs veːtˈ miːɐ̯ fɔn deːɐ̯ ˈblyːtˈə nɪçtˈ heːɐ̯.
und es weht mir von der Blüte nicht her.
and it blows to me from the blossoming not hither.
(and the scent of the blossoms does not blow my way.)

ɪç gəˈnɔs lae̯nstˈ, loː liːɐ̯ ˈtʰoːtˈən, lɪç gəˈnɔs lɛs lae̯nstˈ mɪtˈ lɔͤøçˈ!
Ich genoss einst, o ihr Toten, ich genoss es einst mit euch!
I enjoyed once, O you dead ones, I enjoyed it once with you!
(I enjoyed such things, O spirits of my beloved dead, I once enjoyed such things with you!)
[*poem:* **Ich genoss einst, o ihr Toten, es mit euch!]**

viː lʊmˈveːtˈən lʊns deːɐ̯ dʊftˈ lʊnt di ˈkʰyːlʊŋ,
Wie umwehten uns der Duft und die Kühlung,
How wafted around us the fragrance and the cooling breeze,
(How the fragrance and the cooling breeze once wafted around us,)

426

viː fɛɐ̯'ʃøːntʰ vaːɐ̯stʰ fɔn dem 'moːndə duː, loː 'ʃøːnə na'tʰuːɐ̯!
wie verschönt warst von dem Monde du, o schöne Natur!
how beautified were from the moon you, O beautiful nature!
(O beautiful nature, how transfigured you were in the moonlight!)

[Klopstock wrote the poem after the death of his beloved wife. Schubert made two versions, only slightly different, both mainly in the style of recitative.]

di 'ʃpʰɪnərɪn
Die Spinnerin
The Spinster

Op. 118, No. 6 [1815] (Johann Wolfgang von Goethe)

als lɪç ʃtʰɪl lʊntʰ 'ruːɪç ʃpʰan, 'loːnə nuːɐ̯ tsu 'ʃtʰɔkʰən,
Als ich still und ruhig spann, ohne nur zu stocken,
As I quietly and calmly spun, without even to stop,
(As I was quietly and calmly spinning, without even stopping,)

tʰraːtʰ laen 'ʃøːnɐ 'jʊŋɐ man 'naːə miːɐ̯ tsum 'rɔkʰən.
trat ein schöner junger Mann nahe mir zum Rocken.
stepped a handsome young man near to me to the distaff.
(a handsome young man came up to me at the distaff.)

'loːpʰtʰə, vas tsu 'loːbən vaːɐ̯, 'zɔltʰə das vas 'ʃaːdən?
Lobte, was zu loben war, sollte das was schaden?
(He) praised what to praise was, should that something harm?
(He praised what there was to praise,—was there any harm in that?—)

maen dem 'flaksə 'glaeçəs haːɐ̯/haːr lʊnt den 'glaeçən 'faːdən.
mein dem Flachse gleiches Haar und den gleichen Faden.
my to the flax similar hair and the similar thread.
(praised my hair, so like the flax, and the thread, so like my hair.)

'ruːɪç vaːɐ̯/vaːr leːɐ̯ nɪçt da'bae, liːs lɛs nɪçtʰ baem 'laltʰən;
Ruhig war er nicht dabei, liess es nicht beim Alten;
Calm was he not in doing so, left it not by the old;
(In so doing he did not stay calm; he did not leave it at that;)

ʊnt deːɐ̯ 'faːdən rɪs lɛntʰtsvae, deːn lɪç laŋ lɛɐ̯'haltʰən.
und der Faden riss entzwei, den ich lang' erhalten.
and the thread ripped in two, which I long (had) held.
(and the thread that I had been holding so long snapped in two.)

ʊnt dɛs 'flaksəs 'ʃtʰaengəvɪçtʰ gaːpʰ nɔx 'viːlə 'tsaːlən;
Und des Flachses Steingewicht gab noch viele Zahlen;
And the flax's stone-weight gave still many numbers;
(And the stone weight that pulled down the flax kept producing plenty of thread;)

'aːbɐ(r) lax! lɪç 'kʰɔntʰə nɪçtʰ meːɐ̯ mɪtʰ 'liːnən 'pʰraːlən.
aber ach! ich konnte nicht mehr mit ihnen prahlen.
but ah! I could not any more with them boast.
(but, ah, I could not take the credit for that any more.)

als lıç zi: tsʊm 'veːbɐ tʰruːkʼ, fyːltʼ lıç vas   zıç 're:gən,
Als ich sie zum Weber trug, fühlt' ich was   sich regen,
As I   them to the weaver carried, felt   I   something itself stir,
(As I was taking the thread to the weaver, I felt something stirring,)

ʊntʼ maen 'larməs 'hɛrtsə ʃluːkʼ mıtʼ gə'ʃvındɐn   'ʃleːgən.
und mein armes Herze schlug mit geschwindern Schlägen.
and my   poor heart beat   with faster   beats.
(and my poor heart beat faster.)

nuːn, baem 'haesən 'zɔnənʃtʼıç,   brıŋ   lıçs lɑof di 'blaeçə,
Nun, beim heissen Sonnenstich, bring' ich's auf die Bleiche,
Now, in the hot   sunstroke,   bring I   it to the bleaching-ground,
(Now, in the scorching sun, I bring it to the bleaching-ground,)

ʊntʼ mıtʼ 'myːə bʏkʼ lıç mıç   naːx   dem 'nɛːçstʼən 'tʰaeçə.
und mit Mühe bück' ich mich nach   dem nächsten Teiche.
and with effort bend I   myself toward the   nearest   pool.
(and with considerable effort I bend over the nearest pool.)

vas   lıç lın dem 'kʰɛmɐlaen   ʃtʼıl   lʊntʼ faen gə'ʃpʼɔnən,
Was ich in dem Kämmerlein still   und fein   gesponnen,
What I   in the   little chamber quietly and finely (have) spun,
(What I have spun so quietly and so finely in my little room,)

kʰɔmtʼ, viː kʰan lɛs 'landɐs   zaen?'lɛntʼlıç   lan di 'zɔnən.
kommt, wie kann es anders   sein? endlich   an die Sonnen.
comes—how can it otherwise be?— in the end to the suns.
(will in the end—how can it be otherwise?—come out into the light of day.)

[The spinning motion is shared between the voice and the piano, and Schubert has caught in this attractive strophic song the folk tone of Goethe's racy poem that must have brought a blush to the cheek of many a proper *Biedermeier* maiden. Let's hope the young man will do his duty!]

Die Stadt see *Schwanengesang*

di 'ʃtʼɛrbəndə
Die Sterbende
The Dying Woman

Posthumously published [composed 1815?] (poem by Friedrich von Matthisson)

hael! diːs lıst di 'lɛtstʼə 'tseːrə, di: deːɐ   'myːdən   'lɑokʼ lɛntʼfɛltʰ!
Heil! dies ist die letzte Zähre, die der   Müden   Aug' entfällt!
Hail! This is the last   tear   that from the weary woman's eye falls!
(Hail! This is the last tear that will fall from the weary woman's eyes!)

ʃoːn   lɛntʼʃatʼətʼ zıç di 'sfeːrə 'liːrɐ 'haemaːtʼlıçən vɛltʰ!
Schon entschattet sich die Sphäre ihrer heimatlichen Welt!
Already de-shadows itself the sphere of her homeland   world!
(Already the sphere of her familiar world is clearing away the shadows!)

428

laeçt', vi: 'fry:lɪŋsneːbəl 'ʃvɪndən, lɪst dɛs 'leːbəns tʰrɑom lɛnt''floːn,
Leicht, wie Frühlingsnebel schwinden, ist des Lebens Traum entflohn,
Lightly, as spring- mists vanish, is the life's dream fled,
(The dream of life has fled as lightly as the mists vanish in spring,)

pʰara'diːzəsbluːmən 'vɪndən 'zeːrafiːm ʦum 'kʰranʦə ʃoːn!
Paradiesesblumen winden Seraphim zum Kranze schon!
Paradise- flowers twine seaphim into the wreath already!
(Already seraphim are twining flowers from Paradise into a wreath!)

[haː! mɪt 'daenəm 'ʃt'ɑop''gəvɪməl flɔøkst', loː 'leːɐ̯də, duː da'hɪn!
[Ha! mit deinem Staubgewimmel fleugst, o Erde, du dahin!
[Ah! With your dust- swarm fly, O earth, you away!
[(Ah! You, O earth, with your swarming dust, are already flying away from her consciousness!)

'neːɐ̯ glɛnʦt deːɐ̯/deːr 'lɔfnə 'hɪməl deːɐ̯ bə'fraet'ən 'dʊldərɪn.
Näher glänzt der offne Himmel der befreiten Dulderin.
Nearer gleams the open heaven for the freed sufferer.
(For the suffering one who has been freed, the open gates of heaven are gleaming nearer.)

'nɔøɐ̯ tʰaːk' lɪst' 'ɑofgəgaŋən! 'hɛrlɪç ʃt'raːlt' zaen 'mɔrgənlɪçtʰ!
Neuer Tag ist aufgegangen! Herrlich strahlt sein Morgenlicht!
New day has dawned! Gloriously beams its morning light!
(A new day has dawned! Its morning light shines gloriously!)

oː dɛs 'landəs, voː deːɐ̯ 'baŋən 'tʰrɛnʊŋ veː kʰaen hɛrʦ meːɐ̯ brɪçtʰ!
O des Landes, wo der bangen Trennung Weh kein Herz mehr bricht!
Oh, of the land where the fearful parting's pain no heart any more breaks!
(Oh, it is the light of a land where no heart will break again from the pain of fearful parting!)

hɔrç! lɪm 'haelgən haen deːɐ̯ 'pʰalmən, voː deːɐ̯ ʃt'roːm dɛs 'leːbəns fliːstʰ,
Horch! im heilgen Hain der Palmen, wo der Strom des Lebens fliesst,
Hark! In the sacred grove of the palms, where the stream of life flows,
(Hark! In the sacred palm grove where the river of life is flowing,)

tʰøːnt' lɛs lɪn deːɐ̯ 'lɛŋəl 'psalmən: ʃvɛst'ɐzeːlə, zae gə'gryːstʰ!
tönt es in der Engel Psalmen: Schwesterseele, sei gegrüsst!
sounds it in the angels' psalms: "Sister soul, be greeted!
(these words are sounding in the angels' psalms: "We greet you, sister soul,)

diː lɛmpʰoːɐ̯ mɪt' 'laːdlɐsʃnɛlə ʦuː dɛs 'lɪçt'əs 'luːɐ̯kʰvɛl ʃt'iːk';
die empor mit Adlerschnelle zu des Lichtes Urquell stieg;
who aloft with eagle-speed to the light's primeval source arose;
(who have risen up with the speed of an eagle to the primeval source of all light;)

tʰoːt'! voː lɪst daen 'ʃt'axəl? 'hœlə! 'ʃt'ɔlʦə 'hœlə! voː lɪst daen ziːk'?
Tod! Wo ist dein Stachel? Hölle! stolze Hölle! Wo ist dein Sieg?]
death! Where is thy sting? Hell, proud hell, where is thy victory?"]
(death, where is thy sting? Hell, proud hell, where is thy victory?")] [*poem:* **Wo dein Sieg?**]

[Schubert set the first verse; the other two, in brackets above, also fit the musical line (with an adjustment for the extra syllable in the very last line, if sung as printed in the *Gesamtausgabe*— the poem lacks that last "*ist*," which breaks the rhythm). The title of the poem was *Die sterbende*

Elisa. The poet's friend Rosenfeld had died before he could marry his fiancée Elisa, who soon after died of a broken heart. Matthisson presents death as a liberating transfiguration.]

di ˈʃtˈɛrnə / duː ˈʃtˈɑonəstˈ, loː mɛnʃ
Die Sterne / Du staunest, o Mensch
The Stars / You Marvel, O Man

Posthumously published [composed 1819 or 1820?] (poem by Friedrich von Schlegel)

duː ˈʃtˈɑonəstˈ, loː mɛnʃ,   vas ˈhɑelɪç   viːɐ̯ ˈʃtˈraːlən?
Du staunest, o Mensch, was heilig   wir strahlen?
You marvel,   O man,   what sacredly we   radiate?
(Do you marvel, O man, at what we are sacredly radiating?)

oː ˈfɔlkˈtˈəst duː nuːɐ̯ den ˈhɪmlɪʃən   ˈvɪŋkˈən,   [den ˈhɪmlɪʃən   ˈmɛçtˈən]
O folgtest   du nur den himmlischen Winken, [*Peters:* den himmlischen Mächten]
Oh, if followed you only the heavenly   signs,   [the heavenly   powers]
(Oh, if you only would follow the heavenly signs,)

fɛɐ̯ˈneːməst   duː ˈbɛsɐ, vas ˈfrɔøntˈlɪç viːɐ̯ ˈblɪŋkˈən,   [viːɐ̯ ˈvɪŋkˈən]
vernähmest   du besser, was freundlich wir blinken, [*Peters:* wir winken]
would perceive you better   what friendlily   we   signal,   [we   signal]
(you would better perceive what we are signaling as your friends;)

viː ˈveːrən fɛɐ̯ˈʃvundən   di ˈlɪrdɪʃə   ˈkʰvaːlən! dan ˈflœsə   di ˈliːbə
wie wären verschwunden die irdische Qualen! Dann flösse   die Liebe
how were   vanished   the earthly   torments! Then would flow the love
(how your earthly torments would vanish! Then love would flow)

lɑos ˈleːvɪgən ˈʃaːlən, lɛs ˈlaːtˈmətˈən   ˈlalə lɪn ˈraenən laˈtsuːrən, das ˈlɪçtˈblɑoə meːɐ̯
aus   ewigen Schalen, es   atmeten   alle in reinen Azuren,   das lichtblaue Meer
out of eternal   vessels,   there would breathe all in pure   azure,   the light-blue sea
(from eternal vessels, all would breathe the pure azure air, the light-blue sea)

ʊmˈʃveːpˈtˈə   di ˈfluːrən, lʊntˈ ˈfʊŋkˈəltˈən   ˈʃtˈɛrnə lɑof den ˈhɑemɪʃən   ˈtʰaːlən.
umschwebte   die Fluren, und funkelten   Sterne auf den heimischen Talen.
would float about the meadows, and would sparkle stars   on   the native   valleys.
(would float about the meadows, and stars would sparkle in your native valleys.)

[*poem:* **und funkelten Stern'** (ʃtˈɛrn)]

ɑos ˈgœtˈlɪçɐ ˈkʰvɛlə zɪntˈ ˈlalə gəˈnɔmən,   lɪstˈ ˈjeːkˈlɪçəs ˈveːzən nɪçtˈ
Aus göttlicher Quelle sind alle genommen, ist   jegliches Wesen nicht
From divine   source   are all taken,   is   each   being not
(All spring from the same divine source; are not all beings)

ˈlɑenəs lɪm ˈkʰoːrə? nuːn zɪntˈ jaː   gəˈlœfnət di ˈhɪmlɪʃən   ˈtʰoːrə,
eines im   Chore? Nun sind ja   geöffnet die himmlischen Tore,
one   in the choir? Now are   indeed opened the heavenly   gates,
(united in one choir? Now indeed the heavenly gates are open;)

vas zɔl den das ˈbaŋə fɛɐ̯ˈtsaːgən nɔx ˈfrɔmən?   loː ˈveːrətˈ liːɐ̯ ʃoːn
was soll denn das bange Verzagen noch frommen? O wäret ihr schon
what shall then the fearful despair   still avail?   Oh were   you already
(of what avail is fearful despair? Oh, if you already)

tsʊr 'tʰiːfə gə'kʰlɔmən, zoː 'zɛːət   das hɑɔp't' liːɐ̯ fɔn 'ʃt'ɛrnən lʊm'floːgən
zur Tiefe geklommen, so sähet   das Haupt ihr von Sternen umflogen
to the depths climbed,   then would see the head   you by stars   flown around
(had plumbed the depths of being, then you would see stars circling around your head)

ʊnt' ʃp'iːlənt' lʊms   hɛrt͜s di 'kʰɪnt'lɪçən 'voːgən, t͜su 'deːnən di 'ʃt'ʏrmə
und spielend ums   Herz die kindlichen Wogen, zu denen die Stürme
and playing around the heart the childlike   waves, to which the storms
(and, playing about your heart, childlike waves, to which the storms)

dɛs 'leːbəns nɪçt' 'kʰɔmən.
des Lebens nicht kommen.
of the life   not   come.
(of life will not come.)

[The stars urge us to read their message of light. Schubert has clothed the poem in long and lovely *cantabile* phrases. The Peters edition prints only the first of the two verses.]

di 'ʃt'ɛrnə / vas 'fʊŋk'əlt' liːɐ̯ zoː mɪlt'
Die Sterne / Was funkelt ihr so mild
The Stars / Why Do You Sparkle So Gently

Posthumously published [composed 1815] (poem by Johann Georg Fellinger)

vas 'fʊŋk'əlt' liːɐ̯ zoː mɪlt' mɪç lan? liːɐ̯ 'ʃt'ɛrnə, hɔlt' lʊnt' heːɐ̯!
Was funkelt ihr so mild mich an? ihr Sterne, hold und hehr!
Why sparkle you so gently me at? You stars,   lovely and lofty!
(Why do you sparkle so gently at me, you lovely, lofty stars?)

vas 'tʰraebət' lɔø̯ç lɑof 'dʊŋk'lɐ baːn lɪm 'lɛːt'ɐblɑoən meːɐ̯?
Was treibet euch auf dunkler Bahn im ätherblauen Meer?
What drives   you on dark   course in the ether-blue   sea?
(What drives you on your dark course through the blue sea of ether?)

viː 'gɔt'əs 'lɑogən ʃɑot' liːɐ̯ dɔrt', lɑos lɔst' lʊnt' vɛst', lɑos zyːt' lʊnt' nɔrt',
Wie Gottes Augen schaut ihr dort, aus Ost und West, aus Süd und Nord,
Like God's eyes   gaze you there, from east and west, from south and north,
(Like the eyes of God, you are gazing down, up there, from east and west, from south and north,)

zoː 'frɔø̯nt'lɪç lɑof mɪç heːɐ̯. lʊnt' 'lyːbə(r)lal lʊm'blɪŋk't'   liːɐ̯ mɪç
so freundlich auf mich her. Und überall umblinkt ihr mich
so friendlily at   me   hither. And everywhere surround-gleam you me
(in such a friendly way at me. And everywhere you gleam all around me)

mɪt' 'zanft'əm 'dɛmɐlɪçtʰ, di 'zɔnə heːp't' lɪn 'mɔrgən zɪç,
mit sanftem Dämmerlicht, die Sonne hebt in Morgen sich,
with soft   twilight glow, the sun   raises in morning itself,
(with a soft glow of twilight. The sun rises in the morning,)

dɔx liːɐ̯ fɛɐ̯'last' mɪç nɪçtʰ; vɛn kʰɑom deːɐ̯/deːr 'laːbənt' 'niːdɐgrɑot',
doch ihr verlasst mich nicht; wenn kaum der Abend niedergraut,
but you desert me not; when scarcely the   evening down- greys,
(but you do not desert me; when the evening has scarcely begun to darken,)

zoː blɪk' t' liːɐ̯ miːɐ̯, zoː frɔm lʊnt tʰrɑot' ʃoːn 'viːdɐ(r) lɪns ɡə'zɪçtʰ.
so blickt ihr mir, so fromm und traut schon wieder ins Gesicht.
then look you to me, so innocent and dear already again into the face.
(then already you look into my face again, so innocent and so dear to me.)

vɪl'kʰɔmən dɛn, vɪl'kʰɔmən miːɐ̯/miːr, liːɐ̯ 'frɔʏndə, ʃt'ɪl lʊnt' blɑeç!
Willkommen denn, willkommen mir, ihr Freunde, still und bleich!
Welcome then, welcome to me, you friends, quiet and pale!
(Welcome then, I bid you welcome, you friends, quiet and pale!)

viː 'lɪçt'ə 'ɡɑest'ɐ̯ 'vandəlt' liːɐ̯ dʊrç 'lɔʏɐ̯ 'vɑet'əs rɑeç, lʊnt' lax!
Wie lichte Geister wandelt ihr durch euer weites Reich, und ach!
Like light spirits wander you through your broad realm, and ah!
(Like luminous spirits you wander through your broad realm, and ah!)

fi'lɑeçt' bə'ɡryːsət' mɪç lɑen 'leːdlɐ, deːɐ̯ tsu fryː fɛɐ̯'blɪç,
vielleicht begrüsset mich ein Edler, der zu früh verblich,
perhaps greets me a noble being, who too early passed away,
(perhaps a noble soul that passed away too soon is greeting me,)

ɑen 'tʰrɔʏɐ̯ frɔʏnt' lɑos lɔʏç! fi'lɑeçt' vɪrt' lɑenst' mɑen 'lɑoflɛnt'halt'
ein treuer Freund aus euch! Vielleicht wird einst mein Aufenthalt
a faithful friend out of you! Perhaps becomes one day my dwelling place
(perhaps a faithful friend of mine, from among you! Perhaps one day my dwelling place will be)

lɪm 'hɛlən 'ziːrius, vɛn 'diːzə 'kʰlɑenə 'vʊrmɡəʃt'alt di 'hʏlə 'vɛksəln mʊs;
im hellen Sirius, wenn diese kleine Wurmgestalt die Hülle wechseln muss;
in the bright Sirius, when this little worm-shape the outer covering change must;
(on bright Sirius, when this little wormlike frame must change its outer shell;)

[*poem:* **der helle** (deːɐ̯ 'hɛlə, the bright) **Sirius**]

fi'lɑeçt' lɛɐ̯'heːp't deːɐ̯ 'fʊŋk'ə ɡɑest', vɛn 'diːzə 'ʃvaxə fɔrm tsɛɐ̯'rɑest',
vielleicht erhebt der Funke Geist, wenn diese schwache Form zerreisst,
perhaps raises the spark spirit, when this weak form tears apart,
(perhaps the spark we call the spirit will rise, when this weak form of flesh tears apart,)

zɪç lɑof tsʊm 'luːranʊs! loː 'lɛçəlt' nuːɐ̯/nuːr, loː 'vɪŋk'ət' nuːɐ̯ miːɐ̯ ʃt'ɪl tsuː lɔʏç hɪ'nan!
sich auf zum Uranus! O lächelt nur, o winket nur mir still zu euch hinan!
itself up to the Uranus! Oh smile only, oh beckon only to me quietly to you upward!
(will rise up to the starry heaven! Oh, just smile, just beckon me quietly to come up to you!)

mɪç 'fyːrət' 'mʊt'ɐ(r) 'lalnaˌtʰuːɐ̯ naːx 'liːrəm 'ɡroːsən pʰlaːn;
Mich führet Mutter Allnatur nach ihrem grossen Plan;
Me guides Mother All-Nature according to her great plan;
(Mother Nature is guiding me according to her own great plan;)

mɪç 'kʰʏmɐt' nɪçt deːɐ̯ 'vɛlt'ən fal,
mich kümmert nicht der Welten Fall,
me troubles not the worlds' fall,
(the downfall of worlds does not trouble me,)

432

venn ıç nuːɐ dɔrt di ˈliːbən ɑl feɐˈlaenət`/ferˈlaenət` ˈfɪndən kʰan.
wenn ich nur dort die Lieben all' vereinet finden kann.
if I only there the loved ones all united find can.
(if only I can find all my loved ones there, reunited.)

[Uranus was the primeval god of the sky in Greek mythology; the planet named after him was discovered in 1781, too faint to be seen by the naked eye unless one knows exactly where to look for it. The poem was written in 1812. Schubert wrote out only the first verse, but placed repeat signs at the end of his setting. The stars twinkle in the treble octave leaps of the accompaniment.]

di ˈʃtˈɛrnə / viː ˈblɪtsən di ˈʃtˈɛrnə
Die Sterne / Wie blitzen die Sterne
The Stars / How Brightly the Stars

Op. 96, No. 1 [1828] (Karl Gottfried von Leitner)

viː ˈblɪtsən di ˈʃtˈɛrnə zoː hɛl dʊrç di naxtʰ!
Wie blitzen die Sterne so hell durch die Nacht!
How flash the stars so brightly through the night!
(How brightly the stars are flashing through the night!)

bɪn ɔftˈ ʃoːn daˈryːbɐ fɔm ˈʃlʊmɐ(r) ɛɐˈvaxtʰ.
Bin oft schon darüber vom Schlummer erwacht.
Am often already over that from the slumber awakened.
(I have already been often awakened from slumber because of that.)

dɔx ʃɛltˈ ɪç di ˈlɪçtˈən gəˈbɪldə drʊm nɪçtʰ,
Doch schelt' ich die lichten Gebilde drum nicht,
But reproach I the luminous creatures for that not,
(But I do not reproach the luminous creatures for that,)

ziː ˈyːbən ɪm ˈʃtˈɪlən manç ˈhaelzaːmə pflɪçtʰ.
sie üben im Stillen manch heilsame Pflicht.
they perform in the silence many a beneficial duty.
(for they perform in silence many a beneficial duty.)

ziː ˈvalən hoːx ˈloːbən ɪn ˈɛŋəlgəʃtˈaltʰ, ziː ˈlɔøçtˈən dem ˈpʰɪlgɐ
Sie wallen hoch oben in Engelgestalt, sie leuchten dem Pilger
They wander high above in angel-form, they light for the pilgrim
(They wander high above us in the form of angels, they light the pilgrim's way)

[*poem:* **und** (ʊntˈ, and) **leuchten**]

dʊrç ˈhaedən ʊntˈ valtˈ. ziː ˈʃveːbən ɑls ˈboːtˈən deːɐ ˈliːbə ʊmˈheːɐ,
durch Heiden und Wald. Sie schweben als Boten der Liebe umher,
through heath and forest. They hover as messengers of the love around,
(through heath and forest. They hover about as messengers of love,)

ʊnt ˈtʰraːgən ɔftˈ ˈkʰʏsə vaetˈ ˈyːbɐ das meːɐ.
und tragen oft Küsse weit über das Meer.
and carry often kisses far over the sea.
(and often carry kisses far across the sea.)

zi: 'blɪk'ən dem 'dʊldɐ rɛçt' mɪlt' ɪns gə'zɪçt^h,
Sie blicken dem Dulder recht mild ins Gesicht,
They look to the sufferer right mildly into the face,
(They look very gently into the face of the sufferer,)

ʊnt' 'zɔ̷ømən di 't^hrɛːnən mɪt' 'zɪlbɐnəm lɪçt^h.
und säumen die Tränen mit silbernem Licht.
and border the tears with silvery light.
(and rim his tears with silvery light.)

ʊnt' 'vaeːzən fɔn 'grɛːbɐn gaːɐ̯ 't^hrø̷ːst'lɪç ʊnt' hɔlt' ʊns 'hɪnt'ɐ das 'blɑ̈ɔ̈ə
Und weisen von Gräbern gar tröstlich und hold uns hinter das Blaue
And point from graves very comfortingly and graciously us behind the blue
(And comfortingly and graciously they point us away from the grave and beyond the blue)

                                                           [*poem:* **Sie** (ziː, they) **weisen**]

mɪt' 'fɪŋən fɔn gɔlt'. zoː zae dɛn gə'zeːgnət, du: 'ʃt'raːlɪgə ʃaːɐ̯!
mit Fingern von Gold. So sei denn gesegnet, du strahlige Schar!
with fingers of gold. Therefore be then blessed, you radiant host!
(with fingers of gold. Therefore I bless you, radiant host!)

ʊnt' 'lɔ̷øçt'ə miːɐ̯ 'laŋə nɔx 'frɔ̷ønt'lɪç ʊnt' k^hlaːɐ̯! ʊnt' vɛn lɪç laenst' 'liːbə,
Und leuchte mir lange noch freundlich und klar! Und wenn ich einst liebe,
And shine for me long still friendly and clear! And if I one day love,
(And long may you still shine for me, friendly and clear! And if one day I fall in love,)

zaet' hɔlt dem fɛɐ̯'laen/fɛr'laen, ʊnt' 'lɔ̷øɐ gə'flɪmɐ last' 'zeːgən ʊns zaen!
seid hold dem Verein, und euer Geflimmer lasst Segen uns sein!
be gracious to the union, and your glimmer let blessing for us be!
(be gracious to our bond, and let your glimmer be a blessing upon us!)

[The stars are dancing in Schubert's cheerful music. Each verse starts out with the same melody, makes an unexpected modulation in its third line, and returns to a similar closing phrase.]

di 'ʃt'ɛrnə / viː voːl lɪst' miːɐ̯ lɪm 'dʊŋk'əln!
Die Sterne / Wie wohl ist mir im Dunkeln!
The Stars / How Well I Feel in the Dark!

Posthumously published [composed 1815] (poem by Ludwig Kosegarten)

viː voːl lɪst' miːɐ̯/miːr lɪm 'dʊŋk'əln! viː veːt di 'lɑ̈ɔ̈ə naxt^h!
Wie wohl ist mir im Dunkeln! Wie weht die laue Nacht!
How well is for me in the darkening! How blows the lukewarm night!
(How well I feel in the dark! How mildly the warm night breezes blow!)

di 'ʃt'ɛrnə 'gɔt'əs 'fʊŋk'əln lɪn 'faeɐlɪçɐ p^hraxt^h! k^hɔm, 'liːda, k^hɔm lɪns 'fraeə,
Die Sterne Gottes funkeln in feierlicher Pracht! Komm, Ida, komm' ins Freie,
The stars of God sparkle in ceremonial splendor! Come, Ida, come into the open air,
(God's stars sparkle in ceremonial splendor! Come, Ida, come out into the open air,)

ʊnt' las lɪn 'jeːnə 'blɔ̈ɔ̈ə ʊnt' las tsuː 'jeːnən hø̷ːn ʊns 'ʃt'ɑ̈ɔ̈nənt' 'lɑ̈ɔ̈fvɛrts zeːn.
und lass in jene Bläue und lass zu jenen Höhn uns staunend aufwärts sehn.
and let in that blue and let to those heights us wondering upwards see.
(and let us gaze in wonder into that blue and up to those heights.)

ziː, viː di ˈlaɐ ˈʃɪmɐtʰ!   ziː, viː deːɐ/deːr ˈlaːdlɐ glyːtʰ! ziː, viː di ˈkʰroːnə
Sieh, wie die Leier schimmert! Sieh, wie der   Adler glüht! Sieh, wie die Krone
See how the lyre shimmers! See how the   eagle glows! See how the crown
(See how Lyra shimmers! See how Aquila glows! See how Corona Borealis, Ariadne's crown,)

ˈflɪmɐtʰ, ʊntʰ ˈgɛma ˈfʊŋkʰən ʃpʰryːtʰ! di ˈhɛlən ˈvɛçtʰɐ ˈvɪŋkʰən,
flimmert, und Gemma Funken sprüht! Die hellen Wächter winken,
glimmers, and Gemma sparks sprays! The bright guardians beckon,
(glimmers, and how Gemma is emitting sparks! The bright guardians are beckoning,)

di ˈgɔldnən ˈvaːgən ˈblɪŋkʰən, ʊntʰ ˈʃtʰɔlts dʊrçˈʃvɪmt   deːɐ ʃvaːn   den ˈblaʊən ˈloːtseaːn.
die goldnen Wagen blinken, und stolz   durchschwimmt der Schwan den blauen Ozean.
the golden wagons gleam,   and proudly through-swims the swan   the blue   ocean.
(the golden Dippers gleam, and Cygnus swims proudly through the blue ocean of the sky.)
　　　　　　　　　　　[*poem:* **und prächtig** (ˈpʰrɛçtʰɪç, magnificently) **schwimmt der Schwan**
　　　　　　　　　　　　　　　　　　　　　　　im (ɪm, in the) **blauen Ocean**]

oː ˈʃtʰɛrnə ˈgɔtʰəs, ˈtsɔøgən ʊntʰ ˈboːtʰən   ˈbɛsrɐ   vɛltʰ, liːɐ haest den ˈlaʊfruːɐ
O Sterne Gottes, Zeugen und Boten   bessrer Welt, ihr heisst den Aufruhr
O stars   of God, witnesses and messengers of better world, you bid the tumult
(O stars of God, witnesses and messengers from a better world, you bid the tumult)

ˈʃvaegən, deːɐ/deːr ˈlʊnzən ˈbuːzən ʃvɛltʰ. lɪç zeː hrˈnaof, liːɐ ˈheːrən, tsuː ˈlɔørən
schweigen, der   unsern Busen schwellt. Ich seh' hinauf, ihr Hehren,   zu euren
be still,   that   our   bosom swells. I look up,   you lofty ones, to your
(be still that swells our bosom. I look up, you lofty ones, to your)
　　　　　　　　　　　[*poem:* **der unsre** (ˈlʊnzrə) **Brust** (brʊstʰ, breast) **erschwellt** (lɛɐˈʃvɛltʰ)]

ˈlɪçtʰən ˈsfeːrən, ʊntʰ ˈlaːndʊŋ   ˈbɛsrɐ   lʊstʰ   ˈʃtʰɪlt di lɛmˈpʰøːɐtʰə brʊstʰ.
lichten Sphären, und Ahndung   bessrer Lust   stillt die empörte Brust.
light spheres, and premonition of better pleasure quiets the indignant breast.
(bright spheres, and a premonition of greater pleasure quiets my indignant heart.)
　　　　　　　　　　　[*poem:* **und Ahnung** (ˈlaːnʊŋ)—"*Ahndung*" is an older form (in this sense)]

oː ˈliːda, vɛn di ˈʃveːɐmuːt daen ˈzanftʰəs ˈlaʊgə hyltʰ, vɛn diːɐ   di vɛltʰ
O Ida, wenn die Schwermut dein sanftes Auge hüllt, wenn dir   die Welt
Oh Ida, when the melancholy your gentle eye   veils, when for you the world
(Oh Ida, when melancholy veils your gentle eyes, when for you the world)

mɪtʰ ˈveːɐmuːt den ˈleːbənsbeçɐ fʏltʰ: zoː geː hrˈnaos ɪm ˈdʊŋkʰəln, ʊntʰ ziː di
mit Wermut   den Lebensbecher füllt: so geh' hinaus im Dunkeln, und sieh die
with wormwood the life's goblet fills: then go out   in the darkening, and see the
(fills the goblet of life with bitter gall: then go out in the dark and see the)

ˈʃtʰɛrnə ˈfʊŋkʰəln, ʊntʰ ˈlaezɐ vɪrt   daen ʃmɛrts, ʊntʰ ˈfraeɐ ʃleːkʰtʰ daen hɛrts.
Sterne funkeln, und leiser wird   dein Schmerz, und freier schlägt dein Herz.
stars sparkle, and softer becomes your pain,   and freer beats your heart.
(stars sparkling, and your pain will be eased, and your heart will beat more freely.)
　　　　　　　　　　　[*poem:* **und freier schlägt das** (das, the) **Herz**]

ʊntʰ vɛn ɪm ˈløːdən ˈʃtʰaobɐ deːɐ/deːr ˈlɪrə gaestʰ lɛɐˈkʰraŋkʰtʰ; vɛn tʰiːf ɪn diːɐ
Und wenn im öden Staube der   irre Geist erkrankt;   wenn tief in dir
And when in the empty dust the   straying spirit sickens;   when deep in you
(And when the straying spirit sickens amid the empty dust; when deep inside you)

deːɐ̯ 'glɑ͜obə ǀan gɔt' ǀʊnt 'tsuːkʰʊnft' ʃvaŋk'tʰ: ʃɑ͜o ǀɑ͜of tsuː 'jeːnən 'fɛrnən,
der Glaube an Gott und Zukunft schwankt: schau auf zu jenen Fernen,
the faith in God and future wavers: look up to those distances,
(your faith in God and in the future wavers: look up into those distances,)

tsuː 'jeːnən 'leːvgən 'ʃt'ɛrnən! ʃɑ͜o ǀɑ͜of, ǀʊnt' glɑ͜op' ǀan gɔt', ǀʊnt' 'zeːgnə graːp' ǀʊnt tʰoːt'.
zu jenen ew'gen Sternen! Schau auf, und glaub' an Gott, und segne Grab und Tod.
to those eternal stars! Look up, and believe in God, and bless grave and death.
(to those eternal stars! Look up, and have faith in God, and bless the grave and death.)

oː 'liːda, vɛn di 'ʃt'rɛŋə dɛs 'ʃɪk'zaːls ǀa͜enst' ǀʊns tʰrɛntʰ, ǀʊnt' vɛn das
O Ida, wenn die Strenge des Schicksals einst uns trennt, und wenn das
Oh Ida, if the severity of the fate once us parts, and if the
(Oh Ida, if the severity of our fate should part us one day, and if the)

'vɛlt'gədrɛŋə nɪçt' blɪk' nɔx kʰʊs ǀʊns gœntʰ: zoː ʃɑ͜o hɪ'nɑ͜of ǀɪns 'fra͜eə,
Weltgedränge nicht Blick noch Kuss uns gönnt: so schau hinauf ins Freie,
world-buffeting not glance nor kiss us grants: then look up into the free air,
(buffeting of the world begrudges us a glance or a kiss: then look up into the free air,)
[*poem:* **wenn uns das Weltgedränge nicht Blick noch Kuss vergönnt** (fɛɐ̯'gœntʰ)]

ɪn 'jeːnə 'va͜et'ə 'blɔ͜ø̯ə! ǀɪn 'jeːnə 'lɪçt'ən høːn, dɔrt, dɔrt' ǀɪst' 'viːdɐzeːn!
in jene weite Bläue! In jene lichten Höhn, dort, dort ist Wiedersehn!
into that vast blue! Into those light heights, there, there is reunion!
(into that vast blue! In those bright heights, there, *there* we shall meet again!)

ʊnt' vɛn ǀɪç ǀa͜enst', loː 'tʰɔ͜ø̯rə, fɔn 'ǀaləm kʰampf ǀʊnt' kʰriːk' ǀɪm 'ʃt'ɪlən 'graːbə 'fa͜erə,
Und wenn ich einst, o Teure, von allem Kampf und Krieg im stillen Grabe fei're,
And when I once, O dear one, from all battle and war in the quiet grave rest,
(And when one day, O dear one, I am resting in a quiet grave from all battle and war,)

zoː ʃɑ͜o ǀɛm'pʰoːɐ̯(r) ǀʊnt' ʃp'rɪç: ǀɪn 'jeːnən 'hoːən 'fɛrnən, ǀɑ͜of 'jeːnən 'gɔldnən 'ʃt'ɛrnən,
so schau empor und sprich: "In jenen hohen Fernen, auf jenen goldnen Sternen,
then look up and say: "In those high distances, on those golden stars,

dɔrt', voːs ǀam 'hɛlst'ən blɪtst', valt' ma͜en fɛɐ̯'loːrnɐ(r) ǀɪtstʰ.
dort, wo's am hellsten blitzt, wallt mein Verlorner itzt!"
there, where it at the brightest lightens, wanders my lost one now!"
(there where it flashes most brightly, my lost one is now wandering!")

oː 'ʃt'ɛrnə 'gɔt'əs, 'boːt'ən ǀʊnt' 'bʏrgɐ 'bɛsrɐ vɛltʰ, diː liːɐ̯
O Sterne Gottes, Boten und Bürger bessrer Welt, die ihr
O stars of God, messengers and denizens of better world, who you
(O stars of God, messengers and denizens of a better world, you who)

di naxt deːɐ̯ 'tʰoːt'ən tsuː 'mɪldɐ 'dɛmrʊŋ hɛltʰ! ǀʊm'ʃɪmɐt' zanft di 'ʃt'ɛt'ə,
die Nacht der Toten zu milder Dämmrung hellt! Umschimmert sanft die Stätte,
the night of the dead to mild twilight brighten! Shimmer around gently the place
(brighten the dark night of the dead to a mild twilight! Shimmer gently around the place)

voː ǀɪç ǀɑ͜os 'ʃt'ɪləm 'bɛt'ə ǀʊnt' 'zyːsəm ʃlaːf ǀɛɐ̯'vax tsuː 'leːdəns 'ʃøːnɐm tʰaːk'!
wo ich aus stillem Bette und süssem Schlaf erwach' zu Edens schönerm Tag!
where I out of quiet bed and sweet sleep awake to Eden's more beautiful day!
(where out of a quiet bed and a sweet sleep I shall awaken to Eden's more beautiful day!)

436

[In the above song a lovely modulation gives interest and expression to Schubert's otherwise rather conventional hymn tune. Eight verses are at least three too many.]

di ˈʃtˈɛrnənˌnɛçtˈə / ˈʃtˈɛrnənˌnɛçtˈə
Die Sternennächte / Sternennächte
The Starry Nights / Starry Nights

Op. 165, No. 2 [1819] (Johann Mayrhofer)

ɪn ˈmoːntˈhɛlən   ˈnɛçtˈən
In Monderhellten Nächten
In moon-brightened nights
(On moonlit nights)

mɪt dem gəˈʃɪkˈ   t͡suː ˈrɛçtˈən hat ˈdiːzə brʊstˈ fɛɐ̯ˈlɛrntʰ.
mit dem Geschick zu rechten hat diese Brust verlernt.
with the fate   to litigate has this breast unlearned.
(this heart of mine has learned not to argue with fate.)

deːɐ̯ ˈhɪməl,   raɛ̯ç bəˈʃtˈɛrntʰ, ʊmˈvoːgətˈ mɪç mɪtˈ ˈfriːdən   [gəˈʃtˈɪrntʰ]
Der Himmel, reich bestern, umwoget mich mit Frieden,   [*Peters:* **gestirnt** (no rhyme)]
The sky,   richly starred, bathes me with peace,   [starred]
(The sky, rich with stars, bathes me in peace,)   [*"umwogen"* = to surround with waves]

daː dɛŋkˈ ɪç, ɑ̯ox hiˈniːdən   gəˈdaɛ̯tˈ ˈmançə ˈbluːmə;
da denk' ich, auch hienieden gedeihet manche Blume;
then think I,   also here below flourishes many a flower;
(then I think: here on earth, too, many a flower can flourish;)

ʊntˈ ˈfrɪʃɐ   ʃɑ̯ot deːɐ̯ ˈʃtˈʊmə, zɔnst ˈtʰryːbə   blɪkˈ hɪˈnɑ̯of
und frischer schaut der stumme, sonst   trübe   Blick hinauf
and fresher looks the silent,   formerly melancholy gaze upwards
(and my silent gaze, melancholy until then, looks up refreshed)

t͡suː ˈleːvgɐ ˈʃtˈɛrnə lɑ̯of.   [t͡sʊm ˈleːvgən ˈʃtˈɛrnənlɑ̯of]
zu ew'ger Sterne Lauf.   [*Peters:* **zum ew'gen Sternenlauf**]
to   eternal stars' course.   [to the eternal course of the stars]
(at the course of eternal stars.)

ɑ̯of ˈliːnən ˈbluːtˈən ˈhɛrt͡sən, ˈlɑ̯of ˈliːnən ˈkʰvɛːlən ˈʃmɛrt͡sən,
Auf ihnen bluten Herzen, auf ihnen quälen Schmerzen,
On them bleed hearts, on them torment pains,
(Hearts are bleeding on those stars, pains are tormenting on them, as here on earth;)
                    [*poem:* **Auf ihnen quälen Schmerzen, auf ihnen bluten Herzen**]

ziː ˈlaːbɐ   ˈʃtˈraːlən ˈhaɛ̯tˈɐ. zoː ʃliːs   ɪç ˈzeːlɪç   ˈvaɛ̯tˈɐ:
sie aber   strahlen heiter. So schliess' ich selig   weiter:
they however beam   serenely. So conclude I blissfully further:
(the stars, however, go on beaming serenely. So I blissfully draw a further conclusion:)

ɑ̯ox ˈlʊnzrə ˈkʰlaɛ̯nə ˈleːɐ̯də, fɔl   ˈmɪstʰoːn lʊntˈ gəˈfɛːɐ̯də,
auch unsre kleine Erde, voll Misston und Gefährde,
also our   little   earth, full of discord and danger,
(our little earth, too, so full of discord and danger,)

zɪç ˌals ˌaen ˈhaet'ɐ lɪçt' ˌɪns diaˈdeːm fɛɐ̯ˈflɪçt^h;

zɪç ˌals ˌaen ˈhaet'ɐ lɪçt' ˌɪns diaˈdeːm fɛɐ̯ˈflɪçtʰ;
sich als ein heiter Licht ins   Diadem verflicht;
itself as a   serene light into the diadem interweaves;
(is interwoven into the celestial diadem as a serene light;)

zoː ˈveːɐ̯dən ˈʃt'ɛrnə dʊrç di ˈfɛrnə!
so werden Sterne durch die Ferne!
so become stars   through the distance!
(that is how stars are seen at a distance!)

[The philosophical poet draws comfort in contemplating the pains and trials of life from the perspective of the celestial stars. Seen from afar, all is serene; and so seems the earth when viewed from space. The original title of the song, as of the poem, was simply *Sternennächte*; publication added the article. The *Gesamtausgabe* prints the original key (D flat major); Peters offers the more comfortable key of the first published version (B flat).]

di ˈʃt'ɛrnənvɛlt'ən
Die Sternenwelten
The Starry Worlds

Posthumously published [composed 1815] (original poem in Slovenian by Urban Jarnik)
(German translation by Johann Georg Fellinger)

ˈoːbən ˈdreːən zɪç   di ˈgroːsən ˈlʊnbəkʰant'ən ˈvɛlt'ən dɔrt',
Oben drehen sich   die grossen unbekannten Welten dort,
Above revolve themselves the great   unknown   worlds there,
(Up there above us the great unknown worlds revolve,)

fɔn dem ˈzɔnənlɪçt' lʊmˈflɔsən ˈkʰraezən ziː di ˈbaːnən fɔrtʰ!
von dem Sonnenlicht umflossen kreisen sie die Bahnen fort!
by the sunlight   bathed   circle   they the course forth!
(bathed in sunlight, they circle onwards in their course!)

ˈtʰraolɪç ˈraeət' zɪç deːɐ̯ ˈʃt'ɛrnə ˈtsaːlənloːzəs heːɐ̯ rɪŋsˈlʊm,
Traulich reihet sich der Sterne zahlenloses Heer ringsum,
Familiarly ranges itself the stars' numberless host all around,
(The numberless host of stars is ranged familiarly all around;)

ziːt' zɪç ˈlɛçəlnt dʊrç di ˈfɛrnə lʊnt' fɛɐ̯ˈbraet'ət' ˈgɔt'əs ruːm.
sieht sich lächelnd durch die Ferne und verbreitet Gottes Ruhm.
sees itself smiling through the distance and spreads   God's glory.
(smiling, they gaze at each other through the distance and spread the glory of God.)

ˈaenə ˈlɪçt'ə ˈʃt'raːsə ˈglaet'ət dʊrç das ˈvaet'ə blao heˈraof,
Eine lichte Strasse gleitet durch das weite Blau herauf,
A   luminous street glides through the broad blue up,
(A path of light [the Milky Way?] glides upwards through the broad blue sky,)

ʊnt di maxt deːɐ̯ ˈgɔt'haet' ˈlaet'ət' ˈʃveːbənt' hiːɐ̯ den ˈʃt'ɛrnənlaof;
und die Macht der Gottheit leitet   schwebend hier den Sternenlauf;
and the power of the Godhead guides hovering here the star-   course;
(and here, hovering in heaven, the power of God guides the course of the stars;)

ˈaləs hatˈ zɪç ˈʦuːɡəryndətˈ, ˈaləs voːkˈtˈ ɪn glanʦ ʊntˈ brantˈ,
alles hat sich zugeründet, alles wogt in Glanz und Brand,
everything has itself to-rounded, all surges in radiance and fire,
(all the individual parts have become rounded into a whole, all surge in radiance and fire,)

ʊnt diːs ˈɡroːsə lal fɛɐ̯ˈkʰyndətˈ ˈlaɛnə ˈhoːə ˈbɪldnɐhantˈ.
und dies grosse All verkündet eine hohe Bildnerhand.
and this great universe proclaims a high sculptor-hand.
(and this great universe proclaims the hand of a supreme sculptor.)

ˈjeːnə ˈʃtˈɛrnənheːrə ˈvaɛzən ˈʃœpfɐ! ˈdaɛnə majɛsˈtˈɛːtˈ!
Jene Sternenheere weisen Schöpfer! deine Majestät!
Those star- hosts show, Creator, thy majesty!
(Those starry hosts reveal thy majesty, Creator!)

ˈzeːlɪç kʰan nuːɐ̯ deːɐ̯ zɪç ˈpʰraɛzən, ˈdɛsən ɡaɛst ʦuː diːɐ̯/diːr lɛntˈˈveːtʰ;
Selig kann nur der sich preisen, dessen Geist zu dir entweht;
Blessed can only he himself consider, whose spirit to thee wafts away;
(Only he whose spirit wafts up to thee can consider himself blessed;)

nuːɐ̯ daɛn ˈloːpˈliːtˈ vɪrtˈ leːɐ̯ ˈzɪŋən, ˈvoːnən lɔpˈ dem ˈsfɛːrəngaŋ,
nur dein Loblied wird er singen, wohnen ob dem Sphärengang,
only thy praise-song will he sing, dwell above the spheres- movement,
(he will sing only songs of praise to thee, dwell above the moving spheres,)

ˈfrɔødɪç zɪç dʊrç ˈvɛltˈən ˈʃvɪŋən ˈtʰrɪŋkˈəntˈ ˈraɛnən ˈlɛŋəlzaŋ.
freudig sich durch Welten schwingen trinkend reinen Engelsang.
joyously himself through worlds vault drinking pure angel-song.
(soar joyously among the worlds, drinking the pure song of angels.)

[The *Gesamtausgabe* prints only the first verse; but Schubert specifically called for two more in
a note on the autograph. The music has grandeur and simple dignity within its twenty-five bars.]

Die Taubenpost see *Schwanengesang*

di ˈtʰɔøʃʊŋ
Die Täuschung
Illusion

Op. 165, No. 4 [1815] (Ludwig Kosegarten)

ɪm ˈlɛrlənbʊʃ, lɪm ˈtʰanənhaɛn, ɪn zɔn lʊntˈ moːntˈ lʊntˈ
Im Erlenbusch, im Tannenhain, in Sonn- und Mond- und
In the alder thicket, in the pine grove, in sun(shine) and moon(light) and
(In the alder thicket, in the pine grove, by sunshine, moonlight, and)

ˈʃtˈɛrnənʃaen lʊmˈlɛçəltˈ mɪç laen ˈbɪltˈnɪs; [ˈlaːbəntˈ ʃaen]
Sternenschein umlächelt mich ein Bildnis; [*Peters:* **Abendschein**]
star- shine around-smiles me an image; [evening glow]
(starlight, a smiling image hovers around me;)

foːɐ̯ ˈzaɛ̯nəm ˈlɛçəln kʰleːɐ̯tˈ zɪç ʃnɛl di ˈdɛmərʊŋ ɪn ˈhɪməlhɛl, [zɪçs]
vor seinem Lächeln klärt sich schnell die Dämmerung in Himmelhell, [*P:* **sich 's**]
before its smile clears itself quickly the dusk into heaven- bright, [itself it]
(at that smile the shadowy dusk quickly clears into celestial brightness,)

> [*poem:* **ob dessen** (ɔpˈ ˈdɛsən, above whose) **Lächeln**]

ɪn pʰaraˈdiːs di ˈvɪltˈnɪs. [ɛs ˈzɔ͜ø̯zəltˈ ɪn deːɐ̯/deːr ˈlaːbəntˈlʊftʰ,
in Paradies die Wildnis. [Es säuselt in der Abendluft,
into paradise the wilderness. [It whispers in the evening air,
(the wilderness turns into paradise. [It whispers in the evening air,)

ɛs ˈdɛmətˈ ɪn dem ˈmɔrgəndʊftˈ, ɛs ˈtʰantsətˈ ɑ͜ʊ̯f deːɐ̯/deːr ˈɑ͜ʊ̯ə,
es dämmert in dem Morgenduft, es tanzet auf der Aue,
it dawns in the morning fragrance, it dances on the meadow,
(it becomes brighter in the fragrance of the morning, it dances on the meadow,)

ɛs ˈfløːtˈətˈ ɪn deːɐ̯ ˈvaxtˈəl ʃlaːkˈ, ʊntˈ ˈʃpˈiːgəltˈ zɪç ɪm ˈkʰlaːrən bax,
es flötet in der Wachtel Schlag, und spiegelt sich im klaren Bach,
it warbles in the quail's song, and mirrors itself in the clear brook,
(it warbles in the song of the quail, and it is reflected in the clear brook,)

> [*poem:* **in dem** (dem) **Wachtelschlag** (in the quail-song)]

ʊntˈ ˈbaːdətˈ zɪç ɪm ˈtʰɑ͜ʊ̯ə. ɛs naːtˈ ɪn ˈhɔldɐ ˈtʰrɑ͜ʊ̯lɪçkʰaɛ̯tˈ zɪç miːɐ̯/miːr
und badet sich im Taue. Es naht in holder Traulichkeit sich mir
and bathes itself in the dew. It nears in gracious intimacy itself to me
(and bathes itself in the dew. It draws near to me in gracious intimacy,)

ɪn ˈtʰiːfstˈɐ ˈdʊŋkˈəlhaɛ̯tˈ zoː ˈʃʏçtˈɐn ʊntˈ zoː ˈlaɛ̯zə. ɛs lʊltˈ mɪç voːl
in tiefster Dunkelheit so schüchtern und so leise. Es lullt mich wohl
in deepest darkness, so shyly and so quietly. It lulls me well

ɪn ˈzanftˈə ruː, ʊntˈ hɑ͜ʊ̯xtˈ ɪm ʃlaːf miːɐ̯ ˈtʰrɔ͜ø̯mə tsuː fɔn ˈvʊndɐbaːrɐ ˈvaɛ̯zə.]
in sanfte Ruh, und haucht im Schlaf mir Träume zu von wunderbarer Weise.]
into gentle rest, and breathes in the sleep to me dreams to of wondrous manner.]
(into gentle rest, and, in my sleep, breathes into me dreams of a wondrous kind.])

ɪç lœf niːm ˈzeːnəntˈ ˈmaɛ̯nən larm, ʊntˈ ʃtˈreːpˈ
Ich öffn' ihm sehnend meinen Arm, und streb'
I open to it longingly my arm, and strive
(I open my arms to it longingly, and strive)

ɛs tʰrɑ͜ʊ̯tˈ ʊntˈ ˈliːbəvarm lan ˈmaɛ̯nə brʊst tsuː ˈdrʏkˈən; lɪç haʃ ʊntˈ ˈhaʃə
es traut und liebewarm an meine Brust zu drücken; ich hasch' und hasche
it intimately and love-warmly to my breast to press; I snatch and snatch at
(to press it intimately and ardently to my breast; again and again I snatch at)

ˈleːrə lʊftˈ, ʊntˈ ˈnɪçtˈɪç, viː laɛ̯n ˈneːbəldʊftˈ, lɛntˈˈvaltˈ ɛs ˈmaɛ̯nən ˈblɪkˈən.
leere Luft, und nichtig, wie ein Nebelduft, entwallt es meinen Blicken.
empty air, and void, like a mist- vapor, floats away it from my gazes.
(empty air, and, void, it floats away from my gaze like a misty vapor.)

> [*poem:* **entschwimmt** (lɛntˈˈʃvɪmtˈ, swims away) **es meinen Blicken**]

440

[ˈveːɐ̯ bɪst duː, ˈhɔldəs ˈlʊftˈɡəbɪlt, das ˈɛŋəlhɔltʰ ˈʊntʰ ˈɛŋəlmɪltʰ
[Wer bist du, holdes Luftgebild, das engelhold und engelmild
[Who are you, lovely phantom, that angel-graciously and angel-mildly
[(Who are you, lovely phantom, that, in your angelic graciousness and gentleness,)

mɪtʰ ʃmɛrts ʊntʰ lʊstʰ mɪç ˈtʰrɛŋkˈətʰ? bɪst duː ae̯n ˈboːtʰə ˈbɛsrɐ vɛlt,
mit Schmerz und Lust mich tränket? Bist du ein Bote bess'rer Welt,
with pain and pleasure me drenches? Are you a messenger of better world,
(drenches me with pain and pleasure? Are you a messenger from a better world,)

deːɐ̯ mɪç ˈaọs ˈdiːzəm ˈøːdən fɛltʰ ɪn ˈzae̯nə ˈhae̯maːtʰ ˈvɪŋkˈətʰ?]
der mich aus diesem öden Feld in seine Heimat winket?]
who me from this desolate field into its homeland beckons?]
(who beckons me from this desolate plain to your homeland?)]

[*poem:* **fern** (fɛrn, far) **in die** (di, the) **Heimat winket]**

oː fliːkʰ foˈran! ɪç ˈfɔlɡə diːɐ̯, bae̯ diːɐ̯/diːr ɪstʰ ˈzeːlɪçkʰae̯tʰ, nɪçtʰ hiːɐ̯. [flɔøkʰ]
O flieg' voran! Ich folge dir. Bei dir ist Seligkeit, nicht hier. [*GA:* **fleug** (archaic)]
O fly ahead! I follow you. With you is bliss, not here.

[*poem:* **Fleuch, fleuch** (flɔøç) **voran!**

ʃpˈrɪç, voː ɪç dɪç ɛɐ̯ˈfasə, ʊntʰ ˈleːvɪç ˈalɐ pʰae̯n ɛntˈrʏkˈtʰ,
Sprich, wo ich dich erfasse, und ewig aller Pein entrückt,
Say where I you lay hold of, and eternally from all pain carried away,
(Tell me where I may hold onto you, and, eternally removed from all pain,)
    [*poem:* **ewig dicht an dich geschmiegt** (dɪçtʰ lan dɪç ɡəˈʃmiːkʰtʰ, closely against you nestled)]

ʊmˈʃtʰrɪkˈəntʰ dɪç, fɔn diːɐ̯/diːr ʊmˈʃtʰrɪkˈtʰ, dɪç ˈnɪmɐ, ˈnɪmɐ ˈlasə.
umstrickend dich, von dir umstrickt, dich nimmer, nimmer lasse.
ensnaring you, by you ensnared, you never, never leave.
(embracing you, embraced by you, and never, never leave you.)
    [*poem:* **und ewig fest an dich gefügt** (fɛstʰ lan dɪç ɡəˈfyːkʰtʰ, firmly to you joined),]

[The verses in brackets, above, are omitted in the Peters edition. The music is graceful, pretty.]

di ʊntʰˈɐ̯ˈʃae̯dʊŋ
Die Unterscheidung
The Distinction

Op. 95, No. 1 [1828?] (Johann Gabriel Seidl)

di ˈmʊtʰɐ hatʰ mɪç jʏŋstʰ ɡəˈʃɔltʰən ʊntʰ foːɐ̯ deːɐ̯ ˈliːbə ʃtʰrɛŋ ɡəˈvarntʰ.
Die Mutter hat mich jüngst gescholten und vor der Liebe streng gewarnt.
The mother has me recently scolded and against the love sternly warned.
(Mother recently scolded me and sternly warned me against love.)

nɔx ˈjeːdə, ʃpˈraːx ziː, hats ɛntˈɡɔltʰən: fɛɐ̯ˈloːrən ɪstʰ, veːn ziː ʊmˈɡarntʰ!?
"Noch jede," sprach sie, "hat's entgolten: verloren ist, wen sie umgarnt!"
"Still every female," said she, "has it made pay: lost is (she) whom it ensnares!"
("Every woman," she said, "still has to pay for it: she whom it ensnares is lost!")

drʊm lɪst' lɛs 'besɐ, viː lɪç 'maenə, vɛn kʰaens fɔn lʊns daˈfɔn meːɐ̯ ʃpˈrɪçtʰ:
Drum ist es besser, wie ich meine, wenn keins von uns davon mehr spricht:
Therefore is it better, as I think, if none of us of it more speaks:
(Therefore I think it's better if neither of us speaks of it any more.)

lç bɪn tsvaːɐ̯/tsvaːr 'lɪmɐ nɔx di 'daenə,—dɔx 'liːbən, hans, kʰan lɪç dɪç nɪçtʰ!
ich bin zwar immer noch die Deine,— doch lieben, Hans, kann ich dich nicht!
I am of course always still the yours,— but love, Hans, can I you not!
(I am still forever yours, of course,—but *love* you, Hans? That I can *not*!)

foːɐ̯/foːr 'laləm, hans, fɛɐ̯ˈgɪs miːɐ̯ 'nɪmɐ, das duː nuːɐ̯ mɪç tsuː 'liːbən hastʰ.
Vor allem, Hans, vergiss mir nimmer, dass du nur mich zu lieben hast.
Above all, Hans, forget for me never that you only me to love have.
(Above all, Hans, never forget that you have to love only me.)

maen 'lɛçəln zae diːɐ̯ lʊst' nuːɐ̯/nuːr 'lɪmɐ(r), lʊnt' 'jeːdɐ(r) 'landɛn 'lɛçəln lastʰ!
Mein Lächeln sei dir Lust nur immer, und jeder andern Lächeln Last!
My smile be to you pleasure only always, and every other smile burden!
(My smile alone shall always be your pleasure, and the smile of every other girl a nuisance!)

jaː, lʊm deːɐ̯ 'mʊt'ɐ 'naːxtsugeːbən, vɪl lɪç mɪç, tʰrɔø deːɐ̯ 'dɔp'əlpflɪçtʰ,
Ja, um der Mutter nachzugeben, will ich mich, treu der Doppelpflicht,
Yes, in order to the mother to give in, want I myself, true to the double duty,
(Yes, in order to give in to my mother's wish, and faithful to my double duty, I want)

diːɐ̯ tsuː gəˈfalən ʃt'eːts bəˈʃt'reːbən,—dɔx 'liːbən, hans, kʰan lɪç dɪç nɪçtʰ.
dir zu gefallen stets bestreben,— doch lieben, Hans, kann ich dich nicht.
to you to please constantly strive,— but love, Hans, can I you not.
(to strive constantly to please you; but *love* you, Hans, that I can *not*.)

bae 'jeːdəm 'fɛst'ə, das viːɐ̯ 'haːbən, zɔls 'maenə 'grøːst'ə 'vɔnə zaen,
Bei jedem Feste, das wir haben, soll's meine grösste Wonne sein,
At every holiday that we have, shall it my greatest delight be,
(At every holiday that we have it shall be my greatest delight)

flɪçt' 'daenə hant dɛs 'fryːlɪŋs 'gaːbən tsʊm 'ʃmʊk'ə miːɐ̯/miːr lɪns 'miːdɐ (r)laen.
flicht deine Hand des Frühlings Gaben zum Schmucke mir ins Mieder ein.
twines your hand the spring's gifts for the adornment for me into the bodice into.
(if your hand twines spring flowers into my bodice to adorn it.) [*Peters:* **flieht** (misprint)]

bəˈgɪnt deːɐ̯ tʰants, dan lɪst', viː 'bɪlɪç, laen tʰants mɪt' 'greːt'çən 'daenə pflɪçtʰ;
Beginnt der Tanz, dann ist, wie billig, ein Tanz mit Gretchen deine Pflicht;
Begins the dance, then is, as (is) fair, a dance with Gretchen your duty;
(When the dancing starts, then a dance with Gretchen is your duty, as is only fair;)

zɛlpst' 'laefɐzʏçt'ɪç 'veːɐ̯dən vɪl lɪç, dɔx 'liːbən, hans, kʰan lɪç dɪç nɪçtʰ.
selbst eifersüchtig werden will ich, doch lieben, Hans, kann ich dich nicht.
even jealous to become shall I, but love, Hans, can I you not.
(I shall even become jealous; but *love* you, Hans? That I can *not*.)

lʊnt' zɪŋk't deːɐ̯/deːr 'laːbənt' kʰyːl hɛɐ̯ˈniːdɐ(r), lʊnt' ruːn viːɐ̯ dan, rɛçt' mɪlt' bəˈveːk'tʰ,
Und sinkt der Abend kühl hernieder, und ruhn wir dann, recht mild bewegt,
And sinks the evening coolly down, and rest we then, very tenderly moved,
(And when the cool evening descends and we then rest, very tenderly moved,)

halt' 'ımɐ miːɐ̯ di hant' lans 'miːdɐ(r), lʊnt' 'fyːlə, viː maen 'hɛrtsçən ʃlɛːk't'!
halt immer mir die Hand ans Mieder, und fühle, wie mein Herzchen schlägt!
hold always for me the hand on the bodice, and feel how my little heart beats!
(keep holding your hand against my bodice and feel how my little heart is beating!)

ʊnt' vɪlst duː mɪç dʊrç 'kʰYsə 'leːrən, vas ʃt'ʊm daen 'laogə tsu: miːɐ̯ ʃp'rɪçt',
Und willst du mich durch Küsse lehren, was stumm dein Auge zu mir spricht,
And want you me through kisses to teach what silently your eye to me speaks,
(And if you want to teach me with kisses what your eyes are silently telling me,)

zɛlpst das vɪl lıç diːɐ̯ nɪçt' fɛɐ̯'veːrən, dɔx 'liːbən, hans, kʰan lıç dɪç nɪçt'.
selbst das will ich dir nicht verwehren, doch lieben, Hans, kann ich dich nicht.
even that shall I to you not forbid, but love, Hans, can I you not.
(I shall not even stop you from doing *that*; but *love* you, Hans? That I can *not*.)

[This musically charming and verbally amusing song is the first of the "Four Refrain Songs," the others being "*Bei dir allein,*" "*Die Männer sind méchant,*" and "*Irdisches Glück.*" All four poems are by Seidl. In this one the girl is willing to give her admirer every freedom, as long as neither she nor he calls it *love*, since her mother has warned her that love gets a girl into trouble.]

di fɛɐ̯'feːlt'ə 'ʃt'ʊndə
Die verfehlte Stunde
The Unsuccessful Hour

Posthumously published [composed 1816] (poem by August Wilhelm von Schlegel)

'kʰveːlənt' 'lʊngəʃt'ɪlt'əs 'zeːnən pʰɔxt' miːɐ̯/miːr lın ɛm'pʰøːɐ̯t'ɐ brʊst'.
Quälend ungestilltes Sehnen pocht mir in empörter Brust.
Tormentingly unstilled longing beats to me in indignant breast.
(Tormentingly unsatisfied longing is beating within my indignant breast.)

'liːbə, diː miːɐ̯ zeːl lʊnt' 'zınən 'ʃmaeçəlnt' 'vʊst'ə tsu: gə'vınən,
Liebe, die mir Seel' und Sinnen schmeichelnd wusste zu gewinnen,
Love, which from me soul and senses flatteringly knew how to win,
(Love, which knew how to win my soul and senses through flattery,)

viːk't' daen 'tsaobərıʃəs 'veːnən nuːɐ̯/nuːr lın 't'rɔømə 'kʰʊrtsɐ lʊst',
wiegt dein zauberisches Wähnen nur in Träume kurzer Lust,
lulls your magical imagining only in dreams of brief pleasure,
(does your magical illusion lull me only in dreams of brief pleasure,)

ʊnt' lɛɐ̯'vɛk't' tsu: 't'rɛːnən? — zyːs bə'raoʃt' lın 't'rɛːnən
und erweckt zu Tränen? — Süss berauscht in Tränen
and wakens to tears? — Sweetly intoxicated in tears
(and waken me to tears? — Sweetly intoxicated, in tears,)

lan dɛs 'liːbən brʊst' mıç 'leːnən, larm lın larm gə'ʃt'rık't',
an des Lieben Brust mich lehnen, Arm in Arm gestrickt,
on the dear one's breast myself to lean, arm in arm entwined,
(to be leaning on my dear one's breast, our arms entwined,)

mʊnt' laof mʊnt' gə'drʏk't*, das nuːɐ̯ ʃt'ɪlt' maen 'zeːnən!
Mund auf Mund gedrückt, das nur stillt mein Sehnen!
mouth on mouth pressed, *that* alone stills my longing!
(mouth pressed against mouth, *that* alone can still my longing!)

ax, lɪç gaːp' liːm 'kʰaenə 'kʰʊndə, vʊst' les 'zɛlbɐ nɪçt t͡suˈfoːɐ̯;
Ach, ich gab ihm keine Kunde, wusst' es selber nicht zuvor;
Ah, I gave him no notice, knew it myself not beforehand;
(Ah, I gave him no indication, didn't even know it *myself* beforehand;)

ʊnt' nuːn beːp' lɪç zoː bə'kʰlɔmən: vɪrt deːɐ̯ 't'raot'ə, vɪrt' leːɐ̯ 'kʰɔmən?
und nun beb' ich so beklommen: wird der Traute, wird er kommen?
and now tremble I so anxiously: will the beloved, will he come?
(and now I tremble so anxiously: will my beloved, will he come?)

ʃt'ɪl lʊnt' 'ɡʏnst'ɪç lɪst di 'ʃt'ʊndə, 'nɪrɡənt͡s droːt' laen 'hɔrçənt' loːɐ̯
Still und günstig ist die Stunde, nirgends droht ein horchend Ohr
Quiet and favorable is the hour, nowhere threatens a listening ear
(The hour is quiet and favorable; nowhere does a listening ear threaten)

dem ɡə'haemən 'bʊndə. — t'rɔ͡ʏ lɪm 'zeːlɡən 'bʊndə
dem geheimen Bunde. — Treu im sel'gen Bunde
the secret union. — Faithful in the blissful union
(our secret union. — Faithful, in a blissful union,)

lan dɛs 'liːbən brʊst' mɪç 'leːnən,... das nuːɐ̯ ʃt'ɪlt' maen 'zeːnən.
an des Lieben Brust mich lehnen,... das nur stillt mein Sehnen.
on the dear one's breast myself to lean,... *that* alone stills my longing.
(to be leaning on my dear one's breast,... *that* alone can still my longing.)

høːr lç 'laezə 't'rɪt'ə 'raoʃən, deŋk' lɪç: laː, daː lɪst' leːɐ̯ ʃoːn!
Hör' ich leise Tritte rauschen, denk' ich: ah, da ist er schon!
Hear I soft steps rustling, think I: ah, there is he already!
(When I hear the sound of soft steps, I think: "Ah, there he is already!")

'aːndʊŋ ['aːnʊŋ] hat' liːm voːl fɛɐ̯'kʰʏndət, das di 'ʃøːnə t͡saet' zɪç 'fɪndət,
Ahndung hat ihm wohl verkündet, dass die schöne Zeit sich findet,
Presentiment has to him probably announced that the lovely time itself finds,
(Intuition has probably told him that a lovely time has been found)
["*Ahndung*" = "*Ahnung*" in modern German]

vɔn lʊm 'vɔnə frae t͡suː 't'aoʃən. dɔx ziː lɪst' ʃoːn halp' lɛniˈfloːn
Wonn' um Wonne frei zu tauschen. Doch sie ist schon halb entflohn
rapture after rapture freely to exchange. But it is already half fled
(for us freely to exchange rapture after rapture. — But that hour is already half spent)

bae fɛɐ̯'ɡeːbnəm 'laoʃən. — mɪt' lɛnt't͡sʏk't'əm 'laoʃən
bei vergebnem Lauschen. — Mit entzücktem Lauschen
in futile listening. — With enraptured listening

lan dɛs 'liːbən brʊst' mɪç 'leːnən,... das nuːɐ̯ ʃt'ɪlt' maen 'zeːnən.
an des Lieben Brust mich lehnen,... das nur stillt mein Sehnen.
on the dear one's breast myself to lean,... *that* alone stills my longing.
(to be leaning on my dear one's breast,... *that* alone can still my longing.)

'tʰɔøʃən   vɪrt' fi'laɛçt' maen 'zeːnən, hɔft' ɪç, dɛs gə'zaŋəs lʊstʰ.
Täuschen wird vielleicht mein Sehnen, hofft' ich, des Gesanges Lust.
Deceive   will perhaps   my   longing, hoped I   the song's   pleasure.
(I had hoped that the pleasure of singing would perhaps delude my longing:)

'ʊngə'ʃt'yːmɐ 'vʏnʃə   'glyːən 'lɪndɐn 'zanft'ə melo'diːən.
Ungestümer Wünsche Glühen lindern sanfte Melodien.
Turbulent   wishes' burning mitigate gentle   melodies.
(gentle melodies can sometimes mitigate the burning pain of turbulent desires.)

dɔx das liːt' lɛnt''hoːp' mɪt' 'ʃt'øːnən tʰiːf lɛɐ'laːt'mənt' zɪç deːɐ   brʊstʰ,
Doch das Lied enthob   mit Stöhnen tief eratmend   sich der   Brust,
But the song removed with moaning deep breathing   itself from the breast,
(But the song left my heart with moaning and deep panting)

ʊnt' lɛɐ'ʃtarp' lɪn 'tʰrɛːnən. — zyːs   bə'rɑʊʃt' lɪn 'tʰrɛːnən
und erstarb in Tränen. — Süss   berauscht in Tränen
and died   in tears.   — Sweetly intoxicated, in tears,

lan dɛs 'liːbən   brʊst' mɪç 'leːnən,... das nuːɐ ʃt'ɪlt' maen 'zeːnən.
an des Lieben   Brust mich lehnen,... das nur stillt mein Sehnen.
on the dear one's breast myself to lean,... *that* alone stills my   longing.
(to be leaning on my dear one's breast,... *that* alone can still my longing.)

[An amorous lady waits anxiously for a lover who fails to show up. Each of the four verses of the
poem starts with seven four-footed lines followed by a refrain of five lines, of which four are
three-footed. Schubert's strophic setting reflects the shift: the first part a plaintive melody in F
minor, the second and last, at a faster tempo, a passionate surge in optimistic A flat major toward
a double climax, as the hopeful but frustrated lady imagines the reunion that fails to take place.]

di fiːɐ 'vɛlt'lalt'ɐ
Die vier Weltalter
The Four Ages of the World

Op. 111, No. 3 [1816?] (Friedrich von Schiller)

voːl 'pʰɛrlət' lɪm 'glaːzə deːɐ 'pʰʊrp'ʊrnə vaen, voːl 'glɛntsən di 'lɑʊgən deːɐ 'gɛst'ə;
Wohl perlet   im   Glase der purpurne Wein, wohl glänzen die Augen der   Gäste;
Surely sparkles in the glass the purple   wine, surely shine   the eyes of the guests;
(Purple wine sparkles in the glass, the eyes of the guests are shining;)

ɛs tsaek't' zɪç   deːɐ 'zɛŋɐ(r), leːɐ tʰrɪt' hɛ'raen, tsuː dem 'guːt'ən brɪŋt' leːɐ das 'bɛst'ə;
es zeigt sich   der Sänger, er tritt herein, zu dem Guten bringt er das Beste;
there shows himself the singer, he steps inside, to the good   brings he   the best;
(the singer appears, he enters, to that which is good he brings that which is best;)

dɛn 'loːnə di 'laeɐ(r) lɪm 'hɪmlɪʃən   zaːl lɪst di 'frɔødə gə'maen lɑox baem
denn ohne   die Leier im   himmlischen Saal ist die Freude gemein auch beim
for   without the lyre   in the heavenly   hall is the joy   common even at the
(for without the lyre joy is ordinary in the heavenly hall, even at the)

'nɛk‘t‘armaːl. liːm ‘gaːbən di ‘gœt‘ɐ das ‘rae̯nə gə'myːt‘, voː di vɛlt‘
Nektarmahl. Ihm gaben die Götter das reine Gemüt, wo die Welt
nectar-meal. To him gave the gods the pure mind, in which the world
(nectar banquet. To the singer the gods have given a pure mind in which the world,)

zɪç, di ‘leːvɪgə, ‘ʃp‘iːgəlt‘; leːɐ̯ hat‘ ‘laləs gə'zeːn, vas lao̯f ‘leːɐ̯dən gə'ʃiːt‘, [‘leːvgə]
sich, die ewige, spiegelt; er hat alles gesehn, was auf Erden geschieht, [_P:_ ew'ge]
itself, the eternal, reflects; he has everything seen that on earth happens,
(the eternal world, is reflected; he has seen everything that happens on earth,)

ʊnt‘ vas lʊns di ‘t͡suːk‘ʊnft fɛɐ̯'ziːgəlt‘; leːɐ̯ zaːs lɪn deːɐ̯ ‘gœt‘ɐ(r) luːɐ̯(r)‘lɛlt‘əst‘əm raːt‘
und was uns die Zukunft versiegelt; er sass in der Götter urältestem Rat
and what to us the future seals; he sat in the gods' most ancient council
(and what the future keeps sealed to us; he has sat in the most ancient council of the gods)

lʊnt‘ bə'hɔrçt‘ə deːɐ̯ ‘dɪŋə gə'hae̯mst‘ə zaːt‘. leːɐ̯ ‘brae̯t‘ət‘ lɛs ‘lʊst‘ɪç lʊnt‘ ‘glɛnt͡sənt‘ lao̯s,
und behorchte der Dinge geheimste Saat. Er breitet es lustig und glänzend aus,
and listened to the things' most secret seed. He spreads it merrily and splendidly out,
(and listened to the most secret seed-thoughts of all things. He merrily, splendidly spreads out)

das t͡su'zaməngəfalt‘ət‘ə ‘leːbən; t͡sʊm ‘t‘ɛmp‘əl ʃmʏk‘t‘ leːɐ̯ das ‘lɪrdɪʃə hao̯s,
das zusammengefaltete Leben; zum Tempel schmückt er das irdische Haus,
the together- folded life; to the temple beautifies he the earthly house,
(the tightly furled fabric of life; through his art he transforms our earthly house into a temple,)

iːm hat‘ lɛs di ‘muːzə gə'geːbən; kʰae̯n dax lɪst‘ zoː ‘niːdrɪç, ‘kʰae̯nə ‘hʏt‘ə zoː kʰlae̯n,
ihm hat es die Muse gegeben; kein Dach ist so niedrig, keine Hütte so klein,
to him has it the muse given; no roof is so low, no hut so small,
(the muse has given it to him; no roof is so low, no hut so small,)

leːɐ̯ fyːɐ̯t‘ ‘lae̯nən ‘hɪməl fɔl ‘gœt‘ɐ hɪ'nae̯n. lʊnt‘ viː deːɐ̯/deːr lɛɐ̯'fɪndəndə zoːn
er führt einen Himmel voll Götter hinein. Und wie der erfindende Sohn
he leads a heaven full of gods into it. And as the inventive son
(but that he can lead a whole heaven full of gods into it. And as Hephaestus, the inventive son)

dɛs t͡sɔø̯s lao̯f dɛs ‘ʃɪldəs ‘lae̯nfaxəm ‘rʊndə di ‘leːɐ̯də, das meːɐ̯/meːr lʊnt den
des Zeus auf des Schildes einfachem Runde die Erde, das Meer und den
of the Zeus on the shield's simple round the earth, the sea, and the
(of Zeus, on the simple disk of Achilles' shield had portrayed the earth, the sea, and the)

‘ʃt‘ɛrnənkʰrae̯s gə'bɪldət‘ mɪt‘ ‘gœt‘lɪçɐ ‘kʰʊndə, zoː drʏk‘t‘ leːɐ̯/leːr lae̯n bɪlt‘
Sternenkreis gebildet mit göttlicher Kunde, so drückt er ein Bild
star-circle fashioned with divine knowledge, so presses he an image
(circle of the stars with divine ingenuity, so can the singer compress an image)

dɛs lʊn'lɛnt‘lɪçən lal lɪn dɛs ‘lao̯gənblɪks ‘flʏçt‘ɪç fɛɐ̯'rao̯ʃəndən ʃal.
des unendlichen All in des Augenblicks flüchtig verrauschenden Schall.
of the infinite universe into the moment's fleetingly dying-away sound.
(of the infinite universe into the fleetly fading sound of a single moment.)

eːɐ̯ kʰɔmt‘ lao̯s dem ‘kʰɪnt‘lɪçən ‘lalt‘ɐ deːɐ̯ vɛlt‘, voː di ‘fœlk‘ɐ
Er kommt aus dem kindlichen Alter der Welt, wo die Völker
He comes from the childlike age of the world, in which the peoples

zıç 'juːgənt'lıç 'frɔøt'ən; leːɐ̯ hat' zıç, laen 'frøːlıçɐ 'vandrɐ, gə'zɛlt'
sich jugendlich freuten; er hat sich, ein fröhlicher Wandrer, gesellt
themselves youthfully gladdened; he has himself, a cheerful wanderer, associated
(were youthfully happy; he has associated himself as a cheerful wanderer)

tsuː 'alən gə'ʃlɛçt'ɐn lʊnt 'tsaet'ən. fiːɐ̯ 'mɛnʃənˌalt'ɐ hat' leːɐ̯ gə'zeːn
zu allen Geschlechtern und Zeiten. Vier Menschenalter hat er gesehn
with all races and times. Four ages of mankind has he seen
(with all races and times. He has seen four ages of mankind)

lʊnt' lɛst' ziː lam 'fʏnft'ən fo'ryːbɐgeːn. leːɐ̯st re'giːɐ̯t'ə za't'ʊrnʊs ʃlıçt'
und lässt sie am fünften vorübergehn. Erst regierte Saturnus schlicht
and lets them at the fifth pass by. First reigned Saturn simply
(and lets them pass by in the fifth. First Saturn reigned, simply)

lʊnt' gə'reçth, daː vaːɐ̯/vaːr lɛs 'hɔøt'ə viː 'mɔrgən, daː 'leːp't'ən di 'hɪrt'ən, laen
und gerecht, da war es heute wie morgen, da lebten die Hirten, ein
and justly; then was it today as tomorrow, then lived the shepherds, a
(and justly; at that time one day was very much like the next; the shepherds lived at that time, a)

'harmloːs gə'ʃlɛçt', lʊnt' 'braoxt'ən fyːɐ̯ gaːɐ̯ nıçts tsuː 'zɔrgən; ziː
harmlos Geschlecht, und brauchten für gar nichts zu sorgen; sie
harmless race, and needed for at all nothing to worry; they
(harmless kind of people, and they did not need to worry about anything at all; they)

'liːp't'ən lʊnt 't'aːt'ən 'vaet'ɐ nıçts meːɐ̯, di 'leːɐ̯də gaːp' 'laləs 'fraevılıç heːɐ̯.
liebten und taten weiter nichts mehr, die Erde gab alles freiwillig her.
loved and did further nothing more, the earth gave everything voluntarily hither.
(loved and did little else: the earth provided them voluntarily with everything that they needed.)

draof khaːm di 'larbaet, deːɐ̯ khampf bə'gan mıt' 'lʊngəhɔøɐn lʊnt 'draxən, lʊnt di
Drauf kam die Arbeit, der Kampf begann mit Ungeheuern und Drachen, und die
Next came the work, the battle began with monsters and dragons, and the
(Next came the age of work; the battle with monsters and dragons began, and)

'hɛldən 'fıŋən, di 'hɛrʃɐ(r), lan, lʊnt den 'mɛçt'ıgən 'zuːxt'ən di 'ʃvaxən.
Helden fingen, die Herrscher, an, und den Mächtigen suchten die Schwachen.
heroes started, the rulers, up, and the powerful [object] sought the weak [subject].
(heroes emerged and became rulers, and the weak sought the protection of the powerful.)

ʊnt deːɐ̯ ʃt'raet tsoːk lın dɛs sk'a'mandɐs fɛlt'; dɔx di 'ʃøːnhaet' vaːɐ̯/vaːr 'lımɐ
Und der Streit zog in des Skamanders Feld; doch die Schönheit war immer
And the strife drew into the Scamander's field; but the beauty was always
(And the battle came to Scamander's fields, the site of the Trojan War; but always beauty was)

deːɐ̯ gɔt deːɐ̯ vɛlth. laos dem khampf gıŋ 'lɛnt'lıç deːɐ̯ ziːk' hɛɐ̯'foːɐ̯/hɛɐ̯'foːr,
der Gott der Welt. Aus dem Kampf ging endlich der Sieg hervor,
the god of the world. Out of the battle went finally the victory forth,
(the god of the world. Out of the battle victory finally came forth,)

ʊnt deːɐ̯ khraft' lɛnt''blyːt'ə di 'mıldə, daː 'zaŋən di 'muːzən lım 'hımlıʃən
und der Kraft entblühte die Milde, da sangen die Musen im himmlischen
and from the strength blossomed the gentleness, then sang the muses in the heavenly
(and gentleness blossomed out of strength; then the muses sang in the heavenly)

kʰoːɐ̯, daː lɛɐ̯ˈhuːbən zɪç 'gœt'ɐgəbɪldə; das ˈalt'ɐ deːɐ̯ 'gœt'lɪçən fant'aˈziː,
Chor, da erhuben sich Göttergebilde; das Alter der göttlichen Phantasie,
choir, then raised themselves gods- images; the age of the divine imagination,
(choir, and images of the gods arose; but that age of divine imagination)

lɛs lɪst' fɛɐ̯ˈʃvʊndən, lɛs ˈkʰeːrət' niː. di 'gœt'ɐ 'zaŋk'ən fɔm 'hɪməlstʰroːn,
es ist verschwunden, es kehret nie. Die Götter sanken vom Himmelsthron,
it has vanished, it returns never. The gods sank from the heaven- throne,
(has vanished and will never return. The gods fell from their heavenly throne,)

ɛs 'ʃt'ʏrt͡st'ən di 'hɛrlɪçən 'zɔø̯lən, lʊnt gəˈboːrən 'vʊrdə deːɐ̯ 'jʊŋfrɑo̯ zoːn,
es stürzten die herrlichen Säulen, und geboren wurde der Jungfrau Sohn,
there collapsed the glorious columns, and born was the virgin's son,
(the glorious columns tumbled down, and the son of the virgin was born)

di gəˈbrɛçən deːɐ̯/deːr 'leːɐ̯də t͡suː 'haɛ̯lən; fɛɐ̯ˈbant' vart deːɐ̯ 'zɪnə 'flʏçt'ɪgə lʊst',
die Gebrechen der Erde zu heilen; verbannt ward der Sinne flüchtige Lust,
the infirmities of the earth to heal; banned was the senses' fleeting pleasure,
(to heal the infirmities of the earth; the fleeting pleasure of the senses was banned,)

lʊnt deːɐ̯ mɛnʃ grɪf 'dɛŋk'ənt' lɪn 'zaɛ̯nə brʊstʰ. lʊnt deːɐ̯/deːr 'laet'lə,
und der Mensch griff denkend in seine Brust. Und der eitle,
and the human being grasped *thinking* into his breast. And the vain,
(and the human being began consciously to dig into his own breast. And the vain,)

deːɐ̯/deːr 'lʏp'ɪgə raɛ̯t͡s lɛnt''vɪç, deːɐ̯ di 'froːə 'juːgənt'vɛlt 't͡siːɐ̯t'ə; deːɐ̯ mœnç
der üppige Reiz entwich, der die frohe Jugendwelt zierte; der Mönch
the voluptuous charm disappeared, which the happy youth- world adorned; the monk
(the voluptuous charm that once adorned the happy youth of the world disappeared; the monk)

lʊnt di 'nɔnə t͡sɛɐ̯ˈgaɛ̯səlt'ən zɪç, lʊnt deːɐ̯/deːr 'laɛ̯zənə 'rɪt'ɐ tʰʊɐ̯ˈniːɐ̯t'ə. dox
und die Nonne zergeisselten sich, und der eiserne Ritter turnierte. Doch
and the nun flagellated themselves, and the iron knight jousted. But
(and the nun flagellated themselves, and the knight, covered with iron armor, jousted. But)

vaːɐ̯ das 'leːbən lɑox 'fɪnst'ɐ(r) lʊnt' vɪlt', zoː bliːp' dox di 'liːbə 'liːp'lɪç lʊnt' mɪlt'.
war das Leben auch finster und wild, so blieb doch die Liebe lieblich und mild.
was the life even dark and wild, so remained though the love lovely and gentle.
(even though life was dark and wild, nevertheless love remained lovely and gentle.)

ʊnt' 'laɛ̯nən 'haɛ̯lɪgən, 'kʰɔø̯ʃən lalˈtʰaːɐ̯ bəˈvaːɐ̯t'ən zɪç 'ʃt'ɪlə di 'muːzən;
Und e i n e n heiligen, keuschen Altar bewahrten sich stille die Musen;
And *one* holy, chaste altar preserved for themselves quietly the muses;
(And the muses quietly preserved for themselves *one* holy, chaste altar:)

ɛs 'leːp't'ə, vas 'leːdəl lʊnt' 'zɪt'lɪç vaːɐ̯/vaːr, lɪn deːɐ̯ 'frɑo̯ən 't͡syçt'ɪgəm 'buːzən;
es lebte, was edel und sittlich war, in der Frauen züchtigem Busen;
there lived, what noble and moral was, in the women's modest bosom;
(all that was noble and moral was kept alive in the modest bosom of women;)

di 'flamə dɛs 'liːdəs lɛnt''brant'ə nɔø̯ lan deːɐ̯ 'ʃøːnən 'mɪnə lʊnt' 'liːbəstʰrɔø̯.
die Flamme des Liedes entbrannte neu an der schönen Minne und Liebestreu.
the flame of the song flared up anew in the beautiful courtly love and constancy.
(the flame of song flared up anew in beautiful courtly love and constancy.)

448

drʊm zɔl lɑox laen 'leːvɪgəs 'ʦaːɐ̯t'əs bant di 'frɑɔən, di 'zɛŋɐ lʊm'flɛçt'ən;
Drum soll auch ein ewiges zartes Band die Frauen, die Sänger umflechten;
Therefore shall also an eternal delicate bond the women, the singers entwine about;
(Therefore an eternal delicate bond shall exist between women and singers;)

ziː 'vɪrk'ən lʊnt' 'veːbən, hant' lɪn hant, den 'gʏrt'əl dɛs 'ʃøːnən lʊnt' 'rɛçt'ən.
sie wirken und weben, Hand in Hand, den Gürtel des Schönen und Rechten.
they work and weave, hand in hand, the girdle of the beautiful and right.
(together, hand in hand, they work to weave the girdle of that which is beautiful and right.)

gə'zaŋ lʊnt' 'liːbə lɪn 'ʃøːnəm fɛɐ̯(r)'laen zi: lɛɐ̯'halt'ən dem 'leːbən den 'juːgənt'ʃaen.
Gesang und Liebe in schönem Verein, sie erhalten dem Leben den Jugendschein.
Song and love in beautiful union, they preserve for the life the youth- shine.
(Song and love in beautiful union, they preserve for life the glow of youth.)

[Schiller's poem is a poetic history of the world in twelve verses; Schubert set it as a catchy little drinking song, ignoring the lofty philosophical fantasies. He copied out only the first verse, then added repeat marks. The performer is faced with a daunting problem: singing all twelve musically identical verses would invite boredom; but leaving out almost any verse would impair the continuity of Schiller's concept. The Peters edition, unlike the *Gesamtausgabe*, prints all the verses under the vocal line, with frequent adjustments to fit varied verbal rhythms to the music.]

di 'føːgəl
Die Vögel
The Birds

Op. 172, No. 6 [1820] (Friedrich von Schlegel)

viː 'liːp'lɪç lʊnt' 'frøːlɪç, ʦu 'ʃveːbən, ʦu 'zɪŋən,
Wie lieblich und fröhlich, zu schweben, zu singen,
How lovely and merry, to soar, to sing,

fɔn 'glɛnʦəndɐ 'høːə ʦur 'leːɐ̯də ʦu 'blɪk'ən! [ɪn]
von glänzender Höhe zur Erde zu blicken! [*Peters:* in glänzender Höhe]
from radiant heights to the earth to look! [in]
(to look down at the earth from radiant heights!)

di 'mɛnʃən zɪnt 't'øːrɪçt', ziː 'kʰœnən nɪçt' 'fliːgən. zi: 'jamɐn lɪn 'nøːt'ən,
Die Menschen sind töricht, sie können nicht fliegen. Sie jammern in Nöten,
The humans are silly, they can not fly. They lament in miseries,
(Human beings are silly: they can't fly. They are always in distress, complaining;)

viːɐ̯ 'flat'ɐn gɛn 'hɪməl. deːɐ̯ 'jeːgɐ vɪl 't'øːt'ən, deːm 'frʏçt'ə viːɐ̯ 'pʰɪk't'ən;
wir flattern gen Himmel. Der Jäger will töten, dem Früchte wir pickten;
we flutter toward heaven. The huntsman wants to kill, from whom fruits we pecked;
(*we* flutter up to heaven. The huntsman whose fruit we pecked wants to kill us;)

viːɐ̯ 'mʏsən liːn 'høːnən lʊnt' 'bɔøt'ə gə'vɪnən.
wir müssen ihn höhnen und Beute gewinnen.
we must him mock and spoils win.
(we should mock him and carry off our spoils.)

[A charming, twittery *Ländler* (a slowish countrified waltz), for a charming, chirpy soprano.]

di 'valfaːɐ̯tʰ
Die Wallfahrt
The Pilgrimage

Discovered 1968, published 1968, 1969 [composed 1822-3?] (poem by Friedrich Rückert)

'maɛ̯nə 'tʰreːnən lɪm   'buːsgəvant'
Meine Tränen im   Bussgewand
My   tears   in the penitential garb
(My tears, in penitential garb,)

di 'valfaːɐ̯t'   'haːbən ʦʊr   'kʰaːba deːɐ̯   'ʃøːnhaɛ̯t'   'langətʰreːt'ən;
die Wallfahrt haben zur   Kaaba der   Schönheit angetreten;   [*errors:* **Wahlfahrt, Aula**]
the pilgrimage have   to the Kaaba of the beauty   set out upon;
(have set out upon the pilgrimage to the Kaaba of Beauty;)

ɪn deːɐ̯ 'vyːst'ə 'brɛnəndəm   zant' zɪnt' ziː   bə'graːbən,
In der Wüste   brennendem Sand sind sie   begraben,
In the   desert's burning   sand are   they buried,
(they are buried in the burning sand of the desert,)

nɪçt' 'hɪngəlaŋt'ən   ziː   'lanʦubeːt'ən.
nicht hingelangten   sie   anzubeten.
not   arrived at or reached the goal they to worship.
(they never got near enough to worship.)

[This song was discovered in 1968 by Reinhard van Hoorickx, who published it privately. In 1969 Bärenreiter included it in their *Ausgewählte Lieder* (*Selected Songs*) album, with some mistakes that have since been corrected, namely "*Wahlfahrt*" for "*Wallfahrt*" and "*Aula*," a misreading of Schubert's handwriting, for "*Kaaba*," which is the small building in Mecca that houses the holy Black Stone, the chief object of pilgrimage for the Islamic world. The words are from the first edition of Rückert's *Östliche Rosen*. Schubert set it as a song for the bass voice.]

Die Wehmut see *Die Herbstnacht*

Die Wetterfahne see *Winterreise*

dit'y'rambə
Dithyrambe
Dithyramb

Op. 60, No. 2 [1824?] (Friedrich von Schiller)

'nɪmɐ,   das glɑ̯op't'   miːɐ̯/miːr, lɛɐ̯'ʃaɛ̯nən di   'gœt'ɐ, 'nɪmɐ(r) la'laɛ̯n.
Nimmer, das glaubt   mir,   erscheinen die Götter, nimmer allein.
Never,   that believe me,   appear   the gods,   never   alone.
(Never, believe me, never do the gods appear alone.)

kʰɑ̯om das lɪç 'baxʊs,   den 'lʊst'ɪgən,   'haːbə, kʰɔmt' lɑ̯ox ʃoːn   'laːmoːɐ̯,
Kaum   dass ich Bacchus, den Lustigen,   habe, kommt auch schon Amor,
Scarcely that I   Bacchus, the   merry one, have, comes   also already Cupid,
(No sooner have I the company of merry Bacchus, then along comes Cupid too,)

deːɐ̯ ˈlɛçəlndə ˈkʰnaːbə, ˈføːbʊs,　　　　deːɐ̯ ˈhɛrlɪçə,　　ˈfɪndət‘ zɪç　ˈlaen.
der lächelnde Knabe, Phöbus,　　　　der Herrliche,　findet sich　ein.
the smiling　　boy,　　Phoebus Apollo, the　glorious one,　finds　himself in [= appears].
(the smiling boy, and glorious Phoebus Apollo puts in an appearance, wine, love, and music!)

ziː ˈnaːən, ziː ˈkʰɔmən, di ˈhɪmlɪʃən　ˈlalə,
Sie　nahen, sie　kommen, die Himmlischen alle,
They near,　they come,　the　heavenly ones all,
(They approach, they come, all the immortals,)

mɪt‘ ˈɡœt‘ɐn lɛɐ̯ˈfʏlt‘ zɪç di ˈlɪrdɪʃə　ˈhalə.
mit Göttern erfüllt sich die irdische Halle.
with gods　fills　itself the terrestrial hall.
(the terrestrial hall is filled with celestial gods.)

zaːk‘t‘, viː bəˈvɪrt‘ lɪç, deːɐ̯/deːr ˈleːɐ̯dəgəbɔːrnə, ˈhɪmlɪʃən　kʰoːɐ̯? ˈʃɛŋk‘ət miːɐ̯/miːr
Sagt, wie bewirt ich, der　　Erdegeborne, himmlischen Chor? Schenket mir
Say,　how entertain I,　the　　earth-born,　heavenly　choir? Give　　to me
(Tell me how I, earth-born, should entertain a heavenly choir? Give me)

ˈlɔɐ̯(r) lʊnˈʃt‘ɛrp‘lɪçəs ˈleːbən, ˈɡœt‘ɐ! vas　kʰan lɔɐ̯ç　deːɐ̯ ˈʃt‘ɛrp‘lɪçɐ ˈgeːbən?
euer　unsterbliches Leben, Götter! was　kann euch der　Sterblicher geben?
your　immortal　　life,　gods!　What can　to you the　mortal one　give?
(your immortal life, gods! What can a mortal give to you?)

ˈheːbət t͡suː ˈlɔørəm loˈlʏmp‘　mɪç lɛmˈpʰoːɐ̯! di ˈfrɔødə, ziː voːnt‘ nuːɐ̯/nuːr lɪn ˈjuːp‘it‘es ˈzaːlə,
Hebet zu eurem Olymp　mich empor! Die Freude, sie wohnt nur　in Jupiters Saale,
Lift　to your Olympus me up!　　The joy,　it dwells only　in Jupiter's halls,
(Lift me up to your Olympus! Joy dwells only in Jupiter's halls:)

loː ˈfʏlət‘ mɪt‘ ˈnɛk‘t‘ar, loː ˈraeçt miːɐ̯ di ˈʃaːlə!　—raeç liːm di ˈʃaːlə!
o füllet mit Nektar, o reicht mir　die Schale! —Reich ihm die Schale!
oh fill　with nectar,　oh pass　to me the cup!　—Pass　him the cup!
(oh fill the cup with nectar, oh pass me the cup! [Jupiter speaks:] "Pass him the cup!")

loː ˈʃɛŋk‘ə dem ˈdɪçt‘ɐ, ˈheːbə, nuːɐ̯/n　ˈ　ˈ l! nɛt͡s　liːm　di ˈlɑogən
o schenke dem Dichter, Hebe, nur　ein! Netz' ihm　die Augen
O pour　for the poet,　Hebe, just　in! Moisten for him the eyes
(O Hebe, cupbearer to the gods, pour nectar for the poet! Moisten his eyes) *[poem: without "o"]*

mɪt‘ ˈhɪmlɪʃəm ˈtʰɑoə, das　leːɐ̯ den ʃtʏks/ʃt‘ʏks, den fɛɐ̯ˈhast‘ən, nɪçt‘ ˈʃɑoə,
mit himmlischem Taue, dass　er den Styx,　den verhassten, nicht schaue,
with heavenly　　dew,　so that he the Styx,　the hated,　not see,
(with heavenly dew, so that he may not see the Styx, the hated river of death,)

ˈlaenɐ deːɐ̯/deːr ˈlʊnzɐn zɪç　ˈdʏŋk‘ə t͡suː zaen. ziː ˈrɑoʃət‘, ziː ˈpʰɛrlət‘,
einer der　Unsern sich　dünke zu sein. Sie rauschet, sie perlet,
one　of the　ours　himself imagine to be.　It　murmurs,　it　bubbles,
(and may imagine himself to be one of us. It murmurs, it bubbles,)

di ˈhɪmlɪʃə　ˈkʰvɛlə, deːɐ̯ ˈbuːzən vɪrt‘　ˈruːɪç, das ˈlɑogə vɪrt‘　ˈhɛlə.
die himmlische Quelle, der Busen wird　ruhig, das Auge wird　helle.
the heavenly　spring; the bosom becomes calm, the eye　becomes bright.

[A dithyramb is a lyric poem in honor of Dionysus (Bacchus), god of wine and uninhibited natural instincts. The *Gesamtausgabe* follows Schubert's original (undated) manuscript, with the vocal part in the bass cleff; Peters prints the version that was first published, presumably with Schubert's corrections, which included a shorter postlude. The song calls for a powerful voice that can hold its own in the lower register against a boisterously Dionysian accompaniment. The last verse, be it noted, is sung by Zeus (Jupiter), king of the gods, and should be differentiated from the first two in tone and expression, as recommended by Dietrich Fischer-Dieskau.]

dɔn gae̯ˈseros, ḷae̯ns

Don Gayseros I

Don Gayseros I

Posthumously published [date disputed; 1815?] (Friedrich de la Motte Fouqué)

— dɔn gae̯ˈseros, dɔn gae̯ˈseros, ˈvʊndɐlɪçɐ,   ˈʃøːnɐ   ˈrɪtˈɐ,
—**"Don Gayseros, Don Gayseros, wunderlicher, schöner Ritter,**
— "Don Gayseros, Don Gayseros, strange,   handsome knight,

hastˈ   mɪç ḷao̯s deːɐ̯ bʊrkˈ bəˈʃvoːrən, ˈliːpˈlɪçɐ,   mɪt ˈdae̯nən ˈbɪtˈən.
hast   mich aus der Burg beschworen, Lieblicher, mit deinen Bitten.
(you) have me out of the castle entreated,   lovely one, with your   pleas.
(you have enticed me out of the castle, charmer, with your pleas.)

dɔn gae̯ˈseros, diːɐ̯/diːr ḷɪm   ˈbʏntˈnɪs ˈlɔkˈtˈən valtˈ ḷʊntˈ ˈḷaːbəntˈlɪçtˈɐ.
Don Gayseros, dir   im   Bündnis lockten Wald und Abendlichter.
Don Gayseros, with you in the league lured forest and evening lights.
(Don Gayseros, the forest and the evening light, in league with you, lured me out.)

ziː   mɪç hiːɐ̯ nuːn, zaːkˈ nuːn ˈvae̯tˈɐ, voˈhɪn ˈvandəln viːɐ̯, du ˈliːbɐ?
Sieh' mich hier nun, sag' nun weiter, wohin wandeln wir, du Lieber?"
See   me   here now; say now further, whither wander we, you dear one?"
(Here I am; now tell me further: where shall we go walking, my dear?")

— ˈdɔna   ˈklara, ˈdɔna   ˈklara, duː bɪstˈ ˈhɛrɪn,   ḷɪç deːɐ̯ ˈdiːnɐ,
—**"Donna Clara, Donna Clara, du bist Herrin,   ich der Diener,**
— "Doña   Clara, Doña   Clara, you are mistress, I the servant,
(—"Doña Clara, Doña Clara, you are the mistress, I am the servant,)

duː bɪstˈ ˈlɛŋkˈrɪn, ḷɪç pʰlaˈneːtˈ nuːɐ̯, ˈzyːsə maxtˈ, ḷoː vɔlstˈ   gəˈbiːtˈən!
du bist Lenk'rin, ich Planet   nur, süsse Macht, o woll'st   gebieten!"
you are guide,   I planet   only, sweet power, O may (you) want to command!"
(you set the course, I am only your planet; sweet ruler, give your command!")

— guːtˈ, zoː ˈvandəln viːɐ̯ den ˈbɛrkˈhaŋ dɔrtˈ ḷam kʰruʦiˈfɪksə ˈniːdɐ;
—**"Gut, so wandeln wir den Berghang dort am Kruzifixe nieder;**
— "Good; then wander we the hillside   there at the crucifix down;
(—"Good; then let us wander down the hillside over there to the crucifix,)

ˈvɛndən drao̯f ḷan deːɐ̯ kʰaˈpʰɛlə ˈhae̯mvɛrts ḷʊns,   ḷɛntˈlɛŋs den ˈviːzən.
wenden drauf an der Kapelle heimwärts uns,   entlängs* den Wiesen."
turn   then at the chapel   homewards ourselves, alongside the meadows."
(then turn homewards at the chapel, walking alongside the meadows.")

*[*Fouqué:* **entlängst** (lɛntˈlɛŋst—*not usual*) **die** (di—*accusative, more usual*) **Wiesen**]

— ax, vaˈrʊm lan deːɐ̯ kʰaˈpʰɛlə? lax, vaˈrʊm bae̯m kʰrutsiˈfɪksə?
—"Ach, warum an der Kapelle? ach, warum beim Kruzifixe?"
—"Ah, why to the chapel? Ah, why by the crucifix?"

— ʃpˈrɪç, vas hast du: nuːn tsuː ʃtˈrae̯tˈən? mae̯ntˈ lɪç jaː, du: vɛːɐ̯stˈ mae̯n ˈdiːnɐ.
—"Sprich, was hast du nun zu streiten? Meint' ich ja, du wärst mein Diener."
—"Speak, why have you now to argue? Thought I, after all, you were my servant."
(—"Tell me why you have to argue now! I thought, after all, that you were my servant.")

— jaː, lɪç ʃrae̯tˈə, jaː, lɪç ˈvandlə, ˈhɛrɪn, gants naːx ˈdae̯nən ˈvɪlən.
—"Ja, ich schreite, ja, ich wandle, Herrin, ganz nach deinen Willen."
—"Yes, I walk, yes, I wander, mistress, entirely according to your will."
(—"Yes, I shall walk, yes, I shall stroll with you, mistress, entirely according to your will.")

ʊntˈ ziː ˈvandəltˈən tsuˈzamən, ˈʃpˈraːxən fiːl fɔn ˈzyːsɐ ˈmɪnə.
und sie wandelten zusammen, sprachen viel von süsser Minne.
and they wandered together, spoke much of sweet love.
(and they wandered on together, talking much about sweet love.)

— dɔn gae̯ˈseros, dɔn gae̯ˈseros, ziː, viːɐ̯ zɪntˈ lam kʰrutsiˈfɪksə,
—"Don Gayseros, Don Gayseros, sieh', wir sind am Kruzifixe,
—"Don Gayseros, Don Gayseros, look, we are at the crucifix;

hast du: nɪçt dae̯n hao̯pˈtˈ gəˈboːgən, foːɐ̯ dem hɛrn viː ˈlandrə ˈkʰrɪstˈən?
hast du nicht dein Haupt gebogen, vor dem Herrn wie andre Christen?"
have you not your head bowed before the Lord like other Christians?"
(have you not bowed your head before the Lord like other Christians?")

— ˈdɔna ˈklara, ˈdɔna ˈklara, kʰɔntˈ lɪç lao̯f vas ˈlandrəs ˈblɪkˈən,
—"Donna Clara, Donna Clara, konnt' ich auf was andres blicken,
—"Doña Clara, Doña Clara, could I at something else look,
(—"Doña Clara, Doña Clara, could I look at anything else)

als lao̯f ˈdae̯nə ˈtsaːɐ̯tˈən ˈhɛndə, viː ziː mɪt den ˈbluːmən ʃpˈiːltˈən?
als auf deine zarten Hände, wie sie mit den Blumen spielten?"
than at your delicate hands, as they with the flowers played?"
(than at your delicate hands as they were playing with the flowers?")

— dɔn gae̯ˈseros, dɔn gae̯ˈseros, ˈkʰɔntˈəst du: den nɪçts lɛɐ̯ˈviːden,
—"Don Gayseros, Don Gayseros, konntest du denn nichts erwidern,
—"Don Gayseros, Don Gayseros, could you then nothing answer,
(—"Don Gayseros, Don Gayseros, could you then not give any response)

　　　　　　　　　　　　　　　　[*poem:* **konntest du denn nicht** (nɪçtˈ, not) **erwidern**]

als deːɐ̯ ˈfrɔmə mœnç dɪç ˈgryːstˈə, ʃpˈrɛçəntˈ: ˈkʰrɪstˈʊs geːɐ̯ˈ diːɐ̯ ˈfriːdən?
als der fromme Mönch dich grüsste, sprechend: 'Christus geb' dir Frieden?'"
when the pious monk you greeted, saying: 'Christ give to you peace'?"
(when the pious monk greeted you, saying: 'May Christ give you peace'?")

— ˈdɔna ˈklara, ˈdɔna ˈklara, dʊrftˈ lɪns loːɐ̯/loːr lae̯n lao̯tˈ miːɐ̯ ˈdrɪŋən,
—"Donna Clara, Donna Clara, durft' ins Ohr ein Laut mir dringen,
—"Doña Clara, Doña Clara, might into the ear a sound to me penetrate,
(—"Doña Clara, Doña Clara, could a sound penetrate my ear,)

'ɪrgənt' nɔx ‖aen ‖ɑot' ‖ɑof 'leːɐ̯dən, ‖als duː 'flʏst'ɐnt' ʃp'raːxst': ‖ɪç 'liːbə?
irgend noch ein Laut auf Erden, als du flüsternd sprachst: 'Ich liebe'?"
any other a sound on earth when you whispering said: 'I love'?"
(any other sound on earth, when you were whispering: 'I love you'?")

— dɔn gae'seros, dɔn gae'seros, ziː, foːɐ̯ deːɐ̯ kʰa'pʰɛlə
—"Don Gayseros, Don Gayseros, sieh', vor der Kapelle
—"Don Gayseros, Don Gayseros, look, in front of the chapel

[*GA:* **von der Kapelle** (fɔn deːɐ̯ kʰa'pʰɛlə), from the chapel]

'blɪŋk'ətʰ dɛs gə'vaet'ən 'vasɐs 'ʃaːlə! kʰɔm ‖ʊnt tʰuː viː ‖ɪç, gə'liːp't'ɐ!
blinket des geweihten Wassers Schale! komm' und tu' wie ich, Geliebter!"
gleams the consecrated water's bowl! Come and do as I, beloved!"
(the holy water font is gleaming! Come and do as I do, beloved!")

— 'dɔna 'klara, 'dɔna 'klara, 'gɛntsʁlɪç mʊs ‖ɪç jɛt͡st' ‖ɛɐ̯'blɪndən,,
—"Donna Clara, Donna Clara, gänzlich muss ich jetzt erblinden,
—"Doña Clara, Doña Clara, totally must I now grow blind,
(—"Doña Clara, Doña Clara, I must now be growing totally blind,)

dɛn ‖ɪç ʃɑot' ‖ɪn 'daenə 'ɑogən, kʰan mɪç zɛlpst' nɪçt' 'viːdɐ 'fɪndən.
denn ich schaut' in deine Augen, kann mich selbst nicht wieder finden."
for I looked into your eyes, can me myself not again find."
(for I looked into your eyes and cannot find myself again, lost since I looked into your eyes.")

— dɔn gae'seros, dɔn gae'seros, tʰuː miːɐ̯s naːx, bɪst duː maen 'diːnɐ!
—"Don Gayseros, Don Gayseros, tu' mir's nach, bist du mein Diener!
—"Don Gayseros, Don Gayseros, do me it after, are you my servant!
(—"Don Gayseros, Don Gayseros, do after me as I do, if you are my servant!)

tʰɑox ‖ɪns 'vasɐ 'daenə 'rɛçt'ə, t͡saeç naen kʰrɔ͡øts ‖ɑof 'daenə 'ʃt'ɪrnə!
Tauch' ins Wasser deine Rechte, zeichn' ein Kreuz auf deine Stirne!"
Dip into the water your right hand, draw a cross on your forehead!"
(Dip your right hand into the holy water and make the sign of the cross on your forehead!")

dɔn gae'seros ʃviːk' ‖ɛɐ̯'ʃrɔk'ən, dɔn gae'seros floː fɔn 'hɪnən;
Don Gayseros schwieg erschrocken, Don Gayseros floh von hinnen;
Don Gayseros was silent, frightened; Don Gayseros fled from there;

'dɔna 'klara 'lɛŋk't'ə 'beːbənt t͡suː deːɐ̯ bʊrk' di 'ʃɔ͡øən 'tʰrɪt'ə.
Donna Clara lenkte bebend zu der Burg die scheuen Tritte.
Doña Clara directed trembling to the castle the timid steps.
(Doña Clara, trembling, directed her timid steps back to the castle.)

[This song is an experiment: to vary the strophic form, the repetitions of the melodies recur in different keys. This is the first in a cycle of three songs; the poems come from the novel *Der Zauberring* ("The Magic Ring") by the author of *Undine*. A Spaniard sings songs of his homeland, accompanying himself on the lute. "Don Gayseros" is a Moorish king in disguise.]

dɔn gae̯ˈseros, ʦvae̯
Don Gayseros II
Don Gayseros II

Posthumously published [date disputed; 1815?] (poem by Friedrich de la Motte Fouqué)

ˈnɛçtˈəns kʰlaŋ   di ˈzyːsə ˈlao̯tˈə, voː   ziː lɔft   ʦuː naxtˈ gəˈkʰlʊŋən,   [viː]
Nächtens klang   die süsse Laute, wo   sie oft   zu Nacht geklungen, [*poem:* **wie sie oft**]
By night sounded the sweet lute   where it often by night (had) sounded,   [as]
(By night the sweet lute sounded, where it often had sounded by night,)

ˈnɛçtˈəns zaŋ deːɐ̯ ˈʃøːnə   ˈrɪtˈɐ, voː   leːɐ̯/leːr lɔft   ʦuː naxtˈ gəˈzʊŋən.
nächtens sang der schöne Ritter, wo   er   oft   zu Nacht gesungen.
by night sang the handsome knight where he   often by night (had) sung.
(by night the handsome knight sang where he had often sung by night.)

ʊnt das ˈfɛnstˈɐ ˈkʰlɪrtˈə ˈviːdɐ, ˈdɔna ˈklara ʃao̯tˈ heˈrʊntˈɐ,
Und das Fenster klirrte wieder, Donna Clara schaut' herunter,
And the window rattled again, Doña   Clara looked down,

ˈaːbɐ ˈfʊrçtˈzaːm ˈliːrə ˈblɪkˈə ˈʃvae̯ftˈən dʊrç   das ˈtʰao̯gə ˈdʊŋkˈəl.   [ˈʃvae̯fənt]
aber furchtsam ihre Blicke schweiften durch das tau'ge Dunkel.   [*poem:* **schweifend**]
but fearfully her glances swept   through the dewy darkness.   [sweeping]
(but her glances, full of fear, swept through the dewy darkness.)

ʊntˈ ʃtˈatˈ   ˈzyːsɐ ˈmɪnəliːdɐ, ʃtˈat   deːɐ̯ ˈʃmae̯çəlvɔrtˈə   ˈkʰʊndə
Und statt   süsser Minnelieder, statt   der Schmeichelworte Kunde
And instead of sweet love songs, instead of the flatter-   words' tidings
(And instead of sweet love songs, instead of tidings in flattering words,)

[*poem:* **Minnereden** (ˈmɪnəreːdən, talk of love)]

huːpˈ ziː lan lae̯n ʃtˈrɛŋ bəˈʃvøːrən: zakˈ, veːɐ̯ bɪst duː, ˈfɪnstˈrɐ ˈbuːlə?
hub sie an ein streng Beschwören: "Sag, wer bist du, finstrer Buhle?
raised she up a   stern adjuration: "Say, who are you, dark   lover?
(she brought forth a stern adjuration: "Tell me, who are you, dark lover?)

zakˈ, bae̯ dae̯n lʊntˈ ˈmae̯nɐ ˈliːbə, zakˈ, bae̯ ˈdae̯nɐ ˈzeːlənruːə,
Sag, bei dein' und meiner Liebe, sag, bei deiner Seelenruhe,
Say, by your and my   love, say, by your soul- peace,
(Say, by your love and mine, say, by the peace of your soul,)

bɪstˈ lae̯n kʰrɪst   duː, bɪstˈ lae̯n ˈʃpˈaːni̯ɐ? ˈʃtˈeːst duː lɪn deːɐ̯ ˈkʰɪrçə   ˈbʊndə?
bist ein Christ   du, bist ein Spanier? Stehst du in der Kirche Bunde?"
are a   Christian you, are a   Spaniard? Stand you in the church's covenant?"
(are you a Christian, are you a Spaniard? Are you a member of the church?")

— ˈhɛrɪn,   hoːx hast duː bəˈʃvoːrən, ˈhɛrɪn,   jaː, duː zɔlsʦ lɐɐ̯ˈkʰʊndən.
—"Herrin,   hoch hast du beschworen, Herrin, ja, du sollst's erkunden.
— "Mistress, high have you adjured,   Mistress, yes, you shall it ascertain.
(—"Mistress, you have solemnly adjured; Mistress, yes, you shall have that information.)

ˈhɛrɪn, lax, lɪç bɪn kʰa͜en ˈʃpˈaːnɪ̯ɐ, nɪçtˈ lɪn ˈda͜enɐ ˈkʰɪrçɐ ˈbʊndɐ.
Herrin, ach, ich bin kein Spanier, nicht in deiner Kirche Bunde.
Mistress, ah, I am no Spaniard, not in your church's covenant.
(Mistress, ah, I am not a Spaniard; I am not a member of your religion.)

ˈhɛrɪn, bɪn la͜en ˈmoːrənkʰøːnɪç, glyːntˈ lɪn ˈda͜enɐ ˈliːbə ˈgluːtˈən,
Herrin, bin ein Mohrenkönig, glüh'nd in deiner Liebe Gluten,
Mistress, (I) am a Moorish king, burning in your love's fires,
(Mistress, I am a Moorish king, burning in the fire of my love for you,)

groːs lan maxtˈ lʊntˈ ra͜eç lan ˈʃɛtsən, ˈzɔndɐ gla͜eç lan ˈtʰapfrəm muːtʰ.
gross an Macht und reich an Schätzen, sonder gleich an tapfrem Mut.
great in power and rich in treasures, without equal in valiant courage.
[*poem:* **tapferm** (ˈtʰapfɐm) **Mute** (ˈmuːtˈə)]

ˈrøːtˈlɪç blyːn graˈnaːdas ˈgɛrtˈən, ˈgɔldən ʃtˈeːn lalˈhambras ˈbʊrgən,
Rötlich blühn Granadas Gärten, golden stehn Alhambras Burgen,
Reddish bloom Granada's gardens, golden stand Alhambra's castles,
(The gardens of Granada bloom red, the castles within the Alhambra are golden,)

ˈmoːrən ˈharən ˈliːrɐ ˈkʰøːnɪgə, flɔø̯ç mɪtˈ miːɐ̯ dʊrçs tʰa͜ogə ˈdʊŋkˈəl.
Mohren harren ihrer Königin, fleuch mit mir durchs tau'ge Dunkel."
Moors are waiting for their queen, fly with me through the dewy darkness."
[*poem:* **Kön'gin** (ˈkøːngɪn)]

— fɔrt, duː ˈfalʃɐ ˈzeːlənrɔøbɐ, fɔrt, duː fa͜entˈ! —ziː vɔltˈ lɛs ˈruːfən,
—"Fort, du falscher Seelenräuber, fort, du Feind!" —sie wollt' es rufen,
—"Away, you false soul- robber, away, you enemy!"—she wanted it to cry out,
(—"Away, you false robber of souls, away, you enemy!"—that is what she wanted to cry out,)

dɔx bəˈfoːɐ̯ ziː fa͜entˈ gəˈʃpˈrɔxən, lɔʃ das vɔrtˈ liːɐ̯/liːr la͜os lɪm ˈmʊndə.
doch bevor sie Feind gesprochen, losch das Wort ihr aus im Munde.
but before she "enemy" (had) spoken, died the word to her out in the mouth.
(but before she could say "enemy," the word died out in her mouth.)

ˈoːnmaxtˈ hiːltˈ lɪn ˈdʊŋkˈlən ˈnɛtsən liːɐ̯ den ˈʃøːnən la͜epˈ lʊmˈʃlʊŋən.
Ohnmacht hielt in dunklen Netzen ihr den schönen Leib umschlungen.
(A) fainting fit held in dark nets, for her the beautiful body entwined.
(She fainted; unconsciousness held her beautiful body entwined in its dark toils.)
[*poem:* **dunkeln** (ˈdʊŋkˈəln)]

eːɐ̯/eːr lalsˈbalt tʰruːkˈ ziː tsuː ˈrɔsə, raʃ dan fɔrtˈ lɪm ˈnɛçtˈgən fluːkˈ.
Er alsbald trug sie zu Rosse, rasch dann fort im nächt'gen Flug.
He forthwith carried her to horse, swiftly then away in the nocturnal flight.
(He then immediately carried her swiftly away on his horse in a nocturnal flight.)
[*poem:* **Fluge** (ˈfluːgə)]

[This is a continuation of the story begun in *Don Gayseros I*.]

456

dɔn gae̯ˈseros, drae̯
Don Gayseros III
Don Gayseros III

Posthumously published [date disputed; 1815?] (poem by Friedrich de la Motte Fouqué)

an dem ˈjʊŋən ˈmɔrgənhɪməl   ʃtˈeːt di ˈrae̯nə ˈzɔnə kʰlaːɐ̯,
An dem jungen Morgenhimmel steht die reine Sonne klar,
In the young morning-sky   stands the pure sun   clear,
(In the early morning sky the sun is shining pure and clear,)

ˈaːbɐ bluːtˈ kʰvɪltˈ lɑo̯f deːɐ̯ ˈviːzə,   lʊntˈ lae̯n rɔs, des   ˈrae̯tˈɐs baːɐ̯,
aber Blut quillt auf der Wiese, und ein Ross, des   Reiters bar,
but blood flows on the meadow, and a horse, of the rider   devoid,
(but blood is flowing on the meadow, and a horse without a rider)

tʰraːpˈtˈ fɛɐ̯ˈʃʏçtˈɐtˈ lɪn deːɐ̯ ˈrʊndə, ʃtˈar   ʃtˈeːt ˈlae̯nə ˈrae̯zgə   ʃaːɐ̯.
trabt   verschüchtert in der Runde, starr   steht eine reis'ge   Schar.
trots scared   in the circle, motionless stands a   mounted knights' troop.
(is trotting around in a circle, frightened, and a troop of mounted knights looks on, motionless.)

ˈmoːrənkʰøːnɪç,   bɪstˈ lɛɐ̯ˈʃlaːgən fɔn dem ˈtʰapfɛn ˈbryːdɐpʰaːɐ̯,
Mohrenkönig,   bist erschlagen von dem tapfern Brüderpaar,
Moorish king, (you) are slain   by the valiant brother-pair,
(Moorish king, you have been slain by her two valiant brothers,)

das dae̯n ˈkʰyːnəs ˈrɔøbɐvaːkˈnɪs   naːm lɪm ˈgryːnən ˈhɔrstˈə vaːɐ̯!
das dein kühnes Räuberwagnis   nahm im   grünen Horste wahr!
which your bold   robber- hazardous venture took in the green   thicket notice of!
(who observed in the green thicket your bold, hazardous theft!)
                    [*poem:* **Forste** (ˈfɔrstˈə), forest; "*wahrnehmen*" = to perceive, observe, notice]

ˈdɔna ˈklara kʰniːtˈ bae̯m   ˈlae̯çnaːm, ˈlɑo̯fgəløːstˈ liːɐ̯ ˈgɔldnəs haːɐ̯,
Donna Clara kniet beim   Leichnam, aufgelöst ihr goldnes Haar,
Doña   Clara kneels beside the corpse,   loosened   her golden hair,
(Doña Clara kneels beside the corpse, her golden hair undone,)

ˈzɔndɐ ˈʃɔøə nuːn bəˈkʰɛnəntˈ, viː liːɐ̯ liːpˈ deːɐ̯ ˈtʰoːtˈə   vaːɐ̯.
sonder Scheue nun bekennend,   wie ihr   lieb der Tote   war.
without shyness now acknowledging how to her dear the dead man was.
(now acknowledging without shyness how dear to her the dead man was.)

ˈbryːdɐ ˈbɪtˈən, ˈpʰriːstˈɐ ˈleːrən, lae̯ns   nuːɐ̯ blae̯pˈtˈ liːɐ̯/liːr ˈlɔfənbaːɐ̯.
Brüder bitten, Priester lehren, eins   nur bleibt ihr   offenbar.
Brothers plead, priests instruct, one thing only remains to her manifest.
(Her brothers plead with her, priests try to instruct her, but only one thing remains clear to her.)

ˈzɔnə geːtˈ, lʊntˈ ˈʃtˈɛrnə ˈkʰɔmən, lɑo̯f lʊntˈ ˈniːdɐ ʃveːpˈtˈ deːɐ̯/deːr laːɐ̯,
Sonne geht, und Sterne kommen, auf und nieder schwebt der   Aar,
Sun   goes, and stars   come,   up and down soars   the   eagle,
(The sun sets and the stars come out; the eagle soars up and down;)

'aləs   lɑof deːɐ̯ vɛltʼ lɪstʼ 'vandəl, ziː la'laɛn   lʊn'vandəlbaːɐ̯.
alles   auf der Welt ist Wandel, sie allein   unwandelbar.
everything in   the   world   is   change; she alone (is) unchangeable.
(everything else in the world is in a state of flux; she alone is constant.)

'entʼlɪç bɑon di 'tʰrɔɸən 'bryːdɐ dɔrtʼ kʰaʼpʰɛl liːɐ̯/liːr lʊntʼ lalʼtʰaːɐ̯,
Endlich bau'n die treuen Brüder dort Kapell' ihr   und Altar,
Finally   build   the   faithful brothers there chapel   for her and   altar,
(Finally her faithful brothers build a chapel and altar there for her,)

'beːtʼəntʼ nuːn fɛɐ̯'rɪntʼ   liːɐ̯ 'leːbən, tʰaːkʼ fyːɐ̯ tʰaːkʼ lʊntʼ jaːɐ̯ fyːɐ̯ jaːɐ̯,
betend   nun verrinnt   ihr Leben, Tag für Tag und Jahr für Jahr,
praying   now trickles away her life,   day   after day   and   year after year
(her life now is spent in prayer; day after day and year after year)

brɪŋtʼ fɛɐ̯'hɑoxəntʼ ziː lals 'lɔpfɐ   fyːɐ̯ dɛs 'liːpʼstʼən   'zeːlə daːɐ̯.
bringt verhauchend sie als Opfer   für des Liebsten   Seele dar.
offers   pining away   she as   sacrifice for   the dearest one's soul ... . ["*darbringen*" = to offer]
(are offered by her as a sacrifice for the sake of the soul of her dearest one, as she pines away.)

[This concludes the story told in a mini-cycle of three songs.]

draŋ lɪn di 'fɛrnə
Drang in die Ferne
The Urge toward Distant Places

Op. 71 [1823?] (poem by Karl Gottfried von Leitner)

'faːtʼɐ, duː glɑopstʼ lɛs nɪçtʼ, viːs   miːɐ̯ tsʊm 'hɛrtsən ʃpʼrɪçtʼ,
Vater, du glaubst es nicht, wie's mir   zum Herzen spricht,
Father, you believe it   not,   how it to me to the heart   speaks,
(Father, you wouldn't believe how it speaks to my heart)

vɛn lɪç di 'vɔlkʼən zeː 'loːdɐ(r) lam   'ʃtʼroːmə ʃtʼeː!
wenn ich die Wolken seh' oder   am   Strome steh'!
when I   the clouds   see or   by the river   stand!
(when I look at the clouds or stand by the river!)

'vɔlkʼəngɔltʼ, 'vɛləngryːn 'tsiːən zoː laɛçt daʼhɪn,   'vaɛlən lɪm 'zɔnənlɪçtʼ,
Wolkengold, Wellengrün ziehen so leicht dahin,   weilen im   Sonnenlicht,
Cloud- gold, wave- green move   so easily onwards, stay   in the sunlight,
(Golden clouds, green waves move onwards so easily; they stay in the sunlight,)

'laːbɐ baɛ 'bluːmən nɪçtʰ, 'tsøːgɐn lʊntʼ 'rastʼən niː,
aber bei Blumen nicht, zögern und rasten nie,
but   by   flowers not,   hesitate and rest   never,
(but do not linger by the flowers; they never hesitate and never rest;)

'laɛlən. lals 'vʏstʼən ziː,   'fɛrnə lʊntʼ 'lʊngəkʰantʼ, 'lɪrgəntʼ laɛn 'ʃøːnrəs   lantʼ.
eilen, als wüssten sie, ferne und ungekannt, irgend ein schön'res   Land.
hasten, as if knew   they, distant and   unknown,   some   ... more beautiful land.
(they hurry on, as if they knew of some more beautiful land, far away and unknown to us.)

["*irgend ein*" = some]

ax! fɔn gə'vœlk' lʊnt' fluːt' hat' lɑox maen 'vɪldəs bluːt'
Ach! von Gewölk und Flut   hat auch mein wildes Blut
Ah! from clouds   and stream has also   my   wild   blood
(Ah, from cloud and stream my wild blood has also)

'haemlıç gə'lɛrp't den draŋ, 'ʃt'ʏrmət di vɛlt' lɛnt'ˈlaŋ!
heimlich geerbt   den Drang, stürmet die Welt entlang!
secretly   inherited the urge,   storms   the world along!
(secretly inherited the urge to storm through the world!)

'faːt'ɐlants 'fɛlzənthaːl vɪrt'   miːɐ t͡su: lɛŋ,   t͡su: ʃmaːl;
Vaterlands Felsental   wird   mir   zu eng,   zu schmal;
Native land's rocky valley becomes for me too confined, too narrow;
(The rocky valley of my native land is becoming too confining, too narrow for me;)

dɛn 'maenɐ 'zeːnzʊxt   thrɑom 'fɪndət da'rɪn nɪçt' rɑom.
denn meiner Sehnsucht Traum findet darin nicht Raum.
for   my   yearning's dream finds therein not   room.
(for there is no room in that valley for my yearning dream.)

last' mıç! lıç mʊs, lıç mʊs 'fɔrdɐn den 'ʃaedəkhʊs.
Lasst mich! ich muss, ich muss fordern den Scheidekuss.
Let   me!   I   must, I   must ask for   the   parting kiss.
(Let me go! I must, I *must* ask you for the parting kiss.)

'faːt'ɐ(r) lʊnt' 'mʊt'ɐ maen, 'mʏsət   nıçt' 'bøːzə zaen! haːp' lɔøç ja: 'hɛrtslıç liːp';
Vater   und Mutter mein, müsset   nicht böse sein! Hab' euch ja   herzlich lieb;
Father   and   mother mine, (you) must not   angry be! (I) have you, you know, sincerely dear;
(Father and Mother, you must not be angry! I love you sincerely, as you know;)

["*liebhaben*" = to love]

'laːbɐ(r) laen 'vıldɐ thriːp' ja:k't' mıç valt'ˈlaen, valt'ˈlɑos, vaet' fɔn dem 'faːt'ɐhɑos.
aber   ein wilder Trieb   jagt   mich waldein, waldaus,   weit von dem Vaterhaus.
but   a   wild   instinct drives me   woods-in, woods-out, far   from the   father-house.
(but a wild instinct drives me into woods, out of woods, and far away from home.)

zɔrk't' nıçt, dʊrç 'vɛlçəs lant' 'laenzaːm maen veːk' zıç vant';
Sorgt nicht, durch welches Land einsam   mein Weg sich wand;
Worry not,   through which   land   lonely   my   way   itself wended;
(Do not worry through which land my lonely way was wended;)

'moːndən lʊnt' 'ʃt'ɛrnənʃaen 'lɔøçt'ət lɑox dɔrt' hı'naen.
Monden- und   Sternenschein leuchtet auch dort hinein.
moon   and   starslight   shine   also   there into.
(the moon and stars shine down upon there as well as here.)

'yːbɐ(r)lal vœlp't͡s   gə'fɪlt'   zıç den la't͡suːɐnən ʃılt',
Überall   wölbt   's Gefild'   sich den azurnen   Schild,
Everywhere arches [verb] the field [subject] (above) itself the azure   shield [object],
(Everywhere the fields of earth project in an arch above themselves the azure shield of the sky,)

deːn lʊm   di 'ganţsə vɛlt' 'ʃɪrmənt   deːɐ̯ 'ʃœpfɐ hɛltʰ.
den um   die ganze Welt schirmend der Schöpfer hält.
which around the whole world protectingly the Creator   holds.
(which the Creator holds protectively around the whole world.)

ax! lʊnt' vɛn 'nɪmɐmeːɐ̯/nɪmɐmeːr lɪç ţsuː lɔøç 'viːdɐkʰeːɐ̯,
Ach! und wenn nimmermehr   ich zu euch wiederkehr,
Ah! and if   nevermore   I   to you return,
(Ah, and if I never come back to you again,)

'liːbən,   zoː dɛŋk'tʰ: leːɐ̯ fant' 'glʏk'lɪç das 'ʃøːnrə   lant'.
Lieben, so denkt: er fand glücklich das schön're   Land.
dear ones, then think: he found happily   the more beautiful land.
(my dear ones, then think this: he has happily found that more beautiful land he was seeking.)

[This song was first published in a magazine, in March 1823. It is full of energy and eagerness, with a touch of poignancy. Much as he loved Vienna, Schubert would have gladly followed the clouds and the waves to other lands, and he does so in this music which is practically sky-borne.]

Drei Gesänge von Metastasio see *L'incanto degli occhi* (*Die Macht der Augen*)

duː bɪst di ruː
Du bist die Ruh
You Are Repose

Op. 59, No. 3 [1823] (Johann Michael Rückert)

duː bɪst di ruː,   deːɐ̯ 'friːdə mɪlt', di 'zeːnzʊxt duː, lʊnt' vas ziː ʃt'ɪltʰ.
Du bist die Ruh,   der Friede mild, die Sehnsucht du, und was sie stillt.
you are the repose, the peace mild, the yearning you, and what it stills.
(You are repose, gentle peace; you are both yearning and that which stills it.)

ɪç 'vaeə   diːɐ̯ fɔl lʊst'   lʊnt' ʃmɛrţs
Ich weihe   dir voll Lust   und Schmerz
I consecrate to you full of pleasure and pain

ţsuːɐ̯ 'voːnʊŋ   hiːɐ̯ maen lɑok' lʊnt' hɛrţs.
zur Wohnung hier mein Aug und Herz.
to the dwelling   here my eye and heart.
(my eyes and my heart as a dwelling place here.)

kʰeːɐ̯/kʰeːr laen bae miːɐ̯/miːr, lʊnt' 'ʃliːsə   duː ʃt'ɪl 'hɪnt'ɐ diːɐ̯   di 'pfɔrt'ən ţsuː.
Kehr   ein bei mir,   und schliesse du still hinter dir   die Pforten zu.
lodge   ... by me,   and close   you quietly behind yourself the gates [to].
(Come live with me, and quietly close the gates behind you.)
            ["*einkehren*" = to enter, to put up at (usually an inn); "*Einkehr*" = lodging]

tʰraep' 'landɐn ʃmerţs lɑos 'diːzɐ brʊstʰ! fɔl zae diːs hɛrţs fɔn 'daenɐ lʊstʰ.
Treib andern Schmerz aus dieser Brust! voll sei dies Herz von deiner Lust.
Drive other pain   out of this breast! full be this heart of your pleasure.
(Drive any other pain out of this breast of mine! May this heart be full of your pleasure.)

diːs ˈlɑogəntselt ˈ,   fɔn ˈdaenəm glants   laˈlaen lɛɐˈhɛltʰ,   loː fʏl lɛs gants!
Dies Augenzelt,   von deinem Glanz   allein erhellt,   o   füll es ganz!
This eye-tabernacle, by   your   radiance alone illumined, oh fill   it completely!
(This tabernacle of my eyes, illumined by your radiance alone, oh fill it completely!)

[Schubert's original manuscript of this justly famous song has been lost. The Peters edition follows the first published version, with two F flats for the soprano or tenor in bar 70, instead of the D flats of bar 56, a variation that could be analogous to the small differences between bars 20 and 43 in the piano part as well as in the vocal line. The *Gesamtausgabe*, on the assumption that F flat was a misprint, opted for D flat in bar 70, rejecting the expressive variation.]

duː liːpstˈ mıç nıçtʰ
Du liebst mich nicht
You do not Love me

Op. 59, No. 1 [1822] (August Graf von Platen)

maen hɛrts lıst tsɛɐˈrısən, duː liːpstˈ mıç nıçtʰ! duː ˈliːsəstˈ mıçs ˈvısən,
Mein Herz ist zerrissen, du   liebst mich nicht! Du   liessest mich's wissen,
My   heart is torn,   you love me   not! You let   me it know,
(My heart is torn apart, you do not love me! You let me know it,)

duː liːpstˈ mıç nıçtʰ! viˈvoːl   lıç diːɐ ˈfleːəntˈ   lʊntˈ ˈvɛrbəntˈ lɛɐˈʃiːn,
du   liebst mich nicht! Wiewohl ich dir flehend   und werbend erschien,
you love me   not!   Although I to you imploring and wooing   appeared,
(Although I appeared before you, imploring and wooing,)

ʊntˈ ˈliːbəbəˌflısən,   duː liːpstˈ mıç nıçtʰ! duː hastˈ lɛs gəˈʃpˈrɔxən,
und liebebeflissen, du   liebst mich nicht! Du   hast es gesprochen,
and   love-diligent,   you love me   not!   You have it   spoken,
(and lovingly devoted, you do not love me! You have told me that,)

mıtˈ ˈvɔrtˈən gəˈzaːkˈtʰ, mıtˈ ˈlaltsuː gəˈvısən,   duː liːpstˈ mıç nıçtʰ!
mit Worten gesagt,   mit allzu gewissen,   du liebst mich nicht!
with words   said,   with all too certain ones, you love   me   not!
(have put it into words, into all too unambiguous words: you do not love me!)

zoː zɔl lıç di ˈʃtˈɛrnə, zoː zɔl lıç den moːnt, di ˈzɔnə fɛɐˈmısən?
So soll ich die Sterne, so soll ich den Mond, die Sonne vermissen?
So shall I   the stars,   so shall I   the   moon, the sun   miss?
(Must I then forgo the stars, the moon, the sun?)

duː liːpstˈ mıç nıçtʰ! vas blyːtˈ miːɐ di ˈroːzə? vas blyːt deːɐ jasˈmiːn?
du   liebst mich nicht! Was blüht mir   die Rose? Was blüht der Jasmin?
you love me   not!   Why blooms for me the rose? Why blooms the jasmine?
(You do not love me! What is it to me that the rose is blooming, or the jasmine?)

vas blyːn di narˈtsısən? duː liːpstˈ mıç nıçtʰ!
was blühn die Narzissen? du   liebst mich nicht!
why bloom the narcissuses? You love   me   not!
(Why should the narcissus bloom? You do not love me!)

[The form of the above poem is derived from the Persian *ghazal*, in which one rhyme reappears in each couplet (and twice in the first). It is partly an exercise in ingenuity. But Schubert takes the sentiment very seriously, and—probably—very personally: the song has deep emotional intensity, and moving sincerity, in its expressive modulations. Schubert left two slightly differing versions, one in G sharp minor, the other in A minor; both are printed in the *Gesamtausgabe*.]

e'doːnə
Edone
Edone

Posthumously published [composed 1816] (poem by Friedrich Gottfried Klopstock)

daen 'zyːsəs bɪlt', leˈdoːnə, ʃveːp't' ʃt'eːts foːɐ̯ 'maenəm blɪkʰ;
Dein süsses Bild, Edone, schwebt stets vor meinem Blick;
Your sweet image, Edone, hovers constantly before my gaze;

aˈlaen liːn 'tʰryːbən 'tseːrən, das duː lɛs zɛlpst' nɪçt' bɪstʰ.
allein ihn trüben Zähren, dass du es selbst nicht bist.
but it (my gaze) dim tears, that you it yourself not are.
(but tears dim my eyes, because it is an image and not you yourself.)

ɪç zeː lɛs, vɛn deːɐ̯/deːr 'laːbənt' miːɐ̯ 'dɛmɐt', vɛn deːɐ̯ moːnt' miːɐ̯ glɛntst',
Ich seh' es, wenn der Abend mir dämmert, wenn der Mond mir glänzt,
I see it, when the evening for me darkens, when the moon for me gleams,
(I see it when twilight is falling around me, when the moon is gleaming,)

zeː lɪçs lʊnt' 'vaenə, das duː lɛs zɛlpst' nɪçt' bɪstʰ.
seh' ich's und weine, dass du es selbst nicht bist.
see I it and weep, that you it yourself not are.
(I see it and weep because it is not you yourself.)

bae 'jeːnəs 'tʰaːləs 'bluːmən, diː lɪç liːɐ̯ 'leːzən vɪl, bae 'jeːnən
Bei jenes Tales Blumen, die ich ihr lesen will, bei jenen
Among that valley's flowers, which I for her to gather want, among those
(Among the flowers in that valley, the flowers which I want to gather for her, among those)

'myrt'əntsvaegən, diː lɪç liːɐ̯ 'flɛçt'ən vɪl, bəˈʃvøːr ɪç dɪç, lɛɐ̯ˈʃaenʊŋ, laof,
Myrtenzweigen, die ich ihr flechten will, beschwör' ich dich, Erscheinung, auf,
myrtle sprigs, which I for her to entwine want, conjure I you, apparition: up
(myrtle sprigs which I want to entwine into a wreath for her, I conjure you, apparition: arise)

lʊnt' fɛɐ̯ˈvandlə dɪç! fɛɐ̯ˈvandlə dɪç, lɛɐ̯ˈʃaenʊŋ, lʊnt' veːɐ̯d e'doːnə zɛlpstʰ!
und verwand'le dich! Verwand'le dich, Erscheinung, und werd' Edone selbst!
and transform yourself! Transform yourself, apparition, and become Edone herself!

[This exquisite song exists in two authentic keys; Peters follows the original edition in B minor, the *Gesamtausgabe* an earlier manuscript in C minor. Schubert copied it out, in the latter key, for the songbook of Therese Grob, his first love. It is hard to imagine how Dietrich Fischer-Dieskau could write that the song portrays the thoughts of a young *lady* for her absent lover, when the pronoun "*ihr*" in two of the phrases makes it utterly clear that the words are those of a man!]

Edward see *Eine altschottische Ballade*

462

Eifersucht und Stolz see *Die schöne Müllerin*

ˈaɛnə ˈlaltˈʃɔtˈɪʃə baˈlaːdə
Eine altschottische Ballade
An Old Scottish Ballad

Op. 165, No. 5 [1827] (German translation by Johann Gottfried Herder)

daɛn ʃveːɐtˈ, viː lɪsts̱ fɔn bluːtˈ zoː roːtˈ, ˈleːdu̯artˈ, ˈleːdu̯artˈ,
Dein Schwert, wie ist's von Blut so rot, Eduard, Eduard,*
Your sword,   why is it with blood so red, Edward, Edward,
(Why is your sword so red with blood, Edward,)   [*Peters (in error):* **vom** (fɔm, from the) **Blut**]
         [**poem, translation, GA (2nd version) & Peters:* **Edward** (ˈlɛtˈvartˈ); *Schubert:* **Eduard**]

ʊntˈ   geːstˈ zoː ˈtʰrɑorɪç daːʔ loː! —ɪç haːpˈ gəˈʃlaːgən ˈmaɛnən ˈgaɛɐ tʰoːtˈ,
und   gehst so traurig da? O! —Ich hab' geschlagen meinen Geier tot,
and (you) walk so sadly   there? O! —I have struck   my   hawk dead,
(and why do you walk there so sadly? O! —I have killed my hawk,)

ˈmʊtˈɐ, ˈmʊtˈɐ, ʊnt das, das geːtˈ miːɐ naː, loː! —ˈdaɛnəs ˈgaɛɐs bluːtˈ
Mutter, Mutter, und das, das geht   mir nah'. O! — Deines Geiers Blut
Mother, Mother, and that, that grieves me. ...   O! —Your   hawk's blood
         [*1st version & Herder:* **Dein's** (daɛns); *"nahegehen"* = to grieve, to affect]

lɪstˈ nɪçtˈ zoː roːtˈ, ˈleːdu̯artˈ! maɛn zoːn, bəˈkʰɛn miːɐ fraɛ. loː!
ist nicht so rot, Eduard! Mein Sohn, bekenn' mir frei. O!
is   not so red, Edward! My   son,   confess to me freely. O!

—ɪç haːpˈ gəˈʃlaːgən maɛn ˈroːtˈrɔs tʰoːtˈ, ˈmʊtˈɐ, ʊntˈ s vaːɐ zoː ʃtˈɔlts ʊnt tʰrɔø.
—Ich hab' geschlagen mein Rotross tot, Mutter, und 's war so stolz und treu.
—I   have struck   my   red horse dead, Mother, and it was so proud and faithful.
(—I have killed my red-roan horse, Mother, and it was so proud and faithful.)

—daɛn rɔs vaːɐ/vaːr lalt ʊntˈ   hasts nɪçtˈ noːtˈ, dɪç drʏkˈtˈ laɛn ˈlandʁ ʃmɛrts.
—Dein Ross war   alt und   hast's nicht not, dich drückt ein andrer Schmerz.
—Your horse was   old and (you) have it not need, you presses an other pain.
(—Your horse was old and you have no need of it; another pain is afflicting you.)
         [*Herder:* **ein ander** (ˈlandɐ) **Schmerz**]

—ɪç haːpˈ gəˈʃlaːgən ˈmaɛnən ˈfaːtˈɐ tʰoːtˈ, ʊnt das, das kʰveːltˈ maɛn hɛrts!
—Ich hab' geschlagen meinen Vater tot, und das, das quält   mein Herz!
—I   have struck   my   father dead, and that, that torments my   heart!
(—I have killed my father, and that torments my heart!)

—ʊntˈ vas vɪrst duː nuːn lan diːɐ   tʰuːn?   [lan miːɐ]
—Und was wirst du nun an dir   tun? [*Peters (error):* **an mir**]
—And what will   you now to yourself do?   [to me]
(—And what penance will you now do?)

maɛn zoːn, das ˈzaːgə miːɐ.   [maɛn zoːn, bəˈkʰɛn miːɐ meːɐ.]
Mein Sohn, das sage mir. [*GA, from Herder:* **Mein Sohn, bekenn' mir   mehr.**]
My   son, that tell me.   [My   son,   confess to me more.]
(My son, tell me that.)

—ɑ͜of ˈleːɐ̯dən zɔl mɑ͜en fuːs nɪçtˈ ruːn, vɪl ˈvandɐn ˈlyːbɐs meːɐ̯.　　[ˈlyːbɐ]
—**Auf Erden soll mein Fuss nicht ruhn, will wandern übers Meer.** [*Herder:* **über**]
—On earth　shall my　foot not　rest, (I) want to wander over the sea.
(—My foot shall not rest upon the earth; I will wander over the sea.)

—ʊntˈ vas zɔl ˈveːɐ̯dən dɑ͜en hoːf　　ʊntˈ hal, zoː ˈhɛrlɪç zɔnstˈ　　ʊntˈ ʃøːn?
—**Und was soll werden dein Hof　　und Hall, so herrlich sonst　　und schön?**
—And what shall become your court-yard and hall, so splendid otherwise and beautiful?
(—And what shall become of your country house, till now so splendid and beautiful?)

—ax, ˈɪmɐ ʃtˈeːs ʊntˈ zɪŋkˈ ʊntˈ fal!
—**Ach, immer steh's und sink' und fall'!**
—Ah,　always stand it and sink　and fall!
(—Ah, for all I care it can stand or sink and fall!)

ɪç veːɐ̯tˈ ɛs ˈnɪmɐ　zeːn!　　　　　　　　　　[makˈ niː　ɛs ˈviːdɐ zeːn!]
Ich werd' es nimmer sehn! [*GA, from Herder's last version:* **Mag nie　es wieder sehn!**]
I　shall it never　see!　　　　　　　　[(I) want never it again　to see!]
(I shall never see it!)　　　　　　　　　　[[(I never want to see it again!)]

—ʊntˈ vas zɔl ˈveːɐ̯dən dɑ͜en vɑ͜epˈ ʊntˈ kʰɪntˈ vɛn duː geːstˈ ˈlyːbɐs　meːɐ̯?　[ˈlyːbɐ]
—**Und was soll werden dein Weib und Kind wenn du gehst übers Meer?** [*H:* **über**]
—And what shall become your wife and child when you go　over the sea?
(—And what shall become of your wife and child when you go over the sea?)

—di vɛltˈ ˈɪstˈ groːs, las ziː ˈbɛtˈəln drɪn, ˈɪç zeː ziː　ˈnɪmɐmeːɐ̯!
—**Die Welt ist gross, lass sie betteln drin, ich seh' sie nimmermehr!**
—The world is　big,　let them beg　in it, I　see them nevermore!
(—The world is big; let them go begging in it. I shall never see them again!)

—ʊntˈ vas zɔl ˈdɑ͜enə ˈmʊtˈɐ tʰuːn? mɑ͜en zoːn, das ˈzaːgə miːɐ̯!
—**Und was soll deine Mutter tun? Mein Sohn, das sage mir!**
—And what shall your mother do? My　son,　that tell　me!
(—And what shall your mother do? My son, tell me that!)

—deːɐ̯ fluːx deːɐ̯ hœlə zɔl lɑ͜of lɔ͜øç ruːn, ˈmʊtˈɐ, ˈmʊtˈɐ,
—**Der Fluch der Hölle soll auf Euch ruhn, Mutter, Mutter,**
—The curse of the hell　shall upon you rest, Mother, Mother,
(—May the curse of hell rest upon you, Mother,)

dɛn liːɐ̯/liːr, liːɐ̯ ˈriːtˈəts　　miːɐ̯. loː!
denn Ihr,　Ihr rietet's　mir. O!
for　you,　you counseled it to me. O!
(for it was you who told me to do it. O!)

[Schubert wrote the name as "Eduard"; the publishers changed the spelling to conform to the poem. His first version was conceived as a solo song; his second as a dialogue between a female and a male singer. Carl Loewe and Johannes Brahms also set this famous ballad, which derives from Bishop Percy's *Reliques of Ancient English Poetry*, published in 1765. It is the task of the singers to vary the dramatic expression appropriately in this simple but effective strophic ballad.]

'aenə 'laeçənfant'a'ziː
Eine Leichenphantasie
A Funereal Fantasy

Posthumously published [composed 1811] (poem by Friedrich von Schiller)

mɪt' lɛɐ̯'ʃt'ɔrbnəm 'ʃaenən   ʃt'eːt deːɐ̯ moːnt' lɑof 't^hoːt'ənʃt'ɪlən 'haenən,
Mit erstorbnem Scheinen steht der Mond auf totenstillen Hainen,
With died away   shining   stands the moon on   dead-still   groves,
(With its light nearly extinct, the moon hovers above deathly still groves;)

'zɔøftsənt' ʃt'raeft deːɐ̯ 'naxt'gaest dʊrç   di lʊft' — 'neːbəlvɔlk'ən 'ʃɑoɐn,
seufzend streift der Nachtgeist durch die Luft — Nebelwolken schauern,
sighing   streaks the night- spirit through the air —   mist- clouds shiver,
(sighing, a nocturnal ghost streaks though the air — the clouds of mist quiver at its passing;)
                                                  [*poem:* **Seufzend streicht** (ʃt'raeçt, moves quickly past)]

'ʃt'ɛrnə 't^hrɑoɐn blaeç hɛ'rap', viː 'lamp'ən lɪn deːɐ̯ grʊft^h. glaeç gə'ʃp'ɛnst'ɐn, ʃt'ʊm lʊnt'
Sterne trauern bleich herab, wie Lampen in der Gruft. Gleich Gespenstern, stumm und
stars   mourn palely down, like lamps in the tomb. Like   ghosts,   silent and
(pale stars shine down mournfully, like lamps in a tomb. Like ghosts, silent and)

hoːl   lʊnt' 'haːgɐ, tsiːt'   lɪn 'ʃvartsəm   't^hoːt'ənp^hɔmp'ə dɔrt' laen gə'vɪməl
hohl   und hager, zieht in schwarzem Totenpompe   dort ein Gewimmel
hollow and gaunt, moves in black   funeral pomp   there a   crowd
(hollow and gaunt, a crowd in black funeral pomp is proceeding there)

naːx   dem 'laeçənlaːgɐ(r) 'lʊntɐm 'ʃɑoɐfloːɐ̯   deːɐ̯ 'graːp'naxt' fɔrt^h.
nach   dem Leichenlager unterm Schauerflor der   Grabnacht fort.
toward the graveyard   beneath horror- crape of the grave-night forth.
(on its way toward the graveyard, beneath the mourning veil of the burial night.)

'tsɪt'ɐnt'   lan deːɐ̯ 'k^hrʏk'ə, veːɐ̯ mɪt 'dyːst'ɐm, 'rʏkgəzʊŋk'nəm 'blɪk'ə.
Zitternd   an der Krücke, wer mit düsterm, rückgesunknem Blicke,
Trembling at the   crutch,   who with gloomy,   back-sunken   gaze,
(Who is that, who, trembling on his crutch, with gloomy, backward-sunken gaze,)

'lɑosgəgɔsən lɪn laen 'hɔølɛnt' lax, ʃveːɐ̯ gə'nɛk't' fɔm   'laezɐnən gə'ʃɪk'ə,
ausgegossen in ein heulend Ach, schwer geneckt vom   eisernen Geschicke,
poured out into a   howling moan, heavily tormented by the iron   fate,
(his soul poured out in a howl of misery, cruelly tormented by an iron fate,)

ʃvaŋk't dem 'ʃt'ʊmgət^hraːgnən 'zargə naːx? flɔs   lɛs 'fat'ɐ fɔn dɛs 'jʏŋlɪŋs 'lɪp'ə?
schwankt dem stummgetragnen Sarge nach? floss   es "Vater" von des Jünglings Lippe?
totters   the silently carried   coffin after? Flowed it "Father" from the youth's   lip?
(is tottering after the silently carried coffin? Did the word "Father" flow from the youth's lips?)

'nasə 'ʃɑoɐ 'ʃɑoɐn 'fʏrçt'ɐlɪç dʊrç zaen 'graːmgəʃmɔltsənəs gə'rɪp'ə, 'zaenə
Nasse Schauer schauern fürchterlich durch sein gramgeschmolzenes Geripp, seine
Damp shudders shiver   frightfully   through his   grief-melted   frame,   his

'zɪlbɐha:rə 'bɔɡˀmən zɪç.　　'lɑofgərisən 'zɑenə 'fɔɡɐvundə!
Silberhaare bäumen sich.　　Aufgerissen seine Feuerwunde!
silver hairs rear　　themselves. Ripped open his　　fire- wounds!
(silver hair stands on end. His burning wounds are torn open!)

dʊrç　di 'ze:lə 'hœlənʃmɛrts!　'fa:tˀɐ flɔs　lɛs fɔn dɛs 'jʏŋlɪŋs　'mʊndə,
Durch　die Seele Höllenschmerz! "Vater" floss　es von des Jünglings Munde,
Through the soul　hellish pain!　　"Father" flowed it from the youth's　mouth,
(Hellish pain shoots through his soul! The word "Father"flowed from the dead boy's mouth,)

zo:n　gə'lɪspˀəltˀ hat das 'fa:tˀɐhɛrts.　'lɑeskʰaltˀ li:kˀtˀ le:ɐ hi:ɐ/hi:r lɪm　'tʰu:xə, lʊnt dɑen
"Sohn" gelispelt hat das Vaterherz. Eiskalt liegt er hier　im　Tuche, und dein
"Son," whispered has the father-heart. Ice-cold lies　he　here　in the shroud, and your
("Son," whispered the father's heart. Ice-cold he lies here in the shroud, and your)

tʰrɑom, zo: 'gɔldən lɑenstˀ, zo: zy:s!　zy:s lʊntˀ 'gɔldən, 'fa:tˀɐ, di:ɐ　tsʊm 'flu:xə!
Traum, so golden einst,　so süss! Süss und golden, Vater, dir　zum Fluche!
dream, so golden once,　so sweet! Sweet and golden, father, for you to the curse!
(dream, once so golden, so sweet! Sweet and golden, father, now turned for you into a curse!)

'lɑeskʰaltˀ li:kˀtˀ le:ɐ hi:ɐ/hi:r lɪm　'tʰu:xə, 'dɑenə 'vɔnə,　lʊnt dɑen pʰara'di:s!
Eiskalt liegt er hier　im　Tuche, deine Wonne, und dein Paradies!
Ice-cold lies　he　here　in the shroud, your　joy　and your paradise!
(Ice-cold he lies here in the shroud, your joy and your paradise!)

mɪltˀ, vi: lʊm've:tˀ　fɔn le'ly:zi̯ʊms̩lʏftˀən, vi:, lɑos lɑo'ro:ras lʊm'larmʊŋ gə'ʃlʏpftʰ,
Mild, wie umweht　von Elysiumslüften, wie, aus　Auroras Umarmung geschlüpft,
Gentle, as　about-wafted　by Elysian breezes, as,　out of Aurora's embrace　slipped,
(Gently, as if caressed by Elysian breezes, as if, having just slipped out of Aurora's embrace,)

'hɪmlɪʃ　lʊm'gʏrtˀətˀ mɪtˀ 'ro:zɪçtˀən 'dʏftˀən,　'flo:ras zo:n 'ly:bɐ das 'blu:mənfɛltˀ hʏpftʰ,
himmlisch umgürtet　mit rosigten Düften,　Florens Sohn über das Blumenfeld hüpft,
celestially girded　with roseate　fragrances, Flora's son　over the flower- field leaps,
(celestially girded with roseate fragrances, Flora's son were leaping about in a field of flowers,)

flo:kˀ leɐ/le:r lɑen'he:ɐ lɑof den 'laxəndən 'vi:zən, 'na:xgəʃpˀi:gəltˀ fɔn 'zɪlbɐnɐ flu:tʰ,
flog er　einher　auf den lachenden Wiesen, nachgespiegelt von silberner Flut,
flew he　along　on the laughing　meadow, reflected　by silver　waters,
(he flew over the smiling meadow, mirrored in silver waters,)

'vɔlʊstˀflamən　lɛntˀ'ʃpˀry:tˀən　den 'kʰʏsən, 'ja:kˀtˀən di 'mɛ:tˀçən lɪn 'li:bəndə glu:tʰ.
Wollustflammen entsprühten　den Küssen, jagten die Mädchen in liebende Glut.
voluptuous flames sprayed out from the kisses, drove　the girls　into loving　fire.
(flames of sensual pleasure sprang from his kisses and drove the girls to burning passion.)

'mu:tˀɪç ʃpˀraŋ le:ɐ/le:r lɪm　gə'vy:lə de:ɐ 'mɛnʃən,　vi: lɑen 'ju:gəntˀlɪç re:;
Mutig sprang er　im Gewühle der　Menschen, wie ein　jugendlich Reh;
Bravely leapt he　in the throng　of the people,　like a　youthful　deer;
(Bravely he leapt about among masses of people, like a young deer;)

　　　[*poem:* **wie auf Gebirgen** (vi: lɑof gə'bɪrgən, as on mountains) **ein jugendlich Reh**]

466

ˈhɪməlʊm   floːkˈ leːɐ̯/leːr ɪn ˈʃvaɛ̯fəndən   ˈvʏnʃən,   hoːx viː deːɐ̯/deːr ˈlaːdlɐ
himmelum   flog er   in schweifenden Wünschen, hoch wie der   Adler
around heaven flew he   in roving   wishes,   high as the   eagle
(he flew around heaven with soaring desires, high as the eagle)

[*poem:* **die** (diː, the—plural) **Adler** (eagles)]

ɪn ˈvɔlkˈɪçtˈɐ høːˑ;   ʃtˈɔlts viː di ˈrɔsə zɪç   ʃtˈrɔɔ̯bən ʊntˈ ˈʃɔɔ̯mən, ˈvɛrfən
in wolkigter Höh'; stolz   wie die Rosse sich   sträuben und schäumen, werfen
in clouded   heights; proudly as the horses themselves rear up and foam,   toss
(in cloudy heights; proudly, as horses rear up and foam, toss)

ɪm ˈʃtʏrmə di ˈmɛːnən ʊmˈheːɐ̯, ˈkʰøːnɪkˈlɪç ˈviːdɐ den ˈtsyːɡəl zɪç   ˈbɔɔ̯mən,
im Sturme die Mähnen umher, königlich wider den Zügel sich   bäumen,
in the storm   the manes about,   regally   against the reins   themselves stand on hind legs,
(their manes about in the storm, rise up on their hind legs, regally resisting the reins,)

tʰraːtˈ   leːɐ̯ foːɐ̯ ˈskˈlaːfən ʊntˈ ˈfʏrstˈən daˈheːɐ̯. ˈhaɛ̯tˈɐ, viː ˈfryːlɪŋstʰaːkˈ,
trat   er vor   Sklaven und Fürsten daher. Heiter, wie Frühlingstag,
stepped he before slaves   and princes along. Serene, as spring   day,
(he went his way before slaves and princes. As serenely as a spring day)

ʃvantˈ liːm   das ˈleːbən, floːkˈ liːm   foˈryːbɐ(r) ɪn ˈhɛspˈerʊs glants,
schwand ihm   das Leben, flog ihm   vorüber in Hesperus' Glanz,
vanished for him the life,   flew for him past   in Herperus's glitter,
(life slipped by for him, flew by for him in the glitter of Hesperus,)

ˈkʰlaːɡən lɛɐ̯ˈtʰrɛŋkˈtˈ leːɐ̯/leːr ɪm ˈɡɔldə deːɐ̯ ˈreːbən, ˈʃmɛrtsən fɛɐ̯ˈhypftˈ leːɐ̯/leːr
Klagen   ertränkt er   im Golde der Reben, Schmerzen verhüpft' er
Complaints drowned he   in the gold of the vines, sorrows   hopped away he
(he drowned complaints in the gold of the vine, he danced away his sorrows)

ɪm ˈvɪrbəlndən tʰants. ˈvɛltˈən ˈʃliːfən ɪm ˈhɛrlɪçən ˈjʊŋən,
im wirbelnden Tanz. Welten schliefen im herrlichen Jungen,
in the whirling   dance. Worlds slept   in the splendid young man,
(in a whirling dance. Whole worlds lay dormant in that splendid young man,)

ha! vɛn leːɐ̯/leːr ˈlaɛ̯nstˈən tsʊm man   ɡəˈraɛ̯ftʰ— ˈfrɔɔ̯ə dɪç,   ˈfaːtˈɐ(r), ɪm
Ha! wenn er   einsten zum Mann   gereift— Freue dich,   Vater,   im
Ah! when he   one day   to the man (has) matured— Gladden yourself, father, in the
(Ah, when he has matured one day to manhood... Rejoice, father, in the) [*poem:* **Manne** (ˈmanə)]

ˈhɛrlɪçən ˈjʊŋən, vɛn laɛ̯nst di ˈʃlaːfəndən ˈkʰaɛ̯mə   ɡəˈraɛ̯ftʰ! naɛ̯n dɔx, ˈfaːtˈɐ—
herrlichen Jungen, wenn einst die schlafenden Keime   gereift! Nein doch, Vater—
splendid   youth,   when once the sleeping   seeds (have) ripened! No   though, father—
(splendid young man, when once the sleeping seeds have ripened! But no, father—)

hɔrç! di ˈkʰɪrçhoːftʰyːrə ˈbraɔ̯zətʰ, ʊnt di ˈleːɐ̯nən ˈlaŋəl ˈkʰlɪrən lɔof—
Horch! Die Kirchhoftüre   brauset, und die eh'rnen Angel klirren auf—
Hark! The churchyard door booms, and the brass   hinges creak open—

viːs hɪˈnaɛn ɪns ˈgraːpˈgəvœlbə ˈgraʊozətʰ!— naɛn dɔx, las den ˈtʰreːnən ˈliːrən laʊof!
Wie's hinein ins Grabgewölbe grauset!— Nein doch, lass den Tränen ihren Lauf!
How it inside into the tomb shudders!—No though, let the tears their course!
(How one shudders to enter the tomb! — But no, let the tears flow!)

geː, duː ˈhɔldɐ, geː ɪm ˈpfaːdə deːɐ̯ ˈzɔnə ˈfrɔødɪç ˈvaɛtˈɐ deːɐ̯ fɔlˈlɛndʊŋ tsuː,
Geh, du Holder, geh im Pfade der Sonne freudig weiter der Vollendung zu,
Go, you gracious one, go in the path of the sun joyfully farther the perfection to,
(Go, gracious youth, go in the path of the sun, joyfully further toward perfection,)

[*poem:* **im Pfad** (pfaːt)]

ˈlœʃə nuːn den ˈleːdlən dʊrstˈ naːx ˈvɔnə,
lösche nun den edlen Durst nach Wonne,
quench now the noble thirst for ecstasy,

ˈgraːmlɛntˈbʊndnɐ, ɪn ˈvalhalas ruː! ˈviːdɐzeːn — ˈhɪmlɪʃɐ gəˈdaŋkˈə!
Gramentbundner, in Walhallas Ruh! Wiedersehn — himmlischer Gedanke!
(from) grief-released, in Valhalla's rest! To see again — heavenly thought!
(released from grief, rest in the peace of Valhalla! Reunion — heavenly thought!)

[*poem:* **Wiedersehen** (ˈviːdɐzeːən), *for the rhythm*]

ˈviːdɐzeːən dɔrtˈ lan ˈleːdəns tʰoːɐ̯! hɔrç! deːɐ̯ zarkˈ fɛɐ̯ˈzɪŋkˈtˈ mɪt ˈdʊmpfəm,
Wiedersehen dort an Edens Tor! Horch! der Sarg versinkt mit dumpfem,
to see again there at Eden's gate! Hark! The coffin sinks with dull,
(to see each other again there at the gates of Eden! Hark! The coffin is lowered with dull,)

[*Schiller:* **dumpfigem** (musty), *Schubert* (first time only): **dumpfem** (dull or musty)]

mɪt ˈdʊmpfɪgəm gəˈʃvaŋkˈə, ˈvɪmɐntˈ ʃnʊrt das ˈtʰoːtˈənzaɛl lɛmˈpʰoːɐ̯!
mit dumpfigem Geschwanke, wimmernd schnurrt das Totenseil empor!
with musty rocking, whining whirs the dead- rope upwards!
(musty rocking, the ropes whirr upwards, whining!)

daː viːɐ̯ ˈtʰrʊŋkˈən lʊm laɛˈnandɐ ˈrɔltˈən, ˈlɪpˈən ˈʃviːgən lʊnt das ˈlaʊogə ʃpraːx—
Da wir trunken um einander rollten, Lippen schwiegen und das Auge sprach —
When we drunkenly around each other rolled, lips were silent and the eye spoke —
(When we rolled over each other, intoxicated, our lips were silent but our eyes spoke:)

ˈhaltˈətˈ! daː viːɐ̯ ˈboːshaftˈ ˈgrɔltˈən — ˈlaːbɐ ˈtʰreːnən ˈʃtˈyrtstˈən ˈvɛrmɐ naːx.
Haltet! da wir boshaft grollten — aber Tränen stürzten wärmer nach.
Stop! when we maliciously were resentful — but tears fell warmer afterwards.
("Stop!" when we maliciously harbored resentment... but our tears fell more warmly afterwards.)

Mit erstorbnem Scheinen... Lampen in der Gruft. [*repeated in both poem and song*]

ˈdʊmpfɪç ˈʃɔlɐts ˈlyːbɐm zarkˈ tsʊm ˈhuːgəl. loː
Dumpfig schollert's überm Sarg zum Hügel. O
Musty tumbles it over the coffin to the grave mound. Oh
(Musty clods tumble down with dull thuds, as a mound is piled up over the coffin. Oh)

lʊm ˈleːɐ̯tˈbals ˈʃɛtsə nuːɐ̯ nɔx ˈlaɛnən blɪkʰ! ʃtˈar lʊntˈ ˈleːvɪç ʃliːst dɛs ˈgraːbəs ˈriːgəl,
um Erdballs Schätze nur noch einen Blick! Starr und ewig schliesst des Grabes Riegel,
for earth's treasures only still one look! Rigid and eternal closes the grave's bolt,
(for one more glimpse of the earth's treasures! The bolts of the grave close rigidly and eternally;)

'dʊmpfɐ 'ʃɔlɐts   'lyːbɐm zark' t͡sʊm 'hyːgəl,   'nɪmɐ   gip't das graːp' t͡su'rʏkʰ.
dumpfer schollert's überm Sarg zum Hügel,   nimmer gibt das Grab zurück.
duller   thuds   it over the coffin to the grave mound, never   gives the grave back.
(the thudding is duller now in the mound over the coffin; the grave never gives back its own.)

[Schiller wrote the poem after the death of his friend, August von Hoven. Schubert was fourteen when he composed the striking music, reveling in the macabre details like any young boy, but revealing a depth of compassionate empathy with father, son, and friend, that far transcends the more gruesome elements. The song is eighteen pages long. (Aurora was the goddess of the dawn, Flora of flowers; Elysium, the Grecian version of paradise; Hesperus, the evening star; Valhalla is the name of the sky-castle of the Teutonic gods, where heroes were welcomed after death.)]

'aɛnzaːmkʰaetʰ / giːp' miːɐ̯ di 'fʏlə deːɐ̯ 'laenzaːmkʰaetʰ
Einsamkeit / Gib mir die Fülle der Einsamkeit
Solitude / Give Me the Fullness of Solitude

Posthumously published [composed 1818] (poem by Johann Mayrhofer)

giːp' miːɐ̯ di 'fʏlə   deːɐ̯/deːr 'laenzaːmkʰaetʰ. lɪm   tʰaːl, fɔn 'blyːt'ən lyːbɐʃnaetʰ,
"Gib mir die Fülle der   Einsamkeit." Im   Tal, von Blüten überschneit,
"Give me the fullness of the   solitude."   In the valley, by blossoms over-snowed,
("Give me a full experience of solitude." In the valley, covered with snowy blossoms,)

daː raːk't' laen doːm,   lʊnt' neːbən'bae lɪn 'hoːəm 'ʃt'iːlə/st'iːlə di lap't'ʰaeː:
da ragt ein Dom,   und nebenbei in hohem Stile   die Abtei:
there towers a   cathedral, and beside it   in high   style   the abbey:
(a cathedral towers over its surroundings, and next to it is an abbey, in "high style" architecture:)

viː liːɐ̯ bə'grʏndɐ, frɔm lʊnt' ʃt'ɪl, deːɐ̯ 'myːdən   'haːfən lʊnt' la'zyːl.
wie ihr Begründer, fromm und still, der Müden   Hafen und Asyl.
like its founder,   devout and quiet, the weary ones' haven and refuge.
(devout and quiet like its founder, a haven and a refuge for the weary.)

hiːɐ̯ kʰyːlt' mɪt' 'haelɪgɐ bə'tʰaoʊŋ, deːɐ̯ niː   fɛɐ̯'ziːgəndən — bə'ʃaoʊŋ.
Hier kühlt mit heiliger Betauung, der nie   versiegenden — Beschauung.
Here cools with holy   bedewing, the never drying up —   contemplation.
(Here contemplation refreshes with a holy dew that is inexhaustible.) [(*the wording of the poem*)]
["**der nie versiegenden**" *refers to* "**Betauung**"]

[di niː   fɛɐ̯'ziːgəndə]
[*GA:* **Hier kühlt...   die nie   versiegende Beschauung.**]
[here refreshes...the never depletive   contemplation.]
(Here an inexhaustible contemplation refreshes with a holy dew. [*not the sense of the poem*])
["**die nie versiegende**" *modifies* "**Beschauung**"]

dɔx den 'frɪʃən   'jʏŋlɪŋ   'kʰveːlən zɛlpst' lɪn 'gɔt'gəvaet'ən 't͡sɛlən 'bɪldɐ,
Doch den frischen Jüngling   quälen selbst in gottgeweihten Zellen Bilder,
But the fresh   youth [obj.] torment, even   in God-consecrated cells, images [subj.],
(But even in cells consecrated to God, images torment the fresh-blooded youth,)

'foːørɪgɐ   feɐ̯'jʏŋtʰ; lʊnt' laen 'vɪldɐ ʃt'roːm ɛnt'ʃp'rɪŋt' laos deːɐ̯ brʊst,
feuriger   verjüngt; und ein wilder Strom entspringt aus der Brust,
more ardently rejuvenated; and a   wild   torrent streams forth from the breast,
(ever more ardently regenerated; and a wild torrent streams forth from his breast,)

diː   leːɐ̯/leːr lʊm'dɛmtʰː lʊnt' lɪn 'laenəm 'laogənblɪk' lɪst deːɐ̯ 'ruːə   'tsaːɐ̯t'əs glʏk'
die   er   umdämmt: und in einem Augenblick ist der Ruhe   zartes Glück
which he   dams up: and in one   moment   is the tranquility's delicate happiness
(which he tries to suppress: and in one moment the delicate happiness of tranquility)

fɔn den 'vɛlən 'vɛkgəʃvɛmtʰ.   giːp' miːɐ̯ di 'fʏlə   deːɐ̯ 'tʰɛːt'ɪçkʰaetʰ.
von den Wellen weggeschwemmt. "Gib mir die Fülle der   Tätigkeit."
by the waves washed away.   "Give me the fullness of the activity."
(is swept away by the waves. "Give me a full experience of the active life.")

'mɛnʃən 'vɪməln   vaet' lʊnt' braet', 'vaːgən 'kʰrɔøtsən zɪç   lʊnt' 'ʃt'ɔøbən,
Menschen wimmeln weit und breit, Wagen kreuzen sich   und stäuben,
People   swarm   far and wide, wagons cross   each other and scatter dust,
(People are swarming everywhere, wagons cross in front of each other and scatter dust,)

'kʰɔøfɐ zɪç   lʊm 'leːdən 'tʰraebən, 'roːt'əs gɔlt' lʊnt' 'helɐ ʃt'aen lɔk't di
Käufer sich   um   Läden treiben, rotes Gold und heller Stein lockt die
Buyers themselves around shops drive,   red gold and bright stone lures the
(Customers crowd around the shops, red gold and bright gems lure the)

'tsøːgɐndən hɪ'naen; lʊnt' lɛɐ̯'zats   fyːɐ̯ 'landəsgryːnə 'biːt'ən 'mask'ənbal lʊnt' 'byːnə.
Zögernden hinein; und Ersatz   für Landesgrüne bieten Maskenball und Bühne.
hesitating inside; and substitute for country-green offer masked ball and stage.
(hesitant inside; and masked balls and the theater offer a substitute for the green countryside.)

dɔx lɪn 'p'raŋəndən p'a'lɛst'ən, bae deːɐ̯ 'frɔødə   'laot'ən 'fɛst'ən,
Doch in prangenden Palästen, bei der Freude   lauten Festen,
But in resplendent palaces,   at the pleasure's loud festivities,
(But in resplendent palaces, at loud festivities devoted to pleasure,)

ʃp'riːst' lɛm'p'oːɐ̯ deːɐ̯ 'ʃveːɐ̯muːt' 'bluːmə, zɛŋk't' liːɐ̯ haop't tsʊm 'haelɪçt'uːmə 'zaenɐ
spriesst empor der Schwermut Blume, senkt ihr Haupt zum Heiligtume seiner
sprouts up   the   melancholy's flower, lowers its head to the sanctuary   of its
(the flower of melancholy sprouts up, bends its head toward the sanctuary of its)

'juːgənt' 'lʊnʃʊlt'lʊstʰ,   tsuː dem 'blaoən 'hɪrt'ənlant' lʊnt deːɐ̯ 'lɪçt'ən 'kʰvɛlə rant'.
Jugend Unschuldlust,   zu dem blauen Hirtenland und der lichten Quelle Rand.
youth's innocence-pleasure, to the blue   shepherd land and the light   spring's edge,
(innocent youthful pleasure, toward the blue land of shepherds and the edge of the bright spring,)

ax! das leːɐ̯ hɪn'vɛk gə'mʊstʰ! giːp' miːɐ̯ das glʏk'   deːɐ̯ gə'zɛlɪçkʰaetʰ.
Ach! dass er hinweg gemusst! "Gib mir das Glück   der Geselligkeit."
Ah! that he away had to! "Give me the happiness of good fellowship."
(Alas, that he had to leave all that! "Give me the happiness of good fellowship.")

gə'nɔsən, 'frɔønt'lɪç 'langəraet deːɐ̯ 'tʰaːfəl, 'ʃt'ɪmən 'kʰoːrʊs lan
Genossen, freundlich angereiht der Tafel, stimmen Chorus an
Comrades, friendlily seated   at the table, strike   chorus up
(Comrades, seated in friendship at the table, strike up a chorus)

470

ʊntˈ ˈleːbənən di ˈfɛlzənbaːn.   zoː geːts ʦʊm ˈʃøːnən ˈhyːgəlkʰranʦ
und ebenen die Felsenbahn. So geht's zum schönen Hügelkranz
and   smooth the rock-pathway. So goes it to the beautiful hill- wreath
(and smooth life's rocky path. So they go up to the beautiful wreath of hills)

ʊntˈ ˈlapˈverʦ   ʦuː dɛs ʃtˈroːməs tʰanʦ; ʊntˈ ˈlɪmɐ   meːɐ̯
und abwärts   zu des Stromes Tanz; und immer mehr
and downwards to the stream's dance; and ever   more
(and down to the dancing stream; and, ever more,)

bəˈfɛstˈɪgətˈ zɪç ˈna_egʊŋ   mɪt tʰrɔø̯ɐ ˈkʰrɛftˈɪgɐ fɛɐ̯ˈʦvaegʊŋ.
befestiget   sich Neigung   mit treuer kräftiger Verzweigung.
strengthens itself inclination with faithful powerful branching.
(liking is strengthened with a powerful branching out of mutual interests and faithful bonding.)

dɔx,   vɛn di gəˈnɔsən ˈʃiːdən,   ˈɪsʦ gəˈtʰaːn ʊm ˈʦaenən ˈfriːdən.
Doch, wenn die Genossen schieden, ist's getan um seinen Frieden.
But,   when the comrades parted,   is it done with his   peace.
(But when comrades have parted his peace is gone.)
    [*Peters:* **wenn die Zeitgenossen** (ˈʦaetˈgənɔsən, contemporaries) **schieden** (*music altered*)]

iːn bəˈveːkˈt deːɐ̯ ˈzeːnzʊxtˈ ʃmɛrʦ, ʊntˈ leːɐ̯ ˈʃao̯ətˈ ˈhiməlverʦː   das gəˈʃtˈɪrn
Ihn bewegt der Sehnsucht Schmerz, und er schauet himmelwärts: das Gestirn
Him moves the yearning's pain,   and he looks   heavenwards: the constellation
(the pain of yearning moves him, and he looks heavenwards: the constellation)

deːɐ̯ ˈliːbə ʃtˈraːltʰ. ˈliːbə— ruːft di ˈlao̯ə lʊftʰ, ˈliːbə— ˈlaːtˈmət ˈbluːməndʊftʰ,
der Liebe strahlt. Liebe—ruft die laue Luft, Liebe—atmet Blumenduft,
of the love   radiates. Love— calls the balmy air, love— breathes flower- fragrance,
(of love is shining. The warm air cries out: "Love," the fragrance of flowers breathes out love,)

ʊntˈ zaen ˈɪnrəs   ˈliːbə haltʰ.   giːp miːɐ̯ di ˈfʏlə   deːɐ̯ ˈzeːlɪçkʰaetʰ!
und sein Innres   Liebe hallt. "Gib mir die Fülle   der Seligkeit!"
and his inner being love echoes. "Give me the fullness of the bliss!"
(and his inner being reverberates "love." "Give me a full experience of bliss!")

nuːn ˈvandəltˈ leːɐ̯/leːr ɪn tʰrʊŋkˈənhaetˈ lan ˈliːrɐ hantˈ ɪn ˈʃvaegəndən   gəˈʃpˈrɛçən,
Nun wandelt er   in Trunkenheit an ihrer Hand in schweigenden Gesprächen,
Now wanders he   in intoxication   at her hand in silent   conversations,
(Now he wanders with her, hand in hand, in silent conversation,)

ɪm ˈbuːxəngaŋ,   lan ˈvaesən ˈbɛçən, ʊntˈ mʊs leːɐ̯/leːr lao̯x dʊrç vyːstˈəˈnaeən,
im Buchengang,   an weissen Bächen, und muss er   auch durch Wüsteneien,
in the beach-tree walk, at white   brooks, and must he   also through wildernesses,
(along the beach-tree walk, by foaming brooks; and if he must pass through wildernesses,)

liːm   ˈlɔø̯çtˈətˈ ˈzyːsɐ(r) ˈlao̯gən ʃaen;   ʊntˈ ɪn deːɐ̯ ˈfaentˈlɪçstˈən fɛɐ̯ˈvɪrʊŋ
ihm   leuchtet süsser Augen Schein; und in der feindlichsten Verwirrung
for him shines   sweet eyes'   light;   and in the most hostile confusion
(the light of her sweet eyes will shine for him; and in the most hostile confusion)
    [*GA:* **ihm   leuchtet süsser Augenschein**]
       [for him shines   sweet eye- light (*same meaning, but not the syntax of the poem*)]

fɛɐ̯'tʰrɑoət‘ leːɐ̯ deːɐ̯ 'hɔldən 'fyːrʊŋ. dɔx di 'zɛrgə 'groːsɐ(r) 'laːnən,
vertrauet er der holden Führung. Doch die Särge grosser Ahnen,
trusts he the gracious guidance. But the coffins of great forebears,
(he puts his trust in that gracious guidance. But the coffins of great forefathers,)

[*GA:* **vertrauet er der Holden Führung**]
[trusts he the gracious one's guidance]

'ziːgɐkʰroːnən, 'ʃt‘ʊrməsfaːnən 'lasən iːn nɪçt‘ 'fʏrdɐ ruːn: ʊnt‘ leːɐ̯ mʊs
Siegerkronen, Sturmesfahnen lassen ihn nicht fürder ruhn: und er muss
victor's crowns, storm- banners let him not further rest: and he must
(the crowns of victory, the banners of war, let him rest no more: and he must)

laen 'glaeçəs tʰuːn, ʊnt‘ vi zi: ʊn'ʃt‘ɛrp‘lɪç zaen. zi:, leːɐ̯ ʃt‘aek‘t‘ lɑofs
ein Gleiches tun, und wie sie unsterblich sein. Sieh, er steigt aufs
a similar thing do, and as they immortal be. See, he mounts onto the
(do the same, and become as immortal as they are. See, he mounts a)

'hoːə pfeːɐ̯t‘, ʃvɪŋt‘ ʊnt‘ pʰryːft das 'blaŋk‘ə ʃveːɐ̯t‘, 'raet‘ət‘ lɪn di ʃlaxt‘ hɪ'naen.
hohe Pferd, schwingt und prüft das blanke Schwert, reitet in die Schlacht hinein.
tall horse, swings and tests the shining sword, rides into the battle into.
(tall horse, swings and tests his shining sword, rides into battle.)

giːp‘ miːɐ̯ di 'fʏlə deːɐ̯ 'dyːst‘ɐkʰaetʰ, da: 'liːgən zi: lɪm 'bluːt‘ə hɪngə'ʃt‘rɔʉ̯tʰ, di
"Gib mir die Fülle der Düsterkeit." Da liegen sie im Blute hingestreut, die
"Give me the fullness of the gloom." There lie they in the blood scattered hence, the
("Give me the full experience of gloom." There they lie, scattered about in their blood, their)

[*GA:* **Düsterheit** ('dyːst‘ɐhaetʰ) = *Düsterkeit*]

'lɪp‘ə ʃt‘ar, das 'lɑogə vɪlt‘ gə'brɔxən, di: leːɐ̯st dem 'ʃrɛk‘ən tʰrɔts gə'ʃp‘rɔxən.
Lippe starr, das Auge wild gebrochen, die erst dem Schrecken Trotz gesprochen.
lip rigid, the eye wild broken, which just to the fear defiance (had) spoken.
(lips rigid, those eyes wild and dimmed that had just before expressed defiance to fear.)

kʰaen 'faːt‘ɐ kʰeːɐ̯t den 'zaenən meːɐ̯/meːr, ʊnt‘ 'haemvɛrts kʰeːɐ̯t‘ laen 'landɐ heːɐ̯;
Kein Vater kehrt den Seinen mehr, und heimwärts kehrt ein ander Heer;
No father returns to the his (family) more, and homewards turns a different army;
(No father will return to his family again, and a different army turns homewards;)

ʊnt 'deːnən kʰriːk‘ das 'tʰɔʉ̯ɐst‘ə gə'nɔmən, bə'gryːsən nuːn mɪt‘
und denen Krieg das Teuerste genommen, begrüssen nun mit
and those from whom war the dearest (has) taken, greet now with
(and those from whom war has taken their dearest possession now greet the survivors with)

'ʃmɛrtslɪçəm vɪl'kʰɔmən. zo: dɔʉ̯çt‘ liːm des 'faːt‘ɐlandəs 'vɛçt‘ɐ
schmerzlichem Willkommen. So däucht ihm des Vaterlandes Wächter
painful welcome. So seems to him the fatherland's guardian
(a painful welcome. So the guardian of the fatherland seems to him to be)

aen lɛɐ̯'grɪmt‘ɐ 'bryːdɐʃlɛçt‘ɐ, deːɐ̯ deːɐ̯ 'fraehaet‘ 'leːdəl guːtʰ dʏŋt‘ mɪt‘
ein ergrimmter Brüderschlächter, der der Freiheit edel Gut düngt mit
an angered brothers-butcher, who the freedom's noble good fertilizes with
(a furious butcher of his brother humans, who fertilizes the noble blessing of freedom with)

ˈroːtʼəm ˈmɛnʃənbluːtʰ.　ˈʊntʼ leːɐ fluːxt dem ˈtʰɔlən ruːm, ʊntʼ ˈtʰɑ̯ɔʃətʼ
rotem Menschenblut. Und er flucht dem tollen Ruhm, und tauschet
red　　　human　　blood. And he curses the　insane glory,　and　exchanges
(red human blood. And he curses insane glory, and trades)

ˈlɛrməndəs ɡəˈvyːl　mɪt dem ˈfɔrstʼə, ɡryːn ʊntʼ ˈkʰyːl, mɪt dem ˈziːdlɐleːbən　ʊm.
lärmendes Gewühl mit dem Forste, grün und kühl, mit dem Siedlerleben um.
noisy　　　tumult　for the　forest,　green and　cool,　for the　hermit's life ... .

[*"umtauschen"* = exchanges, trades]

　ɡiːpʼ miːɐ di ˈvaɛə　　deːɐ/deːr ˈlaɛnzaːmkʰaetʰ! dʊrç　ˈdɪçtʼə ˈtʰanəndʊŋkʼəlhaetʰ
"Gib mir die Weihe　　der　　Einsamkeit!" Durch　dichte Tannendunkelheit
"Give me　the consecration of the　solitude!"　　Through dense fir-tree darkness
("Give me the consecration of solitude!" Through the darkness of dense fir-trees)

drɪŋtʼ　　ˈzɔnənblɪkʼ　　nuːɐ halpʼ ʊntʼ halpʼ, ʊntʼ ˈfɛrbətʼ ˈnaːdəlʃɪçtʼən　falpʼ.
dringt　　Sonnenblick nur halb und halb, und färbet Nadelschichten falb.
penetrates sun-　　glance only half　and　half,　and　tints　needle-layers　pale yellow.
(the sun only half penetrates, and tints the layers of needles a pale yellow.)

deːɐ ˈkʰʊkʼʊkʼ　ruːftʼ ʔɑ̯ɔs ˈtsvaɛkɡəfleçtʰ, ʔan ˈɡrɑ̯ɔɐ ˈrɪndə　pʰɪkʼt deːɐ ʃpʼɛçtʰ,
Der Kuckuck ruft aus Zweiggeflecht, an grauer Rinde pickt der Specht,
The cuckoo　　calls from branch-mesh,　at　grey　　bark　pecks the woodpecker,
(The cuckoo calls from the interweaving branches, the woodpecker pecks at grey bark,)

ʊnt ˈdɔnɐnt　　ˈlyːbɐ ˈkʰlɪpʼənhɛmʊŋ　　lɛɐˈɡeːt dɛs ˈɡiːsbaxs　　　ˈkʰyːnə ˈʃtʼrøːmʊŋ.
und donnernd über Klippenhemmung ergeht des Giessbachs　　kühne Strömung.
and thundering over rock-　restraint　issues the mountain torrent's bold　stream.
(and the bold stream of a mountain torrent gushes, thundering, over the rocky barriers.)

vas　leːɐ ˈvynʃtʼə,　vas　leːɐ ˈliːpʼtʼə, liːn lɛɐˈfrɔɔtʼə, liːn bəˈtʰryːpʼtʼə,
Was er wünschte, was er liebte, ihn erfreute, ihn betrübte,
What he wished for, what he loved,　him pleased,　him troubled,
(What he wished for, what he loved, what pleased him, what troubled him—)

ʃveːpʼtʼ mɪtʼ ˈzanftʼɐ ˈʃvɛrmərɑ̯ɛ　viː lɪm　ˈlaːbəntʼroːtʼ foːɐˈbaɛ.
schwebt mit sanfter Schwärmerei wie im　Abendrot　vorbei.
floats　with gentle　rapture　　　as in the sunset　　by.
(all of that floats by with gentle rapture as at sunset.)

ˈjynlɪŋs　　ˈzeːnzʊxtʼ, ˈlaɛnzaːmkʰaetʼ, vɪrt　　dem　ˈɡraɛzən nuːn tsuˈtʰael,
Jünglings　Sehnsucht, Einsamkeit,　wird　　dem　Greisen nun zuteil,
young man's yearning,　solitude,　　becomes for the old man now lot,
(Solitude, which the young man had once yearned for, now becomes the old man's lot,)

ʊntʼ zaɛn ˈleːbən rɑɔ　ʊntʼ ʃtʼael ˈfyːɐtʼə dɔx　　tsʊr　ˈzeːlɪçkʰaetʰ.
und sein Leben rauh und steil führte doch　zur　Seligkeit.
and his　life,　rough and steel, led　　after all to the bliss.
(and his life, rough and arduous, has led him after all to bliss.)

[Schubert was very pleased with this composition and considered it his best up till then. Similar to Beethoven's *An die ferne Geliebte* in form, it is really a small song cycle. Schubert made many changes in the wording of his friend's poem, too numerous to indicate here (often those words of the published poem that differ from Schubert's text do not fit the music). The *Gesamtausgabe* includes a twelve-bar repeat that is omitted in the Peters edition.]

Einsamkeit / Wie eine trübe Wolke see *Winterreise*

'ɛləns 'leːɐ̯stʼɐ gəˈzaŋ / ˈrastʼə, ˈkʰriːgɐ! kʰriːkʼ lɪstʼ lɑos
Ellens erster Gesang / Raste, Krieger! Krieg ist aus
Ellen's First Song / Rest, Warrior! War is Over
(from Sir Walter Scott's *The Lady of the Lake*)

Op. 52, No. 1 [1825] (German translation by Adam Storck)

'rastʼə 'kʰriːgɐ! kʰriːkʼ lɪstʼ lɑos, ʃlaːf   den ʃlaːf, nɪçts   vɪrt dɪç 'vɛkʼən.
Raste, Krieger! Krieg ist aus, schlaf' den Schlaf, nichts wird dich wecken.
Rest, warrior! War is over; sleep the sleep, nothing will you wake.
(Rest, warrior! War is over; sleep your sleep, nothing will wake you.)

'tʰrɔø̯mə nɪçtʼ fɔn 'vɪldəm ʃtʼrɑos, nɪçtʼ fɔn tʰaːkʼ lʊntʼ naxtʼ fɔl   ʃrɛkʼən.
Träume nicht von wildem Strauss, nicht von Tag und Nacht voll Schrecken.
Dream not of wild   battle, not of day and night full of terror.
(Do not dream of wild battle, nor of days and nights full of terror.)
                    [*Storck (each time):* **vom wilden** (fɔm 'vɪldən, of the wild) **Strauss**]

ɪn deːɐ̯/deːr 'ɪnzəl 'tsɑobɐhaləln   vɪrtʼ lɑen 'vaeçɐ 'ʃlaːfgəzaŋ
In der   Insel   Zauberhallen wird ein weicher Schlafgesang
In the   island's magic halls will a   soft   sleep- song
(In the island's magic halls a soft lullaby will)

lʊm   das 'myːdə hɑopʼt diːɐ̯ 'valən tsu: deːɐ̯ 'tsɑobɐharfə kʰlaŋ. 'feːən
um   das müde Haupt dir   wallen zu der Zauberharfe Klang. Feen
around the weary head for you float to the   magic harp's sound. Fairies
(float about your weary head to the sound of the magic harp. Fairies)

mɪtʼ 'lʊnzɪçtʼbaːrən 'hɛndən 'veːɐ̯dən lɑof daen 'laːgɐ hɪn 'hɔldə 'ʃlʊmɐbluːmən   'zɛndən,
mit unsichtbaren Händen werden auf dein Lager hin   holde Schlummerblumen senden,
with invisible   hands   will   to your couch hence lovely slumber- flowers send,
(will send with invisible hands lovely flowers of sleep to your couch,)

di: lɪm 'tsɑobɐlandə blyːn. 'rastʼə, 'kʰriːgɐ! kʰriːkʼ lɪstʼ lɑos...
die im   Zauberlande blüh'n. Raste, Krieger! Krieg ist aus...
which in the magic land bloom. Rest, warrior! War is over...
(flowers that bloom in their enchanted land. Rest, warrior! War is over...)

nɪçt deːɐ̯ 'tʰrɔməl 'vɪldəs 'raːzən, nɪçt dɛs kʰriːks gə'biːtʼəntʼ   vɔrtʰ,
Nicht der Trommel wildes Rasen, nicht des Kriegs gebietend   Wort,
Not   the drum's   wild   raging, not the war's commanding word,
(Neither the drum's wild raging, nor the commands of war,)
            [*Storck (variant):* **des Kriegs Kommandowort** (kʰɔ'mandovɔrtʰ, word of command)]

nɪçt deːɐ̯ 'tʰoːdəshœrnɐ 'blaːzən 'ʃɔø̯çən   'daenən 'ʃlʊmɐ   fɔrtʰ.
nicht der Todeshörner Blasen scheuchen deinen Schlummer fort.
not   the   death-horns' blaring scare   your   slumber   away,
(nor the blaring of death's horns will scare away your slumber,)

nıçt das 'ʃt'ampfən 'vɪldɐ 'pfeːɐ̯də, nıçt deːɐ̯ 'ʃrɛk'ənsruːf deːɐ̯ vaxtʰ,
Nicht das Stampfen wilder Pferde, nicht der Schreckensruf der Wacht,
not the stamping of wild horses, not the fright- cry of the watch,

nıçt das bɪlt' fɔn 'tʰaːksbəʃveːɐ̯də 'ʃt'øːrən 'daɛnə 'ʃt'ɪlə naxtʰ.
nicht das Bild von Tagsbeschwerde stören deine stille Nacht.
not the vision of day's difficulties disturb your quiet night.
(nor the vision of the day's difficulties will disturb your quiet night.)

dɔx deːɐ̯ 'lɛrçə 'mɔrgənzɛŋə 'vɛk'ən zanft daɛn 'ʃlʊmɐnt' loːɐ̯,
Doch der Lerche Morgensänge wecken sanft dein Schlummernd Ohr,
But the lark's morning songs wake gently your slumbering ear,
(But the lark's morning songs will gently wake your slumbering ear,)

ʊnt dɛs 'zʊmpfgəfiːdɐs 'kʰlɛŋə 'ʃt'aɛgən laos gəʃɪlf ʊnt roːɐ̯. 'rast'ə, 'kʰriːgɐ...
und des Sumpfgefieders Klänge steigen aus Geschilf und Rohr. Raste, Krieger...
and the marsh birds' sounds rise up from rushes and reeds. Rest, warrior....

[In *The Lady of the Lake* these words precede the song: "She sung, and still a harp unseen / Filled up the symphony between"; they give a clue to the opening accompaniment of Schubert's lovely lullaby. The pianist must be discreet when martial rhythms invade the musical fabric; the words tell us that the sleeper must not hear such sounds. The original English text is as follows:

> Soldier, rest! thy warfare o'er, / Sleep the sleep that knows no breaking:
> Dream of battled fields no more / Days of danger, nights of waking.
> In our isle's enchanted hall, / Hands unseen thy couch are strewing,
> Fairy strains of music fall / Every sense in slumber dewing.
> Soldier, rest! thy warfare o'er / Dream of fighting fields no more:
> Sleep the sleep that knows no breaking, / Morn of toil, nor night of waking.
> No rude sound shall reach thine ear, / Armour's clang, or war-steed champing,
> Trump nor pibroch* summon here / Mustering clan or squadron tramping.
> Yet the lark's shrill fife may come / At the daybreak from the fallow,
> And the bittern* sound his drum, / Booming from the sedgy shallow.
> Ruder sounds shall none be near, / Guards nor warders challenge here,
> Here's no war-steeds neigh and champing, / Shouting clans, or squadrons stamping.
>   (*"pibroch" = bagpipe; "bittern" = small heron with a loud call)]

'ɛləns ' tsvaet'ɐ gə'zaŋ / 'jɛːgɐ, 'ruːə fɔn deːɐ̯ jaːk't'
Ellens Gesang II / Ellens zweiter Gesang / Jäger, ruhe von der Jagd
Ellen's Song II / Huntsman, Rest! Thy Chase is Done
(from Sir Walter Scott's *The Lady of the Lake*)

Op. 52, No. 2 [1825] (German translation by Adam Storck)

'jɛːgɐ, 'ruːə fɔn deːɐ̯ jaːk't'! 'vaeçɐ 'ʃlʊmɐ zɔl dɪç 'dɛk'ən;
Jäger, ruhe von der Jagd! Weicher Schlummer soll dich decken;
Huntsman, rest from the hunt! Soft slumber shall you cover;
(Huntsman, rest from the hunt! Gentle slumber shall cover you;)

'tʰrɔømə nıçt', vɛn zɔn lɛɐ̯'vaxt, das 'jaːk't'hœrnɐ dıç lɛɐ̯'vɛk'ən. ['laofvɛk'ən]
träume nicht, wenn Sonn' erwacht, dass Jagdhörner dich erwecken. [*Storck:* **aufwecken**]
dream not, when sun awakes, that hunting horns you awaken.
(do not dream, when the sun rises, that hunting horns are waking you.)

ʃlaːf! deːɐ̯ hɪrʃ ruːt‘ ɪn deːɐ̯ ‘høːlə, ba̯e diːɐ̯ zɪnt di ‘hʊndə vax;
Schlaf! der Hirsch ruht in der Höhle, bei dir sind die Hunde wach;
Sleep! The stag rests in the cave, with you are the hounds awake;
(Sleep! The stag rests in his cave, your hounds are awake beside you:)

ʃlaːf, nɪçt‘ kʰveːl ɛs ‘da̯enə ‘zeːlə, das da̯en ‘leːdləs rɔs ɛɐ̯‘laːk‘.
schlaf, nicht quäl' es deine Seele, dass dein edles Ross erlag.
sleep, not torment it your soul, that your noble steed succumbed.
(sleep, let it not torment your soul that your noble steed has died.)

vɛn deːɐ̯ ‘jʊŋə tʰaːk‘ ɛɐ̯‘vaxt‘, vɪrt‘ kʰa̯en ‘jeːɡəhorn dɪç ‘vɛk‘ən.
Wenn der junge Tag erwacht, wird kein Jägerhorn dich wecken.
When the young day awakes, will no huntsman's horn you waken.
(When the new day dawns no huntsman's horn will wake you.)

[Schubert set seven excerpts from *The Lady of the Lake*, five as solo songs, two as choruses (male quartet, female trio). Ellen's Second Song comes from the end of the first canto of Scott's novel in verse. The piano part imitates hunting horns. The original English words are as follows:

Huntsman, rest! thy chase is done, / While our slumbrous spells assail ye,
Dream not, with the rising sun / Bugles here shall sound reveille.
Sleep! the deer is in his den; / Sleep! thy hounds are by thee lying;
Sleep! nor dream in yonder glen, / How thy gallant steed lay dying.
Huntsman, rest; thy chase is done, / Think not of the rising sun,
For at dawning to assail ye, / Here no bugles sound reveille.]

Ellens Gesang III see *Ave Maria*

e‘lyːzi̯ʊm
Elysium
Elysium

Posthumously published [composed 1817] (poem by Friedrich von Schiller)

fo‘ryːbɐ di ʃt‘øːnəndə ‘kʰlaːɡə! le‘lyːzi̯ʊms ‘frɔɪ̯dəngəlaːɡə ɛɐ̯‘zɔɪ̯fən ‘jeːk‘lɪçəs lax!
Vorüber die stöhnende Klage! Elysiums Freudengelage ersäufen jegliches Ach!
Past the moaning lament! Elysium's joy- feasts drown every sigh!
(The moaning lament is past! Elysium's joyous feasts drown every sigh!)

le‘lyːzi̯ʊms ‘leːbən ‘leːvɪɡə ‘vɔnə, ‘leːvɪɡəs ‘ʃveːbən, dʊrç ‘laxəndə ‘fluːrən
Elysiums Leben ewige Wonne, ewiges Schweben, durch lachende Fluren
Elysium's life eternal bliss, eternal soaring, through laughing meadows
(Elysium's life is eternal bliss, eternal soaring, through smiling meadows)

laen ‘fløːt‘əndɐ bax. ‘juːɡənt‘lɪç ‘mɪldə bə‘ʃveːp‘t di ɡə‘fɪldə ‘leːvɪɡɐ ma̯e;
ein flötender Bach. Jugendlich milde beschwebt die Gefilde ewiger Mai;
a fluting brook. Youthfully mild hovers over the fields eternal May;
(a fluting brook is flowing. An eternal May, youthfully mild, hovers over the fields;)

di ‘ʃt‘ʊndən lɛnt‘‘fliːn ɪn ‘ɡɔldənən ‘tʰrɔɪ̯mən, di ‘zeːlə ʃvɪlt‘ laɔs ɪn lʊn‘lɛnt‘‘lɪçən
die Stunden entflieh'n in goldenen Träumen, die Seele schwillt aus in unendlichen
the hours fly away in golden dreams, the soul swells out into infinite
[*poem:* **entfliehen** (lɛnt‘‘fliːən)]

'rɔømən. 'vaːɐ̯haet' ɾaest' hiːɐ̯ den 'ʃlaeɐ(r) lɛnt'tsvae. lʊn'lɛnt'lɪçə 'frɔødə
Räumen. Wahrheit reisst hier den Schleier entzwei. Unendliche Freude
spaces. Truth tears here the veil in two. Endless joy
(space. Here truth rends her veil. Endless joy)

dʊrç'valət das hɛrts. hiːɐ̯ 'maŋəlt deːɐ̯ 'naːmə dem 'tʰraoɐndən 'laedə,
durchwallet das Herz. Hier mangelt der Name dem trauernden Leide,
flows through the heart. Here lacks the name for the mourning grief,
(flows through the heart. Here there is no name for mourning grief:)

'zanft'əs lɛnt'tsʏk'ən nuːɐ̯ 'haesət' hiːɐ̯ ʃmɛrts. ['haesət' man ʃmɛrts]
sanftes Entzücken nur heisset hier Schmerz. [GA: heisset man Schmerz]
gentle rapture only is called here pain. [calls one pain]
(here a gentle rapture is the extent of one's concept of pain.)
              [*poem:* **sanfter** ('zanft'ɐ, gentler) **Entzücken nur heisset hier Schmerz**]

hiːɐ̯ 'ʃt'rɛk'ət deːɐ̯ 'valəndə 'pʰɪlgɐ di 'mat'ən, 'brenəndən 'gliːdə
Hier strecket der wallende Pilger die matten, brennenden Glieder
Here stretches the wandering pilgrim the exhausted, burning limbs
(Here the wandering pilgrim can stretch out his exhausted, burning limbs)

ɪm 'zɔøzəlndən 'ʃat'ən, leːgət di 'bʏrdə lɑof 'leːvɪç da'hɪn.
im säuselnden Schatten, leget die Bürde auf ewig dahin.
in the murmuring shadow, lays the burden for ever away.
(in the murmuring shadow, can lay down his burden for good.)

'zaenə 'zɪçəl lɛnt'felt' hiːɐ̯ dem 'ʃnit'ɐ, 'laengəzʊŋən fɔn 'harfəngətsit'ɐ,
Seine Sichel entfällt hier dem Schnitter, eingesungen von Harfengezitter,
His sickel falls away here from the reaper, sung to sleep by harp- quivering,
(The sickel falls from the hand of the reaper, lulled to sleep by quivering harps,)

tʰrɔømt' leːɐ̯ gə'ʃnit'ənə 'halmə tsuː zeːn. 'dɛsən 'faːnə 'donɐʃtʏrmə 'valt'ə,
träumt er geschnittene Halme zu seh'n. Dessen Fahne Donnerstürme wallte,
dreams he cut [past part.] stalks to see. (He) whose banner thunderstorms flutterd,
(he dreams that he sees the stalks already cut. He whose banner waved through thunderstorms,)

'dɛsən 'loːrən 'mɔrt'gəbrʏl lʊm'halt'ə, 'bɛrgə 'beːp't'ən 'lʊnt'ɐ 'dɛsən 'donɐgaŋ,
dessen Ohren Mordgebrüll umhallte, Berge bebten unter dessen Donnergang,
whose ears murder-roar around-echoed, mountains quaked beneath whose thunder-gait,
(around whose ears murderous roars echoed, beneath whose thundering steps mountains quaked,]

ʃlɛːft' hiːɐ̯ 'lɪndə bae des 'baxəs 'riːzəln, deːɐ̯ viː 'zɪlbɐ 'ʃp'iːlət' 'lyːbɐ 'kʰiːzəln,
schläft hier linde bei des Baches Rieseln, der wie Silber spielet über Kieseln,
sleeps here gently to the brook's rippling, which like silver plays over pebbles,
(he now sleeps here gently by the rippling brook that plays over the pebbles like flowing silver,)

iːm fɛɐ̯'halət' 'vɪldɐ 'ʃp'eːrə kʰlaŋ. hiːɐ̯/hiːr lʊm'larmən zɪç gə'tʰrɔøə 'gat'ən,
ihm verhallet wilder Speere Klang. Hier umarmen sich getreue Gatten,
for him dies away wild spears' sound. Here embrace each other faithful spouses,
(for him the clang of violent spears dies away. Here faithful spouses embrace each other,)

'kʰʏsən zɪç lɑof 'gryːnən, 'zamt'nən 'mat'ən, 'liːp'gəkʰoːst' fɔm 'balzaːmvɛstʰ;
küssen sich auf grünen, sammtnen Matten, liebgekost vom Balsamwest;
kiss each other on green, velvety meads, caressed by the balmy west wind;

'iːrə 'kʰroːnə 'fɪndət' hiːɐ̯ di 'liːbə, 'zɪçɐ foːɐ̯ dɛs 'tʰoːdəs 'ʃt'rɛŋəm 'hiːbə,
ihre Krone findet hier die Liebe, sicher vor des Todes strengem Hiebe,
its crown finds here the love, safe from the death's severe blows,
(here love finds its crown; safe from the severe blows of death,)

'faeɐt' ziː lᴀen 'leːvɪç 'hɔxt͡saet'fɛstʰ. ['hɔxt͡saet͡sfɛstʰ]
feiert sie ein ewig Hochzeitfest. [*Schiller:* Hochzeitsfest]
celebrates it [love] an eternal wedding feast.
(love celebrates an eternal wedding feast.)

[This view of Elysium, the Grecian paradise, followed directly upon *Gruppe aus dem Tartarus*, inspired by a Greek view of hell. More a sequence of individual musical movements—often very lovely—than a song, this is a sort of solo cantata, ten pages long in the *Gesamtausgabe* (nine in Peters). The performer will need exceptional breath control: one syllable is held without a breath for ten bars in the final twelve-bar phrase. Studying with Salieri, Schubert had already set several of the stanzas to music in 1813; but this version, four years later, is entirely new.]

Entra l'uomo allor che nasce see *Aria di Abramo*

ɛnt'ts ʏk'ʊŋ
Entzückung
Rapture

Posthumously published [composed 1816] (poem by Friedrich von Matthisson)

tʰaːk' fɔl 'hɪməl! daː lᴀos 'lᴀoras 'blɪk'ən
Tag voll Himmel! da aus Lauras Blicken
Day full of heaven! When from Laura's glances

miːɐ̯ deːɐ̯ 'liːbə 'haelɪçst'əs lɛnt'ts ʏk'ən lɪn di 'vɔnətʰrʊŋk'nə 'zeːlə draŋ!
mir der Liebe heiligstes Entzücken in die wonnetrunk'ne Seele drang!
to me the love's holiest rapture into the bliss- drunk soul surged!
(love's holiest rapture surged into my bliss-intoxicated soul,)

ʊnt', fɔn 'liːrəm 'tsᴀobɐ 'hɪŋərɪsən,
Und, von ihrem Zauber hingerissen,
and, by their (or her) magic carried away,
(and, carried away by the magic of those glances,)

ɪç deːɐ̯ 'hɔldən, 'ʊnt'ɐ 'fᴐøɐkʰʏsən, lan den 'zyːsbɛkʰlɔmnən 'buːzən zaŋkʰ!
ich der Holden, unter Feuerküssen, an den süssbeklommnen Busen sank!
I to the lovely one, amid fire- kisses, on the sweetly-anxious bosom sank!
(I sank, amid fiery kisses, onto the sweetly anxious breast of my lovely one!)

'gɔldnɐ zaː lɪç 'vɔlk'ən zɪç bə'zᴐømən,
Goldner sah ich Wolken sich besäumen,
More golden saw I clouds themselves rim,
(I saw the clouds rimmed with brighter gold,)

'jeːdəs 'blɛt'çən lᴀof den 'fryːlɪŋsbᴐømən ʃiːn tsuː 'flʏst'ɐn:
jedes Blättchen auf den Frühlingsbäumen schien zu flüstern:
each little leaf on the spring- trees seemed to whisper:
(each little leaf on the trees of springtime seemed to whisper:)

478

ˈleːvɪç, ˈleːvɪç daẹn! ˈglʏkˈlɪçɐ(r), ɪn ˈzɔlçɐ ˈtʰaọməlfʏlə,
"Ewig, ewig dein!" Glücklicher, in solcher Taumelfülle,
"Eternally, eternally yours!" Happier, in such giddy-ecstasy-fullness,
("Eternally, eternally yours!" Happier, in such a fullness of giddy ecstasy,)

veːɐd ɪç, nax fɛɐˈʃtˈɔφpˈtˈɐ(r) ˈleːɐdənhʏlə, kʰaọm ɪn ˈleːdəns ˈmʏrtˈənlaọbən zaẹn.
werd' ich, nach verstäubter Erdenhülle, kaum in Edens Myrtenlaube n sein.
shall I, after reduced-to-dust earth- shell, scarcely in Eden's myrtle- arbors be.
(I shall scarcely be in the myrtle arbors of Eden, after my earthly shell has turned to dust.)

[Schubert repeats the first three lines of the poem at the end, after a brief recitative. The music is
exultant, with some effective harmonies, and the vocal line is strenuously high, but grateful.]

eˈpʰɪstˈl̩ fɔn kʰɔˈliːn / hɛrn ˈjoːzɛf ˈʃpʰaọn, aˈsɛsoːɐ ɪn lɪnts / muziˈkʰaːlɪʃɐ ʃvaŋkʰ
Epistel von Collin / Herrn Josef Spaun, Assessor in Linz / Musikalischer Schwank
Epistle from Collin / To Herr Joseph Spaun, Assessor in Linz / A Musical Prank

Posthumously published [composed 1822] (poem by Matthäus von Collin)

Recitativo:
ọntˈ ˈnɪmɐ ˈʃraẹpst duː? blaẹpstˈ ọns fɛɐˈloːrən, laẹn ʃtˈar fɛɐˈʃtˈọmtˈɐ,
Und nimmer schreibst du? Bleibst uns verloren, ein starr Verstummter,
And never write you? Remain (you) to us lost, a motionless mute,
(And will you never write? Do you remain lost to us, a motionless mute,)

nuːn fyːɐ/fyːr ˈleːvgə tsaẹtʰ? fiˈlaẹçtˈ, vaẹl ˈnɔφə ˈfrɔφndə duː lɛɐˈkʰoːrən?
nun für ew'ge Zeit? Vielleicht, weil neue Freunde du erkoren?
now for eternal time? Maybe because new friends you (have) chosen?
(now for all time to come? Maybe because you have chosen new friends?)

vartst duː laˈsɛsoːɐ dɛn lam tʰɪʃ zoː braẹtˈ, voˈran
Wardst du Assessor denn am Tisch so breit, woran
Became you assessor then at the table so wide, at which
(Have you become an assessor at such a wide desk, at which)

baẹm ˈlakˈtˈənʃtˈoːs zɔφftstˈlaŋəvaẹlə, lọm ˈlapˈtsuʃtˈɛrbən ˈlalɐ ˈfrɔφdɪçkʰaẹtʰ?
beim Aktenstoss seufzt Langeweile, um abzusterben aller Freudigkeit?
before the pile of documents sighs boredom, in order to withdraw from all jollity?
(boredom is sighing before a pile of documents, in order to withdraw from all jollity?)

dɔx naẹn, nuːɐ viːɐ zɪnts, nuːɐ/nuːr lọns vart tsuˈtʰaẹlə diːs ˈʃvaẹgən,
Doch nein, nur wir sind's, nur uns ward zuteile dies Schweigen,
But no, only we are it, only to us became as share this silence,
(But no, *we* are the only ones, this silence has only fallen to *our* lot,)

["*zuteile werden*" = to fall to one's lot]

diːs fɛɐˈʃtˈọmən lọntˈ fɛɐˈgesən. ˈlarmuːtˈ lọntˈ noːtˈ zɛlpstˈ
dies Verstummen und Vergessen. Armut und Not selbst
this muteness and oblivion. Poverty and need, even

lan deːɐ ˈkʰlaẹnstˈən ˈtsaẹlə! fyːɐ ˈjeːdən bɪst duː ˈʃrɪftˈkʰarkˈ nɪçtˈ gəˈzesən;
an der kleinsten Zeile! Für jeden bist du schriftkarg nicht gesessen;
to the smallest line! For everyone have you writing-miserly not sat (= remained);
(deprivation of the smallest line! You have not remained miserly with your pen to *every*one;)

fyːɐ̯ ˈmançən   ˈkʰaːmən ˈbriːfə ˈlaŋəfloːɡən, lʊntˈ naːx deːɐ̯/deːr ˈlɛlə
für manchen   kamen Briefe angeflogen, und nach der   Elle
for many a person came letters flying,   and by the   ell
(for some letters have come flying in, and by the yard)

hast duː ziː ɡəˈmɛsən; dɔx lʊns, barˈbaːɐ̯, hast duː da̯ɛn hɛrts lɛntˈtsoːɡən!
hast du sie gemessen; doch uns, Barbar, hast du dein Herz entzogen!
have you them measured; but from us, barbarian, have you your heart withdrawn!
(you have measured them; but from us, you cruel man, you have withdrawn your heart!)

Aria:
ʃvɪŋtˈ lɔɸç   kʰyːn, tsuː ˈbaŋə ˈkʰlaːɡən, la̯os lɛmˈpʰøːɐ̯tˈɐ brʊstˈ hɛɐ̯ˈfoːɐ̯,
Schwingt euch   kühn, zu bange Klagen, aus empörter Brust hervor,
Soar yourselves boldly, too anxious laments, from indignant breast forth,
(Soar boldly forth, you too anxious laments, from our indignant breast,)

[*Peters (in error)*: **zu bangen Klagen**]

ʊntˈ fɔn meloˈdiːn* ɡəˈtʰraːɡən vaːkˈtˈ lɔɸç   lan dɛs ˈfɛrnən loːɐ̯! [*normally* meloˈdiːən]
und von Melodien getragen wagt euch   an des Fernen Ohr!
and by melodies borne   dare yourselves to the far one's ear!
(and, borne by melodies, dare to fly to the ear of the distant one!)

vas leːɐ̯/leːr ˈlɪmɐ maːkˈ lɛɐ̯ˈviːdɐn, ˈdiːzəs hiːɐ̯ ˈzaːɡət dɔx:
Was er   immer mag erwidern, dieses hier saget doch:
What he   ever may reply, this here say nevertheless:
(Whatever he may reply, *do* say this:)

tsvaːɐ̯ fɛɐ̯ˈɡɛsən, ˈjeːnəs ˈbiːdɐn   ˈdɛŋkˈən viːɐ̯/viːr lɪn ˈliːbə nɔx.
"Zwar vergessen, jenes Biedern   denken wir in Liebe noch."
"Though forgotten, of that good fellow think we   with love still."
("Though we are forgotten, we still think of that good fellow with love.")

[This is a letter in the style of a hilarious opera parody, with a *fermata* on high C, followed by a descending chromatic scale, on the reproachful word "*Barbar!*", plenty of melodramatic *Sturm und Drang*, and two more high Cs (edited out of the Peters version) in the agitated *finale*. Collin was a cousin of Josef von Spaun, who had left Vienna to take up the post of assessor in Linz.]

Erinnerung see *Die Erscheinung*

ɛɐ̯ˈlɪnərʊŋən
Erinnerungen
Memories

Posthumously published [composed 1814] (poem by Friedrich von Matthisson)

am ˈzeːɡəʃtˈaːtˈ, lɪn ˈla̯oən ˈfɔlmoːntˈnɛçtˈən, dɛŋkˈ lɪç nuːɐ̯ dɪç!
Am Seegestad', in lauen Vollmondnächten, denk' ich nur dich!
At the lake-shore, in tepid full-moon-nights, think I only you!
(By the shore of the lake, on warm nights, when the moon is full, I think only of you!)

tsuː ˈda̯enəs ˈnaːməns ˈɡɔldnəm tsuːkˈ fɛɐ̯ˈflɛçtˈən di ˈʃtˈɛrnə zɪç.
Zu deines Namens goldnem Zug verflechten die Sterne sich.
To your name's golden trait entwine the stars themselves.
(The stars entwine themselves to spell your name in golden light.)

di ˈvɪltˈnɪs glɛntst ˈ ɪn ˈ ʊngəvoːntˈɐ ˈhɛlə, fɔn diːɐ̯/diːr ˈɛɐ̯ˈfʏltʰ;
Die Wildnis glänzt in ungewohnter Helle, von dir erfüllt;
The wilderness gleams in unaccustomed brightness, by you filled;
(The wilderness gleams with unaccustomed brightness, filled with you;)

ɑof ˈjeːdəs blatˈ, ɪn ˈjeːdə ˈʃatˈənkʰvɛlə maːltˈ zɪç daen bɪltˈ.
auf jedes Blatt, in jede Schattenquelle malt sich dein Bild.
on every leaf, in every shadow- spring paints itself your image.
(on every leaf, in every shady spring your image is painted.)

gɛrn vael ɪç, ˈgraːtsiə, voː du deːn ˈhyːgəl hɪˈnapˈgəʃveːpˈtʰ,
Gern weil' ich, Grazie, wo du den Hügel hinabgeschwebt,
Gladly linger I, Grace, where you the hill (have) down-floated,
(I gladly linger, you personification of grace, where you once floated down from the hill,)

laeçtˈ, viː laen ˈroːzənblatˈ lɑof ˈtseːfyːɐ̯s ˈflyːgəl foˈryːbɐbeːpˈtʰ.
leicht, wie ein Rosenblatt auf Zephyrs Flügel vorüberbebt.
lightly, as a rose- petal on Zephyr's wing past quivers.
(lightly, as a rose petal quivers by on the wings of a zephyr.)

am ˈhʏtˈçən dɔrtˈ bəˈkʰrɛntstˈ lɪç diːɐ̯, lʊmˈflɔsən fɔn ˈlaːbəntˈgluːtʰ,
Am Hüttchen dort bekränzt' ich dir, umflossen von Abendglut,
At the little hut there garlanded I for you, bathed in evening glow,
(At the little hut there, while you were bathed in sunset glow, I once garlanded)

mɪtˈ ˈlɪmɐgryːn lʊnt ˈjʊŋən ˈblyːtˈənʃpˈrɔsən den ˈhalmənhuːtʰ.
mit Immergrün und jungen Blütensprossen den Halmenhut.
with evergreen and young blossom-sprouts the straw hat.
(your straw hat with evergreen and fresh new blossoms.)

bae ˈjeːdəm ˈlɪçtˈvʊrm lɪn den ˈfɛlzənʃtˈʏkˈən, lals lɔpˈ di ˈfeːən
Bei jedem Lichtwurm in den Felsenstücken, als ob die Feen
With each glowworm in the rock- pieces, as if the fairies
(Each time a glowworm would light up among the rocks, as if fairies)

daː ˈtʰɛntsə ˈveːpˈtˈən, riːfst duː fɔl lɛntˈtsʏkˈʊŋ: viː ʃøːn! viː ʃøːn!
da Tänze webten, riefst du voll Entzückung: "Wie schön! wie schön!"
there dances were weaving, called you full of delight: "How lovely! How lovely!"
(were dancing there, you cried out, full of delight: "How lovely! How lovely!")

voˈhɪn lɪç blɪkˈ lʊnt geːˌ lɛɐ̯ˈblɪkˈ lɪç ˈlɪmɐ den ˈviːzənpˈlaːn,
Wohin ich blick' und geh', erblick' ich immer den Wiesenplan,
Wherever I look and go, see I always the meadow-plain,
(Wherever I look, wherever I go, I always see the meadow)

voː viːɐ̯ deːɐ̯ ˈbɛrgə ʃneː mɪtˈ ˈpʰʊrpˈʊrʃimɐ bəˈlɔɵ̯çtˈətˈ zaːn.
wo wir der Berge Schnee mit Purpurschimmer beleuchtet sahn.
where we the mountains' snow with crimson shimmer illumined saw.
(where we once saw the snow on the mountains illumined by the sunset with a purple shimmer.)

iːɐ̯ ˈʃmɛltsəntˈ ˈmaeliːtˈ ˈvaentˈə filoˈmeːnə lɪm ˈluːfɐhaen;
Ihr schmelzend Mailied weinte Philomele im Uferhain;
Her melting May-song wept Philomela in the shore-grove;
(Philomela* wept her melting May song in the grove by the shore;)

da: fle:t' lıç di:ɐ̯/di:r, ım blık' di 'gantsə 'ze:lə: gə'deŋk'ə maen!
da fleht' ich dir, im Blick die ganze Seele: Gedenke mein!
there implored I to you, in the gaze the whole soul: "Think of me!"
(there I implored you, with my whole soul in my gaze: "Think of me!")

[*Philomela was a king's daughter who, according to Ovid, was transformed into a nightingale. In Schubert's song the first three verses, and the last two, are musically identical; the fourth is pure recitative, and the fifth has a different melody that builds to a climax at *"Wie schön!"*]

'ɛrlafze:
Erlafsee
Lake Erlaf

Op. 8, No. 3 [1817] (Johann Mayrhofer)

mi:ɐ̯/mi:r lıst' zo: vo:l, zo: ve: lam 'ʃt'ılən 'lɛrlafze:.
Mir ist so wohl, so weh am stillen Erlafsee.
To me is so well, so sad by the quiet Erlaf Lake.
(I feel so happy, yet so sad, by quiet Lake Erlaf.)

'haelıç 'ʃvaegən ın 'fıçt'əntsvaegən, 're:gʊŋslo:s de:ɐ̯ 'blaoə ʃo:s, ['dʊŋk'lə]
Heilig Schweigen in Fichtenzweigen, regungslos der blaue Schoss, [*poem:* **dunkle Schoss**]
Holy stillness in pine- branches, motionless the blue lap, [dark]
(A holy stillness in the pine-branches, the blue water motionless.)

nu:ɐ̯ de:ɐ̯ 'vɔlk'ən 'ʃat'ən fli:n 'ly:bɐm 'glat'ən 'ʃp'i:gəl hın. ['dʊŋk'əln]
nur der Wolken Schatten fliehn überm glatten Spiegel hin. [*Peters:* **dunklen Spiegel**]
only the clouds' shadows flee over the smooth mirror hence. [dark]
(Only the shadows of the clouds move across the smooth mirror of the lake.)

'frıʃə 'vındə 'kʰrɔ̜øzəln 'lındə das gə'vɛsɐ,
Frische Winde kräuseln linde das Gewässer,
Fresh winds ruffle gently the waters,
(Fresh breezes gently ruffle the water,)

ʊnt de:ɐ̯ 'zɔnə 'gyldnə 'kʰro:nə 'flımɐt' 'blɛsɐ.
und der Sonne güldne Krone flimmert blässer.
and the sun's golden crown glitters paler.

mi:ɐ̯/mi:r lıst' zo: vo:l, zo: ve: lam 'ʃt'ılən 'lɛrlafze:.
Mir ist so wohl, so weh am stillen Erlafsee.
To me is so well, so sad by the quiet Erlaf Lake.
(I feel so happy, yet so sad, by quiet Lake Erlaf.)

[This was the first of Schubert's songs to appear in print. He left out more than half the poem, concentrating on those lines that provided the atmosphere he wanted for his song. Mayrhofer must have forgiven the cuts, for he shared lodgings with Schubert for two years, after the song had been composed. Lake Erlaf is near Mariazell, about sixty miles Southwest of Vienna.]

ˈɛrlkʰøːnɪç
Erlkönig
The Erl-King

Op. 1 [1815] (Johann Wolfgang von Goethe)

veːɐ̯ ˈraet̯ˈət̯ zoː ʃpˈɛːt dʊrç naxtˈ ʊntˈ vɪntˈʔ ɛs lɪst deːɐ̯ ˈfaːt̯ˈɐ mɪtˈ ˈzaenəm kʰɪntˈ;
Wer reitet so spät durch Nacht und Wind? Es ist der Vater mit seinem Kind;
Who rides so late through night and wind? It is the father with his child;
(Who is riding so late through the windy night? It is the father with his child;)

eːɐ̯ hat den ˈkʰnaːbən voːl lɪn dem larm, leːɐ̯ fastˈ liːn ˈzɪçɐ. leːɐ̯ hɛltˈ liːn varm. —
Er hat den Knaben wohl in dem Arm, er fasst ihn sicher, er hält ihn warm. —
He has the boy well in the arm, he grasps him securely, he holds him warm. —
(He holds the boy firmly in his arms, he clasps him securely, he keeps him warm.)

maen zoːn, vas bɪrkst duː zoː baŋ daen ɡəˈzɪçtʰʔ —ziːstˈ, ˈfaːt̯ˈɐ, duː den ˈlɛrlkʰøːnɪç nɪçtʰʔ
Mein Sohn, was birgst du so bang dein Gesicht?—Siehst, Vater, du den Erlkönig nicht?
My son, why hide you so afraid your face? —See, Father, you the Erl-King not?
(—My son, why do you hide your face so anxiously? —Father, do you not see the Erl-King?)

den ˈlɛrlənkʰøːnɪç mɪtˈ kʰroːn lʊntˈ ʃvaefʔ —maen zoːn, lɛs lɪstˈ laen ˈneːbəlʃtˈraef.
den Erlenkönig mit Kron und Schweif?—Mein Sohn, es ist ein Nebelstreif.
the Erl-King with crown and tail? —My son, it is a mist- streak.
(the Erl-King with his crown and his tail? —My son, it is a streak of mist.)

—duː ˈliːbəs kʰɪntˈ, kʰɔm, ɡeː mɪtˈ miːɐ̯ ! ɡaːɐ̯ ˈʃøːnə ˈʃpˈiːlə ʃpˈiːl lɪç mɪt diːɐ̯;
—"Du liebes Kind, komm, geh mit mir! gar schöne Spiele spie ich mit dir;
—"You dear child, come, go with me! very lovely games play I with you;
(—"you dear child, come away with me! I shall play very lovely games with you;)

manç ˈbʊntˈə ˈbluːmən zɪntˈ lan dem ʃtrantˈ, ˈmaenə ˈmʊtˈɐ hatˈ manç ˈɡyldən ɡəˈvantˈ.
manch bunte Blumen sind an dem Strand, meine Mutter hat manch gülden Gewand."
many bright flowers are on the shore, my mother has many a golden garment."

—maen ˈfaːt̯ˈɐ, maen ˈfaːt̯ˈɐ, lʊntˈ ˈhøːrəst duː nɪçtʰ, vas ˈlɛrlənkʰøːnɪç miːɐ̯ ˈlaezə fɛɐ̯ʃpˈrɪçtʰʔ
—Mein Vater, mein Vater, und hörest du nicht, was Erlenkönig mir leise verspricht?
—My father, my father, and hear you not what Erl-King to me softly promises?
(—My father, my father, and do you not hear what the Erl-King is softly promising me?)

—zae ˈruːɪç, ˈblaebə ˈruːɪç, maen kʰɪntˈ; lɪn ˈdyrən ˈblɛtˈən ˈzɔʏzəlt deːɐ̯ vɪntˈ. —
—Sei ruhig, bleibe ruhig, mein Kind; in dürren Blättern säuselt der Wind. —
—Be calm, stay calm, my child; in dry leaves rustles the wind. —
(—Be calm, stay calm, my child; the wind is rustling in the dry leaves.)

vɪlstˈ, ˈfaenɐ ˈkʰnaːbə, duː mɪtˈ miːɐ̯ ɡeːn? ˈmaenə ˈtʰœçtˈɐ ˈzɔlən dɪç ˈvartˈən ʃøːn;
"Willst, feiner Knabe, du mit mir gehn? meine Töchter sollen dich warten schön;
"Want, fine boy, you with me to go? my daughters shall you wait on beautifully;
(—"Fine boy, do you want to come with me? My daughters will look after you beautifully;)

ˈmaenə ˈtʰœçtˈɐ ˈfyːrən den ˈnɛçtˈlɪçən raen
meine Töchter führen den nächtlichen Reihn
my daughters lead the nocturnal dance

ʊnt' 'viːgən ʊnt 'tʰantsən ʊnt' 'zɪŋən dɪç ḁen,
und wiegen und tanzen und singen dich ein,
and rock and dance and sing you to sleep,
(and will rock you and dance and sing you to sleep,)

ziː 'viːgən ʊnt tʰantsən ʊnt' 'zɪŋən dɪç ḁen. —
sie wiegen und tanzen und singen dich ein." —
they rock and dance and sing you to sleep." —
(they will rock you and dance and sing you to sleep.")

mḁen 'faː'ɐ, mḁen 'faːt'ɐ, ʊnt' ziːst duː nɪçt dɔrtʰ 'ɛrlkʰøːnɪks 'tʰœçt'ɐ ḁam 'dystʰɐn ɔrtʰ?
Mein Vater, mein Vater, und siehst du nicht dort Erlkönigs Töchter am düsterm Ort?
My father, my father, and see you not there Erl-King's daughters at the dark spot?
(—My father, my father, and don't you see Erl-King's daughters in the dark spot over there?)

—mḁen zoːn, mḁen zoːn, lɪç zeː ḁes gə'nḁo, ḁes 'ʃḁenən di 'ḁaltʰən 'vḁedən zoː grḁo.
—Mein Sohn, mein Sohn, ich seh es genau, es scheinen die alten Weiden so grau.
—My son, my son, I see it exactly, there shine the old willows so grey.
(—My son, my son, I see it clearly: it is the old willows that are gleaming so grey.)

—ɪç 'liːbə dɪç, mɪç rḁetst 'dḁenə 'ʃøːnə gə'ʃtʰaltʰ,
—"Ich liebe dich, mich reizt deine schöne Gestalt,
—"I love you, me allures your beautiful form,
(—"I love you, your beautiful form allures me,)

ʊnt' bɪst duː nɪçt' 'vɪlɪç, zoː brḁox lɪç gə'valtʰ.
und bist du nicht willig, so brauch ich Gewalt."
and are you not willing, so use I force."
(and if you are not willing, then I shall use force.")

—mḁen 'faːt'ɐ, mḁen 'faːt'ɐ, jɛtst' fast' lḁeɐ mɪç ḁan!
—Mein Vater, mein Vater, jetzt fasst er mich an!
—My father, my father, now seizes he me ... !   ["*anfassen*" = to seize]
(—My father, my father, now he is seizing me!)

'ɛrlkʰøːnɪç hat' miːɐ/miːr ḁen lḁets gə'tʰaːn! —
Erlkönig hat mir ein Leids getan! —
Erl-King has me an injury done! —
(Erl-King has hurt me! —)

deːm 'faːt'ɐ 'grḁozəts, lḁeɐ 'rḁet'ət gə'ʃvɪnt', lḁeɐ hɛlt' ḁɪn 'ḁarmən das 'ḁɛçtsəndə kʰɪnt',
Dem Vater grauset's, er reitet geschwind, er hält in Armen das ächzende Kind,
To the father horrifies it, he rides fast, he holds in arms the groaning child,
(The father is horrified, he rides fast, he holds in his arms the groaning child,)

ɐɐ'rḁeçt den hoːf mɪt' myː ʊnt' noːtʰ; ḁɪn 'zḁenən 'ḁarmən das kʰɪnt' vḁaɐ tʰoːtʰ.
erreicht den Hof mit Müh und Not; in seinen Armen das Kind war tot.
reaches the courtyard with effort and distress; in his arms the child was dead.
(he reaches the courtyard with a great effort and in dire distress; in his arms the child was dead.)

[*poem:* **mit Mühe** ('myːə)]

[This marvelous, gripping song is all the more remarkable in that the composer was only eighteen years old when he wrote it. The name *Erlkönig* is derived from the Danish *Ellekonge*

484

(elf-king), but as it was translated into German it became "king of the alder trees" instead of "king of the elves." There are four speakers: the narrator, the father, the child, and the erl-king.]

'ɛrnt'əli:t'
Erntelied
Harvest Song

Posthumously published [composed 1816] (poem by Ludwig Hölty)

'zɪçəln 'ʃalən, 'ɛːrən 'falən 'ʊnt'ɐ 'zɪçəlʃal;
Sicheln schallen, Ähren fallen unter Sichelschall;
Sickels resound, ears of corn fall beneath sickel-sound;
(Sickels are sounding, ears of corn are falling to the sound of the sickels;)

ɑof den 'mɛːt'çənhyːt'ən 'tsɪt'ɐn 'blɑoə 'blyːt'ən, frɔøt' lɪst' 'yːbɐ(r)lal.
auf den Mädchenhüten zittern blaue Blüten, Freud ist überall.
on the girls' hats tremble blue blossoms, joy is everywhere.
(on the girls' hats blue blossoms are quivering; joy is everywhere.)

'zɪçəln 'kʰlɪŋən, 'mɛːt'çən 'zɪŋən 'ʊnt'ɐ 'zɪçəlkʰlaŋ,
Sicheln klingen, Mädchen singen unter Sichelklang,
Sickels resound, girls sing beneath sickel-ring,
(Sickels are sounding, girls are singing to the ringing sound of the sickels,)

bɪs fɔm moːnt' bə'ʃɪmɐt', rɪŋs di 'ʃt'ɔp'əl 'flɪmɐt', tʰøːnt deːɐ/deːr 'ɛrnt'əzaŋ.
bis vom Mond beschimmert, rings die Stoppel flimmert, tönt der Erntesang.
till by the moon be-shimmered, all around the stubble glitters, sounds the harvest song.
(till, bathed in moonlight, the stubble is glittering all around, the harvest song is sounding.)

'aləs 'ʃp'rɪŋət', 'aləs 'zɪŋət', vas nuːɐ 'lalən kʰan.
Alles springet, alles singet, was nur lallen kann.
All leaps, all sings, whatever (whoever) only babble can.
(Everyone is leaping, everyone who can babble at all is singing.)

bae dem 'ɛrnt'əmaːlə lɪst' lɑos 'laenɐ 'ʃaːlə kʰneçt' lʊnt' 'bɑoɐsman.
Bei dem Erntemahle isst aus einer Schale Knecht und Bauersmann.
At the harvest meal eats out of one bowl farm-hand and farmer.
(At the harvest feast the farmer and his farm-hand eat out of the same bowl.)

'jeːdɐ 'ʃertsət', 'jeːdɐ 'hertsət dan zaen 'liːbəlaen.
Jeder scherzet, jeder herzet dann sein Liebelein.
Everyone jokes, everyone cuddles then his sweetheart.

naːx gə'leːɐt'ən 'kʰanən, 'geːən ziː fɔn 'danən, 'zɪŋən lʊnt' jʊx'haen!
Nach geleerten Kannen, gehen sie von dannen, singen und juchhei'n!
After drained tankards, go they from there, sing and shout with high spirits!
(After the tankards have all been emptied, they go home, singing and shouting with spirits high!)

[The four-bar prelude, possibly spurious, does not appear in the *Gesamtausgabe*. Schubert omitted the fourth of five verses. A little song cycle of the seasons in folksong-style could consist of *Frühlingslied, Erntelied*, and *Winterlied,* as Dietrich Fischer-Dieskau has suggested.]

Erstarrung see *Winterreise*

'eːɐ̯stʰɐ fɛɐ̯'lʊstʰ
Erster Verlust
First Loss

Op. 5, No. 4 [1815] (Johann Wolfgang von Goethe)

ax, veːɐ̯ brɪŋt di 'ʃøːnən 'tʰaːgə, 'jeːnə 'tʰaːgə deːɐ̯/deːr 'leːɐ̯stʰə 'liːbə,
Ach, wer bringt die schönen Tage, jene Tage der ersten Liebe,
Ah, who brings the beautiful days, those days of the first love,
(Ah, who will bring back the beautiful days, those days of first love?)

ax, veːɐ̯ brɪŋtʰ nuːɐ̯/nuːr 'aenə 'ʃtʰʊndə 'jeːnɐ 'hɔldən tsaet tsu'rʏkʰ!
ach, wer bringt nur eine Stunde jener holden Zeit zurück!
ah, who brings just one hour of that lovely time back?
(Ah, who will bring back even one hour of that lovely time?)

'aenzaːm nɛːr ɪç 'maenə 'vʊndə,
Einsam nähr' ich meine Wunde,
In solitude nurse I my wound,
(In my solitude I nurse my wound,)

ʊntʰ mɪtʰ ʃtʰeːts lɛɐ̯'nɔøtʰɐ 'kʰlaːgə tʰrao rɪç ʊms fɛɐ̯'loːrnə glʏkʰ.
und mit stets erneuter Klage traur' ich ums verlorne Glück.
and with constantly renewed lament mourn I for the lost happiness.
(and with a constantly renewed lament I mourn my lost happiness.)

ax, veːɐ̯ brɪŋt di 'ʃøːnən 'tʰaːgə, veːɐ̯ 'jeːnə 'hɔldə tsaet tsu'rʏkʰ!
Ach, wer bringt die schönen Tage, wer jene holde Zeit zurück!
Ah, who brings the beautiful days, who that lovely time back?
(Ah, who will bring back the beautiful days, that lovely time?) [*poem: without the second* "**wer**"]

[Goethe wrote the poem for a Singspiel, *Die ungleichen Hausgenossen* ("The Dissimilar Housemates"), and, short as it is, Schubert's setting is a masterpiece, touching, sweet and sad.]

evaŋ'geːli̯ʊm jo'hanɪs / ɪn deːɐ̯ tsaetʰ ʃpʰ'raːx deːɐ̯ hɛr 'jeːzʊs
Evangelium Johannis / In der Zeit sprach der Herr Jesus
The Gospel According to St. John (vi. 53-8) / Then Jesus said unto them

First published in 1902 in *Franz Schubert* by Richard Heuberger, Vienna
[composed 1818] (text from the German Bible, modified by Schubert himself)

ɪn deːɐ̯ tsaetʰ ʃpʰ'raːx deːɐ̯ hɛr 'jeːzʊs tsuː den 'ʃaːrən deːɐ̯ 'juːdən:
In der Zeit sprach der Herr Jesus zu den Scharen der Juden:
At that time spoke the Lord Jesus to the multitudes of the Jews:
(At that time the Lord Jesus spoke as follows to the multitude of Jews:)

maen flaeʃ ɪstʰ vaːɐ̯'haftʰɪç 'aenə ʃpʰ'aes, maen bluːtʰ ɪstʰ vaːɐ̯'haftʰɪç aen tʰraŋkʰ!
mein Fleisch ist wahrhaftig eine Speis, mein Blut ist wahrhaftig ein Trank!
my flesh is truly a food, my blood is truly a drink!

veːɐ̯ maen flaeʃ 'ɪsət' ʊnt 'tʰrɪŋk'ət' maen bluːt, deːɐ̯ blaep't' ɪn miːɐ̯/miːr ʊnt' ɪç
Wer mein Fleisch isset und trinket mein Blut, der bleibt in mir und ich
Whoever my flesh eats and drinks my blood, he remains in me and I
(Whoever eats my flesh and drinks my blood will remain in me and I)

ɪn liːm. viː mɪç gə'zant deːɐ̯ le'bɛndɪgə 'faːt'ɐ(r), ʊnt' ɪç 'leːbə ʊm dɛs 'faːt'ɐs
in ihm. Wie mich gesandt der lebendige Vater, und ich lebe um des Vaters
in him. As me (has) sent the living Father, and (as) I live for the Father's
(in him. As the living Father has sent me, and as I live for the Father's)

'vɪlən: 'alzo veːɐ̯ mɪç 'ɪsət', vɪrt' ɑox 'leːbən ʊm 'maenət'vɪlən.
Willen: also wer mich isset, wird auch leben um meinetwillen.
sake: thus whoever me eats, will also live for my sake.
(sake: thus whoever eats me will also live for my sake.)

'diːzəs ɪst das broːt, das fɔm 'hɪməl 'kʰɔmən ɪstʰ. nɪçt' viː 'lɔɸrə 'fɛːt'ɐ
Dieses ist das Brot, das vom Himmel kommen ist. Nicht wie eure Väter
This is the bread that from the heaven come is. Not as your fathers
(This is bread that has come from heaven. Not as your forefathers)

'haːbən 'hɪməlbroːt' gə'gɛsən, ʊnt' zɪnt' gə'ʃt'ɔrbən. veːɐ̯ fɔn 'diːzəm broːt' ɪstʰ,
haben Himmelbrot gegessen, und sind gestorben. Wer von diesem Brot isst,
have heaven- bread eaten, and have died. Whoever of this bread eats,
(ate manna from heaven and are dead. Whoever eats of this bread,)

deːɐ̯ vɪrt' 'leːbən ɪn 'eːvɪçkʰaetʰ.
der wird leben in Ewigkeit.
he will live in eternity.
(will have eternal life.)

[Reinhard van Hoorickx has edited and privately published this song, and has identified the text as coming from the Gospel pericope for the Mass for the Feast of Corpus Christi.]

faːɐ̯t t͡sʊm 'haːdəs
Fahrt zum Hades
Journey to Hades

Posthumously published [composed 1817] (poem by Johann Mayrhofer)

deːɐ̯ 'naxən drøːnt', t͡sy'pʰrɛsən 'flʏst'ɐn, hɔrç, 'gaest'ɐ 'reːdən ʃɑorɪç draen;
Der Nachen dröhnt, Zypressen flüstern, horch, Geister reden schaurig drein;
The boat creaks, cypresses whisper, hark, spirits speak gruesomely thereinto;
(The boat creaks, cypresses whisper; listen! Spirit voices mingle gruesomely with those sounds;)

balt' veːɐ̯d ɪç ʔam gə'ʃt'aːt, dem 'dyːst'ɐn, vaet', vaet' fɔn deːɐ̯ 'ʃøːnən 'eːɐ̯də zaen.
bald werd' ich am Gestad', dem düstern, weit, weit von der schönen Erde sein.
soon shall I at the shore, the dark one, far, far from the beautiful earth be.
(soon I shall be at that dark shore, far, far from the beautiful earth.) [*poem: just one* **"weit"**]

da: 'lɔɸçt'ən 'zɔnə nɪçt' nɔx 'ʃt'ɛrnə, da: tʰøːnt' kʰaen liːt, da: ɪst' kʰaen frɔɸnt'.
Da leuchten Sonne nicht noch Sterne, da tönt kein Lied, da ist kein Freund.
There shine sun not nor stars, there sounds no song, there is no friend.
(There neither sun nor stars are shining; no song sounds there, no friend is there.)

ɛmˈpfaŋ di ˈlɛtstˈə ˈtʰrɛːnə, loː ˈfɛrnə! diː ˈdiːzəs ˈmyːdə ˈaͮogə vaͮentʰ.
Empfang' die letzte Träne, o Ferne! die dieses müde Auge weint.
Receive the last tear, O distance! which this weary eye weeps.
(Receive the last tear, distant earth, which these weary eyes will weep.)   *[poem: no "o"]*

ʃoːn ʃaͮo lɪç di ˈblasən danaˈiːdən, den ˈfluːxbəlaːdnən ˈtʰantˈalʊs;   [ˈʃaͮoə]
Schon schau' ich die blassen Danaiden, den fluchbeladnen Tantalus; *[poem: schaue]*
Already see I the pale Danaids, the curse-laden Tantalus;
(Already I see the pale Danaids,* and curse-laden Tantalus;*)   *[poem: without "blassen"]*

ɛs ˈmʊrməlt ˈtʰoːdəsʃvaŋən ˈfriːdən, fɛɐ̯ˈgɛsənhaͮetˈ, daͮen ˈaltˈɐ flʊs.
es murmelt todesschwangern Frieden, Vergessenheit, dein alter Fluss.
it murmurs death-pregnant peace, Oblivion, your old river.
(your ancient river, Oblivion, murmurs a peace that is pregnant with death.)

fɛɐ̯ˈgɛsən, nɛn lɪç ˈtsviːfax ˈʃtˈɛrbən. vas lɪç mɪtˈ ˈhøːçstˈɐ kʰraftˈ gəˈvan,
Vergessen, nenn' ich zwiefach Sterben. Was ich mit höchster Kraft gewann,
Oblivion, name I twofold dying. What I with highest strength won,
(Oblivion, to forget, forgotten, I call that twofold death. What I have won with my utmost effort,)

fɛɐ̯ˈliːrən, ˈviːdɐ(r) lɛs lɛɐ̯ˈvɛrbən— van ˈlɛndən ˈdiːzə ˈkʰvaːlən, van?
verlieren, wieder es erwerben— wann enden diese Qualen, wann?
to lose, again it to obtain— when end these torments, when?
(to *lose* that, and then to try to win it once more... When will these torments be ended? When?)

[Hades was the underworld land of the dead. Lethe, or "Oblivion," was one of its rivers. *The Danaids, daughters of King Danaus, were doomed to the endless task of carrying water in jugs that were perforated like sieves, because they had—all but one—murdered their bridegrooms on their wedding night, having been warned beforehand that their husbands were ordered to murder *them*. *Tantalus had invited the gods to a banquet; when the supply of food became insufficient, he cut up his son and served the pieces in a stew. His punishment was to hang from a fruit tree above a lake, doomed to eternal hunger and thirst. Whenever he bent down to drink, the water would recede. Whenever he reached for a fruit, the wind would blow the branch too far away. The word "tantalize" is derived from his name. Schubert's song, for a bass voice, is beautiful and less well known than it deserves to be. A few bars of dramatic recitative begin with the word "*Vergessen*"; after the last "*wann?*" Schubert repeats the words of the opening, to similar music.]

ˈfɪʃɐliːtˈ
Fischerlied
Fisherman's Song

Two different settings (both in the *Gesamtausgabe*)
Posthumously published [composed 1816?, 1817] (poem by Johann Gaudenz von Salis-Seewis)

das ˈfɪʃɐgəvɛrbə giːpˈtˈ ˈrʏstˈɪgən muːtˈ! viːɐ̯ ˈhaːbən tsʊm ˈlɛrbə
Das Fischergewerbe gibt rüstigen Mut! Wir haben zum Erbe
The fisherman-trade gives vigorous mettle! We have as the inheritance
(The fisherman's trade gives us a hale and hearty spirit! We have as our inheritance)

di ˈgyːtˈɐ deːɐ̯ fluːtʰ. viːɐ̯ ˈgraːbən nɪçtˈ ˈʃɛtsə, viːɐ̯ ˈpflyːgən kʰaͮen fɛltˈ;
die Güter der Flut. Wir graben nicht Schätze, wir pflügen kein Feld;
the goods of the waters. We dig not treasures, we plow no field;
(the wealth of the waters. We do not dig for treasure, we do not plow a field;)

488

viːɐ̯/viːr ˈlɛrntʼən ɪm ˈnɛt͡sə, viːɐ̯/viːr ˈlaŋəln ɪʊns gɛltʼ. [tra la la la]
wir ernten im Netze, wir angeln uns Geld. [*first version adds* **Tra la la la**]
we harvest in the net, we fish ourselves money. [Tra la la la]
(we gather our harvest in our nets, we fish ourselves money. [Tra la la la.])

viːɐ̯ ˈheːbən di ˈrɔɪ̯zən den ˈʃɪlfbax ɛntʼˈlaŋ, ʊntʼ ruːn baɛ̯ den ˈʃlɔɪ̯zən,
Wir heben die Reusen den Schilfbach entlang, und ruhn bei den Schleusen,
We lift the weir-baskets the reed- brook along, and rest at the sluices,
(We lift the fish traps along the reed-lined stream, and rest at the sluice-gates ,)

t͡suː ˈzɔndɐn den faŋ. gɔltʼˈvaɛ̯dən bəˈʃatʼən das ˈmoːzɪɡə dax;
zu sondern den Fang. Goldweiden beschatten das moosige Dach;
to sort the catch. Golden willows shade the mossy roof;

viːɐ̯ ˈʃlʊmɐn ɪaʊ̯f ˈmatʼən ɪm ˈkʰyːlən ɡəˈmax. mɪtʼ ˈroːtʼən kʰoˈralən
wir schlummern auf Matten im kühlen Gemach. / Mit roten Korallen
we sleep on mats in the cool chamber. / With red corals

pʰraŋtʼ ˈʃpʼiːɡəl ʊntʼ vantʼ, den ˈlɛstʼrɪç deːɐ̯ ˈhalən dɛkʼtʼ ˈzɪlbɐnɐ zantʼ.
prangt Spiegel und Wand, den Estrich der Hallen deckt silberner Sand.
are decked mirror and wall, the stone floor of the halls covers silver sand.
(the mirror and the wall are decorated; silver sand covers the stone floor of the halls.)

das ˈɡɛrtʼçən daˈneːbən ɡryːntʼ ˈlɛntʼlɪç ʊmˈt͡sɔɪ̯ntʼ fɔn ˈkʰrɔɪ̯t͡səndən ˈʃtʼɛːbən
Das Gärtchen daneben grünt ländlich umzäunt von kreuzenden Stäben
The little garden next to it grows rurally fenced with crossing rails
(Next to the house a little garden is growing, rustically fenced with crossed rails,)

mɪtʼ ˈbastʼə fɛɐ̯ˈlaɛ̯ntʰ/fɛrˈlaɛ̯ntʰ. ɪm ˈlantʼlɪt͡s deːɐ̯ ˈbuːbən laxtʼ ˈmuːtʼɪɡɐ zɪn.
mit Baste vereint. / Im Antlitz der Buben lacht mutiger Sinn,
with bast joined together. / In the face of the boys laughs plucky inclination,
(joined together with cords made of bark fiber. / A plucky spirit glows in the faces of the boys;)

ziː ˈmaɛ̯dən di ˈʃtʼuːbən baɛ̯ ˈtʰaːɡəsbəɡɪn; ziː ˈtʰaʊ̯xən ʊntʼ ˈʃvɪmən
sie meiden die Stuben bei Tagesbeginn; sie tauchen und schwimmen
they avoid the rooms at day-beginning; they dive and swim
(they are out of their rooms by daybreak; they dive and swim)

ɪm ˈlaɛ̯zɪɡən zeː, ʊntʼ ˈbaːɐ̯fuːs lɛɐ̯ˈkʰlɪmən ziː ˈkʰlɪpʼən fɔl ʃneː. [fɔn]
im eisigen See, und barfuss erklimmen sie Klippen voll Schnee. [*poem:* **von Schnee**]
in the icy lake, and barefoot climb they crags full of snow. [of]
(in the icy lake, and climb, barefoot, crags covered with snow.)

di ˈtʰœçtʼɐ lɛɐ̯ˈɡœt͡sən zɪç ˈlaːbənt͡s baɛ̯ lɪçtʰ,
Die Töchter ergötzen sich abends bei Licht,
The daughters amuse themselves evenings by light,
(Our daughters amuse themselves in the evening by lamplight,)

vɛn ˈlaləs lan ˈnɛt͡sən ʊntʼ ˈmaʃənvɛrkʼ flɪçtʰ. [van]
wenn alles an Netzen und Maschenwerk flicht. [*poem:* **wann alles**]
when all at nets and network mends.
(when all are mending nets and netting.)

ɔft' vɪrt' mɪt' gə'lɛçt'ɐ dʊrç'mʊst'ɐt das dɔrf; di 'mʊt'ɐ(r), ǀals 'vɛçt'ɐ,
Oft wird mit Gelächter durchmustert das Dorf; die Mutter, als Wächter,
Often is with laughter passed in review the village; the mother, as guard,
(Often they gossip with much laughter about everyone in the village; their mother, on guard,)

ʃyːɐt' 'nɪk'ənt den tʰɔrf. ɔft' 'ruːdɐn viːɐ 'fɛrnə ǀɪm 'viːgəndən kʰaːn;
schürt nickend den Torf. / Oft rudern wir ferne im wiegenden Kahn;
stirs up nodding the peat. / Often row we far out in the rocking boat;
(stirs up the peat, nodding. / Often we row far out in the rocking boat;)

dan 'blɪŋkən di 'ʃt'ɛrnə zoː 'frɔøɲt'lɪç ǀʊns ǀan; deːɐ moːnt' ǀɑos den 'høːən,
dann blinken die Sterne so freundlich uns an; der Mond aus den Höhen,
then twinkle the stars so friendly us at; the moon from the heights,
(then the stars twinkle down at us in a friendly way; the moon in the sky,)

deːɐ moːnt' ǀɑos dem bax, zoː ʃnɛl viːɐ/viːr ǀɛnt'fløːən, ziː 'glɑet'ən ǀʊns naːx.
der Mond aus dem Bach, so schnell wir entflöhen, sie gleiten uns nach.
the moon from the brook, as fast (as) we might flee, they glide us after.
(the moon in the stream, no matter how fast we row, they both keep gliding after us.)

viːɐ 'tʰrɔtsən dem 'vɛt'ɐ, das 'fɪnst'ɐ(r) ǀʊns droːtʰ, vɛn 'ʃœpfəndə 'brɛt'ɐ
Wir trotzen dem Wetter, das finster uns droht, wenn schöpfende Bretter
We defy the weather, that ominously us threatens, when bailing boards
(We defy the weather that ominously threatens us, when bailing ladles) [*poem:* **wann** (van)]

kʰɑom 'hɛmən den tʰoːt'. viːɐ 'tʰrɔtsən ǀɑox 'voːgən ǀɑof 'kʰraxəndəm ʃif,
kaum hemmen den Tod. Wir trotzen auch Wogen auf krachendem Schiff,
(scarcely hinder the death. We defy also waves on crashing ship,
(scarcely can slow the advance of death. We also defy the waves, on a foundering ship,)

ǀɪn 'tʰiːfən gə'tsoːgən, gə'ʃlɔødɐt' ǀans rif! deːɐ hɛr, deːɐ/deːr ǀɪn 'ʃt'ʏrmən
in Tiefen gezogen, geschleudert ans Riff! / Der Herr, der in Stürmen
into depths drawn, hurled onto the reef! / The Lord, who in storms
(drawn down into the depths, dashed against a reef! / The Lord, who during storms)

deːɐ 'mɪt'ɐnaxt' blɪtstʰ, fɛɐ'maːk' ǀʊns tsuː 'ʃirmən, ǀʊnt' kʰɛnt', vas ǀʊns nʏtstʰ.
der Mitternacht blitzt, vermag uns zu schirmen, und kennt, was uns nützt.
to the midnight flashes, has the power us to shield, and knows, what to us is of use.
(lights the midnight sky with lightning, has the power to shield us and knows what we need.)

glɑeç 'ǀʊnt'ɐ dem 'flyːgəl dɛs 'leːvɪgən ruːt deːɐ 'raːzəngrʊft' 'hyːgəl,
Gleich unter dem Flügel des Ewigen ruht der Rasengruft Hügel,
Equally under the wing of the Eternal One rests the grass- tomb mound,
(Under the wing of the Eternal One rest equally both the grave under a grass-covered mound)
[*poem:* **den Flügeln** (den 'flyːgəln, the wings)]

das graːp' ǀɪn deːɐ fluːtʰ.
das Grab in der Flut.
the grave in the waters.
(and the grave beneath the waters.)

[The two versions are very different: the first has a vigorous swing to it and some jolly tra-la-las at the end of the verses; the second is marked "moderate, calm," suggests a reflective mood, and, with other words, could do good service as a cradle song (at least the first eight bars).]

490

'fɪʃɐvaezə
Fischerweise
Fisherman's Tune

Op. 96, No. 4 [1826] (Franz Xaver von Schlechta)

den fɪʃɐ 'fɛçtʼən 'zɔrgən lʊntʼ graːm lʊntʼ laetʼ nɪçtʼ lan;
Den Fischer fechten Sorgen und Gram und Leid nicht an;
The fisherman attack cares and grief and sorrow not at; ["*anfechten*" = attack]
(Cares and grief and sorrow do not attack the fisherman;)

eːɐ løːstʼ lam 'fryːən 'mɔrgən mɪtʼ 'laeçtʼəm zɪn den kʰaːn.
er löst am frühen Morgen mit leichtem Sinn den Kahn.
He unties in the early morning with light mind the boat.
(In a light-hearted mood he unties his boat in the early morning.)

daː 'laːgɐtʼ rɪŋs nɔx 'friːdə laof valtʼ lʊntʼ fluːɐ/fluːr lʊntʼ bax,
Da lagert rings noch Friede auf Wald und Flur und Bach,
There rests all around still peace on woods and meadow and brook,
(All around there is still peacefulness in the woods, in the meadow and the brook;)

eːɐ ruːftʼ mɪtʼ 'zaenəm 'liːdə di 'gɔldnə 'zɔnə vax.
er ruft mit seinem Liede die goldne Sonne wach.
he calls with his song the golden sun awake.
(with his song he wakes the golden sun.)

eːɐ zɪŋt tsu 'zaenəm 'vɛrkʼə laos 'fɔlɐ 'frɪʃɐ brʊstʰ,
Er singt zu seinem Werke aus voller frischer Brust, [*poem:* **Und** (lʊntʼ, and) **singt...**]
He sings at his work out of full fresh breast,
(He sings at his work from a full, fresh heart;)

di 'larbaetʼ giːpʼtʼ liːm 'ʃtʼɛrkʼə, di 'ʃtʼɛrkʼə 'leːbənslʊstʰ.
die Arbeit gibt ihm Stärke, die Stärke Lebenslust.
the work gives him strength, the strength life- pleasure.
(the work gives him strength, his strength gives him zest for life.)

baltʼ vɪrtʼ laen bʊntʼ gə'vɪməl lɪn 'lalən 'tʰiːfən laotʰ,
Bald wird ein bunt Gewimmel in allen Tiefen laut,
Soon becomes a many-colored swarm in all depths loud,
(Soon a colorful swarm starts to make noises at all depths,)

ʊntʼ 'pʰlɛtʃɐtʼ dʊrç den 'hɪməl, deːɐ zɪç lɪm 'vasɐ baotʰ.
und plätschert durch den Himmel, der sich im Wasser baut.
and splashes through the sky that itself in the water constructs.
(and splashes through the sky that is reflected in the water.)

[ʊntʼ ʃlʏpftʼ laof 'glatʼən 'ʃtʼaenən lʊntʼ 'baːdətʼ zɪç lʊntʼ ʃnɛltʰ,
[Und schlüpft auf glatten Steinen und badet sich und schnellt,
[And slips on smooth stones and bathes itself and leaps up,
[(And slips over smooth stones, and bathes, and leaps up,)

deːɐ 'groːsə frɪst den 'kʰlaenən, viː laof deːɐ 'gantsən vɛltʰ.]
der Grosse frisst den Kleinen, wie auf der ganzen Welt.]
the big one devours the little one, as in the whole world.]

dɔx veːɐ̯/veːr lae̯n nɛt͡s vɪl   ˈʃtˈɛlən, braoxtˈ ˈlaogən kʰlaːɐ̯/kʰlaːr lʊntˈ guːtʰ,
Doch wer   ein Netz will   stellen, braucht Augen klar   und gut,
But   whoever a   net   wants to cast, needs   eyes   clear   and good,
(But whoever wants to cast a net needs to have good clear eyes,)

mʊs ˈhae̯tˈɐ glae̯ç den ˈvɛlən lʊntˈ frae̯ zae̯n viː di fluːtʰ;
muss heiter gleich den Wellen und frei sein wie die Flut;
must cheerful like the waves and free be   as the water;
(must be cheerful like the waves and as free as the water;)

dɔrtˈ ˈlaŋəltˈ lao̯f deːɐ̯ ˈbrʏkˈə di ˈhɪrtˈɪn,   ˈʃlao̯ɐ vɪçtʰ!
dort angelt auf der Brücke die Hirtin,   schlauer Wicht!
there fishes on the bridge the shepherdess, sly   creature!
(there on the bridge the shepherdess is fishing, the sly creature!)

giːpˈ lao̯f nuːɐ̯ ˈdae̯nə ˈtʰʏkˈə, deːn fɪʃ bəˈtʰryːkst duː nɪçtʰ!   [lɛntˈzaːgə ˈdae̯nɐ ˈtʰʏkˈə]
Gib auf nur deine Tücke, d e n Fisch betrügst du nicht! [*var.:* Entsage   deiner Tücke]
Give up only your trick, *this* fish deceive   you not!   [Renounce   your   trick]
(Just give up your tricks: *this* fish you won't deceive!)

[The *Gesamtausgabe* prints both the first draft and the fair copy (Peters the latter only); there are some differences. Schubert omitted the fifth verse (in brackets above) for the sake of musical symmetry; for the last verse he altered the vocal line, to make a verbal point, but kept the accompaniment the same. This famous song is overflowing with energy, humor, and charm.]

ˈflɔːri̯o (t͡svae̯ ˈʃt͡seːnən. ˈleːɐ̯stˈə)
Florio (Zwei Szenen. I.)
Florio (from "Two Scenes." I.)
(from the play *Lacrimas*)

Op. 124, No. 2 [1825] (Christian Wilhelm von Schütz)

nuːn, daː ˈʃatˈən ˈniːdɐglae̯tˈən, lʊnt di ˈlʏftˈə ˈt͡sɛːɐ̯tˈlɪç ˈveːən,
Nun, da   Schatten niedergleiten, und die Lüfte zärtlich   wehen,
Now, when shadows down- glide,   and the airs   tenderly blow,
(Now, when shadows are gliding down and the breezes blow tenderly,)

ˈdrɪŋətˈ ˈzɔ͡ʏft͡sən lao̯s deːɐ̯ ˈzeːlə lʊntˈ lʊmˈgɪrt   di ˈtʰrɔ͡øən ˈzae̯tˈən.
dringet Seufzen aus der Seele und umgirrt   die treuen Saiten.
presses sighing out of the soul and around-coos the faithful strings.
(sighs are pressed out of my soul and coo around the faithful strings.)

ˈkʰlaːgət, das liːɐ̯ mɪtˈ miːɐ̯ ˈʃtˈɛrbətˈ ˈbɪtˈɐn tʰoːtˈ, vɛn diː nɪçtˈ ˈhae̯lətˈ,
Klaget, dass ihr mit mir sterbet bittern Tod, wenn die nicht heilet,
Lament that you with me die (a) bitter   death, if *she* not   heals,
(Lament, strings, that you will die a bitter death with me if *she* does not heal me,)

diː   den ˈbɛçɐ miːɐ̯ gəˈrae̯çətʰ, ˈfɔlɐ gɪft, das lɪç lʊntˈ liːɐ̯ fɛɐ̯ˈdɛrbətʰ.
die   den Becher mir gereichet, voller Gift, dass ich und ihr verderbet.*
(she) who the cup   to me offers   full of poison, so that I   and you perish.
(she who offers me a cup full of poison, so that I—and you—will perish.)

[*original text:* **voller Gift in süssem Scherbet** = full of poison in sweet sherbet (*now* **Sorbet**)]

eːɐ̯st' mɪt 'tʰøːnən, zanft' viː 'fløːt'ən, gɔs ziː ʃmɛrts ɪn 'maenə 'laːdɐn;
Erst mit Tönen, sanft wie Flöten, goss sie Schmerz in meine Adern;
First with tones gentle as flutes poured she pain into my veins;
(First, with tones as gentle as flutes, she poured pain into my veins;)

'zeːən 'vɔlt'ə ziː deːɐ̯ 'kʰraŋk'ə, ʊnt' nuːn vɪrt' liːɐ̯ raets liːn 'tʰøːt'ən.
sehen wollte sie der Kranke, und nun wird ihr Reiz ihn töten.
to see wanted her the sick man, and now will her charm him kill.
(the sick man wanted to see her, and now her charms will kill him.)

naxt', kʰɔm heːɐ̯, mɪç tsuː ʊm'vɪndən mɪt dem 'farbənloːzən 'dʊŋk'əl!
Nacht, komm her, mich zu umwinden mit dem farbenlosen Dunkel!
Night, come hither, me to encircle with the colorless darkness!
(Night, come and encircle me with your colorless darkness!)

'ruːə vɪl lɪç bae diːɐ̯ 'zuːxən, di: miːɐ̯ noːt tʰuːt', balt tsuː 'fɪndən.
Ruhe will ich bei dir suchen, die mir not tut, bald zu finden.
rest want I in you to seek, which for me necessary is, soon to find.
(In you, night, I shall seek rest, which I need to find soon.) ["*not tun*" = to be necessary]

[Schubert composed music for two songs from the play *Lacrimas* ("Tears") by Christian Wilhelm von Schütz, mistakenly believing the author to have been A. W. Schlegel (who had in fact been the editor of the printed text), and the first edition of these songs perpetuated the error. The words alone might wrongly suggest a rather somber mood, but Schubert's music makes it clear that they are not to be taken seriously in this charming serenade.]

fraɡ'mɛnt' ɑos dem 'ɛʃylʊs
Fragment aus dem Aeschylus
Fragment from Aeschylus
(from *The Eumenides*)

Posthumously published [composed 1816] (translated by Johann Mayrhofer)

zoː vɪrt deːɐ̯ man, deːɐ̯ 'zɔndɐ tsvaŋ ɡə'rɛçt' lɪst', nɪçt' ʊn'ɡlʏk'lɪç zaen,
So wird der Mann, der sonder Zwang gerecht ist, nicht unglücklich sein,
So will the man, who without coercion just is, not unhappy be,
(Thus the man who is just without coercion will not be unhappy;)

fɛɐ̯'zɪŋk'ən ɡants ɪn 'leːlənt' kʰan leːɐ̯ 'nɪmɐ; ɪn'dɛs deːɐ̯ 'freːfəlndə fɛɐ̯'breçɐ(r)
versinken ganz in Elend kann er nimmer; indess der frevelnde Verbrecher
sink completely into misery can he never; while the wanton criminal
(he can never sink completely into misery; whereas the wanton criminal)

ɪm 'ʃt'roːmə deːɐ̯ tsaet' ɡə'valt'zaːm 'ʊnt'ɐɡeːtʰ, ['ʊnt'ɐzɪŋk'tʰ]
im Strome der Zeit gewaltsam untergeht, [*Schubert's first version:* **untersinkt**]
in the stream of the time violently goes under, [sinks under]
(perishes violently in the stream of time,)

vɛn lam tsɛɐ̯'ʃmɛt'ɐt'ən 'mast'ə das 'vɛt'ɐ di 'zeːɡəl lɛɐ̯'ɡraeftʰ.
wenn am zerschmetterten Maste das Wetter die Segel ergreift.
when at the shattered mast the storm the sails seizes.
(when the storm seizes the sails at the shattered mast.)

eːɐ̯ ruːftʰ,   fɔn ˈkʰaɛnəm loːɐ̯ fɛɐ̯ˈnɔmən,   kʰɛmpftʰ lɪn dɛs ˈʃtʰruːdəls ˈmɪtʰə,
Er ruft,   von keinem Ohr vernommen, kämpft in des Strudels   Mitte,
He cries out, by no   ear   heard,   struggles in the whirlpool's middle,
(He cries out, unheard by any ear, and struggles in the midst of the whirlpool,)

ˈhɔfnʊŋsloːs. dɛs ˈfreːflɐs laxt di ˈgɔtʰhaɛtʰ nuːn,   [jɛtstʰ]
hoffnungslos. Des   Frevlers lacht die Gottheit nun,   [*Schubert's first version:* jetzt]
hopelessly. At the evil-doer laughs the godhead now,   [now]
(hopelessly. The deity laughs at the evil-doer now,)

ziːtʰ liːn, nuːn nɪçtʰ meːɐ̯ ʃtʰɔlts, lɪn ˈbandən deːɐ̯ noːtʰ   fɛɐ̯ˈʃtʰrɪkʰtʰ,
sieht ihn, nun nicht mehr stolz, in Banden der   Not   verstrickt,
sees him, now no   longer proud, in bonds of the distress entangled,
(sees him, now no longer proud, entangled in bonds of distress,)

ʊmˈzɔnst di ˈfɛlsbaŋkʰ fliːn; lan deːɐ̯ fɛɐ̯ˈgɛltʰʊŋ fɛls ˈʃaɛtʰɐtʰ zaɛn glʏkʰ,
umsonst die Felsbank fliehn; an der Vergeltung Fels scheitert   sein Glück,
in vain   the rocky reef escape; on the requital's   rock is wrecked his fortune,
(escape in vain the rocky reef: his fortune is wrecked on the rocks of retribution,)

ʊntʰ ˈlʊnbəvaɛntʰ fɛɐ̯ˈzɪŋkʰtʰ leːɐ̯.
und unbeweint versinkt   er.
and unwept   sinks   he.
(and unmourned he sinks.)

[The *Gesamtausgabe* prints two versions of this short, powerfully dramatic song, the first derived from Schubert's original draft, the second, somewhat longer, from the fair copy. The words in brackets, above, are from the first draft and were later corrected. The text is a translation from the original Greek, an excerpt from a speech by the Chorus in *The Eumenides*.]

Fragment aus Schillers Gedicht see *Die Götter Griechenlands*

ˈfraɛvɪlɪgəs fɛɐ̯ˈzɪŋkʰən
Freiwilliges Versinken
Voluntary Sinking

Posthumously published [composed 1817?] (poem by Johann Mayrhofer)

voˈhɪn, loː ˈheːlios? lɪn ˈkʰyːlən ˈfluːtʰən vɪl lɪç den ˈflamənlaɛpʰ fɛɐ̯ˈzɛŋkən,
Wohin, o Helios? "In kühlen Fluten will ich den Flammenleib versenken,
Whither, O Helios? "In cool   waters want I   the flame-   body to sink,
(Whither, O Helios, god of the sun? —"I want to immerse my flaming body in cool waters,)
                              [*poem: without the word* "**kühlen**"]

gəˈvɪs lɪm ˈlɪnɐn,   ˈnɔɣ̊ə ˈgluːtʰən deːɐ̯/deːr ˈleːɐ̯də ˈfɔɣ̊ɐraɛç tsuː ˈʃɛŋkʰən.
gewiss im   Innern,   neue Gluten der   Erde feuerreich zu schenken.
certain in the inner being, new warmth to the earth fire- rich to give.
(inwardly certain that I, rich in fire, can continue to bestow new warmth upon the earth.)
            [*poem:* **der Erde nach Bedarf** (naːx bəˈdarf, according to need) **zu schenken**]

494

ɪç 'neːmə nɪçtˈ, lɪç 'pfleːgə   nuːɐ̯ t͜suː 'geːbən; lʊntˈ viː fɛɐ̯'ʃvɛndərɪʃ   maen
Ich nehme nicht, ich pflege   nur zu geben; und wie verschwenderisch mein
I   take not, I   am accustomed only to give; and as prodigal   my
(I do not take, I am accustomed only to give; and, as prodigal as my)
          [*poem:* **Ich nehme nichts** (nɪçt͜s, nothing), **gewohnt** (gə'voːnt, accustomed) **zu geben**]

'leːbən, ʊm'hʏltˈ maen 'ʃaedən 'gɔldnə pʰraxtʰ, lɪç 'ʃaedə 'hɛrlɪç,   naːt di naxtʰ.
Leben, umhüllt mein Scheiden goldne Pracht,   ich scheide herrlich,   naht die Nacht.
life,   surrounds my   departure golden splendor: I depart gloriously, nears the night.
(life is, so is my departure bathed in golden splendor: I depart gloriously when night is nearing.)

viː blas deːɐ̯ moːntˈ, viː mat di 'ʃtˈɛrnə, zoː laŋ   lɪç 'kʰrɛftˈɪç mɪç bə'veːgə;
Wie blass der Mond, wie matt die Sterne, so lang   ich kräftig   mich bewege;
How pale the moon, how faint the stars, as long (as) I powerfully myself bestir;
(How pale the moon, how faint the stars, as long as I am in powerful motion;)
          [*poem:* **wie bleich** (blaeç, pale) **der Mond**]

eːɐ̯stˈ vɛn lɪç laof di 'bɛrgə   'maenə 'kʰroːnə 'leːgə,
erst wenn ich auf die Berge   meine Krone lege,
first when I   upon the mountains my   crown lay,
(not until I lay my crown down upon the mountains)
          [*poem:* **erst wenn ich ab** (lapˈ, down) **die** (di, the) **Krone lege**]

gə'vɪnən ziː lan muːtˈ   lʊntˈ kʰraftˈ lɪn 'vaetˈɐ 'fɛrnə.
gewinnen sie an Mut   und Kraft in weiter Ferne."
gain   they in courage and power in far   distance."
(do they gain courage and strength in the far distance.")
          [*poem:* **wird ihnen** (vɪrtˈ 'liːnən, is given to them) **Mut und Glanz** (glant͜s, radiance)
                                    in ihrer ('liːrɐ, their) **Ferne**]

[Schubert made numerous changes in the text of the poem, as indicated above. Schubert set more
than forty poems by his friend Mayrhofer; many of them were inspired by nostalgia for ancient
Greece, as it was imagined by young romantic Germans at the time. In this poem, the sun god,
freely giving light and warmth, is a symbol of the artist and his mission. The title is prophetic:
Mayrhofer took his own life. The music is remarkably adventurous, far in advance of its era.]

'frɔɪ̯də deːɐ̯ 'kʰɪndɐjaːrə
Freude der Kinderjahre
Joy of Childhood

Posthumously published [composed 1816] (poem by Friedrich von Köpken)

'frɔɪ̯də, diː lɪm 'fryːən 'lɛnt͜sə 'maenəm 'haoptˈə 'bluːmən vantˈ,
Freude, die im   frühen Lenze meinem Haupte Blumen wand,
Joy,   that in the early   spring for my head   flowers wreathed,
(Joy, that in early spring wreathed flowers for my head,)

ziː, nɔx 'dʊftˈən   'daenə 'kʰrɛnt͜sə, nɔx geː lɪç lan 'daenɐ hantˈ.
sieh', noch duften   deine Kränze, noch geh' ich an deiner Hand.
see, still are fragrant your garlands, still walk I   at   your   hand.
(see, your garlands are still fragrant, I still walk with your hand in mine.)

[*published poem:* **sieh', im Schmucke deiner Kränze wall' ich noch an deiner Hand.**]
[see, in the adornment of your garlands I still wander with you hand in hand.]

zɛlpst deːɐ̯ 'kʰɪnt'hae̯t' 'kʰnɔsp'ən 'blyːən lao̯f lɪn 'mae̯nɐ fant'aˈziː;
Selbst der Kindheit   Knospen   blühen auf in meiner Phantasie;
Even the childhood's buds   bloom open in my   fantasy;
(Even the buds of childhood bloom open in my fantasy;)

[*poem:* **Selbst der Kindheit Knospen blühen meinem Geiste noch einmal,**
(even the buds of childhood bloom in my spirit once again)]

ʊnt' mɪt' 'frɪʃəm   'rae̯tsə ˈˈglyːən nɔx lɪn 'mae̯nəm 'hɛrpst'ə ziː   ['frɪʃən 'roːzən]
und mit frischem Reize glühen noch in meinem Herbste sie. [*Peters:* mit frischen Rosen]
and with fresh   charms glow still in my   autumn they.   [fresh   roses]
(and with fresh charms they still are glowing in the autumn of my life.)

[*poem:* **und im Abendschimmer glühen sie mir all' im Morgenstrahl.**
(and in the glimmer of my evening they all glow as if in morning sunlight)]

Verses two through five from the Gesamtausgabe *(different from those in the printed poem):*

[fryː ʃoːn kʰant' lɪç dɪç! duː 'veːt'əst' froː   bae̯ 'jeːdəm ʃp'iːl lʊm   mɪç,
[Früh schon kannt' ich dich! du wehtest froh   bei jedem Spiel um   mich,
[Early already knew I   you! you wafted   happily at   every game around me,
[(Already in early childhood I knew you! You hovered about me whenever I was playing,)

ʃp'raŋst'   lɪn 'mae̯nəm 'balə, 'dreːt'əst' lae̯çt' lɪn 'mae̯nəm 'kʰrae̯zəl dɪç;
sprangst   in meinem Balle, drehtest leicht in meinem Kreisel dich;
(you) bounced in my   ball, spun   easily in my   top   yourself;
(you bounced in my ball, you spun easily in my top;)

liːfst' mɪt' miːɐ̯ dʊrç   graːs lʊnt' 'hɛk'ən 'flʏçt'ɪç 'ʃmɛt'ɐlɪŋə   naːx,
liefst mit mir durch Gras und Hecken flüchtig Schmetterlinge nach,
ran with me   through grass and hedges hastily butterflies   after,
(you ran with me through grass and heges, chasing after butterflies,)

'rɪt'əst' mɪt' lao̯f 'bʊnt'ən   'ʃt'ɛk'ən,   'vɪrbəlt'əst' lɪm   't'rɔməlʃlaːk'.
rittest mit auf bunten   Stecken,   wirbeltest im   Trommelschlag.
rode   with on bright-colored hobby horses, rolled   in the drum- beat.
(you rode with me on brightly painted hobby horses and rolled the drum with me.)

'ʃt'ʏrmt'ə mɪt' bəˈlae̯st'ən 'lɔk'ən lao̯x deːɐ̯ 'vɪnt'ɐ vɪlt   daˈheːɐ̯:
Stürmte mit beeisten   Locken auch der Winter wild   daher:
Stormed with ice-covered curls   also the winter fiercely hither:
(Likewise, if winter came storming this way with ice-covered curls:)

oː lɪn 'zae̯nəs ʃneːs   'flɔk'ən zaː lɪç nuːɐ̯ deːɐ̯ 'ʃp'iːlə meːɐ̯;
o in seines Schnees Flocken sah ich nur der   Spiele mehr;
oh, in its   snow's flakes   saw I only of the games more;
(oh, in its snowflakes I only saw more chances to play;)

[*poem (fits the rhythm better)*: **o in seinen Silberflocken** (oh, in its silvery flakes)]

duː, duː 'zɛlbə 'ʃp'raŋəst' 'mɪt'ən   dʊrç gəˈt'ʏrmt'ən ʃneː miːɐ̯ foːɐ̯,
Du, du selber sprangest mitten   durch getürmten Schnee mir vor,
You, you yourself jumped   in the middle through piled-up   snow me before,
(You, you yourself, jumped before me into the midst of piled-up snow,)

ˈzaːsəstˈ mɪtˈ ɪm ˈkʰlaɛnən ˈʃlɪtˈən, ˈloːdɐ ʃpˈantˈəst dɪç daˈfoːɐ̯.
sassest mit im kleinen Schlitten, oder spanntest dich davor.
sat with in the little sled, or hitched yourself in front of it.
(you sat with me on the little sled, or hitched yourself in front to pull it.)

ˈkʰaːmən lɑox tsuˈvaɛlən ˈzɔrgən: ˈkʰɪndɐzɔrgən zɪntˈ nɪçtˈ groːs!
Kamen auch zuweilen Sorgen: Kindersorgen sind nicht gross!
Came also at times cares: children's troubles are not big!
(If at times cares came along too—children's troubles are not big ones!—)

froː hʏpftˈ lɪç lam ˈlandɛn ˈmɔrgən, ˈʃɑokˈəltˈə di ˈzɔrgən loːs;
froh hüpft' ich am andern Morgen, schaukelte die Sorgen los;
happily hopped I on the next morning, swung the cares away;
(the next morning I would be skipping around happily and easing my cares away on the swing;)

ˈkʰletˈɐtˈə diːɐ̯ naːx lɑof ˈbɔømə, ˈveltstˈə myːtˈ lɪm ˈgraːzə mɪç;
kletterte dir nach auf Bäume, wälzte müd' im Grase mich;
climbed you after on trees, rolled tired in the grass myself;
(I climbed trees after you, rolled about in the grass, tired;)

ʊntˈ lentˈʃliːf lɪç: ˈzyːsə ˈtʰrɔømə ˈtsaɛkˈtˈən miːɐ̯/mːr lɪm ˈbɪldə dɪç!
und entschlief ich: süsse Träume zeigten mir im Bilde dich!
and fell asleep I: sweet dreams showed to me in the effigy you!
(and if I fell asleep, then sweet dreams showed me you in effigy!)

ˈzeːlɪç ˈfloːən tʰaːkˈ lʊntˈ ˈjaːrə zoː lan ˈdaɛnɐ hantˈ miːɐ̯ hɪn!
Selig flohen Tag' und Jahre so an deiner Hand mir hin!
Blissfully flew days and years thus at your hand for me by!
(Thus days and years flew blissfully by, as you led me by the hand!)

blaɛçt deːɐ̯ herpstˈ lɑox ˈmaɛnə ˈhaːrə: dɔx blaɛpˈtˈ miːɐ̯ daɛn ˈfroːɐ zɪn.
Bleicht der Herbst auch meine Haare: doch bleibt mir dein froher Sinn.
Bleaches the autumn even my hairs: nevertheless remains to me your happy nature.
(Even though autumn whitens my hair: nevertheless your happy nature remains with me.)

kʰɔmtˈ maɛn ˈvɪntˈɐ(r): ˈlʊnfɛɐ̯gesən zaɛ lɑox dan daɛn frɔøntˈ fɔn diːɐ̯;
Kommt mein Winter: unvergessen sei auch dann dein Freund von dir;
Comes my winter: unforgotten be also then your friend by you;
(When my winter comes, may you not forget your friend;)

nɔx lʊm ˈmaɛnəs graːps tsyˈpʰrɛsən ˈʃlɪŋə ˈdaɛnə ˈroːzən miːɐ̯!]
noch um meines Grabs Zypressen schlinge deine Rosen mir!]
still around my grave's cypresses twine your roses for me!]
(twine your roses even around the cypresses that shade my grave!)]

A second verse, by Max Kalbeck, printed in the Peters edition:

[ˈyːbɐ ˈmaɛnɐ ˈzeːnzʊçtˈ ˈbrʏkˈə vand lɪç ʃtˈɪl tsʊr ˈaltˈən tsaɛtʰ,
[Über meiner Sehnsucht Brücke wandl' ich still zur alten Zeit,
[Over my yearning's bridge wander I quietly to the old time,
[(I quietly wander back to that good old time over the bridge of my yearning,)

tsu: deːɐ̯ ˈjuːgənt̚ ˈlɔfnəm ˈglʏk̚ə   tʰraːk̚ lɪç ma̯en fɛɐ̯ˈʃlɔsnəs   laet̚.
zu der Jugend offnem Glücke   trag' ich mein verschloss'nes Leid.
to the youth's open   happiness carry I   my   locked   sorrow.
(back to the open happiness of youth I carry my locked-up sorrow.)

dan viː ˈtʰrɔø̯ə ˈmʊt̚ɐhɛndə ryːɐ̯t̚   lɛs lan mɪç zanft̚ ʊnt̚ lɪnt̚,
Dann wie treue Mutterhände rührt es an mich sanft und lind,
Then like faithful mother-hands touches it at me   softly and   gently,
(Then it touches me softly and gently, like the hands of a faithful mother,)

ʊnt̚ lɪç zɪŋk̚ lao̯fs   kʰniː lam ˈlɛndə, lax lʊnt̚ va̯en lʊnt̚ bɪn laen kʰɪnt̚.]
und ich sink' aufs   Knie am   Ende, lach' und wein' und bin ein Kind.]
and I   sink onto the knee in the end,   laugh and cry   and am a   child.]
(and, in the end, I sink down on my knees, laugh and cry, and become a child again.)]

[Schubert copied out only the first verse, followed by repeat marks. Either he made extensive changes or the variants (indicated above) derive from another version of the poem than the published one. The second, third, and fourth verses in the *Gesamtausgabe* are clearly referring to boyhood memories, whereas the two verses in the Peters edition could be sung by a woman or a man with equal appropriateness. Both versions differ considerably from the poem as printed in the collection of Schubert song texts researched and edited by Maximilian and Lilly Schochow. The *Gesamtausgabe* gives the song in the key of C, as in the first draft; the Peters version is transposed down to A major. Kalbeck's verse adds a note of pathos not explicit in the original.]

ˈfrøːlɪçəs ˈʃae̯dən
Fröhliches Scheiden
Cheerful Parting

Unfinished [composed 1827 or 1828] (poem by Karl Gottfried von Leitner)

gaːɐ̯ ˈfrøːlɪç   kʰan lɪç ˈʃae̯dən, lɪç hɛt̚   lɛs nɪçt̚ gəˈmae̯ntʰ;
Gar fröhlich   kann ich scheiden, ich hätt'   es nicht gemeint;
Very cheerfully can I   leave,   I   would have it not   thought;
(I can leave very cheerfully; I never would have thought so:)

di ˈtʰrɛnʊŋ   brɪŋt̚ zɔnst̚ ˈlae̯dən, dɔx ˈfrøːlɪç   kʰan lɪç ˈʃae̯dən;
die Trennung bringt sonst Leiden,   doch fröhlich   kann ich scheiden;
the separation brings usually suffering, yet   cheerfully can I   leave;
(separation usually brings suffering; yet I can leave cheerfully:)

ziː hat̚ lʊm mɪç gəˈva̯entʰ. viː   tʰraːk̚ lɪç diːs lɛntˈtsʏk̚ən
sie hat um mich geweint. Wie   trag' ich dies Entzücken
she has for me   wept.   How bear I   this delight
(because — she *cried* for me! How can I bear this delight)

lɪn ˈʃt̚ʊmɐ   brʊst̚ fɛɐ̯ˈlae̯ntʰ/fɛrˈlae̯ntʰ? lɛs vɪl mɪç fast̚   lɛɐ̯ˈdrʏk̚ən,
in stummer Brust vereint?   Es will mich fast   erdrücken,
in silent   breast united?   It   will me   nearly crush,
(silently when we are together? Trying to hide my happiness nearly kills me!)

viː tʰraːk̚ lɪç diːs lɛntˈtsʏk̚ən? ziː hat̚ lʊm mɪç gəˈva̯entʰ!
wie trag' ich dies Entzücken? Sie hat um mich geweint!
how bear I   this delight?   She has for me   wept!
(How can I bear this delight? She cried because I told her I had to leave!)

iːɐ̯/iːr ˈalpˈən, ˈzeːən lʊntˈ ˈlaọən,　　du: moːnt, deːɐ̯　zi: bəˈʃaẹntʰ,
Ihr Alpen, Seen und Auen,　　du Mond, der　sie bescheint,
You alps,　　lakes, and　meadows, you moon,　which her shines on,
(You alps, lakes, and meadows, you, moon, who shine down on her,)

ɔ͜øç　vɪl　lɪç mɪç　fɛɐ̯ˈtʰraọən: iːɐ̯/iːr ˈalpˈən, ˈzeːən lʊntˈ ˈlaọən!
euch will　ich mich　vertrauen: ihr　Alpen, Seen und Auen!
to you want I　myself to confide: you　alps,　　lakes, and　meadows!
(I want to confide in you: you alps, lakes, and meadows,)

zi: hatˈ lʊm mɪç　gəˈvaẹntʰ. ʊntˈ ʃtˈɛrb ɪç　lɪn deːɐ̯ ˈfrɛmdə,
sie hat um mich geweint. Und sterb' ich in der Fremde,
she has for me　wept.　　And die　I　in the　foreign land, [*"in der Fremde"* = abroad]
(she cried for me! And if I should die while I am away in a foreign land,)

miːɐ̯ dʏŋkˈtˈ nɪçtˈ ˈfʏrçtˈɐlɪç　deːɐ̯ ʃlaːf lɪm　ˈlaẹçənhɛmdə;
mir dünkt　nicht fürchterlich der Schlaf im　Leichenhemde;
to me seems　not　frightening　the sleep　in the shroud;
(the long sleep in a shroud does not seem frightening to me;)

dɛn, ʃtˈɛrb ɪç　lɪn deːɐ̯ ˈfrɛmdə,　zo: vaẹntˈ zi: voːl　lʊm mɪç.
denn, sterb' ich in der Fremde,　so　weint sie wohl　um mich.
for,　die　I　in the　foreign land, then weeps she probably for me.
(because if I die in a foreign land she will probably weep for me.)

[Only the vocal line was complete; the accompaniment was left as a sketch. The song has been edited and privately published by Reinhard van Hoorickx.]

ˈfroːzɪn
Frohsinn
Cheerfulness

Posthumously published [composed 1817] (poem by Ignaz Franz Castelli)

ɪç bɪn fɔn ˈlɔkˈərəm ˈʃlaːgə,　gəˈniːs ˈloːnə　ˈtʰryːpˈzɪn　di vɛltʰ,
Ich bin von lockerem Schlage, geniess' ohne　Trübsinn　die Welt,
I　am of　easy-going character, enjoy　　without melancholy the world,
(I am an easy-going sort; I enjoy the world without any melancholy,)

mɪç drʏkˈtˈ kʰaẹn ʃmɛrts, ˈkʰaẹnə ˈpʰlaːgə,　maẹn ˈfroːzɪn　vʏrtstˈ miːɐ̯ di ˈtʰaːgə,
mich drückt kein Schmerz, keine Plage,　mein Frohsinn　würzt mir　die Tage,
me　presses no　pain,　no　　annoyance, my　cheerfulness spices for me the days,
(no pain oppresses me, no annoyance; my cheerfulness spices my days,)

liːn haːb ɪç tsʊm ʃilt　miːɐ̯　gəˈveːltʰ. [ɪç ˈgryːsə froː　ˈjeːdən ˈmɔrgən,
ihn hab' ich zum Schild mir　gewählt. [Ich grüsse froh　jeden Morgen,
it　have I　as a　shield for me chosen. [I　greet　gladly every　morning,
(I have chosen it as my shield. [I gladly greet every morning,)

deːɐ̯　nuːɐ̯ ˈnɔ͜øə ˈfrɔ͜ødən miːɐ̯ brɪŋtʰ, feːltˈ gɛltˈ　miːɐ̯, mʊs lɪç voːl　ˈbɔrgən,
der　nur neue Freuden mir　bringt, fehlt Geld　mir, muss ich wohl　borgen,
which only new joys　　to me brings, lacks money to me, must I　probably borrow,
(which only brings me new joys; if I lack money, I must probably borrow some,)

dɔx diːs maxt' 'niːmaːls miːɐ̯ 'zɔrgən, vael ʃt'eːts 'jeːdɐ vʊnʃ miːɐ̯ gə'lɪŋtʰ.
doch dies macht niemals mir Sorgen, weil stets jeder Wunsch mir gelingt.
but that makes never for me troubles, because always every wish for me succeeds.
(but that is never any trouble for me, since I always get what I wish for.)

bae 'mɛːt'çən 'gɛrnə gə'zeːən, kʰvɛːlt' 'laefɐzʊxt' 'niːmaːls maen hɛrt͡s; ʃmɔlt' 'laenə,
Bei Mädchen gerne gesehen, quält Eifersucht niemals mein Herz; schmollt eine,
Among girls gladly seen, plagues jealousy never my heart; pouts one,
(Girls like to see me; jealousy never plagues my heart; if one of them pouts,)

las ɪç zi: 'ʃt'eːən, foːɐ̯ 'liːbəsgraːm t͡suː fɛɐ̯'geːən, das 'vɛːrə laen 'bɪt'ɐʀ ʃɛrt͡s.]
lass ich sie stehen, vor Liebesgram zu vergehen, das wäre ein bitterer Scherz.]
let I her stand, for love- grief to waste away, that would be a bitter joke.]
(I let her be; to waste away for love-sickness, that would be a bitter joke.])

[Schubert's manuscript of the song has only one verse, since only that one verse was printed in the almanac where he presumably found it; nevertheless he did add repeat marks, implying that other verses should be sung as well. After his death, the publisher Diabelli brought out the song, with a different piano introduction, with some variants in the vocal line, and with two additional verses (in brackets, above), that are not, however, part of Castelli's poem as it was eventually published in full. The *Gesamtausgabe* prints Schubert's song as he left it (one verse only); the Peters edition follows Diabelli's version (three verses), as it was published in 1850.]

'fryːlɪŋsglaobə
Frühlingsglaube
Faith in Spring

Op. 20, No. 2 [1820] (Ludwig Uhland)

di 'lɪndən 'lʏft'ə zɪnt' lɛɐ̯'vaxtʰ, zi: 'zɔ͜øzəln lʊnt' 'veːbən tʰaːk' lʊnt' naxtʰ,
Die linden Lüfte sind erwacht, sie säuseln und weben Tag und Nacht,
The gentle breezes are awakened, they murmur and stir day and night,

zi: 'ʃafən lan 'lalən 'lɛndən.
sie schaffen an allen Enden.
they are at work at all ends.
(they are at work everywhere.) ["*an allen Ecken und Enden*" = everywhere]

o: 'frɪʃɐ dʊftʰ, lo: 'nɔ͜øɐ kʰlaŋ! nuːn, 'larmɛs 'hɛrt͡sə, zae nɪçt' baŋ!
O frischer Duft, o neuer Klang! Nun, armes Herze, sei nicht bang!
Oh fresh fragrance, oh new sound! Now, poor heart, be not afraid!

nuːn mʊs zɪç 'laləs, 'laləs 'vɛndən.
Nun muss sich alles, alles wenden.
Now must itself everything, everything turn around.
(Now everything will surely turn around for the better.)

di vɛlt' vɪrt' 'ʃøːnɐ mɪt' 'jeːdəm tʰaːk',
Die Welt wird schöner mit jedem Tag,
The world becomes more beautiful with every day,
(The world becomes more beautiful with every passing day,)

500

man vaes nıçt‘, vas nɔx ‘verɐdən maːk‘,
man weiss nicht, was noch werden mag,
one knows not what still become may,
(one does not know what still may come to be,)

das ‘blyːən vıl nıçt‘ ‘lɛndən, ɛs vıl nıçt‘ ‘lɛndən;
das Blühen will nicht enden, es will nicht enden;
the blossoming wants not to end, it wants not to end;
(there is no end to the blossoming;) [*poem: without* "**es will nicht enden**"]

ɛs blyːt das ‘fɛrnst‘ə, t‘hiːfst‘ə t‘haːl : nuːn, ‘arməs hɛrts̪, fɛɐ‘gıs deːɐ k‘hvaːl!
es blüht das fernste, tiefste Tal: nun, armes Herz, vergiss der Qual!
there blossoms the farthest, deepest valley: now, poor heart, forget the torment!
(the farthest, deepest valley is in blossom: now, poor heart, forget your pain!)

nuːn mʊs zıç ‘aləs, ‘aləs ‘vɛndən.
nun muss sich alles, alles wenden.
now must itself everything, everything turn around.
(now everything will surely turn around for the better.)

[The heart is comforted by the coming of spring: now everything will change for the better!]

‘fryːlıŋsliːt‘
Frühlingslied
Spring Song

Posthumously published [composed 1816] (poem by Ludwig Hölty)

di lʊft‘ lıst‘ blɑo, das t‘haːl lıst‘ gryːn, di ‘k‘hlaenən ‘maeənglɔk‘ən blyːn,
Die Luft ist blau, das Tal ist grün, die kleinen Maienglocken blühn,
The air is blue, the valley is green, the little lilies of the valley are blooming,

lʊnt‘ ‘ʃlʏsəlbluːmən ‘drʊnt‘ɐ; deːɐ ‘viːzəngrʊnt‘ lıst‘ ʃoːn zoː bʊnt‘,
und Schlüsselblumen drunter; der Wiesengrund ist schon so bunt,
and cowslips among them; the meadow-ground is already so colorful,

lʊnt‘ maːlt‘ zıç ‘t‘hɛːk‘lıç ‘bʊnt‘ɐ. drʊm ‘k‘hɔmə, veːm deːɐ mae gə‘fɛlt‘,
und malt sich täglich bunter. Drum komme, wem der Mai gefällt,
and paints itself daily more colorful. Therefore come, whomever the May pleases,
(and becomes more so every day. Therefore whoever likes May should come)

lʊnt‘ ‘ʃɑoə froː di ‘ʃøːnə vɛlt‘ lʊnt‘ ‘gɔt‘əs ‘faːt‘ɐgyːt‘ə,
und schaue froh die schöne Welt und Gottes Vatergüte,
and look at happily the beautiful world and God’s fatherly kindness,
(and look with happiness at the beautiful world and at the signs of God’s fatherly kindness,)

diː ‘diːzə p‘hraxt‘ hɛɐ‘foːɐgəbraxt, den bɑom lʊnt‘ ‘zaenə ‘blyːt‘ə.
die diese Pracht hervorgebracht, den Baum und seine Blüte.
which this splendor brought forth, the tree and its blossom.
(which brought forth this splendor, the tree and its blossoming.)

[Before composing this attractive little *Lied*, Schubert had already set the poem as a partsong for first and second tenor and bass. With *Erntelied* and *Winterlied* this makes a garland of seasons.]

502

504

508

512

From **Terresa Berganza**
Plaza San Lorenzo del Escorial
Madrid Spain
February 25, 1980

La competencia profesional del señor BEAUMONT GLASS me es conocida desde hace muchos años. Su profunda experiencia musicológica, sus dotes personales, su variado dominio lingüistico y su inigualable capacidad en el trabajo diario han sido para mí en repetidas ocasiones, el mejor apoyo y el mejor estímulo para mi propio trabajo...

...su extraordinaria labor en el Festival Internacional de Opera de Aix-en-Provence 1978, cuando en mi interpretación del personaje "Ruggiero" de la ópera "ALCINA" de Haendel pude y debí recurrir a él a fin de lograr una mejor y más perfecta elaboración artística de mi personaje.

Así mismo, mi debut en el personaje de "Charlotte" de la ópera "WERTHER" de Massenet, en la ópera de Zürich, debut que estuvo acompañado de un extraordinario éxito, sólo fué posible gracias a su eficaz trabajo y asistencia. Sus insinuaciones y consejos me fueron siempre de inestimable valía.

Podría citar, por último, mis largas sesiones de refinadísimo trabajo en la preparación de la obra "Frauenliebe und Leben" de Schumann, destinada a figurar en mi repertorio de recitales. Y no puedo dejar de hacer observar que fué también el señor Beaumont Glass quien cuido de escoger entre los Liedern de Brahms, aquellos que mejor se adecuaban a mis especiales cualidades vocales...

English Translation

"The professional competence of Mr. BEAUMONT GLASS has been known to me for many years. His profound musicological experience, his personal talents, his command of various languages and his matchless capability in the daily routine have been for me on repeated occasions the greatest support and the greatest stimulation for my own work...

...his extraordinary work in the International Opera Festival of Aix-en-Provence 1978 when for my interpretation of the character, Ruggiero, in the opera, *Alcina* by Handel I was able to turn to him in order to achieve a better and more perfect artistic working-out of my role...

Similarly, my debut in the part of Charlotte in the opera *Werther* by Massenet at the Zurich Opera, which was accompanied by an extraordinary success, was only possible thanks to his efficacious work and assistance. His suggestions and advice were always of inestimable value to me...

I could cite, finally, my long sessions of most detailed work in the preparation of the cycle *Frauenliebe und Leben* by Schumann, destined to be featured in my recital repertoire. And I must mention that it was also Mr. Beaumont Glass who chose among the Lieder of Brahms those which were best suited to my particular vocal qualities..."

Teresa Berganza